Managerial Applications
of Information Technology

A Customized Version of

Managing Information Technology: What Managers Need to Know

Second Edition

E. Wainright Martin • Daniel W. DeHayes

Jeffrey A. Hoffer • William C. Perkins

Graduate School of Business
Decision and Information Systems
Indiana University, Bloomington, Indiana

&

Decision Support and Expert Systems: Management Support Systems

Fourth Edition

Efraim Turban

California State University, Long Beach
and
Nanyang Technological University, Singapore

Edited by

Donald R. Carter

SIMON & SCHUSTER CUSTOM PUBLISHING

Printed in the United States of America

10   9   8   7   6   5   4   3   2   1

ISBN   0–536–59264–0
BA   95009

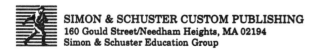

SIMON & SCHUSTER CUSTOM PUBLISHING
160 Gould Street/Needham Heights, MA 02194
Simon & Schuster Education Group

Table of Contents

The following chapters are taken from
Managing Information Technology:
What Managers Need to Know
Second Edition, Martin, DeHayes,Hoffer and Perkins

1

The Growing User-Manager Role in Information Management

The 1980s witnessed a revolution in how data processing, office automation, telecommunications, and other applications of information technology were being used and how they improved business performance in large and small organizations. The diversity of new technology applications during the decade was almost as broad as the industries that were affected. The nature of these new uses of technology has often led to increased responsibility for managing certain information systems (IS) functions by the user-manager of the information. As a result, managers and professionals in the sales, human resources, manufacturing, financial, and legal departments are finding more of their time and attention consumed by these "computing" activities.

In the 1990s, organizations began using information technology where such applications would not have been considered only a few years earlier. Grocery stores routinely use scanning machines for customer checkout, inventory updating, and stock replenishment. Banks increasingly use automatic teller machines as a primary interface with their retail customers. Voice mail now greets callers at many firms.

In many organizations, the IS organization has assumed new roles and responsibilities, often under new and more business-oriented leadership, as it learns to deal with the changing environment. This revolution in applications is also pushing senior management to include information technology on the strategic issues agenda of companies for the first time. For the same reasons, many professionals in organizations are finding that the new capability brought by these technologies is having a significant effect on their jobs and careers.

This chapter outlines the scope of the book, describes the breadth of impact of the application of information technology on business operations and performance, and suggests a range of current user perceptions of information systems—perceptions of both the IS organization and IS people. The historical and developing reasons for some of these attitudes are then explained. The attributes of an evolving system for using and managing technology are briefly outlined. Finally, the objectives of the book are presented.

FOCUS OF THE BOOK

This book describes both traditional and more recent uses of information technology in organizations, reviews the outlook for developments in the

2

future, and proposes some new roles for user-managers in managing the information resources of the organization. The authors believe that the 1990s environment requires both user-managers and IS professionals to assume new roles. The authors assume that the reader is, or intends to be, a professional or a manager in a large or small business or government organization. Like most large and small businesses, the reader will be asked to use information in electronic form to help perform a job that is increasingly dependent on technology.

The authors have written the text for readers who do not consider themselves IS professionals. We approach information management issues from the point of view of the user-manager—often called the *user* by the professional IS organization. While the reader may not be interested in making a career in information systems, we are convinced that all managers must be proactive in utilizing electronic information to help increase personal efficiency, improve departmental effectiveness, and perhaps even achieve a sustainable strategic advantage for the entire organization.

This book has been written with the hope that the user-manager will gain personal, as well as organizational, benefit from the improved use of information technology. Traditionally, an understanding of human resources, sales, finance, operations, and marketing principles has been critical for advancement into general management. We believe that during the 1990s and beyond a core comprehension of IS fundamentals will also be essential for professional advancement in most organizations, both small and large.

Finally, we sincerely hope that the reader recognizes that active involvement by user-managers in the management of information technology is required for the organization to be able to take advantage of new opportunities. Before the mid-1980s, it was common and appropriate for the typical user-manager to be only passively involved in issues relating to IS. Developing and supporting systems was clearly seen as a complex process requiring substantial technical knowledge. Moreover, the technology options were limited. Most systems were designed for large, central computing resources and were developed and operated by

IS personnel. The typical manager in the typical company was not involved and did not want to be involved.

During the 1980s, the quickening pace of technology and the growing awareness of the strategic value of IS created a new situation. Desktop microcomputers now house critical systems for larger companies, and smaller firms may use microcomputers exclusively and may not even have an IS specialist. A passive IS role for the manager is no longer sufficient. The user-manager cannot allow the central IS organization or an outside service bureau to perform most, if not all, of the functions of discovering, defining, developing, maintaining, and terminating systems without active user involvement. Managers in all functional areas must take on more information management responsibility and exercise their authority over the information technology area. While the need for user-manager involvement is clear, the appropriate policies and procedures that the large or small company should use to manage its information technology resources are not, and effective ways to manage these resources is the subject of this book.

THE GROWING IMPACT OF INFORMATION TECHNOLOGY
....

The opportunities for information systems applications brought about by new technology are greater than ever before. Faced with an ever-increasing demand for services, most IS departments have done an admirable job of delivering systems in both new and traditional application areas. A comprehensive list of information technology applications developed during the 1980s and early 1990s is beyond the scope of this book. A sampling is included here to show the diversity and significance of information technology applications. (Additional examples are provided in Chapters 2 and 3.) The examples range from large organizations to small ones, from solely domestic companies to global ones, from manufacturing firms to those in the service sector, and from single applications to total company transformations.

MAC ATTACK ON BIG IRON

HOPS International, a small software firm in Miami, says its HOPS product will boost the performance of an Apple Computer, Inc. Macintosh to big iron levels. According to president Harry Goodman, HOPS—an object-oriented software environment that combines the functions of a network operating system, applications development tool, and database—can sort 1 million hundred-byte records in less than three minutes and scan those same records in 17 seconds—similar to mainframe applications speed.

Is HOPS really as fast as the vendor claims? An official at Liberty Mutual Insurance Co., so far the only commercial customer, declined to comment. However, according to sources close to Liberty Mutual, the company recently swapped out several Teradata computers from its data center—$36 million worth of the number-crunching machines from NCR Corp.—and replaced them with a handful of Macintosh Quadra 950 computers running the HOPS software program.

LifeScan, Inc., a Milpitas, California-based manufacturer of medical equipment, is testing HOPS. According to Rod Alleman, HOPS is outperforming transaction processing systems on machines such as the IBM 3090 mainframe, Digital Equipment Corporation VAXs, and the Mips 6260 server from Mips Computer Systems, Inc. In one comparison, HOPS searched 760,000 customer records in 45 seconds. On a Mips server, the same feat took 45 *minutes*. "It's a jump in technology above what the other people have," Alleman says.

(Kelly, 1992)

Collectively, they illustrate the successes that have been obtained through the creative use of information technology.

Decreasing Product Development Time and Manufacturing Cost

By adopting the industry standard manufacturing automation protocol (MAP) as well as computer-integrated manufacturing (CIM) techniques, Deere & Company, the farm implement manufac-turer, was able to achieve some impressive business benefits. Officials at Deere credit information technology with helping reduce the time needed to bring a new product idea to market from five to two years. Likewise, Deere was able to reduce a product's manufacturing breakeven point by 50 percent in ten years. The application of these technologies also helped reduce space needs and factory equipment investment requirements. A metal-stamping process for component parts that required ten machines and five to six operators in 1984 could be accomplished with two machines and one operator only two years later (Bozman, 1986).

Cross-Selling Banking Services

Competition in the financial services industry greatly intensified during the 1980s because of deregulation, global competition, and information technology. In order to compete, banks were required to cross-sell products to enhance revenue and market share. These cross-selling efforts were aided by automation of branch operations. First Wisconsin Bank had been operating a simple on-line terminal network for branch tellers since the late 1970s. In 1986, First Wisconsin implemented a sophisticated new information system, first with tellers and then with other customer services personnel. The system gave these employees full access to the bank's database, greatly increasing the ability of branch personnel to determine other customer needs and thereby cross-sell bank services. The new system also greatly reduced the amount of time needed to perform certain services, such as opening a new account. This systems upgrade not only increased cross-selling opportunities but also led to estimated productivity increases of 10 percent for tellers and an estimated 30 to 40 percent for customer services personnel (*ABA Banking Journal*, 1988).

Improving Retail Merchandising

Merchandisers at Hallmark Cards began using a new supercomputer-based inventory management system in the early 1990s. When a holiday item suddenly became popular and the stocks of some retailers were reported dangerously low, the system located inventory of the item throughout Hallmark's extensive retailer network. This powerful supercomputer also searched vast amounts of data to assist management with inventory repositioning, pricing, purchasing, and a myriad of other information-dependent tasks. Questions that only a few years ago would not be asked could now be answered quickly and accurately, leading to improved decisions. When discussing the role of information technology in retailing, Wayne Hood of Prudential Securities concluded, "It is going to separate the winners from the losers in retailing in the 1990s" (Wilke, 1992).

Increasing Customer Information Access

Akzo Coatings, the paint division of the large Dutch company Akzo, worked with a sister subsidiary, Akzo Systems, to develop a totally new way to work with their customers. The IS department created a system that enables auto repair shops to obtain instant electronic access through a personal computer to warehouse spare parts inventory status, new repair procedures, and labor-hour standards for several thousand car models and repair types. The system helped allay the worries of auto shop customers and gave shop managers better control over repair costs. As a result, Akzo Systems expected a 50 percent sales growth rate in Germany alone for its new system from 1985 to 1988, and Akzo Coatings is experiencing better gross margins on its coating products (Harris, 1985).

Allowing Automated Dictation

Automated speech-recognition systems make fast, accurate dictation possible without the intervention of a human operator. In 1992, Clinical Information Advantages began selling a system to radiologists so they can dictate analyses of X rays. The radiologist dictates into a computer that has been "trained" to recognize the person's voice. Early tests verified a dictation rate of 160 words per minute with the new system. While applications were limited by the size of the recognized vocabulary, improved algorithms and larger dictionaries

are being developed. Users credited the new system with significant increases in both accuracy and productivity (Bulkeley, 1992).

Integrating All Value-Added Functions

In ocean shipping, as in most global businesses, companies have had to alter the way they do business to survive. American President Lines, the shipping subsidiary of American President Companies (APC), succeeded in establishing itself as a leader in shipping containerized freight by investing heavily in information technology. The new system made it possible for APC staff to access extensive data files, enabling management to analyze the company's market share in transporting various products. The new capability allowed the sales force to focus efforts in those areas where higher margins can be obtained for carrying time-critical or high-value products. In addition, APC installed a data interpretation system that provides management reports in thirty minutes (versus several weeks before the installation of the automated system). Software to streamline the loading and unloading of ships is also being used. APC was the first carrier to implement a computerized cargo clearance system that allows U.S. customs agents to begin screening cargo while it is still at sea. APC's customers can now track the progress of their shipments twenty-four hours a day via direct access to the shipment database. APC management concluded that information technology improved the quality of its decisions and provided more value-added services for its customers (McCusker, 1988).

Contributing to Overall Competitiveness

The J. C. Penney Company, the department store and cataloging giant, has made major investments in electronic data interchange with suppliers and in helping store managers make merchandising decisions through satellite closed-circuit television broadcasting. Management asserts that these uses of information technology have played a significant role in Penney's steady increase in earnings during the early to mid-1980s and in achieving the rank of second place among department stores in sales per employee (Alper and Daly, 1988).

6

PERCEPTIONS OF THE INFORMATION SYSTEMS FUNCTION

The revolution in the applications of information technology during the 1980s has produced a major change in the perception of the role of information technology and the IS organization in some companies. Executives in these companies credit information technology with making major strategic and operational contributions to the company. Consider this typical comment:

> Our information resources department makes a major contribution to our profitability. We expect our vice president of information resources to provide ideas for improving the business just as we rely on the heads of sales, manufacturing, and engineering for their contributions.

Despite all the advances, however, many managers are not totally comfortable with the revolution that is taking place. They recognize the potential value of new information technology applications but are not sure how the company can take advantage of more investment in these information systems. Consider this representative statement:

> Information systems is our top strategic concern—not because it outweighs everything else, but because we are unsure what to do with it. Although we understand the other parts of our business strategy, information systems issues keep eluding us. We make good technical decisions, our systems work well, and we have good project management, but we just can't seem to grasp the bigger picture.

This comment recognizes that the IS area is a major management concern in many organizations. Managers have read how a small hospital supplies wholesaler, American Hospital Supply Corporation (AHSC), gained a large market share with a new electronic order-entry system called ASAP. The system involved placing terminals in the buying offices of major hospitals and hooking them into AHSC computers. They have also heard how American Airlines developed the SABRE reservation system to capture the travel agency business on major air routes. Executives know that if their

company is not trying to introduce information technology into its products and services, a rival is probably doing so. They remember that many competitors were caught flat-footed when Merrill Lynch introduced its Cash Management Account, which combined information on many financial products and accounts into one easy-to-read statement for the customer. There is agreement in these firms that information technology can have a positive business impact, but something is missing.

Despite all the attention given to computing and telecommunications in the business and popular press during the 1980s, many managers do not truly understand the fundamental principles of information technology and information management. They do realize that they need to comprehend this critical area in which a company may be spending 5 percent or more of sales. Such a lack of understanding can cause some management to lose trust in the IS organization, especially if user-managers do not relate well to the person in charge of IS. As a result, some companies have replaced the professional IS director with an executive who has more line management experience—someone with a user background. While changing people often can help (but not always), a full understanding of the building blocks of information technology, how IS can be used to benefit the firm, and how it should be managed in the 1990s is required to achieve bottom line results.

Another statement that describes a totally different management perception of IS is:

> We have shaped up data processing very nicely since the mid-1980s. We have developed many new systems to support our operations. When computing costs come down, we think more systems development projects will be justified and implemented.

This statement demonstrates a cost-only view of information technology. Some managers see the IS area as basically a utility for the company, a support activity managed by technical specialists that must be managed on a strict cost basis. While cost management of IS is indeed critical, managers should not be satisfied with this view. They should worry about what is being missed by not seeing information technology as an area to exploit for strategic advantage by the organization.

The person quoted above also seems to believe that all information technology activities must be cost justified. In his view, evaluating a new automation venture should be treated as any other standard capital investment, such as expanding basic plant capacity. This manager has failed to see that there might be an aspect to the development of information technology that is more like investing in a high-risk research project. Companies dominated by this thinking may only make IS investments that reduce costs—and never see the chances to use information technology to increase revenue or market share.

Another frequent observation about IS managers provides yet another perception about the state of information management in certain organizations:

> *Our data processing manager does a fine job for the firm. He handles all those technical details no one else understands quickly and without complaining. We can always count on Charlie.*

This statement reflects an impression about the people in the information technology areas of many companies. IS people are often a mystery to others in the firm. They speak a different language, one too often consisting of acronyms and specialized terms. They are considered separate from the mainstream management team. IS people are to be respected but viewed as part of the middle/lower management group. They are appreciated but are not really expected to contribute to the strategic vitality of the company. As a result, IS people in these firms are not included in business planning deliberations.

All but the first of these four perceptions reflect a limited understanding of the potential of information technology in an organization. While each of the perceptions may accurately reflect company history, all but the first hide the possible contribution of information technology in a company. Despite substantial educational efforts by the IS organization, perceptions that underestimate what is possible to achieve through information technology are common among user-managers. We hope to shed light on information

technology and information management in a way that will result in greater understanding among management. Our hope is that more managers would agree with Alexander Giacco, president and CEO of Hercules, Inc., when he said:

> *Computer technology is allowing us as managers—I should say forcing us—to move to new and different organization types so that we can better meet competitive needs. And the people who can best harness these new technologies in the future will be the most successful. Information becomes the key to success only with an information system that causes information to flow up to top management where we can make decisions and where we can effectively communicate back down so our decisions can quickly be put into action. (Harvard Business School Case 91-863-05).*

THE TRADITION OF INFORMATION SYSTEMS

To understand the sources of these varied impressions of information technology and to gain some insight into an improved management system for information technology, it is helpful to look back to when information technology and information management responsibilities were quite different.

Sole Source Position

Not many years ago, the central data processing organization in most firms was the sole source of data and computing capacity. With very few exceptions, such as using an outside service bureau to generate payroll checks, most business computing in larger companies was done by the central computing organization. Smaller companies usually did not even use computers, which were very expensive and considered specialized equipment.

As the sole source of computing services, many IS organizations knowingly or unknowingly began to act like a monopoly inside their company. Typically, services were priced on a cost-plus basis. The cost to perform a task was estimated, overhead was added, and a price was quoted. The choices for the user were either to accept the price for the service or to forego development of the system. While generally high service levels were provided, responses to requests for new services were quite slow and costs often grew unreasonably if not controlled. The focus of the monopolistic IS organization was often on meeting standardized needs that could be fulfilled with standard equipment and full cost recovery rather than a market-driven focus.

Most monopolists tend to be very committed to what they perceive the job to be. Unfortunately, outside forces sometimes change the nature of the job unexpectedly. IS professionals were committed to the job as it was defined to them, but changes in computing and communications technology during the 1980s caused significant upheavals in many IS organizations, quite often resulting in the loss of this monopoly position.

Mission of Improving Efficiency

IS organizations traditionally reported through the financial organization and had a clear mission of operational efficiency improvement. Automation of routine business functions, such as maintaining the general ledger, producing a payroll, and operating the order-entry function, were typical tasks. Controlling operational expenses and reducing staff were seen as the basic roles of new systems development. The standard criterion used to decide whether an IS development project should be undertaken was whether the firm could reduce its cost by the installation of this new automated transaction processing system. Such a cost-reduction discipline made good sense in many situations, especially when companies experienced intense competitive pressures, but it provided a narrow scope for appropriate applications of information technology.

Professional Orientation

IS people have traditionally maintained a strong professional orientation in their work. Standards for carrying out certain computing tasks were often established by outside professional societies, much like the accounting profession. Few executives in the typical business or government organization outside the IS organization understood the complex task of computer programming or operating telephone switches. In addition, the IS professional took pride in applying the most advanced technical tools to develop elegant solutions to company problems. Completing the last small portion of a new IS (which often took a large percent of the time) was considered crucial to the quality of the project by the IS professional.

FORCES OF CHANGE

The 1980s brought major changes in the information technology environment within organizations. The cumulative effect of these changes was significant enough to demand the creation of entirely new management systems. Many companies responded aggressively to these changes and created new approaches to information management, while other organizations either responded to these external changes slowly or in ways that tended to address only the symptoms rather than the causes of their problems. Let's review some of these changes.

Microcomputer Technology

Since 1980 the options available in computing technology have skyrocketed. The development that ranks at the top of the list is the microcomputer. The raw processing power in a personal computer today, measured in MIPS (million instructions per second), can match the entire processing capacity in a central computer center of only a few years ago. The cost of storage on a microcomputer is also very low; large data files, containing more than 100 million characters, can routinely be kept on microcomputers. The effectiveness of microcomputer hardware has been enhanced by the simultaneous development of user-friendly software. Powerful software, such as Excel, Lotus 1-2-3, Paradox, and dBase, made using computers understandable to the nonexpert for the first time. The development of the microcomputer also added tension to the relationship between the user-managers and the IS organization because now IS customers could develop their own information systems on a personal computer rather than being forced to use a mainframe solution. As a result, many important information systems have been developed on personal computers and are independent from other systems used to support the organization.

Commercial Software

The applications systems development backlog during the 1980s in many IS organizations created a major new industry. Software companies began to offer complete applications packages written especially for a particular need. For example, assume that the manager of the trust department in a bank needed an information system to improve operations. The manager's choices were to design and develop the system through the IS organization of the bank or to buy commercially available software that might operate only on certain particular hardware. What was the likely decision? The IS organization quoted several years of development time and a programming cost that seemed outrageously high. The alternative was to buy a minicomputer (made by IBM, Hewlett-Packard, Digital Equipment Corporation, or Data General) and a special software package. The salesperson of the commercial software company seemed to understand customer needs and was anxious to please the trust manager. The promise of "just turn the key and it will run" seemed compelling. Many functional managers applied this logic and bought the "turnkey" commercial system. While perhaps satisfactory for this particular operation, such a packaged solution separated trust department operations data from all other data at the bank. The repeated selection of packaged solutions, often on different hardware, led to the often-used term "islands of automation."

Growing User-Manager Computer Competency

During the 1980s, many business graduates began to expect to use personal computing routinely in their jobs because they had used it in their university courses. Graduates in other fields as well were exploiting computers in their courses, and they expected the capability to be available in their companies. Some of these young people displayed

extensive knowledge about some computing applications and technology. Others did not really internalize more than a mechanical understanding of how certain inputs yield certain outputs from systems. The increasing capability of graduates has created many positive results for IS development. Nevertheless, a little knowledge, especially when it was confined to a few personal computing applications, also caused unreasonable expectations (for example, in terms of complex systems development time) for the IS department.

Upheaval in Telecommunications

The 1980s began a new era for telecommunications in business organizations. The separation of responsibilities between American Telephone & Telegraph (AT&T) and seven regional telecommunications organizations that earlier were all part of the Bell System, combined with the deregulation of the long-distance communications and telephone switch markets, created significant new opportunities—and problems—for companies. Most companies can no longer rely on a single supplier for telecommunications services. Several competing firms must be considered, and it is often unclear exactly how their services fit with others. New competitors have entered the market, offering a vast array of new products and services. Most business organizations, however, have little internal experience in managing the variety of complex telecommunications activities.

Business Cost Pressures

The 1980s witnessed severe pressures to reduce operating costs in most U.S.–based organizations. Global competition reduced margins and forced fundamental reviews of company cost structures. Corporate headcounts have been reduced in many organizations. Business practices and processes have been reviewed and reengineered. As a result, the IS manager in many organizations was under increasing pressure to justify charges. In addition, many users of information technologies in major companies expressed concern about IS overhead costs over which they had little control. Some user-managers claimed that the methods and procedures built into how the IS department conducted its business created an unnecessarily large cost infrastructure, leading to high prices.

Competitive Turbulence

The information industry has undergone significant restructuring, and most experts forecast that the turbulence will continue into the next century. Before the mid-1980s, the supply situation was much clearer. For telecommunications products and services, IS managers contacted AT&T to meet their needs. For computing needs, the manager bought most products from International Business Machines (IBM) Corporation. For reprographic problems, the manager often contacted Xerox for solutions. Many more companies now exist to serve information needs. Each year organizations enter or leave the information business; new suppliers of specialized technology seem to appear almost weekly. Some stalwarts disappear or are reduced in size. In early 1993, the stock value of Microsoft (a relatively new software firm) was reported to be higher than IBM.

In addition, many established information technology firms are undergoing significant changes in their focus. One of the most rapidly growing areas at IBM since the late 1980s has been based around a powerful workstation originally designed for engineering work, although IBM was always best known for its large mainframes and its administrative processing capability. Administrative applications is a rapidly growing business area at Digital Equipment Corporation (DEC), long prominent as a scientific computing supplier. With the acquisition of National Cash Register, AT&T is now a major computer company. These changes have created a myriad of new products that somehow must be made to fit into an integrated information system for the company.

New Ways of Managing

In order to deal with increased competition in diversified markets, many companies have decentralized their various operations into separate business units. New divisions and business teams have been formed and empowered to achieve results based on a more concentrated business focus. As more is discovered about these niche markets, urgent demands for new and different systems are placed on the IS organization. Likewise, companies have introduced total quality management programs that generate new data requirements as well as more frequent reporting of key data, all creating major new tasks for the IS department.

MANAGING INFORMATION IN THE 1990s

Many IS organizations responded aggressively and positively to business changes during the 1980s by revising their approach to managing information technology. One of these responses has been the increased involvement of user-managers on policy-making committees for the IS department. Such groups have helped IS deal with the distributed (and sometimes disjointed) array of computing and data services that has been created in many companies so they may be better linked together through the corporate network. Computing by user-managers now consumes a substantial part, if not a majority, of the resources and services provided by many IS departments.

Second, some IS departments have grown more effective at using technology to improve their own productivity, especially in the development of major new systems. Not only are some user-managers more involved in designing systems through such techniques as joint applications development, but some programmers now have such software tools as CASE (computer-aided software engineering), which can significantly reduce the time needed to develop a new application program.

Third, some companies have involved senior management in a comprehensive process of evaluating the direction of the company and how information technology can help the organization move in the desired direction. Sometimes this discussion leads to a fundamental review of how the daily

WHITE-COLLAR COMPUTERS

Intelligent machines are increasingly being used to hide the brain-numbing complexity of modern business's products and processes, letting people concentrate on customers. In addition to providing better service, this redistribution of work should give new (and unsexist) meaning to the phrase "man's work."

One of the most ambitious efforts to employ intelligent machines is being undertaken in the credit-card operations of American Express. The firm is building a "knowledge highway" in which bright computers will help people with every step of the job of managing credit, from card applications to collecting overdue accounts. The business goal is to use the machines to shield both credit-card holders and employees from the bureaucracy needed to manage American Express's vast business, so leaving employees free to devote their efforts to building relationships with customers.

The machines help in several ways. The latest addition to the "knowledge highway" is designed to help with overdue accounts. It leaves humans in charge of collection, but protects them from error at every step. The system automatically pulls together all of the information needed to analyze an account. Previously analysts had to make 22 queries on average—to computers spread across the whole of the company—each time they looked at a problem account. Now they typically make only one. The computer keeps track of which state or national laws might affect the account. It files all the paperwork. And it automatically reminds the analyst if the account needs to be looked at again.

Thanks to such automated assistance, American Express is gradually changing the sort of people it recruits to manage credit. Instead of hiring people good at number-crunching and applying complex rules, it is turning to people who know how to deal with people. And it is giving them more scope to use their skills. Previously the sheer complexity of the work meant that jobs had to be narrowly defined in order to be manageable. With that complexity largely hidden, American Express reckons it can define jobs more broadly—so giving generalists more freedom to make their customers happy.

(The Economist, 1992)

work of clericals, professionals, managers, and executives can change with the use of information technology. This vision of the ideal information environment for a company can in turn lead toward a technical and managerial information technology architecture and long-term plan for the IS department.

Another frequent step is to make all parts of the information technology area the responsibility of one person, often called a chief information officer, or CIO. This organizational focus can facilitate coordination of all computing and communications issues and the determination of the best role of information technology throughout the organization.

These actions, and others to be outlined in later chapters, form the basis of a new system for managing information technology, but not all steps make sense in every organization. There are no simple formulas for making information technology effective in an organization. Certain principles and concepts are becoming clear, and these ideas are the basis for this entire book. Before learning more about IS applications, however, it is important to review some of the changes induced by information technology that have occurred in business.

IMPACT OF INFORMATION TECHNOLOGY

In 1958 a landmark article in the *Harvard Business Review*, "Management in the 1980s," provided a vision of the impact of information technology in the last part of the twentieth century (Leavitt and Whisler). The authors foresaw a fundamental change in the use of computing and management science tools. They imagined a future business environment that was information rich and a set of decision science tools (such as linear programming, statistics, and simulation) that would be commonplace within many firms. They envisioned individuals with the skills to operate in such a rich information environment and the ability to use advanced management science tools. They also suggested that more and more business firms would recentralize their operations because fewer people with more data and greater analytical capability could make the same number of decisions. This centralization would in turn mean the removal of a significant number of middle-manager positions, either those that were no longer needed or because the manager could not join this new analytical cult. Finally, they believed that the typical company in the 1980s would maintain a significant barrier (glass ceiling) between top management and everyone else in the company. They suggested that a class distinction, much like what had occurred in the industrial age between worker and first-line supervisor, would be created between the information worker and others.

Many commentaries have been made on the extent to which information technology has helped create the vision foretold by Leavitt and Whisler. While the conclusions may vary, it is clear that technology has made it possible for trained people to utilize data and analytical tools more easily. Whether developed on the job or through a formal educational program, the skill of making information-based decisions is a distinguishing characteristic of a small group of people in many organizations. In addition, most people would agree that technology has been one of the contributing factors toward a significant reduction in the number of middle managers.

The typical user-manager job has also been changed significantly by technology. Clearly, the availability of more data and analytical tools, such as statistical software packages and electronic spreadsheets, has made capital expenditures, budgets, and marketing plans much more susceptible to analysis by a professional. "What if" analysis can now be a common part of the typical decision-making process in all companies, regardless of size, because of the availability of these tools. Some people would claim that such a richness of analytical capability can often lead to a paralysis in making decisions, but the increased ability of an individual to understand many aspects of a problem and test more alternatives is clear.

Several companies have noted that the use of information technology has reduced wasted time by executives. Studies confirm that a significant amount of a typical manager's day is spent in nonproductive activities, such as "telephone tag." The use of information technology tools, such as electronic mail, group support systems, interactive video teleconferencing, and voice messaging, all help reduce wasted time.

The extensive use of information technology tools also serves to extend the workday and make it more flexible. Some companies employ a significant number of people who work from their homes and interact electronically with other people in the company. Similarly, the use of electronic mail can allow an individual who works best in the early mornings to conduct work before the regular workday begins in a much more time-effective manner than if interrupted on a constant basis.

Companies are also demonstrating that the use of information technology improves collaboration among work groups. For example, because insights into common problems come at random times, an electronic bulletin board within a group of design engineers or product planners can be the place to post an idea at any time. Group support systems can help speed complex decision-making among several individuals.

Finally, electronic technology has provided a basis for the redesign of clerical and professional jobs. The expanded capability for word processing and other automated functions offers an individual a much richer work experience and, in many cases, increased responsibility.

Clearly, a knowledge of information technology can have a positive influence on an individual's career, but the person must become actively involved in learning the technology to be able to operate in the electronic environment. Obviously, the depth of knowledge required will vary with the personality and job needs of the individual. While some organizations attempt to predefine a particular technology training program, the reader is cautioned to be more attentive to personal needs and comfort level and to go beyond the recommended level or stop short, depending on the individual's situation. We also recommend strongly that the reader engage actively in work with the company's IS department. With the knowledge gained from this book and other experiences, active participation in the joint development of systems and the shared management of data can have positive effects in terms of both immediate job assignments and longer-term careers.

OBJECTIVES OF THE BOOK

After studying and discussing this book, you should feel prepared to manage information technology resources in your area of responsibility and to cope with continual technology-based change. You should also be able to identify ways in which to exploit information technology in business. Tapping this skill requires that you become familiar with the opportunities for application of information technology in various industries and functional areas. You then should be able to guide the development of an effective, reliable, secure, and changeable information system for your area of responsibility. You should be able to communicate effectively with IS specialists, a skill requiring a basic understanding of computer hardware, applications software, networks, databases, and fundamental systems concepts. In addition, you should be able to choose among different ways to procure an information system, based on the type of application and your technological and organizational environment.

In a broader sense, you should be able to identify potential strategic applications of information technology and be prepared to contribute to the development of a vision and strategic plan for information technology in your company. You should be familiar with the alternative technical and managerial architectures for supporting such a plan.

Finally, you should be able to evaluate the effectiveness of the IS organization in a company and understand how to use this organization effectively to obtain the systems needed in your particular area of responsibility. We hope that you will be able to develop a clear vision of the future impact of information technology on managers, organizations, the economy, and society.

REVIEW QUESTIONS

1. What areas does the field of information technology include in addition to data processing?
2. What common factors seem to account for success in the example applications of information technology cited in the chapter?
3. What options did a small retailer have for applying information technology before 1980? How have the technology developments of the 1980s changed these options?
4. What factors account for the varying perceptions that the user-managers quoted in the chapter have about their information systems department?
5. How has the rapid development of commercial software during the 1980s changed the role of the information systems department? The user-manager?

DISCUSSION QUESTIONS

1. Briefly cite examples that show the impact the information/technological revolution has had on the business functions of marketing, production, finance, and human resources. What future benefits do you envision in these areas?
2. What other factors not cited in the text have contributed to the need for a new system for managing information technology today?
3. Discuss the statement, "To be successful, the information system of an organization must reflect the culture and values of the organization." Why do you feel this is true or false?
4. Experts argue that organizations now have the ability to capture more data than ever before, but the information needs of senior managers are still not being met as effectively as the needs of operational managers. Discuss why this is so. What are the implications for management?
5. Cost control and budget-cutting have characterized much of the business environment of

14

the 1980s. In light of this reality, what potential problems might be encountered by a user-manager requesting a new information system? How would you address these problems?

6. "Tomorrow's user-managers will have to be more than computer literate; they will have to be information systems literate." Discuss the factors that have contributed to the need for managers to possess a high degree of computer sophistication. Will it be possible for user-managers of the future to be successful without being information systems literate?

REFERENCES

1988. "In search of the big payoff." *ABA Banking Journal* 80 (August): 51–56.

1992. "White-collar computers." *The Economist* 61 (August 1): 57, 58.

Alper, Alan, and James Daly. 1988. "Penney cashes in on leading edge." *Computerworld* 22 (June 20): 2, 62–66.

Bozman, Jean S. 1986. "Deere reaps MAP, CIM benefits." *Computerworld* 20 (June 6): 43–44.

Bulkeley, William M. 1992. "Hands full? Just keep talking and this computer types for you." *Wall Street Journal* 74 (December 21): B1.

Harris, Catherine L. 1985. "Information power." *Business Week* (October 14): 108–114.

Harvard Business School. "Hercules, Inc.: Anatomy of a Vision." Harvard Business School Case 91-863-05.

Kelly, Rob. 1992. "Mac attack on big iron." *Information Week* 21 (November 16): 24.

Latamore, G. Burton, and John Bush. 1987. "Lots of tunnel, a little light." *Computer and Communications Decisions* 19 (September): 58–61, 67–68.

Leavitt, Harold J., and Thomas L. Whisler. 1958. "Management in the 1980s." *Harvard Business Review* 36 (November–December): 41–48.

McCusker, Tom. 1988. "Allen-Bradley tries to fight competition by tooling up." *Datamation* 34 (March): 33, 36.

————. 1988. "Ocean freighters turn to high tech on the high seas." *Datamation* 34 (March): 25–26.

Wilke, John R. 1992. "Supercomputers manage holiday stock." *Wall Street Journal* 74 (December 23): B1.

1

Midsouth Chamber of Commerce

It was 10 PM and Leon Lassiter, vice president of marketing with the Midsouth Chamber of Commerce, was in his office, reflecting on the day's frustrations. Lassiter had met with four territory managers, his marketing support supervisor, and a number of staff representatives. All were upset about their lack of access to the computer system and the problems they were having with the new software. Lassiter assured them that their problems were being addressed. He stressed that patience was needed during the ongoing conversion. Now, during his private moment late in the evening, Lassiter was beginning to recognize the problems and complexities he faced with the current software conversion. The sales and funding system represented by his marketing staff had ground to a halt, unable to access the computer system to handle their accounts. All communications processing was frozen, and access to the computer for conference registrations was unavailable. These inconveniences, however, were minor compared to Lassiter's uneasy feeling that there were problems with Simon Kovecki, Midsouth Chamber of Commerce's systems analyst. Lassiter knew that time was of the essence and that he might have to step in and manage the conversion, even though he had no management information systems background.

General Background on MSCC

In the early 1900s, economic development in the Midsouth area was almost totally dependent on transportation systems. As a result of legislative decisions, many communities in the Midsouth area were cut off from reasonable transportation access, thus retarding business and economic development. With no one to

represent their concerns to the legislative branch of Midsouth's government, a group of powerful businessmen formed the Midsouth Chamber of Commerce to research and lobby the state government on the issue of transportation.

MSCC dealt with this single issue until the 1930s, when its charter was reorganized to include a broad range of issues affecting the business community, including state banking laws, transportation, industrial development, and taxes. By the late 1970s and early 1980s, the MSCC, under the leadership of Jack Wallingford, became an aggressive advocacy organization for the business community.

Wallingford's shift in the MSCC aggressiveness brought substantial change to the organization. In 1978 the MSCC had a staff of 14, a membership of 4,000, and an annual budget of $720,000. Over the years, the MSCC had been able to develop a reserve account of just over $1 million.

By 1982 the staff had grown to 24, the $1 million cash reserve had been drawn down to $250,000, and membership had dropped to 2,300, largely because of the recession of the early 1980s. The reserve reduction, supported by the board of directors, had fueled considerable internal growth in terms of staff and capabilities. During this time the MSCC moved into larger offices and began implementation of a new computer system.

By 1982 the MSCC was considered to be the most powerful business advocacy organization in the Midsouth area and one of the most innovative in its approaches and techniques in dealing with problems facing the business community. The greatest problem facing the MSCC was the growing concern that its aggressive changes in focus and capabilities might have to be curtailed because it could no longer fund its annual operating budget.

In mid-1982 Wallingford was faced with a serious dilemma. The MSCC was projecting a $330,000 deficit for the 1983 fiscal year. Wallingford realized he was going to have to cut staff and reduce the number of programs the MSCC was involved in or find some way to more aggressively fund the organization. Wallingford called in his vice president of public affairs and operations, Ed Wilson, and asked him to find someone of experience to replace the sales manager in whom Wallingford had lost confidence.

Leon Lassiter came to MSCC in December 1982 with six years of experience in sales management and marketing with American Brands, where he had recently turned down a promotion to regional sales manager. MSCC, he reasoned, offered an opportunity to be much more involved than he had been with American Brands.

Lassiter then began quickly making dramatic changes. His analysis suggested that the marketing support functions were better coordinated and managed than the sales functions. Additionally, although the MSCC had recently purchased a computer and had installed custom software, Lassiter could not gain the information necessary to determine what was possible on the system and what was not. With these facts, Lassiter began to develop an entirely new sales and marketing system based on solid goals, objectives, standards, operating procedures, and training programs. Within four months, Lassiter had developed standards of operation that were based on paper systems with some integration of computer capacity.

Early Systems Integration

Ed Wilson performed a variety of duties at the MSCC. He was responsible for coordinating the legislative lobby team, managing Midsouth's operations, and, during the interim when there was no vice president of marketing, managing that function as well. Wilson had been with MSCC for 20 years.

Beginning in 1978 Wilson began introducing MSCC to the world of database management. Most of the staff was fearful of change and reluctant to accept computers, but with the help of a consultant, Wilson determined that the MSCC needs would best be satisfied by hiring a programmer to write custom software.

Marketing Division Wilson and the consultant identified three primary users. One user was the marketing division whose primary need was to track the activity and changes occurring in membership. Primary uses of the computer system would include the following:

Development of a membership database
Development of a prospective member database
Making daily changes to the member database
Generating a wide series of letters for personalized mail contact
Generating prospect and member lists and labels by standard industrial classification (SIC) numbers, firm size (sales, employment), zip code, mailing designator, and other criteria
Processing call-record activity by the territory managers
Tracking member activities and concerns through a comment field
Audit trails for reviewing changes
Word processing

The huge amount of data was managed primarily by the marketing support area. All requests for labels, lists, and changes were filled by the marketing division. Requested changes to the member database sometimes backed up as much as two weeks. Lassiter felt this was unacceptable and required a three-day turnaround on member-change activity.

The marketing division was staffed by four territory managers, a marketing support supervisor, and two clerical people. The managers generated 75 to 80 call records per day that required changes, letters, and invoice processing. It generally took both clerical people a total of twelve hours to process these activities. In addition, the clerical staff also tracked payments, commissions, member cancellations, and list maintenance. List maintenance included prospect lists, delinquent lists, and renewal lists. The clerical staff also handled special-letter requests from the territory managers and all normal secretarial duties (see Exhibit 1).

The marketing support supervisor was responsible for the day-to-day management of the support functions and the management of the computer resources as they directly related to the marketing support area. She was also administrative assistant to Lassiter and assisted in all his projects and activities.

The marketing support functions had been either revised or designed by Lassiter. In addition, the sales and direct marketing functions had been created by Lassiter. He instituted a number of cross-checking functions within the system, but they were labor intensive. He also felt software enhancements could significantly lower his costs of labor and dramatically increase his division's productivity.

EXHIBIT 1
Index of MSCC Clerical Tasks

I. Morning Mail
  A. Mail
  B. Processing current member payments
  C. Processing new member payments
  D. Processing teleblitz payments
  E. Cancel requests
  F. Final steps with morning mail
II. Record Maintenance
  A. Membership inquiry
  B. Adding a new member
  C. Corporate screen (sample)
    1. firm name and alpha key
    2. street address
    3. sample address problems
    4. city, zip code, telephone, mailing address, description
    5. SIC, employees, senate, house, union
    6. payment history screen
  D. Sample affiliate screen
  E. Affiliate screen instructions
    1. member name
    2. alpha name, formal salutation, nickname
    3. address, county, contact, PAC rep., bill to, congress, district, state house and senate
  F. Affiliate designator screen
  G. Changes on current members
  H. Members who pay semiannually
  I. Rollovers (semiannuals)
  J. Cancelled member rejoining
  K. Cross-reference

III. Call Record Procedures
  A. Counting call records
  B. Delinquents
  C. Cancels
  D. Upgrades
  E. Processing call records—New members or prospects
  F. Contact file entry
  G. Entering billing comments
  H. Processing "special" call-record letters
  I. Processing letters to prospects
  J. Sending invoices to upgrades
  K. Printing miscellaneous invoices
  L. Finishing call records
  M. Directors letters
  N. Filing call records
IV. Receipt Letters
  A. Preparing receipt statements
  B. Gathering receipt letters
  C. Company mailing list
  D. Printing envelopes or labels
  E. Filing receipt statements
V. Printing Labels from Request Form
VI. Membership Printout by County
VII. Billings
VIII. Delinquents
IX. New Members for Outlook
X. Cancellations
XI. Projected Billing Report
XII. Weekly Follow-ups for Prospects
XIII. Glossary

Operations Division In developing an initial hardware and software system for the MSCC, Wilson had conscientiously involved key managers and support people on staff to develop an idea of what was needed in software. Wilson was manager of the operations division and had 14 managers and support people. Wilson was primarily interested in building a software system capable of providing financial and accounting controls, because all payment histories and financial and accounting transactions were handled on a ledger system and were tracked by hand.

Wilson and his accounting manager set out a series of needs for the system to meet. These included:

Ledger system
Fund balances
Accrual accounting functions
Payment histories tracking
Commission schedules
Cancellation tracking
Report generation

In addition, Wilson wanted the system to be able to track legislative bills from their introduction through passage or veto by the governor. This information would be processed into the system manually and updated as changes occurred. The information would then be printed and sent to members on a daily basis.

Human Resources Division The human resources division, with two managers and two support people, was primarily interested in developing a conference and seminar tracking and reporting mechanism that would also have the capability of printing out badges for conference or seminar attendees.

The human resources division was the most active of the five major divisions of the MSCC in the area of conferences and seminars and could be expected to contribute approximately $90,000 to the bottom line net of expenses annually. Although not a major financial contribution, it was an indication of what other MSCC divisions might do if they became more active.

With this information in hand, Wilson selected an outside programmer to assist in more clearly identifying needs and selecting appropriate hardware. The programmer, Ted Vassici, selected a Wang system after a careful study. In early 1981 the VS-80 system was ordered with five terminals and two daisy-wheel character printers. These were to be strategically located throughout the office to provide equal access to the system once up and running.

Vassici further developed MSCC's software for sale to other membership-related organizations. Wilson actively promoted the software, and MSCC earned a royalty on these sales.

....
Changing Times

By 1984, as a result of Lassiter's marketing and sales reorganization and Wilson's management of expenses, MSCC was experiencing spectacular financial growth. While the two men were primarily responsible for the turnaround, Wilson and Lassiter had clashed on innumerable occasions. Lassiter felt that a large percentage of his territory managers' work and his marketing support activities could be automated to provide MSCC with much higher productivity with a significant reduction in labor and allied costs. Lassiter believed that a full-time systems analyst should be hired to meet the growing needs of the MSCC.

Wilson struggled with the issue of control. He felt that by maintaining the relationship with Vassici, he could control the rapidly growing demand for computer capabilities by not hiring a full-time systems analyst. He knew that there were limited funds for expansion of computer capabilities, and by adding a full-time systems analyst to the staff, it would be significantly more difficult to contend with growing staff demands. Continuing the relationship with Vassici provided Wilson with an ability to control what Vassici worked on and what should be tabled until there was time to get to it. Wilson had total control of what was worked on and what should wait.

Although Lassiter and Wilson continued to clash, Lassiter understood Wilson's desire to control growth in light of the limited resources of the MSCC. Lassiter knew that the slowly growing sophistication of the staff would explode once the tap was fully opened. However, Lassiter felt this was a management problem that should be allowed to manifest itself, and he felt confident that it could be dealt with effectively once the MSCC determined the extent of the staff's needs.

In 1985 Lassiter and Wilson joined forces on a concept where the MSCC would offer health insurance to its members, now numbering more than 4,000. Although the proposal was rejected by the board of directors, Wilson and Lassiter, as a result of the study, determined there were a myriad of other income-related opportunities to pursue that would require a much higher level of information management and computer use. Wilson soon hired a systems analyst to increase the MSCC's capabilities.

Simon Kovecki, a bright, brash, and technically competent systems analyst, had no experience on a Wang system and spent the first six months of 1986 learning the system. He began working exceptionally long hours as he struggled to understand a software system for which there was no documentation. Calls to Vassici went unanswered because his business had closed.

Through mid-1988, Wilson continued to manage the computer system and had done a credible job in upgrading the hardware with new CPUs, memory upgrades, disk drives, and additional monitors. The software system continued to work relatively well with Kovecki's constant attention. From 1986 to 1988, Wilson, with Kovecki's assistance, had developed an on-line legislative information system that was considered state-of-the-art in the chamber of commerce industry. With this application, and the addition of a research librarian who was tied into a number of on-line databases, MSCC's software had reached its ceiling.

As Wilson was developing the legislative service and other smaller applications for the public affairs and operations areas, Lassiter, frustrated with the lack of aggressiveness in determining alternatives for the MSCC, had begun seeking information on a number of software packages compatible with the Wang system. With annual dues approaching $2.3 million, and approximately 4,500 member firms, MSCC was among the largest statewide chambers in the country. By 1988 the staff had swelled to 42 and the financial reserve was nearly $2 million. Although Lassiter felt some satisfaction with the growth and financial strength, he was bothered with the lack of systems planning or vision as to how MSCC might develop a comprehensive plan to use information as a competitive advantage. Wilson, too, was beginning to recognize the enormous potential of information systems to an organization in the business of gathering, analyzing, and using information to affect legislative outcomes.

Catalyst for Change

By 1988, MSCC had reached a point where change had to occur (see Exhibit 2). Wallingford, at the urging of the board of directors, assigned Lassiter the additional areas of communications, graphic arts, and printing operations. Controller duties were assigned to Harry Taska, and Jeff Hedges, vice president of public finance, was assigned the responsibilities of computer operations. Wilson retained his public affairs activities and was asked to focus his effort in developing an important public affairs project.

Just after the staff changes took place, Kovecki confided to Lassiter that he was disillusioned over the changes in staff responsibility. He felt he should have been placed in the role of manager over the computer operation. Hedges, who had little computer background, was also placed in charge of the research area. Kovecki felt concerned that Hedges would have difficulty spending the time needed to properly manage the growing computer operations.

Although the changes took place in early 1988, Lassiter had anticipated the changes in late 1987. He had sent out requests for information to a number of firms servicing the software needs of organizations like MSCC. Primarily interested in sales and account tracking software, he focused on software systems from Cameo, MEI Colorado Association of Commerce and Industry, Connecticut Business and Industry Association, TelePro 2000, and Data Link. During this

time, Lassiter sent along the information to other key people but received little interest or response. Wilson was involved in his new project, Taska was learning his new duties as controller, and Hedges showed little interest and had little time to examine the computer activities.

In August 1988, Lassiter attended a national association meeting where a presentation of management software led to Lassiter's discovery of a small software firm called Unitrak, which had developed software that Lassiter was convinced would meet MSCC's needs. He based his assessment on the MSCC current and anticipated future divisional use of its computer capabilities (see Exhibit 3).

Planning the New Data Processing System

Lassiter had identified a number of areas where he felt a more powerful software system would provide MSCC with a number of efficiencies. He also identified several key factors for the automation he had in mind. These would allow for:

staff members to input member information into a notes field

territory managers to access all their account information from computer terminals on their desks

territory managers to request letters and attachments from the computer rather than the current paper system

marketing support to correct and process changes and requests from territory managers and staff instead of typing in the information from paper generated by staff

telemarketing scripts that would allow tree scripting based on various sales objections

reports menu to provide activity recaps and sales management reporting

a statistical inquiry feature that would provide quantitative analysis of sales activity figures.

The Unitrak system, Lassiter determined, not only met his needs but was also powerful and flexible enough to provide MSCC with the room to grow into the software over the next five to eight years. The software also appeared to be user friendly, which Lassiter believed was the key to freeing up Kovecki's time. Lassiter showed the software to Wilson, who believed that the current accounting system should be left intact but agreed that now was the time to move forward in finding a more powerful software solution to MSCC problems. One of Wilson's last acts as

EXHIBIT 2
MSCC Organization Structure

EXHIBIT 3
MSCC Software Needs

Information Systems Capabilities	Marketing Division	Operations Division	Public Affairs Division	Public Finance Division	Economic Development Division	Human Resources Division	Executive Division
Word Processing	X		X	X	X	X	X
Record Maintenance	X						
Legislative Services			X				
On-line Publications			X			X	
List Processing	X						
Label Generation	X						
Database Management	X		X			X	X
Financial Controls		X					
Conference Registration	X	X				X	X
Seminar Registration	X	X	X				X
Billings/Invoicing	X	X					
Publication Processing	X	X		X			
Data Search/Research					X		
Inventory Tracking	X	X					
Desktop Publishing	X						
Project Management	X	X	X		X		

controller was a significant upgrade in the Wang hardware system from a VS-80 to a VS-7110.

In October 1988, Lassiter contacted Greg Ozzuzo, president of the Unitrak Software Corporation, and invited him to MSCC for a demonstration. Wilson observed about 45 minutes of the three-hour demonstration and told Lassiter, "I'll support it if you want it. It will work for my project for public affairs, and free up Kovecki's time to get more involved in planning and systems development." Kovecki's comments were different. "Yeah, the software has its strengths and weaknesses and it probably would save some of my time. . . . But I don't like the idea of the staff creating their own lists and labels. I think I should keep doing that to control what's being used."

The Proposal

Lassiter, surprised by Wilson's and Kovecki's casual support, decided to move ahead quickly.

Lassiter developed simple flow charts (see Exhibits 4 and 5) that showed the hours it took to process under the current system versus the time it would take to process with the new software. Lassiter knew that the Executive Committee would require some justification to approve an off-budget expenditure. He had also done some calculations to show that if the software performed as he hoped, the territory managers would be able to increase production in terms of number of contacts to produce up to $100,000 in increased sales. Although Lassiter knew this was aggressive and very difficult to quantify, he wanted to be able to fall back on a less-than-six-month payback if challenged by the Executive Committee.

Lassiter knew that Unitrak would deal on the software. The software was new and Unitrak had sold it to only one other statewide chamber organization, the Northern State Chamber of Commerce. Jeff Fritzly, vice-president of marketing and development of the NSCC, said, "I looked at quite a few software packages as well as writing our own custom software, but our consultant chose Wang hardware and Unitrak software. We purchased the hardware and software from Unitrak Software Corporation. They have been very helpful and supportive of our needs."

A week prior to the Executive Committee meeting, Ozzuzo and Lassiter had agreed on a price. Lassiter was elated that the price was 60 percent less than NSCC had paid and felt this was another justification for approval of the project. Lassiter also made it a point to meet with both Wilson and Kovecki to keep them abreast of the negotiation and seek advice. He felt that by increasing the level of communication with Kovecki and Wilson, he would be able to garner their interest and support, which he felt was important to the success of the project.

When the Executive Committee met in November 1988, Lassiter explained that MSCC had reached its limits with the current software and an investment was needed to allow the MSCC to meet current and future opportunities for growth. During his presentation, Lassiter said:

While MSCC has made significant and appropriate investments in the hardware necessary for MSCC to increase its operational sophistication, we have not evaluated or made any

EXHIBIT 4
Marketing/Membership Sales Flow

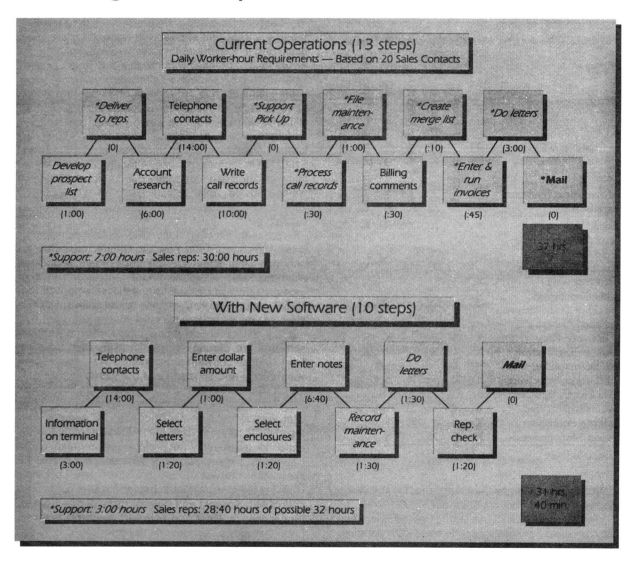

capital expenditures for over ten years in the software needed to drive the hardware. With the spectacular growth [Exhibit 6] we've enjoyed over the last six years, our requirements and demands on our software have increased dramatically. Without an immediate investment in increased software capability, MSCC's continued growth will be in jeopardy.

In response to challenges from the Executive Committee regarding what the new software would mean to the bottom line, Lassiter responded, "I believe we will see a 5 percent increase in sales and a 20 percent increase in productivity once the software is operational." With these assurances, the Executive Committee complimented Lassiter on his work and approved the purchase of the software.

EXHIBIT 5

Marketing/Membership Sales Flow

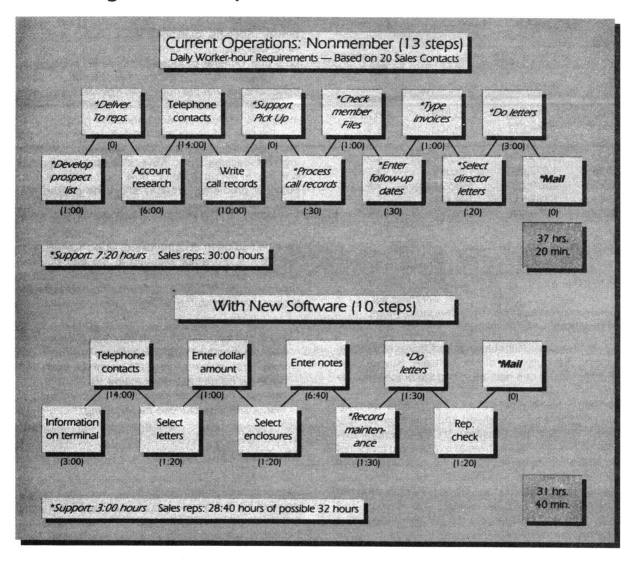

Current Operations: Nonmember (13 steps)
Daily Worker-hour Requirements — Based on 20 Sales Contacts

*Deliver To reps. (0) — Telephone contacts (14:00) — *Support Pick Up (0) — *Check member Files (1:00) — *Type invoices (1:00) — *Do letters (3:00)

*Develop prospect list (1:00) — Account research (6:00) — Write call records (10:00) — *Process call records (:30) — *Enter follow-up dates (:30) — *Select director letters (:20) — *Mail (0)

*Support: 7:20 hours   Sales reps: 30:00 hours

37 hrs. 20 min.

With New Software (10 steps)

Telephone contacts (14:00) — Enter dollar amount (1:00) — Enter notes (6:40) — *Do letters (1:30) — *Mail (0)

Information on terminal (3:00) — Select letters (1:20) — Select enclosures (1:20) — *Record maintenance (1:30) — Rep. check (1:20)

*Support: 3:00 hours   Sales reps: 28:40 hours of possible 32 hours

31 hrs. 40 min.

Implementation

Greg Ozzuzo of Unitrak was ecstatic over the order and promised unlimited support at no charge to get the software up and running. Kovecki had skimmed through the software documentation and agreed that the software would be a significant enhancement to MSCC. But Kovecki continued to express concern about staff members using the computers for anything other than word processing and inquiry. He said:

I know that Lassiter expects this new software to be user friendly, but I'm uncomfortable with how strongly he feels about training the staff to use as many of the features as possible. He thinks that training the staff on whatever they want to learn will make the MSCC more

EXHIBIT 6
....
MSCC Income/IS Expense/ IS Growth

Year	Income	IS Expenses	IS Expense as Percent of Total Income
1982	$ 790,596	$ 85,000	10.75%
1983	954,652	80,600	8.4
1984	1,298,196	88,800	6.8
1985	1,473,317	88,040	6.0
1986	1,572,000	90,090	5.7
1987	1,620,230	158,922	9.8
1988	1,905,952	104,418	5.5
1989	2,150,000	119,797	5.6

effective, but I disagree. We would be opening Pandora's box and I would lose control over what was going on. The last thing we need is for people to be getting into things they don't need to be in.

By February 1989 Lassiter had heard nothing regarding the purchase of the software. Kovecki told Lassiter that no one had approved the purchase. Lassiter then questioned Hedges, who responded that he had heard nothing more and had been busy with legislative problems. "Go ahead and purchase the software," Hedges told Lassiter. "It's your system anyway." Although Lassiter tried to explain that it was not his responsibility to implement the purchase or conversion, he felt the project would not move forward without his purchasing the software. After signing the purchase order, Lassiter handed it to Kovecki and said, "You and Hedges are the project managers. I shouldn't be involved at this point. It's up to you guys to complete the project."

Around March 30 Lassiter asked Kovecki how the project was proceeding. Kovecki stated that he was busy with a project of Wilson's and didn't have time to work on the new software. Lassiter went to Wilson to inquire about the anticipated length of the project Kovecki was working on and Wilson indicated it should be finished by mid-April.

Although Lassiter felt uncomfortable about pushing Hedges and Kovecki, he was beginning to feel that he would have to use his influence to get things

moving. As a result of Lassiter's intervention, the staff was informed that new software had been approved that would improve operations in several areas. Several staff members were upset that they had not been consulted or informed of the process before its approval. Specific questions were asked regarding word processing, conference and seminar registration, and general processing. Lassiter, anticipating that Kovecki had studied the documentation, asked Kovecki to answer the questions. Kovecki was unable to answer the questions and indicated he needed more time to study the documentation guide.

Lassiter set up an appointment for three days of training for Kovecki and himself. After a positive training visit, Lassiter asked Kovecki to spend half a day with him to set up a project flow chart and anticipate potential problems, but May and June passed with little forward progress on the conversion. Lassiter had told the Executive Committee that the project would be completed by the end of the first calendar quarter, yet little had been accomplished. Upon Kovecki's return from a two-week vacation at the end of June, Lassiter asked Wallingford to intervene and to strongly urge Hedges and Kovecki to complete the project. Lassiter stated:

It really bothered me that I had to go over Hedges' head but we were coming up on the seventh month of what should have been an easy three-month project. It's partly my fault because I didn't establish teamwork up front, nor did I make clear early in the process the responsibilities of those participating.

....
The Final Phase

With Hedges and Kovecki's agreement, Lassiter set up two days of staff training for the third week in July (see Exhibit 7). Kovecki had assured Lassiter that the system would be up by the last day of training so that the staff could immediately use the new system. Lassiter broke the training into major segments and had Kovecki set up training sites in two separate conference rooms for staff. Unitrak sent a two-person team that would act as project managers and trainers.

The training went well with the exception of the conference and seminar segment of the software. Significant complaints were brought up by the users that the new software segment representing this area was not as functional and user friendly as the old custom-written software. Although Lassiter suspected that a large part of the problem was that the new software

EXHIBIT 7
Staff Training

TO: **All Staff Members**
FROM: **Leon Lassiter**
DATE: **July 12, 1989**
RE: **Computer Training Schedule**

The following schedule has been designed to train all staff members on the new software system:

July 18, 1989

9:30–11:30 Marketing Support
Susan Devine
Ann Triplett
Dianne Hippelheuser

11:30–12:30 Lunch

12:30–2:30 Territory Managers
Mitch Guiet
Jim Wagner
Gayle Roberts
Dave Girton

2:30–3:00 Break

3:00–3:30 General Staff
1. _____
2. _____
3. _____
4. _____
5. _____

3:30–4:00 Staff
1. _____
2. _____
3. _____
4. _____
5. _____

4:00–4:30 Staff
1. _____
2. _____
3. _____
4. _____
5. _____

July 19, 1989

8:30–9:00 Staff
1. _____
2. _____
3. _____
4. _____
5. _____

9:30–10:30 Conferences
Joyce Jones
Kathy Neeb
Carolyn Hosford
Dianne Hippelheuser
Gini Raymond
Marge Price
Amy Kerrick

10:30–11:00 Staff
1. _____
2. _____
3. _____
4. _____
5. _____

11:00–11:30 Staff
1. _____
2. _____
3. _____
4. _____
5. _____

11:30–12:30 Lunch

12:30–1:30 Accounting
Darla Barnett

1:30–2:30 Labels/Lists
Joyce Jones
Dianne Hippelheuser
Gini Raymond
Jean Wiles
Carolyn Hosford
Amy Kerrick
Kathy Neeb
Kathleen Johnson

2:30–3:00 Break

3:00–5:00

OPEN

was different, he asked Unitrak to work with the users in adapting the Unitrak software to better meet their needs. Ozzuzo commented, "Because our software was relatively new to the market place, we were open to adjusting and changing certain aspects of the software without rewriting major portions. We feel we could learn a great deal from MSCC which would make our software more marketable."

On the final day of training, Lassiter told Kovecki to roll over the data in the old system to the new system. Kovecki told Lassiter that he was having a few problems and would conduct the rollover after work, and it would be ready first thing in the morning. The next morning Kovecki, in responding to Lassiter's query as to why the system was not up, said, "When I attempted the rollover last night, less than 25 percent of the data rolled over into the proper assignments. With no documentation to refer to, it will probably take me a week to work out the bugs. In the meantime, the new system won't work and the old system won't work."

Although the marketing division had anticipated the problems and had initiated a fall-back paper system, the rest of MSCC was basically inoperable. Requests for lists and labels for mailings could not be fulfilled. Word processing, payment and invoice posting, changes, list management, and so forth were all inoperable or partially inoperable. Unitrak was finding it difficult to help because Kovecki had forgotten

to order or install a new modem that would allow Unitrak experts access to the system.

Lassiter was finding it very difficult to gain information from Kovecki as to the progress and status of the system. Kovecki, frustrated with the problems he was having and irritated with the staff coming to him to ask for assistance, was going out of his way to avoid staff. Lassiter said, "I explained to Kovecki that I wasn't trying to grill him for information, but because the staff now considered me to be the project director, I needed information with which to make decisions affecting the work flow of the staff and determine what kind of help we could request from Unitrak." Although Lassiter knew that the staff felt he was responsible for the new software, he felt frustrated that there was little he could do in managing the conversion. Hedges remained aloof, and Kovecki did not report to Lassiter.

. . . .

The Future

It was in that situation Lassiter found himself sitting in his office at 10 PM six weeks later. Kovecki had promised that the system would be up on each of the last six Mondays. Each Monday brought disappointment and compounded frustration to each staff member. Lassiter knew that the two days of training had been wasted because the staff had long forgotten how to use the new system. Something had to be done—but what?

2

Applications of Information Technology

Information technology continues to have a major impact on organizations of all sizes, both public and private. This impact may be positive or negative, but it is almost always present. Businesses and other organizations are not the same as they were a decade ago. They are more complex but have fewer layers of management; they tend to offer more diversified products and services; they are increasingly international in scope; and they are heavily dependent on the accurate and timely flow of information. And this change in organizations is accelerating, not decelerating.

As a current or future manager, you must be aware of information technology and its potential impact on your job, your career, and your organization. You cannot afford to leave consideration of information technology solely to the information systems (IS) specialists. As a user-manager, you must perform many critical roles if you and your organization are to be successful: conceptualize ways in which information technology can be used to improve performance; serve as a consultant to the IS specialists who are developing or modifying applications for your organization; manage the change that is wrought by the information technology; use the technology applications and help maintain them; and evaluate the success of the applications.

Where do we start getting you ready for your new roles? We start with an awareness of where information technology is being used in a variety of organizations. Chapter 1 has already begun this process of building information technology awareness, and this chapter and Chapter 3 provide a systematic introduction to a wide variety of information technology applications. Most of the obvious applications are already in place. Nearly every organization uses a computer to handle its payroll, keep inventory records, and process accounts receivable and payable; almost every organization uses a telephone system and copying machines. But many applications remain to be discovered, most likely by managers like you.

APPLICATION AREAS

To consider a topic as broad as information technology applications, some type of framework is needed. As a first cut, we have divided applications into those which are *interorganizational systems* (and the largely overlapping category of strategic information systems) and those which are *intraorganizational systems*. The ASAP system at American Hospital Supply and the SABRE system at American Airlines (see Chapter 1) represent obvious examples of interorganizational systems—systems that span organizational boundaries. In the case of ASAP, SABRE, and other systems to be

Management Support Application Areas
  Transaction Processing Systems
  Decision Support Systems
  Group Support Systems
  Geographic Information Systems
  Executive Information Systems
Functional Support Application Areas
  Office Automation
  Factory Automation
  Computer-Integrated Manufacturing
Technology-Based Application Areas
  Artificial Intelligence
  Virtual Reality
Architecture-Based Application Areas
  Distributed Systems
  Client/Server Systems

FIGURE 2.1 Types of Application Systems

explored later, these interorganizational systems have had a major strategic impact; in such instances, the applications are also called strategic information systems. In our view, the idea of interorganizational systems (and strategic information systems) is so important to you as a manager that we have chosen to devote all of Chapter 3 to this topic.

To provide some structure to the broad range of intraorganizational systems, we have divided these applications into those that directly support some level of management (e.g., transaction processing systems and executive information systems); those that support a particular function within an organization (e.g., factory and office automation); those that are based on new technologies (e.g., expert systems and virtual reality); and those that are based on the information technology architecture of an organization (e.g., distributed processing). The architecture, which will be explored in depth in Chapter 12, describes the overall approach that will be used by the organization in making use of information technology.

Figure 2.1 lists these four major categories, along with application areas that fall within each category. This figure provides the primary framework for the consideration of information systems

applications in this chapter. Please note that the individual application areas are neither unique nor exhaustive. Some specific applications may fall into two or more application areas (such as transaction processing systems and client/server systems), while others may not fit in any of these categories. The application areas given in the figure, however, do encompass the overwhelming majority of specific applications, and the terminology employed generally represents standard usage.

CRITICAL CONCEPTS

Before we turn to specific examples of the various application areas, a number of important concepts that are intertwined throughout all the applications must be considered. An understanding of these concepts is a prerequisite to an understanding of the applications.

Batch Processing versus On-Line Processing

One of the fundamental distinctions for computer applications is **batch processing** versus **on-line processing**. In the early days of computers, all processing was batched. An organization accumulated a batch of transactions and then processed the entire batch at one time. For example, all inventory transactions (in and out) were recorded on paper during the day. After the close of business for the day, the transactions were keyed into some computer-readable medium, such as magnetic tape. The medium was then physically carried to the computer center, and the entire inventory was updated by processing that day's batch against the master inventory file on the computer. By the beginning of the next business day, the master inventory file was completely up to date and appropriate inventory reports were printed. Figure 2.2 represents this batch processing approach in a simplified form.

The major problem with batch processing is obvious—the time delays involved before the master file is updated. Only at the beginning of the business day, for example, will the master inventory file be up to date. At all other times, the company does not really know how many units of each product it has in stock.

As the technology improved, on-line processing was developed to avoid the time delays in batch processing. With a fully implemented on-line system, each transaction is entered directly into the computer when it occurs. For example, in an on-line inventory system a shipping clerk or sales clerk enters the receipt or sale of a product

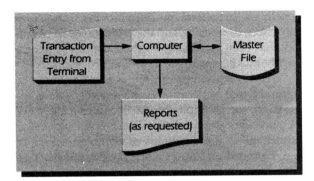

FIGURE 2.3 On-line Processing

into a terminal (perhaps a sophisticated cash register), which is connected by a telecommunications line to the main computer, which holds the inventory master file. As soon as the entry is completed, the computer updates the master file within a fraction of a second. Thus, the company always knows how many units of each product it has in stock. Figure 2.3 depicts such an **on-line system.**

A fully implemented on-line system is also called an **interactive system** because the user is directly interacting with the computer. The computer will provide a response to the user very quickly, usually within a second. Not all on-line systems, however, are interactive. Some systems, often called **in-line systems,** provide for on-line data entry, but the actual processing of the transaction is deferred until a batch of transactions has been accumulated.

A fully on-line system has the distinct advantage of timeliness. Why then aren't all present-day systems on-line? There are two reasons—cost and the existence of so-called natural batch applications. In most cases, batch systems are much less expensive to operate than their on-line counterparts. There are usually significant economies associated with batching both in the data-entry function and the transaction processing. But if the data-entry function can be accomplished when the original data are captured (such as with a sophisticated cash register), an on-line data entry/batch processing system may be less expensive than a straight batch system. The decision of batch versus on-line becomes a trade-off between cost and

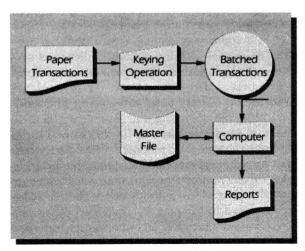

FIGURE 2.2 Batch Processing (simplified)

timeliness. In general, on-line costs per transaction have been decreasing and the importance of timeliness has been increasing, so there continues to be a steady movement toward on-line processing.

The exception to this movement has been the natural batch applications. The payroll of an organization, for example, might be run once a week or once every two weeks. There is no particular advantage to the timeliness of on-line processing; the organization knows when the payroll must be run. Even in this instance, there may be advantages to on-line data entry, to permit convenient changes in employees, exemptions, deductions, and wage rates. Thus, hybrid on-line data entry/batch processing systems will continue to exist.

Functional Information Systems

Instead of considering applications within the four major categories of Figure 2.1, it is possible to create a framework strictly on the basis of the primary business functions of the organization—a **functional information systems** framework. For example, consider an organization in which the primary business functions are production, marketing, accounting, personnel, and engineering. Applications may then be categorized as part of the production information system, or part of the marketing information system, or part of the accounting information system, and so on. This functional approach is simply an alternative way of classifying applications.

In this alternative view, the overall IS is composed of multiple subsystems, each providing information for various tasks within the function. In turn, each functional subsystem consists of a possibly interrelated series of subsubsystems. For example, the production information system is likely to include interrelated subsystems for sales forecasting, production planning, production scheduling, material requirements planning, capacity requirements planning, personnel requirements planning, materials purchasing, and inventory. The marketing information system may include subsystems for promotion and advertising, new product development, sales forecasting (hopefully tied into the production sales forecasting subsys-

tem), product planning, product pricing, market research, and sales information. The accounting information system, which is generally the oldest and most fully developed functional system, is likely to include computerized versions of the entire journal and ledger system, plus a cost or responsibility accounting system and a financial reporting system for preparing reports for stockholders and other external groups.

Vertical Integration of Systems

Another important characteristic of some systems is that they operate across levels of the organization or, in some instances, across independent firms occupying different levels in an industry hierarchy, such as an automobile manufacturer and the associated independent dealers. (More on these interorganizational systems will be covered in Chapter 3.) Such a system that serves more than one vertical level in an organization or an industry is called a **vertically integrated information system**. For example, in a single firm, a vertically integrated sales information system may capture the initial sales data and produce invoices (acting as a transaction processing system), summarize these data on a weekly basis for use by middle managers in tracking slow- and fast-selling items as well as productive and unproductive salespeople (acting as a decision support system), and further analyze this data for long-term trends for use by top managers in determining strategic directions (acting as an executive information system).

In a somewhat similar way, a national fast-food chain may develop a sales information system with modules both for operating units (company stores and franchises) and for the national organization. Thus, data collected at the store level using the operating unit module are already in the appropriate form to be processed by the national organization module. These basic data may be either transmitted via telecommunication lines to the national organization each night or mailed each week on a floppy disk. (These choices are discussed in Chapter 6.) Therefore, the extent of vertical integration is an important characteristic of applications.

Value of Information

In the information technology area, **information** is defined as data (usually processed data) that are useful to a decision-maker. In theory, therefore, the value of a particular piece of information is the net benefits obtained in a decision situation (total benefits minus total costs) when the information is known, less the net benefits that would have been obtained in the same decision situation without the information. In practice computing this **value of information** is very difficult if not impossible. The organization rarely knows all the costs and benefits involved before a decision is made, and it often does not know them after a decision is made.

It is useful to view the value of information as consisting of two parts—a tangible part and an intangible part. The tangible portion can be quantified, using historical experience and educated guesses. It is usually possible to estimate the reduction (or increase) in manpower required to operate a new system, to estimate the computer time required to run the system, and to estimate the reduced inventory costs resulting from the new system. The intangible portion, however, defies estimation. It is difficult to estimate the value of better decisions made because the manager has better information or to estimate the value of improved customer goodwill because backorders will be reduced with the new system. Historically, the tangible portion of the value of information has been used to justify most transaction processing systems. As information technology moves into new arenas, however, such as decision support systems and artificial intelligence, it will become increasingly necessary for organizations to justify new applications based on both the tangible and the intangible portions of the value of information. We will revisit the issue of tangible and intangible costs and benefits in Chapter 8.

TRANSACTION PROCESSING SYSTEMS
....

Let us begin our survey of applications with the "granddaddy" applications, the ones that started it all—**transaction processing systems.** These sys-

tems process the thousands of transactions that occur every day in most organizations, including sales; payments made and received; inventory shipped and received; hiring, firing, and paying employees; and paying a dividend. In addition to producing the documents and updated records that result from the transaction processing (such as invoices, checks, and orders), these systems produce a variety of summarized reports that are useful for upper levels of management.

Transaction processing systems are life-or-death systems for "paperwork" organizations, such as banks and insurance companies, and critical systems for the overwhelming majority of medium and large organizations. These were the first computerized systems, and they still use the majority of computing time in most organizations. For the most part, these transaction processing systems were and are justified by means of traditional cost-benefit analysis. These systems are able to process the transactions more rapidly and more economically (and certainly more accurately) than by a manual (human) system.

As a manager, you do not need to know the details of these systems. You only need to know the general nature and importance of such systems and that they are more complex than an outsider might imagine. Therefore, we will limit our discussion to two representative transaction processing systems—payroll and order entry.

Payroll System

The first impression of a payroll system is that it seems fairly simple. Operators input the number of hours worked for each employee (using either batch or on-line data entry), and the system batch processes these transactions to produce payroll checks. While this one-sentence description is correct, it represents only the tip of the iceberg because it involves only about 10 percent of the system. The payroll processing subsystem must keep year-to-date totals of gross income, social security income, individual deductions, various categories of taxes, and net income; it must incorporate the ability to compute federal, state, and local taxes as well as social security contributions; and it must handle both mandatory and voluntary deductions.

What other subsystems are necessary? Figure 2.4 lists the primary subsystems in most payroll systems and what these subsystems must accomplish. Thus, the payroll system is both commonplace and complex. The payroll system is usually easy to justify on a cost-benefit basis because it would take an incredible number of payroll clerks to turn out a modern payroll and keep all the associated records.

Order Entry System

Today's order entry systems may be either batch or on-line, but the movement to on-line systems is so strong that we will consider only this type of system. The basic idea behind an order entry system is simple. As orders are received (whether in person, by mail, or by telephone), the sales representative enters the information into the computer. This data entry may be via a terminal or microcomputer on the person's desk, or it may be through a point-of-sale transaction recording system (a sophisticated cash register that doubles as a

terminal). The computer then updates the appropriate files and prints an invoice, either at the point-of-sale terminal, the sales representative's desk, or in the computer center.

Once again, this basic idea tells only a small part of the story. Figure 2.5 provides a more complete version and shows how each transaction (each sale) interacts with as many as six different files on the computer system. In addition to the invoice itself, more than a dozen additional types of computer output may be generated. For example, the computer will check the credit status of the customer and may reject the sale if the credit limit would be exceeded. If the item ordered is in stock,

---

Subsystems to accomplish:
  Payroll processing, including updating year-to-date master file
  Capture hours-worked data
  Add/delete employees
  Change deduction information for employees
  Change wage rates and salaries
  Creation of initial year-to-date master file
  Calculate and print payroll totals for pay period, quarter, and year
  Calculate and print tax reports for pay period, quarter, and year
  Calculate and print deduction reports for pay period, quarter, and year
  Calculate and print W-2 forms at end of year
  Interface with human resources information system
  Interface with budget information system

FIGURE 2.4 Components of a Payroll System

ANDERSEN CONSULTING'S SMART STORE 2000

Andersen Consulting has created a prototype of the checkout system (transaction processing system) for tomorrow's retail store through its SMART Store 2000. The SMART (Super Marketing through Applied Retail Technology) Store has been set up on one floor of an Andersen facility to serve as a demonstration and test laboratory for new hardware, software, and systems. It features approximately 75 pieces of technology from about 30 vendors.

At the SMART Store, when an item is scanned by the checkout counter's bar code reader, the data are not only used in computing the bill, but also become a data point in several interconnected data systems: an inventory tracking database, an electronic demographic profile of store patrons, and an exception reporting system that alerts the store manager to buy more of certain items. From the basic checkout data, a "store manager's workbench" module produces reports on operating results, customer traffic patterns, and personnel; a "merchandising workbench" coordinates the store's inventory based on actual sales and customer data; and a "marketing workbench" analyzes sales information from the store in contrast to external demographic data to develop an appropriate, profit-maximizing product mix for the store.

(Adapted from Booker, 1989)

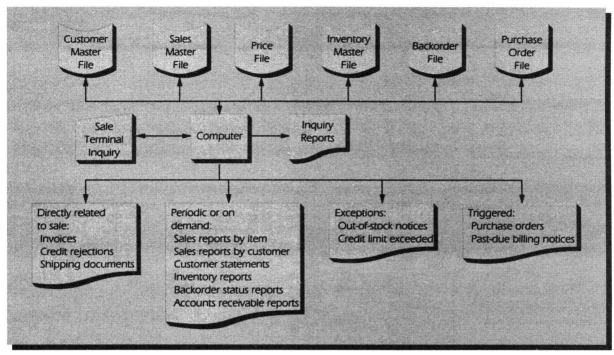

FIGURE 2.5 On-line Order Entry System

a multipart shipping document is printed; if it is not in stock, a message is sent (via the terminal) to the customer to ask if he wants to backorder the item. Periodically or on demand, the order entry system will print out sales reports organized by item or by customer, customer statements, inventory reports, backorder status reports, and accounts receivable reports. The system will also generate reports when exception conditions occur, such as when an item is out of stock or a customer attempts to exceed the established credit limit. In these cases, management action may be necessary. The order entry system may automatically print out purchase orders when an item is out of stock; it may also print out past-due billing notices for customers. A primary advantage of such an on-line system is that inquiries will be answered in a few seconds.

The American Hospital Supply ASAP system (and other order entry systems that have emulated it) carries this on-line approach one major step further. The order entry terminal is placed on the

customers' premises, and customers place orders themselves. The convenience of this type of interorganizational order entry system has been a major strategic plus.

DECISION SUPPORT SYSTEMS

A **decision support system** (DSS) is a computer-based system, almost always interactive, designed to assist a manager (or another decision-maker) in making decisions. A DSS incorporates both data and models to help a decision-maker solve a problem, especially an unstructured problem. The data would often be extracted from a transaction processing system, but that is not always the case. The model may be simple (e.g., a profit-and-loss model to calculate profit given certain assumptions) or complex (e.g., an optimization model to suggest loadings for each machine in a job shop). DSSs (and many of the systems discussed in the

A POTPOURRI OF DSS EXAMPLES

Virtually every issue of *Interfaces* contains a discussion of one or more new DSSs. To illustrate, we briefly describe three quite different decision support systems presented in the March–April 1992 issue of *Interfaces*.

The lead-off article, "Scheduling Ambulances" (Aubin), describes a DSS built by Urgences Sante, the public agency responsible for coordinating ambulances in the Montreal area. This DSS consists of two major components, one for the long-term scheduling of ambulances and the second for the scheduling of technicians. Urgences Sante does not own the ambulances but rents them from fifteen private owners. The DSS is run on a quarterly basis. Based on the demand forecast for the quarter, the DSS uses mathematical programming to determine the number of required vehicles for each hour of a typical week and then equitably distributes the required coverage among the fifteen firms. The second component of the DSS then builds individual schedules for the technicians, based largely on rules set by the union contract.

Shannon and Minch describe the development of a DSS for evaluating motor vehicle legislation in the state of Idaho. The DSS, which relies on extensive data and numerous statistical models, permits users to evaluate the impact of changes in fixed vehicle registration fees and weight-distance taxes on state revenue collections and trucking industry costs. The system, which was used in 1987 and again in 1989–90, allowed interested government officials and industry groups to predict the effects of particular taxation proposals. Shannon and Minch report that, "Partially because of information provided by the system, the state of Idaho avoided what could have been a multi-million dollar adverse economic impact due to proposed legislation affecting the structure of motor vehicle taxation."

The third example falls in the marketing area, or media planning to be precise (Rathnam et al.). Media planning consists of choosing from the advertising vehicles available and deciding on the number of insertions to place in each vehicle. This DSS uses a multiphase mathematical programming approach to solve the media planning problem for print media. Using the DSS for a large advertising agency in India resulted in a cost saving of 20 to 30 percent over the previous trial-and-error methods.

following sections) are rarely justified by a traditional cost-benefit approach; for these systems, it is necessary to incorporate the intangible benefits into the analysis to arrive at a justification.

One example of a DSS driven by transactions data is a police-beat allocation system used by a California city. This system enables a police officer to display a map outline and call up data by geographic zone, which shows police calls for service, types of service, and service times. The interactive graphics capability of the system permits the officer to manipulate the maps, zones, and data to consider a variety of police-beat alternatives quickly and easily and takes maximum advantage of the officer's judgment.

Other DSS examples include an interactive system for capacity planning and production scheduling in a large paper company. This system employs detailed historical data and forecasting and scheduling models to simulate overall performance of the company under differing planning assumptions. A major oil company developed a DSS to support capital investment decision-making. This system incorporates various financial routines and models for generating future plans; these plans are then displayed in tabular or graphic form to aid in decision-making.

All the DSS examples cited are more properly called **specific DSS**. These are the actual applications that assist in the decision-making process. In contrast, a **decision support system generator** is a system that provides a set of capabilities to build a specific DSS quickly and easily (Sprague and Carlson, 1982). The DSS generator is a package of computer programs (software) designed to be run on a particular computer system. For example, the Interactive Financial Planning System (IFPS), produced by Execucom Systems, is a financial-modeling language that permits the construction of specific financial models for use in decision-making.

Thus, IFPS is a DSS generator, while an IFPS model produced to represent a particular division of a company is a specific DSS.

Group Support Systems

Group support systems (GSSs) are an important variant of DSSs in which the system is designed to support a group rather than an individual. These systems, sometimes called group decision support systems (GDSSs) or electronic meeting systems (EMSs), strive to take advantage of the power of a group to make better decisions than individuals acting alone. Managers spend a significant portion of their time in group activity (meetings, committees, conferences); in fact, some researchers have estimated that middle managers spend 35 percent of their work week in meetings and that top managers spend 50 to 80 percent of their time in meetings. GSSs represent an attempt to make these group sessions more productive.

GroupSystems, developed at the University of Arizona (and now marketed by Ventana Corporation), is an excellent example of GSS software (Nunamaker et al., 1989; Nunamaker et al., 1991). GroupSystems is in use in forty-five internal IBM sites as well as at least twelve other corporations and twenty-two universities. In a typical implementation, a computer-supported meeting room is set up containing a microcomputer for each participant, all linked by a local area network (see Chapter 6). A large public screen facilitates common viewing of information when this is desired. GroupSystems, which is installed on each machine in the network, provides computerized support for idea generation (e.g., brainstorming), organizing ideas, prioritizing (e.g., voting), and policy development (e.g., stakeholder identification).

Each participant in a group session (for example, a brainstorming session) has the opportunity to provide input anonymously and simultaneously via the microcomputer keyboard. This should encourage creative thinking, since no one can be ridiculed for a "stupid idea." Each idea or comment is evaluated on its own merits rather than in light of the person who offered it. Similarly, in a voting session the participants will not be swayed by how someone else votes. Thus, a GSS such as GroupSystems should generate more high-

---

GSS WORKS FOR MARRIOTT, BOEING

"We're having the quietest, least stressful, most productive meetings you've ever seen," says Carl DiPietro, vice president human resources at Marriott Corp.'s architecture and construction division. Marriott, which uses a program called VisionQuest from Collaborative Technologies Corp., Austin, Texas, finished a computerized meeting room last fall. In two months, 1,000 people used the room to generate and organize 10,000 ideas, he says. Mr. DiPietro and his associates estimate traditional meetings would have taken nine to 12 times longer to accomplish as much.

Boeing Co. analyzed 64 groups using a meeting room equipped with personal computers and TeamFocus software sold by International Business Machines Corp. It found that total time in meetings was cut 71%. The calendar time required for team projects involving meetings was cut a whopping 91%.

(Bulkeley, 1992)

---

quality ideas and decisions that truly represent the group.

Recent work in the GSS area has moved beyond support of the traditional group session as described above. The new focus is to support the work team in all its endeavors, whether the team is operating in a same time–same place traditional meeting or in a different time–different place mode.

GEOGRAPHIC INFORMATION SYSTEMS

A **geographic information system** (GIS) is a computer-based system designed to collect, store, retrieve, manipulate, and display spatial data. In simpler terms, a GIS links data to maps so that the spatial characteristics of the data can be easily comprehended. GISs have often been used as DSSs to perform such tasks as fast-food restaurant site selection and the establishment of routes for delivery people.

A GIS usually includes either a microcomputer or a workstation (more will be said about this in Chapter 4, but a workstation is considerably more powerful—and more expensive—than a microcomputer), a mouse for interacting with the system, a digitizing tablet for translating a paper map to computer-understandable form, a plotter for producing maps, a large computer storage device, and GIS software. The GIS software permits maps to be stored in digitized form, and then it links a wide variety of other data to the maps.

The police-beat allocation system described in the DSS section is an example of a GIS. Arby's, the roast beef fast-food chain, uses a GIS to locate new stores. Chemical Bank uses a GIS to ensure that it lends money equitably to both high-income and low-income neighborhoods. A GIS package is available for insurance companies to enable them to assess the risks for homeowner insurance more efficiently and equitably. To use this package, the underwriter enters the home address into the computer. The GIS searches its digitized city street maps to locate the address, then computes the distance from the address to the nearest fire hydrant, police station, and body of water to provide an almost-instant risk assessment.

The key to these examples is the existence of a digitized map and then the ability to link other data—police call statistics, projected fast-food expenditures, and income, for example—to the map. Terance Moloney, a product manager at Tydac Technologies Corporation, which produces GIS software, says, "In mapping there are three basic axes, X for latitude, Y for longitude, and Z for elevation. Substitute income or some other demographic measure for elevation, and you have a commercial GIS" (Churbuck, 1992). Figure 2.6 illustrates the use of the Tydac software to show the impact a new competitor will have on an existing store's customers.

The GIS examples given could be viewed as spatially based DSSs. Without a doubt, the GIS and DSS categories have considerable overlap. GISs, however, can also be used in other application areas, such as executive information systems to display summarized data (e.g., sales by region) in a more easily understandable form. Because of this wider role for GISs, and because of their rapidly growing popularity, we have elected to consider GISs as a separate category of applications.

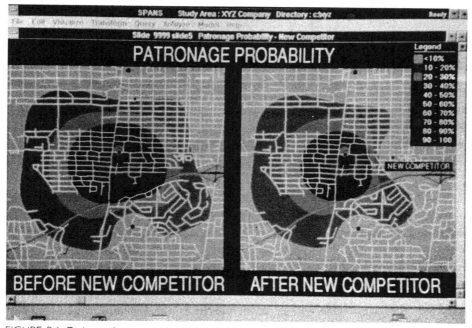

FIGURE 2.6 Tydac software used to visualize the impact of a new competitor. (Courtesy of Intera Tydac Technologies, Inc.)

EXECUTIVE INFORMATION SYSTEMS

The key concept behind an **executive information system** (EIS) is that such a system delivers current information about business conditions directly to senior executives. An EIS is designed to be used directly by top managers without the assistance of intermediaries. An EIS uses state-of-the-art graphics, communications, and data storage methods to provide the executive easy on-line access to current information about the status of the organization.

Dating back only to the late 1980s in most cases, EISs represent the first real attempt to deliver relevant information to top management. EISs employ transactions data that have been fil-

tered and summarized into a form useful for the top executives in the organization. A successful EIS, however, also requires the use of large quantities of soft data, such as assessments, rumors, opinions, and ideas. Comshare, Inc., the vendor of Commander EIS, a leading commercial product, defines an EIS as "a hands-on tool which focuses, filters, and organizes an executive's information so he or she can make more effective use of it."

Comshare's Commander EIS permits customization of a number of easy-to-use and easy-to-interpret displays to present key information to top managers. Examples of Commander EIS displays are shown in Figure 2.7. Other leading commercial EIS products include Command Center from Pilot Executive Software, Executive Edge

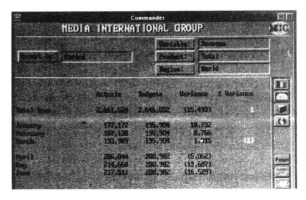

FIGURE 2.7 Comshare's Commander Executive Information System Displays. (Screens courtesy of Comshare, Inc. © 1993)

from Execucom, and Executive Decisions from IBM.

In 1988 an authority on EISs indicated that he was not aware of any successful EIS that had been cost justified, nor was he aware of any successful EIS that had been developed by the IS organization. Six years later, it is doubtful that those particular statements are still true, but they still point out some important truths about EISs. An EIS requires a sponsor or champion who is highly placed in the organization, preferably the president or CEO. This sponsor must decide that the organization needs the EIS and that cost justification is not required. A special staff must then be created to develop the EIS, with that staff reporting to the sponsor or another top executive. The special staff will rely on the IS organization for technical support—and may include several IS specialists on loan from the IS organization—but the staff members themselves must analyze the information requirements of the executives who will use the system.

Perhaps the most talked-about EIS developed to date is the management information and decision support (MIDS) system at the Lockheed-Georgia Company (Houdeshel and Watson, 1987). The sponsor for MIDS was the Lockheed-Georgia president, and a special staff reporting to the vice president of finance developed the system. An evolutionary approach was used in developing MIDS, with only a limited number of displays developed initially for a limited number of executives. (A display might show, for example, prospective customers for a particular type of aircraft or might graphically depict both forecast and actual sales over the past year.)

Over time, more displays were developed and more executives added to the system. The initial version of MIDS in 1979 had only thirty-one displays developed for fewer than a dozen senior executives. By 1985, 710 displays had been developed and the system was being used by thirty senior executives and forty operating managers, and the mean number of displays viewed per user per day was up to 5.5. Many factors had to come together for MIDS to be successful, but perhaps the most important was that the system delivered

the information (based on both hard and soft data) that senior executives needed for them and their company to be successful. The system provided information relevant to the critical success factors of top management.

More recently, Phillips Petroleum, a $31 billion company, has installed a highly successful EIS that may well be part of the reason for its recent turnaround (Goff, 1989). The champion of the EIS at Phillips was the executive vice president, Bob Wallace, who felt the future of the company depended on the key people having all the information they needed—delivered in an effective format—all the time. Wallace handpicked a team to develop the system and set it up outside the IS organization. EISs are also being used successfully in other large companies such as Analog Devices,

---

THE NEW ROLE FOR EIS

The purpose of an EIS is to allow nontechnical executives to access data of interest, easily create useful information from it, package the results in a clear form, then deliver it to PC [personal computer] monitors and printers. This report [from which this quotation was taken] analyzes the results of our research into how EIS are now being designed and used. We have found that many EIS today are effectively meeting their stated purpose, and are well-accepted tools for access to critical information, particularly in the areas of customer service and competitive action.

EIS were formerly considered to be just for the two top executive levels, but that caused many problems of data disparity between the layers of management. The most useful data are generated under the control of lower managers, dealing with customers, and they must be cognizant of what is being reported higher up. Most successful EIS today are available in consistent detail to all levels in an organization, and sometimes even to managers in customer and supplier organizations, depending upon what data is in the system.

*(I/S Analyzer,
January 1992)*

Inc., Dun & Bradstreet Software, Coca-Cola Company, Fisher-Price, Conoco, Inc., and CIGNA Corporation.

OFFICE AUTOMATION
. . . .

We now turn from applications that directly support some level of management to those that support a particular function within an organization (see Figure 2.1). We start with **office automation**, which involves a set of office-related functions that may or may not be integrated into a single system. The most common functions are electronic mail, word processing, and copying, with document preparation, document storage and imaging, voice mail, desktop publishing, and electronic calendaring also receiving a great deal of attention.

Trade journals and popular magazines have been talking about the "office of the future" for years, but in many organizations management has become so disillusioned with office automation that they are not sure the "future" will ever arrive. Nevertheless, office technology has taken major strides since World War II. Document preparation has moved from manual typewriters, to electric typewriters with a moving carriage, to IBM Selectric typewriters with the "golf ball" typing elements, to memory typewriters, to expensive terminals connected to a minicomputer, to stand-alone microcomputers, and now to microcomputers linked via a local area network (LAN). Copying has moved from mimeograph machines to fast photocopiers and facsimile machines. The telephone has moved from a simple instrument with no dial or keys to a rotary dial telephone, then from a simple touch-tone telephone to a versatile touch-tone instrument with such features as automatic redial, call forwarding, call waiting, and multiparty calling. For the most part, however, all of these devices still do not talk to each other. The office of the future, if it ever arrives, will have these devices and others connected via an integrated voice/data/image network as shown in

Figure 2.8. In our discussion of the components of this figure, we will mention those connections that exist today.

Workstations and Word Processing

Professional/executive workstations and secretarial workstations will be the most numerous items in a fully automated office. Because of their relatively low cost and high power, and because extensive software has been developed for these machines, the microcomputer will be the predominant workstation for both categories of use. As of this writing, the IBM Personal System/2 and its clones are the standard office workstations, with the Apple Macintosh also an important contender.

A number of excellent and inexpensive word-processing packages have been developed for microcomputers, including WordPerfect, Microsoft Word, AmiPro (from Lotus), and WordStar. Coupled with an inexpensive dot-matrix printer (near-letter quality for less than $300) or a somewhat more expensive laser printer ($1,000–$2,000), the microcomputer makes an excellent document preparation device. Most organizations are not willing to put a letter-quality printer with each microcomputer, so some form of communication is necessary between the workstation where the document is created and a workstation with a letter-quality printer. At present, that communication often consists of hand-carrying a floppy disk from one microcomputer to another (jokingly referred to as "sneakernet"). An increasing number of LANs are being installed in today's offices so that a document can be electronically sent from the preparing workstation to the letter-quality printer, as depicted in Figure 2.8.

Integrated Office Systems

If the various workstations are linked together, either by a LAN or by attaching them directly to a minicomputer or mainframe computer (distinctions that will be explored in Chapters 4 and 6), a number of other office automation features become possible. Perhaps the most important of these features is electronic mail. The primary

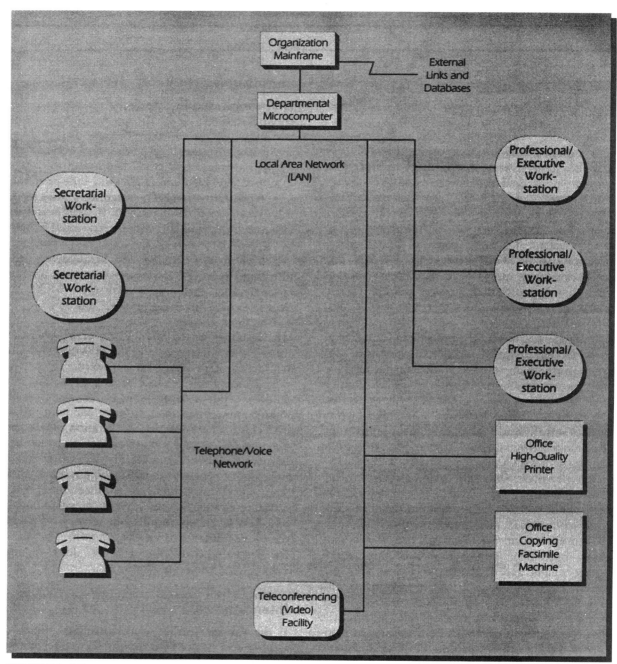

FIGURE 2.8 Office of the Future Network

mainframe and minicomputer vendors have developed electronic mail systems, and they are usually quite easy to use. More recently, a number of excellent electronic mail packages have been developed for use with LANs.

For both mainframes/minicomputers and LANs, electronic mail is sometimes packaged with other related features to create a type of total office system. Examples are Digital Equipment's ALL-IN-ONE and IBM's OfficeVision and PROFS (Professional Office System) for larger machines, and WordPerfect Office and Lotus Notes for

LANs. For the mainframe/minicomputer environment, users are encouraged to log their workstations into the integrated office system anytime they are in the office. The integrated office system is actually running on the mainframe or minicomputer, with the workstation being used as a terminal. The main menu usually includes a calendar with the current date highlighted, a clock, a message area where other users can directly communicate with this workstation, and a menu of other choices. The main menu for the PROFS system from IBM is shown in Figure 2.9. For a LAN

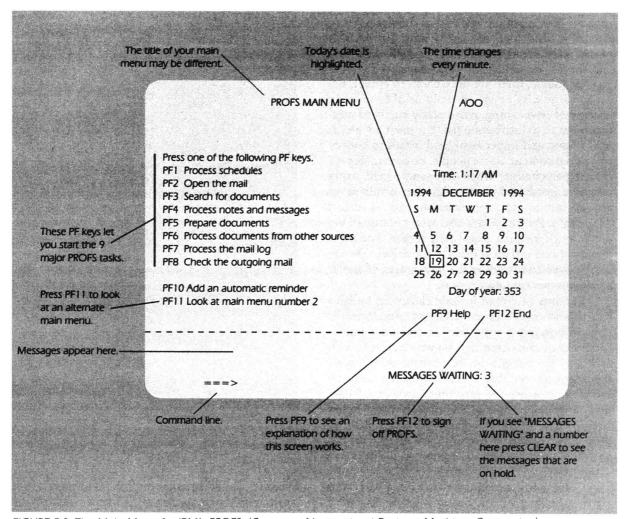

FIGURE 2.9 The Main Menu for IBM's PROFS. (Courtesy of International Business Machines Corporation)

42

environment, the integrated office system can also be active all of the time when users are in their offices, but the system is now actually running on the microcomputer (as well as on a server—often a high-end microcomputer—elsewhere on the LAN).

Electronic Mail

Electronic mail systems (**e-mail**) permit rapid but asynchronous communication between workstations—no more telephone tag. Most systems incorporate such features as sending a note to a distribution list, resending a note to someone else with an appended message, replying to a note without reentering the address, and filing notes in electronic file folders for later recall. The authors of this book use electronic mail many times a day, and we feel we could not do without it.

Of course, there are drawbacks to e-mail. Because it is so easy to use, the volume of e-mail may become overwhelming, particularly standard messages sent to a distribution list. For most people, e-mail is cold and impersonal, and it fails to convey emotional content. Some people, however, seem to change personalities when they send e-mail, using offensive words and phrases that they would never use in face-to-face conversation (this is called "flaming"). Privacy issues also arise because of the difficulty of keeping passwords secure. For most organizations and most users, these drawbacks are totally overshadowed by the advantages of rapid, asynchronous communication.

Variants of e-mail include electronic bulletin boards and computer conferencing. An electronic bulletin board is a repository (a disk on a microcomputer or minicomputer) on which anyone with access to the bulletin board (anyone who knows the telephone number or the computer account) can post messages and read other messages. Bulletin boards can be operated within an organization (employing the usual communication links), or they may require a long-distance telephone call to hook your workstation into someone else's computer.

Computer conferencing works in a way similar to a bulletin board, but it is set up around a particular topic. For example, a computer conference might be set up by a professional society to

E-MAIL SMILEYS FOR ALL OCCASIONS

As E-mail has spread throughout corporate America and around the world, new conventions for communication have been created. Perhaps the most humorous of these conventions is the digital smiley face, and the numerous variations that have evolved from the original smiley. When you tilt your head to the left and use your imagination, the original digital smiley :-) looks like a little face with a colon for eyes and a hypen for a nose. The use of this digital smiley at the end of an E-mail message means something like "just kidding," as in the following message copied from an electronic bulletin board. The subject is uncontrollable scalp-flaking, and one writer is proposing a new remedy: "I find that rinsing my scalp with vinegar will cut down on it for a while, if you don't mind smelling like a salad :-)"

The variants are even more fun. Here are some of them and their interpretations:

```
:-(            I'm unhappy
:-D            I'm laughing
B-)            I'm cool
:*)            I'm drunk
{(:-)          I have a toupee
}(:-(          I have a toupee
               and it's windy
:-&            I'm talking out
               of both sides
               of my mouth
[:-)           I'm wearing a
               Walkman
d:-)           I'm a baseball
               player
:-?            I'm smoking a
               pipe
<<<<(:-)       I'm a hat
               salesman
':-)           I accidentally
               shaved off one
               eyebrow
```

Try creating your own smileys, and spice up your own E-mail messages!

(Adapted from Miller, 1992)

consider the advantages and disadvantages of the various microcomputer spreadsheet packages on the market. The announcement of the topic and the telephone number of the computer on which the conference will be held are published in the society's newsletter. Anyone can participate in the conference by calling up, entering an opinion of Lotus 1-2-3 or Quattro Pro or Microsoft Excel, and reading the opinions of other participants. Both bulletin boards and computer conferencing tend to be entertaining and educational.

PROFS and the other integrated systems also provide a calendaring function. Individuals can keep their daily appointment calendars on the system and, if they wish, allow other system users to access the calendar. Calendars can also be kept for scheduling conference rooms or departmental events. The integrated systems also provide a document-preparation facility (a word processor) and have the ability to distribute these documents electronically. The mainframe/minicomputer-based integrated word processors, however, are not usually as easy to use as the microcomputer-based packages mentioned above, and it is often difficult (or impossible) to print the resulting documents on a printer connected to the microcomputer. Thus, these integrated word processors are often of little use. In contrast, the LAN-based systems are designed to work closely with the same vendor's word processing package.

Future Developments

Today, the telephone/voice network in most companies is totally independent of the computer/data network. In the office of the not-so-distant future, these networks will be combined into one integrated office network. A bit further in the future, the functions of today's telephones are likely to be subsumed by the workstation itself, that is, the workstation will include a voice receiver and a voice speaker, as well as appropriate connections to the office and external integrated networks.

Most offices today have facsimile machines to receive electronically transmitted documents and produce a hard copy version. Conventional copying machines are, however, still stand-alone devices. At some point in the future, the copying machine will be incorporated into the office network and will absorb the function of the facsimile device. Single or multiple copies of a document may be printed either at the copying machine,

---

LAW FIRM USES FREESTYLE

Steel Hector & Davis, one of Florida's largest law firms, has achieved an efficiency breakthrough by using Freestyle, an office imaging system developed and sold by Wang Laboratories. Freestyle is an advanced office automation system for creating, annotating, and sending document images over an office network. Users have told Pat Cash, MIS director for the law firm, that they gain at least half an hour daily by using Freestyle. Potentially, this would add up to a savings for the firm of $1.2 million per year based on its average billing rate.

Freestyle begins with a document preparation facility, but it is much more than that. First, the document can be electronically distributed to an appropriate distribution list. Then recipients of the document (or the originator) can annotate the document either by means of a voice mail message accompanying the document or by handwritten comments. In the latter case, the comments are scanned and electronically sent along with the document. One attorney with the firm indicated that Freestyle "saves steps" and "speeds up deal making."

(Adapted from Johnson, 1989)

---

from a workstation in the same office or from a remote site.

Document storage is another evolving area of office automation. It is not unusual today for organizations to store some of their business documents on-line to the computer, often using magnetic or optical disk technology (to be discussed in Chapter 4). More and more of these documents will be stored on-line, particularly with the growing use of imaging technology. With imaging, any type of paper document—including reports, graphs, and photographs—can be read by a digital scanner and translated into digital form so that it can be stored in the computer system. Later this process can be reversed, so that the digitized image stored in the computer system can be printed on paper, displayed on a video display unit, or transmitted to another workstation.

A facility that only a few organizations possess today—a video teleconferencing facility—is shown at the bottom of Figure 2.8. Such facilities (in multiple locations) would permit face-to-face, or more properly image-to-image, meetings and conferences to take place without the need for costly and time-consuming travel. By tying the teleconferencing facility into the integrated office network, computer-generated reports and graphics could also be shared during the conferences. Such teleconferencing facilities are quite expensive today, but the prices are going down and the capabilities of such systems are going up. For example, a roll-about videoconferencing system from PictureTel Corporation, one of the leaders in this area, runs from $20,000 to $50,000 per unit. At present, virtually all videoconferencing takes place in special conference rooms, but this barrier is likely to fall soon. The goal is to permit videoconferencing from the desktops of individuals, utilizing the same wiring connections shown in Figure 2.8 (Hindus, 1992).

The ideal office network shown in Figure 2.8 does not exist. Offices have the secretarial and professional/executive workstations in ever-increasing numbers, and links of some type are being created between these machines in most offices. Historically, the links were most often directly to a mainframe or minicomputer, but LANs are gaining rapidly in popularity as organizations learn more about them. There are still problems in transferring data in the most convenient form between microcomputers and mainframes/minicomputers, but these compatibility problems are gradually being resolved.

As organizations have moved toward office automation, they have learned some important lessons. First, the process of office automation must be coordinated—each office unit cannot go its own way. The various islands of automation must be made compatible. In most organizations, the IS organization has been given the responsibility for corporatewide office automation. Second, the emphasis must be on the information requirements—the problem(s) being solved—in office automation as in other information technology applications. Third, training and education of all parties involved is a necessary prerequisite for a successful system. Fourth, office automation should be an evolutionary process, moving toward

the mythical office of the future, but not expecting to get there overnight. Fifth, the redefinition of the function of the office and the restructuring of individual roles may be required to achieve the maximum benefits of office automation.

FACTORY AUTOMATION

The roots of **factory automation** lie in (1) numerically controlled machines, which use a computer program, or a tape with holes punched in it, to control the movement of tools on sophisticated machines, and (2) **material requirements planning** (MRP) systems, which rely on extensive data input to produce a production schedule for the factory and a schedule of needed raw materials. The newer **computer-integrated manufacturing** (CIM) combines these basic ideas not only to let the computer set up the schedules (as with MRP) but to carry them out through control of the various machines involved (as with numerically controlled machines).

Computer-integrated manufacturing is one of the primary ways by which manufacturers are facing the challenges of global competition. Through the various components of CIM, manufacturers are increasing productivity and quality while simultaneously reducing the lead time from the idea stage to the marketplace for most products. An executive at John Deere & Company has been quoted as saying: "CIM is the only way to maintain competitiveness. Just take a look at our competitors—they're not there anymore" (Francett, 1987). A list of strong proponents of CIM reads like a who's who of manufacturing—General Motors, John Deere, Ford, Weyerhauser, FMC, and Kodak, among others.

CIM systems fall into three major categories: engineering systems, manufacturing administration, and factory operations. Table 2.1 lists the acronyms used in this section on factory automation. The engineering systems are aimed at increasing the productivity of engineers and include such systems as computer-aided design and group technology. Manufacturing administration includes systems that develop production schedules and monitor production against these schedules; these

TABLE 2.1   Abbreviations Used in Factory Automation

Acronym	Full Name
CIM	Computer-integrated manufacturing
CAD	Computer-aided design
GT	Group technology
MRP	Material requirements planning
MRP II	Manufacturing resources planning
CAM	Computer-aided manufacturing
CAE	Computer-aided engineering
CAPP	Computer-aided process planning
AGV	Automated-guided vehicle
MAP	Manufacturing automation protocol
SFC	Shop floor control

systems are usually termed manufacturing resources planning systems (MRP II). Factory operations include those systems that actually control the operation of machines on the factory floor. Computer-aided manufacturing and shop floor control are examples of such systems.

Engineering Systems

Computer-aided design (CAD) is perhaps the most familiar of the engineering systems. CAD involves the use of computer graphics—both two-dimensional and three-dimensional—to create and modify engineering designs. **Computer-aided engineering** (CAE) is a system designed to analyze the functional characteristics of a design and used to simulate the product performance under various conditions in order to reduce the need to build prototypes. CAD and CAE permit engineers to conduct a more thorough engineering analysis and to investigate a wider range of design alternatives. Advanced CAD/CAE systems store the information they generate in a database that is shared with the other components of CIM, such as CAM.

Group technology (GT) systems logically group parts according to physical characteristics, machine routings through the factory, and similar machine operations. On the basis of these logical groupings, GT is able to identify existing parts that engineers can use or modify rather than design new parts, simplifying the design and manufacturing processes. **Computer-aided process planning** (CAPP) systems plan the sequence of

processes that produce or assemble a part. During the design process, the engineer retrieves the closest standard plan from a database (using the GT classification of the new part) and modifies that plan rather than starting from scratch. The resulting plans are more accurate and more consistent, thereby reducing process planning and manufacturing costs.

Manufacturing Administration

Manufacturing resources planning (MRP II) systems usually have three major components: the master production schedule, material requirements planning, and shop floor control. The master production schedule component sets the overall production goals based on forecasts of demand. The MRP component then develops a detailed production schedule to accomplish the master schedule, using parts explosion, production capacity, inventory, and lead-time data. The shop floor control component releases orders to the shop floor based on the detailed production schedule and the actual production accomplished thus far. Using the buzzwords of the 1990s, MRP II systems attempt to implement just-in-time (JIT) production. Note that MRP II does not directly control machines on the shop floor; it is an information system that tries to minimize inventory and employ the machines effectively and efficiently.

Factory Operations

Factory operations systems go a significant step further than MRP II—they control the machines. By definition, **computer-aided manufacturing** (CAM) is the use of computers to control manufacturing processes. CAM is built around a series of computer programs that control automated equipment on the shop floor. In addition to computer-controlled machines such as automated drill presses and milling machines, CAM systems employ automated guided vehicles (AGVs) to move raw materials, in-process materials, and finished products from one workstation to another. AGVs are loaded using robotlike arms and then follow a computer-generated electronic signal (often a track under the floor that has been activated) to

Hamilton Standard's commercial aircraft electronics plant, in Colorado Springs, Colorado, has set up high-performance work teams to achieve its goals and is using CIM to support the work teams. Hamilton Standard chose a software package called Linkage, which might be termed a CIM generator (see our discussion of a DSS generator), developed by CIMLINC, Inc. Linkage was used to develop two systems, CAPP and factory floor data collection. In addition, Linkage was able to interface with existing finance, general ledger, purchasing, MRP, inventory tracking, and general management systems.

The entire set of systems is being designed and used to support the high-performance work teams. For example, the factory floor data are used for several purposes. One purpose is to build proactive processes, so that the data let the workers see how to improve the product they are manufacturing. Another purpose is to enable Hamilton Standard to move from *identifying* defects to *preventing* them. In Hamilton Standard's view, the Linkage-based CIM systems increase the capabilities of the work teams to do things as they determine it is best to do them. The work teams can reorganize product line flow, change the manner in which a product is built, retool a product, or change how a machine is used; they use CIM to collect the data used for analyzing the processes. Hamilton Standard believes it is "weaving quality into the work environment, not simply putting in a set of checks to compare against the environment."

(Adapted from *I/S Analyzer,* August 1992)

As this brief description has implied, a CAM system is very sophisticated and requires a great deal of input data from other systems. Product design data would come from CAD, process design data from CAPP, and the master production schedule and material requirements from MRP II. The CAM system also must be able to communicate electronically with the machines on the shop floor.

The manufacturing communications network is likely to employ the **manufacturing automation protocol** (MAP), pioneered by General Motors and now accepted by nearly all major manufacturers and vendors. MAP is a communications protocol (a set of rules that must be used) to ensure an open manufacturing system. With conformance to MAP by all vendors, seamless communication between all equipment on the factory floor—regardless of the vendor—will be possible. MAP is a user-driven effort, and the details of the concept are evolving over time. Nevertheless, MAP is a reality in factory automation upon which future systems will be based.

Within factory operations applications, **shop floor control** (SFC) systems are less ambitious than CAM but are still important. These systems provide on-line, real-time (immediate) control and monitoring of machines on the shop floor. For example, the SFC might recognize that a tool on a particular milling machine is getting dull (by measuring the metal that the machine is cutting per second) and signal this fact to the human operator on duty. The operator can then take corrective measures, such as instructing the SFC to change the tool or changing it himself (depending on the system).

their next destination. Workers are used only to provide maintenance on the equipment and to handle problems. Because job setups (preparing a machine to work on a new part) are automated and accomplished in minimum time, CAM permits extremely high machine utilization. With the low setup time, very small batches (even as small as one) can be produced efficiently, shortening production lead times and reducing inventory levels.

Robotics

Outside the broad area of CIM, robotics is one other aspect of factory automation that deserves mention. Robotics is, in fact, one branch of the artificial intelligence tree. With robotics, scientists and engineers are building machines to accomplish coordinated physical tasks in the manner of humans. Robots have been important in manufacturing for more than a decade to accomplish simple but important tasks, such as painting and welding. Robots are tireless in performing repetitive tasks, produce more consistent high-quality output than humans, and are not subject to the dangers of paint inhalation or retinal damage. Newer robots incorporate a certain amount of visual perception and thus are able to perform assembly tasks of increasing complexity. Industrial robots are very expensive, but they are becoming economically viable for a wider range of tasks as their capabilities are extended. Robots and CIM are producing a vastly different "factory of the future" based on information technology.

ARTIFICIAL INTELLIGENCE

The third major category of information systems applications encompasses applications based on new technologies (see Figure 2.1). The idea of **artificial intelligence** (AI), the study of how to make computers do things that are presently done better by people, is about thirty years old, but only recently have computers become powerful enough to make AI commercially attractive. AI research has evolved into five separate but related areas— natural languages, robotics, perceptive systems (vision and hearing), expert systems, and neural networks.

The work in natural languages (primarily in computer science departments in universities and vendor laboratories) is aimed at producing systems that translate ordinary human instructions into a language that computers can understand and execute. The topic of robotics was considered in the previous section. Perceptive systems research involves creating machines possessing a visual or aural (or both) perceptual ability that affects their physical behavior. In other words, this research is aimed at creating robots that can "see" or "hear" and react to what they see or hear. The final two branches of AI are the ones of greatest interest to us. **Expert systems** is concerned with building systems that incorporate the decision-making logic of a human expert. The newest branch of AI is **neural networks,** which is named after the study of how the human nervous system

works, but in fact uses statistical analysis to recognize patterns from vast amounts of information by a process of adaptive learning.

Expert Systems

How does one capture the logic of an expert in a computer system? To design an expert system, a specialist known as a knowledge engineer (a specially trained systems analyst) works very closely with one or more experts in the area under study. Knowledge engineers try to learn everything they can about the way in which the expert makes decisions. If one is trying to build an expert system for estate planning, for example, the knowledge engineer works with experienced estate planners to see how they carry out their job. The knowledge gained by the knowledge engineer is then loaded into the computer system in a specialized format, in a module called the knowledge base (see Figure 2.10). This knowledge base contains both the inference rules that are followed in decision-making and the parameters (facts) relevant to the decision.

The other major pieces of an expert system are the inference engine and the user interface. The inference engine is a logical framework that automatically executes a line of reasoning when supplied with the inference rules and parameters involved in the decision. Thus, the same inference engine can be used for many different expert systems, each with a different knowledge base. The user interface is the module used by the end-user—for example, an inexperienced estate planner. Ideally, the interface is very easy to use, or user-friendly. The other modules include an explanation subsystem to explain the reasoning that the system followed in arriving at a decision, a knowledge acquisition subsystem to assist the knowledge engineer in recording inference rules and parameters in the knowledge base, and a workspace for the computer to use as the decision is being made.

Obtaining an Expert System

Is it necessary to build all these pieces each time your organization wants to develop and use an expert system? Absolutely not. There are three general approaches to obtaining an expert system,

48

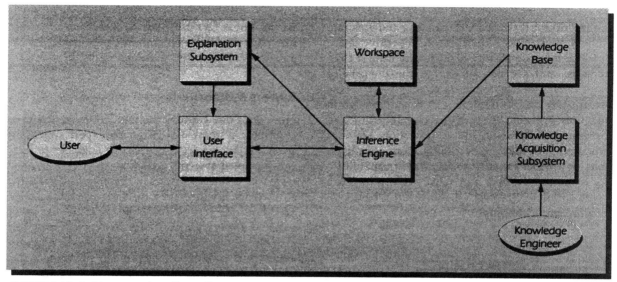

FIGURE 2.10 Architecture of an Expert System

and only one of them requires construction of all these pieces. First, an organization can buy a fully developed system that has been created for a specific application. For example, Syntelligence, Inc., has developed an expert system called Lending Advisor to make commercial lending decisions for banks and other financial institutions. Lending Advisor incorporates the multiplicity of factors involved in approving or rejecting a commercial loan. Several banks have installed Lending Advisor, including Wells Fargo Bank in San Francisco and First Wachovia Corporation in Winston-Salem, North Carolina (Wilder, 1987).

Second, an organization can develop an expert system itself using an **artificial intelligence shell** (also called an **expert systems shell**). The shell, which can be purchased from a software company or a computer vendor, provides the basic framework illustrated in Figure 2.10 and a limited but user-friendly special language with which to develop the expert system. With the basic expert system functions already in place in the shell, the system builder can concentrate on the details of the business decision being modeled and the development of the knowledge base.

Third, an organization can have internal or external knowledge engineers custom-build the expert system. In this case, the system is usually

programmed in a special-purpose language such as Prolog or Franzlisp. This final approach is clearly the most expensive, and it can be justified only if the potential payoff from the expert system is quite high and no other way is possible.

Examples of Expert Systems

Perhaps the classic example of an expert system is MYCIN, which was developed at Stanford University in the mid-1970s to diagnose and prescribe treatment for meningitis and blood diseases. General Electric created an expert system called CATS-1 to diagnose mechanical problems in diesel locomotives, and AT&T developed ACE to locate faults in telephone cables. Schlumberger, Ltd., an international oil company, developed an expert system named Dipmeter to provide advice when a drill bit gets stuck while drilling a well. These examples and others are concerned with diagnosing problem situations and prescribing appropriate actions, since experts will not always be present when a problem occurs.

Some expert systems specialize in sifting through massive sets of rules or other data. The Human Services Agency of Merced County, California, employs an expert system called Magic, which incorporates six thousand government regulations relating to welfare, food stamps, medicaid, foster care, and so on. Magic determines if an applicant qualifies for benefits and then calculates the type and amount of benefits. The entire process from application to final decision now takes three days or less, whereas it used to take as long as three months. In addition, the clerks who process the applications do not require the extensive training that was previously required—all they need to be able to do is lead applicants through a series of questions posed by the computer (Schwartz, 1992). The Credit Clearing House (CCH) division of Dun & Bradstreet has developed an expert system to respond to requests from subscribers seeking information about businesses in the apparel industry. The CCH expert system incorporates about eight hundred rules and cost $1 million to develop. When a subscriber calls in requesting credit information on a business, the system analyzes the payment history, financial statement, and overall strength of the business, arrives at a credit rating and recommendation, and sets a recommended credit limit in dollars (LaPlante, 1991).

Scheduling is another important area for expert systems. Expert systems currently in use include a truck routing and scheduling system that determines the sequence of stops on a route to provide the best service and a factory design system that organizes machines and operators to provide an efficient flow of materials through the factory and use the resources efficiently. American Airlines uses an expert system called MOCA (Maintenance Operations Center Advisor), which runs on a Macintosh microcomputer, to schedule routine maintenance for all 622 planes in American's fleet. MOCA incorporates five thousand rules that have been gleaned from thirty aircraft-routing experts. Aircraft must undergo routine maintenance at least once every sixty hours of flying time, and MOCA's job is to set up a schedule that meets this rule, covers all of American's routes, and avoids the cost of flying empty planes to regional maintenance centers. American estimates that MOCA saves the company $500,000 a year, compared to human schedulers (LaPlante, 1991; Schwartz, 1992).

Neural Networks

Whereas expert systems try to capture the expertise of humans in a computer program, neural networks attempt to tease out meaningful patterns from vast amounts of data. Neural networks can recognize patterns too obscure for humans to detect, and they adapt as new information is received.

The key to neural networks is that they learn! The neural network program is originally given a set of data consisting of many variables associated with a large number of cases (or events) in which the outcomes are known. The program analyzes the data and works out all the correlations, then selects a set of variables that are strongly correlated with particular known outcomes as the initial pattern. This initial pattern is used to try to predict the outcomes of the various cases, and these predicted results are compared to the known results. Based on this comparison, the program changes the pattern by adjusting the weights given to the variables or even by changing the variables. The neural network program then repeats this process over and over, continuously adjusting the pattern in an attempt to improve its predictive ability. When no further improvement is possible from this iterative approach, the program is ready to make predictions for future cases.

This does not end the story. As more cases become available, these data are also fed into the neural network and the pattern is once again adjusted. The neural network learns more about cause-and-effect patterns from this additional data, and its predictive ability usually improves accordingly.

Commercial neural network programs (actually, these are shells) are available for a reasonable price, but the difficult part of building a neural network application is often the data collection and data maintenance effort. Still, a growing number of applications are being deployed. BankAmerica uses a neural network to evaluate commercial loan applications. American Express uses a neural system to read handwriting on credit card slips. The state of Wyoming uses a neural system to read hand-printed numbers on tax forms.

PICKING STOCKS BY NEURAL NETWORK

Bradford Lewis, the fund manager for the Fidelity Disciplined Equity Fund, gives much of the credit for the extraordinary success of his fund to the neural network programs he uses to select stocks. Fidelity Disciplined Equity Fund has beaten the Standard & Poor's 500 stock index by 2.3 to 5.6 percent in the years 1989–1991, and was doing so by 5.8 percent through ten months of 1992. This is particularly unusual because of the nature of the Disciplined Equity Fund, which invests in the same industries in the same proportions as the S & P 500 index. Thus, the key for the Disciplined Equity Fund is the particular stocks picked in these industries.

Mr. Lewis' neural network program uses eleven different variables for each of two thousand stocks as data input. "The computer," Mr. Lewis hopes, "will detect patterns in stock prices that are too subtle or too diffuse for a human to discover. And if the computer can 'learn' which patterns are driving the stock market, it can also find those 'undervalued' stocks where those patterns remain unrewarded." The neural network program tends to select little-known stocks trading at below-average multiples of earnings or book value, but with higher than average rates of earnings growth. The impressive performance of the fund suggests that the neural system certainly works most of the time.

(Adapted from McGough, 1992)

Mellon Bank is working on a system to speed up recognition of fraudulent credit-card transactions by monitoring such factors as the frequency of credit-card use and the size of charges relative to the credit line. The oil giants Arco and Texaco are using neural networks to help pinpoint oil and gas deposits below the earth's surface. Spiegel, which depends on catalogs to generate sales for its mail-order business, is experimenting with the use of a neural network as a way of pruning its mailing list to eliminate those who are unlikely to order from Spiegel again (Field, 1992; Schwartz, 1992).

The list of potential expert systems and neural networks is endless, but it is uncertain how many items on this list can be economically justified. Nevertheless, expert systems and neural networks are currently "in" topics in corporate America and around the world. In 1991, U.S. computer and software companies sold about $200 million in expert systems and neural networks, according to International Data Corporation (Schwartz, 1992). Many major businesses are currently devoting significant resources to investigate ways in which expert systems, neural networks, and artificial intelligence in general can be used to help them cope with problem situations and make better and more consistent decisions.

VIRTUAL REALITY

Virtual reality is an "extra" application area—one that is not important enough yet, from a business perspective, to list as a major application area but is so fascinating that we feel compelled to include it. **Virtual reality** refers to the use of computer-based systems to create an environment that seems real to one or more senses (usually including sight) of the human user or users. The ultimate example of virtual reality is the holodeck aboard the U.S.S. *Enterprise* on the television series "Star Trek: The Next Generation," where Data can be Sherlock Holmes in a realistic setting with realistic characters, and where Captain Jean-Luc Picard can play the role of a hard-boiled private eye in the early 20th century.

Virtual reality exists today, but with nowhere near the reality of the *Enterprise*'s holodeck. You may have played a video game where you don a head-mounted computer display and a glove to get directly into the action. In a more serious setting, the U.S. Army is beginning to use virtual reality to train tank crews. Through multiple large video screens and sound, the soldiers are seemingly placed inside a tank rolling across the Iraqi desert, and they have to react as if they were in a real tank battle. In a research project at the University of North Carolina, virtual reality has been used to provide a three-dimensional model of a tumor inside a patient's body. A radiologist, after donning special eyeglasses, is able to get inside this model of the patient's body and adjust radiation beams so that they intersect at the heart of the tumor and yet avoid radiosensitive tissue such as the spinal cord and esophagus (Rheingold, 1992).

Chrysler and IBM are developing a virtual reality system to assist in the design of automobiles. With this system, an automotive engineer, wearing special glasses and a special glove to be able to interact with the system, is able to sit in the driver's seat of a future automobile. He turns the steering wheel and uses buttons and knobs as though he were in a real car. By letting the engineer get the feel of this future car, Chrysler hopes that problems in the dashboard and controls design can be corrected before actual—and expensive—prototypes are built (Hamilton et al., 1992). The development of virtual reality is in its infancy, and it will be a long time before anything remotely approaching the *Enterprise*'s holodeck is possible. For the short run, there may be some niche commercial products developed, but most of the work will be carried out in the research and development laboratories.

DISTRIBUTED SYSTEMS AND CLIENT/SERVER SYSTEMS

Finally, we turn to our fourth major category of information systems applications—application areas based on the information technology architecture of an organization (see Figure 2.1). Within this broad category, we will consider only distributed systems and client/server systems. Our discussion will be brief because of this area's overlap with all the other areas. All the previous applications that have been addressed can be (and have been) carried out in a distributed mode or a client/server mode, using telecommunications lines to link the various components of the system. Also, the technical details of telecommunications will occupy all of Chapter 6.

Distributed systems, sometimes called **distributed data processing,** refers to a mode of delivery rather than a more traditional class of applica-

tions, such as transaction processing or decision support systems. With distributed systems, the processing power is distributed to multiple sites, which are then tied together via telecommunications lines. We should note that there are a variety of operational functions that can be distributed, including data collection and entry, data editing and error correction, file location, and processing. In our view, only the last function—processing—represents distributed systems. Whether or not the processing power is distributed, it is often appropriate to distribute data collection and entry as well as data editing and error correction to the sites at which the transactions occur (for example, the sales floor in a department store and the loading dock in a warehouse). File location, however, would never be distributed unless at least some processing power is also distributed.

Thus, we are defining distributed systems as systems in which computers of some size (microcomputers, minicomputers, mainframes, and so forth) are located at various physical sites at which the organization does business (headquarters, factories, stores, warehouses, office buildings), and these computers are linked by telecommunication lines of some sort in order to support some business process. This mode of computing has become the norm for American business firms, although there are both pluses and minuses for distributed systems (see Table 2.2).

The economics of distributed systems are not perfectly clear, but tend to favor distribution. For the most part, communication costs go up with distributed systems, while computer costs go down. Without distributed systems, noncentral sites will have to communicate by other means (mail, telephone, courier) to the central site, while with such systems rather expensive telecommunications links are required. Placing smaller microcomputers and minicomputers at noncentral sites is generally less expensive than expanding the capacity of a large mainframe at the central site. Of course, the economics will depend on the particular situation for the particular organization. Whatever the disadvantages of distributed systems, the advantages must outweigh them in most instances, because distributed systems are here to stay.

VIRTUAL STORE LAYOUT

One intriguing and not-so-distant application of virtual reality is its use for retail store layout. Using a software package called Virtus Walkthrough (with a purchase price of under $500) on a Macintosh microcomputer, a national women's-apparel retailer has saved time and money in designing store layouts and storefronts. This package provides a three-dimensional image on the computer screen (no special glasses required—see Figure 2.11). The user can, in effect, walk through the image of a store and view the layout from a variety of perspectives. With the package, fixtures can be easily changed, the color scheme can be modified, and the placement of walls, doors, and windows can be moved.

(Adapted from Bandrowski, 1992)

In the 1990s, a particular type of distributed system known as a **client/server system** has received a great deal of attention. With this type of system, the processing power is distributed between a central server computer, such as a minicomputer or a powerful workstation, and a number of client computers, which are usually desktop microcomputers. The split in responsibilities between the server and the client varies considerably from application to application, but the client often handles data entry and the immediate output, while the server maintains the larger database against which the new data are processed. For example, in a retail client/server application, the client may be the sophisticated cash register on the sales floor, while the server is a minicomputer in the back office. When a credit sale is made, the data are entered at the register and transmitted to the server, the server retrieves the customer's re-

FIGURE 2.11 Virtus Walkthrough Used for Virtual Store Layout. (Courtesy of Virtus Corporation)

THE PROMISE OF CLIENT/SERVER TECHNOLOGY

Client/server technology promises many things to many people: to end users, easier access to corporate and external data; to managers, dramatically lower costs for processing; to programmers, reduced maintenance; and to corporate planners, an infrastructure that enables business processes to be reengineered for strategic benefits. Whether client/server lives up to these promises will depend in large part on how carefully it is planned for and how intelligently policies are put forth to manage it.

(*IS Analyzer*, April 1992)

cord and updates it based on the sale, the server returns a credit authorization signal to the register, and the sales document is printed at the register. At the close of the billing cycle, the server prepares the bills for all of the customers, prints them, and produces summary reports for store management.

TABLE 2.2 Advantages and Disadvantages of Distributed Systems

Possible Advantages

Increased service and responsiveness to local users

Improved local morale because of local involvement

Ability to adapt to the organizational structure

Less vulnerable to downtime or catastrophe at central site

Increased manageability because the pieces of the system are smaller

Reduced computing costs

Possible Disadvantages

Very dependent on high-quality telecommunication lines, which are quite vulnerable

Utilizes technologies that are relatively new and not well understood

Greater security risk because of easy accessibility

Local sites may deviate from central standards, making an integrated system impossible

Greater required coordination across organizational boundaries and geographic locations

Increased communication costs

Laptop Computers for Sales Forces

One of the more interesting recent developments in distributed systems involves the outfitting of entire sales forces with laptop or notebook computers. Laptop and notebook computers (notebooks are smaller versions of laptops), which are portable battery-powered microcomputers weighing from five to twenty pounds, constitute the fastest-growing computer market in the first half of the 1990s. The number of portable computers in use is doubling every four years, from 6 million units in 1992 to a projected 8.5 million in 1994 and more than 12 million in 1996 (Bachus and Longsworth, 1993).

One of many examples of the use of laptops by salespeople is the experience of Jansen Pharmaceutica, a subsidiary of Johnson & Johnson (Fersko-Weiss, 1987). Jansen has 120 salespeople, each having a territory containing several thousand doctors. The sales representatives cannot possibly visit every doctor, so they decide which doctors to see and then manage follow-up visits. Once a sale is made, the order is transmitted back to Jansen's headquarters. Laptop computers have made both the front end (selecting the physicians) and back end (placing the orders) of the sales process much easier to accomplish.

The front end of the job is made easier because the salespeople have access to a large database of market and demographic data on the physicians in their territory. The IS organization has created an individual database for each sales representative and stored these data on a disk. Using the laptop, the salesperson can then access this database as the week's itinerary is planned. After the visit, the salesperson can record information discussed with the doctor, including products used and samples that were left. Thus, over time the sales representative builds up a valuable profile of each customer.

The back end of the job is also made easier. At least twice a week, the sales representative dials up the central corporate computer and transmits orders from the laptop computer to the mainframe, giving management better information on what is selling and permitting customer orders to be filled more quickly. For Jansen, the distributed system using laptops has been a major success. The national sales manager reports a 15 percent increase in business because of the system.

Client/Server Applications

To illustrate the diversity of client/server systems, two quite different applications will be briefly reviewed. Client/server accounting applications are becoming quite popular. A recent addition is a software package with the awkward name of SeQueL to Platinum General Ledger, developed by Platinum Software Corporation. This general ledger accounting package is designed to run with a desktop microcomputer as the client and either a high-end microcomputer or a workstation as the server. With SeQueL to Platinum, the data entry takes place on the client machine but most computations are carried out by the server. SeQueL to Platinum incorporates a 32-digit chart-of-accounts number that can be expanded, and it permits users to track nonfinancial data, such as ratios and statistics, as well as general ledger data. The software package is priced starting at $15,000, and it has already been adopted by Federal Mogul's chassis products operations division (Ferranti, 1992).

In the real estate area, CB Commercial Real Estate Group, Inc., a Los Angeles firm, is moving its commercial real estate database—a collection of key variables on every piece of commercial real estate in Los Angeles—to a client/server system. The client machines will be microcomputers which may be located in CB Commercial offices or in customer offices; thus, this system is designed to be an interorganizational system (more on this in Chapter 3). When information is requested, it will be retrieved from the database stored on the server, and then will be presented on the client screen in an easy-to-understand manner (see Figure 2.12 for an example). Eventually, CB Commercial hopes to have data in its database on every piece of commercial real estate in the United States (Moser, 1992).

PITFALLS IN APPLYING INFORMATION TECHNOLOGY

We have now considered information technology applications in eight major areas: transaction processing, decision support systems, geographic information systems, executive information systems,

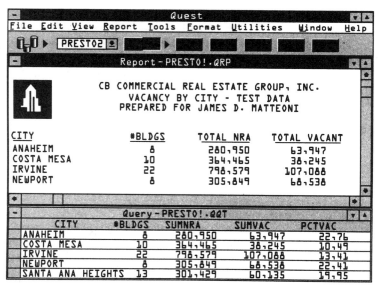

FIGURE 2.12 Client/server real estate database developed by CB Commercial Real Estate Group. (Courtesy of CB Commercial Real Estate Group, Inc.)

office automation, factory automation, artificial intelligence, and distributed and client/server systems. It is hoped that we have created an awareness of information technology applications—the primary goal of this chapter and the next. In our view, it is not too early to lay some groundwork for another goal: a realistic assessment of the pitfalls in applying information technology.

The first pitfall can be the difficulty of conceptualizing how technology can be used to improve performance and then identifying the appropriate information technology applications. As a user-manager, you must play an active role in identifying applications; this job cannot be left to the IS organization alone. Your role is to define applications that will produce benefits to your organization and then to assist in the development and to oversee the use of these applications to ensure that the benefits actually occur.

Justification of an information technology application is laden with possible pitfalls. In some organizations there is a tendency to insist on hard numbers on both benefits and costs before any application will be approved. This is an unrealistic and potentially disastrous approach, for very few applications, except transaction processing systems, can be so justified. Successful organizations have been willing to recognize the potential value of soft benefits, such as improved decision-making, better customer service, better organizational morale, and more up-to-date and complete information. On the opposite side of the issue, some organizations have been willing to try anything new just to be the first in the industry to use some new technology. As a user-manager you have an important role in avoiding both extremes. Once a new application has been identified that lies in your area of expertise, it is your job to analyze the business case for the application, which should be a thorough, unbiased assessment of both hard and soft benefits and costs associated with the application.

Another possible pitfall is to let the IS organization develop the new application in a vacuum, without input from you and other user-managers. The role of the user-manager in the development process is a crucial one that will be explored in depth in Chapters 8, 9, 10, and 11. The lack of

managerial input at any stage of the process from conceptualization to justification to development to implementation to assessment virtually guarantees failure of the application.

Perhaps the most devastating pitfall can occur at any time—the lack of communication among the various players in the information technology game. Communication is everyone's responsibility, and that especially means the user-manager. When you are involved with information technology in any role, do not let your questions go unanswered or your views go unexpressed. Take the lead in communication, both with your fellow managers and with information specialists. Your role in communication and other aspects of an information technology application is likely to be critical to the success of the application.

REVIEW QUESTIONS

1. Consider the application areas listed in Figure 2.1. Which types of information technology applications are likely to be used at the operating, middle, and upper management levels of an organization?
2. Describe the fundamental differences between batch processing and on-line processing.
3. What is a vertically integrated information system? Give an example.
4. Explain the difference between a specific decision support system (DSS) and a DSS generator. Give an example of each.
5. What is the purpose of a group support system (GSS)? What are the potential advantages and disadvantages of using a GSS?
6. What are the distinguishing characteristics of an executive information system (EIS)?
7. What aspects of the automated office are you most likely to encounter today? In the future, what additional features are likely to be added to the automated office?
8. Some of the most important acronyms used in the factory automation area are listed below.

Provide the full names for each of these acronyms.

CIM	MAP
CAD	GT
MRP	MRP II

9. Consider again the six acronyms listed in question 8. Give a one-sentence explanation of each term, and then describe the interrelationships among the terms.

10. Briefly describe the five areas of artificial intelligence (AI) research. Indicate why we in business are most interested in the expert systems and neural networks areas.

11. What are the three general approaches to obtaining an expert system? What are the pluses and minuses of each approach?

12. Discuss the advantages and disadvantages of client/server systems. In your opinion, what are the primary factors causing the present movement toward client/server systems?

DISCUSSION QUESTIONS

1. In this chapter, payroll and order entry were used as examples of transaction processing systems. Another example with which all of us are somewhat familiar is the check-processing system employed by your bank. Consider how the check-processing system is similar to (and different from) the two examples in this chapter. Is the check-processing system likely to be batch or on-line or some hybrid of the two? What subsystems would be required to operate the check-processing system?

2. Two of the important topics in this chapter are decision support systems (DSSs) and expert systems. Based on your reading of this chapter, you have undoubtedly noticed that these two application areas have a great deal in common. What are the primary distinctions between DSSs and expert systems?

3. Several examples of expert systems were mentioned in the chapter. Consider an industry or a company with which you have some familiarity, and identify at least one possible applica-

tion of expert systems in the industry or company. Explain why you think this is a good prospect for an expert system application.

4. Consider an office environment with which you are somewhat familiar. What changes have occurred in the preparation of documents (such as reports and letters) over the past five years? Why do you think these changes have occurred? Have they been technology- or people-driven or some of both?

5. The terminology employed in factory automation is often confusing, in part because the names are so similar and in part because the subareas overlap. Carefully distinguish among CIM, CAD, CAE, CAM, and CAPP, indicating any overlaps.

6. Consider a factory environment with which you are somewhat familiar. Can you suggest a possible use of a robot in this setting? How might the robot be economically justified?

7. All of us come into contact with distributed systems almost every day, even if it is only while shopping at Sears or J. C. Penney. Describe a distributed system with which you have come in contact. In your view, what are the advantages and disadvantages of this system?

8. We concluded this chapter by listing several possible pitfalls in applying information technology: the difficulty of conceptualizing appropriate applications, the justification of applications, the lack of managerial input in application development, and the lack of communication among those concerned about information technology. Using your knowledge of organizations (either from personal experience or from other courses), expand this list of pitfalls. Be creative!

REFERENCES

1989. "Applications for the 1990s." *I/S Analyzer* 27 (September): 1–16.

1992. "The new role for 'executive' information systems." *I/S Analyzer* 30 (January): 1–16.

1992. "Plans and policies for client/server technology." *I/S Analyzer* 30 (April): 1–12.

1992. "Redefining computer-integrated manufacturing." *I/S Analyzer* 30 (August): 1–10.

Arthur Andersen & Co. 1987. *Trends in Information Technology: A Handbook for Senior Management Who Must Understand Information Technology in a Competitive Context*, 3rd ed. Chicago: Arthur Andersen & Co.

Aubin, Jean. 1992. "Scheduling ambulances." *Interfaces* 22 (March–April): 1–10.

Bachus, Kevin, and Elizabeth Longsworth. 1993. "Road Nodes." *Corporate Computing* 2 (March): 54–61.

Bandrowski, Paul. 1992. "Try before you buy: virtually real merchandising." *Corporate Computing* 1 (December): 209–211.

Booker, Ellis. 1989. "A supermarket with SMARTs." *Computerworld* 23 (September 11): 25, 31.

Bulkeley, William M. 1992. "'Computerizing' dull meetings is touted as an antidote to the mouth that bored." *Wall Street Journal* 73 (January 28): B1, B8.

Churbuck, David. 1992. "Geographics." *Forbes* 149 (January 6): 262–267.

Ferranti, Marc. 1992. "Platinum ships first module in high-end line." *PC Week* 9 (November 2): 35, 40.

Fersko-Weiss, Henry. 1987. "Tools of the sales trade." *Personal Computing* 11 (August): 78–88.

Feuche, Mike. 1989. "Retailer develops EIS application and speeds management response." *MIS Week* 10 (December 18): 14.

Field, Roger. 1992. "Figuring out those neural networks." *Beyond Computing* 1 (August–September): 38–42.

Francett, Barbara. 1987. "MAP confronts the real world." *Computer and Communications Decisions* 19 (November): 99–102.

Franklin, Carl. 1992. "An introduction to geographic information systems: Linking maps to databases." *Database* (April): 12–21.

Glover, Harry, Hugh J. Watson, and Rex Kelly Rainer, Jr. 1992. "20 ways to waste an EIS investment." *Information Strategy: The Executive's Journal* 8 (Winter): 11–17.

Goff, Leslie. 1989. "User acceptance key for system that aided Phillips turnaround." *MIS Week* 10 (October 16): 36.

Hamilton, Joan O'C., with Emily T. Smith, Gary McWilliams, Evan I. Schwartz, and John Carey. 1992. "Virtual reality: How a computer-generated world could change the real world." *Business Week* (October 5): 97–105.

Hindus, Leonard A. 1992. "What MIS should know about videoconferencing." *Datamation* 38 (August 15): 60–64.

Houdeshel, George, and Hugh J. Watson. 1987. "The management information and decision support (MIDS) system at Lockheed-Georgia." *MIS Quarterly* 11 (March): 127–140.

Johnson, Maryfran. 1989. "Miami law firm shows its Freestyle." *Computerworld* 23 (December 18): 25.

LaPlante, Alice. 1991. "Using your smarts." *CIO* 5 (December): 54–58.

McGough, Robert. 1992. "Fidelity's Bradford Lewis takes aim at indexes with his 'neural network' computer program." *Wall Street Journal* 74 (October 27): C1, C19.

Miller, Michael W. 1992. "A story of the type that turns heads in computer circles." *Wall Street Journal* 73 (September 15): A1, A8.

Moser, Karen D. 1992. "Real-estate firm bets on rapid downsizing." *PC Week* 9 (August 17): 51, 54.

Nunamaker, J. F., Jr., D. R. Vogel, A. R. Heminger, B. Martz, R. Growhowski, and C. McGoff. 1989. "Experiences at IBM with group support systems: A field study." In *Decision Support Systems*, Vol. 5. Amsterdam, The Netherlands: North-Holland, 183–196.

Nunamaker, J. F., Alan R. Dennis, Joseph S. Valacich, Douglas R. Vogel, and Joey F. George. 1991. "Electronic meeting systems to support group work." *Communications of the ACM* 34 (July): 40–61.

Rathnam, Sukumar, M. R. Arun, Abhijit Chaudhury, and P. R. Shukla. 1992. "MUDRAPLAN—a DSS for media planning: From design to utilization." *Interfaces* 22 (March–April): 65–75.

Rheingold, Howard. 1992. "How real is virtual reality?" *Beyond Computing* 1 (March–April): 26–29.

Schwartz, Evan I., with James B. Treece. 1992. "Smart programs go to work." *Business Week* (March 2): 97–105.

Shannon, Patrick W., and Robert P. Minch. 1992. "A decision support system for motor vehicle taxation evaluation." *Interfaces* 22 (March–April): 52–64.

Sprague, Ralph H., Jr., and Eric D. Carlson. 1982. *Building Effective Decision Support Systems*. Englewood Cliffs, NJ: Prentice-Hall, Inc.

Watson, Hugh J. 1992. "How to fit an EIS into a competitive context." *Information Strategy: The Executive's Journal* 8 (Winter): 5–10.

Wilder, Clinton. 1987. "BankAmerica cozies up to AI to assist lending procedure." *Computerworld* 21 (August 10): 17.

2

Midstate University
Business Placement Office: Part I

Midstate University is a major state university with about 35,000 students on its main campus. It is internationally known for its programs in the arts, sciences, music, engineering, education, business, and languages. The Midstate University School of Business has outstanding undergraduate, M.B.A., doctoral, and executive programs. Its faculty is renowned for research, teaching, and service to the state and the business community.

The Business Placement Office (BPO) is among the handful of placement operations in the country that conduct over 20,000 interviews each year and has an outstanding reputation among company recruiters and other business schools. Arnold Worthy, dean of the School of Business, notes that the BPO is very important to the mission of the school:

It is our marketing arm, and a very good one. We get good students at least partly because they know that they can get good jobs. Our school is in the top twenty in all the national rankings of business schools, but we rank highest where those who do the ranking are businessmen. That is quite a tribute to our BPO.

The director of the BPO, James P. Wine, is known among his peers as an energetic and innovative director. He is a past president of the Midwest College Placement Association and is a frequent speaker at placement conventions nationwide. Wine has a degree in electrical engineering, an M.B.A. in personnel management, and a Ph.D. in industrial relations. He is

This case was prepared by Professor E. W. Martin as the basis for class discussion, rather than to illustrate either effective or ineffective handling of an administrative situation.

Copyright © 1988 by E. W. Martin.

the author of four textbooks that are widely used in placement and career-planning courses.

The primary mission of the BPO is to help Midstate students get appropriate jobs, but, as Wine notes, "We must also serve our corporate clients, for if they don't come back year after year, there won't be any jobs for our students." In 1987 the BPO served about 2,500 students and more than 500 employers. More than 22,000 interviews were conducted in the BPO's 34 interview rooms, an average of more than 1,400 each week of the interviewing season.

The matchmaking required to schedule 2,500 students for 22,000 interviews with 500 companies so that the students talk with their desired companies and the companies interview students with the desired qualifications is a very complex, high-volume logistical problem. It is particularly difficult because the students want to talk with the companies offering the best jobs, and the companies have strict requirements concerning the qualifications of the students they want to interview. Some companies have far more students seeking interviews than there are interview times available, while the interview schedules of other companies may not be filled.

To handle the problem of fairly allocating interviews to qualified students, the BPO uses a bidding system, where students submit bids for interviews with the companies of their choice. Each student is given an allotment of bids with different levels of priority for use each semester: two "A" bids, two "B" bids, two "C" bids, and 24 regular bids. When many students are bidding for slots on the same schedule, a complex process (designed to be fair to the students given their qualifications, their time availability, when they are graduating, and the bid priority) is used to decide which students get the interview slots. Since the BPO receives up to 7,000 bids during a peak week, interview scheduling can only be handled with the aid of computers.

The BPO Computer System

The BPO has developed a comprehensive computer system to support its day-by-day operations and provide management information to Wine and the Business School faculty and administration. This system supports the high-volume interview process, helps communicate with employer clients throughout the year, and provides many valuable analysis reports for Wine and the Business School.

As depicted in Exhibit 1, the system takes a variety of inputs from client companies and students, and provides outputs for the companies, students, and BPO and Business School management. The system maintains a number of important databases, schedules student interviews, supports coordination with client companies, and produces a wide variety of analysis reports for management.

The Computer Network   The BPO system is run on a network, with both data and processing distributed over many computers. This network, depicted in Exhibit 2, is used to transfer files between the various computers. The local network includes 18 XT-compatibles (most with hard disks), three laser printers, five dot-matrix printers, and an optical card reader. The file server is an NCR MODUS with a 60-megabyte disk that stores the master copy of the database that is used to produce the output reports. Files are transferred via an Apple microcomputer over telephone lines to and from the IBM mainframe computer at the University Data Processing Center.

The system includes over 100 dBASE III+ programs that run on the microcomputers, and 10 COBOL and seven FOCUS programs that run on the IBM mainframe computer using the System 2000 DBMS.

In brief, the BPO system is a distributed processing system where the local area network and micro-

EXHIBIT 1

BPO Computer System Context Diagram

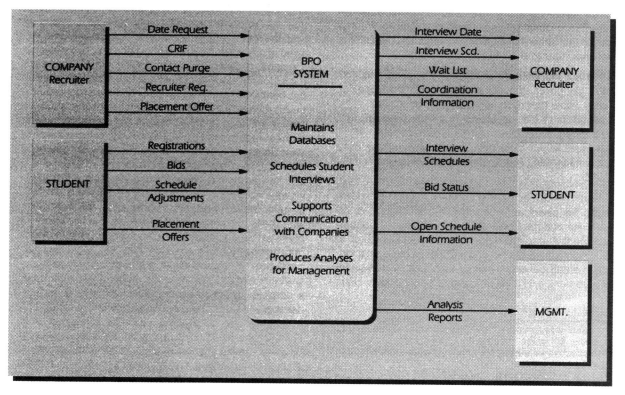

EXHIBIT 2
....
BPO Computer Network

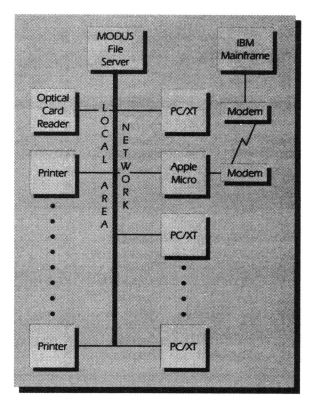

computers are used to maintain the databases, process the daily work, and produce the analysis reports. Once a week, however, the IBM mainframe is used for the long, complex scheduling process and for printing the reports detailing the results of the interview scheduling.

Maintenance of the Database   The heart of this system is a comprehensive database that is managed by the relational microcomputer DBMS dBASE III+. There are eight major tables in this database, and since the BPO people refer to these tables as databases, that is what we will call them. There are over 150 tables in the BPO database, but most of the others are derived from these eight and are used for producing the various reports from the system.

The data elements contained in each of these databases are shown in Exhibit 3. Unfortunately, the

data names do not always adequately define the data elements for someone unfamiliar with the system, but they do give a pretty good idea of the contents of the databases.

The Company database contains name and address information on each of the BPO's client companies. It is updated whenever BPO managers enlist a new client or when there is some change in the data

EXHIBIT 3
....
BPO Databases

Company

Structure for database :   E:\COMPANY.DBF
Number of data records: 1336
Date of last update   :   03/07/88

Field	Field Name	Type	Width	Dec
1	COMNAME	Character	35	
2	COMNUM	Character	4	
3	ADDRESS1	Character	25	
4	ADDRESS2	Character	25	
5	CITY	Character	15	
6	STATE	Character	2	
7	ZIP	Character	10	
8	PHONE	Character	13	
9	CPCTYPE	Character	4	
10	UPDATE	Character	8	
Total			142	

Contact

Structure for database :   C:\CRIS\CONMASTE.DBF
Number of data records: 5313
Date of last update   :   02/23/88

Field	Field Name	Type	Width	Dec
1	COMNUM	Character	4	
2	LASTNAME	Character	20	
3	FIRSTNAME	Character	20	
4	ADDRESS1	Character	25	
5	ADDRESS2	Character	25	
6	CITY	Character	15	
7	STATE	Character	2	
8	ZIP	Character	10	
9	TITLE	Character	25	
10	PHONE	Character	13	
11	TYPE	Character	5	
12	UPDATE	Character	8	
13	SALUT	Character	4	
Total			177	

(exhibit continued on next page)

EXHIBIT 3 *(continued)*
....

Company Schedule

Structure for database :   E:\COMSCH87.DBF
Number of data records: 2223
Date of last update   :   03/07/88

Field	Field Name	Type	Width	Dec
1	COMNUM	Character	4	
2	INTDATE	Character	8	
3	NUMSCHEDS	Numeric	2	
4	CRFRCVD	Logical	1	
5	UPDATE	Character	8	
6	ROOMONLY	Logical	1	
Total			25	

CRIF

Structure for database :   C:\CRIS\CRFMASTE.DBF
Number of data records: 3877
Date of last update   :   02/23/88

Field	Field Name	Type	Width	Dec
1	SCHEDNUM	Character	6	
2	INTDATE	Character	8	
3	MAJORS	Character	34	
4	DEGREE	Character	1	
5	GRADDATE	Character	1	
6	CITIZEN	Character	1	
7	POSITION	Character	2	
8	DESCRIPT	Character	25	
9	LENGTH	Character	2	
10	START	Character	5	
11	END	Character	5	
12	SLOTS	Numeric	2	
13	INVITE	Logical	1	
14	UPDATE	Character	8	
15	INTERVIEWS	Numeric	2	
16	REGTYPE	Character	1	
Total			105	

Student

Structure for database :   C:\CRIS\REGMASTE.DBF
Number of data records: 2820
Date of last update   :   02/23/88

Field	Field Name	Type	Width	Dec
1	REGNUM	Character	11	
2	LASTNAME	Character	20	
3	FIRSTNAME	Character	20	
4	INITIAL	Character	1	
5	MAJORS	Character	8	

Field	Field Name	Type	Width	Dec
6	UDGMAJ	Character	4	
7	DEGREE	Character	1	
8	GRADDATE	Character	5	
9	REGTYPE	Character	1	
10	GPA	Numeric	4	2
11	UDGGPA	Numeric	4	2
12	BIRTHYR	Character	2	
13	SEX	Character	1	
14	RACE	Character	1	
15	CITIZEN	Character	1	
16	COUNTRY	Character	10	
17	POSITIONS	Character	8	
18	WRKEXP	Numeric	3	
19	SKILLS	Character	14	
20	LOCATIONS	Character	14	
21	DATEAVAIL	Character	8	
22	SALMIN	Numeric	5	
23	SALMAX	Numeric	5	
24	EMPLOYER	Character	35	
25	EXPDATE	Character	8	
26	NOSHOW	Character	8	
27	BIDS	Character	10	
28	UPDATE	Character	8	
29	CAMPUS	Character	1	
30	REFERRALS	Logical	1	
31	SALUT	Character	4	
32	OFPSTATUS	Character	1	
33	VAXNUM	Character	9	
Total			237	

Placement Offers

Structure for database :   C:\CRIS\OFPMASTE.DBF
Number of data records: 1515
Date of last update   :   02/22/88

Field	Field Name	Type	Width	Dec
1	REGNUM	Character	11	
2	COMNUM	Character	4	
3	COMNAME	Character	35	
4	POSITION	Character	2	
5	SALARY	Numeric	5	
6	STATE	Character	2	
7	OFPSTATUS	Character	1	
8	UPDATE	Character	8	
9	DESCRIPT	Character	25	
10	INDATE	Character	8	
11	ABBREV	Character	4	
12	COUNTRY	Character	15	
13	REGION	Character	15	
14	OFPCPCRP	Logical	1	
15	COMSICCODE	Character	4	
Total			141	

EXHIBIT 3 *(continued)*

. . . .

Interview Schedule

Structure for database : F:\TRNMASTE.DBF
Number of data records: 27555
Date of last update   : 03/07/88

Field	Field Name	Type	Width	Dec
1	SCHEDNUM	Character	6	
2	TIME	Character	5	
3	REGNUM	Character	11	
4	POSITION	Character	2	
5	BID	Character	1	
6	SPECIAL	Logical	1	
7	REGTYPE	Character	1	
Total			28	

Waitlist

Structure for database : F:\BIDWAIT.DBF
Number of data records: 0
Date of last update   : 08/05/85

Field	Field Name	Type	Width	Dec
1	LASTNAME	Character	15	
2	FIRSTNAME	Character	15	
3	STUNUM	Character	11	
4	MAJOR1	Character	4	
5	MAJOR2	Character	4	
6	DEGREE	Character	1	
7	GRADDATE	Character	1	
8	GPA	Character	4	
9	CPHONE	Character	8	
10	POSITION	Character	2	
Total			66	

on a current client. There is relatively little maintenance activity on this database.

The Contact database contains data on individual recruiters who have interviewed at Midstate through the BPO. It is updated with data from the registration forms that recruiters fill out when they arrive at the BPO to interview. Each summer the BPO sends a list of current contacts to each company and asks it to return the list after crossing off the names of those who are no longer recruiting for the company. This list is then used to purge names from the Contact database.

The Company Schedule database has an entry for each interview date scheduled for the company.

Companies usually schedule interview dates a year ahead of time, and schedules are entered into the database when they are received. Changes to planned schedules occur, and when they are approved by the BPO manager in charge of the schedule, they are entered into the database.

The CRIF database contains data from the companies describing the positions offered through each of their interview schedules and the qualifications they require of students to get on that schedule. This data is provided via the Campus Recruiting Information Form (CRIF) that is submitted by the companies at least eight weeks before the interview date. The CRIFs are entered into the database on a daily basis, and any changes to this data (such as positions available or required qualifications) are made as they occur. Examining the data elements for the CRIF database, one may wonder why company number (COMNUM) is not included. Actually it is, but it is hidden as a part of the schedule number (SCHEDNUM) that is made up of company number plus digits identifying individual schedules.

The Student database contains data on the students served by the BPO. Each such student must register with the BPO, and the data from the registration form is entered into the database. During the year changes to this data may occur, and they are entered into the database.

The Placement Offers database contains data on job offers received by the students, who are asked to fill out and submit a placement offer form when they receive an offer and/or accept a job. These forms are used to enter this important data into this database.

The Interview Schedule database contains the data for a line on an interview schedule. The entries to this database are produced by the schedule processing system. However, during the time between when the schedule is posted and when the interview occurs, changes (such as cancelling an interview or signing up for an open interview slot) may be made by BPO personnel. These manual transactions are entered on the bid card form, read into the system, and used to update this database.

The Waitlist database contains the data for the unsuccessful bidders for interview slots. This data is also created by the schedule processing system. If someone cancels an interview and a waitlisted person is given that slot, both the Interview Schedule and the Waitlist databases must be updated.

Changes to these databases take place quite frequently, so each of them is maintained on a daily basis. Responsibility for each of these databases is assigned to a BPO manager. A copy of the database resides on the hard disk of a PC/XT under control of that manager, and all changes to that database are made through that PC/XT. Not only is that local database updated, but a transaction record is also created in a file that is sent to the MODUS file server at the end of the day and is used to update the master database on the MODUS disk.

Interview Scheduling Subsystem   The Midstate BPO bidding process to allocate interview slots to students could not be used without the support of a computer system, so from the perspective of the student, this is the heart of the BPO system.

A seven-page section of the BPO Placement Manual describes BPO policies relating to interviews, how the student interacts with the system, and how the bids are processed to schedule the interviews. The following description of the sign-up process as

the student sees it discusses the inputs to and outputs from the system.

On Friday of each week, descriptions of the positions available through interviews for the week beginning 17 days later appear in the BPO newsletter, *Career Street Journal*, along with an index to the positions by position code (see Exhibit 4). These descriptions and the listing are produced by the system and are entered via floppy disk directly into the desktop publishing system that composes the *Career Street Journal* pages.

On Monday and Tuesday of the week after the schedule is printed in the *Journal*, students may submit bids for any of the interviews on that schedule. These bids are submitted by marking bid/transaction cards (see Exhibit 5) and placing the cards in a box outside the BPO. The bid cards are read into the computer system, and the interview schedule is produced.

(text continues on p. 68)

EXHIBIT 4
. . . .
BPO *Career Street Journal* Job Listings

Career Street Journal CRIF Corner

Schedules Available For 02/29/88 Thru 03/04/88

AETNA LIFE & CASUALTY COMPANY

23 Bond Representative Trn   Schedule # 88851

Production, acceptance, modification, rejection and servicing of all Bond Department lines of business (Surety, Fidelity, Burglary and Bond Liability) within the branch office territory and other territories assigned to the branch office. Interviewing for location in Indianapolis with possibility for relocation in another Midwest area office.

Graduation Month: 05-06 Degree Level: B Citizenship: C,P
Registrant Type: R Majors: BUS, MATH
Schedule(s) - 2, Each With 10–30 Minute Interviews, 08:30 TO 02:30

| Dates - | Interview | :03/04/88 | Posting | :02/19/88 TO 02/25/88 |
| | Bidding | :02/15/88 TO 02/16/88 | Transactions | :02/26/88 TO 03/01/88 |

AETNA LIFE & CASUALTY COMPANY

30 Marketing Rep. Trainee   Schedule # 88851

Promotes the production of profitable Commercial Lines business in an assigned territory. Interviewing for location in Indianapolis with possible relocation in another Midwest area office.

Graduation Month: 05-06 Degree Level: B Citizenship: C,P
Registrant Type: R Majors: BUS, MATH
Schedule(s) - 2, Each With 10–30 Minute Interviews, 08:30 TO 02:30

| Dates - | Interview | :03/04/88 | Posting | :02/19/88 TO 02/25/88 |
| | Bidding | :02/15/88 TO 02/16/88 | Transactions | :02/26/88 TO 03/01/88 |

EXHIBIT 4 *(continued)*

....

AETNA LIFE & CASUALTY COMPANY
72 Underwriter Trainee   Schedule # 88851

Determines acceptability and/or continuation of business subject to delegated authority in accordance with company goals and profit objectives. Interviewing for locations in Indianapolis with a possibility of relocation in another Midwest area office.

Graduation Month: 05-06 Degree Level: B Citizenship: C,P
Registrant Type: R Majors: B.EC,MGMT,FIN,INS,D.S.,MATH
Schedule(s) - 2, Each With 10–30 Minute Interviews, 08:30 TO 02:30

| Dates - | Interview | :03/04/88 | Posting | :02/19/88 TO 02/25/88 |
| | Bidding | :02/15/88 TO 02/16/88 | Transactions | :02/26/88 TO 03/01/88 |

AETNA LIFE & CASUALTY COMPANY
99 Claim Representative Trn   Schedule # 88851

Investigates, evaluates, negotiates and disposes of all assigned claims. Interviewing for location in Indianapolis with possibility of relocation in another Midwest area office.

Graduation Month: 05-06 Degree Level: B Citizenship: C,P
Registrant Type: R Majors: B.EC,MGMT,FIN,INS,D.S.,MATH
Schedule(s) - 2, Each With 10–30 Minute Interviews, 08:30 TO 02:30

| Dates - | Interview | :03/04/88 | Posting | :02/19/88 TO 02/25/88 |
| | Bidding | :02/15/88 TO 02/16/88 | Transactions | :02/26/88 TO 03/01/88 |

AMERICAN GREETINGS CORPORATION
30 Sales Representative   Schedule # 20451

Representative has selling responsibility for an average of 60 retail outlets which represent the major retail chains of America as well as smaller chains in the territory. Rep will present and sell product and programming from National or Regional Managers who give Rep programs in differing degrees of completeness. Merchandisers will help the Rep execute these programs.

Graduation Month: 05-06 Degree Level: B Citizenship: C,P
Registrant Type: R Majors: BUS
Schedule(s) - 1, Each With 13–30 Minute Interviews, 08:30 TO 04:30

| Dates - | Interview | :02/29/88 | Posting | :02/19/88 TO 02/25/88 |
| | Bidding | :02/15/88 TO 02/16/88 | Transactions | :02/22/88 TO 02/24/88 |

AMERICAN GREETINGS CORPORATION   ** INVITE ONLY **
30 Sales Representative   Schedule # 20452

Representative has selling responsibility for an average of 60 retail outlets which represent the major retail chains of America as well as smaller chains in the territory. Rep will present and sell product and programming from National or Regional Managers who give Rep programs in differing degrees of completeness. Merchandisers will help the Rep execute these programs.

Graduation Month: 05-06 Degree Level: B Citizenship: C,P
Registrant Type: R Majors: BUS
Schedule(s) - 1, Each With 13–30 Minute Interviews, 08:30 TO 04:30

| Dates - | Interview | :02/29/88 | Posting | :02/19/88 TO 02/25/88 |
| | Bidding | :02/15/88 TO 02/16/88 | Transactions | :02/22/88 TO 02/24/88 |

(exhibit continued on next page)

EXHIBIT 4 *(continued)*
....

Career Street Journal Position Requirements Listing

Schedules Available For 02/29/88 Thru 03/04/88

SEE FULL DESCRIPTIONS FOR SCHEDULE NUMBER, INTERVIEW DATE, ETC.

Position					Employer
REG	Invite?	DL	GD	CIT	Major(s)
11 Internal Auditor					Amsted Industries
R	Open	B	05–06	CP	ACCT
11 Accountant					Army & Air Force Exchange Service
R	Open	B	05–08	CP	BUS
11 Accountant					Army & Air Force Exchange Service
R	Open	B	05–08	CP	BUS
11 Auditor Trainee					Defense Contract Audit Agency
R	Open	B	05–06	CP	ACCT
11 Cost Engineering/Account					Eastman Kodak Company
R	Invite	B	05–08	CP	ACCT
11 Cost Engineering/Account					Eastman Kodak Company
R	Open	B	05–08	CP	ACCT
11 Cost Engineering/Account					Eastman Kodak Company
R	Invite	B	05–08	CP	ACCT
11 Cost Engineering/Account					Eastman Kodak Company
R	Open	B	05–08	CP	ACCT
11 Cost Engineering/Account					Eastman Kodak Company
R	Invite	B	05–08	CP	ACCT
11 Cost Engineering/Account					Eastman Kodak Company
R	Open	B	05–08	CP	ACCT
11 Accounting Staff					General Motors Corp-A.C. Spark Plug
R	Open	M	05–06	CP	ACCT,FIN
11 Entry Level Accounting					Harlan Sprague Dawley, Inc.
R	Open	B	05–08	CP	ACCT,FIN
11 Accountant					Monsanto Research Corporation
R	Open	BM	05–08	CP	ACCT,FIN
11 Staff Auditor					National Futures Association
R	Open	B	05–06	CP	ACCT,FIN
11 Accounting Trainees					Parker Hannifin Corporation
R	Open	B	05–08	CP	ACCT
11 Accounting Associate					Quaker Oats—Operations
R	Open	B	05–06	CP	ACCT
11 Corporate Accounting					Square D Company—Lexington
R	Open	B	05–06	CP	ACCT
11 Corporate Accounting					Square D Company—Lexington
R	Open	B	05–06	CP	ACCT
11 Corporate Internal Audit					Teledyne, Inc.
R	Open	B	05–06	CP	ACCT,FIN
13 Acct & Fin'l Devel Prog					Electronic Data Systems Corp.
R	Open	BM	05–06	CP	ACCT,FIN
13 Acct & Fin'l Devel Prog					Electronic Data Systems Corp.
R	Invite	BM	05–06	CP	ACCT,FIN

EXHIBIT 4 *(continued)*

Position					Employer
REG	Invite?	DL	GD	CIT	Major(s)
13 Acct/Fin Entry Level					Harlan Sprague Dawley, Inc.
R	Open	B	05–08	CP	ACCT,FIN
13 Comptrollers Dept-Var Pos					Prudential-Corp. Emplmt. Ctr.
R	Open	B	05–08	CP	ANY
13 Comptrollers Dept-Var Pos					Prudential-Corp. Emplmt. Ctr.
R	Invite	B	05–08	CP	ANY
13 Quantitative Analyst					The State Teachers Retirement of OH
R	Open	B	05–06	CP	BUS,ECON
20 Financial Analyst					Eastman Kodak Company
R	Invite	M	05–08	CP	BUS
20 Financial Analyst					Eastman Kodak Company
R	Open	M	05–08	CP	BUS
20 Financial Analyst					Eastman Kodak Company
R	Invite	M	05–08	CP	BUS
20 Financial Analyst					Eastman Kodak Company
R	Open	M	05–08	CP	BUS
20 Financial Analyst					Eastman Kodak Company
R	Invite	M	05–08	CP	BUS
20 Financial Analyst					Eastman Kodak Company
R	Open	M	05–08	CP	BUS
20 Research Analyst					Houlihan, Lokey, Howard & Zukin Inc
R	Open	B	05–06	CP	BUS,ECON
20 Financial Analyst					Pfizer, Inc.—Terre Haute
R	Invite	M	05–08	CP	BUS
20 Security Analyst					The Principal Financial Group—Des Moines
R	Open	M	05–08	CP	BUS
21 Retail Banking					NCNB Corporation
R	Open	B	05–08	CP	ANY
21 Prof'l/Banker Devel Prog					Southeast Bank, N.A.
R	Open	B	05–08	CP	ANY
21 Credit Analyst					Summit Bank
R	Open	B	05–06	CP	BUS
23 Bond Representative Trn					Aetna Life & Casualty Company
R	Open	B	05–06	CP	BUS,MATH
23 Analyst					Dean Witter Reynolds
R	Open	B	05–06	CP	ACCT,FIN
23 Customer Assistance Rep					Electronic Data Systems Corp.
R	Open	B	05–06	CP	MKTG
23 Customer Assistance Rep					Electronic Data Systems Corp.
R	Open	B	05–06	CP	MKTG
23 Capital Analyst					G. D. Searle Company
R	Open	M	05–08	CP	FIN,ACCT
23 Personal Financial Plan					IDS Financial Services—Louisville
R	Open	M	05–08	CP	ANY
23 Investment Advisor/St Bro					Karmire Financial Group
R	Open	BM	05–06	CP	FIN,MKTG,ACCT

On Thursday or Friday of that same week the results of the bidding process for interviews in the week beginning 10 days later are posted on bulletin boards outside the BPO (see Exhibit 6 for an example of a posted schedule produced by the computer). The system also produces a report showing the results of the bidding process by student name, which is posted outside the BPO for student reference. A listing of input errors by student number is also posted with the student listing. Both of these are shown in Exhibit 7.

About 15 percent of the bid cards have errors, but some of these errors are corrected by the system and those bids can still be processed. Although most

EXHIBIT 5
....
BPO Bid/Transaction Card

Bid/Transaction Card

A sample bid/transaction card is shown here. The same form is used for both bids and transactions, although some fields of the card are used only for bids or only for transactions (see below). The major portion of the information required is completed by filling out the blank spaces along the top of the card and filling in the spaces below by darkening the circle within the appropriate square. When filling in the boxes, please note:

—Use a number 2 pencil. Anything else will not be read by the computer.

—Darken the circle only in each square indicated. DO NOT fill in the complete box. Your pencil markings should not touch the lines forming the box.

—Complete the additional information in the lower right portion of the card by writing in your name, the company name, and the other information requested.

When using the card for bidding, DO NOT put anything in the columns marked SCHED TIME or AC. These fields are used for counter transactions only. At the counter, the graduate assistant will add the time scheduled, and you will note whether you are adding to or canceling from a schedule in the "AC" column.

When using the card for transactions, DO NOT complete the "Times Available" section. As you complete the transaction at the BPO counter, you will then complete the "BID SUF" section.

EXHIBIT 6
....
BPO Interview Schedule

```
SCHEDULE # 13153A          Arthur Andersen & Company
INTERVIEW DATE: 02/18/88                              AS OF 2/16/88
ROOM #:        RECRUITER NAME:
SCHEDULE STARTS:   08:30    LAST INTERVIEW AT:   04:30
10 Staff Account
   ACCT                   ANY DEGREE   MAY, JUNE, AUG      US OR PRV ONLY
12 Tax Consultant
   ACCT                   ANY DEGREE   MAY, JUNE, AUG      US OR PRV ONLY
```

TIME	STUDENT NAME		STUDENT #	MAJOR(S)	DEGREE	GRAD	POS	PHONE
08:00		CHECK IN AT ROOM P100 WAITING ROOM						
08:30	Diane	Weingold	317-82-6802	ACCT MKTG	B	05/88	12	(812)331-7211
09:00	John	Lundey	317-84-0918	ACCT	B	08/88	10	(812)339-7745
09:30	Vicki	Wilt	312-86-9611	ACCT	B	06/88	12	(812)333-5310
10:00		COFFEE BREAK						
10:30	Gregory	Jones	308-70-1370	ACCT	B	05/88	10	(812)339-7153
11:00								
11:30	David	Smith	315-84-8945	ACCT	B	05/88	10	(812)333-5057
12:00		LUNCH IN ROOM P109						
12:30		LUNCH IN ROOM P109						
01:00	Craig	Lee	320-46-0854	ACCT	B	05/88	10	(812)339-6305
01:30	Steven	Brown	317-78-3022	ACCT	B	05/88	10	(812)332-0675
02:00	Gerald	Ransom	346-52-7320	ACCT	B	05/88	10	(812)336-4721
02:30		COFFEE BREAK						
03:00	Gerald	Martin	316-68-0696	ACCT	B	05/88	10	(812)339-3626
03:30	Robert	Hogg	314-66-5551	ACCT	B	08/88	10	(812)333-5681
04:00	Daniel	Kite	316-68-8229	ACCT	B	05/88	10	(812)339-0122
04:30	Deborah	Hale	315-80-2959	ACCT	B	05/88	10	(812)339-1905
05:00		CHECK OUT WITH GRADUATE ASSISTANT						

**PLEASE SEE THE GRADUATE ASSISTANT IN THE P100 WAITING ROOM IF YOU HAVE
ANY QUESTIONS, OR IF A STUDENT FAILS TO APPEAR FOR AN INTERVIEW**

of these errors are caused by students mismarking their bid cards, these input errors are still very frustrating to students because they result in losing the opportunity to interview with a company. Particularly frustrating are errors in the student number, for the error listing only shows the erroneous number and thus the student may not even be able to find his problem on the error listing. The BPO attempts to reduce these frustrations by having people to talk to when the students have problems and to encourage the students to come in and discuss what is going wrong.

Since the students know their interview schedules at least 10 days ahead of time, it is possible to make changes to the schedules before the interview date. If the student does not want to take a scheduled interview, or wants to sign up for a vacant time slot on an interview schedule, or if action can be taken to overcome an input error, adjustments can be made via over-the-counter transactions approved by BPO counselors during this 10-day period. As noted in Exhibit 5, the handmarked bid cards are also used to enter adjustment transactions.

Other outputs from the system that are posted for the students to examine include a listing of all active schedules with three or more openings (that students are encouraged to sign up for without using up a bid), and a report showing all changes in the future interview schedules.

The flow chart in Exhibit 8 depicts the BPO interview schedule processing system. The bid cards marked by the students are read into the bid file

(text continues on p. 72)

EXHIBIT 7
Bid Results by Students

```
                    BID RESULTS AS OF 01/25/88, FOR INTERVIEW WEEK
                            02/08/88 THRU 02/12/88
*****************************************************************************
ABRAMS, STEVEN
                COMPANY NAME              SCHED   BID           RESULTS
         ------------------------------  -----   ---   ---------------------
         MACY'S                          35952    1    SCHEDULED ON 35952A AT 03:00
         MACY'S                          35954         ALREADY SCHEDULED
         NUMBER OF BIDS USED AS OF 01/25/88:   A=00      B=01      C=00      R=05
*****************************************************************************
ACKERMAN, JOSEPH
                COMPANY NAME              SCHED   BID           RESULTS
         ------------------------------  -----   ---   ---------------------
         UNPROCESSED                     96551         INVALID SCHED NO.
         THE PRINCIPAL FINANCIAL GROUP   85852    R    WAITLISTED
         PEPSI-COLA BOTTLING CO. - INDPLS. 92451  R    WAITLISTED
         FORD MOTOR COMPANY              26652    R    WAITLISTED
         NUMBER OF BIDS USED AS OF 01/25/88:   A=00      B=00      C=00      R=04
*****************************************************************************
ADAMS, JULIE
                COMPANY NAME              SCHED   BID           RESULTS
         ------------------------------  -----   ---   ---------------------
         LEO BURNETT-MEDIA DEVELOPMENT PROG. 94551 R   WAITLISTED
         THE PRINCIPAL FINANCIAL GROUP   85852    R    WAITLISTED
         NUMBER OF BIDS USED AS OF 01/25/88:   A=00      B=00      C=00      R=02
*****************************************************************************
ADAMS, SHELLIE
                COMPANY NAME              SCHED   BID           RESULTS
         ------------------------------  -----   ---   ---------------------
         HALLMARK CARDS, INC.            28855    A    SCHEDULED ON 28855A AT 03:30
         OSCAR MAYER FOODS CORPORATION   42554    R    WAITLISTED
         NUMBER OF BIDS USED AS OF 01/25/88:   A=02      B=01      C=00      R=05
*****************************************************************************
ADAMS, WILLIAM
                COMPANY NAME              SCHED   BID           RESULTS
         ------------------------------  -----   ---   ---------------------
         JOHNSON & JOHNSON - SALES       65451    A    SCHEDULED ON 65451A AT 08:30
         FORD MOTOR COMPANY              26652    B    SCHEDULED ON 26652A AT 09:00
         GENERAL ELECTRIC COMPANY        26951    R    WAITLISTED
         ALCOA - SALES & MARKETING       23251    R    WAITLISTED
         BP AMERICA, INC/THE STANDARD OIL CO 95351 R   WAITLISTED
         NUMBER OF BIDS USED AS OF 01/25/88:   A=01      B=02      C=00      R=03
*****************************************************************************
AHEARN, ABIGAIL
                COMPANY NAME              SCHED   BID           RESULTS
         ------------------------------  -----   ---   ---------------------
         OSCAR MAYER FOODS CORPORATION   42554    R    WAITLISTED
         HALLMARK CARDS, INC.            28855    R    WAITLISTED
         HALLMARK CARDS, INC.            28856    I    SCHEDULED ON 28856A AT 08:30
         NUMBER OF BIDS USED AS OF 01/25/88:   A=00      B=02      C=00      R=03
*****************************************************************************
ALEMAN, JUAN
                COMPANY NAME              SCHED   BID           RESULTS
         ------------------------------  -----   ---   ---------------------
         IRWIN UNION CORPORATION         31551    R    WAITLISTED
         OSCAR MAYER FOODS CORPORATION   42554    R    WAITLISTED
         HALLMARK CARDS, INC.            28855    R    WAITLISTED
         NUMBER OF BIDS USED AS OF 01/25/88:   A=00      B=00      C=00      R=08
```

EXHIBIT 7 *(continued)*

BPO BID ERROR LISTING FOR BID WEEK STARTING ON: 01/25/88

     If you submitted a bid, your name should appear on one of three lists: 1) ALPHABETICAL LIST 2) BPO BID ERROR LIST 3) BID ERROR LIST from Information Services. "P" bids will not appear on the alpha or either error list. A P bid error list will be posted at a later date. If your name is not on that list, it has been forwarded to the company.

     If your name does not appear on any list, the card reader was unable to read your card. Your only recourse is manual transactions.

     If this happens two times, there is a chance that your SDS is invalid or a more serious problem exists. Submit a trouble log request at the counter. We will check out your situation and contact you.

     ERROR EXPLANATION: If there is a duplicate bid, the computer picks the last one and processes it. If there is an invalid position code (or more), the computer randomly assigns a valid code, but it may or may not be one for which you are qualified. Invalid bid levels (or missing bid levels) are automatically assigned an "R" bid level. All of these bids are then processed so your name will appear on the alpha list.

STUDENT NUMBER	SCHEDULE NO.	PROBLEM
011-76-0687	38251	INVALID OR MISSING POSITION CODE
025-62-3244	88551	INVALID OR MISSING POSITION CODE
040-58-2093	65451	INVALID OR MISSING BID
040-58-2093	65451	ALL TIMES ARE AVAILABLE
042-46-1754	26654	INVALID OR MISSING POSITION CODE
045-62-3876	94551	ALL TIMES ARE AVAILABLE
045-62-3876	97251	ALL TIMES ARE AVAILABLE
048-46-9107	57650	INCORRECT SCHEDULE NUMBER
048-46-9107	75051	INVALID OR MISSING BID
049-58-9993	75051	ALL TIMES ARE AVAILABLE
060-64-4926	59951	INVALID OR MISSING POSITION CODE
062-48-1312	42554	INVALID OR MISSING BID
079-56-6182	75051	INVALID OR MISSING BID
080-64-4664	38251	INVALID OR MISSING POSITION CODE
087-50-1006	28855	DUPLICATE BID
101-60-1022	52657	INVALID OR MISSING POSITION CODE
106-60-2869	75051	INVALID OR MISSING BID
121-52-1828	42554	INVALID OR MISSING POSITION CODE
121-52-1828	42554	DUPLICATE BID
138-66-1654	17651	ALL TIMES ARE AVAILABLE
138-66-1654	26953	ALL TIMES ARE AVAILABLE
138-66-1654	38251	ALL TIMES ARE AVAILABLE
141-50-6964	59950	INCORRECT SCHEDULE NUMBER
145-48-1526	17552	INVALID OR MISSING POSITION CODE
145-64-9937	25355	ALL TIMES ARE AVAILABLE
146-72-2776	26954	INVALID OR MISSING POSITION CODE
148-58-7670	49352	ALL TIMES ARE AVAILABLE
148-66-7618	28851	INVALID OR MISSING POSITION CODE

through an optical card reader. Then the bid file and the transactions created as a by-product of updating the CRIF, Student, and Company databases are sent via the Apple to the IBM mainframe at the Data Processing Center.

At the Data Center these transactions are used to update copies of the CRIF, Student, and Company databases that are maintained using the System 2000

DBMS. Then the updated CRIF and Student databases are used to screen the bids to detect bad student numbers, bad schedule numbers, duplicate bids, bad position codes, bid priority levels that are invalid or not available to the student, and so on. This screening produces an error summary report, an error file that is sorted to produce the error listing by student number, and the valid bid file that is sorted by

EXHIBIT 8
. . . .
BPO Interview Schedule Processing System

EXHIBIT 8 *(continued)*

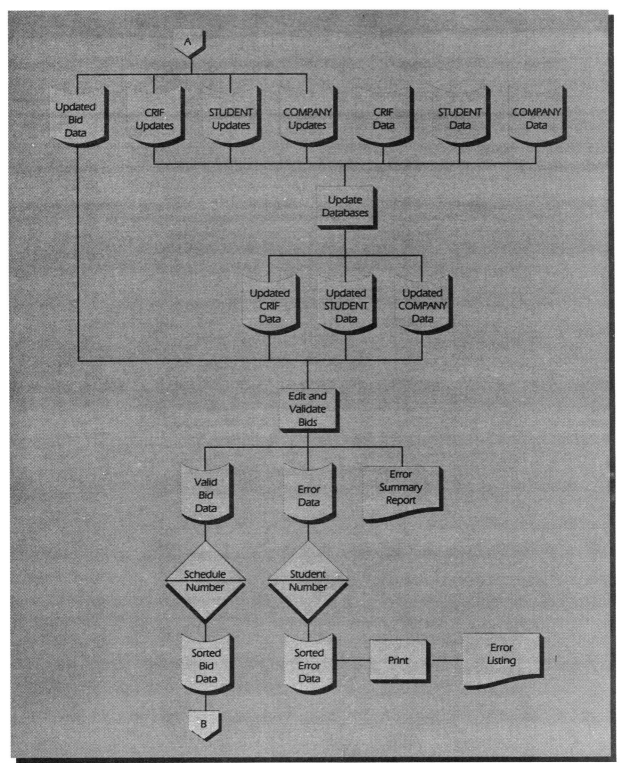

(exhibit continued on next page)

EXHIBIT 8 *(continued)*

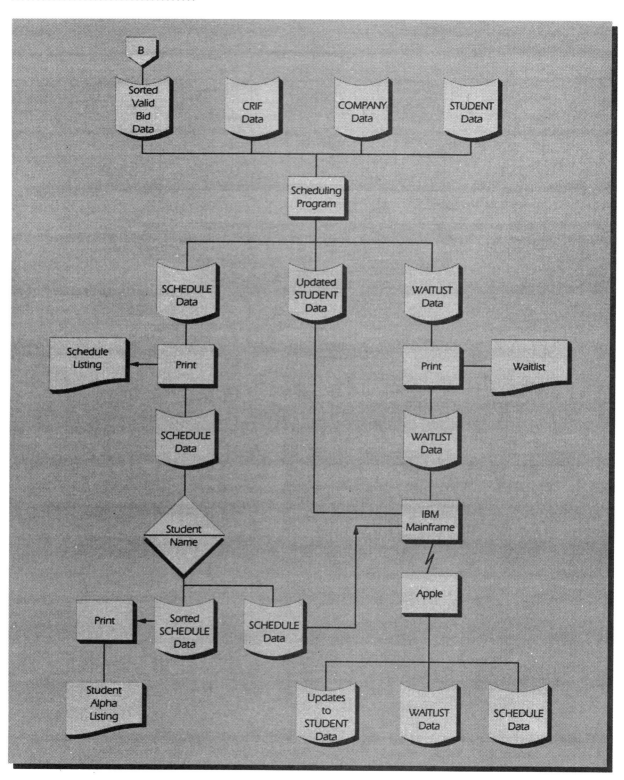

schedule number before it goes into the scheduling program.

The scheduling program takes the valid bid data in schedule number sequence, combines it with data from the CRIF, Student, and Company databases, and applies complex logical processes to determine which students to place on the interview schedule. This program sometimes takes over seven hours to run on the IBM mainframe.

The outputs from this program include the Student database (updated to reflect the bids that were successfully used), a Waitlist file that is printed to produce a list of those students that were unsuccessful bidders on each schedule, and the Interview Schedule database that is used for many purposes, including printing the schedules. A copy of this file is sorted to produce the student alphabetical listing of bid results. All of these listings are printed by the high-speed printers at the Data Center and sent back to the BPO via courier. Finally, the Schedule and Waitlist databases and updates to the Student databases are transmitted back to the BPO, where they are used to update the master databases on the MODUS file server.

Coordination with the Companies A valuable function of the BPO system is to foster better relationships with client companies by facilitating the interviewing process and by supporting year-round communication with recruiters.

Making sure that client companies are scheduled for interviews each year is very important to the BPO. To identify slipups, the system compares next year's Company Schedule database with this year's and last year's versions and produces a report showing previous clients who have not rescheduled. Next year's database can also be used to identify dates that still have openings, as well as any dates that may be overbooked. Thus, the system helps the BPO managers to get in touch with laggard clients and to get them scheduled for the following year.

The system uses the Company Schedule and Contact databases to support the interviewing process by sending out reminder notices a few weeks before scheduled visits and by providing interviewers with updated interview schedules and waitlists shortly before their visits. This helps recruiters prepare for their visits and sometimes leads to last-minute additions of waitlisted students. It also gives the recruiter a better idea of the student demand for interviews with his company that may be useful in planning next year's schedule.

The Contact database is used extensively to prepare periodic mailings to the recruiters to keep them aware of the Midstate University School of Business. The system produces mailing labels for the BPO yearly report sent out in August, the Midstate recruiter newsletter twice yearly, and a yearly recruiting information packet.

At the end of each season the BPO sends each of the companies an extensive packet of information, including a report of their recruiting activities. This includes a review of the past year's interview dates and a listing of next year's scheduled dates. If the company is not yet scheduled for next year, dates are suggested. The packet includes an alphabetic listing of all the students the company interviewed, accompanied by a note asking them to fill in blanks for offers and hires and return it to the BPO. This is used to update the Placement Offers database. The packet also includes a list of the contacts from that company, along with a request to return it after deleting the names of any persons who no longer work for the company (used to purge them from the Contact database).

Management Reporting The databases of this system are maintained by the dBASE III+ DBMS, which makes it relatively easy to produce a large number of standard analysis reports that are prepared on a weekly basis, at the end of a semester, and yearly. Additional ad hoc reports can be produced as desired.

As mentioned above, the Placement Offers database contains data on job offers and acceptance from both the companies and the students. This data is incomplete because neither the companies nor the students can be required to furnish it, but even incomplete data provides valuable management information.

From its data on students, companies, interview activity, and job offers, the system produces a host of tables for the BPO annual report. Exhibit 9 includes a sample of these tables from the BPO annual report for 1987.

. . . .

Summary

The BPO computer system is a distributed system, with both processing and data distributed over a network of microcomputers in the BPO and the IBM mainframe at the University Data Processing Center.

The system is both an operational system and a management information system. It was designed

(text continues on p. 79)

EXHIBIT 9
....
BPO 1987 Annual Report
Sample Tables

Recruiting Activity

This year has continued the plateau of recruiting activity experienced over the last two years. This plateau has shown a significant increase in activity over previous years and stabilized due to both internal and external factors.

Large corporations are decreasing the number of new hires, due to downsizing, mergers, and economic conditions. Accommodations have been made to increase BPO recruiting capacity, by three rooms. In spite of this fact, we are still nearing recruiting capacity.

We will be actively seeking to attract medium and small employers to recruit on campus. These employers represent a large market for future job opportunities, which students are becoming increasingly interested in pursuing.

	1983–84	1984–85	1985–86	1986–87
Different employers	500	508	508	514
Number of schedules	1,980	2,243	2,208	2,106
Number of interviews	19,823	21,500	21,907	21,824
Registrants	2,183	2,460	2,549	2,497
Interviews per student	9.08	8.75	8.8	8.74

MBA Student Profile

The majority of our MBAs continue to enroll in either the Finance or Marketing areas of concentration. Over the past four years both of these programs have witnessed steady enrollment increases. Women increased their representation in the graduating class from 31% to 32%.

Numbers appearing below reflect the total number of MBA registrants in the BPO, not total class size. Included in this total registrant number are 19 foreign nationals. Based upon previous years' distribution of majors we anticipate this year's supply of MBA graduates to approximate 1986–87.

Major	Graduating Registrants*	Female	Male	Minority	Interns
Accounting	4	2	2	0	3
Decision Sciences	5	0	5	0	0
Finance	168	35	130	14	103
Management	11	5	6	1	5
MIS	13	8	5	1	13
Marketing	79	33	46	3	69
Operations	7	2	5	1	10
Personnel	7	3	4	1	3
Other (Non-business combined)	14	9	5	2	1
TOTAL	308	97 (32%)	211 (68%)	23 (7%)	208

* MBA graduates are not required to register for placement services. About 10% more graduates actually earned the MBA degree. The category marked "other" includes non-MBAs, largely from Public Administration and Computer Science.

Interview Frequency Report

The opportunity to interview at the BPO is one of the best in the U.S. Some students aggressively plunge into the interviewing season, while others just test the waters. The figures below represent only an overall average; however, an aggressive BS candidate can interview 10–20 times, while an MBA can have 20–30 opportunities to interview during the year. A number of students, both undergraduate and graduate, were able to reach 50 interviews at the BPO. The most industrious student was able to set this year's record with 55 interviews. Students are not limited in the number of interviews they may have.

	Number of Registrants	Number of Interviews	Average Number of Interviews Per Student
BS	1,980	16,889	9.48
MBA	308	4,156	14.68
Interns	209	779	4.60
Overall	2,497	21,824	9.77

EXHIBIT 9 *(continued)*

Undergraduate Interview Frequency

Business Major	Total Interviews	Modal Range of Interviews	Average Interviews Per Student*
Accounting	3,544	11–15	12.84
Business Economics	93	1–5	7.15
Decision Sciences	1,077	11–15	12.10
Finance	2,679	6–10	10.30
Management	960	1–5	8.20
Marketing	5,031	6–10	11.10
Operations	409	11–15	11.68

Non-Business Major	Total Interviews	Modal Range of Interviews	Average Interviews Per Student*
Computer Science	126	1–5	6.30
Economics	156	1–5	4.45
Fashion Merchandising	669	1–5	7.43
Journalism	117	1–5	3.90
Psychology	61	1–5	4.35
SPEA	895	1–5	5.84
Telecommunications	406	1–5	5.97

Averages differ from modal ranges since some students have targeted employers in mind when they register with the BPO. Thus, averages are sometimes skewed by those students who either interview very selectively or do not interview at all.

MBA Interview Frequency

Major	Total Interviews	Modal Range of Interviews	Average Interviews Per Student*
Accounting	29	6–10	9.66
Decision Sciences	55	11–15	11.00
Finance	2,612	21+	16.96
MIS	116	1–5	9.66
Marketing	1,152	21+	15.15
Operations	75	6–10	12.50
Personnel	46	6–10	6.57

* These averages and modals are computed with spring/summer graduates only. Total number of interviews reflects all graduation dates.

Starting Salaries

BS/BA Placement Salary Summary

Starting salary information is the most requested statistic, and yet it tends to be the most misused and misunderstood. Salaries can be greatly inflated by benefits, automobile allowance, commissions, COLA, discounts, and overtime. We report base salaries only. The BPO collects salary data from two sources—reports sent to us by employers and student self-reports. Wide swings between universities may exist, depending on what is included in annual earnings. Nonetheless, the following figures can be used as a very rough guide. Note the wide swings in ranges.

Summarizing the Results

Telecommunications graduates received the largest salary increase (9.9%). Marketing graduates pulled in the largest salary increase, 7.3%, of any business major. Accounting majors reversed last year's situation by retaking the salary advantage over Finance majors. After last year's huge salary increase of 13%, this year's Fashion Merchandising salaries decreased 4.6%. Decision Sciences majors commanded the highest salaries of the undergraduate business majors. The overall average salary for non-business undergraduates is skewed towards the high side, since this figure includes Computer Science majors, who drew the highest salaries of all undergraduates.

The tables below and on the next page give the figures.

Business Major	# Placed, Reporting Salary	Average Annual Salary	Salary Low	Range High
Accounting	175	22,300	12,000	36,000
Decision Sciences	38	23,850	14,400	36,000
Finance	106	22,050	12,000	36,000
Management	28	20,600	15,000	30,000
Marketing	146	20,700	12,000	35,000
Operations	11	20,200	13,500	24,000
All business majors combined	512	21,684	12,000	36,000

(exhibit continued on next page)

EXHIBIT 9 *(continued)*

Non-Business Majors	# Placed, Reporting Salary	Average Annual Salary	Salary Low	Range High
Computer Science	10	25,700	21,000	29,100
Fashion Merchandising	31	17,260	12,000	24,000
SPEA (Public and Environmental Affairs)	33	20,330	12,120	36,000
Telecommunications	9	20,660	12,900	25,500
Non-business majors combined	118	19,970	12,000	36,000
All BS/BA majors combined	630	21,360	12,000	36,000

Salary information (like placement status) is self-reported. Average salaries are only reported for those sample sizes over 10.

MBA Placement Salary Summary

Many employers have voiced concern over spiraling MBA salaries. These salaries reflect some of the best career assignments in the nation. Most MBAs have previous work experience which enhances their earning potential. This year approximately 320 firms sought our 290 MBA candidates—an intense competition that also drives MBA salaries higher. We have excluded offers that exceed $60,000 from these averages, because they tend not to be representative.

Major	Number Reporting Salary	Average Salary	Salary Low	Range High
Finance	85	37,180	21,000	60,000
MIS	14	33,990	26,500	40,000
Marketing	38	36,670	24,920	46,000
Operations	5	36,130	30,160	40,000
Personnel	5	35,610	25,500	42,000
Overall average	147	36,620	21,000	60,000

Salary information (like placement status) is self-reported. Average salaries are only reported for those sample sizes of 5 or over.

Salary Information by Functional Field

Degree	Average Annual Salary	Salary Low	Range High
BS			
Accounting			
Public accounting	22,070	15,600	27,500
Corporate accounting	22,680	14,400	26,400
Tax accounting	22,540	21,000	23,000
Finance			
Financial analysis	23,820	15,600	36,000
Banking	20,140	12,000	30,000
Investment banking	21,528	15,000	25,200
Marketing			
Sales	22,020	12,000	36,000
Brand management	21,120	17,600	28,000
Retailing	18,770	12,000	24,000
Management			
Management training	21,400	17,000	35,000
Management consulting	23,800	21,000	27,000
Other			
Operations	23,136	13,500	26,500
Systems analysis	25,570	15,600	29,000
MBA			
Accounting (corporate and public combined)	31,420	24,000	36,000
Finance			
Financial analysis	36,600	26,500	48,000
Banking	39,370	24,000	50,000
Marketing			
Market research/product management	38,930	31,500	46,000
Sales	37,370	21,000	60,000
Management			
Management consulting	37,400	25,500	50,000
Management training	33,400	24,925	40,000
Other			
Operations	37,750	27,000	50,000
Systems analysis	33,110	26,500	38,000

from the beginning to support the critical operations of the placement office and to produce the analyses and reports needed to manage the placement office and to report the results to university management. The system benefits students, recruiters, BPO staff, faculty, Jim Wine, and Dean Worthy, and it has produced unanticipated side benefits in cultivating addi-tional financial support for the Business School and the University.

Jim Wine is understandably pleased with the system. "Nobody has a system in their placement office that is doing anything close to what we are doing, particularly with the volume that we deal with," he notes.

3

Strategic and Interorganizational Systems

In Chapter 2 we reviewed a wide variety of information technology (IT) applications that can significantly improve the operation and management of an organization. Such technologies as office automation, factory automation, transaction processing systems, and database management systems have clearly impacted the quality of organizations. An organization, however, does not exist in isolation. An organization operates in a marketplace of customers, suppliers, competitors, partners, and regulators. Can an organization use IT to reach these important stakeholders to improve its position?

In this chapter we address various applications of IT that extend the boundaries of information systems beyond the core organization. In this discussion we cover the use of IT as part of gaining a competitive advantage. We address key determinants, examples, alternative arrangements, and risks of such IT use. Further, we outline the use of IT to link different organizations through electronic data interchange (EDI). EDI and other forms of interorganizational systems suggest significant changes in the way organizations communicate, interact, and compete.

THE REACH AND RANGE OF IT

Peter G. W. Keen (1991) suggests that the scope of the use of information technology by an organization can be summarized via three key features:

1. **IT platform,** which is the set of hardware, software, and standards an organization uses to build its information systems; the IT platform influences what IT-related products and services an organization can deliver in its marketplace.
2. **information reach,** which shows who (both internal and external to the organization) can access information through an organization's IT platform.
3. **information range,** which shows the information and information-based services that can be directly shared through an organization's IT platform.

We discuss the concept of an IT platform in Chapter 12 as part of an IT architecture for an organization. An IT platform that

- uses the standard and commonly available technologies
- provides telecommunication connections to/from outside the organization
- is designed with an emphasis on the needs, requirements, and characteristics of other organizations in its marketplace

can create an opportunity for extensive market advantage.

Figure 3.1 illustrates the dimensions of reach and range supported by an IT platform. Chapter 2 focused on applications in the lower three levels of this graph—those inside the organization.

According to Keen, the goal is IT ubiquity, that is, IT should be able to reach anyone, anytime with any information, similar to the ease of use of the telephone system. A seamless blending of technologies and systems across this scope is not a reality today. A lack of coherent platforms, incompatible hardware, software, and telecommunications technologies, and narrow organizational philosophies on the role of IT limit the reach and range of systems. As Keen points out, however, the "reach and range of the IT platform will significantly affect the degree of freedom a firm enjoys in its business plans."

What we will see in the remainder of this chapter are concepts and examples of how an organization can take advantage of extending the range and reach of its IT-based products and services.

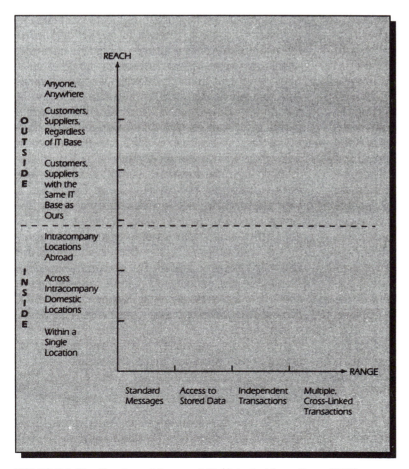

FIGURE 3.1 The Reach and Range of IT. (Adapted from Keen, 1991)

IT FOR STRATEGIC ADVANTAGE

Since the mid-1980s, there has been considerable attention given to possible strategic and competitive advantages through the use of IT as an element of business strategy. We review in this section various ways businesses have used IT strategically. We also address if and when such applications can have a sustainable advantage for an organization.

One of the most publicized and dissected examples of gaining strategic advantage through IT is the experience of American Airlines. The U.S. Department of Transportation has estimated that in 1986 the American Airlines SABRE computerized reservation system achieved a profit of $178 million, which represented a 76 percent rate of return on its investment. This was roughly 63 percent of the total net income for AMR, the parent company, in that year. In the same year, the United Airlines Apollo reservation system brought in $136 million (a 52 percent rate of return) in profits (net income for the parent Allegis Corporation that year was only $11.6 million). Such systems have completely changed the nature of the passenger air travel industry, including air carriers, travel agencies, and rental car and hotel chains. These systems force all American and United competitors to build similar systems or pay to be included in SABRE or Apollo. Further, these systems have directly generated sizable income and profits, which were not present in financial plans before the installation of the systems.

On an indirect level, such airline reservation systems provide an opportunity to influence buying behavior. Association with the reservation system creates a perception of airline service in the minds of passengers and travel agents. Further, some have claimed there is inherent bias in reservation screen displays for the airline providing the system, which can result in a significant competitive advantage. For example, an airline can create a favorable bias by placing its flights at the top of the display, by making electronic links to a competitor's reservation system difficult, and by capturing a large market share of travel-agent workstations. Thus, SABRE and Apollo are not just order-entry and transaction processing systems as

discussed in Chapter 2 (which have existed since the late 1950s), but are also an element for gaining advantage in the marketplace and growth in stockholder equity. These systems are vehicles of corporate strategy.

The astute recognition of business opportunities made available by information technology (including data communications, computers, software, data, artificial intelligence, and factory automation) has transformed companies, such as American Airlines, and entire industries. Such transformations do not occur overnight. It took American Airlines thirty years to craft its systems into such a major market force (Hopper, 1990). SABRE began as a simple seat inventory management tool. It evolved as its reach and range expanded to travel agents, individual travelers, and other travel industry organizations.

Competitors can often duplicate strategic applications, but being the first to market and utilizing proprietary data where possible (for example, using passenger travel history in targeted telemarketing) can make it difficult for the competition to achieve the same level of gains. The initial advantage can be fleeting. According to Hopper, a travel agent can replace SABRE in no more than thirty days, so how can SABRE create a long-term advantage for American Airlines? The key is that SABRE is not a constant. Today, American Airlines is installing the early phase of InterAAct, a new platform, to link it with other players in "an electronic travel supermarket." InterAAct merges data processing, office automation, personal computing, and networking to extend even further the reach and range to knowledge workers in and outside American Airlines. As summarized by Freedman (1991), such strategic systems as SABRE achieve their benefits "over a period of years as the organization learned to reshape the way they did business based on higher quality and quantity of information" provided by these systems.

Who Can Gain Advantage Through IT?

Does it take the resources of an American Airlines to use IT strategically? No, there are many examples of small and medium-sized firms that use IT for market advantage. For example, Lindsey et al.

PROPRIETARY vs. OPEN PLATFORMS

The SABRE reservation system was built from homegrown, proprietary technologies at American Airlines. Today, the push in all organizations, including American Airlines, is to lower IT costs by using standard technologies that permit easy connection of different hardware and software (so-called open systems). Thus, organizations today tend not to compete based upon unique, basic technologies that require long lead-time and specialized skills to develop. Rather, because all competitors have access to basically the same technology, the key is being smarter at using IT in ways that lead from the strengths and unique capabilities of your organization.

(1990) report on the Plains Cotton Cooperative Association, which grew from a $50 million to a $500 million business in fifteen years through an IT application, TELCOT. Any organization with the vision and leadership (or strong champion) can use IT wisely. The overriding theme in this and other examples is that the use of IT must mesh with the strategic direction and plans of the organization if significant gains are to be achieved. An organization must leverage IT with its own strengths as part of an overall business strategy. Unless an organization follows this guideline, others can duplicate or improve upon the use of IT, and any temporary advantage is exactly that—temporary.

WHAT ARE STRATEGIC INFORMATION SYSTEMS?

Very simply, **strategic information systems** (*SISs*) are vehicles for implementing business strategy that use information, information processing, and/or the communication of information. Frequently, such systems extend beyond the bounds of the organization itself, to the customers or clients, suppliers, and competitors. Thus, the use of telecommunications is often central to the implementation of an SIS.

Strategy can have a broad and persistent impact upon an organization, a market, or an entire industry. Strategy can be used to redefine an organization. *An information system is strategic if it enables or supports changes in an organization's product or service or the way it competes in its industry.* Important in this statement is that IT is the enabler. IT must be used as part of an overall business plan, usually to meet customer needs. When this occurs, an SIS can help create, at least temporarily, a competitive advantage for the organization. Usually this competitive advantage will concern a particular product and a particular market. There are also special risks associated with an SIS, which we will explore later in the chapter.

From a strategic viewpoint, a product or service is the entire package of physical goods, support services, and information the organization provides to create value for its customers. In banking, for example, the checking account product/service includes the monthly statement you receive concerning your transactions and account balances and the ability to pay bills by phone and electronically transfer funds. Another example is an elevator service and repair company that could link each elevator via telephone and modem, even those in remote locations, to a central diagnostic computer. This telecommunications link could be used to diagnose a problem and either recommend which plug-in parts can be replaced by local personnel or automatically dispatch a service technician. Convenience, efficiency, and unique features, as well as direct benefit from use of the product, all contribute to the value of the product or service.

Information Intensity

For some firms, a wide range of information is an integral part of the business. **Information intensity** is the amount of dependence a product or firm has on information and information technology. Insurance, banking, stock brokerage, and many government agency organizations are said to have high information intensity. Information systems will almost always play a major role in implementation of strategy in such firms.

For example, Merrill Lynch recognized that there were inconveniences for customers associated with transferring investments between different instruments and accounts and with receiving multiple statements of holdings. Such inconveniences inhibited trading transactions. In response, Merrill Lynch (in cooperation with Bank One) created an integrated information-based financial service, the Cash Management Account (CMA). The CMA consolidates customer accounts (and their associated information systems), such as a brokerage account, checking and credit card account, credit line service, and money market fund, into one account with one monthly statement. Cash that accumulates from the individual accounts (for example, dividends and interest) can be automatically invested in a variety of money accounts. The individual investment products have not changed. The information service that links them is the distinguishing feature.

Figure 3.2 is an example of the summary page from a CMA monthly statement; other pages list the detailed transactions, estimated market values, and other pertinent information for the individual accounts. Merrill Lynch claims that having all this information on one form saves time for tax preparation, budgeting, expense planning, and record keeping. CMA provides a competitive advantage, through an integration of information on these various securities and banking services, that other investment service organizations have never been able fully to overcome as they have duplicated the CMA.

Being first with this service was very important. By some estimates, Merrill Lynch has attracted 450,000 new customers with the CMA service. This SIS also helped to change one of the

Summary Page

Account No. 123-45678	Taxpayer No. 333-22-4444	Page 1 OF 6	Statement Period 02/23/92 TO 03/29/92
Your Financial Consultant ROBERT SEARS FC# 9977 1-800-555-0040	Office Serving Your Account 800 SCUDDERS MILL ROAD YOURTOWN, NY 08536	Questions? CALL 1-800-CMA-INFO OR YOUR FINANCIAL CONSULTANT	

MR. THOMAS ANDERSON
456 NORTH ROAD
ANYTOWN, USA 12345-0987

Account Status

	As of 02/23/92	As of 03/29/92
CMA MONEY ACCOUNTS	$ 11,765.00	$ 30,869.00
CASH	$ 0.55	$ 0.46
SUBTOTAL	$ 11,765.55	$ 30,869.46
PRICED INVESTMENTS	$ 13,566.00	$ 45,346.00
ESTIMATED ACCRUED INTEREST	$ 0.00	$ 282.00
Priced Portfolio	$ 25,331.55	$ 76,497.46
BORROWING POWER	$ 17,945.00	$ 17,682.00
PURCHASING POWER	$ 29,710.00	$ 48,510.00

Account Activity

Credits	This Statement	Year-to-Date
INVESTMENTS SOLD	$ 9,214.05	$ 10,000.05
DIVIDEND/INTEREST INCOME	$ 439.71	$ 3,765.12
FUNDS RECEIVED	$ 31,341.83	$ 52,565.10
OTHER CREDITS	$ 0.00	$ 0.00
TOTAL CREDITS	$ 40,995.59	$ 66,330.27
Debits		
INVESTMENTS BOUGHT	$ 13,698.22	$ 20,453.58
CMA CHECKS	$ 7,431.46	$ 11,147.19
VISA CARD TRANSACTIONS	$ 762.00	$ 1,912.61
INTEREST CHARGED	$ 0.00	$ 0.00
OTHER DEBITS	$ 0.00	$ 0.00
TOTAL DEBITS	$ 21,891.68	$ 33,513.38
Net Activity	+$ 19,103.91	+$ 32,816.89

Dividend and Interest Income

	This Statement	Year to Date
DIVIDENDS (REPORTABLE)	$ 439.71	$ 589.71
INTEREST (REPORTABLE)	$ 0.00	$ 1,175.41
DIVIDENDS (NOT REPORTABLE)	$ 0.00	$ 0.00
INTEREST (NOT REPORTABLE)	$ 0.00	$ 2,000.00
Total Dividend and Interest Income	$ 439.71	$ 3,765.12

EFFECTIVE YIELD FOR THE PERIOD FROM 02/22/92 TO 03/28/92
CMA MONEY FUND: 4.50%

CMA News

LOOK HERE FOR ALL THE LATEST NEWS AND INFORMATION ABOUT YOUR ACCOUNT, INVESTMENT OPPORTUNITIES, THE MARKET, ECONOMIC CONDITIONS, AND MORE.

March 1992

Please advise your Financial Consultant immediately of any discrepancies in securities transactions or investment activity on your statement of account or if you contemplate changing your address. Send all correspondence relating to these matters to the office serving your account. For all other questions about your statement, direct inquiries by telephone to 1-800-CMA-INFO (1-800-262-4636) or in writing to Merrill Lynch CMA Operations, New Brunswick, N.J. 08989-0566. When making inquiries, please give your account number. See back of page for definitions of key terms.

Merrill Lynch, Pierce, Fenner & Smith Inc.
Member, Securities Investor Protection Corporation (SIPC)
We urge you to keep this statement with your investment records.

FIGURE 3.2 Summary Page from a Merrill Lynch CMA ® Statement. (Adapted by permission of Merrill Lynch, Pierce, Fenner & Smith Inc. © Copyright 1992)

DATABASE CATALOG MARKETING

Computerized databases that link location characteristics, individual demographics, and prior buying behavior with marketing channel management may do for the direct sales industry what the Merrill Lynch CMA has done to financial services. Today, major catalog marketers such as Land's End, L. L. Bean, and Spiegel can custombind a catalog for potentially every customer. An artificial intelligence–based information system scans past communication with a customer plus the data in databases mentioned above to predict purchase probabilities for different products, which then drives the catalog construction.

(Adapted from Blattberg and Deighton, 1991)

most basic relationships in the investment industry, that between investor and broker. The existence of the CMA discourages investors from switching to another brokerage firm when individual brokers change firms. Key to this application, as with many that help to achieve a strategic advantage, is a strong focus on the customer and customer service.

SISs and Sustaining a Competitive Advantage

SISs can be used to achieve a competitive advantage for the organization. As outlined by Mc-Farlan (1984) and Porter and Millar (1985), an organization can use information systems to change its balance of power with current competitors, potential competitors, suppliers, firms with substitute products, and customers. Each of these competitive forces will be discussed later in this chapter and in Chapter 13.

Some firms have a vision for SISs. These firms aggressively seek applications of IT that gain competitive advantage for the organization. As documented by Wiseman (1985), in 1978 Dun and Bradstreet (D&B) was a diversified information services company with interests in credit and collection services, insurance, publishing, marketing

services, and broadcasting. Then, from 1979 to 1990, D&B acquired National CSS (a leading computer services and software firm), McCormick and Dodge (a major supplier of software for financial and human resources management), A. C. Nielsen (a leading consumer research organization), and MSA (a major computer services organization). These acquisitions have given D&B expertise in all aspects of the collection, distribution, and analysis of business information. Many of the seven Regional Bell Operating Companies (RBOCs) are now in the process of similar acquisitions in order to be able to both move and manage vast amounts of data for business and residential applications.

How can an organization sustain the impact of IT on its competitive situation? Three key sources that need to be present for sustainability are:

1. **Preempting the competition by being first in the market and respecting your competition by continuing to lead (this is the key to the success of SABRE and CMA).**
2. **Intimidate would-be duplicators by an innovation that is risky, complex, and costly to replicate.**
3. **Leverage your organization's existing strengths (such as proprietary data, size, and costs) with IT, rather than forging new territory.**

Sustainable advantage places a barrier in front of competitors. The core element of placing such a barrier is a solid IT platform and an overall architecture that links IT strategy with business strategy.

Why So Much Interest in SISs Today?

As managers hear and read about the SIS successes in other firms, such as American Airlines, American Hospital Supply, and Merrill Lynch, they may develop similar expectations for their own situations. Beyond this halo effect, however, several factors are working together to create considerable interest in using IT for strategic advantage: economics of technology, entrepreneurial spirit,

86

foreign and domestic competition, and a quest for quality.

First, the diminishing price and increased availability of information and communication technologies (hardware, software, and data networks—see Chapters 4, 5, and 6 for more details) make possible new applications. These trends reduce the risk associated with applications that have benefits that are difficult to quantify. Applications can be prototyped and built rapidly, in essential form, to test for strategic significance. The first business to introduce a valuable strategic application may have a real advantage by being the initial entrant. Thus, there is a noticeable technology push behind such systems.

Second, senior management in many organizations is becoming more entrepreneurial and intrapreneurial, creating a demand for uses of all organizational resources (people, land, capital, and information) for competitive advantage. According to *Business Week* (October 14, 1985), "Business is beginning to reconfigure things from the ground up—this time with the computer in mind." As part of this intrapreneurial spirit, managers are exploring every possible way to take advantage of the vast warehouse of data and systems now in place. With most of the basic transaction processing systems in place, much of an organization's data is computerized. Those who recognize that IT is not a necessary expense but rather a resource that can be applied creatively and advantageously can outline systems of strategic importance to the organization. The key is making these data, along with appropriate presentation and analysis tools, available upon demand (that is, extending IT reach and range).

Third, foreign and domestic competitive pressures are forcing organizations to use every resource to advantage. Factory automation, robotics, just-in-time inventory methods, and other approaches revitalizing U.S. manufacturing industries are all information-intensive applications. For example, just-in-time and zero inventory methods require the linkage of information systems between manufacturers and their suppliers. The foreign and domestic pressures also include non–North American firms using technology for a

IT IN ECONOMIC DEVELOPMENT

Cities worldwide now are using IT to lure corporate headquarters and to provide new "trade routes" for goods and services produced in their area. Amsterdam, London, and Singapore are strengthening their economic position by:

- being major nodes in global electronic trading networks
- providing help to multinationals to set up international communications links

This makes it easier for companies to establish their back-office operations in these cities, increasing the local economic base.

(Adapted from *ICIT Advance*, 1988)

competitive worldwide advantage. Telecommunications drastically reduce the barriers of national boundaries and tend to open global markets.

Fourth, competitive advantage relates strongly to the quality of the products and services provided by an organization. High quality may mean lower costs, lower prices, more reliable service, and greater market share. Quality means, in part, doing things right the first time. For example, consider six different product managers who want to share market research data. If each uses separate information systems with different customer identification codes, poor quality data and misinformation will occur, or, even worse, these managers will not be able to share their collective intelligence.

One major computer and communications supplier estimated that poor quality data were costing the organization $3 billion annually in wasted effort and lost sales from inaccurate or confusing communication with customers. This poor quality was due to three factors—inconsistent record systems, duplicate processing and unsynchronized updating of data in separate systems, and the use of the wrong data because the correct data could not be easily distinguished. Thus, the quality of information systems can be of strategic importance to organizations.

Information Sharing—A Central Philosophy

According to Cole (1985), a philosophy of information sharing is central to the achievement of competitive advantage through information technology. SISs support communication between employees, contractors, customers, suppliers, lines of business, functional areas, and so on. To do so, two fundamental philosophical changes have to occur in many organizations:

1. Information systems must be opened to external organizations.
2. Information must be made available to anyone who has a need to know.

Obviously, such information sharing is built on trust, which must be a part of the organizational value system. As we will discuss in Chapter 16, organizational politics can use IT as a vehicle for internal gain. Some organizational units and individuals, especially those already supported by IT, may resist such openness, since they may see it as diluting their own competitive advantage. Experience has shown, however, that competitive advantage for the organization can be achieved by such information sharing, and these individual values must be managed to reach this broader goal.

To be effective, shared information must be useful, valuable, and secure. Customers will not enter orders directly into your computer systems unless doing so means lower prices, faster delivery, improved support, or some other advantage. Further, customers expect that data about their interactions with your organization cannot be seen or manipulated by other organizations.

Such an information-sharing philosophy allows organizations not only new ways to compete, but also new ways to cooperate. For example, American Airlines and Citibank share information on customers—frequent flyer credits are earned for purchases made on Citibank's credit cards. Both American Airlines and Citibank customers have an additional reason to be loyal to each company (Konsynski and McFarlan, 1990). Cooperation can even occur between competitors, as in the case of ATM banking networks. In this case, those banks in partnership share the high costs and risks to develop technology that has become a necessary element in banking competition. Each participating bank then differentiates itself based upon fees and the information content of ATM transactions and account summary statements. Later in this chapter we will address another major example of IT cooperation, the electronic exchange of documents between customers and suppliers.

THE IMPACT OF STRATEGIC APPLICATIONS

One way to understand the nature of strategic information systems and to identify possible applications in an organization is by studying existing successful applications. Tables 3.1 and 3.2 outline many of the ways in which SISs have affected individual organizations and whole industries. This scheme has two general categories:

1. Applications that directly affect the competitive environment of an organization.
2. Applications that change the nature of products and markets of an industry.

The categories are not mutually exclusive, but they still represent a useful way to group similar applications. Many examples fit into several categories; in fact, applications with multiple impacts are some of the most successful applications.

Competitive Impacts

Competitive impacts of SISs (see Table 3.1) are those that directly affect the ability of competitors to operate. This class of SIS often creates alliances with customers. Such alliances make it difficult or costly for a customer to switch to a competitor or raise the cost for a new competitor to enter the marketplace (for example, by forcing competitors to provide additional features that are difficult or time-consuming to duplicate).

88

TABLE 3.1 Competitive Impacts of Strategic Information Systems

Impact	Definition
Product development cycle	Reduce research and development, production, or physical distribution time
Product quality enhancement	Make product/service more reliable or more rapidly repairable or have less down time
Sales force and selling support	Identify customers and support sales activities
Order cycle automation	Reduce effort/cost of submitting and processing order or make possible anytime buying
Office cost reduction	Reduce time in clerical and back-office functions
Channel and inventory management	Reduce inventory and make inventory more attractive to customers
Reduction of management levels	Eliminate middleman and functions that filter, transcribe, and manipulate data
Product features enhancement and threat of substitution	Ability to be flexible and meet new demands

TABLE 3.2 Industry Impacts of Strategic Information Systems

Impact	Definition
Nature of products and services	Create or change products/services by adding information or technology
Product life cycle	Extend life of product/service
Geographical scope	Reduce geographical or market limitations on product/service
Economies of scale in production	Increase volume of production without comparable increase in cost or shift in production mix
Shift in value-added locus	Change product/service content and value by adding information-based dimensions
Bargaining power of suppliers	Ability to control marketplace on price, availability, delivery, or quality of purchased materials/components
New business creation	Create new products or markets

Product Development Cycle Computer-aided design (CAD) and computer-aided manufacturing (CAM) systems make it possible to develop and produce new, improved, or custom products rapidly, thus beating the competition to the marketplace.

Product Quality Enhancement Microelectronics in automobiles have allowed for more rapid diagnosis of problems and simpler maintenance by replacement of modules. Digital Equipment's artificial intelligence system, XCON, uses decision rules to develop custom computer configurations, which dramatically reduces the time required to fill orders and increases accuracy.

Sales Force and Selling Support McKesson Corporation uses hand-held computer terminals with bar-code readers to scan stock on drugstore shelves and to reorder when supply becomes low. In addition, this system knows where products are shelved in the store so that items can be packaged together to reduce the work of restocking. Chevron Chemicals Fertilizer Division uses laptop computers for its sales force to pass order, pricing, and product information back and forth. In addition, a skeleton spreadsheet allows field sales staff to help farmers develop their own business plans, which breeds customer loyalty and provides useful data for future sales activities.

Order Cycle Automation Computers installed in participating car dealerships are linked to the bank's host computer to transmit the information needed for review directly to the loan officer's desk. The appropriate credit bureau review is retrieved and sent with the report to a credit analyst for further processing. If necessary, the system can also generate a letter of refusal on the bank's letterhead. Turnaround time is about 10 to 15 minutes and may be especially useful for the Monday morning crunch when applications are backed up from Saturday car buyers.

Office Cost Reduction Point-of-sale terminals and the associated computer systems have saved tedious and costly office and clerical time for implementing price changes, collecting and analyzing

COMPETING IN REAL-TIME: THE WAL-MART SUCCESS

Wal-Mart has used IT as part of its business strategy to become the largest U.S. retailer. IT pervades the business. Wal-Mart has twice the return on sales and three-quarters the overhead of K-mart. Many IT applications make this possible. One in-store system constantly tracks sales from point-of-sale and automatically triggers replenishment orders through satellite data communication to corporate headquarters. This system links manufacturers, distribution centers, Wal-Mart headquarters, and stores into a just-in-time physical distribution system. Through this system, Wal-Mart shares valuable sales data with 2,000 vendors. This system drastically reduces inventory costs, which leads to lower prices and more customers. Stocking the right amount of just what is needed reduces lost sales.

(Adapted from Freedman, 1992)

sales summaries, and making price decisions. Beyond cost reductions, these data have also given the stores a new business, that of selling sales data to manufacturers and distributors. Sales can be easily summarized by store location, association with coupons, day of week, package, and price. Point-of-sale systems have changed stores into on-line market research labs, feeding sales activity to manufacturers and distributors within a day after sales promotions take effect.

Channel and Inventory Management   A system at Red Lion Inns tracks occupancy rates at specific inns and by types of rooms. The system then automatically sends messages to its hotels and SABRE offering discounts designed to stimulate demand. As a result, Red Lion has a more than 70 percent occupancy rate, which is 2 to 3 percentage points above the national average. Bringing in business has lasting value to Red Lion, which claims a repeat business rate of 85 percent, which is very high for the industry.

Reduction of Management Levels   Systems that automate order processing or billing can elim-

inate whole classes of jobs in expediting, order entry, credit authorization and management, and vendor selection. Integrated systems that make marketing, financial, product, and production data available to individual managers reduce the need for layers of managers to combine, filter, reconcile, and interpret data from multiple sources. Such use of IT results in significant cost reduction and a more nimble organization that is more responsive to changes in its markets.

Product Features Enhancement and Threat of Substitution   Flexible manufacturing systems and other manufacturing technologies reduce the threat of competitors providing substitute products or new features because the ability of the firm to react quickly is improved. Desktop publishing technology has made it less expensive for such firms as duplicating services to compete economically with print shops (who use bulky and expensive equipment), and thus to enter new markets.

Industry Impacts

Industry impacts of SISs (see Table 3.2) are those that permanently change the nature of doing business in a particular industry. The American Airlines SABRE reservation system is one such example. These impacts affect the whole industry, not just relationships between certain competitors or between one supplier and some customers. These impacts redefine the business and may come about because of the integration of information technologies with products/services.

Nature of Products and Services   Many products have both a physical and an information component. Information may be useful in buying, using, or repairing the product, or information may be integral to the operation of the product or service. For public information data banks, such as Dow Jones News Retrieval Service or The Source, information and information technology are central to their business (see Chapter 14 for more information on public data banks). Microelectronics in appliances and automobiles are transforming the nature of these products.

Product Life Cycle Computer-controlled machine tools and microprocessor boards that add functionality and capacity represent ways to give existing products longer lives. Computer programs and plug-in boards make products flexible, easier to upgrade and repair, and more current, all of which extend a product's life cycle.

Geographical Scope Telecommunications has made possible the delivery of the newspaper *USA Today* into all U.S. and even international markets. Computer-based kiosks in the aisles of shopping malls that display products and take orders have allowed stores to compete without renting additional space.

Economies of Scale in Production Flexible manufacturing systems make it economically possible to produce products in smaller batches, thus carrying less inventory, and to be able to switch from the manufacture of one product to another as demand warrants.

Shift in Value-Added Locus Information systems for real estate brokers assist them in advising clients on available mortgage packages and their eligibility for financing. Such systems shift the focus from brokering properties to a broader range of steps, all of which are necessary for a prospective buyer to acquire a home, land, or a building.

Bargaining Power of Suppliers A manufacturer that forces suppliers to participate in electronic exchange of orders shifts the balance of power in the manufacturer's favor.

New Business Creation Information and information technology can stimulate the birth of completely new businesses. This can occur by:

- making new businesses technologically feasible (telecommunications technology has made facsimile services possible).
- creating demand for new products (the proliferation of personal computers and modems has created the demand for electronic bulletin boards and mail systems, magazines, and tutorial books/manuals).

ALLOWING THE COMPETITION TO LEAPFROG

The Bank of America's experience with their Trust Department is one example of a one-time leader that allowed the competition to leapfrog. In the 1950s and 1960s, BOA was recognized as a leader in the use of information technology, including being involved in the invention of magnetic ink characters. By 1981, BOA had fallen woefully behind after a decade of redirecting funds into projects that created short-term profits. In 1981 and several times later, BOA tried to introduce an advanced application for trust reporting and accounting that would again allow the bank to be competitive in this specific market. In the rush to catch up with the competitors in the use of information technology in trust management, compromises were made and shortcuts were taken to try to reduce system development times, but these efforts failed. BOA had lost its leadership position and was not able to recover. In 1987, after spending about $80 million on hardware and systems development in the unsuccessful efforts to become competitive again, BOA sold its trust business to Wells Fargo for $100 million.

- creating new businesses within existing ones (a company that develops a network for moving its own data, for example, a bank that creates an automated teller machine network, may spin off a subsidiary to sell excess network capacity to other companies).

The Potential Hazards of Using IT Strategically

Even though information technology can provide strategic advantages when it is appropriately applied and managed, it can also cause disasters (or at best no advantage) when it is misapplied, neglected, or ignored. As with any basis for competition, if the firm is not willing or able to sustain the investment, then changing the focus of competition is not advantageous. Competitors will react and attempt to duplicate and leapfrog (some estimate that the second firm to implement a particular strategic application can develop it in one-half the time and cost it took the pioneer). Thus, if you do not continue to be the leader, you may simply have opened the door for a competitor more willing or able to compete on new grounds (see the box "Allowing the Competition to Leapfrog").

Electronic home-shopping services are an interesting example of an information service with which many companies have experimented. Most companies have decided to wait to implement them, however, because of the associated risks. Firms unwilling or unable to make sustained investments in the development of an SIS and in stimulating recognition of its value should be extremely cautious about starting to develop an SIS.

SISs are very visible, not hidden inside the organization. Thus, operational problems (such as malfunctioning telecommunication lines, poor human interfaces, and incorrect data) can cause serious public embarrassment to the firm. Also, because many SISs are built using state-of-the-art technology, such technology may not be infallible. SISs that rely on partnerships and cooperation across organizations may be difficult to coordinate. Computer system changes in any of the partners can affect the whole effort. One organization does not control all the pieces. Thus, SISs can be fragile, complex systems that require concentrated attention to be effective. A thorough understanding of an SIS may require someone who can conceptualize the operation of several organizations and anticipate the interorganizational problems.

The resounding conclusion is that any advantage from an attempt at a strategic application is most likely to occur if the system exploits some unique strength of the organization. Clemons and Row (1991) suggest that an organization look at its plant and equipment, proprietary knowledge, brand name recognition, and other unique resources it might possess. For example, Merrill Lynch leveraged an existing strength in its retail presence and money market funds expertise into the Cash Management Account discussed earlier. When IT is combined with such strengths, the value of these already advantageous resources are enhanced. If this approach is not taken, the organization runs the risk of not being able to sustain any initial advantage.

Summary of SIS Applications

The conventional perspective on information systems has focused on support of critical operational and decision-making tasks *within* an organization; the goal was usually cost reduction or incremental revenue generation. This focus has been on internal, operational levels of the organization where technology can substitute for labor or less efficient technology. Automated warehouse systems, production scheduling programs, and automated financial accounting systems are prime examples. In general, such systems were not related to the strategic direction of the firm (a notable exception has been production planning and control systems necessary to make a manufacturing company competitive).

Today, companies are recognizing that information systems (in fact, often the same type of systems previously developed) can be used strategically when emphasis is placed on other dimensions besides internal efficiency or incremental gains. An information system can be considered strategic if its purpose is to accomplish any of the following:

Achieve a low-cost leadership position in an industry by reducing internal costs or by raising the costs for competitors or potential competitors.

Provide product/service *differentiation* and greater value to customers.

Create alliances between the firm and its suppliers and customers, thus reducing costs for a supplier or providing special support to customers.

Enhance a product/service by providing innovative features or support.

Assist in bringing a product to a *target* or *niche market.*

Provide *growth in existing markets* by geographical or volume expansion.

A common characteristic of many of the examples described in this chapter is the strategic use of telecommunications technology. The more that telecommunications bond a customer's processes to the firm, the greater the costs for the customer to switch to a substitute or alternative supplier.

92

This bonding is through data that cannot be provided by another supplier. The combination of telecommunications and data can help the customer to perform some analysis or reporting that is otherwise costly and time-consuming. A customer becomes dependent on these features and, consequently, on the supplier.

REACHING OUT THROUGH EDI AND INTERORGANIZATIONAL SYSTEMS

Preparing and sending a single paper purchase order can cost up to $25. It is very expensive and requires much human time to enter the data for purchase orders or invoices, to verify prices and discounts, to translate from one format or media to another, and to track down the errors induced by this manual handling of data in two different organizations. Figure 3.3 depicts this highly manual document interchange process. In this process, delay and costs are incurred for mailing hardcopy documents, errors are introduced from multiple data entries, and inconsistencies occur because of multiple copies of documents at different points in the process. According to *Business Week* (August

26, 1985), a typical U.S. auto manufacturer spends as much as $200 of the cost of each vehicle on processing bills, orders, inquiries, and other intercompany paperwork. This $200 represents not only postage and handling costs, but also the cost to correct errors in the documents.

Similar to systems built to reduce internal paper handling (for example, from order entry to production), interorganizational systems can reduce this communications cost across organizational boundaries. More important, such interorganizational systems, by extending IT reach, can be vehicles to bond electronically two organizations. Such bonding makes it costly for either partner to break up the relationship or for others to penetrate it.

An **interorganizational information system (IOS)** is an integrated data processing and data communications system used by two or more participant organizations. These organizations may be part of a cooperative (such as a banking network) or may be in a customer-supplier relationship. The most common type of IOS involves electronic exchange of business documents.

Electronic data interchange (EDI) is a set of standards and hardware and software technology that permits computers in separate organizations

FIGURE 3.3 Manual Handling of a Purchase Order. (Adapted with permission of *Datamation*, 1990, © 1990 by Cahners Publishing Co.)

to transfer data electronically (such as purchase orders, invoices, medical claims, and price lists). EDI, as the basis for an IOS, can reduce the cost of producing a purchase order from the $25. level down to $5, and with much less hassle and shorter lead time. These savings are in addition to the potential benefits from lower inventories and more responsive customer service possible with this application of EDI. For example, Navistar International has cut its truck inventory from a thirty-three-day supply to a six-day supply. Further, computer systems can be designed to absorb the peaks and valleys in the volume of data transfers, which can reduce pressure on and interruptions of clerical and managerial staff when handling overload situations (for example, Monday mornings, just before closing, or after plant shutdowns). Costs are also reduced because data entry errors, which result from rekeying data as they pass from organization to organization, are eliminated.

Many experts believe that the real value of EDI comes not from automating the exchange of paperwork between companies, but from integrating stand-alone EDI systems in such areas as purchasing with accounts payable and electronic funds payments. This integration practically eliminates duplicate data entry and the errors and inconsistencies created by separate incompatible systems. As a supplier, your customers are interested in the entire business process of ordering, order status, and payment, not just one of these individually.

How EDI Works

Figure 3.4 outlines the EDI approach to document interchange (compare this to Figure 3.3). With EDI a customer sends a supplier a purchase order or release to a blanket order via a standard electronic document (usually via computer-to-computer communication, but EDI can occur by passing magnetic tapes or disks). There is no manual shuffling of paperwork and little if any reentering of data. Standard document formats can be set between the partners in the EDI relationship, selected from industry agreements, or chosen from the ANSI (American National Standards Institute) X.12 committee standards. The supplier checks

FIGURE 3.4 EDI Handling of a Purchase Order. (Adapted with permission of *Datamation*, 1990, © 1990 by Cahners Publishing Co.)

94

that the message is in an acceptable format and sends an electronic acknowledgment to the customer. The electronic order then feeds the supplier's production planning and shipping systems to schedule the shipment. Elapsed time is short, errors are not introduced, and documents are not lost in transit.

When the order is ready to ship, the supplier sends the customer an electronic notice of the pending shipment. The customer's computers will check that the shipment information corresponds to the order and returns a message authorizing the shipment. The supplier then sends a message that includes the truck number, carrier, approximate arrival time, and bill of lading. The customer's computer alerts the receiving dock of the expected arrival; receiving personnel visually verify the shipment upon arrival for quality and the shipment is accepted.

The customer's accounts payable system is then triggered to issue payment. Today, because banks are not usually included in EDI, a physical check, not an electronic funds transfer, is produced. EDI is more than electronic mail because the exchanges of documents are also linked into business operating systems. Very little manual data entry is required, and the customer carries less inventory because the ordering cycle is significantly reduced by the elimination of mail and paper processing.

EDI is usually implemented by computer-to-computer communication between organizations. Documents may be exchanged over a private telecommunications network of leased lines created by one of the parties, over public networks, or via a third-party value-added network (VAN). A VAN would provide not only the network paths between the organizations, but might also provide software to support EDI. Some VANs concentrate in specific industries (for example, GE Information Services in apparel, automotive, and petrochemical, among others, and British Telecom/Tymnet in grocery, transportation, chemical, and electronics).

The first generation of EDI places documents in an electronic mailbox until the recipient picks it up, much like electronic mail. Second-generation EDI drastically reduces delays in such a passive system by immediately forwarding messages

placed in the mailbox. Today's most advanced third-generation EDI systems are interactive, in which documents, messages, and queries are sent directly between partners, bypassing store and forward mailboxes.

EDI AND LEVILINK

Levi Strauss provides a variety of services to customers through its Electronic Data Interchange Services group and its LeviLink services. These services help retail store customers in merchandising, ordering, payments, and other aspects of the whole apparel manufacturing and marketing cycle. The services include preticketing of items with Uniform Product Code tickets, various stock and management reports showing sales and profitability by item and period, and electronic purchase orders and packing slips. These services allow retailers to replenish stock in three days instead of the previous fourteen. Captured sales data help Levi Strauss (and retailers) analyze sales by color, style, size, location, and time to keep the retailer stocked with the right goods and to feed production schedules. LeviLink cost more than $1 million to develop.

(Adapted from *I/S Analyzer*, 1989)

DEPARTMENT OF DEFENSE AND EDI

The U.S. Department of Defense (DOD) is implementing an EDI application for exchange of technical product documentation with defense contractors. Computer-aided acquisition and logistics support (CALS) will provide technical manuals and engineering drawings in electronic, rather than paper, form. Before CALS, cost estimates for delivery of technical data ranged from 10 percent to 30 percent of total contract costs. For example, the B-1B bomber has one million pages of documentation. The DOD estimates that CALS will reduce technical documentation authoring costs by 20 percent to 30 percent, provide annual savings to the U.S. Air Force of $135 million for documentation, and result in an overall 20 percent reduction in weapon system life-cycle costs.

According to Kavan and Van Over (1991), EDI has been implemented in organizations with annual sales of $1.8 million and higher. As much as 90 percent of interbusiness transactions are conducted via EDI in some firms. The overriding reason for implementing EDI is to improve relationships between customers and suppliers. The annual growth rate of EDI users is roughly 75 percent, with 21,000 users listed in the 1992 *EDI Yellow Pages*.

Why is EDI Important Today?

According to Cash and Konsynski (1985) and Senn (1992), EDI has developed from six technological, economic, and organizational changes:

1. *The need for fast, reliable information exchange in response to rapidly changing markets, products, and services.* Internal processes cannot be the only way a company can react quickly to changing markets; the whole chain of activities from production of raw materials to final product delivery to the customer must be considered. Processes like just-in-time manufacturing demand more rapid data flows.
2. *The evolution of guidelines, standards, and protocols.* Such standards as the Uniform Product Code, optical and magnetic ink characters, and data transmission schemes make it easier for different organizations to exchange data without having to expend effort and dollars to make systems compatible.
3. *Penetration of information systems into internal business processes.* Most business units depend on computer processing of data, so data about the movement of materials, products, orders, and the like between these units are already in electronic form. Because of the relative changes in labor and information technology costs in today's world, it simply makes good business sense to exchange data electronically rather than reenter this data.
4. *Technical quality and capability of information technology.* The greater reliability of information technology permits organizations to use this technology in areas of greater risk to reputation and external perception, such as in direct contact with customers or suppliers.
5. *Differentiation of products/services via information technology.* Computer systems themselves can become valuable components of a firm's product or service. The access to order status, product availability, prices, and shipment schedules, for example, can make a customer reluctant to switch to another supplier.
6. *The globalization of organizations.* To compete on an international scope requires an organization responding like a competitor in the same neighborhood. A common method of communication through EDI simplifies what would otherwise be an intractable communication problem.

Each EDI partner must sign contracts outlining each other's responsibilities and liabilities. A contract resolves, for example, when an electronic order is legally binding (when it is delivered, after the message is read, or after it has been checked) and whether all messages must be acknowledged. Usually, the customer must guarantee that if it issues a correctly formatted and acknowledged order, then the customer is obliged to accept and pay for the requested goods. Less time is available to correct ordering errors because EDI reduces the ordering lead time. In such a tightly coupled system, an error can cascade from a customer through a chain of suppliers before it is detected. Thus, all parties must agree to the exact point at which a message becomes binding in the electronic chain of events. Transactions should be encrypted for security, especially when public telecommunication facilities are used.

EDI Applications

EDI has been implemented most widely in the transportation, manufacturing, and retail sectors. Digital Equipment Corporation claims to have reduced order processing costs for components by more than 50 percent with EDI. Service Merchandise, a national catalog warehouse retail chain, has used EDI to reduce the time to process a purchase order from ten days to two, with faster inventory turnover and better customer service. The benefits of EDI are so significant for some companies—such as R. J. Reynolds Tobacco Company, Ford, and General Motors—that they are discontinuing

96

EDI IN SINGAPORE

Singapore introduced a National IT Plan in 1986, in which EDI plays a prominent role. Among the many EDI applications spawned by this national initiative is MediNet. MediNet links pharmacies, clinics, hospitals, insurance companies, and a central health care system board. The system facilitates a national exchange of various medical documents: medical records, patient bills and claims, supplier orders and invoices, and national medical research data.

(Adapted from Liang, 1992)

EDI INTERNATIONAL STANDARDS

The Consultative Committee on International Telephony and Telegraphy (CCITT) is setting worldwide data communication standards for EDI. These include:

- X.400 for general store-and-forward electronic messaging (like e-mail).
- X.435 for EDI messages, which will allow sending such messages directly between business partners rather than through a VAN; X.435 automatically verifies message receipt and allows broadcasting of EDI messages (for example, to send new price lists to all customers).
- X.500 is a directory function that centralizes all the demographics of customers and suppliers needed to initiate an EDI message (X.500 is like an automated telephone directory of all organizations capable of participating in EDI).

Besides CCITT, ANSI X.12 in the United States and Edifact in the European Community are setting standards. Unfortunately, three standards can mean no standard. Today, international EDI requires software bridges to interface EDI applications across systems built on different standards.

suppliers who do not adopt EDI. Other organizations simply give EDI partners favorable treatment.

As more and more organizations (including the Internal Revenue Service) start interorganizational systems, they will be in a better position to force customers and suppliers to participate. A study by Coopers & Lybrand (Booker and Fitzgerald, 1990) predicted that organizational spending on EDI would quadruple between 1990 and 1993.

Organizational Requirements for Using EDI

Gesellschaft für Mathematik und Datenverarbeitung (1991) reports on case studies of twelve EDI pilot projects throughout Europe (see box "EDI in Europe" for a synopsis of several of these projects). The study concluded that a wide variety of EDI applications are possible if:

- partners cooperate, trust each other, and work to overcome initial obstacles.
- a suitable technical infrastructure of hardware, software, and telecommunications experts is available.
- an application promoter and a technical promoter are in place in participating organizations.

Technical Standards for EDI

The technical success of EDI depends on standards. Standards for EDI are necessary because computer file formats, forms, data and transaction definitions, and the overall methods of processing data vary considerably across companies, and especially across countries. Standards provide a way to decouple the different EDI participants as much as possible, yet still facilitate data exchange. Among business transactions alone, EDI requires standard formats for (Senn, 1992):

- purchase order
- purchase order acknowledgment
- purchase order change request
- invoice
- request for quote
- reply to request for quote
- price and sales catalog
- request for information about EDI participants

Individual companies, industrial consortia, and international technical standards bodies have worked to establish the standards of data interchange. Standards are needed for computers, terminals, data communications, business forms, and

---

EDI IN EUROPE

PUSHED and PRODEC are just two examples of extensive EDI development in Europe.

PUSHED

Montedipe and Montfluos, two major companies in the Italian chemical industry, initiated an EDI application with their customers and suppliers. The main objective of the project was a pragmatic approach to electronic data interchange in small and medium-sized companies. The first step was the development of an EDI workstation that could be used by all participants. It was intended to gain practical experience to prove the feasibility of EDI and heighten awareness of the strategic and organizational issues among the companies.

PRODEC

PRODEC is part of the EUROSELECT initiative to establish a price/product catalog for the exchange and comparison of product information in the wholesale grocery industry throughout Europe. This system increases the market transparency and the chance to buy products with the highest value for the money. It was developed to strengthen the market position of small and medium-sized wholesalers in relation to large food producers and large supermarket chains.

(Adapted from *Gesellschaft für Mathematik und Datenverarbeitung,* 1991)

---

error or problem detection and management. Currently, one common international set of document standards does not exist for EDI. One legal complication to EDI is that some countries limit or tariff so-called transborder data flow, including some EDI business documents. International EDI requires considerable cooperation today among the EDI partners.

Ford, General Motors, and Chrysler, along with 300 large suppliers, have created the Automotive Industry Action Group to set standards for transmitting forms among companies. To be a supplier to these auto manufacturers, a company must comply with these standards. The nature of doing business has changed between the auto companies and their suppliers, and hence the balance of power between them has also shifted. The lower production costs of foreign vehicle manufacturers are forcing such cost-cutting measures.

HOW TO IDENTIFY AND JUSTIFY OPPORTUNITIES TO EXTEND IT REACH

Many SISs are discovered almost by accident, when a manager recognizes an opportunity to extend an existing information service or to create a new, simple, innovative application. That is, many SISs result from simply broadening the reach and range of current systems or using them to support interactions with customers, suppliers, or business partners. Data that are captured as part of the business may be valuable to other organizations (for example, point-of-sale data, product documentation, or business documents). Services that report and summarize such data can extend IT reach into the marketplace.

Various frameworks and procedures have been developed for aiding a manager in identifying strategic applications. Our purpose in these early chapters is to review a wide range of applications for information technology, not to discuss how to plan or develop these applications. Chapters 12 and 13 provide detailed discussions of such approaches.

The Need for Champions

Any of several processes for identifying strategic systems can be effective. Whether identified by accident or by one of these processes, however, a key element in translating suggested applications into truly competitive weapons is follow-up. Active and creative managers easily recognize ideas for the strategic application of information technologies; the hangup often comes when no one steps forward to champion an idea and see it through to implementation.

An ideal champion is a successful manager whose opinions (especially on the value of business decisions) are implicitly trusted and who has all the contacts necessary to muster the resources required to build the SIS. To create the SIS, the initial idea has to be tested, developed, and approved through multiple departments and levels of management. As the managers who originated the idea are promoted or transferred, it is very easy to drop the ball without such a champion. The development and execution of good ideas is where most organizations lose competitive advantage opportunities.

A champion may provide executive level leadership and support or actually take charge in carrying through on the idea. Also, less bureaucratic (organic) organizations in which intrapreneurship is encouraged can be helpful for implementing innovations like an SIS. An SIS can be difficult to justify (to be discussed in the next section). The rapid development of a prototype of the system (prototyping will be discussed in detail in Chapter 10) can be critical for mustering the necessary enthusiasm and resources. Some organizations have also formed councils for new ideas that sort through various new concepts, such as an SIS, set priorities to ensure proper support, and identify and empower a champion for the system.

Justifying SISs

According to John A. Cunningham, manager of General Management Systems Development at General Electric (Cunningham, 1985), you know that you have gained a competitive advantage when competitors start spending money they did not know they had to spend. In other words, the market will tell your competitors that your actions have made a difference. This is the ultimate test of the justification of a strategic application.

Parker and Benson (1988) suggest that strategic applications provide six kinds of value, an analysis of which can be the basis for the justification of an SIS:

1. Return on Investment: traditional quantitative, financial cost-benefit analysis that estimates a development and operating cost stream, and a business cost reduction and revenue generation stream, to determine a net benefit over time.
2. Strategic Match: direct support of a stated business strategy by the system.
3. Competitive Advantage: a value created from a new business or product, or increased market share.
4. Management Information: providing information about critical aspects of the business: those aspects that must be done well for the business to succeed.
5. Competitive Response: information technology activities aimed at catching up with the competition or possibly even leapfrogging over them in ways that will be difficult for them to duplicate or overcome.
6. SIS Architecture: a basic and necessary investment that enables subsequent strategic applications to occur.

SISs are often justified incrementally, as a nonstrategic system expands its range to more strategic services or reach outside the organization. Some SISs are imperative, in response to a competitor's strategic information system.

Many SISs, by their nature, are speculative, and their success depends heavily on many organizational programs well beyond the system itself. Thus, an accurate estimate of the worth of a proposed strategic application may be unattainable. One viable option is to develop rapidly the essentials of the system using advanced programming languages (this technology, fourth-generation languages, and process, prototyping, are explained in Chapter 10). This prototype, which can be iteratively improved, can then be used to judge the potential of a fully working system.

SUMMARY

For information systems to be strategic weapons of an organization, the information and systems that move and manage information must be recognized as resources to be exploited (see Chapter 14, which elaborates on this concept). This recognition often means changing management's thinking about information technology. Management first thought about IT as a way to automate labor-intensive tasks (such as financial and inventory accounting jobs). Then management considered applications of IT that would cut costs and improve productivity. Next, managers and engineers determined ways to build computers and micro-electronics into products and factory processes. Although progressively more sophisticated and integral to the business, such applications usually did not reach beyond the business and often did not make a pervasive impact upon the firm. Today, an increasing number of managers recognize that real strategic advantage can be achieved from integrating information into the business strategy.

Not all strategic information systems come from well-planned and orchestrated analyses of opportunities. Frequently, one event, one customer contact, reading about one application somewhere else, or some other spontaneous thought is the seed for a strategic application. Not all SISs result in a home run; many just keep hitting singles with a very high batting average. SISs often build on existing expertise and capabilities to provide that one additional feature that customers find compelling.

A key to identifying useful strategic applications is simply the awareness that information technology can be used for strategic advantage. Managers throughout the business (certainly not just in the information systems area) can be the source and champion for these ideas. The role of each general, line, and staff manager has now changed and a new dimension has been added, that of seeking new and extended applications of IT that reach beyond the organization's boundaries. Managing information for strategic advantage is not a spectator sport.

To be a strategic information system, the system must relate to business strategy. Frequently, the system will focus outside the firm to manage those forces (customers, suppliers, competitors, potential entrants) critical to business success. For example, consider a firm whose strategy is expansion into new markets. It may use IT to find and support niche markets or to add features to existing products that make them attractive to additional markets.

Strategic systems are built on a series of partnerships. First, managers and system developers must work together to identify the features of such systems and to apply the most appropriate technology. Second, customers and/or suppliers need to cooperate by agreeing to certain electronic and procedural linkages between firms. Third, executives and line managers must be alert to opportunities for creative applications that:

- yield low cost production.
- create innovative new products or services of value to customers.
- provide access to new markets.
- create barriers to entry of new competitors.
- shift the balance of power between the firm and its customers or suppliers.
- increase the cost for customers to switch to competitors or substitutes.

We have covered in this chapter many interorganizational applications that have made a difference for certain businesses. Some applications have yielded outstanding successes; by contrast, ignoring opportunities has yielded disasters. Information technology is a weapon to be used for strategic advantage and is a resource unlike any other in the organization. Understanding information technology is crucial to your success as a manager. Building on the appreciation for strategic applications and the other types of systems outlined in these first three chapters, the following three chapters present the basic technology concepts crucial for your exploitation of information technology in your organization and in your career.

REVIEW QUESTIONS

1. List the strategic impacts of the American Airlines SABRE computerized reservation system.

2. Explain why being first with a competitive application can have lasting value, even when the application can be duplicated by your competitors.

3. Discuss the importance of a data-sharing philosophy in the success of strategic information systems.

4. Explain how an SIS can be used to change the scope of competition for a company.

5. What are the potential benefits of interorganizational information systems?

6. What information technologies are used in EDI?

7. What organizational and technical factors are necessary for a successful EDI application?

8. What is it that an interorganizational system does that can reduce the cost of a purchase order from $25 to $5?

9. Whose responsibility is it to identify strategic applications?

10. In what ways can information technology be applied in supplier relationships?

11. Discuss the value of proprietary data for strategic information systems.

12. On what basis can an SIS be justified?

13. Discuss the concept of information reach as it applies to interorganizational systems.

DISCUSSION QUESTIONS

1. What distinguishes a strategic information system from a transaction processing system? Give examples. Give an example that illustrates where one system would be both a transaction processing system and a strategic information system.

2. What questions should a user-manager ask to evaluate the feasibility and potential advantages of developing and implementing an SIS?

3. As a manager responsible for the decision to implement an SIS that would be an industry first, what situations might exist where it would be better to adopt a wait-and-see or follow-the-leader approach? Be specific.

4. Assume you are a general manager of a steel fabrication firm. In addition to the obvious technical considerations, what might you wish to consider before you enter into an EDI program with a supplier? With a customer?

5. As a marketing/sales manager of a small retail goods manufacturing firm, you are faced with the loss of your most important account, a nationwide discount store chain, unless you adopt its EDI standard. For the size of your firm, this would entail a substantial invest-

ment. What options might be available to you? Is such an ultimatum from your customer legal?

6. Recall your experiences with any financial institution, restaurant chain, department store, or your university. Can you think of any new uses of information technology that these organizations might implement to capture a competitive advantage? Be brief but creative. Explain the "hook" each example has.

7. Given the definition of an SIS and the many examples noted in this chapter, what should be your expectations for the results of implementing such a system?

8. One of your competitors has just introduced an SIS that poses an immediate and potentially lasting threat to your market position. What steps might you take to counter such a development?

9. Discuss the organizational barriers to the development of an SIS. How might you address each of these obstacles?

10. In your opinion, can an organization implement an SIS without having (or before having) all of its operational systems in place? Explain. If so, what is the likelihood of success of an SIS?

11. How might a small to medium-sized firm without a sizable or sophisticated IS department go about developing an SIS? Where is more of the responsibility for the development likely to rest?

12. "We pride ourselves on undertaking only projects that we can definitely quantify as having a direct, positive impact on the bottom line, so as not to squander shareholder value." Counter this statement for evaluating an SIS.

13. One type of SIS, computer program trading, has received much attention since the stock market crash of October 1987. While the exact role that computer trading played in the crash is not clear, it raises many questions about the use of computers in ways that impact on society. What guidelines or standards should a firm consider/establish before implementing any SIS?

14. Computer-aided software design, reusable code, prototyping, and so on have helped to reduce the time frame for developing and implementing a new system. With this in mind, will firms still be able to capture a sizable competitive advantage by being the first in the market with such a system? In your opinion, will any such advantage be sizable or last long enough to warrant the risks inherent in such an endeavor? Explain.

15. Suppose that you have come up with what appears to be a great idea for an SIS. What hazards might exist, or what cautions should you evaluate, before you charge full steam into implementation of this system that has clear benefits?

REFERENCES

1985. "Detroit tries to level a mountain of paperwork." *Business Week* (August 26): 94, 96.

1985. "Information power: How companies are using new technologies to gain a competitive edge." *Business Week* (October 14): 108–114.

1988. "How cities compete: Changing the rules of the game." *ICIT Advance* (August): 2.

1989. "The strategic value of EDI." *I/S Analyzer* 27 (August): entire issue.

1991. "Technical organizational and managerial aspects of implementing EDI." *Gesellschaft für Mathematik und Datenverarbeitung* (September).

Babcock, Charles. 1987. "Financial adviser goes on-line." *Computerworld* 21 (November 9): 23, 33.

Blattberg, Robert C., and John Deighton. 1991. "Interactive marketing: Exploiting the age of addressability." *Sloan Management Review* 33 (Fall): 5–14.

Booker, Ellis, and Michael Fitzgerald. 1990. "Retailers try EDI hard sell." *Computerworld* 24 (July 9): 1, 8.

Cash, James I., Jr., and Benn R. Konsynski. 1985. "IS redraws competitive boundaries." *Harvard Business Review* 63 (March–April): 134–142.

Clemons, Eric K., and Michael C. Row. 1991. "Sustaining IT advantage: The role of structural differences." *MIS Quarterly* 15 (September): 275–292.

Cole, Robert E. 1985. "Target information for competitive performance." *Harvard Business Review* 63 (May–June): 100–109.

Cunningham, John A. 1985. "Information technology stirs GE marketing renaissance." *Infosystems* 32 (December): 32–37.

Freedman, David. 1991. "The myth of strategic I.S." *CIO* 4 (July): 42–48.

———. 1992. "Retailing in real time." *CIO* 5 (August): 34–42.

Hopper, Max D. 1990. "Rattling SABRE: New ways to compete on information." *Harvard Business Review* 68 (May–June): 118–124.

Kavan, C. Bruce, and David Van Over. 1991. "Electronic data interchange: An analysis of current adopters." University of Georgia, College of Business Administration, Department of Management, working paper #49.

Keen, Peter G. W. 1991. *Shaping the Future: Business Design Through Information Technology.* Boston, MA: Harvard Business School Press.

Konsynski, Benn R., and F. Warren McFarlan. 1990. "Information partnerships—shared data, shared scale." *Harvard Business Review* 68 (September–October): 114–120.

Liang, Thow-Yick. 1992. "Electronic data interchange systems in Singapore: A strategic utilization." *International Business Schools Computing Quarterly* 4 (Spring): 43–47.

Lindsey, Darryl, Paul H. Cheney, George M. Kasper, and Blake Ives. 1990. "TELCOT: An application of information technology for competitive advantage in the cotton industry." *MIS Quarterly* 14 (December): 347–357.

McFarlan, F. Warren. 1984. "Information technology changes the way you compete." *Harvard Business Review* 62: (May–June): 98–103.

Parker, Marilyn M., and Robert J. Benson. 1988. *Information Economics: Linking Business Performance to Information Technology*. Englewood Cliffs, NJ: Prentice-Hall, Inc.

Porter, Michael E., and Victor E. Millar. 1985. "How information gives you competitive advantage." *Harvard Business Review* 63 (July–August): 149–160.

Schatz, Willie. 1988. "EDI: Putting the muscle in commerce & industry." *Datamation* 34 (March 15): 56–59, 62, 64.

Senn, James A. 1992. "Electronic data interchange: The elements of implementation." *Information Systems Management* 9 (Winter): 45–53.

Wiseman, Charles. 1985. *Strategy and Computers: Information Systems as Competitive Weapons*. Homewood, IL: Dow Jones Irwin.

3

Ameritech Publishing, Inc.

Ameritech Publishing, Inc., a subsidiary of Ameritech Corporation, publishes *Ameritech PagesPlus* telephone directories for the Ameritech Bell telephone companies in Indiana, Michigan, Ohio, and Wisconsin. Ameritech Publishing also has subsidiaries that produce fourteen Ameritech Industrial Yellow Pages books covering thirty-three states and publish about seventy directories in ten states outside the Ameritech area, English language directories for Tokyo and Osaka, and German, Austrian, and Swiss industrial directories. Publishing and distributing approximately 40 million copies of 484 different directories in 1990, Ameritech Publishing had $866.4 million in revenues and provided about one-fourth of Ameritech's profits in 1990.

Ameritech Publishing's primary business is publishing yellow pages telephone directories. Yellow pages advertising does not generate demand, but a person who has decided to buy something often looks in the yellow pages to decide where to buy it. Because almost everyone has access to the yellow pages, and the average person uses them about 100 times each year to decide where to obtain something he already wants, it can be a very productive form of advertising.

As shown in Exhibit 1, there are two different types of yellow pages advertising. The entries in the column in the upper left of Exhibit 1 are in-column ads, which vary in size and form, as described in Exhibit 2. The large ads in Exhibit 1 are display ads,

and (although it is not apparent in this black-and-white reproduction) they may be black on yellow or contain several colors. For example, the elaborate border of the "Fields of Flowers" ad is green, while the name Fields of Flowers and the telephone number are bright red. Display ads are more completely described in Exhibit 3. The yearly cost of a full-page display ad is about $11,000 in a city the size of Bloomington, Indiana, but can range up to almost $30,000 in Detroit or Cleveland.

Ameritech Publishing is in a very competitive business, with other companies publishing similar directories in every one of its markets. Moreover, Ameritech Publishing must compete with newspapers, radio, television, cable TV, and direct mail for a portion of each customer's advertising budget. It has a sales force of about 700 people who are paid on a commission basis.

History of Ameritech Publishing

Ameritech Corporation was formed in 1984 as one of seven regional holding companies created from the divestiture of AT&T. Prior to divestiture, each of the Bell companies was responsible for its own telephone directories and yellow pages, but Ameritech quickly decided that there was great potential for growth in yellow pages revenues and that this potential could best be exploited by separating the directory operations from the local telephone company's responsibilities and centralizing them in a wholly owned subsidiary. Therefore, in 1984 Ameritech Publishing was formed by combining the directory publishing organizations from Indiana Bell, Michigan Bell, Ohio Bell, and Wisconsin Bell. Illinois Bell (which is part of Ameritech) was excluded because Ameritech decided to handle directory operations in Illinois through a joint venture with R. H. Donnelly. Although the telephone directory part of the

This case was prepared by Professor E. W. Martin as the basis for class discussion rather than to illustrate either effective or ineffective handling of an administrative situation. Its development was supported by the Institute for Research on the Management of Information Systems (IRMIS), School of Business, Indiana University.

EXHIBIT 1

Ameritech Yellow Pages In-Column and Display Ads

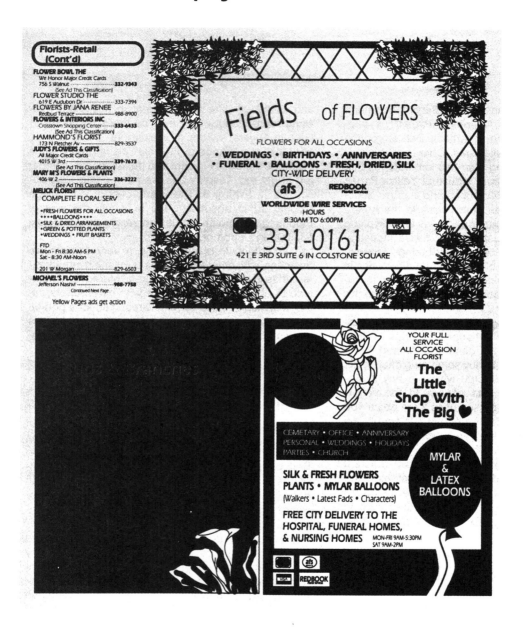

EXHIBIT 2
. . . .
Ameritech Yellow Pages
In-Column Ad Descriptions

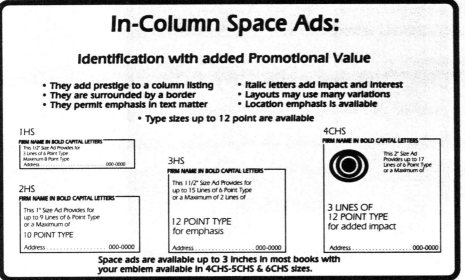

EXHIBIT 3
. . . .
Ameritech Yellow Pages
Display Ad Descriptions

When you want to get
ATTENTION
this Half-Page ad size will get your business
NOTICED!

Be sure to describe all of your products, services, or special feature information for your potential customers.

Also use an attractive illustration to catch the eye! Remember that the more you tell, the more you sell.

(8QCH)

DISPLAY ADS:
The **Ultimate** in Yellow Pages

Advantages of Display Ads
- Complete flexibility in layout
- Pictures-speaking a universal language
- Great variety of type styles
- White space to assure interest
- Benday panels
- Selection of border styles

ANCHOR LISTING provided with each display ad. Special phrase follows address line, designed to lead column user to a more complete message in the display ad.

Firm Name in **BOLD** or Regular Type
Address 000-0000
             or
             000-0000
See Advertisement This Classification

DISPLAY ADS ARE AVAILABLE IN OTHER STANDARD SIZES
IF YOU WISH TO BE CONTACTED FOR COMPLETE INFORMATION CALL (317)685-7800, INPLS. IN. OR CALL 1-800-382-1929

One Large or Several Small Illustrations May Be Used In This Size Ad

This is a Triple Half Column Display Ad.

The shape and size of this ad offers designers the greater flexibility. It holds more information. Several illustrations may be used. Greater white space encourages readership. In past studies, Yellow Pages users have said that they consider the size of ad to be an indication of the size and reliability of the firm.

SPECIFIC INFORMATION TO ENCOURAGE YOUR CUSTOMERS
VISIT - HOURS - MAPS

BOLD FIRM NAME & HEADINGS

(6QCH)

Ameritech business was centralized, the five state telephone companies continued to operate as standalone entities.

Leo Egan, a general manager from Michigan Bell, was the first president of Ameritech Publishing. His mission was to build an organization while at the same time improving the profitability of the ongoing directory operations. To mold an organization out of the pieces of four previous groups, Egan organized the company functionally, with most of the field personnel reporting to publishing and sales vice presidents. He also established staff positions in the finance, information services, human resources, and legal areas.

The four Bell companies from which the Ameritech Publishing personnel were drawn had been typical telephone companies with typical telephone company attitudes, but each had its own distinct corporate culture. Each of the Bell companies did things its own way, which carried over to the yellow pages as well. The layouts of the pages, the pricing, the contracts with advertisers, and the sales compensation plans were all different from one Bell company to another.

The new publishing vice president, Donald J. Frayer, was convinced of the need to standardize the publication of the directories. He felt that this required standard computer systems to support the publication and sales functions. Egan agreed on the need for these systems and supported their development, but his main focus was on the profitability of current operations, not on standardizing them. Having accomplished his mission of creating a new company from fragments of four Ameritech telephone companies and getting it off to a profitable start, Egan retired in 1986. He was replaced by Barry Allen, a young, energetic executive from Ameritech with marketing experience and an MBA from the Darden School at the University of Virginia.

Allen took over a young company that was going well in terms of profitability, but not much effort had been put into defining its long-range role and goals. He felt that Ameritech Publishing's culture was still essentially that of the old bureaucratic, monopolistic telephone companies from whence it came. Allen's vision for the company was that of a lean and mean, customer-focused, competitive tiger. Allen's first priority was to get the company focused on the customer and customer responsiveness. Thus, he wanted to move decision-making down so that it was very close to the customer. His second priority was to get the bureaucratic fat out of the organization. He believed

that one of the best ways to remove this fat was to break down the business into many smaller pieces and to assign each piece to a manager empowered to manage that piece as if it were his own business.

Soon after he took over, Allen reorganized the company from a functional to a profit center organization (as shown in Exhibit 4). As before, there were staff positions concerned with human resources, finance, corporate planning, information services, and legal affairs. The line organization was no longer functional, but rather had a general manager for each state who was responsible for the bottom line profitability in his state. Each state manager had his own publishing and sales responsibilities, and bottom line responsibility was also pushed down to the district and even the office. In mid-1989, when Allen was transferred to become head of Wisconsin Bell, Ameritech Publishing had become more efficient and was even more profitable than before.

Ameritech Publishing's new president and CEO was Gary G. Drook, a dynamic executive in his mid-forties who was vice president of marketing at Ameritech. Prior to this job, Drook had been with Indiana Bell, where he had served in several assistant vice president positions in information systems and marketing. Drook found that the organization had not made as much progress toward becoming customer-focused as he desired, and that there had been little progress in replacing the individual state cultures with a unified company vision. Also, the development of the new computer systems to support the sales and publications functions had bogged down.

Drook's Vision for Ameritech Publishing

In late 1991 Drook's primary goals for Ameritech Publishing were growth and quality. He wanted continual growth in terms of market share, revenues, and profits. "Being quick and flexible is what is going to help us grow the business," Drook says. "We must be able to quickly introduce new products, new enhancements, new pricing strategies. And we must become more customer-oriented and easier to do business with."

Drook also wanted better and better quality as perceived by his customers. According to Drook, "Quality involves better and more effective products and services, but it also means a mistake-free yellow pages book where each advertisement looks exactly like the customer intended it to look."

EXHIBIT 4
Ameritech Publishing 1987 Reorganization

Drook's Concerns

Even after eight years, the heritage of being a part of the old Bell System telephone companies still persisted. According to Drook:

> Before divestiture the telephone companies had a tremendous internal focus—on processes, procedures, and profitability. Customers were something that they just tolerated. They sold the yellow pages more on fear and intimidation than on value and service. We still have too many traces of these old attitudes.
>
> We are perceived as being hard to do business with. One problem is that our products are different from one state to another. Consider South Bend, Indiana, and Niles, Michigan. These two towns are almost one town, but the state line runs down a street between them. Ads cost one thing on one side of this street and something else on the other side. Ads are vertical on one side and horizontal on the other side. It is very hard for me to explain to customers in the Niles–South Bend market why we cannot be more customer-focused.
>
> Although the yellow pages are considered to be a local medium, we do about 12 percent of our business with national advertisers like General Motors, Ford, Chrysler, Roto Rooter, GE, and Westinghouse. The marketing department for General Motors, for example, defines and lays out all the yellow pages ads for General Motors dealers nationwide. Someone has estimated that for General Motors to place ads in our four hundred directories, they need about fifty-seven different pieces of artwork. This is partly because they have different size ads in different books, but the primary cause is that each of our states does things differently—for example, three-

quarter page ads that are horizontal in Michigan are vertical in Ohio.

As a result, General Motors finds it very difficult to do business with us. They cannot just consider the market and decide which size ad they should have. Instead we have to get into long discussions about how we do our book in Detroit, and then another discussion about how we do it in Cleveland, etc. Kmart, for example, spends $300 million on advertising, but they do not advertise in the yellow pages. They, and a number of other large advertisers, have told us that we are tough to do business with, that we are expensive, that we have a lot of funny rules, that they cannot make a national buy that makes cohesive sense to them.

In order to increase business, Drook wants to be able to quickly develop, test, and introduce new products. New products may be new pricing plans, but they also include significant changes, such as the availability of colors. It is very difficult for Ameritech Publishing to introduce new products when its products are not standard across states, because it may have to have different versions of the new product in each state. Also, because other things differ so much between states, market research and customer attitude surveys on new products are suspect unless they are replicated in each state, which increases costs and slows things down tremendously.

Drook knows that the quality of his product is not what he would like it to be. One measure of quality is the number of claims that they must deal with. A claim is a request by an advertiser for compensation because there was a problem with the advertisement—the wrong phone number, a misspelled name, the wrong color of ink, and so on. "We pay out about $20 million a year in claims because of mistakes in the books," Drook notes. Today a lot of these claims go to court. "We make so many mistakes that we have to be very careful about what we give out in compensation for claims or we could bankrupt the business," Drook laments. "We want to get the claims level down to where it is much more reasonable," asserts Drook. "Then for the few customers who have a problem we could do almost anything to make them happy."

One reason there are so many mistakes today is that, because of the time pressure in preparing ads to meet publication deadlines, Ameritech Publishing is often unable to allow customers to proofread their ads before they are published.

Drook's Strategies for Improving

Drook knows that changing people's attitudes is not easy and that there is no quick fix. He is continually working to communicate his vision to everyone in the company. He designated 1991 as "The Year of the Customer" and publicized this widely within the company. Drook also has focused the attention of Ameritech Publishing on his goals by announcing and repeatedly emphasizing an "Advertiser's Bill of Rights," which states that every advertiser can expect from Ameritech Publishing:

- a simple contract that permits them to understand what we will do and how much our services and product will cost.
- the opportunity to see what their advertising will look like before the advertisement is made public.
- an account executive that is knowledgeable about OUR products and THEIR business.
- an advertisement "delivered," designed and produced as we promised.
- an accurate bill that is understandable.
- immediate, effective, and courteous resolution if a problem should arise.
- guaranteed products.

Drook has also aligned the company reward system with his customer-service vision by basing 20 percent of each salesman's compensation on service performance as perceived by the salesman's customers. The company does telephone surveys that measure the customer's perception of the timeliness and accuracy of the ad, concern and helpfulness, and quality of service. The results produce a service index for each salesman on a scale of one to ten. "At the start," reports Drook, "the results were all over the map, but they have been moving up and becoming more uniform. We now have sales groups that average a nine. We are very happy with the results."

Another of Drook's strategies is to standardize Ameritech Publishing's products and operations so that they are uniform from state to state. Not only will this make them much less confusing to large customers, but it will enable the company to introduce new products much more quickly and to better control the quality of its products and services.

Finally, Drook is counting on new computer systems that are under development to provide the accuracy and flexibility that are so lacking today in the sales and publishing operations. These systems will accept orders for advertising, assist employees in creating the artwork for the ads, and store the ads in computer files. Once the ads are created and stored, the copy for a telephone book will be created by the computer and sent to the printer with no manual processes required.

· ·
New Computer Systems

The interrelated computer systems being developed to support Ameritech Publishing's sales and publishing operations are depicted in Exhibit 5.

ARIES (Ameritech Regional Information Exchange System) is a large, complex system that maintains the customer database and provides many services to the sales organization. The database contains information on customers, including their history of advertising buys and their current contract. One of its major functions is to support the salesman when he calls on the customer to sell advertising in next year's book. The system produces a report that shows the customer's past history and the contract terms for

EXHIBIT 5
· · · · · · · · · · · · · · · ·
Publication Systems

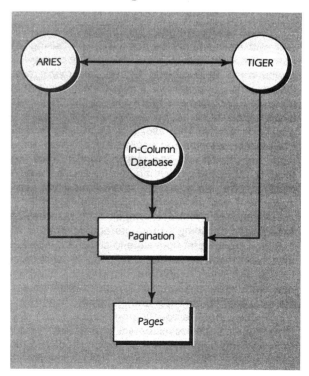

this year's products. It accepts orders and updates the database, calculates the salesman's commission, and notifies the TIGER graphics system that the ad must be included in the book. It also keeps track of claims and reflects their impact on the compensation of salesmen. The ARIES database contains the data for producing virtually any sales reports that management might desire.

TIGER (Total Integrated Graphics Entry and Retrieval) is a large graphics and database system that can be used to create and store advertisements that will be printed in the book. The TIGER processing center is located in Troy, Michigan, and contains several rooms full of Sun workstations networked to the large VAX computer that manages the database—about $10 million worth of hardware (see Exhibit 6).

At a TIGER workstation an artist has access to a catalog of about 50,000 pieces of "clip art" that can be incorporated into any advertisement, a scanner through which he can transfer images into the computer, and a high quality color printer for producing advertising layouts. As with most desktop publishing systems, the artist can use his mouse to draw, bring in clip art, move or rotate images, change the size of all or part of the ad, determine the color of images, modify previous versions of the ad, and store the result in the computer's digital graphical database. Thus, the artist can produce a new ad or modify last year's ad, and the result is stored in the database so that it can be used to produce the yellow pages book. The final ad can also be electronically sent to the sales office to show to the customer.

TIGER can enforce standards concerning the size and shape of ads, and it also notifies ARIES that the ad that the customer ordered has been created. If an ad is published with a mistake, this results in a claim that is entered into ARIES. ARIES then notifies the TIGER database to tag the ad for correction before it can be used in next year's book. Thus, there should be no mistakes in the old ads that are used in the new book. Likewise, ads that require revision each year can be tagged to make sure that the required revision has been made before the ad is reused.

The in-column database has traditionally been maintained by the printer, but Ameritech Publishing has decided to bring this function in-house so that this material can be combined with the display ads to electronically produce the yellow pages.

As shown in Exhibit 5, the final component of this system is an automatic pagination system. When it is time to produce one of the telephone books, the pagi-

EXHIBIT 6
. . . .
Using a TIGER Workstation

nation system receives the orders from ARIES the in-column material from that database, and the display ads from the TIGER database. The pagination system then applies rules to design and create electronic page images that can be fed to a computer controlling the press to print the pages without manual intervention.

Consider how the yellow pages have traditionally been produced. It all started with the canvassing function, when Ameritech Publishing's salesmen contacted customers to sell advertising in the next yellow pages directory. The creation of a new display ad was contracted out to an artist working for a local ad agency. The completed artwork was placed in a brown envelope and filed with the other ads appearing in the new book. About two and a half months

before the deadline for distributing the new book, the sales office would stop selling and send these envelopes containing the hand-done artwork to the printer, along with a printout of the advertising orders from the computer. The printer would obtain the in-column information from the local telephone company, and then would lay out the pages by hand and print the book.

This process was slow, expensive, and mistake-prone. Because of the tight deadlines, there was no time to show the new ads to customers before they were sent to the printer, so errors and misunderstandings often appeared in the book. Also, when there were mistakes in the current book, someone might get confused and send the old artwork to the printer instead of the corrected version, which infuriated the advertiser.

With the new system, the display ads will be created by in-house artists using TIGER and stored in the TIGER database. Because the manual layout will be eliminated, Ameritech Publishing expects to save about $6 million of the $10 million per year that it pays the printer for these services. It also expects to save around $5 million a year on printing costs because tests indicate that the automatic pagination system is more efficient in the use of space, thus reducing the number of pages printed.

But Drook sees the main benefits of the new systems to be speed, flexibility, and accuracy. Because the company will be able to drastically compress the time required to produce a telephone book, it will be able to make sure that every ad is seen and approved by the advertiser before it appears in the book. Since the ads will have been approved by the customer (and corrected if necessary) and stored in the graphics database, there should be very few errors in the book when it is printed. Fewer errors should drastically reduce claims and enable the company to generously compensate customers for the few problems that remain. Thus, Drook is counting on these new computer systems to enable Ameritech Publishing to live up to the ideals expressed in his Advertiser's Bill of Rights.

Unfortunately, these systems, which were started in 1985, are still not completed and installed throughout Ameritech Publishing. While initial versions of components are being used in some states, and it has been demonstrated that the systems can perform adequately, the date when they will be completely operational throughout Ameritech Publishing keeps receding.

The Development of ARIES and TIGER

When Ameritech Publishing was formed in 1984, it had no information systems organization. Daniel J. Harmon, who had started out at Bell Labs as a systems analyst and worked in both information systems and the directory business at Michigan Bell, was designated to build an information services organization for Ameritech Publishing. Harmon started with a staff of two, which had grown to 160 by 1991.

Each of the Ameritech states had its own customer/contract system that was being run at that state's Bell Telephone data center. Harmon's first task was to bring them into the new Ameritech Publishing data center in Troy, Michigan, which was accomplished by the end of 1984. Ameritech Publishing management quickly decided that the company needed a single customer/contract system to serve all of Ameritech Publishing.

Management first thought that the most efficient way to get to this single system would be to take the best of the existing systems, move the other three states to that system, and then enhance it over time to include all the needed capabilities. After extensive investigation and negotiation, however, management found that each of the four existing state systems was unacceptable to the other three states. Therefore, they decided to develop a new system (ARIES) that would combine the best features of each of the existing systems.

At that time (1985), Ameritech Publishing still had a very small information services organization with little systems development capability. Therefore, the company opted to contract the development of this system to the Indiana Bell information services organization that had developed the Indiana Contract System. Ameritech Publishing planned to complete and install ARIES in the four states by the middle of 1988 at a cost of about $5 million.

During 1985, Donald J. Frayer, vice president of publishing, was developing a vision of how to run publishing in the future. He envisioned an "integrated publishing environment" that corresponds to the systems depicted in Exhibit 5 and serves the needs of both sales and publishing. Thus, the company began to envision the graphics system for producing and storing display ads that became TIGER.

The Ameritech Publishing IS organization had no experience with or capability for graphics systems, so it began to look for a system to purchase. After some investigation, Ameritech Publishing signed a system integration contract with Janus Systems to produce the TIGER system, including responsibility for both software and hardware. Development and installation of TIGER was projected to take two years and cost less than $6 million. According to Harmon, "We had originally intended to build and convert our operations to ARIES, and then schedule the graphics system to come in behind. However, the economics of TIGER were so compelling that we decided to develop the two systems in parallel, with TIGER lagging about six months behind ARIES."

The requirements analysis and system design for ARIES were almost completed when Barry Allen took over as president in 1986 and reorganized the company into profit centers. In 1987, when IS was trying to get final sign offs on the system design so that coding could begin, it found that previously agreed upon decisions were no longer acceptable. IS could not get final agreement on the form of the contract, what the system was to provide to the salesmen, and hundreds of other standardization issues. "Our standardization committees were up against the wall because they could not get the states to agree," reports Harmon. "Each profit center was insisting that we do it their way, and since IS had no power to say no, we ended up trying to satisfy everyone." Needless to say, this resulted in a complex, unwieldy system, and in continual delays.

Indiana was to be the first state for ARIES, and management established the target date of February 1989 to begin installation, almost a year after it had originally planned to have this system operational in all four states. In order to make this deadline, whenever it got bogged down trying to make a standardization decision, the Indiana Bell IS organization had to go on and make a decision, usually based upon what was wanted by Ameritech Publishing's Indiana profit center. IS knew that these decisions would cause problems in the other states, but it had no alternative.

When Gary Drook took over as president in mid-1989, he found that Ameritech Publishing had already spent double its original $11 million development budget for ARIES and TIGER. The original plan was to install these systems throughout the company in 1988, but the company was just converting Indiana to these systems. It looked as if it would be at least three more years before the new systems would be in company-wide use.

Things were not going well in Indiana. The company had problems cleaning up the existing data and converting to ARIES. The salesmen and clerks who used the systems had to change what they did and how they did it and were not adequately trained. The Indiana profit center also was approaching its most difficult time of the year, when it was to publish its Indianapolis book. Furthermore, the other states were watching Indiana, seeing a system that was not what they wanted and increasingly questioning what the system was going to do for them.

One of Allen's last moves was to replace the user project manager, who was responsible for obtaining agreement on what the system was to do, with Walter E. Smolak, who had worked for Harmon as director of the Ameritech Publishing data center. Smolak had come from Michigan Bell, where he had run data centers and served as an internal auditing manager, and before divestiture had headed AT&T's Development and Research Center in Orlando, Florida. Given how things were going in Indiana, Smolak was very uncomfortable with the planned conversion schedule for the other states.

After reviewing the history of the ARIES and TI-GER projects with Harmon and Smolak, Drook concluded that, in addition to the normal difficulties associated with developing large systems, the major problem was that Ameritech Publishing had not faced the standardization issues inherent in these systems.

"We were trying to build a car with four engines in it, one for each state," Drook recalls. "You do not see many cars with four engines because they do not work very well. Furthermore, they are expensive to build and even more expensive to maintain." Drook coined the phrase "one car, one engine" to express his determination to "standardize our products, standardize our processes, standardize our procedures, and standardize the computer systems that support these standardized processes."

To get the development of ARIES and TIGER back on track, Drook asked Smolak to make a list of the standardization issues that were holding up progress. Smolak came up with a list of thirty-nine issues, and Drook called his state general managers together and divided these issues up among them. For example, he told the Ohio manager: "You are responsible for sales reports. You should get input from your peers, but you are going to define the sales re-

ports that everyone is going to get." He gave another manager the responsibility for defining the standard order form, and so on.

"This was a big help," reports Smolak, "but we always had a flock of new issues coming up, so we continued to be bogged down in resolving them. Moreover, although under pressure the managers would finally agree to standardize, in their heart of hearts they really did not want to do it. They would delay as long as possible before agreeing, and then insist that it would take them two years to make the change." Progress continued to be frustratingly slow.

After finishing the Indiana conversion to ARIES and TIGER, Ameritech Publishing started converting Michigan in September 1990. Because Michigan was organized and managed differently from the other states, Michigan had even more difficulty converting to the system than Indiana.

. . . .

Present Status

In August 1991, Ameritech Publishing had almost completed the Michigan conversion. The company purchased a pagination system that is very flexible in that it allows the company to insert its own rules on allocating space. Since page layout is still different in each state, however, the company is having difficulty defining these rules and has not yet started pagination in any state. Ameritech Publishing has invested several times its original $11 million development budget in these systems, and because most of the anticipated savings lie in automatic page layout, it has yet to obtain any substantial return on this investment. Furthermore, Ohio is scheduled to begin conversion soon, and the Ohio general manager is pressing to postpone it for another year.

Because these systems are essential to achieving his vision for Ameritech Publishing, Drook has been increasingly frustrated that his efforts to promote standardization and get these systems back on track have not been successful. For some time he has been considering his alternatives, and he intends to act soon.

4

Computer Systems

Chapters 1 to 3 have set the stage for the detailed study of information technology and your role in harnessing that technology. We can now take a closer look at the building blocks of information technology and the development and maintenance of information technology systems.

Our definition of information technology is a broad one, encompassing all forms of technology involved in capturing, manipulating, communicating, presenting, and using data (and data transformed into information). Thus, information technology includes computers (both the hardware and the software), peripheral devices attached to computers, communications devices and networks, photocopiers, facsimile machines, computer-controlled factory machines, robots, video recorders and players, and a host of other related devices. All of these manifestations of information technology are important, and you need to be aware of their existence and their present and potential uses in an organizational environment. There are, however, two broad categories of information technology that are critical for the manager in a modern organization—computer technology and communications technology. Both of these technologies have had and are continuing to have a gigantic impact on the structure of a modern organization, the way it does its business, the scope of the organization, and the jobs and careers of the managers in the organization.

Perhaps the first important point to be made in this chapter is that the division between computer and communications technology is arbitrary and somewhat misleading. Historically, computer and communications technologies were independent, but they have grown together over the years, especially in the 1980s and early 1990s. Distributed systems (discussed in Chapter 2) exist in virtually every industry, and these systems require the linking of computers by telecommunication lines. An increasing proportion of managers at all levels have a terminal or microcomputer on their desks connected by telecommunication lines to a corporate computer. Often the information systems organization now has responsibility for both computing and communications. Even the historically dominant firms in the computer and communications industries, namely International Business Machines (IBM) and American Telephone and Telegraph (AT&T), are now major players in each other's industry. AT&T moved into the computer business in a big way with its purchase of the NCR Corporation in 1991. It is still convenient for us to discuss computing technology as distinct from communications technology, but the distinctions are becoming even more blurred as time passes. In reality, there is computer/communications technology being developed and marketed by the computer/communications industry.

This chapter concentrates on computer **hardware**, as distinct from computer **software**. Computer hardware refers to the physical pieces of a computer system that can be touched, such as a central processing unit, a printer, and a terminal. Software, by contrast, is the set of programs (instructions) that control the operations of the

116

computer system. For the most part, our consideration of software will be deferred until Chapter 5, but the central idea behind today's computers—the stored-program concept—will be explored here to aid in our understanding of how a computer system works.

EVOLUTION OF COMPUTER SYSTEMS

At present, in the middle of the last decade of the twentieth century, the computer/communications industry is easily the largest industry in the world in terms of dollar volume of sales. This is a remarkable statement, given that the first large-scale electronic computer was completed in 1946. The ENIAC (Electronic Numerical Integrator And Computer), which was built by Dr. John W. Mauchly and J. Presper Eckert, Jr., at the Moore School of Electrical Engineering at the University of Pennsylvania, was composed of more than 18,000 vacuum tubes, occupied 15,000 square feet of floor space, and weighed more than 30 tons (see Figure 4.1). Its performance was impressive for its day—the ENIAC could perform 5,000 additions or 500 multiplications per minute.

First Generation of Computers

The ENIAC ushered in the so-called First Generation of Computers, extending from 1946 through 1959. Vacuum tubes were the distinguishing characteristic of the First Generation machines. After several one-of-a-kind laboratory machines, the first production-line machines—the Sperry Rand Univac followed shortly by the IBM 701—became available in the early 1950s. The major success story among First Generation machines, however, was the IBM 650, introduced in 1954. The 650 was designed as a logical move upward from existing punched-card machines, and it was a hit. IBM expected to sell fifty of the 650s, but, in fact, installed more than one thousand, which helped IBM gain its position of prominence in the computer industry.

Second Generation of Computers

The invention of the transistor led to the Second Generation of Computers. Transistors were smaller, more reliable, less expensive, and gave off less heat than vacuum tubes. The Second Generation machines generally used magnetic cores (minute magnetizable washers strung on a lattice of

FIGURE 4.1 The ENIAC. (Courtesy of UPI/Bettmann)

wires) as their primary memory, compared to the vacuum tubes or magnetic drums, where spots were magnetized on the surface of a rotating metal cylinder, that were used in the First Generation. Memory sizes were increased considerably, perhaps by a factor of twenty, and execution speeds increased as well, again perhaps by a factor of twenty. IBM again dominated this era, largely on the strength of the popular 7000 series large machines and the record-breaking sales of the 1400 series small machines.

Third Generation of Computers

The beginning of the Third Generation has a specific date—April 7, 1964—when IBM announced the System/360 line of computers. The System/360, as well as Third Generation machines from other vendors, was based on the use of integrated circuits rather than individual transistors. Early in the Third Generation, magnetic cores were still used as primary memory; later, cores were replaced by semiconductor memories. Memory sizes and execution speeds continued to climb dramatically. With the Third Generation, the notion of

upward compatibility was introduced, that is, when a customer outgrew (ran out of capacity with) one model in a product line, he could trade up to the next model without any reworking of implemented applications. Perhaps the most drastic change was that the Third Generation machines relied on revolutionary, sophisticated operating systems (complex programs), such as IBM's OS, to actually control the actions of the computer. As one might expect, the System/360 and the System/370 that followed were the dominant computers of the late 1960s and the 1970s (see Figure 4.2).

Fourth Generation of Computers

Unfortunately, there is no neat dividing line between the Third and Fourth generations of computers. Most experts and vendors would agree that we are now in the Fourth Generation, but they do not agree on when this generation started or how soon we should expect the Fifth Generation. Changes since the introduction of the System/360 have tended to be evolutionary, rather than revolutionary. New models or new lines based on

FIGURE 4.2 A Configuration of the IBM System/360. (Courtesy of International Business Machines Corporation)

new technologies were announced by all major vendors on a regular basis in the 1970s and 1980s, and this has continued into the 1990s (although many of the players have changed). Memory sizes have continued to climb and speeds have continued to increase. The integrated circuits of the Third Generation became LSI (large-scale integration) circuits and then VLSI (very-large-scale integration) circuits. Through VLSI the entire circuitry for a computer can be put on a single silicon chip smaller than a fingernail. Communication between terminals and computers, and between computers themselves, first began during the Third Generation, but the use of this technology came of age during the Fourth Generation. With the spread of distributed systems and various local and long-distance network arrangements, some commentators refer to communication as the distinguishing feature of the Fourth Generation.

The Development of Minicomputers

Parallel with the Third and Fourth generations, there was an important splintering within the computer industry. As IBM and the other major vendors, such as Sperry Rand, Burroughs, NCR, Honeywell, and Control Data, competed for industry leadership with more powerful, larger machines, a number of smaller, newer firms recognized a market niche for small machines aimed at smaller businesses and scientific applications. Successful firms in this minicomputer market included Digital Equipment Corporation (DEC), Data General, and Hewlett-Packard. These minicomputers were just like the larger machines (which came to be called mainframes), except that they were less powerful and less expensive. The minicomputer vendors also worked very hard at developing easy-to-use applications software. As the minicomputer market evolved, many of the mainframe vendors, such as IBM, moved into this area.

The Development of Microcomputers

Another splintering within the industry took place in the late 1970s and 1980s with the introduction and success of the microcomputer, which is based on the computer on a chip (see Figure 4.3), or microprocessor. Apple and other companies pio-

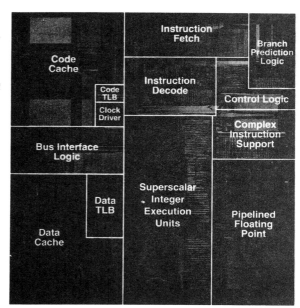

FIGURE 4.3 Intel Pentium Microprocessor Chip. (Courtesy of Intel Corporation)

neered the microcomputer business, finding a market niche below the minicomputers for home use, in very small businesses, and in the public school system. Then, in late 1981, IBM entered the market with its Personal Computer, or PC, which quickly became the microcomputer standard for the workplace. In fact, the PC became so much of a standard that most people use the terms microcomputer, Personal Computer, and PC interchangeably (and we will do so in this book, as well). Subsequent developments have included the greatly increased speed and capabilities of microcomputers, as well as the introduction of a variety of IBM clones in the marketplace by other vendors. The widespread acceptance of microcomputers in the business world has placed significant computing power at the fingertips of virtually every manager.

BASIC COMPONENTS OF COMPUTER SYSTEMS

For completeness, we should note that there are really two distinct types of computers—digital and analog. Digital computers operate directly on numbers, or digits, just as humans do. Analog computers manipulate some analogous physical quantity, such as voltage or shaft rotation speed, which represents (to some degree of accuracy) the numbers involved in the computation. Analog computers have been most useful in engineering and process-control environments, but they have been largely replaced by digital machines even in these situations. Thus, all of our preceding discussion referred to digital computers, as will that which follows.

Underlying Structure

Today's computers vary greatly in size, speed, and details of their operation—from hand-held microcomputers costing around $100 to supercomputers with price tags of more than $10 million. Fortunately, as we try to understand these machines, they all have essentially the same basic logical structure (as represented in Figure 4.4). All computers, whether they are sold by Radio Shack or by Cray (the dominant manufacturer of supercomputers), are made up of the same set of six building blocks: input, output, memory, arithmetic/logical unit, control unit, and files. (Some of the very smallest microcomputers may not have files.) Our discussion of how computers work will focus on these six blocks and their interrelationships.

FIGURE 4.4 The Logical Structure of Digital Computers

In addition to the blocks themselves, Figure 4.4 also includes two types of arrows. The broad arrows represent the flows of data through the computer system, and the thin arrows indicate that each of the other components is controlled by the control unit. A dashed line encircles the control unit and the arithmetic/logical unit. These two blocks together are often referred to as the **central processing unit,** or CPU, or just the **processor.** (Historically, the memory was also considered part of the CPU because it was located in the same physical cabinet, but with changes in memory technologies, memory is increasingly regarded as a separate entity from the CPU.)

Input/Output

To use a computer, we must have some means of entering data into the computer for it to use in its computations. There are a wide variety of input devices, and we will mention only the most commonly used types. The input device that you as a manager are most likely to use is a keyboard on a terminal or a microcomputer. We will talk more about microcomputers (PCs) later, but they include all of the building blocks shown in Figure 4.4. A **terminal** is a simpler device than a PC—it is designed strictly for input/output and does not incorporate a processor (CPU). Most terminals consist of a keyboard for data entry and a video display unit (a television screen) to show the user what has been entered and to display the output from the computer. The terminal is connected to a computer via some type of telecommunication line. In addition to their use by managers, terminals are widely used by clerical personnel involved in on-line transaction processing (see Chapter 2).

Special types of terminals are also in widespread use as computer input devices. Point-of-sale terminals have largely replaced conventional cash registers in major department stores, and automatic teller machines (ATMs) are commonplace in the banking industry. These devices are simply terminals modified to serve a specific purpose. Like the standard terminals described above, these special-purpose devices serve as both input and output devices, often incorporating a small built-in printer to provide a hard-copy record of the transaction.

Terminals allow users to key data directly into the computer. By contrast, some input methods require that data be recorded on a special input medium before they can be entered into the computer. Until a dozen years ago, the most common form of computer input involved punched cards and a punched-card reader. Users keyed in data at a punched-card keypunch machine, which translated the key strokes into holes in a punched card (employing a coding scheme known as Hollerith code). Then the punched cards were hand carried to a punched-card reader directly attached to the computer; the reader then read the cards one at a time, interpreting the holes in the cards and transmitting the data to the memory, as indicated in Figure 4.4. Until early in the 1980s, U.S. government checks, many credit-card charge slips, and class enrollment cards at most universities were punched cards. Computers often had a card punch attached as an output device to produce checks, enrollment cards, and other punched-card output. Punched cards were a nuisance to handle and store, and they have disappeared because of the communications developments of the past decade and a half.

Other input methods employing special input media have not disappeared, although their importance is shrinking. With a key-to-tape system or a key-to-disk system, data entry personnel key in data at a microcomputer or a workstation attached to a minicomputer. The small computer records the data as a series of magnetized spots (using some type of coding scheme) on the surface of a magnetic tape (similar to the tape used in a home VCR) or a magnetic disk (similar in appearance to a phonograph record). After a significant quantity of data has been recorded, an output magnetic tape is created and hand carried to the primary computer system, where it is mounted in a magnetic tape unit. This unit then reads the tape, interpreting the magnetized spots on the surface of the tape and transmitting the data to the memory.

Some input methods read an original document (such as a typed report or a check or deposit slip) directly into the memory of the computer. Check processing is handled this way in the United States through the **magnetic ink character recognition**, or MICR, input method. Most checks have the account number and bank number preprinted at the bottom using strange-looking numbers and a special magnetizable ink. After a check is cashed, the amount of the check is recorded in magnetizable ink at the bottom of the check by the bank that cashed the check. A computer input device called a magnetic ink character reader magnetizes the ink, recognizes the numbers, and transmits the data to the memory of the bank's computer. **Optical character recognition**, or OCR, is an input method that directly scans typed, printed, or hand-printed material. A device called an optical character reader scans and recognizes the characters and then transmits the data to the memory or records them on magnetic tape.

Imaging goes even further than optical character recognition. With imaging, any type of paper document—including business forms, reports, charts, graphs, and photographs—can be read by a scanner and translated into digital form so that it can be stored in the computer system. This process can be reversed, so that the digitized image stored in the computer system can be displayed on a video display unit, printed on paper, or transmitted to another computer or workstation. The individual characters in the image, however, cannot be easily processed as numbers or letters. Imaging is often accomplished through a specialized image management system, which is a microcomputer-based system attached to the organization's primary mainframe or minicomputer.

Just as we must have a way of entering data into the computer, the computer must have a way of producing results in a usable form. We have already mentioned displaying results on a video display unit, printing a document on a small printer built into a special-purpose terminal, and punching cards. Output can also be written on a magnetic tape or a magnetic disk, which may be useful if the data will be read back later either into the same or another computer.

The dominant form of output, however, is the printed report. Computer printers come in a variety of sizes, speeds, and prices. At the lower end are serial printers, which are usually employed with microcomputers. They may be impact dot-matrix printers or nonimpact ink-jet printers, and they typically operate in a speed range of 50 to 500 characters per second. Line printers operate at a higher speed and print one line at a time, usually

VOICE INPUT TO COMPUTERS

Voice input to computers is becoming more of a reality, although we cannot converse with today's machines as easily as Starfleet officers can talk with the computer system on the U.S.S. *Enterprise*. Consider the following examples. By the end of 1994, AT&T will have installed voice-recognition systems in long-distance offices throughout the United States. These systems can recognize words like "collect" and "person to person," and will replace up to one-third of AT&T's long-distance operators. The U.S. Postal Service uses voice-recognition systems in thirty of its larger postal centers to sort packages that cannot be processed by its automated equipment. An employee reads the zip codes off the label, and the system recognizes the codes and directs the packages to the proper chute.

American Express is employing voice recognition for charge-card authorizations. Retailers who do not have electronic approval equipment must call American Express for charge authorization; in some cases, computers handle these calls. The computer answers the phone, asks for the account number and purchase amount, checks the cardholder's account, and provides a verbal response. As a final example, stockbrokers trading U.S. government securities for six major brokerage houses can now place buy and sell orders by speaking into a special telephone connected to a computer system. The trades are carried out almost instantaneously and displayed on the brokers' computer screens at their desks.

(Adapted from Elmer-DeWitt, 1992)

On the research side, IBM is now experimenting with a prototype voice-recognition system called Tangora (named after the world's fastest typist in the *Guinness Book of World Records*). Tangora currently recognizes about 60,000 words, and IBM is trying to make it easy to use. Tangora allows the user to dictate a letter and review it almost instantly; it also enables the user to correct an error in a document, such as a misspelled name—and Tangora automatically learns from its mistake so that it will spell the name correctly the next time. IBM's Carl Kessler believes that "voice holds the promise of bringing some of the last holdouts of the computer revolution into the fold. It will be fantastic for the inexperienced computer user, and could·have a dramatic impact on the workday of medical professionals, attorneys, and others who do a lot of dictation in their job."

(Adapted from Kaplan, 1992)

employing an impact printing mechanism in which individual hammers force the paper and ribbon against the appropriate print characters (which are embossed on a rotating band or chain). These higher-cost printers typically operate at 500 to 5,000 lines per minute. Page printers have wide variations in speed, from around 8 pages per minute for desktop units used with microcomputers to 250 pages per minute for printers used with large mainframes and supercomputers. Page printers print one entire page at a time, often employing an electrophotographic printing process (like a copying machine) to print an image formed by a laser beam.

In part to counteract the flood of paper that is threatening to engulf many organizations, micro-film increasingly is being used as a computer output medium. The output device is a **computer output microfilm** (COM) recorder that accepts the data from the memory and prepares the microfilm output at very high speeds, either as a roll of microfilm or as a sheet of film called a microfiche that contains many pages on each sheet. **Voice response units** are gaining increasing acceptance as providers of limited, tightly programmed computer output. Cable television shopping services and stock price quotation services often use voice output in conjunction with touch-tone telephone input.

The newest buzzword used to describe computer output is **multimedia**. A multimedia system uses a microcomputer system to coordinate many types of communications media—text, graphics, sound, still images, animations, and video. The purpose of a multimedia system is to enhance the quality of and interest in a presentation, whether it is a corporate briefing, a college lecture, an elementary school lesson, or self-paced instruction. The sound may come from a compact disk player controlled by the computer or from digital sound files stored within the computer's files. Graphics or photographs used as part of the presentation may have been scanned via an imaging system, and artwork may have been created with a graphics program on the computer. The video portion usually comes from a video disk player, but may come from the computer's files. In any case, the entire multimedia presentation is controlled by the microcomputer.

To summarize, the particular input and output devices attached to a given computer will vary based on the uses of the computer. Every computer system will have at least one input device and at least one output device. On the computers you will be using as a manager, keyboards, video display units, and printers will be the most common input/output devices.

Computer Memory

At the heart of the diagram of Figure 4.4 is the **memory**, also referred to as main memory or primary memory. All data flows are to and from memory. Data from input devices always goes into memory; output devices always receive their data from memory; two-way data flows exist between files and memory, and between the arithmetic/logical unit and memory; and a special type of data flows from memory to the control unit to tell the control unit what to do next (this latter flow will be the focus of the section "The Stored-Program Concept").

In some respects, the computer memory is like human memory. Both computers and humans store data in memory in order to remember them, or use them, at a later time, but the way in which data are stored and recalled differs radically between computer memory and human memory. The computer memory is divided into cells, and a fixed amount of data can be stored in each cell.

Further, each memory cell has an identifying number called an address that never changes. An older microcomputer, for example, might have 65,536 memory cells, each capable of storing one character of data at a time. These cells have unchanging addresses varying from 0 for the first cell up to 65535 for the last cell.

A useful analogy is to compare computer memory to a wall of post office boxes (see Figure 4.5). Each box has its own sequential identifying number printed on the door to the box, and these numbers correspond to the addresses associated with memory cells. In Figure 4.5 the address or identifying number of each memory register is shown in the upper left corner of each box. The mail stored in each box changes as mail is distributed or picked up. In computer memory, each memory cell holds some amount of data until it is changed. For example, memory cell 0 holds the characters MAY, memory cell 1 holds the characters 1994, memory cell 2 holds the characters 700.00, and so on. The characters shown in Figure 4.5 represent the contents of memory at a particular point in time; a fraction of a second later the contents may be entirely different as the computer goes about its work. The contents of the memory cells will change as the computer works, while the addresses of the cells are fixed.

Computer memory is different from the post office boxes in several ways, of course. For one thing, computer memory operates on the principle of destructive read-in, nondestructive read-out. This principle means that as a particular piece of data is placed into a particular memory cell, either by reading it from an input device or as the result of a computation in the arithmetic/logical unit, it destroys (or erases) whatever data item was previously in the cell. By contrast, when a data item is retrieved from a cell, either to print it out or to use it in a computation, the contents of the cell are unchanged.

Another major difference between post office boxes and memory cells is in their capacity. A post office box has a variable capacity depending upon the size of the pieces of mail and how much effort is spent by postal employees in stuffing the mail in the box. A memory cell has a fixed capacity, with the capacity varying from one computer model to

0	1	2	3	4	5	6	7
MAY	1994	700.00	4	OSU	17	321.16	3
8	9	10	11	12	13	14	15
C	OMPU	TER	32	0	MARY	71.3	L
16	17	18	19	20	21	22	23
27	18	103.0	7	JOHN	41	100.00	0
24	25	26	27	28	29	30	31
0	0	0	37	B	0	62	1

FIGURE 4.5 Diagram of Computer Memory

another. A memory cell that can store only one character of data is called a **byte,** while a memory cell that can store two or more characters of data is called a **word.** In order to provide comparability, it has become customary to describe the size of memory (and the size of direct-access files) in terms of the equivalent number of bytes, even if the cells are really words.

An alternative related definition of a word in computer jargon is the amount of data handled by the central processing unit (CPU) as a single unit. It is quite common, for instance, for machines with byte-sized memory cells to process four bytes at a time through the CPU. On these machines, four bytes equals one word.

Leaving our post office analogy, we can note that there are several important differences between the memory of one computer model and that of another. First, the capacity of each cell may differ. In a microcomputer, each cell may hold only one digit of a number, while a single cell may hold fourteen digits in a mainframe. Second, the number of cells making up memory may vary from a few thousand to more than 500 million. Third,

the time involved to transfer data from memory to another component may differ by an order of magnitude from one machine to another. The technologies employed in constructing the memories may also differ, although most memory today is based on some variation of VLSI circuits on silicon chips.

Bits and Coding Schemes   Each memory cell consists of a particular set of circuits (a small subset of the VLSI circuits on a memory chip), and each circuit can be set to either "on" or "off." Since each circuit has just two states (on and off), they have been equated to 1 and 0, the two possible values of a binary number. Thus, each circuit corresponds to a *bi*nary digi*t*, or a **bit.** In order to represent the decimal digits (and the alphabetic letters and special characters) with which we want the computer to deal, several of these bits (or circuits) must be combined to represent a single character. In most computers, eight bits (or circuits) represent a single character. And a memory cell containing a single character, we know, is called a byte. Thus, eight bits equals one byte in most machines.

Let's consider a particular example. Assume that we have a computer where each memory cell is a byte (can contain one character). Then memory cell number 327, for example, will consist of eight circuits or bits. If these circuits are set to on-on-on-on-on-off-off-on (or, alternatively, 1111 1001), this may be defined by the coding scheme to represent the decimal digit 9; if these bits are set to 1111 0001, this may be defined as the decimal digit 1; if these bits are set to 1100 0010, this may be defined as the letter B; and so on, with each character we wish to represent having a corresponding pattern of eight bits.

There are two common coding schemes in use today. The examples given above are taken from the Extended Binary Coded Decimal Interchange Code (commonly known as EBCDIC, pronounced eb'-si-dic). EBCDIC was originally developed by IBM in the 1950s, and it is still used by IBM and other vendors. The other common code in use is the American Standard Code for Information Interchange (ASCII), which is employed in data transmission and in microcomputers. Figure 4.6 compares the ASCII and EBCDIC codes for the alphabet and decimal digits. You do not need to know these codes—only that they exist!

The bottom line is that a coding scheme of some sort is used to represent data in memory and in the other components of the computer. In memory, circuits in a particular cell are turned on and off—following the coding scheme—to enable us to store the data until a later time. It turns out that circuits are also used to represent data in the control and arithmetic/logical units. In the input, output, and files, the coding scheme is often expressed through magnetized spots (on and off) on some media, such as tape or disk. In data transmission, the coding scheme is often expressed through a series of electrical pulses or light pulses. In all cases, the coding scheme is vital to permit the storage, transmission, and manipulation of data.

Arithmetic/Logical Unit

The **arithmetic/logical unit**, like memory, usually consists of VLSI circuits on a silicon chip. In fact, the chip pictured in Figure 4.3 is the Intel Pentium

Character	EBCDIC Binary	Character	ASCII-8 Binary
A	1100 0001	A	1010 0001
B	1100 0010	B	1010 0010
C	1100 0011	C	1010 0011
D	1100 0100	D	1010 0100
E	1100 0101	E	1010 0101
F	1100 0110	F	1010 0110
G	1100 0111	G	1010 0111
H	1100 1000	H	1010 1000
I	1100 1001	I	1010 1001
J	1101 0001	J	1010 1010
K	1101 0010	K	1010 1011
L	1101 0011	L	1010 1100
M	1101 0100	M	1010 1101
N	1101 0101	N	1010 1110
O	1101 0110	O	1010 1111
P	1101 0111	P	1011 0000
Q	1101 1000	Q	1011 0001
R	1101 1001	R	1011 0010
S	1110 0010	S	1011 0011
T	1110 0011	T	1011 0100
U	1110 0100	U	1011 0101
V	1110 0101	V	1011 0110
W	1110 0110	W	1011 0111
X	1110 0111	X	1011 1000
Y	1110 1000	Y	1011 1001
Z	1110 1001	Z	1011 1010
0	1111 0000	0	0101 0000
1	1111 0001	1	0101 0001
2	1111 0010	2	0101 0010
3	1111 0011	3	0101 0011
4	1111 0100	4	0101 0100
5	1111 0101	5	0101 0101
6	1111 0110	6	0101 0110
7	1111 0111	7	0101 0111
8	1111 1000	8	0101 1000
9	1111 1001	9	0101 1001

FIGURE 4.6 EBCDIC And ASCII Computer Coding Schemes

processor chip used in today's top-of-the-line microcomputers. In many respects, the arithmetic/logical unit is very simple. It has been built to carry out addition, subtraction, multiplication, and division, as well as to perform certain logical operations, such as comparing two numbers for equality or finding out which number is bigger.

The broad arrows in Figure 4.4 represent the way in which the arithmetic/logical unit works. As indicated by the broad arrow from memory to the arithmetic/logical unit, the numbers to be manipulated (added, subtracted, etc.) are brought from the appropriate memory cells to the arithmetic/logical unit. Next the operation is performed, with the time required to carry out the operation varying with the computer model. The speeds involved vary from thousands of operations per second up to many millions of operations per second. Then, as indicated by the broad arrow from the arithmetic/logical unit to memory in Figure 4.4, the result of the operation is stored in the designated memory cell or cells.

Computer Files

As applications are being processed on a computer, the data required for the current computations must be stored in the computer memory. The capacity of memory is limited, however (although it may go over a billion bytes on some large machines), and there is not enough space to keep all of the data for all of the applications in memory at the same time. Adding additional memory may be possible, but memory is very expensive for large computers. In addition, memory is volatile—if the power goes off, anything stored in memory is lost. To keep vast quantities of data accessible within the computer system, in a nonvolatile medium but at more reasonable costs than main memory, file devices—sometimes called secondary memory or secondary storage devices—have been added to all but the tiniest computer systems.

The broad arrows in each direction in Figure 4.4 illustrate that data can be moved from particular cells in memory to the file, and that data can be retrieved from the file to particular memory cells. The disadvantage of files is that the process of storing data in the file from memory or retrieving data from the file to memory is quite slow relative to the computation speed of the computer. Depending upon the type of file, the store/retrieve time may vary from a very small fraction of a second to several minutes. Nevertheless, we are willing to live with this disadvantage to be able to store enormous quantities of data at a reasonable cost per byte (or character).

Sequential Access Files   Computer files fall into two basic types—sequential access and direct access. With sequential access files, all of the records that make up the files are stored in sequence according to the control key of the file. For example, a payroll file will contain one record for each employee. These individual employee records are stored in sequence according to the employee identification number. There are no addresses within the file; to find a particular record, the file device must start at the beginning of the sequential file and read each record until it finds the desired one. It is apparent that this method of finding a single record might take a long time, particularly if the sequential file is a long one and the desired record is near the end. Thus, we would rarely try to find a single record with a sequential access file. Instead, we would accumulate a batch of transactions and process the entire batch at the same time (see the discussion of batch processing in Chapter 2).

Sequential access files are usually stored on magnetic tape. A magnetic tape unit or magnetic tape drive is the file device that stores (writes) data on tape and that retrieves (reads) data from tape back into memory. Even with batch processing, retrieval from magnetic tape tends to be much slower than retrieval from the direct access files, to be discussed below. Thus, if speed is of the essence, sequential access files may not be suitable. On the other hand, magnetic tapes can store vast quantities of data economically. For example, a tape cartridge that can store up to 400 million bytes of data can be purchased for under $50.

Until the mid-1980s, the magnetic tape used with computers was all of the reel-to-reel variety, like old-style home tape recorders. Then 1/2-inch tape cartridges were introduced, and in 1988 the sales of magnetic tape cartridge drives overtook the sales of reel-to-reel drives for the first time (Savage, 1988). The tape cartridges are rectangular and thus easier to store than round reels, and, more important, the cartridges can be automatically loaded and ejected from the tape drives. With reel-to-reel, an operator must mount each individual tape; with cartridges, an operator can place an entire stack of cartridges into a hopper at one time and let the drive load and eject the individual cartridges. Thus, fewer operators are needed to handle a cartridge-based tape system.

Direct Access Files   A direct access file, stored on a direct access storage device or DASD, is a file from which it is possible for the computer to obtain a record immediately, without regard to where the record is located in the file. A typical

DASD for a large computer consists of a continuously rotating stack of disks resembling phonograph records (see Figure 4.7). A comb-shaped access mechanism moves in and out among the disks to record on and read from hundreds of concentric tracks on each disk surface. As an example of a very large DASD, an IBM 3390 Model B3C can store up to 34.05 billion bytes (or, to use the shorthand notation, 34.05 gigabytes), with a transfer rate from disk to memory of 4.2 million bytes (megabytes) per second. The cost of such a file is under $10 per million bytes of capacity.

In contrast to these fixed-disk, large-capacity, fairly expensive files, direct access files can also be removable, relatively small, and quite inexpensive. For example, a removable 3.5-inch high density disk for a microcomputer can store up to 1.44 million bytes (1.44 megabytes) of data and costs under $1. The disk drive itself costs under $100. These 3.5-inch disks are protected by a permanent hard plastic case, but they are sometimes called floppy disks. Although a misnomer for today's disks, their 5.25-inch predecessors for microcomputers were made of flexible plastic and were in fact "floppy."

The key to the operation of direct access files is that the physical file is divided into cells, each of which has an address. The cells are similar to memory cells, except that they are much larger—usually large enough to store several records in one cell. Because of the existence of this address, it is possible for the computer to store a record in a particular file address and then to retrieve that record by remembering the address. Thus, the computer can go directly to the file address of the desired record, rather than reading through sequentially stored records until it encounters the desired one.

How does the computer know the correct file address for a desired record? For example, assume that an inventory control application running on the computer needs to update the record for item number 79032. That record, which is stored somewhere in DASD, must be brought into memory for processing. But where is it? At what file address? This problem of translating from the identification number of a desired record (79032) to the corresponding file address is the biggest challenge in using direct access files. Very sophisticated software, to be discussed in Chapter 5, is required to handle this translation.

On-line processing (discussed in Chapter 2) requires direct access files. Airline reservation clerks, salespeople in a department store, or managers in their offices cannot afford to wait the several minutes that may be required to mount and read the appropriate magnetic tape. On the other hand, batch processing can be done with either sequential access files or DASD. Sequential access files are not going to go away, but all the trends are pushing organizations toward increased use of direct access files. First, advancements in magnetic technology and manufacturing processes keep pushing the costs per byte of DASD down. Second, the newer optical disk technology (see the box "Optical Disk Storage") provides drastically lower costs per byte of DASD for applications where slower data retrieval speeds are acceptable. Third, and most important, today's competitive environment is forcing organizations to focus on speed in information processing—and that means an increased emphasis on on-line processing and direct access files.

Many major computer installations today have so many DASD units that they are collectively referred to as a disk farm. It is not unusual for a large installation to have more than a trillion

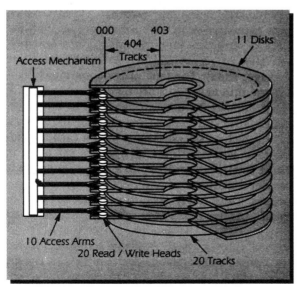

FIGURE 4.7 A Schematic Diagram of a Magnetic Disk Drive

OPTICAL DISK STORAGE

The newest type of file storage for computer systems is the optical disk. The disk is made of plastic coated with a thin reflective alloy material. Data are recorded on the disk by using a laser beam to burn microscopic pits in the reflective surface (or in some cases alter the magnetic characteristics of the surface), employing a binary coding scheme. Optical disks have a tremendous capacity advantage over magnetic disks, but they are typically much slower. There are three primary types of optical disks in use today: CD-ROM (compact disk–read only memory) disks, WORM (write once, read many) disks, and rewritable disks.

CD-ROM can only be read and cannot be erased. CD-ROM is much like a phonograph record in that a master disk is originally created, and then duplicates can be mass-produced for distribution. CD-ROM is particularly useful for distributing large amounts of relatively stable data (such as a manual or multimedia material) to many locations. As an example, a 4.72-inch CD-ROM can hold 680 megabytes of data.

As distinct from CD-ROM, a WORM disk can be written on by the user—but only once!

Then it can be read many times. As implemented on IBM's 3995 Optical Library Dataserver Model 132, one 5.25-inch removable disk cartridge can hold 652 megabytes of data. The Model 132 handles 144 cartridges at a time, giving a total on-line capacity of 94 gigabytes. WORM technology is quite appropriate for archiving documents, engineering drawings, and records of all types.

Rewritable disks are the most versatile form of optical storage because the data can be altered. Writing on a rewritable disk involves the use of laser heat to erase the recording surface and a combination of laser and magnetic technology to write on it. This type of optical disk may be an appropriate choice for supporting an on-line transaction processing system. Model 131 of the IBM 3995 Optical Library Dataserver uses rewritable disks. The specifications on these disks are the same as those given above for Model 132, so the total on-line capacity for this unit is 94 gigabytes. A mixture of write-once and rewritable units may be attached to a single large IBM computer to provide more than 5.2 terabytes (5.2 trillion bytes) of optical storage.

(Adapted from Hoskins, 1992 and IBM, 1992)

bytes (1,000 gigabytes, or 1 terabyte) of disk storage on line.

Control Unit

We have considered five of the six building blocks represented in Figure 4.4, but we would not have much if we stopped our discussion at this point. Thus far we have no way of controlling these various components, no way of taking advantage of the tremendous speed and capacity we have described. The **control unit** is the key. It provides the control that enables the computer to take advantage of the speed and capacity of its other components. The thin arrows in Figure 4.4 point out that each of the other five components is controlled by the control unit.

How does the control unit know what to do? Someone must tell the control unit what to do by devising a precise list of operations to be performed. This list of operations, which is called a program, is stored in the memory of the computer just like data. One item at a time from this list is moved from memory to the control unit (note the broad arrow in Figure 4.4), interpreted by the control unit, and carried out. The control unit works through the entire list of operations at electronic speed, rather than waiting for the user to tell it what to do next. What we have just described is the **stored-program concept**, which is the most important idea in all of computing.

THE STORED-PROGRAM CONCEPT

Some person must prepare a precise listing of exactly what the computer is to do. This listing must be in a form that the control unit of the computer has been built to understand. The complete listing of what is to be done for an application is called a **program**, and each individual step or operation in the program is called an **instruction**. The control unit then carries out the program, one step or instruction at a time, at electronic speed.

When a particular computer model is designed, the engineers build into it (more precisely, build into its circuitry) the capability to carry out a certain set of operations. For example, a computer may be able to read a line of data keyed in at a terminal, print a line of output, add two numbers, subtract one number from another, multiply two numbers, divide one number by another, compare two numbers for equality, and several other operations. The control unit of the computer is built to associate each of these operations with a particular instruction type. Then the control unit is told which operations are to be done by means of a program consisting of these instructions. The form of the instructions is peculiar to a particular model of computer. Thus, each instruction in a program must be expressed in the precise form that the computer has been built to understand. This form of the program that the computer understands is called the **machine language** for the particular model of computer.

Not only will the form of the instructions vary from one computer model to another, so will the number of different types of instructions. For example, a small computer may have only one add instruction, while a large one may have a different add instruction for each of several classes of numbers (such as integer, floating point or decimal, and double precision). Thus, the instruction set on some machines may contain as few as 20 types of instructions, while other machines may have more than 200 instruction types.

In general, each machine language instruction consists of two parts—an operation code and one or more addresses. The operation code is a symbol (for example, A for add) that tells the control unit what operation is to be performed. The addresses refer to the specific cells in memory whose contents will be involved in the operation. As an example, for a hypothetical computer the instruction

Operation Code	Addresses
A	470 500

means add the number found in memory cell 470 to the number found in memory cell 500, storing the result back in memory cell 500. Therefore, if the value 32.10 is originally stored in cell 470 and the value 63.00 is originally stored in cell 500, the sum, 95.10, will be stored in cell 500 after the instruction is executed. Continuing our example, assume that the next instruction in the sequence is

$$M \quad 500 \quad 200$$

This instruction means move (M) the contents of memory cell 500 to memory cell 200. Thus, 95.10 will be placed in cell 200, erasing whatever was there before. (Because of nondestructive read-out, 95.10 will still be stored in cell 500.) The third instruction in our sequence is

$$P \quad 200$$

which means print (P) the contents of memory cell 200 on the printer, and 95.10 will be printed.

Our very short example contains only three instructions and obviously represents only a small portion of a program, but these few instructions should provide the flavor of machine language programming. A complete program would consist of hundreds or thousands of instructions, all expressed in the machine language of the particular computer being used. The person preparing the program (called a programmer) would have to look up each operation code and remember what data he has stored in every memory cell. Obviously, machine language programming is very difficult and time-consuming. (As we will learn in Chapter 5, programs may be written in languages that are easier for us to use and then automatically translated into machine language, so almost no one programs in machine language today.)

Once the entire machine language program has been prepared, it must be entered into the computer, using one of the input methods already described, and stored in the memory of the computer. This step of entering the program in memory is called loading the program. The control unit then is told (somehow) where to find the first instruction in the program. The control unit fetches this first instruction and places it in special storage cells called registers within the control unit. Using built-in circuitry, the control unit interprets the instruction (recognizes what is to be done) and causes it to be executed (carried out) by the appropriate components of the computer. For example, the control unit would interpret the add instruction above, cause the contents of memory cells 470 and 500 to be sent to the arithmetic/logical unit, cause the arithmetic/logical unit to add these two numbers, and then cause the answer to be sent back to memory cell 500.

After the first instruction has been completed, the control unit fetches the second instruction from memory. The control unit then interprets and executes this second instruction. The control unit then fetches and executes the third instruction. The control unit proceeds with this fetch-execute-fetch-execute-fetch-execute cycle until the program has been completed. Usually the instruction that is fetched is the next sequential one, but machine languages incorporate one or more branching instructions that, when executed, cause the control unit to jump to a nonsequential instruction for the next fetch. The important point is that the control unit is fetching and executing at electronic speed; it is doing exactly what the programmer told it to do, but at its own rate of speed.

One of the primary measures of the power of any computer model is the number of instructions that it can execute in a given period of time. Of course, some instructions take longer to execute than others, so any speed rating represents an average of some sort. These averages may not be representative of the speeds that the computer could sustain on the mix of jobs carried out by your organization or any other organization. Furthermore, some machines operate on one or two bytes at a time (many microcomputers), while others operate on words (most mainframes). Thus, the speed rating for a micro is not at all comparable to the speed rating for a larger machine. Nevertheless, the various speed ratings serve as a rough measure of the processing power of various machines.

The most commonly used speed rating is **MIPS**, millions of instructions per second executed by the control unit. MIPS ratings range from approximately 0.5 for a microcomputer based on Intel's 80286 chip, to 1 for a low-end IBM AS/400 minicomputer, to 5 for a midrange IBM 4381, to 10 for an 80486-based microcomputer, to 59 for a DEC VAX 9000 Model 420, to 242 for an IBM ES/9000 Model 900.

Another speed rating used is **MegaFLOPS** or **MFLOPS**, millions of floating point operations per second. These ratings are derived by running a particular set of programs in a particular language on the machines being investigated. The ratings are therefore more meaningful than a simple MIPS rating, but they still reflect only a single problem area. In the so-called LINPACK ratings, the problem area considered is the solution of dense systems of linear equations using the LINPACK software in a FORTRAN environment (Dongarra, 1992). MFLOPS ratings vary from 0.12 for an Apple Macintosh IIsi and an IBM PS/2 Model 70, to 0.71 for a Hewlett-Packard 9000 Series 850, to 1.2 for a DEC VAX 6000 Model 410, to 43 for a DEC 10000 Model 610, to 60 for an IBM ES/9000 Model 520, to 479 for a Cray Y-MP Model C90.

These published speed ratings may be useful as a very rough guide, but the only way to get a handle on how various machines would handle your organization's workload is **benchmarking**. Even benchmarking is quite difficult to do, but the idea is to collect a representative set of real jobs that you regularly run on your computer, and then for comparison actually run this set of jobs on various machines. The vendors involved will usually cooperate because they want to sell you a machine, but there may be severe problems in getting existing jobs to run on the target machines and in comparing the results once you get them.

Again, processing speeds will vary across machines, but all computers use the stored-program concept. On all computers a machine language program is loaded in memory and executed by the control unit. There is a great deal more to the story of how we get the machine language program, but suffice it to say at this point that we let the computer do most of the work in creating the machine language program. Neither you nor programmers working for your organization will write in machine language; any programs will be written in a language much easier to understand, much closer to English. Chapter 5 is primarily concerned with the software, or programs, used to control computer systems.

TYPES OF COMPUTER SYSTEMS

In our earlier discussion of the various generations of computers, we introduced some terminology—microcomputers, minicomputers, and mainframes—that has been applied to different types of computer systems. Now we want to expand our taxonomy of computer types to include the full range of computer systems available today. In our discussion, we will indicate the primary uses of each type of system as well as the major vendors. Our discussion must begin with a significant caveat. While there is general agreement on the terms we will be using, there is no such agreement on the parameters defining each category or the computer models that belong in each type. Even if there were such agreement today, there would not be tomorrow, as new technologies are employed and new computer models are introduced.

Generally speaking, the boundaries between the categories are defined by a combination of cost, computing power, and purpose for which a machine is built. Listed in order of generally in-

creasing cost and power, the categories we will use are microcomputers, workstations, minicomputers, mainframes, minisupercomputers, and supercomputers (see Table 4.1). You will note that the ranges of cost and power in Table 4.1 are often overlapping, which reflects the differences in purposes for which the machines have been designed. Remember also that MIPS is not a good comparative measure of power. One MIPS on one machine may represent considerably more (or less) computing power—in terms of the actual job mix to be run on the computer—than one MIPS on another machine.

Microcomputers

Microcomputers, often called micros or personal computers or just PCs, cost from $1,000 to $5,000. They generally have less power than minicomputers, but the dividing line between these two categories is faint. In general, microcomputers can be carried or moved by one person, and they usually have only a single keyboard and video display

TABLE 4.1 Types of Computer Systems

Category	Cost	MIPS	Primary Uses
Microcomputers	$1,000–$5,000	0.5–20	Personal computing Terminal attached to large computers Client in client/server applications Small business processing
Workstations	$5,000–$100,000	20–400	Server in client/server applications Server for local area network Specific applications (CAD, other graphics)
Minicomputers	$10,000–$750,000	1–50	Departmental computing Specific applications (office automation, CAD) Midsized business general processing Universities Server in client/server applications
Mainframes	$500,000–$20,000,000	20–400	Large business general processing Widest range of applications
Minisupercomputers	$500,000–$5,000,000	200–4000	Numerically intensive scientific calculations
Supercomputers	$5,000,000–$30,000,000	400–10000	Numerically intensive scientific calculations

unit (which is why they are called personal computers). Most microcomputers consist of the computer itself (a medium-sized box containing the memory, arithmetic/logical unit, and control unit), a keyboard for input, a video monitor, perhaps a small printer for output, and one or more floppy or hard disk drives (files) in the same box with the computer. Laptop models combine all these pieces except the printer in a small briefcase-like package weighing under fifteen pounds; notebook models are smaller, often weighing only five or six pounds; and the newer hand-held or palmtop models are smaller yet, weighing in at two pounds or less. Desktop models are not so trim or so easy to transport, but they can be moved by a single person.

In the second half of the 1980s, the most popular microcomputer for business use was the IBM Personal Computer (and its big brothers, the XT and the AT), designed around microprocessor chips built by Intel and the PC-DOS operating system (a software package) created by Microsoft. By the early 1990s, the IBM Personal Computer line had been largely replaced by the various models of the IBM Personal System/2. As we move into the middle of the 1990s, IBM-compatible machines still dominate the business marketplace, but more and more of these machines are being sold by vendors other than IBM. Compaq has been very successful by building top-of-the-line IBM-compatible machines. Mail-order vendors such as Dell and Gateway 2000 have captured significant market shares by extremely competitive pricing. In response to competitive pressures, both Compaq and IBM have lowered their prices and introduced multiple microcomputer lines.

The IBM and IBM-compatible machines in use today employ predominantly Intel 80386 chips in the less powerful models and 80486 chips in the more advanced models. Most of these machines still use the PC-DOS operating system, although IBM is pushing its newer OS/2 operating system (originally developed by Microsoft) for the more powerful models. Microsoft Windows, a graphical user interface (GUI) that works with and extends the PC-DOS operating system, is being used with an increasing proportion of these IBM and IBM-compatible machines.

HAND-HELD COMPUTERS

The smallest microcomputers—hand-held machines weighing one or two pounds and costing $500 to $3,000—are proving to be extremely versatile business tools. Many companies are now equipping their field staff with these small micros to improve employee productivity and enhance communication between the field staff and the office. For example, both Hertz and Avis use hand-held computers to generate receipts and speed up car rental returns at busy locations. These devices, which hang on a strap around the agent's shoulder, include a small printer to produce the receipt right at the rental car as it is being turned in. Utility company workers use hand-held computers to read meters. Frito-Lay has provided hand-held machines to all of its 10,000 delivery people. With these computers, the delivery person enters the orders at each store and then attaches the computer to a printer in his truck to print an itemized invoice. At the end of the day, the machine generates a sales report and—via a hookup in the local warehouse—transmits the report to company headquarters.

(Adapted from Fuchsberg, 1990)

Another major contender in the business environment is the Apple Macintosh. Initially, the Macintosh found tough-going in the business world against the entrenched IBM microcomputers, but its easy-to-use graphical interface won it many converts in the late 1980s and early 1990s. The continued growth in the Macintosh market, plus the splintering of the IBM-compatible market as described above, pushed Apple past IBM in dollar value of microcomputer sales in 1992 for the first time since IBM entered this market. The microcomputer market is extremely competitive and should remain so for the rest of this century.

Microcomputers have been put to a myriad of uses. In the home, they have been used for record-keeping, word processing, and games; in the public schools, for computerized exercises, educational games, and limited programming; in colleges, for word processing, spreadsheet exercises (more on this in Chapter 5), and programming; and in the corporate environment, for word processing, spreadsheets, and programming, as a terminal into a larger computer, and, most recently, as a client in a client/server application. Stand-alone microcomputers in a large organizational setting are rapidly becoming a thing of the past. For managers to do their jobs, they need microcomputers linked into the corporate computer network in order to access data and applications wherever they exist. Microcomputers have also become important for small businesses, where they do operate as stand-alone machines or on small local area networks. The growing supply of software developed for a particular type of small business (for example, a general contractor, hardware store, or farmer), coupled with the relatively low price of microcomputers, has opened up the small business market.

Workstations

Here is one example of the confusing terminology that abounds in the computing field. The term **workstation** was used in Chapter 2 and is in standard usage in industry to mean any type of computer-related device at which an individual may work. Thus, a personal computer is a workstation, and so is a terminal. More recently, workstation has been used to describe a more powerful machine, still run by a microprocessor, which may or may not be used by a single individual. This more powerful type of workstation is the subject of our next category.

As the numbers in Table 4.1 indicate, this category of machines is a very broad one, with prices ranging from $5,000 to more than $100,000 and an equally wide range in terms of power. Workstations are, in fact, grown up, more powerful microcomputers. Workstations at the lower end of the range tend to have only one "station"—a keyboard and a high-quality video monitor—at which to "work", although that is not necessarily true for the upper-end machines. Workstations are based on the microprocessor chip, but more powerful ones than those used in microcomputers. Workstations were originally deployed for specific applications demanding a great deal of computing power and/or high-resolution graphics, but more recently have been used as servers in client/server

applications and in network management. In fact, because of their very strong price-performance characteristics compared to minicomputers and mainframes (see Table 4.1), workstations are beginning to make inroads into the traditional domains of minicomputers (departmental computing, midsized business general processing) and mainframes (large business general processing).

The development of the **RISC** (reduced instruction set computing) chip is largely responsible for the success of this class of machines. You will recall from our earlier discussion that some computers have a large instruction set (mainframes), while others have a considerably smaller instruction set (microcomputers). The designers of the RISC chips based their work on already-existing microprocessor chips, not mainframe chips. By working with a reduced instruction set, they were able to create a smaller, faster chip than had been possible previously. Variations of these RISC chips power many of the machines in this category, including those in Hewlett-Packard's HP 9000 family, IBM's RISC System/6000 family, and Sun's SPARCsystem family. IBM, the world's largest computer company, experienced serious problems during the early part of the 1990s, but one of the bright spots for IBM was the strong acceptance of its RISC System/6000 machines.

Minicomputers

Minicomputers represent one step up in cost and power from microcomputers, ranging in price from $10,000 to $750,000. Minicomputers overlap in price and power with workstations but tend to have less power for the same price. Minicomputers are bigger than microcomputers, and tend to be bigger than workstations as well; they are usually placed in an office or a small room. Numerous terminals or microcomputers acting as terminals (say, up to 200 for top-end minicomputers) can be handled by a single minicomputer. These machines are often regarded as departmental computers and may be devoted to a specific task, such as office automation or computer-aided design. Many midsized businesses use one or more minicomputers to handle their corporate data processing.

Major vendors include Digital Equipment Corporation (DEC), Hewlett-Packard, Unisys, Data General, and, of course, IBM. In the 1980s, IBM's System/34, System/36, and System/38 became the most popular business computers (not including microcomputers) of all time. Many of these machines have now been replaced by IBM's Application System/400, which was first introduced in 1988 and has been a major success for IBM. DEC has ridden the success of its VAX series of minicomputers to the number two spot in the computer industry in the United States, behind IBM. In addition to good price-performance ratios for its machines, another reason for the success of DEC has been its easy-to-use and powerful VMS operating system, which runs on all the VAXes.

The larger minicomputers are sometimes called **superminicomputers**, which is a strange name, using both super and mini as prefixes. A supermini usually requires a small room and calls for a professional staff of operators and programmer/analysts. (By contrast, smaller minicomputers may or may not have a professional staff.)

Some commentators have suggested that minicomputers may be a dying breed, squeezed between increasingly powerful microcomputers from the bottom and entrenched mainframe systems from above—and with workstations offering considerably better price-performance figures. Certainly DEC's troubles in the early 1990s are partly the result of this situation, but we do not expect minicomputers to disappear in the near term, although their market share may shrink. Minicomputers offer much better input/output capabilities than workstations, and an extensive array of easy-to-use commercial applications software has been developed for these machines. In addition, extensive specialized software has been developed by thousands of organizations to run on minicomputers, and these "legacy" systems cannot easily be converted to run on other types of machines.

Mainframe Computers

The **mainframes** are the "bread-and-butter" machines of information processing that are the heart of the computing systems of most major corporations and government agencies. Our earlier discus-

---

DON'T WRITE OFF THE MINI

IBM has sold over 200,000 AS/400s since its announcement four and a half years ago. If the group within IBM responsible for the AS/400 separated from the rest of IBM, it would end up being the second-largest computer company in the country, second only to the rest of IBM. There are tens of thousands of . . . applications written, installed, fully debugged, and still being enhanced on the AS/400.

Just last week I called on two very different customers who have IBM minis. They're running industry-specific applications that they're unable to find in the PC market, either because they don't exist yet or because the products out for the PC are unreliable and untested. Both customers are very happy with their applications.

I could go on with many more of the minicomputer's strong points, such as its integrated database, security (when was the last time you had a virus on your AS/400?), and connectivity. The point is, the mini is not dead (especially not the AS/400). It's part of the corporate strategy for many Fortune 500 companies as well as small to medium-sized firms, and it will continue to be for many years to come. More and more systems are being integrated into networks, with users having the ability to seamlessly access PC, mini, and, in some cases, mainframe applications all from one [microcomputer].

(White, 1993)

---

sion on the evolution of computing dealt primarily with the various generations of mainframe computers. The range of mainframe power and cost is wide, with MIPS varying from 20 to 400 and costs from $500,000 to $20 million. Hundreds of terminals (or microcomputers acting as terminals) can be handled by a mainframe, and the machine requires a good-sized computer room and a sizable professional staff of operators and programmer/analysts. The strength of mainframes is the versatility of applications they can handle—on-line and batch processing, standard business applications, engineering and scientific applications, network control, systems development, and more. Because of the continuing importance of mainframes in corporate computing, a wide variety of peripheral

134

equipment has been developed for use with these machines, as has an even wider variety of applications and systems software. This development, by the way, has been carried out by computer vendors, other equipment manufacturers, and companies that specialize in writing software, known as software houses.

Competition has been fierce in the mainframe arena because of its central role in computing. The dominant vendor has been IBM ever since the overwhelming success of the 650 in the late 1950s. The current generation of IBM mainframes is the Enterprise System/9000 series, first introduced in 1990. As of this writing, the smallest ES/9000 that is truly a mainframe is the air-cooled, single-processor Model 180 and the largest is the water-cooled Model 900, a six-processor machine (see Figure 4.8). IBM has maintained its preeminent position in the mainframe arena through solid technical products (but not necessarily the most technologically advanced), excellent and extensive software, reliable machines and unmatched service, and aggressive marketing.

Other major players in the mainframe arena are Unisys (the merger of Burroughs and Sper-

ry), NCR (formerly National Cash Register, and now part of AT&T), Control Data Corporation (CDC), Amdahl, and a trio of Japanese manufacturers—Fujitsu, Hitachi, and NEC. Amdahl and Hitachi are both interesting cases because they have succeeded by building machines that are virtually identical to IBM's—often with slightly newer technology—and then selling them for a lower price. The newest major player on the block is Digital Equipment Corporation, whose newest and largest machines have moved out of the minicomputer category into the mainframe arena.

All of the major mainframe vendors fell on hard times in the early 1990s, including IBM. The ES/9000 and its counterparts from other vendors are solid machines technically, but their price-performance ratios are much weaker than other classes of machines, especially microcomputers and workstations. Thus, the primary focus of new systems development in the first half of the 1990s has been on client/server applications designed to run on these more cost-effective platforms. This does not mean that mainframes are going away—far from it! It means that there will be little if any growth in the mainframe market, with most new

FIGURE 4.8 The IBM ES/9000 Mainframe Series. (Courtesy of International Business Machines Corporation)

THE ROLE OF THE MAINFRAME

Mainframes are definitely not "dead." Nor is most of their current work usurped by the millions of new PCs and workstations that are flooding into organizations. In most larger companies, the powerful, new, little computers are exponentially increasing the capabilities of people to do useful analytical work that is in addition to the accounting and operational work that is best ground out by the mainframes. The mainframes are the trucks, carrying huge, predetermined loads, while the workstations are the cars, scattering swiftly out to new destinations.

The mainframe is no longer simply the central accounting computer, churning out voluminous periodic reports. It is changing to several new roles. One new role is that of the super network controller, interconnecting worldwide corporate operations. Another new role is that of the central data warehouse, where huge amounts of useful information are readily accessed by any user, with a consistent level of accuracy and control. A third new role is that of powerful client/server, where complex questions can be asked through sophisticated applications that tap into a wide array of data storage media.

Mainframes will be further developed in such new roles, in concert with PCs and networks, to attain strategic visions that may not have even been formulated yet.

(I/S Analyzer, January 1993)

sales simply replacing older machines. The role of the mainframe will continue to evolve in the last half of the 1990s, with more emphasis on its roles as keeper of the corporate data warehouse, server in sophisticated client/server applications, and controller of worldwide corporate networks (see "The Role of the Mainframe").

Minisupercomputers

Minisupercomputers make up the newest group of computer systems, as well as the most innovative. As distinct from superminicomputers, which are simply big minicomputers, minisupercomputers are small supercomputers. Most of the firms work-

ing in this area are relatively new firms, trying to take advantage of the newest and most advanced technology. As a consequence, the machines differ widely in their architecture (general approach to computing) and in their power and cost. Many of these machines employ parallel processing, and some utilize massively parallel processing (more on this topic later in this chapter). The MIPS ratings of the minisupercomputers are often higher than those of mainframes, but their costs are considerably lower. For example, MIPS of the minisupercomputers vary from 200 to more than 4000, with prices in the $500,000 to $5 million range. A typical minisupercomputer might operate at 500 MIPS and cost $1 million. These machines seem like a bargain compared to mainframes, but they do not offer the versatility and (in most cases) the usable power of the mainframes because they do not have well-developed input/output capabilities, and there is no existing base of applications and systems software. At this point, they are not suitable for use in most business and government information processing centers. They are primarily employed in university and research laboratory settings for numerically intensive calculations.

Most of the vendors in the minisupercomputer market are probably unfamiliar names—Alliant, Convex, Floating Point Systems, Intel Paragon, and Thinking Machines, among others.

Supercomputers

Supercomputers are the true number-crunchers, with MIPS ratings in excess of 400 and price tags from $5 million to $30 million. A typical midlevel supercomputer might cost $10 million and operate at nearly 1,000 MIPS. Supercomputers are specifically designed to handle numerically intensive problems, most of which are generated by research scientists, such as chemists, physicists, and astronomers. Thus, most of the supercomputers are located in government research laboratories or on major university campuses (even in the latter case, most of the machines are largely supported by grants from the National Science Foundation or other government agencies). Major business firms do occasionally need time on a supercomputer for their research and development efforts, but they usually buy time on a machine at a convenient research laboratory or university (see box on Eli Lilly's supercomputer for an exception).

The acknowledged leader in the supercomputer arena is Cray Research, based in Minneapolis. Cray has supplied well over half of the world's supercomputers. In late 1992, *Business Week* estimated that Cray held 67 percent of the world market in large supercomputers (Gross, 1992). A poor second at 20 percent is a Japanese firm, Fujitsu, followed by another Japanese firm, NEC, in third with 6 percent. Noticeably absent among the leaders is IBM, although the top-of-the-line ES/9000 models are considered supercomputers by some. IBM, however, is actively moving back into the high-end scientific computation realm that it ignored for several years. In addition to internal efforts, IBM bankrolled Steve Chen, a leading supercomputer designer and a former Cray vice president, who set up his own company (Supercomputer Systems, Inc., or SSI) to develop a machine 100 times as fast as any currently on the market. IBM pulled the plug on SSI in early 1993, however, and now appears to be relying entirely on its internal efforts. Cray, of course, is not sitting still and continues to develop and market bigger, faster machines. With the number of major players involved, competition in the supercomputer arena seems destined to continue to be strong.

THE INFORMATION SYSTEMS INDUSTRY

We have spent significant portions of this chapter discussing computer hardware manufacturers, providing a good start in understanding a portion of the information systems industry. The hardware vendors, however, represent only a part of a much broader information systems industry. In this section, we want to explore the global makeup of that industry and identify the major players.

The authors of this book would like to be able to provide statistics for the total computer/communications industry, but they are not readily available for such a broad industrial grouping. We have had to settle for the information systems in-

---

A SUPERCOMPUTER AT ELI LILLY

In a gamble that startled the conservative pharmaceutical industry, Indianapolis-based Eli Lilly & Company, the Number 4 U.S. drug maker, recently became the first pharmaceutical company to install its own supercomputer—a $12 million Cray-2, one of the most powerful machines made by industry-leading Cray Research, Inc. The Cray-2 is a powerful tool for research scientists at Eli Lilly to use in their cutting-edge drug research.

Through the use of desktop terminals tied into the Cray-2, scientists are now able to manipulate images of large, complex human proteins and enzymes and watch them interact with other substances. The Cray-2 allows researchers to replace slow, near-random laboratory testing of hundreds of substances with more rapid theoretical screening. The new technology also holds out the hope of streamlining human tests of experimental compounds. By helping researchers analyze test data for a wider range of doses on more patient groups, for example, a supercomputer could help identify safer doses of the compounds.

Eli Lilly's purchase of a Cray-2 has touched off an industry-wide spending spree for big machines. Merck & Company has signed a pact with IBM to utilize a giant IBM computer; Monsanto has leased a supercomputer; and both Abbott Laboratories and Schering-Plough have upgraded their big machines. All these companies believe that computing power is one possible key to speeding up the discovery process for new drugs.

(Adapted from Shellenbarger, 1990)

---

dustry, as defined by *Datamation* magazine. *Datamation*'s definition of the IS industry includes information systems hardware, software, services, maintenance, and data communications, so this is a reasonable subset of our preferred broader construct. In 1992 (the last complete year for which data are available), *Datamation* estimated that the global IS revenues of the world's 100 leading IS companies (Schlack, 1993) were $318 billion, up 9.7 percent over the prior year (see Figure 4.9). Based on estimates by Arthur D. Little, Inc., of global IS sales for all companies, *Datamation*'s top

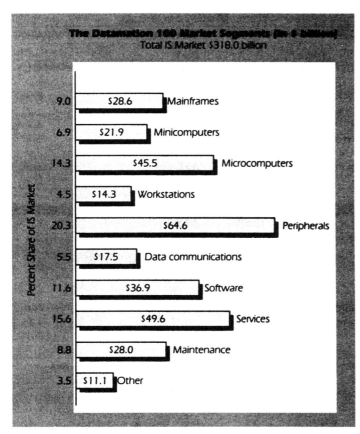

FIGURE 4.9 Breakdown of the Information Systems Market
(*Datamation* 39 [June 15, 1993]: 23.)

100 appear to represent more than 80 percent of the world IS industry (Hedges, 1988).

A breakdown of the total IS market in 1992 may be instructive. Computer hardware (not including data communications) constituted 55.0 percent of the total, with mainframes (including what we have called mainframes, minisupercomputers, and supercomputers) accounting for 9.0 percent of the total ($28.6 billion); minicomputers, 6.9 percent ($21.9 billion); microcomputers, 14.3 percent ($45.5 billion); workstations, 4.5 percent ($14.3 billion); and peripherals (printers, disk drives, tape drives, and so on), a sizable 20.3 percent ($64.6 billion). Data communications brings in 5.5 percent ($17.5 billion); software, 11.6 percent ($36.9 billion); services such as consulting, 15.6 percent ($49.6 billion); and maintenance, 8.8 percent ($28.0 billion).

Another way of looking at the IS industry is to check the home bases of the top 100 IS firms. Sixty-three of the top 100 are based in the United States, two in Canada (Northern Telecom and SHL Systemhouse), fifteen in Europe, sixteen in Japan, three in Taiwan, and one in South Korea. As an aside, Northern Telecom specializes in telephone switches, a specialized type of computer. Until five years ago the number of non-U.S. companies in the top 100 was slowly rising, but it now appears to have stabilized. The IS industry is clearly global and extremely competitive.

Now let us look at the top ten firms in each of the nine major market sectors—mainframes, minicomputers, microcomputers, workstations, peripherals, data communications, software, services, and maintenance. In Table 4.2, the market share represents each firm's percentage share of

138

TABLE 4.2 The Top Ten Firms In Various Information Systems Market Segments

Mainframes	Percent	Minicomputers	Percent	Microcomputers	Percent
IBM	29.1%	IBM	26.7%	IBM	17.2%
Fujitsu	15.8	Digital Equipment	11.6	Apple	12.1
Hitachi	14.4	Fujitsu	11.2	Compaq	9.2
NEC	11.0	NEC	9.2	NEC	8.9
Unisys	7.0	Hewlett-Packard	6.2	Fujitsu	5.9
Amdahl	5.3	Toshiba	5.9	Toshiba	4.4
Nihon Unisys	3.7	Siemens Nixdorf	4.8	Dell	4.1
Siemens Nixdorf	3.4	Tandem	3.9	Olivetti	3.0
Groupe Bull	3.0	ICL	3.3	AST	2.6
Cray Research	2.0	Mitsubishi	2.6	Gateway 2000	2.5

Workstations	Percent	Peripherals	Percent	Data Communications	Percent
Sun	17.4%	IBM	12.6%	AT&T	19.5%
IBM	13.7	Hewlett-Packard	7.3	Northern Telecom	12.6
Hewlett-Packard	11.1	Canon	6.2	IBM	12.0
Fujitsu	11.0	Hitachi	5.4	Nippon T&T	10.2
Digital Equipment	8.1	Fujitsu	4.9	Matsushita	6.9
Matsushita	8.1	Seagate	4.9	Ricoh	5.6
Silicon Graphics	5.3	Digital Equipment	4.7	Motorola	4.4
Unisys	4.7	Xerox	4.3	Racal	4.1
Intergraph	4.5	AT&T	3.6	Mitsubishi	3.8
Siemens Nixdorf	2.8	Conner	3.5	Hewlett-Packard	3.7

Software	Percent	Services	Percent	Maintenance	Percent
IBM	31.9%	IBM	13.3%	IBM	27.7%
Fujitsu	9.9	EDS	8.8	Digital Equipment	16.1
Microsoft	8.3	Computer Sciences	5.1	AT&T	6.2
NEC	5.2	Andersen Consulting	5.1	Unisys	6.1
Computer Associates	5.0	ADP	4.3	Siemens Nixdorf	5.7
Siemens Nixdorf	3.0	Fujitsu	4.0	Groupe Bull	5.2
Novell	2.8	Cap Gemini	3.9	Olivetti	4.1
Hitachi	2.8	TRW	3.7	ICL	3.5
Lotus Development	2.3	Digital Equipment	3.2	NEC	3.1
Digital Equipment	2.2	Unisys	2.8	Wang	2.3

Note: Percents all refer to share of *Datamation* 100 revenues.

Source: *Datamation* 39 (June 15, 1993): 22–23.

total revenues in the appropriate category by all of the *Datamation* 100 firms. Perhaps the first thing one notices in the table is that IBM heads seven of the nine lists, but the IBM market share only tops 30 percent once—for software. The second interesting fact is the presence of many non-U.S. firms in these top ten lists—six in the mainframes list, six in minicomputers, four in microcomputers, three in workstations, three in peripherals, six in data communications, four in software, two in

services, and five in maintenance. These lists underscore once again the global nature of the IS industry.

Missing from this data is the true impact of information technology on those firms that are not directly a part of the IS industry. For example, these data do not reflect the growing reliance on information technology by firms who have been investing in strategic information systems (see Chapter 3). It does not reflect the importance of

SEMICONDUCTOR CHIP WARS

In 1992, the U.S. semiconductor industry forged back into the lead in terms of worldwide sales, edging out the Japanese by a narrow margin of 43.8 percent to 43.1 percent. In terms of all types of chips, Intel (U.S.) led with revenues of $5.1 billion, followed by NEC (Japan) with $5 billion, Toshiba (Japan) with $4.8 billion, and Motorola (U.S.) with $4.6 billion. These numbers represent a drastic turnaround from just a few years prior, when U.S. chip production dropped to just over 35 percent of the world market. Why the reversal? There are several reasons, but perhaps the most important is the healthy demand for U.S. products built with chips—especially microcomputers, which may contain as many as 125 chips in one machine. By contrast, Japan's chipmakers rely more on sales to consumer electronics manufacturers, where the 1992 demand was lackluster. A longer-term reason for the turnaround has been the work of the U.S. government–sponsored Sematech, a consortium of U.S. chipmakers that has helped improve the quality of chipmaking equipment and thus the chip yield (percent of usable chips). As an example, Motorola's chips now contain fewer than 4 defects per million, a yield that cannot be matched by the Japanese.

The Japanese still have a healthy lead in sales of the memory chips used in most microcomputers. But in the critical microprocessor category— the chips that run the microcomputers—the overwhelming leader is Silicon Valley–based Intel Corporation. In 1991, Intel controlled 66 percent of the world 32-bit microprocessor market (those microprocessors used in mid-level and top-of-the-line microcomputers). Motorola occupied second place with 13 percent (these are the chips used in the Apple Macintosh). Intel's most popular chip today is the 80486, which has more than 1 million transistors on a thumb-tack-size sliver of silicon. The circuit lines on the 80486 are 1 micron wide—roughly 1 percent of the diameter of a human hair. Intel's new Pentium chip has approximately 3 million transistors and operates at about three times the speed of the 80486. And this is only the beginning: Intel is well underway on a microprocessor chip to be introduced in 1996 containing 20 million transistors and operating at 10 times the speed of the 80486.

(Adapted from Hof, 1992; Brandt, 1993; Moore, 1993; and Schneidawind, 1993)

computer-integrated manufacturing and robotics to a long list of manufacturing companies. Further, these statistics do not reflect the many noncomputer products that now incorporate microprocessor chips, such as automobiles, refrigerators, stoves, and airplanes. The IS industry is not only large by itself, but it has a disproportionate impact on other industries, and that impact will continue to grow through the rest of this century and into the next.

EXTENSIONS TO THE BASIC MODEL[1]

Earlier in this chapter we considered the underlying logical structure of all digital computers, and we found that all computers are made up of the set of six building blocks shown in Figure 4.4. Note that Figure 4.4 is an accurate but incomplete picture of many of today's computers. To be complete, the figure should be extended in two ways. First, today's computers (both microcomputers and larger machines) often have multiple components for each of the six blocks rather than a single component. Machines may have multiple input devices, or multiple file devices, or multiple central processing units (CPUs). Second, the architecture of today's machines often includes several additional components to interconnect the basic six components. For example, magnetic disk file devices usually have a disk controller that interfaces with a data channel connected to the central processing unit. In this section, we want to extend our basic model to incorporate these additional ideas and thus present a more complete picture of today's (and tomorrow's) computer systems.

Communications Within the Computer System

Controller   As a starting point for the extended model, let us note that appropriate controllers are needed to link input/output devices such as

[1] The material in this section is more technical than the rest of the chapter, and it is not essential to a general understanding of computer systems. It is included to provide the manager with an overview of the technical advances taking place in computer systems in the mid-1990s.

terminals, direct access storage devices (DASD), and sequential access devices to the CPU and memory of large computer systems. The exact nature of the controller will vary with the vendor and the devices being linked, but the controller is usually a highly specialized microprocessor attached to the CPU (through another new component called a data channel) and to the terminals or DASD or other devices (see Figure 4.10). The controller manages the operation of the attached devices to free up the CPU (and the data channel) from these tasks.

For example, a DASD controller receives requests for DASD read or write activity from the data channel, translates these requests into the proper sets of operations for the disk device, sees that the operations are executed, performs any necessary error recovery, and reports any problems back to the data channel (and thus to the CPU). A communications controller has the job of managing near-simultaneous input/output from an attached set of terminals, ensuring that the messages from each terminal are properly collected and forwarded to the data channel, and that responses from the data channel are properly sent to the right terminal.

Data Channel   The **data channel** is just as critical as the controller. A data channel is a specialized input/output processor (yet another computer) that takes over the function of device communication from the CPU. The role of the data channel is to correct for the significant mismatch in speeds between the very slow peripheral devices and the fast and expensive CPU. When the CPU encounters an input/output request (including requests for disk or tape reads and writes) during the execution of a program, it relays that request to the data channel connected to the device in question (the number of data channels varies with the machine). The CPU then turns to some other job while the data channel oversees input/output.

The data channel often includes some amount of buffer storage (a special type of memory), so that it may move large blocks of data into and out

FIGURE 4.10 Data Channels and Controllers

of main memory at one time. In this way, the data channel only has to interrupt the CPU when it is ready to move a large data block; during most of the time the CPU can continue to process another job. The data channel, on the other hand, must wait on data transmitted from the controller as it gathers an input block, or it must wait for a block of output data to be accepted by the controller.

Another way in which the data channel may operate is by cycle stealing. In this variation, the data channel has only a small amount of buffer storage in which it receives data. For example, when this small buffer fills up during a disk read, the channel steals a cycle from the CPU and places the contents of the buffer in main memory. This operation has minimal impact on the CPU (it loses only one cycle out of thousands) and allows the data channel to employ an area of main memory as its buffer.

Communications Bus   A third component often involved in the internal communication is a communications **bus**. The idea of a bus gained popularity in microcomputers, but is increasingly being employed in larger machines. A bus is a flexible way of handling communications among the components of the system. Rather than having individually designed wiring or cabling connections among the various components, all of the components are simply attached to a bus, which may be a conventional wiring cable or a fiber optics cable. Thus, it is a simple matter to add additional components (such as an additional CPU, DASD, or controller) to the bus. Of course, the bus must have sufficient data-path width (the number of bits that can be transmitted at the same time) and speed to avoid becoming a bottleneck for the entire computer system.

A Hierarchy of Storage Devices

Thus far, we have considered two (or perhaps three) levels of storage devices: main or primary memory, which is very fast and quite expensive; and secondary memory, which we can subdivide into not-so-fast and not-so-expensive direct access storage devices (DASD) and slow and inexpensive sequential access storage devices (magnetic tapes). In addition to these levels, we can add two more

levels and suggest that even more levels may be created in the future.

Cache Memory   Cache memory was originally employed as a very high-speed, high-cost storage unit used as an intermediary between the control unit and the main memory (Grossman, 1985). The term *cache*, by the way, is taken from the French word for a hidden storage place. The cache was intended to compensate for one of the speed mismatches built into computer systems, in this case, that between fetching data from main memory (to the arithmetic/logical unit or other internal registers) and executing an instruction. The CPU can execute an instruction much faster than it can fetch data (which requires electronically moving the data from memory to the arithmetic/logical unit). Thus, in a conventional architecture the expensive CPU often waited for the completion of a data fetch.

With cache memory, an entire block of data is moved at one time into the cache, and then most data fetches take place from the higher-speed cache to the arithmetic/logical unit. The success of cache memory depends upon two characteristics of the data to be used by the CPU—locality of reference and data reuse. Locality of reference means that if a given piece of data is used, there is a high probability that a nearby piece of data will be used shortly thereafter. Data reuse means that a block of data will be kept in the cache until it has not been recently referenced; then it will be replaced by a block of data that has been requested. The use of cache memory should optimize the use of the costly CPU.

After its successful use as an intermediary between the CPU and main memory, cache memory was incorporated into DASD controllers. The basic idea is similar, except the speed mismatch is greater—between the relatively slow DASD and the much faster data channel. Again, the keys to success of the cache are locality of reference and data reuse. A large block of data is moved from DASD to the cache, and then (hopefully) most data fetches take place from the cache rather than DASD itself. A microprocessor in the DASD controller manages the cache memory, keeping track of the frequency of reference to the data in the cache and moving blocks of data into and out of the cache in an attempt to optimize the use of the data channel (and, indirectly, the CPU). Figure 4.11 illustrates the use of cache memory both in the CPU and in a DASD controller.

Expanded Storage Whereas cache memory (when used in the CPU) is faster and more expensive than main memory, **expanded storage** is a slower and less expensive variation. Both cache and expanded storage are implemented using semiconductor memory (integrated circuits on silicon chips), as is main memory. As implemented by IBM, expanded storage is designed for electronic transfer of blocks of 4,096 bytes (defined as a page) between expanded storage and main memory. With the IBM ES/9000 mainframe, the transfer of each page from expanded storage to main memory takes about 75 microseconds (75 millionths of a second), which is typically from 200 to

300 times faster than data transfers from DASD controller cache. The use of expanded storage is transparent to application programs, so there are no required software changes. Expanded storage provides performance similar to additional main memory at a greatly reduced cost. On the top-of-the-line ES/9000, the Model 900, up to 1,024 megabytes of main memory are available and up to 8,192 megabytes of expanded storage.

Cache memory (in the CPU and in the DASD controller) and expanded storage represent three ways in which the conventional storage hierarchy has been extended. Cache memory is becoming a part of many components of the hardware, including high-speed communication modules and special purpose CPUs such as array processors. Thus, more layers may be added to the storage hierarchy as system designers seek to balance cost, capacity, and performance.

Multiple Processor Configurations

One of the most intriguing extensions to the basic model is the use of multiple CPUs or processors as part of a single computer system. Without using the multiple processor terminology, we actually considered such a system when we discussed the use of data channels (which are themselves processors) with a single primary CPU. Sometimes the term *front-end processor* is used instead of data channel, but in either case the additional processor (or processors) is used to offload handling of input/output from the primary CPU.

Multiprocessors An increasing number of larger machines (from minicomputers up) now make use of multiple processors as a way of increasing their power (usually measured by throughput). In these cases, two, three, or more CPUs are installed as part of the same computer system. The term **multiprocessor** usually means that each processor or CPU operates independently of the others. The multiple CPUs share main memory and the various peripherals, with each CPU working in its own allotted portion of memory. One CPU might handle on-line transaction processing, while another deals with engineering calculations and a third works on a batch pay-

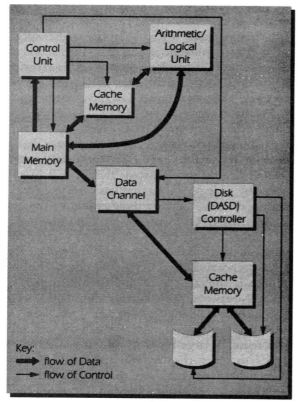

FIGURE 4.11 *Partial Logical Structure of Computer Incorporating Cache Memory*

roll system. The IBM ES/9000 Model 900 employs six multiple processors in this manner.

Vector Facilities   A **vector facility** is a specialized multiple processor configuration to handle calculations involving vectors. For these calculations, the same operation is to be performed on each element of the vector. By installing a number of parallel, relatively inexpensive microprocessors (operating under control of a primary control unit and thus a single program), all these operations can be performed simultaneously. The keys to whether a vector facility is worthwhile are the percentage of the total calculations that involve vectors and the lengths of the vectors themselves. The higher the percentage and the longer the vectors, the more valuable the vector facility. For research and development activities, vector facilities are often worthwhile, but their value for most business information processing is limited.

Parallel Processors   A **parallel processor** (PP) has two major differences from a vector facility. First, there is no single primary CPU in a parallel processor, and, second, the various CPUs are not always performing the same operation at the same time. For example, a parallel processing machine may have 16, 64, 256, or more processors, each of which would work on a separate piece of the same program. In order to use a parallel processing approach, the program must somehow be divided up among the processors and the activities of the various processors must be coordinated. Some of the minisupercomputers, such as those produced by Paragon and Floating Point Systems, employ a parallel processing architecture.

The term **massively parallel processor** (MPP) is used to describe machines with some large number of parallel CPUs. There is no firm guideline to distinguish between a PP and an MPP; in general, however, 32 or more parallel CPUs would be considered an MPP if the different CPUs are capable of performing different instructions at the same time, or a thousand or more parallel CPUs would be considered an MPP if the different CPUs must all carry out the same instruction at the same time. A machine like the Intel Paragon, a 56-processor MPP, can be used in various ways. It can run a

single, parallel job using all or most of the 56 processors; it can run a separate job on each processor (this is multiprocessing); or it can perform a combination of parallel processing and multiprocessing by dividing the CPUs up into partitions and running a separate job on each partition.

Needless to say, we are just beginning to learn how to take advantage of the incredible power of the parallel processing machines. The major drawback to these machines is the lack of software to permit users to easily take advantage of the processing power. At present, users must specifically tailor their programs to utilize the parallel CPUs effectively. For the short term, parallel processors will be most useful in universities and research laboratories, and in a few specialized applications that demand extensive computations, such as extremely high volume transaction processing.

SUMMARY

There is a lot more to information technology than the digital computer, but there is no doubt that the computer is the key technological development of the 20th century. The computer has had an astounding impact on organizations and on our lives, and it has captured our imaginations like no other recent development.

To summarize, all computer systems are made up of some combination of six basic building blocks: input, output, memory, arithmetic/logical unit, files, and control unit. All of these components are controlled by a stored program, which resides in memory and is brought into the control unit one instruction at a time, interpreted, and executed. The basic model has been extended in several directions over the years, such as by adding controllers and data channels to interface the slower peripheral devices (input, output, disks, tapes) with the much faster central processing unit. Communications buses have been added to permit flexible and easy configuration of systems, and a multilevel hierarchical memory involving cache and expanded storage has been adopted on some machines. To gain more power, multiple processors have been employed in a single computer system in a variety of configurations. Whatever the machine configuration, the computer system is still controlled by stored programs, or software. Chapter 5 explores computer software, concentrating on the programs that are most critical in running the computer system and the applications that you are most likely to encounter.

Let us end this chapter with the caveat that the numbers and specific details covered in the chapter will quickly become outdated, while the basic material should be valid for the foreseeable future.

REVIEW QUESTIONS

1. What are the distinguishing characteristics of the present, or Fourth Generation, computers?

2. Distinguish between microcomputers, minicomputers, mainframes, and supercomputers. Give approximate speeds (millions of instructions per second, or MIPS), and costs.

3. List the six building blocks that make up digital computers, and describe the flows of data that occur among these blocks.

4. Distinguish between the *contents* of a memory cell and the *address* of a memory cell. Distinguish between a *byte* and a *word*. Distinguish between a *bit* and a *byte*.

5. What are the advantages and disadvantages of using direct access files versus using sequential access files?

6. Explain in your own words the importance of the stored-program concept. Include the role of the control unit in your explanation.

7. Define the expressions in italics in the following sentence copied from this chapter: "In general, each *machine language* instruction consists of two parts: an *operation code* and one or more *addresses*."

8. Provide the full names for the following acronyms or abbreviations used in this chapter.

DEC	MIPS
CPU	MPP
MFLOPS	DASD
WORM	CPU

9. Six categories of computer systems were considered in this chapter: microcomputers, workstations, minicomputers, mainframes, minisupercomputers, and supercomputers. Provide the name of at least one prominent vendor in at least five of these categories (and you can use IBM only once).

10. Describe what is meant by benchmarking. When and how would you carry out benchmarking?

11. What is cache memory? Where would it be used and why?

12. Distinguish between a multiprocessor computer and a parallel processor computer. Which is the most important now for business information processing and why?

DISCUSSION QUESTIONS

1. From the discussion in this chapter and your own knowledge from other sources, what do you think is the most important advancement in computer hardware technology in the past five years? Why?

2. Some writers have suggested that the minicomputer may be squeezed out of existence in the next few years, with the incredible advances in the capabilities of microcomputers and workstations and the versatility of mainframes combining to divide up the present minicomputer market. What do you think? Why?

3. As this chapter has indicated, IBM has been the dominant force in the computer industry since the late 1950s. Why do you think this is the case? More specifically, why are so many large U.S. corporations seemingly committed to "Big Blue" (as IBM is affectionately known)?

4. Building on your answer to question 3, why has IBM suffered serious reverses in the early 1990s? Do you think that IBM will retain its dominant position as we move into the latter half of the 1990s? Why?

5. With one dominant firm controlling 50 percent (or more) of the mainframe hardware

market in the United States, has the computer industry truly been competitive over the past three decades? Support your position.

6. List possible uses of a supercomputer in a business setting.

7. MIPS and MegaFLOPS were mentioned in this chapter as measures of the power of computer systems. If you were in charge of buying a new computer system (and you may be some day), what measures of power would you want to find out? How would you go about determining these measures of power?

8. The following are *Datamation*'s top ten information systems companies in the world in 1992, along with their estimated information systems revenues. Either from your own knowledge or from library research, list the products and services that are primarily responsible for these companies making the top ten list.

1992 Rank	Company	1992 IS Revenue
1	IBM	$64.5 billion
2	Fujitsu	$20.1 billion
3	NEC	$15.4 billion
4	Digital Equipment	$14.2 billion
5	Hewlett-Packard	$12.7 billion
6	Hitachi	$11.4 billion
7	AT&T	$10.5 billion
8	Siemens Nixdorf	$ 8.3 billion
9	Unisys	$ 7.8 billion
10	Toshiba	$ 7.4 billion

9. For most business information processing, what do you believe are the critical or limiting characteristics of today's computing systems—CPU speed, memory capacity, DASD capacity, data channel speed, input speed, output speed, other factors, or some combination of these factors? Justify your answer.

10. In your opinion, is it important to the national welfare of the United States that we have a strong and viable information systems industry, especially in terms of technology? If so, what measures (if any) should the federal government take to encourage and support

such high-tech development? In particular, do you believe that we need a national high-tech industrial policy? Support your position.

REFERENCES

1993. "Global leaders in nine product categories." *Datamation* 39 (June 15): 22–23.

1993. "The changing role of the mainframe." *I/S Analyzer* 31 (January): 16.

Brandt, Richard. 1993. "A power surge in chips." *Business Week* (January 11): 80.

Dongarra, Jack J. 1992. "Performance of various computers using standard linear equations software." Computer Science Department, University of Tennessee, and Oak Ridge National Laboratory, No. CS-89-85 (December 15).

Elmer-DeWitt, Philip. 1992. "The machines are listening." *Time* 140 (August 10): 45.

Fuchsberg, Gilbert. 1990. "Hand-held computers help field staff cut paper work and harvest more data." *Wall Street Journal* 71 (January 30): B1, B6.

Gross, Neil. 1992. "Why Cray's number cruncher got crunched in Japan." *Business Week* (November 2): 154.

Grossman, C. P. 1985. "Cache-DASD storage design for improving system performance." *IBM Systems Journal* 24: 316–334.

Hedges, Parker. 1988. "Charting the champs." *Datamation* 34 (June 15): 14–24.

Hof, Robert D. 1992. "Inside Intel." *Business Week* (June 1): 86–94.

Hoskins, Jim. 1992. *ES/9000: A Business Perspective.* New York: John Wiley & Sons.

IBM. 1992. *Systems and Products Guide.* Spring. White Plains, NY: IBM.

Kaplan, Michael. 1992. "Tracking technologies." *Beyond Computing* 1 (August-September): 50–55.

Moore, Mark. 1993. "U.S. chip makers bounce back." *PC Week* 10 (February 1): 107, 114.

Savage, J. A. 1988. "Tape storage." *Computerworld* (July 11): 98.

Schneidawind, John. 1993. "In the chips: Explosive growth ahead for industry." *USA Today* (January 22): 1B–2B.

Schlack, Mark. 1993. "The new IT industry takes shape." *Datamation* 39 (June 15): 12–23.

Shellenbarger, Sue. 1990. "Lilly's new supercomputer spurs a race for hardware to quicken drug research." *Wall Street Journal* 71 (August 14): B1, B6.

White, Bradley. 1993. "Don't write off the mini, especially the AS/400." *PC Week* 10 (February 1): 57.

4

IMT Custom Machine Company, Inc.
Selection of a Hardware Platform

Darrin Young saw a late summer storm coming from the west across the open Indiana cornfields as he peered through the glass wall of his second-story executive office. He knew how helpful the rain would be for the farmers and for his dry lawn. Turning to a growing stack of paperwork, he also thought of the dark cloud hanging over his information systems (IS) area. He knew something had to be done. Committee after committee had analyzed various systems needs and proposed solutions. Young's trust in his staff invariably led him to approve the recommendations. But some "glitch" always seemed to pop up and put the solution on hold. "Something was missing; there is no real direction here—we don't know where we are going," he thought to himself. "We have to get our arms around our information systems once and for all."

Young was a vice president and division manager in a subsidiary company of International Machine and Tool–USA (IMT-USA). Building multimillion dollar, large custom machines for the automotive industry and delivering them on time while making a profit was the primary goal of Young's division. Under his charge, Young had two factories, which built about 150 custom machines per year. His division also included a third unit that made smaller machined parts for the two factories. A service and spare parts group within the division supported the repair and maintenance business for any custom machines, including machines built by IMT's competition. The

Fort Wayne, Indiana, plant, where Young was located, was the largest custom machine factory in the Western Hemisphere. As shown in Exhibit 1, Young had an executive staff and two plant managers reporting to him.

Young recognized that he had selected a nonconventional strategy to get to the heart of his division's IS problems when he called Charles Browning into his office on September 3, 1991. Browning was an experienced staff engineer with an extensive background in computers who was finishing his MBA. Browning reported to the development engineering manager at the Fort Wayne plant. Young explained his concerns to Browning and commissioned him to "survey the big IS picture and give me three basic options which will satisfy our IS needs. I expect you to report your findings in six weeks, and I plan to review the findings with you and incorporate one of the alternatives into my business plan." Young made it clear to Browning that he wanted "the true picture." He further stated that, "there should be no limits on the type of recommendations you provide, Charlie." By using Browning, Young hoped to cut through the layers of management that may have been "filtering" the root causes of IMT's IS problems.

. . . .

Background

The Automotive Industry Exhibit 2 summarizes the market capacity for U.S. suppliers of custom machines. The graphic shows increasing production capacity additions until the 1974 Arab oil embargo, when Americans began a long-term trend toward energy conservation. Spare production capacity suddenly became a reality to the custom machine industry. Underutilized plants were easy targets for closing, and plans for scores of new plants were canceled. As the U.S.-based automobile makers' market

EXHIBIT 1

IMT Custom Machine
Company Organization Chart

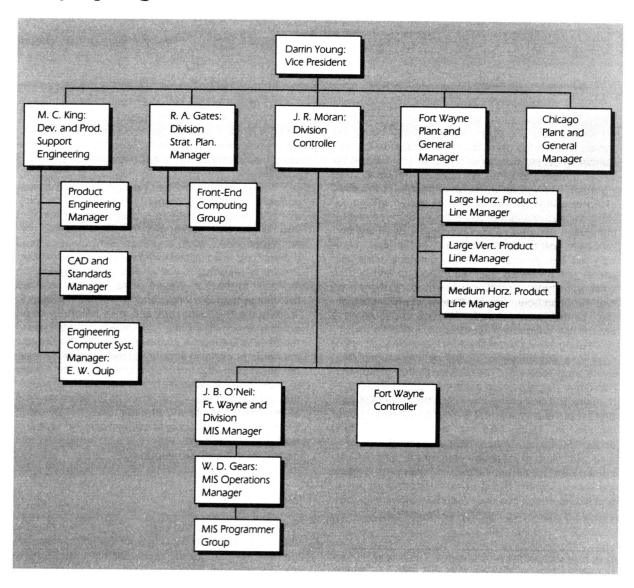

share declined, resulting demand decreases rippled through to the U.S. custom machine design industry. Annual capacity additions declined after 1974. By 1989, they had reached a level near that of the early 1960s.

The industry slowdown caused Williamson Machines and Engineering Corporation (WILMEC), which held about 30 percent of the market, to close its "medium horizontal"-type machine factory in Cleveland, Ohio, in 1983 and move medium horizontal production capability to its one remaining custom machine factory in Fort Wayne, Indiana. The Fort Wayne facility was constructed in the early 1960s specifically to manufacture a similar, but technically different, type of custom machine called a "large vertical."

In 1986, General Engineering, Inc., which in previous years had been an equal market rival to WILMEC, abandoned its custom machine business by closing its Detroit, Michigan, plant. General Engineering (GE) sold its technology to WILMEC, and GE's production equipment was moved to WILMEC's Fort Wayne plant. The result of WILMEC's technology

EXHIBIT 2
....
U.S. Custom Machine Production Capacity Additions

Production Capacity Additions from 1966 and Forecasted to 1995

acquisition from GE was that a third, and very different, technology called "large horizontal" was also manufactured in Fort Wayne. At this time, WILMEC also expanded a custom machine reconditioning operation in Chicago, Illinois to handle the assembly of one-third of its medium horizontal machines. Fort Wayne continued to produce all three machine types: large horizontal, large vertical, and medium horizontal.

In late 1989, WILMEC refocused its strategy away from the automotive industry into various service industries. WILMEC sold all of its custom machine engineering, manufacturing, and sales operations to International Machine and Tool (IMT) of Bonn, Germany. IMT was itself the result of a 1987 merger between Europe's two largest machine manufacturers—International Machine (English translation) of Germany, and Tools of Commerce (English translation) of Italy. Numerous plant closings and shakeups had rippled through Europe as well in the late 1980s.

By 1991, the production capacity for custom machines in the U.S. market had nearly stabilized at the level of demand. A significant increase in demand would have caused capacity problems and resulted in delayed deliveries. Some evidence suggested that the custom machine industry, which had been reducing spare capacity, might have to return to a robust building program by the mid-1990s.

International Machine and Tool   International Machine and Tool used a matrix style of management throughout its global operations. IMT's matrix organization was modeled after the structure of other large, European-based global companies. Dr. Wilhelm Schlein, chairman of IMT, summarized the organization as "a federation of national companies with a global coordination center—a distributed organization which has many homes." Schlein's strategy for building a decentralized, multidomestic enterprise included the critical responsibilities of IMT's business group leaders and its national holding company presidents toward IMT's goal to "Think global, act local."

One side of IMT's matrix organization was country-based. Each country manager (president of the national holding company) was responsible for financial targets for all products and services in that country. Country presidents coordinated synergistic relationships across IMT operations within the country (e.g., distribution and service networks). They were also responsible for maintaining relationships with national government officials.

The second side of IMT's matrix was technology-based (product classes) and reported through a separate transnational technology management group, called a business group (BG). The mission of each BG was to support shared knowledge and operations among many international factories. BG leaders served as business strategists who set global "rules of the game" and then let local managers pilot the execution.

In early 1991, IMT had eight international custom machine factories; two were located in the United States. Exhibit 3 displays a rough measure of the

EXHIBIT 3
Annual Custom Machine Production by Country

amount of available manufacturing capacity for the main countries in which IMT operated custom machine factories. The combined capacity of the Chicago and Fort Wayne plants was by far larger than that of any of the other countries.

Darrin Young Darrin Young reported to two managers in the matrix—the U.S. country manager and a BG manager. Young often felt the pressure of conflicting goals. On one hand, he was striving to increase return on assets. On the other hand, he was being encouraged to maintain a leading technology development process with the BG. As was true for all custom machine factories, Young's division "repatriated" about 1 percent of its sales to the BG for R&D projects.

With over thirty years of custom machine engineering experience, Young was widely known and highly respected throughout the industry. While working for WILMEC, he worked his way up through numerous engineering and manufacturing management positions. He had always been active in the industry by chairing and working on technical committees of various professional associations. Young's personal use of a computer was limited to a remote interest in an Apple Macintosh at home. His daily managerial

demands at work had made it impossible to use his personal computer on his desk.

In 1990, Young was appointed vice president of IMT Custom Machines Company, Inc. (CMCI), the newly created IMT subsidiary in the United States. On the country side of the matrix, CMCI reported through the IMT-USA holding company in New York, which in turn reported to IMT's world headquarters in Bonn. On the BG side of the matrix, Young reported to the managing director of the Custom Machine BG. The headquarters for CMCI's business group was in Milan, Italy.

Shortly after taking the job, Darrin and other division managers worked with the IMT-USA president to develop mission, principles, and vision statements. The statements, applying to all IMT-USA companies, appear in Exhibit 4; they were taken from a presentation by the IMT-USA president on March 26, 1990.

The Fort Wayne Plant The work environment of the Fort Wayne plant from 1975 to 1990 was extremely dynamic, to say the least. The plant transitioned from a busy single-product, focused factory to a factory that was nearly shut down (due to a lack of orders) and employed only a few hundred workers. It then evolved into a facility that supported three technically

EXHIBIT 4
IMT-USA Mission, Guiding Principles, and Vision Statements

Mission
- Serve the needs of U.S. customers to give them total satisfaction.
- Create an organizational environment that allows all IMT-USA's employees to add value.
- Promote an atmosphere of thirst and eagerness to perform, which allows delegation of responsibility to the lowest possible organizational level and attracts good people.
- Generate a sense of urgency and results orientation in the deployment of capital and human resources to ensure proper return for both our employees and our shareholders.
- Expand the horizon of the organization to share in and contribute to our worldwide core competencies.

Guiding Principles
- Create a sense of urgency—concentrate on priority actions rather than procedural issues.
- Promote a unifying culture: "can do—do it."
- Remove barriers to performance.
- Shift organizational focus to servicing the customers and beating competition.

Vision
- Demonstrate leadership in serving the U.S. marketplace in its transition to cleaner industry, where products are more efficiently produced, distributed, and applied.

different products (large horizontal, large vertical, and medium horizontal custom machines), which had originated from three different factories with three different engineering design systems. In 1991, IMT's Fort Wayne facility was producing near optimal capacity and was fully staffed with about 1,200 employees.

From 1984 to 1990, all of the engineering and marketing operations for the Fort Wayne and Chicago plants were located in Cleveland, Ohio (200 miles from Fort Wayne and 350 from Chicago). In mid-1990, IMT finished closing the Cleveland site by transferring all the engineering and marketing staffs to either Fort Wayne or Chicago.

As the Fort Wayne plant evolved to support multiple product lines, numerous informal systems emerged to handle day-to-day situations. The undocumented systems worked despite the incompatibilities among the three different technologies, which used three separate drafting systems as well as unique manufacturing processes. Very little capital had been invested to upgrade the operations during the last several years of WILMEC's ownership. Not until IMT had completed the purchase of the technology and the factories in 1990 had a major capital upgrade program been considered.

In 1990 the plant was also reorganized into three product lines. Each of the three technologies was considered a separate product line and profit center.

CMCI's mission statement appears in Exhibit 5. It was developed by the Fort Wayne plant quality assurance manager, Edward Fortesque, and issued throughout the Fort Wayne plant on June 25, 1991.

CMCI's Information System

Browning began his investigation shortly after receiving his charge from Young. By mid-September 1991, he had uncovered considerable data about the information systems at Fort Wayne and Chicago.

Organization   The support for Fort Wayne's IS was divided into two groups, an engineering systems group and a management information systems (MIS) group (see Exhibit 1). The engineering systems group consisted of eight of the twenty-five people who reported to Dr. Michael King, Fort Wayne's development engineering manager. Dr. King was trained as an engineer and was known as an industry-wide expert on the design of automated fabrication technologies. When asked about his use of the personal computer in his office, King responded in jest that he would soon start to use it.

Twenty MIS support staff members reported directly to Bill Gears, who in turn reported to Joe O'Neil, the division MIS manager. O'Neil reported through the division controller's organization. O'Neil was a former IBM employee with good experience on the

EXHIBIT 5
CMCI Mission/Goals/Vision Statement

Mission

To be recognized as the outstanding custom machine manufacturer in the world.

Goals

Provide market leadership

- Customer satisfaction
    Quality
    Reliability
    Delivery
    Service
- Serve the market with optional products and services
- Be the technology leader

Achieve business (operational) excellence

- Zero failures
- On-time performance
- Low throughput time
- High productivity
- Physical capital turnover > 2.5
- Financial capital turnover > 9
- Return on capital employed > 29%
- Revenue/total compensation + 5%/year

Vision

To be perceived by each of our customers as superior to the best competition in the overall quality of our products and services.

IBM AS/400 hardware platform. He had been the MIS manager at another IMT site before coming to Fort Wayne in 1988. Exhibit 6 summarizes O'Neil's direction and objectives for Fort Wayne's MIS group. It was taken from a memo issued to top division and plant management on July 30, 1991. In an interview, O'Neil said he did not have a formal mission for the MIS group, but offered the following: "Basically it [the mission] would be to provide an adequate, responsive, and economical network structure of data processing support for all sites within the division."

The Chicago plant used Fort Wayne's mainframe, but had its own one-person MIS "group," which reported through the Chicago controller.

Hardware Browning found that hardware had been used in a variety of ways.

Mainframe: The division operated an IBM mainframe that could be used by anyone in the division with no direct charge. All operating and lease costs for the mainframe were covered in the division's overhead. New engineers were "automatically" supplied with a mainframe user account, a personal computer (PC) equipped with a board to enable it to communicate with the IBM mainframe, and several PC software packages when they joined the firm. The current mainframe was an IBM model 3090-200 with 128 megabytes (MB) of main memory, 256MB of extended memory, and 55 gigabytes of disk storage.

Exhibit 7 illustrates that the mainframe was configured with two operating systems: VM/CMS-XA and DOS VSE. Exhibit 8 contains a brief description of those operating systems. Exhibit 7 also shows the operating system that was used for each of the functional groups at Fort Wayne. Transferring data between the two operating systems was not easily achieved. Most exchanges were done by "pulling" data from one side to the other. Although an operating system routine (called AMSERV) was available to "push" data to the other operating system, its use was not fully understood—or desired.

AMSERV was not used because the receiver's data file could be updated without the user's knowledge. Thus, the resolution of data security issues had slowed the practice of sharing data between operating systems. In sequential applications, where data was created under one operating system and used under another, identical data files with the same data were needed and maintained under each operating system.

From 1988 to 1991, the heaviest use of the mainframe was from the computer-aided drafting (CAD) and engineering users. IMT Fort Wayne used IBM's CADAM™ CAD product. CADAM, along with additional engineering and drafting programs, represented about 65 percent of the current mainframe use. Total usage in 1991 was projected at approximately 60 percent of the 3090's capacity.

EXHIBIT 6
....
CMCI Fort Wayne MIS Direction and Objectives

Direction

· Pursue a more structured MIS strategy with a reasonable and manageable level of risk that will be consistent with our being a leader in the custom machine industry.
· Develop and execute a plan that will continually upgrade our hardware, software, applications, database, and network environments to accomplish the above.

Objectives

· Recognize our business is designing and producing custom machines, not chasing ever-changing computer technology and theories.
· Coordinate MIS strategy with our business objectives of:

Zero defects
TPT of 0.9 (throughput time)
ROCE of 30% (return on capital employed)
EAD of 10% (earnings after dividends)
· Control our own destiny.
· Get out from under old lease obligations.
· Minimize risk and hidden costs.
· Work from total systems architecture plan:
  Develop applications architecture
  Select the hardware plan required to best accomplish our goals
· Maintain an integrated environment that supports the various functions of our division.

EXHIBIT 7
CMCI Functional Use of the Mainframe Computer

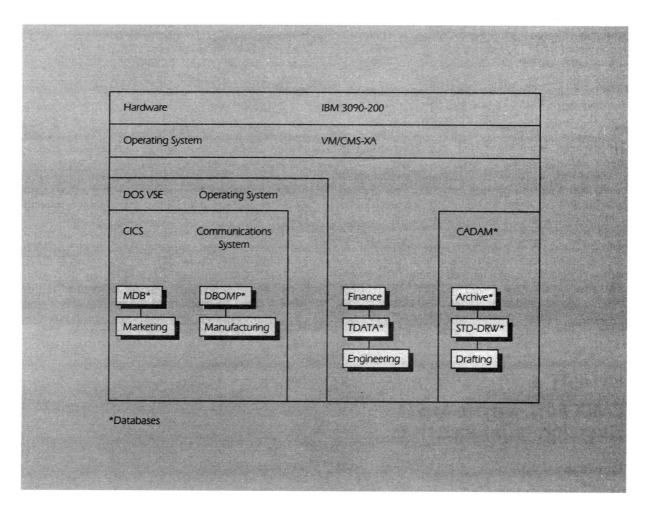

Exhibit 9 displays the past history of mainframe configuration and usage at Fort Wayne. Recent mainframe upgrades had been driven by the need for improvements in CAD response time and an increasing number of users. There were also about ninety IBM-type terminals throughout the factory and front offices. The 3090 had twelve 32-port controllers on-line—not including the CAD units that were directly connected through separate high-speed controllers. The mainframe lease in 1991 was $175,000 per month. IMT was in the second year of a five-calendar-year agreement. The net value of all leased hardware was estimated to be $10 million.

Personal Computers: The unofficial policy at Fort Wayne was that anyone who needed a PC could get one. Financial justification was not necessary. PCs were considered a tool, like the necessity for a special hammer on the shop floor. Fort Wayne's standard PC configuration was an IBM PS/2 model 55—a 386-based CPU with a 40 or 70MB hard disk—and an IBM Proprinter. A spreadsheet and a word processing program were standard issue with all new PCs. PCs

EXHIBIT 8
CMCI Operating System Descriptions

Exhibit 7 illustrates that the IBM mainframe was configured with two operating systems: VM/CMS-XA and VSE. An operating system is a very complex program (software) that controls the operation of the computer hardware and coordinates all the other software.

In most cases, a computer system operates under control of a single operating system. In this case, however, overall control of the mainframe rests with the primary or *host* operating system, IBM's VM/CMS-XA. VM stands for *virtual machine* (the remainder of the letters indicate the particular variation of VM), and this operating system permits the partitioning of the computer into several "virtual machines," each of which can be controlled by its own operating system. IBM's VSE operating system, working as a *guest* operating system, controls such a virtual machine in this instance. Thus, the two operating systems work together in a guest-host relationship, each controlling applications within its own virtual machine, its own portion of the entire computer system.

---

were issued under a three-year lease from IBM. Microsoft's Windows system was installed on most machines, but used regularly by only about 20 percent of the users.

Many users felt that the lack of sufficient software support and development from the MIS group had been partially circumvented by the use of PCs. For example, scheduling in various major work centers in the factory was done with a spreadsheet on "souped-up" PCs. The principle use for nearly all PCs was as a "dumb" terminal to the mainframe. However, all secretaries who performed typing used PCs, and engineers routinely used the word processor to write memos. Of the 350 users on Fort Wayne's mainframe, about 200 were accessing it through PCs.

Workstations: Exhibit 9 also shows the historical use of workstations at Fort Wayne and Chicago. As of 1991, Fort Wayne had three RS/6000 AIX workstations[1], which were used in the development engineering group for special projects but not for active production tasks. They were connected through a local area network (LAN). A Digital MicroVAX and IBM PCs were also to be linked into the LAN within the year. As of 1991, the Chicago facility used eighteen RS/6000 workstations for normal CAD production. Exhibit 10 contains the typical costs to IMT for a RS/6000 workstation. RS/6000 workstations in Chicago used the AIX version of CADAM which had a "look and feel"

---

[1] AIX was IBM's derivative of the UNIX operating system, which was typically run on workstations. IMT used the term "workstation" to mean a computer that was more powerful than a conventional PC (e.g., IBM's RS/6000 workstation).

identical to the mainframe version of CADAM used in Fort Wayne.

Drawings made in Chicago on workstations were stored on Fort Wayne's mainframe and uploaded and downloaded over a high-speed dedicated line. Chicago's designers liked their CAD stations, but were having trouble with the connection between the IBM mainframe and the Chicago LAN. Tom Goodman, the MIS support person in Chicago, said the following about IBM and their lack of AIX and network support: "I feel like we are a beta site for IBM as they learn networks."

Data Flow and Functional Responsibilities

Exhibit 11 illustrates the generalized data flow among the main functional areas of the Fort Wayne operation. Of the seven processes, only human resources (HR) was not interconnected with the main flow of the information. The remaining six organizational areas participated in a continuous sequential flow process of information.

Marketing   Exhibit 11 shows that the flow of business information started from the interaction between marketing and the customer. Information originated from the customer when a technical description or specification (a "spec") was sent to IMT for a new machine. The length of the spec could be from ten pages to over an inch thick. A marketing engineer would then read the spec and enter his interpretation of it into a mainframe negotiation program. The negotiation program operated under the DOS VSE

EXHIBIT 9
. . . .
CMCI Use of Mainframes and Workstations at Fort Wayne and Chicago

Mainframe

Year	CAD Response (seconds)	Number of CAD Users	Mainframe	Operating Systems	Other Users
1962–68	—	0	IBM 1440	VSE	Acct
1969–78	—	0	IBM 360-30/40	VSE	Acct, BOM, Eng
1979	—	0	IBM 360-40	VSE	Eng, BOM, Acct
1980	n/a	4	IBM 370-135	VM, VSE, OS/VS1	Eng, BOM, Acct
1981	n/a	8	IBM 370-135	VM, VSE, OS/VS1	Eng, BOM, Acct
1982	n/a	10	IBM 370-135	VM, VSE, OS/VS1	Eng, BOM, Acct
1983	n/a	16	IBM 4341	VM, VSE, OS/VS1	Eng, BOM, Acct
1984	n/a	24	IBM 4341	VM, VSE, OS/VS1	Eng, BOM, Acct
1985	n/a	22	IBM 4341	VM, VSE, OS/VS1	Eng, BOM, Acct
1986	n/a	18	IBM 4381	VM, VSE	Eng, BOM, Acct
1987	n/a	23	IBM 4381	VM, VSE	Eng, BOM, Acct
1988	0.40	48	IBM 3090-150E	VM, VSE	Eng, BOM, Acct
1989	0.26	65	IBM 3090-150E	VM, VSE	Eng, BOM, Acct
1990	0.32	73	IBM 3090-200E	VM, VSE, MVS	Eng, BOM, Acct
1991	0.12	85	IBM 3090-200E	VM, VSE	Eng, BOM, Acct

Workstations

Year	Chicago No. Users	Ft. Wayne No. Users	Hardware	Operating Systems	Uses
1986	—	1	MicroVAX	VMS	Dev
1987	—	1	MicroVAX	VMS	Dev
1988	5	2, 1*	IBM RT, mv*	UNIX(AIX), VMS*	CAD, Dev*
1989	10	2, 1*	IBM RT, mv*	UNIX(AIX), VMS*	CAD, Dev*
1990	12	2, 1*	IBM RS/6000, mv*	UNIX(AIX), VMS*	CAD, Dev*
1991	18	3, 1*	IBM RS/6000, mv*	UNIX(AIX), VMS*	CAD, Dev*

* = References to the one MicroVAX
Eng = Engineering
Dev = Development engineering
CAD = Computer-aided drafting
BOM = Bill-of-materials and manufacturing information
Acct = Accounting applications
mv = MicroVAX with the VMS operating system
n/a = not available

EXHIBIT 10

CMCI Cost of UNIX Workstation to Support CAD

Item	IMT Price
IBM RS/6000 with	$18,855
800MB Disk	
3270 Card	
Ethernet Card	
Keyboard/Mouse	
150MB Tape	1,532
CD-ROM Drive	1,302
Display	2,765
AIX (UNIX)	1,262
Other Support Software	1,300
Total Hardware	$27,016
CADAM CAD Software	3,000
Total Hardware and Software	$30,016

operating system and required the input of about fifty computer screens of data.

If a marketing engineer had a question about specs, he called a design engineer or another local expert. Most estimates had to be turned around in ten working days. Because of the volume of requests and a staff of only two engineers covering all of the United States, negotiations were sometimes very hectic. Gary Goruni, a marketing engineer, stated, "We do the best we can, but we will miss some things from time to time. Almost always after winning the order, we will go back and negotiate with the customer over what we missed."

Marketing also used a spreadsheet and a graphics program for presentations. Another frequently used application was an IBM mainframe package called Info Center, an early 1970s mainframe version of a database and spreadsheet combination that ran under the VM operating system. Info Center was automatically linked to data from the negotiation program. It was used to analyze data from ongoing negotiations as well as contracts after they were won or lost.

Administration and Finance The administration and finance group was the home for most business support systems. The purchase order, accounts payable, and accounts receivable systems were ap-

plications used by purchasing, receiving, and other groups. All three systems were custom developed in COBOL at the Fort Wayne facility. Although wages and salaries were totaled locally, they were maintained on an external data service company's computer.

EXHIBIT 11

CMCI Data Flow Among Basic Functional Areas and Support Groups

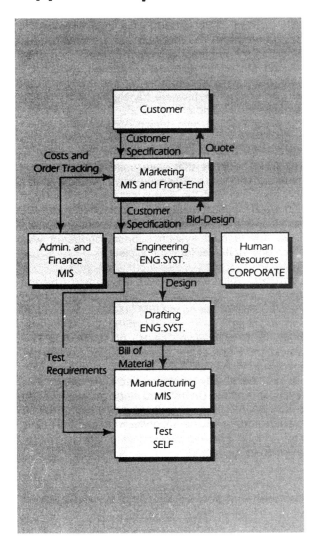

Engineering   Each machine was electrically and mechanically custom designed to a customer's exact specifications. Customization requirements, when mixed with the complexities of the economic and engineering limits, required sophisticated computer programs for modeling and design work. In 1991, Fort Wayne had three separate design systems, one for each of the three types of custom machines. Design engineers for each product line were experts on their own programs.

The first step in design engineering was to electronically receive the data previously entered into the negotiation program. The process entailed pulling the data records from the negotiation database under DOS VSE to VM/CMS-XA. The engineer then reread the customer's spec and decided which additional data needed to be added to the input files for the design program. The program then generated a design that the engineer reviewed in detail and often revised. Once the design was accepted by the engineer, the electronic computer file and a paper folder with completed forms were transferred to a drafting supervisor for completion.

All of Fort Wayne's design systems were written in the FORTRAN programming language and ran under the VM/CMS-XA operating system. The number of FORTRAN routines that were used by each of the three systems was used as a relative measure of size and complexity of the systems. Large vertical had about 500 routines, medium horizontal had about 400 routines, and large horizontal had about 2,400 routines. The annual system support budgeted was about one staff-year for each system.

Drafting   All drafting at Fort Wayne and Chicago was performed on a CAD applications system. At Fort Wayne, CADAM ran on the IBM 3090-200 mainframe, and in Chicago it ran on IBM RS/6000 workstations. There were eighty-five "seats" of CADAM at Fort Wayne and eighteen at Chicago.[2] During the last five years, additional FORTRAN programs had been written to automatically take output from the design programs and create CADAM drawings or references to drawings with standard parts. About 60 percent of the average 4,000 parts per machine were created in this way. All jobs were reduced to drawings prior to being released to the factory.

---

[2] A "seat" was one hardware CAD setup with a high-resolution screen, keyboard, function button box, and a pointing device that functioned like a mouse.

A standard part drawing included the material specification on the drawing. Assembly drawings contained the bill of material (BOM). Having CADAM and the custom machine design programs under the same operating system environment made the development of the automatic drawing programs very convenient. Jenny Velan, an engineer in the development group, said, "There are things we have been able to do with this operating system setup that would be impossible if the jobs were split between the two separate operating systems."

Manufacturing   When all the drawings for a custom machine were completed, the BOM was manually transferred from the drawings into the BOM database system, called DBOMP. DBOMP was originally written by IBM and extensively modified for Fort Wayne in the early 1970s to handle BOM for the vertical type machines. When production of the medium and large horizontal custom machines was transferred to Fort Wayne in the 1980s, DBOMP's limitations forced many "work-arounds." For example, when the General Engineering large horizontal technology was moved to Fort Wayne, it was discovered that DBOMP could not handle the longer General Engineering drawing numbers. Moreover, there was no one at Fort Wayne who knew the DBOMP code well enough to make a change.

The work-in-process (WIP) tracking system for the shop floor at Fort Wayne was very limited and worked only for items required for the "main aisle assembly" area. It could only handle unique made-to-order parts, not stock items. The system worked by having a main aisle supervisor request a "pull" from the storeroom to get parts delivered. The tracking systems for items within feeder aisles were either manual or used custom spreadsheets. Each item's information was maintained by its respective aisle. This WIP main aisle tracking system resided on DOS VSE, and the data was loaded by hand from the DBOMP.

The parts inventory system was very limited and similar to the tracking system except that it worked off of all stocked inventory items for the main and all feeder aisles. It used an identical process to the WIP system.

The systems group was backlogged in supporting the rapid changes that were occurring at the Fort Wayne plant in the late 1980s. When a computerized system failed to provide needed functionality, paper systems were created to support the information needs.

Test   Since each custom machine was a significant investment—between $2 million and $8 million—all machines were fully tested and personally witnessed at Fort Wayne or Chicago by an employee or agent of the customer company. The test department, along with the witness, certified that every machine met the customer's test requirements set forth in the specification. Scheduling information and other test details were forwarded to the test department by hand. Test information was written on a form that was interpreted or copied from the customer specification in marketing and engineering. The biggest complaint from the test department had been the necessity for marketing to properly interpret the customer's test requirement specifications. A failed or unnecessary test that resulted from misinterpreting a customer's specification could cost IMT well over $100,000.

The test department had several personal computers but no local area network (LAN). However, they had plans to install a LAN among their four test stations and a central PC. While the test department continued to wait for the LAN installation, all test information was written on paper at each test station and hand-carried to a central PC for processing.

Although all PCs in the test department were connected to the mainframe, the connections were used only occasionally. The test department was a part of the quality assurance organization at Fort Wayne, which was responsible for the data and production of the test reports sent to customers. Electronic test result data, however, remained on the test department's PCs only. The test department maintained its own PC applications.

Human Resources   As of early 1991, human resources had no networked computers. HR had plans to install a LAN with a server that would operate customized corporate programs for handling HR functions, including benefits and pension/investment plans. There were no plans to interconnect the LAN with Fort Wayne's mainframe due to security concerns.

. . . .

Other Information

Browning discovered other information and relevant developments in IMT's use of information technology.

Information Systems Personnel   The programmers in MIS had extensive backgrounds in COBOL and system control languages (i.e., IBM's JCL). However, none of them knew the UNIX operating system or the C programming language. Of the fourteen programmers, four had over twenty-five years experience at Fort Wayne, two had about twelve years, and the remaining eight had two years or less.

Engineers who supported the engineering system in the development group had significant backgrounds in FORTRAN and one had some experience in C. Each engineer had more than ten years experience with the company. One of the new programmers in the engineering systems group knew UNIX very well.

Browning heard many comments during his investigation that suggested that MIS and engineering systems staff at Fort Wayne always made the systems work—despite the high degree of constant change.

Management Systems   Browning concluded that by employing informal systems, work-arounds, and an extraordinary amount of human effort, Fort Wayne was profitable in 1990—its first profitable year since 1985. Slowly, things were stabilizing at Fort Wayne—the informal systems were being corrected and formalized. Restructuring into three product lines helped clarify the focus and purpose of operations systems and procedures. The primary reason for progress cited by many staff was that each product line was allowed independent control and responsibility.

However, computer systems support had remained an issue. In addition to showing the data flow, each box in Exhibit 11 indicates the systems group that supported each functional area. (The engineering systems group supported engineering and drafting, and the MIS group supported everything else.) The HR organization was not considered a local support issue because its applications were supported from the corporate MIS group in New York. A small group within MIS maintained all PCs and miscellaneous computer hardware for all the functional groups across the plant.

Placement of Support for Engineering and Drafting Systems   Browning discovered that there was an ongoing debate over where the support for engineering and drafting systems should be located. Browning summarized the three alternatives that seemed to be in constant debate:

1. In the engineering support systems group: Arguments for leaving support for engineering and drafting in the development engineering line of authority were strong. The design and drafting programs

produced models of the three dynamic product line technologies. The three principle people supporting these design systems were engineers with strong computer backgrounds. Two of the three had masters degrees in engineering. Support for these programs required a balance of custom machine design knowledge, creativity, and programming. By keeping program support close to the design engineers, code updates could occur more rapidly by working closer to the user engineer in the product line. As for MIS programmers taking responsibility, the engineers feared that they had little understanding of the implicit design technology. Some speculated that they might make coding changes that "would cost millions to correct once a design was committed and the parts were made."

2. In the product lines: Arguments for product line support of engineering systems included the fact that these engineers had extensive firsthand use of the system. Therefore, feedback on problems would be more obvious to those who supported the system. Ultimate control of the software should be in the hands of each of the profit centers. They should have the option to regulate the level of computer support based on their own strategy. However, if the engineering systems support responsibilities were located with the product lines, a programmer would need to be transferred from the engineering support systems group to each of the product lines.

3. In the MIS group: Arguments for MIS-based support of engineering and drafting systems included an alignment of all computer-related functions in one functional group—thus providing a common responsibility point for all computer support and integrated applications. Product line and development engineering would have to submit change requests that were more completely documented. Support through MIS would guarantee that coding changes would be documented. If support were the responsibility of the product line engineers, MIS people argued that the end result may be "spaghetti code," which no one but the original programmer could understand.

The Move to a Common Custom Machine Design System

About six months into Young's new position, he received instructions that his subsidiary would have to use a redeveloped set of custom machine design programs from Germany. The BG management team believed it was appropriate to institute a common custom machine design system across all factories. The BG's strategy was based on porting the

German programs onto a UNIX workstation platform and then distributing and supporting it worldwide. The design system would be based on an Ingres relational database. In 1990, when the announcement was made that the German programs would be used, none of the programs existed under UNIX. Nor did the German FORTRAN developers possess more than a few years in total experience in the UNIX environment.

A New Marketing and Negotiation System

The existing negotiation program was seen by marketing and engineering as inefficient and ineffective. Two years of studying how the IMT division should do business with its customers led the marketing group to propose a reengineered "Front-End Information" system. The proposed system was to include capabilities to optically scan in all customer proposals, including text. Customers' specs could then be analyzed and processed more quickly.

The proposed system had an initial price tag of over $1 million. Hardware included 110 networked PCs. The original idea for the system was conceived in the marketing department, which employed two staff engineers and an independent outside consultant as its own IS expert. MIS was only recently involved with planning the system. Top division management was providing direct support for the project. The project was being led by the division strategic planning manager, which isolated the project from division MIS and engineering biases. Hardware purchases were to begin in November 1991 and the system was to be completed and operational by the end of 1992.

CMCI's Interface to Field Sales.   IMT's field sales group had been planning a new system for transferring order information to the factories. The new system, called SPEC, was planned to come on line in late 1992. By mid-1992, each factory was to have installed a LAN to accommodate the data downloaded from field sales personnel. As of September 1991, SPEC had been plagued with delays because staff could not arrive at a consensus on the exact information that should be transmitted to each of the factories.

New Software Design Tools   Repatriation from Fort Wayne and Chicago accounted for 25 percent of the funds used for the BG's R&D development budget. IMT's MIS group felt that about 30 percent of its investment was received back in the form of useful information technologies; the remaining 70 percent benefited production hardware improvements. The BG was definitely committed to additional investments in UNIX application tools. Various software engineering and applications development tools had been mentioned, but the specific software and the number of seats that would be leased or purchased had not been finalized as of August 1991.

Bill of Material (BOM) System Replacement

The DBOMP system was nearly twenty years old and could not handle the new IMT drawing system that was to replace the three older systems. To support the new drawing system and its subsequent BOM structure, a new BOM system was required. Fort Wayne systems staff had identified a system that would run under DOS VSE and could be acquired at no cost. The program, called PUFR, was free because it was in the process of being obsoleted by IMT-USA's corporate MIS group. The only requirement was that Fort Wayne MIS staff had to support PUFR.

By August 1991, over 7,000 staff hours had been consumed by Fort Wayne MIS personnel trying to make PUFR operational. Projections suggested that approximately 10 percent more work had to be done in order to get PUFR in a test mode. To get this far, Fort Wayne systems had purchased additional modules that were not originally included free in the IMT corporate version of PUFR. The effort had also included converting some of the approximately 400 auxiliary programs that used the old DBOMP format. Occasional discussions of replacing PUFR "in a few years" were heard in the halls.

....

Browning's Options

Near the end of his investigation, Browning summarized his findings:

The best way to characterize the current information systems situation at Fort Wayne is as a lot of manual points where data is transferred between a patchwork of old, semiautomatic, outdated processes. The result is that since each place where information is transferred had a probability of introducing a new error, checking and rechecking becomes necessary to ensure integrity. And since the outdated processes require constant attention with fixes and work-arounds, the newer processes never move ahead. What we really need is a clear vision to guide our decisions today, so we can be ready for tomorrow.

After his six-week study, Browning envisioned three potential IS options for Fort Wayne. "Besides considering these alternatives," Browning told Young, "Fort Wayne needs to develop a mission statement for its IS group which is consistent with our business objectives."

Option 1: Mainframe Computing

Commit to staying with the mainframe for all important applications and discourage the use of UNIX workstations, PCs, and LANs. Maximize the use of a fixed-cost mainframe.

Commitment to the mainframe would be a long-term venture. To continue to maintain a large central mainframe and acquire new applications and full access for all users would require a systematic plan. The plan would include porting all of the major PC applications for scheduling up to the mainframe in order to assure central usage, support, and control. Major mainframe packages would be reviewed for upgrades that could handle Fort Wayne's current capacity and requirements. Older packages that were used in Fort Wayne would be phased out over the next five years.

PCs would be allowed where needed, but dumb terminals connected to the mainframe would be encouraged. LANs would be strongly discouraged or disallowed because of the redundant nature of the networking available through the mainframe.

Option 2: Distributed Computing

Follow a strategy whereby the mainframe is phased out completely. At the same time, make investments in UNIX workstations, PCs, and LANs.

Plans for a long-term shift to a distributed UNIX workstation environment would include migration of all applications to the new environment. As demand grows, a high-speed network would be installed. Data and application servers would be distributed by functional area and profit centers (e.g., marketing, development engineering, human resources, test). CAD seats would be slowly transferred from the mainframe to dedicated workstations. During the transition period, the mainframe would be connected to the network and available for access from all workstations.

One database would serve the entire UNIX network system, but local databases could also exist as necessary. PCs would be encouraged as network terminals, but no separate LANs would be employed. If a separate LAN was necessary, then gateways would be installed to bridge between networks.

As CAD and other major applications were shifted off the mainframe, it would be downsized to a smaller, compatible mid-range mainframe. The process should be expected to take approximately ten years and two mainframe downgrades before all of Fort Wayne's applications would be migrated to UNIX workstations.

Option 3: Watch Carefully Do not act yet. Wait and see what develops; decide only as circumstances force key issues.

Following the "watch carefully" option means that each decision would be made in response to immediate demands. Decisions would be based on the lowest risk and least expensive alternative at decision time. While no long-term commitment would be made to either the mainframe or distributed strategy, only technically adequate solutions would be acceptable. As a result of incurring lower risk, faster payback was expected and additional opportunities would be available to evaluate new technology.

....

A Decision and Direction for IMT IS

Young's feeling was confirmed when he received Browning's report; change was going to be painful. Years of neglect, restructuring, and a growing organization had finally caught up with Fort Wayne's information systems. Young also recognized that changes in Fort Wayne's IS architecture may require organizational changes as well. A decision had to be made soon. Or did it? "Things have worked themselves out in the past," Young said to himself. "After all, why fix something if it is at least working? Our top-notch staff always finds a way to solve problems when we really need it. Should I really be spending lots of money here?"

5

Computer Software

In many respects, this chapter is merely a continuation of Chapter 4, which concentrated on computer hardware, the physical pieces of a computer system. We learned that all the hardware is controlled by a stored program, which is a complete listing (in a form that the computer has been built to understand) of what the computer is to do. Such a stored program is an example of computer software, the topic of this chapter. Software is the set of programs (made up of instructions) that control the operations of the computer system. Computer hardware without software is of little value (and vice versa). Both are required for a computer system to be a useful tool for you and your organization. Thus, this chapter will explain more fully the symbiotic relationship between computer hardware and software.

Computer software does not seem to hold the same mystique as hardware for most of us, but it is even more important for you as a manager to understand software. First, appropriate software is required before hardware can do anything at all. Second, most organizations spend at least twice as much money on software as they do on hardware. This ratio of software to hardware costs is rapidly increasing over time. In the mid-1990s, a software company, Microsoft Corporation, is arguably the most successful and most influential company in the entire computer arena.

Third, and most personally relevant, you will be dealing directly with a number of important software packages—such as spreadsheets and word processing—while the only hardware you are likely to deal with is a workstation (most likely a microcomputer, not one of the higher-powered workstations discussed in the previous chapter). Whatever your job within an organization, you are also likely to be involved in software development or acquisition efforts as a member of a project team or as an end-user. If your field is marketing, you may well be involved with the creation of a new sales reporting system; if your field is finance, you may develop a computer model to evaluate the impact of a possible merger; if you are an operations manager, you may participate in the development of a new inventory reporting system. (The role of the manager in software development and acquisition is discussed more fully in Chapters 8, 10, and 11.) For a variety of reasons, therefore, it is important that you understand the various types of computer software and the ways in which it is used within an organization.

EVOLUTION OF COMPUTER SOFTWARE

First- and Second-Generation Languages

Computer software has, of course, been around as long as computer hardware. Initially, all software was written in machine language, as described in "The Stored-Program Concept" section of Chapter 4. Each instruction in a machine language program must be expressed in the precise form that the particular computer has been built to understand. If, for instance, we want to subtract the number found in memory cell 720 from the number found in memory cell 600, storing the result in cell 600, then the machine language instruction (for a hypothetical computer) would be

Operation Code	Addresses
S	720 600

A complete program to carry out a particular application (e.g., compute the payroll or prepare a management report) would consist of hundreds or thousands of similar instructions expressed in the machine language of the particular computer. The programmer would have to look up (or memorize) each operation code and remember what data have been stored in every memory cell. Machine language programming was (and is) an exacting, tedious, time-consuming process, but it was the only option available on the earliest computers.

Computer software developers quickly created **assembly languages** that used the computer itself to perform many of the most tedious aspects of programming. For example, easily remembered mnemonic operation codes are substituted for the machine language operation codes (e.g., SUB for S or SUB for something as unintelligible as 67 on some machines). Symbolic addresses are substituted for a memory cell address (e.g., GPAY for 600). Thus, if our single instruction above is part of a payroll program where we want to subtract deductions (DED) from gross pay (GPAY), we can write

SUB   DED GPAY

Writing instructions such as this is much easier (and more error-free) than writing machine language instructions, particularly when we consider that there are likely to be fifty different operation codes and hundreds of memory cell addresses to remember in even a moderate-sized program.

The entire assembly language program is written using instructions similar to the one above. Then the computer, under the control of a special stored program called an **assembler**, converts these mnemonic operation codes and symbolic addresses to the machine language operation codes and memory cell addresses. The assembler pro-

gram simply keeps a table of conversions for operation codes and addresses and makes the substitutions as necessary. Figure 5.1 illustrates this translation process from the assembly language program—the program containing mnemonic codes and symbolic addresses—to the machine language program. The assembly language program is also called the **source program**, while the resulting machine language program is the **object program**. Once the translation process has been completed, the outcome machine language program is loaded into memory and carried out by the control unit (as described in Chapter 4). The machine language for a particular computer is referred to as the first-generation language, or 1 GL, while the assembly language—which came along later—is called the second-generation language, or 2 GL.

Assembly language programming was popular for business applications for many years (until about 1970), and assembly language is still used by a few major firms (including Sears) and by some computer professionals.[1] Popular assembly languages have included SOAP (Symbolic Optimization Assembly Program), Autocoder, and BAL (Basic Assembly Language). Assembly language programming is much easier than machine language programming, but it still requires the programmer to employ the same small steps that the computer has been built to understand; it still re-

---

[1] The primary reason for the continued use of assembly language is computer efficiency. A well-written assembly language program will require less memory and take less time to execute than a well-written third- or fourth-generation language program.

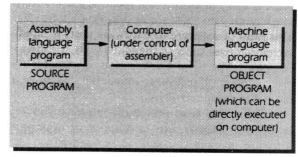

FIGURE 5.1 Assembler Translation Process

quires one assembly language instruction for each machine language instruction.[2] Thus, even after the advent of assembly languages, efforts continued to make it easier to tell the computer what the user wanted done. The results are today's third- and fourth-generation languages (3 GLs and 4 GLs).

Third- and Fourth-Generation Languages

The third- and fourth-generation languages represent a radical departure from the first two generations. Both machine language and assembly language programming require the programmer to think like the computer in terms of the individual instructions. With 3 GLs and 4 GLs, the programmer uses a language that is relatively easy for humans to learn and use, but has no direct relationship to the machine language into which it must eventually be translated. Thus, the 3 GLs and 4 GLs are designed for humans, not computers! Typically, each 3 GL or 4 GL instruction will be translated into many machine language instructions (perhaps 10 machine language instructions per 3 GL instruction, or 100 machine language instructions per 4 GL instruction). Further, while each type of computer has its unique 2 GL, the 3 GLs and 4 GLs are largely machine independent. Thus, a program written in a 3 GL or 4 GL can be run on many different types of computers, which is often a significant advantage.

Third-generation languages are also called **procedural languages** because they express a step-by-step procedure devised by the programmer to accomplish the desired task. The earliest procedural language was FORTRAN (an abbreviation for FORmula TRANslator), which was developed by IBM in the mid-1950s. Other popular procedural languages include COBOL (COmmon Business Oriented Language), PL/1, BASIC, PASCAL, ADA, and C. A source program in any one of these

languages must be translated into the machine language object program before it can be carried out by the computer. These third-generation languages—particularly COBOL, FORTRAN, BASIC, and C—are still very important today, and a later section of this chapter will expand on these introductory remarks. Estimates vary, but it is likely that at least 75 percent of the programs written today employ the 3 GLs.

Fourth-generation languages, also called **productivity languages** and **nonprocedural languages**, are even easier to use than the third-generation languages. To employ a 3 GL, the programmer must devise a step-by-step procedure to accomplish the desired result and express this procedure in the form of 3 GL statements. With a 4 GL, the computer user merely gives a precise statement of what he or she wishes to accomplish, not how to do it. Thus, the order in which statements are given in a 4 GL is usually inconsequential. Further, each 4 GL statement is usually translated into significantly more machine language instructions—sometimes by a factor of 100—than a single 3 GL statement. Thus, 4 GL programs are easier to write, shorter, and less error-prone than 3 GL programs, which in turn have these same advantages over their 2 GL predecessors.

With these advantages, why aren't all programs written in 4 GLs today? First, some of the 4 GLs—like IFPS and SAS—are not general purpose languages and cannot be used easily for many types of programs. On the other hand, FOCUS, RAMIS, and NOMAD are indeed general purpose 4 GLs. More important, many programs are not written in 4 GLs because of concern for efficient use of the computer resources of the organization. For the most part, 4 GL programs translate into longer machine language programs that take much longer to execute than the equivalent programs written in a 3 GL. (Similarly, 3 GL programs often translate into longer machine language programs that take more time to execute than the equivalent 2 GL programs.) The upshot of these arguments is that an increasing number of one-time programs or infrequently used programs (such as a decision support system or a specialized management report) are being written in 4 GLs, while most production programs—those that will be run

---

[2] To be complete, assembly languages often provide for macroinstructions, where one macroinstruction may correspond to five, ten, or more machine language instructions. A programmer writes a set of assembly language instructions that he expects to use repeatedly and then gives this set a label (or a macroinstruction name). Then each time the macroinstruction is used in a program, the entire set of assembly language instructions is substituted.

every day or every week—are still written in 3 GLs. In the case of infrequently used programs, human efficiency in writing the program is more important than computer efficiency in running it; for production programs, the opposite is often the case. The increasing costs of personnel and decreasing costs of computer systems (on a per instruction basis), however, are gradually tilting the balance in favor of 4 GLs for a wider variety of applications.

In the mid-1990s, both 3 GLs and 4 GLs are in use in most organizations, with the trend toward an increasing use of 4 GLs. If you as a manager are ever involved in programming, and perhaps 25 percent of you will be—you are likely to use a 4 GL. We will look at two fourth-generation languages in more detail in a later section.

Operating Systems and Support Software

All of the software for computers is written using one of the four generations of languages. Most programs have been designed to accomplish specific purposes for an organization or an individual, such as keeping track of accounts receivable, scheduling production, or evaluating a proposed acquisition. Some programs, however, have been designed to support these activities behind the scenes, rather than directly produce output of value to the user. The most important of these support programs is the operating system, which originated in the mid-1960s and is now an integral part of every computer system.

The **operating system** is a very complex program that controls the operation of the computer hardware and coordinates all the other software, so as to get as much work done as possible with the available resources. Before operating systems, human computer operators had to physically load programs and start them running by pushing buttons on the computer console. Only one program could be run at a time, and the computer was often idle while waiting on the operator. Now the operator's job is much easier and the computer is used more efficiently, with the operating system controlling the starting and stopping of individual programs and permitting multiple programs to be run at the same time. Because of the importance of

the operating system, we will consider its functions in more detail shortly. We will also discuss other support software, including language translators, communications interface software, database management systems, and utility programs.

With our overview of software evolution completed, we can concentrate on the key types of computer software in the 1990s. We will find that third-generation languages, fourth-generation languages, operating systems, and other support software all have an important role in today's and tomorrow's computer systems.

KEY TYPES OF SOFTWARE IN THE 1990s

Two Kinds of Software

To begin our look at the key elements of computer software, let us step back from the details and view the big picture. It is useful to divide software into two major categories:

1. Applications software
2. Support software

Applications software includes all programs written to accomplish particular tasks for computer users. In addition to our payroll computation example, applications programs would include an inventory record-keeping program, a word processing package, a spreadsheet package, a program to allocate advertising expenditures, and a program producing a summarized report for top management. Each of these programs produces output needed by users to accomplish their jobs.

By contrast, **support software** (also called **systems software**) does not directly produce output needed by users. Instead, support software provides a computing environment in which it is relatively easy and efficient for humans to work; it enables applications programs written in a variety of languages to be carried out; and it ensures that the computer hardware and software resources are used efficiently. Support software is usually obtained from computer vendors and from specialized software development companies called software houses.

The relationship between applications software and support software may be more readily understood by considering the software iceberg depicted in Figure 5.2. The above-water portion of the iceberg is analogous to applications software; both are highly visible. Applications software directly produces results that you as a manager require to perform your job. But just as the underwater portion of the iceberg keeps the top of the iceberg above water, the support software is absolutely essential for the applications software to produce the desired results. (Please note that the iceberg analogy is not an accurate representation of the numbers of applications and support programs—there are usually many more applications programs than support programs.) Your concern as a manager will be primarily with the applications software—the programs that are directly relevant to your job—but you need to understand the functions of the primary types of support software to appreciate how the complete hardware/software system works.

The Operating System

Clearly the single most important piece of software of any type in a modern computer system is the operating system. Every computer, from a small microcomputer to a giant supercomputer, is controlled by its operating system. Human users

deal with the operating system, not the hardware, and the operating system in turn controls all hardware and software resources of the computer system.

There are two overriding purposes for an operating system—to maximize the work done by the computer system (the throughput), and to ease the work load of human operators and system users. In effect, the operation of the computer system has been automated through the use of this sophisticated program. Figure 5.3 illustrates some of the ways in which these purposes are advanced by the operating system. This somewhat complex diagram presents the roles of the operating system in a reasonably large computer system. To make these roles more understandable, we will concentrate on the individual elements of the diagram.

First, note that the human operator at the top of the diagram interfaces only with the operating system, the local input job stream, and the local output job stream. The interface with the operating system is usually by entering simple commands at an operator console (a specialized terminal); the interface with the local input job stream is usually mounting tapes or changing removable disk packs; and the interface with the local output job stream means separating and distributing printed output.

The operating system, either directly or indirectly through other support software, controls everything else that takes place in Figure 5.3. It controls the inflow and outflow of communications with the various terminals and microcomputers (often through a specialized communications interface program). Using priority rules specified by the computer center manager, the operating system decides when to initiate a particular job from among those waiting in the input queue; similarly, the operating system decides when to terminate a job (either because it has been completed, an error has occurred, or it has run too long). The operating system decides which job to print next, again based on priority rules. It stores and retrieves data files, keeping track of where everything is stored (a function sometimes shared with a database management system). The operating system also manages the software library, keeping track of both support and applications programs.

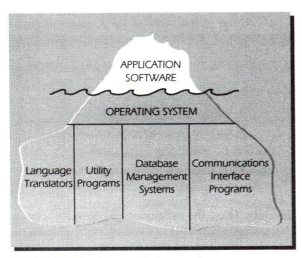

FIGURE 5.2 The Software Iceberg

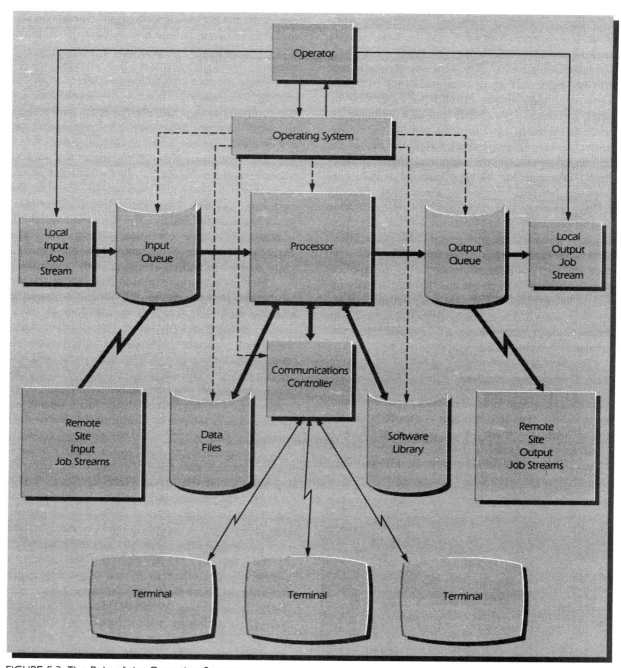

FIGURE 5.3 The Role of the Operating System

The advantage of letting the operating system perform all the above tasks is that it can react at electronic speed to select the next job, handle multiple terminal sessions, select the appropriate software from the library, and retrieve the appropriate data file. Thus, the expensive and powerful central processing unit (CPU) can be kept as busy as possible, and the throughput from the system can be maximized. Further, the operating system can create a computing environment—in terms of what operators and other users see on their terminal screens and what they need to key in to instruct the operating system what to do—in which it is relatively easy to work.

Job Control Language   As noted, it is necessary for computer users to communicate with the operating system, usually by keying in instructions at a terminal. These instructions must be expressed in the particular **job control language**, or JCL, that is understood by the operating system being used. This job control language varies significantly from one operating system to the next, both in terms of the types of instructions and the detailed syntax. For example, with the PC-DOS or MS-DOS operating systems (IBM and IBM compatibles), to change directories one types CD\ followed by the name of the new directory; to list the current directory one types DIR; to copy a file named MEMO from the A drive to the B drive one types COPY A:MEMO B:. These are examples of the job control language. The JCL is even simpler for a Macintosh or a PC operating under Windows—the user may click or double-click on an icon to start an application or retrieve a file. The JCL is much more complex for a larger machine, but the ideas are the same. To run a payroll program, for example, JCL will be used to tell the operating system the name of the program to be run, the names of the data files that are needed, instructions for output of data, and the account number to be charged, among other things.

Multiprogramming   The operating systems for larger machines (as well as the newer, more powerful microcomputers and workstations) often incorporate several important concepts—multiprogramming, time-sharing, and virtual memory—in order to increase the efficiency of the computer's operations. All these concepts are concerned with the management of the memory and the CPU time of the computer system.

By means of **multiprogramming**, the operating system makes it possible to overlap input and output operations with processing time. This is very important because the time required for the computer to perform an input/output operation (such as reading from disk) is quite large compared to the time required to execute an arithmetic instruction. In fact, a typical computer might execute 10,000 arithmetic instructions in the time required to read a single record from a disk. Thus, it would be quite inefficient to let the CPU remain idle while input/output operations are being completed. Multiprogramming keeps the CPU busy by overlapping the input/output operations of one program with the processing time of another program.

For multiprogramming, several programs (say five to ten) must be located in memory at the same time. Then the operating system supervises the switching back and forth among these programs so that the CPU is almost always busy. When the currently executing program encounters an input/output instruction, an interrupt occurs and the operating system takes control. The operating system stores the contents of the various CPU registers (which contain all the information describing the status of the interrupted program—the current instruction, its address, the results of the most recent calculation, and so on) in memory so that this information will be available when the interrupted program gets another shot at the CPU. The operating system then decides which of the waiting programs should be executed next, and it resets the CPU registers with the status of the new program. Then the operating system gives control to the new program, which executes until it encounters an input/output instruction. Thus, the operating system controls the switching back and forth among programs that is involved in multiprogramming.

Time-Sharing   **Time-sharing** is very similar to multiprogramming in that the operating system again controls the switching back and forth among programs stored in memory. Whereas the switching is triggered by an event in multiprogramming (the occurrence of an input/output instruction), it is time driven (as well as event driven) in time-sharing. Time-sharing is the usual mode of operation when large numbers of users are simultaneously using a computer (minicomputer or larger) from terminals or microcomputers serving as terminals. In this environment, each user is allocated a small slice of CPU time (a few milliseconds). When a particular user's turn arises, his or her program runs for those few milliseconds (or until an input/output instruction is encountered), carrying out thousands of instructions. Then a time interrupt occurs, and the operating system transfers control to the next user for a slice of time. Unless the number of concurrent users becomes excessively high, these bursts of available time occur so rapidly that it appears to the user that he or she is the only person who is using the computer.

Virtual Memory While multiprogramming and time-sharing are primarily concerned with the management of CPU time, **virtual memory** is concerned with the management of main memory. Virtual memory makes it appear to the user that he has an unlimited amount of main memory available, meaning that individual programs can be much larger than the actual number of memory cells. More important, virtual memory permits multiprogramming to operate more efficiently. How does this work?

The trick is the creative use of direct access storage devices (DASD), with the operating system switching portions of programs (called pages) between main memory and DASD. Unless all the programs are small, it is difficult to get enough programs stored in memory for multiprogramming to operate efficiently. For example, three large programs may occupy all of memory, and it may be common for all three programs to be processing input/output instructions at the same time, leaving the CPU idle, which is undesirable. The cost of adding enough real memory to store ten programs at a time—to permit efficient multiprogramming—may be prohibitive. The virtual memory concept recognizes that only one segment of a large program is being executed at a time, while the bulk of the program is inactive. Therefore, with virtual memory, only a few pages of the program (perhaps only one) are kept in main memory, with the rest relegated to DASD. Since only a small portion of each program is located in memory, portions of a sufficient number of programs can be stored in memory to permit efficient multiprogramming.

Of course, it is often necessary for the operating system to bring new portions of program (new pages) into memory so they can be executed. This swapping of pages between DASD and main memory is called, appropriately enough, paging. The size of pages varies, but each is often a few thousand bytes. When one combines the concepts of multiprogramming (switching among pages of programs already in memory) with virtual memory (requiring frequent page switches from DASD to memory), then we begin to realize the incredible complexity of tasks carried out by the operating system.

Multiprocessing Despite the similarities between the terms, multiprocessing is quite different from multiprogramming. **Multiprocessing** refers to the processing, or work, that takes place when two or more CPUs are installed as part of the same computer system. Each CPU works on its own job or set of jobs (often using multiprogramming), with all the CPUs under control of a single operating system, which keeps track of what the various CPUs are doing. This is complexity piled on complexity! It is easy to see that computer systems of the 1990s would be much less efficient and of very limited use to us without the powerful operating systems that exist and are continually being upgraded.

Sources of Operating Systems For the most part, operating systems are obtained (by purchase or lease) from the manufacturer of the hardware. Most of the popular operating systems are **proprietary systems** that were written expressly for a particular computer system. Examples are PC-DOS and MS-DOS, which are the same operating system written by Microsoft for IBM microcomputers and IBM compatibles, respectively; MVS and VM, which are the two alternative large machine operating systems offered by IBM; OS/400, which is the operating system for the IBM AS/400 line of minicomputers; and VMS, which is the operating system offered by Digital Equipment Corporation for its popular line of VAX computers.

In contrast to these proprietary systems, the increasingly popular UNIX operating system is an **open system**. UNIX is not tied to a particular computer system or hardware manufacturer. UNIX was originally developed by Bell Laboratories, with subsequent versions created by the University

THE ALLURE OF UNIX

What is the allure of UNIX? The primary reason is software portability. Applications developed to run under a UNIX operating system should be easily transportable to run under any other UNIX operating system. Thus, by choosing UNIX, users are not tied to a particular hardware vendor. The secondary reason for the move to UNIX is to take advantage of price-performance savings offered by the new UNIX-based computer systems developed by vendors such as Hewlett-Packard, NCR, Unisys, and IBM (the RS/6000). A few corporations, such as the Burlington Coat Factory and Tootsie Roll Industries, have decided to convert their data centers to UNIX. Most companies, however, are doing nothing about UNIX or are merely testing the water by trying pilot projects and running specific applications using UNIX.

This latter approach is consistent with the recommendations of the consulting firm McKinsey & Company. McKinsey believes the cost implications of going to UNIX are quite different for different types of users. For small businesses and corporate departmental users considering new applications, McKinsey argues that UNIX may make economic sense because these users have little existing investment in vendor-based systems, and conversion and retraining costs will be low.

But for large users planning major extensions to existing systems and those considering total conversion to UNIX, McKinsey feels that the costs of rewriting and replacing applications, retraining staff, and modifying databases and networks rule out any wholesale moves to UNIX. In the corporate world, at least for the next several years, UNIX seems to be destined for niche applications—either at the departmental level or for specific distributed applications.

(Adapted from Moad, 1989)

The movement to UNIX will be aided by the recent appearance of systems management software tools to assist the IS organization in running a UNIX-based computing center. These support software tools, which are really add-ons to the underlying operating system, handle such tasks as job scheduling, tape management, job accounting, security, backup, and configuration management. Such support software has been available for vendor-based systems for years but first became available for UNIX systems in 1992 and 1993 with such packages as Unicenter from Computer Associates International and OmegaCenter from Candle Corporation.

(Adapted from Ricciuti, 1992, 1993)

---

of California at Berkeley and a variety of hardware manufacturers. Even Digital Equipment Corporation and IBM have developed their own versions of UNIX—ULTRIX for Digital and AIX for IBM. Many of the newer computers, such as high-powered workstations and minisupercomputers, run only UNIX.

UNIX is powerful and easy to use, and many computer professionals would like to see UNIX become the standard operating system for all computer systems. That may happen, but it will not happen overnight (see the box "The Allure of UNIX"). The use of UNIX will continue to spread, particularly among universities and research laboratories and in niche applications in large corpora-

tions. Some organizations have even adopted a strategy of carrying out all new applications software development in a UNIX environment, and gradually moving existing applications to UNIX. For the next several years, however, UNIX is unlikely to replace vendor operating systems like MVS and VMS in major corporate and government data processing centers.

At the microcomputer level, UNIX is not a serious contender at this time. For those users who need a more powerful operating system than PC-DOS or MS-DOS, the choice is between Microsoft's Windows and IBM's OS/2 (which was, interestingly, originally developed by Microsoft). Windows operates in conjunction with PC-DOS or MS-DOS, while OS/2 is a stand-alone operating system. Both Windows and OS/2 feature a powerful **graphical user interface**, or GUI (pronounced gooey). With a GUI, the user selects an application or makes other choices by using a mouse to click on an appropriate icon or label appearing on the screen. Both Windows and OS/2 also permit multiple "windows" to be open on the video screen, with a separate application running in each window. As of this writing, Windows has a large lead in terms of number of copies sold, but OS/2 has been adopted for many critical applications in large organizations. In summary, all of the widely used operating systems in use today will continue to evolve over the next several years, with each becoming more powerful and more complex, but the movement toward UNIX for larger machines and Windows or OS/2 for microcomputers will get stronger.

In Chapter 3, the idea of an information technology platform was introduced, and it was noted that the platform is defined by a combination of hardware, software, and communications. Now we are in the position to point out that the operating system is often the single most critical component of the platform. Thus, it is common to discuss a VAX/VMS platform, an MVS (mainframe) platform, a VM (mainframe) platform, a UNIX platform, a Windows platform, or an OS/2 platform.

Other Support Software

As illustrated in Figure 5.2, the underwater portion of the software iceberg includes other support software in addition to the critical operating system. It is useful to divide this support software into four major categories—communications interface software, utility programs, language translators, and database management systems.

The operating system itself contains some rudimentary data management capabilities, primarily for dealing with programs and files of data. For more sophisticated data management capabilities, including storing, retrieving, and combining individual data elements, a specialized database management system (DBMS) is usually employed. Because of the importance of these DBMSs—and the fact that you as a manager are likely to directly use

a DBMS in your job—we have chosen to devote an entire section to database management systems later in this chapter. For now, we will concentrate on the other three categories of support software.

Communications Interface Software This category of support software has become increasingly important with the explosion in the number of workstations (terminals and microcomputers) attached to large computers and the advent of local area networks (LANs). Discussion of LAN software will be deferred until Chapter 6. Two types of communications interface software will be considered now—large computer (minicomputer and larger) communications packages and microcomputer communications packages.

The large computer communications packages have the awesome task of controlling the communications of a large number of terminals with the central computer. This software collects the messages from the terminals, processes them as necessary, and returns the responses to the proper terminals. These packages are often designed to work closely with a particular operating system. For example, IBM's CICS (Customer Information Control System) and TSO (Time Sharing Option) are communications packages designed to work with IBM's MVS operating system. Similarly, IBM's CMS (Conversational Monitor System) is designed to work with the VM operating system. Digital Equipment Corporation has its communications package embedded within its VMS operating system. In an interesting development, IBM has recently announced a version of CICS which works with AIX, IBM's UNIX operating system. This AIX/CICS combination will make it much easier for IBM customers to move their applications to UNIX and provides further evidence of the growing importance of UNIX.

The microcomputer communications packages have the much simpler task of making the microcomputer act as if it were a particular type of terminal that can be handled by the large computer communications package. Popular microcomputer communications packages include KERMIT (developed at Columbia University) and PROCOMM (Datastorm Technologies). When paired with an appropriate program in the large computer (such as a mainframe version of KERMIT), these microcomputer communications packages can also upload and download files between the microcomputer and the large computer.

Utility Programs   This is obviously a catchall category, but an important one nevertheless. Utility software includes programs that load applications programs into an area of memory, link together related programs and subprograms, merge two files of data together, sort a file of data into a desired sequence (e.g., alphabetical order on a particular data item), and copy files from one place to another (e.g., from DASD to magnetic tape). Utility programs also give the user access to the software library. In most cases, the user communicates with these utility programs by means of commands in the job control language.

Language Translators   As noted, a program written in any language except machine language must be translated into machine language before the computer can carry out the program. The translation into machine language is done by the computer under control of a support program written specifically for the source language and the computer model. If the source language is assembly language (2 GL), the language translator program is called an assembler (as we already know). For third- and fourth-generation languages, the language translator is called a **compiler** if the entire program is translated into machine language before any of the program is executed, or an **interpreter** if each source program statement is executed as soon as that single statement is translated.

Figure 5.4 depicts the process of compiling and running a compiled procedural language program, such as FORTRAN, COBOL, or PASCAL. This process is quite similar to that used for assembly language programming (see Figure 5.1), with the labels changed as appropriate. The key is that the entire program is translated into an object program, and then the object program is loaded and executed. Dealing with the entire program in this manner has the advantage that an efficient machine language program (one that executes rapidly) can be produced because the interrelationships among the program statements can be

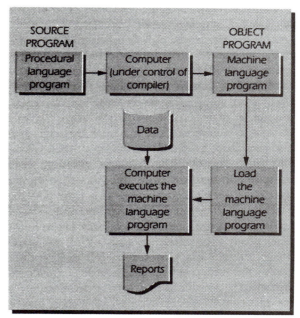

FIGURE 5.4 Compiling and Running a Procedural Language Program

considered during the compilation process; dealing with the entire program has the disadvantage that the programmer does not learn about his errors until the entire program has been translated.

Figure 5.5 shows the process of interpreting and running an interpretive language program, such as BASIC. With an interpreter, only one statement from the source program is considered at a time. This single statement is translated into machine language, and—if no errors are

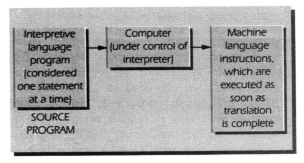

FIGURE 5.5 Interpreting and Running an Interpretive Language Program

174

encountered—immediately executed. The process is repeated, statement after statement. This interpretive process lends itself to interactive programming, where the programmer composes the program at a workstation, keys in one statement at a time, and is almost immediately provided feedback if an error is made. If there are no errors, output is produced immediately after the last statement is entered. The machine language program resulting from the interpretive process is usually much less efficient than one resulting from compilation because only one source program statement is being considered at a time. On the other hand, program development may be speeded up because of the immediate feedback to programmers when they make an error. With an interpreter, there is often no true object program because the machine language instructions are discarded as soon as they are executed. Further, if the program is executed repeatedly, each source statement is translated again each time it is executed, which is quite inefficient as compared to compilation.

The BASIC language is usually interpreted, while most other 3 GLs are usually compiled. However, BASIC compilers exist for some computers, while interpreted COBOL is sometimes used during program development. Fourth-generation languages, for the most part, use an interpreter to translate the source program into machine language. Please note that the 3 GLs and 4 GLs are essentially the same from one computer model to the next, but the translation programs (compilers and interpreters) must be specific to the particular computer model.

Applications Software

Applications software is a much wider, much more diverse category than support software. Applications software includes all programs written to accomplish particular tasks for computer users. Portfolio management programs, general ledger accounting programs, sales forecasting programs, material requirements planning (MRP) programs, electronic mail programs, and desktop publishing packages are all examples of applications software. Each of you will be using applications software as part of your job, and many of you will be involved in developing or obtaining applications software to fulfill the needs of your organization.

Because applications software is so diverse, it is difficult to divide these programs into a few neat categories. Instead, we will begin with a brief look at the sources of applications software, then we will discuss the various ways in which applications software can be written (3 GLs, 4 GLs, DBMSs, CASE) and a set of personal productivity packages for handling many common applications (e.g., word processing, spreadsheets, statistics). Following that, we will give an example of a PC-based accounting package to illustrate the type of commercial packages that are available for purchase.

Where do we obtain software? Support software is almost always purchased or leased from a hardware vendor or a software house. Only the very largest IS organizations would even consider writing utility programs or modifying operating systems or compilers. Applications software, however, is sometimes developed within the organization and sometimes purchased from an outside source. Standard applications packages, such as word processing, graphics, electronic mail, and spreadsheets, are almost always purchased. Applications that are unique to the organization—a one-of-a-kind production control system, a proprietary foreign exchange trading program, a decision support system for adoption/nonadoption of a new product—are always developed within the organization (or by a consulting firm under contract to the organization). The vast middle ground of applications that are quite similar from one organization to the next, but may have some features peculiar to the particular organization, may be either purchased or developed.

These middle-ground applications include payroll, accounts payable, accounts receivable, general ledger, inventory control, MRP, sales analysis, and personnel reporting. In these areas the organization must decide whether its requirements are truly unique. Does the organization have the capability of developing this application in-house? What are the costs and benefits of developing in-house versus purchasing a package? This make-or-buy decision for applications software is an important one for almost every organization, and this topic will be addressed in Chapter 10. Let us note at this point that the rising costs of software development tend to be pushing the balance toward more purchased software and less in-house development.

In 1985 virtually all software development done within an organization was done by the formally constituted information systems organization. The exceptions were engineers, scientists, and a few computer jocks[3] in other user departments. A revolution called end-user computing has occurred in the past several years, and now much of the internal software development is done by end-users such as you. There are at least three reasons for the end-user computing revolution. First, the IS organization was unable to keep up with the demand for new applications software, and significant backlogs of jobs developed. Second, a more knowledgeable, more computer-oriented group of users was created through the hiring of college graduates and the use of various internal and external training programs. Third, and perhaps most significant, relatively easy-to-use tools were developed by software vendors that made it possible for interested, but not expert, users to carry out significant software development. These tools include the fourth-generation languages and the query languages associated with database management systems. This trend toward end-user computing will continue, in our view, with many of you becoming involved in software development early in your careers. Chapter 11 explores this phenomenon of user development.

Of course, not all internal software development is now or should be done by users. For the most part, IS organizations have not shrunk because of end-user computing; they simply have not grown as rapidly as they might have otherwise. The large, complex applications continue to be developed and maintained by the IS organization. They also tend to develop applications that apply to multiple areas within the organization and those applications for which efficiency is paramount (such as sales transaction processing). The

IS organizations employ the same tools used by end-users, but they also do a substantial portion of their work using COBOL and other 3 GLs and are beginning to use CASE (computer-aided software engineering) tools. Chapters 8 to 11 explore the various ways in which applications systems are developed or procured.

Third-Generation Languages

The third-generation languages, which are more commonly called procedural or procedure-oriented languages, are and will continue to be the workhorses of the information processing field. The procedural languages do not enjoy the near-total dominance of a decade ago, but they are still largely the languages of choice for most computer professionals, scientists, and engineers. During the first half of the 1990s, the 4 GLs, DBMSs, and application generators have gained ground on the 3 GLs (largely because of the growth of end-user computing), but they will not replace the 3 GLs in the next few years. There are several reasons why the procedural languages will remain popular. First, most computer professionals are familiar with one or more procedural languages and will be reluctant to change to something new. Second, the procedural languages tend to produce more efficient machine language programs (and thus shorter execution times) than the 4 GLs and other newer alternatives. Third, new versions of the procedural languages continue to be developed, each generally more powerful and easier to use than the previous version.

Using a procedural language requires logical thinking, because the programmer must devise a detailed step-by-step procedure to accomplish the desired task, and, of course, these steps in the procedure must be expressed in the particular statement types available in the given procedural language. Writing a procedural program is generally viewed as just one stage in the entire program development process. Table 5.1 provides one possible listing of the various stages in the program development process. Note that writing the program does not occur until stage four. Stage eight is debugging, which literally means to get the bugs or errors out of the program. The most difficult

---

[3] This is not meant as a term of derision. "Computer jock" is a common term used to indicate a person who spends great quantities of time and effort working with a computer.

TABLE 5.1 Stages in the Program Development Process

Stage 1	Problem identification
Stage 2	Algorithm development
Stage 3	Conversion of algorithm to computer-understandable logic, usually in form of structure chart or pseudocode
Stage 4	Program preparation
Stage 5	Keying program into computer
Stage 6	Program compilation
Stage 7	Execution of program with test data
Stage 8	Debugging process using test data
Stage 9	Use of program with actual data

stages in this program development process tend to be one and two—the proper identification of the problem and the development of an algorithm, which is a step-by-step description (in English) of the actions necessary to perform the task. In stage three, the algorithm is converted into a structure chart, which is a pictorial representation of the algorithm (to be discussed in Chapter 7), or pseudocode, which is an English-language-like version of the program. Throughout the entire process, logical thinking and a logical progression of steps are required to effectively use a procedural language.

Perhaps the most significant change in the newer versions of procedural languages is that they are more amenable to **structured programming**. A structured program is one that is divided into modules or blocks, where each block has only one entry point and only one exit point. When a program is written in this form, the program logic is easy to follow and understand, and thus the maintenance and correction of such a program should be easier than for a nonstructured program. The consequence of structured programming is that few if any transfer statements (often implemented as a GO TO statement) are required to transfer control to some other portion of the program. Therefore, structured programming is often referred to as GO TO-less programming, although the modular approach is really the central feature of a structured program. The newer versions of BASIC, FORTRAN, and COBOL all encourage highly structured programs, and some of the other procedural languages have adopted a totally structured approach.

BASIC BASIC is a good place to begin a brief look at the four most popular procedural languages because it is the simplest of the four languages and the one to which you were most likely exposed in high school or early in your college career. BASIC, which is an acronym for Beginner's All-purpose Symbolic Instruction Code, was developed in the early 1960s by John Kemeny and Thomas Kurtz at Dartmouth College. Their purpose was to create an easy-to-learn, interactive language for college students that would let the students concentrate on the thought processes involved in programming rather than the syntax. BASIC is the most popular programming language on college campuses (with the exception of the computer science, engineering, and science departments) and is also very popular on microcomputers.

Most versions of BASIC are interpreted rather than compiled, but some BASIC compilers have popped up in the past decade. Unfortunately, there are many versions of BASIC—developed by various computer manufacturers and software houses—and they are often incompatible with one another. This lack of standardization of BASIC is one reason why businesses have been loath to adopt it. Also BASIC has historically lacked the mathematical capabilities, data management capabilities, and control structures necessary to carry out business and scientific processing efficiently. Newer versions of BASIC have addressed these shortcomings, however, which may lead to a greater role for BASIC in the future.

To illustrate BASIC, consider the following sample problem: Write a BASIC program that will find the average of a set of numbers input by the user. Use a negative number to indicate the end of the data. A BASIC program to solve this problem is shown in Figure 5.6, together with the screen dialog that occurred when the program was run on a microcomputer using a simple data set. While the details of programming are not important, you will note that most of the instructions are quite intuitive, that is, even the uninitiated would correctly guess the meaning of most instructions.

C The granddaddy of the procedural languages is FORTRAN. Originally introduced by IBM in the mid-1950s, it quickly became the standard for

BASIC PROGRAM

```
10    REM   THIS PROGRAM FINDS THE AVERAGE OF A SET OF NUMBERS
20    REM      INPUT BY THE USER. A NEGATIVE NUMBER IS USED
30    REM      TO INDICATE THE END OF THE DATA.
40    PRINT "ENTER AS MANY POSITIVE NUMBERS AS YOU WISH,"
50    PRINT "WITH ONE NUMBER ENTERED PER LINE."
60    PRINT "WHEN YOU HAVE ENTERED YOUR ENTIRE SET OF NUMBERS,"
70    PRINT "ENTER A NEGATIVE NUMBER TO SIGNAL THE END OF DATA."
80    LET COUNT = 0
90    LET TOTAL = 0
100   INPUT NUMBER
110   IF NUMBER < 0 GOTO 150
120   LET TOTAL = TOTAL + NUMBER
130   LET COUNT = COUNT + 1
140   GOTO 100
150   LET AVG = TOTAL / COUNT
160   PRINT "THE AVERAGE OF YOUR NUMBERS IS"; AVG
170   PRINT "YOU ENTERED"; COUNT; "NUMBERS TOTALING"; TOTAL
180   END
```

SCREEN DIALOG WITH ABOVE BASIC PROGRAM
(Responses keyed in by user are underlined; computer responses are not underlined.)

```
OK
RUN
ENTER AS MANY POSITIVE NUMBERS AS YOU WISH,
WITH ONE NUMBER ENTERED PER LINE.
WHEN YOU HAVE ENTERED YOUR ENTIRE SET OF NUMBERS,
ENTER A NEGATIVE NUMBER TO SIGNAL THE END OF DATA.
?23
?45
?1
?78.6
?-9
THE AVERAGE OF YOUR NUMBERS IS  36.9
YOU ENTERED  4  NUMBERS TOTALING  147.6
OK
```

FIGURE 5.6 BASIC Program and Accompanying Screen Dialog

scientific and engineering programming. FORTRAN is still widely used today, in good part because of the significant investment made in the development of FORTRAN scientific software. The newest challenger to the supremacy of FORTRAN for scientific and engineering programming is C, which was introduced in 1983.

C is a very powerful language, but hard to use because it is less English-like and closer to assembly language than the other procedural languages. The C programming language features economy of expression, versatile data structures, modern control flow, and a rich set of operators. Because of these strengths, C is widely used in the development of microcomputer packages such as word processing, spreadsheets, and database management systems, and it is gaining on FORTRAN for scientific applications. Further, C has better data management capabilities than FORTRAN and other scientific languages, so it is also being used in traditional business data processing tasks, such as payroll, accounting, and sales reporting.

C was originally developed for and implemented on the UNIX operating system, and its use is growing as UNIX spreads. C programs have a high level of portability from one computer system to another—even from a mainframe to a microcomputer—with only minor changes. C has been adopted as the standard language by many college computer science departments, and it is widely used on microcomputers. On large research computers, it is not unusual for C and FORTRAN to be the only languages ever used.

The strengths of C are its control structures and its mathematical features. To illustrate, suppose that the result of one trial of a simulation experiment is an estimated profit for the firm for the next year. Twenty such trials have been made, each producing an estimated profit for the next year. Write a C program to compute the mean and variance of the estimated profit figures, entering in the data from the keyboard, one estimated profit figure per line.

A C program to solve this problem is given in Figure 5.7. The statements beginning and ending with /* and */ are comments. The *for* statement near the top of the program is a C statement to control repeated execution of a set of instructions. Some of the mathematical statements are obvious and some are not—but the program gets the job done.

COBOL COBOL, which is an acronym for COmmon Business-Oriented Language, is a language specifically devised for traditional business data-processing tasks. It was developed by a com-

puter industry committee (originally the short-range committee of the Conference on Data Systems Languages or CODASYL, later the COBOL Committee of CODASYL) in order to provide an industry-wide common language, closely resembling ordinary English, in which business data-processing procedures could be expressed. Since its inception in 1960, COBOL has gained widespread acceptance because it is standardized, has strong data management capabilities (relative to the other 3 GLs), and is relatively easy to learn and use. COBOL is by far the most popular language for programming mainframe computers for business applications.

COBOL programs are divided into four distinct divisions. The first two divisions are usually fairly short. The IDENTIFICATION DIVISION gives the program a name and provides other identifying information, and the ENVIRONMENT DIVISION describes the computer environment in which the program will be run. The ENVIRONMENT DIVISION is also the portion of the program that has to be changed to transport the program from one computer model to another. The DATA DIVISION, which is often quite lengthy, defines the entire file structure employed in the program. The PROCEDURE DIVISION corresponds most closely to a BASIC, FORTRAN, or C

(*text continued on p. 185*)

```
#include <stdio.h>
/* C program to compute means and variances
   of simulated profit figures */
main()
{
   /* Variable declaration and initialization */
        int index;
        float sum=0.0,sumsq=0.0,trial,mean,var;
   /* Control repeated execution using for statement */
        for (index = 1; index <=20; ++index)
        {
            printf(" Enter a profit figure: \n");
            scanf("%f",&trial);
            sum += trial;
            sumsq += trial*trial;
        } /* End control for */
        mean = sum/20.0;
        var = (sumsq/19.0) - (sum*sum)/(19.0*20.0);
        printf(" Mean Value is = %f \n",mean);
        printf(" Variance is = %f \n",var);
}   /* End of program */
```

FIGURE 5.7 C Program

```
1    8    12
     IDENTIFICATION DIVISION.
     PROGRAM-ID. COMMISSIONS-COMPUTE.
     AUTHOR. JOE PROGRAMMER.
     ENVIRONMENT DIVISION.
     CONFIGURATION SECTION.
     SOURCE-COMPUTER. IBM-4381.
     OBJECT-COMPUTER. IBM-4381.
     INPUT-OUTPUT SECTION.
     FILE-CONTROL.
         SELECT SALES-FILE ASSIGN DA-3380-S-IPT.
         SELECT COMMISSIONS-FILE ASSIGN DA-3380-S-RPT.
     DATA DIVISION.
     FILE SECTION.
     FD SALES-FILE
         LABEL RECORD OMITTED
         RECORD CONTAINS 80 CHARACTERS
         DATA RECORD IS IN-RECORD.
     01  IN-RECORD               PICTURE X(80).
     FD  COMMISSIONS-FILE
         LABEL RECORD OMITTED
         RECORD CONTAINS 132 CHARACTERS
         DATA RECORD IS PRINT-RECORD.
     01  PRINT-RECORD            PICTURE X(132).
```

FIGURE 5.8 COBOL Program

(continued on next page)

```
1      8  12
       WORKING-STORAGE SECTION.
       01  SALES-RECORD.
           05  NAME                 PICTURE A(30).
           05  FILLER               PICTURE X(10).
           05  SALES                PICTURE 9(8)V99.
           05  FILLER               PICTURE X(30).
       01  COMMISSION-RECORD.
           05  FILLER               PICTURE X(10).
           05  NAME-OUT             PICTURE A(30).
           05  FILLER               PICTURE X(10).
           05  SALES-OUT            PICTURE $$$,$$$,$$$.99.
           05  FILLER               PICTURE X(10).
           05  COMMISSION           PICTURE $$$$,$$$.99.
           05  FILLER               PICTURE X(47).
       77  TEMP-COMMISSION          PICTURE 9(6)V99.
       77  TOTAL-COMMISSIONS        PICTURE 9(10)V99    VALUE 0.
       77  TOTAL-COMM-EDITED        PICTURE $$,$$$,$$$.99.
       01  MORE-DATA                PICTURE X           VALUE 'Y'.
           88  THERE-IS-MORE-DATA                       VALUE 'Y'.
           88  THERE-IS-NO-MORE-DATA                    VALUE 'N'.
```

FIGURE 5.8 (continued)

180

```
1       8   12
PROCEDURE DIVISION.
MAIN-CONTROL.
    PERFORM INITIALIZATION.
    PERFORM READ-PROCESS-PRINT UNTIL THERE-IS-NO-MORE-DATA.
    PERFORM COMPLETE.
    STOP RUN.
INITIALIZATION.
    OPEN INPUT SALES-FILE, OUTPUT COMMISSIONS-FILE.
    MOVE SPACES TO COMMISSION-RECORD.
READ-PROCESS-PRINT.
    READ SALES-FILE INTO SALES-RECORD
        AT END MOVE 'N' TO MORE-DATA.
    IF THERE-IS-MORE-DATA
        MOVE NAME TO NAME-OUT
        MOVE SALES TO SALES-OUT
        IF SALES GREATER 50000
            COMPUTE TEMP-COMMISSION = .01*50000+.02*(SALES-50000)
        ELSE
            COMPUTE TEMP-COMMISSION= .01*SALES
        MOVE TEMP-COMMISSION TO COMMISSION
        WRITE PRINT-RECORD FROM COMMISSION-RECORD
            AFTER ADVANCING 1 LINES
        ADD TEMP-COMMISSION TO TOTAL-COMMISSIONS.
```

(continued on next page)

FIGURE 5.8 (continued)

```
1       8    12
        COMPLETE.
            MOVE TOTAL-COMMISSIONS TO TOTAL-COMM-EDITED.
            DISPLAY 'TOTAL-COMMISSIONS ARE ' TOTAL-COMM-EDITED.
            CLOSE SALES-FILE, COMMISSIONS-FILE.
```

FIGURE 5.8 (continued)

program; it consists of a series of operations specified in a logical order to accomplish the desired task. The combination of all these divisions, especially the DATA DIVISION, makes COBOL programs quite long compared to other procedural languages. COBOL has been correctly described as a verbose language.

Our sample COBOL program is designed to compute and print monthly sales commissions for the salespersons of a large corporation. Each salesperson earns a 1 percent commission on the first $50,000 in sales during a month and a 2 percent commission on all sales in excess of $50,000. The data have already been keyed in and are stored as a data file on a magnetic disk. One record has been prepared for each salesperson, containing the person's name and sales for the month. The output is to be a line for each salesperson, showing the name, monthly sales, and sales commission. In addition, the program is to accumulate the total commissions for all salespersons and to print this amount after all salespersons' records have been processed.

Figure 5.8 provides a COBOL program to accomplish this processing. Again, the details are not important, but note the four divisions of the program and the sheer length of this relatively simple program.

Other Procedural Languages   There are many other procedural languages in addition to BASIC, FORTRAN, C, and COBOL. PL/1 (Programming Language One) was developed by IBM in the mid-1960s as a language to do both mathematical and business-oriented processing. IBM hoped that PL/1 would replace both FORTRAN and COBOL, but it obviously did not do so. Some companies switched from COBOL to PL/1 and have remained staunch PL/1 users, but their numbers are limited.

In the 1980s, PASCAL was often the favorite language of college computer science departments, and it was widely used on microcomputers. PASCAL has greater mathematical capabilities than BASIC, and it handles data files better than FORTRAN. PASCAL never caught on outside universities, however, except as a microcomputer language, and its popularity is now waning in favor of C.

ADA is a language developed under the direction of the U.S. Department of Defense as a potential replacement for COBOL and FORTRAN. It was first introduced in 1980 and does have strong scientific capabilities, but thus far has not been widely adopted outside the federal government.

Special-purpose procedural languages have also been developed. For instance, SIMSCRIPT, GPSS, and SLAM are all special-purpose languages designed to help simulate the behavior of a system, such as a production line in a factory. Our listing of procedural languages is incomplete, but it is sufficient for our purposes. The bottom line is that these workhorse languages are still important, for they are the primary languages used by computer professionals.

Fourth-Generation Languages

There is no generally accepted definition of a fourth-generation language, but there are certain characteristics that most 4 GLs share. They generally employ an English-like syntax, and they are predominantly nonprocedural in nature. With a 4 GL, the user merely gives a precise statement of what is to be accomplished, not how to do it (as would be done for a procedural language). For the most part, then, the order in which instructions are given in a 4 GL is unimportant.

The 4 GLs employ very high-level instructions not present in 3 GLs, and thus 4 GL programs tend to require significantly fewer instructions than their 3 GL counterparts. Fewer instructions make 4 GL programs shorter, easier to write, easier to modify, easier to read and understand, and more error-free than 3 GL programs. Fourth-generation languages are sometimes called very high-level languages in contrast to the high-level third-generation languages.

The roots of fourth-generation languages date back to 1967, with the introduction of RAMIS (originally developed by Mathematica, Inc., and now sold by Computer Associates International). Other entries by the mid-1970s were NOMAD (originally from National CSS, and now from MUST Software International) and FOCUS (from Information Builders, Inc.). Initially, these products were primarily available on commercial time-sharing networks (like Telenet and Tymnet), but

184

direct sales of the products to customers took off around 1980 (earlier in the case of RAMIS). By the mid-1980s, FOCUS was estimated to command about 20 percent of the market, with RAMIS following with 16 percent and NOMAD with 10 percent (Jenkins and Bordoloi, 1986).

In the late 1980s and early 1990s, the 4 GL market became even more splintered as new versions of the early 4 GLs were rolled out and a wide variety of new products entered the marketplace. The emphasis of the products appearing in the mid-1990s is on portability—the ability of the 4 GL to work with different hardware platforms and operating systems, the ability to work over different types of networks (see Chapter 6), and the ability to work with different database management systems (Lindholm, 1992).

Some of the 4 GL products are full-function, general purpose languages like RAMIS, NOMAD, and FOCUS and have the complete functionality necessary to handle any application program. Thus, they are direct competitors with the 3 GLs. Other products are more specialized, with only limited functionality. These 4 GLs have been designed to handle a particular class of applications, such as graphics or financial modeling. IFPS (from Execucom) and SAS (from SAS Institute) are examples of limited purpose 4 GLs that focus on decision support and modeling. To gain a better perspective on general purpose and limited purpose 4 GLs, we will take a brief look at a representative from each type.

FOCUS FOCUS is an extremely versatile general purpose 4 GL. Versions of FOCUS are available to operate under the control of all the major operating systems mentioned earlier in this chapter, including a microcomputer version of FOCUS called PC/FOCUS, which operates under MS-DOS and PC-DOS. FOCUS consists of a large number of integrated tools and facilities, including a FOCUS database management system, a data dictionary/directory, a query language and report generator, an interactive text editor and screen painter, and a statistical analysis package. Of particular importance, FOCUS has the ability to process data managed both by its own DBMS (FOCUS files) and by an external DBMS or external file system (non-FOCUS files). We will concentrate on per-

KAWASAKI U.S.A. GOES WITH 4 GL OVER COBOL

In 1986 Kawasaki Motors Corporation, U.S.A., made a decision to use a 4 GL rather than COBOL for nearly all applications development of on-line systems. This decision came after an extensive study in which Kawasaki estimated that the particular 4 GL it adopted—Pro-IV from McDonnell Douglas Corporation—yielded a programmer productivity gain of 22 to 1 relative to COBOL. In the years since the decision to go with Pro-IV was made, more than 800 new applications have been developed using the 4 GL. Kawasaki believes that its use of Pro-IV has resulted in more real-time access to information, reduced applications backlogs, and improved programmer productivity.

Kawasaki U.S.A. manufactures motorcycles and Jet Ski watercraft, and demand for its products has been high with the growing role of leisure activities in the United States. For its first Pro-IV application, Kawasaki chose to develop an extensive decision support system/reporting system to allocate a limited number of vehicles to dealers in an equitable manner. This initial 4 GL-developed system was completed on time and under budget, and this highly visible success led the way for further use of Pro-IV. At present, Kawasaki is using Pro-IV to develop an innovative and comprehensive claims administration and product registration system.

(Adapted from Kador, 1989)

haps the most widely used of the FOCUS capabilities, the query language and report generator.

Consider the following problem situation. A telephone company wants to prepare a report for its internal management and its regulatory body showing the difference between customer bills under two different bill computation approaches. One of these bill computation methods is the traditional flat rate based on the size of the local calling area; the other is so-called "measured service," where the customer pays a very small flat rate for a minimum number of calls and then pays so much per call ($.21 in the example) for calls above this minimum. Massive FOCUS data files already exist containing all the necessary raw data for an extended test period, with each record including customer number, area, type of service, number of calls during the time period, and the length of the time period (in months). The telephone company wants a report for present flat rate customers in area two only, showing the difference between the two billing approaches for each customer and the total difference over all flat rate customers in area two.

Figure 5.9 shows a FOCUS program (more commonly called a FOCEXEC) to produce the desired report. As with our 3 GL examples, the individual instructions are not important, but let us consider the major pieces of the program. After some initial comments, the program begins with the TABLE command, which calls the query/report generator function of FOCUS. The data file is called TEST. Up to the first END, the instructions

FOCUS PROGRAM

```
                         (FOCEXEC)
-*
-*    THIS FOCEXEC GIVES THE BILL DIFFERENCES FOR ALL
-*    CUSTOMERS WITH FLAT RATE SERVICE IN AREA TWO, AS WELL
-*    AS THE TOTAL OF THESE BILL DIFFERENCES.
-*
TABLE FILE TEST
SUM TOT_CALLS MONTHS AND COMPUTE
AVG_CALLS/D12.2=TOT_CALLS/MONTHS;
BY CUST BY AREA IF SERV CONTAINS FL
ON TABLE HOLD AS BDATA
END
DEFINE FILE BDATA
FRATE/D4.2=IF AREA CONTAINS 'ON' THEN 12.10
          ELSE IF AREA CONTAINS 'TW' THEN 13.40
          ELSE 14.51;
MRATE/D4.2=7.35;
K/I1=IF AVG_CALLS GT 30 THEN 1 ELSE 0;
MESSRU/D12.2=(AVG_CALLS-30)*.21*K;
BILL_DIFF/D12.2=FRATE-(MRATE+MESSRU);
END
TABLE FILE BDATA
HEADING CENTER
"1993 -- TWO"
"SERV = FL"
SUM BILL_DIFF NOPRINT MONTHS NOPRINT AND COMPUTE
    AVG_BILL_DIFF/D12.2=BILL_DIFF/MONTHS;
IF AREA EQ TWO ON TABLE COLUMN-TOTAL BY AREA BY CUST
END
```

FOCUS OUTPUT

```
                          1993 -- TWO
                            SERV = FL
          AREA        CUST           AVG_BILL_DIFF
          TWO         4122                4.87
                      4125                8.28
                      4211               -5.33
                        .                   .
                        .                   .
                        .                   .
          TOTAL                         2,113.88
```

FIGURE 5.9 FOCUS Program and Output

sum the variables TOT_CALLS and MONTHS for each customer in each area if the type of service is FL, then divide one sum by the other to get an average number of calls per month AVG_CALLS. The DEFINE FILE BDATA computes the rates by the two approaches, as well as the difference between the two rates, storing these computed values in the temporary file BDATA. Finally, the TABLE FILE BDATA computes the average bill difference AVG_BILL_DIFF and prints the report shown at the bottom of Figure 5.9.

Note that the FOCUS program is not particularly intuitive, but it is quite short for a reasonably complex problem. It is also largely nonprocedural in that the order of most statements does not make any difference. Of course, the conditional IFs and BYs must be appropriately placed.

IFPS The Interactive Financial Planning System, or IFPS, is among the most popular of the limited function fourth-generation languages. IFPS, which was developed by Execucom Systems Corporation, is primarily known as a financial modeling language, but it has wider capabilities that make it quite similar to FOCUS. The structure of IFPS includes an overall executive level under which operate a modeling language to create financial models, a reporting language to prepare presentations, a data manipulation language to create, change, and query a database, and a command language. We will concentrate on the popular modeling language, which is nonprocedural so the instructions can be placed in any order.

The IFPS modeling language makes it easy to build financially oriented models. These models are representations of reality, containing the assumptions and relationships that the model builder believes will hold true in the real situation. With IFPS, the model builder (who is often a manager) can quickly build a model, verify its accuracy, change it if required, and test alternative assumptions. An IFPS model is a decision support system for its user.

To illustrate IFPS, consider a high-technology riding lawn mower manufacturer that is developing its financial plan for the years 1995–2000. Demand for 1995 is expected to be 20,000 units and is expected to grow by 1,200 units per year. The price of the lawn mower in 1995 is $1,295

per unit and is expected to remain constant through 1997, after which it will rise by 5 percent per year.

The unit manufacturing cost (labor and materials) is $947 per unit in 1995 and is expected to rise by 3 percent per year through 1997, after which it is expected to rise by 8 percent per year. Administrative costs in 1995 are $4.2 million. These costs will be reduced by 10 percent per year through 2000. Advertising costs are estimated to be 7 percent of sales revenue throughout the 1995–2000 period. The company calculates its income before taxes as sales revenue minus its manufacturing, administrative, and advertising expenses. Income is taxed at a 50 percent rate. The company wants to determine its income after taxes for each year in the six-year period.

An IFPS model to produce the financial plan for the lawn mower manufacturer for the years 1995–2000 is shown at the top of Figure 5.10. This model has been written using the IFPS/Personal version of the language, which is designed to run on PCs. At the bottom of the figure is the output from the IFPS model. Within the IFPS model, the statements could have been placed in any order, but it is desirable to place them in some logical order because the output appears in the same order. The backwards slash (\) at the beginning of a line denotes a comment. Each noncomment line defines the variable on the left-hand side of the equal sign. The right-hand side indicates what will happen to the variable over the time period under study. For example, the PRICE variable will remain at $1,295 for the first three years (1995–1997), then increase at 5 percent per year for the next three years (1998–2000).

The model in Figure 5.10 may be useful as given, but the power of the IFPS approach comes from experimentation with the model. Once the model is built, it takes only a few seconds to change an assumption and see the resulting impact. (This employs the IFPS **What_if** command.) The user can also set a goal, such as a yearly income after taxes of $750,000, and determine the sales level that would be required to achieve this goal. (This uses the **gOal_seek** command.) For the type of financial planning represented by our example, the power and ease of use of IFPS should be obvious.

IFPS MODEL

```
COLUMNS 1995 THRU 2000
\      HIGH-TECH LAWN MOWER CORPORATION
\      ----- REVENUE -----
DEMAND = 20000, PREVIOUS + 1200 FOR 5
PRICE = 1295 FOR 3, PREVIOUS * 1.05 FOR 3
SALES REVENUE = DEMAND * PRICE
\      ----- EXPENSES -----
UNIT MFG COST = 947, PREVIOUS * 1.03 FOR 2, PREVIOUS * 1.08
TOTAL MFG COST = UNIT MFG COST * DEMAND
ADMIN COSTS = 4200000, PREVIOUS * .90
ADVERTISING COSTS = SALES REVENUE * .07
TOTAL COSTS = TOTAL MFG COST + ADMIN COSTS + ADVERTISING COSTS
\      ----- INCOME -----
INCOME BEFORE TAXES = SALES REVENUE - TOTAL COSTS
TAX = .50 * INCOME BEFORE TAXES
INCOME AFTER TAXES = INCOME BEFORE TAXES - TAX
```

IFPS OUTPUT

	1995	1996	1997	1998	1999	2000
HIGH-TECH LAWN MOWER CORPORATION						
----- REVENUE -----						
DEMAND	20000	21200	22400	23600	24800	26000
PRICE	1295	1295	1295	1360	1428	1499
SALES REVENUE	25900000	27454000	29008000	32090100	35407890	38977234
----- EXPENSES -----						
UNIT MFG COST	947	975.4	1005	1085	1172	1266
TOTAL MFG COST	18940000	20678692	22504660	25607088	29061874	32905542
ADMIN COSTS	4200000	3780000	3402000	3061800	2755620	2480058
ADVERTISING COSTS	1813000	1921780	2030560	2246307	2478552	2728406
TOTAL COSTS	24953000	26380472	27937220	30915195	34296047	38114006
----- INCOME -----						
INCOME BEFORE TAXES	947000	1073528	1070780	1174905	1111843	863228
TAX	473500	536764	535390	587453	555922	431614
INCOME AFTER TAXES	473500	536764	535390	587453	555922	431614

FIGURE 5.10 IFPS Model and Output

Future Developments The fourth-generation languages are evolving even more rapidly than those in the third generation. Both large computer and microcomputer versions of the 4 GLs are continually being improved in terms of both capabilities and ease of use. Progress is also being made in terms of the efficiency of execution of 4 GL programs vis-à-vis 3 GL programs. For these reasons and others mentioned earlier (increasing computer sophistication of managers, continuing backlogs in the information systems department), the use of 4 GLs will continue to grow through the rest of this century. The strongest element of growth will come from end-user computing, but information systems departments will also shift toward 4 GLs, especially for infrequently used programs.

Fifth-generation languages will also emerge in the 1990s, although it is too soon to be very specific about their form and functionality. We suspect that the fifth-generation languages will be **natural languages**, in which users write their programs in ordinary English (or something very close to it). Users will need little or no training to program using a natural language; they simply write (or perhaps verbalize) what they want done without regard for syntax or form (other than that incorporated in ordinary English). At present, there are no true natural languages. There are,

WHAT MAKES OOP RUN?

Objects are self-contained software modules that perform a given set of tasks on command. By connecting a number of these objects, a software engineer can create a complete, working application almost as easily as assembling a stereo system by plugging together a receiver, tape deck, and CD player.

The difficulty arises in creating an object that works properly and is robust enough to be used in a variety of applications. However, once a given object exists in finished, working form, other programmers need know nothing about how it accomplishes its task. Instead, it's enough to send the object the right commands, or messages.

This makes the object-oriented approach ideal for the large-scale, team development cycle typical in the corporate setting. When, like stereo components, an object can be moved as a complete unit to a new program, the object is, in the lingo of OOP, encapsulated. A quintessential black box, the object always does its job the same way, independently of the application in which it's used.

Perhaps most important, objects are defined both by the data and by the methods that act on the data—in other words, by what function the object is to perform. This feature is critical in allowing managers to define objects in terms of real-world attributes. A customer object, for example, can be defined by what it must do to calculate an account balance and what it should do with it once it does.

(Cummings, 1992)

however, some rudimentary natural language-like products, such as Artificial Intelligence Corporation's INTELLECT, which can be used with a variety of database management systems (including IBM's SQL/DS) and 4 GLs (including FOCUS), and Microrim's Clout, which interfaces with Microrim's R:base database management system. Future developments in the natural language area will be fascinating to watch.

Object-Oriented Programming

In the mid-1990s, the hottest programming languages (at least in terms of interest and experimentation) are not 4 GLs or natural languages, but object-oriented programming (OOP) languages. OOP is not new—it dates back to the 1970s—but it has received renewed attention in the 1990s because of the increased power of workstations and the excellent graphical user interfaces (GUIs) that have been developed for these workstations. OOP requires more computing power than traditional languages, and a graphical interface provides a natural way to work with the OOP objects.

OOP is neither a 3 GL nor a 4 GL, but an entirely new paradigm for programming with roots in both the procedural 3 GLs and the non-procedural 4 GLs. Creating the objects in OOP is somewhat akin to 3 GL programming in that the procedures (called methods) are embedded in the objects, while putting the objects together to create an application is much closer to the use of a 4 GL. The most popular OOP language is C++, a modified version of C (a 3 GL); one of the advantages of C++ is that a C programmer can learn to use it quickly. The first OOP language, Smalltalk, which was originally developed by Xerox, is also a popular choice for OOP. More recently, object-oriented development environments (software), such as Borland's ObjectVision, are being marketed that are much easier to use than C++ and Smalltalk.

According to Tom Chavez of Apple Computer, OOP technology is quickly becoming the standard in situations where large programs must be developed (see box "What Makes OOP Run?"). "Forward-thinking companies are now taking the financial hit—sometimes millions of dollars for retraining and reengineering—and are using OOP for procedural programming. They realize that they'll actually save money in the long run. If it ordinarily takes six months to develop a piece of software, you can do it in three months when you're using OOP. All the end-user will see is that new features are coming down the pike quicker, cheaper, and more efficiently than they would have before OOP" (Kaplan, 1992).

Database Management Systems

A database management system (DBMS) is support software that is used to create, manage, and protect organizational data. A DBMS works with the operating system to store and modify data and to make data accessible in a variety of meaningful and authorized ways. For most computer systems, the DBMS is separate from the operating system, although the trend appears to be to place some DBMS functions either in the operating system or in separate attached computer processors called database servers. The purpose of this trend is to achieve greater efficiency and security.

A DBMS adds significant data management capabilities to those provided by the operating system. The goal is to allow a computer programmer to select data from disk files by referring to the content of records, not their physical location, which makes programming easier, more productive, and less prone to errors. This also allows systems professionals responsible for database design to reorganize the physical organization of data without affecting the logic of programs, which significantly reduces maintenance requirements. These objectives are given the umbrella term *data independence*. For example, a DBMS would allow a programmer to specify retrieval of a customer record based only on knowledge of the customer's name or number. Further, once the customer record is retrieved, a DBMS would allow direct reference to any of the customer's related order or shipment records (even if these records are relocated or changed). Thus, a DBMS allows access to data based on content (e.g., customer number) as well as by association (e.g., orders for a given customer).

A **database** is a shared collection of logically related data, organized to meet the needs of an organization. The DBMS is the software that manages a database. There are several different types of DBMSs in use today:

Hierarchical: characterized by the IBM product Information Management System (IMS)— data are arranged in a top-down organization chart fashion.

Network: a good example is Integrated Database Management System (IDMS) from Computer Associates International—data are arranged like the cities on a highway system, often with several paths from one piece of data to another.

Relational: many such products exist, including dBASE IV and Paradox by Borland, SQL/DS

and DB2 by IBM, and INGRES[4]—data are arranged into simple tables, and records are related by storing common data in each of the associated tables.

An organization almost always purchases a DBMS, rather than developing it in-house, because of the extensive development cost and time. A DBMS is a very complex and costly software package, ranging in price from approximately $500 for a personal computer product to $200,000 for a DBMS on a large mainframe computer. By purchasing a DBMS, an organization is able to draw upon a larger pool of programmers and systems designers who are familiar with the package, which then reduces training costs and gives them more choices for hiring database professionals.

File Organization The computer files are stored on the disk using the file organization provided by the operating system and special structures added by the DBMS. Although their exact details can be treated as a black box in most cases, it is useful to know some of the terminology and choices. Three general kinds of file organizations exist—sequential, direct, and indexed (see Figure 5.11).

A **sequential file organization** arranges the records so that they are physically adjacent and in order by some sort key (usually the unique key that distinguishes each record from one another). Thus, a sequential customer file would have the records arranged in order by customer name or identifier. Sequential files use very little space and are fast when the records are to be retrieved in order, but they are inefficient when searching for a particular record since they must be scanned front to back. Also, when records are added or deleted, the whole file must be rearranged to accommodate the modifications, which can be a time-consuming task.

A **direct file organization** also uses a key for each record, but records are placed and retrieved so that an individual record can be rapidly

---

[4] INGRES is the name of the company as well as the software product. For the remainder of this chapter, the name of the company offering a software product will not be given if the company name is essentially the same as the product name.

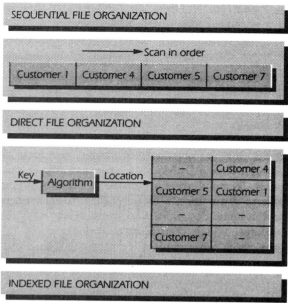

SEQUENTIAL FILE ORGANIZATION

Scan in order

| Customer 1 | Customer 4 | Customer 5 | Customer 7 |

DIRECT FILE ORGANIZATION

Key → Algorithm → Location

–	Customer 4
Customer 5	Customer 1
–	–
Customer 7	–

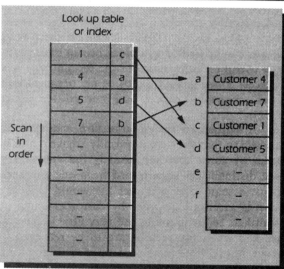

INDEXED FILE ORGANIZATION

Look up table or index

Scan in order

1	c
4	a
5	d
7	b
–	
–	
–	
–	
–	

a	Customer 4
b	Customer 7
c	Customer 1
d	Customer 5
e	–
f	–
	–

FIGURE 5.11 File Organizations

It is possible that several keys can "collide" to the same location, but such synonyms are easily resolved. Direct files are extremely fast for accessing a single record, but because which keys exist at any point in time is usually arbitrary, sequential processing of direct files requires a long and tedious scan and usually sorting of the records.

Indexed file organizations provide a compromise between the sequential and direct-access capabilities. The record keys only are arranged in sequence in a separate table, along with the location of the rest of the data associated with that key (this location field in the table is called a pointer). This lookup table or index is similar to a card catalog in a library, in which the author's name, book title, and topics are different types of keys and the book catalog number is a pointer to its location in the library. To access the records sequentially, the table is completely scanned one entry at a time, and as each entry is encountered, its associated data record is retrieved. To access the records individually, the table is scanned until a match with the desired key is found and only the desired record is retrieved; if no match is found, an error is indicated. Because the table is quite small (just enough space for the key and location of every record, compared to possibly hundreds or thousands of characters needed for the entire record—remember the analogy of the card catalog in a library), this scan can be very fast (certainly considerably faster than scanning the actual data). For a very large table, a second table can be created to access the first table (which is, of course, nothing more than a specialized file itself). Popular names for such methods of indexes on top of indexes are indexed sequential access method (ISAM) and virtual storage access method (VSAM).

Finally, because in a database we want to be able to access records based upon content (e.g., by customer number) as well as by relationship (e.g., orders for a given customer), a DBMS along with the operating system must also provide a means for access via these relationships. Record keys and location pointers are these means. For example, we could store pointers in a customer record and its associated order records to link these related records together (see Figure 5.12). Such a scheme

accessed. The records are located wherever they can most quickly be retrieved, and the space from deleted records can be reused without having to rearrange the file. The most typical method employed is a hashing function. In this case, the record key, such as the customer number, is mathematically manipulated (by some algorithm) to determine the location of the record with that key.

FIGURE 5.12 Schemes for Relationships Between Files

is called chaining or a list structure. Alternately, we could store the customer number in each of its associated order records and use tables or hashing functions to locate the related record or records in other files. This scheme is used by relational DBMSs.

Database Programming Data processing activity with a database can be specified in either procedural programs written in a 3 GL or via special-purpose languages developed for database processing. In the case of a 3 GL program, additional and more powerful instructions are added to the vocabulary of the programming language. For example, in a customer and order database the storage of a new order record not only necessitates storing the order data itself, but also updating various linkages that tie together a customer record with its associated order records. In a regular 3 GL program, instructions to write new data to the customer record, its index, the order record, and its indexes would have to be provided individually. With the commands available through the special enhancements to the language provided by the DBMS, only one instruction is needed in the program and all the associated indexes and records are updated automatically, which makes the programming task more productive and error free.

A DBMS also frequently provides a 4 GL, nonprocedural special-purpose language for posing queries to the database. For example, the query in the SQL/DS command language

```
SELECT ORDER#, CUSTOMER#,
CUSTNAME, ORDER-DATE
  FROM CUSTOMER, ORDER
  WHERE ORDER-DATE > '04/12/95'
  AND CUSTOMER.CUSTOMER# =
  ORDER.CUSTOMER#
```

is all that is required to request the display of the order number and date from each order record, plus the customer number and name from the associated customer record, for orders placed after April 12, 1995. The equivalent COBOL program might require ten or more procedural division instructions. The popularity of such products as dBASE IV (Borland), Paradox (Borland), R:base (Microrim), INGRES, and several SQL-based language products (a standard created by the American National Standards Institute, or ANSI) is due in great measure to the existence of such easy-to-use query languages.

Not all query languages are quite this simple to use, but they are still quite powerful. In some cases, the manager writing a query needs to know more about the contents of the database than is implied above. In the programming language provided with dBASE III+, for example, the programmer must know how the files are linked. For the previous example, this would typically be done by storing the customer number in both the order and customer files and using this data to logically join the two tables together. In the dBASE programming language, the instructions equivalent to the SQL/DS commands above would be:

```
SELECT 2
USE CUSTOMER
SELECT 1
USE ORDER
JOIN WITH CUSTOMER TO RESULT
  FOR ORDER-DATE>'04/12/95'
  FIELDS ORDER#, CUSTOMER#,
  B->CUSTNAME, ORDER-DATE
DISPLAY RESULT
```

Managing the Data Resource   A DBMS is a software tool to help an organization manage its data. In Chapter 14 we will discuss data resource management, and a DBMS is an important tool for this management function. From a managerial point of view, a DBMS helps manage data by providing the functions of:

Data Storage, Retrieval, Update: provide a variety of commands that allow easy retrieval/presentation and modification of data.
Backup: automatically making copies of the database and the updates made to it to protect against accidental damage or deliberate sabotage.
Recovery: ability to restore the database after damage, or after inaccurate data have gotten into the database.
Integrity Control: ensuring that only valid data are entered into the database (so that, for example, data values only in a permissible range are entered).
Security Control: ensuring that only authorized use (reading and updating) is permitted on the database.
Concurrency Control: protecting the database against anomalies that can occur when two or more programs attempt to update the same data at the same time.
Transaction Control: being able to undo changes to a database when a program malfunctions, a user cancels a business transaction, or the DBMS rejects a business transaction that updates several database records.

Along with the DBMS, many organizations also use a **data dictionary/directory**, or DD/D, which is a repository of data definitions that is shared among all the users. Such a central catalog is used by the DBMS and system users whenever the meaning, storage format, integrity rules, security clearances, and physical location of data need to be discovered. The DD/D is similar to an inventory accounting system for a parts warehouse—in this case for a data warehouse, or database. Many modern DBMSs have a built-in DD/D capability.

A DBMS and a DD/D are tools, and user-managers and database professionals in the information systems organization must use these and other tools wisely if data are to be readily accessible to all who have a need to know. The manager must:

- understand his data, the meaning of the data, and quality requirements, so that accurate definitions of data can be developed and shared with all who need access to them.
- understand how data will be used and communicate this to database designers so that efficient structures can be built to provide rapid and secure access to these data.
- recognize that data such as customer number and credit balance, part number and description, and product bill-of-materials are organizational data, the value of which is multiplied by sharing and ensuring accuracy.
- learn to make intelligent choices between developing local databases on personal computers or using central, shared databases (Chapters 7 and 14 will provide further insights).

Today, most organizations are highly computerized and vast databases exist. The issue often is not whether the data are available, but rather which of several alternative versions of the data to use and how to gain access to these data. A DBMS with a variety of methods to store data and easy-to-use programming and query languages is essential for such access. Although not as widely understood as spreadsheets or word processors at present, DBMSs, are the means for connecting a highly interrelated organization. Being able to use prewritten database processing routines and to write original database queries are necessary skills of today's general manager.

CASE Tools

In this section we will introduce the software that is likely to have a major impact on computer professionals in the 1990s and beyond. CASE, an acronym for computer-aided software engineering, is actually a collection of software tools to help automate all phases of the software development life cycle. (The life cycle for software development is discussed in detail in Chapter 8.) In those firms that have adopted CASE tools—and there are a growing number of them—CASE is changing the jobs of systems analysts and programmers in radical ways. In particular, the job of the analyst or programmer involves more up-front work in

clearly defining the problem and expressing it in the particular specifications required by the CASE tool. Then the tool assists in the back-end work of translating the specifications to the required output, such as a data flow diagram (see Chapter 7) or a COBOL program.

We will defer a more complete treatment of CASE software until Chapter 8, where the variety of CASE tools and their role in the systems development process will be explored. For now, note that the impact of CASE is only beginning to be felt. CASE may well change the way in which the IS organization in your company does business, and thus CASE is indirectly important to you. CASE has the potential of providing a productivity boost to an area of the company (the IS organization) that needs such a boost.

Personal Productivity Software

From your personal standpoint as a manager, the category of applications software that we have chosen to call personal productivity software is probably the most important of all. These are the packages that you and your fellow managers will use on a regular basis—word processing, spreadsheets, presentation graphics, electronic mail, desktop publishing, microcomputer-based database management systems, statistical packages, and other similar easy-to-use and extremely useful packages. Most of these packages are microcomputer-based, and they have been developed with a friendly, comfortable user interface.

Exciting things are happening in the personal productivity software area. A few of the packages date back to the 1970s, but the true beginning of this area came in 1979 with the introduction of VisiCalc, the first electronic spreadsheet. With VisiCalc, microcomputers became a valuable business tool, not just a toy or a hobby. The financial success of VisiCalc convinced many individuals that there was money to be made in developing software packages that individuals and companies would buy and use. Within a few years a deluge of products appeared—a mixture of good ones and bad—that has not stopped flowing. The results have been truly marvelous for the businessperson with a willingness to experiment and a desire to

194

become more productive. Most of the microcomputer products are quite reasonably priced (often a few hundred dollars) because the successful products can expect to reap large rewards on their volume of sales. Furthermore, a number of excellent publications have appeared (such as *PC/Computing*, *Byte*, and *PC Week*), which carefully review new products to assist us in choosing the right packages. Hardly a month goes by without the announcement of an exciting new package that may become the new VisiCalc, Lotus 1-2-3, or WordPerfect.

Word Processing Word processing may be the most ubiquitous of the personal productivity software packages. In many organizations, the first users of microcomputers were the secretaries using early word-processing packages (often WordStar). As secretaries learned the advantages of word processing—particularly the ability to make corrections in a draft without retyping the entire document—managers began to think that it might be more convenient for them, too, to have a microcomputer on their desk so that they could draft letters and reports directly at the keyboard rather than writing them out longhand. There is an art to composing at the keyboard, but once a person has the hang of it, his productivity (in terms of written output) can easily be doubled, as compared to writing longhand. Thus, word processing has made major inroads into the corporate world at the managerial level.

The newest versions of the popular word-processing packages make it easy to get addicted to them. For example WordStar Professional 7.0 incorporates automatic hyphenation at the end of a line, spell-checking against an extensive dictionary, a thesaurus to aid a writer searching for the right word, the ability to incorporate drawings or figures directly into the text, page preview to check the layout of the page, and the ability to draw boxes and horizontal and vertical lines. Another popular capability is mail merge—the ability to automatically print the same letter (with the address and salutation changed, of course) to everyone on a mailing list. Other popular word-processing packages include WordPerfect, Microsoft

Word, Ami Pro (from Lotus Development), Professional Write (Software Publishing), MultiMate (Borland), and DeScribe Word Processor. All these packages try to achieve "what you see is what you get," or WYSIWYG, and all succeed to a great extent. The idea is that the text you see on the microcomputer screen should be as close as possible to the resulting printed text. The choice of a word processor is a complex decision based on many factors in addition to WYSIWYG. Most of us tend to prefer whichever word processor we worked with first. The important thing is not which word processor, it is forcing yourself to choose and use any one of the better word processors in order to improve your personal productivity in writing.

Spreadsheets Second only to word processing in popularity are electronic spreadsheet packages, the most widely used of which is Lotus 1-2-3. Other popular spreadsheet packages are Excel (from Microsoft), Quattro Pro (Borland), Wingz (Informix), and SuperCalc 5 (Computer Associates International). The so-called integrated packages such as Symphony (Lotus) and Microsoft Works include spreadsheet capabilities as well as word processing and database. The idea of the electronic spreadsheet is based on the accountant's spreadsheet, which is a large sheet of paper divided into many columns and rows on which the accountant can organize and present financial data. The spreadsheet approach can be used for any application that can fit into the rows and columns framework, such as budget summaries for several time periods, profit and loss statements for various divisions of a company, sales forecasts for the next twelve months, an instructor's gradebook, or computation of various statistics for a basketball team.

The intersection of a row and a column is called a cell. Each row in the spreadsheet is given a label (1, 2, 3, and so on, from the top down), as is each column (A, B, C, and so on, from left to right), and a cell is identified by combining the designations of the intersecting row and column (see Figure 5.13). In a budget summary spreadsheet, for example, cell C4 might contain $32,150,

	A	B	C	D	E	F	G
1			SECOND COMPANY PROJECTED PROFIT				
2							
3			1996	1997	1998	1999	2000
4							
5	Quantity sold		2000	2100	2205	2315	2431
6	Price		$50.00	$54.00	$58.32	$62.99	$68.02
7							
8	Total income		$100,000	$113,400	$128,596	$145,827	$165,368
9							
10							
11	Fixed costs:						
12	Rent		$1,000	$1,100	$1,200	$1,300	$1,400
13	Salaries		$20,000	$22,000	$24,200	$26,620	$29,282
14	Equipment leases		$4,000	$4,200	$4,410	$4,631	$4,862
15	Utilities		$5,000	$6,000	$7,200	$8,640	$10,368
16	Office supplies		$500	$475	$451	$429	$407
17							
18	Total fixed costs		$30,500	$33,775	$37,461	$41,619	$46,319
19							
20	Variable costs:						
21	Unit material cost		$8.00	$10.00	$12.00	$14.00	$16.00
22	Unit labor cost		$4.00	$4.16	$4.33	$5.11	$5.62
23	Unit supplies cost		$1.00	$1.00	$1.00	$1.00	$1.00
24							
25	Total material cost		$16,000	$21,000	$26,460	$32,414	$38,896
26	Total labor cost		$8,000	$8,736	$9,540	$11,820	$13,652
27	Total supplies cost		$2,000	$2,100	$2,205	$2,315	$2,431
28							
29	Total variable costs		$26,000	$31,836	$38,205	$46,548	$54,979
30							
31	Total costs		$56,500	$65,611	$75,666	$88,168	$101,298
32							
33							
34	Profit before taxes		$43,500	$47,789	$52,930	$57,660	$64,070
35							
36							
37							
38							

FIGURE 5.13 Lotus 1-2-3 Spreadsheet

the budgeted sales income for the second quarter. Similarly, cell C2 might contain the heading information "Second Quarter." To enter data into a cell, the cursor is positioned on that cell and the user merely keys in the appropriate data.

The power of a spreadsheet program does not come from keying numeric data into particular cells, although that is certainly done. The power comes in part from the use of formulas to combine the contents of other cells, letting the program do the calculations rather than doing them by hand.

For example, let us assume that cell C9 in our budget summary example is to contain the total income for the second quarter, which is the sum of cells C4, C5, C6, and C7. Rather than total C4 through C7 by hand, the user enters a formula in cell C9 that tells the program to total the contents of those four cells. One way to express that formula in Lotus 1-2-3 is +C4+C5+C6+C7. Then the sum is computed by the program and placed in cell C9. More important, if a change has to be made in one of the numerical entries—say in cell

C5—then the sum in cell C9 is automatically corrected to reflect the new number. This feature makes it very easy to modify assumptions and conduct "what if" analyses using a spreadsheet package.

Among the spreadsheet packages, Lotus 1-2-3 is the generally accepted standard, with most of the other packages modifying or extending the Lotus approach. The normal display when using 1-2-3 is a portion of the spreadsheet (a window) with control information at the top of the screen. Using the arrow keys, the user navigates around the spreadsheet to the cell where the entry is to be made (the window automatically changes to keep the cursor cell visible). As numerical or heading information is keyed in, it appears both in the control area at the top of the screen and in the desired cell. If a formula is keyed in, however, the formula appears in the control area while the resulting numerical value is placed in the cell. The various commands in 1-2-3 are controlled by a multilevel menu system, which is initially accessed by keying in a slash (/). This causes the menu to appear at the top of the screen. To choose from any level of the menu, the user keys in the first letter of a command or moves the cursor to the desired command and then taps the "Enter" key. If a particular string of commands is likely to be used repeatedly, it is possible to create a macro (a program). The user then employs a few keystrokes to call the macro rather than entering the entire string of commands.

Projecting profit for a hypothetical company will serve as a specific spreadsheet application. The Second Company wishes to project its profit for the years 1996 through 2000, given a set of assumptions about quantity sold of its product, selling price, fixed expenses, and variable expenses. For example, quantity sold of the only product is assumed to be 2,000 units in 1996, increasing 5 percent per year for each year thereafter. Price is assumed to be $50 per unit in 1996, increasing at 8 percent per year. Rent is $1,000 in 1996, growing at $100 per year. Similar assumptions are made for each of the other categories of fixed and variable costs. The resulting spreadsheet is shown in Figure 5.13, which indicates that the Second Company is projected to make $43,500 in profit before taxes in 1996 and $64,070 in 2000.

How were these numbers in the spreadsheet determined? Many of the numbers in the 1996 column were keyed directly in as initial assumptions, but eight of the numbers in the 1996 column and all of the numbers in the remaining columns were determined by formulas, letting the program perform the actual calculations. For example, 2000 was actually keyed into cell C5 and 50.00 into cell C6. Cell C8, however, contains a formula to multiply quantity sold times price +C5*C6. Figure 5.14 shows the formulas behind the numbers in Figure 5.13. If the cursor is positioned on cell C8 in the spreadsheet, the number 100,000 will appear in the spreadsheet but the formula +C5*C6 will appear in the control area at the top. Similarly, cell C18 contains a formula to add the contents of cells C12, C13, C14, C15, and C16; one way of expressing this formula is @SUM(C12..C16). Cell D5, the quantity sold in 1997, also contains a formula. In this case, the quantity sold in 1997 is to be 5 percent greater than the quantity sold in 1996, so the formula is +C5*1.05. Not surprisingly, the formula in cell E5 is +D5*1.05. Thus, any changed assumption about the quantity sold in 1996 will automatically impact both total income and profit in 1996 and quantity sold, total income, and profit in all future years. Because of this cascading effect, the impact of alternative assumptions can be easily analyzed after the original spreadsheet has been developed. This is the power of a spreadsheet package.

Microcomputer-Based Database Management Systems After word processing and spreadsheets, the next most popular category of personal productivity software is microcomputer-based database management systems. The most widely used packages are dBase III+ and IV (from Borland) and Paradox (Borland), but other popular packages include Microsoft Access, Approach, CA-dBFast (Computer Associates International), SQLWindows (Gupta Technologies), Superbase and Windowbase (Software Publishing), FileMaker (Claris), and DataEase. All these packages are based on the relational data model and all meet our ease-of-use criterion. The basic ideas be-

SECOND COMPANY PROJECTED PROFIT

	1996	1997	1998	1999	2000
Quantity sold	2000	+C5*1.05	+D5*1.05	+E5*1.05	+F5*1.05
Price	50.00	+C6*1.08	+D6*1.08	+E6*1.08	+F6*1.08
Total income	+C5*C6	+D5*D6	+E5*E6	+F5*F6	+G5*G6
Fixed costs:					
Rent	1000	+C12+100	+D12+100	+E12+100	+F12+100
Salaries	20000	+C13*1.1	+D13*1.1	+E13*1.1	+F13*1.1
Equipment leases	4000	+C14*1.05	+D14*1.05	+E14*1.05	+F14*1.05
Utilities	5000	+C15*1.2	+D15*1.2	+E15*1.2	+F15*1.2
Office supplies	500	+C16*0.95	+D16*0.95	+E16*0.95	+F16*0.95
Total fixed costs	@SUM(C12..C16)	@SUM(D12..D16)	@SUM(E12..E16)	@SUM(F12..F16)	@SUM(G12..G16)
Variable costs:					
Unit material cost	8.00	+C21+2	+D21+2	+E21+2	+F21+2
Unit labor cost	4.00	+C22*1.04	+D22*1.04	+E22*1.18	+F22*1.10
Unit supplies cost	1.00	+C23	+D23	+E23	+F23
Total material cost	+C5*C21	+D5*D21	+E5*E21	+F5*F21	+G5*G21
Total labor cost	+C5*C22	+D5*D22	+E5*E22	+F5*F22	+G5*G22
Total supplies cost	+C5*C23	+D5*D23	+E5*E23	+F5*F23	+G5*G23
Total variable costs	+C25+C26+C27	+D25+D26+D27	+E25+E26+E27	+F25+F26+F27	+G25+G26+G27
Total costs	+C18+C29	+D18+D29	+E18+E29	+F18+F29	+G18+G29
Profit before taxes	+C8-C31	+D8-D31	+E8-E31	+F8-F31	+G8-G31

FIGURE 5.14 Cell Formulas for Lotus 1-2-3 Spreadsheet

hind these packages are the same as those discussed for large machine DBMSs.

Apple Computer's HyperCard is a graphically based data management software package for the Macintosh line of microcomputers. HyperCard employs the concept of hypertext—text, images, and data that are linked to other text, images, and data by buttons. Using a mouse to click on a designated button causes the linked items to be displayed on the screen. HyperCard uses a collection of stacks consisting of cards to organize information in a way that makes sense to the user. HyperCard enthusiasts believe that this package will change the way most people use computers.

Presentation Graphics   Presentation graphics is yet another important category of personal productivity software. Most of the spreadsheet packages incorporate some graphics capabilities, but they are often quite rudimentary. Borland's Quattro Pro and Microsoft's Excel (both spreadsheet packages), however, provide capabilities such as three-dimensional effects, vivid colors, and multiple type styles. The special-purpose presentation graphics packages, such as Harvard Graphics (Software Publishing), Charisma (Micrografx), Freelance Graphics (Lotus), Aldus Persuasion, CA-Cricket Graph (Computer Associates International), Claris Hollywood, and Power Point (Microsoft) provide additional features, such as finer control over fonts and colors, the ability to incorporate clip art images, and the ability to add a related graphic from an image library.

Other Personal Productivity Packages   Desktop publishing gives the user the ability to design (and eventually print) an in-house newspaper or magazine, a sales brochure, or an annual report. The more advanced word-processing packages, such as Microsoft Word and WordPerfect, provide the capability to arrange the document in appropriate columns, import figures and tables, and use appropriate type fonts and styles. Popular specialized desktop publishing packages are Ventura Publisher, Aldus PageMaker, FrameMaker (Frame Technology), Publisher for Windows (Microsoft), and Express Publisher (Power Up Software), all of which incorporate these features and more.

198

In the late 1980s Price Waterhouse, the number six accounting firm in the nation, found itself with a major problem in terms of internal communication and sharing of information. Symptoms of the problem included: "Highly paid associates shuttling between floors with stacks of paperwork, desperately trying to get sign-offs on top-priority projects. Partners in regional offices struggling to decipher complex accounting rules without the aid of centralized databases. And out-of-town partners growing frustrated when they couldn't use local offices to print out data from their 3.5-inch disks." After studying the problem the Price Waterhouse IS manager, Sheldon Laube, decided that Lotus Notes was the answer to PW's information bottleneck. In 1989, he purchased 10,000 copies of Notes—while it was still in beta testing.

It wasn't easy, but three years later Lotus Notes has fundamentally altered the way PW does business. "With the combination E-mail, database management, and bulletin board application, senior executives adopted the technology with a zeal seldom seen among bosses who typically leave word processing to their secretaries and spreadsheets to their subordinates." Notes has changed the availability and the sharing of information within PW. For example, PW partners and associates can now view, from a database, a collection of the firm's analyses of IRS rulings and opinions. Within hours of a court ruling, they can share all information about the ruling and can read the ruling itself on-line. They can now access every business proposal PW has submitted since 1989, which reduces preparation time and improves the chances of winning future contracts.

PW's success with Notes has attracted the attention of the other Big 6 firms. Arthur Andersen has purchased 20,000 copies of Notes, and will eventually license another 40,000 copies. Ernst & Young is currently engaged in a 100-copy test of Notes. And two other major firms are reportedly considering Notes as well. For Price Waterhouse, Notes has provided increased personal productivity *and* organizational productivity.

(Adapted from Mehler, 1992)

There are a number of both microcomputer and large machine statistical packages that are quite easy to use. For IBM-compatible microcomputers, Execustat (from Strategy Plus, Inc.) is easy to learn and use and has excellent graphics. Minitab is also popular and operates on IBM-compatible, Macintosh, UNIX, and VAX/VMS platforms. The most popular and powerful statistical packages are SPSS and SAS, with versions available for both microcomputers and a wide variety of larger machines.

Certainly the office automation packages mentioned in Chapter 2 qualify as personal productivity software. Both the mainframe-based packages, such as IBM's PROFS and Digital Equipment Corporation's ALL-IN-ONE, and the LAN packages, such as WordPerfect Office and Lotus Notes, provide a convenient interface for both electronic mail and scheduling.

The list of personal productivity software presented here could certainly be extended, but today's most important categories have been mentioned. New packages and new categories will most assuredly be introduced in the next few years. Software vendors, especially those operating in the microcomputer arena, will continue development of new personal productivity software packages.

Applications Packages: An Example

In our survey of key applications software, we have covered a variety of tools that may be used by an individual or an organization to develop

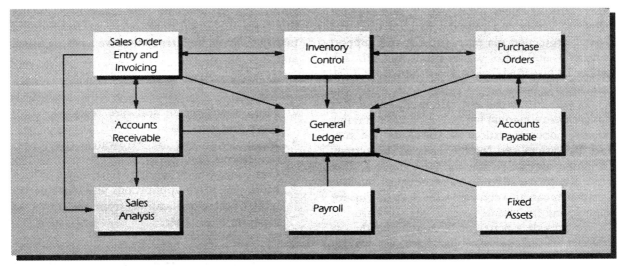

FIGURE 5.15 Modules of a Typical PC Accounting Package

needed applications—3 GLs, 4 GLs, object-oriented programming, database management systems, personal productivity software, and CASE. Often, however, applications software will be purchased from an outside source. To conclude our look at applications software, we will consider one category of purchased software—PC accounting packages—as a representative of the many categories that exist.

A typical PC accounting package includes quite a number of interrelated modules centered around the general ledger (see Figure 5.15). A special issue of *DBMS Magazine*[5] describes the characteristics of more than 100 accounting packages that run on IBM-compatible microcomputers (PCs). These packages range in price from $50 to more than $25,000 and include accounting packages designed for small manufacturers, retailers, distributors, consultants, building contractors, manufacturers representatives, physicians, and other professional service providers.

For example, the Accounting Plus™ package from Systems Plus, Inc.,[6] which claims more than 60,000 installations, is a general accounting package designed to serve retail, wholesale, and service companies. This package runs on IBM PCs or compatibles and requires at least 256,000 bytes of memory and a hard disk. Modules available (at $495 each) include General Ledger, Accounts Receivable, Accounts Payable, Inventory, Order Entry, Purchase Orders, Sales Analysis, Fixed Assets, and Payroll. It provides 200 standard reports, 20 exception reports, and 30 management reports, many of which can be customized with user-defined sorting. All modules are fully menu-driven and feature on-line data entry with error checking, on-line updating of data files, automatic file backup and recovery, and mandatory creation of a hard-copy audit trail.

There are seventy-five parameters that may be used to configure the system to individual needs, and Systems Plus will contract to customize a system to meet special requirements. The system will

---

[5] "PC accounting: CEO's guide to accounting software," compiled by the publishers and editors of *DBMS Magazine* (Winter, 1988–1989).

[6] The information on this package is taken from "PC accounting: CEO's guide to accounting software", *DBMS Magazine* (Winter, 1988–1989), and sales literature from Systems Plus, Inc., Mountain View, California.

export files in Lotus 1-2-3, ASCII, and comma-delimited forms and provides systems-level and layered protection via passwords. It will support as many as 600 linked workstations under the following LANs: IBM Token Ring, Novell, 3COM, and IBM PC Net.

In addition to the software itself, Accounting Plus includes a manual for each module containing extensive documentation for installing and running the system and for the users of the system. Telephone support is free for three months, after which it is provided for $150 per year per module. Companies can also contract with Systems Plus for training and for maintenance of the software.

To provide a better understanding of the capabilities of such software packages, we provide details on the sales order entry module of the Accounting Plus system. This module captures order data and prints customer acknowledgments, as well as updating the sales order file and allocating quantities in the inventory file. The system accepts orders from customers in the customer file for items either in the inventory file or nonstock items. Customer addresses, pricing, extensions, and item descriptions are supplied automatically and need not be keyed in (but the computer-supplied data can be overridden if desired).

When an order is ready to be shipped, the sales order file is updated with the quantity shipped, and the inventory file's allocated and on-hand quantities are reduced. Miscellaneous charges, discounts, freight, and sales tax are then entered and the invoice is printed and posted to the accounts receivable file. Shipping papers are also printed. Reports produced include customer acknowledgments, sales order listings, sales order backlog report, invoices, shipping papers, and sales analyses by customer number, part number, product group, and vendor.

THE CHANGING NATURE OF SOFTWARE

In the process of investigating the various categories of computer software for the 1990s, we have noted many of the important trends in the software arena. Building on our earlier discussions, we can explicitly identify the significant developing

patterns in the software field, emphasizing those that have the most direct relevance to you as a manager. Seven key trends that we have identified are:

1. More hardwiring of software and more microcode.
2. More sophisticated software tools for computer professionals.
3. More complexity of hardware/software arrangements.
4. Less concern with machine efficiency.
5. More purchased applications and more portability of these applications from one computer platform to another.
6. More user development.
7. More use of personal productivity software on microcomputers, especially packages with a graphical user interface (GUI).

More Hardwiring of Software and More Microcode

In their efforts to make their machines run more efficiently, hardware manufacturers will convert more of the present software—especially operating systems and other support software—into hardwiring and microcode. Hardwiring simply means building into the circuitry of the machine the same steps that were previously accomplished by carrying out a portion of a machine language program. Microcode accomplishes a similar function, in that the machine language instructions are permanently stored in read-only memory (ROM) microchips. In both cases, portions of key programs are removed from regular memory, freeing it for other purposes. Hardwiring also speeds up execution because instructions do not have to be moved to the control unit and interpreted before execution. This first trend has little direct impact on you as a manager; it is simply one way in which computers will be made more powerful.

More Sophisticated Software Tools for Computer Professionals

Extensive development work will continue on CASE tools, fourth-generation languages, object-oriented programming, and other productivity tools for computer professionals. Work on fifth-generation or natural language programming will progress. Gradually, business and government information systems organizations will adopt and employ these tools, and as they do their productivity will increase. The result should be IS organizations that are more responsive to your needs as a manager.

More Complexity of Hardware/Software Arrangements

To a much greater extent, varying configurations of hardware will be tied together by sophisticated software packages. We discussed multiprocessing and parallel processing, which involve multiple CPUs in one machine controlled by the operating system. Another way of configuring machines is to cluster several computers together, sharing common disk devices, all under control of their separate operating systems. Increasingly, separate computers are being used as front-end communication controllers and back-end file or database servers for large mainframe computers. The coordination of these various hardware resources must be handled by the mainframe operating system and complementary software in the communications machine or database server. Even applications software is being split among machines as organizations move to client/server arrangements. These more complex hardware/software arrangements are additional ways that computers may be able to assist in the efficient and effective running of a business.

Less Concern with Machine Efficiency

The cost per instruction on computers will continue to drop dramatically, as it has for the past three decades—that is, machine cycles will continue to get cheaper. On the other hand, personnel costs, both for computer professionals and managers, will continue to climb. Thus, as time passes, we will be more concerned with human efficiency and less concerned with machine efficiency. This reduced concern for machine efficiency has both direct and indirect impacts on you as a manager. It means that software tools that improve human effi-

ciency, such as 4 GLs, query languages, and CASE tools, will become more popular for computer professionals and, where appropriate, for managers. It also will lead to the development of executive workstations with voice and natural language interfaces, which are terribly inefficient from the machine standpoint.

More Purchased Applications

The higher personnel costs for computer professionals mean higher costs for in-house development of new applications software. In addition, the present backlogs for internal development of new applications are not going to disappear in the short run. The demand for new applications is also not going to slacken, particularly with the infusion of an increasing number of computer-literate managers into organizations. Add to this mix a healthy, growing, vigorous software industry marketing both developed packages (off-the-shelf software) and customized packages, and it is easy to predict a continuing growth in purchased software. Furthermore, more of the purchased applications will be portable from one computing platform to another, or will work with a variety of support software (especially database management systems). This gives organizations more flexibility in their choice of computing platforms. The advantage to you of the trend toward more purchased applications is that you will be able to get needed new applications implemented more quickly; the disadvantage is that the purchased software may not be able to do precisely what you want done in the exact way you want it done.

More User Development

The trend toward increased user development hits close to home because you and your fellow managers will carry out more software development efforts yourselves. For the most part, you will work with 4 GLs and query languages that are easy to learn and use. Why will this increase in user development occur? Because it is easier and faster for you to develop the software than to go to the information systems organization and work with them on the development (often after an extensive wait). This will be the case for many situations where you need a one-time or infrequently used report, or a decision support system to help you with a particular decision. Managers will continue to rely on the IS organization (or on purchased software) for major ongoing systems, such as production control, general ledger accounting, and human resource information systems. Because of its importance to you as managers, we have devoted all of Chapter 11 to user application development.

More Use of Personal Productivity Software on Microcomputers

This final trend is the most important one for most of you. The use of personal productivity software, especially microcomputer-based packages, will grow for managers and other professionals. Packages with a well-designed graphical user interface will increasingly be the software of choice, because a GUI makes the software easier to learn and use. Your microcomputer, linked to a mainframe computer and possibly to other microcomputers (see Chapter 6), will become as indispensable as your telephone. Unless you are out of the office, you will use it almost every hour of every day—for electronic mail, word processing, spreadsheets, database management, presentation graphics, and perhaps for desktop publishing and statistical work. For some of your jobs you will find the microcomputer so essential that you will carry a notebook version with you when you are out of your office.

THE SOFTWARE COMPONENT OF THE INFORMATION SYSTEMS INDUSTRY

Many software products have been mentioned in this chapter, as well as many software vendors, but we lack a frame of reference in which to view the software subindustry. Some of that frame of reference was provided in "The Information Sys-

tems Industry" section of Chapter 4, but that section looked at only the giants in the software sector. The "Software" column in Table 4.2 listed the top ten firms in the world in terms of software revenues: IBM, Fujitsu, Microsoft, NEC, Computer Associates International, Siemens Nixdorf, Novell, Hitachi, Lotus, and Digital Equipment Corporation. As a percentage share of total software revenues by all of the *Datamation* top 100 firms, IBM had 31.9 percent of the market, Fujitsu 9.9 percent, Microsoft 8.3 percent, NEC 5.2 percent, Computer Associates 5.0 percent, down to Digital at 2.2 percent (*Datamation*, 1993).

There are three primary groups of players in the software arena—hardware manufacturers, software houses or vendors, and consulting firms. The hardware and software vendors dominate the top ten list, with six hardware vendors and four software houses. The six hardware vendors—IBM and Digital (U.S.); Fujitsu, NEC, and Hitachi (Japan); and Siemens Nixdorf (Germany)—all have a major presence in the mainframe/minicomputer market. In this big machine market, customers usually buy their operating systems and much of their support software from their hardware vendors, but the strength of the hardware manufacturers on this list indicates that customers must also purchase a large proportion of their applications software from the hardware vendors as well.

The software houses form an interesting and competitive group. The largest and most influential is Microsoft, based in Redmond, Washington, and headed by Bill Gates, who is reportedly the richest person in America. Microsoft's 1992 revenues jumped 43 percent to a whopping $3.25 billion on the strength of a broad range of microcomputer software products, especially Windows. Other Microsoft products include PC-DOS, MS-DOS, Word, Excel, Works, Access, Foxbase, and Mail. Number two among the software vendors is Computer Associates International, based in Islandia, New York, with estimated 1992 revenue of $1.77 billion. Computer Associates produces a variety of software packages, with particular strength in mainframe database, job scheduling, security, and systems management software. The next largest software house is Novell Inc., with

1992 sales of $989 million. Novell is the leader in providing local area network management software with its NetWare line. Fourth largest is Lotus Development Corporation, developers of Lotus 1-2-3, Ami Pro, Notes, and cc:Mail, with 1992 sales of $900 million. Another large software house, which did not quite make the top ten, is Oracle, which specializes in mainframe DBMSs, with 1992 sales of $782 million. Both Computer Associates and Oracle achieved their status by building software to run on proprietary big machine platforms. Interestingly, both now view UNIX-based systems as their major growth area. Other major players are WordPerfect ($550 million), Borland ($464 million), and Legent ($446 million). For the most part, Microsoft, Novell, Lotus, WordPerfect, and Borland work in the microcomputer arena, while Computer Associates, Oracle, and Legent work predominantly with larger machines. In addition to these big software houses, there are a multitude of medium-sized to small-sized software firms. Many of the smaller firms tend to rise and fall rapidly based on the success or failure of a single product, and many small firms have gone bankrupt when they attempted and failed to develop additional products.

Consulting firms constitute the third group in the software subindustry. Within this group, the leaders are the so-called "Big Six" public accounting firms, led by Andersen Consulting. For the most part, the software developed and sold by these firms has been an outgrowth of their consulting practices and thus tends to be applications software geared to particular industries in which they have consulted extensively. There are also many smaller firms in the information systems arena that are difficult to categorize as a software house or a consulting firm because they truly operate as both. Their consulting jobs often involve writing or modifying software for a particular firm, then moving to another firm within the same industry to do a similar job.

To complete the software story, we should mention that some excellent software can be obtained from noninformation systems companies that have developed software for their own use and then later decided to market the product. The software business is dominated, however, by the

hardware manufacturers, software houses, and consulting firms, each having its own special niche. In Chapter 10, we will discuss the option of purchasing applications software.

SUMMARY

Both computer hardware and software are required for a computer system to perform useful work. The hardware actually does the work—adding two numbers, reading a record from disk, printing a line—but the software controls all of the actions of the hardware. Thus, an understanding of software is critical to comprehending how computer systems work. From a financial perspective, most organizations spend at least twice as much money on software as they spend on hardware. Further, managers will be directly dealing with a variety of software packages, while they rarely deal with hardware other than their own workstation. For all these reasons, the topic of software is a vital one for aspiring managers.

Figuratively speaking, software comes in a variety of shapes and sizes. Applications software consists of all programs written to accomplish particular tasks for computer users; support software establishes a relatively easy-to-use computing environment, translates programs into machine language, and ensures that the hardware and software resources are used efficiently. The most important piece of support software is the operating system that controls the operation of the hardware and coordinates all of the other software. Other support software includes language translators, communications interface software, database management systems, and utility programs.

Applications software is often developed within the organization using third-generation procedural languages, such as COBOL or FORTRAN, or fourth-generation nonprocedural languages, such as FOCUS or IFPS. Historically, nearly all the internal software development has been carried out by computer professionals in the information systems organization. Recently, however, more of the development has been done by end-users (including managers), using 4 GLs and DBMS query languages. The trend that impacts managers even more is the growing availability and use of personal productivity software, such as spreadsheets and microcomputer-based database management systems. We anticipate that these trends toward more user development of software and more use of personal productivity packages will continue and strengthen.

Almost all of an organization's support software and an increasing proportion of its applications software is purchased from outside the firm. The hardware manufacturers appear to supply the bulk of the support software and some of the applications programs for larger computers. Independent software houses (not associated with hardware manufacturers) are particularly important sources of mainframe applications software and microcomputer software of all types. Consulting firms are also a valuable source of applications software. When purchasing software, the organization must consider the quality and fit of the software package and the services and stability provided by the vendor.

It is hoped that this chapter has provided you with sufficient knowledge of computer software to begin to appreciate the present and potential impact of computers on your organization and your job.

REVIEW QUESTIONS

1. Briefly describe the four generations of computer programming languages, concentrating on the major differences among the generations.

2. What are the purposes of an operating system? What are the primary tasks carried out by a mainframe operating system?

3. Differentiate between multiprogramming and multiprocessing.

4. Explain the concept of virtual memory. Why is it important?

5. List the five major categories of support software.

6. Explain the concept of structured programming. Why is it important?

7. IFPS and Lotus 1-2-3 can both be used to solve the same types of problems. If you have prior experience with Lotus 1-2-3 (or one of its clones), prepare a 1-2-3 spreadsheet to present the financial plan for the years 1995–2000 for High-Tech Lawn Mower Corporation (see Figure 5.10 and associated text for the problem description). Which approach (IFPS or 1-2-3) most appeals to you?

8. IFPS and Lotus 1-2-3 can both be used to solve the same types of problems. If you have prior experience with IFPS, prepare an IFPS model to project the profit for the Second Company for the years 1996–2000 (see Figure 5.14 and associated text for the problem description). Which approach (IFPS or 1-2-3) most appeals to you?

9. What are the primary advantages of a fourth-generation language over a third-generation language? What are the primary disadvantages?

10. Three general types of file organizations were described in the text: sequential, direct, and indexed file organizations. In general terms, describe how each type of file organization works. It may be helpful to draw a diagram to depict each type of file organization.

11. Three different types of database management systems were described: hierarchical, network, and relational. Briefly describe how the data are arranged in each type of database.

12. List at least five categories of personal productivity software packages. Then concentrate on one of these categories, and describe a representative product in that category with which you are somewhat familiar. Provide both strong points and weak points of the particular product.

13. For what does the CASE acronym stand? In general, what is the purpose of CASE tools? What types of individuals are most likely to use CASE tools?

14. List at least three computer vendors that are major players in the software component of the information systems industry. List at least three independent software houses (not associated with a computer vendor) that are major players in the software component of the information systems industry. List any software products that you regularly use and indicate the firm that developed each product.

15. Some of the acronyms used in this chapter are listed below. Provide the full names for each of these acronyms.

JCL	DD/D
4 GL	BASIC
DBMS	DASD
COBOL	CASE

DISCUSSION QUESTIONS

1. From the discussion in this chapter and your own knowledge from other sources, what do you think is the most important advancement in computer software in the past five years? Why?

2. In the mid-1980s, a movement developed within the information systems industry to "stamp out COBOL" and replace it with 4 GLs and other productivity tools. Manifestations of this movement included the slogan to "Kill the COBOL programmer" (not literally, of course) and T-shirts bearing the word COBOL within the international symbol for "not permitted" (a red circle with a red line diagonally across the word COBOL). Do you think the movement will be successful in the 1990s? At some time in the future? Why?

3. You probably have had experience with at least one procedural (3 GL) language, either in high school or college. What are the strengths and weaknesses of the particular language that you know best? Based on what you have gleaned from the text, what primary advantages would be offered by a nonprocedural 4 GL over the 3

GL that you know best? What disadvantages? What primary advantages would be offered by a natural language or an object-oriented programming language over the 3 GL that you know best? What disadvantages?

4. List the pros and cons of the involvement of managers in the end-user computing revolution. What strengths and weaknesses do managers bring to the software development process? Is it appropriate for managers to be directly involved in applications software development?

5. According to the statistics quoted from *Datamation* magazine, IBM controls more than 30 percent of the software market worldwide (among the top 100 companies). With this degree of dominance by one firm, has the software subindustry truly been competitive, particularly over the past decade? Support your position.

6. Which one category of personal productivity software is of most value to you now as a student? Why? Within this category, what is your favorite software package? Why?

7. Which one category of personal productivity software do you expect to be of most value to you in your career? Why? Is this different from the category you selected in the previous question? Why or why not?

8. Based on your own computing experience and your discussions with other computer users, which one category of personal productivity software needs the most developmental work to make it useful to managers? What type of development is needed?

REFERENCES

1993. "Global leaders in nine product categories." *Datamation* 39 (June 15): 22–23.

Cummings, Steve. 1992. "Gearing up for the object-oriented express." *Corporate Computing* 1 (June-July): 285–287.

Jenkins, A. Milton, and Bijoy Bordoloi. 1986. "The evolution and status of fourth-generation languages: A tutorial." Institute for Research on the Management of Information Systems (IRMIS) Working Paper #W611, Indiana University Graduate School of Business.

Kador, John. 1989. "Kawasaki prefers 4 GL over COBOL for on-line development." *MIS Week* 10 (October 16): 22, 24.

Kaplan, Michael. 1992. "Tracking technologies." *Beyond Computing* 1 (August-September): 50–55.

Lindholm, Elizabeth. 1992. "The portable 4 GL?" *Datamation* 38 (April 1): 83–85.

Mehler, Mark. 1992. "Notes fanatic." *Corporate Computing* 1 (August): 160–164.

Moad, Jeff. 1989. "The allure of UNIX." *Datamation* 35 (September 15): 20–24.

Ricciuti, Mike. 1992. "Industrial strength UNIX management tools." *Datamation* 38 (May 1): 71–74.

———. 1993. "Other UNIX systems tools are on the way." *Datamation* 39 (February 1): 57–60.

Wohl, Amy D. 1992. "Playing the GUI card." *Beyond Computing* 1 (December): 54–55.

5

Batesville Casket Company

Batesville Casket Company is a subsidiary of Hillenbrand Industries, Inc., a diversified holding company headquartered in the small southern Indiana town of Batesville. Other Hillenbrand subsidiaries include: American Tourister, Inc., a major U.S. luggage manufacturer; Medeco Security Locks, a leading producer of high security locks; Hill-Rom Company, the leading U.S. producer of electric hospital beds, patient room furniture, and patient handling equipment; SSI Medical Services, a leading provider of wound care and other therapy units and services; Block Medical, a leading producer of home infusion therapy products; and Forethought, an insurance company that offers specialized funeral planning products through funeral homes.

In its twenty years of operation as a publicly held company, Hillenbrand Industries has had exponential growth in revenues, cash flow, and profits. Revenues have grown from about $75 million in 1971 to almost $1.2 billion in 1991, and earnings per share have increased from about 10 cents to $1.22. Highlights of Hillenbrand Industries financial performance for 1989–91 are presented in Exhibit 1.

Headquartered in Batesville, Indiana, Batesville Casket Company, Inc., is the world's largest producer of metal and hardwood burial caskets, having a significant percentage of the U.S. market for its products. Batesville Casket serves more than 16,000 funeral homes in the continental United States, Canada, and

Puerto Rico. It operates six manufacturing plants that are specialized by product line. To provide optimum customer service, it has 66 strategically located distribution warehouses (called Customer Service Centers) from which it delivers caskets to funeral homes using its own truck fleet.

Batesville Casket's managers believe that long-term success will result from listening to their funeral director–customers and responding to their needs better than anyone else. Batesville is committed to listening to these customers in their plants, their offices, their Customer Service Centers, their sales organization—literally everywhere they do business. Another key element in Batesville Casket's strategy for achieving total customer satisfaction is to continually improve all processes and methods so that the company can serve its customers more effectively.

The MIS Department

The MIS department is responsible for providing information systems and services to Batesville Casket. As shown in Exhibit 2, applications development is basically organized functionally, with teams serving logistics, sales and marketing, and manufacturing. The Computer Aided Manufacturing group is responsible for interfacing manufacturing systems with the machines in the factories. The Data Center operates an IBM 4381 mainframe. Last year Batesville Casket spent only .73 percent of its revenue on MIS.

James J. Kuisel, who reports to the senior vice president and chief financial officer, has been director of MIS for fourteen years. Until recently the MIS department has had most of the responsibility for systems projects, but it is now sharing more of this responsibility with the users. Another major thrust of the department is toward use of client/server networks rather than the mainframe. This is not just a matter of less costly processing on personal computers (PCs), but it also takes advantage of the competitive

This case was prepared by Professor E. W. Martin as the basis for class discussion rather than to illustrate either effective or ineffective handling of an administrative situation. Its development was supported by the Institute for Research on the Management of Information Systems (IRMIS), School of Business, Indiana University.

EXHIBIT 1
·················
Hillenbrand Industries Financial Highlights

Dollars in thousands except per share data

Results of Operations	Fiscal Year			Percent Change	
	1991	1990	1989	1991/90	1990/89
Net revenues:					
Industrial					
Durables	$ 146,973	$ 159,872	$ 161,479	(8.1%)	(1.0%)
Health Care	592,998	523,846	469,408	13.2	11.6
Caskets	396,894	384,217	350,217	3.3	9.7
Total	1,136,865	1,067,935	981,104	6.5	8.9
Insurance	62,009	38,627	19,677	60.5	96.3
Total net revenues	1,198,874	1,106,562	1,000,781	8.3	10.6
Operating profit by segment:					
Industrial					
Durables	(2,721)	7,613	14,638	(135.7)	(48.0)
Health Care	91,883	73,453	81,143	25.1	(9.5)
Caskets	78,792	68,270	56,891	15.4	20.0
Total	167,954	149,336	152,672	12.5	(2.2)
Insurance	2,552	(1,397)	(5,009)	282.7	72.1
Total operating profit by segment	170,506	147,939	147,663	15.3	.2
Other items	(24,847)	(21,599)	(26,297)	15.0	(17.9)
Income taxes	56,472	50,662	50,048	11.5	1.2
Net income	89,187	75,678	71,318	17.9	6.1
Earnings per common share*	1.22	1.02	.96	19.6	6.3
Dividends per common share*	.29	.275	.25	5.5	10.0
Return on average equity	19.7%	18.2%	19.5%	N/A	N/A
Average shares outstanding (000's)*	72,885	73,971	74,377	(1.5)	(.5)
Shareholders	11,000	9,800	9,500	12.2	3.2
Employees	10,500	9,500	9,000	10.5	5.6

* Reflects two-for-one stock split effective February 28, 1992

environment for a whole array of software products. "Software products for the mainframe are very expensive—$250,000 for a Human Resource System," Kuisel explains. "There are only a few mainframe suppliers who have developed highly complex systems that cost an arm and a leg. But for the client/server environment there are hundreds of developers, all competing with aggressive pricing."

With the help of an outside consultant, Batesville Casket is concentrating on reducing cycle time of business processes. The MIS department is heavily involved in process mapping the company and in analyzing each process to take "non–value added"

time out of it. Kuisel is the head of the "Make to Market" team that is leading this process, and many others from MIS are involved in the other teams that are working on this project.

Kuisel is proactive in the use of new technology. "We want to be leaders," he asserts, "but not heat seekers. Where we can make a tremendous gain by getting on the bleeding edge, then we will go ahead and take the risk. But when the business is not going to benefit greatly, then we will let the technology mature so that we do not waste resources. We want the business need, not the technology, to drive us, and we try to minimize the risk."

EXHIBIT 2
Organization of MIS Department

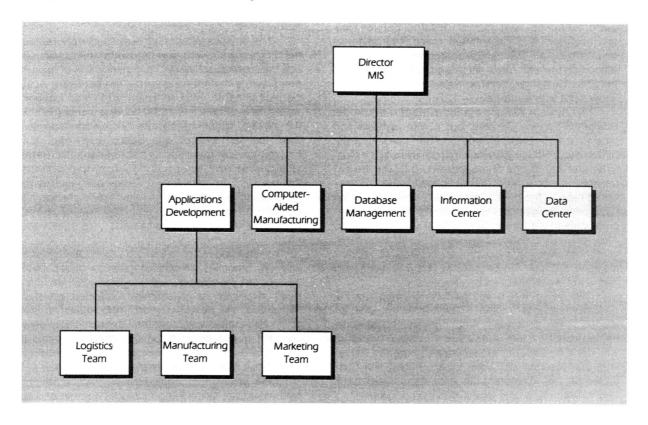

··
The Distribution System

Logistics is an important area at Batesville Casket. Caskets are bulky and heavy items, so transportation costs are significant when distributing them on a national basis. Furthermore, when a funeral director has a demand for a specific casket that he does not have in his relatively limited stock, he must have that casket in time for the family visitation and funeral, a matter of a day or two at most. So the ability to deliver a specific model quickly is essential to good customer service.

As mentioned above, Batesville Casket distributes its products through 66 Customer Service Centers. The typical Customer Service Center has a manager and a small staff of warehouse–worker/drivers, most of whom are out of the Customer Service Center much of the time delivering caskets. Although the

Batesville Casket product line includes several hundred models, the typical Customer Service Center stocks only a portion of these, depending upon the preferences of the funeral directors it serves.

In the early 1980s, Batesville Casket was a pioneer in the development of PC-based distributed systems. Working together, the MIS and logistics departments developed a PC-based system that was installed in each of the Customer Service Centers. This system served most of the operational needs of the Customer Service Center, including order entry from the customer, maintaining the Customer Service Center inventory by model and serial number, and keeping track of where each casket was located in the warehouse. It included a routing model that accepted the delivery requirements for the day, determined the route that each truck should take in order to deliver the caskets most efficiently, and printed out the routing and the sequence in which the truck should be loaded so that the first casket to be delivered was the last casket on the truck.

Through a dial-up network, each night the Customer Service Center PC transmitted that day's orders to the central computer in Batesville that handled customer billing, kept track of Customer Service Center inventory, and determined inventory replenishment schedules. The central computer then sent information on the next day's shipments back to the PC so that the Customer Service Center manager would know what was en route.

This system replaced a lot of paperwork in the Customer Service Centers, but it was justified and paid for on the basis of reducing the time to get the billing out. With the previous manual system the Customer Service Center managers would fill out the paperwork, batch it, and mail it to Batesville, so they would receive the billing information from three to ten days after the casket was delivered. With the computer system they could get the bills out the next day. Also, the system enabled the centers to respond more quickly to demand and, through centralized replenishment, reduced the probability that a desired item would not be available when needed.

This system was developed using a then-new PC development tool, called Knowledge-Man, that included a 4th generation language and a database management system. Since some of the processing was done by the central mainframe system in Batesville and the rest was done by the PCs in the Customer Service Centers, with data transmitted back and forth at night, this was a distributed system.

When the system was installed, most of the Customer Service Center managers had never even seen a computer, did not know what a floppy disk was, and had no experience with a computer keyboard, so they were initially reluctant to become hands-on computer users. But with a lot of help and training they converted to the new system, and soon they became enthusiastic users of the new computer system.

The Decision to Replace the Customer Service Center System

The hardware for the PC-based Customer Service Center system was an early IBM PC with the 8086 chip, plus a 10-megabyte hard disk. Although the system had been enhanced over the years and was working well, by 1990 Batesville Casket had reached the limit of what could be done with this first-generation hardware, and there were a number of things that the logistics people wanted to do in the near future to improve Customer Service Center operations. But the major problem was that the equipment was so old and obsolete that some maintenance contractors were not willing to continue to service some of the components of the hardware. It was clear that the hardware was on its last legs.

One obvious alternative was to merely replace the old hardware with new hardware and continue to use the existing software. The functionality of the system would remain the same, but the hardware would be maintainable, and sufficient additional capacity would be available to support future enhancements of the system. Unfortunately, the Knowledge-Man software that the system was based upon had gone through several releases, and the version that Batesville Casket was using was no longer supported by the vendor. Even if Batesville Casket continued to use the existing software, they would have to change it to conform to the current version of Knowledge-Man, which would involve a substantial reprogramming effort.

In 1990 Jan Holm, a senior systems analyst, and Jerry W. Munchel, an MIS program manager, spent several months working with the logistics area to explore expectations concerning logistics developments over the next five years. "We looked at their goals and objectives, how they expected Batesville Casket's manufacturing and distribution systems to evolve, and projects they were anticipating that might impact the needs of the system," Holm reports.

One idea under consideration was to identify each casket by bar-coding its model number and serial number so that the casket could be automatically tracked through the production and distribution system. Logistics managers expected to place a hand-held bar-code reader on the loading dock at each Customer Service Center and connect it to the Customer Service Center PC through a radio-frequency link. Then they could automatically enter the identification of each casket into the computer as it was received into or sent out of the Customer Service Center. Also, in order to further reduce cycle times, they wanted to send orders to the factory several times a day rather than sending them all at night. Furthermore, they wanted to replace the routing software package that was part of the system with a more powerful version.

Batesville Casket's increased emphasis on total customer satisfaction was also leading logistics to plan significant additions to the system to enable them to capture data on service quality and improve customer service. For example, many funeral directors order by description rather than model number, so a Customer Service Center manager sometimes misunderstands and sends the wrong casket to the funeral home. Therefore, logistics would like to have a system that maintains a history of orders and allows for improved identification of the models being ordered.

Therefore, in early 1991 the MIS department set up a team to investigate alternatives and recommend what should be done. Munchel headed the team, and the other members were Holm, Kenneth D. Fairchild, director of Technical Support, and Delbert Rippeltoe, manager of Database Administration. Munchel and Holm had been instrumental in the development of the old system, and Fairchild was responsible for the communications between the office and the Customer Service Centers.

....

Deciding What Technology to Use

The logistics study convinced the team that they needed to significantly revise the software in addition to replacing the hardware, and it also provided the basis for a number of critical decisions relating to the future technological platform. "Once we decided to replace the hardware, we had to determine how big and how fast the computers should be and what operating system to use," Fairchild explains, "and when we decided to redo the software we had to determine what database manager and development environment to use."

The hardware and operating system decisions were relatively straightforward. The plan to place barcode readers at the loading dock and enter data from them directly into the computer determined that the new computers must be multi-tasking. Otherwise, the Customer Service Center manager would have to interrupt his work with the computer whenever the barcode reader was used. Another reason for multi-tasking was that logistics managers wanted to be able to transmit orders to Batesville during the day without interrupting computer support of normal Customer Service Center operations.

They concluded that an IBM-compatible 386-based computer would have all the processing power that the Customer Service Centers were likely to need during the next few years, and they wanted computers that could be upgraded if needs expanded even more than they planned. They chose an IBM PS/2 Model A16 with 4 megabytes of memory, a math co-processor, a color monitor, a mouse, and a 160-megabyte hard disk. They chose a Hayes 9600 Ultra external

modem for communications with Batesville and an Epson LQ1170 printer. In order to minimize error and downtime problems, they decided to install an uninterruptible power supply at each site. The total hardware cost for each site was over $8,000.

The operating system had to support multi-tasking, and they only considered IBM's OS/2 and UNIX. Windows was not considered because its DOS base was not considered robust enough for the Customer Service Center operations. They chose OS/2 primarily because they were concerned that there would be a shortage of business software packages that operated under UNIX. In particular, they knew of no routing packages that would run under UNIX.

The database manager and development environment were related decisions, for the development environment had to support the chosen database manager. One critical issue that strongly influenced their decisions at this point was the choice of a user interface. Intuitively they felt that the new system should be based on a graphical user interface, where system functions would be controlled by using a mouse to select options by pointing and clicking on icons, buttons, decision bars, and pull-down menus. The Apple Macintosh, Microsoft Windows, and OS/2 Presentation Manager employ graphical user interfaces.

"We did not know how the Customer Service Center managers would react to using a mouse," Holm explains, "but when we looked at the interactive software packages that were becoming available, they were mouse-driven, windowing, graphical. The upgrade to our router package that logistics was considering has a mouse-driven, windowing user interface. We knew that the managers were going to have to learn how to interact with those packages anyway, so we decided that we needed to be graphical as well."

As an example of such a graphical interface, the order update screen from the new system (shown in Exhibit 3) allows a Customer Service Center manager to update an existing order. This order is from the ABC FUNERAL HOME for product number 7878. A casket, serial number WA7915, has been allocated to this order, and other information on this order is shown on the screen. The buttons along the right show the things a manager can do to this order by using the mouse to point to the button and click. The top two buttons allow him to navigate to the next and prior orders. Other buttons allow him to change data on the order, cancel the order, allocate or unallocate a specific casket to the order, assign it to a route for

EXHIBIT 3
....
Order Update Screen

```
┌─────────────────────────────────────────────────────────────────┐
│                          Order-Update2                           │
├─────────────────────────────────────────────────────────────────┤
│  Location - 0001   ABC FUNERAL HOME                    DELIVER    │
│                    1001 MAIN STRE, HOMETOWN, INDI    05-20-92 08:51│
│  Product -7878   Order Type -  D  Manifest -          [ Next Ordr ]│
│  Serial -  [ WA7915                              ]    [ Prior Ordr]│
│  Route -  [ LOCAL ]                                   [ Change ]   │
│  Okay to Deliver - [Y]   To Their Whse - [N]          [ Cancel ]   │
│  Delv Comm - [ DELIVER BY NOON ON 5/25          ]     [ Allocate ] │
│  Pick Comm - [                                  ]     [ Unallocate]│
│  Bill Comm - [                                  ]     [ Assign ]   │
│  One Time Bill to - [ ]   Open Tm1 - [  :  ]          [ Remove ]   │
│  Discount - [T254]        Close Tm1 - [  :  ]         [ Chg Route ]│
│  PO# - [        ]         Open Tm2 - [  :  ]          [ Quit ]     │
│  Norm Whse - [  ]         Close Tm2 - [  :  ]                      │
│  Deceased - [                      ]                              │
└─────────────────────────────────────────────────────────────────┘
```

delivery, remove it from an assigned route, change the route, or quit the order update process.

Once they decided to use a graphical interface, the development environment had to support the easy creation (or "painting") of graphical screens. This led them to consider Object/1, a tool that Holm knew supported object-oriented programming and that claimed to allow a developer to paint dozens of graphical screens in a day. Object/1 was a product of MDBS, Inc., a small software house located in Lafayette, Indiana, which furnished the Knowledge-Man system that had been used to support the original Customer Service Center system. Since Batesville Casket had a long and favorable experience with

MDBS, it was natural for the team to take a hard look at Object/1.

They did not know much about object-oriented programming at the time, but they were aware that it was creating a lot of excitement in the industry. Software industry gurus such as William H. Gates, Microsoft's chairman, Philippe Kahn, president of Borland International, and Steven P. Jobs, who founded Apple Computer and Next, were predicting that object-oriented technology would have a revolutionary impact on the future use of computers.

Object-oriented programming was extolled as a way to increase development productivity by creating programs composed of completely independent components (code modules). These building blocks are freely interchangeable among different programs, so as an organization builds up more and more such modules, new systems require creating less and less new code. Also, maintenance is much easier because functions are isolated in modules and thus easy to locate, and once a module is corrected in one system it can easily be corrected in all the other systems which use that module.

The team did not do an extensive search of development environments. "We did not have a lot of time to search," Fairchild reports, "so we looked at the products that we had in house that we had used before, and we looked at object-oriented programming and made the decision."

They chose Object/1 for a number of reasons in addition to its reputed development and maintenance efficiency. First, it would provide outstanding support for the graphical user interface approach that they wanted to use, and it could access a database manager that provided the backup and recovery capability that they needed with multi-tasking. Second, industry seemed to be heading that way, and to keep near the leading edge was important to them. Finally, as Holm notes, "We could have used one of our familiar tools, but there would have been no learning experience for the department, and we enjoy the challenge!"

"The team wanted to do something new and exciting, and I knew that they would dedicate themselves to making it a success," Kuisel explains. "Since we knew exactly what the system was to do, and the old system was working well in the short run, there was little risk other than the new technology. Object-oriented programming looked like it might be very important to us as we use PC platforms more extensively, so this was an investment in the future."

Learning to Use Object-Oriented Programming

Object-oriented programming appears to be simple because there are only a few basic terms to learn: object, method, class, inheritance, and encapsulation. But it is also a new paradigm or way of thinking about programs, and it is not easy to explain.

An *object* can represent anything of interest—a number, a date, a screen, a casket, a customer—anything that involves data. An object includes *both* the data describing the object and all of the *methods* that can operate on that object. Each method, then, is a code module that does something to or with the data of the object. *Encapsulation* refers to the binding together of the data and the methods that operate on the object; the only way that an object can be operated on is by means of its methods. Thus, the object is protected from actions performed by other parts of the program, or from actions of other programs that may use that object. Objects are the building blocks from which all programs are built, and because of encapsulation the same objects can be used by many different programs. Once the methods of an object are correct, they are correct everywhere that object is used. When one changes a method, it is changed everywhere that object is used.

"A mortgage is an example of an object," Holm explains. "There are things that you want to do against a mortgage. You might want to calculate a present value, or determine the return on investment. The mortgage has some data associated with it—interest rate, payment amount, amount owed, etc. Then there are routines that you perform against that mortgage when you ask questions about current balance, or the effect on payment amount of a change in interest rate. In object-oriented terminology, these routines are called methods, and they are encapsulated in the object. So when you ask a question of an object, you don't know or care how it gets the answer. If there are ten other systems that need to ask that question, they all ask that same object. And if you decide that you want to change how you calculate the answer, you change the method in the one object and it is changed in all the systems."

The concept of a *class* is closely related to the concept of an object. A class is an abstract object that includes the characteristics (both data and methods) that are common to the objects that comprise it. For example, automobiles might be a class, and Ford Mustang and Buick Skylark might be the objects of that class. Classes are hierarchical—if vehicles were a class, then automobiles would be a subclass and trucks might be another subclass. What makes this concept powerful is *inheritance*. If one creates a new object in a class, it automatically inherits all of the properties of that class, and it is only necessary to add the data and methods that are unique to the new object.

"For example," explains Fairchild, "data might be a class, with alphanumeric data being one subclass and numeric data being another subclass. Then an integer might be a sub-subclass within that subclass of numeric data, and a decimal number might be another sub-subclass and a binary number might be another sub-subclass. Integers and decimal numbers and binary numbers would all inherit certain methods from the numeric data subclass, which would also inherit common methods from the data class."

One of the things that makes Object/1 so powerful is that it comes with some 300 classes and 3,000 methods already defined and ready for use. And whenever you create new objects or classes they become available for use in all subsequent programs.

As has been previously noted, Object/1 already includes the objects necessary to create graphical screens, so they may be painted with no traditional programming. The screen painting utility displays a blank screen (called a *canvas*) along with a set of symbols denoting the various things that can be placed on a screen—buttons, list boxes, data entry boxes, display boxes, labels, etc. To create the button "Next Ordr" on the screen in Exhibit 3, for example, one would use the mouse to point and click on the symbol for push buttons. Then you use the mouse to point to the position on the screen where you want this button to appear and click again. This brings up a screen that allows you to enter the name of the push button and the method to be invoked when this button is selected. To create the entry field labeled "Serial," you would click on the symbol for entry field, point to where it should appear, and click to bring up a screen that allows you to enter the name of the field, and so forth. If you do not like where you have placed an object, the mouse can be used to "drag" it to another position. When finished, you give the screen a name and it becomes an object that inherits all the methods that have been created for the screen class of objects.

As an example of object-oriented programming, Exhibit 4 presents the code invoked by clicking on the *Change* button on the order update screen shown in Exhibit 3. Methods are invoked to operate on ob-

jects by the following notation:

```
MethodName(ObjectName, P1, P2,...)
```

When a pair of parentheses encloses a list of symbols separated by commas, the left-most symbol is the name of an object, and the other symbols in the list (if any) designate parameters that are used by the method. The name of the method to be applied to the object precedes the left parenthesis.

Consider line 8 of Exhibit 4:

```
found=
returnValueOf(new(OrdrChg, self));
```

This nested pair of methods would execute from the inside out, so the method *new* would be applied to the object *OrdrChg* with the parameter *self*. But the object *OrdrChg* is the screen shown in Exhibit 5, which has methods that allow the manager to point to any box and enter or change the data in that box. In this example, we have typed **pick comment** in the box labeled *Pick Comm*.

When the manager is through making changes to the data shown on this screen, he uses the mouse to click on the *Accept* button on this screen. This button is an object, and clicking on it invokes a method that completes the change process and returns to the method *new*, which creates a new version of the object *OrdrChg* (and completes the actions enclosed within the parentheses in line 8). Then the method *returnValueOf* is applied to this new version of the object *OrdrChg* to store a returned value into the object *found*. The result of the entire process shown in Exhibit 4 is to display the screen shown in Exhibit 6.

In the above, the object *OrdrChg* is an instance of a class that comes from Object/1, and the methods *new* and *returnValueOf* were inherited from existing objects in Object/1. All of the button objects are instances of the button class from Object/1, and all the screens are instances of a screen class from Object/1.

Although these basic concepts may seem relatively straightforward, the team found that it was not easy to learn to use them effectively. "We had a much longer learning curve than we expected," Munchel reports. "We had a training problem. When we decided on Object/1, the next vendor training class was scheduled for two months later, and we couldn't wait that long. So we brought in a consultant to do an abbreviated version of the training, and we did not get the training we needed. We ended up working through tutorials while we were trying to get started with coding the system."

EXHIBIT 4
Code for Change Button

```
/* Handle change pushbutton. */
method OrdrUpd2::change(self, mp1, mp2)
{
        local found;
        show(self, false);
        beginTransaction(session);
        getCurrent(self);
        found = returnValueOf(new(OrdrChg, self));
        commitTransaction(session);
        if(found != MBID_CANCEL)
        {
         get(recordHandles[0], subString(textOf(locIdName), 0, 4));
         fillScreen2(self);
         setText(message, "Order information changed");
        }
        else
        {
         setText(message, "Order information change bypassed");
        }
        nullCurrencies(session);
        show(self, true);
        focusOn(self);
        return nil;
}
```

This lack of formal training was critical because object-oriented programming is so different. "Object-oriented really is a totally different mind-set," Fairchild notes. "I couldn't find anything to relate it to in my twenty-five years of programming experience. In fact, my past experience often led me astray!"

"We didn't really understand the terminology," Holm explains. "It sounded like doubletalk—we laugh now. But once in a while the light would pop on and we'd think we understood. And then we would go on and find that we did not completely understand that, and we would have to go back to the beginning again. It was a highly repetitive process."

Not only did they have to learn the concepts, but they also had to learn how to use the Object/1 tool. Object/1 provides many classes and objects that one can use, but it takes some time to become familiar with what is there. "MDBS, Inc. provides a big book that contains descriptions of all these classes and methods," Fairchild explains, "and we had to learn whether to use one of theirs or write one of our own. It

took us a long time to figure out what classes we were creating and maintaining. And we had to teach the other programmers (and ourselves) to look for existing methods before starting to code something new."

Object/1 supports the programmer by providing an on-line list of all the available objects and classes. When the programmer selects a class or object, a list of all the methods that apply to it appears on the screen. When a new object or method is created, it is automatically added to this on-line display. Object/1 also includes an on-line editor that enables a programmer to create code on the screen, and edit it to make changes. Thus Object/1 provides powerful assistance for on-line programming.

Developing the System

The team was scheduled to install the system in December 1991. They planned to train the Customer Service Center managers in December, when they

EXHIBIT 5
Order Change Screen

```
                                    Order-Change

    Location - 0001    ABC FUNERAL HOME                    Product - 7878


    Serial -  [ WA7915                                                    ]

    Okay to Deliver - [Y]   To Their Whse - [N]

    Delv Comm - [ DELIVER BY NOON ON 5/25                                 ]

    Pick Comm - [ pick comment                                           ]

    Bill Comm - [                                                         ]

    One Time Bill to - [    ]   Open Tm1 - [  :  ]

    Discount - [T254]          Close Tm1 - [  :  ]

    PO# - [           ]        Open Tm2 - [  :  ]                [ Accept ]

    Norm Whse - [    ]         Close Tm2 - [  :  ]               [  Quit  ]

    Deceased - [                ]
```

were to be in Batesville for a national meeting, thus saving about $70,000 that it would cost to fly them in at another time. Although the team had decided on Object/1 in early June, because of their long learning curve they did not produce any usable code until early September.

By working seventy-hour weeks, Holm, Fairchild, and two additional programmers were able to complete about 80 percent of the functionality of the system—the day-to-day operations necessary to run a Customer Service Center—by the training date in December, so they were able to train the Customer Service Center managers at the scheduled time. But the system was far from ready to install—they still had to complete the remaining 20 percent of the functionality and take care of fundamental system operations like transaction logging and record locking. They also had to develop a system to convert the data files in the present system to the form required by the new system.

They also had to redo the data model of the old system. "Although about 95 percent of the data were there in the old system," Holm recalls, "the new model does not look like the model we had in the old system. We had to rethink the data in terms of object-oriented concepts."

EXHIBIT 6
Changed Order Update Screen

```
                          Order-Update2

   Location - 0001   ABC FUNERAL HOME                        DELIVER

                     1001 MAIN STRE, HOMETOWN, INDI          05-20-92 08:51

   Product -7878   Order Type -  D   Manifest -              [ Next Ordr ]

   Serial -  [ WA7915                                  ]     [ Prior Ordr ]

   Route -   [ LOCAL   ]                                     [ Change ]

   Okay to Deliver -[Y]   To Their Whse -[N]                 [ Cancel ]

   Delv Comm - [ DELIVER BY NOON ON 5/25               ]     [ Allocate ]

   Pick Comm - [ PICK COMMENT                          ]     [ Unallocate ]

   Bill Comm - [                                       ]
                                                             [ Assign ]
   One Time Bill to - [  ]  Open Tm1 - [ : ]
                                                             [ Remove ]
   Discount - [T254]       Close Tm1 - [ : ]

   PO# - [          ]      Open Tm2 - [ : ]                  [ Chg Route ]

   Norm Whse - [  ]        Close Tm2 - [ : ]

   Deceased - [                 ]                            [ Quit ]

   Order information changed
```

The final system includes about forty data objects, such as an order object, a customer object, and a casket object. There are many other objects, such as input and output screen objects. And they have created about ten "utility" classes, such as the *print* class that their programmers always use when printing a report. This print class includes methods that take care of the date, positioning column headers,

page counts, spacing, accumulating and printing totals, and all the other things that are necessary to
create a printed report.

Converting to the New System

Rather than the team going to each Customer Service
Center to assist them in converting to the new system,
the team devoted about two man-months to the creation of an elaborate conversion system to guide the
Customer Service Center manager through the forty-
odd steps necessary to install the new OS/2 operating
system, load the new software on the hard disk, and
convert the files from the old to the new system. It
takes between six and twelve hours to complete the
conversion process at each Customer Service Center.
And since there had been such a long time between
the training in December and the actual installation of
the system in April, the team also prepared and sent
out a training version of the system in March so that
the Customer Service Center managers could practice installing the system and play with it to refamiliar-
ize themselves with the operation of the new system.

In mid-March 1992, they tested the system in the
Customer Service Center in Indianapolis, and they
began to convert to the new system in the rest of the
Customer Service Centers in early April. When they
converted the first four Customer Service Centers,
they encountered a mysterious bug that set them
back for a while. On rare occasions the system would
mysteriously lock up and they would have to shut it
down and reload the software. With new hardware, a
new operating system, the Object/1 development system, and the new application system, they were in
totally unfamiliar territory and had to call in experts
from IBM and the software vendor MDBS to help them
diagnose and correct the problem, which turned out
to be a bug in OS/2. As of June 1992, the system was
successfully installed in all the Customer Service
Centers.

Batesville Casket had purchased fifteen of the
new computers in late 1990 and installed them in
Customer Service Centers early in 1991, running the
old software on them. The system really flew! But the
new system operates slower on the new hardware
than the old system does, and the Customer Service
Center managers that had used the old system on the
new hardware have noticed this slowdown. The new
system is slower because Object/1 programs are interpreted rather than compiled in this first generation
version of the software.

Evaluation of This Experience

Although the team learned a tremendous amount
about the object-oriented approach, they realize that
they still have more to learn. "We need to change our
approach to design as well as to writing code," Holm
asserts. "We think we are in pretty good shape in
object-oriented analysis, but we need to go back and
work more on system and program design." Fairchild
recalls that: "As part of the tool they say that a method
should probably not exceed fifteen to twenty lines of
code, but we have some with a couple of hundred. We
need to go back with what we have learned and rethink some of the things we have done."

They obviously did not meet the original December 1991 deadline for installing the system. After getting through the long learning curve, it took them
about five months to code the system. "We did a lot
of work in a short amount of time, even including
the learning curve," Fairchild notes. "Without the
Object/1 tool, I do not know how we could have produced a system with the graphical interface that we
now have."

"The first system you develop using object-oriented programming may take about the same amount
of time that it would using traditional approaches,"
Fairchild continues. "But where you are really going
to make hay is on the next and succeeding systems.
You don't have to go back and rewrite any of the
things that you have already done. You can use the
objects and methods that you have created, and they
will port right into any new system. For example, we
can use our print class in any new system, and there
are many objects like that."

Holm notes that there are even wider implications. "One inventory control system, no matter what
the industry, is much like any other. The object-oriented approach allows us to take advantage of that
commonality. I would be comfortable taking this system to any company that is running a distribution
warehouse, and it could be easily modified to suit its
needs.

"Tools like Object/1 will eventually have an inventory control set of classes and methods that will
allow any organization to easily put together an inventory control system to suit its needs. You will be able
to make changes to reflect the uniqueness of your
organization, while still taking advantage of all the
commonality. You will be able to quickly create a
working system from common objects, try it, and
quickly modify it to suit your special needs."

Kuisel evaluates the project as follows: "It has taken longer than we planned, and a late project is always a disappointment. But the new system appears to be just what we wanted, and there is a lot of excitement about using it. The old system was getting to be a little shaky, but I'm confident that the new one is a solid foundation for what we want to do in the future.

"Moreover," Kuisel continues, "we have learned a lot about the object-oriented approach and how to use it. After this is over, we will evaluate this and other tools available in the marketplace and see what fits our needs best. I suspect that the object-oriented approach is going to come out ahead, but our development people will make that decision. They are the ones that must go through the very difficult learning curve to adapt to the object-oriented approach, so they must make their own commitment if we are to adopt this new technology for widespread use."

6

Telecommunications and Networking

This chapter is the last of a trio of chapters devoted to the building blocks of information technology. If every computer were a stand-alone unit with no connections to other computers, and there was no way of receiving input from or sending output to workstations or sites physically removed from the computer, then hardware and software would be the end of the story as far as computers are concerned. In fact, until about two decades ago, that was the end of the story. Today, however, virtually all medium- and large-scale computers and a rapidly increasing proportion of microcomputers communicate directly with other workstations or computers by means of an incredible variety of networks. In addition to computer (or data) communications, today's organizations also depend heavily on voice (telephone) and image (video and facsimile) communication. This chapter explores the increasingly important topic of telecommunications and networking.

The goal of this chapter is to cover only the telecommunications and networking technology that you as a user-manager need to know. You need to understand the roles and general capabilities of various types of transmission media and networks, but you do not need to know all the technical details. You certainly need to know the important terminology and concepts relating to telecommunications and networking. Most important, you need to understand the interrelationships between hardware, software, and telecommunica-

tions and networking so that you can use the full gamut of information technology to increase your personal productivity and the effectiveness of your organization.

Change is everywhere in the information technology domain, but nowhere is this change more evident and more dramatic than in the realm of telecommunications and networking. A communications revolution is taking place that is directly or indirectly affecting the job of every manager.

The breakup of American Telephone & Telegraph (AT&T) in 1984 created an environment in which a large number of firms are now competing to develop and market telecommunications equipment and services. Partially because of this increased competition, innovation in the telecommunications and networking arena has been at an all-time high. Digital networks, fiber optic cabling, and the ability to send both voice and data over the same wires at the same time have contributed to the revolution.

At the same time, most large American businesses have restructured internally to reduce layers of middle management and create a leaner organization. They have also tended to decentralize operations in order to respond more quickly to market opportunities and competitors' actions. The net result of these internal changes is that communication has become more important than ever for the remaining, often geographically dispersed,

> ## "THE NETWORK IS THE COMPUTER"
>
> "The network is the computer" seems to be the catch phrase of the computer industry these days, with good reason. Our conventional notion of a computer system has been considerably altered by new technologies in the 1980s. The network is emerging as the core around which to build information systems into the next decade and beyond.
>
> (*I/S Analyzer,*
> **December 1989**)

managers. They need rapid, reliable voice and data communication with other parts of the company and with suppliers and customers. Small businesses are also more dependent upon communication than ever before, and developments such as local area networks and increased functionality of the public telephone network have helped fill this need. Internal needs and external competition and innovation have combined to create a late twentieth century communications revolution. The aim of this chapter is to help you become a knowledgeable participant in the communications revolution.

THE NEED FOR NETWORKING

Let us be more precise in justifying the need for networking among computers and computer-related devices such as terminals and printers. Why do managers or other professionals working at microcomputers need to be connected to a network? Why are small computers often connected to larger machines? Why are laser printers often attached to a local area network? In our judgment, there are four primary reasons for networking: sharing of resources, sharing of data, distributed data processing and client/servers systems, and enhanced communications.

Sharing of Resources

Networking permits the sharing of critical (and often expensive) resources among the various users (machines) on the network. For example, by

putting all of the microcomputers in an office on a local area network (LAN), the users can share a variety of resources, including a single laser printer that is a part of the network or a single facsimile machine on the network. The users can also share software that is electronically stored on a file server (another microcomputer designated for that particular purpose). All these devices are connected by wiring and are able to communicate with one another under control of a LAN software package. When a particular user wants to print a document or send a facsimile, it is sent electronically from the user's machine to the requested device, where it is printed or dispatched.

The sharing of resources is also important for larger computers. It is quite common for mainframe or minicomputers to share magnetic disk devices and high-speed line printers or laser printers. Further, so-called wide area networks permit the sharing of very expensive resources such as supercomputers. The National Science Foundation has funded five national supercomputer centers across the country, and researchers from other universities and research laboratories are able to share these giant machines by going through their local computer network into a national network known as NSFNET.

Sharing of Data

Just as important as the sharing of resources is the sharing of data. Either a LAN or a wide area network permits users on the network to get data (if they are authorized to do so) from other points called nodes on the network. It is very important, for example, for managers to be able to retrieve overall corporate sales forecasts from the corporate database to use in developing spreadsheets to project future activity in their departments. Similarly, accountants at corporate headquarters need to be able to retrieve summary data on sales and expenses from each of the company's divisional computer centers. The chief executive officer, using an executive information system (see Chapter 2), needs to be able to access up-to-the-minute data on business trends from the corporate mainframe computer. In some instances, data may be retrieved from a commercial, public database external to the firm, such as Dow Jones News Retrieval, Prodigy, and CompuServe (see Chapter 15).

Distributed Data Processing and Client/Server Systems

Distributed data processing (first discussed in Chapter 2) is totally dependent upon networking. The information technology architecture, which is the focus of Chapter 12, defines the role of networking and distributed data processing within the organization. With distributed data processing, the processing power is distributed to multiple sites, which are then tied together via telecommunications lines. Client/server systems are a variant of distributed systems in which the processing power is distributed between a central server system, such as a minicomputer or a powerful workstation, and a number of client computers, which are usually desktop microcomputers. Perhaps the two most important advantages of distributed and client/server systems are reduced computing costs because of reliance on more cost-effective microcomputers and workstations and increased service and responsiveness to local users, resulting in improved local morale. On the other hand, such systems are dependent upon high-quality telecommunications lines, which are often quite vulnerable.

Chapter 2 contained three examples of distributed systems. One involved the use of laptop computers by the sales force, where orders and sales data are transmitted over the telephone network to the corporate computer center. The second was a client/server application for general ledger accounting, with desktop microcomputers as the clients and either a high-end microcomputer or a workstation as the server. In most cases, this package would be implemented over a LAN in a single building or a cluster of buildings (a "campus"). The third example, which was also a client/server system, involved the creation of a commercial real estate database on a server located at the real estate firm's main office. The client machines are microcomputers located in the firm's branch offices or customer offices, with the clients and server linked via the public telephone network. In any case, it is the existence of a telecommunica-

tions network that makes distributed data processing a feasible and often attractive arrangement.

Enhanced Communications

Networks enhance the communications process within an organization (and between organizations) in many important ways. The telephone network has long been a primary means of communication within and between organizations. Electronic mail sent over the corporate computer network has become a mainstay of communication in many major organizations in the past decade or so. Linkups between networks, such as linking a corporate network to NSFNET, have provided an even broader audience for electronic communication. Electronic bulletin boards, including internal, regional, and national bulletin boards, permit multiparty asynchronous communication on an incredible array of topics. Video communication, especially videoconferencing, provides a richer medium to permit more effective communication.

Direct data communication links between a company and its suppliers and/or customers have

---

"NETWORKS WILL CHANGE EVERYTHING"

Paul Saffo, a fellow at the Institute for the Future, has developed a fascinating set of forecasts about the effect of information technologies on the way we will work, play, and conduct business in the years to come. "The short answer is that networks will change everything," says Saffo. "In the next five years, networks will be supporting a shift to business teams from individuals as the basic unit of corporate productivity. In the ten-year time frame, we'll see changing organizational structures. In twenty to thirty years, we'll see a shift so fundamental, it will mean the end of the corporation as we know it." Saffo believes that organizations have already started down the path to a pervasive interconnectivity of workstations that will result in an entirely new "virtual" corporate structure.

(Adapted from Wylie, 1993)

been successfully used to give the company a strategic advantage (see Chapter 3). The SABRE airline reservation system is a classic example of a strategic information system that depends upon communication provided through a network. Recent developments to be discussed later in this chapter, such as ISDN, permit both voice and data communications to occur over the same telecommunications line at the same time. Starting with "plain old telephone service" (POTS) networks and continuing with today's computer, local area, wide area, and private branch exchange (PBX) networks and tomorrow's truly integrated networks, networks have enhanced the communication process for individuals and organizations.

AN OVERVIEW OF TELECOMMUNICATIONS AND NETWORKING

Networking—the electronic linking of geographically dispersed devices—is critical for modern organizations. To participate effectively in the ongoing communications revolution, managers need to have a rudimentary understanding of the various telecommunications and networking options available to their organizations.

The prefix tele- simply means operating at a distance. Therefore, **telecommunications** is communications at a distance. There are a number of other terms or abbreviations that are used almost interchangeably with telecommunications: data communications, datacom, teleprocessing, telecom, and networking. We prefer telecommunications because it is the broadest of these similar terms. It includes both voice (telephone) and data communications (including text and image). Teleprocessing means the computer processing is taking place at a distance from where the data originate, which obviously requires telecommunications. Networking is the electronic linking required to accomplish telecommunications.

To begin a detailed consideration of telecommunications, first consider the primary functions performed by a telecommunications network, as listed in Table 6.1. The most obvious of these functions is the transmission of voice and/or data,

TABLE 6.1   Functions of a Telecommunications Network

Function	Brief Description
Transmission	Movement of voice and/or data using network and underlying media
Processing	Ensuring that error-free communication gets to right destination
Editorial	Checking for errors and putting communication into standardized format
Conversion	Changing coding system or speed when moving from one device to another
Routing	Choosing most efficient path when multiple paths are available
Network control	Keeping track of status of network elements and checking to see if communications are ready to be sent
Interface	Handling interactions between users and the network

using the network and the underlying media. The processing involves making sure that the error-free message or data packet gets to the right destination. Subfunctions of processing include editorial, conversion, and routing. Editorial involves checking for errors and putting the communication into a standardized format, while conversion includes any necessary changes in the coding system or the transmission speed when moving from one device on the network to another. In networks where alternative paths are possible between the source and the destination of a communication (particularly wide area networks), routing—choosing the most efficient path—is an important task. Closely related to the processing function is network control, which includes keeping track of the status of various elements of the system (e.g., which elements are busy or out of service) and, for some types of networks, checking each user periodically to see if the user has a communication to send. A not-so-obvious but critical function is the provision of an interface between the network and the user; hopefully this interface will make it easy and efficient for a manager or any other network user to send a communication. The next major section explores the variety of ways in which the functions listed in Table 6.1 can be delivered.

KEY ELEMENTS OF TELECOMMUNICATIONS AND NETWORKING

We believe that you as a user-manager need to understand certain key elements about telecommunications and networking to participate effectively in the communications revolution—to know what your options are. These key elements include certain underlying basic ideas, such as analog versus digital signals and switched versus private lines; the variety of transmission media available; the topology (or possible arrangements) of networks; the various types of networks, including LANs and wide area networks; and the network protocols employed on these networks. This section will be quite technical and will involve a number of difficult concepts, so it may require some effort on your part to keep sight of the big picture of telecommunications.

Analog and Digital Signals

Perhaps the most basic idea about telecommunications is that the electronic signals sent on a network may be either analog or digital, depending on the type of network. Historically, the telephone network has been an **analog network**, with voice messages sent over the network by having some physical quantity (e.g., voltage) continuously vary as a function of time. This analog transmission worked fine for voice transmission because it re-quired the significant variations provided by an analog signal (corresponding to variations in human speech characteristics) and was insensitive to minor degradations in the signal quality. On the other hand, computer data consist of a string of binary digits, or bits—a string of zeros and ones to represent the desired characters. The form of this computer data does not mesh well with analog transmission. First, only two distinct signals—representing zeros and ones—need to be sent, and second, the data are extremely sensitive to degradations in signal quality. Noise in a telephone line could easily cause a zero to be interpreted as a one or vice versa, and the entire message may become garbled. Because of this problem with noise, data cannot be sent directly over the analog telephone network.

Two solutions are possible to the problem of transmitting computer data. The original solution, and one that is still widely used, is to convert the data from digital form to analog form before sending it over the analog telephone network. This conversion is accomplished by a device called a **modem**, an abbreviation for a *mo*dulator/*dem*odulator (see Figure 6.1). Of course, the data must be reconverted from analog form back to digital form at the other end of the transmission line, which requires a second modem. The conversion (or modulation) carried out by the modem may be of different types. Figure 6.2 illustrates the use of amplitude modulation (two different voltage levels to represent 0 and 1), frequency modulation (two different frequencies of oscillations to represent 0 and 1), and phase modulation (the use of a phase shift to represent the change from a 0 to a 1 or vice versa). The use of modems and the analog telephone network is an acceptable way to transmit

FIGURE 6.1 The Use of Modems in Analog Network

1 0 0 1 0 1 0 1 1 0 1 0 0 1

(a)
Digital
Signal

(b)
Amplitude
Modulation

(c)
Frequency
Modulation

Phase changes

(d)
Phase
Modulation

FIGURE 6.2 Digital and Analog Signals

data for many applications, but it is severely limited in terms of transmission speeds and error rates.

The second and longer-term solution to the problem of transmitting computer data is to develop **digital networks** specifically designed to directly transmit zeros and ones, as in Figure 6.2(a). Digital networks have the advantages of potentially lower error rates and higher transmission speeds, and modems are no longer necessary. Because of these advantages, the networks that have been created for the purpose of linking computers and computer-related devices are digital. Furthermore, the telephone network is gradually being shifted from an analog to a digital network.

This shift of the telephone network from analog to digital is due in part to the increasing volume of data being transmitted over the network,

but there is also a significant advantage to transmitting voice signals over a digital network. Digital voice transmission can provide higher quality transmission—less noise on the line—just as digital recording provides higher fidelity compact disks. Most of our telephone instruments are still analog devices, so the signal sent from the instrument to the nearest switching center (which may be operated either by the telephone company or your own organization) is still an analog signal. These telephone switches, however, are rapidly being converted from analog to digital switches. When the analog voice signal arrives at a digital switch, it is converted to a digital voice signal for transmission to a digital switch somewhere else, which may be across town or across the country. Thus, an increasing proportion of the voice transmission between switching centers is digitized. In the future, our telephone instruments will also be digital devices, so the entire telephone network will eventually become digital.

Speed of Transmission

Whether the signal is digital or analog, another basic question is the speed of transmission. Terms such as bandwidth, baud, and Hertz (Hz) are used to describe transmission speeds, whereas a measure such as bits transmitted per second (bits per second) would be more understandable. Happily, the three terms mentioned above are all essentially the same as bits per second in many circumstances. **Bandwidth** is the difference between the highest and the lowest frequencies (cycles per second) that can be transmitted on a single medium, and it is a measure of the capacity of the medium. (Sometimes it is necessary to divide the bandwidth up into multiple channels, all carried on a single medium, to utilize the entire capacity. Thus the transmission speeds we discuss are really data rates for the one or more channels carried on the single medium.) **Hertz** is simply cycles per second and **baud** is the number of signals sent per second. If each cycle sends one signal that transmits exactly one bit of data, which is often the case, then all these terms are identical. To minimize any possible confusion, we will talk about bits per second (bps) in this chapter. In information technology publications, baud is often used for relatively slow speeds, such as 1,200 baud (1,200 bps) or 2,400 baud (2,400 bps), while Hertz (with an appropriate prefix) is often used for higher speeds such as 33 megaHertz (33 million bps) or 500 megaHertz (500 million bps).

The notion of bandwidth, or capacity, is an important one for telecommunications. For example, approximately 50,000 bits (0s and 1s) are required to represent one page of data. To transmit this page using a 1,200 bps modem over an ordinary analog telephone line would take 42 seconds. If one were transmitting a large data file (such as customer accounts), that bandwidth or capacity would be unacceptably slow. On the other hand, to transmit this same page over a 64,000 bps (64 kbps) digital voice line would take only eight-tenths of a second. For graphics, approximately 1 million bits are required for one page. This would require almost 14 minutes for transmission at 1,200 bps over an analog telephone line, or about 16 seconds over a 64 kbps digital voice line. Full-motion video transmission requires the enormous bandwidth of 12 million bps, and thus data compression techniques must be employed to be able to send video over the existing telephone network. The bandwidth determines what types of communication—voice, data, graphics, stop-frame video, full-motion video—can reasonably be transmitted over a particular medium.

Types of Transmission Lines

Another basic distinction is between private (or dedicated) communication lines and switched lines. The public telephone network, for example, is a switched-line system. When a communication of some sort (voice or data) is sent over the telephone network, the sender has no idea what route the communication will take. The telephone company (or companies) computers make connections between switching centers to send the communication over the lines they deem appropriate, based on such factors as the length of the path, the amount of traffic on the various routes, and the capacity of the various routes. This switched-line system usually works fine for voice communications. Data communications, however, are more sensitive to the differences in line quality over different routes and to other local phenomena, such as electrical storms. Thus, a data communication sent from Minneapolis to Atlanta over the telephone network may be transmitted perfectly at 11 A.M., but another communication sent from Minneapolis to Atlanta fifteen minutes later (a different connection) may be badly garbled because they were sent via different routes.

One way to reduce the error rate is through private lines. Most private lines are dedicated lines leased from a common-carrier company such as MCI or AT&T. A company may choose to lease a line between Minneapolis and Atlanta to ensure the quality of its data transmissions. Private lines also exist within a building or a campus. These are lines owned by the organization for the purpose of transmitting its own voice and data communications. Within-building or within-campus lines for computer telecommunications, for example, are usually private lines.

The last basic idea we wish to introduce is the difference among simplex, half-duplex, and full-duplex transmission. With **simplex transmission**, data can travel only in one direction. This one-way communication is rarely useful but might be employed from a monitoring device at a remote site (monitoring power consumption, for example) back to a central computer. With **half-duplex transmission**, data can travel in both directions but not simultaneously. **Full-duplex transmission** permits data to travel in both directions at once and, therefore, provides greater capacity and costs more than half-duplex lines.

Transmission Media

A telecommunications network is made up of some physical medium (or media) over which communications are sent. There are five primary media in use today: twisted pair of wires, coaxial cable, wireless, satellite (which is a special form of wireless), and fiber optic cable.

Twisted Pair   When all uses are considered, the most common transmission medium is a **twisted pair** of wires. Most telephones are connected to the local telephone company office or the local private branch exchange (PBX) via a twisted pair. Similarly, many LANs have been implemented by using twisted-pair wiring to connect the various microcomputers and related devices. A twisted pair consists of two insulated copper wires, typically about 1 millimeter thick, twisted together in a long helix. The purpose of the twisting is to reduce electrical interference from similar twisted pairs nearby. If many twisted pairs will run parallel for a significant distance—such as from a neighborhood to a telephone company office—it is common to bundle them together and enclose them in a protective sheath.

The transmission speeds attainable with twisted pairs vary considerably, depending upon such factors as thickness of the wire and the distance traveled. On the voice telephone network without modification, speeds from 300 to 9,600

bps are commonplace. Telephone twisted pairs can be conditioned, which means subjected to extensive testing, to support speeds from 56,000 bps to 144,000 bps for distances up to several miles. Much higher speeds—up to 16 million bps—can be obtained when twisted pairs are used in LANs. So-called shielded twisted pairs (special shielding to minimize interference) can support speeds up to 100 million bps when used in a Fiber Distributed Data Interface (FDDI) LAN (more on this later).

Coaxial Cable   **Coaxial cable**, or **coax** for short, is another common transmission medium. A coaxial cable consists of a heavy copper wire at the center, surrounded by insulating material. Around the insulating material is a cylindrical conductor, which is often a woven braided mesh. Then the cylindrical conductor is covered by an outer protective plastic covering. Figure 6.3 illustrates the construction of a coaxial cable. Because of its construction, coaxial cable provides a good combination of relatively high transmission speeds and low noise or interference. Two kinds of coaxial cable are in widespread use—a 50-ohm[1] cable used for digital transmission called **baseband coax**, and a 75-ohm cable used for analog transmission called **broadband coax** (Tanenbaum, 1988).

Baseband coax is simple to use and inexpensive to install, and the required interfaces to microcomputers or other devices are relatively inexpensive. Baseband offers a single digital transmission channel with data transmission rates ranging from 10 million bits per second (10 mbps) up to 264 mbps, depending primarily on the distances involved (longer cables mean lower data rates). Baseband coax has been widely used for LANs and for long-distance transmission within the telephone network.

Broadband coax uses analog transmission on standard cable television cabling. Higher transmission speeds are possible—up to 550 mbps—over much longer distances. Furthermore, a single broadband coax can be divided into multiple channels, so that a single cable can support simultaneous transmission of data, voice, and

---

[1] An ohm is a measure of electrical resistance and therefore varies with the diameter of the wire.

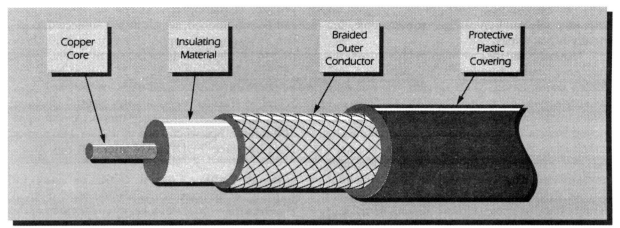

FIGURE 6.3 Construction of a Coaxial Cable

television. Broadband cable systems require analog amplifiers to boost the signals periodically. In general, broadband systems are more difficult to install and considerably more expensive than baseband systems. Engineers are required to plan the cable and amplifier layout and install the system, and skilled technicians are needed to maintain the system over time. Thus, the choice between broadband and baseband hinges upon whether the additional capacity and multiple channels provided by broadband are worth the corresponding complexity and expense. Unless there are special requirements (such as the need to transmit both video and data simultaneously), the choice is usually the less expensive baseband.

Wireless   Strictly speaking, wireless is not a transmission medium. **Wireless** is broadcast technology in which radio signals are sent out into the air. Wireless communication is being used in a variety of circumstances, including cordless telephones, cellular telephones, wireless LANs, and microwave transmission of voice and data.

A **cordless telephone** is a portable device that can be used up to about 1,000 feet from its wired telephone base unit. This permits the user to carry the telephone to various rooms in a house or take it outdoors on the patio. By contrast, a **cellular telephone** (installed in a car or carried in a pocket or briefcase) may be used anywhere as long as it is within range—about 8 to 10 miles—of a cellular

switching station. At present, these cellular switching stations are available in all metropolitan areas of the United States and most rural areas. The switching stations are low-powered transmitter/re‹ ‹vers that are connected to a cellular telephone switching office by means of conventional telephone lines or microwave technology. The switching office, which is computer-controlled, coordinates the calls for its service area and links the cellular system into the local and long distance telephone network.

Wireless LANs are growing in popularity. They have the obvious advantage of being reasonably easy to plan and install. A wireless system provides networking where cable or wire installation would be extremely expensive or impractical, such as in an old building. They tend to be more expensive than a wired LAN, they are certainly less secure, and their speeds are usually slower. For example, most radio signal LANs operate in the range of 2 to 4 mbps.

Microwave has been in widespread use for long distance wireless communication for several decades. Microwave is line-of-sight transmission—there must be an unobstructed straight line between the microwave transmitter and the receiver. Because of the curvature of the earth, microwave towers (see Figure 6.4) have to be built, typically about 25 to 50 miles apart, to relay signals over long distances from the originating transmitter to the final receiver. These require-

FIGURE 6.4 Microwave Tower (Courtesy of AT&T Archives)

WIRELESS MOBILE DATA NETWORKS

A variety of wireless mobile data networks are being used to keep track of both equipment and cargo in the transportation industry. In a typical implementation, microchip-based radio-frequency tags are attached to each truck trailer, railroad car, or cargo container. When the equipment or cargo passes a stationary antenna or scanning device, the tag is activated and transmits its unique identification code containing information about the shipment, including destination, weight, and customer. This information is then transmitted from the scanning device to a nearby microcomputer, which in turn transmits the information to the corporate mainframe computer, usually over the public telephone network. Thus, these networks use short-range radio broadcasting to collect the data on equipment and cargo, and then use the telephone network for long-distance transmission.

As an example of such a system, New Jersey-based Sea-Land Service, Inc., a large container shipping company, has installed radio-frequency tags on 42,000 pieces of equipment and containers. Sea-Land chose its Anchorage, Alaska, port for its initial test of the technology. When any one of these tagged units enters or exits the Anchorage port, it passes an antenna that picks up the unique identification code, transmits it to an Anchorage microcomputer local area network and eventually to Sea-Land's New Jersey mainframe computer. The system performed perfectly in its initial tests and will be implemented in all of Sea-Land's 80 worldwide ports. Such a system will provide Sea-Land, and other transportation companies, with the ability to keep better track of equipment and cargo, allowing them to operate more productively and to provide better customer service.

(Adapted from Conlon, 1990)

ments for towers, transmitters, and receivers suggest that microwave transmission can be expensive, and it is, but long-distance microwave may still be less expensive than burying coaxial cable or fiber optic cable in a very long trench. Microwave is widely used for long distance telephone communication and for corporate voice and data networks; transmission speeds of 50 mbps or more are possible.

Other line-of-sight transmission methods exist in addition to microwave. For short distances (such as from one building to another), laser or infrared transmitters and receivers, mounted on the rooftops, are often an economical and easy

230

way to transmit data. The fastest wireless LANs, operating at speeds from 4 to 16 mbps, use line-of-sight infrared light as their medium.

Satellite   A special variation of microwave transmission employs **satellite communication** to relay signals over very long distances. A communications satellite is simply a big microwave repeater in the sky; it contains one or more transponders that listen to a particular portion of the bandwidth, amplify the incoming signals, and retransmit back to earth. A typical satellite may have a dozen transponders, each of which can handle a 50-mbps data transmission, 800 digital voice channels of 64 kbps each, or other combinations of data channels and voice channels. Transmission via satellite is still line-of-sight transmission, so a communication would have to be relayed through several satellites to go half way around the world (see Figure 6.5).

One interesting and annoying aspect of satellite transmission is the substantial delay in receiving the signal because of the large distances involved in transmitting up to the geostationary satellite and then back down to earth. The minimum delay is about one-third of a second, which is an order of magnitude larger than on coax connections or earth-bound microwave covering the same ground distance.

Interest in the use of satellites by corporations has been heightened by the development of KU-band satellite technology and the new very small aperture terminals (VSATs). VSATs are small satellite dishes (4 to 10 feet in diameter), which are much less costly than their bigger cousins. A VSAT dish can cost from $5,000 to $15,000. KU-band broadcasts at a higher radio frequency than the older C-band and thus can be received by a smaller antenna. KU-band data transmission rates are generally in the 56 kbps range, although speeds up to 1.544 mbps are possible.

Fiber Optics   The last and newest transmission medium—**fiber optic** cabling—is a true medium, not broadcast technology. Advances in optical technology have made it possible to transmit data by pulses of light through a thin fiber of glass or fused silica. A light pulse can signal a 1 bit, while the absence of a pulse signals a 0 bit. An optical transmission system requires three components: the light source, either an LED—a light-emitting diode—or a laser diode; the fiber optic cable itself; and a detector (a photodiode). The light source emits light pulses when an electrical current is applied and the detector generates an electrical current when it is hit by light.

The speeds possible with fiber optics are much faster than the other media and the space requirements are much less because the fiber optic cable is very small in diameter. Fiber optic cables are more secure because the cables emit no radiation and thus are very difficult to tap. They are also highly reliable because they are not affected by power-line surges, electromagnetic interference, or corrosive chemicals in the air. All of these reasons are leading telephone companies to use fiber optics in all of their new long-distance telephone lines and lines connecting central office sites and most of their new local lines from central office sites to terminals located in subdivisions. (The

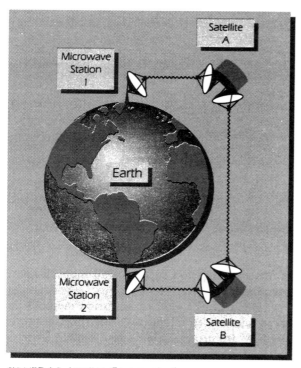

FIGURE 6.5 Satellite Communications

FIRE IN FIBER OPTIC TELEPHONE GATEWAY

The extensive reliance on fiber optic cabling for the telephone network sometimes has a downside. On May 8, 1988, a small electrical fire broke out in an unattended Illinois Bell telephone switching office in Hinsdale, Illinois, a suburb of Chicago. The fire, which blazed out of control for an hour and was not put out for another five hours, essentially destroyed this fiber optic telephone hub. Thirty-five thousand local telephone lines were wiped out, as were 118,000 fiber optic long distance circuits and 13,000 circuits carrying computer-to-computer connections. Essentially all telephone-based communications in Chicago suburbs west and south of the hub office were disrupted for up to several days.

Perhaps the most critical problem came at O'Hare, the nation's busiest airport, where computer links went down between the control tower and the Federal Aviation Administration center directing incoming traffic. Without essential flight data, controllers stretched the distances between flights to 20 miles instead of the usual five, causing air traffic backups across the nation. About 20 percent of O'Hare's 2,300 daily flights were cancelled on the day of the fire. Thousands of cash machines in the Chicago area also went dead, and banks were unable to cash checks because their computer lines to central check-clearing stations were out. Car telephones were out all over the area, and Sears sent their telephone marketing personnel home on indefinite leave. United Airlines reported that some 7,000 telephone calls to their reservation service went unanswered because the airline's computer system receives calls through Hinsdale.

(Adapted from Bozman, 1988, and Richards, 1988)

advantages of speed and security are obvious; the size is important because many of the cable ducts already installed lack room for more coax but could hold more of the thinner fiber optic cabling.) The high cost of the required equipment and the difficulty of dealing with the tiny fibers make this medium inappropriate for most LANs, with the

TABLE 6.2 Telecommunications Transmission Speeds

Transmission Medium	Typical Speeds
Twisted pair—voice telephone	300 bps–9600 bps
Twisted pair—conditioned	56 kbps–144 kbps
Twisted pair—LAN	4 mbps–16 mbps
Coaxial cable—baseband	10 mbps–264 mbps
Coaxial cable—broadband	10 mbps–550 mbps
Radio frequency wireless LAN	2 mbps–4 mbps
Infrared light wireless LAN	4 mbps–16 mbps
Microwave	56 kbps–50 mbps
Satellite (microwave)	56 kbps–50 mbps
Fiber optic cable	500 kbps–30 gbps

KEY: bps = bits per second
kbps = thousand bits per second, or kilo bps
mbps = million bits per second, or mega bps
gbps = billion bits per second, or giga bps

possible exceptions of its use to connect several LANs and where very high speeds or high security needs exist.

Transmission speeds for fiber range up to 500 mbps for a large diameter fiber (50 to 100 micron[2] core, which does not count any protective covering) to as high as 30 billion bits per second (30 giga bps or 30 gbps) for a small diameter fiber (10 microns or less). The fact that the smaller diameter fiber has much larger capacity may be surprising, but light reflections are greatly reduced with a smaller fiber—there is much less bouncing around of the light ray—which permits higher transmission speeds. One major telephone company is currently installing either 8.3 micron single-mode fiber—single mode meaning that the light propagates essentially in a straight line without bouncing—with an average transmission speed of 2.5 gbps, or 62.5 micron multimode fiber with an average speed of 150 mbps. Single-mode fiber, unfortunately, requires higher cost laser light sources and detectors than multimode fiber. The outside diameter (including protective covering) of both these fibers is only 125 microns, which is about one-fiftieth the outside diameter of a typical coaxial cable. Thus, both the speed and size advantages of fiber optics are significant.

---

[2] A micron is one-millionth of a meter or one-thousandth of a millimeter.

232

Topology of Networks

The starting point for the understanding of networks is to recognize that all telecommunications networks employ one or more of the transmission media discussed above. But what do the networks look like in terms of their configuration or arrangement of devices and media? The technical term for this configuration is the topology of the network. There are four basic network topologies—bus, ring, star, and hierarchical or tree (see Figure 6.6)—plus an unlimited number of variations and combinations of these four basic forms.

Bus The simplest topology is the linear or **bus topology**. With the bus, a single length of cable (coax, fiber, or twisted pair) is shared by all network devices. One of the network devices is usually a file server with a large data storage capacity. An obvious advantage of the bus is the wiring simplicity. A disadvantage is its single point failure characteristic. If the bus fails, nodes on either side of the failure point cannot communicate with one another.

Ring The **ring topology** is similar to the bus except that the two ends of the cable are connected. In this case, a single cable runs through every network device, including (usually) a file server. The wiring for the ring is slightly more complicated

than for the bus, but the ring is not as susceptible to failure. In particular, a single failure in the ring still permits each network device to communicate with every other device.

Star The **star topology** has a mainframe or minicomputer, a file server (usually a microcomputer), or a PBX at its center, with cables (or media of some type) radiating from the central device to all the other network devices. This design is representative of many small-to-medium computer configurations, with all workstations and peripherals attached to the single minicomputer. It is also encountered in LANs and in networks built around a PBX. Advantages of the star include ease of identifying cable failure because each device has its own cable; ease of installation for each device, which must only be connected to the central device; and low cost for small networks where all the devices are close together. The primary disadvantage of the star is that if the central device fails, the whole network fails. A cost disadvantage may also be encountered if the network grows, because a separate cable must be run to each individual device, even if several devices are close together but far from the central device.

Tree The **tree topology,** or hierarchical, is sometimes called an hierarchical star, because with some rearrangement (spreading the branches out around the central device), it looks like an extension of the star. The configuration of most large and very large computer networks is a tree, with the mainframe at the top of the tree connected (through data channels) to terminal controllers, such as multiplexers and concentrators[3], and perhaps to other smaller computers. These terminal controllers, or smaller computers, are in turn connected to other devices such as terminals, microcomputers, and printers. Thus, the tree gets "bushy" as one traverses it from top to bottom.

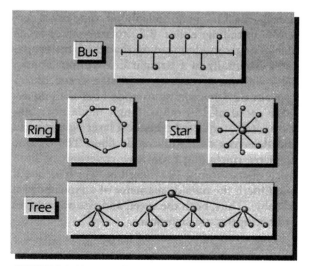

FIGURE 6.6 Network Topologies

[3] A multiplexer and a concentrator are similar devices, usually located at a site remote from the mainframe, whose function is to merge ("multiplex" or "concentrate") the data streams from multiple low-speed input devices, such as terminals and microcomputers, so that the full capacity of the transmission line to the mainframe is utilized.

The tree has the same primary disadvantage as the star. If the central device fails, the entire network goes down. On the other hand, the tree arrangement possesses a great deal of flexibility. The cost disadvantage of the star may not appear when devices are added to the network, for the use of intermediate devices (multiplexers, small computers) removes the necessity of connecting every device directly to the center.

More Complex Networks   Now the fun begins, for the above four network topologies can be combined and modified in a bewildering assortment of networks. For example, it is quite common to attach a bus or a ring LAN to the tree mainframe computer network. Two ring LANs may be attached via a microwave channel, which is in effect a very simple bus network.

National networks are much more complex than those we have considered thus far because the designers have intentionally built in a significant amount of redundancy. In this way if one transmission line goes out, there are alternative routes to almost every node or device on the network. As a simple example without much redundancy, the high-speed **backbone** (the underlying foundation of the network, to which other elements attach) for NSFNET is shown in Figure 6.7. NSFNET is based upon a ring connecting the east and west coasts, with spurs going off the ring to several cities such as San Francisco, Salt Lake City, and Washington, D.C. The long distance telephone network has much more redundancy, with numerous paths possible to connect most metropolitan areas.

Types of Networks

Thus far we have considered two key elements of telecommunications networks: the transmission media used to send the communications and the arrangement or topology of the networks. Now we turn to the categorization of networks into basic types. Please note that the categories employed here are somewhat arbitrary—but we believe extremely useful—and may differ from those used in

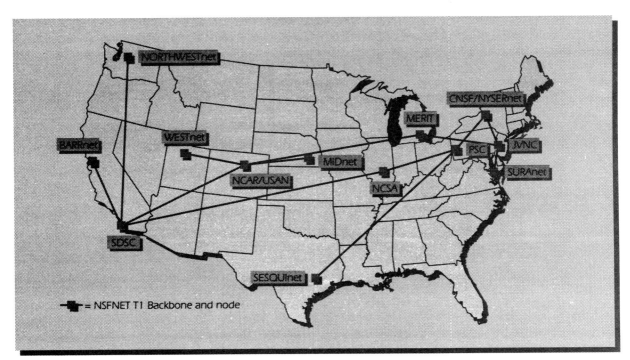

FIGURE 6.7 NSFNET Backbone and Nodes

other references. The types of networks to be described include computer telecommunications networks, PBX networks, local area networks (LANs), and wide area networks (WANs).

Computer Telecommunications Networks
A **computer telecommunications network** is the network emanating from a single medium, large, or very large computer or a group of closely linked computers. This type of network usually is arranged as a tree (see Figure 6.6) with coaxial cable and twisted pair as the media. Until a decade ago, this was usually the only type of network (except for the telephone network) operated by an organization that did business in one building or a group of adjacent buildings (a campus). Even today the predominant communication with the central computer is through the computer telecommunications network. This type of network is controlled by the central computer, with all other devices (e.g., terminals, microcomputers, and printers) operating as "slaves" on the network. IBM's mainframe architecture is based on this type of network.

This is not a bad arrangement, but it puts a tremendous communications control burden on the central computer. For this reason, it is quite common to add a front-end processor or communications controller to the network—between the central computer and the rest of the network—to offload the communications work from the central computer (see Figure 6.8). A front-end processor or communications controller is another computer with specially designed hardware and software to

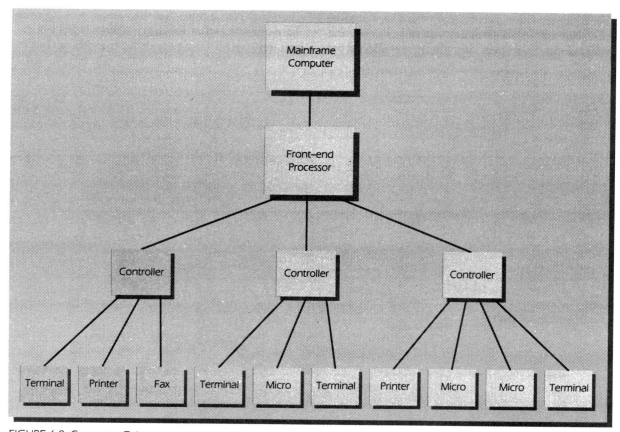

FIGURE 6.8 Computer Telecommunications Network

handle all aspects of telecommunications, including error control, editing, controlling, routing, and speed and signal conversion.

PBX Networks Private branch exchanges, or PBXs, have been around for many years, but today's digital **PBX networks** have extensive capabilities not possessed by their predecessors. First-generation PBXs were switchboards run by human operators to operate an internal telephone system within an organization. Second-generation PBXs worked in the same way except that electromechanical relays were used to perform the switching rather than human operators. Today's third-generation PBX consists of a digital switch operated by a built-in computer, and the PBX has the capability of simultaneously handling communications with internal analog telephones, digital microcomputers and terminals, mainframe computers, and the external telephone network. Figure 6.9 provides a schematic representation of a PBX.

It is obvious from Figure 6.9 that a PBX can serve as the central device in a star or a tree network. The media used are typically some combination of coax, twisted pair, and fiber (if high speeds are essential). If a mainframe computer is

attached to the PBX, then the PBX can function as the front-end processor for the mainframe. In terms of the telephone network, the PBX will have to translate analog telephone signals to digital form before sending them over the digital network. Except for telephone instruments, all the devices shown in Figure 6.9 are digital, including the ISDN devices to be discussed later.

A PBX has several advantages. It can connect all, not just some, of the telecommunications devices in a building or campus; it can use existing telephone wiring; it can carry voice and data over the same network; it can connect in a transparent way to the external telephone network; and it has an incredible potential throughput of over 500 mbps. On the negative side, the maximum speed for a single channel (as distinct from overall throughput) is only 64 kbps, which is plenty for telephone and most terminal traffic but is painfully slow for shipping a large computer file from the mainframe to a remote disk unit. PBXs are also complex and expensive pieces of equipment.

Local Area Networks A **local area network (LAN)** is first and foremost a *local* network—it is completely owned by a single organization and generally operates within an area no more than two or three miles in diameter. LANs are data networks that generally have a high data rate of several million bps or more.

A LAN differs from a computer telecommunications network in that a LAN contains a number of intelligent devices (usually microcomputers) capable of data processing rather than being built around a central computer that controls all processing. In other words, a LAN is based on a peer-to-peer relationship, rather than a master-slave relationship. A LAN differs from a PBX network in that a LAN handles only data, is not part of the telephone system, and requires new wiring. A LAN does have a great deal in common with a PBX network in that both are aimed at establishing communication between a variety of devices in order to share data and resources and to facilitate office or factory automation. Thus, PBXs and LANs are often seen as competing technologies.

LANs employ both bus and ring topologies, and standards have been developed for three

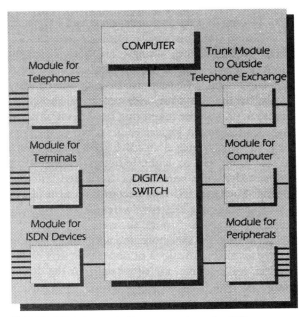

FIGURE 6.9 Schematic Representation of a PBX

widely adopted configurations. These three LAN standards, which were developed by the Institute for Electrical and Electronic Engineers (IEEE) and subsequently adopted by both national and international standards organizations, are officially designated as IEEE 802.3 (contention bus design), IEEE 802.4 (token bus design), and IEEE 802.5 (token ring design).

The **contention bus** design was originally developed by Xerox and subsequently adopted by Digital Equipment Corporation and Novell, among others. This design is usually referred to as **Ethernet**, named after the original Xerox version of the design. The contention bus is obviously a bus topology (see Figure 6.6) and usually is implemented using coaxial cable or twisted pair wiring. The interesting feature of this design is its contention aspect—all devices must contend for the use of the cable.

With Ethernet, devices listen to the cable in order to pick off communications intended for the particular device and to see if the cable is busy. If the cable is idle, any device may transmit a message. Most of the time this will work fine, but what happens if two devices start to transmit at the same time? A collision will occur and the messages will become garbled. The devices must recognize that this collision has occurred, stop transmitting, wait some random period of time, and then try again. This method of operation is called a **CSMA/CD protocol**, an abbreviation for carrier sense multiple access with collision detection. In theory, collisions might continue to occur and thus there is no upper bound on the time a device might wait to send a message. In practice, a contention bus design is simple to implement and works very well as long as traffic on the network is fairly light (and there are few collisions).

The **token bus** design also employs a bus topology with coaxial cable or twisted pair wiring, but it does not rely on contention. Instead, a single token (a special communication or message) is passed around the bus to all devices in a specified order, and a given device can only transmit when it has the token. Thus, a particular microcomputer must wait until it receives the token before transmitting a message; when it has completed sending the message, it sends the token on to the next de-

vice. After some deterministic period of time, it will receive the token again.

The token bus design is central to **MAP** (**Manufacturing Automation Protocol**), which was developed by General Motors and has been adopted by many manufacturers. MAP is a factory automation protocol (or set of standards) designed to connect robots and other machines on the assembly line by a LAN. In designing MAP, General Motors did not feel it could rely on a contention-based LAN with a probabilistic delay time before a message could be sent. An automobile assembly line moves at a fixed rate, and it cannot be held up because a robot has not received the appropriate message from the LAN. Therefore, General Motors and many other manufacturers have opted for the deterministic token bus LAN design.

The third LAN standard is IBM's **token ring**, which combines a ring topology (see Figure 6.6) with the use of a token as described for the token bus. A device attached to the ring must seize the token and remove it from the ring before transmitting a message; when the device has completed transmitting, it releases the token back into the ring. Thus, collisions can never occur, and the maximum delay time before any station can transmit is deterministic.

The token ring is a unidirectional ring, with data flowing in only one direction around the ring. If the ring were physically implemented as suggested in Figure 6.6, a single break anywhere in the ring would disrupt communication for the entire ring. This potential problem is solved very nicely by the use of a wire center as shown in Figure 6.10, and the token ring becomes a physical star but remains a logical ring. In the IBM token ring, the wire center is an IBM 8228 Multistation Access Unit. Up to eight individual devices are connected to the wire center using twisted pair wiring. Each twisted pair becomes an arm of the physical star, but the two wires in the pair are joined with others through the wire center to form a logical ring. Furthermore, the wire center is built to bypass automatically a nonoperative arm of the star (if, for example, the ring breaks or the device fails).

As implied by Figure 6.10, reconfiguring a token ring is as easy as plugging in a new device or

FOUR DEVICES CONNECTED VIA A WIRE CENTER.

FIGURE 6.10 Physical Star, Logical Ring. (Andrew S. Tanenbaum, *Computer Networks*, 2 ed © 1988, p. 156. Reprinted by permission of Prentice Hall, Inc., Englewood Cliffs, New Jersey.)

unplugging an old one. Because of the physical **star arrangement, it is easy to diagnose and correct any communications problems that arise. The IBM token ring network operates at either 4 mbps or 16 mbps and can accommodate up to 260 de-**vices per ring. In a very active LAN, both the token ring and the token bus will significantly outperform the contention bus in terms of the actual data rate delivered for any potential data rate (see Figure 6.11). Thus, the token bus and ring seem to

238

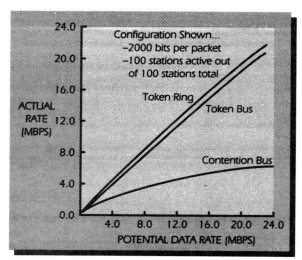

FIGURE 6.11 Performance Comparison of the LAN Technologies

have significant factors in their favor. Nevertheless, contention bus LANs are well established and perform satisfactorily in many situations. All three types of LANs are widely used today, with token bus dominating the manufacturing scene and contention bus leading token ring in office applications.

Newer, faster types of LANs are being developed and deployed in the middle of the 1990s. While the top speed of a contention bus is 10 mbps and the similar figure for a token ring is 16 mbps, the newer LANs operate at 100 mbps or faster. Of course, these faster LANs cost a great deal more. The two primary contenders among high-speed LANs are Fast Ethernet and FDDI. Fast Ethernet makes use of new equipment to run Ethernet at speeds as fast as 100 mbps, using existing twisted pair wiring. Further along in development is **FDDI**, or **Fiber Distributed Data Interface**. FDDI, which is an ANSI (American National Standards Institute) standard, offers both 100 mbps performance and fault tolerance because of its doubling-ring architecture. In FDDI, the primary ring is active until a fault is detected, at which time the secondary ring is activated. FDDI utilizes either fiber optic cabling or shielded twisted pair wiring. In a test conducted by *PC Week*, "FDDI offered slightly more than 10 times the performance of

Ethernet at slightly less than 10 times the price" (Chernicoff, 1993). As development of these fast LANs continues and acceptance of them increases, their prices should drop.

Wide Area Networks The more complex, more widely dispersed organizations of the late 1990s need **wide area networks** (**WANs**), also called long-haul networks, to communicate both voice and data across their far-flung operations. A WAN differs from a LAN in that a WAN spans much greater distances (often entire countries), has slower data rates (usually below 2 mbps), and is usually owned by several organizations (including both common carriers and the user organization). In addition, a WAN employs point-to-point transmission (except for satellites), whereas a LAN uses a multiaccess channel (such as the bus and ring). We will note some exceptions, but for the most part WANs rely on the public telephone network.

DDD and WATS. The easiest way to set up a WAN is to rely on ordinary public telephone service. **Direct Distance Dialing** (**DDD**) is available through the local telephone company and a long distance carrier—AT&T, MCI, Sprint, or others—and can be used for voice and data communications between any two spots served by the telephone network. Of course, the speed for data transmission is quite limited (up to 14,400 bps, depending upon the modem), data error rates are relatively high, and the cost per hour is very expensive (approximately $20 to $40). **Wide Area Telephone Service** (**WATS**) is also available, in which the organization pays a monthly fee for (typically) unlimited long distance telephone service using the ordinary voice circuits. WATS has the same advantages and disadvantages as DDD, except that the cost per hour is somewhat less ($15 to $25), but the customer pays for WATS whether it is used or not, while DDD is paid for only when it is utilized. DDD may be appropriate for intermittent, limited-volume data transmission at relatively slow speeds, while WATS might be used for more nearly continuous, somewhat larger volumes of data to be transmitted at relatively slow speeds.

Leased Lines. Another, often quite attractive, alternative is to lease dedicated communications lines from AT&T or another carrier. If a manufacturing company has three plants geographically separated from corporate headquarters (where the mainframe computer is located), it may make sense to lease lines from each of the three plants to headquarters. These leased lines are generally coaxial cables or microwave (sometimes fiber) of very high capacity, and they are less prone to data errors than ordinary voice lines. The leased lines are expensive, ranging from hundreds of dollars per month for distances of a few miles up to tens of thousands of dollars per month for cross-country lines.

The most common leased lines operate at a data transmission rate of 1.544 mbps and are referred to as **T-1 lines**.[4] All of the links in NSFNET, shown in Figure 6.7, are T-1 communication lines. In order to effectively use this huge data transmission rate, organizations must employ multiplexers at each end of a T-1 line to combine (or separate out) a number of data streams that are, individually, much less than 1.544 mbps. These multiplexers vary in price depending upon their functions, with a range from $20,000 to $100,000 each.

Leased lines with capacities higher than T-1 are now available. Four T-1 lines are combined to create a T-2 trunk, with a capacity of 6.312 mbps, but T-2 trunks have largely been bypassed in favor of T-3 trunks (consisting of seven T-2s), with a data transmission capacity of nearly 45 mbps. T-3 links are available between major cities, although the costs are much higher than for T-1s. A Denver-Chicago T-1 line would cost $20,000 per month, while a T-3 link between the same two cities would be about $200,000. T-4 trunks are in the offing (made up of six T-3s), with a staggering capacity of 274 mbps.

Satellite. Satellite microwave communication is being used by an increasing number of organizations setting up a WAN. The satellite or satellites involved are owned by companies such as RCA and AT&T, and the user organization leases a

---

[4] The T-1 terminology originated when leased lines were all analog. For the newer digital technology lines, the correct designation is DS-1 for a 1.544 mbps line, but T-1 is commonly used to refer to both analog and digital lines operating at 1.544 mbps.

SATELLITE NETWORKS PAY OFF

Nine hundred Porsche, Audi, and Volkswagen dealerships throughout the United States have enjoyed fixed-price network service since V-Crest Systems, a member of the Volkswagen Group, installed a VSAT network in 1990. "If you look at what we've done here, it's pretty amazing," brags Mike Glovis, network manager at V-Crest. "We've got end-to-end control, we've got video, and we've got disaster recovery."

Charging dealerships the equivalent cost of its former multidrop terrestrial lines, $395 per month, V-Crest provides them with all their vital information-service needs. The hub in Auburn Hills, Michigan, handles order placement, warranty processing, parts and vehicle location, customer tracking, financing, insurance, accounting, inventory control, and service management.

Glovis expects his VSAT network to pay for itself in five years, based on projected increases in telecommunications charges. But, he happily points out, the equipment has an estimated life span of ten years, giving V-Crest a national network over the second five years for the price of its operating costs.

The Farm Credit Bank of Austin, Texas, has branches in small towns where the phone service is run on "baling wire, barbed wire, whatever they can find," says Rodney Gilson, vice president of Computer Services. Without reliable land-based carriers, Gilson gladly abandoned his multidrop circuits in favor of a 70-site VSAT network from AT&T/Tridom. VSAT allowed the bank to stabilize costs, Gilson explains, eliminating concerns about increases in the carrier tariff. His payback for the network, installed in May 1989, was less than three years, he says.

(Johnson, 1992)

portion of the satellite's capacity. In addition, the user organization either provides its own ground stations or leases time on a carrier's ground stations, as well as communication lines to and from those ground stations. Satellite data transmission rates vary from 56 kbps for KU-band transmission to more than 50 mbps for the older C-band. The use of KU-band transmission with relatively inexpensive VSAT ground stations ($5,000 to $15,000 each) is making satellite transmission very popular for organizations with many remote locations and moderate volumes of data to transmit. Both Kmart and Walmart, for example, use VSAT networks to link their thousands of stores with their corporate headquarters.

Value Added Networks. With the WAN alternatives described above, the user organization is responsible for managing all aspects of the telecommunications function. Some pieces of the network (a T-1 line, satellite capacity) may be leased from a carrier, but the user must fit all the pieces together, including such details as the routing of communications, error checking and editing, and speed and format conversion of the data. If the organization wants someone else to handle these telecommunications management functions for it (for a fee, of course), then a **value added network**, or **VAN**, is the way to go.

The VAN may use T-1 lines, earthbound microwave, or satellite microwave, but this is all transparent to the user. Assume, for example, that the user has computers in Seattle, Dallas, and Boston that need to communicate with one another. To use a particular VAN, connections from the computers to the VAN nodes in the three cities would be made via the local telephone network or a dedicated cable. The user does not care how these three VAN nodes communicate with one another, as long as the data are transmitted in a timely and error-free manner. The user is buying a service, or, alternatively, the VAN operating company is adding value to the basic network (which consists of some assortment of media and WANs) by managing the entire process so that it is transparent to the user.

A VAN is a data-only, private, nonregulated telecommunications network. The NSFNET is a VAN; the scientists who use it do not need to know the types of lines used or the routing of messages. Some VANs, like NSFNET, serve a limited audience, while others are available to any organization that wishes to buy the networking service. This second type of VAN is called a public network; in the United States these public networks are operated by private companies, such as AT&T, General Electric, Tymnet, GTE, and IBM. In much of the rest of the world, these public networks are operated by government-owned postal, telephone, and telegraph companies (PTTs). Each of these VANs is computer-controlled, and they usually involve multiple media and multiple paths between points on the network.

VANs also employ **packet switching**. Communications sent over the VAN are divided into packets of some fixed length, often 300 characters. Control information is attached to the front and rear of this packet, and it is sent over a communications line in a single bundle. This is quite different from usual voice and data communications, where the entire end-to-end circuit is tied up for the duration of the session. With packet switching, the network is used more efficiently because packets from various users can be interspersed with one another. The computers controlling the network will route each individual packet along the appropriate path. (Packet switching is not limited to VANs; some of the user-organization WANs use the packet switching strategy.)

ISDN. The newest way of implementing a WAN is an **Integrated Services Digital Network**, or **ISDN**. ISDN is an emerging set of international standards by which the public telephone network will offer extensive new telecommunications capabilities, including simultaneous transmission of both voice and data over the same line, to telephone users worldwide. So-called narrowband ISDN is available in many areas of the world, with the areas served by ISDN growing every year. ISDN is digital communication, using the same twisted pairs already used in the present telephone network. Because the entire system is digital, modems are not required, but new ISDN telephone instruments are required that produce a digital rather than an analog signal.

ISDN capabilities are made possible by hardware and software at the local telephone company office and on the organization's premises (such as a digital PBX) that divide a single telephone line (twisted pair) into two different types of communication channels. The B, or bearer, channel transmits voice or data at rates of 64 kbps, considerably faster than today's rates of 14,400 bps using a modem. The D, or data, channel is used to send signal information to control the B channels and to carry packet-switched digital data.

Two narrowband ISDN services have been offered so far. The basic rate offers two B channels and one 16 kbps D channel (a total data rate of 144 kbps) over a single twisted pair. Each basic rate line is capable of supporting two voice devices and six data devices, any two of which can be operating simultaneously. The primary rate provides twenty-three B channels and one 64 kbps D channel (for a total data rate of 1.544 mbps) over two twisted pairs. In the future, broadband ISDN, using fiber optic cabling, will be available with total data transmission rates of over 100 mbps. Thus, ISDN provides a significant increase in capacity while still using the public telephone network.

Further, the D channel brings new capabilities to the network. For example, the D channel can be used for telemetry, enabling remote control of machinery, heating, or air conditioning at the same time the B channels are being used for voice or data transmission. The D channel can also be used for single-button access to a variety of telephony features, such as call-waiting and display of the calling party's number.

A number of innovative uses of ISDN are already being implemented or considered. For example, in a customer service application, an incoming call from a customer might come in over one of the B channels. The D channel might be used to automatically signal the mainframe computer to send the customer's record to the service representative's workstation over the second B channel. In a marketing application, a salesperson could send alternative specifications or designs to a potential buyer's video screen over one B channel while simultaneously talking to the buyer over the second B channel.

The developments in ISDN are exciting, and they promise a bright future for the public telephone network. At present, the regional Bell operating companies (RBOCs) and other local companies are providing local ISDN service as described above. In 1991, ISDN service availability among the RBOCs varied from 8.3 percent of the lines in the NYNEX territory to 37.9 percent in Bell Atlantic's area. By 1994, these numbers will range from 16.3 percent in Southwestern Bell's area to Bell Atlantic's 87 percent (Kerr, 1992a). With time, a national and international ISDN network

---

THE QUIET SUCCESSES OF ISDN

For the leading edge of customers, ISDN has had some quiet successes. It has allowed some users to replace private branch exchanges (PBXs), modems, and expensive leased lines. Its usefulness is also being explored for backing up private lines, providing on-demand bandwidth to supplement overused private networks, handling videoconferencing and graphics applications, and for handheld PC communications.

Perhaps the best known ISDN application is automatic number identification, or ANI, which is widely used in customer service operations and telemarketing. ANI displays the caller's phone number even before the phone is picked up. This allows businesses to tie their phone systems into customer databases to speed call processing.

Supporters now say that it is likely there may never be another application as dependent on ISDN as ANI, and the emphasis should be on additional ways ISDN can save users money and time. "To a telecom person, ANI is no big Watusi," comments Lisa Hoesel, senior telecommunications specialist for U.S. Bancorp in Portland, Oregon. "What I like about ISDN and other technologies are the bandwidth and network management features."

According to a July 1991 survey of 200 computer-assisted telephony users conducted by Business Research Group, a subsidiary of Cahners Publishing Company in Newton, Massachusetts, 7 percent of respondents currently use ISDN and 56 percent will potentially use it over the next two years. Most interesting is the discovery that 42 percent intend to attach local area networks to ISDN. These users won't replace LANs with ISDN. Rather, they'll use ISDN to connect LANs to other devices, such as packet-switched networks, PBXs, workstations, and host computers.

(Kerr, 1992a)

---

will develop that will provide answers to the wide area telecommunications problems of many organizations.

Network Protocols

There is only one more major piece to our network puzzle. How do the various elements of these networks actually communicate with one another?

The answer is by means of a **network protocol,** an agreed-upon set of rules or conventions governing communication among elements of a network or, to be more precise, among layers or levels of a network. In order for two network elements to communicate with one another, they must both be using the same protocol. Thus, the protocol truly enables elements of the network to communicate with one another.

Without actually using the protocol label, we have already considered several protocols. LANs, for example, have three widely accepted protocols—contention bus, token bus, and token ring. The standard plug-in interface between a microcomputer and a modem is the protocol RS-232-C. These are only a few of the many protocols; in fact, the biggest problem with protocols is that there are too many of them (or, to look at the problem in another way, not enough acceptance of a few of them). IBM has created its own set of protocols, collectively termed Systems Network Architecture or SNA. Digital Equipment Corporation has developed DECNET as its set of protocols, and other vendors have also created their own proprietary protocols. IBM equipment and DEC equipment cannot communicate with each other unless both employ the same protocols—IBM's, DEC's, or perhaps another set of "open systems" protocols. The big problem involved in integrating computers and other related equipment from many vendors into a network is standardization so that all use the same protocols.

In the past few years, progress has been made in standardization (and acceptance) of a set of protocols. The International Standards Organization (ISO) has developed a model called the **OSI or Open Systems Interconnection Reference Model,** which deals with connecting all systems that are open for communication with other systems (i.e., systems that conform to certain minimal standards). The OSI model defines seven layers (see Figure 6.12), each of which will have its own protocol (or perhaps more than one). Happily, all major computer and telecommunications vendors—including IBM—have announced their support for the OSI model. The OSI model is only a skeleton at this point, with standard protocols in existence for some layers (the three LAN protocols are part

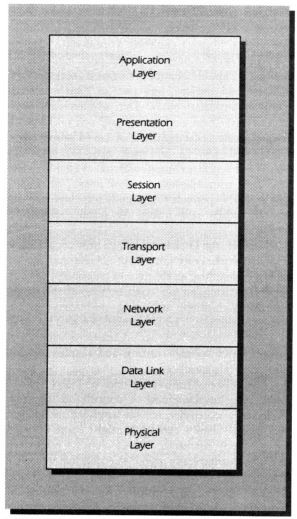

FIGURE 6.12 Seven Layers of the OSI Reference Model

of the data link layer), but with only rough ideas in other layers. Thus, the OSI model is evolving, and the vendors are modifying and expanding their products to more nearly match the changing OSI model.

OSI Reference Model Because of the growing importance of the OSI model, and because it will give us a conceptual framework to understand how communication takes place in networks, we will briefly discuss each of the layers in the OSI model and an example of how data can be transmitted using the model (see Figure 6.13). This is a very complex model because it must support many types of networks (e.g., LANs, WANs) and many types of communication (e.g., E-mail, EDI, EIS).

Physical Layer. The physical layer is concerned with transmitting bits (a string of zeros and ones) over a physical communication channel. Electrical engineers work at this level. Typical design issues involve such questions as how many volts should be used to represent a 1 and how many for a 0.

Data Link Layer. For the data link layer to work, data must be submitted to it (by the network layer) in the form of data frames of a few hundred bytes. Then the data link adds special header and trailer data at the beginning and end of each frame, respectively, so that it can recognize the frame boundaries. The data link transmits the frames in sequence to the physical layer for actual transmittal and also processes acknowledgement frames sent back by the data link layer of the re-

ceiver and makes sure that there are no transmission errors.

Network Layer. The network layer receives a packet of data from the transport layer and adds special header data to it to identify the route that the packet is to take to its destination. This augmented packet becomes the frame passed on to the data link layer. Thus, the primary concern of the network layer is the routing of the packets. The network layer often contains an accounting function as well in order to produce billing information.

Transport Layer. Although not illustrated by Figure 6.13, the transport layer is the first end-to-end layer encountered. In the lower layers of the OSI model, the protocols are between a sending device and its immediate neighbor, then between the neighbor and its immediate neighbor, and so on until the receiving device is reached. Starting with the transport layer and continuing through the three upper layers, the conversation is directly

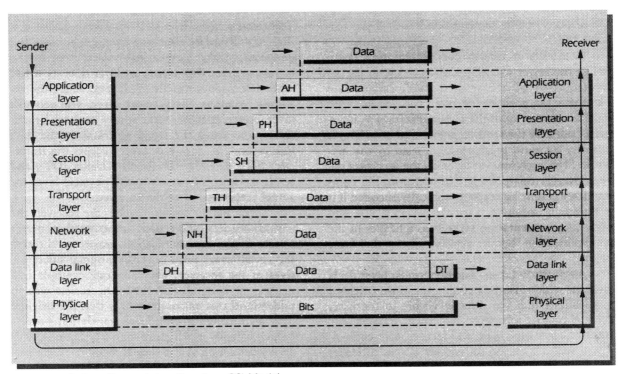

FIGURE 6.13 Data Transmission Based on OSI Model

between the layer for the sending device and the corresponding layer for the receiving device. Thus, the upper four layers are end-to-end protocols.

The transport layer receives the communication (of whatever length) from the session layer, splits it into smaller blocks if necessary, adds special header data defining the network connection(s) to be used, passes the packet(s) to the network layer, and then checks to make sure that all the packets arrive correctly at the receiving end. If the network connection requires multiplexing for its efficient use, this is also handled by the transport layer (and in a manner transparent to the higher layers).

Session Layer. Through the session layer, users on different machines may establish sessions between them. For most applications, the session layer is not used, but, for example, it would allow a user to log into a remote interactive computer or to transfer a file between two computers. The session layer may provide several services to the users, including dialogue control (if traffic can only move in one direction at a time) and synchronization (so that a portion of a communication received need not be retransmitted even if the network fails).

Presentation Layer. The presentation layer, unlike the lower layers, is concerned with the information to be transmitted itself, rather than viewing it as a string of bits. The presentation layer accepts as input the communication as internally coded by the sending device and translates it into the standard representation used by the network. (The presentation layer on the receiving device reverses this process.) In addition, the communication may be cryptographically encoded if it is especially sensitive. Like the layers below and above, the presentation layer adds a header to the communication before sending it to the layer below.

Application Layer. The uppermost layer deals with the wide variety of communications-oriented applications that are directly visible to the user, such as remote job entry, document transfer, file transfer, electronic mail, and factory floor control. There will always be differences across different terminals or systems, and a protocol is required for each application (usually implemented in soft-

ware) to make each of these devices appear the same to the network. For a group of users to communicate using e-mail, for example, the devices they employ must all use the same application layer/e-mail protocol. The OSI e-mail protocol, known as MOTIS, is gaining significant acceptance.

Data Transmission Using the OSI Model. Figure 6.13 provides an illustration of data transmission based on the OSI model. The sender has some data to be transmitted to the receiver. The sender, for example, may be a manager at a workstation who wishes to transmit a query to the corporate executive information system located on a mainframe in another state. The manager types in a query, which is temporarily stored in the workstation in electronic form. When the manager hits the enter key, the query (data) is given to the application layer, which adds the application header (AH) and gives the resulting augmented data item to the presentation layer.

The presentation layer converts the item into the appropriate network code, adds a presentation header (PH), and passes it on to the session layer. The session layer may not do anything, but if it does, it will end by attaching a session header (SH) and passing the further augmented item to the transport layer. The transport layer does its work, adds a transport header (TH), and sends the resulting packet to the network layer. The network layer in turn does its work, adds a network header (NH), and sends the resulting frame to the data link layer. The data link layer accepts the frame, adds both a header (DH) and a trailer (DT), and sends the final bit stream to the physical layer for actual transmission to the receiver.

When the bit stream reaches the receiver, the various headers (and trailer) are stripped off one at a time as the communication moves up through the seven layers until only the original query arrives at the receiver, which in our example is a mainframe computer. Perhaps the easiest way to understand this entire process is that the original data go through a multilevel translation process (which is really much more than translation), with each layer acting as if it were directly communicating with the corresponding receiving layer. Most important, the entire process should take place in a device/system-independent way that is totally transparent to the user.

SNA and SAA   The OSI reference model clearly represents the future in terms of network protocols, as indicated above. In the short term, however, IBM's **Systems Network Architecture (SNA)** remains an important standard. SNA, like OSI, is really a suite or grouping of protocols. SNA was created by IBM to allow its customers to construct their own private networks. In the original 1974 version of SNA, only a simple tree topology emanating from a single mainframe was permitted. By 1985, however, arbitrary topologies of mainframes, minicomputers, and LANs were supported.

SNA is a very complicated suite of protocols because it was designed to support the incredible variety of IBM communication products, teleprocessing access methods, and data link protocols that existed before SNA. We do not need to explore the details of these protocols, but it may be useful to note that the newer OSI model was patterned after SNA in several ways. Both employ the concept of layering, have seven layers, and incorporate essentially the same functions. The contents of the two sets of layers, however, are quite different, especially in the middle three layers (called the network, transport, and session layers in OSI).

In 1987 IBM announced **Systems Application Architecture (SAA)** as the basis for creating common applications and distributing them across networks connecting all IBM computers from mainframes through microcomputers. SAA is more a direction or a philosophy than a reality, although SAA software packages began to appear in the early 1990s. SAA is an evolving set of specifications defining programming, communications, and a common end-user interface that will allow applications to be created and moved among the full range of IBM computers. The three foundation layers of SAA are common communications support, which provides for interconnection across a network; common user access, which defines the user interface; and common programming interface, which provides the tools, languages, and services for developing applications.

Under the common communications support, IBM explicitly has stated its intention of supporting both SNA and OSI protocols in its future efforts under the SAA umbrella. This is one more major piece of evidence that OSI is becoming the single set of protocols to permit the disparate elements of a network to communicate with one another.

Other Protocols   There are a number of other network protocols, two of which are important enough to merit special mention. First, most value added networks (VANs) employ the X.25 protocol for the physical, data link, and network layers of the seven-layer model. X.25 has been formally adopted by the ISO as part of the OSI model. Because VANs are based on packet switching, some sources use X.25 networks and packet-switching networks interchangeably, although there are certainly other ways to implement packet switching besides X.25.

Another important protocol is **TCP/IP**, or **Transmission Control Protocol/Internet Protocol.** TCP/IP is not part of the OSI reference model, although it roughly corresponds to the network and transport layers. TCP/IP is used in several private VAN networks, including NSFNET and ARPANET[5], as well as in many versions of the UNIX operating system, so it is very popular today, particularly among universities and research laboratories. The IP portion of the protocol corresponds roughly to the network layer of the seven-layer model, while the TCP portion corresponds approximately to the transport layer. TCP/IP accepts messages of any length, breaks them into pieces less than 64,000 bytes, sends the pieces to the designated receiver, and makes sure that the pieces are correctly delivered and are placed in the right order (because they may arrive out of order). TCP/IP does not know the path the pieces will take, and it assumes that communication will be unreliable—thus, substantial error-checking

---

[5] ARPANET is a creation of the Advanced Research Projects Agency of the U.S. Department of Defense. Much of the pioneering work on networking is the result of ARPANET, which was a network designed to link the computer science departments of a number of leading universities. TCP/IP was originally developed as part of the ARPANET project.

246

capabilities are built into TCP/IP itself to ensure reliability.

We now have all the pieces of the network puzzle. Network protocols provide the means by which various elements of telecommunications networks can communicate with one another. Thus, networks consist of physical media, arranged according to some topology, in a particular type of network, with communication throughout the network permitted through the use of particular protocols.

THE EXPLODING ROLE OF TELECOMMUNICATIONS AND NETWORKING

We have already stressed the critical role of telecommunications and networking several times, but to make the point even stronger, we will discuss how the role of telecommunications and networking is exploding in organizations today, particularly in medium-sized and large firms and agencies. In fact, some authorities suggest that the network (not the computer) is the most critical and most important information technology of the future. To illustrate this explosion, we will consider four areas of operation in which telecommunications networks are of critical and growing importance.

On-Line Operations

The dominant activities of many organizations have now been placed on-line to the computer via a network. For banks and other financial institutions, most teller stations (as well as automated teller machines) are now on-line. Tellers directly update your account when you cash a check or when you make a deposit. The bank does not care what branch in what city you use, because your account is always up-to-date. Not quite as obviously, insurance companies have much of their home office and branch office activities on-line. When an insurance claim is made or paid, when a premium is paid, or when a change is made to a policy, those activities are entered on-line to the

insurance company computer. These and other financial institutions (such as brokerage firms and international banks) simply could not operate as they do without telecommunications networks.

The computerized reservations systems of the major airlines are another example of an indispensable use of on-line systems. Of the nearly 40,000 travel agencies in the United States, more than 90 percent were on-line to one of these systems in 1988 (Belitsos, 1988), and the on-line proportion is approaching 100 percent in the mid-1990s. Further, studies show that the airline that provides an agency's computerized reservation system is up to 30 percent more likely to gain bookings on its flights. Thus, all the major airlines are making strong efforts to get their systems installed in as many agencies as possible and to maintain a strong customer relationship after the systems are installed (see Chapter 3 for further discussion).

Connectivity

Connectivity is a very popular buzzword among major U.S. and international corporations. Many organizations have major efforts underway to provide every managerial and professional employee with a personal workstation (usually a microcomputer) and to connect these workstations to a network structure so that each of these employees has access to every person and every system with which he might conceivably need to interact. Of course, it will take a long time and many resources to achieve this connectivity goal. The first steps are usually the installation of workstations and the provision of much more limited connectivity; often E-mail is the initial widely available application.

Connectivity to persons and organizations outside the firm is also important. American Hospital Supply Corporation created a strategic advantage by providing connectivity with the hospitals it served. Chrysler Corporation has installed a system to tie its dealers to the corporation so that deviations from expected sales are spotted quickly. All the automobile manufacturers are stressing connectivity with their suppliers so that they can adjust orders efficiently. Thus, connectivity

---

Kmart USING "RADAR" TO TRACK SHOPPER TRAFFIC

Kmart Corp., in an effort to improve service and sales at its discount stores, is testing a new radar-like system that tracks customer traffic. The system, developed by the Datatec Industries unit of Tytronix Corp., Fairfield, N.J., uses beams of infrared light to count customers as they pass under sensors mounted over the store entrance and on the ceiling at certain locations inside the store.

In the test at its Westwood, N.J., store, Kmart hopes to use the so-called Shopper-Trak system to improve service by sending salespeople to crowded departments and opening more checkout lanes before long lines form. The retailer, based in Troy, Mich., also expects to be able to determine for the first time what percentage of shoppers actually make purchases. Until now, the company has only tracked transactions, using the scanner system it finished installing last year at checkout counters at its 2,200 discount stores.

(Schwadel, 1991)

VOICE RESPONSE WORKS FOR SHOPPING CLUB

The Home Shopping Club is a television-based sales organization. The club offers a wide ranging merchandise selection—from personal computers to diamonds—on its own cable television channel. In order to handle the resulting flood of telephone calls, the club has installed a voice response system named "Tootie." Tootie consists of software written by Precision Software to run on an IBM Personal Computer AT or compatible. One AT can handle up to 64 telephone lines. Tootie has been highly successful and now handles about a million calls a month, which is more than one-third of the club's monthly calls.

The club offers only one item at a time—the item that is on display for the home television audience. All the items being sold are in-stock items at the club's warehouse, so selling continues until all items have been sold or the rate of sales becomes too slow. All the callers who wish to buy the merchandise call in on a toll-free 800 number and are directly routed to Tootie. Tootie answers by saying, "Hi! This is Tootie. We are now taking orders for the diamond necklace [or whatever]." The caller then uses a touch-tone telephone as a computer terminal to communicate with Tootie. If the caller wants to talk with a human operator, she punches in a zero. If the caller knows what she wants and has all the appropriate numbers handy, Tootie will prompt the customer to enter the numbers as needed. According to the Home Shopping Club, a human operator takes between 50 percent and 100 percent longer than Tootie to handle a call.

(Adapted from Ryan, 1988)

---

throughout the customer-manufacturer-supplier chain is a critical element.

Marketing

Telecommunications is being used for many exciting projects in the marketing area. Two examples are the use of laptop microcomputers by salespersons and the use of telecommunications for telemarketing and customer support. All business organizations sell products and services, although the distribution channels vary widely. The sales function is often performed either by sales representatives employed by the firm or by independent agents aligned with the firm (e.g., an insurance agent). In either case, telecommunications is being widely used to provide support for the sales personnel.

This sales support is not always as direct as the two examples above. Such support often takes the form of on-line information describing product or service characteristics and availability. This up-to-the-minute information makes the sales representative or agent more competitive and should increase profitability of the organization (as well as increasing the chances of retaining productive sales personnel). The importance of this instantaneous information is apparent for a St. Louis–based Merrill Lynch stockbroker talking to a client who is considering the purchase of a stock on the New York Stock Exchange, but it is almost as critical for a parts clerk at a Honda dealership in

Oregon dealing with a disgruntled customer. The parts clerk can use his terminal to check the availability of a needed part in ten Honda regional warehouses in the United States, and can immediately place the order from the closest warehouse that has the part.

Electronic Data Interchange

Electronic data interchange, or EDI, was defined in Chapter 3 as a set of standards and hardware and software technology that permits business documents (such as purchase orders, invoices, and price lists) to be transferred electronically between computers in separate organizations. For the most part, the transmission of EDI documents takes place over public VANs. The automobile industry is probably further along in introducing EDI than other industries, but many firms and industries are now moving to implement this exciting technology.

It has been estimated that one-half of all interorganizational business documents will be transmitted by EDI by the year 1995 (Senn, 1992). Certainly the evidence favoring EDI is impressive. For example, RCA recently estimated that each purchase order it processes by conventional means costs approximately $50, while each purchase order processed by EDI costs $4 ($1 of which is communications costs). An Arthur D. Little study performed for the grocery industry concluded that if only half of the firms in the industry implemented EDI, the industry would save $300 million per year. Lithonia Inc., a manufacturer of lighting fixtures, has cut in half the time it takes to receive and fill orders from customers by incorporating EDI in the process.

The challenge with EDI, as with many other telecommunications applications, is the development of a set of widely accepted standards or protocols to govern EDI transmissions. The American National Standards Institute (ANSI) has taken the lead in setting up EDI standards by charging its X12 Committee "to develop standards to facilitate electronic interchange relating to such business transactions as order placement and processing, shipment and receiving, invoicing, payment and cash application data associated with the provi-

sion of products and services" (*X12 Standards*, 1989). Thus far, standards exist for such documents as an invoice, price/sales catalog, request for quotation, purchase order, order status inquiry and report, and payment order/remittance advice; work is continuing to develop standards for additional transactions and to refine existing standards. The ANSI X12 Committee is also working closely with the ISO to ensure the eventual development of a worldwide standard for EDI.

THE TELECOMMUNICATIONS INDUSTRY

We would like to discuss the telecommunications component of the computer/communications industry in this section, but the statistics on such a broad industrial grouping as the computer/communications industry are not readily available. In fact, statistics on the entire telecommunications industry (including both carriers and equipment vendors) are not readily available either. Estimates for the entire industry could be determined for the United States, but they would be considerably more difficult to obtain for the rest of the world, where many of the carriers are government-owned and operated. We are forced to pursue our consideration of the telecommunications industry in a more segmented fashion.

There are two major segments of the telecommunications industry (or the telecommunications segment of the computer/communications industry): (a) carriers, who own the physical plant (cabling, satellites, and so forth) and provide the service of transmitting communications from one location to another; and (b) equipment vendors, who manufacture and sell a wide range of telecommunications-related equipment, including LANs, digital PBXs, multiplexers, and modems.

As an important historical footnote, the entire complexion of the telecommunications industry changed in 1984 with the breakup of AT&T into the long-distance telephone and equipment-centered AT&T and the regional Bell operating companies (RBOCs). Although the various pieces that resulted from the divestiture were still large, there was no longer a single monolithic entity in control of most telecommunications in the United States. Just before the AT&T breakup, technological developments in long-haul communications (microwave, satellites, and fiber optics) made economically feasible the development of long distance networks to compete with those of AT&T. Thus came the rise of MCI, Sprint, and other long distance carriers. Furthermore, court decisions and management policies served to split effectively AT&T (and each of the RBOCs) into two businesses—regulated and nonregulated. The original carrier portion of the business was still regulated, but the nonregulated portion could now compete actively in the computer/communications equipment market. AT&T, and to a lesser extent the operating companies, became major players as equipment vendors.

The AT&T divestiture also had significant managerial implications for the telecommunications function in a user organization. Prior to 1984 the telecommunications manager had a relatively easy job, dealing with AT&T for almost all telecommunications needs and receiving high quality, reliable service for a regulated price. After divestiture, the job got much tougher. The manager now has to deal with a variety of carriers and equipment vendors (often including AT&T), and the manager has the responsibility to make sure that all the various pieces fit together.

The carriers, as noted, are government-owned in much of the world, although links between countries (such as transatlantic and transpacific links) are often privately owned. In the United States the carriers are dominated by AT&T and the RBOCs, such as Ameritech and BellSouth, but there is significant competition in the long distance arena, with AT&T being severely pushed by MCI and Sprint. The carriers are regulated in terms of what they can charge for their various transmission services by federal and state regulatory agencies. Thus, rates for local telephone, long distance telephone, leased line, T-1, T-3, and ISDN services are all subject to review by the appropriate regulatory bodies.

To provide a rough picture of the major players in the U.S. telecommunications industry, the top ten telecommunications companies in sales of equipment and services, according to the 1993

TABLE 6.3   Top Ten Firms in Telecommunications: Equipment and Services, United States

Company	Sales (millions)
AT&T	$64,904
MCI Communications	10,562
Sprint	9,230
McCaw Cellular Communications	1,743
Pacific Telecom	705
Scientific-Atlanta	677
Lin Broadcasting	573
Communications Satellite	564
DSC Communications	536
Telephone & Data Systems	454

Source: "The 1993 Business Week 1000," *Business Week* (April 2, 1993): 195.

Business Week 1000, are listed in Table 6.3. Please note that in every case the services component (long distance or cellular) dominates the equipment component. Table 6.4 lists the top ten telephone companies (local service) according to *Business Week*. Neither list contains any real surprises, with the equipment and services list dominated by AT&T, MCI, and Sprint (in that order), and the telephone companies list dominated by GTE and the RBOCs.

In the hotly contested long distance market, AT&T's market share had dropped to 66 percent in 1992, compared to 17 percent for second-place MCI (Lewyn, 1993). In terms of the 800 number

TABLE 6.4. Top Ten Firms in Telecommunications: Telephone Companies, United States

Company	Sales (millions)
GTE	$19,984
BellSouth	15,202
NYNEX	13,155
Bell Atlantic	12,647
Ameritech	11,153
US West	10,281
Southwestern Bell	10,015
Pacific Telesis Group	9,935
Alltel	2,092
Southern New England Telecommunications	1,614

Source: "The 1993 Business Week 1000," *Business Week* (April 2, 1993): 195.

market share in the United States, AT&T led the way with 85 percent, followed by MCI with 6 percent and Sprint with 3 percent (*Communications News*, 1993).

For a closer look at the equipment vendor segment of the telecommunications industry, we shall rely on the statistics gathered by *Datamation* (1993). *Datamation* calls the relevant category data communications, and it explicitly includes the global sales of communications processors, LANs, digital PBXs, multiplexers, modems, and facsimile machines but excludes central office telephone switches and analog PBXs as well as data transmission services. Thus, the *Datamation* figures are not quite as inclusive for communications equipment as we would prefer, but they should provide a reasonable overall picture of this segment of the industry.

In 1992 (the last complete year for which data are available), *Datamation* estimated the global data communications revenues of the world's top 100 information systems (IS) companies as $17.5 billion, or 5.5 percent of the total IS revenue of these 100 firms. Table 6.5 lists the top ten firms in data communications, their sales, and their market shares expressed as a percentage of total revenues in data communications by all of the *Datamation* top 100 firms.

These top ten firms are an interesting set. Four of them are American (AT&T, IBM, Mo-

torola, and Hewlett-Packard); one is British (Racal), one Canadian (Northern Telecom), and four are Japanese. (By contrast, only one of the next five firms—3Com—is based in the United States.) Most of the top ten firms in data communications are also computer vendors, but computer hardware is the primary business only for IBM and Hewlett-Packard. AT&T and Nippon T&T are primarily providers of telephone service; Northern Telecom produces communications equipment; Motorola is a diversified manufacturer of semiconductor chips and other electronics gear, including modems and wireless LAN products; Ricoh is a major supplier of copiers, facsimile, and other office equipment; and Matsushita, Racal, and Mitsubishi all produce a wide variety of electronics products. Racal has a major contract to operate the Government Data Network in the United Kingdom, which is designed to link all government departments across the country.

In addition to the two primary segments, there are other smaller but important segments of the broadly defined telecommunications industry: the manufacture and sale of twisted pair, coaxial, and fiber optic cabling; the installation of cabling, microwave, and satellite stations; and the development of standards and software for telecommunications.

SUMMARY

The telecommunications and networking area has existed for considerably longer than computer hardware and software, but the developments in all three areas have merged in the past several years to put more emphasis on telecommunications than ever before. The decade of the 1990s may well become known as the era of networking. Networks provide enhanced communication to organizations and individuals, as well as permit the sharing of resources and data. They are also essential to implement distributed data processing and client/server systems. The exploding role of telecommunications and networking is evident in many organizational activities, including on-line operations, marketing, and EDI. There is an

TABLE 6.5   Top Ten Firms in Data Communications Segment of Information Systems Industry, World

Company	Sales (millions)	Market Share (percent)
AT&T	$3,315	19.5%
Northern Telecom	2,300	12.6
IBM	2,200	12.0
Nippon T&T	1,872	10.2
Matsushita	1,262	6.9
Ricoh	956	5.6
Motorola	745	4.4
Racal	691	4.1
Mitsubishi	647	3.8
Hewlett-Packard	630	3.7

Note: Percents refer to share of *Datamation* 100 revenues.

Source: *Datamation* 39 (June 15, 1993): 23.

intense desire to improve organizational communications through universal connectivity. A communications revolution is underway, with networking at the heart of it.

The technology of telecommunications and networking is extremely complex, perhaps even more so than computer hardware and software. By concentrating on a number of key elements, we have attempted to develop a managerial-level understanding of networks. Communication signals may be either analog or digital. It is easier to transmit data digitally, and there is a concerted movement toward digital transmission today. Networks employ a variety of transmission media (such as coaxial and fiber optic cable) and are configured in various topologies (such as rings and trees). Major network types include computer telecommunications networks, emanating from a mainframe computer; digital PBX networks for both voice and data; LANs for high-speed communication within a restricted area; and WANs for lower-speed communication over a long haul. The WANs in particular are highly dependent upon facilities owned and operated by the telephone companies and other carriers. To enable the devices attached to any type of network to communicate with one another, protocols (or rules of operation) have to be agreed upon. Happily, there is general movement toward the establishment and acceptance of a suite of protocols known as the OSI model.

This marks the end of the three-chapter technology component of this book. We have tried very hard to cover only the technology that you as a manager need to know. Whatever your personal managerial career entails, you are likely to be working both directly and indirectly with hardware, software, and telecommunications. Knowledge of information technology is essential for understanding its present and potential impact on your organization and your job.

REVIEW QUESTIONS

1. What are the primary reasons for networking among computers and computer-related devices?

2. Explain the difference between analog and digital signals. Is the trend toward more use of (a) analog or (b) digital signals in the future?

3. What is a modem? When and why are modems necessary?

4. List the primary types of physical media in use today in telecommunications networks. Which of these media has the fastest transmission speed? The slowest transmission speed?

5. Describe the similarity between the bus and the ring topology; then describe the similarity between the star and the tree topology.

6. Identify the following acronyms or initials:

    | LAN | WATS | PBX |
    | WAN | VAN | ISDN |

7. Explain how packet switching works.

8. List the seven layers of the OSI reference model, and give a description of the role of each layer in a single sentence.

9. In addition to the OSI model, other important protocols include SNA, X.25, and TCP/IP. In one or two sentences per protocol, tell what these names stand for (if anything) and describe the basic purposes of these three protocols.

10. Name the top firm in the world (in terms of market share) in the data communications sector of the information systems industry (as defined by *Datamation*). Also name three other firms in the top ten. In what countries are most of the top ten firms based?

11. Considering the telecommunications industry in the United States as defined by *Business Week*, name three of the top firms in the equipment and services segment and name three of the top firms in the telephone companies segment.

DISCUSSION QUESTIONS

1. Review Question 2 refers to the trend toward more digital (rather than analog) communication. In your judgment, what are the primary causes of this trend?

2. Discuss the advantages and disadvantages of the three primary types of local area networks—contention bus, token bus, and token ring.

3. A PBX network is often viewed as an alternative to a local area network. What are the advantages and disadvantages of a PBX network vis-à-vis a local area network?

4. As noted in the chapter, the most common transmission medium is the twisted pair. What recent development is likely to ensure that twisted pair will continue to be the most common transmission medium? Why?

5. Why is the idea of a standard network protocol, such as the OSI reference model, important? What are the advantages and disadvantages of developing a single standard protocol?

6. Consider an industry with which you are somewhat familiar (because of your own work experience, a parent's work experience, a friend's work experience, or your study of industry performance). Use your imagination to suggest new ways in which electronic data interchange could be used in this industry.

7. The current status of the telecommunications industry was described near the end of this chapter. Using your personal crystal ball (and the knowledge you have picked up from reading the business news and from other classes), speculate on likely important future trends in the telecommunications industry. What firms do you think are likely to do well over the next decade? Which firms may stumble? What new developments may reshape the industry?

8. Consider a particular small business with which you are familiar (as a customer, as a current or former employee, as a relative of the owner). Describe the current telecommunications employed by the business (every business uses a telephone). In what ways might telecommunications and networking be used to improve the profitability of this business? Consider, as appropriate, such ideas as the use of facsimile communication, telemarketing, enhanced communication through an in-house local area network, and WATS.

REFERENCES

1987. "Tomorrow's role for tele-communications." *I/S Analyzer* 25 (May): 1–11.

1988. "Exploiting tele-communications benefits." *I/S Analyzer* 26 (April): 1–14.

1988. "ISDN: The new telephone network." *Fortune* 118 (October 24): 179–208.

1989. "The strategic value of EDI." *I/S Analyzer* 27 (August): 1–14.

1989. "Networking management: The key to better customer service." *I/S Analyzer* 27 (December): 1–11.

1993. "Global leaders in nine product categories." *Datamation* 39 (June 15): 22–23.

1993. "800 number market share." *Communications News* 30 (March): 52.

1993. "The 1993 Business Week 1000." *Business Week* (April 2): 195.

American National Standards Institute. 1989. *Electronic Data Interchange X12 Standards* (Draft Version 2 Release 4, Document Number ASC X12S/89-647).

Belitsos, Byron. 1988. "MIS pilots the air wars." *Computer Decisions* 22 (March): 36–41.

Bozman, Jean S. 1988. "Fire KOs Chicago networks." *Computerworld* 22 (May 16): 1, 121.

Catlett, Charles E. 1989. "The NFSNET: Beginnings of a national research internet." *Academic Computing* 3 (January): 18–22, 59–64.

Chernicoff, David P. 1993. "Wired for the future." *PC Week* 10 (March 15): 49–51.

Conlon, Theresa. 1990. "Mobile networks keep transportation rolling." *MIS Week* 11 (February 12): 1, 17, 20.

Johnson, Amy H. 1992. "Pennies from heaven: VSAT nets pay off." *Corporate Computing* 1 (December): 33.

Kerr, Susan. 1992a. "One last chance for ISDN." *Datamation* 38 (May 1): 65–68.

———. 1992b. "How IBM is rebuilding SNA." *Datamation* 38 (October 1): 28–31.

Lewyn, Mark. 1993. "MCI is coming through loud and clear." *Business Week* (January 25): 84, 88.

Richards, Bill. 1988. "Fire in fiber-optic 'gateway' sparks flight delays, problems in brokerages." *Wall Street Journal* 69 (May 11): 24.

Ryan, Alan J. 1988. "Shopping club finds a bargain." *Computerworld* 22 (February 8): 14.

Schwadel, Francine. 1991. "Kmart testing 'radar' to track shopper traffic." *Wall Street Journal* 72 (September 24): B1, B7.

Senn, James A. 1992. "Electronic data interchange: The elements of implementation." *Information Systems Management* 9 (Winter): 45–53.

Strauss, Paul. 1992. "IBM legitimizes FDDI?" *Datamation* 38 (August 15): 87–88.

Tanenbaum, Andrew S. 1988. *Computer Networks*, 2nd ed. Englewood Cliffs, N.J.: Prentice-Hall.

Wylie, Margie. 1993. "Will networks kill the corporation?" *Network World* 10 (January 11): S9, S12.

6

Pacific Financial Services, Inc.

Pacific Financial Services, Inc. (PFS), was formed in 1986 when a mutual health insurance company formally transformed itself from a single-state health care insurer into a diversified company providing financial and insurance services to clients in many states. That transformation was still under way in 1988, when PFS had divisions and subsidiaries in five states and was serving clients throughout the western half of the country.

In its traditional health insurance business, PFS provides individual and group health insurance and managed health-care products for more than one million clients. Its managed health-care plans include more than 50 percent of the hospitals and 70 percent of the physicians in the states participating as health-care providers, and membership in these plans grew by 25 percent in 1987 to more than 200,000 persons.

PFS also has a life insurance subsidiary that offers a growing portfolio of life and disability insurance products, including payroll deduction products. Another subsidiary provides administration and consultation for benefit plans, retirement plans, and group insurance arrangements. Another subsidiary offers risk-management services and property and casualty insurance.

....

PFS Strategic Thrusts

In 1988 PFS was in the process of changing its fundamental corporate culture from a rather staid mutual

insurance company to a dynamic, growth-and-profit-oriented competitive tiger. As stated in the 1987 PFS Annual Report:

Our corporate mission is to provide financial products and services of outstanding value and quality to a wide variety of clients.

This corporate mission provides a framework for a new corporate culture that has permeated this growing organization: A commitment to exploring new market opportunities . . . a heightened sensitivity to customer needs . . . a new spirit of entrepreneurship . . . a confidence that we can provide exceptional value to our clients.

At Pacific Financial Services we are committed to new and higher levels of performance as we develop new ways to serve more clients by helping them maximize their rewards and control their risks.

PFS has three major strategic thrusts: diversification, decentralization, and providing the very best service of any financial services company.

PFS president Daniel B. Harton has been the champion of these new directions and strategies:

Our primary customers are organizations that seek to provide a range of benefits to their employees, one of which is health insurance. We can serve these customers better by providing other benefit packages such as retirement plans and life insurance. Moreover, it is getting harder and harder to make decent profits in the health insurance business. Thus we intend to grow by creating or purchasing new financial services operations wherever we see a product or service need

---

that has an attractive profit potential and fits into our marketplace.

We also believe in decentralization, both organizationally and geographically. A business is most effective when it is comprised of small, well-focused units with clear missions. We also need diversity in our organizational forms—we need both a mutual company and stock companies working together. We've found that having semi-autonomous operating companies works better than having more divisions of our big mutual company. And as we grow we intend to expand into attractive smaller communities with favorable labor markets.

Health care insurance has gotten to the point where it is virtually a commodity product. Thus the only competitive edge is service, and we are committed to getting that competitive edge! In order to use service as our competitive edge we must provide the very best service, and a major component of that service is providing convenient access to us no matter who you are or where you may be.

Harton recognizes that the new PFS organization will be in continual change. "I want to be able to react instantly to both opportunities and problems!" he asserts. "We must be able to create and deliver new products, acquire new businesses, and divest ourselves of nonperformers with a minimum of delay and disruption."

Harton is convinced that communications technology is a key to the success of the new PFS:

We've been highly automated for years, but diversification and decentralization will only work if we can tie things together with effective communications networks. And providing outstanding service means giving everyone— our customers, policyholders, health care providers—convenient access to us. That means that each person must be able to contact us through a single local telephone number, no matter what line of business they are concerned with or what their purpose may be.

....
Telecommunications at PFS

John Scott is the director of corporate communications for PFS. Before joining PFS in 1987, Scott had

experience managing customer services for a hospital and running the information services organization for a large regional bank in Denver, where he had experience with voice and data integration. He reports to senior vice president Arthur K. Wilson, who is responsible for the decentralization of PFS.

Scott is responsible for running the telecommunications organization, both voice and data, but his major responsibilities center on supporting the PFS strategic thrusts with computer/communications technology. He reports,

My biggest challenge has been development of our strategic communications directions and relating that to the business strategic thrusts. I have to show President Harton how we can improve our service. That takes every bit of my customer service background, for I have to understand customer service as a product that you sell and manage as a product. I have to be able to take a business problem and visualize how it could be handled by blending technology and manual efforts into a system to solve the business problem. And I have to be able to communicate this to managers at all levels, including the board of directors.

When Scott joined PFS the telecommunications area reported to the director of operations of information services. Information services was a very traditional data processing department that operated a pure IBM shop with centralized processing on a huge IBM 3090-600 located in the headquarters building. The department was wary of minicomputers, having had a bad experience about 10 years ago with several minis that could not talk to each other, and it did not understand office automation, equating it with word processing. The department was committed to IBM's IMS DBMS and had never even investigated relational databases.

Furthermore, data communications was committed to IBM's Systems Network Architecture—if you wanted to communicate with the mainframe you had to come in through SNA and could not use the standard ASYNCH approach that is commonly used with PCs. That didn't make sense to Scott. He asserts,

My philosophy is just the opposite of that! If the corporate objective is service and if a provider wants to send in electronic claims from a PC, my job is to find a way for them to do so without them having to spend major amounts of money.

As a result of the new directions at PFS, there have been many changes in both the telecommunications and data processing areas. For example, they are taking much work off the IBM mainframe and putting it on networked DEC VAXes, and they have installed AT&T's 3B2 UNIX processor to control communications and do protocol conversion so that people coming in ASYNCH can get into the mainframe through SNA.

The Telecom Organization   Scott has seven former technicians who are taking on new roles as consultants and product managers. He has a voice product manager, an office systems product manager, and a data systems product manager that market and manage the technology in their areas. He has a trainer for office automation and installers who program the PBXs and work with clients on designing applications. There is a controls person who runs the monitoring systems and prepares reports on system performance, and there is a system architect who consults with users and helps Scott develop his technical architecture. In addition, he has 10 people in the back room who control and operate the networks.

The Voice Network   PFS is in an information-intensive business. It supplies information to member customers, physicians, pharmacies, state insurance commissioners, and other government agencies. Its corporate telephone bill is about $350,000 a month, which is the largest corporate operating expense.

PFS supplies 800 numbers (inbound WATS) for all its customers to call when they have problems or questions. For example, if you get a statement reporting how much your health insurance paid on an outpatient surgical procedure, the statement will include an 800 number for you to call for any questions that you have when you try to understand why they did not pay more of the costs. They have almost 300 inbound WATS lines going into 37 groups, each of which handles a specific class of users or problems. They have between 300 and 400 customer service people who do nothing but handle these calls.

A few years ago, when the health care insurance business was less competitive, service was not a major priority, and its service in handling telephone questions was terrible. When PFS began to be concerned with providing good service, it had no way to measure the quality of its call-handling service. Therefore, PFS added an Automatic Call Distributor

(ACD) to monitor the incoming lines and distribute the calls to the customer service personnel. The ACD also provides statistics on how long callers wait before talking to a customer service person.

The ACD at PFS runs on an AT&T minicomputer that attaches to DIMENSION PBX. When you call one of the 800 numbers the ACD routes your call to any free customer service representative in the group serving you. If all the service representatives are busy, the ACD plays you a message saying "All our customer service representatives are busy right now. Please hang on and someone will be with you as soon as possible." Then your call is put in a queue, and when your turn comes, you are connected to the next available representative.

A major value of the ACD lies in the information that it collects about the volume of calls, length of calls, time customers are on hold, the number of calls abandoned while on hold, and so on. These statistics can be reported by phone number, operator, group, time of day, or (since the basic data are stored in a relational database) in any way you want them summarized. Several typical reports from an ACD are included as Exhibit 1.

When PFS got its first reports after installing the ACD the company was shocked to learn that service was so bad. For some groups the average waiting time was almost 10 minutes, and about 60 percent of the calls were abandoned. Today, PFS has very stringent performance standards that are taken very seriously by everyone—they are used when determining people's performance pay increases, merit pay, and bonuses. The current standards require that the average speed of answering not exceed 20 seconds and that the percentage of abandoned calls not exceed 15 percent. A current management report shows that all but four groups are meeting these standards. Most of the groups have abandoned calls down to less than 5 percent and are answering over 80 percent of their calls in less than 20 seconds.

In its headquarters location PFS has a DIMENSION 2000 PBX switch with automatic route selection for outgoing calls that serves about 2,000 telephones. It has smaller PBXs in its other locations throughout the country.

Data Networks   PFS uses quite a variety of data networks. Its backbone network connecting its major operations in the metropolitan area has just been converted to use T-1 circuits. As it continues its

(text continued on p. 262)

EXHIBIT 1
....
Automatic Call Distributor Reports

```
                   ECD-4000EX AGENT ACTIVITY REPORT

ARCHIVE DAILY REPORT              TELCOM TECHNOLOGIES
                                    AGENT ACTIVITY
AGENT GROUP 5:    OVERFLOW GRP                REPORT INTERVAL: 24:00
Period Covered:   May/04/87    Mon 12:00 AM to May/05/87   Tue 12:00 AM
-----------------------------------------------------------------------
          ------TOTAL CALLS----------------- ----AVERAGE DURATION-------------
                                                         Min:Sec
AGENT      Incoming Outgoing Internal Transfer Incoming Outgoing Internal Wrapup
          -------- -------- -------- -------- -------- -------- -------- ------
FINDLEY C     53       10       1        0      1:59     3:27     0:11    2:10
GURULE R      40        6       0        0      1:54     2:25     0:00    1:38
GOMEZ D       34        0       1        1      2:24     0:00     0:02    0:29
HERNANDEZ D  165       16       3        3      1:28     1:13     0:02    0:00
LEONARD MN   137        2      12        2      1:30     2:58     0:02    0:00
MARTINEZ A    24        7       1        0      2:34     1:58     0:01    0:25
SIBILLA S     90        0       2        2      1:30     0:00     0:02    0:00
HOLMAN D     121       16       7        1      2:17     1:47     0:04    2:30
GOINGS C      92       13       0        0      2:41     1:57     0:00    1:14
SHARPY L      59        3       0        0      2:22     2:21     0:00    0:27
MCMILLAN N    44        5       1        1      1:48     1:11     0:01    0:00
BURR J       102       16       4        2      3:04     3:14     0:37    0:00
LEE L         96        5       1        1      3:18     3:10     1:03    3:10
CATES T        0        0       0        0      0:00     0:00     0:00    0:00
SIERRA M     122       11       3        3      2:11     0:58     0:02    2:06
ZUMBRO R     177        7      10        2      1:47     0:43     0:40    0:33
MIRANDA S     46        0       1        1      2:56     0:00     0:03    1:03
          -------- -------- -------- -------- -------- -------- -------- ------
TOTAL       1402      117      37       19      2:08     2:02     0:16    1:33


                        ALLOCATION OF TIME
                             Hr:Min
           Signed-in
AGENT      Duration Incoming Outgoing Internal  Wrapup Available Unavailable
-----      -------- -------- -------- -------- ------ --------- -----------
FINDLEY C    7:26     1:45     0:35     0:01     0:04    4:44      0:17
                     23.6%     7.7%     0.0%     0.9%   63.6%      3.8%
GURULE R     7:25     1:16     0:15     0:00     0:23    5:29      0:02
                     17.1%     3.2%     0.0%     5.1%   74.0%      0.4%
GOMEZ D      1:50     1:22     0:00     0:00     0:01    0:24      0:03
                     74.4%     0.0%     0.0%     0.8%   21.6%      2.9%
```

(continued on next page)

EXHIBIT 1 *(continued)*

ECD-4000EX AGENT ACTIVITY REPORT (Continued)

ARCHIVE DAILY REPORT   TELCOM TECHNOLOGIES
                               SYSTEM ACTIVITY

AGENT GROUP 1: P.O.T.S.   REPORT INTERVAL: 24:00
Period Covered: May/04/87   Mon 12:00 AM to May/05/87   Tue 12:00 AM

	Answered before Message	Answered after Message	Handled	Abandoned	Offered	Over-flowed	Night Service	OUTGOING CALLS
12:00-12:30 AM	1	0	1	0	1	5	0	0
12:30-01:00 AM	0	0	0	0	0	3	0	0
01:00-01:30 AM	0	0	0	0	0	1	0	0
01:30-02:00 AM	0	0	0	0	0	3	0	0
03:30-04:00 AM	0	0	0	0	0	3	0	0
04:30-05:00 AM	0	0	0	0	0	1	0	0
05:00-05:30 AM	0	0	0	0	0	3	0	0
05:30-06:00 AM	0	0	0	1	1	15	0	0
06:00-06:30 AM	17	8	25	6	31	13	0	0
06:30-07:00 AM	46	23	69	8	77	10	0	4
07:00-07:30 AM	47	67	114	22	136	30	0	2
07:30-08:00 AM	39	127	166	50	216	31	0	12
08:00-08:30 AM	146	92	238	20	258	74	0	13
08:30-09:00 AM	197	139	336	40	376	125	0	39
09:00-09:30 AM	101	195	296	43	339	108	0	32
09:30-10:00 AM	152	144	296	34	330	86	0	34
10:00-10:30 AM	165	74	239	16	255	90	0	37
10:30-11:00 AM	264	40	304	15	319	90	0	45
11:00-11:30 AM	220	14	234	4	238	54	0	33
11:00-12:00 PM	250	0	250	3	253	31	0	22
12:00-12:30 PM	136	53	189	16	205	20	0	27
12:30-01:00 PM	54	145	199	41	240	46	0	34
01:00-01:30 PM	50	142	192	73	265	45	0	17
01:30-02:00 PM	47	162	209	45	254	43	0	30
02:00-02:30 PM	121	109	230	22	252	39	0	49
02:30-03:00 PM	96	107	203	27	230	76	0	27
03:00-03:30 PM	121	81	202	24	226	63	0	23
03:30-04:00 PM	152	64	216	13	229	62	0	23
04:00-04:30 PM	166	23	189	3	192	54	0	13
04:30-05:00 PM	72	116	188	36	224	57	0	19
05:00-05:30 PM	54	68	122	25	147	37	0	16
05:30-06:00 PM	58	65	123	12	135	49	0	9
06:00-06:30 PM	130	5	135	4	139	4	0	14
06:30-07:00 PM	133	0	133	6	139	0	0	8
07:00-07:30 PM	116	0	116	7	123	0	0	7
07:30-08:00 PM	91	14	105	6	111	0	0	6
08:00-08:30 PM	68	17	85	6	91	0	0	14
08:30-09:00 PM	65	1	66	5	71	0	0	1
09:00-09:30 PM	47	7	54	2	56	0	0	3
09:30-10:00 PM	42	14	56	1	57	0	0	2
10:00-10:30 PM	30	9	39	5	44	0	0	3
10:30-11:00 PM	15	1	16	3	19	0	0	0
11:00-11:30 PM	13	4	17	0	17	0	0	2
11:30-12:00 AM	4	1	5	0	5	0	0	0
TOTAL CALLS	3526	2131	5657	644	6301	1371	0	620

EXHIBIT 1 *(continued)*

....

ECD-4000EX AGENT ACTIVITY REPORT (Continued)

ARCHIVE DAILY REPORT   TELCOM TECHNOLOGIES
                           SYSTEM ACTIVITY
--------------INCOMING CALLS----------------------
                    Min:Sec

	Average Sign-in Agents	Average Talk Time	Average Queue	Longest Queue	Average Wait to Abandon	Longest Wait to Abandon	OUTGOING CALLS Average Duration
12:00-12:30 AM	0	1:41	0:02	0:02	0:00	0:00	0:00
12:30-01:00 AM	0	0:00	0:00	0:00	0:00	0:00	0:00
01:00-01:30 AM	0	0:00	0:00	0:00	0:00	0:00	0:00
01:30-02:00 AM	0	0:00	0:00	0:00	0:00	0:00	0:00
03:30-04:00 AM	0	0:00	0:00	0:00	0:00	0:00	0:00
04:30-05:00 AM	0	0:00	0:00	0:00	0:00	0:00	0:00
05:00-05:30 AM	0	0:00	0:00	0:00	0:00	0:00	0:00
05:30-06:00 AM	0	0:00	0:00	0:00	2:01	2:01	0:00
06:00-06:30 AM	2	1:25	0:15	1:19	0:30	1:26	0:00
06:30-07:00 AM	6	1:36	0:30	3:25	0:33	1:02	2:14
07:00-07:30 AM	10	2:01	0:28	1:42	0:19	0:53	2:05
07:30-08:00 AM	13	1:56	1:28	3:52	1:03	3:05	1:29
08:00-08:30 AM	21	2:10	0:21	1:53	0:24	0:49	0:59
08:30-09:00 AM	30	2:11	0:30	2:05	0:31	1:20	1:26
09:00-09:30 AM	31	2:24	0:32	1:41	0:29	1:19	2:51
09:30-10:00 AM	28	2:07	0:42	2:43	0:34	1:51	2:03
10:00-10:30 AM	25	2:30	0:15	1:13	0:19	0:47	1:20
10:30-11:00 AM	28	2:00	0:08	1:34	0:12	0:58	1:27
11:00-11:30 AM	26	2:25	0:03	1:08	0:01	0:02	1:52
11:30-12:00 AM	22	1:51	0:01	0:06	0:01	0:03	1:01
12:00-12:30 PM	20	2:23	0:13	1:26	0:24	1:19	1:12
12:30-01:00 PM	19	2:21	1:07	3:55	0:47	3:07	1:02
01:00-01:30 PM	20	2:26	1:47	4:55	0:55	4:50	2:38
01:30-02:00 PM	21	2:17	1:03	2:45	0:35	2:19	1:25
02:00-02:30 PM	24	2:19	0:24	1:32	0:30	1:23	1:07
02:30-03:00 PM	21	2:20	0:24	1:21	0:19	1:04	1:57
03:00-03:30 PM	20	2:30	0:16	1:11	0:21	1:00	1:20
03:30-04:00 PM	22	2:21	0:14	1:20	0:25	0:53	1:57
04:00-04:30 PM	21	2:32	0:05	0:42	0:03	0:04	2:18
04:30-05:00 PM	17	2:18	0:35	2:09	0:29	1:34	1:09
05:00-05:30 PM	14	2:37	0:35	2:02	0:18	0:58	1:41
05:30-06:00 PM	11	1:59	0:23	1:49	0:17	0:51	2:17
06:00-06:30 PM	16	1:52	0:03	0:21	0:05	0:14	2:42
06:30-07:00 PM	12	1:24	0:01	0:14	0:02	0:04	1:27
07:00-07:30 PM	13	1:48	0:01	0:05	0:01	0:04	2:55
07:30-08:00 PM	10	1:53	0:06	1:05	0:07	0:36	0:38
08:00-08:30 PM	9	1:50	0:11	1:32	0:17	1:12	1:14
08:30-09:00 PM	8	1:45	0:02	0:18	0:05	0:23	2:15
09:00-09:30 PM	7	1:45	0:05	1:14	0:01	0:02	4:24
09:30-10:00 PM	5	1:31	0:17	1:55	0:15	0:15	1:36
10:00-10:30 PM	4	1:31	0:13	1:52	0:01	0:02	1:12
10:30-11:00 PM	3	1:10	0:06	0:27	0:15	0:35	0:00
11:00-11:30 PM	2	1:25	0:15	1:46	0:00	0:00	1:02
11:30-12:00 PM	2	0:55	0:09	0:26	0:00	0:00	0:00
TOTAL	13	2:10	0:26	4:55	0:32	4:50	1:38

(continued on next page)

259

EXHIBIT 1 *(continued)*

ECD-4000EX AGENT ACTIVITY REPORT (Continued)

ARCHIVE DAILY REPORT   TELCOM TECHNOLOGIES
                                          SYSTEM ACTIVITY
                                          SERVICE LEVELS
                       Number of Calls Handled within XX Seconds

0	10	20	30	40	60	180	240	OVER
0	3198	442	375	312	442	805	72	11
0.0%	56.5%	7.8%	6.6%	5.5%	5.5%	7.8%	14.2%	0.1%

ABANDON LEVELS
Number of Calls Abandoned within XX Seconds

5	10	20	30	60	120	180	240	OVER
162	33	52	112	205	57	16	5	2
25.1%	5.1%	8.0%	17.3%	31.8%	8.8%	2.4%	0.7%	0.3%

decentralization, it plans to expand this network to include all locations nationwide.

PFS has an extensive 800 number dial-in network for its providers. Of the 35,000 providers in the area PFS serves, almost 13,000 of them use this network to send in electronic claims. These providers have PC software that allows them to fill out the claim form on the PC screen, and when it is completed the computer automatically dials a PFS 800 number and transmits the claim to the PFS computer.

Some of these providers also make inquiries to obtain information on the status of claims from the PFS claims processing system. Querying the claims processing system is rather cumbersome at present, but PFS has plans to develop a user-friendly front end to it that will encourage providers to make more direct inquiries through the system.

PFS also has an 800-station office automation network that provides word processing and document preparation, spreadsheets, electronic mail, maintaining calendars and scheduling meetings, and other executive support functions. This network also provides access to the mainframe for those stations.

PFS is a node in the national network that ties together many mutual health insurers with 56-kbps circuits so that they can talk to each other and share data. PFS also has a company-wide FAX network.

Current Directions

Scott is a strong believer in twisted pair and in using the PBX to provide both voice and data networks.

We've stopped running COAX in our buildings. We have a big patchboard in this building that allows us to move telephones and terminals with only an hour's notice. It used to take us at least three weeks to make the simplest change.

PFS is providing a PC environment for workstations at all levels. It has a standard hardware and software setup for executives, another setup for professional people, and another for clerical people. These are all connected to the network that provides access to the mainframe and the office automation system.

PFS's commitment to decentralization includes getting everything that it can off the huge mainframe and onto DEC VAXes located with the units and networked together. Scott notes that,

EXHIBIT 2
PFS Corporate Site Example

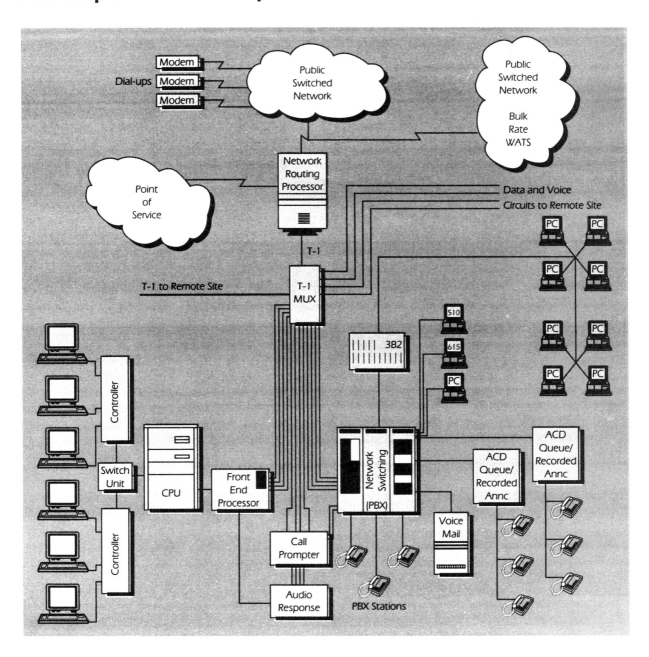

EXHIBIT 3
. . . .
PFS Operating Company
Example: Future Environment

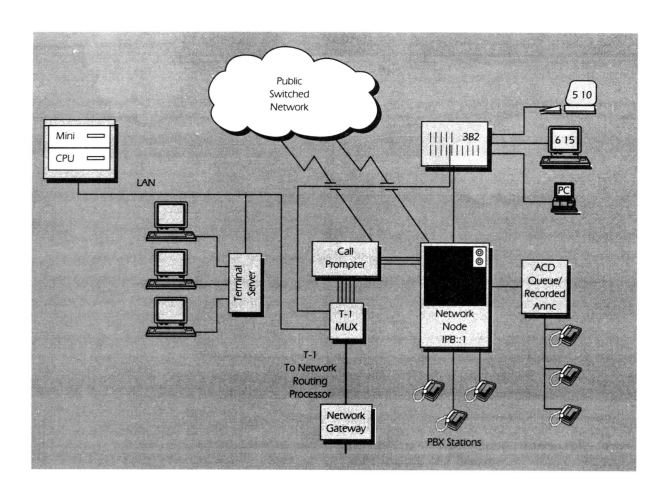

There's a tremendous difference in the networking needs between an SNA network and an ASYNCH network. So other than the backbone components, we're just waiting to see how things are going to shake out before we make any big commitments.

Reliability is an overriding concern for systems that are so crucial for PFS operations, so Scott believes in conservative design.

We overdo our circuitry and provide at least 35% spare capacity on everything. It's been my experience that if you give people bandwidth, they're going to find some way to utilize it, and we would rather they do it this way rather than taking it on themselves to run individual circuits.

I'm very proactive when it comes to maintenance and fixing things before they're broken. And we reduce our problems by keeping our vendor list short—we only deal with established firms with outstanding track records. I insist that we keep our products compatible, which in the PBX market means virtually the same. With all this, we don't have many operational problems. Our goal on availability is 99.6 percent, and we often hit 99.9 percent.

PFS will be using voice response, but very carefully and in a limited domain. PFS will use call prompters with its providers where the system is dealing with clerical people that can be trained, and otherwise use ACD units with human operators. A call prompter is like an automated attendant that asks you what you are calling for and routes you to the proper unit or operating company that provides the service you need. It answers the phone and asks you to push the "1" button if you're inquiring about a claim, the "2" button if you wish to process a claim, the "3" button if you want to check on the eligibility of a patient, the "4" button if you wish to check the eligibility of a procedure, and so on.

The PFS Technical Architecture The network architecture that Scott is working toward is depicted in Exhibit 2 for the corporate site and other major hubs, and in Exhibit 3 for remote operating units. "We're not quite there yet," John reports, "but at the corporate site we're very close."

This network will have a good deal of built-in intelligence, with computers incorporated in the network routing processors, the mainframe front-end pro-

cessor, 3B2 UNIX boxes, ACD units, call prompters, PBXs, voice mail unit, and the T-1 MUX (multiplexer), in addition to the regular computers the network serves.

This intelligence serves several purposes. It provides flexibility—it can easily be added to or reconfigured whenever PFS decides to acquire an operating unit or restructure its operations. It also allows PFS to present a unified entry point to each client—the client need have no concern for where his call is going because the network connects him to the right person or processor without his knowing that it isn't all in the headquarters building. It also allows PFS great flexibility in protocol conversion so that the network can adapt to various types of equipment in the providers' offices.

In Exhibit 3, PFS is insisting on on-premise PBXs because Scott believes that the PBX of tomorrow is going to be a much more powerful device than it is today.

I think that the System 75 will become a virtual front-end processor. It will be a minicomputer that will also serve as a network routing device and they will integrate a lot of different technologies into that one box.

....

Plans for the Future

The blockbuster strategic development PFS is working toward is the "smart card," a plastic card that contains a powerful computer chip. The company is working with AT&T to design a smart card that will record the member's entire medical history, blood type, insurance coverage information, credit information, and even a list of the pharmacies and the prescriptions the member has received.

Scott believes that before long each health insurance member will be issued a smart card. When you go to the doctor's office, he or she will insert your card into a machine that will give all your insurance and medical information. All the doctor has to do is enter the procedure and prescription codes, and the system will automatically generate the claim, which will be electronically shipped to PFS. The doctor will be paid automatically through electronic funds transfer. If you get a prescription it will be on the card, and you will give the card to your pharmacist, and he will insert it into his reader to determine exactly what the doctor wants and what other medications you are taking that may interact with that drug. If your insurance pays for the prescription, your claim will be generated and handled electronically, just as in the doctor's office.

PFS isn't alone in development of the smart card—several mutual health insurance organizations are looking into this together. PFS is participating in the technical design and implementation of a pilot smart card program that will take place in the near future. It plans to implement the pilot slowly and carefully to make sure that the major bugs are worked out. It expects to have some problems deploying it because of the differences from state to state in the reporting requirements and in what you can and cannot do with confidential medical information.

Another technology of the future that PFS is experimenting with is the Integrated Services Digital Network (ISDN), a service obtainable from AT&T that provides very flexible digital networking capabilities. PFS anticipates that an early use of ISDN will involve asking the caller to key in his member number through the telephone and the system will automatically connect him with the appropriate customer service representative.

The communications area has already developed a simple expert system to do telephone system configurations. If you need a new phone system you can sit down at a PC and the expert system will walk you through some simple business questions, and it then creates an order for the system that describes how many trunks you need and the system configuration. A technician checks it over before ordering the system, but it usually does a very good job. Scott believes that AI will have a growing impact on PFS.

Communication Management Problems

The communications industry has been in continual turmoil since the divestiture of AT&T. According to Scott,

The divestiture of AT&T has been a disaster from the standpoint of people like me. No one has the responsibility for ensuring that vendors work together, agree to standards for end-to-end connectivity, and finally implement those standards when the users need them. We need them desperately right now, but things are moving very slowly!

Scott's problem is that one organization can no longer take responsibility for the entire network, so the users have to assume this responsibility. With the competition between the vendors created by the divestiture, it is difficult to get the close cooperation that is needed to make things work well. Add to that the fact that the technology is changing all the time—new products and even new companies are continually coming into the market—and "it's a circus out there!"

Another problem has been trying to change an organization with a traditional IBM mind-set.

It's just been in the last three or four months that we can say ASYNCH out loud without being challenged. IBMers have their own way of doing things. It's very procedure-driven, and we bog ourselves down with things like change management and version control, and in the meantime the normal lead time from when a request for change was submitted to when it actually happened was in the two-month time frame for the most trivial change. With UNIX and intelligence in the network, you can make changes easily and quickly— the power is in the box, not in the head of the person who is doing it.

There have been even more fundamental problems at PFS in the process of changing corporate culture so that it is not doing the same things the same old way. Scott notes:

In order to gain the advantages we seek from dispersing into smaller local units, users have to give up their reliance on the large data processing support staffs and services currently in place that are causing tremendous overhead expense. It's difficult for users to give up their security blankets!

Scott has also had some problems associated with the PFS philosophy of decentralization.

The overall tone and the personality of the corporation is that an operating company president is quite autonomous and completely responsible for his bottom line. What happens then when an operating company president insists that his unit doesn't need a communications system that conforms to our architecture, and that they're not going to get one? I've tried to sell top management on the concept that there are some things that everyone has to do for the good of the whole organization.

So Scott's biggest challenge has been relating to top management of the company. His critical role is to interact with the president and the board of directors to formulate strategic directions for the company, not just for the technology:

President Harton is convinced that technology *is crucial to his success. But he's not used to talking with and relating to real true techies. Trying to be the person who bridges that gap has been the most difficult part of my job— when I go to a board meeting I have to be careful to keep my management hat on at all times.*

7

Basic Systems Concepts

"It's the SYSTEM's fault."

"I have a SYSTEM that can't lose!"

"Don't buck the SYSTEM."

"The SYSTEM is down."

These and other familiar phrases suggest that everything and anything can be thought of as a system, and it can in fact. Two problems arise with this universal nature of systems: which system we mean and what actually defines the extent of the system are both unclear. Thus, we need some concepts that will help us to understand systems, to deal realistically with the design of information systems (IS), and to diagnose systems problems. The purpose of this chapter is to present these concepts.

Practically all of management is about systems. Any management action (for example, lowering prices, introducing a new product, changing an accounting method) creates a chain reaction throughout the business and the marketplace that causes other changes to occur, which create other changes. Systems concepts help us to understand the intricate networks of related events and actions so we can make positive changes in the business. The ability to view organizations as systems is an essential skill of an effective manager.

Chapters 4, 5, and 6 dealt with the three major technology components of information systems—hardware, software, and telecommunications. We will see in this chapter that technology is one of the four major elements in the systems view of organizations. The principles, techniques, and notations for systems analysis and design introduced in this chapter are central to understanding how to analyze a business situation and logically apply information technology to meet business needs.

It is obvious that these principles must be mastered by an IS professional. But why do you, as a business manager, need to understand them? First, business managers frequently develop their own systems. To build quality end-user systems, you will have to apply these same principles without the aid of a systems professional. Second, you may hire or work with internal or consulting IS professionals to analyze, design, and build a system. In these cases, an understanding of systems concepts will significantly help you communicate your needs and confirm that the system addresses those needs. Knowing about systems concepts will also help you to understand various processes IS professionals use for systems development.

Third, you must understand basic systems concepts to comprehend ISs. ISs are structured and operate based on certain fundamental principles of systems. You can greatly enhance your ability to grasp the basics of a new IS or deal with problems in an existing IS by viewing systems in light of these basic principles. Last, you can apply systems concepts in a wide variety of business situations, not just IS analysis and design. The principles presented in this chapter also introduce you to an effective approach to problem-solving that you will find useful in many aspects of your work.

268

THE SYSTEMS VIEW

The systems view is a template for describing, analyzing, and designing all aspects of any system. We will describe this view in organizational terms here because this is the viewpoint of a business manager. Reporting structures, sequences of work steps, information and material flows between work steps, and the organization of data are modeled using the systems view.

What Is a System?

A **system** is a set of interrelated components that must work together to achieve some common purpose. Even when each component is well-designed,

efficient, and simple, the system will malfunction if the components do not work together. Further, a change in one component may affect other components. For example, suppose marketing (one component of the system that is the organization) sells more than expected of some product, then production (another component) would have to special-order materials or pay overtime to produce more than the planned amount. The likely result would be a rise of the costs of goods sold and the company might actually lose money from this apparently successful selling spree.

An example of what happens when system components do not work together appears in Figure 7.1. This house has all the components necessary for a functioning home, but the rooms,

FIGURE 7.1 Poorly Designed House

plumbing, electrical wiring, and other components just do not fit together. The functional relationships among these components are simply not right. For example, front steps exist, but not where needed.

An **information system (IS)** is the collection of computer hardware and software, procedures, documentation, forms, and people responsible for the capture, movement, management, and distribution of data and information. As with any system, it is crucial that the components of an IS work together, that is, the components must be consistent, minimally redundant, complete, and well connected with each other.

The process we follow to develop a good system is called **systems analysis and design (SA&D)**. SA&D processes are based on a systems approach to problem solving that is driven by several fundamental principles:

- You must know *what* a system is to do before you can specify *how* a system is to operate.
- Choosing an appropriate scope for the situation you will analyze greatly influences what you can and cannot do to solve a problem.
- A problem (or system) is actually a set of problems; thus, an appropriate strategy is to recursively break a problem down into smaller and smaller problems, which are more manageable than the whole problem.
- The solution of a problem is not usually obvious to all interested parties, so alternative solutions representing different perspectives should be generated and compared before a final solution is selected.
- The problem and your understanding of it continues to change while you are analyzing the problem, so you should take a staged approach to problem-solving in which you reassess the problem and your approach to solving it at each stage; this allows an *incremental* commitment to a particular solution, with a "go" or "no-go" decision after each stage.

We outline various systems analysis and design methodologies based on these principles in Chapters 8 through 11. In the following sections of this chapter we elaborate on some of these important systems fundamentals.

Function Before Form in Systems

Systems are described in various, and necessarily separate, ways. These different ways concentrate on separate aspects of systems (for example, what the system does versus how it operates) or represent systems in different levels of detail. Consider a good example of a system—a house. As any architect knows, function precedes form with the design of a new house. Before the house is designed, we must determine how many people will live in it, how each room will be used, the lifestyle of the family, and so on. These requirements comprise a functional, or logical, specification for the house. It would be premature to choose the type of materials, color of plumbing fixtures, and other physical characteristics before we determine the purpose of these aspects. We are often anxious to hurry into building (form) before we determine needs (functions), but the penalty for violating the function before form principle is increased costs—the cost to fix a functional specification error grows exponentially as you progress through the systems analysis and design process.

Thus, the requirements of the house (or system) must be well defined and clearly understood. Architects use blueprints and other drawings to depict and communicate the design specifications for these requirements. A blueprint is an abstract representation of the house, which masks many of the detailed and physical features of the house. We will see in this chapter several types of blueprints for various aspects of information systems.

Scope of Systems

Often the fatal flaw in conceiving and designing a system centers on choosing an inappropriate system scope. Apparently the designer of the house in Figure 7.1 outlined each component separately, keeping the boundaries narrow and manageable; he did not see all the necessary interrelationships among the components. Turning to a business situation, when a salesperson sells a cheaper version of a product to underbid a competitor, that salesperson has defined the limits of the system to be this one sale. However, the costs of handling customer complaints about inadequacy of the

THE NINE-DOT PROBLEM

Consider the figure above, which is the basis for the classical nine-dot problem. Without taking your pencil off the page, can you draw four straight lines that together cross each dot in the figure? Many people will define the boundary of this system (scope in which to find a solution) of dots to be delineated by the square formed by the outermost eight dots. However, to accomplish the task, lines have to extend beyond the outside edges of the box of dots, as shown below.

product, repeated trips to install upgrades, and other possible problems make this narrow definition of scope inadequate.

The system boundary indicates the system scope. Defining the boundary is crucial to designing any system or solving any problem. For example, we could install more efficient computer equipment that can process banking transactions much faster, but if tellers are confused by the new equipment or if the human factors of using the equipment are not also considered as part of the system, any benefit from the new equipment may be lost. Therefore, tellers and their capabilities should be included within the boundaries of the system being considered.

Too narrow a scope may cause you to miss a really good solution to a problem. Too wide a scope may be too complex to handle. Choosing an appropriate scope is difficult but crucial in viewing an organization as a system.

AN ORGANIZATIONAL FRAMEWORK FOR SYSTEMS

Several useful frameworks exist to view how information systems fit into the whole organization, and one such framework is illustrated in Figure 7.2. This figure indicates four general key components of the organization that must work in concert for the whole organization to be effective—people, technology, tasks/procedures, and organization structure.

The important point is that each time we change characteristics of one or more of these four components, we must consider compensating changes in the others. For example, when technology—such as computer hardware and software—changes, people may have to be retrained, methods of work may have to be redesigned, and old reporting relationships may have to be modified. These changes must be considered together, or we may find that the compensating changes are infeasible or enacting them will take too long. Further, we should not consider introducing a new product without considering how to bill sales of the product, how to keep track of inventory, and how to monitor production. Many organizations, however, wait to consider the information technology component until the new product is designed and ready to go into production (which may then delay the deployment of the product).

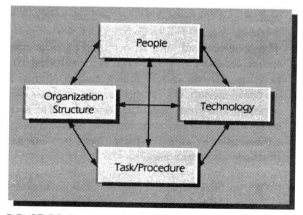

FIGURE 7.2 Fundamental Components of an Organization

Universities provide another practical example of these kinds of compensating changes. Before modern computers, the head of IS frequently reported to the university registrar. Today, computer systems integrate registration with bursar and other functions. Hence, in some universities, the registration office is part of the systems organization, inverting the historical relationship.

This framework raises an interesting question concerning making changes to organizations. In which of the four components do we start? There is no universal answer to this. Issues of organizational politics can play a role in answering this question (see Chapter 16). When technology changes, we must consider compensating changes in the other three components, we can use this change to force other components to change, and we can use the technology change to make possible other innovations in organizations. Later in this chapter we discuss a process called business reengineering, which utilizes information technology as an enabler for significant changes throughout the system that is the entire organization.

The Human Element in Information Systems

Humans, especially as providers and consumers of information, are an integral part of an information system, as suggested by the framework of Figure 7.2. Human factors (for example, ergonomics, health and safety, and stress brought on by computer systems) and how people interact with systems are important considerations in the design of any system. Two individuals may not react in the same manner or may not have the same needs for an IS. Understanding the human element helps in understanding why one system may not fit all. For example, a purchased application software package may have to be changed and any system may have to be customized to satisfy characteristics of individuals.

Humans are constantly receiving stimuli from all of our operating senses. We take these stimuli, or input, digest them, compare them to what we know and remember, and produce some type of response. Newell and Simon (1972) outlined this in their model of **human information processing** (see Figure 7.3). This model, with its four components (reception of stimuli, effecting actions, processing, and memory) is also the basis for the model of an IS as input, output, process, and storage, which is presented later in this chapter.

Newell and Simon have shown in various experiments that humans use three different memories, or storage systems:

Long-term memory: a vast storehouse of facts and relationships contained in the human brain.

FIGURE 7.3 Newell-Simon Model of Human Information Processing

Short-term memory: a limited amount of space (possibly with five to nine pieces of data at a time) where the brain manipulates data.

External memory: paper, chalkboards, computer screens, and so on, which extend the capacity of long- and short-term memory

Computer systems are extensions of human information-processing capabilities and are used frequently as memory aids.

Besides limited human short-term memory, other characteristics of human information processing have been identified:

Just Noticeable Differences: The ability of a given person to identify variations and errors is in the same proportions for different situations, so larger differences are needed in situations involving larger numbers; for example, an individual who can identify a budget variance when there is a $10,000 variation in a $100,000 line item will need a $100,000 variation for a $1 million line item.

Deficiencies in Handling Probabilities: Humans are poor at understanding causation, integrating and synthesizing data, and dealing with sample size and variance (see box "Probabilistic Outcomes" for an interesting exercise to demonstrate this human trait).

Recency Effect: The most recent data we have heard, felt, tasted, or seen carries far more weight than does other data in forming our opinions.

Bounded Rationality: Humans are, because of limited capacities, only able to cope with so much data before they become overloaded—thus we have a tendency to restrict problems and the way we view the world to a manageable size; we do this by eliminating some data or some possible actions, and we seek satisfying, not optimal, solutions.

Cognitive Style: Different individuals use different processes for organizing and changing data during decision-making and other tasks; some are more analytical, others more intuitive, some concentrate on details, others on the big picture.

Left Brain–Right Brain: The brain contains two hemispheres and each person appears to have a dominant hemisphere; the left brain is ana-

---

PROBABILISTIC OUTCOMES

Divide your class or any group in half. Explain to both groups that there has been an outbreak of a deadly disease on a remote tropical island. There are two known treatments, A and B, to cope with the disease. Only one treatment can be applied, and it is the group's responsibility to pick the treatment. Based on experience with the treatments, we can predict the effects of each treatment on the island's population of 600 inhabitants. To the first group explain the predicted effects as follows:

Treatment	Expected Outcome
A	200 lives saved
B	probability 1/3 that 600 are saved
	probability 2/3 that 0 are saved

And to the second group explain the predicted effects as follows:

Treatment	Expected Outcome
A	400 people die
B	probability 2/3 that 600 die
	probability 1/3 that 600 do not die

If the group members understand probabilities and carefully consider each option, both groups should pick treatment A and B similarly, but, usually 75 percent of the first group will pick A and 25 percent will pick treatment B, whereas in the second group roughly 15 percent will pick treatment A and 85 percent will pick treatment B. Wording changes interact with the probabilities to create different perceptions of the probabilistic outcomes.

---

lytical, sequential, realistic, and highly organized, and the right brain is intuitive, simultaneous, imaginative, and impulsive.

Individual Differences: Concepts of dogmatism, risk-taking propensity, tolerance for ambiguity, quantitative and verbal abilities, age, gender, experience, and position in the organization all influence the way people process data or the way data contributed by one person are perceived by others who interpret that data.

These human characteristics plus many more interact to determine the information-processing

LEFT-HANDED DISCRIMINATION

Woodridge, Ill.—A dispute between a left-handed clerk and a grocery chain's work rules has resulted in a jury's judgment for the clerk. "It didn't make sense," said Crystal Sagen that she be required to check out groceries with her right hand. "It was discrimination against left-handers." Miss Sagen claimed that she was one of the fastest clerks in the store until the computerized check-out scanners were installed. All the clerks were told to check right-handed after this installation. After a year and a half at the store, Miss Sagen quit. She sued and a jury, all right-handers, awarded her $136,700.

(Adapted from Seligman, 1985)

style and capabilities of individuals. Information systems need to be designed to tolerate such individual differences, to help people overcome biases, and to complement and supplement human capabilities. Some research suggests that certain types of individuals are attracted to certain types of jobs. Other research has shown there still may be significant enough variations in information-processing style among people in similar jobs that systems must be developed with sensitivity to such human factors.

Decision-Making

Because decision-making is such a common managerial task, there has been considerable study of how people make decisions in organizations. Understanding the decision-making process is, of course, critical for decision support, group support, and executive information systems, which were outlined in Chapter 2.

A useful model of decision-making appears in Figure 7.4, which depicts decision-making as a six-phase cycle, with feedback (the inner loop), that involves the following phases:

Intelligence: searching the environment for conditions that suggest the need to make a decision, and the collection of relevant data.
Design: developing and finding alternative solutions or actions, and testing the feasibility of these solutions/actions.

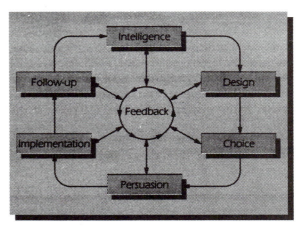

FIGURE 7.4 Decision-making Process

Choice: selecting among the alternatives the one that best (or at least satisfactorily) addresses the problem.
Persuasion: influencing others who are involved in the implementation of the decision so that they accept and follow the chosen solution.
Implementation: managing the installation of the new solution so that it is done in a timely and efficient manner.
Follow-up: monitoring the solution to be sure it works as expected and modifying or refining the solution.

Information systems can replace or support human beings in one or more of these steps. For example:

- Mathematical techniques like linear programming are used in the choice phase.
- Computer simulation is used to test alternative solutions in the design phase.
- Ad hoc data retrieval makes the intelligence and follow-up phases more efficient.
- Collaborative work or group support tools (see Chapter 2) help in the intelligence and persuasion phases.
- Project management programs help in the implementation phase.

Some organizations have human-factors experts who are involved in system design to consider human information-processing characteristics. These system specialists assess the amount of information presented, its format, the effects of

274

color and graphics on understanding data, consistency in screen and report layouts, compliance with sound principles of report and screen designs, the design of special equipment, and hazards in the workplace from computer equipment (such as video display terminals and special inks). Unfortunately, many organizations take for granted the humans in data processing systems. It is important, however, that high-tech systems have a human touch so that clerks and managers can be satisfied, rather than frustrated users of the system.

CHARACTERISTICS OF SYSTEMS

One approach to illustrating a system is shown in Figure 7.5, where a system is the interrelated set of activities used to transform input into output. There are seven general system elements:

1. Boundary: the delineation of which elements (such as components and storages) are within the system being studied and which are outside; it is assumed that elements within the boundary are more easily changed and controlled than those outside.
2. Environment: everything outside the system; the environment provides assumptions, constraints, and inputs to the system.
3. Inputs: the resources (data, materials, supplies, energy) from the environment that are consumed and manipulated within the system.
4. Outputs: the resources or products (information, reports, documents, screen displays, materials) provided to the environment by the activities within the system.
5. Components: the activities or processes within the system that transform inputs into intermediate forms or that generate system outputs; recursively, components may be considered as

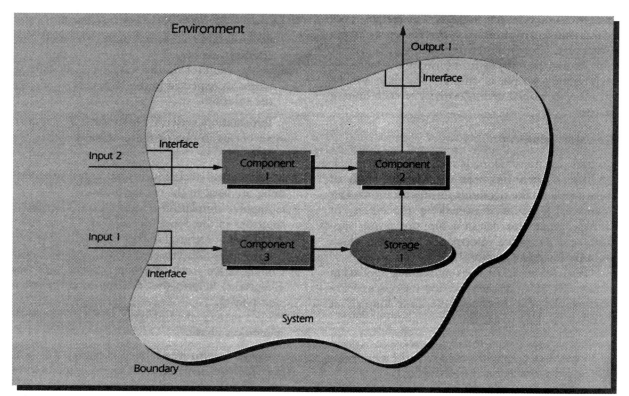

FIGURE 7.5 General Structure of a System

systems themselves, in which case they are called subsystems.

6. Interfaces: the place where two components or the system and its environment meet or interact; systems need special subcomponents at interfaces to filter, translate, store, and correct whatever flows through the interface.

7. Storage: holding areas used for the temporary and permanent storage of information, energy, materials, and so on; storage provides a buffer between system components to allow them to work at different rates or at different times and to allow different components to share the same data; storage is especially important in IS because data are not consumed with usage, so the organization of storage is crucial to handle the potentially large volume of data maintained there.

Table 7.1 illustrates two business systems and examples of system elements for each.

An important distinction in many organizational contexts is the difference between formal and informal systems. The **formal system** is the way an organization was designed to work. By contrast, when workers tape bills-of-materials with years of annotated changes to workbenches, an informal system has replaced the formal information system that prints a materials list for each shop order. When there is resistance to the system by those who work within it, when there are flaws in the system, or when the system adapts in practice to changing stimuli, an **informal system** develops that is the way the organization actually works. The "real" system is, of course, the informal system. Recognizing that the formal system, often designed in the abstract, may not match the real system is crucial to analyzing a business situation for improvement in system operations and design.

Logical and Physical Systems

Any description of a system will be abstract, since it is not the system itself, but different system descriptions can emphasize different aspects of the system. Two important general kinds of system descriptions are logical and physical, which correspond to system function and system form.

A **logical system (description)** depicts the function and purpose (the what) of the system without reference to or implications for the physical way in which the system will be implemented, that is, a logical system is a representation independent of technology. We must get the logical or functional specifications right to understand how to choose among alternate physical implementations. Further, the cost and effort to change systems grows exponentially as we implement more and more of the physical reality of the system.

A **physical system (description)** is also an abstraction, but it uses symbols and a notation that imply the physical form (the how) in which the system operates. As an example of the difference between a logical and a physical system, consider a class registration system. A logical system description would show such steps as submitting a request for classes, checking class requests against degree requirements and prerequisites, and generating class registration lists. A physical system description would show whether the submission of a request for classes is via computer punched cards or a computer terminal, whether the prerequisite checking is done manually or by electronic comparison of transcript with course descriptions, and so on.

TABLE 7.1 Examples of Systems

System	Payroll	Sales Tracking
Inputs	Time cards	Customer orders
	Vouchers	Customer returns of goods
Outputs	Paychecks	Monthly sales by product
	W-2 forms	Monthly sales by territory
Components	Calculate total pay	Accumulate sales by product and compare to forecast
	Subtract deductions	
Interfaces	Match time cards to employees	Translate customer zip code into territory code
	Sort paychecks by department	
Storage	Employee benefits	Product list
	Pay rates	Sales history
		Sales forecasts

One important aspect of the difference between logical and physical systems is the geographical location of tasks and the technology used to perform the tasks. The same logical system may be physically centralized, decentralized and independent, or distributed and linked. For example, a company could implement its logical payroll system in any of these three physical modes. The payroll system could be centralized, with all checks and reports generated on the corporate computer system from data entered into the information system by a headquarters data entry staff. Alternatively, the system could be distributed, with, for example, time-accounting and data-entry functions located at plants and in divisions, but with record-keeping centralized. Finally, the payroll system could be decentralized, with each plant or division processing all aspects of payroll independently. Combinations are also possible. For example, the people and management of payroll might be distributed throughout the company, and the operations of the payroll information system could be centralized at the headquarters computer.

The System of Systems

As stated earlier, a system is a set of interrelated components. What principles should influence grouping activities into components? How do we show what goes on inside one component relative to other components? What steps does the component follow to accomplish its task? Yes, components can be viewed as systems, too. Each component must have a well-defined function and we need to know exactly how the different components cooperate to accomplish the system functions. This cooperation among system components to achieve an overall system goal is called **functional cohesion**.

A component of a system that is itself viewed (at some level of analysis) as a set of interrelated components is called a **subsystem**, or a module. The components of a subsystem can be further broken down (or what systems analysts call decomposed) into more detailed subsystems. The process of breaking down a system into successive levels of subsystems, each of which shows

---

NASA USES FUNCTIONAL DECOMPOSITION

Consider, for example, the intricate system built for placing a man on the moon. NASA and the other organizations broke this complex system into the subsystems of launch, lunar landing, lunar ascent, spacecraft, life support, and so on. With clearly defined interconnections between each subsystem, contractors were able to work independently to understand the needs for and the design of each subsystem. When each was done, all the parts fit together. Functional decomposition made this intricate system manageable.

---

more detail, is called **hierarchical (or functional) decomposition**.

Hierarchical Decomposition Hierarchical decomposition of a system helps us to accomplish five important goals:

1. To cope with the complexity of a system, because it allows us to break the system down into understandable pieces (see box "NASA Uses Functional Decomposition").
2. To analyze or change only part of the system; decomposition allows us to focus on just those components at just the right level of detail for the job.
3. To design and build each subsystem at different times, as business needs and resources permit.
4. To direct attention only to the components of interest of a certain target audience, without forgetting about the whole system.
5. To allow systems to operate, as much as is possible, as independent components; hence, complicated coordination can be avoided, problems in one area can be isolated, and components can be switched with minimal impact on other components.

Figure 7.6 illustrates the hierarchical decomposition of a sales reporting system. At the highest level of abstraction, this system simply accepts as input customer orders, sales histories, and other data about customers, products, and markets and produces various summary reports. More detailed

(a) SALES SUMMARY SYSTEM

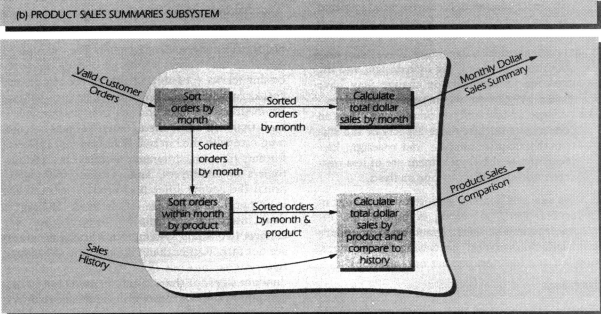

(b) PRODUCT SALES SUMMARIES SUBSYSTEM

FIGURE 7.6 Sales Reporting System and Subsystem

descriptions of each component reveal the inner workings of the system (Figure 7.6(b) describes one of the subsystems at an additional level of detail). This hierarchical decomposition is a functional breakdown, not a structural outline, that is, as a functional specification, there is no presumption of how or with what technologies tasks are done.

System Boundaries

As defined earlier, a **boundary** marks the inside and the outside of a system. A boundary segregates the environment from the system, or segregates one subsystem from other subsystems. A boundary in the systems world is often arbitrary, that is, we can choose to include or exclude any component in the system. The choice of where to "draw the boundary" depends on the following three factors:

What can be controlled. Usually, elements outside our control are part of the environment. Thus, what is in the environment is assumed and places constraints on the system (for example, if the billing system is treated as part of the environment of the product management system, the product management system will be constrained to devise products that can be priced and billed only in ways now supported).

What is manageable. Large, unwieldy systems may take too long to analyze or redesign, and the need for the analysis or change may have passed by the time the analysis is complete.

The purpose of the analysis or redesign. We can concentrate on just those aspects of the system that require analysis and redesign. Elements put in the environment are of less concern and not subject to our analysis.

We saw in Chapter 3 an interesting change in the general trend in setting IS boundaries. Interorganizational systems expand an IS boundary to include information processing in customer, supplier, and business partner organizations.

Interfaces

Where a system meets its environment or where one subsystem interacts with another subsystem there exists an interface. An interface is the point of contact between two subsystems or a system and its environment. An example of such a component is a clutch subsystem that supports the interface between the engine and the transmission subsystems in a car. In general, the functions of an interface component in an IS are:

- filtering: disposing of useless data (or noise).
- coding/decoding: translating data in one format into another (for example, switching between two part number schemes, one used by marketing and another used in engineering).
- error detection and correction: checking for compliance to standards and for consistency; by isolating this task in interfaces, other components can concentrate on their more essential responsibilities.
- buffer: allowing two subsystems to work together without being tightly synchronized, for example, by having the interface collect data until the next component is ready to accept the data.
- security: rejecting, for example, unauthorized requests for data.
- summarizing: condensing a large volume of input into aggregate statistics or even mathematical parameters to reduce the amount of work needed by subsequent subsystems.

Frequently, organizations decide to link two historically independent systems. For example, a company may contract with an outside data-processing service (possibly a bank) to process payroll checks or with a market research firm to capture competitor sales data. In each case, an interface is built that will allow the external systems to communicate with the internal data systems. Different formats for data, different identifications for customers or employees, and various other definitional and coding differences need to be translated to support this linkage of systems. Sometimes these interfaces are called bridges because they connect two island systems. Such bridge programs are not rare. Rather than take the time to redesign two systems into one (for example, to reduce redundant steps, to share common data, and to discontinue duplicate processing and calculations), the two systems are simply bridged. Such bridges are an expedient way to accomplish the goal of expanding the capabilities of any one system, but this is not a lasting or efficient way to accomplish the merging or integration of systems.

Another important purpose of an interface is the **decoupling of system components.** Two highly coupled system components require frequent and rapid communication, thus creating a dependence and bottleneck in the system. If one of the components fails, the other cannot function; if one is modified, the other may also have to be modified. Appropriately designed interfaces help to decouple system components. The principal methods of decoupling system components are:

Slack and flexible resources: providing alternative paths to follow when one component breaks down or slows down (for example, if the company's private data communications network becomes busy, an interface could re-route data transmissions to public carriers).

Buffers: storing data in a temporary location as a buffer or waiting line that can be depleted as the data can be handled by the next component (for example, collecting customer orders over the complete day and allowing an order-filling batch program to allocate scarce inventory to highest-need jobs).

Sharing resources: creating shared data stores with only one program (part of the interface component) maintaining the data, thus avoiding having to synchronize multiple step updating or having multiple copies of data being inconsistent.

Standards: enforcing standards that reduce the need for two components to communicate (for example, business policy that requires all interunit transfer of information about customers to be done using the company standard customer identification code).

Decoupling allows one subsystem to remain relatively stable while other subsystems change. Because business is in constant change and the need to maintain systems in response to this change is essential, decoupling subsystems significantly reduces the burden on systems maintenance (see Chapter 9).

Decoupling helps to achieve simplicity of design. A system with n components can potentially have $n(n-1)/2$ interfaces. By clustering components into subsystems and by applying various de-coupling techniques, the amount of design and maintenance effort can be significantly reduced. Figure 7.7 illustrates the result of clustering a six-component system into two three-component subsystems. The design in Figure 7.7(b) is much simpler, but the system depends heavily on the proper operation of components 2 and 5 because the redundant connections of Figure 7.7(a) have been eliminated.

The Systems Design and Change Effort

Almost everyone in a business or public administration curriculum today learns some form of computer programming. You have probably written (or will soon write) a program using a programming language (BASIC, COBOL, or FORTRAN) or a problem-solving language (IFPS, Lotus 1-2-3, or SPSS). A system might be composed of hundreds of individual programs, with inputs and outputs passing from one program to the next. When a system of programs is developed, the effort you have expended in the design of one system component can grow in unexpected proportions.

This exponential increase in effort in systems design over individual component design is due to several factors. First, when many interconnections between components exist, careful testing is conducted to ensure that each interaction, under all combinations of interactions, will work properly. For example, a banking system may work perfectly when only one customer at a time tries to withdraw money from the same account. When both joint-account holders try to withdraw money simultaneously, however, the system may not properly debit their account by both withdrawals unless designed and tested for this combination of activities.

Second, the design of or change to a system involves consideration of many technical and organizational factors, for which subtle interactions may exist. Suppose that a company has been using two separate billing systems, one for products and one for services (such as repair). Because some customers were confused by receiving two bills and because it was difficult for the company to get a complete picture of the total business generated by each customer, the company decides to combine

(a) ALL COMPONENTS CONNECTED WITH EACH OTHER.

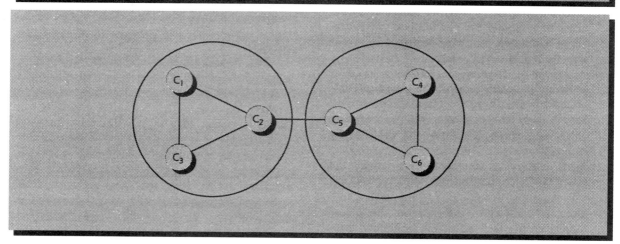

(b) TWO SUBSYSTEMS WITH SINGLE CONNECTION BETWEEN SUBSYSTEMS.

FIGURE 7.7 Simplifying a System

the two billing systems. To combine these two systems (including computer programs, data processing equipment, procedures, forms, and offices) into one consolidated system requires identifying duplicate processing, deciding on a consistent customer identifier, agreeing on a common bill format, and so forth. The redesign of the billing system must coordinate many people, forms, programs, equipment, and databases. For any reasonably important and sizable system, this will be a complex political and technical effort.

The point of these observations is that the amount of work required to design or modify a whole system versus one system component is

THE DIFFICULT JOB OF CREATING SOFTWARE

The business of creating new computer software—the programs that make computers work—is one of the most complex, painstaking, even exasperating jobs around. It is as if someone is writing *War and Peace* in code, puts one letter out of place and turns the whole book into gibberish. So difficult is the process that it can baffle even such industry stars as Mitch Kapor, the founder of Lotus Development Corp., and Peter Miller, a well-known software veteran. In November 1987, the two men formed ON Technology Inc. with the announced intention of making personal computers much easier to use.

Besides the inherent complexity of the work, there are other problems. Most software-development planning stinks: A joke in the industry is that programmers spend 90% of their time on the first 80% of a project, then 90% of the remaining time on the final 20%. And most design stinks, too: Programmers either don't understand their customers well enough or load up products with features that please themselves but perplex everyone else.

[A computer graphics designer] started what the team called the product's choreography, figuring out how the user would use the product and anticipating all the errors he might make. It's a daunting task. [The designer] went through more than 200 versions of how the program should look on a monitor. The office became intense, with programmers sometimes working in bursts and then falling asleep in their offices, sometimes working well into the night at home. Spirits were high; the pingpong games turned fierce. [One manager] instituted a Friday-afternoon party, whose start was signaled by blasting music over the intercom and then by the sound of beer glug-glugging into a glass.

But the schedule kept slipping further and further. As the shipment date headed toward the end of last year, Mr. Kapor worried the ON would miss the Christmas selling season. "It's like a Russian doll," [another project manager] says. "Every time we finally crack open one problem, we find there's another one inside."

He, and all the others, vow to do better with their next project. But there's another software axiom that usually proves true. Called Hofstadter's law, it's circular: It says, software development always takes longer than you think, even when you take into account Hofstadter's law.

(Adapted from Carroll, 1990)

quite different. In a system, we have to make sure that each component works by itself (that is, we have to design it and test it as a process of transforming inputs into outputs). In addition, we also have to make sure that all outputs from one subsystem are acceptable inputs to another related subsystem and that changes in one component do not affect other components in unexpected ways. Designing systems in a top-down, hierarchical decomposition fashion, as well as the decoupling of components, can greatly simplify system design, but the level of effort for designing and maintaining a large system is much greater than that required for designing a set of unrelated small systems. Much of the time spent in the design, testing, and documentation of a system addresses the interrelationships among components. Put another way, it may be difficult for you to extrapolate from your experience in writing a single simple computer program to understand the effort required to create an entire information system.

DESCRIBING INFORMATION SYSTEMS

An essential skill required to analyze or design a system, including an information system, is to be able to model, that is, describe the system of interest. Thus, many of the various steps in the different methods for systems development, to be discussed in Chapters 8 to 11, involve capturing the essence of certain aspects of an IS. This essence is depicted in unambiguous textual and/or graphical models of the IS and the organization in which it operates.

In this section we present an overview of a variety of notations used to describe an IS. You need a basic understanding of these notations so that you can review system designs developed by IS professionals and you can clearly describe your information processing requirements. Before we introduce these notations, however, we overview the IS development process and a universally used model of an IS. These topics are introduced first so that you can better understand the role and context of each systems description notation.

An Overview of Systems Development

We will more thoroughly explain the process of systems development in Chapter 8. For our purposes here, we need to overview this process to motivate the various notations introduced in the remainder of this chapter.

Two approaches dominate systems development methods used today. The first, the **process-oriented approach**, concentrates on the flow, use, and transformation of information in an IS. Techniques and notations used under this approach show the movement of data from their source, through various intermediate processing steps, and finally reaching some destination. For example, the process model in Figure 7.6 shows data coming into a system, the flow of data between several processing steps involved in handling the data, and eventually the distribution of information out of the system. A process-oriented technique can also show where data are stored (or "data at rest") in a system to compensate for the different speeds at which the various processing components work.

The second approach to systems development is the **data-oriented approach**. Techniques and notations in this approach depict the ideal organization of data, independent of how or where they are used within a system. These techniques produce a data model, which describes the kinds of data needed in a system and the business relationships between these data. For example, a customer order entry system might contain data about customers, products, orders, invoices, and shipments. Further, one customer could have zero or many associated orders, and each order is for exactly

one customer. A data model describes the rules and policies of the business. Some people believe that a data model is more permanent than a process model because a data model describes the inherent nature of the business, independent of the changing way the business operates.

Process and data views are complementary and both are essential for a complete picture of an IS. Thus, we will introduce notations for both kinds of views in this chapter. Today, most systems development methodologies used in organizations utilize a combination of process- and data-oriented approaches.

In Chapters 8 to 11 we will describe in detail the major methodologies for systems development. Most of these methodologies follow a variation on a general cycle for systems development that has been used for decades. This cycle is called the **systems development life cycle (SDLC)**. There are many descriptions of the SDLC, each involving a different number of phases and stages and using different names for them. There is general agreement, however, on the generic activities that are involved. This general SDLC model appears in Figure 7.8.

The three main phases of the SDLC are definition, construction, and implementation, with various stages under each. The analysis and design of a business problem and IS solution is reviewed after each phase and often after each stage. The SDLC follows the principles of function before form, hierarchical decomposition, and incremental commitment outlined earlier in this chapter. A variety

---

Definition Phase
    Feasibility Analysis
    Requirements Definition
Construction Phase
    System Design
    System Building
    System Testing
Implementation Phase
    Installation
    Operations and Maintenance

FIGURE 7.8 The Systems Development Life Cycle

of systems description notations are used throughout the SDLC.

In the *definition phase*, end-users and systems analysts conduct a multistep analysis of the current business operations and IS in the area of concern. Current operations and systems are described via both process- and data-oriented notations. Problems with current operations and opportunities for business gain through new system capabilities are identified. A business case is made for the feasibility of new systems, and one solution is chosen. This solution is detailed in a requirements statement agreed to by all parties. This stage of the SDLC is very much a cooperative effort between business and systems professionals. You must review descriptions of current business operations for accuracy. Because these descriptions are done using systems notations, it is essential that you be able to read both process and data modeling notations. Doing this stage right can have significant impact on reducing long-term system costs. One crucial element of this stage is proposing a system that fits into the business strategy and the information technology architecture for the organization. We cover these important topics in Chapters 12 and 13.

In the *construction phase*, IS professionals, with the oversight of business managers, design a system that satisfies the stated requirements. The system first is detailed functionally (at a "look and feel" level), and then its physical design is specified. Programs and computer files are designed, computer technology is chosen, and business procedures are redesigned. Business forms, computer screens, and printed reports are laid out. You must approve all of these designs as providing the data and information content you need, being readable and easy to use, and being produced when you need the information. Again, understanding various notations that describe a system is essential for your role in the construction phase. After the physical design is accepted as feasible (technically and economically) by all parties, the computer software is programmed and tested. Users are ultimately in charge of acceptance testing, to verify that the system does what was intended.

In the *implementation phase*, business managers and IS professionals work together to install the new system, which often involves converting data and procedures from an old system. The installation of a new system can occur in a variety of ways, such as in parallel with operation of the old system or in a total and clean cutover. How to convert is an important business and technical decision. Finally, implementation includes the operation and continued maintenance of the system. Maintenance is the longest stage of the SDLC, lasting throughout the life of a system, and it includes all the changes made to a system. Changes result from flaws in the original design, changing business needs or regulations, recognized system improvements, or technological advancements. The principles of system decoupling, hierarchical decomposition, function before form, and other system-structuring ideas can drastically reduce the costs for ongoing system maintenance.

Basic Model of an Information System

Figure 7.9 summarizes the typical components—input, output, process, and storage—that are the focus of IS development. Any IS at any level of descriptive detail is a network of processes interconnected by inputs and outputs, with access to data storage at appropriate points.

Figure 7.10 illustrates a typical macro systems process view of the functional components and general information flows between them for a hypothetical inventory information management system and related systems for a manufacturing company. This figure shows the relationship between major system components (such as handle customer order), not the detailed logic of any one

FIGURE 7.9 Information System Components

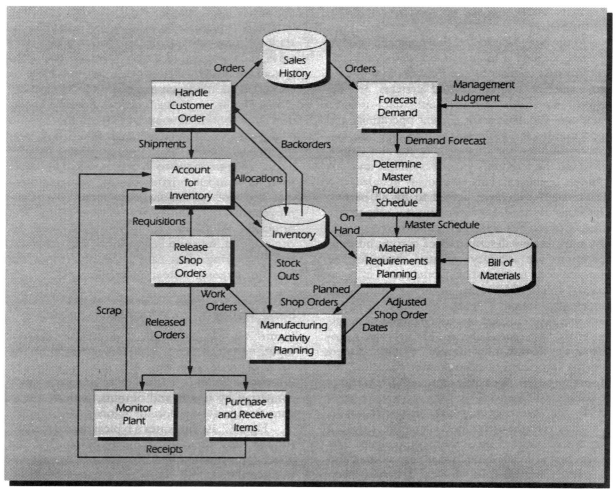

FIGURE 7.10 Inventory Information Management System

step; therefore, this type of figure is called a **system flow chart**. It depicts information movement and use, so the line labeled "scrap" refers to information about scrap, not scrap material itself.

Such process flow charts explain the movement of data between different system functions, but the data themselves are an organizational resource. Understanding the business relationships between categories of data is also important in comprehending the capabilities of a data processing system. Figure 7.11 shows a general database diagram for an inventory information management system and the inherent interrelationships between data, not how or where they are used. For example, the line between inventory and supplier

indicates that these two entities are related, because suppliers supply inventoried items. Further, purchase orders are related to both inventory and supplier because a purchase is of something from someone. This view is independent of how we process new purchase orders but is inherent in the way the business operates.

Finally, there is the distinction between describing the IS and describing the operation of a particular program within the system. Figure 7.12 shows one type of program level chart, a **structure chart**, that explains the logic of the processing performed in an inventory accounting program. Compared to system level charts, a structure chart is more detailed, shows the hierarchical relation-

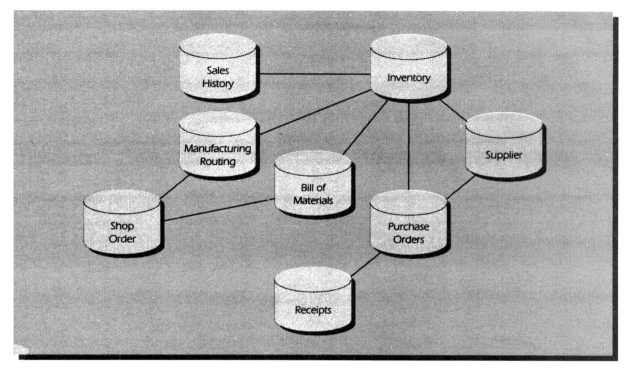

FIGURE 7.11 Inventory Information System Database Diagram

ship of the modules in the program, and is a form of pseudocode that permits a relatively simple translation into a computer programming language. Modules are presumed to execute in a top-down, left-to-right sequence. Labeled arrows pointing up and down the hierarchy show the flow of data (open circle on arrow, called *data couple*) or control (filled-in circle on arrow, called a *control flag*) between modules. A control flag informs a higher-level module that a special condition has occurred (such as not finding data in a computer file) or informs a lower-level module to follow a given option (such as process data as an add new record transaction).

The purpose of this section has been to introduce the need for a wide variety of information description notations useful for concentrating on different aspects of an IS. There is no one set of standard notations used by all organizations. Conversely, every organization uses at least some of these standard notations. The next section, which describes an example information system, introduces some of the most typical forms. Since busi-

ness managers review and approve systems designs, and these formats are often used to communicate the results of a systems analysis or a proposed design, you need to learn how to interpret such notations. Further, you can use many of these notations to analyze a wide variety of problems, so you should find such analytical tools helpful for business analysis and problem-solving.

INFORMATION SYSTEM DESCRIPTION NOTATIONS

Systems professionals use literally hundreds of different system description notations, but we will illustrate only a selected variety that you may encounter as a user-manager. Frequently, as a user or requester of a proposed system, systems professionals will ask you to review systems descriptions that use these notations. These notations certainly are not mystical or magical. You can use these same notations, when appropriate, to analyze and

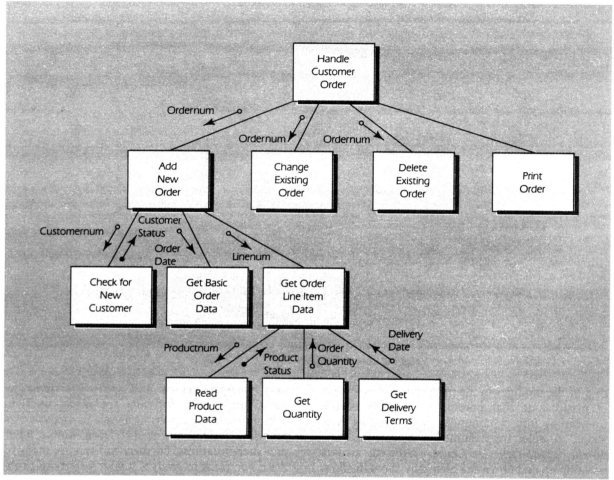

FIGURE 7.12 Program Structure Chart

explain your data processing needs. These notations are used to describe:

- data flow, both in a technology independent (organizational) and in a technology dependent (system) fashion.
- the format of input transactions in printed/hardcopy forms, computer terminal video displays, and other computer readable media.
- the layout of printed output.
- the logic of processing and manipulating data within an individual computer program.
- files and databases used to store data for repeated use.

The business situation we will use to illustrate these system notations is an accounts payable (AP) application. AP is responsible for paying vendor invoices promptly and for keeping credit balances with vendors at a reasonable level. The AP application must make such decisions as when to pay, the amount to pay, whether to accept a cash discount, and whether the invoice is correct. Crucial to AP, as with most accounting applications, are data processing controls that ensure accurate and secure processing.

It is important with any system to understand the organizational context. Often the first diagram developed for an application is a context diagram, which shows the business area of concern, with the major data flows in and out of the system, along with the people or organizations that send or receive these data. A context diagram for our AP application is shown in Figure 7.13.

This context diagram shows that AP interacts with three other systems—external vendors and the company's accounting and purchasing functions. Because these are external to the system (that is, outside the AP system boundary), we assume that these entities cannot be changed and that they may impose restrictions on the design of the AP system.

Organizational Data Flow

Describing organizational data flows is important for several purposes. First, documenting data flows can identify bottlenecks and workload through different processing steps. Second, it clearly shows all the steps involved in data processing and, hence, all the business units that must be involved in the more detailed design of specific procedures for the system. Finally, it helps to identify redundant and missing steps. Often several data flow charts are developed for the design of a new IS, each describing options or alternative methods for the flow of data in the organization. Managers then need to work with system builders to determine which alternative makes the most business sense. The builders will provide advice on the costs to develop and operate systems to support each alternative.

A common diagrammatic technique for showing data flow is the (logical) **data flow diagram**, or DFD (see Kozar, 1989, for a thorough discussion of DFDs). This notation is technology independent, that is, all the symbols have no association to the type of equipment or the humans that might perform the component activities or store the data. DFDs describe the logic and sequencing of processing steps (that is, a logical system), not the physical way in which they will be performed. Two DFDs for the accounts payable application of Figure 7.13 are shown in Figure 7.14.

In Figure 7.14(a), a top level diagram shows the overall view of this business application. This system includes four processing components. Data stores internal to this system (D2, D3, and D4) serve as buffers between the components (for example, to compensate for different processing rates of the components or to permit batch processing of transactions). The dashed line delineates the boundary of this business system, consistent with the context diagram of Figure 7.13. A top level DFD, as a macro view, does not show many of the details that appear on lower level DFDs. For example, the top level diagram does not show what happens to invoices that do not match purchase orders or shipment receipt records.

Four types of symbols appear in this chart:

External Entity: a square indicates some element in the environment of the system that sends or receives data. External entities may not directly access data in the system, but must get data from processing components of the system. No data flows between external entities are shown. External entities have noun labels.

Data Flow: arrows indicate data in motion, that is, data moving between external entities and

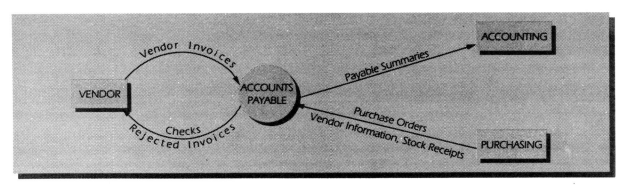

FIGURE 7.13 Accounts Payable Context Diagram

288

system processes or between system processes. Timing and volume of data are not shown. Data flows have noun labels.

Process: circles represent processing components of the system. Each process has to have both input and output (whereas an external entity

FIGURE 7.14 Accounts Payable System Data Flow Diagrams

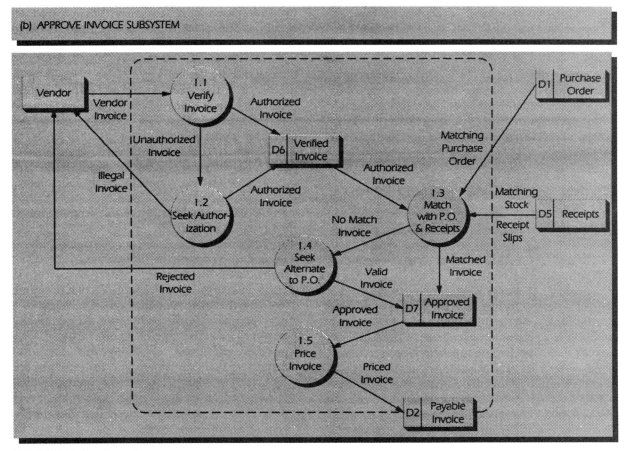

FIGURE 7.14 (continued)

must have either input, output, or both). Processes have verb-phrase labels as well as a numerical identifier.

Data Store: open rectangles depict data at rest; that is, data temporarily or permanently held for repeated reference by one or more processes. Use of a data store implies there is a delay in the flow of data between two or more processes. Each data store contained within the system must have both input and output (that is, be populated and be used) within the system. Data stores may also appear outside the system in which case only input or only output is possible. Data stores have noun labels and an alphanumeric identifier.

Figure 7.14(b) shows a second level diagram of the approve invoice process component from the top level diagram. This is the same type of subsystem decomposition discussed earlier, and all the rules outlined there for decomposition also apply to data flow diagrams. For example, the vendor invoice data flow and the payable invoice data store are interfaces of this subsystem to its environment. Which higher level process is being decomposed is indicated by numerical process labels.

From reviewing these DFDs, we see, for example:

1. Other systems maintain the purchase orders and shipment receipt records (these are accessed from external data sources).
2. The "Payable Invoice" process temporarily stores and groups invoices after approval before subsequent vendor account updating and check writing.

These two statements describe the business AP organizational data flows as we want to implement them. None of the symbols used in this chart implies computerization or any other form for implementing this system. The charts, however, indicate some design decisions; for example, approved invoices are temporarily held before vendor account updating, which is done possibly for economies of scale in the update vendor account process.

Physical Systems Data Flow and Structure

Once the "what" of the processing is designed, DFDs can be translated into a style that conveys the exact "how" of data processing. System flow charts and program structure charts (explained earlier) explain such details.

Figure 7.15 shows a system flow chart for the same AP system in Figure 7.14. This system flow chart indicates that vendor invoices will be entered on-line via a computer terminal as they are received, then matched against the associated purchase order and vendor shipment receipt records stored in on-line files (these files act as interfaces between the AP system and purchasing and receiving systems). The work files correspond to data stores D6 and D7 from Figure 7.14(b). A printed error report lists the rejected invoices. The system creates no other paperwork until checks are sent to vendors, done in batch mode in the process "Prepare Vendor Check" using the "Payable Invoice" computer magnetic tape. The system periodically produces summary reports (the check register and the general ledger account summary) from the most recent vendor account tape and the on-line checking account file. It would be typical that more detailed system flow charts, called run charts, would also be drawn to show each stage of this chart in more detail. Individual run charts would show each summary report program, including how exception and error conditions are handled by each program.

Input Transactions

The purpose of describing input transactions is to document the format of data, so managers and systems analysts can evaluate ease of use, readability, and efficiency of data entry. When a transaction is to appear on a machine readable medium (computer terminal screen, mark sense or magnetic ink document, or the like), the best way to understand the design is to develop a mock-up or prototype of the form or screen. Today there are tools that help in quickly laying out video terminal forms, which managers and clerical personnel can check for workability.

Figure 7.16 illustrates a mock-up of a computer terminal video screen for entering the data on a vendor invoice. Typically, each screen has:

- a title that uniquely identifies this screen from all other types of screens.
- an indication if the screen is one page of several needed to complete the transaction.
- instructions on what keyboard keys to press for what functions (it is desirable to use the same keys for the same functions on all screens).
- data pertinent to the transaction (for example, vendor invoice number in Figure 7.16).
- possibly additional, nonchangeable data that helps to explain the other data; for example, for the screen in Figure 7.16, vendor address, which is retrieved from the vendor master file, helps data entry personnel to check that the proper vendor number was entered.
- an indication of the maximum length, data type, and format of data (9 means numeric only and X means either numbers or alphabetic characters).

Printed Output Layout

The documentation of printed output layout is very similar to that of computer terminal screen displays. The goal is to be sure that the printed report is readable and contains all the necessary data, that data used together are near each other on the page, that data are clearly labeled, and that the date the report is generated and the date the data were current are explicitly shown. Figure 7.17 illustrates the standard kind of report layout developed by systems builders before programs are written.

Printed reports such as that shown in Figure 7.17, as well as on-line screen displays, are the most frequent types of output from computer systems. In addition, computer systems may generate

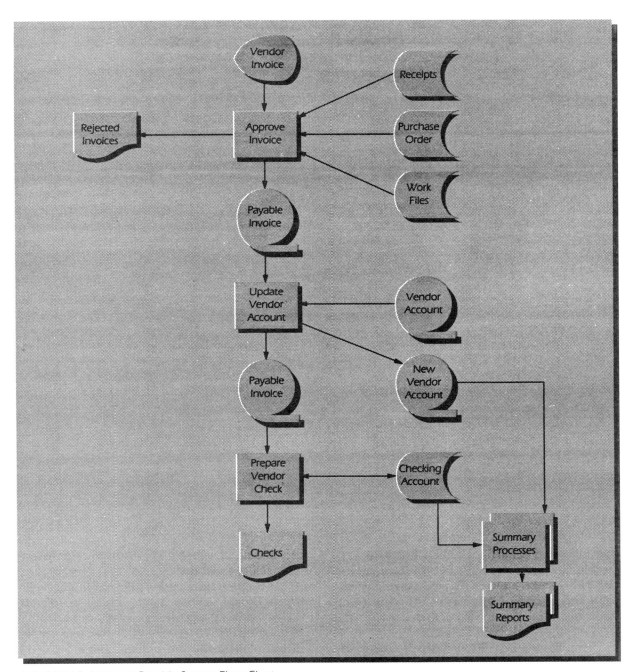

FIGURE 7.15 Accounts Payable System Flow Chart

voice responses, print universal product codes and bar codes for merchandise tickets and other applications, send electronic messages to numerically controlled manufacturing tools, and produce various other types of output.

Process Logic and Structure

As a manager you may not care how a computer system electronically calculates a sales forecast, the value of an investment decision, or the net pay

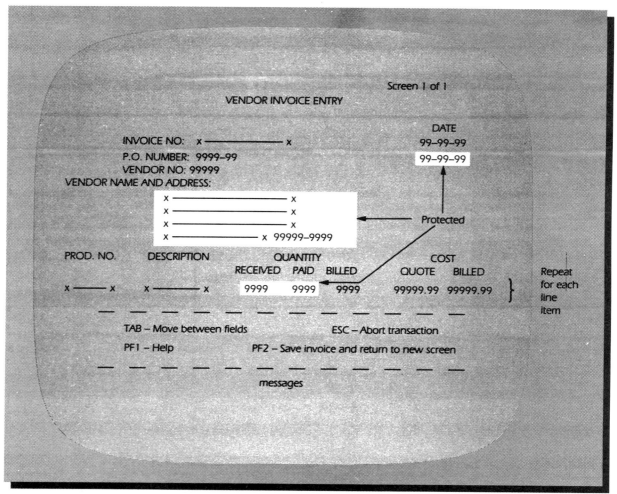

FIGURE 7.16 Enter Vendor Invoice Screen Layout

after taxes and deductions (unless it is your paycheck!). However, you must be able to communicate with systems builders the rules, special conditions, and business logic behind the work being automated, and you must be able to verify the accuracy of systems built for you.

You and the systems analysts designing systems for you need documentation tools to unambiguously and clearly describe the business conditions that lead to certain actions. Three forms of process logic documentation are frequently used for these purposes: decision tables, decision trees, and structured English. For simplicity, we will illustrate only decision tables to provide a basic understanding of representing business rules in systems analysis and design.

A decision table outlines the conditions under which certain actions are to be taken. (Figure 7.18(a) shows the general structure and a sample of the rules that govern the validation of a vendor invoice. Potentially one column exists for every unique combination of conditions (columns are combined using the '-' symbol or ELSE column when the action is the same for different sets of conditions). Actions can also be numbered when the sequence of actions needs to be specified.

Decision tables are a concise way to outline the overall logic of a business decision. They have

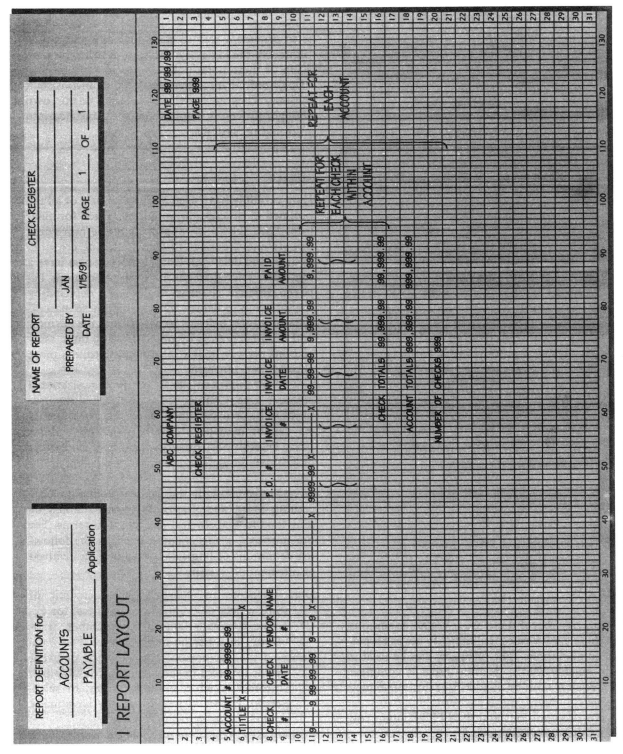

FIGURE 7.17 Accounts Payable Check Register Report Layout

294

(a) GENERAL STRUCTURE OF DECISION TABLE

	1	2	3	...
Condition Statements		Rules		
Action Statements		Action Indicators		

(b) VENDOR INVOICE VALIDATION DECISION TABLE

	1	2	3	4	Else
Invoice P.O. No. matches with P.O. on file	Y	Y	N	Y	
Quantity received minus quantity paid at least as large as quantity billed for all items	Y	N	–	N	
Invalid invoice override	–	Y	Y	N	
Store vendor invoice	X	X	X		
Add invoice to override list		X	X		
Reject invoice and put on error list				X	X

FIGURE 7.18 Decision Table

the property that if there are *n* yes/no conditions, then there are 2*n* rules (columns) to cover all possible combinations. This property can be used to check quickly that a decision table is complete. The decision table in Figure 7.18(b) is complete because columns 1 and 3 each combine two separate sets of conditions and the ELSE column covers all other combinations.

The purpose of a decision table (as well as a decision tree and the structured English notation)

is to provide a way to state concisely and unambiguously the logic of a decision or other process. Each of these notations helps to identify missing steps, redundant operations, and inconsistent actions. They each help us to analyze our own thought processes before these are translated into information systems.

Describing Data

Data certainly have been an integral part of all the outlined IS description notations. These formulations have shown, as appropriate, the movement of data and the usage of data (retrieval, creation, update, and deletion). Data, however, also have a structure, related to the natural associations between different elements of data, not depicted by the previous schemes. Describing these natural data structures helps us to understand the business and business policy. By understanding these associations we can make information storage more efficient and powerful.

More important, data are an organizational resource (see Chapter 14). Thus, this resource needs to be managed and, hence, described (just as we cannot manage materials inventory without parts descriptions, quantity on hand, and other descriptive data). Therefore, we need data about data.

Consistent with the earlier discussion concerning logical and physical systems, data must be described in both logical and physical terms. For our purposes in this chapter, consider the following definitions of (logical) classes of data involved in information systems:

Data Element: an elementary characteristic of some object or event of the business; for example, customer name, vendor number, or inventory quantity on hand.

Entity: a type of person, place, object, or event that is inherent in the business; for example, customer, vendor, purchase order, or salesperson. Each entity will typically have many data elements associated with it.

Primary Key: one or more data elements, values for which uniquely identify instances of an entity; for example, for a vendor entity the primary key would be vendor number, and for a price quotation entity the primary key would be the combination of inventory number and vendor number.

At the physical, computer system level, such logical terms often have an associated implementation term. Figure 7.19 lists the terms used to describe the physical versions of many of these logical terms for data and shows the relationships between the physical level terms.

Two different approaches to managing data have been used in data processing—file processing and database processing (see McFadden and Hoffer, 1994, for a discussion of database processing). In **file processing** each application system (for example, accounts payable system, purchasing system, and shipping and receiving system) separately maintains its own set of computer files containing the data that it needs. Although this permits each system to be individually optimized, redundant and inconsistent data will arise across systems, which makes it difficult to reconcile reports gener-

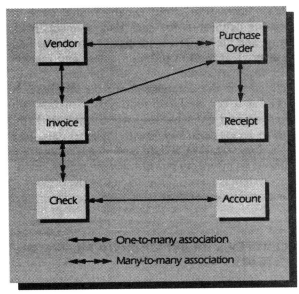

FIGURE 7.20 Example Accounting Database

ated by each system and causes confusion in the business.

The database approach is used in most modern IS. A database is a shared collection of files and associations between these files. Thus, accounts payable, purchasing, and shipping and receiving would share a single copy of common data, such as the vendor file, as part of a database. Figure 7.20 is a database schematic showing some of the typical files that would support a variety of accounting applications. Arrows between files (rectangles) do not represent data flows, but rather explain the natural relationship between records in the files. For example, a vendor issues many invoices, but an invoice is for only one vendor (a so-called one-to-many relationship). The relationship between the vendor and invoice files explains how the business operates. In the same company, one check may be used to pay many invoices and one invoice might be paid by several checks (for example, for split payment between accounts, so each check is associated with only one account). This association between invoice and check is called a many-to-many relationship.

One additional tool used in documenting data is the data dictionary (introduced in Chapter 4). A **data dictionary** is an inventory of definitions and

FIGURE 7.19 Data Terminology

other information about organizational data. It contains definitions for each data element, field, entity, and file, as well as formats, coding schemes, security clearances, validation rules, and ownership designations for each piece of data. A data dictionary is the database about the database. It serves as a consolidated source that anyone can access to find out what and where data are kept, how to access data, and how to interpret data. Just as an organization would not want to operate without an inventory control system, a data dictionary system is essential for managing the organizational inventory of data.

CONTROLS IN INFORMATION SYSTEMS

Suppose you and your spouse or a friend with whom you have a joint savings account both separately go to the bank one day to each withdraw your shared $500 in savings. Or suppose a data entry trainee forgets to include the decimal point in all the new inventory burden rates developed by the cost accountants. Or suppose an inventory accounting clerk enters a wrong, but legitimate, part number to record the issue of an item from the storeroom; this depletion results in an out-of-stock status, which automatically generates a purchase order to a vendor, who then begins production, and so on. These situations illustrate just some of the ways in which errors and unsafe conditions can arise in information systems. These also suggest possible wasted work, customer and employee confusion, and added expenses. For the integrity of the organization, protection (detection, prevention, and correction) against such breaches must be built into information systems.

Control is an integral part of systems. Negative feedback reduces the effect of variances from the desired system state. For example, the variance of a sales forecast from actual sales triggers adjustment of variables and formulas used to predict sales. Positive feedback is used to encourage a system to repeat its actions. For example, rewards are used to encourage sales staff to continue to exceed

quotas. Of course, many IS provide support for such organizational controls.

Controls are also needed to make sure that IS work properly. Procedures, either automated or manual, are needed to make sure that the right data are entered, all the necessary data are present for processing, and only authorized information processing occurs.

It is the user-manager's responsibility to identify potential violations of proper data processing. Systems builders will include some standard controls irrespective of the application, but specifying checks and balances to ensure accurate data entry and handling is a management responsibility. Managers must carefully define what are valid data, what errors might be made while handling data, what security risks are present, and what potential business losses could result from inaccurate or lost data. Since the identification of potential IS controls is a managerial responsibility, we include a discussion of controls in this chapter on systems concepts. It is during IS analysis and design that the needs for specific controls are identified and measures are developed to address the needs.

Many procedures have been developed to control data processing and to protect against the harm caused by data processing errors, malfunctions of software and equipment, power outages and natural disasters, and abuse of computer resources, including intentional crimes. Some of the more common of these controls are described in the following sections.

Backup

The following story has been told about a secretary in the office of the president of a major university. By the end of the first week of using a new computer-based word processing system, he had created many diskettes. As was office policy, the secretary decided to tidy up the office and erased all the data from each diskette so he could start fresh on the following Monday morning. On a more personal level, have you used a personal computer and asked to have a new, blank diskette formatted (electronically organized so it can be used)? With just a minor keystroke error, it is easy to misspecify this command and have an existing disk with current data formatted instead, thus erasing all previous work saved on this disk. Or, have you ever had a previously readable diskette become unreadable?

The ultimate protection against such errors is to have a backup copy. Periodically a file can be copied and saved in a separate location (companies may store backup files in bank vaults or at another computer site). Then, when a file becomes contaminated or destroyed, the most recent version can be restored. Of course, any changes since the last copy was made will not appear. Thus, organizations often also keep transaction logs (a chronological history of changes to each file), so these changes can be automatically applied to a backup copy to bring the file up to current status. Some organizations can operate only if computer systems are working (such as airlines, banks, and telephone networks). These organizations will create "hot site" data centers, to which they automatically switch operations in case of the breakdown of the primary data center (due to power failure, earthquake or fire, or failure of a critical computer component). These centers must have duplicate copies of the "live" data to reduce the transition time.

On-line computer files are especially critical to backup. Files stored on tape have an automatic copy made when data is updated (since data cannot be overwritten on tape, the previous tape file becomes a backup). On-line disk files must be periodically copied for protection. As part of the transaction log for disk files, some organizations also keep before and after images of disk records that are updated. This is a form of selective backup, which saves the time and delay of copying whole files, when only a small percentage of the contents have changed.

Information systems and computer equipment are now distributed throughout business departments and in small businesses where IS professionals are not present. Thus, making backup copies of files is becoming more of a user-manager responsibility. Further, management must help determine how frequently backup copies are needed,

the business cost of recovering files from backup copies, and the cost for delays in the business during restoration from backups. For example, hourly backups may be very secure, but the lost computer time to make the backups can slow down other processing and make certain data inaccessible during business hours.

Standards

One way to avoid errors is to develop standard, repeatable, and possibly reusable ways to do certain data processing. Use of standard programming languages and equipment means that systems developers will be more familiar with the tools and will be less likely to make mistakes. Also, it is more cost efficient to support training and consulting on a few standard tools than a host of infrequently used technologies. A common method also employed is to create a library of frequently used functions (such as calculation of net present value or a sales forecasting model) that can be used by many different information systems. Such a function can then be developed with great care and reused each time it is needed, saving development time and reducing the likelihood of design and programming flaws.

Managers need to cooperate with IS professionals in choosing and using standard languages, packages, data, and function libraries. Autonomy to be able to use whatever tools a manager wants must be balanced with the costs to support such diversity.

Edit Rules

Each time a data element is updated, the new value can be checked against a legitimate set or range of values permitted for that data. This check can be performed in each application program (for example, in a payables adjustment program that modifies previously entered vendor invoices) that changes this data. It is better, however, to check using special software, called a database management system (see Chapter 5), that changes the data value in computer files. This ensures that the checks are made the same way for all programs and that checks are not forgotten. Edit rules are also used to ensure that data are not missing, that data are of a valid size and type, and that data match with other stored values.

Simply visually displaying associated data can be a very useful edit check. For example, when a vendor number is entered, the program can display the associated name and address. The person inputting or modifying data can then visually verify that not only is this an existing vendor number (within the valid range of values), but it is also the correct vendor. Edit rules can also ensure that only numbers are entered for numeric data, that only feasible codes are entered, or that some calculation made from a modified data value is valid (for example, that quantity times price is still legitimate when either quantity or price changes on a vendor invoice). These edit checks are integrity rules that control the validity of data.

Managers and their staff are responsible for defining the legitimate values for data. Further, management must set policy to specify if checks can be overridden and who can authorize overrides. Edit rules should permit business growth and expansion, yet reduce the likelihood of erroneous data.

Security

The unauthorized use of data may result in a material loss, such as the embezzlement of funds, or an intangible loss, such as the unauthorized use of a computer or the disclosure of sensitive data. In any case, security of data and computers is necessary so that employees, customers, shareholders, and others can be confident that their interactions with the organization are confidential and the assets of the business are safe.

Many security methods are employed. For example, see Hoffer and Straub (1989) for details on administrative practices that deter computer security and abuse threats. Backup copies of data and program files are helpful in recovery from breaches of security that damage these critical resources. To prevent security breaches, passwords can be associated with programs, files, and terminals. Different passwords are required by different users and possibly for different operations for the

same user. For example, you might need one password to have the right to read certain computer files and a different password to be able to change the contents of these files. Encryption is used to encode data so that copies of data cannot be made, taken to another computer, and accessed. Unless you know the decryption formula, an unauthorized copy will be unreadable and uninterpretable.

Physical security of computer centers and of specific workstations limits contact with data. Badge readers, voice and retina recognition, or combination locks are common. Computer ethics statements raise awareness to the sensitivity of data privacy and the need to protect organizational data.

Since no security system is foolproof, detection of security breaches is also needed. Some detection methods are:

- analysis of the amount of computer time used by individuals.
- hiding special instructions in sensitive programs that log identifying data about users.
- periodic logging of all system users and what information system data and equipment they are currently using.

EDP Auditing

EDP auditing is a field that is a combination of data processing and accounting. EDP auditors use a variety of methods to ensure the correct processing of data, including compliance tests, statistical sampling, and embedded auditing methods.

Compliance tests check that systems builders use high quality systems development procedures that lead to properly functioning systems. Statistical sampling of a portion of databases identifies abnormalities that indicate more systematic problems or security breaches. Embedded auditing methods are triggers that are activated when certain events occur in a data processing system. These records are analyzed to determine if errors or security breaches are occurring in the system.

Probably the most used EDP auditing technique is an **audit trail**. An audit trail is a list of references (for example, invoice numbers, batch numbers, transaction numbers, program names, user names, dates, and times) that allow a transaction to be traced from the time of input through all the reports in which the transaction data is used. External auditors and tax authorities use an audit trail to check computer records. An audit trail can help identify where errors are introduced into computerized data or where security breaches might have occurred. Managers are needed to identify what data should be included in the audit trail so that errors can be detected and the organization stays in compliance with all the various laws and regulations.

System Testing

Certainly the most common of all IS controls is complete system testing. Each program must be tested individually and in combination with the other programs in the IS. Managers develop test data that have known results. Programs are run with typical and atypical, correct and erroneous data, and the actual results are compared to what should be produced. Testing occurs not only when systems are initially developed, but also repeatedly when systems are modified for enhancement or fixing errors. (See Chapter 8 on the role of managers during system testing.)

Control Calculations

Various calculations can be performed to validate data processing. **Batch totals** that calculate the sum of certain data in a batch of transactions can be computed both manually before processing and by the computer during processing; discrepancies suggest the occurrence of data entry errors such as transposition of digits. For example, in the accounts payable application, the manual total of a batch of vendor invoice total amount fields can be calculated and compared against the same total after data entry. This is not foolproof because offsetting errors can be made and the manual and computer batch totals will still match, but it will catch most errors.

A **check digit** can be appended to critical identifying numbers (such as general ledger account numbers or vendor numbers); the value of this check digit has some mathematical relationship to the other digits in the number. This can be used to quickly verify that at least a valid, if not proper, code has been entered, and it can catch most common errors.

As in the other controls, the manager has considerable input into the design of useful and efficient control calculations. The user can identify natural batches of data on which batch totals can be calculated. Also, managers must verify that those totals that appear on CRT screens and in printed reports can be used by their staff. The design of manual procedures to trace errors to their source will also be the responsibility of supervisors and managers.

REENGINEERING THE BUSINESS SYSTEM

For many years, as outlined in Chapter 1, we used information technology (IT) only to automate current business operations. Although some productivity gains occurred from mechanizing old ways of doing business, we really did not take advantage of IT to enable us to redesign the business for major improvement. Recently, organizations have taken a more systems-oriented approach in which they analyze business operations from the ground up, eliminating old processes, controls, reporting relationships, and compensation/reward systems that have outlived their utility. This radical business redesign to achieve dramatic improvements in business processes by taking advantage of information technology is called **business process reengineering**.

Business process reengineering questions the assumptions about how we organize and conduct business that may have been in place for decades. It searches for new business rules that make more sense given current market conditions and the capabilities of IT. The goal is to achieve an order of magnitude improvement, rather than incremental gains, from automating current processes.

The origins of business process reengineering are in manufacturing. Innovations such as concurrent engineering and just-in-time inventory

DROWNING IN PAPER

Connecticut Mutual Life Insurance used to store policyholder data in a warehouse the size of a football field, with dedicated vehicles shuttling paper between the office and warehouse every hour. By reengineering the process of handling policyholder questions, Connecticut Mutual reduced response time to queries from five days to a few hours with 20 percent fewer people. The assumption that was broken in this reengineering was that policy data had to be kept on original, paper forms. Connecticut Mutual uses a combination of "smart" electronic forms that have edit controls built in and optical disk storage to make policyholder data readily accessible to any office worker.

(Adapted from Symonds, 1992)

controls created profound changes in manufacturing management. In such innovations, tasks previously isolated in one department are now integrated with work across departments.

Two notable reports of business process reengineering are Ford Motor Company and Mutual Benefit Life Insurance (Hammer, 1990). The Ford situation deals with their accounts payable function. During an early design of a new accounts payable system, Ford concluded that they could reduce head count by 20 percent in this department. They were reasonably proud of their plans until they discovered that Mazda accomplished the same function with just five people. The difference was that Ford based their planned new system on old business assumptions:

- Problems with coordinating purchase orders, shipment documents, and invoices were inevitable, so an accounts payable system should help clerks investigate mismatches between purchasing documents; a reengineered system would, instead, help prevent mismatches.
- Ford could not pay a vendor without an invoice; a reengineered system would, in contrast, use negotiated prices to pay immediately upon receipt of validated goods, without an invoice.

The result of taking a reengineering view was a 75 percent improvement gain, not the original 20 percent.

Similarly, Mutual Benefit Life reengineered its insurance application processing. Rather than automate what was a thirty-step process covering five departments and nineteen people, they created a whole new way of processing applications. The result was the use of an advanced PC workstation through which one person had complete control over all tasks related to processing an application.

Consider the case of interorganizational systems from Chapter 3. Prior to such systems, organizations assumed that "Customers won't enter their own orders," "Vendors won't let us check about the status of our orders," and "Vendors own the specifications for components they make for us." By questioning and ultimately breaking these assumptions, artificial constraints are relaxed and radically new system solutions are possible. With interorganizational systems, the assumptions in question are those that define system boundaries, which is often the case in reengineering. *Impertinence is the basis for business process reengineering.* Simple questions like "why," "what if," "who says so," and "what would you rather do" can lead to breakthrough insights to totally new business processes.

Business process reengineering involves a thorough reassessment of people, procedures, organizations, and technologies—the four elements of the organization as a system outlined earlier in this chapter. The enabler is technology, which allows new, not just automated, processes. According to Hammer (1990), reengineering involves certain principles for analyzing and dramatically reorganizing business as a system. We have consolidated these into six key principles:

1. *Organize business processes around outcomes, not tasks.* This principle implies that one person should perform all the steps in a given process, as in the case of Mutual Benefit Life, where one manager handles the whole application approval process. Information technology is used to bring together all the information and decision-making resources needed by this

one person. Often this principle also means organizing work around the customer, not the product. For example, in Chapter 3 we discussed the Merrill Lynch Cash Management Account. This information service integrated all investment activities to focus on the customer, not individual investment products.

2. *Assign those who use the output to perform the process.* The intent of this principle is to make those most interested in a result accountable for the production of that result. For example, Hammer reports the case of an electronics equipment manufacturer that reengineered its field service function to have customers perform simple repairs themselves. This principle causes a reduction in nonproductive overhead jobs, including liaison positions. Principles 1 and 2 yield a compression of linear steps into one step, greatly reducing delays, miscommunication, and wasted coordination efforts. Information technologies, like expert systems and databases, allow every manager to perform functions traditionally done by specialty managers.

3. *Integrate information processing into the work that produces the information.* This principle states that information should be processed at its source. For example, at Ford this means that the receiving department, which produces information on goods received, should also enter this data, rather than sending it to accounts payable for processing. This puts data capture closest to the place where data entry errors can be detected and corrected, thus minimizing extra reconciliation steps. This principle also implies that data should be captured once at the primary source, thus avoiding transmittal and transcription errors. All who need these data work from a common and consistent source. For example, the true power of EDI comes when all information processing related to an EDI transaction works from a common, integrated database.

4. *Create a virtual enterprise by treating geographically distributed resources as though they were centralized.* This principle implies

that the distinction between centralization and decentralization is artificial with information technology. Technologies such as teleconferencing, group support systems, e-mail, and others can create an information processing environment in which time and space are compressed. Hammer reports about the experience of Hewlett-Packard, which treats the purchasing departments of fifty manufacturing units as if they were one giant department by using a shared database on vendor and purchase orders. The result is 50 percent to 150 percent improvement in key purchasing function performance variables.

5. *Link parallel activities instead of integrating their results.* This principle says that related activities should be constantly coordinated rather than waiting until a final step to ensure consistency. For example, Hammer suggests that different kinds of credit functions in a financial institution could share common databases, use communication networks, and employ teleconferencing to coordinate their operations constantly. This would ensure, for example, that a customer is not extended a full line of credit from each unit.

6. *Have the people who do the work make all the decisions, and let controls built into the system monitor the process.* The result of this principle is the drastic reduction of layers of management, the empowerment of employees, and the shortcutting of bureaucracy. This principle emphasizes the importance of building controls into a system from the start, rather than as an afterthought. The controls discussed earlier in the chapter, as well as expert systems, allow people to make decisions within a limited and validated environment.

Business process reengineering is a cooperative effort between IS professionals and business managers. Managers know the details of current operations and where wasted steps appear to exist. IS professionals bring systems analysis methodologies, analysis tools, and technologies that enable prior assumptions about business operations to be broken.

SUMMARY

This chapter presents the basic systems concepts on which modern information systems are built and the notations used to describe these systems. The existence of such concepts and standards for documentation suggests that the design of systems is not totally an art, but is based upon principles and good design practices.

Neither you nor a systems builder can sort through these concepts individually and arrive at the exact design for your system; remember, each of you has your own experience and human information processing characteristics that will lead you to possibly different conclusions. Thus, systems design is a partnership in which managers and system professionals each contribute to meeting information processing needs.

This chapter introduces concepts of systems that will be used throughout this book and for the design of information systems. We have seen that management itself can be viewed as a system involving technology, people, tasks, and organization structures. Important system design issues are reviewed, such as where to draw the system boundary and selecting the scope of a system, the distinction between logical and physical systems, and the consideration of human factors in systems design.

The hierarchical decomposition of systems is shown to be very useful in the analysis and design of systems, including information systems. Although there are accepted elements of good systems design that make systems easier to develop and maintain, the chapter also addresses the significant effort that an organization and individuals often expend to design information systems. A wide variety of notations are introduced so that you as a user-manager can unambiguously communicate your information needs and understand the systems built to satisfy them. The chapter also reviews a variety of controls to improve the likelihood that systems operate correctly and securely.

The chapter concludes with a discussion of the application of systems principles in the reengineering of an organization. This section shows the significant impact systems thinking can have on a business and how information technology is an enabler of business change.

REVIEW QUESTIONS

1. Define the term *system*. Give an example of a business system and identify for this example the boundary, environment, components, and objective.

2. Define the term *subsystem*. Give an example of a business subsystem and identify the other subsystems with which it relates.

3. What are the six phases of the decision-making process?

4. Contrast logical and physical system descriptions.

5. Outline the factors to consider when choosing a system boundary.

6. What are the functions of an interface component of a system?

7. Define the term *decoupling*. Grocery and other retail stores have decoupled pricing from the display of products in the store. Why?

8. Contrast the use and content of data flow diagrams versus system flow charts.

9. What is a data dictionary?

10. Inaccurate data and security breaches threaten the viability of information systems. List and briefly explain the nature of four data processing controls that help in either the detection, prevention, or correction/recovery from errors in data processing.

11. What is an audit trail? How is an audit trail used for controlling an information system?

12. What is a check digit? Give a personal example of one that you have encountered.

13. Outline the phases and stages of the systems development life cycle.

14. Define the term business process reengineering.

DISCUSSION QUESTIONS

1. Explain and give an example that supports the following statement: "Each time we change characteristics of one or more of the components of the organization (organization structure, people, task/procedure, and technology), we must consider compensating changes in the other components."

2. Explain the function of hierarchical decomposition in systems analysis and design and discuss the reasons for viewing and analyzing systems in this way.

3. In Chapter 8 we will discuss the costs to develop systems and the costs at different stages of systems development to correct errors made in the system design. From the material presented in Chapter 7 concerning logical and physical systems, discuss the consequences of making a change in the functionality or capabilities of a system during definition versus construction phases of the SDLC.

4. Why do informal systems arise?

5. Explain why the amount of work required to write programs for one computer system of ten programs is not simply ten times the work to write one program.

6. Explain the differences in purpose and type of content between system flow charts and logical data flow diagrams.

7. Study the process followed at your university for registering for classes. Represent this as a single level logical data flow diagram.

8. Midstate Community Hospital is a typical in- and out-patient medical center in a medium-sized midwestern town. Data entities for this hospital include patient, bed, patient-room, medical-procedure, physician, charge, and drug/item (for example, a television rented for the patient). Draw a database diagram, as was done for an accounts payable application in Figure 7.20, for these entities in this hospital.

9. For each of the six phases of the decision-making process outlined in Figure 7.4, give examples of information system capabilities that would help or support a manager.

10. Describe a situation in which the recency effect played a role in your processing of information.

11. Discuss the benefits of modularity in systems design.

12. Contrast the purpose of a data flow diagram to that of a database structure diagram. Why is it now accepted that data and process need to be documented separately?

13. Discuss the similarities between the systems development life cycle of Figure 7.8 and the decision-making process of Figure 7.4. Why are these two processes similar?

14. Discuss the relationship between business process reengineering and the fundamental components of an organization as a system as outlined in Figure 7.2.

REFERENCES

Carroll, Paul B. 1990. "Creating new software were agonizing tasks for Mitch Kapor firm." *Wall Street Journal* 71 (May 11): A1, A4.

Fites, Philip, Peter Johnston, and Martin Kratz. 1989. *The Computer Virus Crisis.* New York: Van Nostrand Reinhold.

Hammer, Michael. 1990. "Reengineering work: Don't automate, obliterate." *Harvard Business Review* 68 (July–August): 104–112.

Hoffer, Jeffrey A., and Detmar W. Straub, Jr. 1989. "The 9 to 5 underground: Are you policing computer crimes?" *Sloan Management Review* 30 (Summer): 35–43.

Kozar, Kenneth A. 1989. *Humanized Information Systems Analysis and Design.* New York: McGraw-Hill Book Company.

McFadden, Fred R., and Jeffrey A. Hoffer. 1994. *Modern Database Management*, Menlo Park, Calif.: Benjamin Cummings Publishing Company.

Newell, Allen, and Herbert A. Simon. 1972. *Human Problem Solving*. Englewood Cliffs, N.J.: Prentice-Hall.

Seligman, Daniel. 1985. "Handism" in "Keeping Up" column. *Fortune*. (March 18): 165, 168.

Symonds, William C. 1992. "Getting rid of paper is just the beginning." *Business Week* (December 21): 88–89.

7

Digital Equipment Corporation

"I'm convinced that we're on the verge of something big," remarked Peter Campbell, newly appointed manager of Order Administration for Digital Equipment Corporation's U.S. Manufacturing Group (USMG),

> but I can't tell you I know exactly what to do next. When I was a plant manager I learned a lot from the boneyard.[1] I'd look there to find out what was wrong with a process. Here in order administration, the boneyard is someone's desk drawer or a tiny slice of some data storage disk, where some order could be sitting without our knowing it. With that order resides a great opportunity to improve the process and better meet our customers' expectations.

It was the summer of 1989 and Campbell was addressing Edward Nicholas, manager of the Order Quality Group, whom he had appointed to improve the USMG's administrative processes, and Chris Couch, a summer associate from a well-known eastern business school hired in the spring to assess the effectiveness of the company's order management system.

---

[1] "Boneyard" is slang for a storage room for defective components from a manufacturing process. Detailed analysis of these parts often led to valuable improvements in the process.

Product Background

Digital Equipment Corporation (Digital) was founded in 1957 by Kenneth Olsen, who had graduated from MIT in 1950 with a degree in electrical engineering. Digital's inaugural product entry, the $18,000 PDP-8, was the world's first inexpensive minicomputer. Credited by many with changing forever the world of computing, it laid the groundwork for the personal computer revolution that was to follow.

In 1989, thirty-two years after its founding, Digital was deriving revenues of $12.7 billion and a net income of $1.1 billion from the design, manufacture, and marketing of minicomputers, workstations, and a full line of computer components and peripherals. In addition, Digital sold many "third-party" (externally manufactured) accessories such as paper, printer ribbons, and plotter pens. For purposes of order management, the company segregated its product line and built specially designed order fulfillment systems for each product category.[2] For example, products such as printer ribbons or plotter pens that were likely to be held in inventory rather than built to order were fulfilled through DECDirect, a process "built for speed." Ninety-five percent of DECDirect orders were shipped within 24 hours. Other product categories having separate order management processes included software, spare parts, third-party supplies, and sophisticated products, which constituted Digital's "complex orders."

Digital computers were organized into distinct product lines on the basis of the computer's central processing unit or CPU. CPUs were differentiated by processing speed, maximum number of users, and a variety of other parameters. A typical computer system comprised a CPU, one of several different

---

[2] The administration of customer orders, from submitting quotes to the customer to shipping equipment, is referred to as order management.

options for communications, internal memory expansion, disk and tape drives, and other components. Even the simplest product had an enormous number of feasible combinations of components; and most components were compatible with multiple products.

Every computer configuration was subject to constraints. There was a physical limitation on the number of options each CPU could accommodate; some options were not compatible with some CPUs; certain options required other options. This backdrop of practically limitless variation led Digital to develop a complex order fulfillment system with complex rules for option selection.

Components of the Complex Order Management Process: Summary

Digital's complex order process circa spring 1989 had roughly six phases. One, salespeople collected orders from the field. Two, Customer Administrative Services (CAS) personnel verified customer data, including billing addresses and credit limits. Three, the Operations Business Group (OBG) routed the orders. Four, Technical Editing verified the technical accuracy of the orders. Five, Common Scheduling assigned production dates to orders, based on production schedules from Digital's thirteen plants. Six, Headers, Plant, and Consolidation administered, built, and shipped orders to the customers (see Exhibit 1a).

In the summer of 1989, Digital management eliminated Technical Editing and reassigned former technical editors as configuration technical specialists (CTSs) to Customer Administrative Services. Salespeople, because they believed that the advent to CTSs would mean better and faster customer service, liked the change. CTSs welcomed the closeness to customers, whom they helped directly by solving configuration problems and explaining the concepts of order configuration. CTSs were also responsible for detecting defects in customer orders. The complex order management process after the creation of CTSs consisted of the stages depicted in Exhibit 1b.

Sales   Customer needs for Digital products were relayed to the company by 6,000 sales representatives in 500 sales offices (see Exhibit 2) who made routine sales calls and initiated customer contacts. Digital's sales reps were responsible for translating

customers' needs into "solutions" built from Digital products.

When talking to customers, sales reps would develop sets of notes that subsequently had to be converted into official price quotations. Sales reps had two ways of doing this. Using a computer terminal located in their sales office, they could type the information into Digital's Automated Quoting System (AQS), which helped them organize information into a standard format, print quotations to be submitted to customers, and track outstanding quotations. Because sales reps were not familiar with the details of all Digital products, it was possible for them to generate quotations that were not technically correct, for example, that contained incompatible components. A customer order from such a quotation could put the sales rep in the embarrassing position of having to inform the customer that the quote was incorrect. Alternatively, sales reps could provide customer information in verbal, written, or electronic (E-mail) form to a Customer Administrative Services (CAS) representative. Although this required more work (e.g., telephone calls to CAS reps who were usually located in separate offices), the CAS reps could help to ensure that quotes were "clean" before they went to customers.

Digital's downstream complex order management process required that each order contain only CPUs from a single product line. If a customer needed more than one type of CPU, the quotation was split into multiple quotations. (Exhibit 2 depicts the entire complex order management process.)

Customer-Administrative Services   Each of the 370 CAS reps supported several sales reps and had access to a number of powerful electronic resources. Centrally located customer master files, component code and specification files, and other resources were accessible from CAS reps' desktop computer terminals.

Upon receiving the details of a quotation, a CAS rep used the AQS in the same way a sales rep would. But the CAS rep would also ask a CTS to check the quotation. Each CAS site had at least one CTS specially trained in the technical details of all Digital products and the use of XSEL (eXpert SELling system), an expert system invoked by AQS that alerted the CTS to technically inconsistent or invalid options in the quotation (e.g., options that were incompatible, that exceeded a CPU's power supply capacity, and so forth). The CTS was trained to correct errors, either

EXHIBIT 1

Complex Order Management
Process System

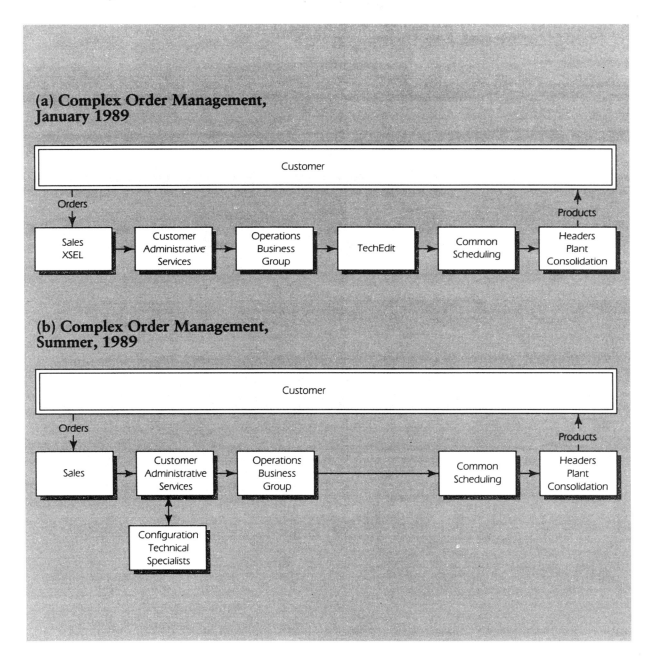

(a) Complex Order Management, January 1989

(b) Complex Order Management, Summer, 1989

EXHIBIT 2
. . . .
Information Technology Support
of Complex Order Management

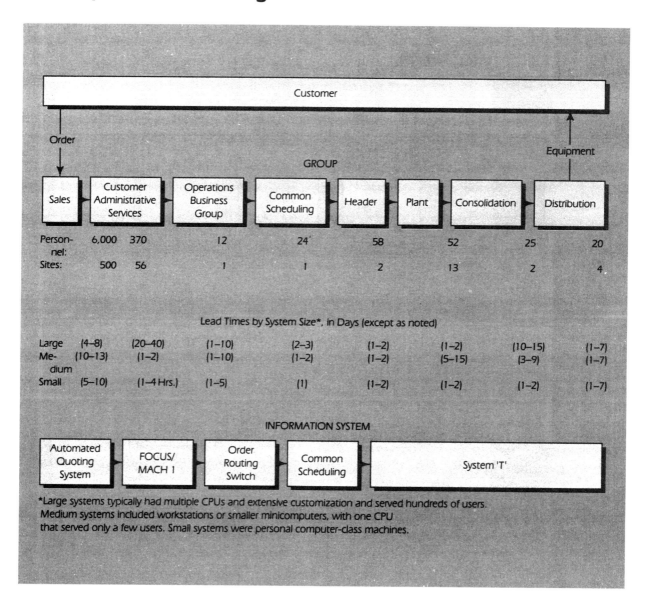

	Sales	Customer Administrative Services	Operations Business Group	Common Scheduling	Header	Plant	Consolidation	Distribution
Personnel:	6,000	370	12	24	58	52	25	20
Sites:	500	56	1	1	2	13	2	4

Lead Times by System Size*, in Days (except as noted)

Large	(4–8)	(20–40)	(1–10)	(2–3)	(1–2)	(1–2)	(10–15)	(1–7)
Medium	(10–13)	(1–2)	(1–10)	(1–2)	(1–2)	(5–15)	(3–9)	(1–7)
Small	(5–10)	(1–4 Hrs.)	(1–5)	(1)	(1–2)	(1–2)	(1–2)	(1–7)

INFORMATION SYSTEM

Automated Quoting System	FOCUS/ MACH 1	Order Routing Switch	Common Scheduling	System 'T'

*Large systems typically had multiple CPUs and extensive customization and served hundreds of users. Medium systems included workstations or smaller minicomputers, with one CPU that served only a few users. Small systems were personal computer-class machines.

by editing the order or by recommending changes to the sales rep or customer.

Once a quotation was "clean," the CAS rep provided it to the customer, either directly or via the sales rep. Depending upon the sales office and the product line, the ratio of quotations to orders fell between 5 : 1 and 10 : 1. Acceptable quotations generally resulted in official purchase orders for equipment.

CAS reps processed customer purchase orders through a computer system called FOCUS/MACH I, an automated order administration system and the vehicle by which CAS reps accessed their electronic resources. If an arriving order referenced an AQS quotation number, the CAS rep would have FOCUS/MACH I retrieve the quotation from AQS, eliminating the need to retype the order. CAS reps used FOCUS/MACH I to check three classes of order information in strict sequence: administrative, technical edit, and credit. Orders that failed one of these checks were put "in suspense" until the error was cleared. For example, a customer code that was not found in the customer master file would result in an administrative error. CAS reps were responsible for correcting errors that held orders in administrative suspense. This could involve editing the order or calling the department responsible for having the master file edited. About 4 percent of orders were held in administrative suspense.

Errors that placed orders in tech-edit suspense had to be corrected by a CTS. Digital standards required the use of XSEL within the AQS procedure, but a CTS could manually tech-edit orders on FOCUS/MACH I. Experienced CTSs could tech-edit some orders faster manually than with XSEL. Tech-edited orders cleared tech-edit suspense. Quotations tech-edited on AQS and passed to FOCUS/MACH I (identified by a "Q" in the unique quotation number used to track the AQS quotations) were not subject to tech-edit suspense. Credit checks to verify customer creditworthiness involved accessing the customer master file. Risk of nonpayment would place an order in credit suspense.

CAS reps were measured on several parameters: the time it took to respond to sales and customer requests; the average time orders remained in suspense; and order cleanliness (i.e., the technical validity and administrative correctness of orders). For one eastern region CAS office, the statistic for all suspenses per order was two hours. Orders that were clean and accepted, which digital referred to as certifications, or "certs," counted toward company sales goals. As an order cleared credit suspense, FOCUS/

MACH I passed it immediately to the Order Routing Switch (ORS), a computer system monitored by the OBG.

Operations Business Group   The twelve people in the Merrimack, New Hampshire-based OBG were responsible for correcting all orders that the ORS was unable to pass to the next step in the order management process, about five per day. (ORS processed between 600 and 800 "complex" orders per day. If all went well, OBG never examined an order; the ORS electronically checked each order's part codes and routed it to the proper order management system. Like most systems of this nature, ORS was dependent on many different databases for valid part codes, customer addresses, plant codes, and so forth. Orders rejected by ORS for invalid part codes were resolved by OBG through interaction with the organization supervising the appropriate database or with the CAS office that submitted the order. OBG routed orders to Common Scheduling (the name of a group of people as well as of a computer program) in two batches, the first between 5 P.M. and 6 P.M. and the second at midnight to capture sales activity in later time zones.

Common Scheduling   Different parts of a complex order were likely to be produced at different plants. The Burlington, Vermont, plant might build the CPU, the Colorado Springs plant the disk drives, and the Puerto Rico plant the terminals. Common Scheduling allocated orders among plants. Upon receiving a batch of orders from ORS, the Common Scheduling software program used a weekly production schedule to assign each order a planned ship date as close as possible to the customer request date. Each morning, Common Scheduling personnel reviewed reports and checked for problems. Seventy-five to 80 percent of orders would "autoload" and be scheduled reasonably close to the customer request date. In the event of a production shortfall that prevented scheduling an order close to the customer request date, Common Scheduling personnel resolved the problem by telephone with the Material Operations Group in Marlboro, Massachusetts.

Common Scheduling personnel used their computer system to release autoloaded orders manually to the Headers group. They believed manual release, which triggered information that flowed both backward and forward, caused fewer errors than releasing orders electronically. Released orders and scheduled ship dates were communicated via the ORS back to FOCUS/MACH I, which printed acknowledgments for customers, and forward to the Headers' computer system, System "T," which received orders twice daily, at 1 P.M. and 8 P.M. System "T" was also used by the plants and by the consolidation organization.

Headers Headers were Digital headquarters groups that monitored plant orders. Headers were assigned to complex system orders: the Mid-Range Systems Header (in Salem, New Hampshire) was responsible for mid-range and large systems; the Small Systems Header (in Boxborough, Massachusetts) was responsible for workstation and personal computer class machines.

The Headers monitored order flows and participated in the resolution of problems that arose in the course of business. It was the Header's responsibility to ensure that shipments were uninterrupted when production moved from one plant to another. The Headers also helped the plants forecast and manage changing volumes as products moved through dramatically shortened life cycles.

System "T" released orders to plants based on standard lead times (see Exhibit 2), which included an administrative buffer, the time required to build the product and ship it from plant to Consolidation. The Header managed lead times carefully. If they were too short, plants would not have enough time to make shipments as scheduled; if they were too long, Digital would carry excessive inventories.

Lead times were sensitive to location. The Colorado plant, for example, would be advised if an order's final destination was in the east slightly earlier than eastern plants. To System "T," "releasing" the order to the plant meant allowing the order information to be accessed by plant order administrators.

Plants Digital plants used System "T" to track orders in production and shipment. When its portion of an order was complete, the plant notified the Header by sending a "Built Confirm." Once all the plants responsible for different pieces of an order had "Built Confirmed," the Header issued a "Ship Authorization" to each simultaneously. Upon receipt of a "Ship Authorization," a plant shipped its components to the appropriate consolidation facility.

Consolidation Because shipments consumed receiving dock space and required careful site preparation and installation planning, most customers required all components of a complex order to arrive at the same time. Rather than ship directly to customers from multiple points and risk incomplete arrivals, Digital maintained two consolidation points, one in Westminster, Massachusetts, and the other in Colorado Springs, Colorado.

A third-party distribution management software package helped direct the components of arriving shipments to the appropriate location within the consolidation facility. Aisles of heavy duty storage racks, two stages high, were divided into numeric slots, or "pigeon-holes," in which the components of an order were held. Forklifts moved product components from receiving to the slots designated by the distribution software and from the slots to the shipping dock when the order was complete and scheduled for shipment.

Exception Handling Exceptions to the order management process arose from both external sources, such as changing customer needs and shipping failures by freight companies, and internal sources, such as product holds for engineering and quality control. Two groups were responsible for exceptions. Area manufacturing managers resolved exceptions in the early part of the process, from initial customer contact through the OBG activities. Exceptions during the rest of the process were handled by the Order Execution Group, which took calls from customers and communicated with other organizations as necessary to meet customer's needs.

. . . .
An Example of Complex Order Management

Consider a hypothetical customer order for, say, four workstations, video terminals, memory expansions, printers, and software. These being standard items in a simple configuration, the sales rep would likely choose to enter the data into AQS and produce the quotation and provide it to the customer directly, delivering it to a CAS rep later.

Seeing the quotation number, the CAS rep would retrieve the necessary information from the AQS via FOCUS/MACH I, review the order, and, if it was "clean," alert CTS. CTS would examine the order, and, it being a simple order, advise FOCUS/MACH I that it had cleared tech-edit suspense. A CAS rep would then clear the order's credit status by ensuring that the customer had no credit problems and that the order did not exceed credit limits. Upon clearance, the order would go immediately to the ORS, which, if it found no errors, would route it to Common Scheduling in the 6 P.M. batch. Common Scheduling attempted to autoload all orders. Common Scheduling personnel noted in the following morning's reports whether customer request dates and planned ship dates were the same and, later in the morning, released the orders to System "T," which picked them up in the 1 P.M. transfer. (This flow is depicted in Exhibit 2.)

System "T" released an order when the lead time window opened[3] for the plant that had been allocated components from the order. The Header, upon being informed of build completion by all of the plants involved, would issue a Ship Authorization to each plant. Components would then move to Consolidation, where they would be accumulated in a slot and eventually shipped to the customer.

Scheduling of orders that contained exception items, such as critical parts, was based on available allocations and schedule confirmation transmitted back to the sales office at the point of order. Orders that contained noncritical items that were unavailable to meet the committed delivery date were sent to a plant that could provide the needed item. Altered orders were routed through the sales office, which would inform the consolidation center of the changes.

....

The 3,000 Configuration Workstation

Digital product managers were responsible for talking with customers and engineers about product characteristics and establishing options for product lines. A product manager, for example, was involved in the decision that certain digital personal computers would have storage options including 20-, 40-, and 80-megabyte disk drives. Digital product managers advanced their careers by assuming greater responsibility for product releases. Managing a product through ramp-up, maturity, and end-of-life was considered being "put out to pasture." Successful product managers released many different products during the early to mid-1980s, most of them six-figure minicomputers.

During the summer of 1989,[4] product managers proposed the creation of a low-end workstation with options for 3,000 configurations. Digital's competitive advantage, product managers argued, lay in its "à la carte" configuration capability, its ability to build different machines with different options for different customers. Given the wide variations in the parameters associated with VAX minicomputers (e.g., terminals, memory disks, tapes, multiplexers), 3,000 possible configurations were not uncommon. With prices for minicomputers running about $100,000 and gross margins exceeding 50 percent, Digital had the resources necessary to support processing costs of more than $500 per order.

For workstations, which characteristically had much less variation and many fewer parameters, 3,000 configurations was a large number. With prices for workstations running about $10,000, and competitive pressure to increase margins, $500 order administration costs would significantly impact net margins.

Other possible disadvantages to the 3,000 configuration workstation included confusing the customer and increasing costs and delays in orders. Custom confusion was not considered a major concern because most Digital customers were experienced in ordering complicated minicomputers. Increased costs and profit and loss responsibility did not rest directly with Digital product managers, but with the company's CEO. Delays in customer orders, product managers argued, would be ameliorated by the XCON and XSEL expert systems. (The former was used for computer configuration, the latter for parts tracking and price quoting.)

Under pressure by senior management to reduce their ranks and simplify their work, Headers favored a workstation with fewer than 3,000 configurations. Although they were not responsible for profit and loss, Headers responded to the corporate mandate to increase competitiveness and decrease staff by examining many different aspects of product definition, release, and management from ramp-up through maturity and end-of-life. As they studied these issues, the Headers assumed profit and loss responsibility that had not been granted by Digital senior management and concluded that 3,000 options were overkill and that product management should limit the options to reduce costs.

An envoy from the Headers scheduled a meeting with product management and a workstation expert to help establish the appropriate product for the workstation order management channel. If the number of configurations were reduced to fit on a single page configuration sheet, DECDirect telephone personnel could take orders for the product at a cost per order of about $300. If the product were fulfilled through the complex order channel, the per order cost would exceed $500. Moreover, ordering through the DEC-

---

[3] A lead time window opened when the current date equaled the ship date minus the lead time. For example, the lead time window for an order with a ship date of February 15 and a lead time of ten days would open on February 5.

[4] Dates have been changed for the purpose of discussion.

Direct order channel was fast, with more than 95 percent of orders shipped within 24 hours. Furthermore, inasmuch as SUN's, Hewlett Packard-Apollo's, and IBM's equivalent product offerings were limited compared to Digital's, many fewer than 3,000 options would still be competitive.

Auditing the Complex Order Management Process

While the Header envoy and project managers debated the 3,000-configuration workstation, Chris Couch was given the summer project of auditing the complex order management process. With only eleven weeks to complete the audit, Couch and Edward Nicholas had to narrow the topic of study. Nicholas' instincts for where opportunities for improvement might lie led them to settle on the direct labor component, defined as labor expended by direct order handlers as distinct from their supervisors or support personnel.

Couch interviewed various members of management and staff in the order processing department in order to better understand the process and establish a measurement system for the cost of quality. An example of the procedure he followed for all departments was used in the CAS area.

At Digital's Bedford, New Hampshire, CAS site, CAS Supervisor Lisa Jackson and her staff described the elements of their work in detail. They identified four activities, the most basic being data entry, entering and changing orders. CAS reps also expedited orders for customers who needed equipment shipped sooner than anticipated, resolved customer problems that arose, and handled return authorizations that allowed customers to ship trial or incorrect equipment back to the company. CAS reps used various media in their work, including telephone calls, electronic mail, and face-to-face meetings.

Having determined what CAS reps did, the next step was to determine roughly what percentage of time they spent at each task. Given a twenty-workday month, CAS reps reported their time as follows:

Entering, changing orders	2 days
Expediting	4 days
Solving problems	6 days
Authorizing returns	4 days

Nonorder-processing activities such as staff meetings and training averaged an additional four days per month.

Subsequently asked to estimate what proportion of each task was created by internal failures (e.g., poorly trained sales reps, confusing catalogs, incorrect databases), CAS reps estimated the total amount of waste caused by Digital at four days per CAS rep per month. A number of CAS reps produced detailed information that provided an objective measure of the source of problems.

At four days per month across 370 CAS representatives, and given thirteen twenty-day months per year and an average annual salary of $50,000 per person, the total cost of quality for the CAS area was $3.7 million. "If all of Digital's people and systems were to perform without errors within the current context of the complex order administration process," Couch concluded, "the CAS group's yearly budget could be reduced by $3.7 million."

Couch, following this procedure for all of the departments that participated in the complex order management process, estimated the amount of wasted direct labor in the entire process at $6 million per year. This, as noted above, was only the beginning of the total cost of quality; additional elements included management time, freight costs incurred for incorrect shipments, potential lost business when customers were dissatisfied, and more.

On August 10, 1989, Couch presented his findings to Peter Campbell's staff, several managers from the next supervisory level, and a few people from other areas of Digital, such as Jane Murphy, who helped to oversee the entire CAS organization. The total audience for the presentation numbered about thirty.

In addition to describing the model for cost of quality and outlining the results, Couch offered opinions as to why such waste continued to exist and several recommendations for improving the situation. Among his recommendations were:

· begin measuring process performance
· refuse to be intimidated by process complexity
· get more people to understand the entire process
· be willing to make changes.

The same presentation was given twice more: once to the programming group in charge of Common Scheduling and System "T," and once, in abbreviated form, to Campbell's manager, Art Hatch, vice president for the U.S. Manufacturing Group.

EXHIBIT 3
Digital Equipment Corporation Organization Chart: Summer 1989

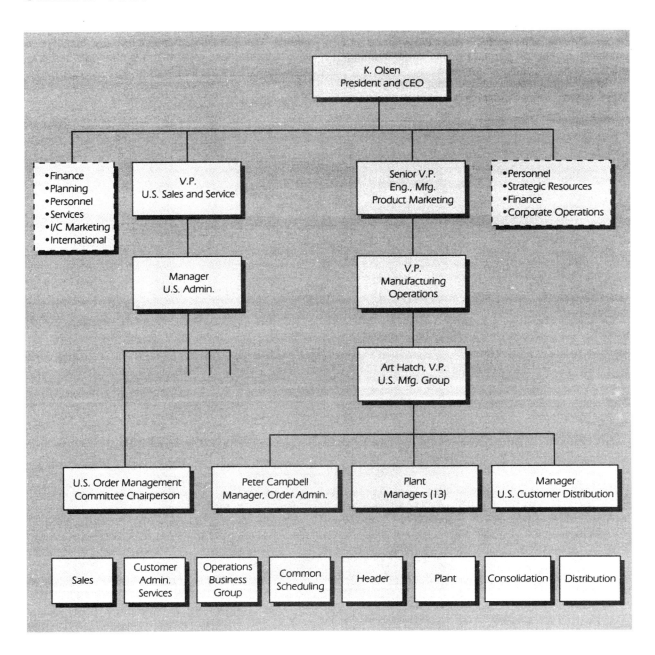

. . . .
How to Proceed?

In September 1989, Campbell, Nicholas, and Couch met in Campbell's office with Dorothy Simmons, manager of administration responsible for Common Scheduling, the Headers, and Order Execution. "It's time," Simmons said, "we start with a clean sheet of paper, consider what we know about the process, and establish, at least on paper, the ideal order management process for complex systems."

"OK," Nicholas responded, "but, even given an ideal system, we can't just rip out what we have now and replace it with something new. That would create even more work."

Campbell considered their input. Given that we have eight groups involved in our complex order management process, "it will still be helpful," he offered, "to understand where we'd like to be if we could start over" (see Exhibit 3 for an organization chart). "But the difficult questions are: first, 'given where we are now, what needs to change?' and second, 'how do we make it happen?' "

8

The Information Vision and Architecture

In previous chapters, the technical and operational groundwork crucial to understanding the major issues associated with managing information technology in an organization has been established. The reader should now be familiar with many of the issues of computing hardware and operating system software, the telecommunications function and networking, the development and maintenance of application software systems, and some of the operations of an information systems organization. The successful management of information technology in the 1990s must combine this knowledge with a thorough understanding of the future business direction to provide an effective set of information resources for the firm.

This chapter deals with the fundamental component of managing information technology in a firm—an information vision and architecture. The development of an overall management system for information technology for an organization is not complete without a technical and managerial framework for future decisions that are business driven.

The notion of a vision and architecture for information technology is a concept only recently discussed in nontechnical terms in most firms and in the literature. This chapter points out some of the reasons companies should think about vision and architecture, defines information vision and architecture, and focuses on the issues that should be addressed. Because different companies will have different business visions, there is no

attempt to indicate precisely what the vision and architecture for a company should be. The chapter ends with some guidelines for developing a vision and architecture and outlines the benefits to users and the IS organization of having a vision and architecture.

THE NEED FOR VISION AND ARCHITECTURE

Organizations need an information vision and architecture for several reasons. In some firms, the applications of information technology are not, and never will be, all organized under a single person. Discussion and agreement on a common structure for the varied applications of information technology in a firm can provide a shared understanding among IS professionals of what the company needs to create with its information resources.

Settling on an architecture for a company's information resources helps communicate the future to others and provides a consistent rationale for making individual decisions. Sometimes an architecture is created because user-managers have expressed concern about whether there is some grand scheme within which to make individual decisions. The architecture provides the grand scheme. The decentralization of IS decisions and resources makes the establishment of a well-understood vision and architecture critical in the 1990s.

Architectural discussions often help in making basic decisions about how the IS business will be conducted—defining the basic style and values of the organization. Such discussions may be part of comprehensive programs that attempt to define or refine the style of the overall company. In 1993, for example, a major health-care company felt it necessary to install a stronger attitude toward quality in the entire business to compete more effectively in the global marketplace. The effort led the IS director of that company to consider more precisely the values to be embraced by the IS organization. For the first time, the IS organization began to consider the role of quality and the shared beliefs of people within the IS organization. Discussion focused on various IS quality issues such as excessive rework in the design of the major systems.

Traumatic incidents often cause the creation of an information architecture. In early 1989, telecommunications network redundancy was a significant architecture discussion topic among IS directors within the banking industry. A major fire had destroyed much of a critical switching center of a telephone company near Chicago. The extensive damage reduced data and voice circuit availability for several days. As a result, banks and other organizations that depend on the constant availability of the public telephone network for certain operations, such as automatic teller machines (ATMs), were forced to reexamine contingency plans associated with the nonavailability of telecommunications service. Some organizations realized that IS management had not thought seriously about what to do when faced with such a loss. The result in many firms was an extended set of discussions on network architecture.

UNDERSTANDING INFORMATION VISION AND ARCHITECTURE

The task of formally developing and communicating an information vision and architecture is relatively new to most organizations. Few have more than a few years experience in developing such

outputs. As a result, the terms take on different meanings from organization to organization.

In a recent poll of IS directors, the following ideas emerged about the meaning of the information technology vision and architecture concept. Some executives described the term as a "shared understanding on how computer technology was to be used and managed in the business." Others reported that they generate a "comprehensive statement that is part philosophy and part blueprint." The group felt that a vision and architecture must be "specific enough to guide planning and decision-making but flexible enough to withstand restatement each time a new information system is developed." Finally, several in the group felt that a "vision and architecture should provide the long-term goal for the IS planning effort"—vision and architecture represent the overall design target.

Definition

Several ideas common in these statements suggest a definition. First, vision and architecture is an ideal view of the future and not the plan on how to get there (the information technology plan is discussed in Chapter 13). Second, vision and architecture must be flexible enough to provide a context for individual decisions but more than just fluff. Finally, deliberation about vision and architecture must focus on the long term, but usually exact dates are not specified.

While these ideas help describe the concepts, our operational definition of vision and architecture is as follows:

> **Information vision** is a written expression of the desired future for information use and management in the organization. The **information technology architecture** depicts the way information resources should be deployed to deliver that vision.

Much like the design of a complex aircraft or a skyscraper, an information vision and an information technology architecture together translate a mental image of the desired future state of information use and management into a comprehensive set of written guidelines, policies, pictures, or

Importance

The management of electronic information is strategically important for us to be successful in the future. In an increasingly competitive environment characterized by the need for quick decision-making, cross-functional and easily accessed information processing and services are crucial. Information will be managed and developed as a critical asset of our company. Usage of this asset will be structured based on the needs of the entire client population and, at the same time, control over its security will be of the highest priority.

Participation

Direct and active participation by senior management will be a continuing process. The rapid changes in hardware and software and the substantial capital needed to develop the required information system must receive the full support of senior management. Our active participation and understanding is recognized as imperative to our company's future success. In addition, it must be acknowledged that the use of our Information Services and Systems organization will reflect our shared value of team work. All critical information will be shared so that ra-

tional, informed, and timely business decisions can be made. All developers and users of information must consider the requirements of the company as a whole, as well as their individual needs. Information Services and Systems' role will be to enhance the efficiency and effectiveness of each individual's contribution to the company. Computer proficiency training must and will become an integral part of our culture. Information Services and Systems will take the lead in seeing that these concepts become realities.

Applications Development

The growth of information needs is a trend that is sure to continue in a competitive business environment. In our business, cross-functional systems are becoming increasingly important as competitive weapons. The traditional differentiation between business and scientific applications will become less distinguishable. As the environment evolves, the consolidation of voice and data information within our firm will become increasingly significant. Information Services and Systems' leadership and technical expertise will be instrumental in the coordination and development of these new technologies within our company and all client groups. It will be of

(continued on next page)

FIGURE 12.1 Information Vision Example

mandates within which an organization should operate and make decisions. Vision and architecture may take the form of a set of doctrinal requirements (like the Ten Commandments). Other organizations create architectural blueprints much like a building architect uses to represent their mental image of the future. As is true for a business vision, the information vision and architecture also may be a written statement. For example, one organization found it sufficient to define its vision by stating, "We must provide quality data and computing products and services that meet our clients' needs in a timely and cost-effective manner." Regardless of the form, vision and architecture should provide the business, managerial, and technical platform for planning and executing IS operations in the firm.

Some Examples

Figure 12.1 presents one version of an information vision and some elements of an architecture. It is a statement of what the officers of a $750 million

energy company would like to see created with information technology. It poses an "ideal state" at some unspecified date in the future. The statement is clear on several applications development issues as well as various network matters. The statement does not, however, draw specific conclusions on all the possible aspects of how to manage the information resources of the firm.

Figure 12.2 is an industrial manufacturing example of one part of a vision for information technology. This pictorial representation depicts the overall business information system that this company's senior and IS management wants for its information resources. Upon close inspection, the picture implies some very interesting attributes about the desired future state for information use and management at this company. For example, the company has defined the expected users for the system (shown on the right). The traditional user of IS, often assumed to be a clerical person, has been supplanted by other types. Indeed, one significant user in the company's architecture of the future is the decision-maker. Such a change in user significant importance that people throughout the organization be responsible for the development of various information applications that tie into the overall network. Technological coordination and guidance from Information Services and Systems will be imperative for this effort to succeed.

The Corporate Network and Database

The creation of a network of information processing resources and a strong database management function is a high priority of senior management. The database must be secure, yet generally shareable throughout the organization. Easily accessible data must be made an integral part of the system's design and the company's overall value system. While the integration of this network is critical and the elements of the database are to be located throughout the network, development of this network and database will be accomplished mindful of end-user requirements. It is recognized that this physically distributed network and database will require an elaborate security system. Information originators will have a greater responsibility and obligation to better manage, verify, and validate information inputs and changes. Information Services and Systems will play an integral part in the application standards development needed to ensure a functional and secure network system and database.

Achieving the Vision

The information network developed will be responsive to a variety of different end-users and different types of ap-

plication development, both inside and outside of our company. In addition to meeting the needs of current clients, another main criteria of Information Services and Systems will be to expand the scope of electronic information clients. This will be done through continuing system proficiency training. It is obvious new applications that offer strategic advantages will be necessary in order for the company to remain successful and competitive in the future. New applications development will be widespread but most prolific in the areas of marketing, finance, operations, and engineering. With the changing nature and needs of the business, most traditional paper files will ultimately be replaced by electronic filing capability and usage. The cost-effective automation of paper files is critical to our future evolutionary transition into our increasingly competitive industry. Timely information gathering, processing, and usage that is adequately safeguarded and controlled is absolutely essential to the company's decision-making process. In order to capitalize on our available opportunities, it is imperative that we create an information environment in which senior management and all other clients can make informed quantitative and qualitative business decisions on a timely basis. Reliable information gathering and dissemination systems that contain adequate safeguards are the key to our future. We have the utmost confidence in our Information Services and Systems personnel to provide the tools needed to successfully compete.

FIGURE 12.1 (continued)

definition should have a profound impact on the future design of application systems.

The figure also implies that this company will develop a set of tools for use by customers on an integrated company database. At present, most application systems in this company require that a user be thoroughly familiar with the application to make use of the data. In the human resources system, for example, the user must understand the workings of the payroll system before being able to make good use of personnel data. This architectural diagram promises something very different—a data warehouse, in which part of the "inventory" is easily available to both internal and external constituents. The future environment will provide a set of "friendly" tools to access data with responses coming via a variety of delivery mechanisms.

The picture also postulates facilities that archive, retrieve, validate, and edit data and perform other housekeeping functions. Notice also that computer-integrated manufacturing is a commitment for this company. Electronic data interchange is another significant area for its information technology capability. There will also be a link to external data and computing services. When this statement was written, the typical user at this firm could not easily access external data from a personal workstation. The future promises to be very different at this company.

Attributes of a Vision and Architecture

A vision and architecture adds more value to an organization when it is comprehensive rather than detailed and when it is clearly communicated. The

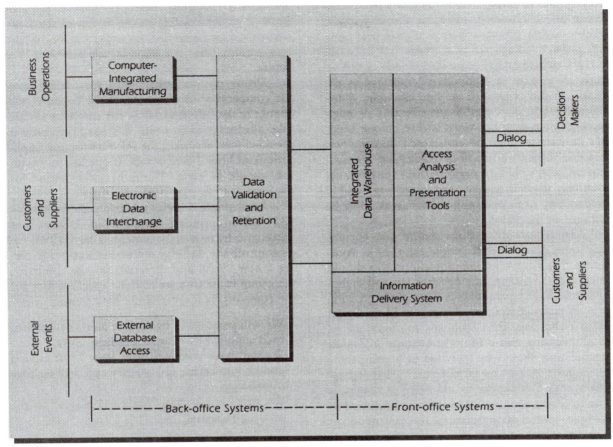

FIGURE 12.2 Information Technology Architecture

purpose of a vision and architecture statement should not be to specify the exact action that someone should take when faced with a particular technology issue. In the fast-moving world of technology, specifying exact answers to every problem would be impossible. Instead, a vision and architecture should create as clear a picture as possible on the desired future state of information use and management. The statement(s) should offer a benchmark against which people inside and outside the IS organization can consider individual decisions. Practically speaking, IS staff do not have the time or the expertise to make every technology decision in the company. Vision and architecture statements should combine to paint a picture of what is hoped to be created rather than defining specific outcomes.

An information vision and architecture is best designed when all the information resources in a firm have been conceptualized as a complex system. In explaining such a system, it is possible to describe the future operations of the system and the rules by which the system should function. Designing the ideal information system for the future is best done by thinking about all the information resources within an organization as a single system, which is influenced by people's attitudes and behavior, changing technology, and future business needs.

The information architecture for a company should be more comprehensive than any technology component, such as mainframe systems, microcomputer applications, or telecommunications. An overall vision can and should help eliminate existing islands of automation at many firms (Mc-Farlan and McKenney, 1983). It should include, when possible, all applications of electronic technology being considered in the firm. The information vision and architecture statements should include all aspects of computing important to the future of the organization. For example, many manufacturers have significant scientific or engineering computing functions whose unique needs and operations must be considered. Information systems, incorporating both traditional transaction processing within organizations (payroll, accounting, general ledger, and inventory) and a wide variety of newer applications areas, must be included in the vision.

Architecture discussions should also encompass areas outside what people think of as computing. The voice telecommunications area should be considered—especially because fax and digital telephone-based technologies are rapidly growing areas in many companies. Because of likely digital image technology developments, the reprographics (duplicating and printing) functions within an organization should be included in a company's information vision and architecture. Some organizations may also choose to add video communications to discussions on vision and architecture. For example, several major financial services organizations are acquiring interactive video teleconferencing systems as a way to conduct meetings rather than consuming time in travel from one city to another. For companies heavily dependent on external electronic information (e.g., law firms), the consideration of vision and architecture should include resources (such as commercial databases) that exist outside the firm.

In short, all business applications of information technology now and in the future should be considered in the development of an information vision and architecture.

CREATING AN INFORMATION VISION

Before outlining the architecture by which information resources will be deployed, the shared business and IS leadership expectations of how information will be used in the business should be specified. Developing these expectations requires both an understanding of the future of the business or organization and an understanding of the role information can play in competing in the future.

Vision creation starts with speculating how the competitive environment of the business will change in the future and how the company should take advantage of it. Once this business vision is specified (and written), the information use implications of how a firm wants to operate in the future should be clear. The information vision for the organization may then be written.

An example is useful to explain the process. A $35 million printing company in Atlanta was taken over by new management in early 1993. After four off-site, full-day discussion sessions to create a new vision and direction for the company, the group came to a set of basic specifications for the company as it entered the next century:

- We will compete in five major market segments, each supplied by distinct business units.
- We will have revenues of at least $100 million and be known for our quality and leading edge technology.
- We will be a leading "national player" in the printing industry.
- We will exploit new business lines or market niches via acquisition or joint ventures or by spinning off existing operations.
- Our administrative units (personnel, accounting, purchasing, etc.) will operate in support of all business units.
- We will achieve strategic advantage in each market via our "information-based" decisions.
- Our profit margins will exceed 10 percent.

These fundamental propositions about the company in the future led to some basic business strategy decisions for the 1990s:

- We must improve gross margins and lower overhead costs while achieving a moderate sales growth.
- We must increase the productivity of every person in the company.
- We must shorten the job fulfillment cycle time (from customer order to delivery).
- We must strive toward "zero defects" in all we

do (quality objectives and monitoring systems will exist).

- We must be able to receive jobs electronically from our customers.
- We must improve companywide internal management systems (e.g., budgeting, personnel evaluation).

These business priorities were then reviewed along with the business vision by senior management and members of the IS department. After several sessions, they jointly arrived at a shared vision for information use and management in the company. They chose to represent this vision via a set of points:

- Our corporate network will be able to service a large number of remote nodes at high speed.
- User demand on our information system each year will experience:
  1. Medium growth in transaction volume on existing shared systems.
  2. High growth in ad hoc requests for information on all shared and personal systems.
  3. High growth in transaction volume from new applications on shared and personal systems.
- New data fields will be defined and managed each year.
- The entire job acquisition and fulfillment cycle will be supported by an integrated, comprehensive, and accurate data base.
- Our corporate network will be able to send and receive large files from customers at high speed.
- Users will know how to use information to make decisions and how to use the capabilities of our information resources effectively.
- Each business unit and functional department will manage its information resources within an overall information technology architecture.
- All existing business support processes (e.g., purchase order processing) will be automated via expert systems to free up time of critical human resources.
- Users will have workstation tools to make all information easily accessible.

Taken together, these statements represent a specification of how information will be used in the future. These statements do not represent a plan—how the IS department will create this environment must still be determined. In addition, these statements are also only a vision of what is desired. The architectural decisions on how to deploy the company's data, software, people, and other IS resources are not all specified. That is the next step.

DESIGNING THE ARCHITECTURE

Now that a vision for future information use has been formulated, the IS organization, often in cooperation with user-managers, must design an information technology architecture. This architecture specifies how the resources available to users and the IS organization must be deployed to meet the information vision. Again, the plan for migrating from the current deployment of resources to the architecture is developed later (Chapter 13 explains the planning process).

Components of Architecture

Several views have been expressed about what elements make up an architecture for information technology. Traditionally, the treatment takes on a very technical definition of a computing architecture. Later models have expanded the dimensions to include more managerial, less technical aspects of information resources. Some alternatives are given here.

Stefferud, Farber, and Dement (1982) postulate that the design of a computing architecture consists of four elements—processors, networks, services, and standards. Their architecture has come to be known as SUMURU, meaning single-user (e.g., personal workstation), multiple-user (e.g., departmental mini), remote utility (e.g., company mainframe). Figure 12.3 illustrates these elements. The architecture outlines the hardware, network, and software resources of a system that includes local area networks, workstations, and central and remote hardware hosts. This conceptual framework can be used to guide the acquisition and use of needed computing and communications equipment for a company that believes in a client/server structure. Versions of this architecture have been adopted by the Federal

322

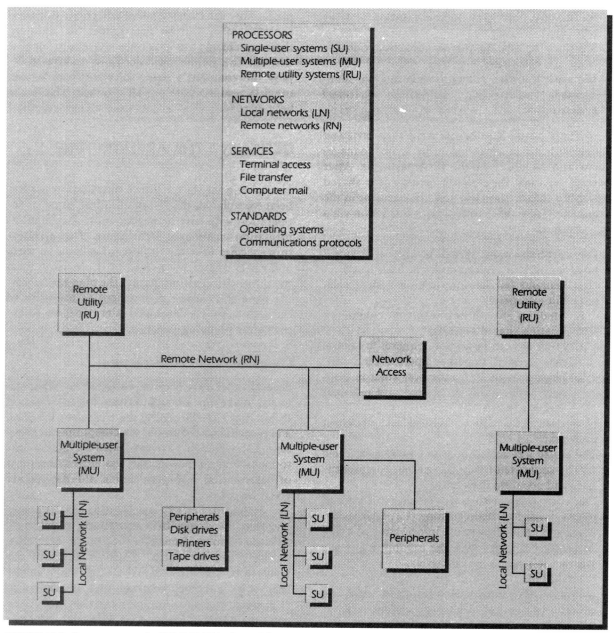

FIGURE 12.3 Components of a SUMURU Distributed System Architecture. (Copyright 1982 by Mini-Micro Systems, Cahners Publishing Company, division of Reed Publishing U.S.A. Used with permission.)

Communications Commission and several other agencies of the U.S. government.

Another model that defines the components of an information technology architecture was proposed by Nolan (1983). Figure 12.4 displays his version of what should be contained in an overall information technology architecture. He divides an architecture into data, applications, and

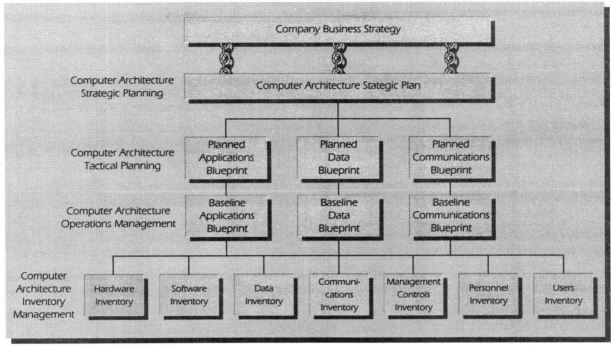

FIGURE 12.4 Computer Architecture. (Courtesy of Richard L. Nolan, "Building the company's computer architecture strategic plan." *Stage by Stage*, Vol. 2, Winter 1983)

communications components. The figure clearly shows the link to the company's business strategy. He also suggests that the process of building an architecture starts by assessing current hardware, software, data, communications, management controls, personnel, and user elements of the system.

A few companies have defined their own conceptual model of an information technology architecture. One notable example is American Standard (1988), shown in Figure 12.5. It specified a three-dimensional model of a computing architecture. The vertical dimension identifies three levels in the hardware architecture—data utility, functional processors, and intelligent workstations. The horizontal dimension identifies the business portfolios that need support—institutional systems, factory automation (manufacturing), professional support services, and external support services. The front-to-back dimension defines applications, data, and communications components of the architecture.

Devlin and Murphy (1988) present yet another view of an architecture to support the transaction processing environment of a major vendor of information technology components. Figure 12.6 shows how IBM intends to organize its efforts for IS support in its regional office for Europe, the Middle East, and Africa. IBM has identified four elements of an information processing architecture—applications, data, network, and support systems.

These examples demonstrate the multidimensional nature of an information technology architecture. While there is some disagreement as to the best dimensions by which to describe an architecture, there are several common elements to each of these models. For our purposes, an information technology architecture should specify a structure in two major categories—managerial and technical—divided into five areas. Within the managerial category, the most important area concerns people—their values and beliefs. Another part of the managerial architecture is the management

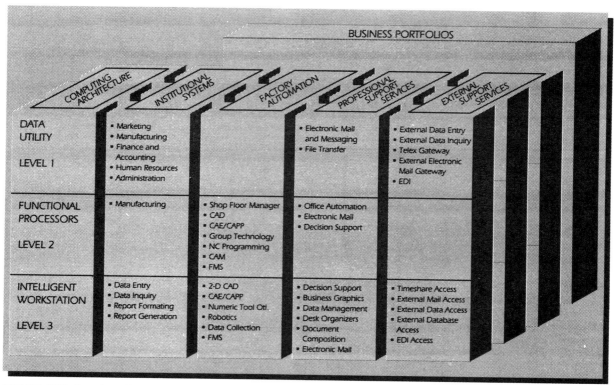

FIGURE 12.5 American Standard Architectural Model for Computing. (Reprinted from *Datamation*, 1988. © 1988 by Cahners/Ziff Publishing Associates, LP.)

systems used for guiding information resources. The most frequently discussed technical area of architecture is the hardware and network infrastructure. The data architecture for the organization is another element in the technical category. A design for the software or applications architecture is the final area in the technical category. Decisions about these five areas collectively specify the information technology architecture for an organization.

Specifying the Managerial Architecture: Values

This module of the overall architecture states basic human beliefs that should guide IS decision-making. Figure 12.7 shows a **values architecture** for a company. Note that these statements could create a major challenge for some people on how infor-

mation will affect their jobs. Collectively, these values also can have a significant influence on other components of the architecture. The following sections discuss some of the most difficult issues to be addressed in creating a values architecture.

Role of the User-Manager The architecture needs to specify the roles and responsibilities of the user. How active users are expected to be involved in both the operations and strategy deliberations of the IS organization should be made explicit. End-user computing efforts seem to reflect a decision that users should have a very active role in building systems. Too often, however, such efforts were initiated under budgetary pressure rather than on a long-term vision of what activities users should be undertaking. Not surprisingly, some users wonder why they are engaged in

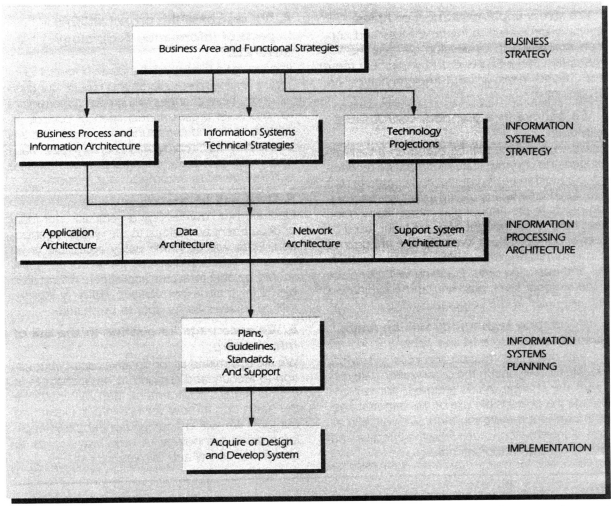

FIGURE 12.6 Information Processing Architecture. (Copyright 1988 International Business Machines Corporation. Reprinted with permission from *IBM Systems Journal*, Vol. 27, No. 1)

activities (such as programming) they consider best done by the specialists.

The architecture can decide as well what control mechanisms the IS organization should expect from users. For example, user committees at some organizations review the IS budget before it is sent to senior management for approval. In some companies, users are involved in testing new vendor products. For example, when a vendor is interested in testing a new video teleconferencing system, some IS organizations actively try to involve their users in the test. There is no single best answer to these or other issues discussed here. Each organization must specify what role user-managers are expected to play.

Technological Leadership Role Some firms clearly put themselves on record as striving to be leaders in the area of information technology. Other companies have decided to be "fast followers." Still others consider the decision to adopt

330

1. We stress implementation of ideas.

We have generated many new ideas and concepts that will help us develop our systems. We must refine these concepts and implement these ideas. Good ideas without implementation are insufficient.

2. We believe in a planned, coordinated approach.

Individual decisions will be based on a well-developed and communicated information technology plan within each regional and corporate staff area. Each area will explicitly recognize information needs in the annual plan. Since many good ideas have been thought of or are being used by areas of our operations, we stress the importance of communicating these ideas to other individuals and operating units. Planning will take place at the regional level; planning and coordination will take place at the corporate staff level.

3. Information technology will be made a valuable resource in our jobs.

We will make information technology services valuable to everyone in the organization. We recognize the change that is required. We will encourage the responsible use of this important asset throughout the organization. We will help all users of information understand the effective and responsible use of the technology.

4. We welcome the organizational impacts of information technology advances.

Improving technology will provide potential to increase service to our clients and reduce our overall cost. These changes will create opportunities to reconsider organizational span of control, reporting lines, and communication paths. We will assess potential improvements on a regular basis and implement those changes that demonstrate enhancements to accomplish our mission.

5. Data will be shared.

Data are not "owned" by a particular individual or department but belong to the whole organization. Data will be made easily accessible to all authorized users. Individuals within our company should be able to access appropriate information based on their responsibilities. Policy guidelines will be established for data to be shared.

6. We encourage innovation in the use of information.

We are committed to the creative use of information to identify and respond to basic changes in the company's environment. We will challenge the status quo in how we use information to do our jobs. We will encourage our people to apply information technology in new ways so as to benefit our clients and owners.

FIGURE 12.7 Values Architecture Example

new technology to be purely a financial one. The choice of a leadership role is not easy.

There are often problems with being on the leading edge of technology, but there are also major benefits. One New York-based insurance company was among the first in the world to experiment with a sophisticated new product that scans documents such as newspapers and translates text to a machine-readable representation. After a successful trial, all typed applications for insurance in this company were read by this device, decreasing cost significantly. Being on the leading edge immediately generated a productivity improvement and gave them a two-year lead on competition. On the other hand, the same company could have failed miserably in another trial.

Some companies choose explicitly to be followers in the adoption of information technology. For example, some banks are known for wanting only proven solutions and credit their posture with positive bottom-line results. The leadership role decision is not easy, but a company should make an explicit decision.

Productivity and Quality Emphasis Another value issue that should be resolved involves the emphasis to be placed on IS staff productivity and the quality of IS staff work. Some firms see a trade-off between these two worthwhile objectives. If there is an effort to increase productivity within an IS organization, the tools to accomplish the goals may not be available, causing reductions in output quality. Others argue that if productivity among a group of programmers is measured by lines of code produced per hour, an emphasis on increasing productivity may be accomplished without an increase in rework effort. While there is argument on which view is correct, basic beliefs about the importance of these two objectives should be made explicit.

Service Orientation and Professionalism A strong service orientation for an IS organization is a value that can provide great user benefits, but it often causes substantial personnel concern within the IS organization. In many companies, IS people are a group greatly respected for their technical skills. They have deep knowledge of the systems design process, know a great deal about how complex systems work, and take a great deal of pride in their work. If this same group is told to be "service-oriented," they may see such an emphasis as decreasing the professional nature of their job. Sometimes, a service orientation is perceived to be simply putting on a "happy face," demeaning the professionals who perform the service. Pride and quality of work can suffer if such a service orientation is mandated, but the importance of high-quality service to internal users is clear. The trade-off between service and professionalism is a difficult one to tackle but should be made explicit where possible.

Supporting Diversity versus Achieving Integration The issue of how much diversity to support should also be dealt with in an architecture. Freedom of expression in the use of informa-

tion technology is critical to the health of many organizations. In research facilities (for example, scientific laboratories and universities), diversity may well provide the platform for creativity. In a research-based organization, many scientists believe that they must have the freedom to select the hardware and software to do their job—regardless of the standard in the firm. The cost of such freedom, however, can be high. Supporting many different technologies is very costly and makes enterprise-wide integration very difficult. Early in the discussion of values, users and IS staff must decide on the level of diversity and the level of integration that the organization expects to be able to sustain in its information technology system.

These basic values and others must be discussed and agreed upon early in the development of an architecture for information technology. The biggest challenge in developing the values component is being specific enough to provide some direction for individual activities and decisions while being general enough to allow for needed flexibility. Without these shared values, however, the other elements of the architecture will be incomplete.

Specifying the Managerial Architecture: Management Systems

The organizational architecture for information is not complete without specifying the future management system for information technology activities via a **management systems architecture**. Further discussion on this topic is contained in Chapter 15, but some of the issues that should be addressed are covered here.

Role of the IS Organization There should be a decision as to the general role of the IS organization. Some companies frame this issue as, "What mix of leadership and support does the company want from its IS organization?" Some companies want the IS organization to make strategic business breakthroughs. In such a company, senior management may expect the IS department to make direct contributions to the profitability of the company. They expect business leadership from the person who heads IS. On the other hand, there are successful companies that expect the IS organization primarily to support the key line functions of the business. IS people should understand the business but not attempt to suggest major changes in how the business is conducted. There is no suggestion here as to which choice should be made. Instead, it is important that a signal be given on the general role of the IS function. (See the example in Figure 12.1 on one management's conclusion in this area.)

Breadth of Media and Application Another issue revolves in part around the media for which the IS organization is responsible. Is the organization responsible for all types of electronic media—voice, data, video, and image? In some hospitals, for example, the IS department is not involved with image processing. Instead, all image processing is controlled by users in various labs. In others, all media included within all areas of application are the responsibility of the IS group. Other questions include, should the IS organization be responsible for office automation? What about factory automation? Should automated manufacturing systems be managed by the IS organization? Decisions on the applications scope of the IS organization must be part of the architecture exercise.

Linking Mechanism with the Business Plan This issue has to do with how to link the company's IS plan with the organization's business plan. What is the mechanism by which the IS organization learns about its challenges to support the business? In some cases, there is not a very good link. Some IS managers do not interface well with senior business managers. Sometimes IS people are not informed of major changes in business direction until they read about it in the annual report. Too often, IS interfaces only with lower-level managers rather than senior vice presidents. (More about this issue is included in Chapter 13.)

Corporate versus Division IS Responsibilities A company should also delineate the roles of the corporate IS organization versus divisional or departmental IS organizations. In many organizations, the role of the IS department is moving away from direct control of operations to one of architecture and policy development, but the roles of each group and the users must be clear. (More on this issue is included in Chapter 15.)

Strategic and Commodity Vendors Some organizations divide information technology vendors into two types—commodity and strategic. Commodity vendors provide the routine components of the IS system, such as spreadsheet software, personal computers, word-processing software, telephones, and fiber capacity. The company buys these products mostly on price.

It is possible as well to identify a few strategic vendors of hardware, software, or communication networks. It is these strategic vendors with which the company will work to build a partnership. The posture of the company on the issue of strategic partnering with its information technology vendors needs to be clear.

Funding The architecture discussion should determine how the company intends to fund information technology growth. Should the firm fund all or part of the IS budget via a user chargeback system? If so, what should be the design of that chargeback system? Because the funding system influences user behavior and no one chargeback mechanism works best in all situations, some general scheme should be created (see Chapter 15 for more description of funding systems).

Mechanisms for IS Planning and Control The planning and control system for information technology should be specified. Some organizations use committees for coordinating the efforts of many different technology organizations. One diversified industrial products company created an information technology policy group to focus on major issues. Members included several key users, the IS director for each division, the corporate telecommunications director, and the head of corporate IS. At a major toy manufacturing firm, the vice president for information technology chairs a committee composed of the IS directors from each product division. The group meets four times a year to establish policy and coordinate strategic plans.

Issue-focused user committees can also be created by organizations as a planning and control system. As an example, one committee could be responsible for the overall design of systems available for the sales and marketing functions. In addition, temporary task forces can be created on topical issues. For example, a task force can be created to select a desktop publishing system. The general scheme by which users interact with the IS organization on operational and policy matters should be designed in the architecture statement.

A sample management systems architecture for a $100 million wholesaler of medical/surgical supplies is shown in Figure 12.8. The statement was developed in early 1993 by the IS department

---

1. All departments will be fully accountable for their use of information resources, including the skill level of people in using information technology.
2. Departments will pay an annual fee for workstations to include capital, software, and maintenance costs.
3. The IS department will set and enforce standards for user workstation hardware, software, and network connection.
4. Departments will pay for use of shareable IS resources through a fair division of overhead.
5. Senior management will be kept engaged in information technology issues via regular communications by IS staff.
6. The IS department will actively initiate communication with user departments.
7. The IS department will build its plan and budget with full knowledge of company business plans.
8. Members of the IS department will serve as internal business process consultants.
9. The IS department will be represented on issue-oriented or business planning teams where information definition and/or collection is crucial.
10. Policy affecting users will be determined by the IS Policy Committee.

FIGURE 12.8 Management Systems Architecture for the 1990s

with four user-representatives and approved by senior management. It addresses several of the matters outlined here and in the values discussion.

Specifying the Technical Architecture: Infrastructure

The second major set of decisions in an information technology architecture concerns the technical aspects of information resources. One technical area is the technology platform or infrastructure, i.e., the design of the network and the attributes of the physical nodes (the hardware) that exist in the network. The following are some of the issues that must be resolved in an **infrastructure architecture.**

Location   Clearly, most organizations operate or are planning to operate a distributed computing environment, but the physical location of the hardware on a network can be a critical issue from cost, control, and security standpoints. Physically distributing equipment, other than microcomputers and some minicomputers, can create additional costs for managing the hardware and safeguarding the data. Computers and telecommunications switches benefit significantly from being housed in a secure, environmentally sound location. Quite often, however, physical location connotes a sense of control to many users. A division general manager may be comforted by locating the division's three minicomputers in a room on divisional premises rather than in the IS data center in corporate headquarters only a few blocks away.

The Workstation   The future design and role of the information technology workstation should be determined as part of a discussion on architecture. Is the workstation of the future to have intelligence or be a device enslaved to some central computer? Should it be able to receive a fax over telephone lines? Should the telephone and computer components of the workstation be physically integrated? Should video teleconferencing capability be integrated into the workstation? Should most work be done at a workstation, at a central mainframe, at a remote hardware resource, on a local area network, or at some departmental mini-computer?

General-Purpose versus Single-Purpose Nodes Traditionally, many central or host computers performed a variety of tasks. In the 1970s, WANG and other vendors demonstrated the value of dedicating particular hardware to a specific function—word processing. Now some computers only perform computer-aided design. What is the vision for the future of hardware nodes or the network? Are most resources to be general-purpose machines or perform a special purpose? If some nodes are going to be special purpose, which purposes are most appropriate? An explicit statement about what functions will be segregated onto specialized nodes helps greatly in future hardware sizing and network capacity decisions.

Supported Operating Systems Many vendors of technology hardware maintain a proprietary operating system. How many and which operating systems will the organizations support? For example, each new computer brand can mean supporting a different operating system, creating more difficulty in linking them together, and costs increase rapidly as new operating systems are added. Confining the company to one telecommunications or computing vendor, however, reduces bargaining power and may limit access to the best software. For example, should all workstations be required to operate with Windows by Microsoft, the company's future now partially depends on Microsoft's success.

Some agreement on standards should be established to allow for the needed flexibility and the required integration level and cost control. Some organizations represent this part of the architecture through a supported equipment list, containing the operating systems the IS organization will support through training, connectivity, repair, and other services.

Some experts see UNIX as the solution to the problem of multiple operating systems. In concept, all supported suppliers would support UNIX, a common operating system designed originally by Bell Labs. Customers would only be required to support one operating system. Most major suppliers of computing equipment have announced support for UNIX as one possible operating system. Several companies have in turn committed to UNIX as their only supported operating system.

Path and Node Redundancy How much redundancy should there be in the design of the network? Should there be full redundancy of all major switching nodes and high-volume pathways? The cost for full redundancy can be very expensive because there must be at least two different paths to every node in the network from any other node. The lack of redundancy, however, can be very expensive in terms of lost user-time if the network is not available for some period. Remember the banking example cited in this chapter.

Hierarchical versus Peer-to-Peer Should the network design be constructed according to some type of hierarchy, where a certain node is assigned overall control functions, or should the relationship be peer-to-peer, where all nodes have equal functionality? There are a number of tradeoffs in this decision. Hierarchical networks generally reduce internode access times, allowing the user to accomplish more work. Peer-to-peer networks, however, connote greater local control, and this type of architecture can often increase network participation rates, especially in cooperative supplier/customer situations.

Supported Communications Protocols As with operating systems, many hardware vendors support their own proprietary communications protocols as well as some mix of standard communications protocols. For example, most vendors support the ASCII file transfer protocol through every hardware type. Most vendors support the ETHERNET protocol, originally developed by Xerox, DEC, and Intel. More and more are supporting TCP/IP. There are many other protocols (see Chapter 6). While the selection process is complex, some set of communications protocols should be established as standards in the firm.

An information technology infrastructure through which video, voice, data, image, and text information may be created, accessed, manipulated, and transmitted electronically will allow our company to enhance its position in the industry. The continued enhancement of such an integrated network must be a key priority into the late 1990s and requires policies.

The specifications are:

A standard workstation shall be uniformly used in offices, laboratories, meeting rooms, and all other facilities.

A common set of physical distribution facilities shall be used throughout the company.

Each physical distribution subsystem shall be designed in such a way that it can be replaced or modified without affecting the performance of the other subsystems.

Each divisional chief executive shall designate the organization responsible for the design, operation, maintenance, and allocation of the appropriate physical distribution facilities.

Strong consideration shall be given to the installation of adequate pathways and substantial reserve transmission capacity when new physical distribution facilities are installed or existing ones enhanced.

The public network will be used among locations for voice, data, and video, and a private data network will be developed at each site.

FIGURE 12.9 *The Infrastructure of the Information Technology System*

Public versus Private Networks
Should the company create a private data or voice network or use the public communications network provided by local and long-distance telecommunications

carriers? Perhaps some mix is appropriate. Service and cost differences can be substantial. Some overall architecture is therefore important. See Figure 12.9 for a statement on infrastructure architecture that contains a decision on public versus private networks.

Bandwidth What bandwidth, or transmission capacity, should be provided between hardware nodes in the network? Is 9,600 bits per second sufficient for the data user? Many image and graphical applications require much greater transmission rates for effective use. Should a company provide excess capacity to allow users to try applications? Or should circuits be designed to meet only current needs? Specifications about the desired technical infrastructure to meet the company's vision for information use are critical to help drive individual decisions.

Specifying the Technical Architecture: Data

The second major area for agreement in the development of a technical architecture is that of data. This critical subject is dealt with in detail in Chapter 14, but this section raises a few of the critical **data architecture** issues.

Ownership and Sharing One major issue to settle in determining a data architecture is that of ownership. Some departments in organizations assume that, "If our people generate the data, we own it." Such an attitude helps ensure security but can cause problems if the information needs of some organizational units include the data elements collected by others. Figure 12.10 shows the data architecture for an organization that had recently experienced the data ownership problem. The statement attempts to establish data as an asset of the total organization. Both shareable data and private data are recognized, and a set of specifications for shareable data are outlined.

Stewardship Recently, several organizations have recognized the need for formalized responsibility for stewardship of the data asset—much like

Data are a corporate resource. Much of our corporate data is stored electronically. Excellence in data management is a key to achieving many of our business goals.

The following statements constitute our electronic data access architecture:

Corporate data will be shared internally. Data are not owned by a particular individual or organization, but by the whole organization.

Data will be managed as a corporate resource. Data organization and structure will be planned at the appropriate levels in an integrated fashion.

Data quality will be actively managed. Explicit criteria for data accuracy, availability, accessibility, and ease of use will be written by the IS department.

Data will be safeguarded. As a corporate asset, data will be protected from deliberate or unintentional alteration, destruction, or inappropriate disclosure.

Data will be defined explicitly. Standards will be developed for data representation.

Databases will be logically designed to satisfy broad business functions.

FIGURE 12.10 Data Access Architecture

the stewardship responsibility for the financial assets of an organization. A company's position on stewardship should be resolved in a discussion on architecture. Do we need such a function? Who should be responsible for the data stewardship function—the IS organization or the user? What are the exact responsibilities of the stewardship function for data? Figure 12.11 shows how one organization chose to deal with these issues. This statement lays out the responsibilities of the data

steward and charges each lay steward to work with other users and the IS department in carrying out these responsibilities. (More discussion on data stewardship will be found in Chapter 14.)

Security versus Ease of Access If steps are taken to make critical electronic data more secure, quite often the result is to reduce user ease of access to that data. In a number of companies, for example, users cannot dial-in directly to the data center from home because of security concerns. Instead, a user calls the data center and an operator calls the user back after verification. At other organizations, data can be much more easily accessed from the desk or from home. Some trade-off between security and access ease is being made by either procedure. Organizations should make an explicit decision to operate somewhere along the spectrum between maximum ease of access and maximum security.

Breadth of Data Access How ubiquitous should access to data be? Should everyone in the organization have access to corporate data? Or should access to the data be restricted to those who have a need to know? Some organizations have gone on record as striving for data access by all personnel (see Figure 12.10). As soon as such a commitment is made, however, training and other support requirements increase significantly. Some statement on this issue should be made in the architecture.

Access to External Data Services What should be the range of data services that a user may receive via the network? Should access to customer and supplier databases be allowed? How active will the company be in electronic data interchange with customers and suppliers? Should the network provide access to personal data services? At some firms, results of athletic events are available from the workstation at the desk as a way to demonstrate value of the network. Other organizations provide broad access to the Dow Jones News Service or Prodigy. These issues should be clarified in the architecture statement.

Data stewards are responsible for assessing corporate-wide management information needs and promoting organizational data sharing. Data stewards shall be at the director level or higher. Consulting a committee of interested users of the data entity and a representative of information services, the steward is responsible for:

Establishing procedures governing both initial definition and change of the data elements within their data entity.

Establishing access authorization procedures at information services for their data entity to facilitate access and ensure data security.

Determining the most reliable sources of data and regularly evaluating the quality of the data entity.

Providing the intellectual content of a data dictionary so that all data users may know what shareable data are available, what the data mean, and how to access the data.

Planning the content of the assigned data entity by identifying gaps and redundancies in the data and, to the extent possible, ensuring that only needed versions of each data element exist.

Developing procedures to ensure that any use of the data contains the most appropriate version.

Determining responsibilities for data maintenance to ensure data integrity.

Resolving issues that may arise concerning the assigned portion of the shareable data.

Consulting with users on use of electronic data.

FIGURE 12.11 Data Stewardship Architecture

Specifying the Technical Architecture: Applications

The development and maintenance of IS applications should be subject to some set of architectural guidelines derived from a vision. Figure 12.12 contains a statement that makes a set of conclusions about how applications should be developed in a distributed computing environment at one organization. The statements impose a standard set of management controls on company-critical, personal computer-based applications being developed and supported by all company business units. These guidelines, developed by a committee representing the organization's central IS department, business unit IS groups, and users, define controls that must be applied to critical applications.

Other issues that an **applications architecture** should deal with are the assumed users, applications location, and whether application development will be process-driven or data-driven.

Assumed User In the past, implicit assumptions have often been made about the users of certain applications. Telephone company personnel were assumed to be the users in many telephone network management functions. Data entry operators were assumed to be the users of many transaction processing systems. As users take on more roles and the technology skills of people change, some clarity about likely IS users of the future is required. The design requirements for the user interface are thereby likely to change and should be made explicit (see the diagram in Figure 12.2).

Application Location Where (at what network node) should a particular application be performed? For example, where in the network should word processing normally be done? For many organizations, that decision seems clear. Users find it convenient to do word processing on their personal computers. On the other hand, some organizations do all word processing on department minicomputers, citing the improved ability to share and backup files. There are also many other issues as to where certain applications should be performed in the network.

1. Information systems development in departments is best done on distributed mini- or microcomputers when the object of the analysis (e.g., an asset type or set of transactions) is local and self-contained, has sufficient commitment in the department for funding systems development and operations over the life of the system, has little likelihood to be needed outside the department, and has less total life cycle development and operational cost than on a central resource.

2. Support for the development of distributed information systems is available on a coordinated basis at each division. Support participants include the local IS organization and Corporate Information Services personnel.

3. Distributed information systems development is normally expected to have been identified as a priority in an approved departmental information technology plan.

4. Support software standards for information systems should be used. The list of supported software is determined at the local site in cooperation with information services.

5. The department should be prepared to commit approximately 25 percent of the initial hardware, software, and personnel investment associated with systems development each year for the ongoing support of the system.

6. Documentation standards for distributed information systems are published on a regular basis by the Corporate Information Services organization. These standards may be supplemented by standards published by the local IS organization.

7. The hardware on which the system is developed should be supported by the local IS organization and/or Corporate Information Services and should be attached to either the local network or to the company-wide administrative network or both.

8. Units engaging in centralized or distributed information systems development activity should review internal policies and procedures associated with their targeted activity to determine if changes are appropriate.

FIGURE 12.12 Distributed Applications Development

Process-Driven or Data-Driven Design It must also be determined whether future applications development is going to be data-driven or process-driven. Most past systems have been designed to represent a process and to collect and manipulate only the data necessary to operate the particular process. For example, under the process approach, the job classification information system would be designed to mirror the job of the personnel analyst, who must review a particular job description and make a decision on rank classification. The system would require data input transactions to collect the necessary information to help make that decision. The process approach is efficient for that one particular application.

There are, however, other decisions that require much of the same data, such as hiring. The hiring information system would collect some of the same data, add more data, and store the data in that system. Now there are two different representations of several data fields, each collected for a particular process. The alternative data approach is to collect a broad range of data into a database. Each application would be designed to access this common database and extract only the needed information. (More on data management can be found in Chapter 14.)

HOW TO CREATE A VISION AND ARCHITECTURE

Determining an information vision and architecture, like any visioning process, is a very difficult conceptual task. It requires seeing the ideal future and making some very basic technical and managerial trade-offs without having concrete business cases. For example, many organizations have adopted formal statements on what microcomputer operating systems will be supported in the future. Settling on a standard can be an imposing decision, but it is one critical output of an architectural discussion.

Some people will argue forcefully to avoid deciding such basic matters. They claim that it is easier to avoid an explicit statement on which operating system to support because it is not totally clear which overall choice is correct. By not making some definitive statement, however, the organization may inadvertently develop a collection of separate applications systems that cannot communicate with each other. Part of the task in determining an information vision and architecture is to make as many of these tough decisions as possible.

Prerequisites

The information vision and architecture may be developed in a variety of ways, depending in part on the culture of the firm and the wishes of senior management. In order to ensure success, however, certain prerequisites should be met.

First, the people participating in the design of the vision and architecture should represent a broad range of backgrounds, both from senior management and the IS organization. The key attribute for including any individual is that the person is able to adopt a strategic outside-in view of the information resources of the firm. Only by being able to see the design problem from a total business perspective can the required visionary look forward truly be created. While creative technology visionaries are required on the team, there also must be a representation of business visionaries.

Second, there must be an appreciation of the complexity and breadth of an information technology system. Both the technical aspects and the managerial aspects of IS performance must be recognized. If a technical approach dominates (with the discussion centering only on such issues as technical standards) to the exclusion of more managerial matters, the resulting vision and architecture likely will be incomplete.

Third, some facilitation mechanism must be selected. It is very easy to spend far too much time on each knotty issue. Some organizations choose to use an outside facilitator for the discussion; others operate well without one. The facilitator's role is to ensure that the right issues are dealt with for the appropriate amount of time in the discussion. In any case, there must be some way to ensure that time is spent on the important matters.

Steps in Developing a Vision and Architecture

Whatever mechanism is used, discussion should proceed generally along the following seven steps.

Step 1: Review of the Current Situation Members of the group should review official and unofficial documentation of the current IS architecture. Policy manuals, rationale for particular decisions, prior vision statements, and memos and impressions of users and providers are all important input data. These documents and statements should be compiled, and some sense of the current situation should be documented as a beginning point.

Step 2: Analysis of the Strategic Direction of the Business The strategic vision of the entire business should next be reviewed. This may be represented in a document called the strategic plan. Some firms may not have a written plan, so a discussion with the CEO on her or his vision of the business would be necessary. Care must be taken to ensure that the document being reviewed is for the long term and is comprehensive of the entire business.

Step 3: Recognition of General Technology Trends Available sources should be reviewed to develop a general understanding of the major technology trends in the components of an information technology system. Note that precision about these trends (for example, specific dates) is not critical for an architectural statement. It is sufficient to recognize, for example, that significant advances in the power of workstations and continued price/performance improvements in most components of information technology are expected over the next five to ten years. Consideration of the dates of certain developments and more precise statements should be delayed until the implementation plan. Quite often, university faculty, consultants, or vendors (via nondisclosure statements) can provide valuable input for this step. Figure 12.13 shows the conclusions drawn by one organization on the relevant technology issues in 1993.

DEC will release alpha-based shared processors, offering greater cost effectiveness.

Our major applications software suppliers will migrate products to a relational database management system.

Expert systems technology will be cost-effective for a wide range of functional applications.

Integrated telephone and database technology will be available to stage customer records automatically for individuals handling incoming calls.

Higher speed network technologies will allow cost-effective, multimedia desktop applications.

Digital technology for the entire job completion process will be available.

Major improvements in the cost-effectiveness of personal computing hardware will be made.

FIGURE 12.13 Information Technology Forecast

Step 4: Identification of a Vision for the Role for Information An overall statement should be developed on how information will be used in the firm. This is the information vision. For example, one company identified three basic roles for information—to support business processes, to enhance personal productivity, and to add value to the products and services of the company. Another organization saw the role of information as enhancing product and process quality, improving the efficiency and effectiveness of the business, and sustaining the diversity of the divisions while simultaneously conveying a single image of the whole organization to its customers. Refer to Figures 12.1 and 12.2 for examples of a vision.

Step 5: Determining the Architecture After the first four steps have been accomplished, the determination of an information technology architecture can be made. The issues identified earlier under each architecture component should be raised and as many resolved as possible. It is best to start with the values component.

Step 6: Communication of the Vision and Architecture The decisions on vision and architecture should be documented to allow as many people as needed to see it. Earlier sections of the chapter have reviewed alternative methods for depicting the vision and architecture.

Step 7: Migration Plan The decisions on vision and architecture should be used as input to the information technology planning process. While some movement toward the vision can be made quickly, the overall migration process should be considered a long-term effort. There should be clear criteria or guidelines for major decisions so that the results are in line with the architecture. Care should be taken to make the vision as real as possible by acting in line with the architecture. (Much more information on planning is included in Chapter 13.)

BENEFITS OF A VISION AND ARCHITECTURE

The cost of developing a vision and architecture can be substantial, especially in terms of management time, but companies have found that there are significant benefits from building such statements. Both the resulting document and the process used to create the vision and architecture contribute to these benefits.

Better IS Planning

A vision and architecture provides the basis for more specific IS planning. In most organizations, combinations of users and IS management are charged with creating a set of priorities for the IS organization over the next several years. A vision and architecture answer "what" the group should be trying to create. The plan answers "how" the organization will get there. (Information technology planning is covered in more detail in Chapter 13.)

Communicating with Top Management

Top management insists on a rationale for major capital or staffing investments in the information technology arena. Many IS directors often request significant operating or capital budget increases—well above that available to every department. A vision can help explain the need for such expenditures by showing a nontechnical context for priorities.

Helping Vendors

Having an architecture also helps those from whom the IS organization buys products and services. Most computer and communications vendors have a defined range of products built around their own definitions or conclusions on architecture. The general design of a series of hardware models (for example, the DEC AXP series of computers) is often called an architecture. An explicit information technology architecture is an effective way for the IS director to communicate with vendors on the need for certain capabilities.

Creating a Context for Decisions

Another important function of a vision and architecture is to create a clear context within which providers and users can make individual decisions. In many organizations, it is possible to come to work every day, moving from one meeting to another and from one project to another, not really understanding the overall direction of the organization. It is critical to communicate the overall direction of information use and management widely throughout the firm so everyone can understand that the organization is focused on the same defined target in the future.

Achieving Integration and Decentralization

Most IS organizations are focused on achieving tighter integration of their systems and networks while simultaneously decentralizing the technol-ogy and operational activities. Developing an overall vision and architecture forces discussion on how exactly to go about achieving these seemingly opposite objectives. The issues can then be discussed in much more detail, often without the emotion that a specific decision would provide. Such intense discussions may result in a greater understanding of the trade-offs between autonomy and integration and result in a commitment to a particular course of action. Later, specific issue discussions are more focused and efficient.

Evaluating Options

The range of technology options for solving information technology problems is broad and growing. Both micro-based and mainframe-based solutions to problems may seem feasible and proper. Moreover, the number of vendors is also growing rapidly. A clear architecture can provide guidance in selecting one vendor over another. It allows an organization to take advantage of a range of options and see how they best fit into some overall architecture for the future. Otherwise, the organization runs the risk of being "vendor-driven," as well as responding only to current needs rather than designing long-term solutions to major business problems.

Meeting Expectations of Management

In the 1990s, senior management in many organizations has greater expectations than ever before on what information technology can do strategically for the company. Company executives are looking for new sources of competitive advantage. In a worldwide competitive arena, where many organizations have excellent scientists, design engineers, and new product development specialists, company leaders want to use information technology as another source of distinction in the market. The development of an explicit vision and architecture for information technology generates discussion on the role of this critical resource in meeting the objectives of the firm, thereby defining the strategic role of information technology.

SUMMARY

The definition and development of an information vision and architecture is indeed a difficult conceptual task. Yet the value of an explicit statement over a period of time usually exceeds the creation and maintenance costs. Often organizations create visions or architectures that explicitly deal with only some of the issues mentioned in this chapter. It is not always possible to deal with all critical issues in a short period of time. Therefore, it is important to revisit a vision/architecture statement regularly in order to resolve issues not dealt with earlier and to determine if the information vision still meets the needs of the business. In any case, attention to architecture decisions is critical for the user-manager and the IS organization leadership.

REVIEW QUESTIONS

1. How does the information technology architecture differ from an information vision?

2. List the critical information technology issues about which Figure 12.1 makes an explicit statement. Why do you think these particular decisions were specified?

3. What four important issues (found in the chapter) does Figure 12.1 not address that would normally be part of a complete information vision and architecture? Why do you think these issues were not addressed?

4. How would you respond to the criticism that a particular architecture is not feasible based on today's technology?

5. What are the benefits of stating an architecture via a picture such as Figure 12.2? the problems?

6. In the data stewardship statement shown in Figure 12.11, what functions or responsibilities should remain for the information systems organization to carry out?

7. What are the elements or dimensions common to earlier models of an architecture?

DISCUSSION QUESTIONS

1. In addition to those reasons listed in the chapter, what other issues or events may cause an organization to recognize the need for an information vision and architecture?

2. What are the major implications for the user-manager if a review of current practices indicates substantial inconsistency in the information vision and architecture for the company? for the IS director?

3. How might the values architecture described in Figure 12.7 have an impact on the company's data architecture?

4. What are the user implications of the data access architecture shown in Figure 12.10?

5. What are some of the most important problems that would likely be encountered in working toward the architecture in Figure 12.12?

6. Through which media can an information vision and architecture be represented?

7. Construct an information technology architecture that is consistent with the Atlanta printing company's information vision explained in this chapter.

8. What are the implications for a user-manager of the information vision contained in Figure 12.1?

REFERENCES

1986. "Planning the information systems architecture." *Infosystems* 33 (October): 5–9.

Allen, Brandt R., and Andrew C. Boynton. 1991. "Information architecture: In search of efficient flexibility." *MIS Quarterly* 16 (December): 435–445.

American Standard. 1988. "Architectural model for computing." *Datamation* 34: 88–92.

Couger, J. Daniel. 1986. "E pluribus compu-
tum." *Harvard Business Review* 64 (September–October): 87–91.

Davenport, Thomas H., Michael Hammer,
and Tauno J. Metsisto. 1989. "How executives can shape their company's information systems." *Harvard Business Review* 67 (March-April): 130–134.

Devlin, B. A., and P. T. Murphy. 1988. "An
architecture for a business and information system." *IBM Systems Journal* 27:
60–80.

Gage, Glen. 1991. "IS architecture artistry."
Computerworld 23 (July 29):67–68.

Keen, Peter G. W. 1991. *Shaping the Future:
Business Design through Information
Technology.* Boston: Harvard Business
School Press.

Keim, Robert T. 1992. "Apple's VITAL
statistics for enterprise architecture."
Corporate Computing 1 (October):
173–177.

Kerr, James M. 1989. "A blueprint for information systems." *Database Programming and Design* (September): 60–67.

McFarlan, F. Warren, and James L. McKenney. 1983. "The information archipel-
ago—governing the new world." *Harvard Business Review* 64 (July–August):
91–99.

Nolan, Richard L. 1983. "Building the company's computer architecture strategic
plan." *Stage by Stage* (Nolan, Norton &
Company) 2 (Winter): 1–7.

Stefferud, E., D. Farber, and R. Dement.
1982. "SUMURU: A network configuration for the future." *Mini-Micro Systems*
15 (May): 311–312.

Synnott, William R. 1985. "The building
blocks of IRM architecture." *Information Strategy: The Executive's Journal* 2
(Spring): 4–10.

8

Owens-Corning Fiberglas Corporation Information Systems Architecture

Owens-Corning Fiberglas Corp. (OCF) is the world's leading manufacturer of glass fiber materials and a major producer of polyester resins. Founded in 1938, originally as a joint venture between Owens-Illinois and Corning Glass Works, OCF had an after-tax profit of $172 million on net sales of approximately $3 billion in 1989.

The OCF Construction Products Group manufactures and sells insulation and roofing products for residential, commercial, and industrial construction and remodeling. This group also ranks as the country's largest producer of specialty asphalts and produces a line of windows for new construction and replacement markets.

The OCF Industrial Materials Group produces reinforcements, yarns, and resins for the transportation, marine, aerospace, energy, electronics, and appliance industries.

OCF manufactures and sells reinforcements, yarns, and insulation products in twenty-seven countries through its network of subsidiaries and affiliates. Products are also produced domestically for export.

In addition, a domestic subsidiary, O/C Tanks Corporation, is the world's leading producer of fiberglass-reinforced underground storage tanks.

Headquartered in Toledo, Ohio, OCF employs more than 17,000 people, operates more than 40 manufacturing facilities in the United States, and has sales offices in more than 70 cities and distribution units in 20 locations. Research and development is conducted at the OCF Technical Center complex in Granville, Ohio.

This case was prepared by Professor E. W. Martin as the basis for class discussion rather than to illustrate either effective or ineffective handling of an administrative situation.

Copyright © 1990 by E. W. Martin.

The OCF Information Systems Organization

The OCF IS organization has a history of strong management leadership. Both Paul Daverio, senior vice president for finance and administration, and Frank Glover, vice president of marketing, retail, and distribution for insulation products, are former IS vice presidents. Dennis Barber, vice president of information systems, reports to Daverio.

As shown by the dotted line relationships in Exhibit 1, the OCF IS organization is heavily decentralized, with each operating division and a number of science and technology units having their own IS units. Corporate IS operates the corporate data center and the communications network, develops corporate systems, and provides corporate-wide technical support, training, and planning. A summary of the corporate information systems vision and values is provided in Exhibit 2. The OCF corporate data management mission statement is shown in Exhibit 3.

The IS department is committed to the ideal of a partnership relationship with its clients in the business, whom it refers to as its business partners. OCF believes that information technology must contribute directly to the success of the business, and all IS expenditures must be justified on that basis. All IS services are billed directly to the users, although the OCF management council has occasionally appropriated funds directly to IS for development of systems that were crucial to corporate success.

OCF's Data and Applications Architecture

For the past seven years, OCF has been working on the development of an architecture for data and applications.

Business Objectives OCF views IS as a business within OCF. IS is focused on delivering value to

EXHIBIT 1
. . . .
Information Systems

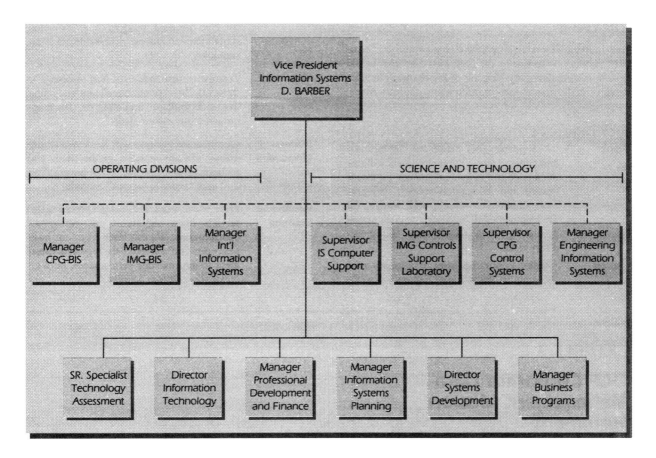

its OCF business partners. It has four business objectives that have motivated the development of the IS architecture:

1. Provide outstanding support to OCF's day-to-day profit making operations.
2. Substantially improve support of OCF management in performing analyses, making decisions, and carrying out actions.
3. Enable OCF management to change the organization freely with only minor delays and expense to change the supporting information systems. OCF is constantly changing in response to external threats and opportunities. In the past, inflexible information systems have seriously constrained OCF's ability to make change within the business because the systems could not change fast

enough and the cost of change was too great. It is strategically important to IS to get out of this bottleneck situation.
4. Improve IS performance in development and maintenance of systems. Vice president Barber set a target of a five-to-one improvement in IS organizational performance in these areas.

What Is an Architecture? According to David Cooper, an IS specialist who is currently leading the development of the OCF architecture:

From our perspective, architecture is an expression of strategy for using information technology. It is a structure of how we do business. It is how we manage the assets of information and information technologies.

EXHIBIT 2
. . . .
OCF CIS Vision and Values

CIS Vision

Each individual or team is dedicated to providing an "error free" product or service to the customer. The goal is 100 percent total quality; anything less does not meet our standards of performance and commitment to the customer.

Values

People	CIS is people: they define our commitment and performance. Our environment will foster change and individual growth. Equitable reward and recognition systems will promote quality, teamwork, and morale. All are empowered to promote a bias for action by making timely decisions and taking necessary risks.
Quality	Quality is our top priority. It starts with focusing on the work of highest value. Error-Free defines a standard of performance; it mandates an attitude that errors are unacceptable.
Teamwork	Teamwork demands trust and respect. The three (3) "In's" dominate all actions: initiative, independence, and integrity. Team approaches are encouraged.
Business Orientation	Our business partners will guide our investments. We are sensitive to the needs and requests of our customers. We have a "can do" and "make it happen" attitude.
Continuous Learning	Pride in our work and creative products and services make significant and recognized contributions. We can learn from our business peers and will make the required investment to improve our performance, both individually and functionally.

EXHIBIT 3
. . . .
OCF Corporate Data Management Mission Statement

The mission of Corporate Data Management (DM) is to be a service organization that is responsible for the management, planning, and control of Corporate Data which is the base element of the "Information Assets." DM provides services to support the Data/Information needs, productivity requirements, and quality guidelines of both Corporate and Division organizations in their quest to build systems that reduce costs, increase productivity, and improve their competitive position. These services include:

1. DM will provide Data Planning and Information Modeling services to support and control the development of integrated "Data Models" that aid management in the strategic use of the Corporation's "Information Assets" through implementation of integrated database systems that support both the operational and informational needs of the Corporation.

2. DM will provide physical database design and consulting services to support the Corporate and Divisional MIS staffs in implementation of integrated IDMS database systems for front and back office systems as well as Data Warehouse applications.

3. DM will provide corporate-wide data dictionary (IDD) services to support the Data Planning, Information Modeling, and physical database design functions. The IDD will provide a "Directory" for the definitions, locations, and uses of Corporate data that reside within it. DM will also provide consultation on the IDD and its uses.

4. DM will implement and maintain the software required to support the database environment. Technical expertise will be maintained in these software products and guidance provided to ensure an efficient and compatible database environment.

EXHIBIT 3 *(continued)*

5. DM will research and implement new development tools and techniques as well as development methodologies required for the development of quality systems and databases with the flexibility needed to improve responsiveness to change and reduce cost to support.
6. DM will develop, coordinate, or otherwise arrange to provide the training necessary to fully implement the use of the "Tools" we have responsibility for and have identified as key to the successful movement to the "Information Age."

7. DM will provide strategic direction guidance and leadership in the evolving areas of Data Planning, Development Center, and Database environment to ensure they support the overall MIS strategy.
8. DM will provide support for the Data Warehouse system. This support includes support for the application programs and databases used by the Warehouse to maintain, store, and deliver data.

We've thought about where technology ought to be going, we've thought about how it ought to be applied in the business environment, and we've set some directions for the corporation and for the IS people in how to leverage it. This says that we move away from making technology decisions on a project-by-project basis as we did in the past. Instead, we define the way we're going to apply technology and the kind of technology we're going to use, and we intend to remain relatively consistent on that regardless of what the apparent demands of individual projects are.

Architecture isn't intended to constrain completely our choices. For an individual project, we look at the needs of that project, assess the architecture, and if the architecture doesn't fit, we do not insist on following the architecture. We're not that smart in developing architecture. But if people can't follow the architecture, then they must explain why not. They must explain what forces them to violate the architecture, and justify the long-term cost to the corporation of that decision. It may turn out that this discussion causes us to alter the architecture because we learn continuously. That's why the architecture is never completely built, or completely accurate. The business conditions change, the technologies are changing, and the architecture has to continue to evolve to represent a target for where we're going, as opposed to a historical perspective of what we've already done.

Breadth of this Architecture   Exhibit 4 shows three dimensions of the OCF concept of architecture. The dispersion axis (projecting forward in the figure) indicates that OCF intends its architecture to impact the entire business, from corporate headquarters out to the customers and suppliers. It intends this architecture to provide ways for it to link with its customers and suppliers.

The horizontal axis presents applications, data, and systems as components of the architecture. Applications refers to a conceptual view of what information systems do for OCF—process transactions and deliver information. Data refers to a logical view of the data that needs to be available to allow OCF to construct and maintain its applications. It provides for a shareable data resource that spans both application and organizational boundaries. Systems refers to the configuration of the hardware, software, and networks that allow the applications to perform.

The vertical axis indicates the five levels of the OCF architecture. The business strategy level deals with what markets the OCF business units will serve and in what ways they will serve their customers. The business design level deals with the processes these business units will employ to serve those markets and customers. It specifies how the business units are organized—who does what, where, and with which customers. The technical facility level deals with the components that must be in place to allow IS to serve the needs identified in the previous two levels. The specification level finally gets down to technology, specifying the technologies and standards that IS will use to provide its services. Finally, the configuration level deals with the specific hardware and software products that will be used to provide applications services, data services, and systems services.

General Conceptual Model

Exhibit 5 depicts the general conceptual model of the OCF applications and data management components of the IS architecture. OCF conceptualizes the

EXHIBIT 4

OCF Data Management Architecture

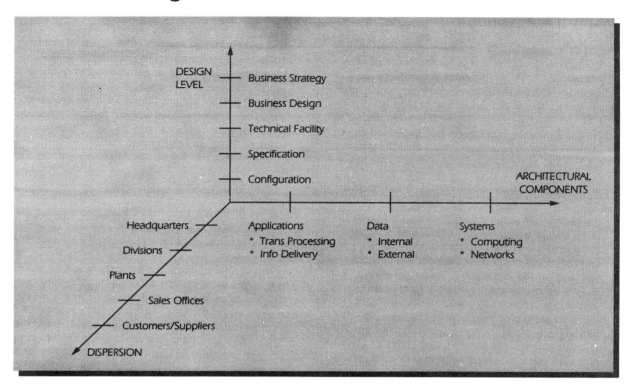

EXHIBIT 5

OCF General Conceptual Model

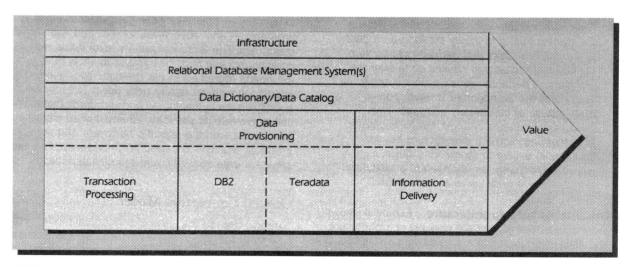

primary IS production activities that produce value for OCF as transaction processing, data provisioning, and information delivery. Today, most applications bundle these activities together, but this architecture proposes to treat each of them separately. The infrastructure components that support this new approach are relational database management systems and a data dictionary/data catalog.

Transaction processing, data provisioning, and information delivery are unusual terms for describing data processing activities. The following explains what they mean and why OCF has separated its processing activities into these three pieces.

Transaction Processing Transaction processing is a limited activity. It collects data—customer number, item number, quantity ordered, and so on. It validates that data using rules defined by the business people. It constructs business transactions from that data and checks that all the data required for a valid transaction are present. Then that validated transaction data is sent to data provisioning.

In addition, transaction processing provides operating information about how the business is performing relative to that set of business transactions. For an order-processing transaction, business people want to know how many of each item have been ordered today, how many of each item are awaiting shipment—the things they need to know in order to decide what to make and what raw materials to order. That is operating information and transaction processing produces it. Transaction processing is routine, predictable, and does not change much from year to year.

One of the architecture's objectives is to simplify transaction processing in order to reduce processing costs, to make it more routine and less subject to change, and to make it easier to change when change is necessary. It simplifies transaction processing by removing the responsibility for maintaining historical data and giving that responsibility to data provisioning. It also removes information delivery responsibility from transaction processing.

Further, the architecture removes from transaction processing all data representing information relationships—all of the codes that represent relationships or allow summarization to produce management reports. OCF refers to such data as fiction because it is not a characteristic of the transactions but is there to allow certain analyses of the transactions and may change when OCF decides it wants to analyze the data in another way. Although this fiction

no longer appears in transaction processing, it is maintained in data provisioning and information delivery so that the desired management information can still be obtained. Relational database technology allows OCF to maintain the fiction data in separate tables, and then combine it with transaction data whenever necessary by joining tables.

Organizational structure data is an example of the fiction that OCF has removed from transaction processing. Organizational structure refers to business units, production departments, sales offices, sales territories, and so on. These are the things that change when OCF reorganizes the business. When this organizational data is collected and stored in transaction files, and the processes for producing reports summarizing this organizational data are incorporated in transaction processing, then transaction processing must be modified whenever OCF reorganizes. It wants to eliminate the cost and delay involved in these changes, so it removes this fictional organizational data from transaction processing and deals with it in data provisioning and information delivery.

As an example of the impact of removing the fiction data from transactions, OCF found that 80 percent of the data that it was collecting on its order forms and entering in order-entry transactions was fiction and only 20 percent of the data was really necessary to identify what was being ordered and who was doing the ordering. By eliminating this fiction OCF could cut its data entered from an order down to 20 percent of what it was before.

Data Provisioning Data provisioning is responsible for receiving, storing, and managing all validated transaction data from transaction processing. In this architecture, transaction processing does not keep any historical data—all it stores is the current data necessary to provide the status of current operations. Data provisioning also receives, stores, and manages information from information delivery. And data provisioning also provides data back to transaction processing and data and information to information delivery when requested.

Data provisioning manages the inventory of data and information, using relational database management systems and a data dictionary and data catalog. These tools keep track of what data exists, where it is stored, what it means, and who has authority to access it. Thus, data provisioning protects the data and provides for convenient access to data and information to those who need it.

Data provisioning is a buffer between transaction processing and information delivery that prevents changes in how people want to look at data from changing the way data is collected and processed on a day to day basis. Data provisioning stores the organizational structure rules in its data dictionary or in tables in the database, so these rules can be readily changed when management decides to modify the organization.

Information Delivery Information delivery requests data and information from data provisioning. It then transforms data into information by applying various models and techniques to perform analyses, identify trends, formulate decisions, develop presentations, and support decision-making.

Data provisioning must provide a rich and responsive database so that whenever someone asks an information delivery question, the data is available. The technology must be fast enough to meet the business needs for responses to the questions. Some questions may require one-second response time, while others are satisfactory with one-day response time.

Responsibility for organizational structure data has been removed from transaction processing and moved to information delivery. Instead of collecting and maintaining organizational data in application programs and storing it in transaction databases, organizational data is stored in tables in data provisioning, and these tables are maintained by business people as part of their information delivery responsibilities. When they want to change the rules, they can go into the tables and change them. If, for example, they want to reorganize and create a new unit that is made up of certain employees reporting to this person, then they simply change the tables that define who reports to whom, and that is all there is to it. Transaction processing is not affected, and the fundamental databases did not change, but different information can be produced.

OCF wants its business people to do their own information delivery. One reason is that the process of analysis is very interactive—a result often suggests another question or another type of analysis. If you introduce the delays involved in having IS people formulate the queries and perform the analyses, then things slow down a lot and the process is much less creative. Often the business person will ask the wrong question the first time, and it is frustrating when the IS person comes back with the answer, but that is not what the manager wanted. If, however, the business person can get the answer by himself in five minutes,

he will figure out that he asked the wrong question and be able to formulate the right question very quickly. He also learns more about the problem than he could when working through someone else.

Since business managers and functional analysts are responsible for their own use of the information delivery facility, the tools that are provided for analysis should be "business seductive." They should be so attractive that they draw the person right into the computer—they cannot leave it alone. The tools need to help the people using them to ask the right questions, not just be easy to use. Furthermore, IS must build partnerships with business people so that they understand how to use these technologies, and even feel ownership of them. This takes a great deal of educating, coaching, and working together.

The Technological Basis for Data Provisioning OCF uses two database technologies to support data provisioning. Data provisioning must store and maintain data in response to transaction processing, and it must also store that data so that people can get information from it. But the performance characteristics of these two demands are quite different. The person seeking information can ask one question that can bring any mainframe computer to its knees for several hours, but transaction processing must have access to data in milliseconds.

Therefore OCF has constructed two environments—one to support transaction processing and another to support information delivery. They are both relational databases. The transaction processing technology is IBM's DB2 running on the mainframe, and it is designed to process high transaction volumes speedily. The information delivery technology is a TERADATA database machine—a combination of hardware and software that is optimized for answering information questions. By applying the right technology to the business needs, OCF optimizes performance on both sides.

. . . .
Evolution of the Information Delivery Architecture

The initial thinking on an "information delivery architecture" was performed by Larry Loehrke, Jerry McColough, and Bill Whitten at the request of Paul Daverio, who was vice president of information systems at that time. Daverio had two motivations for this request. First, he wished to improve the access to data for ad-hoc analysis by business professionals who were becoming PC computer literate and who were under increasing business pressure to reduce significantly the time it took to respond to changes in OCF's markets and operations. Second, he wished to reduce the professional IS resources devoted to modifying systems when OCF wished to change reporting sequences and algorithms. This led the team to the concepts of transaction processing, data provisioning, and information delivery described above.

The Data Warehouse As OCF began to try to implement these concepts, Don Kosanka, who was an early contributor to this effort, initiated the concept of a "data warehouse" in 1984. The data warehouse is part of the data provisioning function depicted in Exhibit 4. As shown in Exhibit 6, the data warehouse is conceptualized as a vast repository for the data that are needed to manage OCF. It must provide interfaces that accept transaction data from all sorts of transaction processing systems and move them into the warehouse environment. In this process that data are carefully examined and validated to assure that only high quality data are accepted. On the output side, there must be interfaces that allow a user to ask

EXHIBIT 6
Corporate Data Warehouse Concept

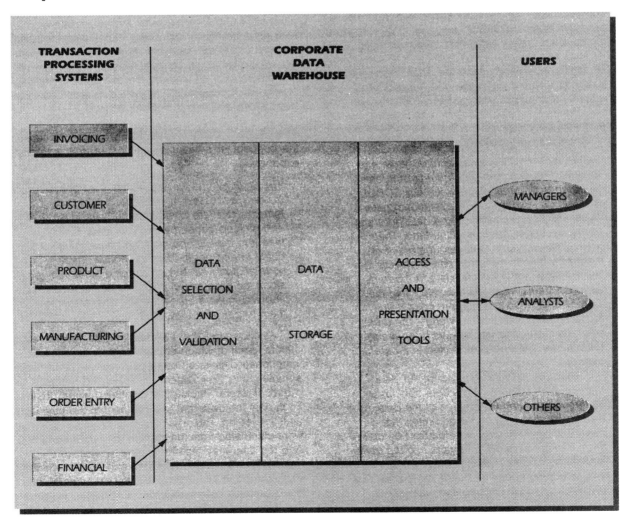

for data from the devices (PCs or terminals) that he ordinarily uses. And the data in the warehouse must be structured, and tools must be provided, so that users can easily obtain answers to their questions and perform analyses on this data.

In the summer of 1985 OCF assigned a project manager and three people to develop a limited data warehouse. After about 18 months they concluded that it was impractical to implement this concept with their existing IDMS/R database management system, so they began a search for more suitable technology. By the summer of 1987 they had selected IBM's DB2 relational DBMS, the SQL query language, and the TERADATA database machine as a suitable combination of technologies to support the data warehouse. They leased a small TERADATA database machine for six months to experiment with this technology.

In about three months they were able to build a data warehouse for the Residential and Commercial Insulation Products (RCIP) division that contained product data, sales data, and customer data. This was received so enthusiastically by RCIP managers that they helped convince the OCF management council to fund the purchase of a larger TERADATA machine and associated software. This move enabled them to expand this data warehouse to serve the other OCF divisions.

Don Kosanka recalls:

In implementing the data warehouse we had to work through some data quality problems. Building the interfaces between our COBOL transaction systems and the relational database warehouse so that all the data got transferred accurately took us some time. There were data problems that were the result of timing problems, and problems that were the result of the fact that some data in the transaction systems were just bad. Now that they were available so people could use it, they found that the codes were wrong—the data were incorrect, and had always been incorrect, but no one had ever looked at it carefully before!

That got us to thinking about our data management strategy. It became obvious to us through the implementation of the data warehouse that a lot of the problems that we had been experiencing were caused by building information delivery aspects into the transaction processing systems. When you build organizational codes and data into transaction processing, you just complicate things. We decided to eliminate this fictional data from

transaction processing. We intend to include in transaction processing only the data that are actually needed to run the business. We introduce fictional organizational codes by storing them in tables in the database that can be joined with the raw data to produce whatever summaries and analyses that you want. These fictional codes, which we change every year, can be easily changed by changing the tables, but we don't have to go back and change the transaction processing systems.

This data warehouse contained cumulative data for the year in both detailed and summary form. The summary data were intended to provide quick, convenient access to all the users, but managers soon found that different users wanted the data summarized in their own way, so the access to the data was often slow and inconvenient. And all of this activity was overloading the database machine and slowing response time for everyone. Further, each user was faced with far too much data, most of which were not of interest, and the users found this to be confusing. These problems led OCF to extend its architecture to include the concept of a "retail outlet."

The Retail Outlet According to Don Kosanka, the concept of a retail outlet comes from common experience.

The analogy that we use is that a warehouse is really accessed by retailers, not by customers. Retailers come into the warehouse and pick up goods by the truckload. They take it to their shops, and their customers come in and get it. The warehouse has all sorts of stuff in it, but if you run a store you stock the products that your customers want, and you make it attractive and convenient for them to get what they want.

As shown in Exhibit 7, there may be several retail outlets, each of which obtains its data from the data warehouse. The retail outlet is a set of data that is selected and "packaged" to serve the needs of a group of users. Packaging involves several things. First, only the data that are pertinent to the business unit is selected. The organizational structure data that were eliminated from the transactions are introduced. And the data may also be summarized according to those organizational categories and by time period. Packaging can also combine different types of data. For example, determining the profitability of a product involves combining sales, cost, freight, adjust-

EXHIBIT 7
....
Retail Outlet Concept

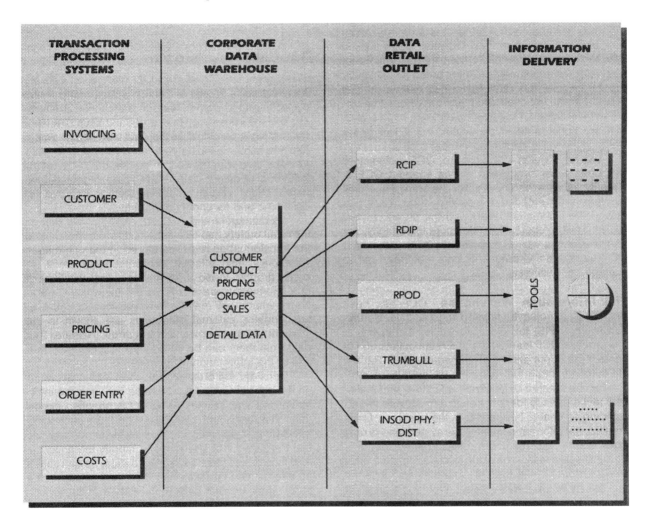

ments, selling expenses, overhead, and so forth. Because the data are small and focused, a person can easily specify what is wanted, and the delay in retrieving the data can be greatly reduced.

A retail outlet may be implemented on several different platforms. It may be a special set of databases on the TERADATA machine, or on a minicomputer, or the data may be moved onto the server of a LAN used by the group of "customers" of that retail outlet. OCF intends the retail outlet concept to be very flexible, and it is trying to provide user-friendly (or

even "business seductive") tools for accessing and analyzing this data.

OCF's first retail outlet was a profitability database for one of its divisions. OCF wanted to be able to look at the profitability of a product, or a sales office, or even a specific customer. In order to develop this retail outlet, managers had to go back and expand the data in the data warehouse. The data warehouse had always contained customer data and price, but it did not contain the detailed cost data required to determine profitability.

The profitability retail outlet was a great success because it addressed a recognized business need. Similar retail outlets have been developed for the other OCF divisions.

The other high priority retail outlet OCF is working on is in the area of pricing. It is a database that provides information to help OCF managers decide how to respond to requests from its distributors for special price adjustments to meet competition. Defining the data for this retail outlet has been a difficult task—it is still not clear what data are needed or how it can be obtained. OCF now has pricing retail outlets that are considered to be useful, but it still has a group working on improving pricing data.

The retail outlet component of OCF architecture has been quite successful. It has enabled OCF to simplify its data warehouse, for the warehouse now contains only detailed transaction data. OCF has moved the summarized data and the organizational tables into the retail outlets. But more importantly, the retail outlet has vastly improved the ease with which OCF managers can obtain the data that they need to manage the business.

The Information Warehouse OCF has been working on a project to develop an Executive Information System (EIS) for one of its senior managers. In this process OCF learned that the retail outlets do not contain the information that managers need. Rather, the outlets contain the data from which this information can be created by applying analytical and statistical techniques to identify trends and provide understanding of what is happening in the business. Once created, the information leaves the system and is only available to those for whom it was created. Not only do these users lose track of the information—the most useful product of the system—but they also lose the process by which it was created. Wouldn't it be great if this information could be returned to the system where it would be available for use by other OCF managers? And wouldn't it be great if the process for creating the information could be preserved so that it could be used again to create similar information in the future?

Thus the concept of an information warehouse was conceived. It is to be another set of databases designed to provide easy access to both management information and the rules and processes used to produce it. Also, the information warehouse provides the tools to turn this information into effective presentations and stores these presentations. This requires that the information warehouse store compound documents that may include image, voice, and graphics information. Incidentally, OCF people believe that the tools needed to support an information warehouse do not exist at this time but that they are being developed.

The Current Architecture

The current version of the OCF information delivery architecture is shown in Exhibit 8. Beginning in the upper left-hand corner, we see transaction processing and the transaction files and databases. Transaction data are delivered to the data warehouse, where they are carefully validated and controlled. Then data from the data warehouse are "packaged" by carefully selecting pertinent data, introducing organizational data (fiction), and summarizing them to improve access time and its understandability.

As managers and analysts transform the data in the retail outlets into information, this information and the transformation rules are stored in the information warehouse. Also, effective presentations (memos, reports, graphs, video presentations, and the like) of this information are stored in the information warehouse where they may be retrieved for use in the future. Finally, external databases are shown in the lower right-hand corner, and the arrow indicates that data from them can be introduced into the retail outlets or the information warehouse.

Consider the business decision-maker depicted on the right of Exhibit 8. The rules built into the information warehouse may bring to his attention conditions that he should consider. If he finds something interesting in an analysis, he can examine the rules that produced that analysis and modify the analysis. And if he needs more background data, he can select an alternative that takes him back to the data in his retail outlet, or even back to the data warehouse. Using this data, he can perform other analyses, ask further questions, and develop decisions and presentations as he sees fit.

The Business Design Level One of the concerns of the business design level of the overall IS architecture shown in Exhibit 4 is organization—who is responsible for what. In this architecture, corporate or divisional IS professionals build the transaction processing systems, which (in new systems) includes delivering the data to the data warehouse. Corporate IS is responsible for the corporate data warehouse, which includes responsibility for developing the bridging interfaces that transfer data from old transaction processing systems into the data warehouse. Corporate IS is responsible for assuring the quality of the data in the data warehouse, and for protecting it from unauthorized access or destruction.

Divisional IS professionals develop the packaging rules that add organizational data, and that summarize and combine data to produce the retail store databases. However, the tables that contain the organizational data are maintained by business people.

Business analysts, not IS professionals, are responsible for converting the data in the retail outlet into information in the information warehouse. The responsibility of IS is to provide business seductive tools and access to data so that these business people can easily create useful information in response to the needs of business management.

The Specification Level As indicated in the above discussion, the technology (both hardware and software) that is available determines the degree to which one can profitably use the concepts of the architecture. The architecture should be driven by business needs, and it may be ahead of current technology. As suitable technology becomes available, it may be used to make the architectural concepts real.

Exhibit 9 shows the specific products in use or under consideration for implementing systems under this architecture. (Those products that are enclosed in rectangles are under consideration.) For example, business people use PC/SQL LINK in various places to retrieve data from the databases. This usage requires them to understand the data well enough to specify what data elements they want and the tables that contain them, and then PC/SQL LINK will retrieve the desired data. To use this technology, business people must concentrate their thoughts on the data rather than on the business problem.

In addition, OCF managers have just decided to purchase another product, INTELLECT, which allows you to say: "Give me all the sales of three-quarter inch Fiberglas roof-deck board sold in the western region last quarter, and tell me what that is in total and by salesman." And it gives you the answer. Or, INTELLECT might come back and say: "I don't understand western region, explain that to me." Since PC/SQL LINK is only user-friendly to an IS professional, INTELLECT will be a vast step in the direction of "user-seductive" tools.

However, OCF does not purchase new technology just because it looks attractive—the decision is made by business people when they are convinced that the business impact of the technology justifies its

cost. It took over a year of study and experimentation to decide to acquire INTELLECT. OCF people are continually evaluating new products to see how they might fit into the architecture, but investments in new technology are carefully evaluated.

....

Impact of the Architecture

OCF has a data warehouse in place containing cost and sales data—customer data, product data, order data, and so forth. OCF has built profitability and pricing retail outlets for individual marketing organizations, and business people are getting experience in using them. As part of its project to develop an EIS for one of the senior OCF managers, OCF is in the process of building an experimental information warehouse.

OCF marketing managers are using their retail outlets on a continuing basis to evaluate product line movement and trends as well as analyze customers and sales areas. And some managers believe that they are doing a much better job of price management. There is wide agreement that the architecture is contributing significantly to business success.

OCF's very limited experience so far indicates that it may obtain the targeted five-to-one increase in IS productivity in developing and maintaining systems that conform to this architecture.

Lastly, OCF is in the process of developing closer relationships with vendors that it considers to be strategic. One unanticipated benefit of the architecture is that it helps provide a framework for interaction with these strategic vendors. Since the architecture describes OCF's strategies in technology, these vendors can better target their products to what OCF is trying to do. That has proved to be helpful in developing mutually beneficial relationships.

Although this architecture is still considered to be experimental, senior OCF management has invested considerable resources in large-scale experiments to develop and evaluate this architecture. The firm is developing most new applications within this architecture. The OCF management council has allocated the necessary resources in 1990 to replace its large, antiquated human resources system with a new system that will be developed under this architecture. That will require adding human resources data to the data warehouse, and developing suitable retail outlets for the human resources department. This will be the first major system in which the "fiction" data will be removed from the transaction data.

EXHIBIT 8

Target Information Delivery Architecture (Business Strategy Level)

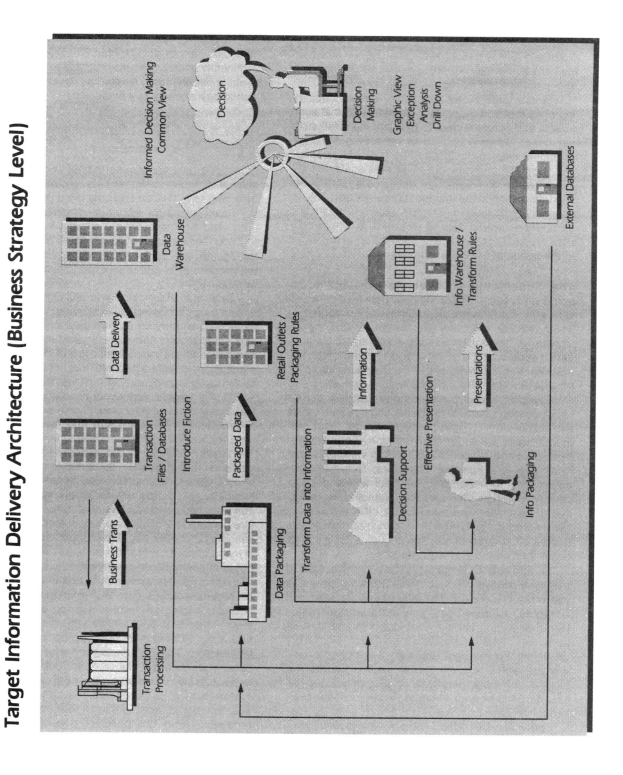

EXHIBIT 9

Target Information Delivery Architecture (Specification Level)

At present, the data warehouse contains only a small fraction of the OCF corporate data, and it will be years (if ever) before all the old mainline transaction systems are converted to conform to this architecture. And the few retail outlets serve only a small percentage of OCF's managers. Since everything is justified on the basis of its bottom-line benefit, change is deliberate.

There have been and there continue to be a number of significant problems in applying this architecture. It is often a struggle to justify adhering to the architecture when developing a new system, for some people may argue that another course of action may be quicker, or less costly, or in some way better for that project. Also, most existing systems do not adhere to the architecture, and there is a tendency to want to expand these systems without converting them to the new architecture. Finally, the new architecture requires significant changes in how IS professionals must think when they design and implement new systems, and a number of IS people are uncomfortable with these changes. The road to adoption of this architecture has been and will continue to be steep and crooked.

9

Managing Organizational Data

As outlined in Chapter 12, the category of data is one component of the information technology architecture. Some IS professionals believe that data are the most important element of the information technology architecture, and they have designed comprehensive IS planning and development methodologies based on data (see Finkelstein, 1989, and Zachman, 1987).

Some IS experts argue that the data architecture shows the inherent nature of the organization, which will stay relatively unchanged over time and space. For example, where the organization operates, how business processes are conducted, and the forces that drive the IS values and mission are constantly changing. These changes cause computer hardware, software, networks, and management to adjust, often radically. As long as what the organization is (that is, a financial institution, a manufacturer, or a human services agency) does not change, the nature of data will remain relatively constant.

In this chapter we overview those concepts, principles, and skills you need to understand to manage organizational data. This chapter presents several topics that are important to a general manager:

1. Data. This chapter makes the case that data are an organizational resource that, like other resources—people, facilities, land—requires general management attention.

2. Notation. This chapter shows you notation you can use to understand and explain the data required in your organization, consistent with business policies and rules.
3. Management. This chapter explains the management roles needed in the IS unit and, in general, management to effectively manage the data resource.

THE DATA RESOURCE

Data are now recognized as a major organizational resource, to be managed like other assets, such as land, labor, and capital. In fact, many observers of trends in business believe that the organizations that will excel in the 1990s will be those that manage data as a major resource, understand the usefulness of data for business decisions, and structure data as efficiently as they do other assets.

Of course, information can be an asset only if it is available when you want it, and this can occur only if an organization purposely organizes and manages its data. Financial resources are available to build a new plant or to buy new raw materials only if a financial manager and other business managers have planned for enough funds to cover the associated costs. A new high-tech product can be built only if engineering and personnel managers have anticipated the needs for certain skills in the work force. A business certainly would not think about not planning and managing land, labor, and capital. Similarly, information must be planned and managed.

This effort to manage organizational data is the responsibility of *every* manager. In addition, a special management unit, called data administration, usually provides organizational leadership. Every manager has some financial, personnel, equipment, and facilities/space responsibilities. Today, we must add information to this list of managed assets.

Why Manage Data?

One way to view the importance of managing the data resource is to consider the following questions:

What would your company do if its critical business data, such as customer orders, class registrations, product prices, account balances, or patient history were destroyed? Could the organization still function? for how long?

What costs would your company incur if its database was damaged? Is the data irreplaceable? How would business operations change without the computerized data?

How much time does your organization spend reconciling inconsistent data? Do account balances in your department agree with those in central accounting? What happens when these figures do not agree? Do marketing and engineering use the same product identifiers? Are there problems with providing custom products because of different specifications by sales and engineering? Can you track a customer order all the way from entry through production to shipping and billing in a consistent and unconfused way?

How difficult is it to determine what information is stored about the part of the business you manage? What data exist about customer sales in a particular market? In what databases do these data reside? What is the meaning of these data (for example, do the data include lost sales, blanket orders, special orders, private label sales)? How can you gain access to these data?

A SEGMENT OF ONE

"We know millions and millions of people intimately—right down to their shorts." (National Demographics & Lifestyles, Inc.)

Mass marketing is dead, and niche marketing is not good enough. The theme for the 1990s is marketing to a "segment of one." This means creating a corporate database full of details about the buying habits of those individual customers and prospects. The trick is to keep the relationship with each customer going from diapers to death. Experts say it often takes wrenching cultural changes for a corporation to pull together data from several far-flung departments. Sixty percent (of the data) comes from the companies' own databases, scattered in such places as the customer-service and billing departments. Information services and service bureaus can overlay company data with lifestyle, financial, and demographic data collected from sources such as new car registrations, magazine subscriptions, the U.S. Postal Service's change-of-address file, credit-card records, and surveys in warranty registration cards.

(Adapted from Betts, 1990)

Although managing information as a resource has many general business dimensions, it is also important for the cost-effective operation and development of information systems. Poor systems development productivity is frequently due to a lack of data management, and some methods, such as prototyping (see Chapter 10), cannot work unless the source of data is clear and the data are present. Systems development is enhanced by the reuse of data and programs as new applications are designed and built. Unless data are cataloged, named in standard ways, protected but accessible by those with a need to know, and maintained with high quality, data and the programs that capture and maintain them cannot be reused.

A key element in this management system is an overall map for business data—a data model. A manufacturing company would never think about building a new product without developing a blueprint and using common components and parts from existing products where appropriate. The same is true for data. The analogy to the components of a blueprint are data entities, such as customer, order, product, vendor, market, and employee, and the relationships between them (see Chapter 7).

Although there are many technical, or engineering, issues about the technology used to manage data (see Chapter 5), the issues to be emphasized in this chapter are managerial. How to plan for data, to control data integrity, to secure access to and use data, and to make data accessible are important to the general business manager. As with any business resource, quality sources for data must be identified and the data acquired; enough space must be available for data storage; obsolete data must be identified, disposed of, or archived; and usage of data must be accounted for, and, if appropriate, usage should be charged to those accessing and storing the data. These are not technical issues—the general business manager should be equipped to deal with these issues.

Problems in Managing the Data Resource

A major source of resistance to managing data as a shared corporate resource is the history of data and system ownership. Traditionally, individual departments or managers have owned application systems and the data locked in them. The philosophy that information is power creates a tremendous inertia that leads to resistance to managing data as a shared resource (see Chapter 16 for a discussion on managing the politics of information systems).

Most organizations do not start from scratch and cannot rebuild every database immediately. Overlapping databases exist in which the same data are stored under different names and in different formats and are updated at different times. It may be impossible to reconcile the differences and inconsistencies between these databases. Further, it will cost a considerable sum to create a new information infrastructure, which may cause managers to question whether managing data is worth the cost.

Until data are planned and managed in a coordinated way, however, systemic problems will continue. For example, joint marketing by two product managers cannot occur until these two managers work from a common pool of customer data. A customer complaint cannot be resolved unless customer service, repair, and product design data are synchronized (see Chapter 13 for methods of information systems planning). Consolidated and coordinated plans for data are needed to rid organizations of miscommunication and open new opportunities that are not possible with blinders on data.

THE PERMANENCE OF DATA

Any organization has customers or clients, whether these are other organizations, individual consumers, patients, or students. Also, no matter whether a company makes to stock or to order, there are vendors or suppliers, orders or reservations, products or services, and employees. Further, irrespective of how accounting, selling, billing, or any other management activity is performed, there still will be data about customers, vendors, orders, products, and employees. Data values may change, new customers added, products discontinued, and employees hired and retired, but we will always have customers, products, and employees about which we need to keep current data. Occurrences of data are volatile, the existence of data is persistent, and the need for data is constant.

Business processes change, and so must information systems. If we decide to change a sales forecasting method, programs will have to be rewritten, but customer, order, and general economic condition data are still needed. In fact, if data are well-managed, the databases will remain relatively unchanged when we change the way we do business. At the same time, programs that analyze, process, and report information may change drastically.

Thus, data are fundamental to the business. Data remain over time and need to be managed over time.

The Data Pyramid

Although the business retains vast amounts of data, there may be relatively few basic classes of data on which to base most information. Figure

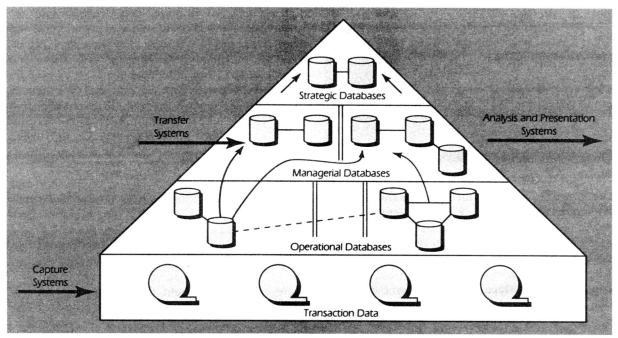

FIGURE 14.1 Organizational Data Pyramid

14.1 depicts the organizational data pyramid. Although new data can enter this pyramid at any level, most new data are captured in the base of the pyramid in operational databases. These databases contain the business transaction history of customer orders, purchases from suppliers, internal work orders, personnel transfers, and other day-to-day business activities. Managerial control and strategic databases are typically subsets, summaries, or aggregations of operational databases, with key external data as supplements. For example, a database for sales forecasting (a managerial control function) can contain monthly summaries of sales by product family or geographical area, derived from customer orders and product data. This might be supplemented with economic indicators and sales force judgments to produce estimates needed for production planning and scheduling.

When managerial databases are constructed from sources other than internal, shared operational databases, there can be significant inconsistencies. For example, a marketing department might track customer sales in a local database before passing these on to order entry. If they use these figures for forecasting final sales, they may not consider canceled orders, orders rejected due to insufficient credit, returned goods, or sales not met because of inadequate production capacity. These information items may not be considered because they enter the business at other points of contact with the customer. A well-run business must coordinate all customer contacts through a common understanding of the customer.

Developing an understanding of the relationships between data in various databases is a critical element of managing the data resource. Ideally, aggregate data will be derived from operational data, not collected separately (and, hence, inconsistently), and different databases will receive data transferred from a common source.

Application Independence

The goal of data resource management is **application independence**, the separation, or decoupling, of data from applications. This concept, embodied in Figure 14.1, is further illustrated in Figure 14.2.

In this figure, the management of data is viewed like the management of the raw and

360

component material resources in a manufacturing company. Raw data are received, inspected, and stored in the warehouse. Data in storage are used in the production of any authorized information product. Data are retrieved from the warehouse when needed but, unlike raw materials, are not consumed from usage. As data become obsolete, they are replaced with new data. As data are processed into information, they are added to the warehouse, similar to the entry of components and subassemblies into storage. The warehouse is used by all information production operations and work centers, but individual work centers (applications) have their own work-in-process inventory and receive a few kinds of data that are not shared among other applications. Thus, data are cataloged, managed, and, at least conceptually, stored centrally, where they can be kept safe and uncontaminated for use throughout the business.

The central point of Figure 14.2 is that data and applications must be treated as separate entities. When treated separately, data are not locked inside applications, where their meaning and structure are hidden from other applications that also require these data.

This metaphor for application independence suggests that different data processing applications can be classified into three groups, based

FIGURE 14.2 Categories of Information Processing with Application Independence

upon their role in managing data—capture, transfer, and analysis and presentation.

Data Capture Applications   **Data capture applications** gather data and populate databases. They store and maintain data in the data pyramid of Figure 14.1. Ideally, each datum is captured once and fully tested for accuracy and completeness. Responsibility for ensuring the quality of data capture systems might be distributed across the organization. Localized data capture applications are developed for data with an isolated use or data for which coordination across units is not required. Still, because localized data might eventually be useful somewhere else in the organization (and they must then be consistent across sites), an inventory (kept in the data dictionary) must be maintained of all database contents.

Data Transfer Applications   **Data transfer applications** move data from one database to another. These applications are often called bridges or interfaces because they connect related databases. Once raw data are captured, they may be copied to various databases where they are stored for specific purposes. For example, customer order data may be stored in multiple subject or target area databases supporting production scheduling, billing, and customer service. Also, this kind of application extracts and summarizes data, as well as distributes copies of original data. Ideally, this transfer would be event triggered, that is, if new basic data are captured or changed in value, messages are sent as needed to all other databases that build on these data to alert these databases that changes have occurred.

Data Analysis and Presentation Applications   **Data analysis and presentation applications** distribute data to authorized persons. Data might be summarized, compared to history, reformulated into graphs, or inserted into documents being developed using a word processor. Data might be input to a decision support system or executive information system (see Chapter 2). Data analysis and presentation applications can draw upon any and all data from databases the manager receiving the presentation is authorized to see. Data and the way they are presented are

independent, and those who determine the format or presentation do not necessarily control the location and format for capture and storage of data.

A significant result of application independence is the creation of **disposable systems**. In many organizations, systems cannot be dropped or easily rewritten because applications and data are so intertwined. When the presentation capabilities of an application system become obsolete, but it maintains data that are essential to the business, an inefficient system may have to be kept alive. With application independence, you can replace the capture, transfer, and presentation modules separately. Presentation modules are the most volatile, and it is from these types of systems that management receives business value. In addition, with modern programming languages and system generators, managers can customize their own presentation and analysis systems to meet personal needs.

Further, data are captured at one source and, even when not shared from one common database, are synchronized across different databases. It is simply too costly for an organization to capture the same data multiple times and reconcile differences across applications. Thus, architecture based on application independence permits a more responsive, flexible, and beneficial approach for managing the data resource.

Figure 14.1 is another way to view the data architecture discussed in Chapter 12. The data architecture in an organization contains an inventory of the uses of data across the business units. The architecture also includes a plan to distribute data to various databases to support the analysis and presentation needs of different user groups. The same data are stored in multiple databases because that is the most efficient architecture to deliver data to users. To ensure that data are current, accurate, and synchronized across the organization, however, key business data are captured once and transferred between databases as needed.

The Need for Data Standards

Because the same and similar data are used in various application systems, data must be clearly identified and defined so that all users know exactly what data they are manipulating. Further, shared

362

databases and data transfer systems require that database contents be unambiguously defined and described. The central responsibility in managing the data resource is to develop a clear and useful way to uniquely identify every instance of data and to give unambiguous business meaning to all data. For example, we must be able to distinguish data about one customer from data about another. Further, the meaning of such data as product description and product specification must be clear and distinct.

Figure 14.3 lists the five types of data standards that must be established for a business—identifiers, naming, definition, integrity rules, and usage rights. Business managers, not information technology managers, have the knowledge necessary to set these standards.

Identifier This is a characteristic of a business object or event (a so-called data entity) that uniquely distinguishes one instance of this entity from every other instance. For example, an employee number is a distinctive feature of each employee, and a unique bill-of-lading number is assigned to each shipment. It is not uncommon to find different units of a business using different identifiers for the same entity. As long as there is a one-for-one match of identifier values across the various schemes, there is not a problem, but usually there is no such compatibility. The ideal identifier is one that is guaranteed to be unique and is stable for a long time. Also, identifiers related to meaningful data tend not to be desirable because they are not stable. For example, a customer identification based on geographical region and standard industrial code (SIC) will no longer be valid if

a customer moves or changes primary businesses. Thus, it is wise to design a meaningless, sequentially assigned code as the identifier, and simply use such data as geographical location and SIC as other descriptive data.

Naming Distinct and meaningful names must be given to each kind of data retained in organizational databases. If two data elements have the same name, their true meaning will be confusing to users. If the same data element is referred to by different names that are never associated, managers will think that these are different pieces of data. Many organizations develop a naming scheme or template for constructing all data names, with common terms to be used for different elements of the scheme. For example, a data name of employee-monthly-pay indicates which entity, which time period, and which type of data. Each of the three components of this data name would be limited to a restricted vocabulary; for example, the time period would have values such as daily and weekly, and abbreviations for each could be assigned. Standard names make naming new data easier and give a user a quick start on knowing what data are on a report or in a certain database.

Definition Each data entity and element is given a description that clarifies its meaning. The definition applies to all business circumstances and users. Terms such as customer, employee, and product may, surprisingly, not have universal meaning. For example, does customer refer to someone who has bought from you or any potential consumer of your products or services? Different parts of the business may have developed over the years their own interpretation of such terms, so definitions must be constructed through review by a broad range of organizational units.

Integrity Rules The permissible range or set of values must be clear for each kind of data. These integrity rules add to the meaning of data conveyed by data definitions and names. For example, a data element of region is probably limited to some set of valid values based upon sales territories or some other artificial construct. In addition,

---

Identifier: unique value for each business entity.
Naming: unique name or label for each type of data.
Definition: unambiguous description of each type of data.
Integrity rule: specification of legitimate values for a type of data.
Usage right: security clearances for a type of data.

FIGURE 14.3 Types of Data Standards

a central and single standard for valid values can be used by those developing all data capture applications to detect mistakes. Also, since exceptions may be permitted, the integrity rules may specify who can authorize deviations or under what circumstances values outside of the valid set can be authorized.

Usage Rights These standards prescribe who can do what and when to each kind of data. Such security standards state for every kind of data (whole databases, individual files in a database, particular records, or data elements in a file) what is permissible use of that data. For example, a manager might be restricted to retrieving only the employee-monthly-pay data element, only during regular business hours, from an authorized terminal, and only about himself and those people he supervises.

These data standards would be retained in a standards database called a data dictionary/directory or data repository (see Chapter 5). This central repository of data about data helps users to learn more about organizational databases. It is also used by database management systems to access and authorize use of data.

TYPICAL ORGANIZATIONAL DATABASES

To gain a more concrete understanding of managing the data resource of an organization, this section presents examples of databases found in personal, departmental, and organizational situations. Notation introduced in Figure 7.20 will be used to describe these databases in graphical form. Later in this chapter a richer notation, called the entity-relationship (ER) notation, will be introduced. (You might review the terminology from Chapter 7 on the concepts of file, data element, relationship, and database, because these terms will be used extensively here.)

Although we will illustrate one database for each example situation, most organizations usually have many databases (see Figure 14.1). Figures 14.4, 14.5, and 14.6 are not meant to show

all the data relevant to any particular manager or organization, but are meant to illustrate how data for a given business situation can be logically organized as part of a data resource management effort. A very early step in data resource management is the clear representation of the data to be managed. Whether a given manager or department uses a separate database or a customized view of a shared database involves many technical and organizational issues, which is usually not the concern of the business manager. The concern of business managers is to understand the nature of their data and to ensure that they have access to quality data.

Personal Databases

Contact history and tracking for a single salesperson is used in this section to illustrate a personal database. This is typical of a database for the personal use of one manager or individual (see Figure 14.4).

The salesperson contact database of Figure 14.4 contains data about the customers who are a given salesperson's responsibility. Because data about region are shown in the figure, this suggests that a salesperson is responsible for customers who are located in several sales regions, although each customer is in only one region. This database might be one database within the data pyramid of

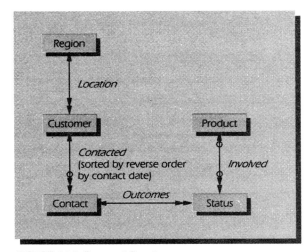

FIGURE 14.4 Personal Database

Figure 14.1 or might be a personal view of a larger, shared database that services several people or departments.

Each customer might be contacted zero, one, or many times; the small circle on the line between Customer and Contact indicates a conditional relationship in which the salesperson might never have contacted some customers. Such conditional relationships are important because this helps us to understand that the database contains data about potential customers, inactive customers, and other customers who have never been contacted, which contributes to the clear understanding of organizational data.

The outcome of discussing each product involved in a contact is called a Status, which could show that an order was placed, the customer has no interest in the product, or any other outcome. The salesperson handles several products, and most contacts involve the salesperson discussing several products with a customer. Sometimes, the contact is general, so no specific product is involved (indicated by the small circle near Product on the line between Product and Status). Some products are never involved in a contact (see the small circle near Status on the line between Product and Status).

This database would allow a salesperson to ask a wide variety of questions:

What customers did I contact last Thursday? This involves a set of contact records selected by date and the customer record associated with each.

When is the last time I contacted customer "Indiana Office Supply?" This involves data from a particular customer record and the most recent contact record for that customer.

When is the last time I contacted customer "Indiana Office Supply" about product "80-column printer enclosure?" This involves a particular customer record, a particular product record, and contact and status records related to each.

Have I sold any "80-column printer enclosures" in the "Northwest" region? This involves a particular product record, a particular region record, and the customer, contact, and status records related to each.

Functional Area Databases

A personnel department and its need to inventory jobs and employees is one example of a functional area or departmental database (see Figure 14.5). As with personal databases, after the consideration of various technical issues, a physically separate database might be developed for a department's needs or customized access into an

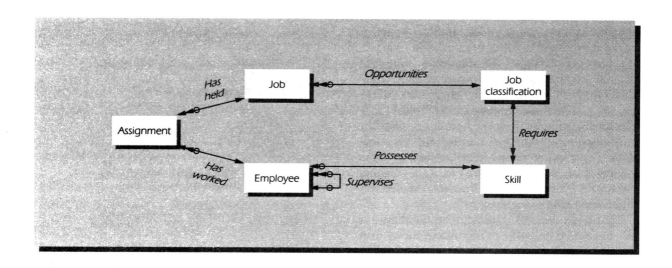

organizational database might be provided. Part of data resource management is to keep track of all such departmental (and personal) database requirements. Then, when separate physical databases are used, data capture and transfer systems can be built to keep these databases consistent and reduce data maintenance expenses for the whole organization.

The personnel department database in Figure 14.5 keeps track of data about employees and jobs. Each employee may supervise many other employees, but in the company depicted, each employee is supervised by at most one employee. A standard job classification scheme is used, and each job classification requires certain skills. Zero, one, or many actual job opportunities might exist in the company under this classification. The history of who has held what jobs is captured in the Assignment. New employees can be hired without a specific assignment (the circle on the Has Worked relationship). A newly listed job may not yet have anyone assigned to it (the circle on the Has Held relationship).

A wide variety of questions can be answered from the data that would likely be stored in such a database:

What jobs are currently unfilled? This would involve accessing each job record and seeing if there has never been any assignment for this job or if the latest assignment has been terminated.

Who are the employees in a particular department? This involves finding the employee record for the head of the department and then accessing all the employee records for which he or she is supervisor (if any).

Does a particular job candidate have all the skills required for an open job? This involves comparing the set of skills held by the job candidate (employee) to those required by the job classification of the open job.

Who are all the employees now in a particular job classification? The Opportunities relationship would be used to find all the jobs in this classification, and then the Has Held relationship would identify (through start and termination dates) if anyone now holds that job. If so, the

Has Worked relationship can be used to find the right employee record for the current holder of each job in the classification.

These queries illustrate the power of relationships in a database. The ability to answer a query depends on knowing not only employee department or job data but also the associations between them.

You can probably imagine many more questions to be answered from this database. Because it is a department resource, career counselors, personnel recruiters, department heads, job designers, and many other managers might use this database. One consequence of this wider use is that it may not be possible to identify all potential uses for the database at one time. A sound design for the database can make it possible for flexible usage and easy expansion (say, to include data about departments in which employees work, external job applicants, or temporary workers and their agencies). Such potential needs should be anticipated.

Organization-Wide Databases

The example we will use to illustrate the potential power of managing an organization-wide database is an outdoor billboard advertising company. Notice that as we describe this database that the business itself is being described. Any database describes *what* is done, not *how* the business operates. The database shows business policy and rules of operation. We will point out examples of how such policy appears in the description of a database.

Figure 14.6 shows the various data entities and relationships that support a variety of functional areas for the operation of a billboard advertising company. A particular billboard has one or more Panels, a kind of frame on the billboard structure on which one ad can appear (some billboards have one, side-by-side, and/or back-to-back panels). A billboard is physically at some Location, in some geographical Market (usually a city). Frequently the land on which a billboard is located is leased from a farmer or other property owner who permits the construction and use of the billboard. As shown by use of the small circle on

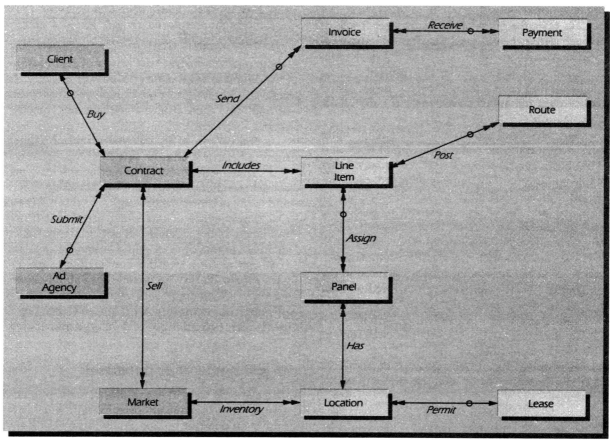

FIGURE 14.6 Billboard Advertiser Database

the Permit relationship near the Lease entity, some Locations do not have a Lease (they are owned by the billboard company).

Billboard rental Contracts are written directly for a Client or submitted through an Ad Agency. Each Line Item included on a Contract is a time-specific rental of some number of panels in a particular Market for the showing of a particular ad. Eventually, specific Panels are assigned for each Line Item. Workers post the paper or painted ads on daily Routes. Based upon a schedule agreed upon in the Contract, Invoices are sent and Payments are received against Invoices. Because this billboard company permits partial payments (many Payments on one Invoice) and a Payment to be applied to many Invoices, Receive is a many-to-many relationship. From this description we can see that this database can support the functions of billing, order entry, (panel) inventory control, lease and property management, posting work scheduling, sales analysis, and others.

Many different applications and queries could be supported from this database. These would include:

- producing invoices, calculating accounts receivables, crediting payments against accounts.
- identifying panels that will be available during certain periods and making sales contacts with previous renters of these panels to encourage new space rentals.
- scanning available panels to find those that match the specifications of a new contract.
- based upon geographical coordinates stored in

location records, determine an optimum routing of trucks for posting new ads that are to begin showing on a particular day.

As with any shared database, a primary benefit is that sales, billing, and other areas can be coordinated with consistent, synchronized data. For example, the sales department can determine, when an ad agency or client submits a new rental contract, the exact status of accounts receivable on that customer. From this information they determine whether to approve the contract immediately or wait for approval to exceed a specified credit limit. Also, a property manager can see the potential sales effect on termination of a lease at a given location. This could be done by analyzing the latest sales figures for past and committed sales on the panels at that location. Phone calls, memos, meetings, business travel, and other forms of costly communication can be avoided by simple inquiries into the shared data resource. The data resource is the glue that holds the organization together.

Efficient and effective coordination of different business functions begins with a foundation of consistent data. Certainly not all organizations can feasibly implement one database for the whole company (although this is quite practical in many small businesses). An organization, however, can develop an organization-wide model of data and then use transfer systems to keep functional area databases synchronized and consistent. The coordination of multiple organizational databases requires a commitment to managing data. The coordination of multiple databases allows business procedures in one area to change without causing problems in other areas of the organization.

DATA MANAGEMENT FUNCTIONS

A student of real estate, personnel, or financial management will be familiar with the basic but essential functions necessary to manage effectively those resources. Figure 14.7 lists the generic functions for managing any business resource, and we briefly overview each of these within the context

Plan	Protect and secure
Source	Account for use
Acquire and maintain	Recover/restore and
Define/describe and	upgrade
inventory	Determine retention
Organize and make	and dispose
accessible	Train and consult for
Control quality and	effective use
integrity	

FIGURE 14.7 Resource Management Functions

of data resource management. An important point to note is that as with land, labor, and capital, every manager is involved, in some way, in almost every one of these functions for data as well.

Plan

Data resource planning (see Chapters 12 and 13) develops a blueprint for data and the relationships between data across business units and functions into the future. As with most plans, there will be a macro-level data plan (typically called an **enterprise data model**) to identify data entities and relationships and more detailed plans to define schedules for the implementation of databases for different parts of this blueprint. The plan says what data are required, where they are used in the business, how they will be used (that is, what they will be used to produce), and how much data is expected. This plan must then be communicated to various other business functions that are involved in aspects of data resource management. For example, computer system capacity planning must be informed of this schedule, along with data and processing volumes, so that adequate computer and network technology can be in place to operate and access these databases.

Source

Decisions must be made about the most timely and highest quality source for each data element required. For example, should customer sales data be collected at point-of-sale or entered later?

Concerns over error rates, frequency of changes, chance of lost paper documents, technology costs, training requirements, and many other factors will influence this decision. Also, for data to be acquired from sources external to the organization, the quality, cost, and timeliness of these sources need to be considered. For example, different market research organizations may collect competitive sales data from retail outlets or telephone surveys. The original source, the reliability of the data, the timing of when the data are needed and when they were collected, precision and detail collected, and other factors should be checked in selecting an external data source.

Acquire and Maintain

Once the best sources for data are identified and selected, data capture systems can be built to acquire and maintain these data. Changes in data need to be broadcast to all databases that store these data. Users of the data need to know when the data are refreshed and possibly automatically informed of exceptional conditions (such as inventory stockout, stock price below a critical level, or receipt of an especially large customer order). Management systems need to be built to track data acquisition and transfer. For example, sup-

pose magnetic tapes of customer list data are sent to telemarketing vendors for a promotional campaign, and results are returned by magnetic tape. A physical distribution system is needed to confirm that all tapes were sent and received, that all customers on the list were called, and that a status is received on each.

Define/Describe

A basic step in managing any resource is defining what it is that you are managing. If you are a real estate manager, each property must be described, standards and scales must be set to define the size and shape of each building and parcel, and terminology must be defined to refer to different pieces of each building. Similarly, in data resource management each data entity, data element, and relationship must be defined, a format for storage and reporting set up, and the organization of the data described so users can know how to access the data. Basically, a data inventory must be maintained, usually using a data dictionary/directory, or data repository. This is where all data definitions and descriptions are kept, volume statistics on data are maintained, and other data about data (such as access rights and integrity rules) are stored. All users can go to the data dictionary to find out what data exist and what the data mean.

Organize and Make Accessible

Databases need to be designed so that data can be retrieved and reported efficiently and in the format required by business processes. Data should be arranged and stored so that information can be produced from it responsively. Although most of the work here is rather technical, this physical arrangement of data cannot be done unless potential uses of the data are well-defined, and this is best done by business managers. Two aspects of data usage need to be known for proper organization—what data are required and how the data are to be selected. For example, database designers need to know if customer data are to be selected by their unique name or code or if customer data will be selected by markets, geographical regions, what products they have bought, through what sales staff they buy, or other criteria. Orders of magnitude improvements in processing speed can be achieved when the data organization is well-tuned to the processing requirements. Of course, significant reductions in the cost to maintain data and to do data processing can similarly be achieved by wise choices for database designs.

Control Quality and Integrity

As with employee certification, audits of financial records, and tests for hazardous materials or structural defects in buildings, quality and integrity controls must be placed on the data resource. The concept of application independence implies that such controls must be stored as part of the data definitions and enforced during data capture and maintenance. In addition, periodic checks of databases will be made as part of the audit of financial records. Thus, the activities of EDP auditing are included in this function.

Protect and Secure

The rights each manager has to each kind of data must be defined. Privileges for use of data might include definition, retrieval, insertion, deletion, update, and retrieval of the datum by itself or in combination with other values. For example, you might be permitted to see the salaries of everyone in your department, but might not be able to match names with salaries. Privileges might be assigned to programs, databases, files, individual records or data elements, terminals, and workstations. Use of other equipment, data, and programs might be limited by time of day or days of the week. The decision on who has the right to do what with data is a delicate balance of two factors. The first factor is the need to protect the quality and integrity of data, by protecting a valuable asset from damage or theft. The second is the rights of individuals to have easy access to the data they need in their jobs. Because security is so important and can be dysfunctional if done improperly, security should be considered when databases and application systems are originally built and not developed as an afterthought.

Account for Use

Because there is considerable cost to capture, maintain, and report data, these costs must be identified and an accounting system developed to report these costs. Further, an organization may choose to distribute these costs to appropriate responsibility centers. Two conditions make accounting for the use of data especially difficult, compared to other resources. First, frequently an organizational unit responsible for acquiring data is not the primary user of the data; and second, usage is shared because data are not consumed from usage. The actual costs of computer disk storage and computer processing time can be captured by the operating system and database management systems. The real issue is to develop a fair chargeback scheme that promotes good management of data and does not deter beneficial use. Because the value of data is so elusive, the linkage of readily identifiable costs to value is difficult. At least the costs for data storage and processing and who uses what data can be determined. This should be separated from how to charge to recover these costs. (The general issue of IS chargeback methods will be addressed in Chapter 15.)

Recover/Restore and Upgrade

When a property becomes old or damaged, it is often renovated and put back into operation. When an employee's skills become obsolete because of new technology or methods, the employee is trained for the new environment. The same is true with organizational data. When a database is damaged because of some hardware or software malfunction, procedures must be in place to restore the database to a clean and uncontaminated condition. Usually, periodic backup copies of the database will be made and an electronic log kept of updates to the database, so the restoration can happen quickly. The user-manager must anticipate what needs to be done in the business when a database is not accessible because of a recovery or upgrading that temporarily takes the database out of action. In addition, the business manager must be able to determine what wrong actions or decisions might have been taken from the bad data

370

and correct these before they cause excess costs or other problems for the business. For example, if an inventory file has been inaccurately changed and inventory replenishment orders have been written, an inventory control manager would immediately have to analyze if work, purchase, or expedited orders should be recalled.

Determine Retention and Dispose

Data are not useful forever, and business managers must decide, on legal and other grounds, how much data history needs to be kept. Some data need to be kept in active databases, while other data can be archived to magnetic tape to be used only if needed. Eventually, data should be summarized and/or eliminated. Keeping data too long not only is costly in terms of storage space, but the use of out-of-date data can also bias forecasts and other analyses.

Train and Consult for Effective Use

Just because data exist, they will not necessarily be effectively used. What data are stored in databases, what they mean, what presentation systems report these data, and how they can be accessed in ad hoc ways all have to be explained to managers who might want to use the data. This training might include review of the contents of the corporate data dictionary, with an emphasis on a particular user group (for example, consumer marketing), or the training might be on how to use a fourth-generation language to access a database for decision support.

MANAGING DOCUMENT AND TEXTUAL DATA

A manager has many potential sources for data. A modern organization has many internal systems that manage and support access to a wide variety of data. Besides the various data and information record processing systems (such as those depicted earlier), there are office automation and document management systems that manage textual data,

such as memos and reports. Office automation systems (see Chapter 2) frequently contain document filing components that permit memos, correspondence, reports, charts, meeting agenda and minutes, and other word-processed matter to be retrieved. Such retrieval might be by key words assigned to these documents, by sender or receiver name, by date or subject, or even by a more complicated analysis of the content of documents.

New technology called **text data management systems (TDMS)** are making the management of textual data more convenient. Systems such as AskSAM, ZyINDEX, and FYI 3000 support rapid searches of documents. Suppose you have received the transcript (on floppy disk) of a litigation involving hazards from a material your firm uses in its manufacturing process. First, you would have the TDMS index the document, a one-time step, which builds references to the words in the transcript. Then, you could pose any of a variety of key word searches (for example, clean-up AND cost NOT asbestos) to locate relevant passages in the text (in this example, words that deal with the cost to rid a site of hazardous materials, except asbestos, which is not of concern to you). Searches can involve many documents. Identified text can then be marked and sent to a word processor where you are preparing a summary of the case.

Public Databases

Also available are public databases that contain news, financial, research, and market data that can be accessed from a workstation on a manager's desk. Three distinct types of organizations are involved in the database business. First, there are suppliers of databases. Such organizations as Mead Data Central produce a series of legal, medical, and general news data banks. Some of these can be purchased on floppy diskette or CD-ROM, and others are available through the second type of organization, on-line information brokers. Second, information brokers include such services as Dow Jones News/Retrieval, Dialog Information Services, Prodigy, and CompuServe. Their services provide historical as well as current data concerning such topical areas as stock and commodity prices, competitor product announcements, market demographics, and research discoveries. The information broker (or utility) provides a single access, via a desktop terminal or personal computer, to a smorgasbord of separate databases from different suppliers. The third type of organization involved is a telecommunications firm (such as Telenet and Tymnet) that provide local telephone numbers (for a fixed hourly connect charge) into different services.

The cost for an on-line database includes the costs for the desktop equipment and software, usually a flat rate per hour connect fee (depending on time of day), a surcharge applied to some databases for each search or for unlimited access per month, data storage space, "postage" for electronic mail, and special charges for premium services.

Using one of the information broker services and a desktop workstation (terminal or personal computer, modem, communications software, and telephone line), a manager can, through a series of electronic searches:

- see a news item announcing a new product by a startup company.
- retrieve financial reports on the firm (if publicly held).
- access patent and other research data about it and competitors.

- send electronic mail to an executive in the company requesting an appointment to discuss exclusive rights to the product.
- book an airline reservation to meet with the executive.

All of this can happen in minutes or a few hours. Andrew C. Gross (1988) refers to this capability as the "information vending machine."

Table 14.1 contains a synopsis of some of the major on-line databases and services. A comprehensive inventory is periodically published by Cuadra Associates, Inc., of Santa Monica, California (*Directory of Online Databases*).

Some of these services can be customized to the individual user, so essentially automatic messages are sent when specified events occur. For example, CompuServe's Executive Option offers stock activity and financial information on selected corporations and display of news on specified topics. Also, many of these services can also download data to the desktop personal computer, where this information could then be included in a spreadsheet for analysis or a memo for distribution.

TABLE 14.1 Synopsis of Popular On-line Databases

Service	Sample Data and Other Services Provided
Mead Data Central	LEXIS, NEXIS, and MEDIS— abstracts of legal, news, and medical information
Dow Jones News/Retrieval Service	Historical stock quotes, corporate information, business articles; *Wall Street Journal* highlights and full text; official airline guide; college selection service; electronic mail; MCI Mail
Dialog Information Service	Abstracts and full-text articles on science, technology, business, and medicine
CompuServe Information Service	On-line shopping; general reference; special interest group bulletin boards; news, sports, and weather news wire; official airline guide; on-line magazines

One additional note is that providing information (as suggested in Chapter 3) can be a profitable product for many organizations. For example, providing a catalog of your products in an "electronic mall" could help you reach new customers. Data that you collect as part of your normal business operations, say on deposits of natural resources or on the chemical properties of nonproprietary materials you use, might be valuable to others. You could sell them via an electronic service or by distribution of floppy diskette or CD-ROM technology. You might also provide programs to display and analyze these data, which would add more value to the consumer of these data. Melissa Data Company of San Juan Capistrano, California, is one broker of such database media.

THE OWNERSHIP OF DATA

Managers can become very possessive of data, for varying reasons:

- The need to protect personal privacy.
- The need to protect trade secrets.
- The requirement to allow only those with a need to know to see sensitive business plans.
- The desire to promote internal competition and to justify the use of scarce resources.
- The desire to promote commitment to and ownership of one's job.
- The desire to use "information as power" for political gain.

This is both good and bad. A commitment to quality data, cost control of data management, and use of data for strategic advantage are essential for obtaining the greatest benefits from managing the data resource. On the other hand, a possessiveness about data can stifle data sharing, which can limit access to data (and, hence, reduce the ability to answer important business questions) and increase data processing costs for the whole enterprise. The culture about data must be managed as part of data resource management.

A **corporate information policy** is the foundation for managing the ownership of data. Figure 14.8 contains an information policy statement similar to ones that have been adopted by many organizations. This policy would be signed usually by both the CEO and the CIO (chief information officer) and would be socialized to all managers through decentralized announcements and staff meetings. Such a policy states that each manager has responsibility for managing data as a resource for the good of the whole enterprise, not just the gain of his area. Some policies will provide a generic way to distinguish classes of data—such as personal, departmental, and organizational—although the trend is to make all data organizational. The responsibilities a manager has for personal, departmental, or organizational data will differ and would be outlined in the policy.

An example that gets to the heart of clarifying what is personal, departmental, or organizational data would be the planning of a new promotion of a product. A promotion would be for a particular (or set of) product(s), in a particular geographical or customer-type market, using certain channels (such as direct mail or telemarketing), and funded from some promotional budget. In total, product, market, channel, financial, data processing, and possibly other managers and departments will eventually have to get involved in this promotion. Any one of these might initiate the idea for this promotion. The information policy issue asks when should the idea and preliminary plans of the

Corporate Information Policy

Data are an enterprise resource. Excellence in data quality and management are key to achieving the mission and goals of our organization. Data management is key to our competitive advantage. Because of the central role of the data as a resource, the following policy statements should be understood by each employee:

Data will be shared internally. Data are not owned by a particular individual or unit, but by the enterprise. Data will be accessible to all authorized employees and systems.

Data are an organizational resource. Data organization and structure will be planned at all levels of the business. Data use will be governed through data stewardship principles that support organizational goals.

Data quality will be actively managed. Explicit criteria for data accuracy, availability, accessibility, and ease of use will be written for all classes of data. Active programs of data quality improvement will be implemented in all units of the organization.

Data will be safeguarded. Data will be protected from deliberate or unintentional alteration, destruction, or disclosure in accordance with established guidelines.

Data will be defined. Standards will be developed to define and describe data. Review processes will be established to assure the completeness and organization-wide applicability of these definitions.

Data will be organized. Databases will be established to satisfy broad enterprise functions, not organizational units. The physical implementation of databases will be based on a logical design and will support the use of data in functional areas.

Goals

Through active data planning, organization, and control, we will:

Maintain a leadership position for our organization in the management of data.

Implement databases that lead to consistent, reliable, and accessible data across the organization.

Be known among our customers, competitors, and associates for excellent data quality and security, and gain their trust and confidence from such data management.

Responsibilities

Every enterprise employee is responsible for implementing and ensuring compliance with this policy and initiating corrective action if needed. Each business unit head is specifically responsible for:

Communicating this data policy to each employee.

Establishing specific goals, objectives, and action plans to implement the data policy and track compliance with the progress in these areas.

Developing data resource plans that support cost effective development of information systems and that satisfy organizational data requirements.

Providing education and training in data management principles to all employees.

Ensuring that each employee makes appropriate use of data and has access to the data he or she needs.

Signed:

_____

Chief Executive Officer

_____

Chief Information Officer

FIGURE 14.8 Sample Corporate Information Policy

promotion be communicated to the other parties? What if different managers are planning similar promotions? What if a market manager is trying to limit promotions because he is concerned about advertising saturation in that market? Without a clear understanding of the point at which a promotion plan becomes shared data, there may be conflict and wasted efforts and resources, but managers should be able to play and experiment with ideas without the organizational machinery rolling into action.

International Ownership Issues

As organizations and the markets they serve become more global, of special concern are issues of international regulations, standards, and cultures about data (see Chapter 15). One specific issue is relevant in our discussion of data resource management—regulation of the flow of data across international boundaries.

Transborder data flows are electronic movements of data that cross a country's national boundary for processing, storage, or retrieval of that data in a foreign country. Data are subject to the laws of the exporting country. There is a wide range of legislation across different countries to control transborder data flows. These laws are in place to:

- *prevent economic and cultural imperialism,* including preventing the change of social values (a kind of antipropaganda mentality) and preventing the usurpation of local decisions by multinational headquarters outside the country.
- *protect domestic industry,* including protecting the local computer hardware, software, and services industry.
- *protect individual privacy,* including protecting individual citizens against storage of personal health, employment, and political affiliation data in databases held in foreign countries.
- *foster international trade,* including measures to make the flow of data easy during desirable international trade and to promote the exporting of information technology and services.

Mechanisms to control transborder data flows include tariffs, ministries of telecommunication and trade to formulate and implement poli-cies, and formal application processes for conducting data processing activities in the country. Often, no one administrative body has overall authority, and there is very little similarity of mechanisms from country to country. International standards bodies on data communications, programming languages, and electronics help to reduce many operational problems, but policy matters still have to be negotiated, often separately with each country.

DATA ADMINISTRATION
....

To better manage data, many organizations have created a unit to lead the efforts in data resource management. Typically this group is called **data administration,** although other terms may be used. This group might report as a staff unit to the IS director or to the head of systems development. Data administration has both operational and planning responsibilities. Data administration helps to design databases to make them efficient for the processing requirements. It works with systems analysts, designers, and users to identify future databases and database technology requirements. Members of the data administration group include both technical and managerial people, often with extensive experience and with considerable respect throughout general and information systems management.

What is important is that the data administration group be a high-level function with responsibility for determining or coordinating data resource management from policy to implementation. A purely technical group, geared to optimization of database structures, is insufficient to deal with the outlined management issues.

The objectives of the data administration group are to:

- *promote and control data sharing.* Basically, this means to encourage all business units to define data and to increase the use of common sources of data for different systems. It also includes working to determine the appropriate ownership for each kind of data and the responsibilities data owners should have to manage for quality data.

- *analyze the impact of changes to programs when data definitions change.* The application independence concept cannot be fully achieved, so some evolution and change to databases requires programming modifications; a schedule of which systems need to be changed and when must be developed considering the needs of all database users.
- *maintain the data dictionary.* When a data dictionary is started, data administration must clean up existing data definitions and write definitions for those that do not exist; and as new data are added or unclear definitions, insufficient formats, and so on are identified, the dictionary needs to be changed.
- *reduce redundant data and processing.* This responsibility includes not only dropping unnecessary copies of data and programs that maintain them, but also helping to synchronize purposefully redundant copies and managing data distributed across the various computer systems within the organization (ranging from mainframe to desktop).
- *reduce system maintenance costs and improve development productivity.* This comes from not only reducing redundant data and programs but also from creating database organizations that are easy to use, selecting database technology that reduces the amount of programming, and training database analysts and programmers in the most current methods.
- *improve quality and security of data.* This is frequently a coordinating role, helping business managers to define data quality standards and to set security clearances and working with data center operations to implement these guidelines.

Within the overall data administration function, two distinct roles have emerged—database administration and data stewardship. **Database administration** (or **DBA**) is responsible for computerized databases and may actually be placed in a technical unit along with staff that supports various system software and hardware. DBA is concerned with:

- tuning database management systems.
- selection and evaluation of and training on database technology.
- physical database design.

DATA RESOURCE ACCOUNTABILITY

A recent report describes numerous examples of incorrect pricing at reputable retail and supermarket chains that use bar-code scanners. The stores had failed to maintain concurrency between shelf prices and database prices. The net result was numerous fines (some nearly $500,000) and an estimate of $2.5 billion in overcharges to the public. What caused the difficulty was poor accountability for the data resource. Data stewardship is a *required*, not an optional component of information resource management.

(Adapted from English, 1993)

- design of methods to recover from damage to databases.
- physical placement of databases on specific computers and storage devices.
- the interface of databases with telecommunications and other technologies.

A **data steward** is a business manager who, in addition to his normal duties, is responsible for, and held accountable for, the quality and viability of a particular data entity or subject area (for example, customer, product, bill, or employee) and the data associated with it. The data architecture of an organization (see Chapter 12) outlines the major data entities, and a data steward would be assigned for each. A data steward coordinates all database and program changes that deal with the entity for which he is responsible, and a data steward initiates quality improvement programs for this data. However, a data steward is not the data's owner; the owner is the enterprise.

A data steward has a major role in setting up data integrity rules, data names and definitions, and security guidelines. A data steward may also lead the effort to create so-called subject area databases around each entity. For example, the customer data steward might organize a managerial or strategic information base useful in tracking customer demographics, buying behavior, sales contacts, and service/repair history.

Although there are different types of data stewards, according to English (1993), typical

376

data stewards also carry out the following tasks:

- develop or review models of data for their subject areas.
- establish data quality standards for data in their areas.
- grant access rights to data under their authority.
- maintain official tables of codes (product, region, customer type) used with data in their areas.

There is often a forum or council of data stewards that meets periodically to coordinate efforts, resolve the inevitable boundary disputes over who controls what data, and coordinate cross-area standards.

A major benefit of data stewardship is that anyone in the organization has only one place to go to handle a data issue. One of the authors of this book worked with an organization that maintained seventeen different customer code tables, each in a different business unit. After creation of a data stewardship program, there was only one code table. Further, other business units could not create new customer codes without clearance by the customer data steward. The steward fostered teamwork, business process reengineering (see Chapter 7), and more rapid and consistent responses to organizational change.

The goal is to anticipate organizational needs for data and to promote sharing of critical data. Usually a data steward comes from a business unit that is the source for or is the primary user of the data and, hence, has the best organizational understanding of the meaning and uses of the data.

Data stewardship is a challenging role, in part because it is a significant departure from the processing control of data and systems of the past. Data administration must ensure, from its position and by what it does, that data center operations, programmers, systems designers, and database administrators, as well as data stewards, all work together. Each must have a clear and recognized role. Each must work at being sensitive to the objectives and backgrounds of each other. See English (1993) for a more complete description of the role of a data steward.

METHODS AND TOOLS FOR MANAGING DATA

In this section we overview the most common methods and tools used by data stewards, administrators, and systems analysts for describing and managing data. As responsibilities for managing the data resource are distributed to the business units, these topics become important to all managers.

Data Planning and Modeling

Data planning and modeling involve both a methodology and a notation. The methodology involves the steps that are followed to identify and describe organizational data entities, and the notation is a way to show, usually graphically, these findings. First, several possible methodologies are discussed, and then a notation (called entity-relationship diagrams) is described.

The role of data planning as part of IS planning and architecture is outlined in Chapters 12 and 13. In practice, two rather different approaches are followed—one top-down, called enterprise modeling, and one bottom-up, called view integration. Many organizations choose to do both because they are complementary methods that emphasize different aspects of data and, hence, check and balance each other.

Enterprise data planning and modeling, which is based on information engineering (see Finkelstein, 1989), involves describing the organization and its data requirements at a very high level, independent of particular reports, screens, or any detailed descriptions of data processing requirements. First, the organization would be divided into approximately fifteen processes (such as selling, billing, manufacturing, and servicing). Each of these functions would then be further divided into about seven processes, and each process into about seven activities. An activity would be rather general and high level (for example, "forecast sales for next quarter"). This three-level decomposition of the business is depicted in Figure 14.9.

Given a rough understanding of each activity, a list of data entities is assigned to each (for

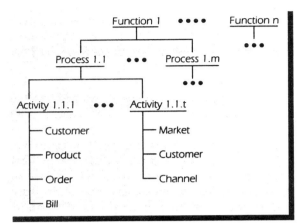

FIGURE 14.9 Enterprise Decomposition for Data Modeling

example, quarterly forecasting activity might have the entities product, customer order history, and work center associated with it). The lists of entities are then checked to make sure that consistent names are used and the meaning of each entity is clear. Finally, based on general business policies and rules of operation, relationships between the entities are identified and a database chart, called a **corporate data model,** is drawn (see Figure 14.6). Priorities are set for what parts of the corporate data model are in need of greatest improvement, and more detailed work (for the data stewards) is defined to describe these more clearly and to revise databases accordingly.

Enterprise modeling has the advantage of not being biased by a lot of details, current databases and files, or how the business actually operates today. It is future-oriented and should identify a comprehensive set of generic data requirements. On the other hand, it can be incomplete or inaccurate because it may ignore some important details. This is where the view integration approach can help.

In **view integration,** each report, computer screen, form, document, and so on to be produced from organizational databases is identified (usually starting from what is done today). Each of these is called a user view. The data elements in each user view are identified, and put into a basic structure called normal form. Normal form is a set of rules that yield a data model that is very stable and useful across many different requirements. In fact, normal form rids data of troublesome anomalies, and databases can evolve with very few changes to the parts that have already been developed and populated.

After each user view has been normalized, they are all combined (or integrated) into one comprehensive description. Ideally, this integrated set of entities from normalization will match those from enterprise modeling, but almost always this is not the case because of the different focuses (top-down and bottom-up) of the two approaches. Therefore, the enterprise and view-integrated data models are reconciled and a final data model is developed.

Concerns with Data Modeling Methods

These data planning and modeling methods are neither simple nor inexpensive to conduct. They require considerable time, organizational commitment, and the assignment of very knowledgeable managers and data specialists. According to Goodhue, Quillard, and Rockart (1988) and Hoffer, Michaele, and Carroll (1989), various pitfalls have to be overcome by a contingency approach customized to the needs of each organization.

An approach to dealing with these pitfalls centers around choosing how to focus on data planning and modeling. These choices concern:

Objective of data modeling: The modeling effort must be justified by some overriding need, such as coordination of operational data processing, flexibility to access data, or effectiveness of data systems.

Scope of data modeling: This concerns the coverage or span of control for a data model; such choices as corporate-wide, division, 80/20 rule of emphasizing particular high-impact needs, and targeting a particularly important or willing business function (for example, selling) are common.

Outcome of data modeling: This deals with the product or deliverable after data modeling is complete; choices here include a subject area database definition (for example, all data about customers), identification of common data capture systems to be shared by several departments (replacing separate databases today), managerial and strategic databases (see Figure 14.1) and access services to support the information needs of these levels of management, and a more nebulous architecture for future databases.

Timing of data modeling: This addresses when to do detailed data modeling studies. It is possible, for example, to do only a high-level data model (with just major data categories), and then fill in details as major systems projects are undertaken. This more evolutionary approach may be more practical, but must be done within the context of an initial overall, general enterprise data model.

Data modeling represents a struggle to resist making short-term fixes to systems and databases. A manager simply wants access to needed data, so why not just add a few more fields and reports to "my system." Unless data management changes are made, however, the inconsistencies and excessive costs will consume the integrity and viability of the data resource.

It should be clear that data planning and modeling is not an issue of centralized versus decentralized control. In fact, the data administration management approach (with database administrators and data stewards) emphasizes placing decision-making power in the hands of those most knowledgeable about data. Some managers (both general and MIS), however, will resist data planning and modeling because they sense a loss of influence. In fact, the result will be more influence over those issues where there is local concern and expertise.

Data Modeling Notation We have used pictures or diagrams to describe organizational databases, but the form used so far has been simple, that is, it has allowed us to show the essence without too much special notation. Today there is an emphasis on modeling as much of the meaning, or semantics, of data as is necessary in order to capture unambiguously the true nature of data. These semantics come from business rules that define the nature of the business. A business rule

would state, for example, whether an employee can exist without being assigned to some department. The most popular notational form used for data modeling is called **entity-relationship (ER) diagramming**.

The original notation was developed in 1976 and has been expanded several times since then to what is now called the extended entity-relationship (EER) form. Several computer-aided software engineering (CASE) products include ER or EER diagramming. Because these diagrams are used so frequently to communicate between a database analyst and users, user-managers need to know how to interpret such charts.

The EER notation uses four symbols, along with lines that connect these symbols together:

Figure 14.10 illustrates the use of this notation. This EER diagram depicts the salesperson contact history and tracking database of Figure 14.4. A "crow's foot" notation shows the type of relationship (for example, Location is one-to-many from Region to Customer, and Status is many-to-many). There are two subclasses of Customers—Prospective and Contacted. Only Contacted Customers participate in the Contacted relationship and have a Purchasing Agent Name data element; all types of customers have Customer ID and Customer Name data elements. Many-to-many relationships, like Status, may also have associated data elements (in this case, a result indicator that specifies the outcome of the contact on that product). The small circles on the lines

from relationship diamonds to entity rectangles are used to indicate that no contacts might be made for a product and that a contact might not concern any particular product. A data element name in an oval is underlined to indicate that datum is a unique identifier for each instance of that entity (for example, Customer ID distinguishes one customer from another).

Database Management Systems

Database management systems (DBMSs) were described in Chapter 5, but two additional points related to data resource management need to be discussed—standards and distributed database management.

DBMS Standards Today the most popular type of DBMS used to develop new systems is relational. In addition, most products use a version of a standard language called SQL for defining and processing data.

A **relational DBMS** allows each entity of the data model to be viewed as a simple table, with the columns as the data elements and the rows as different instances of the entity. Also, simple and high-level relational query languages make programming much simpler than with other types of

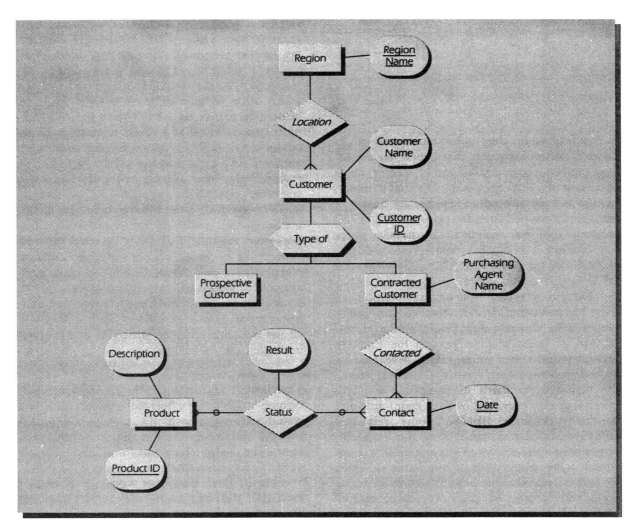

FIGURE 14.10 Salesperson Contact History and Tracking EER Diagram

380

DBMSs (which often used third-generation programming languages). The real power of these systems comes from being able to retrieve easily related data from multiple tables, an operation called a join. Refer to the example in the section on Database Programming in Chapter 5 to see how this is done in SQL.

A special kind of relational system follows a "what you see is what you get" format called **query-by-example (QBE)**. In the QBE format, the manager can simply visually show what data he wants to see. Suppose we wanted to see the customer name and contact date of all customers contacted on April 5, 1994. This query in QBE format would be:

In this format, the data to be displayed is simply checked on the templates that appear on a manager's screen. The restriction for the specific date is entered in the DATE column. The data elements used to join the two tables together are shown by example values of 123 in the two CUSTOMERID columns. QBE has become a very popular query interface and is available in some form in dBASE IV, R:BASE for DOS, PARADOX, SQL/DS, and DB2.

Not all relational systems are identical, so there has been considerable effort to standardize on one style (allowing each DBMS vendor to concentrate on extra features beyond the standard and on performance issues). **SQL**, developed by the independent (of any particular vendor) American National Standards Institute, is a standard query language prevalent in both mainframe and personal computer DBMSs. Some relational DBMSs have been designed from this standard; others permit users to work either with SQL commands or the original set of commands designed for that system. This standard allows an organization to transfer training, experience, and programs more easily between DBMSs, to more easily con-

vert from one DBMS to another, and to make it easier to have a mix of DBMSs without duplicating support groups.

A relatively recent trend is to make the DBMS (using SQL as the standard) a kind of engine on which other support software is built. This can be done by putting the DBMS into a separate computer processor, called a **database machine** or **database server**, or by having system and application software refer to a software DBMS in SQL. For example, the latest version of the IBM personal computer operating system, OS/2, includes an SQL-based DBMS engine that handles the manipulation of data, so DBMS and other software vendors (for example, electronic spreadsheet) can concentrate on issues of user interface, not data management. This standardization of data management functions will hopefully make it easier to share data across different applications and decision support system generators because they will all use the same database structures and processing logic from the engine.

Distributed Databases The second issue concerning database management systems and data resource management is the management of **distributed databases**. Any organization that has been using computer systems for at least ten years probably has developed many separate databases. Frequently, these databases would be physically located on different computer systems. For example, different divisions may have their own data centers, or there may be separate factory and administrative support data centers. Can technology be used to help manage data distributed across different computers?

The answer is, to some limited degree, yes. First, all data can be described in one central, consolidated data dictionary. Many data dictionary systems explicitly support a location designation for each kind of data. From this central repository, data administrators can ensure that the same definitions, formats, integrity rules, security clearances, and so on are assigned to the same data across all computer systems. Even redundant data can be so identified, to the point of recognizing alias names for the same data in different databases.

Second, and more problematic, when the computer systems on which the databases are stored are electronically linked via a data network, then, under some circumstances, data can be conveniently retrieved without being concerned with where they are physically located in the network. Today, to accomplish this location transparency, a single DBMS technology must be established across the organization. Although in the planning stages by several vendors, it is not readily possible today to allow such transparent access in a mixed DBMS vendor environment. Obviously, if an organization could standardize on one DBMS vendor, such distributed database access would be possible. The inertia of managing separate databases independently in the past and the large installed base of data under separate technologies, however, does not make this feasible in the short term for many firms. The trend to a common database engine might help to make this a reality sooner than previously expected.

Data Dictionary/Directory

Very simply, a data dictionary/directory, or DD/D, is a central repository or encyclopedia of data definitions and important usage description. A DD/D is a database about data. Sometimes the DD/D is accessible by a DBMS, in which case it is called an active DD/D. An active DD/D is a common source for data definitions for database software, system developers, and system users.

A DD/D contains a definition of each entity, relationship, and data element of a database. It also retains descriptions of the display format, integrity rules, security restrictions, volume and sizes, physical location, and a list of the programs that use these data.

A DD/D is invaluable to database analysts and users. For example, a marketing manager could query the DD/D to find out what kinds of data are kept in a database about customer market segmentation. By using key words that were assigned to each data definition and by scanning data descriptions, the DD/D would develop a list of data elements that deal with this topic. Users can then determine which of these are most relevant to their needs and then develop queries or report requests to the proper databases to retrieve these data. In a sense, a DD/D acts as a card catalog to the data library. The DD/D is also valuable to assess the impact of planned changes to databases (for example, if we are considering changing the meaning of a data element, what databases need to be modified to reflect this). Physical database designers also use the DD/D to find statistics about data volume, size, and usage needs in order to design efficient data organizations.

Ideally, an organization would acquire a DD/D before or at the same time as its first DBMS, but this is not usually the case. As mentioned earlier, many of the responsibilities of database administrators and data stewards can be facilitated by a DD/D. In fact, not having a DD/D makes it so difficult to coordinate the evolution of databases that it is more likely that independent and inconsistent databases will arise when no DD/D is used. Although a manual DD/D can be used, these are quite insufficient in most circumstances. A DD/D is one of the soundest investments that can be made toward achieving the goals of data resource management.

SUMMARY

The data resource is an organizational asset that must be explicitly and professionally managed, as we manage other assets. This management requires a combination of efforts by data resource specialists and every manager. We will discuss in the next chapter how organizations manage the information systems function as a whole; of course, data resource management is only one part of this total management system—but a very important part.

We have illustrated that organizational data can be described unambiguously in business terms using a blueprint, which we call a data model. Personal, departmental, and organizational data can all be described using this type of graphical model. Being able to interpret such diagrams is essential to communicating a manager's needs for data and for understanding database contents.

An important distinction has been made between three types of data management systems, those that capture, transfer, or present data. It was argued that this separation of data management functions leads to greater flexibility, longer life for some systems and the ability to easily dispose of others, and the benefits of greater sharing of data.

Access to both external and internal data is necessary for many managers. A public database industry has available a wide variety of economic, market, news, research, travel, weather, and other data. Some decision support software supports the downloading of data from these services into spreadsheets, financial models, and other environments. As the information vending machine industry becomes more sophisticated, managers will find it more convenient to access these external sources of data and will find new business opportunities from selling nonproprietary data via such services.

We also reviewed the important position of data administration in an organization. This management effort, which combines technical expertise with organizational savvy, takes the leadership in managing the data resource. In many organizations today, data administration includes a specific role for each user-manager and distributed responsibilities for stewards of major data entities. Rather than considering data to be under the control of some central and technical authority, organizations now recognize the diverse expertise needed to manage the data resource.

REVIEW QUESTIONS

1. What is a data model? What does it contain?
2. Why do organizations often have several databases?
3. Define application independence.
4. Who is a data steward and what does one do?
5. What are the basic functions of managing the data resource?
6. Briefly outline some international issues related to data resource management.
7. What are the objectives of data administration?
8. What is a corporate data model and how is it used?
9. Why are relational database management systems so popular?
10. Are distributed databases a reality today? Why or why not?
11. Explain the significance of "disposable systems" as described in this chapter.

DISCUSSION QUESTIONS

1. Why do some managers resist managing data as an organizational resource? What does an individual manager have to gain or lose from data resource management?
2. By distinguishing between data capture, transfer, and analysis and presentation systems, what capabilities for systems management are possible?
3. What are the different kinds of data standards and why are these an essential part of data resource management?
4. Consider an organization with which you are familiar. Draw an EER diagram for two related departments and one for the organization as a whole. Discuss the opportunities for data sharing across these departments.
5. Discuss the advantages and disadvantages for an organization of setting the types of data standards listed in Figure 14.3.

6. As a manager of a major business unit, what would you do to implement a corporate information policy, such as the one in Figure 14.8?

7. What are the major differences between the two approaches to data planning and modeling outlined in this chapter—enterprise modeling and view integration? Why do these two methodologies usually yield different results?

8. Discuss the problems or pitfalls of doing data planning and modeling. How can these be alleviated?

9. Discuss the data warehouse analogy used in this chapter and its relationship to the organization of data found in the Owens-Corning Fiberglas case in Chapter 12.

10. Consider the operation of your university's library. Develop an EER data model for this organization. Be careful to clearly represent the policies and rules by which the library operates.

REFERENCES

Betts, Mitch. 1990. "Romancing the segment of one." *Computerworld* 24 (March 5): 63–65.

Cuadra Associates, Inc. 1989. *Directory of On-Line Databases*. Santa Monica, CA: Cuadra Associates, Inc.

English, Larry P. 1993. "Accountability to the rescue." *Database Programming & Design* 6 (June): 54–59.

Finkelstein, Clive. 1989. *An Introduction to Information Engineering*. Reading, MA: Addison-Wesley Publishing Co.

Goodhue, Dale L., Judith A. Quillard, and Jack F. Rockart. 1988. "Managing the data resource: A contingency perspective." *MIS Quarterly* 12 (September): 373–394.

Gross, Andrew C. 1988. "The information vending machine." *Business Horizons* 31 (January/February): 24–33.

Hoffer, Jeffrey A., Stephen J. Michaele, and John H. Carroll. 1989. "The pitfalls of strategic data and systems planning: A research agenda." *Proceedings of the 22nd Annual Hawaii International Conference on System Sciences*: 348–356.

Mahmoud, Essam, and Gillian Rice. 1988. "Database accuracy: Results from a survey of database vendors." *Information & Management* 15: 243–250.

Percy, Tony. 1988. "Unfreezing the vital corporate asset—Information." *Chief Information Officer Journal* 1 (Summer): 38–40.

Sullivan-Trainer, Michael. 1989. "Sharing the wealth: Data becomes community property." *Computerworld* 23 (May 22): 71–76.

Zachman, John A. 1987. "A Framework for information systems architecture." *IBM Systems Journal* 26 (March): 276–292.

9

Indiana State Board of Health

Frank Loogootee, director of the Bureau of Administrative Services for the Indiana State Board of Health, walked across the hall to the office of Darrell Fisher, his MIS director. "Darrell, what's this about a data architecture project I hear you want to do? I thought that new system, IDMS, we bought was going to solve our backlog of requests."

"Frank, from a database standpoint, we are kind of at square one and I want to try to grow an integrated database correctly. My goal is to maximize each system development effort as it comes along, rather than have individual systems and databases exist, isolated by themselves. I need to obtain some efficiencies in systems development. With my limited head count, I can't keep up with the tremendous load of requests for new systems from the division and bureau chiefs.

"As you will recall, Frank, we have been designated as a data capture site for all health information for the state. Because of this and other recent changes, I think that every senior manager at the board sees processing and disseminating information as our primary function. We are in the information business. IDMS is the engine to run our information business. But I need some way to understand what all this means, so that when I get a new system request, I don't have to reinvent a totally new system. In fact, I think that maybe once we get organized, most new system requests might be able to be met simply by writing a few report programs. Now our data is so spread across seven or eight major systems and 30 minor ones that I'm better off going ahead and building a new system each time. I can't continue to do this much longer.

"We continue to use the same data over and over again, but I'm convinced we just give it a different name each time. So, we go ahead and build what we think is a unique system for a unique need. Our new vital records system is a great example. The database for this system, our first major one under IDMS, has data in it from many of our other systems, but we couldn't get a handle on this overlap. So we just went ahead and created a whole new database without a road map."

....

Background

The mission of the Indiana State Board of Health (ISBH) is as follows:

> To promote health and wellness activities, to encourage the prevention of disease, and to administer public health programs that promote the availability, accessibility, and quality of health-care services throughout the state of Indiana.

The ISBH is committed to interagency communication, cooperation, and coordination in pursuit of the health and well-being of the citizens of the state.

As early as 1855, the Indiana State Medical Society, a public interest group, was working to secure a public health and vital statistics law for Indiana. After several failed attempts in the legislature, the ISBH was established in 1875. In 1886 the first conference of Indiana state health officers was held in Indianapolis. This conference outlined the needs for statistics and vital records (for example, birth and death) and for ISBH involvement in many health matters in the state (for example, vaccination, and control of diseases, such as cholera and typhoid fever).

By statute the ISBH operates as the superior health board of the state, to which all other boards (such as county departments of health) are subordinate, but do not necessarily report to the ISBH. The

ISBH holds all the powers necessary to bring legal action for the enforcement of health laws and rules. The ISBH keeps vital statistics and cooperates with other state agencies in the sharing of such statistics. It licenses and certifies medical personnel and many different types of health, agriculture, and food services for the purpose of controlling contamination and the spread of disease. The ISBH is a proactive agency involved not only in the control of health-related activities, but also in the prevention of health problems (see Exhibit 1 for a list of the 1987 ISBH strategic initiatives).

The ISBH organization chart appears in Exhibit 2. The state health commissioner, appointed by the governor, oversees the ISBH and serves as chief public spokesperson for health issues in the state. Three commissions, each composed of several bureaus, which in turn are composed of divisions, manage and operate the various programs, laboratories, planning, certification and licensing, surveying and monitoring, public information and publishing, administration, and vital record activities.

The Bureau of Administrative Services includes the Management Information Services Division (MISD), which provides computing and data processing services to all other divisions. This division provides systems analysis and design, programming, data administration, operations and user support, and network management services. The MISD is separate from the central state data processing department and MIS departments in other state agencies. As of July 1, 1987, the division employed twenty-three staff members (four management, eight technical, two operations, and nine clerical or data entry). The director of the MISD is Darrell Fisher.

Traditionally, ISs at the ISBH have been nonintegrated (that is, separate systems and files for each user division and application), using conventional file management technologies, which has meant excessive data storage and processing, as well as incompatible data. The result has made it difficult and costly to answer questions and deal with management issues that cross divisional boundaries. For example, being able to link activities of the Dairy Division with those in the Nutrition Division is almost impossible. Recently, the ISBH purchased IDMS/R from Cullinet Systems. This database management system with integrated dictionary provides the technological basis to support common data stores on keyboard data entities, such as facilities, programs, and individuals.

The MISD also:

- supports the IBM Professional Office System (PROFS) office automation software.
- is testing the development of a statewide "local health network."
- is establishing an information center to support personal computer usage throughout the board.
- has developed a disaster recovery plan for all computer systems in the ISBH.

EXHIBIT 1
1987 ISBH Strategic Initiatives

- AIDS
- Healthy Choices
- Injury Prevention
- Cancer Prevention
- Caring for the Unhealthy Underserved
- Consumer Protection
- Organ Transplantation
- Immunization
- Partnerships for Public Health

The Data Architecture Project

As Fisher explained the goal of his data architecture project idea to Loogootee:

To me, the goal of the project is to build a tool that will help us in two ways in systems development—to identify the overlap in data utilization and to help us be more productive. I can also use the results of this project as a planning tool to identify gaps for new systems as part of our biannual planning and budgeting process. As part of this planning, we do a general survey, division by division, of their information needs for the next two years. A data architecture will help us relate their requests. This could lead to raising the priorities on individual requests when we can see the synergy of multiple needs, which can be supported from a common set of data.

EXHIBIT 2

Indiana State Board of Health Organizational Chart

The data architecture project was undertaken during May-August 1988, at the initiation of Fisher with the full support of Loogootee. The purpose of the project was to develop an inventory of data requirements (not processing), or a logical data architecture, for the board. This architecture was to be independent of how data was or would be managed by specific technology. The general motivation was to provide the logical view of data needed to deploy a more efficient and functional set of systems for ISBH. The premise was that ISBH, from a data viewpoint, needed three types of information systems:

1. Those that capture and maintain data from the various sources of data to the board (such as certification applications, site surveys of regulated facilities, and population and other socioeconomic data from other state agencies).
2. Those that transfer data between separate databases or download data to personal computers for manipulation and display.
3. Those that analyze and report/present summaries and projections for decision-making and policy-making, as well as operational activities.

The goal was to develop an overall design for managing the ISBH data that would make systems of these different types as independent from one another and as efficient as possible. When a new request for a report would be submitted to the MISD, Fisher wanted to be able to identify if and where the data existed to satisfy this request. When new data had to be captured and maintained, the data architecture would be used to help determine logically where this would fit in the overall set of data maintained by ISBH. When standards or the definition of certain data would be changed, the architecture could be used to evaluate the impact of these changes. Subsequently, when a data architecture would be linked with systems and network architectures, a complete management system would exist for planning and control of all ISs in the ISBH.

Organizing the Project It was decided that current MISD employees could not be freed from other responsibilities to conduct this project. The State Office of Systems Technologies (an advisory group, part of the Data Processing Oversight Commission) had initiated a summer internship program to bring students at Indiana universities into state data processing departments. The long-range goal was to attract more highly trained systems professionals into state government. One such student, Jackie Hamon, a computer science masters candidate at Indiana Uni-

versity–Purdue University at Indianapolis, was chosen from this program to be the principal analyst for this project. Neither the ISBH nor any other state agency had ever conducted such a project. Fisher was uncertain what methodology and documentation notation to use. Jerry Douglass, an IS professor from the Indiana University School of Business with a specialty in data management, was hired to help structure the project, set a work plan, and assist in choosing the methods to be used and the form for presenting the results.

It was also decided early that within the summer internship time period, a data architecture that would cover all divisions could not be developed. Therefore, seventeen high-priority divisions were selected by Fisher and Loogootee for analysis. Hamon interviewed and reinterviewed division heads and other employees, studied operating plans and descriptions of the divisions, and analyzed the data defined in current systems for these divisions.

From this work, information was gathered about the persons, places, and things (data entities) about which information is and needed to be stored. The relationships among these entities were also noted. (Relationships are associations, such as a bureau has many employees or a facility has many inspections.) Five products documenting the data architecture were produced from this analysis:

1. A model or view of data, using the generally accepted extended entity-relationship (EER) notation for each of the seventeen divisions (see Exhibit 3 for a sample of three of these seventeen charts).
2. A consolidated data model using EER notation, showing a unified and consistent view across the whole board (see Exhibit 4).
3. Definitions for each of the data entities, along with the primary key (unique identifying data) for each (see Exhibit 5 for an excerpt).
4. Definitions of each relationship, which describe how the board operates and policies on the data (see Exhibit 6 for an excerpt).
5. A cross-reference chart that shows which divisions create, use (retrieve), update/modify, or delete/archive (a so-called CRUD analysis) the data entities (see Exhibit 7).

....

The Extended Entity-Relationship Notation

Early in the project Douglass, Hamon, and Fisher settled on using the extended entity-relationship notation for pictorially describing the data architecture. Because Fisher planned to acquire one of these

CASE tools soon (possibly one supplied by Cullinet Systems that would work with the IDMS/R product), EER diagraming seemed to be an appropriate choice.

Relationships can exist between a pair of entities (for example, between Grant and Budget) or among three or more entities (for example, Budget, Vehicle, and Employee). For each relationship, besides what entities are connected together, the so-called cardinality must be specified. Relationship can be of cardinality one-to-one, one-to-many, or many-to-many.

For the ISBH, an example of a one-to-one relationship is License-to-Facility (named "Legalizes" in the Bureau of Consumer Protection EER diagram in Exhibit 3), for which there must be a one-to-one match of one license for each facility and vice versa.

Numerous one-to-many relationships exist. One is Division-to-Employee (named "Supervises" in the Bureau of Consumer Protection EER diagram in Exhibit 3), a relationship that indicates that an employee must work in one and only one division, but a division can have many employees.

Also, a large percentage of the ISBH data relationships are many-to-many. An example is Budget-to-Contract/Purchase Order (named "Paid From" in the Bureau of Administrative Services EER diagram in

(text continued on page 601)

EXHIBIT 3
....
ISBH EER Notations

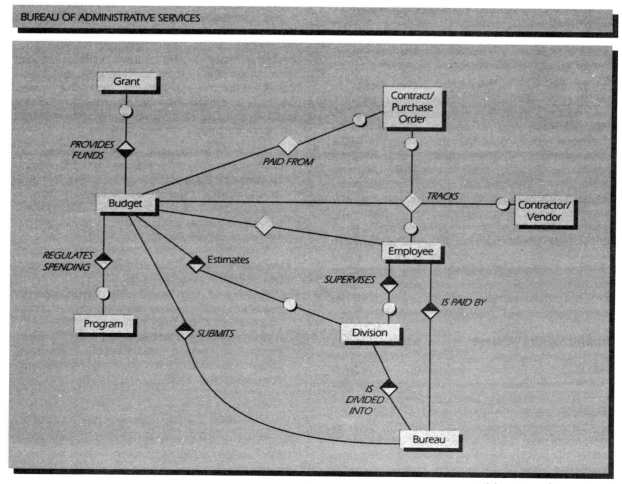

(exhibit continued on next page)

EXHIBIT 3 (continued)

Bureau of Consumer Protection

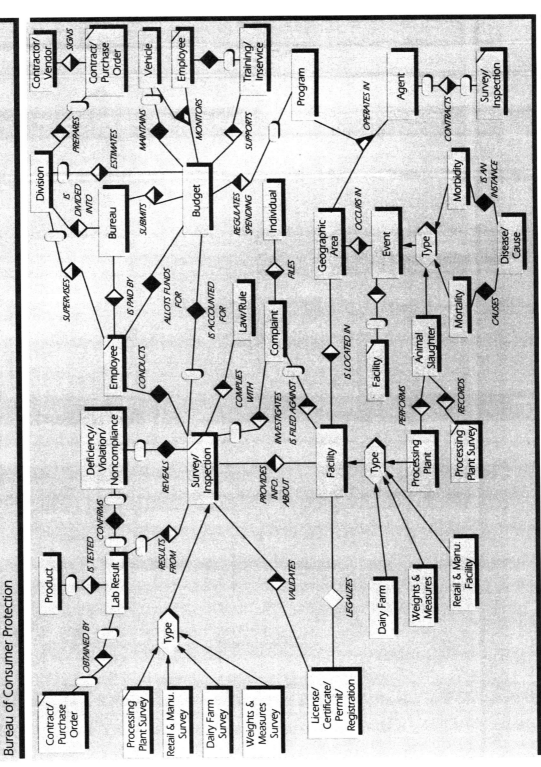

(exhibit continued on next page)

EXHIBIT 3 (continued)

Bureau of Policy Development

EXHIBIT 4
ISBH Composite EER Diagram

EXHIBIT 5

ISBH Entity Definition List

Entity Name	Definition
Agent	Agency or group outside the ISBH that directs a program on the local level. This could be a local health agency, some other such health service location, or a person surveying in a geographical area.
Animal Slaughter	A relative incidence of a slaughter of an animal in a slaughter facility. Used in statistics.
Budget	Information used to estimate the budget for the division or bureau. Includes employee salaries, training fees, in-services, supplies, survey costs, contract allotments, travel expenses, program expenses.
Bureau	A suborganization of the ISBH that directs the activities of one or more divisions within that bureau.
Certificate	Vital records certificate can be one of the following: birth, death, marriage, fetal death, or terminated pregnancy. Certificates are produced by facilities and are recorded in the vital records section of the Bureau of Policy Development.
Class	Course that is certified for aspiring nurses aides and QMAs. Once a student passes this course he or she is ready to take a qualifying exam to become a certified aide.
Complaint	Phoned or written comment about a facility. The complaint is logged and an investigation is conducted if deemed necessary.
Contract/ Purchase Order	Legal agreement or purchase order with a person/company outside the ISBH to receive information or services. Contracts are usually for companies to analyze data from surveys or annual reports. Purchase orders can be for printing, reports, or providing other materials.
Contractor/ Vendor	A person/company hired to do work for the ISBH on a temporary basis under the guidelines of some contract or purchase order.
Deficiency	Aliases: Violation, Noncompliance. A violation of some state or federal law or of a state rule that is discovered in a facility during a survey.
Disease/ Cause	A disease or cause of death. Noted on the birth or death certificate.
Division	Suborganization of a bureau.
Drug Inventory	Inventory of drugs retained in the ISBH for filling prescriptions.

Entity List with Primary Keys

```
PRIMARY KEY
**ENTITY AGENT
AGENT ID
**ENTITY ANIMAL SLAUGHTER
SLAUGHTER ID
**ENTITY BUDGET
DIVISION ID
BUDGET BIENNIUM
PROGRAM ID
GRANT ID
**ENTITY BUREAU
BUREAU ID
**ENTITY CERTIFICATE
CERTIFICATE ID
DATE
**ENTITY CLASS
CLASS NO
```

```
**ENTITY COMPLAINT
INDIVIDUAL ID
FACILITY ID
DATE
**ENTITY CONTRACT/PURCHASE ORDER
CONTRACT NO/ORDER NO
YEAR
**ENTITY CONTRACTOR/VENDOR
CONTRACTOR ID/VENDOR ID
**ENTITY DEFICIENCY
FACILITY ID
DATE
DEFICIENCY CODE
**ENTITY DISEASE/CAUSE
ICDM NO
**ENTITY DIVISION
DIVISION ID
**ENTITY DRUG INVENTORY
INVENTORY NO
```

EXHIBIT 6
ISBH Relationship Definitions and Rules

** Administrative Services

Budget	Allots funds for	Employee	Definition: Each budget allots funds for employee salaries within a bureau or division. Rules: 1. An employee may be associated with more than one budget over a period of several budget periods. 2. A budget may allot funds for more than one employee during the budget period.
Division	Estimates	Budget	Definition: The Division of Finance estimates the amount of money needed for their budget period by recording past usage and estimating future needs. Rules: 1. A budget is associated with only one division. 2. A budget might not be associated with a division, but with a bureau instead. 3. A division may estimate more than one budget.
Bureau	Is divided into	Division	Definition: Each bureau is divided into one or more divisions that are supervised by a bureau director. Rules: 1. Each division is associated with only one bureau. 2. Each bureau may have more than one division.
Employee	Is paid by	Bureau	Definition: An employee is paid from the budget of a bureau or indirectly through the Budget of a division in that bureau. Rules: 1. An employee may be associated with only one bureau at any time. 2. A bureau may have more than one employee asssociated with it at any time.
Contract/ Purchase order	Paid from	Budget	Definition: A contract or purchase order is paid out of a bureau's budget. Rules: 1. A budget may only be associated with one bureau.
Division	Supervises	Employee	Definition: An employee is supervised in the division in which he/she works. Rules: 1. An employee might not be associated with a division (e.g., the bureau director) 2. If an employee is associated with a division, then he can be associated with only one division at a given time. 3. A division may have more than one employee associated with it.
Budget	Tracks	Employee	Definition: This relation is part of a relation with four entities: contract/purchase order, contractor/vendor, employee, and budget. The Division of Finance keeps track of the expenditures for contracts and purchase orders, who the contractors and vendors are, and the employees involved in the transactions for the entire board. Rules: 1. A single budget might not track information for a contract/purchase order, a contractor/vendor, or an employee. 2. A contract/purchase order, a contractor/vendor, or an employee may be associated with one or more budgets over time.
Budget	Tracks	Contractor/ Vendor	See definition for Budget Tracks Employee.
Budget	Tracks	Contract/ Purchase Order	See definition for Budget Tracks Employee.

EXHIBIT 7

ISBH Entity Usage by Division

DIVISION	Agent	Animal Slaughter	Budget	Bureau	Certificate	Class	Complaint	Contract/Purchase Order	Contractor/Vendor	Deficiency	Disease/Cause	Division	Drug Inventory	Employee	Facility	Food Voucher	Geographic Area	Grant	Health Aide	Health Professional	Individual	Instructor	Lab Result	Law	Library Document	License/Certificate	Medical Procedure	Morbidity	Mortality	Natality	Other Vital Events	Prescription	Product	Program	Recipient	Report	Report Section	Survey	Training/Inservice	Vehicle
Dairy	C		C	R			C	C	C	C	R	R		C	C		R				C		R	C		C		C	R					C				C	C	
Retail & Manufactured Food	C	C	C	R			C	C	C	C	R	R		C	C		R				C		R	C		C		C	R				C	C				C	C	
Meat and Poultry	C	C	C	R			C	C	C	C	R	R	C	C	C		R				C		R	C		C		C	C				C	C				C	C	
Weights and Measures	C		C	R	R		C	C	C	C		R	C	C	C		R				C		R	C		C		C	C					C				C	C	C
Acute Disease Control	C		C	R	R	C		C			R	R	C	C	C		R	C		C	C		R	R		R		C	R	R	R	C		C	C	C	C			
Chronic Disease Control	C		C	R	R			C			R	R		C	C		R			C	C		R	R		R		C	R	R	R	C		C	C	C	C	C		
Acquired Disease Control	C		C	R				C			R	R		C	C		R			C	C		R	R		R		C	R	R				C	C	C	C			
Maternal and Child Health	C		C	R			C	C			R	R		C	C		R			C	R		R	R				R	R	R	R			C						
Nutrition	C		C	R			C			C	R	R		C	C	C	R				C			R	C			R	R	R				C						
Dental	C		C	R	R		C				C	R		C	C		R			C	C		R	R	C			C	R	R				C				C		
Public Health Research			C	R				C	C			R		C	R		R	C			C			R		R	R	R	R	R	R				C	C	C		C	
Public Health Statistics			C	R	C			C	C			R		C	R		C				C			R		R	C	C	C	C	C				C	C	C		C	
Health Planning			C	R							R	R		C	C		R		C	C	C			R		R	C	R	R	R	C				C	C	C			
Health Facilities			C	R		C	C	C	C	C		R		C	C		R	C			R			R		R				R										
Acute Care Services			C	R		C	C	C	C	C		R		C	C		R	C			C			R		C												C	C	
Child Care Facilities			C	R		C	C	C		C		R		C	C		R				C			R		C								C				C	C	
Finance			C	R				C	C			R		C				R						R		R								R				C	C	

Exhibit 3). This relationship is many-to-many because a budget can fund many contracts and the total support for a contract can come from several budgets.

The cardinality of each relationship is designated by shading corners of the relationship symbol. The three-way relationship, named "Monitors," between Budget, Vehicle, and Employee (see the EER diagram for the Bureau of Consumer Protection in Exhibit 3) indicates that when an employee uses a particular vehicle, it must be funded from only one budget, but over time a particular budget can fund the use of a certain vehicle by many employees, and one employee can be funded to use many vehicles from the same budget.

One additional notation is the circle placed on a line connecting relationship diamonds and entity rectangles. The circle indicates that there may actually be no entities from time to time associated with the relationship. Consider the EER diagram for the Bureau of Administrative Services in Exhibit 3. This diagram shows that a Grant can supply funds for one or more budgets, and that zero or one grants may support any particular budget.

The EER diagram for the Bureau of Consumer Protection in Exhibit 3 also shows that there are four different types of facilities: Weights and Measures, Dairy Farm, Retail and Manufacturing, and Processing Plant. All facilities have a license, are located in some geographical area, and can be surveyed. Only the processing plant type of entity, however, is associated with animal slaughter event (which is itself a type of the event entity).

To avoid crossing lines and a possibly unreadable chart, a cross-hatch is drawn in the corner of an entity symbol that is repeated on that chart.

Conducting the Project   To gain a broader commitment to the project, to provide a periodic check on project progress, and to begin sharing ideas on data management across the board, Douglass recommended forming a project advisory panel, composed of influential department heads. A panel was formed, including:

Darrell Fisher
Dan Gurney (data administrator)
Joe Fox (director of the Bureau of Policy Development, a bureau which helps each division in its planning and direction setting)
Dave Smith (a consultant working on a new vital records system for one of the divisions)
Frank Loogootee

The panel met every two to four weeks and reviewed interim charts, suggested who should be interviewed from the seventeen priority divisions, suggested ways to present the results for the final report, and accepted responsibility to move forward with the final report findings.

The process that Hamon followed to gather the information needed to produce the data architecture utilized both interviews and the analysis of critical business documents. She started by interviewing various bureau directors to get an idea of the functions of each bureau and who within the bureaus would have the best understanding of the data handled in each group. Then she set up meetings with these people and some division directors.

She described her procedure as follows:

First I explained what I was doing and that I wasn't particularly interested in things that should be processed by a computer, but just the data handled in their unit. I had to use a lot of examples, since they had trouble just talking about data. I also encouraged them to show me lots of examples, like of a survey they took, a report they produced for distribution to the public or other state agencies, or standards on the work in their area. Even the actual laws that define a division's responsibilities were helpful. If I could get my hands on these things before the interview, I'd review them to be better prepared.

They used so many local terms that frequently I had to give examples of the kind of entities I had been formulating, like facility and budget. I wanted to know how they used this data, which was fairly easy for them to talk about. It usually took several interviews, since being new to the organization it took me a long time to understand what I was hearing and to know what questions to ask.

Sometimes I'd hear a term and think that it meant the same as what someone in another division had said, but when I'd go back to my desk and try to draw this into an EER diagram, I'd find inconsistencies and I'd have to ask follow-up questions. Frequently this is when I'd realize that an entity, like facility, had many subclasses or types, and what I was hearing was different because the different types of the same entity were handled in different ways in various divisions.

I also found that the people in the divisions had never really taken the time to conceive of the kind of picture of data I was developing, so a lot of my questions in the first interview didn't generate much. In general, I had to just let them talk about what they do and I had to figure out, and then check with them, what data or relationships they were utilizing.

When I'd go back for a second interview I'd take the preliminary diagrams with me and I would key my questions off the diagram. I was surprised that many of the managers seemed to be able to figure out the diagrams with just a little explanation, and then they could give me the answers I needed. Other times, I'd just refer to the charts myself to pace me through my questions. In either case, the charts were a big help in focusing in on just the information I needed from them. For example, the diagram allowed me to find out if one survey helped a facility to qualify for just one license or if several licenses were being considered. This was very straightforward to them.

The biggest problem I had was to get them to think about all the data they used, not just that computerized. I had to be careful not to say much about our goal of a computer data architecture, since that would really limit what they would talk about.

Another thing was that they often gave me too much detail, much more than I needed. Many people would go on and on and bring up all the problems they ever had with MISD. Yet others were very protective of their data. They felt that nobody else would ever want to use this data, so why should they tell me about it. This was especially true in the divisions that had confidential data on individuals.

Another problem was that I had never done a project like this before and it took me three to four weeks to get comfortable with what I was expected to do. Being new to the board and new to this project made it doubly difficult for me. On the other hand, I was not biased by history or details, so maybe being an outsider had some benefits, too. I was able to see things at a higher level than many of the MISD staff, who have lived through the development of the existing systems, could have.

Also, except for Darrell and one or two other people, nobody had much of an idea of what I was doing. They didn't know if I was actually developing a database for them or what. Maybe if we had a sample of a report and findings from another project to show people quickly, they would have been more on target in what they said to me. One or two people became hostile from some of my questions. I guess that they felt that I was asking some of the same questions that had been asked before and nothing very significant came out of those interviews. These people are very busy and many of them want action, not just planning.

One of the side benefits of this project was that I was able to discover areas that were doing the same thing with data and not realizing it. And I found areas that had systems with so much data that other divisions could use, if they only knew it existed. I was really surprised how little these people knew about what data others had in their systems. People bring in a tape and have it loaded on the MISD computer or on their PC and nobody else ever knows about it. There is so much data here that seems so valuable, but it lies dormant because most people have no way to know it exists or where. They just keep asking for a lot of the same data over and over again.

The other thing that I discovered is that there are a few people who have been around here long enough and are in some rather central positions, like Joe Fox in policy development, who do have a pretty good idea on the total information usage at the board. But these people are swamped with their own jobs and just don't have the time to sort this out for MISD. And when these people leave or retire, their understanding is lost.

Another problem I had was maintaining all the interview data I collected and drawing and redrawing all the EER diagrams and charts. I used dBASE to keep some of the data and a Macintosh to draw the figures, but all of this was brute force. I could have really used better computer tools for organizing the data and maybe even automatically redrawing the EER diagrams when I discovered cardinality changes, entity subclasses, or even new entities. I looked at the data dictionary *from IDMS to help with this, but it was more geared to describing an operating database and it couldn't draw any of the diagrams we wanted. It wasn't very flexible and I didn't have the time to learn how to use it. So, I just did it all my own way.*

Results of the Project Besides producing the five data architecture products outlined, Hamon and the consulting faculty member were able to use these charts and tables as well as the qualitative information collected from the interviews and analyses to develop many general observations and recommendations. These can be summarized as follows:

Even though only selected data elements were documented (because of the limited time of the project and the desire to keep the project at a high data entity and relationship level), the data about each entity and relationship used may be quite different for each division. Thus, the physical design of databases and systems may need to split apart storage of data about a given entity into multiple computer files to handle the large volume and diverse data processing requirements. This emphasizes that this data architecture is strictly a logical prescription, not recommendations on the physical design and organization of data.

The time dimensions of data is not precisely captured in these charts. Many data elements exist and change over time (for example, the address of an employee). Further analysis would be necessary to determine proper archiving and historical record-keeping requirements.

Some apparent flaws in board procedures exist. For example, it is common that several divisions believe that they are responsible for creating instances of a given data entity (such as facility). In some cases, this may be legitimate, since each division is concerned with different types of the entity or different subsets of facility data. In other cases, the historical development of separate systems has encouraged multiple divisions to capture the same data redundantly. Board data policy will need to be established to coordinate this data capture under the new data architecture.

To provide such coordination, Hamon and Douglass recommended establishing a Data Coordinating Committee. This group would be composed of bureau representatives knowledgeable about information needed in their bureaus, along with Dan Gurney, recently appointed to be in charge of the data dictionary of IDMS/R. The duties of this committee are outlined in the recommendations. Briefly, this committee would establish who is responsible for (in a sense, owns) different data, decide how and when data definitions may change, support MISD in acquiring data management staff and software to better manage data as a board resource, and resolve conflicts on data and system plans as it relates to data formats and representations (for example, how to encode the unique identification of a facility, which is now done five different ways across the various systems in place in the ISBH).

Hamon recommended follow-up work to complete the analysis for all thirty-three divisions and to produce an inventory of data that resides in current systems, including a cross-reference of existing locations of data to the elements of the data architecture.

At the final presentation, the advisory panel enthusiastically accepted the products of the project' and decided to move forward with the recommendations. Fisher took responsibility for implementing the recommendations. In looking to the next steps, Fisher said:

We are going to have to set up procedures that will help us standardize how we name and identify data elements so that we can recognize that two elements that are today called by different names are actually the same data The data dictionary will be our tool to accomplish this. There will be a lot of work to populate the data dictionary, but this must be done. We will need also to put more clout behind our data administration function as the way to operationalize the policies and plans of the Data Coordinating Committee. I want to give a copy of this report to every one of my managers so that they better appreciate where I want to go and how each of them fits in. I want them to stop thinking just about the needs of the individual client they serve but to think also in terms of managing the total data resource of the board. This will be a difficult attitudinal change, but a necessary one.

We have a very limited staff. Every time we throw the switch for a new system we better be getting the most for our effort or we will be working against ourselves. We are just not going to get many opportunities to do it right. We need to do a serious inventory of our mainframe systems to see where all this data outlined in the EER diagrams and other charts now reside. I don't see us purposely going out and starting to consolidate these systems, but when they do come up for changes, we can take advantage of the opportunity and roll them into the data architecture. Personal computer systems are more of an issue for such an inventory since people take data in those systems more personally. But if we don't man-

age all data, we are not really managing any data.

Hamon added:

The board has so many divisions using so much of the same information. When I started I thought EER diagrams would be quite distinct from each other, but just look at them! Entities like facility, division, budget, survey, individual, program, employee, and many others are everywhere. There is so much potential here. There is so much more you could do once you realize all the data you have and you can organize it so that everyone can have access to it.

10

Business Management of Information Technology

The management system is one of the key elements in the overall information technology architecture. The purpose of this chapter is to elaborate on this element of the architecture. We will view the information technology (IT) management system in terms of its mission, function, structure, and location, and we will address how you as a business manager can tell if the IT management system is working. Our major theme in this discussion is that *you* hold partial and growing responsibility for IT management because of the critical importance of information and IT in most organizations today.

The way in which the information systems (IS) unit is organized and how its contribution to the organization as a whole is measured are critical issues to the whole organization. Over the years, the response to these issues has changed, and for various reasons (see Chapter 1). Today, information technology is pervasive and requires attention by every organizational unit and manager. Payback from investment, being able to respond quickly to changing requirements, and leveraging technology for competitive advantage are now important in evaluating the contribution

of the IS organization and the data and systems it manages.

Many organizations now are making dramatic changes in IT management. Some organizations are switching from either highly centralized or highly decentralized computing environments to a more cooperative-computing, client/server environment. This trend, called downsizing or rightsizing, is causing changes in IT management. Another common tactic in IT management is the outsourcing of a portion of the IS department to an independent organization. This organization may be a subsidiary of the corporation (this approach is called insourcing), but usually is a separate company in the business of running data centers, telecommunication networks, or systems development groups.

Another major theme in IT management today is helping the organization participate in a global marketplace. As we will see in this chapter, managing global systems raises unique factors and issues for an organization.

As information systems become more pervasive throughout organizations, end-users require more support and guidance as they use and develop systems. The important topic of management, of end-user development is addressed in Chapter 11 and not repeated here. It is nevertheless a critical part of the entire IT management system.

THE INFORMATION TECHNOLOGY MANAGEMENT SYSTEM

The way an organization chooses to manage the IS function and IT overall depends on its mission for systems (see Chapter 12). This mission implies a style and a structure that involves how and where systems are built, run, planned for, and budgeted and where systems professionals are located. The IT management system prescribes the focus of decision-making for IT-related activities within the organization.

The management of IT involves several key decisions. The first is how high the IS function should report in the organization structure. The second is to what degree should the responsibility for IT activities be distributed throughout the organization or centralized in headquarters. This is not simply a matter of moving the pieces around but a matter of deciding on an IS and general management partnership for managing IT. The third decision is what IT management functions should be provided within the organization and which should be purchased from outside consulting and service organizations.

IT management is typically distributed (a combination of centralization and decentralization) in one of several ways. Because no company is totally centralized or decentralized, the real question is not whether to centralize or decentral-

ize, but what and how to distribute. An information vision (see Chapter 12) creates a shared understanding within which an IT management distribution can be designed. Distributed management is a combination of organization-wide coordination and local authority. Technology, people, control, and functional responsibility can each be distributed.

The distribution of IT can be physical, managerial, or both. For example, equipment and IS staff can be physically placed in operating units, but controlled by a central IS organization. In contrast, line units can acquire and manage their own equipment and staff.

Many organizations buy some IS services as needed. Systems may be purchased or developed under contract by outside suppliers. We will discuss other efforts (creating an IS subsidiary and outsourcing) to make IS more competitive and cost effective by reducing fixed costs and gaining economies of scale through outside services.

As an overview of IT management today, Table 15.1 shows a typical distribution of IT management responsibilities.

What Effects Do IT Management Trends Have on You?

One consequence of the trend toward a distributed management for IT is that every business manager may have some authority and responsibility for systems. Today the IS unit is not run by people in sweatshirts and sneakers who work in the basement, which was the image for many years. IS professionals are now expected to be business managers. More important for you, you may hire internal or consulting IS professionals or even manage your own IS staff. Ultimately (as discussed

TABLE 15.1 Typical Distribution of IT Management Responsibilities

Central IS Unit	Business Management
Strategic planning for information technology	Tactical planning for systems
Programming and physical systems design	Systems analysis and logical systems design
Training and consulting	End-user development
Telecom network management	Local data center management
Manage IT for whole organization	Manage IT for business unit
Develop and manage shared and feeder databases	Manage application and local databases
Provide IS professionals to business organizations	Provide business managers to IS units

in Chapter 16), you may be asked to head an IS group in your business unit (what we call an information executive position). Thus, you must learn how to manage IT, just as you must manage the financial, marketing, engineering, and personnel aspects of your job.

The Evolution of IT Management

Why has the evolution of IT management—from highly centralized in a low-level management unit, to a mixture of centralization and decentralization across all units and levels—taken place? Basically, the changes reflect trends in technology, applications, and data; an increased understanding of information technology by managers; and changes in environmental factors. Such trends were described in Chapter 1, and we review a few of them here as a basis for the ideas in this chapter.

Technological Change   Small and inexpensive electronic technologies have made it possible for each manager, department, and small business to acquire computer and communications equipment. In fact, many managers today have more data on floppy disks than in their file cabinets. With this distribution of technology comes a need for local responsibility for operations, backup and recovery, security, development, education, and planning (see Chapter 16 for a discussion of managing your own data center). Even with these decentralized needs to manage the distributed technology, there still is the need to ensure that desktop and departmental technologies do not become islands of automation. A central IS group usually coordinates, standardizes, and inventories distributed technology and the applications and data managed by them.

Applications and Data   To give business units and managers greater control over information support and the allocation of IT and other expenditures, applications and database development have been distributed. In response to this fragmentation, the central IS organization has had to become a support and training group. A current major IS unit mission is to facilitate this distributed development for the good of the whole organiza-

tion. Frequently, the IS organization has been broken apart, with much of the systems analysis and design activities reporting to line organizations. Along with this reorganization, user-managers have had to take more direct roles in IS quality control, managing systems professionals, IS operations, and negotiating with other managers over system interfaces.

Management Understanding   There now is a greater technology awareness and skill among nonsystems professionals, which creates higher and more diverse expectations for new and improved systems and greater confidence that managers can develop and run systems themselves. More use and development of systems by line managers stimulates the need for additional systems (a learning phenomenon - the more you know, the more you want); many of these systems, because they link data across subunits, are natural for a central IS organization to develop and manage. In fact, many IS organizations are evolving into a data warehousing or utility mentality, in which their primary role is the management and transfer of data between data suppliers and consumers within the organization. Many IS organizations, although what they do has changed considerably, are busier than ever and still in critical need of qualified technical and managerial personnel. It seems clear that the IS organization will continue to change, and more so than its counterparts in finance, marketing, and production.

External Factors   External factors have caused major reorganization shock waves throughout the IS organization. For example, the deregulation of the telecommunications industry has forced organizations to manage aspects of data and voice communications previously entrusted to the vendor. International regulations on transborder data flow and vast differences in labor rates have caused organizations to reconsider where systems will be built and operated and where data entry is most economical. The shortage of highly qualified IS professionals (and the faculty to develop them) has encouraged organizations to expect greater productivity from existing IS staff and resulted in the distribution of more systems work to non-IS professionals. Organizations are also relying more on purchased software from the growing application software industry (see Chapter 10).

The following sections cover the essentials of what a general business manager should know about organizing and evaluating the IS organization.

THE ROLE OF THE IS ORGANIZATION

The role of the IS organization is changing, but it is not clear where the function is headed. Although how IT is managed depends on how the organization sees information and IT as a part of the overall business, there are some general trends.

What the IS organization does, how it performs these duties, and how it organizes to get its job done depends in part on what the rest of the organization expects from it. Of course, this will vary from organization to organization. As a general trend, managers expect a future-oriented IS organization that can anticipate their needs, while meeting today's requirements. This means that senior management expects the IS unit to align its activities with the business mission. More specifically, it means:

- demonstrating an understanding of the business, through an awareness of business plans and strategies and close communication with business managers.
- responding quickly with systems to meet changing business conditions (not waiting years for a strategically important system to be built).
- helping to reengineer the business to be more responsive to customers, to bring product to market faster, or to improve business process quality.
- keeping the final customer, not just internal operations, in mind.
- building systems that provide direct and identifiable benefits to the final customer, thus building stronger customer relationships.
- helping managers make better decisions in a constrained amount of time.
- using information technology for sustainable competitive advantage and increased market share.

It is important to note that the traditional dominant expectation of saving money through cost efficiencies (such as work-force reduction) is not included in this set. Although such short-term tangible benefits are still important (yet often difficult to attribute solely to an information system), expectations today are more comprehensive and complex than merely saving money.

From various studies, we know that most CEOs and other senior executives are skeptical that they are getting the most for their investment in information systems. At the same time, these leaders admit that information systems significantly change the way their organizations operate and compete and that good systems are critical to the organization's success.

In general, the role of the IS organization (central and distributed units) is to be the steward of the information and IT resources of the organization, much as the finance organization is for financial resources. More specific roles are to:

- deploy IT resources throughout the organization.
- facilitate the productive and effective use of these resources today, not just in the future.
- lead the development of an architecture and a vision for information and technology that will support the rapid deployment of new and improved services (from both original software development and packaged systems).
- communicate this architecture and vision to the organization in business terms.
- maintain managerial control and integrity over important information and technology.
- administer corporate data and the movement of data between systems.
- make current and new information technology available at the lowest possible cost.
- help business managers become comfortable with information technologies and knowledgeable about their effective use.
- develop a partnership with line management to exploit technology for competitive advantage and to influence the products and services offered by the organization.

These roles must be achieved with as much professional business conduct as is done with any other resource management organization.

Joyce J. Elam et al. (1988) describe this evolving mission for the IS organization as a subtle shift in the types of words associated with IS professionals. Whereas historically we have used such terms as *developer, maintainer,* and *technician,* in the future we will use such terms as *innovator, marketer, consultant,* and *broker* when describing the mission and role of IS professionals and the IS organization, especially the central IS unit. If these semantics are appropriate, then we will see a shift from a doing mission to a helping mission. With this will come a need to measure performance and contributions in different ways.

WHO IS IN CHARGE OF INFORMATION TECHNOLOGY?

Obviously, someone in any organization can be identified as the lowest level manager or executive to whom all other centralized IT management activities report. In some enterprises this person may be an IS department manager, director, or vice president; in other organizations, this person might be a finance or administrative executive. Some organizations have created the role of **chief information officer** (**CIO**) to lead IT management. A true CIO is part of the officer team of the organization, that is, those responsible for the strategic decisions for the whole organization, and is responsible for only information technology. We address this senior general business manager role in this section. We will define this role, discuss the

concerns and perspectives of the CIO, identify the critical success factors of a CIO, and describe the relationships the CIO has with other executives. The role defined for a CIO says much about what you can expect from your IS organization.

The Role of the Chief Information Officer

Above all, the CIO is responsible for guiding and unifying the entire organization's information technology resources—data processing, office automation, telecommunications, and possibly automated factory operations. Although different divisions, lines of business, or subsidiaries may have their own information executives, the CIO is charged with coordinating all the resources. The CIO is a staff function, not a line function; the CIO usually does not have responsibilities for day-to-day IS operations.

CIOs should be business, not technical, managers. They are, however, expected to bridge the gulf between IT and general business managers. Traditional IS managers spent most of their time interacting with other IS professionals and users, focusing on specific user needs. In contrast, CIOs spend the greatest percentage of time interacting with peer general managers as part of managing the business as a whole. CIOs need to be able to see the advantage of technology and where to apply it broadly in the business. CIOs who cannot explain what IT is accomplishing in business terms do not survive long in this role.

Although certainly now a reality, CIOs are still emerging and, therefore, may not yet have all the authority they need for such sweeping responsibilities. According to a study by Coopers & Lybrand (Carlyle, 1988), although 59 percent of the information executives sampled considered themselves CIOs, only 27 percent reported directly into the officer suite. Another study found that only 7.7 percent of CIOs reported directly to the CEO or president (*Business Week*, 1990). Small and medium-sized companies seldom have a CIO. Usually, it is organizations on the frontier of information management that have a true CIO—such information-intensive enterprises as banks, insurance companies, and airlines.

In general, the initial charge to a CIO is to bring IT expenditures under control, through coordination of previously separate, lower-level IS units. The job of a CIO can be frustrating because of differences in perspective with other officers, uncertain job expectations, and a general lack of centralized management in the organization. Equally frustrating, as reported in the Coopers & Lybrand study, was the realization that typically a CIO has little job mobility—he may be hired as CIO and will leave the company from this same job.

Figure 15.1 is a fictitious but possible job advertisement for a CIO. This ad defines the quintessential renaissance person.

Major Concerns of the CIO

Various studies in recent years have tracked the major concerns of IS executives, including the CIO. From these some general patterns have emerged. These concerns represent a set of critical success factors for the CIO and for IS management as a whole. The following is a brief outline of the top concerns frequently cited (see Brancheau and Wetherbe, 1987, and *I/S Analyzer*, 1991):

Improving information and IT planning, especially strategic planning: With rapidly changing businesses and technologies, such planning is not easy, but it is essential to anticipate information needs and manage resources prudently.

Gaining competitive advantage through IT: Strate-

gic systems give the CIO visibility and attention that can help to make many other changes in IT management possible.

Facilitating organizational learning about information technology: This issue is consistent with the evolution of the IS organization into a helping role rather than exclusively a doing role. Training, in particular, is now an important function of the IS organization.

Refining the IS unit's role and position: CIOs are concerned about the future structure for IT management and what responsibilities should be distributed to achieve the greatest payoff for the whole enterprise.

Managing end-user development: The development of systems by end-users directly or by IS staff in line organizations is now a major alternative way to have systems built. Determining the proper standards for programming languages, systems justification procedures, documentation, database management, and the like is a difficult policy challenge for the CIO.

Managing data as a resource: Chapter 14 is devoted to this issue, which has been rising in the list of top concerns for the CIO.

Measuring IS effectiveness: Frequently the strategic and decision support systems being introduced today are difficult to justify with hard benefit numbers. Further, it is difficult to show the contribution of information and IT planning and architecture work. Thus, IT resources may be cut in hard times unless the real contributions can be shown.

Integrating information technologies: The primary role of the CIO is the unification of IS services and technologies. The history of islands of automation, each with strong and protective organizational homes, usually makes integration a difficult political as well as technical problem.

Managing systems personnel: Finding and retaining staff knowledgeable in such strategic technologies as expert systems and telecommunications are of special concern. Motivating systems personnel to be productive and aware of business needs is also of high concern to the CIO and other IS managers.

Wanted

Bright, versatile, industrious individual to manage the aggregate information requirements of a company, including internal and external resources, both technological and human. Person must be able to understand how to apply information and technology to corporate strategy. Must be able to work well under pressure and have strong analytical capabilities. Strong interpersonal and communication skills are required since the individual will interact with all information suppliers and users inside and outside the company. Must add value as a member of the senior management team.

FIGURE 15.1 Example of a CIO Job Advertisement

General Management Leadership for Information Technology

If the CIO is truly an officer of the business, then she will not be the only person at that level concerned with managing IT issues for the business. In many organizations, issues at the officer level are issues for all officers. Team management, where problems are addressed in partnership among peers, is often the culture. Even when a strong consensus or collaborative culture is not present, the CIO cannot address the concerns outlined strictly alone.

It is essential for the CIO (as well as other senior IS managers) to build strong working relationships with other top managers. This cannot be achieved unless the CIO is a peer in authority and responsibility, the CIO's mission and vision are clear, and other managers view IT as an area that cannot be managed by delegation to lower level groups.

What is being defined here is a **partnership**, a cooperative relationship. General managers must welcome such partnerships and overtly communicate this receptivity to their peers and subordinates. The CIO and other senior IS managers must be willing to work on non-IT issues. In many organizations, one senior manager, recognizing the power of such an alliance, has championed the partnership.

Steering Committees for IT Management A **steering committee**, issue forum, or advisory board can be used to make interaction frequent and focused at the CIO and top IS management level. Much discussion of such groups has centered on how they have been misused or abused. Inadequate authority, narrow perspectives, uninformed or improper membership, and a host of other problems can hamper these committees. When properly set up, however, such groups can be used effectively to:

- set priorities for systems development and IS direction.
- check progress against an established direction.
- allocate scarce resources (especially IS staff) to achieve business objectives.

THE MEANING OF PARTNERSHIP

Partnership is a coordinating strategy for IS management. It is based on sustaining a long-term relationship between IS and management. Partners share key common goals. Partners seek benefits not possible to each party individually. Partnership is based on mutual trust. Its goal is to achieve a greater contribution for IS to the organization. Noneconomic factors and shared benefits, responsibilities, and risks form a partnership. Each partner understands and appreciates the critical stakeholders and business processes that influence the performance of the organization. A partner respects the distinctive resources and competencies of other partners. A partnership can be contrasted with a transaction management approach in which each action (for example, new system request) is considered as a separate interaction between IS and management. Pure economics drive transactions. In a partnership, each party influences, but does not control each other.

(Adapted from Henderson, 1990)

- communicate concerns, issues, and possible remedies.
- provide education and the development of shared mind-sets.
- develop shared responsibility and ownership of actions.

Such groups are not a substitute for a good CIO and IS management. Instead, they work best when there is good management for IT already in place. Partnership means cooperation, dealing with problems jointly, and managing the business, not empires. A good steering committee, along with professional IS leadership, can be an effective part of managing information technology for the business.

MANAGERIAL ROLES IN THE IS ORGANIZATION

As a business manager, you will interact with a wide variety of systems professionals, each with certain job responsibilities. The systems field is

TABLE 15.2 Selected IS Management Positions

Position	Brief Description
CIO	Most-senior executive responsible for information technology across the whole organization.
MIS Director	Responsible for the day-to-day operations of all aspects of IS for the whole organization.
IS Executive	Responsible for the day-to-day operations of all aspects of IS in one division, plant, or unit of the business; usually a general manager of that business unit, not the central IS group.
Information Center Manager or Manager of End-user Computing	Oversees the operation of computer hot line and user help desks; training on user development tools and fourth-generation languages; and personal computer installation and support.
Development Manager	Coordinates all new systems development projects, allocates systems analysts and project managers to projects, schedules development work.
Maintenance Manager	Coordinates all systems maintenance projects, allocates systems analysts and project managers to projects, schedules maintenance work; depending on organization structure, development and maintenance manager may be one person or several people responsible for different segments of the business.
IS Planning Manager	Analyzes business and develops an architecture for hardware and software to support systems in the future; may also forecast technology trends.
Operations Manager	Supervises the day-to-day operations of data centers and possibly also data entry, data network, computer file library, and systems hardware and software maintenance staff; schedules computer jobs, manages downtime, and plans computer system capacity.
Programming Manager	Coordinates all application programming efforts: allocates and organizes staff into project teams, acquires tools and languages to improve programmer productivity.
Manager of Emerging Technologies	Evaluates new technologies, fosters experimental projects to test new technologies in the organization, consults with users on appropriate application of new technologies, and approves new technologies for use in the organization.
Telecommunications Manager	Coordinates the installation and operation of the corporate data and voice network.
Systems Programming Manager	Responsible for support and maintenance of systems software (operating system, utilities, programming language compilers, etc.); interacts with vendors to install updates and request changes; may overlap duties with Telecommunications Manager and Database Administrator.
Data or Database Administrator	Plans databases and coordinates use of data management software (duties outlined in Chapter 14).
Project Manager	Supervisor of analysts and programmers working on the development or maintenance of application system.
Quality Assurance Manager or Manager of EDP Auditing	Coordinates activities that set standards and checks compliance with standards to improve the quality and accuracy of systems.
Computer Security Manager	Develops procedures and policies and installs and monitors software to ensure the authorized use of computing resources.

diverse and traditionally specialized. Although senior IS executives are more and more becoming general business managers, most IS professionals, whether based in the IS organization or in line areas, have specific duties.

Table 15.2 lists generic job titles and a brief description for many of the types of systems managers with whom you may have the most frequent contact. Depending on the IS structure in your organization, these positions may be in your business unit or in an IS service unit. All of these roles are essential for the high-quality operation of the systems in the organization. This list does not include the programmers, analysts, computer operators, trainers, and consultants with whom you might have contact. Your possible relationships with these operational people have been discussed earlier in this book.

Each position outlined in Table 15.2 may be held by one or more people (in one staff or possibly distributed across different business divisions), and one person may have several of these roles. In small organizations the same person may assume both managerial and operational duties, and several duties will likely be combined (for example, development and maintenance, quality assurance and security). Frequently in small organizations, development, maintenance, programming, and operations may be the combined duties of one person. Many different talents and skills are needed in an IS organization.

Historically, IS personnel were frequently considered heroes. In fact, it was easy to be a hero. The technology looked like magic and those that could make it work were revered. In the 1990s the aura is gone, and it is down to business for IS professionals, such as those listed in Table 15.2.

ALTERNATIVE STRUCTURES FOR THE IS ORGANIZATION

In this section we consider all IS professionals and business managers with explicit responsibilities for IT management to be called generically the IS organization. A wide variety of IS organization structures can be found in small to large organiza-

> ### AN IS ACCOUNT EXECUTIVE
>
> Federal-Mogul, manufacturer of various parts for the automobile and truck original equipment and after-markets, has created the position of *account executive*. The account executive reports directly to both a line executive (say marketing) and to the IS vice president. An account executive is in charge of all the systems staff who work in the line unit to which he is assigned, with few or no middle level IS managers. The account executive works with each team to help them set their mission, objectives, and work plan. Account executives are charged with keeping their unit's systems plans consistent with the corporation's direction. This includes making decisions on which systems requests are funded. The account executive's performance appraisal and salary are set jointly by the IS vice president and the associated line organization. The goal is better user service, better understanding of line organization needs, and more systems planning in line organizations. Career path management for IS staff, getting agreement on line and IS direction, and finding the right account executives are challenges in this arrangement.
>
> **(Adapted from *I/S Analyzer*, 1989)**

tions and in all kinds of industries. The options are almost endless. We present several structures that demonstrate the range of structures used.

The major organizational elements of an IS function are operations, systems development and maintenance, technical services, and administration. These elements or pieces can be arranged in many ways and located throughout the organization. Although the trend is clearly toward what we call the distributed IS organization, all extremes and hybrids exist.

Operations covers data entry, machine operation, tape and disk file library management, hardware/network maintenance, and job scheduling. *Systems development* includes analysis and design, programming, package acquisition, system installation and conversion, training, and application software maintenance. *Technical services* is responsible for system software maintenance, technology assessment, and data administration.

Administration includes capacity and systems planning, budgeting, personnel management and training, and development of standards and procedures.

Other important IS activities, such as end-user support (for example, an information center) and EDP auditing, are often separate units and may report outside the central IS organization. The new major function of *technology transfer*, which is responsible for researching new technologies, forecasting trends in technology, and diffusing their use throughout the organization, is becoming very important in many organizations. A technology transfer group may have fifteen to twenty employees in a large company that takes an aggressive stance with information technology. This group may become involved in pilot or demonstration projects. Once this group proves that a given technology is viable and has application, further development of uses is turned over to other systems or user groups.

Figure 15.2 illustrates four different generic structures for the IS organization. Each shows a different arrangement for the IS functions and the specific division of responsibility between IS and business managers for IT. These four structures are certainly not inclusive of all possible schemes, but they do highlight some of the choices to be made in organizing the IS function. An organization may have several of these structures, with different operating units organizing their own systems organization in different ways. For example, one division could be running a centralized internal IS organization handling all its IS management, and another division could work within a corporate service structure. Further, these organization designs are presented and explained in the extreme, to highlight the salient features of such arrangements.

Classic IS

The classic IS organization of Figure 15.2 is a highly centralized and task-oriented structure. The IS director is a manager of technical personnel, not a general business manager. A pool of analysts and programmers is used interchangeably as new systems and maintenance projects are approved. Op-

erations, whether centralized or distributed, is managed by the central IS group. Most systems run on a centralized mainframe and use third-generation programming languages. Systems programmers maintain language compilers, the operating systems, telecom software, and other system utilities. Data center and network staff operate and repair the facilities. Batch data entry is performed in-house or by vendors; in this design, the operations group could even handle a telephone order processing center.

The focus of the classic IS organization is on efficiency (low cost) of systems development and operations and skill specialization. The role of IS is to build systems, not solve business problems. IS careers follow through various levels of project administration and lateral moves. There are very few job transfers in and out of this organization. This type of organization can be duplicated, on a smaller scale, in autonomous divisions of a large organization or in a medium-sized business. In smaller businesses, the IS director and head of systems development and maintenance could be the same person, with a computer operator/programmer reporting to him or her.

Functional IS

The functional area IS organization of Figure 15.2 is a precursor to the distributed IS organizations found in many large companies today. Here, the central IS staff is broken into separate development groups for different line units (for example, marketing systems, production systems) and staff units (for example, support services). Particular staff members (either in the development group and/or in user groups) will be appointed to liaison roles with their counterparts in IS or line functions. MBAs with a concentration in IS are prime candidates for these liaison roles because they have the skills to bridge the technical and business areas. Distributed technology may be used, with specialized equipment and software for different user groups, but IS people and IT may not be distributed in identical manners.

The focus of the functional area IS organization is to serve the needs of particular client groups, often at the expense of the management of

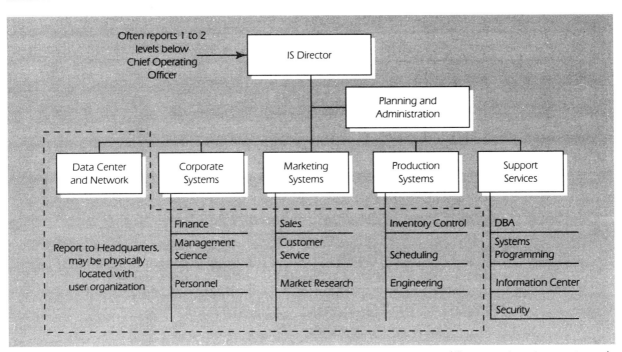

FIGURE 15.2 Alternative IS Organization Structures
(*figure continued on next page*)

(c) SERVICE-ORIENTED IS ORGANIZATION

(d) DISTRIBUTED IS ORGANIZATION

FIGURE 15.2 (continued)

the overall architecture of systems. Considerable negotiation occurs between line managers and IS when resources allocated to them are insufficient to handle all the required systems. A steering committee might be used to allocate resources on the margin. Transfer in and out of the IS organization occurs through the line units. Frequently, IS project management might actually be done by a business line manager on assignment to the IS line organization. Corporate IS support is similarly handled by a corporate functional group.

An extreme case of the functional IS approach is a totally decentralized strategy in which each business unit has a complete IS organization. Such styles are used in some holding companies or other organizations that foster unrelated lines of business diversification, emphasize strong local autonomy, or actively change by acquisition, merger, or divestiture.

Service IS

The service-oriented IS organization of Figure 15.2 recognizes the importance of the functions of data administration and telecommunications management and is, therefore, only relevant to organizations using such technology. The R&D group scans emerging technologies, evaluates alternative products, and sets standards and approved equipment for all of IS and user computing. The information center supports users with personal computers or those using fourth-generation tools on centralized equipment. In this organization, systems development and operations are still centralized, although personal computers are actively used for decision support systems and selected reporting.

The focus of the service-oriented IS organization is responsiveness to the needs for major systems, management of a corporate data and systems architecture, and the support of users doing their own small-scale computing. The IS director is now likely to be a vice president but is still not truly a CIO. Transfer of personnel between systems development, the information center, and line organizations is reasonably frequent.

Distributed IS

The typical distributed IS organization of Figure 15.2 is primarily characterized by the staff nature of the central IS unit. Systems development is responsible for evaluating, acquiring, developing, and training activities concerning tools, methods, and procedures used in systems analysis, design, and programming. Actual systems building is usually done in line division units, with consulting help from the IS group. The IS group may also act as a hired contractor, often in competition with external consulting firms, when the divisional group does not have the capacity or qualifications for parts of projects. Technology is highly distributed, with the central IS group possibly responsible for management of the backbone network, systems security and auditing policies, and technology transfer to the divisions. In the early 1990s, organizations began to consolidate decentralized data centers, while still maintaining distributed IS staff. Client/server technology (see Chapter 2) makes such an approach easier to deploy.

The focus of the typical distributed IS organization is to develop and manage the corporate plan for systems and to assist the divisions in making the best use of information and technology. The IS director in this structure is probably a true CIO. IS organization staff may move between the central and divisional groups and may assume IS specialist or general business manager roles. Central IS may be responsible for career planning of all IS professionals.

A New Role for the Mainframe

It is important to emphasize the distinction between the IT management and hardware/software elements of the IT architecture. In the 1990s, even with a strong trend toward more distributed IS management, many organizations are recentralizing some hardware and software resources. This recentralization is driven by:

- high costs to run multiple data centers (for example, software licensing).
- need to support enterprise-wide systems.

A combination of powerful host (mainframe) computers, intelligent workstations, and client/

server software makes the distinction between centralized and decentralized computing transparent and separable from IT management arrangements. A common term for this combination of technologies is **rightsizing** (*IS/Analyzer*, 1993).

The mainframe in many organizations is not the sole source of computing power. Instead, the mainframe serves as the hub of a cooperative computing environment supporting a distributed IT management structure. The mainframe provides the focal point for data and linkages between business functions. The ability to condense and consolidate data at the mainframe makes rightsizing possible.

The IS Subsidiary

Some organizations have adopted the strategy of making the IS organization a wholly owned subsidiary, responsible for its own financial and market survival. In this structure, IS is treated like a vendor with separate cost and revenue accounting. Creating a subsidiary may be a test to see if contracting out IS is more cost effective than an internal unit. The best-known example of this is the acquisition of Electronic Data Systems (EDS) by General Motors (GM) and the transfer of much of the previous GM IS staff to EDS.

Such a subsidiary is usually put into a competitive position. The parent company units are free to contract with other suppliers for IS services and the subsidiary is allowed to provide services to noncompetitors. This strategy is another method for managing IT more efficiently and for making IS more responsive to user needs. Typically, it is systems development and operations that are moved into the subsidiary; planning, data administration, and other infrastructure functions are retained by the parent company.

DECIDING ON THE RIGHT IT MANAGEMENT SYSTEM

The above IS organization structures illustrate various arrangements of IS activities. Each has a different distribution of IT management functions between a central IS group, distributed IS groups in line organizations, and business managers themselves.

AMERITECH IS

A recent example of the IS subsidiary approach was the formation of Ameritech Services, Inc. This subsidiary of Ameritech, the midwestern regional Bell operating company, became the reporting home for most of the programmers, analysts, and project leaders from the five local operating companies within Ameritech. The staff is still geographically located on-site with clients. The focus of this group is to build common systems, such as billing, that all operating units will use. The expected benefits of this reorganization are reduced development and maintenance costs across the whole organization, and a single point-of-contact for customers doing business in several states. In this case, equipment acquisition (with benefits from bulk purchasing agreements) will be handled by Ameritech Services, but actual operations will remain with the operating company.

The nature of distributed IS operations and some of the operational reasons for such systems is covered in earlier chapters. Not only can IS operations (data collection and processing power) be distributed, but so can the systems development staff and managerial control of IS. It is important to note that the decision on how to distribute IS operations is *separate* from the decision on how to distribute IT management. When these decisions are mixed together, confusion and unproductive discussions occur. Our purpose here is to consider factors affecting the location of the management of the IS function, not the economies of locating data processing operations close to the suppliers and users of data. As noted previously, IS management centralization and decentralization should not be considered absolutes; most organizations today have a mixed approach.

Several key factors affect the structure and location of IS organization functions:

- business characteristics, such as number and size of products or market divisions and their locations.
- level within the organization of the most senior IS manager or officer.
- how the rest of the enterprise is organized, including global operations.

- types of technologies managed by IS.
- the role of IS in the organization.
- the organizational philosophy on the responsibility of business managers for IT.

The following IT management functions are almost always (to some degree) centralized:

- technology transfer.
- support, consulting, and training.
- direction and standards setting and architecture development.
- development and purchase of systems that serve the entire organization (e.g., order entry, personnel, and accounting systems).
- operation of the corporate data center and telecommunications network.
- integration of related but separate systems and technologies.

- research and development into new information technology.
- leadership in exploiting information technology for competitive gain.
- IS professional career path management.

Even these central functions are undertaken with considerable input from distributed IS groups.

Beyond these core functions, there is no generally accepted, normative rule on when IT management (and what parts of it) should be centralized, decentralized, or mixed in some way. Most important is the organizational fit, that is, the management structure for IT should in great measure parallel the general organization structure, mission, strategy, and objectives for IS.

Boynton, Jacobs, and Zmud (1992) have outlined key questions for deciding how to align IS and business management (see Figure 15.3). The

Networking Resources

- To what degree do our business units require networking capabilities?
- Do we need to transport information in the form of data, voice, video, text, graphics, and/or images? Internally or externally?
- Do we need to connect business units internally for electronic mail, access to data, and so forth?
- Do the business units need to connect externally with business partners (i.e., via electronic data interchange)?
- Do we need to reduce costs by sharing networking resources?

Shared Data

- To what extent is data (e.g., product, marketing, and supplier data) shared across any of our business units?
- Do we need standardized subject databases?
- Do the functional areas need to share more than financial data (e.g., customer, market, product, and services data)?
- Do the business units need to share data with customers, suppliers, or buyers?

Common Application Systems

- To what extent do the business units have common application systems requirements?
- Do we need consistent application architecture (e.g., consistent office automation or electronic mail across the firm)?
- Should we have a standardized presence or image with customers or suppliers?
- Do the functional areas need high levels of integration and coordination?
- Do the functional areas need process integration (e.g., order entry, billing, or customer service)?

Human Resources

- To what extent are the people required to run critical systems becoming more difficult to find and more expensive to hire and retain?
- Do we need to increase productivity in building information systems?
- Do we need to maximize critical skills?
- Do we need to support remote operations or provide remote technical support?
- Are critical skills in short supply? Should we have backup people with these skills?

FIGURE 15.3 Questions for Initiating Management Dialogue on IT Management Structure. (Boynton, Jacobs, and Zmud, 1992).

challenge is to evaluate these questions in your organization and to seek the appropriate balance. Not surprisingly, it is common to find frequent reorganizations of IS functions as the answers to these questions inevitably change. Structural shifts occur because of technology, business unit success and failure, a desire to make systems have more strategic value, turnover in key business leaders (and hence business direction), and a tendency to become too central or too autonomous. As the story goes, a good IS organizational consultant only needs two file folders. One contains the boilerplate of the report that recommends centralized IS management to the client, and the other folder contains the skeleton of the decentralization plan. When the one report is submitted, the consultant simply puts a tickler note on his calendar to call the client in about three years. The other report will be needed then to undo the problems of following the first solution in the extreme.

The distribution of IS development is part of the trend toward end-user development of their own systems. (The reasons for end-user development and the management issues related to this trend are discussed in Chapter 11.)

OUTSOURCING IT OPERATIONS AND MANAGEMENT

In the early 1990s a sizable number of medium to large organizations hired outside professional IS services organizations to run part of their IS operations. This approach to IT management is commonly called **outsourcing**. For many companies, internal computer operations have never held a monopoly position. Public data banks, market research data processing firms, and time-sharing and other computing services with special software and data have been around for decades. Recently, there has been renewed interest in outsourcing data center operations (sometimes called facilities management) to external computer centers. Besides the data center, an organization may outsource the management of telecommunications or traditional transaction processing systems programming.

In the early years of computing in businesses, some banks and other aggressive adopters of computer technology performed data processing for other organizations. For example, banks often provided total automation for payroll, receivables, and payables processing under contract for their regular commercial banking customers. As the price of computer equipment fell and the availability of programming talent improved, however, most organizations chose to bring these operations in-house.

The Reason for Outsourcing

According to one study (*Business Week*, June 19, 1989), outsourcing is especially attractive today for organizations because of the significant organizational changes taking place (mergers, acquisitions, and divestitures). With these changes may come sudden shifts in demands for computing power. Moad (1993) claims that the major benefit of the First Fidelity Bancorporation—EDS outsourcing deal has been the speed and efficiency with which FFB can integrate acquired institutions (approximately two to three months). Also, some companies report 10 to 20 percent cost savings from the economies of scale and competitive (rather than captive) pricing provided by the data center suppliers.

Outsourcing allows a company with greatly fluctuating computer time demands to pay for only what it uses, rather than building a data center for peak load (and letting it sit underutilized during other periods). Companies can invest the savings in identifying and developing high-impact applications. The trend toward outsourcing may be related to the establishment of a CIO, who is not tied to the data center and does not feel that the IS function has to manage hardware to prove its value to the firm. A CIO may view data processing much as a manufacturing operation, which is a candidate for outsourcing when demand is highly variable.

Some firms have chosen to outsource IS operations because it is difficult to keep pace with technological change and to hire and retain highly skilled IS staff. Others simply believe that a large outsourcing supplier, with experience in many

First Tennessee National Corp., a Memphis-based banking firm, outsourced its data center to IBM. According to John Kelly, First Tennessee's executive vice president and corporate services group manager, "To compete against larger banks, we either had to become part of a larger bank or find a technology partner. IBM will provide the technology that we need to compete, and they will help us cut costs. [This] will also allow us to spend more time on the strategic part of our jobs than the actual operating part."

(Wilder, 1989)

organizations, can cut costs and provide better service.

The decision to outsource may be viewed as a strategic choice. Eastman Kodak (see Case Study 15) outsourced its data centers to IBM, its telecommunications to Digital Equipment Corporation, and its microcomputer systems to Businessland, Inc. Kodak did not see these areas as central to its vision for information and technologies or a significant strength for competitive advantage. The savings from outsourcing could be used in other parts of the business where Kodak felt a greater return on investment could be achieved.

As discussed in Chapter 10, outsourcing systems development and integration is also possible. Essentially, contracted systems development and programming as well as purchasing of system and application software, both common today, are a form of outsourcing. Because the bulk of IS costs are in personnel, and most personnel are in systems development, major cost-reduction benefits may come from outsourcing.

Cautions About Outsourcing

We have made the case that information technology has strategic value to the firm, so stable and healthy organizations may not see outsourcing, especially of systems development and planning, as a viable option. Security and privacy issues and the strategic value of some data may mean that certain applications cannot be developed or run outside the organization. Computing in support of R&D may be considered too sensitive to outsource. Further, it may be quite difficult to bring systems development or operations back in-house if prices for outsourcing services increase or there is a change in the need for strategic control of these system functions or for technical know-how. Hiring staff and familiarizing them with company operations, building data centers, and setting methods and procedures cannot be done quickly. Organizations with highly variable needs for computing power, however, are increasingly considering the outsourcing option.

An ideal outsourcing arrangement is a partnership between you and your outsourcer (Livingston, 1992). The outsourcer should know and care about your business as much as you do. Sometimes an outsourcer will specialize in particular industries (for example, retail or health care) to gain a depth of knowledge. An outsourcer can also help you make sound technology decisions, not just solutions convenient for the outsourcer. Your outsourcing contract should accommodate growth and expansion in your business. Finally, you want an outsourcer which can operate as geographically dispersed as your operations.

Several key factors in selecting an outsourcing vendor are:

- *vendor reputation*, which includes understanding your business and market and high technology standards.
- *quality of service*, which means a clear comparative advantage over in-house services.
- *pricing*, which means cost effectiveness because, as processing volume increases or new services are added, costs can escalate.

FINANCIAL MANAGEMENT OF IT SERVICES

Measuring the organization's investment in information technology and calculating the impact of this investment on the organization are still not well-understood activities. Most benefits are indirect or confounded by other constant organization changes. In addition, there is no reliable standard for comparing your company to others to see if you are doing better or worse than your competitors.

The typical measures used for tracking IT investment are:

- total IT budget as a percentage of total organization revenues, income, premiums, deposits, or other indicators of overall financial health of the organization.
- total IT budget as a percentage of total organization budget.
- IS personnel costs as a percentage of total organization professional personnel salaries and wages.
- the ratio of hardware and software costs to IS personnel costs.
- the costs for IT hardware and software per managerial or knowledge worker.

No one of these measures is by itself perfect or complete, and most organizations will track several. Sizable changes in these measures might be more significant than the absolute values. Further, high or low values are not by themselves necessarily bad or good. All of these measures require interpretation, matching them with IS and business directions. Organizations that try to be pioneers and leaders should expect, for example, to have higher values on many of these measures than less aggressive firms.

Even in combination, these measures must be used cautiously because of various definitional and measurement problems:

Some IT costs are hidden because of the highly distributed nature of information processing in organizations. Not all costs appear as IT budget line items, and certainly not all are in the IS organization. Further, personal computer hardware, software, training, and services can be purchased as general office expenses or from petty cash—costs that are difficult to track.

No relationship to benefits is directly included in these measures. Costs without benefits give a very incomplete picture.

THE ELUSIVE VALUE OF IT

Just as the accounting system hides many aspects of the costs of IT, it overlooks many of the ways in which IT contributes to business units' performance. The most important contribution IT can make is in avoiding costs. For example, by adding IT costs in year X, a firm might avoid increased business costs in year X plus 5. Looking just at financial records, the business manager sees a growth in IT expenditure and a reduction in business cost growth. IT is now 12 percent of the company's total cost base versus 8 percent previously, while the business units have managed to reduce labor costs as a percentage of sales by 30 percent. What's going on? The business manager's likely conclusion: "IT is out of control!" But what may be going on is that the IT investment generated the labor cost savings by ensuring that the firm could handle larger volumes without adding staff. The accounting system will never tell! Possibly a better measure of the impact of IT investment would be sales per employee, which captures the changes in both benefits and costs.

(Adapted from Keen, 1991)

Benefits happen after many of the development costs occur, and the lag is not considered in these measures. Direct benefits can occur quickly, but secondary benefits of technology diffusion and new ways of doing business may not emerge for years.

There is no simple, reliable way to measure the value-added benefits of information technology. IT costs are easy to see; IT value is typically much more intangible (as is the value of a business education). Thus, organizations must capture and track measures of IS performance over time to utilize best such indicators, so that values can be interpreted, changes explained, and reasonably helpful comparisons made. Some organizations now treat investment in IT like R&D. *No matter how IT investments are valued, it is the job of the business manager, not the IS manager, to justify the investment.*

The IT Budget

A primary mechanism for financial control of IT is the IT budget. Most studies of the IT budget divide costs into four primary groups—personnel, equipment and software, outside services, and overhead. Furthermore, statistics are reported by industry because there is considerable variation by sector. Individual statistics, because of the outlined reporting and measurement issues, can be misleading, but some general observations and trends appear to be valid:

The most common measure, IT expenditures as a percent of revenue (or assets), varies widely by industry and size of firm. Information- and technology-intensive sectors, such as electronics, spend the highest percentage on IT (about 4 percent per year). Smaller firms suffer from a lack of economies of scale and typically spend a higher percentage (all else being equal). Retailing has the lowest IT investment percentage (usually less than 0.5 percent).

Personnel costs have now become the largest piece of the IT budget, about 40 to 50 percent (depending on the industry) of the total (Carlyle, 1990). Although increased productivity aids have helped to keep this percentage from being higher, the demand for new systems makes reduction of IS development staff difficult.

The total IT budget is decreasing as a percentage of revenue, except in public organizations where there now are major efforts to upgrade technology and integrate previously separate data systems.

Even with the distributed nature of IT management, 77 percent of all hardware and software purchases are still made by the IS organization, not user departments (Carlyle, 1990).

Obviously, the IT budget depends on the demand for new systems. As the application portfolio increases, greater budget pressures occur due to enhancement and maintenance requirements. Keen (1991) estimates that every $1 of development causes $4 of ongoing costs over the following five years. Without sizable productivity gains, it is easy to incur double-digit annual IT budget increases.

Accounting and Charging for Information Technology

Many general managers believe that the best way to hold IS and line organizations accountable for the impact of systems on the organization is to have the IS unit operate as a business within a business. In this instance, the IS unit would be a profit or investment center, with a flexible budget and an agreed-upon transfer pricing scheme. This places control of IT in the hands of those who use such services. Control changes from a vague annual negotiation process of capital expenditures approvals and cost allocations into managing to make a profit.

As a general manager, your business unit will be affected directly by an IS chargeback process. Further, you may see chargeback as a way to understand better your true costs, or you may see chargeback as complicating your process of internal budgeting. Certainly there are many positive aspects to charging for IS services, but, as with any profit-center and transfer-pricing scheme, short- and long-term costs and benefits become difficult to balance. You and other managers will adapt behavior to take advantage of the price structure (for example, discounts for overnight processing might cause you to rely less on on-line reporting). Thus, it is important for you to understand why chargeback schemes are put in place and what characterizes a good process.

Organizations adopt a chargeback process for IT services for one or more of the following major reasons:

To assign costs clearly to those who consume and benefit from IT.

To control wasteful use of IT resources by encouraging users to compare the benefits with the costs and eliminate unprofitable use.

To overcome the belief that IT costs may be unnecessarily high.

To provide incentives by subsidizing the price of

certain services or innovative uses of technologies.

- To change the IT budgeting process to be more business driven, thus rewarding the IS organization for improved service and greater efficiency rather than technological change for its own sake.
- To encourage line managers to be knowledgeable consumers of IS because they must directly pay for such support.

A major problem is that many IT costs are joint costs, not easily attributed to one line organization (such as the cost to store and maintain a shared database). Further, some costs are rather fixed (such as systems software and many components of a mainframe). Thus, calculating costs and reducing expenditures as demand varies may not be as easy as one would wish. Also, in applications in which the benefits of IT may be difficult to determine (as in education, research, and customer service), chargeback can limit creative uses of technology.

Transfer prices can be developed for a broad and comprehensive range of IS activities, including charges for:

- personnel time.
- computer usage or wall-clock time (or computer cycles used).
- disk file space.
- magnetic tape storage.
- number of pages or transactions processed.
- number of input and output operations performed.
- amount of computer main memory used (per unit of time).

Charges might be cost-based (to recover all costs) or market-based (to be comparable to market alternatives). A combination might be used of clearly identifiable direct costs plus an allocation of other overhead costs (space, administrative staff, and so on).

Desirable Features of an IT Chargeback System Chargeback systems for IT activities can be a great source of irritation between the IS organization and general managers, unless a mutually agreed-upon structure for charging can be developed. The following are the characteristics you should expect from a successful chargeback system:

Understandable: An understandable chargeback system reports use in business terms that line managers can relate to their own activities, not just computer operations. For example, charges per customer order, invoice, or report relate more to business activity than does the number of computer input/output operations performed or machine cycles used.

Prompt and regular feedback: Charges should be reported soon after the activity to which they are related so that use and cost can be closely linked and total costs can be accurately monitored by those who can control the costs.

Controllable: The activity for which managers are charged must be something they can control (for example, charges for rerun computer jobs because of operator errors would not be controllable). Further, users must have a choice to use alternative services or to substitute one kind of usage with another (for example, switching between two alternative database management systems or trading computer time for data storage).

Accountable: Managers responsible for generating IS activity must be identifiable and must be held accountable for their charges, otherwise the charges are meaningless and useless.

Relate to benefits: Managers must see a link between costs and benefits so they can balance the value of the IS services against what is being spent.

Consistent with IS goals: Charges should be designed to achieve the goals set for the IS organization. Thus, charges should encourage use of important information technology services, efficient use of scarce technology and services, the desired balance of internal and external sourcing of IS services, and development of systems congruent with the accepted architecture for systems.

Chargeback systems must be periodically evaluated to check that the desired results are being achieved.

EVALUATING YOUR
IS ORGANIZATION

A wide variety of sources have suggested that a significant number of organizations are not sure they are getting their money's worth from IT, even after many years of investment. More to the point, many organizations simply do not know what the impact of technology has been. Typically, huge cost savings were never realized, project budgets were exceeded, head count was not reduced or personnel were simply moved to more sophisticated jobs, and the important benefits could not be directly attributed to IT. By contrast, certain general impacts are clear. Some organizations have become very dependent on IT, and it is being used for competitive advantage, so systems must be critical to their success.

Organizations and individual managers need agreed-upon and measurable criteria by which to judge the health and contribution of the IS organization and the systems it manages. IS organizations also need metrics to judge the quality of their work. We concentrate in this section, however, on the measures of most interest to you, the general business manager.

Measures of IS Unit Success

Traditional productivity measurement approaches, such as cost-benefit analysis (CBA) and return on investment (ROI), can be used to justify and evaluate individual systems, as is discussed in earlier chapters. A wide variety of other criteria for evaluating the IS organization are possible, many of which are outlined in Figure 15.4. These criteria are used in combination; no one or two measures adequately provide the complete picture of the contribution of the IS department.

The IS evaluation criteria of Figure 15.4 require specific measures to be useful. Some criteria call for subjective measures. For example, the *Meeting business objectives* criterion could be measured by an opinion survey involving such questions as:

- Does the IT plan support the corporate strategic plan?

- Would our organization be out of business without the IS unit?

Other criteria can be assessed by more quantitative and objective measures. For example, the *Operating reliable and efficient technology resources* criterion could be measured by:

- on-line response time to queries.
- computer up-time as a percentage of total time.
- number of system crashes.

As with any measurement system, you should measure only what is important, what needs improvement, and what is meaningful to some audience. Typically, measures of time, money, and defects are the most useful. Kaplan and Norton (1992) call for using a set of measures that balance various assessment categories, including financial measures as well as the drivers of future performance:

- customer satisfaction (such measures as on-time delivery of new systems, number of defects in a system).
- internal processes (for IS, this could be the productivity of computer system developers, often measured by an industry standard of number of function points per month).
- innovation and learning (education level of IS staff or average age of systems).

Service Level Agreements   The IS organization can be evaluated through a service level agreement (see Chapter 9) similar to one that would be written with an external supplier. This agreement makes expectations, from both IS and management, explicit and defines agreed-upon criteria for a successful system and quality service. The successful use of a service level agreement (SLA) has been described by John P. Singleton et al. (1988) for the Security Pacific Bank.

User Satisfaction Measures   If IS is viewed as a service organization, then user satisfaction is a very important measure of IS success. Such measures are an excellent way for managers to communicate their assessment of IS to senior officers and IS executives.

Meeting business objectives: This means increasing business effectiveness and developing systems that support annual and longer-term business goals and directions.

Responding rapidly and economically to new needs: Reducing the cycle from product idea generation to its market introduction can have tremendous value in research cost reduction, personnel time, earlier revenue generation, and competitive advantage.

Expanding business or services: Reaching new markets, adding features (often information-based) to existing products or services, or improving product service quality can be used for differentiation and revenue generation.

Developing an architecture and plan: An architecture allows line managers to access easily the data now contained in data storage systems and supports the more rapid development and deployment of new systems.

Operating reliable and efficient technology resources: Reliable and efficient operation of both internal systems and external services (such as order entry, reservations, and point-of-sale) is essential for the business to operate.

Focusing on the customer: Better customer support helps the organization to retain customers, gain new customers, and increase sales; the goal is to make it easy for the customer to do business with us and for us to know as much about the customer as he expects us to know.

Providing quality IS staff: Indicators such as a high level of education, low turnover rate, and a large number of employees outplaced to line management jobs all suggest an IS organization of productive and useful people.

Reducing size of backlog: Although a backlog of work indicates a strong demand for IS services, a large backlog can be a source of considerable frustration and unmet business opportunities; with a proper mix of end-user development, use of fourth-generation languages, and purchasing package software, this backlog should be reduced to a manageable and reasonable level.

Satisfying users: In the same spirit of the business focusing on a satisfied customer, the IS organization can be measured by how satisfied line managers are with the technology, systems, and support services provided to them.

FIGURE 15.4 IS Evaluation Criteria

Although not economic in nature and not related directly to business impacts (like reduced inventory, increased customer satisfaction, or improved product quality), user satisfaction measures can be captured easily and compared over time. Your attitudes about systems and the IS department affect your willingness to work with IS professionals in the kinds of partnerships discussed in this book.

Typically, an annual survey would be conducted for each major system, systems that may have problems, IS support organizations (such as the information center), or any area of IS that is receiving criticism; that is, a user satisfaction sur-

vey can be conducted on an application system or on an IS unit. Different levels of managers should be surveyed separately, since their different systems perspectives and roles (for example, direct user, source of funding, supervisor) can affect their evaluation.

Figure 15.5 lists some criteria that can appear on user satisfaction surveys for a specific system and criteria that could be customized to particular IS units, such as systems development or end-user support. The survey could ask you to rate the system or unit on, for example, a one-to-ten scale (low-to-high performance) or ask you to respond on a strongly-disagree-to-strongly-agree scale

User Satisfaction Criteria for Systems

Accuracy of outputs
Quality/readability of output format
Completeness of outputs
Relevance of outputs
Completeness of or accessibility to database
Currency of database
Response time (or other measure of work
    completed)
Availability
Mean time between failures
Downtime or malfunction recovery time
Charges/costs
Quality of system documentation
Number and severity of security breaches
Ease of operation
Ease of making changes
Increased confidence in decisions and actions
    taken due to system
Extent of achieving expected benefits

User Satisfaction Criteria for IS Units

Quality of system specification documents
Size of request backlog or workload
Projects completed on time and within budget
Speed at which requested system changes
    are made
Professionalism of IS staff
Nature of relationships with IS staff
Business knowledge of IS staff
Quality of user training
User feeling of involvement in systems
    management

FIGURE 15.5 Criteria for User Satisfaction Surveys

concerning various statements involving the criteria in Figure 15.5. The survey might also ask you to indicate how important each criterion is, so a weighted assessment can occur. The survey may include some open-ended questions that ask for problems, complaints, praise, particular system features to add or delete, and what you like best or least about the system or IS unit.

MANAGING GLOBAL SYSTEMS

As a business manager you may make decisions on how to organize for global operations, and you may be involved in acquiring foreign subsidiaries or in alliances with international partners. How you will receive IS support should be one aspect you consider in making such decisions. You should realize that information technology and professional practices do not have widely accepted international standards, so expansion of local systems, plans, and IS practices to other countries for a multinational corporation (MNC) is not trivial.

Ives and Jarvenpaa (1991) suggest that there are ten reasons why business managers are requesting the creation of global information systems. These are:

1. *Global Customer Requirements.* Global customers include travelers who require consistent service worldwide and MNCs that demand common worldwide services to support their integrated international business operations.
2. *Global Products.* Worldwide marketing and distribution programs require a global perspective on supporting information systems.
3. *Rationalized Operations.* IT is used to coordinate worldwide manufacturing processes.
4. *Flexible Operations.* Businesses want to be able to move operations between countries as labor rates or skills, raw material availability, laws, trade agreements, and other factors dictate.
5. *Joint Resources.* National subsidiaries may share facilities, people, or materials (for example, oil tankers, warehouses, or consultants).
6. *Duplicate Facilities.* An MNC may operate similar manufacturing plants, refineries, or sales offices in different countries, so common software can be used to support all of these sites.
7. *Scarce Resources.* A unit of an MNC may need to use a unique resource or materials that cannot be made available economically at all sites, and careful coordination of use is

required through integrated materials movement systems.

8. *Risk Reduction.* Care must be taken to account properly for currency conversions, international sourcing of raw materials, or bidding on international projects. A global system is necessary to guarantee that any international site can equally participate without fear of inaccuracy.

9. *Legal Requirements.* A subsidiary that sells in or uses products from multiple countries requires a system that handles laws and accounting practices in all countries involved.

10. *Economies of Scale.* Consolidated data centers and systems can reduce costs, increase reliability and consistency, and ease maintenance and evolution of systems.

Organizing for Global Systems

The choice of how to manage IT internationally is contingent on how the organization as a whole is managed globally. Strong divisional or headquarters mentality will influence the stance on international IT management. The degree of interdependence between international units will suggest the requirements for tight or loose information flows in different functional and staff areas. Size and location of operations will also influence the decision, that is, large groups that are geographically close would suggest a common IS organization, whereas small and highly scattered units would be more difficult to service from one central IS group.

According to Roche (1992), U.S. business has tended to adopt a decentralized strategy for managing IT on a global basis. This tendency was driven by the difficulty of dealing with international differences and the unavailability or lack of uniform quality of IT worldwide. Consequently, only a few truly global applications have been developed. Instead, organizations have deployed systems according to old organization structures, without using IT to reengineer for the global business (see Chapter 7 for discussion of business process reengineering). Thus, IT has tended to follow, not lead, the MNC. Roche cites the case of Ford Motor Company as an example in which global business and IS strategy are meshing, although IS

TAKING IS GLOBAL

Although computers and systems are used worldwide, many differences in technology and general management make global information technology management a special issue. The following are some specific examples of some differences from what is experienced in North American companies.

Danish businesses have to wait several months or more before software introduced in the United States is changed to support their character set.

Word processor macros written to help edit English-language documents may be useless for foreign-language versions of the product.

U.S.-manufactured telecommunications equipment with U.S. standards cannot be used in Germany in order to protect German national firms like Siemens.

Management and executive support systems that assume direct manipulation of data by managers do not work in many European businesses where computer work is associated with only clerical labor force.

PCs are on very few desks in Japan, where computer systems are still considered a shared resource, like copy machines in the United States. There are 202 computers per 1,000 people in the United States. This same ratio is 114 per 1,000 in the U.K., 82 per 1,000 in Germany, and 43 per 1,000 in Italy.

(Adapted from Burnson, 1989, and *Computerworld,* August 12, 1991)

---

strategy is responding to business direction, not leading the business. As part of Ford's efforts to implement the "world car" concept, Ford IS units have installed a second data communications network dedicated to computer-aided design workstations worldwide. Ford insists on common systems in this area, and places the burden of proof on local units for justifying unique systems for a particular engineering center or manufacturing facility. In contrast, because there is no driving business reason to globalize dealers, such systems as order processing are localized.

Robert Reck of the Index Group, a major IS management consulting firm (Reck, 1989), claims that an MNC can choose one of three strategies for global management—imperialistic, multidomestic, and global. Each has different implications for IS management. The imperialistic strategy tightly controls international operations, making them simply extensions of headquarters. In such firms IS management would usually be centralized, there would be a common architecture for IT, computing would hub into one or a few data centers, planning and funding of systems would be centralized, and a strict hierarchical IS organization structure would be used.

The multidomestic style is highly decentralized with only necessary financial ties between subsidiaries and headquarters. In a sense, a multidomestic company is not truly global, but a federation of different companies. Thus, IS management and operations are localized.

The global strategy promotes a high degree of integration, but also a high degree of local control. Reck says that teamwork best describes this style. IS in a global firm will integrate a few key technol-

ogies and resources (as part of the IT architecture), such as data and telecommunications, with dispersal of most planning and control. The IS organization usually follows a matrix structure. Of course, many companies take a mixed strategy, for example with an imperialistic strategy for financial systems, multidomestic for sales, and global for manufacturing.

Another form of the global strategy encourages the development of different types of systems in different international units. "You get the units with the best skills to develop systems for each other. The Germans build the financial systems, the French build the retail systems, and so on" (*Computerworld*, August 12, 1991). One report (Guez, 1992) claims that it can be very advantageous to distribute the building of systems worldwide. Guez states that software development in Europe may take only half the time that it does in the United States. European developers spend more time in analysis and design steps, thus getting the requirements right, compared to their U.S. counterparts.

Barriers to Global IT Management

There are various characteristics of the countries in which an organization operates that influence decisions on global IT management:

Language, character set, and currency differences will influence how easily a central systems development group or common or shared systems can satisfy user needs. Local accounting and securities practices will directly affect the nature of financial systems. The ability and willingness of clerical staff to use systems based in a foreign language or currency must be considered. Fluctuations in exchange rates can drastically affect the cost of distributed IS operations.

The support of operations across *many time zones* may not be possible from one central staff and from centralized systems. For example, central systems will have to be shut down occasionally for maintenance and upgrade, and such scheduling would be tight across various time zones, working hours, holidays, and vacation schedules. On the other hand, a wide geographical telecommunications network can shift work between data centers, order entry offices, telemarketing facilities, and user help desks so that operations can proceed outside of normal local business hours and on local holidays.

Regulations and tariffs for transporting data across international boundaries will dictate the economics of data processing (see Chapter 14 for further discussion of this topic). Laws exist in some parts of the world that require programming and operations to be done locally, thus protecting against perceived threats of imperialism and ensuring that national data resources are not abused by foreign companies. Import restrictions or tariffs may make the use of standard (foreign-developed) software and hardware prohibitively expensive in certain international units. A company must also protect its intellectual property rights for such assets as computer software. Although several international efforts have tried to standardize the process of intellectual property protection, companies are still suffering substantial copyright losses (Deans and Kane, 1992, report statistics from the International Intellectual Property Alliance that show U.S. firms lost $418 million in film, music, books, and computer software in China in 1989 and more than $1 billion worldwide in the same year).

The *cultures and professional practices* of different countries can influence the systems development process (for example, in some European countries IS personnel are unionized) and will suggest whether one or several staffs are needed. Also, differences in accounting practices, tax calculations, and regulations make the deployment of standard application systems for business operations difficult because such systems must support local practices as well as organization standards.

Computer industry standards for computer and telecommunications equipment will influence to what degree operations in different locations can be tightly linked. The existence or strength of computer vendors or representa-

tives to support and maintain local equipment and staff will affect the ability to have common technology (and, hence, common systems) in all countries. Even the availability of quality electrical power will affect the ability to have local operations.

The *cost and availability of reliable voice and data telecommunications networks* will influence the ability to share systems, to transfer electronically data without rekeying, and to build on-line systems in foreign sites. The difficulties of getting telephone lines installed and maintained can significantly increase the costs for on-line systems. The quality of circuits and of telecommunication services varies enormously around the world. Rates for the same services can vary by as much as three times, depending on the country. Thus, where telecommunications services are located matters considerably in deploying IT worldwide. Although there have been many improvements in recent years, there are still some limitations on using the same telecommunications equipment in several countries, and it still may be a challenge to work with highly bureaucratic postal telephone and telegraph (PTT) authorities. Some European countries restrict satellite communication to receive only.

Information technology platforms and systems development approaches vary worldwide. Although many of the same technologies exist around the world, IS professionals may prefer to use (for performance, support, and familiarity) home-grown brands. A country-specific IS unit in an MNC frequently prefers to use its national software development standard method to simplify training, for compatibility with legacy systems, and for reasons of national pride. The deployment of standard application software can be deterred by such differences. According to Steinbart and Nath (1992), hardware and software incompatibility are the top two problems facing companies trying to create global systems.

The *availability and cost of trained local IS professionals and consultants* to provide local management expertise and the costs to relocate

---

IMPATIENT BENETTON S.p.A.

"We can't wait months to connect our new companies—we want our operations to be set up in one month," according to Bruno Zuccaro of Benetton S.p.A. To achieve this service, the Italian apparel company contracted with General Electric Information Services (GEIS) value-added reseller (VAN) service, replacing a collection of leased lines from a host of PTTs. Benetton decided they were in the apparel business, not the telecommunications business. They now let GEIS manage their 75-country communications system that supports sales, cash clearing, and product distribution. Benetton deals with one worldwide supplier, which in turn deals with the fast changing tariffs, regulations, equipment, and services in the international telecommunications industry.

**(Adapted from *Computerworld,*
August 12, 1991)**

STANDARDS AT FEDERAL EXPRESS

Standards are a more important part of IS global policy at Federal Express than are specific technologies. Federal Express updates their five-year plan every six months to incorporate worldwide changes. Core business applications are standardized at all global sites, using a common platform (with greater emphasis on UNIX as an open standard). Core applications may be customized at each site, which allows fast deployment of new systems worldwide, servicing local information needs, and standardizing information flows for integrated business operations.

(Adapted from Runyan, 1989)

---

your personnel to a foreign site are also important. The education level, absenteeism, and other characteristics of the general labor force (clerks, factory workers, and so on) will affect the nature of systems that can be developed or used effectively. Labor rates for IS professionals across the world also vary considerably. Today, some U.S. firms are taking programming assignments offshore to take advantage of these labor rate differences.

Planning for Global Systems

As in other areas of the business, the extension of IT management to other countries should be carefully planned. When considering international mergers or acquisitions, IT management issues should be researched. In fact, the proper conduct of IT management is crucial to the success of MNCs, since systems link units across space and time.

Roche (1992) outlines eight elements of a typical successful global IS plan for a tightly integrated MNC. Although some of these elements are debatable, they suggest a need for comprehensive policies to make global systems successful.

1. *Informatize Strategic Alliances.* Value chain linkages (see Chapter 13) are common practice in MNCs to enhance international competitiveness. Improved information and telecommunication services between alliance partners (such as international EDI) make the coordination between global partners easier. A shared international database, for example containing sales referrals or vendor data, can provide valuable business intelligence.

2. *Develop International Systems Development Skills.* Systems development staff must have a global view of the business, and they must be able to work with foreign cultures and different management styles in different countries. Management of international projects requires a sensitivity to international politics within a foreign unit and within its local business environment. Standards of IS practice vary across countries, and a champion with global influence may be necessary for successful systems deployment.

3. *Building an Anticipative Infrastructure.* It is necessary to build for the future because global systems generally take longer to deploy than single country systems. A goal to build transportable systems requires careful coordination of technology throughout all international operations. Key elements of this strategy are common telecommunications, consistent hardware

and software platforms, and global management of data definitions.

4. *Tear Down the "National" Model.* Totally independent or semiautonomous data centers and systems will never allow an MNC to adequately link business operations worldwide. The tearing down of the national model begins with the hardware and system software standards of strategy 3 above. The second stage is consolidation of application systems to facilitate international workflow automation (for example, production scheduling, inventory control, and order processing).

5. *Capture Residual Value.* The heart of this strategy is the elimination of duplicate facilities and staff and then using the cost savings to invest in improving other international operations. Thus, IT becomes a contributor to international growth of the MNC. Business process reengineering may be necessary for a thorough capture of residual value. As is typical of such reengineering projects, the driving force for consolidation of international IS functions may be customer demands for seamless interaction with the global business.

6. *Exploit the Coming Liberalization in International Telecommunications.* The monopolistic dominance of national PTT organizations is slowly but inevitably breaking apart. Similar to the divestiture of the Bell System in the United States, an MNC must be ready to take advantage of opportunities that will result (such as lower costs, higher quality and more modern services, faster installation). These changes are especially dramatic in Eastern Europe where countries may leapfrog technology stages by installing fully digital telecommunications systems as part of economic revitalization efforts. On the other hand, the lack of qualified people and sufficient capital to support this infrastructure will require considerable investment by the governments and the private sector.

7. *Homogenize Data Structures.* Data elements that are needed to manage the global business must be standardized. National pools of key data make this global management of data as a resource (see Chapter 14) a difficult but necessary task. Without such standards, it is impossible to obtain a global view of an organization (for example, international sales comparisons require common product-class distinctions, units of measure, time units, back-order handling, and booked versus billed designations).

8. *Globalize Human Resources.* Most IS employees take a national and not a global view of systems, which is caused by a lack of training, country-specific experience, and reward systems. Worldwide promotions and relocations can help to overcome such narrow mindsets. Special IS skills found in certain countries can be globalized by focused training programs, careful project team selection to maximize exposure to diverse expertise, language education, and a thorough international IS skills inventory.

As organizations become more global, you will have to consider how to deliver information services to your international operations. You should communicate your international plan to the IS department and work with them to evolve the IT architecture to accommodate the global nature of your business.

SUMMARY

The nature of how organizations manage information systems and technologies is changing. Increasingly, IT is managed like other business units, with expectations for contribution to the organization and with shared responsibility for all managers.

Although some IS professionals initially resisted such management system changes (end-user development, distributed IT management, and so on), the partnership of IS and business managers is now strong in most organizations. A business unit now typically manages the development of systems that support primarily that unit, and the unit is held accountable for the contribution of its systems to its success. The IS unit acts as a technology transfer function, as a consultant to distributed IS units, and as an architect that provides the framework in which other units utilize information technology.

The importance of IT is echoed by the establishment of a chief information officer or other senior IS executive responsible for linking the IT and business plans. A diverse set of other IS management positions exists in central IS departments as well as in line organizations. Career opportunities in IS are plentiful, challenging, and increasingly similar to other general management careers in possible long-term responsibilities and the essentials for success.

Organizations have not settled on one best way to organize the IS unit. The globalization of companies makes structuring this function even more difficult. Although history suggests that the IS function has periodically shifted between centralization and decentralization, today many organizations have very distributed IS functions. At some point in the late 1990s, if history repeats, organizations will decide that they are not achieving some of the advantages of a more centrally managed IT infrastructure, and some functions will be reeled in to headquarters. Thus, the function of the IS unit to develop and communicate a future vision for IT is extremely important. These efforts ease the pain of periodic moves to centralize and distribute responsibilities for IS operations, development, and management.

REVIEW QUESTIONS

1. Why have IT management and structure changed in the past ten years? That is, what changes in IT or the business have caused the IS unit to be restructured or to take on a new mission?

2. Why do some experts believe that the IS department is doomed to extinction, much like the large operations research departments of the 1960s and 1970s? Does this actually seem to be occurring?

3. How have the perspectives of IS professionals changed in the past ten to fifteen years?

4. Why are strictly financial measures like ROI and CBA insufficient for evaluating information systems?

5. What are the major responsibilities of a CIO? How are these different from the traditional IS director?

6. What are the major concerns of a CIO?

7. Name and outline the essential characteristics of the four major generic IS organization structures.

8. What is IT outsourcing?

9. What is the largest cost in the IT budget today?

10. What are the characteristics of a good IT chargeback system?

11. What are some unique issues concerning IT management that arise in multinational firms or firms doing business in many countries?

12. What should be the nature of the partnership between IT and business managers?

DISCUSSION QUESTIONS

1. If you were to write an IS department mission statement, what key words would you have used ten years ago compared to the words you would use today?

2. Develop a chart that takes the major IT functions of operations, development, and management and shows the primary responsibilities in each function for the central IS group, a division-based IS unit, and general managers.

3. What financial measures can be used for the contribution systems make to the business? What are the caveats involved with these measures?

4. What type of person in an organization should be considered for a CIO position? That is, what type of individual would be a prime candidate for such a job?

5. Besides the activities of the CIO, what role do other general managers have in the leadership of IT in organizations?

6. This chapter emphasizes the need for a partnership between IS and general managers for managing IT. Define your concept of a management partnership and relate this to making

people accountable for business operations and functions.

7. Review the various pros and cons of distributing the systems development organization between central IS and line management organizations.

8. What type of organization would benefit most from creating an IS subsidiary? What type of organization would benefit most from outsourcing IS operations?

9. Outline the arguments against using only traditional financial measures for the contribution of IT to the business.

10. Under what circumstances would you recommend an organization to adopt a direct chargeback scheme for IS services?

11. As the manager of a statewide ATM network, how would you evaluate the quality of the IS organization serving you? If you were director of consumer marketing for a major appliance manufacturer, how would you evaluate the quality of the IS services you receive?

12. Consider the IS evaluation criterion of "Focusing on the customer" in Figure 15.4. What precise measures could be used to assess the contribution of IS services to this criterion?

13. What arguments would you use to justify a career in IS management as a way to senior management in an organization?

REFERENCES

1989. "Using the law to rein in computer runaways." *Business Week* (April 3): 70–76.

1989. "More companies are chucking their computers." *Business Week* (June 19): 72–74.

1989. "The evolving systems organization." *I/S Analyzer* 27 (November): 1–27.

1990. "CIO is starting to stand for 'Career Is Over'." *Business Week* (February 26): 78–80.

1991. "Critical issues in information systems management, 1991–1995." *I/S Analyzer* 29 (January): 1–14.

1991. "Adventures in the new Europe." Special supplement to *Computerworld* (August 12).

1993. "The changing role of the mainframe." *I/S Analyzer* 31 (January): 1–14.

Boynton, Andrew C., Gerry C. Jacobs, and Robert W. Zmud. 1992. "Whose responsibility is IT management?" *Sloan Management Review* 33 (Summer): 32–38.

Brancheau, James, and James C. Wetherbe. 1987. "Key issues in information systems—1986." *MIS Quarterly* 11 (March): 23–46.

Burnson, Patrick. 1989. "The perils of going global." *Infoworld* (August 14): 39–40.

Carlyle, Ralph Emmett. 1988. "CIO: Misfit or misnomer?" *Datamation* 34 (August 1): 50–56.

Carlyle, Ralph. 1990. "Recovery!" *Datamation* 36 (April 1): 35–48.

Deans, P. Candace, and Michael J. Kane. 1992. *International Dimensions of Information Systems and Technology*. Boston: PWS–Kent Publishing Company.

Dearden, John. 1987. "The withering away of the IS department." *Sloan Management Review* 28 (Summer): 87–91.

Elam, Joyce J., Michael J. Ginzberg, Peter G. W. Keen, and Robert W. Zmud. 1988. *Transforming the IS Organization*. Washington, DC: International Center for Information Technology.

Guez, Jean-Claude. 1992. "Systems integration for the international company." *The Journal of European Business* 4 (November/December): 10–14.

Henderson, John C. 1990. "Plugging into strategic partnerships: The critical IS connection." *Sloan Management Review* 31 (Spring): 7–18.

Hoffer, Jeffrey A., and Detmar W. Straub, Jr. 1989. "Managing the risk from computer system abuse." *Sloan Management Review* 30 (Summer): 35–43.

Ives, Blake, and Sirkka Jarvenpaa. 1991. "Applications of global information technology: Key issues for management." *MIS Quarterly* 15 (March): 33–49.

Kaplan, Robert S., and David P. Norton. 1992. "The balanced scorecard—measures that drive performance." *Harvard Business Review* 70 (January–February): 71–79.

Keen, Peter G. W. 1991. *Shaping the Future: Business Design through Information Technology*. Boston: Harvard Business School Press.

Livingston, Dennis. 1992. "Outsourcing: Look beyond the price tag." *Datamation* 39 (February 15): 20–27.

Moad, Jeff. 1993. "Inside an outsourcing deal." *Datamation* 39 (February 15): 20–27.

Parker, Marilyn M., and Robert J. Benson. 1988. *Information Economics: Linking Business Performance to Information Technology*. Englewood Cliffs, NJ: Prentice–Hall, Inc.

Reck, Robert H. 1989. "The shock of going global." *Datamation* 35 (August 1): 67–70.

Roche, Edward M. 1992. *Managing Information Technology in Multinational Corporations*. New York: Macmillan Publishing Company.

Runyan, Linda. 1989. "Global IS strategies." *Datamation* 35 (December 1): 71–78.

Singleton, John P., Ephraim R. McLean, and Edward N. Altman. 1988. "Measuring information systems performance: Experience with the management by results system at Security Pacific Bank." *MIS Quarterly* 12 (June): 325–337.

Steinbart, Paul J., and Ravinder Nath. 1992. "Problems and issues in the management of international data communications networks: The experiences of American companies." *MIS Quarterly* 16 (March): 55–76.

Wilder, Clinton. 1989. "Bank hands keys to IBM." *Computerworld* 23 (November 6): 1, 8.

10

Eastman Kodak Company: Managing Information Systems Through Strategic Alliances

Katherine Hudson, vice president of Corporate Information Systems (CIS) at Eastman Kodak Co. (Kodak), surveyed the reports that detailed the performance of her organization over the past year. She was pleased with the progress that had been made but knew that there was much more to be done to achieve her goals of delivering both high-quality and cost-effective information technology (IT) services to Kodak businesses.

When Kodak CEO Colby Chandler created the CIS unit in January 1988 and appointed Hudson head, she became at once the first head of IT and first woman corporate vice president in the company. Hudson was directed to overhaul the existing IT organization to promote the use of IT to improve the competitive position of Kodak businesses while dramatically lowering costs. Despite a lack of IT management experience, Hudson was no stranger to organizational challenges. Her previous job at Kodak had been to dismantle the $239 million instant camera business subsequent to the company's loss of a costly lawsuit with Polaroid.

Upon assuming her position, Hudson reviewed the results of an outside vendor's studies of Kodak's IT services. She supplemented these findings with other internal and external studies. "Every study said we needed help," Hudson recalled, explaining that throughout the organization separate entities were

managing diverse, redundant technology platforms established under different operating standards. "The right hand," she remarked, "had no idea what the left was doing!"

Hudson observed,

The results of the studies generated new questions. For example, should Kodak invest millions of dollars fixing the in-place IT infrastructure or use that money to support our core businesses of imaging, photography, health, and chemicals? We knew that IT was critical to the business but had never stopped to consider which IT functions and services were "core" and which were support. Throughout the company, we were moving toward selling off non-core businesses and services. Why shouldn't we apply that same logic to our IT services?

Throughout 1989, Hudson inaugurated a series of organizational initiatives that not only would dramatically change the IT function within Kodak but would rock the industry. She outsourced data center operations, telecommunications services, and personal computer (PC) support to IBM, Digital Equipment Corporation (DEC), and BusinessLand, respectively. In doing so, she effectively challenged the cultural inertia of the 109-year-old manufacturing company, forced rival IT vendors to collaborate openly before the international press, transformed job descriptions and work environments for more than 2,000 people, and created a new wave of interest in outsourcing that forced IT managers around the world to seriously evaluate its potential for their organizations.

In June 1991, over one year after the last of the strategic alliance contracts had been signed, Hudson surveyed the results of her efforts. While many of the

Professor Lynda M. Applegate and Research Associate Ramiro Montealegre prepared this case as the basis for class discussion rather than to illustrate either effective or ineffective handling of an administrative situation.

original objectives had been achieved, new challenges in managing the alliances required significant attention. The recent announcement by BusinessLand of its decision to merge, be acquired, or declare Chapter 11 drove home the point: clearly, the honeymoon was over.

....

Company Background

The Eastman Kodak Company was founded in 1880 by inventor-entrepreneur-philanthropist George Eastman, a young bank clerk. Since his development of the first snapshot camera in 1888, Kodak had celebrated many creative milestones.

In 1904, Eastman had articulated the company's competitive philosophy: "Nothing is more important than the value of our name and the quality it stands for. We must make quality our fighting argument."[1] Commitment to highest quality products and services led Kodak to adopt a high level of vertical integration. Kodak operated its own laundry service to ensure that the cloth used by personnel in the manufacture of film possessed the requisite softness and was free of detergent residue. The company also ran its own fire department, blacksmith, bank, and cafeteria among many other services. Most of these services were still being run by Kodak as the company entered the 1980s.

Kodak's organization structure also reflected the company's early roots. Although it had become a very large, diversified corporation, Kodak was still organized as a classical hierarchy, with the CEO presiding over a single monolithic, functional structure. "That works fine in a small company or if you have a single product serving a cohesive market," observed Chandler, "but Kodak is no longer operating in that kind of environment."

The solution, undertaken in 1984, was to reorganize the company into 29 separate business units grouped into four lines of business—Photography (PPG), Commercial Imaging Group (CIG), Chemicals (ECC), and Health (HG)—and three international segments—Latin America, Europe, and Asia/Pacific (see Exhibit 1). Each business unit operated as a profit center under a general manager. Centralized corporate functional units downsized considerably as business units assumed control of the functions needed to produce their products, including marketing, manufacturing, and research and development, among

others. Chandler, calling this "a much more decisive structure," observed that "our development time to bring out new products is less than half what it was."

In 1986, as the company faced significant cost pressures secondary to stiff competition and the Polaroid lawsuit, a second, painful organizational change was made. Kodak downsized its core businesses. Employees were cut by 10 percent and the operating budget by 5 percent. Simultaneously, Kodak diversified into new businesses including office equipment and biotechnology, through more than 20 acquisitions and joint ventures. Despite these moves, second-quarter profits plunged 85 percent in 1989 prompting a second round of cost-cutting. More than 4,500 additional jobs were eliminated as unprofitable businesses were consolidated or eliminated. Despite these measures, sales per employee of $140,000 in 1989 were still well below the $380,000 per employee of its arch-rival, Fuji Photo Film Company.[2] A financial summary is provided in Exhibit 2.

....

Information Technology at Kodak

While Kodak fought to regain its competitive position, the Information Systems Division (ISD), a centralized functional unit that managed information and communications technology services for Kodak businesses, also began to restructure in line with the new organization. In 1985, responsibility for development of business applications and management of small-scale computer and network operations (e.g., minicomputers, personal computers, and local area networks) was shifted to each of the 29 business units. ISD remained responsible for management of the large data centers and voice and data communications.

Directed by the CEO to increase efficiency and decrease costs, ISD between 1986 and 1987 began a process of consolidating and standardizing data center and telecommunications operations. (A 1987 *Information Week* study ranked Kodak number 15 among the 100 largest information systems installations.) The creation of the Corporate Information Systems unit in 1988 and appointment of Hudson as head marked the beginning of a more aggressive approach to restructuring the IT organization. Exhibit 3 presents an organization chart for CIS. Hudson described the challenges she faced upon assuming her new position:

(text continued on page 641)

---

[1] "Focus on the Future: A Guide to Kodak's Business Units and Products," Eastman Kodak, 1988.

[2] Ansberry, C., and C. Hymovitz. "Kodak Chief is Trying for the Fourth Time to Trim Firm's Costs." *Wall Street Journal* (July 19, 1989).

EXHIBIT 1

Eastman Kodak Co.: Eastman Kodak Organization—1991

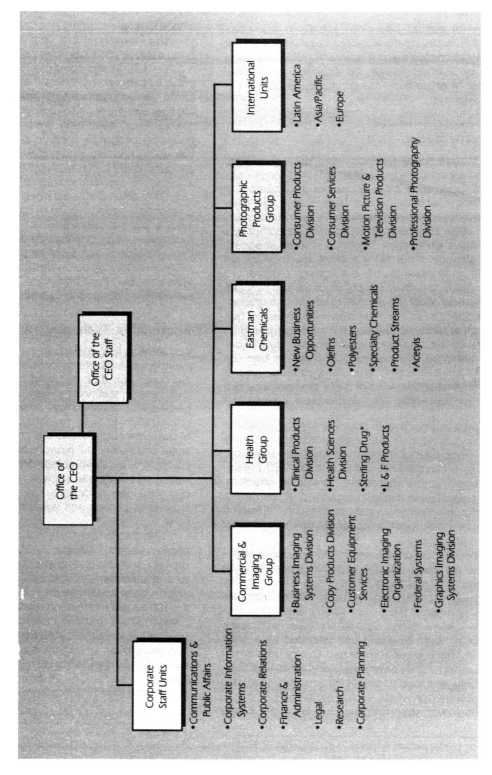

Office of the CEO

Office of the CEO Staff

Corporate Staff Units
- Communications & Public Affairs
- Corporate Information Systems
- Corporate Relations
- Finance & Administration
- Legal
- Research
- Corporate Planning

Commercial & Imaging Group
- Business Imaging Systems Division
- Copy Products Division
- Customer Equipment Services
- Electronic Imaging Organization
- Federal Systems
- Graphics Imaging Systems Division

Health Group
- Clinical Products Division
- Health Sciences Division
- Sterling Drug*
- L & F Products

Eastman Chemicals
- New Business Opportunities
- Olefins
- Polyesters
- Specialty Chemicals
- Product Streams
- Aceyls

Photographic Products Group
- Consumer Products Division
- Consumer Services Division
- Motion Picture & Television Products Division
- Professional Photography Division

International Units
- Latin America
- Asia/Pacific
- Europe

*Sterling Drugs, Inc. was acquired in 1987.

EXHIBIT 2

Eastman Kodak Financial Summary

	1990	1989	1988	1987	1986	1985	1984
Sales	$ 18,908	$ 18,398	$ 17,034	$ 13,305	$ 11,550	$ 10,631	$ 10,600
Earnings from operations	2,844	1,591[b]	2,812	2,078	724[c]	561[d]	1,547
Earnings before income taxes	1,257[a]	925	2,236	1,984	598	530	1,624
Net Earnings	703[a]	529[b]	1,397	1,178	374[c]	332[d]	923
Earnings and Dividends							
Net Earnings—percent sales	3.7%	2.9%	8.2%	8.9%	3.2%	3.1%	8.7%
—percent return on average shareowner's equity[1,2]	10.5%	7.9%	21.8%	19.0%	5.8%	4.8%	12.6%
—per common share[1,2]	2.17	1.63	4.31	3.52	1.10	0.97[d]	2.54
Cash dividends declared—on common shares	$ 649	$ 649	$ 616	$ 572	$ 551	$ 553	$ 578
—per common share[2]	$ 2.00	$ 2.00	$ 1.90	$ 1.71	$ 1.63	$ 1.62	$ 1.60
Common shares outstanding at close of year	324.6	324.4	324.2	324.1	338.7	338.5	350.0
Shareowners at close of year	168,935	171,954	174,110	168,517	172,713	184,231	189,972
Balance Sheet Data							
Current Assets	$ 8,608	$ 8,591	$ 8,684	$ 6,791	$ 5,857	$ 5,677	$ 5,131
Properties at cost	17,648	16,774	15,667	13,789	12,919	12,047	10,775
Accumulated depreciation	8,670	8,146	7,654	7,126	6,643	6,070	5,386
Total assets	24,125	23,652	22,964	14,698	12,994	12,142	10,778
Current liabilities	7,163	6,573	5,850	4,140	3,811	3,325	2,306
Long-term obligations	6,989	7,376	7,779	2,382	981	988	409
Total net assets (shareowners' equity)	6,737	6,642	6,780	6,013	6,388	6,562	7,137
Supplemental Information							
Research and development expenditures	$ 1,329	$ 1,253	$ 1,147	$ 992	$ 1,059	$ 976	$ 838
Wages, salaries, and employee benefits	$ 5,783	$ 5,877	$ 5,469	$ 4,645	$ 4,912	$ 4,484	$ 4,148
Employees at close of year—in the United States	80,350	82,850	87,900	81,800	83,600	89,200	85,600
—worldwide	134,450	137,750	145,300	124,400	121,450	128,950	123,900
Subsidiary Companies Outside the U.S.							
Sales	$ 8,668	$ 8,391	$ 7,748	$ 5,572	$ 4,387	$ 3,429	$ 3,367
Earnings from operations	1,150	771	997	797	400	169	113
Eastman Kodak Company equity in net earnings (loss)	—	—	661	439	167	(9)	25

(exhibit continued on next page)

433

EXHIBIT 2 (continued)

Eastman Kodak Financial Summary

	1983	1982	1981	1980	1979	1978
Sales	$ 10,170	$ 10,815	$ 10,337	$ 9,734	$ 8,028	$ 7,013
Earnings from operations	1,027	1,860	2,060	1,896	1,649	1,646
Earnings before income taxes	1,020	1,872	2,183	1,963	1,707	1,681
Net Earnings	565	1,162	1,239	1,154	1,001	902
Earnings and Dividends						
Net Earnings—percent sales	5.6%	10.7%	12.0%	11.9%	12.5%	12.9%
—percent return on average shareowner's equity[1]	7.5%	16.2%	19.4%	20.2%	19.5%	19.6%
—per common share[2]	$ 1.52	$ 3.17	$ 3.41	$ 3.18	$ 2.76	$ 2.48
Cash dividends declared—on common shares	$ 587	$ 581	$ 566	$ 517	$ 468	$ 376
—per common share	$ 1.58	$ 1.58	$ 1.55	$ 1.42	$ 1.29	$ 1.04
Common shares outstanding at close of year	372.5	372.5	365.6	363.1	363.1	363.1
Shareowners at close of year	200,005	203,788	220,513	234,009	242,227	250,853
Balance Sheet Data						
Current Assets	$ 5,420	$ 5,289	$ 5,063	$ 5,246	$ 4,522	$ 4,000
Properties at cost	10,049	9,344	7,963	6,861	6,041	5,515
Accumulated depreciation	4,801	4,286	3,806	3,426	3,081	2,778
Total assets	10,928	10,622	9,446	8,754	7,554	6,801
Current liabilities	2,182	2,146	2,119	2,247	1,741	1,563
Long-term obligations	416	350	93	79	75	76
Total net assets (shareowners' equity)	7,520	7,541	6,770	6,028	5,391	4,858
Supplemental Information						
Research and development expenditures	$ 746	$ 710	$ 615	$ 520	$ 459	$ 389
Wages, salaries, and employee benefits	$ 4,340	$ 4,446	$ 4,099	$ 3,643	$ 3,177	$ 2,776
Employees at close of year—in the United States	86,000	93,300	91,900	84,400	80,800	79,600
—worldwide	125,500	136,500	136,400	129,500	126,300	124,800
Subsidiary Companies Outside the U.S.						
Sales	$ 3,410	$ 4,279	$ 4,017	$ 4,125	$ 3,305	$ 2,735
Earnings from operations	60	302	450	446	482	411
Eastman Kodak Company equity in net earnings (loss)	(65)	72	188	254	289	220

Note: Dollar figures are expressed in millions except for the "per common share" figures, which are dollars.

[1] Based on average number of shares outstanding.

[2] Data for 1986 have been restated to give effect to the 3-for-2 partial stock split in 1987.

[a] After deducting $888 million for the litigation judgment including post-judgment interest, which reduced net earnings by $564 million.

[b] After deducting restructuring costs of $875 million, which reduced net earnings by $549 million.

[c] After deducting unusual charges of $520 million and certain other special charges of $134 million, which in total reduced earnings from operations by $654 million. Net earnings were reduced by the $373 million after-tax effect of special charges and an additional $50 million from the retroactive repeal of the U.S. investment tax credit as a result of the 1986 tax law change.

[d] After deducting unusual charges of $563 million, which reduced net earnings by $302 million and net earnings per share by $.89. Net earnings were reduced by $373 million because of all special charges and an additional $50 million from the retroactive repeal of the U.S. investment tax credit as a result of the 1986 tax law change.

EXHIBIT 3

Corporate Information Systems—1989

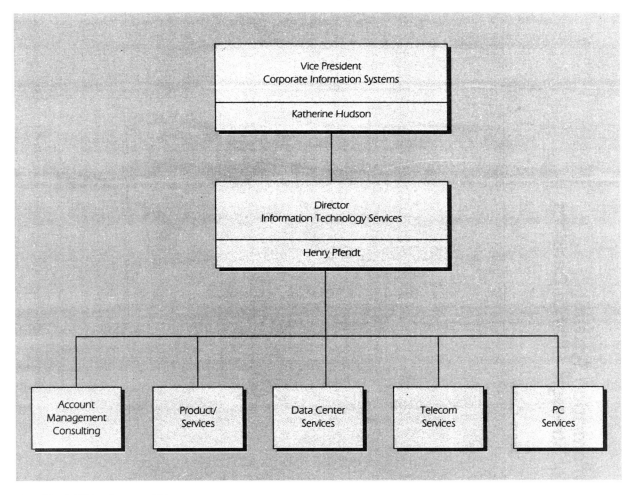

Note: Total CIS headcount = 400.

When we launched CIS at the beginning of 1988, the entire IS management team knew that we had our work cut out for us. I wanted to analyze the IT function using the same criteria·that Kodak was using to analyze our other businesses. In the businesses we had used portfolio analysis to answer the questions: Is there value here? Is this a core function of the company? If the answer was yes, we kept it; if no, we outsourced or eliminated it. I commissioned a number of internal and external studies to help us assess the IT function and provide an overview of our current strengths and weaknesses. See Exhibit 4 for a summary of the IT areas identified as core and non-core. Based on these studies we made the decision to outsource non-core IT services, recognizing that, in the case of IT, non-core IT services would remain inextricably intertwined with core services. Outsourcing IT services, unlike outsourcing laundry services, could not be handled by a simple,

EXHIBIT 4

Corporate Information Systems:
Guidelines for Strategic Alliance Decisions

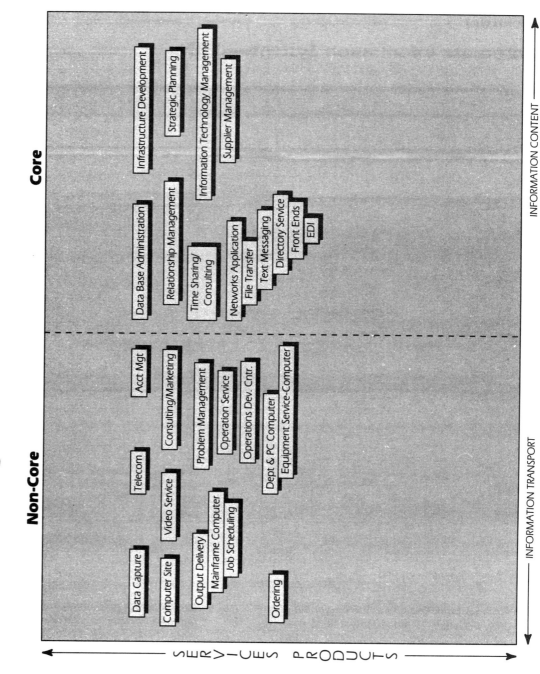

contractual hand-off—the equivalent of throwing the functions over the wall to an outside vendor. Instead, we would have to craft a set of strategic alliances that would allow the relationships to grow and evolve as our needs and our partners' needs changed. We adopted the slogan "Partnership in Innovation Process" (PIP) to capture the philosophy we wanted to communicate as we began implementing the outsourcing decision.

Initially, the strategic alliance agreements were to cover only non-core services in the Photography (PPG) and Commercial Imaging Group (CIG) areas. Kodak's chemical (ECC), health (HG), and international (IG) businesses were to continue to operate their own computing and telecommunications services as they had in the past.

....
The Partnership in Innovation Process

Defining the Change Management Organization
Hudson's first priority was to develop the organization structure and identify key players needed to implement the organization change. She recognized that she would need to provide executive leadership and recruit the assistance of a strong manager who combined both technical and business savvy and was well-known and respected by IT and business unit employees. Hudson chose Henry Pfendt for this key position. During his 32-year tenure with Kodak, Pfendt had worked in a number of key technical and business positions throughout the organization. In 1986, he had been appointed to head a small team of IT professionals charged with defining the IT organization of the future. It was this group that had led the consolidation efforts of 1986–1988.

Two levels of cross-functional teams were created to implement the Partnership in Innovation Process. At the executive level a steering committee, comprising some 25 executives from business units and corporate staff functions, was formed to provide overall business leadership and direction. Douglas Mabon, head of the Financial Planning Department and a member of the steering committee, described its role. "The members of the steering committee were selected," he explained,

because of their special expertise related to business and functional issues that would need to be defined in the outsourcing agreements. For the most part, we were not IT ex-

perts. Our job was to take the broad vision defined by Kathy and to translate it into the business initiatives that would be needed to make it happen. Our role was to communicate the vision and oversee its implementation, but not to implement it directly.

Implementation of the vision rested with the three Partnership in Innovation Process (PIP) teams associated with each major outsourcing initiative. Each team had adopted a code name for its project: data center (BlueStar); telecommunications (TelStar); and personal computer services (MicroBuddy). The PIP teams were to define the specific details and manage the implementation of each outsourcing agreement. PIP teams comprised 8 to 10 Kodak employees, including project and technical leaders, and representatives from the financial, marketing/customer service, business planning, human resources, and legal areas. "All three of the PIP teams reported directly to Kathy and Henry," Mabon explained. "The steering committee provided guidance but had no formal authority over the PIP teams."

Early on, Hudson and Pfendt recognized that defining and managing the outsourcing partnerships was primarily a "relationship" process. Conflict Management, Inc. (CMI), a consulting firm that advises organizations and individuals on the management of critical internal and external relationships and the development of an effective negotiation process, was hired jointly by Kodak and the respective partner organizations to assist with the development of the alliance relationships. CMI's brochure described its philosophy in working with organizations:

Increasingly, organizations have come to realize that how they approach problems, disagreements, and opportunities has an impact on the substantive outcome. Where one must rely on persuasion and influence, the process by which a negotiated agreement is reached affects both the quality and durability of the result, as well as any subsequent relationship between the parties. The ability to negotiate, build, and sustain effective and durable working relationships becomes more critical to "success" in a world that requires agility, innovation, interdependence, and quality decision-making.

CMI President and CEO Elizabeth Gray and two CMI professionals, Mark Smith and Jeff Weiss, worked jointly with Kodak and the respective partner organizations (IBM, DEC, and BusinessLand). They trained team members in effective negotiation and relationship management skills and helped them develop the processes through which the alliance partnerships would be forged and maintained.

Establishing the Process Hudson stated four overarching interests to guide the steering committee and PIP teams in the development of outsourcing alliances: improve shareholder value; create quantum improvements in the quality and productivity of ser-

vices delivered; maintain or improve the quality of employees' worklife; and position Kodak for the IT developments and business challenges of the future. These were translated into specific issues that each vendor was to address in its proposals. Each potential partner was required to identify how it would improve or maintain:

- the transition and development opportunities for employees.
- service quality.
- the cost structure.

EXHIBIT 5
Partnership in Innovation Process

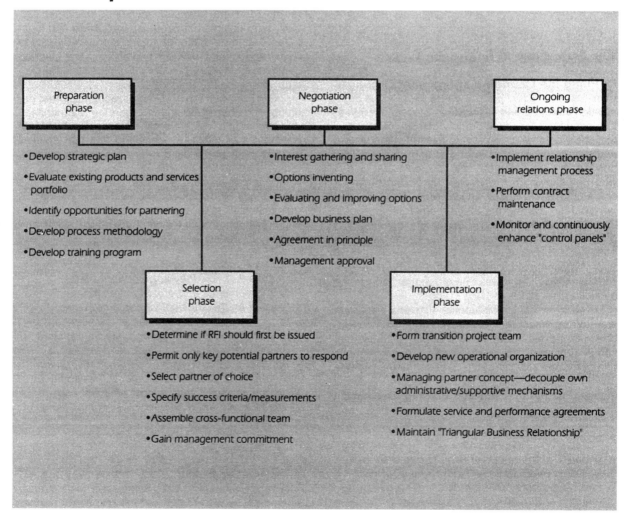

- the identification and assimilation of emerging technologies.
- support systems and management processes.

The PIP teams then developed a five-step process that defined the methodology to be used to identify, select, negotiate, and implement the outsourcing alliances (see Exhibit 5).

Identification and selection Each PIP team began the process with a "preferred partner." Hudson had initially intended to choose vendors for outsourced services based on their reputation in the industry and experience managing similar outsourcing arrangements. Of the three vendors chosen, however, only one, BusinessLand, made it to the contract stage.

Roy Hartwell, a financial analyst working on the BlueStar PIP team, explained:

The preferred partner had extensive experience in managing data center operations for other Fortune 500 firms, and they rapidly developed a proposal that spelled out the relationship in extreme detail. The vendor seemed intent on finding ways to fit us into established practices, resisting many requests to tailor the proposal to meet our requirements. We became very concerned that the detailed proposal would become a detailed contract, and that the inevitable problems that would surely arise would lead to an endless stream of contract renegotiations and additional service charges. The vendor's drive for immediate decisions also conflicted with our focus on developing a relationship, creating considerable tension between the two organizations.

An internal Kodak team had also been commissioned to present the economics of consolidating Kodak's data centers within the company. "Most of the economies of scale that stood to be realized from consolidating our data centers and running them inhouse," Hartwell explained, "could be achieved by creating a data center that operated in the range of 300–400 MIPS. As our consolidated data center would operate at about 600 MIPS, we knew economies of scale could be gained through internal consolidation."

Pfendt elaborated:

We estimated that to offer these services inhouse we would need to spend approximately $30 million for new facilities in the Rochester

area alone and $15–20 million for new systems. And that was just the initial estimate! We questioned whether this was the most appropriate place for Kodak to spend its scarce resources. In the end it was not the economies of scale but the economics that drove our decision. By reengineering the IS value chain, we became convinced that commodity-type IS services could best be procured through alliances and partnerships with world-class service providers, thus allowing the internal resources to be focused on high value-adding IS activities.

Exhibit 6 presents a summary of the key selection criteria used in the final choice of the three alliance partners.

Negotiation The negotiation process was formalized in an alliance contract, in the case of IBM and DEC, and in a business plan in the case of BusinessLand. (BusinessLand's agreement had a much smaller dollar value than the other two and BusinessLand did not have a lawyer on its negotiating team.) Exhibit 7 provides an overview of the categories of agreements covered in the contracts.

It became clear in the course of negotiations that the concept of the contract needed to be reevaluated.

EXHIBIT 6
Key Selection Criteria for Choice of Strategic Partner

Strong technical expertise in the service area but past experience managing the service for outside customers was not required.

Excellent reputation within the industry and strong image as a quality leader.

Solid financial performance.

Reputation as a "good" employer with high quality of work life for employees.

Ability to work together to solve problems; atmosphere of trust and cooperation.

Willing to work together on development of a relationship management process.

Management style and culture similar to Kodak.

EXHIBIT 7
Kodak Outsourcing Alliances: Sample Contract

Table of Contents

The contract needed to support "fluid" and "collaborative" relationships among all alliance partners. No one could specify those relationships in a detailed way in advance. Ideally, the contract would provide a framework for a relationship and the process by which it would be negotiated. Michael Pearlman, a lawyer on the BlueStar team, contrasted two of the contracts developed with alliance partners:

The contract with IBM really fits the company's style. IBM wanted to develop a framework for its future outsourcing business. The contract that resulted is very compact and in plain English. It includes such topics as termination conditions, pricing, personnel, liabilities, warranties, responsibilities of the parties, and the transition process and incorporates in an appendix detailed schedules, timetables, equipment, and software. The DEC contract is much more detailed. The parties found it necessary to attempt to specify issues more rigidly. As we began operations, we found that many of the details just didn't fit with the way things worked.

CMI, according to Pearlman, had suggested a valuable negotiation tool to support contract development:

Before the contract drafting process, both parties would sit down and discuss in detail the specific business concerns to be covered in the contract. From this a single, joint document was prepared and revised as necessary to clarify mistaken assumptions and areas of conflict. This proved to be a very valuable way to ensure that all parties were operating on a common understanding.

Implementation   Contracts were signed with vendors in July 1989 (IBM), September 1989 (BusinessLand), and February 1990 (DEC). Work subsequently began on building the necessary interorganizational structures, work systems, and management processes. But in the end, explained Robert Kordish, Personnel Relations Manager, Kodak and its partners recognized that success in forging the new alliances rested with people. Kordish explained:

Outsourcing is a people process. Transferring our human assets was in many ways more difficult than transferring our physical assets. We knew from the beginning that our success was dependent on how well we managed the transition of the 600-plus Kodak employees

who would be transferring to the alliance partner organizations. We could not afford to lose their knowledge of Kodak's IT systems and how they influenced Kodak's business operations. In each alliance agreement we worked out a human relations package that would provide the employees a quality of work life that was comparable to their current one. The average length of service for the outsourced employees was approximately 18 years. In many cases, their spouses and other family members were also Kodak employees. They did not want to leave Kodak or move from Rochester.

Recognizing that the transition of employees would best be supported by open and honest communication, various members of management met with them approximately every four to six weeks to provide an update on the current status and developments. In addition, a daily electronic news bulletin (questions and answers) was maintained throughout the project. Talks were held on all three shifts to ensure that everyone could attend. For the two largest outsourcing projects there were two major meetings associated with the specific strategic alliance: one when the alliance partner was selected and one before the contract was signed. Kordish recalled DEC's selection:

We had a meeting in the auditorium with all of the Kodak employees who would be moving to DEC. Various DEC vice presidents and employees and Kathy Hudson and I explained the proposal. There was plenty of time to ask questions and discuss concerns. Then we had an informal social hour so that everyone could get acquainted.

Another auditorium meeting was held when the contract with DEC was ready to be signed. At the end of the meeting, DEC management welcomed the Kodak employees to DEC.

Each employee received a manual containing a job description, compensation details, and a comparison of the new benefits package with the previous Kodak benefits package. Generous signing bonuses and guaranteed raises were offered by IBM, DEC, and BusinessLand. Personnel were offered three options: accept and sign the agreement within 60 days; personally find another position within Kodak; retire or resign from Kodak. "Most people made their decision within two weeks," recalled Kordish, adding that, "of

EXHIBIT 8
. . . .
Eastman Kodak IS Organization—1991

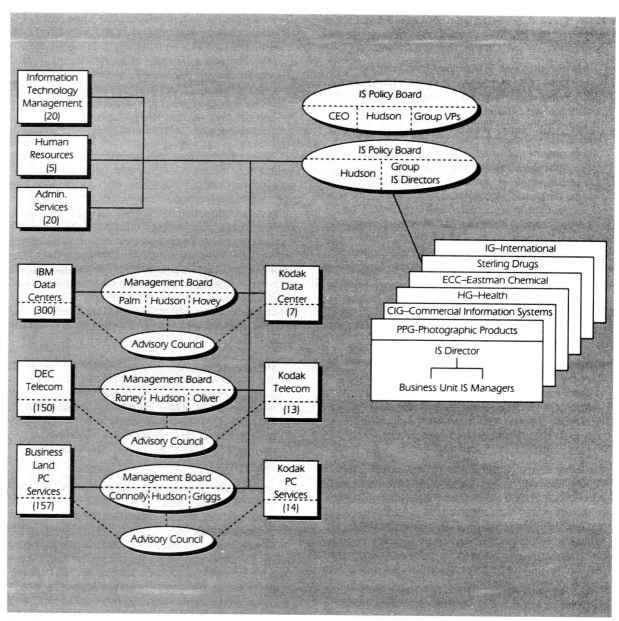

Note: The numbers in parentheses represent lead counts.

the 600 people affected, 586 accepted the strategic alliance offer."

Managing the Ongoing Relationships An alliance organization was defined and managed on two levels; specific alliance organizations were formed for each alliance partner while cross-alliance organizations governed the actions of all three alliance partners with Kodak. Exhibit 8 presents an overview of Kodak's IS organization in 1991. The new organization represented a blending of three distinct organi-zational entities: Kodak's Corporate IS organization; Kodak's Business Group/Business Unit IS organizations; and the alliance organizations. It also represented a complex intermingling of team-based and hierarchical structures. (Team-based structures are represented by circles, and hierarchical structures by boxes in Exhibit 8.) Exhibit 9 summarizes the responsibilities of the three organizations.

Organization structure The hierarchical organization included Kodak's Corporate IS unit and Business Group/Business Unit IS organizations and the

EXHIBIT 9
....
Eastman Kodak IT Roles and Responsibilities—1991

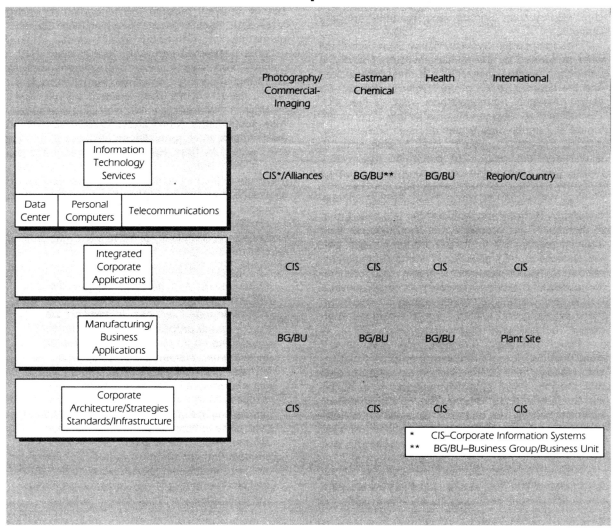

alliance organizations within Kodak and its three alliance partners. Corporate IS, headed by Hudson, included Information Technology Management (a twenty-person unit responsible for technology transfer into the company, standards, and supplier management), Human Resources (a five-person unit), and Administrative Services (a twenty-person organization that supported Kodak end-users of CIS systems and services that were not outsourced).

The alliance organization structure, described as a "networked" organization, was composed of a collection of teams and hierarchical organizational units that helped manage the complex service delivery processes among alliance partners and between the alliances and Kodak end-users. Four types of teams were defined: the Information Systems Policy Board; the Information Systems Executive Council; Relationship Management Boards; and Alliance Advisory Councils.

The Information Systems Policy Board functions were performed by the management council of the company chaired by the CEO. It included Hudson and the heads of each of the business groups and senior functional representatives, such as the CFO. This committee met monthly on a variety of corporate topics. During the outsourcing decision process, significant agenda time was devoted to discussing IS issues and outsourcing in particular. The Policy Board was responsible for setting broad policy guidelines for the use of IT within the company.

The Information Systems Executive Council was chaired by Hudson and included the business group IS directors. The committee met five times per year and was responsible for translating the broad IT policy statements into specific IT strategic initiatives needed to support business strategies and for monitoring Kodak's progress in meeting its corporate-wide IT/Business goals. They relied heavily on input from the IT planning and strategy groups within the Information Technology Management organization.

Policy, strategic direction, and management were provided to each alliance through a Relationship Management Board. Hudson sat on all boards with the respective alliance managers from Kodak and the partner organizations. The Relationship Management Boards met quarterly. Cross-alliance Relationship Management Boards met monthly to define and implement interalliance policy, strategy, and management.

Alliance Advisory Councils, composed of technical professionals from Kodak and the alliance partner organizations, met monthly to define technical standards, plan the evolution of technological platforms, and manage the prioritization and funding of services.

Each Kodak alliance manager was responsible for a hierarchical organization composed of Kodak employees who worked closely with their counterparts in the partner organization to provide data center, telecommunications, and personal computer services. Seven Kodak employees coordinated and controlled the integration of services across alliance partner organizations. Alliance partners provided the outsourced services specified in the alliance contracts, through hierarchical organizations within their companies.

Service delivery process One of the first tasks to occupy the alliance partners was the redesign of the service delivery process. Alliance partners recognized early that this process involved more than each partner working with Kodak independently; all three vendors needed to define the interalliance service delivery processes. For example, a Kodak end-user acquiring a personal computer from BusinessLand had to contact not only BusinessLand, but also IBM to establish a mainframe account and DEC to install network connections. (See Exhibit 10 for a summary of the complex, interorganizational process of fulfilling a PC order.) In 1991, BusinessLand was in the process of developing an automated system to streamline order fulfillment so that a Kodak user could order a personal computer and the attendant account and networking via a single on-line request.

Frank Palm, BlueStar Alliance manager at IBM, explained the complexity of these interorganizational relationships in terms of his organization's relationship with DEC: "One of my managers," he explained,

meets weekly, and sometimes daily, with his DEC counterpart to define the evolving nature of our integrated services. In addition, we have a formal process, called a document of understanding, to define complex problems involving the intersection of our services. So far these mechanisms have worked so well that all problems have been solved through discussions at that level. It has been quite a culture change on the part of DEC and IBM to think of each other as partners rather than competitors. We have taken steps to help promote that collaborative culture. For example, the IBM alliance organization hosted a welcome party for the DEC alliance organization when they won the contract. The most

Process for Acquiring a Personal Computer

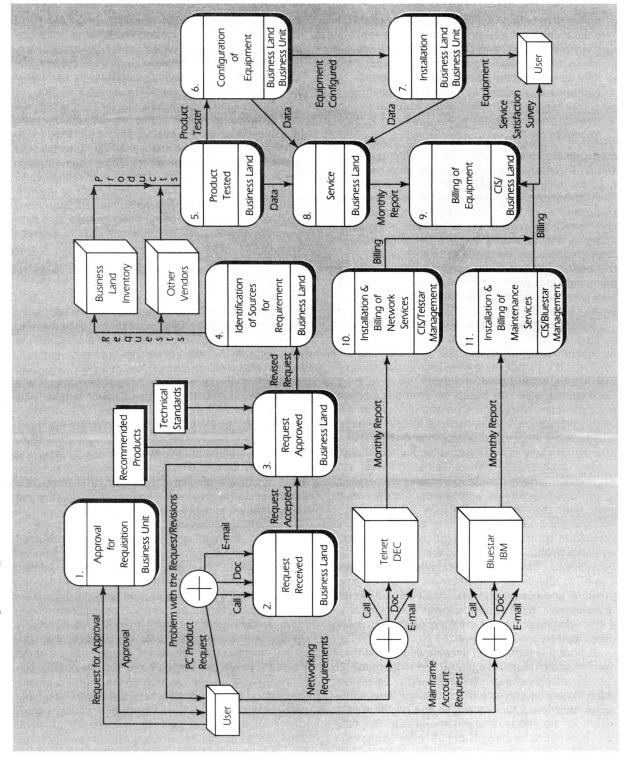

powerful force for helping to forge the collaborative culture, however, has been the background of the IBM and DEC employees working in the alliance organizations. Because they were all former Kodak employees who had lived and worked in Rochester for many years, the conditions for collaboration were already present. As managers, it was up to us to nurture it.

Management control Long-range planning and development of policy and strategic direction were handled by the appropriate Kodak and alliance level management boards. Operational planning was the responsibility of the management of each alliance and varied for each alliance partner. Interalliance planning was handled at the cross-alliance management boards' joint monthly meetings.

Service planning and control systems were implemented to support fulfillment of the contracted service level agreements. Both IBM and DEC followed the same basic procedure for planning and managing service delivery. Annual negotiations with Kodak defined an agreed-upon service level, which could be renegotiated at mid-year and year-end. IBM and DEC would then bill CIS monthly for actual charges. CIS, in turn, billed Kodak end-users.

Planning was still based on customer demand and each alliance organization had evolved its own unique management style. All three alliance partners recognized that they had operated and continued to operate primarily in a "project-oriented" or, in some cases, "crisis-driven" manner. Because formal control systems were still in the process of being developed, customer surveys and request backlogs were used to assess service quality.

The need for a more formal process was addressed in spring 1991, when the interalliance management boards developed a framework, called the Relationship Management Planning and Control Cycle, to guide the development of interalliance planning and control systems. (See Exhibit 11 for the management systems and support tools, many of them automated, that were in the process of being developed.)

Under this framework, alliance and interalliance mission and strategies would be defined through the creation of a business plan that would be revised yearly based on contractual and service level agreements, past and future strategies and plans, and the results of the previous year's operations. The business plan would be used to define goals and specify new projects and service level agreements and would provide a basis for defining alliance activities. An automated system, called the CIS Document Manager, was being developed to help track project progress and problem resolution and develop an historical record of alliance and interalliance activities.

The business plan would also be used to define a set of process and customer service performance measures that would enable alliance managers to control the interalliance service delivery process consistently throughout the year. Formal approaches to measuring the value of IT services were being developed to ensure continuous improvement of the service delivery process, and an automated tool called the Control Panel was being developed to help support the interalliance management control process (see Exhibit 12).

....

Where to Next?

Surveying the performance reports for the past year, Hudson reflected on the significant progress that had been made since 1988. She believed the decision to outsource data center, telecommunications, and personal computer services had been a good one. Cost savings of 15 percent had been realized with one outsourcing function and 3 percent with another. The third partner had experienced some difficulty meeting its cost objectives, but she believed the appropriate service delivery and management processes had been put in place to remedy this situation by the end of the year. Despite initial periods of adjustment, service quality was at least equal and in some cases was superior to previous levels, and valuable lessons had been learned along the way (see Exhibit 13).

But Hudson realized that much more needed to be done. She was comfortable with the networked alliance organization structure, despite its complexity, but recognized that interalliance service delivery processes and planning and control systems needed more attention. Cost, quality, and speed of implementation were critical measures of process performance that needed to be specified in greater detail to fully implement the Control Panel approach to management control, and automated management support systems would be needed to manage the complexity. Although great care had been taken to define a compensation and benefits package that would be beneficial to the former Kodak employees, Hudson knew that new incentive systems and performance evaluation mechanisms that reflected the complexity of the

EXHIBIT 11
....

Proposed Planning and Control Framework

1. The Planning Cycle

2. The Interaction of Process and Tools

TPR = Tactical Project Record
DOU = Document of Understanding

EXHIBIT 12
Proposed Management Control System

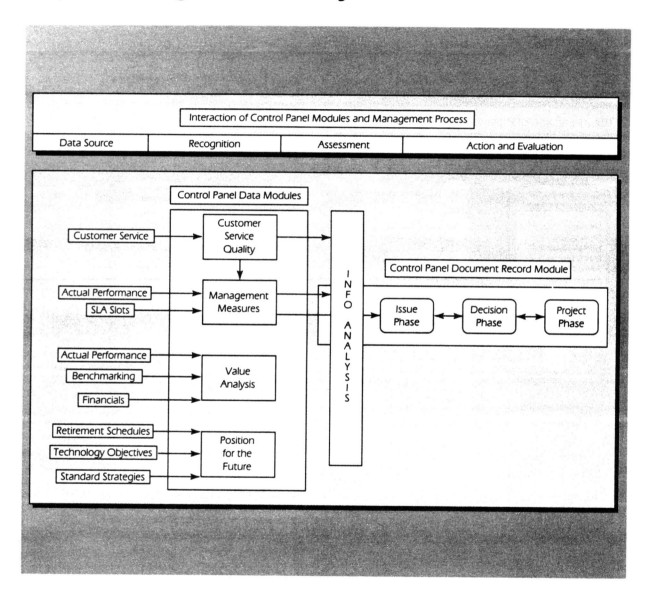

interalliance partnerships would be needed. Career development issues, she knew, would also have to be addressed. Moreover, the same human resource management issues would have to be addressed within Kodak. Hudson was also planning to reduce each Kodak alliance unit to two or three employees within the next year. Finally, managing the interalliance relationships would continue to require considerable time and attention as the various alliance partners faced significant internal and external challenges that were prompting them to undertake their own corporate-wide organizational transformations.

EXHIBIT 13
Lessons Learned

The Outsourcing Decision

Non-core services (Information Transport), not core services (Information Context), are candidates for outsourcing.

Non-core services are inextricably intertwined with core services.

Outsourcing IT is a strategic alliance, not a simple "hand-off."

Previous problems will still remain problems.

Selecting a Partner

Ability to work together over long term is critical.

Begin relationship management process early.

Be sure negotiation team will still be involved in long-term management.

Understand how partner will make money on the deal.

Contract Negotiation

The contract should serve as a framework for the relationship. Don't try to specify everything in detail.

Define ownership of current and future assets (e.g., software, information).

Both sides should write down what they think the contract says and compare understandings before signing.

Long-Term Management

There is significant overhead in coordination and control.

Service delivery and management control processes must be redesigned to incorporate interorganizational nature of alliance.

Both organizations are undergoing significant organization changes. Partners must work together to manage change.

11

Responsibilities of the Manager

We have previously noted that information technology is becoming so pervasive and so important to the success of organizations that most managers now have some responsibility for managing the use of this technology. The purpose of this book has been to prepare you for those responsibilities. We have described many roles of the manager in exploiting this technology, and we will now review some of these responsibilities.

Acquiring new systems is one of the critical activities in exploiting IT. In Chapters 8, 10, and 11 we discussed several ways that one can acquire a new system—have the IS department build it using the systems development life cycle (SDLC) methodology or prototyping, purchase the system, and user application development. In Chapter 11 we highlighted the responsibilities that the sponsoring manager always has, no matter how the system is acquired—obtaining the necessary resources, project management, defining the requirements of the system, implementing the system in the organization, obtaining business benefits, and championing the system.

In Chapters 12 and 13 we emphasized that the IT architecture and IS planning must begin with business strategy and business needs. Thus, business managers, not IS managers, are responsible for determining the role of IT in the business and for making sure that this vision is clearly com-

municated to the IT architects and planners. This requires that business managers participate in determining the values and management systems components of the IT architecture and in IS strategic planning.

We have noted that managers must understand their data if they are to use the data effectively. In Chapter 14 we suggested that managers—not IS specialists—must perform the data stewardship function. Thus, a business manager is responsible for the definition and quality of the data associated with a particular data entity that is important to him and to the business. We also noted that managing data is often quite difficult because information can be very political.

We have repeatedly stated that IT can no longer be managed centrally. In Chapter 15 we described alternatives for decentralizing the management and control of various aspects of IT. It is clear that one of the implications of this decentralization is that most managers, sometime in their careers, will have direct responsibility for managing IS units and IS specialists. In addition, more and more managers are responsible for managing the use of IT within their own organizational units without having the needed IS specialists. Thus, managers themselves often must build and manage their own amateur or semiprofessional IS organizations.

Several of the responsibilities and issues mentioned have not been covered completely. In this chapter we will fill in some of the gaps.

DEALING WITH INFORMATION SYSTEMS POLITICS

Politics is a critical element in the management of information technology. As indicated in the box "Politics of Information," serious difficulties arise when the movement toward the new information-based organization encounters the realities of organizational politics.

The impact of politics is not just an organizational concern; rather, politics may determine success or failure when you attempt to use information technology in your managerial career. Political considerations often arise when you attempt to obtain the resources required for a new system and when managing data. Political considerations may also arise when we attempt to develop or implement a new system, both in dealing with other users and with the IS organization. You may be responsible for dealing with the politics of systems development, the IS organization as a political actor, and the politics of obtaining the systems resources that you need.

The Political View of Organizations

Rob Kling (1980) discusses a number of models that describe how organizations function. We will not explore all of them here, but we will look at two quite different perspectives he presents—the traditional *rational* perspective and the *political* perspective. As depicted in the middle column of Figure 16.1, the rational perspective assumes that the organization has a set of commonly accepted

POLITICS OF INFORMATION

We have studied information management approaches in more than twenty-five companies over the past two years. Many of their efforts to create information-based organizations—or even to implement significant information management initiatives—have failed or are on the path to failure. The primary reason is that the companies did not manage the politics of information. Either the initiative was inappropriate for the firm's overall political culture or politics were treated as peripheral rather than integral to the initiative. Only when information politics are viewed as a natural aspect of organizational life, and consciously managed, will true information-based organizations emerge.

Furthermore, a good argument can be made—and there is increasing evidence for it—that as information becomes the basis for organizational structure and function, politics will increasingly come into play. In the most information-oriented companies we studied, people were least likely to share information freely—as perceived by these companies' managers. As people's jobs and roles become defined by the unique information they hold, they may be less likely to share that information—viewing it as a source of power and indispensability—rather than more so. When information is the primary unit of organizational currency, we should not expect its owners to give it away.

(Davenport, Eccles, and Prusak, 1992)

goals arrived at by consensus, that the predominant value that guides decision-making is the efficiency or effectiveness of the organization, and that decision-makers attempt to maximize the organizational goals by using rational analysis.

	Traditional Rational	Political
Goals	Organizational consensus	Individual with conflicts
Predominant values	Efficiency or effectiveness	Welfare of the decision-maker
Decision criteria	Maximize goals	Resolve the conflicts
Decision mode	Rational analysis	Bargaining and negotiation

FIGURE 16.1 Contrast of the Traditional Rational and the Political Perspectives of Organizations

452

The **political perspective** conceptualizes the organization as a confederation of individuals and groups that are banded together for common ends, each contributing to the organization and each participating in the resulting benefits. The political view assumes that the various individuals in the organization have their own goals that often conflict, that the predominant value that guides decisions is the welfare of the decision-maker, and that decision-makers attempt to arrive at decisions that resolve these conflicts by bargaining and negotiation.

The political perspective does not deny that much of the decision-making in an organization may be rational and motivated by the overall success of the organization, because the organization must survive and prosper if there are to be any rewards to divide. Thus, many bottom-line decisions may follow the rational model. Decisions that affect the distribution of rewards, however, are likely to be made on a political basis and may be the result of conflict and negotiation between the groups that have interests in the decision. The tactics that they can employ are limited, of course, by the common necessity to preserve the organization from which they all receive benefits and by the fact that they have to coexist in the future.

We would not argue that the political perspective depicts the whole truth about how organizations function. Most organizations embody a mix of rational and political decision-making, and the proportion of each varies from one organization to another, but we have never encountered an organization to which the political perspective did not apply to some degree.

The most important factors in the political arena are power and influence. Certainly power and influence are highly valued by most managers. They are important in a political environment because they affect the outcome of any negotiation. In many situations no one manager has sufficient power and influence to determine the outcome, so power must be assembled by forming a coalition of several persons or groups. The different participants often have conflicting preferences, and political skills are required to negotiate the terms under which a winning coalition can be successfully formed. Influence can be especially important in leading the formation of coalitions.

POWER, INFLUENCE, AND POLITICAL CAPACITY

Political capacity—the ability to operate politically—is composed of two ingredients: power and influence. Although these are related concepts that actually affect each other, there are some fundamental differences between them.

Power is the ability to alter the realities of a situation. Stated somewhat differently, power is the ability to change the cause-and-effect relationships within a situation.

Influence is the ability to alter another person's perceptions of a situation, to affect someone else's perceptions of cause and effect.

The sum of someone's power and influence represents that person's capacity for political action.

(Beeman and Sharkey, 1987)

Building Power and Influence

There are a number of ways for a manager to build up power and influence. First, the manager can develop a constituency—a group of loyal supporters who will add their own power and influence. Constituencies are based upon mutual benefit, and building and maintaining a constituency requires one to be helpful and generous to supporters and to always remember and repay favors.

A related way to gain power and influence is to become a member of the constituency of some more powerful person. Because such relationships are reciprocal, one's power and influence are enhanced by the power of those who view him or her as a supporter. This can be a delicate matter, because by becoming a supporter of one person you may become the adversary of others.

Perceptions may be as important as reality in determining power and influence. Whether a person actually has influence or not, that person gains power if people think he or she has influence with a powerful person. Thus, who one plays golf with and what clubs one belongs to may influence his or her power by merely changing perceptions.

An effective long-term way to become powerful and influential is to learn to negotiate win-win solutions to conflicts. Whenever you win and another person loses, you have diminished your power by creating an enemy, but if you can negotiate a compromise where everyone is a winner, then everyone may be in your debt. At the least, it pays to make sure that losers have a face-saving way out. Win-win solutions depend on the fact that the bargaining chips are valued differently by each party to the negotiation. If one clearly understands how each person values each bargaining chip, then it may be possible to arrange for each party to win by giving up chips he values little in exchange for chips he values highly.

Power and influence is best used to reward or persuade, not to punish or coerce. One has a limited amount of power and influence, and it can be used up quickly when it is applied in a negative way. A manager must weigh carefully the costs of using coercive power against the possible gains and decide if the gains are worth the loss. Thus, you may discover that your constituency disappears if you ask it to provide you with coercive power.

One's influence is strongly affected by personal credibility, which is based on a combination of competence and integrity. It is far easier to lose credibility than it is to build it, so it should be carefully protected.

How Information Systems Are Political

Information systems may be intensely political. This is not surprising, for most of us would agree that information is power, and, therefore, that information systems affect the distribution of power in an organization.

According to M. L. Markus (1981), information systems affect organizational power for three reasons. First, individuals who control access to information used to evaluate alternatives in a decision process can influence the outcomes of decisions. Second, information systems are often used as a part of the organization's resource allocation and control system, and thus they can be used to change the behavior of individuals and of organizational units. Third, information systems provide power because they present an image of the ability to influence outcomes, and the perception of power confers power.

INFORMATION SYSTEMS AND POLITICS

Information system development is an intensely political as well as technical process. . . . A strategy for implementation must therefore recognize and deal with the politics of data and the likelihood, even legitimacy, of counterimplementation.

(Keen, 1981)

Resistance to information systems [is explained] as a lack of consonance between the distribution of power implied by an information system and the distribution of power existing in the organization. . . . The origins of resistance are found not in the presence or absence of any particular tactic for introducing change, but in the interaction of the substance of the change with its organizational context.

(Markus, 1981)

Because information systems often affect the distribution of power within an organization, and power is so important to everyone, the development of a new information system is likely to encounter political opposition. Markus asserts that any new information system that changes the power distribution within the organization will be resisted by those who stand to lose power.

Power is usually required to make change happen in an organization. It usually takes less power to prevent change. Not only do entities often possess veto power, but effective counterimplementation activities may disrupt, prevent, or modify the intended change. In particular, the development and implementation of a new information system is especially vulnerable to disruption by various counterimplementation tactics employed by those who may oppose it. Markus (1981, 1983) provides two detailed examples of strong and long-lasting resistance to implementation of new systems for political reasons.

Resistance Tactics

Resistance to IS development may be quite easy. Systems development is a long, complex process that is difficult to manage, and if the system is

COUNTERIMPLEMENTATION

A central lesson to be learned from examples of successful counterimplementation is that there is no need to take the risky step of overtly opposing a project. The simplest approach is to rely on social inertia and use moves based on delay and tokenism. Technical outsiders should be kept outside and their lack of awareness of organizational issues encouraged. ("Why don't you build the model and we'll deal with the people issues later; there's no need to have these interminable meetings.") If more active counterimplementation is needed, one may exploit the difficulty of getting agreement among actors with different interests by enthusiastically saying, "Great idea—but let's do it properly!" adding more people to the game and making the objectives of the venture broader and more ambitious and consequently more contentious and harder to make operational.

(Keen, 1981)

complex or hard to define there is a good chance of failure, even without overt resistance. Systems development projects are often viewed by managers as costly, time-consuming, and disruptive, and therefore they may be quickly abandoned if managers come to believe that they are not going to be successful.

Resistance to a system is almost always concealed or disguised for two major reasons. First, conventional corporate culture denies the legitimacy of political activity. Even in organizations where political considerations are dominant, everyone maintains the pretense that their actions are rational and are solely motivated by a concern for the welfare of the organization. Second, when opposition is recognized it is easier to counter. Thus, some of the most effective resistance strategies are concealed in the guise of support of the new system.

The resister can also take advantage of the entire systems life cycle, from initial requirements definition to the operations and maintenance stage. If resistance is unsuccessful at the requirements stage, it can be continued during systems design, conversion, operations, and maintenance.

Political battles may be won or lost, but the war may go on for a long, long time.

The resister's objectives can often be obtained either by preventing implementation of the system or by obtaining modifications that remove the perceived problems. The resistance tactics employed may be designed to persuade the developer to modify the system in order to avoid the possibility of failure. Thus, the resister may view systems development and implementation as a continuing process of negotiation and may use various tactics as part of this negotiating process.

A classic resistance tactic is to delay the project by raising objection after objection, each of which may be justified in the interest of producing a better system. Resisters who are participants in the process may simply be difficult to pin down on the requirements, changing their minds repeatedly. It is easy to see why organizations that try to manage data find it so difficult to obtain agreement on the definitions of the data elements involved—avoiding agreement is an easy resistance tactic when you have data that you do not want the organization to manage.

Another way to resist a project is to complicate it by expanding its size and complexity. Such a resister may pretend to be an enthusiastic supporter of the system. Also, a resister may attempt to add new participants to the process who have different (and perhaps conflicting) motivations.

Another effective resistance tactic is to withhold resources that are essential for success of the system. This resister may profess complete support, but when the time comes to contribute the necessary resources, they just are not there in the required quantity or quality or at the right time. Often this tactic involves designating a representative on the project team who is not qualified to make the decisions that are needed.

Dealing with the Politics of Systems Development

If you are the sponsor of a new system, it is important to consider the political implications of your system from the very beginning. It is far better to avoid political problems than to become involved in trying to overcome resistance. The astute manager avoids unnecessary political battles, even those he knows he can win. Politics is a long-term game, and the long-term winners are those who have the most effective network of mutually beneficial relationships—it is best to avoid alienating those whose support you may need sometime in the future.

Thus, it is wise to consider how the new system will be perceived by each person or group that it will affect. That includes the people who work for you because they may have immense power to make the system fail. Managers often make the mistake of assuming that they are the experts and that the system belongs to them alone, and acquire systems that fail because of resistance by their clerical people.

If the system can be structured so that it will be viewed as desirable by all those it affects, then one has created a win-win situation that will be supported by all. Because it is sometimes difficult to view a system from another's perspective, one way to create win-win systems is to involve those who will be affected in the development process and to allow them to negotiate the requirements of a system that all can support.

As you analyze the political aspects of the new system, you may find that it cannot be made politically neutral without destroying its value to you—there is no win-win solution. You can then anticipate resistance and should consider how that resistance can be overcome. Do you have the necessary power? Do you want to use it for this purpose? Can you obtain the support of others with the necessary power? How can the system be structured so that you can put together a coalition with sufficient power to make it a success? Or should you just forget it and put your effort into something else?

Looking at this from another perspective, what if you find yourself facing the prospect of a new system that is unacceptable to you? This may occur when someone wishes to computerize information that you now control. Your boss, for example, may suggest a system that will provide him with information about your area that you would prefer to filter first before it gets to your boss. Another example might be a department that feels it needs direct access to data you presently control,

and you know that you will lose some of your power if that data becomes organizational data. You can use all the resistance tactics described, but it is best to lay low and conceal your resistance. At the very least, you must always justify any resistance under the "pure" rational motive of doing what is in the best interests of the organization.

The IS Organization as a Political Actor

The IS department may have power over many aspects of information technology, so it may be a strong political actor.

Depending on the company, the organizational location of IS may provide substantial formal power. Thus, IS people prefer to report as high in the organization as possible—through a chief information officer or a vice president of information systems—and they want their chief to have influence with top management. IS also wants its strategic plans to be blessed by top management—to be integrated into the company's strategic plans. The IS department charter also may confer some formal power over matters pertaining to data and information technology.

The IS organization may also have power derived from the unique expertise possessed by its specialists. Expertise, especially if it enables one to do things that are valuable to others, is a source of power. Because expertise that enables the organization to utilize information technology is valuable to many people, it is a significant source of power for the IS organization.

There are several other sources of IS department power. If there is a steering committee that allocates resources for systems development, IS may have a great deal of power on that committee. Usually all proposals go first to the IS department for analysis and a recommendation, placing IS in a strong position to kill projects or to bless them with its approval. Therefore, the IS representative on the committee, even without voting power, usually has a great deal of influence.

After a system is approved for development, the IS department has a strong influence on the nature of the system that is produced and the success or failure of the project. For example, because the IS department allocates its technical people among all the active projects, it can determine whether a project gets many people or just a few, good people or mediocre ones.

In organizations where IS has monopoly power, the IS organization may employ that power to attempt to preserve its monopoly position. The decentralization of control of information technology that has taken place in many organizations may be viewed as a serious threat by traditional IS management and staff, and they may resist these changes by using their power to reward their supporters and punish those who advocate decentralization. This political struggle usually terminates with the replacement of the director of the IS organization.

The decentralization of control over information technology is usually justified on the basis of fit with the company organizational structure or the assertion that it produces systems that better fit the needs. The major motivation, however, may be that decentralization transfers power from the IS organization to managers, and thus is best understood from the political perspective.

Obtaining the Systems Resources That You Need

No matter how one acquires a new system, it is the manager's responsibility to obtain the necessary resources, and understanding the political environment may be important in obtaining those resources. How you obtain the resources that you need to acquire a new system depends on the organization you are in, what resources you need, what resources you already have, how such decisions are made in your organization, and so on.

In some organizations, for example, you may have profit center responsibility, and you only have to decide how the system will affect your bottom line—you pay the costs and you get the benefits. You have the power to use your resources to get the system, if you decide to do so.

In other organizations you can obtain any resources that you can pay for from your budget, but you negotiate for your budget on a periodic basis. Thus, you have to convince whoever supervises your budget to include the necessary amount.

In many organizations, if you need major resources from the IS area, you must submit a request to IS that eventually goes to a committee that allocates the resources. Your problem is to obtain the approval of that committee.

Whether you are negotiating for your budget or trying to obtain a high priority from a committee, you can view the problem from the rational or the political perspective. If you look at it from the rational perspective, you try to prove that the system you need will be beneficial to the organization by preparing an impressive cost/benefit analysis and making a compelling business case for the proposed system.

If you adopt the political perspective, you still prepare an impressive cost/benefit analysis and make a compelling business case, but you also consider the motivations and power of those who will make the decision. If your boss makes the decision, you may work to understand what his or her "hot buttons" are and make sure that some of them are included in the proposed system.

If the resources you need are allocated by a committee, then adopting the political perspective may be essential to success. You first analyze the membership of the committee. Most such committees are structured so that each major organizational group has a representative on the committee. Who is your representative? Can you get her support? If you have no formal representative, are there persons on the committee you can influence? Can you get the support of the IS department? Even if you have a supporter on the committee, it may be wise to find ways to obtain support from other members.

If IS resources are important enough, you may endeavor to become a member of the committee that allocates the IS resources. Membership on that committee confers a lot of power because there usually is tacit (if not overt) logrolling (mutual support for proposals).

Politically active IS managers will usually try to give outstanding service to those they consider to be powerful supporters, but such managers may neglect those they consider to be less powerful or advocates of change. In such a situation, managers in need of a new system may be motivated to become strong supporters of the status quo and hope to be rewarded by the IS department. Alternatively, such managers may try to go around the IS organization and obtain the system from outside or develop it themselves, or they may try to overthrow the IS department monopoly position by joining those who advocate decentralization.

The Hazards of Being Political

An understanding of information politics is obviously important to any manager who wants to use information technology. The main advantage of this understanding is to prevent political problems and to improve your ability to muster support for needed systems.

Overtly engaging in political activities designed to oppose the interests of others is another matter because that kind of organizational politics is a hazardous game that requires finesse and an understanding of the organizational power structure. Because political power can be very subtle, it may take years of experience in an organization before one understands the power structure, and some people in the organization may never come to understand it.

In the long run those who are recognized as contributing the most to the welfare of the organization are likely to receive the highest rewards, and those who are perceived as being out for themselves are most likely to be out.

MANAGING SYSTEMS IMPLEMENTATION

Implementation is the process of making the new system work in the user organization. Implementation may involve installing new hardware and software, which is usually the responsibility of technical people. But the most difficult aspect of implementation is changing the work behavior of the people who use the system, and this is your responsibility.

In a larger context, it is clear that continual and pervasive change is the defining characteristic of our time. Managers who can cope with and even exploit change will be successful, and those who cling to the past will be left behind.

THE CHANGE IMPERATIVE

On the conference circuit, in the business press, and at business schools, there is nothing quite so insistent as the drumbeat in favor of the virtues of change, of reformation, of the ability to stop on a dime and do something new in response to suddenly altered competitive realities. Change now goes by such value-laden names as flexibility, nimbleness, adaptability, agility, and transformation. Indeed, it is inarguable that organizations that can assume new shapes to fit new circumstances stand a far better chance of thriving than ones that are stuck and rigid. Closer to the truth for some companies is that unless they can change, they will perish.

(Levy, 1991)

Managing change is difficult. When introducing changes into an organization, one cannot assume that people will change just because you tell them to change. Also, one cannot assume that people will change their behavior in the desired or expected way—they often change in ways that are unintended and unexpected.

In the remainder of this section we will introduce some basic ideas that are helpful in managing the behavioral change involved in implementing new systems. Since the ability to manage change is essential for success as a manager, we hope that you will explore this topic more thoroughly through other avenues.

THE DIFFICULTY OF CHANGE

Let it be noted that there is no more delicate matter to take in hand, nor more dangerous to conduct, nor more doubtful in its success, than to set up as a leader in the introduction of changes. For he who innovates will have for his enemies all those who are well off under the existing order, and only lukewarm supporters in those who might be better off under the new.

(Machiavelli, 1513)

Attitudes Toward Change

According to psychologist Kurt R. Student (1978), people do not resist change as much as they resist being changed. Thus, acceptance of change is more likely if those who must change have influence in determining the nature of the new system. People tend to support what they help create, and meaningful participation provides both comfort with the change and a sense of responsibility for the success of the new system.

Contrary to the common saying, familiarity breeds comfort and acceptance, not contempt. Changes in feelings and attitudes do not take place instantaneously—they always take time. Student cites several studies that show that mere exposure to a person, thing, or concept changes attitudes from aversion to acceptance and attachment. Thus, we need to allow plenty of time to overcome initial resistance and for attitudes to change, and we should provide opportunities—such as pilot testing—for persons to become familiar with a new system before acceptance is required.

Student notes that participants often test the soundness of a new system and the degree of support that it has from other important participants. Managers must anticipate some skepticism toward a new system and expect people to test to see if the system is beneficial to them. Furthermore, people often will take some time before accepting a new system to determine whether the organization is serious about the new system or whether it will be sabotaged by a little foot-dragging. It is obvious that omissions and bugs in the new system can create great problems during this psychological testing process and encourage resistance to change. This resistance is one of the reasons why it is so important to thoroughly test new systems before they are installed.

Student also describes a stress factor associated with change. Facing the unknown consequences of change may challenge an individual's sense of adequacy and may seriously threaten self-esteem. Not only do individuals experience stress during change, but organizational units may be under significant tension associated with the resulting individual stress.

There is a relationship between the type of change required by a new system and the difficulty involved in accomplishing the change. Changes in procedures and practices usually involve relatively little stress, but changing role expectations involves more stress, and changing basic orientation and values involves even greater stress. We must be aware that systems that involve changing role expectations are likely to encounter substantial resistance, and systems that require different orientations and values may be quite difficult to implement.

Sociologist Enid Mumford (1969) points out that we all try to meet a number of personal needs through our work. The most obvious of these are money and security, but we also desire status among our peers, satisfying social relationships, interesting work, power, and responsibility. Not all persons have the same degree of need for each of these things, but each of us has some personal bundle of needs that we aspire to satisfy through our work.

Work groups in which the needs of the individuals are being met to a high degree will be stable, in that the members are likely to view any proposed change as undesirable. On the other hand, groups in which individual needs are not being met will be unstable in that there exists an inherent motivation for change.

Work groups tend to be wary of outsiders who may be brought in to analyze the work and introduce changes. If they perceive that changes are being imposed from outside the group, they are likely to resist the changes unanimously. Resistance tactics include absenteeism, poor performance, slowdowns, strikes, sabotage, or employees quitting the firm.

The Lewin/Schein Change Model

The classic **Lewin/Schein model** depicted in Figure 16.2 describes planned change in an organization as consisting of three stages—unfreezing, moving, and refreezing. This perspective is very helpful in planning and managing change due to information systems.

Unfreezing
  Establish a felt need
  Create a safe atmosphere
Moving
  Provide necessary information
  Assimilate knowledge and develop skills
Refreezing

FIGURE 16.2 The Lewin/Schein Change Model

The unfreezing stage includes two aspects. First, a felt need for change must be established in those who will be changing or there is no motivation for changing. Second, because change tends to be viewed as risky, it is helpful to create an atmosphere in which change is safe. Those who will be changing must be convinced that they will not be hurt by giving up the old, safe behavior.

The moving stage also involves two aspects. The first is the provision of the information needed to bring about the changes in attitudes and behavior. Until the knowledge and skills required by the changed roles are available, change cannot take place. This information not only must be available, but it must be assimilated by those who must change, which means that time, motivation, and assistance in learning new skills and attitudes may be required.

The refreezing stage fixes the new behavior as the accepted routine. It involves integrating the new behavior into the larger, ongoing behavior, rather than viewing it as something new and special. Refreezing frequently requires diffusing the change throughout the relevant social system, which may be much larger than the directly involved group of individuals.

In a study of 280 management science projects, D. E. Zand and R. E. Sorenson (1975) correlated the success of each project with the degree to which its implementation followed the precepts of the Lewin/Schein model. Their study showed that activity conducive to the changes required at each stage was associated with project success. They also found that poor performance in the unfreezing activities usually resulted in poor performance in the other stages, and that the refreezing

stage appeared to be very closely related to project success.

L. L. Gremillion (1980) has reported on a process developed for managing the changes required for the installation of packaged software systems. This approach is based upon the Lewin/Schein model and has broad applicability to managing the changes involved in introducing any new application of information technology in which the behavior required for successful implementation can be defined.

Gremillion's conceptual scheme is presented in Figure 16.3. To use this approach, we begin at the bottom of the figure and describe what we mean by successful implementation in terms of the behavior of those using the new system—the events, activities, and outputs that would characterize successful use of the system.

Working upward in the figure, we focus attention on the individual job behaviors that would be required if these events, activities, and outcomes are to occur. Working up to the middle block, this specific job behavior implies specific levels of knowledge, skills, and attitudes of each of the individuals involved in the successful use of the system. The attributes required of each individual are described in this stage.

Jumping to the top block of the figure, for each of the individuals who are involved we investigate the current levels of the same knowledge, skills, and attitudes that were found to be required of these individuals if the use of the new system is to be successful. Comparison of the required and present attributes of each individual defines the requirements of the implementation activities. Then, using everything we know about the change process, the implementation activities are developed to move individuals from their present levels of knowledge, skills, and attitudes to the levels appropriate to successful use of the new system.

The Gremillion approach is conceptually quite simple, but it provides a framework that focuses on precisely defining what must be accomplished with each person who is involved with the change. Thus, it forces us to concentrate on the people changes rather than on the technical changes. Gremillion used this approach

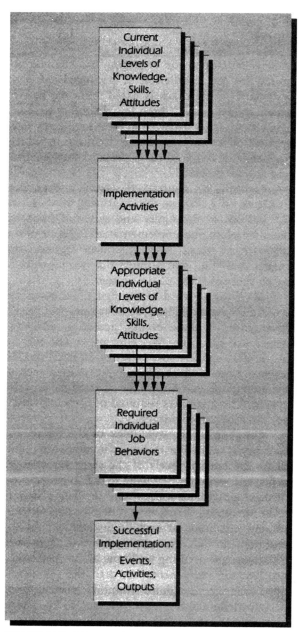

FIGURE 16.3 A Process for Planned Change. (Reprinted by permission from the MIS Quarterly, Vol. 4, No. 4, December 1980. Copyright 1980 by the Society for Information Management and the Management Information Systems Research Center at the University of Minnesota.)

to successfully implement a packaged system planning model in each of the ten forests comprising a region of the U.S. Forest Service.

The Innovation Adoption Perspective

An innovation is an idea or methodology that is perceived as new by an individual. Adoption is a decision to use an innovation. Many of the most important applications of information technology cannot be mandated by the organization; instead, they must be adopted by those who are to use them. Decision support systems, office automation systems, and executive information systems must be adopted by their users because the managers must use them to support their ongoing activities—they do not replace these activities. Strategic systems that serve customers or suppliers cannot be mandated. Many conventional information systems have failed because they were installed but never adopted. Thus, if you want to manage the changes that are involved in using information technology, viewing these changes as innovations that must be adopted provides a valuable perspective.

Everett M. Rogers (1962), a rural sociologist, studied hundreds of research studies on the diffusion of innovations, and produced a general model of the adoption process (see Figure 16.4), which views the adoption process as taking place in five stages. If one is interested in encouraging the adoption of an innovation, it is helpful to understand this process that individuals go through in adopting an innovation.

Awareness Here individuals are exposed to the innovation, but lack complete information about it and are not yet motivated to seek further information.

Interest At this stage individuals become interested in the innovation and seek additional information. Although the individuals are favorably disposed to seek further information, they have not yet judged its personal value. The function of this stage is to increase the potential adopters' information about the innovation.

Evaluation Here individuals mentally try out the innovation, evaluate whether or not it is benefi-

Awareness		Relative advantage	
Interest		Compatibility	
Evaluation		Complexity	
Trial		Divisibility	
Adoption		Communicability	

FIGURE 16.4 Rogers' Stages of the Adoption Process

FIGURE 16.5 Characteristics That Affect Ease of Adoption

cial, and decide whether or not to try it. At this stage individuals are teetering on the brink and may need reinforcement or advice from someone they trust and respect before deciding to try the innovation.

Trial   At this stage individuals tentatively use the innovation, on a small scale if possible, in order to evaluate its value in their own situations. They may need and obtain more information about how to use the innovation at this stage. The individuals are not committed to adoption until they have evaluated the results of the trial. The ease of using (and learning to use) the innovation is crucial here, because if potential adopters find the trial to be difficult and get discouraged, the innovation is likely to be rejected.

Adoption   At this stage the individuals have favorably evaluated the results of the trial and decide to continue full use of the innovation.

Rogers' five-stage process describes the successful adoption, but an innovation may be rejected at any of these stages. The potential adopter may never become aware of the innovation, may never develop interest in it, may lose interest after evaluation, or may reject it after some trial. Furthermore, rejection of an innovation can occur after adoption. Rogers examined many case histories and found a relatively high rate of discontinuance after initial adoption. This seems to relate to the third stage of the Lewin/Schein model—for some reason the refreezing stage failed.

Rogers also presented five characteristics of an innovation that affect its ease of adoption (see Figure 16.5). In dealing with information technology, it may be important to define the system so

that it has characteristics that make it easy to adopt.

Relative advantage is the degree to which an innovation is superior to ideas it supersedes. The perception of this relative advantage is more important than the reality in adoption decisions. As marketing people know, this perception may be altered by information dissemination, education, and promotion programs.

Compatibility is the degree to which the innovation is consistent with the existing values, attitudes, opinions, and past experiences of the potential adopters. It may be possible to design a new system to obtain its major benefits without requiring major changes in the existing values, attitudes, and opinions of its users.

Complexity is the degree to which the innovation is difficult to understand and use. Again, perceived complexity is more important than actual complexity, so a system should appear simple to its users.

Divisibility is the degree to which an innovation can be tried on a limited basis. It is easier to make the decision to try an innovation if it can be tried without much investment of time or expense.

Communicability is the degree to which the results of the innovation can be observed by potential adopters or the ease with which the results can be explained to them.

As an example of how the ease-of-adoption criteria can be useful, consider corporate data modeling as discussed in Chapter 14. If we view corporate data modeling as an innovation that must be adopted and examine the above characteristics that affect its ease of adoption, we find that it fares poorly. Although it may have substantial long-term payoff for the organization, its relative advantage is usually several years in the

462

future, and the benefits to the individual manager are not compelling. It is not compatible with existing values and attitudes because people are used to owning their own data, and most of them prefer not to give up this ownership. It is not easy to understand and use and is often perceived as complex. Its results are not easily observed or explained. No wonder corporate data modeling has been difficult to implement in many organizations.

Diffusion of an Innovation

In many cases one is concerned with the diffusion of an innovation throughout an organization rather than in an adoption of the innovation by any one individual. The diffusion of an innovation throughout a group or an organization is very much a social process. As depicted in Figure 16.6, Rogers reported that diffusion over time usually follows a bell-shaped curve, and this allowed him to categorize individuals in terms of how quickly they adopt an innovation. He calls the first 2.5 percent the innovators and the next 13.5 percent the early adopters; these two groups are critical to success in diffusing an innovation through an organization.

The innovators tend to be quite adventuresome and have more cosmopolitan social relationships and a wider set of sources of information. They are risk-takers who have the ability to understand and apply the technical knowledge required to use the innovation, but they are not usually opinion leaders in the organization or social group because they tend to be viewed as outsiders who are not in tune with the social norms of the group.

The early adopters, on the other hand, tend to be opinion leaders in their groups. Brancheau and Wetherbe (1989) note that opinion leaders are very important in the diffusion of an innovation because they are looked up to as role models by others in the organization. If they reject the innovation, it may get no further in the group, but when they adopt it, most of the rest of the group will go along. It is important in sponsoring a new system to locate opinion leaders and do everything possible to help them to be successful early adopters.

In a study of the diffusion of end-user computing in organizations, Brancheau (1987) found that the innovators tended to be well-educated, professionally active outside the company, very interested in technology, and usually computer opinion leaders. The early adopters had a similar profile, but were less active outside the company, less interested in technology, and often a business opinion leader. He found that the laggards were significantly older, less educated, suspicious of technology, and sometimes slowed adoption through their position in the hierarchy.

Finally, the chances of success of an innovation are greatly improved if it has a **champion**. The champion (perhaps you) probably has a stake in the success of the system and should be an opinion leader in the organization. A manager who is sponsoring a system that must be diffused through an organization should do everything possible to identify opinion leaders and assist them in adopting the system.

MANAGING AN IS UNIT

We have noted that many companies are decentralizing IS responsibilities and people throughout the organization. Thus, line managers may find themselves responsible for managing IS activities and people. We see two IS management roles for the line manager:

1. The head of an IS unit reports to the line manager.
2. A line manager becomes the head of an IS unit or subunit.

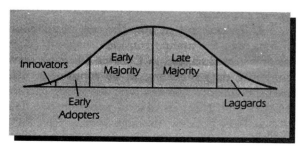

FIGURE 16.6 Rogers Categories of Adopters

When an IS Unit Reports to You

A few years ago, only senior managers (such as the controller, vice president of finance, or vice president of administration) would have an IS unit reporting to them. Today, however, managers at the division, plant, functional area, product line, or even department level may have IS units as part of their responsibilities. Of course, proprietors and senior managers of small businesses often have IS units reporting to them.

When the head of the IS unit reports to you, you do not directly manage the IS specialists. A manager to whom an IS unit reports typically has four major responsibilities (see Figure 16.7). These responsibilities have been difficult for top management when IS has been centralized, so they are not without their challenges, but they become less difficult the smaller the IS unit and the closer the unit is to the people it serves.

Setting Directions   A major reason for decentralization of IS is to assure that IS contributes as much as possible to the bottom line—that IS people focus their attention on things that really matter. The assumption is that line managers are better attuned than IS professionals to the welfare of the business.

If an IS unit reports to you, then it is your responsibility to make sure that the IS unit understands and accepts the business goals of your business unit, and that these goals are faithfully translated into appropriate IS unit goals. Thus, you are responsible for the IS unit's strategic planning. On the other hand, there must be participation by the IS unit in developing its strategic plans because the resulting goals must be accepted by the IS unit if they are to be effective. The head of the IS unit should also participate in your business unit's

---

Setting directions
Allocating resources
Evaluating performance
Resolving conflicts

FIGURE 16.7 Typical Responsibilities of the Manager to Whom an IS Unit Reports

planning so that your planning takes into account the possibilities for effective use of information technology.

Just as the central IS organization needs a mission statement, so does a decentralized IS unit. Chapter 13 describes several ideas that can be very helpful in strategic planning at the business unit level. For example, when you first take over responsibility for an IS unit, a SWOT (strengths, weaknesses, opportunities, and threats) analysis may be helpful, and determining your personal critical success factors may help you ensure that the IS unit is focusing on important things.

Allocating Resources   You may be responsible for allocating resources to the IS unit—determining the IS unit's budget. In order for you to allocate these resources on a rational basis, you must be clear about your IS goals and objectives. You and the IS unit then have a basis for negotiating the level of resources required to achieve these goals. You and the IS unit must translate these long-range goals into specific activities during the planning period. You must understand what goes on in IS well enough to be sure that you are not being overcharged—that the costs for these activities quoted by IS managers are reasonable. It may be helpful to get some outside bids or consulting help to determine how your IS unit's quoted costs compare with the prices of others.

Another approach to funding the IS unit is for it to charge out its services to the organizational units it serves. In this approach you have two responsibilities—to ensure that the charging algorithms are fair and that they lead to desirable user behavior (see Chapter 15), and to ensure that the costs that determine these prices are reasonable and that your IS unit's productivity is in line with other such units, both within and outside your company.

Evaluating Performance   If you have negotiated the IS unit's budget on the basis of plans for what is to be accomplished, then at the end of the period you can determine the performance level of your IS unit. Obviously, you have to evaluate the quantity of the unit's work as well as its quality and timeliness. A number of other criteria for evaluating IS performance were presented in Chapter 15.

Resolving Conflicts Despite efforts to ensure that your IS unit understands and accepts your business goals, conflicts may still arise between your IS unit and its clients. As the person to whom both parties report, it is your responsibility to make sure that these conflicts are resolved in the best interests of your organization.

When You Become an IS Manager

Many organizations now move line managers into IS positions because they believe that IS needs better management or because they believe that information technology is so important to the organization's future that their fast track managers need to have had significant IS experience as part of their preparation for major management responsibilities. Managers in small businesses often have to manage IS as part of their responsibilities because the company cannot afford to devote a full-time manager to IS. When you are an IS unit manager, you may have to deal with the details of what goes on in the IS organization. Thus, a line manager who moves into the IS organization should be a quick learner of the technology.

A decentralized IS unit may carry out some or all of the functions depicted in Figure 16.8. For example, it is not unusual for a company to decentralize development and maintenance of most application systems and centrally manage most of the communications network and computer operations—only local area networks and PC operations would be decentralized. Many aspects of

---

Systems development
Computer operations
Software maintenance
Telecommunications
Technical support
Information center functions
Personnel management

FIGURE 16.8 *Possible Functions Performed by a Decentralized IS Unit*

technical support and personnel management might also remain centralized or be shared between central IS and the local unit.

Chapters 8 through 11 were devoted to ways to acquire, maintain, and operate application systems, but these chapters concentrated primarily on user-manager roles. As an IS manager you need to learn more about the activities of the IS professionals in these processes. You also would be responsible for planning, staffing, motivating, and evaluating your staff, as well as the day-to-day activities of your unit.

Many managers who come up through the IS ranks may be technically oriented, rather than managerially oriented, and may have little managerial training or background, so an experienced line manager may have some advantages when taking over an IS unit. On the other hand, someone who lacks a technical background may be viewed with suspicion by IS people, so managing IS personnel may be a particularly challenging activity for the new IS manager. This lack of technical experience may present particular problems when you must evaluate the performance of technical specialists. A possible solution to this problem is to work with the individuals to jointly set performance objectives that make sense from the perspectives of both the manager and the technical person.

As discussed in Chapter 8, studies have found differences in basic attitudes and values between computer specialists and managers that could be important in managing and motivating IS professionals. Couger and Zawacki (1978) indicate that, relative to other workers, IS professionals have lower needs for social interaction and higher needs for personal growth. Thus, IS professionals may need encouragement and training in interaction skills. Also, they may be motivated by assignments that challenge them to master new technologies and by advanced training opportunities.

Despite these differences, IS specialists are people, too, so everything you are learning about organization theory, organizational behavior, and employee reward and motivation systems can be applied when managing IS specialists. Further, recent research in the insurance industry by Ferratt and Short (1988) found far fewer differences in how IS specialists and other workers are motivated than earlier studies.

The head of an IS unit has both external and internal responsibilities and represents the IS unit to outside management, especially in the negotiation of budgets and evaluation of the unit's performance. This person also represents outside management to the IS people, which can be an especially delicate job if he or she has been placed in the new position as part of the organization's strategy of refocusing IS attitudes and roles.

MANAGING INFORMATION TECHNOLOGY ON YOUR OWN

A manager's business unit may begin to use information technology without having IS professionals to call on. For example, a small business may not have IS professionals on its staff. Even in a large firm your needs may not have sufficient priority within the organization to obtain the professional resources that you need, or the firm may have a policy mandating end-user computing. Therefore, you must manage IS on your own. More precisely, you must develop the necessary IS capabilities within your business unit, which usually involves developing your own small semiprofessional IS unit.

Gerald M. Hoffman (1986) points out that as long as a system is used by only one person, it is the responsibility of that individual. Whenever a system is shared by several people, even if it is only a stand-alone PC system, it is an organizational system, and the manager of that organization has responsibility for it. Thus, Hoffman maintains, you may acquire responsibility for managing information technology without even knowing it and certainly without a lot of thought.

Possible Problems

When you are responsible for managing your own small IS unit, you may have many of the operational problems and responsibilities described in Chapter 9, as well as the problems of managing

development discussed in Chapters 8, 10, and 11. Although these problems may be on a much smaller scale, they may be critical to your organization, and you may not have the people or knowledge to deal with them. Hoffman points out that even if it only involves the use of a few PCs, the operation and management of a user-controlled system may be a complex activity involving some or all of the areas depicted in Figure 16.8.

Managing User Application Development
Although this topic has been discussed extensively in Chapter 11, we will briefly review it in the present context. You (or your people) must select and justify the systems that are developed. Although micro-based systems appear to be inexpensive, the problem here is that you may not understand the true costs of developing and operating such systems. Hoffman points out that there are hidden costs, such as the cost of departmental people doing systems work, the cost of poor quality systems, and the opportunity cost of not being aware of all the available IS opportunities.

A hidden problem in the design of supposedly stand-alone systems is that in the long run there are very few systems that do not need to interface with other systems. As the original system grows in usefulness and functionality, it is highly likely that it will need to obtain data from another system. It is important to recognize this possibility when the system is originally designed and consult with IS people about how to make this interfacing easy. In particular, giving some attention to defining your data in accord with corporate standards and existing data definitions can prevent a lot of problems when you wish to integrate the system into the corporate environment.

Another problem may be failure to consider the full range of options in acquiring the new system. Managers may not consider alternatives, such as purchasing the system or having the IS department build it using the life cycle approach or prototyping.

You should make sure that you do not make the usual amateur mistakes of neglecting testing, controls, security, backup, and documentation. For PC systems, security may mean removing floppy disks and keeping them locked up.

Provision for backup of files should be made (as automatically as possible), and the backup disks or tapes stored in a safe place. Controls, in particular, should be designed into the system, not just grafted on later.

Managing Operations   Your small IS unit may have many of the operations problems discussed in Chapter 9, but there is a tendency to think that microcomputers are so simple that no resources are required to manage them. This assumption is wrong. Managers must organize for and enforce decisions on security and backup. You can recognize the need for security and backup when you design the system, but without constant enforcement of these procedures, they tend to disappear quickly. Hardware maintenance will be required and must be managed. Although the actual maintenance work may be provided by professionals outside your department, some internal person must arrange for it and follow up to see that it is accomplished.

With PCs, hardware security must be considered. Mainframe computers seldom are stolen, but PCs can easily disappear if they are not locked up at night. Laptop and notebook computers, in particular, are tempting targets of thieves.

Operations continuity may be important for PC systems and can be assured through management attention. Uninterruptible power supplies and protection against power surges are not expensive. It may even be prudent to provide extra backup equipment so that a spare is available when a PC is being repaired. If the system is truly critical to your operations, provision should be made for dealing with disasters, such as fire or flood. Donna Raimondi (1986) cites an example where company disaster-recovery planning made it possible to recover from loss of the central data center, but data from PC systems were lost because all backup disks were stored on site.

User-controlled systems tend to grow over time, and they may eventually exceed the capability of the original equipment. Thus, just as with the data center, capacity planning may be an important activity. What capacity do you need, and when will you need it? How can it be obtained,

and (most important) how can you migrate to new hardware without unacceptable disruption?

Managing Software Maintenance   Systems must change over time as the needs of the organization change. Because the bulk of the total costs over the life of a typical system are costs to modify the system to keep it serving the changing needs of the organization, managing this maintenance can be a critical aspect of managing your own small IS department.

One cannot allow individual users to make changes in a system without regard to the other users, so responsibility for maintenance of each system must be assigned, and provision must be made for deciding what changes are to be made and how and when they are to be implemented. There must be provision for testing and complete documentation of the changes and retraining of those using the system when the changes affect their activities.

Even if the system is a purchased system and the vendor is responsible for making upgrades to the system, someone must be responsible for installing the upgrades and for whatever retraining may be required when these changes are made.

Telecommunications Problems   Micro to mainframe communications are usually the responsibility of the IS organization, but the user organization must be aware of and adhere to the established standards.

Local area networks, however, are usually the responsibility of the user organization. The central IS organization may provide engineering support to diagnose and correct the hardware and software problems that will inevitably occur, but the user organization must have someone who is competent to interface with the technical specialists and who is responsible for making sure that the system functions properly.

Experience demonstrates that LANs require someone to serve as the network administrator. In addition to responsibility for coordinating maintenance, the LAN administrator assigns addresses to any new equipment added to the network, admits new users to the system, manages the file server, and may manage any other equipment shared through the LAN.

Managing Technical Support Systems will change over time. The functionality will expand, the amount of data in your files will grow, volumes of transactions may grow, and the technology and organizational standards will change. Thus, technical support will be required for capacity planning, understanding and establishing hardware and software standards, and planning when and how to migrate to upgraded hardware and software.

Your department may have to provide some of this technical support. Even if this support is provided by the central IS organization, your department must have someone who is qualified to interact with and represent your interests to the IS professionals outside your department.

Building Your Own Semiprofessional IS Unit

Assuming that you already have a full-time job, you cannot handle the above responsibilities yourself. Therefore, you must build a group that is capable of handling these responsibilities. This group may be very small—one part-time person—or it may involve several people. Figure 16.9 lists a number of things that should be considered when building your own semiprofessional IS unit.

Designing the Organization Once you have determined which activities are your responsibility, you can design your IS organization. You must define the activities that are required and assign them to individual positions. You must define the specific duties and job descriptions of each posi-

---

Designing the organization
Staffing
Training
Evaluating
Rewarding

FIGURE 16.9 Considerations in Building a Small IS Unit

tion and decide whether it is full-time or combined with other departmental duties. The central IS department can be very helpful in a consulting role to help you design your organization. If necessary, you can employ an outside consultant to assist you in this task.

In designing this organization you may be constrained by the lack of resources available to you for this purpose. You may not be able to justify additional positions, especially because your computer applications are expected to improve the productivity of your unit. At the very least, you may have to build your unit's IS capability over a substantial period of time, and acquiring the necessary resources may have political aspects.

Staffing Obtaining qualified people to fill these positions may be a problem. Qualified people are scarce, and they may command higher salaries than you are paying to other people in your department at comparable levels. Also, you may have little basis for evaluating the qualifications of computer-related people, so you may not hire the best ones available. The central IS department can perform a valuable service by assisting in locating and evaluating possible candidates or even by hiring and training such people and then making them available for transfer into line departments.

Another approach to staffing is to assign existing departmental people, either full- or part-time, to computer-related duties. You may already have a number of amateur computer users in the department who have an interest in the technology and might accept a job assignment that exploits this interest.

Another alternative is to use specialists from consultants or contractor firms to do the most technical work. This may enable you to obtain the services of highly competent people on a short-term basis and thus avoid the problems of developing and managing them yourself.

Training Both the outside people you hire and the department people to whom IS duties are assigned may be amateurs who have an interest in information technology, but they may have quite limited experience in the area. Such people may be very narrow in their backgrounds and interests. They may know programming in a particular language but have no experience with or concept of system design. They may have to learn through experience the need for file backups, documentation, programming standards, controls, and audit trails, as well as the limitations of your hardware and software.

One foresees the problem of each user organization repeating the mistakes that computer professionals have learned to avoid over the past thirty years. Thus, it is very important to make a continuing investment in training to broaden the perspective of your people. Training may be available from your central IS department and from outside the organization through hardware and software vendors (such as IBM), consultants, and universities.

Evaluating   As an amateur yourself, you may have a very limited basis for evaluating the qualifications and performance of your computer specialists. It is important for you to work closely with your computer specialists to define performance objectives that both of you can accept. Also, your central IS department may be helpful to you in evaluating people and in developing evaluation criteria.

Rewarding   To obtain qualified computer specialists, you may have to make exceptions to your existing departmental salary schedule, which can lead to morale problems in the department. The major problem, however, is not salary for computer specialists, but rather how to avoid blighting the careers of people you assign to be the department's computer specialists (Hoffman, 1986).

When you take people already in your department and assign them computer specialist duties, it may reduce their long-term career potential. Many computer specialist jobs in user areas are dead-end jobs because there is no computer specialist career path, so an employee has to get away from the computer in order to be promoted to a higher position within the department. Thus, the more time and effort a person puts into developing specialized computer skills, the more he may fall behind his colleagues in the development of departmental

skills and thus become less qualified for higher positions within the department.

Also, many computer responsibilities in a user department are part-time assignments where people are assigned duties that require the development of computer-related skills. They spend part of their time as departmental computer specialists, but they also retain regular departmental responsibilities. Again, over time, these people's departmental skills may deteriorate relative to those with whom they may be competing for promotion within the department.

How can departmental IS capabilities be built without handicapping those people in the department who contribute by developing specialized computer skills? One way is to bring in people from outside with computer skills and interests who do not aspire to departmental careers. Another approach is to make computer specialist activities a normal part of the department career path—everyone does it for a time, but no one is stuck permanently in a computer specialist job. This approach has the advantage that all employees will then have computer skills that make them better able to exploit the technology in any job. The disadvantage, however, is that some people do not have the special talents required for these computer duties.

Another approach that some companies have found advantageous is to employ IS professionals who work directly for user departments but whose career paths are managed by the IS department, thus giving them satisfying career opportunities as IS professionals.

Sources of Help

If you find yourself in an IS management role, you may need additional help in coping with some of the problems associated with managing information technology. Where can you get this help?

Organizations vary widely in the degree to which they provide support for the manager in satisfying needs for IT. Some organizations will have a well-developed IT architecture designed to support managers while ensuring that the welfare of the overall organization is considered at the same time. Other organizations provide very little support and have not provided a structure that protects the interests of the organization. A few organizations actively discourage user initiative and action in taking advantage of IT. Whatever the degree of support provided by the organization, the manager should be aware of company policy and take advantage of any assistance that is available.

A partnership relationship with a competent IS organization can be highly advantageous, both to the manager and to the overall organization. IS specialists can make a major contribution to user-owned systems through consulting and coaching to reduce the risks associated with inexperience in developing, operating, and managing computer systems. Even when the system is developed by the central IS group, the users and the IS organization should view it as a cooperative venture in which both have important roles.

In organizations where a true partnership between IS and line management exists, providing consulting to the management of decentralized IS units is a major role of the central IS organization. There are also a number of reputable and experienced outside consultants that may be employed when you need help. When you first take over as head of an IS unit, it may be a good idea to bring in an internal or external consultant to perform an independent evaluation of the strengths and weaknesses of the unit.

Another source of help may be associations with colleagues in similar positions. For example, managers with IS responsibilities in your company may have an informal organization that gets together for lunch once a month to discuss common interests. A similar group of managers from various companies may be available within your local area. The IS faculty of your local college or university may be another resource.

The professional literature can also be a valuable source of ideas concerning current issues. There are a number of publications that may be helpful. Weekly publications that are valuable include *Computerworld* and *PC Week*. Two good practitioner magazines are *Datamation* and *Corporate Computing*. Academic-style journals that publish articles useful for managers include *MIS Quarterly, Information and Management*, and *Data Base*. General management magazines, such as *Harvard Business Review* and *Sloan Management Review*, often contain helpful articles.

SUMMARY

A mixture of rational and political considerations govern how most organizations function. We argue that information is inherently political, which explains why it may be difficult to obtain the resources required for a new system, implement a new system, or manage data. The manager is clearly responsible for dealing with the politics of information technology.

We do not intend to imply that the rational model of organizations is wrong or inappropriate. Quite the contrary, organizations are successful to the degree that they are able to establish appropriate objectives and motivate employees to attain them. In the long run, successful business organizations must be rationally oriented, and your long-run success in the organization will depend on how well you perform in achieving the organization's goals. Thus, although you may have employed your understanding of information politics to obtain a new system, you must make sure that the organization obtains the promised benefits.

If a new system is to provide significant benefits to the organization, then it must result in changes in what people do or how they do it. Therefore, most new systems imply such changes. It is the manager's responsibility to make sure that these changes are planned rather than accidental, so you must be involved with organizational redesign while defining the requirements of the new system. Consequently, you are responsible for the impact of the system on your people.

The manager is responsible for managing the behavioral changes—whether planned or not—required to implement the new system in the organization. Both the Lewin/Schein change model and the innovation adoption and diffusion models can help one plan and carry out behavioral changes.

Line managers are likely to have responsibility for an IS unit sometime in their careers. Increasingly, this responsibility is sneaking up on managers when someone in the unit begins to share a personal application with other workers. You then may have to build your own small amateur IS unit to help manage the technology.

The sponsoring manager must provide the vision of how the technology can be used to improve the performance of the business. Without this vision computers seldom produce significant benefits to the organization.

Acquiring and exploiting information technology is a long and hazardous process. Complex technology systems, whether they are information systems or automated production lines, seldom work well when they are first installed. It takes dogged effort to work out the bugs and make incremental improvements before the new system is likely to be successful. If the system's sponsor gives up when serious problems arise, the entire development effort may well be wasted.

Thus, a new system must have a champion who is the instigator and pusher, from the initial vision of the need for the system to the last stage of the change process where the new behavior must be installed as a permanent pattern. New technology is seldom successfully adopted without such a champion.

There are a number of keys to success in exploiting information technology. The first of these is knowledge and understanding of the technology and what it can and cannot do for you, of the systems that make the technology useful, and of the various systems acquisition methods.

Another key is managing the acquisition of systems. Whether the system is purchased, developed by the IS organization, or developed by the user organization, you must manage the process of obtaining and installing the system. Because there may be a substantial personal cost to the sponsoring manager in acquiring a new system, you may wish to evaluate carefully whether your potential personal gain from attempting to acquire a new system is worth your personal cost.

A third key is the development of your own support organization or developing the capability of your people to exploit the technology. Depending on your environment, you may have to do almost everything within your own organization, or you may only need to interface with the IS organization. Your success depends on the overall capability of your group to deal with the technology, not just your personal ability to deal with it.

A fourth key is acquiring the necessary resources. Again, you must understand what resources you need—education, consulting, development assistance, hardware, software, and so on. You also must understand your company information infrastructure (or architecture) to determine where to obtain the needed resources. You also must understand how to obtain these resources—including the politics involved—and actually obtain them.

Most important, you must have the vision of how the technology can enhance the effectiveness of your organization, and you must be the champion of the new system.

REVIEW QUESTIONS

1. Describe the Lewin/Schein model of change.
2. Describe each of Rogers' stages in the adoption process.
3. Contrast the rational and political views of how organizations make decisions.
4. Why is information political?
5. Give three examples of resistance tactics that might be employed by someone who feels that a proposed new information system might cause the individual to lose power.
6. If you were the sponsor of a new information system, how would you evaluate the degree to which it might encounter opposition?
7. If you were the sponsor of a new information system and you anticipated opposition to the new system, what could you do to improve the probability of success of the new system?
8. What are the main responsibilities of a manager to whom a decentralized IS unit reports?

DISCUSSION QUESTIONS

1. A marketing major who is a computer whiz has two job opportunities. One is to be an assistant brand manager in the marketing department of a consumer goods company, and the other is to

be an assistant to the marketing manager whose duties are to be the computer specialist for the department. The second job's starting salary is $3,000 per year more than the first job's starting salary. What questions should this person ask the marketing manager before deciding which of these jobs to accept?

2. Think of a specific organization with which you are familiar. To what degree does this organization operate according to the rational perspective? the political perspective?

3. This chapter asserts that the Gremillion process for installing a complex software package in many locations of the U.S. Forest Service is based on the Lewin/Schein change model. How would you defend this assertion?

4. Consider Rogers' breakdown of innovation adopters into innovators, early adopters, early majority, and so on. It is suggested that innovators are not good candidates to champion the innovation. Do you agree with this statement? Why or why not?

5. This chapter asserted that diffusion of an innovation is a social process. Can you provide an example that supports or refutes this assertion?

6. You have just been assigned to be the manager of a twelve-person decentralized IS unit that is responsible for the IS activities at a location of your company. What would you anticipate to be the top three problems you would face in taking over this responsibility?

7. You submitted a request for a new system to your IS department and were turned down by the IS steering committee. You really need this new system and are convinced that it would be quite beneficial for your company. What are the things that you would consider when deciding how to go about obtaining this system? What would you try next?

8. Why is it important that one redesign the organization at the same time that one is defining the requirements for a new system? How does this affect the manager's role in systems development?

9. Consider the following statement: Sponsoring the development of an application system may be hazardous to your career. Do you agree with this statement? Why or why not?

REFERENCES

Baroudi, Jack J., Margrethe H. Olson, and Blake Ives. 1986. "An empirical study of the impact of user involvement on system usage and information satisfaction." *Communications of the ACM* 29 (March): 232–238.

Beeman, Don R., and Thomas W. Sharkey. 1987. "The use and abuse of corporate politics." *Business Horizons* 30 (March–April): 26–30.

Brancheau, James C. 1987. *The Diffusion of Information Technology: Testing and Extending Innovation Diffusion Theory in the Context of End-User Computing.* Unpublished Ph.D. dissertation. University of Minnesota, Minneapolis, MN.

Brancheau, James C., and James C. Wetherbe. 1989. "Understanding innovation diffusion helps boost acceptance rates of new technology." *Chief Information Officer Journal* 2 (Fall): 23–31.

Cougar, D., and R. Zawacki. 1978. "What motivates DP professionals?" *Datamation* 24 (September): 116–123.

Davenport, Thomas H., Robert B. Eccles, and Laurence Prusak. 1992. "Information politics." *Sloan Management Review* 34 (Fall): 53–65.

Ferratt, Thomas W., and Larry E. Short. 1988. "Are information systems people different? An investigation of how they are and should be managed." *MIS Quarterly* 12 (September): 427–444.

Ginzberg, M. J. 1978. "Steps towards more effective implementation of MS and MIS." *Interfaces* 8 (May): 57–63.

Gremillion, L. L. 1980. "Managing the implementation of standardized computer based systems." *MIS Quarterly* 4 (December): 51–59.

Hoffman, Gerald M. 1986. "Every manager is an information systems manager now, or, managing user-controlled information systems." *Information & Management* 11 (December): 229–235.

Keen, P. G. W. 1981. "Information systems and organizational change." *Communications of the ACM* 24 (January): 24–33.

Kling, Rob. 1980. "Social analyses of computing: Theoretical perspectives in recent empirical research." *Computing Surveys* 12 (March): 61–110.

Levy, Joseph L. 1991. "Letter from the Editor." *CIO* 5 (November): 8.

Machiavelli, Niccolo. ca. 1513. *The Prince.* Translation by Hill Thompson (1988). Palm Springs, CA: ETC Publications.

Markus, M. L. 1981. "Implementation politics: Top management support and user involvement." *Systems, Objectives, Solutions* 1: 203–215.

———. 1983. "Power, politics, and MIS implementation." *Communications of the ACM* 26: 430–444.

Mumford, Enid. 1969. "Implementing EDP systems—A sociological perspective." *The Computer Bulletin* (January): 10–13.

Raimondi, Donna. 1986. "Hot sites: Disaster plan douses flames." *Computerworld* 20 (November 17): 1.

Rogers, Everett M. 1962. *Diffusion of Innovation.* New York: The Free Press.

Student, K. R. 1978. "Managing change: A psychologist's perspective." *Business Horizons* 21 (December): 28–33.

Zand, D. E., and R. E. Sorensen. 1975. "Theory of change and the effective use of management science." *Administrative Science Quarterly* 20 (December): 532–545.

CASE STUDY

11-1

Midstate University
Business Placement Office: Part III
Management of the Computer System

The Midstate University Business Placement Office (BPO) computer system is an integral part of its operations, without which the BPO could not function. Not only is it essential, but it also is somewhat complex, and the computer processing and the activities of the BPO staff are intimately interrelated. Thus, Jim Wine, director of the BPO, is the de facto manager of a miniature information systems department, and his success as BPO manager depends upon how well he manages his IS functions.

The BPO Organization

The organization of the BPO is shown in Exhibit 1. Jim Wine, director of the BPO, is also assistant dean for company relations of the School of Business. Although he is ultimately responsible for all BPO operations, Wine cannot devote all his time to running the BPO on a day-by-day basis.

Elliott Gordon, associate director for administration, manages the day-by-day operations of the BPO. In addition to general oversight of the staff, Gordon supervises the 30 MBA graduate assistants that work in the BPO, and he is the senior counselor of MBA students. Gordon is an excellent manager—he is sensitive to problems, figures out what needs to be done, and organizes things so that they function smoothly year after year.

Jane Meyer, assistant director, is responsible for alumni placement, coordinating company presenta-

tions on campus, and overseeing the BPO back room computer operations. She reports to Gordon.

Margaret Brown, the other associate director, handles the interaction with the company recruiters. She signs them up for their interview dates, corresponds with them to arrange for setting up their schedules via the CRIFs, and markets the BPO to obtain additional client companies.

Stanley Russ, the other assistant director, helps Brown with company relations. He is also responsible for the BPO counter operations, where the students come to make changes in their interview schedules, and for the publications of the BPO.

The BPO also has an office manager and three secretaries.

The BPO Computer Organization Meyer, the BPO manager responsible for the computer system, has been in her present position for two years. Before that she worked as a graduate assistant at the BPO for a year as a practicum for her masters degree in college counseling. Other than an undergraduate course in FORTRAN programming, she had no experience with computers before joining the BPO staff.

The organization of the BPO computer group is shown in Exhibit 2. Dick Greene, computer operations supervisor, is responsible for the day-by-day operations in the back room. He supervises the computer operator who does the production and copying of the computer reports and distributes and posts them as required. Greene has a degree in English and has put a lot of effort into organizing the processing and to getting the system documentation into good shape. He also does some programming, mostly making changes to existing programs.

EXHIBIT 1

Midstate BPO Organization Chart

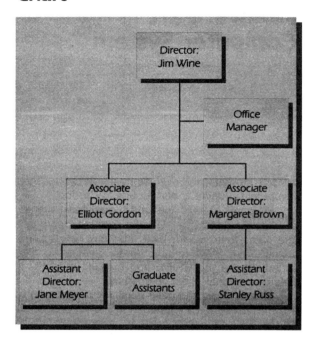

Greene has no formal computer background beyond a FORTRAN programming course several years ago. He became involved with the computer as a hobby. This is his first computer job, and he did not really apply for it—Wine hired him as the result of a casual conversation at a party with a mutual friend.

Ernie McArtor, the chief programmer, supervises the two parttime programmers and is responsible for changes and additions to the system. He has no formal training in computers. He is a musician who plays in a rock band who got interested in amplifiers and electronics that way, and finally drifted into computers.

McArtor is the day-to-day contact with the data processing organization. If data processing has any problems with the input files or with the changes they are making to their part of the BPO system, they call him, and if the BPO has problems with the mainframe output, he calls them. Meyer, however, signs most of the memos that are sent from the BPO to data processing.

One of Meyer's other responsibilities is to check the reports as they come out to catch any errors or problems before the reports are distributed. She is also the intermediary between the other BPO managers and the programmers—she is the one who sits down with the programmers and explains the new projects, makes sure that they are staying on the course that the other directors want, and tries to see that the projects get done on time.

As a novice with computers, supervising the programmers has sometimes been a frustrating experience for Meyer. She reported:

It seemed so simple to me. I'd just tell them to tell the computer to do this simple thing. A month later it wouldn't be done, I'd ask them why, and they'd explain that they'd had these problems. I'd been used to telling a human: Don't do that any more! And they wouldn't do it anymore. But I've had to recognize that with a computer it's a lot more complicated.

Jane has to deal with the students when there are mistakes in the scheduling system, explaining what went wrong and trying to help overcome the difficulties that the computer mistakes have caused for the students, and that puts her on the spot. The students are upset and angry, and sometimes she can only tell them that it is a programming problem. "I can only do

EXHIBIT 2

BPO Computer Group Organization Chart

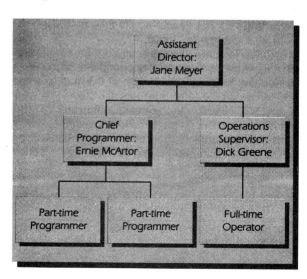

that so many times before I become frustrated," Jane explains. Then she wants to go into the back room and shout at the programmers: "Change it! Change it or I'm not going to open my door tomorrow!" She realizes, however, that that would just frustrate the people in the back room, who are already doing their best.

Development of the Computer Organization Bob Rivers, the brilliant and dedicated MBA halftimer who had helped Wine develop the initial Apple-based system, graduated and left in the spring of 1982, and Wine replaced him with another halftime MBA, Roger Snider. Within a few months both Snider and Wine realized that the job was beyond Snider's capability—there was no way that in 20 hours a week he could do what Rivers had been doing. Of course, Rivers had not been doing the job in 20 hours a week either—he would work 40 or 50 hours a week if necessary to get the job done. Snider did not see it that way, and he was extremely resentful when Wine expected him to work as much as necessary to get the job done, even if he was only being paid for 20 hours and trying to complete a heavy load of MBA classes at the same time.

In January 1983, while Wine was under a great deal of pressure to transfer the scheduling process to the IBM mainframe, Snider abruptly resigned. "That was the straw that broke the camel's back and convinced me that I couldn't handle the computer system with parttime temporary people," recalls Wine. From then on he set out to develop a fulltime professional computer staff.

That was a problem. Wine did not have the authorization to hire people at the level he needed, so he gradually upgraded some of his clerical positions. He would hire someone for $10,000 a year in a clerical position, teach them programming, and then go to the university Personnel Department and have the position upgraded to correspond to what the present occupant was doing. After two or three generations of this, he now has positions that enable him to pay enough to hire and keep good technical people. Wine, however, still has the same number of positions in the BPO that he had before the system was developed.

Until Wine realized that he needed a different type of person in these jobs, there was a great deal of turnover. "People were being burned out very quickly by the magnitude of the job and the chaotic conditions caused by the fact that we had to be ready to bid on Monday, whether the computer worked or not," Wine recalls. After Rivers left, they had a succession of two or three people in that job until they hired Julia Workman, who was a stabilizing force. "Julia was not a workaholic—she did what she could in the eight to nine hours a day that she would give us, and then she was done. But that really was a good thing, because she began to get some things routinized that should have been routinized. She convinced me that we had to have an adequate number of people, and that they had to be organized and managed." Although Workman has left the BPO, it now has three fulltime and two parttime people on the staff, Meyer manages them, and things are quite stable.

....
Managing System Operations

The Back Room Operations During the recruiting season the system is driven by inflexible deadlines set by the bidding process. The bid cards are accepted on Monday and Tuesday, and the results of the bidding have to be available for students on Friday at the latest. Thus, the databases used in the bid processing must be up-to-date, and the bidding file must be complete to send to the data processing center on Tuesday evening to meet the deadlines to complete the processing by Thursday night.

Considerable organization and discipline are required to accomplish the great many things that have to be completed in a specified sequence and by a number of different people. If someone forgets something, or does it wrong, it can cause problems.

Greene is responsible for the day-by-day processing, and he has developed a set of forms to control the processing—a different form for each day of the week that shows every computer program that must be run in the proper sequence. The form has a blank to fill in the time of completion of each program. He also has a set of forms for end-of-month, end-of-semester, and end of the recruiting year.

Greene has also put a good deal of effort into documentation of the system. In addition to his forms for controlling processing, there is a run book that tells how to run each program, with suggestions as to what to do when anything goes wrong. There is also a listing showing the databases and index files that each of the programs uses, and a manual describing the databases and the procedures for initializing them at the beginning of the recruiting year. Thus, the operational aspects of the system are well-documented.

There is, however, little system level documentation, and there is very little documentation of the individual programs beyond that provided by dBASE III. When Greene was revising a program recently, he spent much time creating a program flow chart in order to get an understanding of how the program worked.

There is also a form for controlling backups to the database. The staff learned about the importance of backing up the database soon after they got their first hard disk. Wine remembers:

> A secretary was working with dBASE and accidentally entered a command that cleaned off the entire hard disk—almost 10 megabytes of data. She knew the second she had done it what she had done, but there wasn't a thing she could do to stop it. She came out of that office bawling, and it was a tearful day for everybody in the office because we had to go back and repeat almost a week of data entry work!

Ever since then they have done daily backups.

In addition the system design provides additional security for the databases. The master copy of the database resides on the MODUS fileserver, but a copy of each database also resides on the PC/XT where that database is updated. During the day, only the database on the PC hard disk is updated, and at the end of the day that day's transactions are sent to the MODUS to update the master database and print a transaction log for control purposes. The MODUS database is backed up after it is updated, and everything is ready for the next day's processing. Thus, in addition to the regular backup, the MODUS database is also a backup for the local PC database, and vice versa. Also, all source documents are filed for reference in case there are problems.

The Front Office Operations The computer processing is a critical part of the day-by-day responsibilities of the BPO directors. Brown gets the information from the companies on their interview dates and the specifics of each interview schedule provided by the submitted CRIFs. Meyer is responsible for bid processing, getting the bid cards entered into the system, getting the scheduling processing done at the Data Processing Center, and posting the schedules and the alpha listing for the students. Then Russ is responsible for the changes to the interview schedules that are made over the counter via manual transactions and for preparing the final schedules and sending them to the recruiters prior to their visits.

Two years ago the responsibility for maintaining each of the databases was assigned to a specific director. Brown is in charge of the company, company schedule, contact, and CRIF databases; Meyer is in charge of the student and placement offers databases; and Russ is responsible for changes to the schedule and waitlist databases after they are created by the scheduling system. Of course, each director does not enter all the data, but they do closely supervise their data entry persons.

Prior to this specific assignment of responsibility, they had some problems with the accuracy of the databases. When each director could change any database, there were occasions when a needed change would not be made because it was not entered, and sometimes a director would make a change that should not have been made. Funneling all the changes to each database through one person virtually eliminated these accuracy problems.

Students who have problems with the bidding system come to the BPO counter, where the assistants who staff it are trained to answer the basic questions that occur most frequently. If the graduate assistant at the counter cannot handle the problem, the student fills out a trouble report form. Meyer is responsible for investigating each of these problems and for responding to the students. She can resolve most of them by using the bid status report (which shows the level of bid the student used), the student status listing (which shows the student's degree level, major, graduation date, GPA, and so on), and the error listing. Her life, however, becomes difficult when there are bugs in the programs.

One of Wine's problems is getting his staff to deal with the fact that there are always going to be bugs in the programs:

> Working around the inevitable bugs is a problem to my staff. You want the bugs to be invisible to our students and client companies, so the staff has to deal with the bugs while concealing them from outsiders. You'd like to be able to conceal them from your staff, too, because they hurt staff morale. But you can't, so the question is how you deal with your staff so that they can conceal the bugs from the public while they are frustrated themselves by the problems.

....

Plans for the Future

In 1987 NCR gave the BPO a Tower computer that has the power of a minicomputer—it has 4 megabytes of memory, a 140 megabyte hard disk, and will drive 32 terminals. During the past year the back room staff has been busy converting the system to take advantage of the Tower. They now have it running in parallel with the old system, so next year they will migrate everything to the Tower.

The Tower has given them the computing power to run the interview scheduling process at the BPO, rather than on the IBM mainframe at the university Data Processing Center. They have converted the scheduling programs and have successfully run them on their Tower computer in parallel with the present system.

Relationships with the Data Processing Department   Wine has had a long history of conflict with the university director of data processing, Larry Easterly, who is a traditional conservative data processing manager, very concerned with controlling the university's computer resources and protecting his department's territory.

For example, in 1983 when NCR gave the BPO the MODUS fileserver and the DecisionMate PCs, Easterly was trying to control acquisition of all microcomputers that might be used for data processing. Every purchase of micro components had to be approved by Easterly's office. Although Wine did not have to purchase the NCR equipment, he did have to buy some additional components to make the overall system work, and Easterly would not approve those purchases on the grounds that Wine's equipment was not compatible with the microcomputer standards that data processing had set.

Dean Worthy and Wine called Easterly over to discuss the matter, and the issue of who really had control was laid out on the table. Easterly finally agreed to let the purchases go through because Dean Worthy got tough with him, asking "Who are you to tell the Business School how we run our business and who we get our resources from?" Larry's reply was: "I'll let this through as an exception because of the NCR grant, but in the future I expect Jim to quit circumventing the established university rules and procedures."

Despite this history of conflict, Wine does not intend to transfer the interview scheduling processing back to the BPO unless Easterly forces him to do so. "I certainly plan to continue processing most of the work on my local network," Wine explains, "but we plan to continue to use the Data Processing Center for those things that really ought to be done on the mainframe." The mainframe is more reliable, and its immense power makes it possible to recover and meet the BPO deadlines even if something goes wrong. Furthermore, Wine believes that they should exploit some relationships between the BPO data and the data in other university systems—he is trying to arrange to extract the data for the student database from the university student records system.

The analysts at university data processing would like to make some significant changes in the BPO scheduling system that would simplify their operations and make their processing more efficient. They would like to eliminate the use of the System 2000 DBMS and make the system an on-line rather than a batch system. The issue here is who is going to pay for the changes. The university committee only allocates a very limited number of hours to the Business School for all its needs, and neither Dean Worthy nor Wine is willing to expend those hours just to make the system run more efficiently at Easterly's facility.

Planned Enhancements to the System   Wine has a number of improvements to the student interface in the works. At present, the students provide the BPO with resumes at the beginning of the interview season, and before each interview a student is responsible for furnishing a copy of the resume to be included in the folder given to the interviewer on the day of the interview.

Starting next year the students will use a software system called Resume Expert to guide them in creating their resumes on the computer. They will turn in the resume on a floppy disk to the BPO, it will be stored in the system, and the system will print out copies of the resumes of the students on each interview schedule to place in the recruiter's interview folder. This should make things simpler for both the students and the BPO.

All the MBAs at Midstate University now have accounts on the VAX computer that they use for electronic mail (VAXMAIL) and other things. There are plans to provide VAX accounts to the business undergraduates also, but not until next year. BPO has, however, developed and tested a VAXMAIL interface that will allow the system to automatically send VAXMAIL messages to students notifying them of the results of the bidding and any changes in their appointments, so that they will not have to continuously check the bulletin boards outside the BPO office. Whenever the undergraduate students get their VAX accounts, Wine plans to implement this system.

Wine is also developing a system to use a voice response unit to allow the students to enter their bids directly into the system over their telephones. The student will dial a BPO telephone number and the computer voice response unit will instruct him to enter each data element on the bid card (student number, schedule number, bid priority, and so on) by touching the dialing buttons. After the process is completed, the voice response unit will repeat back what the student entered to verify that it is correct, and if it is not, the student will cancel the bid and repeat the process. Wine believes that this will not only be more convenient to the student, but that it also will reduce the number of input errors in the bidding process.

Jim Wine's Role In the early years of the system, Wine was continuously involved in both the development and operation of the system. Today his role has changed substantially, and he is only involved when there are major operational problems and in exploring new enhancements to the system.

Wine, however, continues to skim the articles in *PC World*, *PC Week*, and *Infoworld*, although he no longer reads them from cover to cover. He explains, "I read these technical publications because I want to see what the major corporations are doing, and I want to know what is happening out there on the fringes where I'm going to have to be in five years."

Wine is always impatient with his rate of progress in improving the system. "There are three constraints that hold you back," he explains. "First, you've got to overcome your budget constraints to get the resources you need. Second, you've got to bring your people up to where they can cope with the changing technology. Finally, you can only move so fast because your organization can only cope with a limited amount of change in a period of time."

CASE STUDY

11-2

State Economic Development Agency

The State Economic Development Agency (SEDA) was established by the state legislature with the mission of fostering economic development throughout the state by supporting the state's existing industry, developing new business enterprises, and attracting new industries to the state.

David Prince, director of SEDA, felt that it would be difficult to assess the economic health of the state and assist in economic development when no one knew what businesses existed, where they were located, what goods and services they provided, how many people they employed, and so on. Therefore, one of Prince's first decisions was to develop a State Enterprise Database (SED) containing data helpful to those interested in economic development in the state.

Rather than building his own data processing department, Prince decided to contract with the State University Center for Business and Economic Research (CBER) to explore the development of the SED. Robert Mixon, SED project director for CBER, began the project in June 1990 with a needs analysis. CBER asked economic developers throughout the state what they needed to know and how they would use that data. CBER found that (among other things) economic developers wanted detailed data on the existing businesses in the state, and they wanted it by location. They wanted the name and address of each business with more than eight employees, the products and services it provides, historical employment by quarter, wage data by quarter, sales data by quarter, whether the business imports or exports, standard industrial classification, and often a product description. They needed an actual local address in addition

This case was prepared by Professor E. W. Martin as the basis for class discussion rather than to illustrate either effective or ineffective handling of an administrative situation.

Copyright © 1993 by E. W. Martin.

to a legal mailing address, which might be the home office rather than the local address.

It quickly became clear that such a database for the entire state would be so massive that they needed to narrow the scope of this initial project. Therefore, Prince and Mixon decided to restrict the initial SED project to Washington county, a typical county in the state that had about 1,800 businesses of interest.

Because it was impractical to collect the needed data directly from the businesses, they began to search for sources that might already collect the data they needed. The Internal Revenue Service (IRS) collects financial data from businesses, but access to this data is heavily restricted by law. They considered the state Department of Revenue, the state Employment Security Department, the state Department of Commerce, the chambers of commerce in the state, and also such business organizations as Dun and Bradstreet.

During this investigation they found that the state Employment Security Department collected much of the data that they needed. So Mixon assigned his senior systems analyst, Ruth Blair, the task of determining what data Employment Security collected and how the data on the businesses in Washington county might be obtained. In early January 1991, Mixon arranged a meeting with James Hogan, executive director of Employment Security, in which he explained the purpose of the SED project, introduced Blair, and requested permission for her to work with Employment Security people to explore what data might be available and how they could be obtained. Hogan was quite agreeable and suggested that Blair start with Jean McAnally, deputy director for Statistical Services.

The mission of the state Employment Security Department is to collect unemployment insurance taxes from businesses in the state and to distribute unemployment benefits to workers who have been laid off. Because the tax rate for a business depends

479

upon its past layoff history, Employment Security must collect and maintain detailed quarterly employment data for each business. Ruth found that Employment Security has highly complex computerized systems that support collecting unemployment insurance taxes and distributing unemployment benefits.

McAnally's Statistical Services unit analyzes some of the data, but this analysis is not the central focus of Employment Security. The systems for supporting operations and for statistical services are quite separate, and just a small part of the data collected for operations goes to statistical services. One reason for this separation is that Employment Security is legally required to protect the confidentiality of the data it collects, and therefore the organization is very security conscious. Upon being hired each employee is required to sign a disclosure form stating that he or she understands that unauthorized disclosure of data is grounds for dismissal and that violators will be prosecuted to the full extent of the law. The law pertaining to Employment Security states in part:

> Information obtained or obtained from any person pursuant to the administration of this article and the records of the department relating to the unemployment tax or the payment of benefits shall be confidential and shall not be published nor be open to public inspection, in any manner, revealing the individual's or the employing unit's identity, except in obedience to an order of a court.
>
> A claimant at a hearing before a referee or the review board shall be supplied with information from such records to the extent necessary for the proper presentation of the subject matter of the appearance, and the director may make such information available to any other agency of the United States or of the state.

Despite this emphasis on confidentiality, Blair was pleased to note that "the director may make such information available to any other agency . . . of the state."

In early February 1991, Blair started working with the Statistical Services unit to determine what data it could provide on businesses in Washington county and to define reports containing that data. During February and March, they negotiated a price and developed a contract between Employment Security and SEDA to produce the desired reports. Blair received the results of the first run at the end of April. It

was full of mistakes caused by programming errors, and Blair requested a rerun, which was completed around the first of June 1991.

As Blair began to work with the data in this report, it became obvious that the data had some severe limitations for the SED. In the first place, there was no unique identifier for each record. For example, if there were two McDonald's restaurants in a county, there would be two records that could only be distinguished by their quantitative data, such as number of employees. Second, she did not understand the meaning of some of the data elements. For example, employment data by quarter was collected, but she didn't know whether this was an average, or at the end of the quarter, or what. Finally, she suspected that there was other data in the Employment Security system that might be quite useful for economic development if she knew what was there. Therefore, Mixon suggested that Blair find out more about the data in the Employment Security operational systems.

Starting the middle of June 1991, Blair began trying to find out details about the data in the Employment Security operational systems. It took two weeks for her to obtain a data dictionary, and when she got it she found that it was a brief programmer's data dictionary that didn't contain the user's data definitions that she needed. It did, however, give her enough hints about the contents of the Employment Security files to indicate that they might contain much useful data for economic development. For example, there was a "foreign ownership code" that might be of tremendous interest. She wasn't sure what it meant, however, because many state departments define foreign ownership to mean that the business is not incorporated in the state.

It took Blair several weeks to locate people who could answer some of her questions about the data in the programmer's data dictionary. These people were very helpful, and she eliminated some possibilities and highlighted others that might turn out to be important. During these discussions Blair found that Employment Security was in the process of adding an ad hoc reporting system to its software. Based on this, she questioned whether SEDA ought to be developing the SED. Perhaps SEDA should simply use the existing Employment Security system to serve the needs of the economic development community.

When Blair suggested this possibility to the Employment Security people that she was working with, they responded positively and invited her to a training session on the new system. After this introduction to the ad hoc reporting system, Blair was even more interested in determining whether the Employment Security system might eliminate the need for much of the proposed SED system.

Blair asked Employment Security to have someone work with her to evaluate the economic development needs and determine whether the Employment Security system could serve some or all of them. Employment Security could not make anyone available to perform that evaluation, so in early October 1991, Blair suggested that perhaps she could perform that evaluation herself. The programmer she had been working with thought that was a good idea. He introduced Blair to a supervisor of data entry who could assign her to a clerk who could walk her through the system, but there was a problem. According to the supervisor, she could not see the system without having a "sign-on" (which was a user number, password, and security authorization to access the system). Blair did not need to access the system; she merely wanted to know in detail what data it contained and how it worked. But the supervisor was adamant that she must have a sign-on to look at the system.

After several weeks of frustration trying to find out how she could get a read-only sign-on, Blair and Mixon decided that she was getting nowhere, and they set up a meeting on November 23, 1991, with Prince and Hogan. In this meeting Mixon explained the objectives of the SED project, the possibility of using the Employment Security system instead, and the difficulties that Blair was experiencing. He asked for Hogan's assistance and support. Hogan assured them of his support and promised that he would facilitate getting a sign-on for Blair. Hogan's memo to Frank Hall, automation project manager of Employment Security, is shown in Exhibit 1.

Exhibit 2 shows Hall's reply to Hogan's memo. As suggested, Blair contacted Harvey Moore and set up a meeting with him on December 11 to discuss her needs and how they could be met. When she arrived at Moore's office for the discussion with him, he told her that he had set up a conference room for the meeting because he had invited a few more people to join them. When she was ushered into the conference room, she found that all the deputy directors of the Employment Security Department were waiting for her.

As soon as the meeting began, it became obvious that the attendees intended to stop Blair from getting her sign-on. They questioned her need for a sign-on, and she explained that she didn't really want a sign-on, just to obtain sufficient understanding of their system and its data to determine whether or not it could be used to support economic development in the state. Pointing out their legal concerns and constraints, they questioned whether Blair should even be allowed to see their system, much less to access it. Blair felt that the meeting was a disaster, and at the end she suggested that they delay processing her request for a sign-on.

After the meeting Blair sent the conciliatory letter shown in Exhibit 3 to Moore, but she was very discouraged. After almost a year of effort working with Employment Security to get access to its data, it seemed that she had made very little progress. And the contract between the CBER and SEDA was coming up for renewal soon.

EXHIBIT 1
Memo to Hall

DEPARTMENT OF EMPLOYMENT SECURITY

TO: Frank Hall
FROM: James Hogan
           Executive Director
DATE: November 27, 1991
SUBJECT: Sign-On Capabilities for Ruth Blair

Please check with DP Security and complete all pertinent forms necessary to give Ruth Blair sign-on capabilities which will allow Ms. Blair to inquire into the new tax system. It would also be a good idea for you to give Ms. Blair a quick review of the new tax system.

Also, please process request forms authorizing Ms. Blair a sign-on for CQS so that she may have access to employment data.

Ms. Blair is aware that she will have access to confidential data and understands the limitations of informed consent.

Thank you for your assistance in this matter.

JH:bj

cc: Ruth Blair

EXHIBIT 2
Hall's Reply

DEPARTMENT OF EMPLOYMENT SECURITY

TO: James Hogan, Executive Director
FROM: Frank Hall, Automation Project Manager
DATE: December 5, 1991
SUBJECT: Sign-on for Ruth Blair

The following is in regard to your memorandum on November 27, 1991, requesting that I provide Ruth Blair sign-ons for the new tax system and CQS.

CQS sign-ons are comprised of two basic parts. One, identifying the user (Ms. Blair) and two, identifying the data accesses. The first is very simple. The second is more complex. Both are needed to have a CQS sign-on.

I talked to Ms. Blair on 11/30/91 to find out what data records or files she needed access to and she informed me that she did not know what records or files she needed. She indicated that she wanted to see the tax inquiry system so that she could determine:

(a) if there was any data she could use
(b) if she would need access to the tax inquiry
(c) if she needed a CQS access.

I have referred her to Harvey Moore so that she can sit down and go through the tax inquiry screens with Mr. Moore and/or a qualified tax employee. I made sure that she understood that I would do everything in my power to get her access to tax inquiry and/or CQS as soon as she could tell me which she needed and in the case of CQS what data she needed.

I did talk to Mr. Moore personally, so that he is aware of the situation. I talked to Ms. Blair on 12/4/91 so that she could schedule a meeting with Mr. Moore as soon as convenient.

cc: H. Moore
     R. Blair

EXHIBIT 3
Letter from Blair

December 19, 1991

Harvey Moore
Department of Employment Security
Street Address
Capital City, State

Dear Harvey,

We discussed several important issues in Monday's meeting. We decided to put a hold on the processing of a sign-on for me. I understand the need for timely consideration of such a precedent setting move.

As I indicated, the purpose of the sign-on request was to facilitate data analysis. It is most likely that the analysis can be accomplished using the existing system documentation, training manuals, and most important, the expertise of those who know the data. I will appreciate your help in providing access to these materials and the expertise, as appropriate.

The ultimate objective of this endeavor is to provide a more efficient and effective system to make information collected by one state agency (Department of Employment Security) available for use by another state agency (Economic Development Agency). It is my understanding that the law permits such interagency sharing and a policy that promotes and facilitates such sharing is critical. I hope that those who were in attendance at Monday's meeting will continue to think strategically toward such an objective.

Sincerely,

Ruth Blair
Ruth Blair

cc: Robert Mixon
     David Prince
     James Hogan

12

The Future of Information Technology in Organizations

More than a generation has passed since Harold J. Leavitt and Thomas S. Whisler (1958) predicted that progress in information technology would thin the ranks of middle management and empower management to focus on more creative, less routine functions. More than a decade has passed since Alvin Toffler's book *The Third Wave* (1980) described the birth of the "information society," predicting a series of fundamental changes in the way we live.

The heralded year 1984 has come and gone without the total fulfillment of the Orwellian vision of a society where the misuse of information is applied to control the populace. Big Brother has not taken control of the entire world, but there are many serious questions about how the awesome capabilities of information technology should be used in the future. How much of the promise of information technology will eventually become reality? How much may soon come to pass? How much will remain conjecture or fiction? These are all difficult questions to answer. This chapter summarizes the many elements pointing toward change introduced throughout the book and weaves them together into an overall vision of the future of information technology in organizations.

THE NATURE OF TECHNOLOGICAL CHANGE

At one time, changes in information technology were somewhat more predictable than today. Monopoly positions held by industry leaders allowed for more regular product life cycles in the information industry. The 1980s, however, halted regularity in the information industry and made prediction of technological change much more difficult. Many of the changes in the industry during that decade were driven by start-up companies, coming seemingly from nowhere. Current industry giants, such as Lotus Development Corporation and Microsoft Corporation, were tiny start-ups in the late 1970s and early 1980s, but they changed the information industry profoundly.

Technological change in the information industry now comes from too many different sources to be predictable with any precision. It is clear that the entertainment industry will greatly impact the look and functionality of the workstation of the future but exactly how is still anyone's guess. Leaps in technology will come from Europe, Japan, North America, and a host of developing countries. Both large companies and two people in a garage will have an impact.

ELECTRONIC VILLAGE

General Magic has also created a kind of command system, called Magic Cap, that simplifies functions for users and is geared to facilitate communication and filter information to fit users' specific needs. Among other things, it allows users to construct their own imaginary town on a touch screen. Touch the post office and you can mail messages. Touch the library to retrieve database information or even a list of books at the real, brick-and-glass library. Touch the bank to make deposits or send checks. Touch a friend's home to send personal messages.

A PC equipped with Magic Cap is based on the concept that its "design center" is the human being, not the technology, says Mr. Porat. Eventually, he says, using it will be like posting "your wants and needs" on a variety of electronic networks, with the PC sending out codes, or "agents," to databases that will grab or wait for the information to answer those wants and needs.

Much of this power won't be available for five to ten years, until service providers such as restaurants and libraries decide to offer Telescript databases. "It's going to take time, a lot of time," says Mr. Porat. "We're doing our planning for two biologic generations."

(Hill and Varada, 1993)

Our predictions about the future are therefore directed toward basic tendencies rather than precise developments. Likewise, the focus here is on the likely impacts that information technology will have on organizations in the future. Clearly, the impact of technology change will be far-reaching and profound, affecting both business strategy and the everyday work of IS professionals and user-managers. Chapter 16 reviewed several issues with which the individual manager must deal, while this chapter looks at the effect of technological change on organizations.

Information technology change in the future may be characterized in the following five ways:

1. *Change will continue at an increasingly rapid pace.* Consider all that society has witnessed in the twentieth century. Yet the majority of technological advances in this century have oc-

curred in the past thirty years. As an example, superfast microprocessors, capable of executing over 100 MIPS (million instructions per second)—a speed not achieved on many of today's mainframes—could be introduced by the mid-1990s (Zorpette, 1989). Such advancements will enable homes to recognize their owners and allow computers to interact with humans through speech and gesture, tasks out of the realm of possibility only a few short years ago. How should work change accordingly?

2. *Change will take many forms.* New types of hardware will appear. Communications advances promise to play a prominent role in a developing networked world. New uses will be found or will become practical for forms of existing technology. Creative new ways to use the corporate database will be suggested more and more frequently. What steps should organizations be taking in order to be better prepared to deal with these changes?

3. *Change will focus attention on the asset value of information.* Information has come to be viewed as a resource by many large organizations. Information will increasingly be considered an asset—with a definite but still unclear value to the organization. Efforts to treat information as an asset may not be effective unless a viable method is developed for determining the actual value of information. If we are in fact an information society, then better methods must be developed to assign information a value, just as manufactured goods are assigned values by the competitive marketplace in an industrial society.

Assigning value to the information produced by a technology system becomes more problematic as the nature of the system progresses from traditional transaction processing systems to more ad hoc decision support and expert systems. This transformation may require that the term "value" be redefined. As reviewed in Chapter 15, Marilyn M. Parker and Robert J. Benson (1988) defined the value of information technology in terms of enabling an organization to achieve improvement in business performance. Additional ideas on practical methods for determining value must be developed. If we can achieve some universal way to define the value of information, will organizations use information as a (the) medium of exchange?

4. *The most important organizational consequence of change will be the effect on its people.* To focus discussion of change only on technological advancements would be a grave error. Hardware and software technology is already far ahead of an organization's ability to develop applications that fully utilize its capabilities. Technology may be the engine that powers change, but unless more emphasis is placed on understanding the impact that more technology and better information can have on humans and business cultures, our efforts will not live up to the promise. In fact, they may even be counterproductive. Those who neglect to explore its impacts will not reap the benefits that technological advancement has to offer. How do we create organizations that can readily exploit technology advances?

5. *Change in the way we use information in the organization must be proactively managed to overcome obstacles.* Because the most important aspect of change is the effect that it will have on individuals, our vision is one that places a premium on user-managers and IS professionals working together in designing a management system for information. They must understand the potential impacts and barriers to change and manage jointly the technology in such a way as to provide benefit to all. How can organizations equip their user-managers to effectively manage information?

CHANGING TECHNOLOGIES

As shown in Figure 17.1, each part of the information technology system is undergoing change, including the hardware and network infrastructure, software applications, and databases. By creatively combining these developments with appropriate management systems, user-managers and IS professionals can make the overall impact ap-

> The genius of the future lies not in technology but in our ability to manage it.
>
> **(Anonymous)**

proach the sum of the individual component impacts. Some of the more significant changes are considered in the following paragraphs.

Infrastructure Developments

Future developments in the technology infrastructure (hardware, operating systems, and network) will influence the way it is used. Existing hardware classifications will continue to evolve, and the types of hardware will likely play very different roles in the information architecture of the organization.

Using a mainframe with a proprietary operating system over a star network was the dominant paradigm of the computing infrastructure in organizations for years. Rapid advancements in the capabilities of workstations during the latter half of the 1980s chipped away at the dominant role of mainframes. There is little doubt that the role of workstation technologies will increase during the

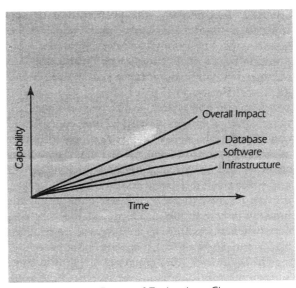

FIGURE 17.1 The Future of Technology Change

1990s, based simply on economics. Even though the cost of mainframe systems is expected to continue to decrease in cost per MIPS, this improvement pales by comparison to the expected cost decrease for personal computers. While a mainframe can do more than a microcomputer, economic differences cause many to wonder whether the mainframe does indeed have a future. It is not hard to argue that much of the difficulty at IBM during the early 1990s is at least partly attributed to the company's reliance on its mainframe products long after their cost/effectiveness was dominated by workstations for many applications.

On the other hand, mainframe computers may remain the preferred hardware solution for certain applications and take on new roles. The installed base of mainframes and their ability to process a large number of data-intense transactions in an efficient manner make them an ongoing valuable resource to many organizations. As the amount of data processed by organizations continues to increase, mainframes could serve as information storehouses if the economics are right. Mainframe computers dedicated solely to database management could also continue. In addition, mainframes, augmented by vector processors or converted to a massively parallel architecture, have the potential of solving some compute-intensive administrative problems currently not being attacked. Alternatively, the proliferation of distributed computer networks may help sustain mainframes. For example, Parker Hannafin Corporation uses a mainframe as its "traffic cop" to manage communications among computers at 160 locations (Verity, 1987).

Minicomputers that today perform such diverse applications as assembly line control and communications network management also face an uncertain future. Some predict that they will be squeezed out of existence by the increasing power and speed available from workstations. However, growth in sophisticated end-user computing, the infusion of computing into more small companies, departmental computing in larger decentralized firms, and specialized processing systems are all logical candidates for minicomputer applications. Superminis may also continue to exist in shared, dedicated applications, such as CAD/CAM.

CLIENT/SERVER AS CORPORATE FARMING

Client/server accepts that the real work of computing will be done in little desktop machines and, for the first time, attempts to get those machines together with real corporate data. "Think of it as corporate farming of data," says Bob Metcalfe, inventor of Ethernet, the dominant computer networking technology. "The move to PCs swung the pendulum—the percentage of available computing power—away from the mainframe and toward the desktop. Local area networks have helped the pendulum swing back toward the server. Sure, we are again dependent on centralized data, but that is not a disadvantage. A century ago we grew our own food, too, but do I feel oppressed by modern farming? I feel liberated."

(Cringely, 1993)

Firms engaged in the development of supercomputers are focusing their efforts not only on faster single processors, but also on the integration of many high-speed processors operating in parallel. Machines incorporating several thousand processors will be able to divide an application program into parts that are processed simultaneously and then reintegrate the results, obviously a very difficult task. It is anticipated that as this technology evolves, it will be able to place a machine possessing the same capabilities as today's supercomputers on a desktop.

It is also likely that the competition for domination in supplying operating systems will heat up in the mid- to late 1990s. This competition, however, will be in a new arena as organizations not only fight for supremacy in workstation operating systems but in offering products that control the developing data and voice and video networks.

Tomorrow's chips and microprocessors, the heart of all classes of computers, will continue to push the technology envelope. There is theoretically still opportunity for significant improvement in size, speed, and number of transistors that can be placed on a silicon chip. Eventually, of course, silicon will have to be replaced by another compound before further advancements can be made. Scientists are working to develop the technology and processes necessary to make large-scale production of gallium arsenide chips both commercially possible and economical.

Faster chips will be of real benefit only if the storage devices that hold the data to be accessed and manipulated can be designed to hold more data and allow faster access time. Until recently, storage usually meant use of a magnetic medium, such as a disk. Optical technology has now emerged, primarily in the form of CD-ROM devices. While earlier CD-ROM devices could read but not write, write capabilities have grown rapidly and this growth is expected to continue. Some experts predict that these optical devices will completely replace traditional magnetic media storage devices.

Voice recognition systems are widely forecasted to grow as well. Detection and correct interpretation of differing speech patterns and accents requires a significant amount of processing power and technical sophistication. Despite these considerable barriers, progress in this area is being made.

Portable data and voice communications equipment is becoming a much more important component of the information technology architecture of the organization. Cellular communication is growing at an explosive rate despite certain health concerns. Portable fax machines have found their way into automobiles to accompany the mobile telephone, providing the driver with a range of useful productivity tools while on the road.

Fiber optic technology will also continue to find its way into individual homes and businesses. Users will be able to create their own video telephones by running the images captured by a video camera in their home through their TV set into the home of another person. Video shopping can also be done on a personalized, interactive basis.

Videoconferencing capabilities allow managers from different regions to meet in a more natural setting than with voice teleconferencing, without requiring expensive, time-consuming travel. Video broadcasting capabilities have found many other business applications, such as new

product showings by large retailers. The cost to participate in full data, voice, and video teleconferencing without leaving your office or home is coming down rapidly. Videotext and videoconferencing applications are becoming economical as a replacement for the internal house organ, memos for distribution, and other paper-bound methods for communicating with employees in organizations (Kusekoski, 1989).

Data communications networks are not a new class of technology, but their use has rapidly expanded, and their strategic importance to increasing numbers of organizations is relatively new. In order for information to be a truly valuable asset, it must be readily transferable between different operating environments both within and between organizations. The communications network forms the electronic highway on which information will be transmitted. Major issues facing those building, managing, and using networks that provide a true information-sharing environment include compatibility and increased linkages between diverse hardware types.

The products of different vendors will likely become better able to communicate with each other. Standards for data transmission are becoming more uniform and accepted. The compatibility issue will be solved for two reasons. First, more hardware and software vendors are active in today's marketplace. As a result, few IS organizations consider themselves as single-vendor dependent. No single vendor can provide the whole range of hardware or software deemed desirable by a customer. Those vendors who can produce products possessing the ability to share information with the products of other vendors stand to benefit in the long run.

Second, organizations are constantly changing their structures. The 1980s trend toward increased numbers of mergers, alliances, acquisitions, divestitures, and partnership formations is likely to continue on both a national and global basis. Those IS organizations serving business units affected by such a change will often be called upon to put together or pull apart information systems in a politically charged environment on relatively short notice. Intervendor compatibility will be of critical importance in such situations.

488

Greater compatibility between the products of competing vendors will lead to greater integration of differing classes of computers, affording end-users the ability to take advantage of the distinct capabilities offered by each of the classes. Integration of the types of computer hardware will lead to more distributed processing and direct data usage by user-managers. This trend will also give rise to greater concern over data security and integrity.

Compatibility, flexibility, shared resources, and development of standards are the central themes of our discussion of the network architecture in Chapter 12. How long it will be until acceptable levels of each attribute are attained is anyone's guess. Some fear that these attributes may never be achieved as new technologies are constantly being introduced. One thing is certain, however—user-managers and IS professionals will, and should, work together to pressure vendors to work toward these goals.

Software Developments

Organizations using information systems for strategic advantage will continue to seek ways to shorten the time from opportunity recognition to system operation. Newer methodologies, such as prototyping and its hybrids, will be used more often, where appropriate. Such methodologies may have the double-edged effect of reducing the time required to develop an individual system, while at the same time unleashing pent-up management demand for more systems, so that the applications backlog facing the organization may not decrease.

Even if not one new system was developed, the software maintenance burden facing many IS organizations is enormous. To address this problem and to cope with the chronic shortage of skilled IS professionals, IS organizations will continue to migrate toward the use of programmer productivity tools.

Software packages that analyze code and structure it in accordance with parameters set by the IS organization are proliferating in the market. These packages may not result in more efficient code, but they do result in more structured code that is easier to maintain. More important, they

TOMORROW'S PHONE NETWORK

Taking their cue from the computer industry, makers of telecommunications equipment are racing to build the gear for a flexible, programmable "intelligent network" that will speed information to wherever it's needed. Here's what the new phone network will do for you.

Video on Demand. You'll be able to watch any movie you want, when you want. Fiber-optic cables to the home—laid by phone or cable television companies—will be able to carry a huge variety of programming, including lots of special-interest channels and localized advertising.

Customized Pricing. Smart phone companies will keep track of your calling patterns and entice you to stick with their service by offering you custom-tailored discounts. If you always call Mom in Tuscaloosa on Sunday nights, the phone company can give you a special rate.

Elastic Bandwidth. Want to send a huge chunk of information from one computer to another? Rapidly? Today you need high-cost circuits that are leased by the month. In the future, you'll just dial a phone number. You'll pay only for the minutes of "bandwidth," or capacity, that you consume.

Never Lose Touch. You'll have one phone number for life. When someone calls it, the network will deliver calls to wherever you go, even in a car or at a neighbor's house—as long as you let the network computer know where you are.

(Coy, 1991)

give the organization the ability to establish standards by which to measure programmer performance and productivity, hopefully leading to better allocation of the scarce programmer resource.

Computer-aided software engineering (CASE) is a much-touted concept that is becoming a reality. Some of the productivity tools that would form the components of an integrated application design workbench are already in existence. More are being designed. Integration of these current and future tools into a package that would allow fully integrated application system design is still on the horizon, but it is a goal that will likely be reached.

Just as fourth-generation languages paved the way for the introduction of the prototyping methodology, future programming languages with imbedded expert systems will lead to the proliferation of manager-developed systems. User-developed systems, if properly managed and audited, will help redistribute the burden of systems development among user-managers and IS programmers or analysts. They will also change the role of many IS professionals from that of analyst to one of consultant or facilitator.

Future programming languages will incorporate many present capabilities into integrated packages that will be powerful but flexible enough to suit the needs of a variety of nontechnical user-developers. More natural interactive/response prompts and instructions may take some of the mystery away from the machine for even the most computer-phobic manager. Future programming languages may support the use of voice input and will surely expand on the use of easy-to-use devices, such as light pens and the mouse, for complex applications.

Graphical user interfaces and icons will be more prevalent in systems for those who wish to use them. Future advances will employ neural networks, learning systems that will modify themselves based on response patterns of the user over time to solve problems. Multimedia applications, in use now, will become easier to use and integrated into more capable workstations. In short, the future developments will make "user-friendly" a legitimate term for larger numbers of unsophisticated users.

Virtual reality offers the promise of a major leap in the application of information technology to a range of problems not heretofore addressed. Virtual reality has promise as a tool for industrial development, design, and testing that "goes far beyond the now familiar computer-assisted design applications" (Bylinsky, 1991). Applications range from industrial product development to space walks to entertainment—anywhere it would be helpful to see and operate as if in the real world as a full participant.

Increased technological and software development capabilities will lead to changes in both traditional applications and in the number and variety of new applications in the late 1990s. One trend springing directly from the advancement of software development capabilities is the increased use of the computer for traditional applications. Reduction in the amount of time and resources needed to develop new applications from start to finish will unleash pent-up demand for more systems. Much of this demand will be in the form of requests for systems that perform many of the same functions that are currently available to users in other areas of the organization or in other organizations. Further, these requests will be for applications that are easier to use by non-IS professionals. Many of the new applications will be augmented by expert systems so that the software makes decisions in much the same fashion as humans possessing years of experience would.

Database Developments

More use of information is one of today's dominant trends, and the implication of this trend is simple—organizations must become better at managing information as an asset or its value will be lessened. Many challenges face the organization seeking to plan for the management of the information asset. Fred R. McFadden and Jeffrey A. Hoffer (1994) highlight several of the salient issues and directions of the management of data in the 1990s. Some of their points deserve mention here.

As introduced in Chapter 14, the choice between distributed and decentralized databases will become a more important issue. Multiple site organizations will decide whether to spread a single logical database across interconnected computers in several locations (distributed databases) or store databases on different computers at different sites without interconnecting them (decentralized databases). Distributed databases are more consistent with our theme of increased information-sharing across organizational lines and represent one of the major challenges for user-managers and IS professionals for the mid-1990s.

Distributed databases will provide location transparency, that is, users at remote sites will be

490

able to easily access information without knowing where it is physically located. This requirement will make network management even more critical.

Data control and integrity will be affected by distributed database configurations. Distributed data will encourage local sites to exercise control over the data for which they are responsible, hopefully leading to improved integrity. Conversely, making the data accessible to more remote parties means that the chances for improper updating and access are increased unless better management policies are developed and implemented.

Complex cost trade-offs will have to be considered in the design of future databases. Storing data closer to local sites of heavy usage helps reduce data communication costs. More complex software will be required to manage data flows if stored remotely or on several machines. Also, multiple sites will have to exchange communications and perform additional data manipulation to ensure proper coordination between sites. Security will become an even larger issue.

Response time for users will be affected by data location decisions. Properly locating data close to heavy usage sites will not only help reduce costs, but also assist in creating a quicker response time. Errors in distributing data will retard response time, potentially to unacceptable levels.

The modular nature of distributed systems will offer additional advantages to database growth. When a centralized system is interrupted, all users are shut off the system. Distributed databases typically can continue to function, albeit at reduced levels of efficiency. Organizations that want to add or delete a new unit to the network in a distributed environment are often able to do so in an easier, more economical fashion, without disturbing all users of the system.

Client/server architectures will play a more important part in database management systems. Rather than centralizing database access on one machine, the task of high-volume database processing may be distributed across many systems. This relatively new approach offers several potential advantages to the organization, such as increased security capabilities and cost performance, but requires much greater willingness for database

sharing. Also being used more and more by companies like Walmart and AT&T are massively parallel computers that greatly decrease access time compared to traditional scalar machines.

The decisions facing organizations concerning the proper way to structure their database management systems are not easy ones. Much technical expertise will be required. Even more important, more and more attention must be devoted to the quality of data management by both large and small organizations. Organizations will have to devise better ways to train and retain exceptional database administration professionals.

CHANGES IN THE NATURE OF WORK

The technological changes described above will generate drastic changes in the nature of work in organizations. One scenario envisions a dramatic change in work habits because of technology. Under this view of the future, integrated workstations capable of sending and receiving data, voice, video, and images will be used by both professional and clerical workers. Information creation, processing, storage, and transfer, in whatever form, will all originate from the same piece of equipment. These systems, whether in the office or in the home, will allow for a wider range of transactions than the current limited workstations. The majority of information sent or received during the work day will be via the workstation. Organizations slow to adopt such integrated workstations will lose competitive advantage.

While the above scenario may seem futuristic, technology developments are not far from being able to achieve such a drastic change. Even if such a dramatic change in the workplace does not occur during the late 1990s, some fundamental changes are coming during this decade which will have a major impact on how we work. The following seven points, while by no means complete, should provide a representative list of the likely impacts of information technology advances on the nature of work inside organizations.

1. Technology will alter the concept of time and space in the work environment. As enhanced

FUTZING AT THE WORKSTATION

SBT Accounting Systems, a Sausalito, California-based maker of business software, estimated that 2 percent of America's gross domestic product, or $97.4 billion, is being diddled away by people who play or tinker with their computers while they're at work. More startling, an estimated 4 percent of clerical and secretarial labor is taken up with trying to get software to function.

According to David Harris, an SBT vice president, futzing has become so widespread that by 1994 it will double to an estimated 4 percent of GDP. "It's become the great time sink of modern technology," says Harris. "Some people use the desktop PC as professional television—something that is just 'on' in a room, so we stare at it without doing anything."

(Jaffe, 1992)

video capability at the workstation allows physical location to become less important to where work is actually performed, better time management should result because people will have much greater control over scheduling of work activities. Teleconferencing, cellular telephones, and satellite technology; more readily available portable equipment; networking (statewide, nationwide, and worldwide); and new mechanisms for data input will transform the physical confines and the operating hours of the workplace as we know it.

2. Maximizing personal productivity can be accomplished. Technology that allows people to work faster (and with more accuracy) will also monitor activities, allowing people to evaluate how well they spend their time. Time wasters will be easily identified.

3. Super workstations will evolve with expert knowledge geared to help a specific user. As new technologies are integrated into these stations, the individual technologies will become separately indistinguishable. Videotext and other services will be available through a single workstation. User-managers will move easily in and out of and between functions.

4. Computers will perform most functions in response to verbal commands. User-managers will be able to obtain information from the computer from remote locations through voice technology. Foreign language translations will be performed automatically. The current difficulty of many older user-managers who did not grow up using computers will be solved via voice command capabilities.

5. Personal intelligent information user profiles will provide decision support information at the time it is needed. For example, a manager's personal workstation software might automatically generate a monthly reminder of all scheduled employee vacation days, holidays, and scheduled retirements for that unit. The computer could likewise call the gift store and order the appropriate present. Other routine data retrieval and update functions will be performed automatically.

6. Document storage will be completely transformed. Alternate forms of data input will exist, including voice and scanning. Sophisticated indexing and retrieval and routing systems will be routinely employed, and easy modification and publication of documents will be typical. Intelligent interfaces will allow construction of documents from a variety of files and sources. Immediate foreign language translation will enhance communications with a worldwide constituency.

7. Management effectiveness will be improved as we move from using the computer to review information to using it for forecasting, planning, and modeling. Communication and knowledge will be enhanced through the use of large databases and increased use of electronic- and voice-mail systems. Decisions will be made on current, reliable information and facts. Systems will be designed so that those people without sophisticated computer skills can utilize the resources needed to enhance their daily work performance.

While it is easy to paint a rosy picture of the marvelous benefits that information technology will provide organizations, some concerns must be mentioned. It is generally believed that the quality

491

492

of life for the majority of workers will be improved by new, imaginative information technology applications. Yet a few caveats are in order.

Information technology will likely have such a profound impact that the very structure of our organizations and cultures will change dramatically. To be sure, banking, shopping, classwork, employment, and other parts of our day will be increasingly made easy through the placement of a workstation in the household. This may save time and energy, reduce congestion, and provide other benefits. It is unclear, however, how the ability to do so much from the home will impact our habits and needs for social interaction. Some fear that we will become a society of isolated individuals and that the resulting quality of business decisions will decrease. Can we make great strategic decisions sitting in front of a screen?

In a less philosophical vein, there are a number of legitimate questions that have been posed by those concerned with the possible misuse of technology. Four such concerns are:

1. Privacy: Simply put, how much do others have the right to know about us without our consent? More about this issue is covered later in the chapter. Closely related to this fundamental concern is the ownership of information concerning individuals. Does one organization have the right to give or sell to another organization data that it has collected about an individual during a legitimate business transaction without obtaining that individual's consent? Again, this issue is discussed in the ethical considerations section of this chapter.

2. Security: Computer hackers who illegally enter systems receive much press and are even romanticized in some circles. Although the actual incidents of such illegal break-ins are relatively few, security is a serious concern. The increased linkages between systems also make huge numbers of systems vulnerable to viruses that travel through communications networks and destroy or alter critical files and programs. The increased use of electronic funds transfer, automated teller machines, and computerized trading systems in the financial markets are also cause for concern.

> **IMPLEMENTING THE INFORMATION-BASED ORGANIZATION**
>
> We are moving rapidly toward the information-based organization. Executives who understand their work in terms of a flow of information are still a very small minority. Today, the big thing to learn is not how to use the computer, or even how to organize information, but how to organize one's own work in the information-based organization. Information is not what the computer delivers, but what executives need to take effective action.
>
> **(Drucker, 1990)**

3. Reliance on faulty information: Incorrect use of CAD (computer-aided design) systems may lead to serious errors in the design of critical components of automobiles, aircraft, buildings, or other products. Bankruptcies occurring from the use of faulty cost-estimate systems have already been documented. Incorrect use of medical diagnostic expert systems could lead to prescribing an incorrect treatment. Rejecting a loan application because of faulty credit information may cause serious economic hardship for the borrower and legal problems for the lender. All are examples of what can occur when information is generated and used without ensuring that the system generating the information is sound. More dangerous than the adage of "garbage in, garbage out" is the idea of "garbage in, gospel out," the blind reliance on computer-generated information.

4. Redefining traditional work roles: The idea of the electronic cottage is not yet a reality. Still, more people are working out of their homes, and more work is being carried home to be done on portable and laptop computers. The economic downturn of the early 1990s created what some call a whole new class of companies termed the "virtual corporation." These firms are made up of individuals who work from home using some type of electronic connection rather than showing up at some location. Fax machines, portable telephones, and other advancements make this type of organization

possible but may also lead to a sense of never being free from work. Quality time spent with family and friends may be reduced. To maintain balance, individuals will have to take steps to ensure that the distinction between home and work does not become hopelessly blurred.

Information technology will also change the global business world. Global markets will become increasingly competitive. Financial markets will remain open around the clock. Increased information sharing may lead to political changes in other countries because it will be increasingly difficult to screen all information flowing into and out of countries. Information technology will be the driving force behind many if not all of these changes.

THE INFORMATION-BASED FIRM

One implication of technology improvements will be the creation of the "information-based" organization. Some firms are moving to embrace this concept now. In the future, it is likely that most firms will find the work day organized more and more around their information technology capability rather than using information technology to augment work that was designed without the technology in mind. In order to understand work in the typical information-based firm of the future, consider the following scenario of a consumer products company near the start of the twenty-first century.

Gary Slick is president of House, Inc., a household products company headquartered in Cleveland. At his terminal, early one Friday morning, Slick reviews the latest updates to the monthly business reports. He chooses the items he will discuss with the Alabama sales manager on Tuesday.

A Monday meeting was also arranged for Slick to meet with the second largest Alabama customer, E-Z Products, who had recently reduced its spring order by 25 percent. On Thursday, Gary had queried the database to determine the other customers included in the top five. By comparing the products used by all five customers, Gary found several common items to refer to during the meeting. He also obtained a list of E-Z Products' competitors and the House, Inc., products they use. He printed the list to take with him on Monday.

As the business reports scroll across his terminal screen, he is concentrating on the issue of the Alabama division gross margins. He identifies each item for discussion by touching the screen. The information is highlighted and electronically captured. As the last item is captured, he types a note for the Alabama sales manager, telling her that this is the information they will discuss on Tuesday. The information package is delivered over the computer network.

With that task completed, Slick begins looking at current news items. He selects the newswire option and the computer connection is made to Reuters. His prearranged format selects items pertaining to the three states he will visit next week.

As he continues to scroll through news items, he notices that a regional competitor in the Southeast has just been acquired by a national competitor of House, Inc., Hunt Industries. Hunt had not heretofore competed in the Southeast. He touches the screen to capture the article then continues with the rest of the newswire items.

After reviewing the rest of his newswire items, he returns to the captured article and prepares a note to send to Bill Parker, one of House, Inc.'s competitive experts. In the note, he mentions that other Hunt acquisitions have caused concern for his company. Hunt has a strategy of acquiring sleepy regional competitors and then unleashing a major marketing program in the territory. He would like Parker's opinion and any information he may be able to dig up. He forwards the note and moves to his electronic-mail in-box.

After reviewing and responding to his mail messages, he packs his briefcase for his trip. He knows that if he has forgotten anything, he can access the system from home on Sunday and print a copy of whatever he may need.

Meanwhile, in Birmingham, Carol Best, Alabama sales manager, has already heard about the acquisition while driving to work. She knows about Hunt's aggressive strategy and is worried that the current House, Inc., marketing plan is inadequate.

When she arrives at her office, she quickly powers up her personal computer and selects the mail option. She prepares a message to Jeff Smith, director of major markets, describing her concerns and asking for assistance. Because the Hunt deal was a closely guarded secret, there was nothing in the Alabama marketing plan to address this strong new competition. She asks Smith if there is anything that can be done at this late date.

In Cleveland, Smith is reviewing the results of the Milwaukee trial of Whiz-Bang, a new House, Inc., offering. The on-line reports include information from the demographic database and usage information from the sales database of House, Inc. Smith stops his review to check an urgent message from Best in Birmingham. After reading the message, Smith decides to have the Alabama marketing plan model rerun with variables showing the strong new threat. He prepares a message to Edley Brown, analysis manager, asking him to rerun the model. He also leaves a voice-mail message for Best to let her know that his staff will be looking at the problem.

Brown receives Smith's request to rerun the model. While he has other work that needs to be done, he recognizes the importance of being on top of this issue in case some action needs to be taken. He accesses the marketing management analysis system and selects Alabama as the market. In this case, he runs a complete profile on the Alabama market while changing the competition variables. He decides to run three versions, each time progressing with a stronger competition variable. The results will be three profiles that include potential product mixes that have proved successful in this type of market. As the models run, Brown types up an activities list of what he will do when the profiles are complete.

First, he requests a report from the customer database that provides the current product mix for the Alabama market. This will be used to determine the level of fit for each of the three new profiles. If the levels of fit do not vary significantly from the original marketing plan, there will be fewer items to adjust.

Another item he asks for is a report that estimates the impact on profitability for each new mix. He schedules the jobs for overnight execution to conserve costs and avoid impacting the daily processing of orders. The reports will be downloaded to his personal computer at home for review Saturday morning. As the profiles continue to process, Brown calls Larry White, pricing manager, and provides him with the Alabama scenario.

Brown may require White's assistance to determine if there are any pricing options that can be utilized. White explains that he can set up a program to produce pricing options if Brown forwards him the profiles. When the profiles are completed, Brown forwards them to Smith and White. The following morning, Brown begins working with the data he has developed. He needs to predict which of the three profiles will be the most successful by determining level of fit. Because there is a great deal of data to go through, the computerized process takes most of the morning. He turns his attention to other matters as the programs execute.

That afternoon, he receives the information from White and combines it with the results of the analysis program. He receives a list of recommendations as output of the combined information. He notes that the number one recommendation includes a strong emphasis on couponing with a cooperative advertising push on selected products. He remembers that two years ago he had worked for a week on a four-person team to develop a new marketing plan for Wisconsin. This recommendation for Alabama was produced in hours through an expert system.

He types up an explanation of the results to create the final marketing action plan. He sends it to Smith and the other marketing directors for their review. The plan provides the recommended product mix and pricing that will optimize company profits. After Smith has approved it, the package is on its way to Birmingham over the computer network.

On Monday, Best finds the action plan waiting for her when she signs on her terminal. She sends a message back to Brown and Smith, thanking them for their quick response. She and the rest of the sales force will be meeting with Slick the next morning. She makes a mental note to let Slick know about the fine work from the staff. She adds the item to the agenda for her Friday crew meeting and then heads for the customer visit with Slick.

After saying how glad he is to be meeting with Best, Slick begins discussing the competitive situation. He explains that Parker indicates that there is a 95 percent probability that Hunt will aggressively pursue House, Inc.'s target market. Parker's research shows that they have done so quickly in every other situation. Best smiles, comforted by the fact that the plan for meeting such a threat has already been devised.

While it may seem fanciful to think of conducting everyday business under such a scenario, four items are worthy of note:

1. All the technology described in the scenario is available now.
2. Many companies are using parts of the technologies implied here. Few use it all. Some are starting to make plans to convert their daily business operations to this format and hire people who are willing and able to participate in such a scenario.
3. Such an intense use of information in a highly sharing and urgent mode is even more uncommon in most businesses. Too often, information sharing is considered to be the opposite of gaining power—everyone knows that one gains organizational power by hoarding information.
4. The companies that can quickly produce information from data as shown above are better able to respond aggressively to external events and thereby should be better able to compete in the future. It is easy to see that data abound in organizations—the data are just not organized in a way that is useful for decision-making.

ETHICAL ISSUES RESULTING FROM TECHNOLOGICAL CHANGE

Information technology improvements have raised and will continue to create a number of ethical issues, both for the individual manager and for the organization as a whole. In an *MIS Quarterly* article, Richard O. Mason (1986) discussed four ethical issues associated with information technol-

---

NOWHERE TO HIDE

Two influential trade groups, the American Business Conference and the National Alliance of Business, have joined with Educational Testing Service, which conducts the Scholastic Aptitude Tests, in creating a pilot program for a nationwide data base of high school records. It would give employers access to a job applicant's grades, attendance history, and the ancient evaluations of teachers. Just like Mother warned you—a ninth-grade report card could follow you for life.

(Lacayo, 1991)

---

ogy: privacy, accuracy, property rights, and access. This section adds a fifth ethical concern—impact on workers.

Privacy

What rights should a person have to keep details about his personal life and his associations from being revealed to others without his permission or even his knowledge? Information technology is making it very easy for businesses, government, and individuals to obtain great volumes of information about individuals without the knowledge of the person involved.

According to Mason, each American citizen has an average of seventeen personally identifiable computer files housed in federal government agencies and several more in state and local governments. We all have other computer files in banks, credit card companies, hospitals, schools, utility companies, businesses we deal with, magazine companies, and companies with mailing lists of all kinds. It also is much easier to access the information from a computer file than from a traditional paper file. In fact, the computer makes it inexpensive as well as easy to obtain information on you from any of these files.

The privacy problem from all this computerization, however, is much more serious than just obtaining information about you from one of these files. Most of them were created for legitimate purposes, and providing information for that purpose usually does not offend us. The problem

496

arises when a person or organization combines the data on a person from all of these files and therefore obtains a very detailed picture of a person's life.

There are companies whose business is gathering data about individuals from various files, combining these data, and selling the resulting package to others. According to Lacayo (1991):

> To get a driver's license, a mortgage, or a credit card, to be admitted to a hospital or to register the warranty on a new purchase, people routinely fill out forms providing a wealth of facts about themselves. Little of it remains confidential. Personal finances, medical history, purchasing habits, and more are raked in by data companies. These firms combine the records with information drawn from other sources—for instance, from state governments that sell lists of driver's licenses, or the post office lists of addresses arranged according to ZIP code—to draw a clearer picture of an individual or a household.
>
> The repackaged data—which often include hearsay and inaccuracies—are then sold to government agencies, mortgage lenders, retailers, small businesses, marketers, and insurers. When making loan decisions, banks rely on credit-bureau reports about the applicant's bill-paying history. Employers often refer to them in making hiring decisions. Marketers use information about buying habits and income to target their mail-order and telephone pitches. Even government agencies are plugging in to commercial databases to make decisions about eligibility for health-care benefits and Social Security.

The danger in this use of computerized information is not so much that an individual's mailbox will be clogged with advertisements and catalogs—one can even argue that such targeting provides a valuable service to the individual as well as to the marketer. Rather, the danger is that unknown persons can use this wealth of information to make important decisions concerning someone without the person's knowledge.

Such easy access to information made possible via technology presents an ethical and legal question for society as a whole as well as organizations. For example, companies have been known to search through e-mail messages that employees

---

E-MAIL PRIVACY

Shouldn't private missives sent over a privately owned computer be sacrosanct? That's what Rhonda Hall and Bonita Bourke thought. . . . A female supervisor heard that some of their e-mail was getting pretty steamy and began monitoring the messages. She soon discovered that the two had some disparaging things to say about her, and the women were threatened with dismissal. When Hall and Bourke filed a grievance complaining that their privacy had been violated, they were fired.

One might think the two employees had a strong case for unlawful termination. But their case was dismissed. . . .

The Electronic Communications Privacy Act of 1986 prohibits "outside" interception of e-mail by a third party—the government, the police or an individual—without proper authorization (such as a search warrant). It does not, however, cover "inside" interception—sneaking a peek at the office gossip's e-mail, for example.

(Elmer-DeWitt, 1993)

---

thought were private. And, as reported by Koepp, Pelton, and Shulman (1986), many employees who work through computer terminals are monitored by the computer, which, in addition to performing the work, records the quality and quantity of that work, even down to recording the time the employee is away from his workstation for breaks.

All of these invasions of privacy are the result of management decisions. Clearly the organization has the ethical responsibility of balancing the worker's right to privacy against the business need to monitor the worker's performance. How can an organization ensure that its managers are making the proper tradeoff?

Accuracy

As mentioned earlier, comprehensive data about individuals are contained in numerous large databases that are used to make important decisions that affect the individual. Unfortunately, much of this data is highly inaccurate.

There is a national computer crime network that serves local and state police by providing information on persons who have been arrested or have arrest warrants outstanding, stolen cars, and other items. Many police agencies have terminals in police cars so that when a policeman stops a car for a traffic violation, he can check whether the driver is potentially dangerous or the car is stolen before he approaches the car. Input into this database comes from thousands of agencies all over the country. Unfortunately, there are few controls on the integrity of this input process, making the accuracy of the data quite low. There have been reports of innocent citizens being shot because they made some motion that the policeman, influenced by information from the computer indicating that the car's occupant was dangerous, interpreted as reaching for a concealed weapon. In other cases, policemen have been injured because the computer did not indicate that the car's occupant was dangerous.

Three large credit reporting services in the United States—TRW, Equifax, and Trans Union—maintain huge databases of data on consumers that are used to determine the credit worthiness of individuals. These services purchase computer records from banks and retailers that detail the financial activities of most Americans, but there is little control on the accuracy of these data. In early 1991, Consumer's Union studied a sample of credit reports and found that almost half contained erroneous data, and that 19 percent had errors serious enough to cause information buyers to deny credit, employment, or insurance.

Horror stories abound. According to Allen (1990), Margaret Holt, who had always paid her bills on time and thought she had good credit, applied for a credit card and was turned down because she had too many delinquent debts. When she obtained a copy of her credit report, it said that she had nearly $40,000 in unpaid charges for items that she had not purchased. Mrs. Holt hired a private investigator to clear her name. He found that the bills had been incurred by a woman with a name similar to Mrs. Holt's. This woman told the investigator that she had gotten Mrs. Holt's Social Security number and other credit data from a man who counseled poor people on repairing their

FAIR CREDIT REPORTING ACT

The Fair Credit Reporting Act, enacted in 1971, gives Americans the right to know what's in their credit file and to challenge information they believe to be inaccurate.

If you're denied credit, you're entitled to know what's in your file within 30 days of receiving a rejection letter. That notice will contain the name and location of the credit-reporting bureau contacted in evaluating your file.

You can also write to or visit the credit bureau to inspect your file for a fee, usually between $5 and $10. The bureau will help you if you don't understand your file.

The law also allows access to your file by those authorized in writing, such as potential employers or lenders to whom you are applying for credit. Every time someone requests a copy of your report, it's noted on your file as an "inquiry."

You can dispute information in your file by providing evidence to prove an error or by insisting on an investigation.

You can also submit statements to your file explaining why negative credit remarks were accumulated. Negative data stays on your report for up to seven years, while bankruptcies are reported for ten years.

(Louisville Courier-Journal, 1989)

credit. Despite this obvious fraud, Mrs. Holt has found it almost impossible to restore her credit rating.

In another example, Lacayo (1991) recounts the saga of Eugene N. Wolfe. When he was turned down for a loan at his local bank, he found that for years a credit bureau had been merging his credit history with that of another Eugene N. Wolfe, who was a bad credit risk. After weeks of work, Wolfe thought that he had cleared up the problem, but a few years later he was turned down for a credit card and found that the debts of the other Wolfe had found their way back into his credit bureau file. In addition to his trouble obtaining credit, Wolfe found that he had unknowingly been charged the highest interest rate on a car loan because the dealer had received an erroneous credit report on him.

When a organization considers the question of accuracy of a database, it becomes clear that the cost of complete accuracy is high. From a business perspective, it makes sense to minimize both the cost of maintaining a given level of accuracy and the cost incurred because of inaccurate data. As long as the company is bearing both of these costs, there is no ethical issue. Ethical issues arise, however, when the manager must balance the costs to the company of maintaining accuracy against the damage to individuals caused by inaccurate data.

Property Rights

Society has long recognized the existence and value of intellectual property. Plagiarism, taking someone else's ideas and presenting them as your own, is considered to be dishonest. Patent and copyright laws are designed to protect intellectual property rights, but the rights associated with information—freedom of expression, freedom of information, privacy rights, and intellectual property rights—are often in conflict with one another. Balancing the public need to know against the rights of the owners of information has always been a problem for society.

Information technology has created new problems for society in defining and protecting intellectual property rights. Information technology separates the information from the media that contains it—one can no longer protect information by controlling the piece of paper on which it is written. An arcane example, taken from Mason (1986), relates to expert systems:

> *Practitioners of artificial intelligence proceed by extracting knowledge from experts, workers, and the knowledgeable, and then implanting it into computer software where it becomes capital in the economic sense. This process of "dis-emminding" knowledge from an individual, and subsequently "emminding" it into machines transfers control of the property to those who own the hardware and software. Is this exchange of property warranted?*

Computer programs are undoubtedly valuable intellectual property, and they are protected by the patent and copyright laws. These laws, however, were written long before present-day information technology could even be imagined, and we are struggling with how to apply them to software.

Consider the problem of protecting the rights to a software package such as Lotus 1-2-3. Because there are many ways of doing the same thing by combining computer codes into a program, forbidding the duplication of the particular series of computer codes does not provide much protection. Several companies have produced clones of Lotus 1-2-3 that, from the standpoint of their use, are virtually identical to the original. This situation has led to a good deal of litigation over copyright protection of software, with confusing results.

Brandt, Schwartz, and Galen (1992) provide several contradictory court rulings. In one case, the court ruled that the basic structure or outline of a computer program cannot be copied. More recently, another court ruled that the basic structure of a program is not copyrightable. In *Lotus vs. Paperback* (1990), the U.S. District Court in Boston ruled that software makers cannot copy screen layouts, menu sequences, and command organization—the "look and feel" of an application. But in *Apple vs. Microsoft and Hewlett-Packard* (1992), the U.S. District Court in San Francisco ruled that only specific screen elements are copyrightable, not overall "look and feel."

Copyright laws do make it illegal to copy a software package without permission of the software vendor. Although this is difficult to enforce against individuals, software vendors have become vigilant in prosecuting large companies who have (knowingly or unknowingly) allowed software to be copied. Many companies have strict policies against copying software, and they may even check periodically to make sure that an individual's office PC hard disk contains only authorized software.

Copying software for personal use is a great temptation for an individual, and it presents serious ethical problems. Consider the following two ways to obtain a word-processing software package—copy the software from a friend's floppy disk, or shoplift the software package from a store. In both cases, one is taking the property of another without permission, and it is hard to argue that one of these is stealing and the other is not. Because there is virtually no chance of getting caught when copying software from a friend, this action is an acid test of one's ethical makeup.

Access

As the world moves toward an information economy, it is clear that the gap between the haves and the have-nots is increasing. Education and information are more than ever the keys to economic security. As a part of this trend, computer literacy—access to information technology—contributes significantly to individual economic success. Few would doubt claims that those with computer knowledge will be earning more in the future than those without it.

Measured by MIPS per dollar, computer power is getting cheaper and cheaper, but taking advantage of this power requires that you have access to a computer and know how to use it. Sadly, access to the computer in American society is largely a privilege of the middle class, and this fact tends to widen the gap between the well-to-do and the poor. From a worldwide perspective, those in the third world have even less access to computer power than the American poor.

Impact on Workers

What is the impact of information technology on people? As noted above, it can make a substantial contribution to one's economic success, but it can also have negative impacts on people.

Strangely, one of these negative impacts may be on the worker's health. People whose jobs require them to work continuously on a computer terminal often develop injuries. According to Horowitz (1992), a three-year study by the National Institute for Occupational Safety and Health found that 111 out of 518 telephone workers who used computers had repetitive stress injuries. To avoid such injuries, companies should provide ergonomic office furniture, provide variety in jobs so that keyboard use is not continuous, and train workers in how to adjust their chairs and

REPETITIVE STRESS INJURIES

As jobs in journalism go, Grant McCool's was a plum assignment. Based in Hong Kong for the Reuters news service, McCool covered breaking news throughout east Asia, traveling to South Korea, China, and Pakistan. But in 1989, after five hectic years, the native of Scotland was ready for a change. That's when his bosses transferred him to New York City to be an editor.

That's also when the trouble started. After typing on his computer keyboard for hours a day over several months, McCool developed excruciating pain in his hands; some mornings he would awake with his arms throbbing and burning. "The doctor told me to stop typing immediately," recalls McCool, 32. He hasn't written or edited a story on deadline since. Nor has he been able to clean house, carry heavy objects, or play squash. He cannot even drive a car; controlling the steering wheel with his injured hands is impossible.

McCool suffers from a severe case of cumulative trauma disorder, a syndrome that results from overusing the muscles and tendons in the fingers, hands, arms, and shoulders. The condition brings pain, numbness, weakness, and sometimes long-term disability. Such problems, more commonly known as repetitive stress injuries (RSI), now strike an estimated 185,000 U.S. office and factory workers a year. The cases account for more than half the country's occupational illnesses, compared with about 20% a decade ago.

(Horowitz, 1992)

posture and use keyboard placement in order to avoid such injuries.

The computer can also be used to monitor people, to invade their privacy, and to dehumanize their jobs. For example, according to Koepp et al. (1986), at one airline company:

The master computer records exactly how long the 400 reservation clerks spend on each call and how much time passes before they pick up their next one. Workers earn negative points for such infractions as repeatedly spending in excess of an average 109 seconds handling a call, and taking any more than twelve minutes in bathroom trips beyond the hour a day they are allotted for lunch and coffee breaks. Employees can lose their jobs if they rack up more than 37 points in a year.

Concerning such practices, Koepp quotes Karen Nussbaum, director of 9 to 5, a national group of working women:

> *The potential for corporate abuse is staggering. It puts you under the gun in the short run and drives you crazy in the long run.*

A work system can be designed in many ways that differ significantly in how computers and people share the work. For example, most manual systems for processing insurance claims break the processing down into small steps and pass the paperwork from person to person. The individual jobs are like jobs on a production line, with each worker performing a small, dull process over and over. When a computer system for processing insurance claims is designed, there are many choices. One can choose to computerize the manual system, keeping the work flow about the same, but supporting each process with the computer. This practice can eliminate some manual steps and simplify the work in others. The result is that the workers' primary tasks are to input data into the computer, and the work becomes even duller and more repetitive than the manual system.

Alternatively, because the computer can easily provide convenient access to all the files to each individual workstation, the system can be designed to support a work system where each worker completes all the claim-processing steps. This approach provides job enrichment because there is more variety to the job, and each worker can see that his or her job is important to the company and to its customers. The work force can be organized into teams according to the type of policy or the geographical area served, and each team can take pride in the quality of service it provides to its group of customers.

What then determines the impact of the technology on the people who use it? The design of the organizational/computer system determines this impact, and user-managers are responsible for designing the organization and determining the requirements of the computer system.

One way to improve the impact of the new system on people is to involve those who will use the system in its development and to challenge them to help devise a work design that will improve both the productivity of the organization and the quality of their work experience.

IMPACTS OF TECHNOLOGY ON WORK ROLES

It is now common to hear that the United States and other developed nations are being transformed into nations of information workers. This transformation has had and will continue to have profound impacts on the nature of jobs for certain individuals in business organizations. The job descriptions and career paths of a wide range of workers have already been greatly altered by the information revolution. As outlined in Chapter 15, changes in individual work roles will continue into the next century for both IS professionals and user-managers alike.

IS Leadership

One of the most important and necessary changes will be at the senior management level through the creation of (or an increased prominence afforded to) the post of senior information officer, or what some firms have termed the chief information officer or CIO. The person filling this position will have to possess all the requisite business skills necessary for success in other functional areas of the organization in addition to a high level of technical expertise. The CIO will be charged with the following responsibilities:

1. Integrating the IS strategic plan with that of the organization: Assuring that the information technology required to support the strategic plans of the organization not only exists but is planned for and can be delivered in a timely fashion will be increasingly important in the future.
2. Planning for strategic information systems: These systems will be essential to the long-term success of the organization. Such systems will often require support from outside the organization and may require skills not normally associated with the internal IS organization. They

will serve both information technology and business needs.

3. Providing guidance for the assessment of the value of information technology: The task of evaluating the worth of information and the technology system necessary to deliver it to the organization will become increasingly problematic as more sophisticated and throwaway-type applications are considered. Someone must make the final decision as to whether expected benefits of a system will merit the cost. This task cannot be done without guidance from high-level IS managers who possess the ability to understand the potential impact of a proposed system on the operational and competitive position of the organization as well as the technological merits of the proposal.

4. Ensuring compliance with government regulations, corporate policy, and ethical standards: It will be the responsibility of the CIO to ensure that systems do not violate regulations, policies, or ethical standards.

5. Assessing the risk of new applications: A firm's reputation, and possibly its existence, will be at risk if incorrect use is made of such information as cost estimates or sales projections, or if errors occur in a multitude of other information processing situations. Moreover, as information technology uses become both more complex and more diverse, the potential for death or serious injury resulting from its use also will increase. Reliance on faulty information from an automated monitoring system of a nuclear power plant, actions resulting from incorrect conclusions reached from the use of expert systems, or failure of computer-controlled machinery are all potential sources of risk. A process for risk analysis using computer-generated information will likely receive more corporate attention. Senior IS management will participate in this process and also be responsible for determining the procedures for system use after the risk analysis is performed.

IS Professionals

IS professionals will continue to be in great demand, although there will be a change in the mix of desired skills. Technical knowledge will still be very important for IS professionals, but possession of a wide range of business reengineering and consulting skills and an increased understanding of the business objectives of the organization will also be necessary. The increasing variety and features of systems now available to users through the advent of workstations will force the IS professional to be skilled in much more than just the COBOL programming language. The need for programmer/systems analysts will not disappear, but there will be a major change in the requisite skills.

The development paths of those selecting IS careers will also change. As the services provided by the IS organization change, so will the paths leading to higher ranks within the organization. Many IS professionals will have to adopt more of an entrepreneurial spirit, anticipating and mastering new technologies as they develop. They must also consider their positions to be at risk; new technologies or competitive pressures will threaten to make positions and skills obsolete at any time. Those possessing the skills to thrive in such an environment will be the ones who climb the career ladder. Being the best programmer will no longer ensure advancement.

User-Managers

Professionals and managers in other functional areas of organizations, as well as attorneys and other specialists, will also be required to adopt a new set of computer skills. Time spent by professionals working with information on computer screens will obviously increase. More important, professionals will have to possess the ability to identify opportunities presented by the adoption of information technology.

Work roles changed by information technology have significant implications for the business user-manager. Managers will have to make greater numbers of decisions on what technologies to select in order to make better business decisions. This seemingly circular process underlines the importance of developing a keen understanding of the capabilities of information technology. This process also highlights the importance of wisely allocating the information technology dollar.

Declining hardware costs per unit of storage or MIPS does not necessarily mean that tomorrow's user-managers will spend fewer total dollars on hardware. More sophisticated applications and the ever-increasing range of available products make it likely that hardware expenditures will continue to increase, even though user-managers will be getting more hardware for their investment. Despite that, there will be a shift in the allocation of the information technology dollar toward increased emphasis on software, training, and support, and greater utilization of externally available data. The more sophisticated applications of the future will cost more to develop, test, and install. Despite great strides in making systems more user-friendly, the success of future systems will ultimately be determined by the quality of the training and support given users. One of the more significant trends will be the integration of information provided by reliable outside data services into the information systems of the organization. Only by obtaining valuable information from such sources will managers be able to make informed business decisions.

Managers will be required to spend more of their time ensuring the reliability of the systems on which they are dependent. In addition to the potential for business or human injury resulting from reliance on defective systems, effective audit techniques already lag behind the development of new types of systems. Managers that elect to blindly accept the soundness of a new system will put much more than their own careers at risk.

Managers will also find themselves managing their work activities through systems—a subtle but important change. At present, systems are one of the many elements under management control. Although they may provide information relevant to the management of the department, they do not actually assist in the management process. Sophisticated systems of the future will be able to make recommendations and even act automatically within certain prescribed limits.

It is obvious, therefore, that the job of user-manager will be markedly different as we move into the future, but in order to take advantage of this opportunity, we must recognize some significant barriers.

BARRIERS TO IMPLEMENTING TECHNOLOGY CHANGE

As discussed in Chapter 16, implementing change made possible by advances in information technology is not easy. Some of the organizational barriers are listed here.

Lack of Standards

Industry-wide agreement to certain communications and operating systems standards is absolutely essential for significant progress to be made in the integration of interorganizational and intraorganizational systems. As uses and vendors continue to proliferate in the marketplace, it will become less and less realistic, or possible, to expect an organization to purchase all of its equipment from one vendor. Interfaces are necessary that allow the integration of existing hardware, operating systems, and data structures.

Data transmission rates, carrier qualities, and regulations for the transfer of data across international boundaries must also become standardized before organizations will be able to take full advantage of data-sharing capabilities. Organizations will find themselves working with governments to resolve issues in data transmission across international boundaries.

Human Resistance to Change

Many theories and models attempt to explain the change process. One common assumption among them is that humans tend to resist change for any number of rational and subjective reasons. The resistance may be brought on by a perceived loss of power or status in the organization, fear of the unknown, the perception that the proposed system will not be effective, or a variety of other reasons. The reasons for resistance may not be known until after the fact. What is important is that the designers and sponsors of the system realize that those expected to use the system may resist its implementation in order to satisfy their own agendas.

To help defuse potential resistance, managers must do a better job of considering needs and possible agendas prior to system implementation.

Perhaps the most important but underused weapons to combat resistance are education and training. Training on information systems is easy to delete when costs must be reduced because of competitive pressures. Lack of training leads to greater levels of uncertainty and by extension discomfort and resistance. Those user-managers who show the ability to arrange for proper training and education will be the ones who benefit the most from the adoption of new information technologies (see other suggestions in Chapter 16).

Financial Justification of Major Advances

Traditional forms of financial evaluation of new ideas in firms, such as cost-benefit analysis or expected rate of return, are no longer adequate for system justification. Benefits expected from the diverse types of systems that will be developed in the future will be extremely difficult, if not impossible, to quantify using traditional methods. A change in orientation on how proposed IS projects are evaluated is necessary.

New system justification methods may take the form of simulations or incorporate tools currently used in long-term market or industry forecasting. In many instances, we suspect that major new advances in the use of technology will continue to be justified primarily through the use of judgment. The important point to remember is that it will be more difficult for managers to get systems approved in tight money periods, unless alternatives to traditional forms of project evaluation are devised (see McKenney and McFarlan, 1982).

Data Issues

Data management issues are some of the most important and problematic concerns facing the development, implementation, and integration of systems. Data security, integrity, and ownership are and will continue to be the three critical issues.

Lack of Top Management Understanding

The most serious obstacle to advancement of the use of information technology in organizations is the lack of understanding and involvement on the part of senior management of organizations. Many executives simply do not possess the vision to foster the organizational culture necessary to embrace the use of information technology in new and creative ways.

Without an understanding of and vision for information technology on the part of senior management, attempts at integrating the strategic IS plan with that of the organization will fail. Such failures will greatly limit the ability of the organization to gain significant competitive advantage through the use of information technology.

SUGGESTIONS FOR MANAGING TECHNOLOGICAL CHANGE

Factors critical to the success of the organization will always vary from organization to organization. When managing technological change, several critical success factors will impact the implementation of a new information technology. Technology selection, vendor selection, development of systems to assist in the selection process, and education and training will play important roles.

When considering a new information technology, managers must consider the role that the new technology will play in relation to existing and other planned systems, its flexibility and room for growth, and its known and potential shortcomings. Integration capabilities should also receive increased attention.

Closely related to the selection of a new technology is the selection of the vendor or vendors to provide and support the technology. The number of players in the technology market will continue to expand, as will the number of casualties. The microcomputer market is an example of this high turnover trend in the marketplace. Organizations that do not consider the future technical, marketing, and financial viability of their suppliers are likely to buy soon-to-be obsolete systems.

Systems will be developed that will help managers plan for, select, and implement new information technologies. These systems for system selection will never take all of the guesswork out of the system change equation, but they will provide valuable information to managers pondering new systems.

We again stress the importance of training and education as being critical to the management of technological change. Poorly trained workers will prevent the achievement of the full potential of a system. As the volume and breadth of data continue to increase, the successful organizations will be those that utilize information technology to work smarter and not harder. To achieve this goal, managers at all levels must adopt a belief in the importance of information technology and be open to serving as a champion for the implementation of new systems in the organization.

A key to the working-smarter approach is the active substitution of information technology for other resources. This philosophy does not necessarily mean the permanent reduction of jobs in the organization. It means that successful organizations will identify opportunities to transfer tasks performed manually or by older technologies to new systems, in order to increase throughput or output and to allow those workers freed from routines to face new, more important challenges for the organization. The approach will also mean, for example, that sophisticated video networks will be used as a substitution for travel or that satellite networks will be utilized to conduct meetings that now require travel.

Savvy managers will manage through their information systems. Information will be gathered, analyzed, and disseminated through the use of information technology, eliminating much wasted time. To maintain an information-intensive approach, managers must stay abreast of technological developments. This task will be jointly shared by business managers and IS professionals. Because it is not realistic to expect the IS professional to be aware of developments specific to every function in the organization (e.g., a new capital asset pricing program), managers must keep pace with developments and share that awareness with the IS professional, so that such developments can be evaluated for possible implementation.

One key to the successful implementation of information technology applications in the organization will be the vision for the role that information technology is to play in the organization espoused by the senior management of the organization. A sense of vision, however, is not enough. That vision must be articulated through an information technology architecture, strategic planning efforts, cultural icons, folklore, and so on, in such a manner that the use of information technology, as an integral part of the functioning of the organization, is embraced by all members throughout the organization.

CONCLUSION

In a sense, almost every major topic covered in this text could be a catalyst for change. There is no doubt that the world in which we live will continue to change, and that technology will be a major driving force of change. The rate of change is also likely to continue to increase. While it is interesting to speculate about what change will entail and what its results will be, the fact is that we know very little for certain. We do know that in order for change to provide meaningful, lasting benefits, the process must continuously be evaluated and, to the extent possible, managed and controlled.

Although change is inevitable and to some degree beyond our control, it is up to all user-managers to attempt to understand the impact that technology will have on their lives and the lives of others, and to act accordingly. Those who elect to go with the flow or to bury their heads in the sand, either in their personal lives or in the workplace, will be drowned or trampled. The heart of any successful attempt to manage change lies in effective planning, education, and training. Only then can one anticipate the possible impacts of technology with a sense of accuracy and reap the benefits of technology.

Up to this point in time, our world has avoided the nightmare of an existence controlled by technology. By the same token, it has failed to reach the utopian state predicted by others. It is our sincere hope that this book has provided you with an appreciation of the benefits offered by the proper use of technology and a realization of the technology issues that will face you in your private and professional life. Whether or not you share all the elements of our vision is irrelevant. What is important is that you develop your own vision of how technology will impact our world and what your place will be in that world. Whatever that vision may be, good luck.

DISCUSSION QUESTIONS

1. What changes in the business climate in the mid-1990s will create new needs for information technology?

2. What changes or advances in the technology for IS do you foresee (in addition to the ones listed) that will have a significant impact on the potential uses of IS?

3. Write a scenario on a "day in the life" of a real estate development company in the year 2000 similar to that given for House, Inc., in this chapter.

4. What new responsibilities do you think the typical user-manager will have regarding information technology by the year 2000?

5. Describe a situation in which the accuracy of a database might raise ethical issues for the user-manager responsible for that database.

6. Although this may invade individual privacy, many companies use information technology to measure the quality and quantity of an employee's work. Analyze the ethical implications of this practice.

REFERENCES

1989. "Fair credit reporting act spells out rights." *Louisville Courier-Journal* 137 (May 23): 4.

Allen, Michael. 1990. "To repair bad credit, advisors give clients someone else's data." *Wall Street Journal* 71 (August 14): A1, A8.

Brandt, Richard, Evan Schwartz, and Michele Galen. 1992. "Bit by bit, software protection is eroding." *Time* 140 (July 20): 86–88.

Bylinsky, Gene. 1991. "The marvels of virtual reality." *Fortune* 63 (June 3): 140–150.

Coy, Peter. 1991. "Super phones." *Business Week* (October 7): 138–144.

Cringely, Robert X. 1993. "Thanks for sharing." *Forbes ASAP* 2 (January): 49–52.

Drucker, Peter. 1990. "Implementing the information-based organization." Speech at an Arthur D. Little conference (March).

Elmer-Dewitt, Philip. 1993. "Who's reading your screen?" *Time* 141 (January 18): 46.

Hill, G. Christian, and Ken Varada. 1993. "Five electronics giants hope General Magic will turn the trick." *Wall Street Journal* 74 (February 8): 1.

Hopper, Max. 1992. "Rattling SABRE—new ways to compete on information." *Harvard Business Review* 70 (May–June): 118–125.

Horowitz, Janice M. 1992. "Crippled by computers." *Time* 140 (October 12): 70–72.

Jaffe, Thomas. 1992. "The futz factor." *Forbes* 150 (September 28): 20.

Koepp, Stephen, Charles Pelton, and Seth Shulman. 1986. "The boss that never blinks." *Time* 135 (July 28): 46–47.

Kusekoski, Gene. 1989. "Corporate videotext: A strategic business information system." *MIS Quarterly* 13 (December): 447–456.

Lacayo, Richard. 1991. "Nowhere to hide." *Time* 139 (November 11): 34–40.

Leavitt, Harold J., and Thomas L. Whisler. 1958. "Management in the 1980s." *Harvard Business Review* 36 (November–December): 41–47.

506

Lewis, Geoff. 1989. "Is the computer business maturing?" *Business Week* (March 6): 68–78.

Mason, Richard O. 1986. "Four ethical issues of the information age." *MIS Quarterly* 10 (March): 5–12.

McFadden, Fred R., and Jeffrey A. Hoffer. 1994. *Modern Database Management.* Menlo Park, CA: Benjamin Cummins Publishing Co.

McKenney, J. L., and F. W. McFarlan. 1982. "The information archipelago-map and bridge." *Harvard Business Review* 60 (September–October): 109–119.

Parker, Marilyn M., and Robert J. Benson. 1988. *Information Economics: Linking Business Performance to Information Technology.* Englewood Cliffs, NJ: Prentice-Hall, Inc.

Pastore, Richard. 1993. "Ethical gray matters." *CIO* 21 (February): 58–62.

Peled, Abraham. 1987. "The next computer revolution." *Scientific American* 257 (October): 57–64.

Toffler, Alvin. 1980. *The Third Wave.* New York: William Morrow.

Verity, John W. 1987. "Mainframes aren't ready for the mothballs yet." *Business Week* (November 30): 121.

———. 1992. "Deconstructing the computer industry." *Business Week* (November 23): 90–100.

Zorpette, Glenn. 1989. "Computing at 100 MIPS: Architecture for success." *The Institute* 13 (April): 1, 8.

The following chapters are taken from
Decision Support and Expert Systems:
Management Support Systems
Fourth Edition, Efraim Turban

Chapter 13

Management Support Systems—An Overview

This book is about emerging computer technologies for supporting the solution of managerial problems: decision support systems, group support systems, executive support and information systems, expert systems, and neural computing. We are already seeing evidence that leads us to believe that these technologies will change the manner in which organizations are being structured, reengineered, and managed. Furthermore, these technologies may create a synergy with even greater potential impact on the effectiveness of managerial decision making. This introductory chapter provides an overview of the book and covers the following topics:

1.1   Managers and Computerized Support

A 1991 study of top corporate executives in large U.S. companies revealed that nine out of ten companies have made information technology a vital part of their business. (See Box 1.1.) About one-quarter of these executives also used computers in their homes. A 1989 study of chief executive officers (CEOs) in the Fortune 500 indicated that 21 percent of them use computers. (See *Personal Computing* 1989.) These figures are only one of many signals indicating that we are indeed in the information age. The impact of computer technology on organizations and society is increasing as new technologies evolve and existing technologies expand. The interaction and cooperation between people and machines is rapidly growing to cover more and more aspects of organizational activities. From traditional uses in payroll and bookkeeping functions, computerized systems are now penetrating complex managerial areas ranging from the design and management of automated factories to the evaluation of proposed mergers and acquisitions.

Box 1.1: Wide Use of Computers in Business

Nine of ten senior executives say U.S. companies have successfully made computers a vital part of their business.

Interviews with 320 chief executives, chief operating officers, and strategic planners, conducted in 1991 under the sponsorship of Digital Equipment Corporation, indicate that computers are now an integral factor in major U.S. corporations.

The results of the survey show that today's top executives believe that computers play significant roles throughout their enterprise. Moreover, executives believe that they personally have a role in the management of their company's computers as a strategic resource.

Among highlights of the poll:

- Nine of ten respondents said U.S. companies have been "somewhat" or "very" successful in integrating computer technology in all areas of their business.
- An overwhelming majority—98 percent—said senior executives *must* understand computers and "their business impact."
- 81 percent said computer networks are "critical" to doing business abroad.
- 88 percent said they are using computers to increase communications, while 87 percent said computers have already cut the time needed to develop products.

Some clerks and business analysts have been using computers for as long as four decades to support routine jobs; in contrast, most managers use computers very infrequently to support their decision-making and other activities. This situation began to change in 1982. The driving forces of this change are the availability of microcomputers, the concepts of distributed computing and client/server computing, and the introduction of relatively easy-to-use software. These innovations enable managers not only to use systems purchased or constructed by the information system department, but also to build their own computerized systems with easy-to-use construction tools. The first construction tool for micros was the spreadsheet technology, which received lots of attention in 1979 because of VisiCalc. Today, spreadsheets, database management systems, word processing, and graphical user interfaces are an integral part of almost any organization.

Computerized systems are assisting managers in building, analyzing, and utilizing models, graphs, and charts; managing time and projects; and electronically writing and transmitting memos and reports. Furthermore, managers can perform these tasks by themselves, on their PCs, instead of waiting for the information systems (IS) department to do it for them. The manager is discovering that the computer is like a very reliable staff assistant; it works endlessly without pay, complaints, mistakes, or criticisms of other people.

Management now realizes that computers are not "just another fad." Executives are recognizing that information systems can provide value-added computing power to the execution of mission-critical tasks and to the business of reengineering. These executives have started asking such questions as "What can we do with all these workstations?" Technological developments in hardware, software, and telecommunications are providing answers to this and similar questions by introducing products that can assist managers in solving difficult problems and allowing companies to compete and sometimes even to survive. Computer applications are moving from transaction (or "backroom") processing and monitoring activities (which dominated the industry in the 1960s and 1970s) to problem analysis and solution applications in the 1990s. There is also a trend to provide managers with information systems that can assist them in their most important task—making decisions.

Computer-based technologies are developed to improve the effectiveness of managerial decision making, especially in complex tasks. Such technologies—decision support systems (DSS),* group support systems (GSS), executive information systems (EIS), expert systems (ES), and artificial neural networks (ANN)—are the subject of this book (see Box 1.2). These technologies appear as independent systems, but the current trend is to integrate

---

*The abbreviations DSS, EIS, ES, and other support technologies are used for both the singular and plural form throughout this text.

Box 1.2: Management Support Systems Technologies

1. Decision Support Systems (DSS)
2. Group Support Systems (GSS), Including Group DSS (GDSS)
3. Executive Information Systems (EIS)
4. Expert Systems (ES)
5. Artificial Neural Networks (ANN)
6. Hybrid Support Systems

them among themselves and with other CBIS. Since the objective of these technologies is to support the solution of management problems, their use, either as independent tools or as hybrid-integrated systems, can be considered as providing management support. The term **management support system** (MSS) refers in this text to the application of any of the technologies, either as an independent tool or in some form of integration, to the solution of management problems.

1.2 Managerial Decision Making and Management Information Systems

To better understand management support systems, let us examine two important topics: managerial decision making and information systems.

Management is a process by which organizational goals are achieved through the use of resources (people, money, energy, materials, space, time). These resources are considered to be inputs, and the attainment of the goals is viewed as the output of the process. The degree of success of the organization and the manager's job is often measured by the ratio between outputs and inputs. This ratio is an indication of the organization's **productivity.**

$$\text{Productivity} = \frac{\text{outputs (products, services)}}{\text{inputs (resources)}}$$

Productivity is a major concern for any organization because it determines the well-being of the organization and its members. Productivity is also one of the most important issues at the national level. National productivity is the sum of the productivity of all organizations and individuals, and it determines the standard of living, the employment level, and the economic well-being of a country.

The level of productivity, or the success of management, depends on the execution of certain managerial functions like planning, organizing, directing, and controlling. To carry out these functions, managers are engaged in a continuous process of making decisions.

All managerial activities revolve around decision making. The manager is first and foremost a decision maker. Organizations are filled with decision makers at various levels (see Box 1.3).

For years, managers have considered decision making a pure art—a talent acquired over a long period of time through experience (learning by trial and error). Management was considered an art because a variety of individual styles could be used in approaching and successfully solving the same type of managerial problems in actual business practice. These styles are often based on creativity, judgment, intuition, and experience, rather than on systematic quantitative methods based on a scientific approach.

Box 1.3: Ability to Make Decisions Rated First in Survey

In almost any survey of what constitutes good management, you are likely to find prominently mentioned the ability to make clear-cut decisions when needed.

It is not surprising, therefore, to hear that the ability to make crisp decisions was rated first in importance in a study of 6,500 managers in more than 100 companies, many of them large, blue-chip corporations.

As managers entered a training course at Harbridge House, a Boston-based firm, they were asked how important it was that managers employ certain management practices. They also were asked how well, in their estimation, managers performed these practices.

It was from a statistical distillation of these answers that Harbridge ranked "making clear-cut decisions when needed" as the most important of ten management practices.

And it was from these evaluations they concluded that only 20 percent of the managers performed "very well" on any given practice.

Ranked second in managerial importance was "getting to the heart of problems rather than dealing with less important issues," a finding that seems to show up in all such studies. Most of the remaining eight management practices were related directly or indirectly to decision making.

(*Source:* Condensed from *Stars and Stripes*, May 10, 1987.)

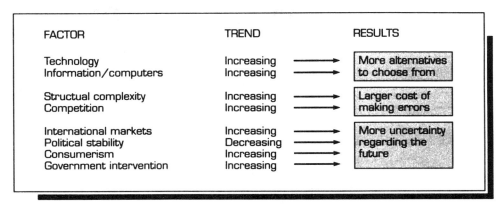

FIGURE 1.1 Factors Affecting Decision Making. (*Source:* Adapted from Turban and Meredith [1994].)

However, the environment in which management must operate today is changing very rapidly. Business and its environment are more complex today than ever before, and the trend is toward increasing complexity. Figure 1.1 shows the changes in major factors (on the left) that have had an impact on managerial decision making. The results (on the right) indicate that decision making today is more complicated than in the past. It is more difficult to make decisions for two reasons. First, the number of available alternatives is much larger today than ever before, owing to improved technology and communication systems. Second, the cost of making errors can be very large, owing to the complexity and magnitude of operations, automation, and the chain reaction that an error can cause in many parts of the organization. By the same token, the benefits can be extremely large if correct decisions are being made.

As a result of these trends and changes, it is very difficult to rely on a trial-and-error approach to management, especially in decisions involving the factors shown in Figure 1.1. Managers must become more sophisticated—they must learn how to use new tools and techniques that are being developed in their field. Many of these techniques use a quantitative analysis approach; they are grouped into a discipline called *management science* (or *operations research*). (For further details, see Turban and Meredith [1994].)

1.3 A Framework for Decision Support

Before defining the specific management support technologies, it will be useful to present a classical framework for decision support. This framework will provide us with several major concepts that are used in the definitions. It will also help us in discussing several additional issues, such as the relationship among the technologies and the evolution of computerized systems. This framework, which is shown as Fig-

514

ure 1.2, was proposed by Gorry and Scott-Morton [1971], who combined the work of Simon [1977] and Anthony [1965]. The details of this framework are as follows:

The left side of the table is based on Simon's idea that decision-making processes fall along a continuum that ranges from highly structured (sometimes referred to as *programmed*) to highly unstructured *(nonprogrammed)* decisions. **Structured** processes refer to routine and repetitive problems for which standard solutions exist. **Unstructured** processes are "fuzzy," complex problems for which there are no cut-and-dried solutions. Simon also described the decision-making process as a three-phase process: intelligence, design, and choice. (Details are given in Chapter 2.)

An *unstructured problem* is one in which none of the three phases are structured. Decisions where some, but not all, of the phases are structured are referred to as **semistructured** by Gorry and Scott-Morton.

	Type of Control			
Type of Decision	**Operational Control**	**Managerial Control**	**Strategic Planning**	**Support Needed**
Structured	Accounts receivable, order entry **1**	Budget analysis, short-term forecasting, personnel reports, make-or-buy **2**	Financial management (investment), warehouse location, distribution systems **3**	MIS, operations research models, transaction processing
Semistructured	Production scheduling, inventory control **4**	Credit evaluation, budget preparation, plant layout, project scheduling, reward systems design **5**	Building new plant, mergers and acquisitions, new product planning, compensation planning, quality assurance planning **6**	DSS
Unstructured	Selecting a cover for a magazine, buying software, approving loans **7**	Negotiating, recruiting an executive, buying hardware, lobbying **8**	R & D planning, new technology development, social responsibility planning **9**	DSS, ES, neural networks
Support Needed	MIS, management science	Management science, DSS, ES, EIS	EIS, ES, neural networks	

FIGURE 1.2 Decision Support Framework.

- Intelligence—searching for conditions that call for decisions.
- Design—inventing, developing, and analyzing possible courses of action.
- Choice—selecting a course of action from those available.

In a structured problem, the procedures for obtaining the best (or at least a good enough) solution are known. Whether the problem involves finding an appropriate inventory level or deciding on an optimal investment strategy, the objectives are clearly defined. Frequent objectives are cost minimization or profit maximization. The manager can use the support of clerical, data processing, or management science models. Management support systems such as DSS and ES can be useful at times. In an unstructured problem, human intuition is frequently the basis for decision making. Typical unstructured problems include planning of new services to be offered, hiring an executive, or choosing a set of research and development projects for next year. The semistructured problems fall between the structured and the unstructured, involving a combination of both standard solution procedures and individual judgment. Keen and Scott-Morton [1978] give the following examples of semistructured problems: trading bonds, setting marketing budgets for consumer products, and performing capital acquisition analysis. Here, a decision support system can improve the quality of the information on which the decision is based (and consequently the quality of the decision) by providing not only a single solution but a range of alternate solutions. These capabilities, which are described later, allow managers to better understand the nature of the problems so they can make better decisions.

The second half of this framework (top of Figure 1.2) is based on Anthony's taxonomy [1965], which defines three broad categories that encompass all managerial activities: (1) strategic planning—the long-range goals and the policies for resource allocation; (2) management control—the acquisition and efficient utilization of resources in the accomplishment of organizational goals; and (3) operational control—the efficient and effective execution of specific tasks.

Anthony and Simon's taxonomies are combined in a nine-cell decision support framework. The right-hand column and the bottom row indicate the technologies needed to support the various decisions. Gorry and Scott-Morton suggested, for example, that for the semistructured and unstructured decisions, the conventional MIS and management science approaches are insufficient. They proposed the use of a supportive information system, which they called a **decision support system** (DSS). Expert systems (ES), which were introduced several years later, are most suitable for tasks requiring expertise.

The more structured and operational control-oriented tasks (cells 1, 2, and 4) are performed by low-level managers, whereas the tasks in cells 6, 8, and 9 are the responsibility of top executives. This means that DSS, EIS, neural computing, and

ES are more often applicable for top executives and professionals tackling specialized, complex problems.

Computer Support for Structured Decisions

Structured and some semistructured decisions, especially of the operational and managerial control type, have been supported by computers since the 1960s. Decisions of this type are made in *all functional areas,* especially in finance and production (operations management).

Such problems, which are encountered fairly repeatedly, have a high level of structure. It is therefore possible to abstract and analyze them and classify them into prototypes. For example, a "make-or-buy" decision belongs to this category. Other examples are capital budgeting (e.g., replacement of equipment), allocation of resources, distribution problems, procurement, planning, and inventory control. For each type of problem, a prescribed solution was developed through the use of some quantitative formulas. This approach is called **management science (MS) or operations research (OR).**

Management Science

The management science approach adopts the view that managers can follow a fairly systematic process for solving problems. Therefore, it is possible to use a scientific approach to managerial decision making. This approach involves the following steps:

1. Defining the *problem* (a decision situation that may deal with some *trouble* or with an *opportunity*).
2. Classifying the problem into a standard category.
3. Constructing a mathematical model that describes the real-life problem.
4. Finding potential solutions to the modeled problem and evaluating them.
5. Choosing and recommending a solution to the problem. This process is centered around *modeling.*

Modeling involves the transformation of the real-world problem into an appropriate prototype structure. As will be seen later, modeling is going to be used also in less structured problems. The use of computers was designed to help in finding the solution for the problem in a quick and efficient manner. Structured problems can be solved with the aid of standard quantitative models, however, the less structured ones can be handled by DSS or other MSS.

1.4   Decision Support Systems

The concepts involved in DSS were first articulated in the early 1970s by Scott-Morton under the term *management decision systems.* He defined such systems as "interactive computer-based systems, which help decision makers utilize *data* and *models* to solve unstructured problems" [1971]. Another classical definition of DSS, provided by Keen and Scott-Morton [1978] follows:

> Decision support systems couple the intellectual resources of individuals with the capabilities of the computer to improve the quality of decisions. It is a computer-based support system for management decision makers who deal with semi-structured problems.

The DSS definition will be revisited and expanded in Chapter 3. It should be noted that DSS, like MIS and other MSS technologies, is content-free expression (i.e., it means different things to different people). There is no universally accepted definition of DSS.

DSS as an Umbrella Term The term DSS is sometimes used to describe any computerized systems. We prefer to use DSS in its narrower definition, and use the term MSS as an umbrella term that describes any type of support.

Now, let us examine a typical case of a successfully implemented DSS, as shown in Box 1.4.

Box 1.4: The Houston Minerals Case

Houston Minerals Corporation was interested in a proposed joint venture with a petrochemicals company to develop a chemical plant. Houston's executive vice president responsible for the decision wanted analysis of the risks involved in the areas of supplies, demands, and prices. Bob Sampson, manager of planning and administration, and his staff built a DSS in a few days by means of a specialized planning language. The results strongly suggested the project should be accepted.

Then came the real test. Although the executive vice president accepted the validity and value of the results, he was worried about the potential downside risk of the project, the chance of a catastrophic outcome. As Sampson tells it, his words were something like this:

> I realize the amount of work you have already done, and I am 99 percent confident with it. However, I would like to see this in a different light. I know we are short of time and we have to get back to our partners with our yes or no decision.

Sampson replied that the executive could have the risk analysis he needed in less than an hour's time. Sampson concluded, "within 20 minutes, there in the executive boardroom, we were reviewing the results of his `what-if?' questions. Those results led to the eventual dismissal of the project, which we otherwise would probably have accepted."

The case demonstrates some of the major characteristics of a DSS. The initial risk analysis was based on the decision maker's definition of the situation using a management science approach. Then the executive vice president, using his experience, judgment, and intuition, felt that the model should be scrutinized. The initial model, although mathematically correct, was incomplete. With a regular simulation system, a modification would have taken a long time, but the DSS provided a very quick analysis. Furthermore, the DSS was flexible and responsive enough to allow managerial intuition and judgment to be incorporated in the analysis.

How can such a thorough risk analysis be performed so quickly? How can the judgment factors be elicited, quantified, and worked into the model? How can the results be presented meaningfully and convincingly to the executive? What is meant by "what-if" questions? The answers to these questions are provided in Chapters 3 through 11.

Why Use a DSS?

Firestone Tire & Rubber Co. explained its reasons for implementing a DSS in *Computerworld* (September 27, 1982). The major reasons were that:

- The company was operating in an unstable economy.
- The company was faced with increasing foreign and domestic competition.
- The company encountered increasing difficulty in tracking the numerous business operations.
- The company's existing computer system did not support the objectives of increasing efficiency, profitability, and entry into profitable markets.
- The DP Department could not begin to address the diversity of the company's needs or management's ad hoc inquiries, and business analysis functions were not inherent within the existing systems.

A survey conducted by Hogue and Watson [1983] identified six main reasons why major corporations started large-scale DSS:

Factors	Cited by percent
Accurate information is needed.	67
DSS is viewed as an organizational winner.	44
New information is needed.	33
Management mandated the DSS.	22
Timely information is provided.	17
Cost reduction is achieved.	6

Another reason for the development of DSS is the end-user computing movement. End-users are not programmers and therefore they require easy-to-use construction tools and procedures. These are provided by DSS.

The overall results of using a DSS can be very impressive, as indicated by the Pfizer case (see Box 1.5).

Box 1.5: DSS at Pfizer Pharmaceutical, Inc.

As of 1973, Rachelle Laboratories, Inc. (Long Beach, CA), a competitor of Pfizer, began selling an antibiotic called Doxychel, which was the same drug as Pfizer's Vibramycin. Pfizer contended that its patent had been violated.

The disagreement came to a head in the winter of 1983 in a district court in Honolulu. Throughout the six-week trial, however, Pfizer had an edge over Rachelle. Pfizer had a DSS. Jeffrey Landau, manager of DSS at Pfizer, recalls: "We put together a team of lawyers, system-staff professionals, and others, and built a model." The model, he says, looked at one key "what-if." If Rachelle hadn't started selling Doxychel, how much more money would Pfizer have made? The answer, of course, depended on two assumptions: One was that all Rachelle's sales were at Pfizer's expense. The other was that, without Rachelle as a competitor, Pfizer could have sold its antibiotic at a higher price.

Armed with these assumptions, the Pfizer team set up, three blocks from the courthouse, a DSS war room, complete with terminals, printers, plotters, and high-speed communication to a DEC System-10 mainframe in Connecticut. With the system in place, the opposition could not stall for time by requesting additional information. Pfizer's system accessed the requested information instantly.

When the trial got underway, however, Pfizer's decision support system was really put to the test. "We could measure the impact of claims witnesses made about the market. Using the information provided, the lawyers would yield on points that were determined to be insignificant. If the other side made a claim that had big monetary implications, our lawyers would fight it." In effect, the Pfizer team used the model to plan its legal tactics.

The result: On June 30, 1983, Judge Martin Pence, who frequently alluded to Pfizer's model, awarded Pfizer $55.8 million. It was the largest judgment on a patent-infringement suit in U.S. history.

(*Source:* Condensed from M. Lasden, *Computer Decisions*, Nov. 1983, pp. 254–58.)

1.5 Group Support Systems

Many major decisions in organizations are made by groups, collectively. Getting a group together in one place and at one time can be difficult and expensive. Furthermore, group meetings can take a long time and the resulting decisions may be mediocre.

Attempts to improve the work of groups with the aid of information technology appear under several names, such as groupware, electronic meeting systems, collaborative systems, and group decision support systems. Of special interest in this book is the area of **group DSS** (GDSS).(See Box 1.6.)

Box 1.6: Total Quality Management (TQM) at IBM

The Malcolm Baldridge National Quality Award is granted annually to those companies and individuals in the U.S. that show excellence in persuing TQM programs. The prestigious award is based on assessment of 32 criteria organized in the following categories: leadership, information and analysis, strategic quality planning, human resource utilization, quality assurance, and customer satisfaction.

At IBM Boulder (Colorado), TQM has a high priority. Although management does not believe that at the present time the organization is ready for the Baldridge Award, they would like to apply for IBM's internal quality award, as well as to identify potential improvement areas. The problem is that there is a diversity of opinion on the current accomplishment level of each of the 32 criteria of quality. Thus, there are disagreements on priorities and the resulting allocation of resources of improving quality.

To arrive at the appropriate decision, IBM used its own decision room and software (TeamFocus) to support the process of group work. This approach, called group DSS, enabled IBM to achieve consensus, to learn more about TQM, to assess where the company is, and to determine where it needs to go to achieve excellence in TQM.

(*Source:* Condensed from R. L. and J. J. Mozeliak, "TeamFocus: Experiences with Malcolm Baldridge Self-Assessment," in *DSS-91 Transactions*, Mahattan Beach, California, June 1991.)

1.6   Executive Information (or Support) Systems

Executive information systems (EIS) are developed primarily for the following objectives:

- Serve the information needs of executives.
- Provide extremely user friendly interface for the executive.
- Meet individual executives' decision styles.
- Provide timely and effective tracking and control.
- Provide quick access to detailed information behind text, numbers, or graphics (drill-down capability).

Box 1.7: Executive Information System at Hardee's

At Hardee's (Rocky Mount, NC), the EIS primarily provides status access, according to John Wilson, chief financial officer. Point of sale terminals at over 3,000 Hardee's restaurants accumulate detailed sales information, which the corporate mainframe collects automatically each night. Financial analysts extract and analyze information from the mass of data using Express (a DSS generator listed in Chapter 7). This information is transformed to the EIS database.

The database also holds information on Hardee's competitors and other financial information from online information services. Five top executives, including the chairman and Wilson, tap the EIS with their own IBM PCs. The executives use a mouse to select graphs and reports from menus. Much of their work with the system involves devising and tracking marketing strategies. For example, if the figures show that sales in a region are falling off during a particular time of day, local advertising might have to be refocused.

At Hardee's, the EIS's analyst is tailoring the information to executives' needs and desires. The analyst puts together a basic package of reports and graphs. As the five users familiarize themselves with the available information and possible formats, they are requesting new reports and modifications of standing ones. Wilson expects to add more sophisticated features that the executives consider critical, like automatic exception reporting and the tracking of situations. The system was developed with the Command Center software (see Chapter 10). "It takes no time at all to learn the system," Wilson says. "Everyone was up to speed in five minutes."

(*Source:* Condensed from *Computer Decisions*, Dec. 17, 1985.)

• Filter, compress, and track critical data and information.
• Identify problems (opportunities).

Executive information systems, which started in the mid-1980s in large corporations (see Box 1.7), are becoming affordable to smaller companies and are serving many managers as *enterprise-wide systems*. (See Watson, et al. [1992].)

1.7 Expert Systems

When an organization has a complex decision to make or problem to solve, it often turns to experts for advice. These experts have specific knowledge and experience in the problem area. They are aware of the alternatives, the chances of success, and the costs the business may incur. Companies engage experts for advice on such matters as which equipment to buy, mergers and acquisitions, and advertising strategy. The more unstructured the situation, the more specialized (and expensive) is the advice. Expert systems are an attempt to mimic human experts.

Typically, an **expert system** (ES) is a decision-making and/or problem-solving package of computer hardware and software that can reach a level of performance comparable to—or even exceeding that of—a human expert in some specialized and usually narrow problem area.

Expert systems are a branch of applied **artificial intelligence** (AI). From applications in medical diagnosis, mineral exploration, and computer configurations, expert systems are spreading into complex business applications like managing assets and liabilities, corporate planning, tax advice, competitive bid preparations, internal control evaluations, and fault analysis.

The basic idea behind ES is simple. **Expertise** is transferred from the expert to the computer. This knowledge is then stored in the computer and users call on the computer for specific advice as needed. The computer can make inferences and arrive at a specific conclusion. Then, like a human consultant, it advises the nonexperts and explains, if necessary, the logic behind the advice. (See Turban [1992].)

Expert systems are used today in thousands of organizations and they support many tasks (see Box 1.8). These capabilities can provide companies with improved productivity levels and increased competitive advantages.

1.8 Neural Computing (Artificial Neural Networks)

The application of all the previous technologies was based on the use of *explicit* data, information, or knowledge, which was stored in a computer and manipulated as needed. However, in the complex real world we may not have explicit data, information, or knowledge. Yet, people must make decisions that are based on partial, incomplete, or inexact information. Such conditions are created, for example, in rapidly changing environments. Decision makers are using their experi-

Box 1.8: How Expert Systems Can Perform Useful Tasks

Suppose you manage an engineering firm that bids on many projects. Each project is, in a sense, unique. You can calculate your expected cost, but that's not sufficient to set up your bid. You have background information on your likely competitors and their bidding strategies. Something is known about the risks—possible technical problems, political delays, material shortages, or other sources of trouble. An experienced proposal manager can put all this together and, generally, arrive at a sound judgment concerning terms and bidding price. However, you do not have that many proposal managers who have the time to concentrate on preparing and negotiating major proposals. This is where expert systems become useful. An expert system can capture the lines of thinking the experienced proposal managers can follow. It can also catalog information gained on competitors, local risks, and so on, and can incorporate your policies and strategies concerning risk, pricing, and terms. It can help your younger managers work through to an informed bid consistent with your policy.

Suppose you are a life insurance agent and you are a very good one; however, your market has changed. You are no longer competing only with other insurance agents. You are also competing with banks, brokers, money market fund managers, and the like. Your company is now pushing a whole array of products, from universal life insurance to venture capital funds. Your clients have the same problems as ever, but they are more inquisitive, more sophisticated, and more conscious of tax avoidance and similar considerations. How can you give them advice and put together a sensible package for them when you are more confused than they are?

Financial planning systems and estate planning guides have been part of the insurance industry's marketing kit for a long time. However, sensible financial planning takes more skill than the average insurance agent has or can afford to acquire. This is one reason why the fees of professional planners are as high as they are. A number of insurance companies are currently investing heavily in artificial intelligence techniques in the hope that these techniques can be used to build sophisticated, competitive, knowledge-based financial planning support systems to assist their agents in helping their clients.

(*Source:* Publicly disclosed project description of Arthur D. Little, Inc.)

Box 1.9: Neural Computing Identifies More Heart Attacks Than Doctors Do

Emergency room doctors instantly identified 78 percent of patients with heart attacks in an experiment involving 331 patients complaining of chest pains at a San Diego hospital emergency room. The sooner a heart attack is diagnosed, the better is the chance of saving the patient's life.

Dr. Baxt of the University of California, San Diego Medical Center, reported in the December 1991 issue of the *Annals of Internal Medicine* that a new computerized technology, called neural computing, instantly and correctly identified 97 percent of the same patients. Furthermore, as compared to the doctors, the computer program did very well when important information was missing.

The capability of neural computing to work despite missing data is one of the greatest advantages of this emerging technology, which has been used successfully in several financial management applications.

---

ences to handle these situations; that is, they are recalling experiences and *learning* from their experiences what to do with new similar situations for which *exact* replicas are unavailable.

In all the previous technologies, there was no element of learning by the computer. A technology that attempts to close this gap is called *neural computing* or **artificial neural networks** (ANN). The technology, which employs a pattern recognition approach, has been used successfully in some business applications (see Box 1.9), but much research and development is still needed. (See Zeidenberg [1990].)

1.9 The Evolution of Computerized Decision Aids

Computers have been used as tools to support managerial decision making for over three decades. Table 1.1 presents a summary of the development of computerized procedures used as aids in decision making.

The computerized tools or decision aids displayed in Table 1.1 can be grouped into seven categories:

- Transaction processing systems (TPS)
- Management information systems (MIS)
- Office automation systems (OAS)
- Decision support systems (DSS) and group DSS (GDSS)
- Expert systems (ES)

TABLE 1.1 Aids in Decision Making.

Phase	Description	Examples of Tools
Early	Compute "crunch numbers," summarize, organize.	Calculators, early computer programs, statistical models, simple management science models.
Intermediate	Find, organize, and display decision-relevant information.	Database management systems, MIS, filing systems. Management science models.
Current	Perform decision-relevant computations on decision-relevant information; organize and display the results. Query-based and user-friendly approach. "What-if" analysis.	Financial models, spreadsheets, trend exploration, operations research models, CAD systems, decision support systems.
	Interact with decision makers to facilitate formulation and execution of the intellectual steps in the process of decision making.	Expert systems; executive information systems.
Just beginning	Complex and fuzzy decisions situations, expanding to collaborative decision making and to machine learning.	Second generation of expert systems, group DSS, neural computing.

- Executive information systems (EIS)
- Artificial neural networks (ANN).

There are several opinions about the evolution of management support systems (MSS) and their relationship to the other systems. A common view is that the recommendations and advice provided by MSS to the manager can be considered as information needed for final decisions made by humans. If we accept this approach, we can consider MSS as sophisticated, high-level types of information systems that can be used in addition to traditional transaction processing systems, office automation, and MIS.

The evolutionary view of computer-based information systems (CBIS), presented in Figure 1.3, has a strong logical basis. First, there is a clear-cut sequence through time: EDP systems appeared in the mid-1950s, MIS followed in the 1960s, OAS was developed mainly in the 1970s, and DSS is a product of the 1970s and expanded in the 1980s. Commercial applications of expert systems and executive information systems emerged in the 1980s. In the 1990s we see group support systems and neural computing emerging, as well as many **integrated computer systems.** Second, there is a common technology linking the various types of CBIS: the computer, which itself has evolved considerably over time. And third, there are systemic linkages in the manner in which each system processes data into information. Additional support for the evolutionary view is presented in Figure 1.4. This figure lists the attributes of TPS, MIS, DSS, EIS, and ES classified into several

FIGURE 1.3 The Evolutionary Path of CBIS. (*Source:* Kroeber and Watson [1988]; modified.)

dimensions. Only the most sophisticated attributes of each level are listed. Several lesser attributes can be found (although not listed) in most of the CBIS.

The relationship among TPS, MIS, DSS, EIS and ES, and other technologies that are not shown in the table, can be summarized as follows:

- The technologies can be viewed as being unique classes of information technology.
- They are interrelated, and they each support some aspects of managerial decision making.
- The evolution and creation of the newer tools help expand the role of information technology for the betterment of management in organizations.
- The interrelationship and coordination between these tools is still evolving.

The classification of CBIS does not imply that real-world computer systems must belong to only one category. On the contrary, an MIS system may be coupled with a transaction processing system. A DSS may be combined with an MIS and integrated with an ES. The interactions among CBIS occur along two dimensions: technology (hardware, software, processes) and applications (personnel management, scheduling, inventory control).

An illustration of CBIS in a personnel department is provided in Appendix A at the end of the chapter.

Dimension	Transactions Processing Systems (TPS)	Management Information Systems (MIS)	Decision Support Systems (DSS)	Expert Systems (ES)	Executive Information Systems (EIS)
Applications	Payroll, inventory, record keeping, production and sales information	Production control, sales forecasting, monitoring	Long-range strategic planning, complex integrated problem areas	Diagnosis, strategic planning, internal control planning, strategies	Support to top management decision, environmental scanning
Focus	Data transactions	Information	Decisions, flexibility, user-friendliness	Inferencing, transfer of expertise	Tracking, control, "Drill down"
Database	Unique to each application, batch update	Interactive access by programmers	Database management systems, interactive access, factual knowledge	Procedural and factual knowledge; knowledge base (facts, rules)	External (online) and corporate, enterprise wide access (to all databases)
Decision capabilities	No decisions	Structured routine problems using conventional management science tools	Semistructured problems, integrated management science models, blend of judgment and modeling	The system makes complex decisions, unstructured; use of rules (heuristics)	Only when combined with a DSS
Manipulation	Numerical	Numerical	Numerical	Symbolic	Numeric (mainly); some symbolic
Type of information	Summary reports, operational	Scheduled and demand reports, structured flow, exception reporting	Information to support specific decisions	Advice and explanations	Status access, exception reporting, key indicators
Highest organizational level served	Submanagerial, low management	Middle management	Analysts and managers	Managers and specialists	Senior executives (only)
Impetus	Expediency	Efficiency	Effectiveness	Effectiveness and expediency	Timeliness

FIGURE 1.4 Attributes of the Major Computerized Support Systems.

1.10 Some Differences Between MIS and DSS

The DSS definitions, performance characteristics, and examples clearly indicate that there are differences between DSS and MIS. We notice that the differences are real and merit our attention. What can be expected from a DSS is less typically possible with an MIS. This does not mean that an MIS cannot have these features; rather, they are simply not common to most management information systems. The Houston Minerals Case (Box 1.4) illustrates these differences.

Specifically, a DSS can be used to address ad hoc, unexpected problems. The proposed joint venture described in Box 1.4 was possibly a once-in-a-lifetime decision-making situation. Most MIS decision support is supplied by structured information flows in the form of summary and exception reports. An exception report singles out items that require special attention. Structured reports are of limited value for unique problems. Either the needed information is not provided or it is in the wrong format.

A DSS can provide a valid representation of a complex real-world system. In this example, the decision maker accepted the validity of the model and the value of the results; the model builders were able to develop a model that could be trusted. The way many models are embedded in an MIS does not engender such trust, because they are frequently built by the management science group and left for the user as the management scientist moves on to other projects. Over time, the models become out-of-date and either are not used or are used and provide potentially misleading, outdated information.

A DSS can supply decision support within a short time frame. A model for the proposed joint venture was completed and working within days. A request for risk analysis was satisfied within one hour. In an MIS, if the model is not already available, the lead time for writing programs and getting answers is often too long to help many decision situations.

A DSS can evolve as the decision maker learns more about the problem. In many cases, managers cannot specify in advance what they want from computer programmers and model builders. In our example, the request for risk analysis occurred *after* the model was built. Many computerized applications are developed in a way that requires detailed specifications to be formalized in advance. This requirement is not reasonable in many semistructured and unstructured decision-making tasks.

A DSS is often developed by non-data processing (DP) professionals. In the Houston case, the planning and administration group created the model with no outside help. This was possible because of the software package that was available. Most MIS applications and systems are developed by data processing professionals.

These distinguishing DSS features are summarized in Table 1.2. Keen and Scott-Morton also have noted the distinctive nature of DSS. Table 1.3 summarizes the differences that they see among MIS, operations research/management science (OR/MS), and DSS.

TABLE 1.2 DSS Features

- A DSS can be used to address ad hoc, unexpected problems.
- A DSS can provide valid representation of the real-world system.
- A DSS can provide decision support within a short time frame.
- A DSS can evolve as the decision maker learns more about the problem.
- DSS can be developed by non-data processing professionals.

Another way to look at the relationships between DSS and MIS is provided by McLean [1982], who uses Anthony's framework. The three levels of organizational activities are shown as a triangle with an added level for transaction processing. Transaction processing is done mainly at the operational level.

MIS, in theory, was to serve all levels of managerial activities. As such, DSS can be considered a subset of MIS (see Figure 1.5). In practice, MIS has fallen far short of this objective. The proponents of decision support systems therefore argued that their approaches were better suited to the upper two layers of decision making.

Similar to McLean's point of view is the notion that MIS is an umbrella that supports all managerial activities. DSS is viewed as the portion that deals with unstructured situations, while management science deals with structured problems.

TABLE 1.3 The Characteristics of MIS, OR/MS, and DSS.

Management Information Systems
- The main impact has been on structured tasks, where standard operating procedures, decision rules, and information flows can be reliably predefined.
- The main payoff has been in improving efficiency by reducing costs, turnaround time, and so on, and by replacing clerical personnel.
- The relevance for managers' decision making has mainly been indirect; for example, by providing reports and access to data.

Operations Research/Management Science
- The impact has mostly been on structured problems (rather than tasks), where the objective, data, and constraints can be prespecified.
- The payoff has been in generating better solutions for given types of problems.
- The relevance for managers has been the provision of detailed recommendations and new methodologies for handling complex problems.

Decision Support Systems
- The impact is on decisions in which there is sufficient structure for computer and analytic aids to be of value but where managers' judgment is essential.
- The payoff is in extending the range and capability of computerized managers' decision processes to help them improve their effectiveness.
- The relevance for managers is the creation of a supportive tool, under their own control, that does not attempt to automate the decision process, predefine objectives, or impose solutions.

Source: Keen and Scott-Morton [1978], p. 1.

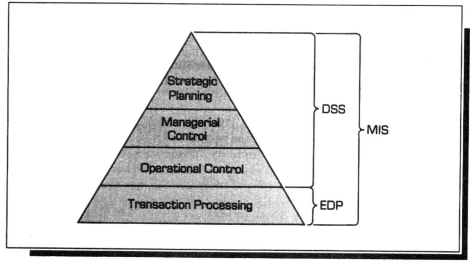

FIGURE 1.5 Relation among EDP, MIS, and DSS. (*Source:* McLean [1982].)

Note: For a discussion on the differences between DSS and EIS, and MIS and EIS, see Chapter 11.

1.11 The Decision Support–Expert Systems Connection

DSS and ES seem to be completely different and unrelated computerized systems. As can be viewed in Table 1.4, there are significant philosophical, technological, and managerial differences between the two tools. These differences are discussed in detail in Chapter 20, when the integration of the tools is examined.

The disciplines of ES and DSS grew up along parallel, but largely independent, paths. Only recently has the potential of integrating the two been recognized. As a matter of fact, because of the different capabilities of the two tools, they can complement each other, creating a powerful, integrated, computer-based system that can considerably improve managerial decision making.

1.12 Support of Decision Making

The technologies discussed in this book can be used to support managers as independent, stand-alone tools, or they can be integrated. The manner in which they are applied depends on the nature of the decision, the nature of the organization, and the individuals involved in the decision making. To show the potential support of the techniques discussed in this book we revisit Simon's decision-making

TABLE 1.4 Differences Between DSS and ES.

	DSS	ES
Objective	Assist human decision maker	Replicate (mimic) human advisers and replace them
Who makes the recommendations (decisions)?	The human and/or the system	The system
Major orientation	Decision making	Transfer of expertise (human-machine-human) and rendering of advice
Major query direction	Human queries the machine	Machine queries the human
Nature of support	Personal, groups, and institutional	Personal (mainly), and groups
Manipulation method	Numerical	Symbolic
Characteristics of problem area	Complex, integrated wide	Narrow domain
Type of problems	Ad hoc, unique	Repetitive
Content of database	Factual knowledge	Procedural and factual knowledge
Reasoning capability	No	Yes, limited
Explanation capability	Limited	Yes

process, discussed earlier. The process is shown in Figure 1.6 (slightly modified). We also show the potential support of MSS technologies.

The steps of the process are:

Step A. Problem (Opportunity) Finding. This step involves the collection of information from various sources in order to identify problems and opportunities.

An ES can help in the design of the flow of information to the executive (e.g., what to monitor, when) and in the interpretation of the collected information. Because some of the information is fuzzy, a combination of ES and ANN can be very helpful. The entire area of scanning, monitoring, forecasting (e.g., trends) and interpretation can be greatly helped by computerization. Also, natural language processors (NLP) can be useful in summarizing information.

Step B. Analysis. Once the problem (opportunity) has been identified, a question is posed: what to do about it? At this step an analysis is called for. The analysis can be qualitative or quantitative (or combined). The quantitative analysis can be supported by a DSS and by structured quantitative analysis tools. The qualitative analysis can be supported by an ES.

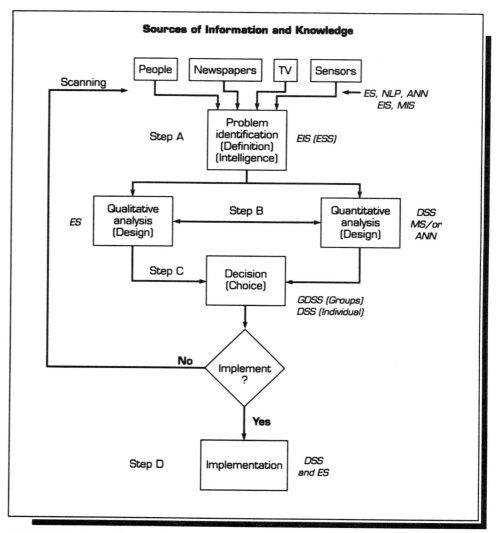

FIGURE 1.6 Computerized Support to the Decision-Making Process.

Step C. Choice. In this step, a decision is made regarding the problem (or opportunity) based on the results of the analysis. The step can be supported by a DSS (if the decision maker is an individual) or by a GDSS (if the decision is made by a group).

Step D. Implementation. In the event that the decision is to implement a proposed solution, a DSS and/or ES can provide the support.

1.13   Hybrid Support Systems

The objective of a CBIS, regardless of its name or nature, is to assist management in solving managerial or organizational problems faster and/or better than what management can do without computers.

The key is the *successful solution* of the managerial problem, and not the tool or technique that was used in the process. A useful analogy is the repair of a machine. The repairperson diagnoses the problem and he (she) is looking for the best tool(s) to execute the repair. Sometimes, there are no tools that can be used; then special tools can be constructed, or the repair is done without any tools. DSS, expert systems, ANN, and other MSS technologies can be considered as tools. Frequently it is necessary to use several tools to get better results (see Box 1.10).

The managerial decision-making process illustrated in Figure 1.6 indicated the possible need for several MSS technologies for the solution of a single problem. And indeed many complex problems require several MSS technologies, as will be

Box 1.10: Solving Complex Urban Traffic Problems with Hybrid MSS

Urban traffic management is a continuous decision process of coordination of all the individual elements (traffic signals, arterial roads, traffic, parking) and the interrelated components of urban transport (private cars, transit, pedestrians, etc.). Its aim is the achievement of maximum efficiency and productivity for the whole system through the application of operating, pricing, regulatory, and service policies. For this purpose, many different specific problems have been addressed and several models developed independently of each other. However, the complexity of urban traffic systems and the presence of a large number of conflicting goals and objectives postulated by various groups emphasizes the need for a hybrid MSS approach in this field. Thanks to this approach, the integration of different methods and techniques (e.g., DSS, management science, and artificial intelligence) and the effective support of public decision making could be obtained. Moreover, the approach and the scenario considered must also take into account the needs arising from the introduction of new information technologies and strategies in urban transport systems, such as route guidance, integrated traffic control, and demand management.

Such a hybrid system is proposed by Bielli [1992]. His hybrid system includes resource optimization models, traffic simulation, and evaluation models.

illustrated in Chapter 20. When a problem solver uses several tools he (she) can use them in different ways. The following are some possible approaches:

- Use each tool in an independent way to solve a different aspect of the problem.
- Use several tools that are loosely integrated. As will be discussed in Chapter 20, such an approach involves mainly transfer of data from one tool to another (e.g., from an EIS to a DSS) for further processing.
- Use several tools in a tightly integrated manner. That is, the tool appears as one hybrid system to the user, where transfer of data and other activities are preprogrammed into a unified MSS.

In addition to performing different tasks in the problem-solving process, tools can be used to support each other. For example, an expert system can be used to enhance the modeling and data management of a DSS. A neural computing system or a GDSS can support the knowledge acquisition process required for building an expert system. In general, expert systems are playing an increasingly important role in supporting the other MSS technologies (making them "smarter"). It is becoming very clear that with the passage of time it will be increasingly economically feasible to build all kinds of hybrid MSS. The components of such systems will include not only MSS but also management science, statistics, and a variety of computer-based tools. These tools can be provided by different vendors. Improved capabilities of the major operating systems, and especially OS/2, Unix, Windows, and Windows NT, will help the process of quickly and accurately building MSS.

1.14 Plan of the Book

The book is composed of 22 chapters organized in six parts (see Figure 1.7).

Part 1—Fundamentals. This part includes two chapters. In Chapter 1 an introduction, definitions, and overview are provided. In Chapter 2 the process of managerial decision making and modeling is described.

Part 2—Decision Support Systems. This part include six chapters. Chapter 3 provides an overview of DSS and its major components. Chapter 4 presents the topics of data, databases, and their management. (Databases are used by other MSS technologies as well.) Chapter 5 deals with models and modeling. Here, a discussion is given about structured models as well as about modeling tools and languages for creating nonstructured models. Chapter 6 deals with the many ways people communicate with computers—the user–machine interface. Chapter 7 describes the process of building DSS both by teams and by end-users. Chapter 8 describes the creation of some special DSS such as large-scale organizational DSS and intelligent DSS.

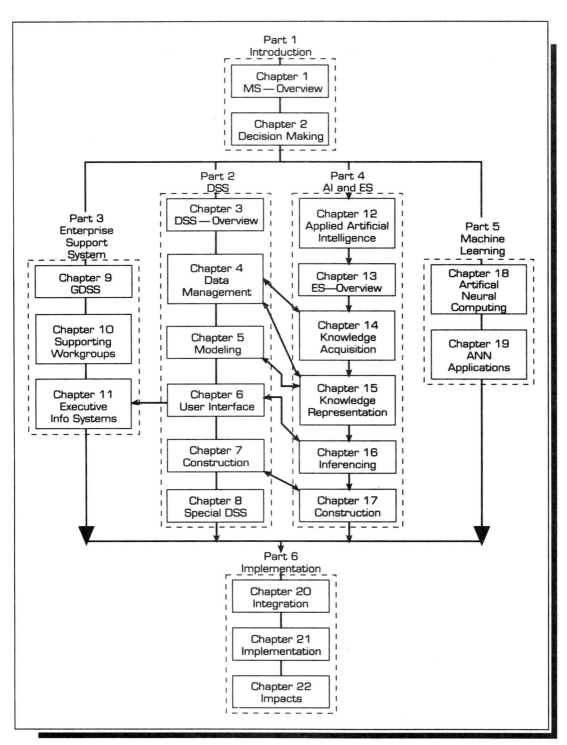

FIGURE 1.7 Plan of the Book

Part 3—Enterprise Support Systems. This part contains three chapters. Chapter 9 deals with GDSS, and especially with the support provided for face-to-face meetings in a decision room. Chapter 10 is dedicated to the support of workgroups whose members are in different locations. This part ends with a description of executive support systems, including enterprise support (Chapter 11).

Part 4—Fundamentals of Artificial Intelligence and Expert Systems. The fundamentals of artificial intelligence are the subjects of Chapter 12, while the overview of AI's most-used technology, expert systems, is provided in Chapter 13. Methods of knowledge acquisition are described in Chapter 14, while representation schemes are the subject of Chapter 15. Inference techniques are presented in Chapter 16. The process of building expert systems is described in Chapter 17.

Part 5—Cutting Edge Decision Support Technologies. The essentials of machine learning and the foundations of neural computing are the subject of Chapter 18, while the applications of neural computing and the essentials of genetic algorithms and fuzzy logic are described in Chapter 19.

Part 6—Integration and Implementation. This concluding part is divided into three chapters. The integration of MSS is described in Chapter 20, while its implementation is the subject of Chapter 21. Finally, the organizational and societal impacts are described in Chapter 22.

Chapter Highlights

- The rate of computerization is increasing rapidly and so is its use by managers.
- Management support systems is a family of technologies that can be used independently or in combination.
- Computerized support for managers is essential, in many cases, for the survival of organizations.
- Managerial decision making is getting complex. Therefore intuition and trial-and-error methods may not be sufficient.
- A framework of decision support divides decision situations into nine categories, depending on the degree of structuredness and managerial activities. Each category is supported differently by computers.
- Structured decisions are supported by standard quantitative analysis methods such as management science and capital budgeting.
- Decision support systems (DSS) is an analytical technology that employs models for the solution of semistructured and unstructured problems.
- Group DSS is a technology that supports the process of making decisions in a group.

- Executive information systems is a technology for supporting executives by providing them with timely, detailed, and easy-to-visualize information.
- Expert systems are advisory systems that attempt to mimic experts.
- The main features of expert systems are the application of knowledge and the use of reasoning.
- Neural computing is a technology that attempts to exhibit learning and pattern recognition.
- All MSS technologies are interactive.
- Most benefits of MSS are intangible.
- MSS technologies can be integrated among themselves and with other CBIS.
- MSS technologies can be deployed in one location or they can distributed throughout the enterprise.

Key Words

artificial intelligence (AI)
artificial neural
    networks (ANN)
decision support
    systems (DSS)
executive information
    systems (EIS)
expertise
expert systems (ES)
integrated computer
    systems

group support
    systems (GSS)
group DSS (GDSS)
management
    information systems
    (MIS)
management science
    (MS)
management support
    systems (MSS)

operations research
    (OR)
semistructured
    decisions
structured decisions
unstructured decisions

Questions for Review

1. What caused the latest revolution in management use of computers? List at least two causes.
2. What is a computer-based information system (CBIS)?
3. List the three phases of the decision-making process (according to H.A. Simon).
4. Define DSS.
5. Discuss the major characteristics of DSS.
6. List five major benefits of DSS.
7. Management is often equated with decision making. Why?
8. Discuss the major trends that impact managerial decision making.
9. Define management science.
10. Define MIS and relate it to the decision-making process.
11. Relate MIS and DSS to the degree of structuredness of managerial decisions.
12. Define structured, semistructured, and unstructured decisions.
13. Categorize managerial activities (according to Anthony).

14. Define expert systems.
15. Define expertise.
16. List the major benefits of ES.
17. Trace the evolution of CBIS.
18. Discuss the major differences between MIS and DSS.
19. Discuss the major differences between DSS and ES.
20. Describe the objectives and characteristics of EIS.
21. Define GSS and GDSS.
22. Define EIS and its major purpose.
23. Define neural computing.
24. Describe a distribution MSS.

Questions for Discussion

1. Give additional examples for each cell in Figure 1.2.
2. Design a computerized system for a brokerage house that trades in securities, conducts research on companies, and provides information and advice to customers (e.g., "buy," "sell," "hold"). In your design, clearly distinguish six parts: transaction processing, MIS, office automation, DSS, ANN, and ES. Be sure to deal with input and output information.
   For extra credit: List the hardware and the software that you recommend. List all your assumptions.
   Note: Assume that the brokerage company is a small one with only 20 branches in four different cities.
3. Survey the literature of the last six months to find one application each of the MSS technologies. Summarize the applications on one page and submit it with a photocopy of the article.
4. Observe an organization that you are familiar with. List five decisions it makes in each of the following categories: strategic planning, management control (tactical planning), and operational planning and control.
5. What capabilities are provided by ANN and not by another MSS?
6. Why are distributed MSS receiving such attention?
7. Why is hybrid MSS useful now and why was it not useful in the late 1980s and early 1990s?

Case Application 1: Manufacturing and Marketing of Machine Devices

Part A: The 1993 Crisis

Durapart is a medium-size manufacturer of specialized mattel devices in Southern California. The company has had an excellent reputation for its quality and customer service. The company formerly made about 30 different products and sold them to several hundred clients, mainly in the food processing industry. The company was successful in competing against several Japanese competitors.

However, the situation changed drastically in the early 1990s. While demand weakened due to the slow economy, customers' requirements for low prices and for customized products increased. Durapart found itself changing and modifying products constantly. In 1992 the number of products grew to 58, and in 1993 to 119. In both years the company reported losses. Futhermore, the Japanese decreased their prices and Durapart lost market share.

The company's problems were created because of two major factors: First, it was difficult to forecast demand due to the frequent introduction of new and modified products. Second, it was difficult to schedule production and change it quickly enough to meet changing market requirements. Attempts to increase productivity and to reduce costs failed.

In an emergency meeting conducted on July 1, 1993, the company decided, as a last resort, to try some MSS. As Jim West, the CEO, put it: "After all, these neural machines and gigabytes should certainly help us to survive."

Nancy Chen, the MIS Director, was less optimistic. She explained that there are different MSS from many vendors, and the technologies are fairly new. She said that it would take several months before a plan could be completed and it would take an additional year to implement it.

Case Questions

1. Which MSS technique is most likely to be selected by Ms. Chen, and why? (If several techniques can be used, rank them by a descending order of likelihood.)
2. Should MSS tool(s) be used in this case at all?

Part B

John Morgan was known as the best production manager in the industry. Mr. Morgan, age 65, retired at the end of 1993 and moved to Long Beach, CA, to enjoy sailing and golf. He had over 40 years of experience working for three companies, including Durapart. He plays golf with Jim West on a regular basis. When Jim told him about the company's problem he came up with the following suggestion: "Listen, Jim, between you and me, you are heading for bankruptcy. What if you hire me on a part-time basis, to help you solve the problem?"

Mr. Morgan started his mission in early 1994. In a few months he was able to change the situation drastically. Not only was he able to predict market demand better than anyone else, he also was able to flexibly schedule production.

At that time he requested an advance of several hundred thousand dollars against his salary for the next five years.

An emergency management meeting was called again.

MR. WEST: I think that we should give John the money and stop messing around with the idea of computers. John promised me that, within several years, he can train two or three of our employees so they can take over his job when he is ready for full retirement.

MS. CHEN: What if he drops dead?

MR. WEST: We will insure him so we will get back the money advanced.

MS. CHEN: I am not worried about the advance, I am worried about the fate of the company in the event that Mr. Morgan dies before his replacements are trained. I feel that we must evaluate the MSS technologies. We will be too dependent on one person who may not be around for a long time.

Case Questions

Examine the following three alternatives:

1. Hire Mr. Morgan; forget MSS.
2. Accelerate the evaluation of MSS technologies; forget Mr. Morgan.
3. Combine alternatives (1) and (2). Be specific.

References and Bibliography

Andriole, S. J. (1989). *Handbook of Decision Support Systems.* Summit, PA: TAB Professional Books.

Anthony, R. N. (1965). *Planning and Control Systems: A Framework for Analysis.* Cambridge, MA: Harvard University Graduate School of Business.

Bielli, M. (1992). "A DSS Approach to Urban Traffic Management." *European Journal of Operational Research,* Vol. 61, pp. 106–113.

Carlson C. (1993). *Decision Support Systems: Myth or Reality?* Oxford: Pergamon Press.

Chung, C. (1988). "A Network of Management Support Systems." *Omega,* Vol. 13, No. 4.

Coll, R., et al. (1991, February). "The Effect of Computerized Decision Aids on Decision Time and Decision Quality." *Information and Management.*

David, S., and B. Davidson. (1991). *2020 Vision.* New York: Simon & Schuster.

Dresner, H. (1993, May 5). *Business Intelligence: Competing Against Time.* Special Report, The Gartner Group, Stamford, CT.

Forgionne, G. A. (1991, Fall). "Decision Technology Systems: A Step toward Complete Decision Support." *Information Systems Management.*

Gorry, G. M., and M. S. Scott-Morton. (1971, Fall). "A Framework for Management Information Systems." *Sloan Management Review.*

Hogue, J. T., and H. J. Watson. (1983, June). "Management's Role in the Approval and Administration of Decision Support Systems." *MIS Quarterly.*

Keen, P. G. W., and M. S. Scott-Morton. (1978). *Decision Support Systems, An Organizational Perspective.* Reading, MA: Addison-Wesley.

Kroeber, D. W., and H. J. Watson. (1988). *Computer-based Information Systems: A Management Approach,* 2nd ed. New York: Macmillan.

McLean, E. R. (1982). *Decision Support Systems and Managerial Decision Making.* Working paper 1-83, Graduate School of Management, UCLA, Los Angeles.

Nagel, S. S. (ed.). (1993) *Computer-Aided Decision Analysis: Theory and Application.* Westport, CT: Quorum Books.

Olson, D. L., and J. F. Courtney. (1992). *Decision Support Models and Expert Systems.* New York: Macmillan.

Rockart, J. F., and D. W. DeLong. (1988). *Executive Support Systems.* Homewood, IL: Dow-Jones, Irwin.

Scott-Morton, M. S. (1971). *Management Decision Systems: Computer-Based Support for Decision Making.* Cambridge, MA: Division of Research, Harvard University.

Simon, H. (1977). *The New Science of Management Decision.* Englewood Cliffs, NJ: Prentice-Hall.

Turban, E., and J. Meredith. (1994). *Fundamentals of Management Science,* 6th ed. Homewood, IL: Irwin.

Turban, E. (1992). *Expert Systems and Applied Artificial Intelligence.* New York: Macmillan.

Watson, H. J., et al. (eds). (1992). *Executive Support Systems.* New York: Wiley.

Zeidenberg, M. (1990). *Neural Computing in Artificial Intelligence.* Englewood Cliffs, NJ: Prentice-Hall.

Personal Computing, April 1989.

Appendix 1-A: Computer-Based Information Systems in a Personnel Department

The purpose of this appendix is to illustrate the content of a typical CBIS in a personnel department. The classification is somewhat arbitrary since we do not have information on the content of each task. In reality these tasks can be placed in different categories or one task can be classified in two categories, since the boundaries of the categories are not precise and several real-life systems combine several of the categories.

Category	Task
Transaction Processing	Keep inventory of personnel. Prepare payroll; compute salaries and incentive plans.
Management Information System	Prepare summary reports (e.g., average salaries in each department). Conduct performance tracking of employees, labor budget. Do preparation, monitoring, and analysis. Perform

Category	Task
	short-term scheduling. Match positions and candidates. Monitor positions control systems. Do fringe benefits monitoring and control.
Decision Support Systems	Prepare special reports (e.g., safety records, equal opportunity achievements). Do long-range planning for human resources. Design a compensation plan. Provide quantitative support of labor-management negotiation.
Expert Systems	Obtain advice on legal and tax implications during management-labor negotiations. Develop a social responsibility plan. Select training media. Design comprehensive training programs. Help in selecting new employees.
Office Automation	Do online job interviews and recruiting, schedule meetings, maintain mailing lists, schedule training, use for electronic mail, receive labor news and statistics online, prepare training materials.
Executive Information System	Exists at the corporate level only. Will measure key performance indicators of the department (such as dollar per employee).
Group DSS	Can be used for supporting the process of making controversial major decisions (e.g., personnel policies).
Neural Computing	Screen applicants for jobs. Analyze reasons why people leave the company (find patterns).

Chapter 14

Decision Making, Systems, Modeling, and Support

The major focus of this book is computerized support of decision making. The purpose of this chapter is to provide the necessary conceptual foundations regarding decision making and systems approach, and how support is provided. This chapter covers the following topics:

2.1 Decision Making*

Decision making is a process of choosing among alternative courses of action for the purpose of attaining a goal or goals. According to Herbert A. Simon [1977], managerial decision making is synonymous with the whole process of management. To illustrate the idea, let us examine the important managerial function of planning. Planning involves a series of decisions, for example, What should be done? When? How? Where? By whom? Hence, planning implies decision making. Other functions in the management process, like organizing and controlling, also involve making decisions.

Decision Making and Problem Solving

Much confusion exists between the terms *decision making* and *problem solving*. One way to distinguish between them is to examine the phases of the decision process. These phases are (1) intelligence, (2) design, (3) choice, and (4) implementation. One school of thought considers the entire process (steps 1–4) as problem solving; the choice step is considered decision making. Another viewpoint is that steps 1–3 constitute decision making that ends with a recommendation—whereas problem solving additionally includes implementation of the recommendation (step 4). The terms decision making and problem solving are used here interchangeably. Problem solving refers not only to the solution of trouble areas but also to the investigation of *opportunities*.

2.2 Systems

The names DSS, GDSS, EIS, and ES include the term *systems*. A **system** is a collection of objects such as people, resources, concepts, and procedures intended to perform an identifiable function or to serve a goal. A clear definition of that function is most important for the design of MSS. For instance, the purpose of an air defense system is to protect ground targets, not just to destroy attacking aircraft or missiles.

The notion of levels (or a hierarchy) of systems reflects that all systems are actually subsystems, since all are contained within some larger system. For example, a bank includes such subsystems as (1) the commercial loan department, (2) the consumer loan department, (3) the savings department, and (4) the operations department. The bank itself may also be a subsidiary of a holding corporation, such as Bank of America, which is a subsystem of the California banking system, which is a part of the national banking system, which is a part of the national economy, and so on. The interconnections and interactions among the subsystems are termed *interfaces*.

---

*Some of the material in this chapter was adapted, with permission, from Turban and Meredith [1994].

The Structure of a System

Systems are divided into three distinct parts: inputs, processes, and outputs. They are surrounded by an environment (Figure 2.1) and frequently include a feedback mechanism. In addition, a human, the decision maker, is considered a part of the system.

Inputs. Inputs. include those elements that enter the system. Examples of inputs are raw materials entering a chemical plant, patients admitted to a hospital, or data input into a computer.

Processes. All the elements necessary to convert or transform the inputs into outputs are included in the processes. For example, in a chemical plant a process may include heating the materials, using operating procedures, employing the materials handling subsystem, and using employees and machines. In a hospital the process may include conducting tests and performing a surgery. In a computer a process may include activating commands, executing computations, and storing information.

Outputs. Outputs describe the finished products or the consequences of being in the system. For example, fertilizers are one output of a chemical plant, cured people are an output of a hospital, and reports may be the output of a computerized system.

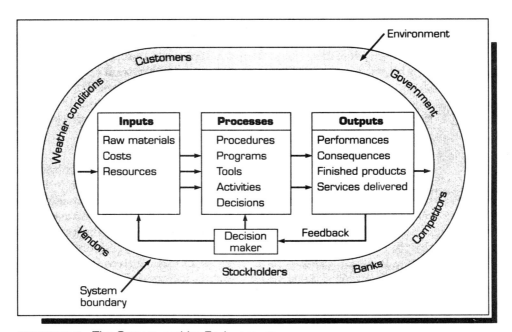

FIGURE 2.1 The System and Its Environment.

Feedback. There is a flow of information from the output component to the decision maker concerning the system's output or performance. Based on this information the decision maker, who acts as a control, may decide to modify the inputs or the processes, or both. This flow, which appears as a closed loop (Figure 2.1), is termed *feedback.*

The Environment. The environment of the system is composed of several elements that lie outside it in the sense that they are not inputs, outputs, or processes. However, they have an impact on the system's performance and consequently on the attainment of its goals. One way to identify the elements of the environment is by answering two questions as suggested by Churchman [1975].

1. Is the element matter relative to the system's goals?
2. Is it possible for the decision maker to significantly manipulate this element?

If and only if the answer to the first question is *yes,* but the answer to the second is *no,* the element should be considered part of the environment. Environmental elements can be social, political, legal, physical, and economical. For example, in the case of a chemical plant the suppliers, competitors, and customers are elements of the environment. In a decision support system that deals with capital budgeting, the Dow-Jones database, the distribution system of the company, a telecommunications network, and the personnel department may represent some elements of the environment.

The Boundary. A system is separated from its environment by a boundary. The system is inside the boundary, whereas the environment lies outside. Boundaries may be physical (e.g., the system is a department in Building C), or the boundary may be some nonphysical factor. For example, a system can be bounded by time. In such a case we may analyze an organization for a period of only one year.

When systems are studied it is often necessary to arbitrarily define the boundaries in order to simplify the analysis. Such boundaries are related to the concepts of closed and open systems.

Closed and Open Systems. Because every system can be considered a subsystem of another, the application of system analysis may never end. Therefore it is necessary, as a matter of practicality, to confine the system analysis to defined manageable boundaries. Such confinement is termed *closing* the system.

A *closed system* represents one extreme along a continuum (the *open system* is at the other extreme), which reflects the degree of independence of systems. A closed system is totally independent, whereas an open system is very dependent on its environment. The open system accepts inputs (information, energy, materials) from the environment and may deliver outputs into the environment.

When determining the impact of decisions on an open system, we must check the relationship with the environment and with related systems. In a closed system, however, it is not necessary to conduct such checks because it is assumed that the system is isolated. Traditional computer systems like transaction processing systems (TPS) are considered to be closed systems. Many management science models are also confined to closed systems.

A special type of closed system is called the *black box*. In such a system inputs and outputs are well defined but the process itself is not specified. Many managers like to treat computer systems as a black box; in other words, they do not care how the computer works. They consider it as they would consider a telephone or an elevator. They use these devices but do not care how they operate.

Decision support systems attempt to deal with systems that are fairly open. Such systems are complex, and during their analysis it is necessary to check the impacts on and from the environment. To illustrate the difference between a DSS and a management science approach, let us look at an inventory system (Table 2.1), which compares a well-known inventory model, the economic order quantity (EOQ) model, with a hypothetical DSS for an inventory system.

System Effectiveness and Efficiency

Systems are evaluated and analyzed with two major classes of performance measurement: effectiveness and efficiency.

Effectiveness is the degree to which goals are achieved. It is therefore concerned with the results or the outputs of a system. These outputs may be total sales of a company or of a salesperson, for example.

Efficiency is a measure of the use of inputs (or resources) to achieve results; for example, how much money is used to generate a certain level of sales.

An interesting way to distinguish between the two terms was proposed by Peter Drucker, who makes the following distinction:

Effectiveness = doing the "right" thing
  Efficiency = doing the "thing" right

An important characteristic of DSS and ES is their emphasis on the effectiveness, or "goodness," of the decision produced, rather than on the computa-

TABLE 2.1 A Closed Versus an Open Inventory System

Management Science, EOQ (Closed System)	DSS (Open System)
Constant demand, constant per-unit cost, constant lead time.	Variable demand influenced by many factors; cost can be changed any day; lead time varies and is difficult to predict.
Vendors and users are excluded from the analysis.	Vendors and users are being considered.
Weather and other environmental factors are ignored.	Weather conditions could determine both demand and lead time.

tional efficiency, which is usually a major concern of a transaction processing system.

In many managerial systems, and especially those involving the delivery of human services (such as education, health, or recreation), the measurement of the system's effectiveness and efficiency is a major problem. The reason for the difficulty is due to the existence of several, often nonquantifiable, conflicting goals. In addition, indirect costs may be involved. For further discussion and references, see Van Gigch [1978].

2.3 Models

A major characteristic of decision support systems is the inclusion of a modeling capability. The basic idea is to execute the DSS analysis on a model of reality rather than on reality itself.

A *model* is a simplified representation or abstraction of reality. It is usually *simplified* because reality is too complex to copy exactly and because much of the complexity is actually *irrelevant* to the specific problem. The characteristics of simplification and representation are difficult to achieve simultaneously in practice (they *contradict* each other). For example, the EOQ model of Table 2.1 is simple but inadequately representative of many real-life inventory systems.

The representation of systems or problems through models can be done at various degrees of abstraction; therefore models are classified, according to their degree of abstraction, into three groups.

Iconic (Scale) Models. An **iconic model**—the least abstract model—is a physical replica of a system, usually based on a different scale from the original. Iconic models may appear to scale in three dimensions, such as that of an airplane, car, bridge, or production line. Photographs are another type of iconic scale model but in only two dimensions. Graphical user interface (Chapter 6) and object-oriented programming (Chapter 15) are other examples of the use of icons.

Analog Models. An **analog model** does not look like the real system but behaves like it. It is more abstract than an iconic model and is considered a symbolic representation of reality. These are usually two-dimensional charts or diagrams: that is, they could be physical models, but the shape of the model differs from that of the actual system. Some examples:

- Organization charts that depict structure, authority, and responsibility relationships
- A map where different colors represent objects such as bodies of water or mountains
- Stock market charts
- Blueprints of a machine or a house

- A speedometer
- A thermometer.

A special class of analog modeling is symbolic logic. This topic is revisited in Chapter 12.

Mathematical (Quantitative) Models. The complexity of relationships in many organizational systems cannot be represented with icons or analogically, or such representation may be cumbersome and time-consuming. Therefore a more abstract model is used with the aid of mathematics. Most DSS analysis is executed numerically with the aid of mathematical or other quantitative models.

The Benefits of Models

The following are the major reasons why an MSS employs models:

1. The cost of the modeling analysis is much lower than the cost of a similar experimentation conducted with a real system.
2. Models enable the compression of time. Years of operations can be simulated in minutes of computer time.
3. Manipulation of the model (changing variables) is much easier than manipulating a real system. Experimentation is therefore easier to conduct and it does not interfere with the daily operation of the organization.
4. The cost of making mistakes during a trial-and-error experiment is much less when models are used rather than real systems.
5. Today's environment involves considerable uncertainty. The use of modeling allows a manager to calculate the risks involved in specific actions.
6. The use of mathematical models enables the analysis of a very large, sometimes infinite number of possible solutions. With today's advanced technology and communications, managers frequently have a large number of alternatives to choose from.
7. Models enhance and reinforce learning and enhance training.

Note: With recent advances in computer graphics, there is an increased tendency to use iconic and analog models to complement mathematical modeling in MSS. For example, visual simulation (see Chapter 6) combines the three types of models.

2.4 The Modeling Process—A Preview

Ma-Pa Groceries is a small neighborhood food store on the West Side of New York City. Bob and Nancy, the owners, are very sensitive to their clients' wishes. They also are concerned with the financial viability of the store. A major product they sell is bread. Bread causes them headaches. Some days there is not enough bread;

other days bread is overstocked so they have to sell it the next day at a loss. Their problem is: How much bread to stock each day?

Bob and Nancy can apply several solution approaches to the problem. Four such approaches are: trial-and-error, simulation, optimization, and heuristics.

a. Trial and Error with the Real Systems. In this approach the owners try to learn from experimentation. Namely, they change the quantities of bread stocked and observe what happens. If they find they are short on bread too often, they will increase the quantities ordered. If they find that too much bread is left, they will decrease the quantities ordered. Sooner or later they will find out how much bread to order.

Although this approach may be very successful for Bob and Nancy, it may fail in many other cases. Trial-and-error may not work if one or more of the following conditions exists:

1. There are too many alternatives ("trials") to experiment with.
2. The cost of making errors (which is part of the trial-and-error approach) is very high.
3. The environment itself keeps changing. Therefore learning from experience is difficult or even impossible. By the time you have experimented with all the alternatives, the environmental conditions have changed—you have a new "ball game" to deal with.

In such cases Nancy and Bob can try modeling approaches; instead of dealing with the real system, they will deal with a model of it. Three common types of modeling approaches they can use are simulation, optimization, and heuristics.

b. Simulation. In this case Nancy and Bob play a make-believe game. They ask themselves a question: *If* we order 300 loaves of bread, *what* will the results be? The results of course will depend on the demand, which may be constant or may vary. Simulation can deal with both situations. The model that represents Ma-Pa Groceries is used to calculate results like total profit (or loss), percentage of unsatisfied customers, and amount of leftovers. A big advantage of modeling is that months of operations can be simulated in seconds (if a computer is used). Next, Nancy and Bob change the order quantity to 350, 400, 200, 250, and so on. They "run the store" on a computer with each order quantity for several months and calculate the results. Finally, they compare the results of each order quantity and decide how much to order.

The problem with the simulation approach is that once the experiment is completed, there is no guarantee that the selected order level is the best one. It will be the best of all levels experimented; but it is possible that the true best level (the optimal one) is 675, a level not checked in the experiment. Another problem with the simulation is that Nancy and Bob will need professional help to design the simulation study, to program it on a computer, and to statistically interpret the results. The cost may not be justified. However, if Nancy and Bob learned DSS they could probably do the job by themselves.

c. Optimization. A more sophisticated solution approach to the problem is to use an optimization model. Ideally such a model will generate in seconds an optimal (best) order level, say, 675. For structured situations there is a very user-friendly software to conduct such an analysis. The limitation of optimization is that it will work only if the problem is structured. Specifically, such a model will specify the required input data, the desired output, and the mathematical relationship in a precise manner. Obviously, if reality differs significantly from the model, optimization cannot be used.

As stated earlier, DSS deals with unstructured problems. Does this preclude optimization? Not necessarily. Many times it is possible to break a problem into subproblems, some of which are structured enough to justify optimization. Also, optimization can be combined with simulation for the solution of complex problems.

d. Heuristics. Nancy and Bob can use some rules of thumb. For example, they can order today the average daily quantity demanded over the last seven days. Another rule that they can use is to order each day the quantity demanded on the same day one week before.

The Decision-Making Process. To better understand modeling, it is advisable to follow the decision-making process, which, according to Simon [1977], involves three major phases: intelligence, design, and choice. A fourth phase, implementation, was added later. A conceptual picture of the decision-making process is shown in Figure 2.2. There is a continuous flow of activities from intelligence to design to choice (bold lines), but at any phase there may be a return to a previous phase. Modeling is an essential part of this process.

The decision-making process starts with the intelligence phase, where reality is examined and the problem is identified and defined. In the design phase a model that represents the system is constructed. This is done by *making assumptions* that simplify reality and by writing the relationships among all variables. The model then is validated and criteria are set for the evaluation of the alternative courses of action that are identified. The choice phase includes a proposed solution of the model (not of the problem that it represents). This solution is tested "on paper" (that is, in the modeling framework). Once the proposed solution seems to be reasonable, it is ready for the last phase—implementation. Successful implementation results in solving the original problem. Failure leads to a return to the modeling process. Detailed discussion of the process is given in the following sections.

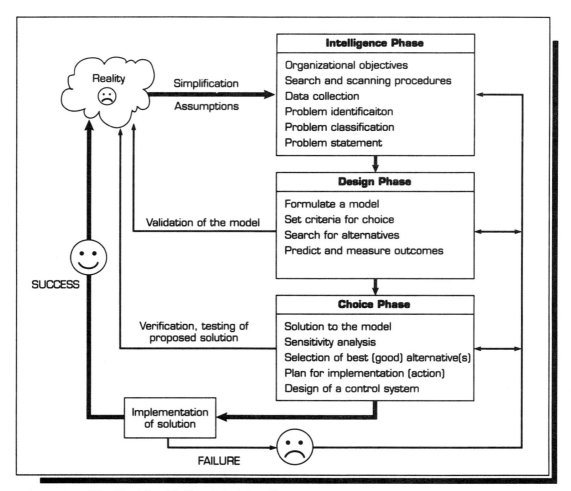

FIGURE 2.2 The Decision-Making/Modeling Process.

2.5 The Intelligence Phase

Intelligence entails scanning the environment, either intermittently or continuously. It includes several activities aimed at identifying problem situations or opportunities.

Finding the Problem. The intelligence phase begins with the identification of organizational goals and objectives. Problems arise out of dissatisfaction with the way things are going. Such dissatisfaction is the result of a difference between what we desire and what is (or is not) happening. In this phase, one attempts to find out if a problem exists, identify the symptoms of the problem, find its magnitude, and define the problem. Often what is described as a problem (e.g., excessive costs) may be only a symptom of a problem (e.g., improper inventory levels). Because so-called real-world problems are usually complicated by many interrelated factors, it is sometimes difficult to distinguish between the symptoms and the real problem.

The existence of a problem in an organization can be appraised by monitoring and analyzing the organization's (or department's) productivity level. The measurement of productivity, as well as the construction of the model, are based on data. The collection of existing data and the estimation of future data is one of the most difficult steps in the analysis. Following are some of the issues that may arise during data collection and estimation:

1. Outcome (or results) may occur over an extended period of time. As a result, revenues, expenses, and profits will be recorded at different points in time. To overcome this difficulty, a present-value approach should be used, if the results are qualifiable.
2. It is often necessary to use a subjective approach to data estimation.
3. It is assumed that future data will be similar to historical data. If not, it is necessary to predict the nature of the change and include it in the analysis.

Once the preliminary investigation is completed it is possible to determine whether a problem really exists, where it is located, and how significant it is (i.e., what is the priority of the problem). In addition, the intelligence phase may involve other activities such as problem classification, problem decomposition, and determination of problem ownership.

Problem Classification. This activity is the conceptualization of a problem in an attempt to classify it into a definable category. An important classification is according to the degree of structuredness evident in the problem.

Programmed versus Nonprogrammed Problems. Herbert A. Simon [1977] has distinguished two extreme situations regarding structuredness of decision problems. At one end of the spectrum are the well-structured problems that are repetitive and routine, and for which standard models have been worked out. Simon termed these *programmed problems.* Examples of such problems are weekly scheduling of employees, monthly determination of cash flow, and selection of an inventory level for a specific item. At the other end of the spectrum are the poorly structured (called *nonprogrammed* by Simon) *problems,* which are novel and nonrecurrent. For example, acquisition and merger decisions, undertaking a complex research and development project, reengineering a corporation, and opening a university are all nonstructured problems.

Problem Decomposition. Many complex problems can be broken apart into subproblems. Solving the simpler subproblems may help in solving the complex problem. Such an approach also facilitates communication between the people involved in the solution process.

Problem Ownership. In the intelligence phase, it is important to establish the "ownership" of the problem. A problem exists in an organization only if the organization has the capability to solve it. For example, many companies feel that they have a problem because interest rates are too high. Since interest rate levels are determined at the national level and most companies can do nothing about them, high interest rates are the problem of the federal government and not of a specific company. The problem that companies face is how to operate in an environment in which the interest rate is high. For the individual company the interest rate level is an uncontrollable factor.

The intelligence phase ends with a problem statement. At that time the design phase can be started.

2.6 The Design Phase

The design phase involves generating, developing, and analyzing possible courses of action. This includes activities such as understanding the problem and testing solutions for feasibility. Also in this phase, a model of the problem situation is constructed, tested, and validated.

Modeling involves the conceptualization of the problem and its abstraction to a quantitative and/or qualitative form. In case of a mathematical model, the dependent and independent variables are identified and the equations describing their relationships are established. Simplifications are made, whenever necessary, through a set of assumptions. For example, a relationship between two variables may be assumed to be linear. It is necessary to find a proper balance between the level of simplification of the model and the representation of reality. A simpler model leads to easier manipulations and faster solution, but is also less representative of the real problem.

The task of modeling involves a combination of art and science. The following topics of modeling are presented here as they relate to quantitative models (mathematical, financial, etc.):

- The components of the model
- The structure of the model
- Selection of a principle of choice (criteria for evaluation)
- Developing (generating) alternatives
- Predicting outcomes
- Measuring outcomes
- Scenarios.

The Components of Quantitative Models

All models are comprised of three basic components (see Figure 2.3): decision variables, uncontrollable variables (and/or parameters), and result (outcome) vari-

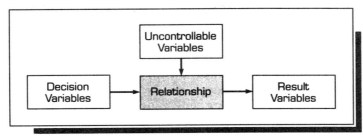

FIGURE 2.3 The General Structure of a Model.

ables. These components are connected by mathematical relationships. In a non-quantitative model the relationships are symbolic or qualitative.

As can be seen in Figure 2.3, the results of decisions are determined by (1) the decision made; (2) other factors that are uncontrollable by the decision maker; and (3) by the relationships among variables.

Result Variables. These variables reflect the level of effectiveness of the system; that is, they indicate how well the system performs or attains its goals. Examples of result variables are shown in Table 2.2. The result variables are considered to be dependent variables. *Note:* A dependent variable means that for the event described by this variable to occur, another event must occur first. In this case the re-

TABLE 2.2 Examples of the Components of Models.

Area	Decision Variables	Result Variables	Uncontrollable Variables and Parameters
Financial investment	Investment alternatives and amounts Period of investment Timing of investment	Total profit Rate of return Earnings per share Liquidity level	Inflation rate Prime rate Competition
Marketing	Advertising budget Product mix	Market share Customer satisfaction	Customers' income Competitors' actions
Manufacturing	Products and amounts Inventory levels Compensation programs	Total cost Quality level Employee satisfaction	Machine capacity Technology Materials prices
Accounting	Use of computers Audit schedule Depreciation schedule	Data processing cost Error rate	Computer technology Tax rates Legal requirements
Transportation	Shipments schedule	Total transport cost	Delivery distance Regulations
Services	Staffing levels	Customer satisfaction	Demand for services

sult variables depend on the occurrence of the decision and the uncontrollable variables.

Decision Variables. Decision variables describe the alternative courses of action. For example, in an investment problem, investing in bonds is a decision variable. In a scheduling problem, the decision variables are people and jobs. The values of these variables are determined by the decision maker. Other examples include the number of tellers to use in a bank (more are listed in Table 2.2). Decision variables are classified mathematically as independent variables (or unknown variables).

Uncontrollable Variables or Parameters. In any decision situation there are factors that affect the result variables but *are not under the control* of the decision maker. These factors can be either fixed, and then they are called parameters, or they can vary, and then they are called variables. Examples are the prime interest rate, a city's building code, tax regulations, and prices of utilities (others are shown in Table 2.2). Most of these factors are uncontrollable because they emanate from the environment surrounding the decision maker. These variables are also classified as **independent variables** since they affect the dependent (result) variables. Some of these variables place limits on the decision maker, and, therefore, are called the *constraints* of the problem.

Intermediate Variables. Intermediate variables are any variables necessary to link the decision variables to the results. Sometimes they reflect intermediate outcomes. For example, in determining machine scheduling, spoilage is an intermediate variable while total profit is the result variable (spoilage is one of the determinants of total profit).

Another example is employee salaries or wages, which is a decision variable. It determines employees' satisfaction (intermediate outcome), which determines productivity level (result).

The Structure of Quantitative Models

The components of a quantitative model are tied together by sets of mathematical expressions such as equations or inequalities.

A simple financial-type model may look like this: $P = R - C$, where P stands for profit, R stands for revenue, and C stands for cost. Another well-known financial-type model is a present-value model, which may look like this:

$$P = \frac{F}{(1 + i)^n}$$

where:

P = the present value
F = a future single payment in dollars
i = interest rate
n = number of years

Using this model, one can find, for example, the present value of a payment of $100,000, to be made five years from today, considering 10 percent interest rate, to be:

$$P = \frac{100,000}{(1.1)^5} = \$62,110$$

A more complex product-mix model is presented next. This model is a management science optimization model that helps determine the best production plan.

Example: The Product-Mix Model

MBI Corporation makes special computers. A decision must be made: How many computers should be produced next month in the Boston plant? Two types of computers are considered: PC-7, which requires 300 days of labor and $10,000 in materials; and PC-8, which requires 500 days of labor and $15,000 in materials. The profit contribution of PC-7 is $8,000, whereas that of PC-8 is $12,000. Currently, the plant has a capacity of 200,000 working days per month while the material budget is $8,000,000 per month. Marketing requires that at least 100 units of PC-7 be produced. The problem is how many units of PC-7 and how many units of PC-8 to produce each month to maximize the company's profits.

Modeling. A standard mathematical model called **linear programming** is used in this case (see Box 2.1). It has three components:

Decision variables: X_1 = units of PC-7 to be produced; X_2 = units of PC-8.
Result variable: The total profit.

Box 2.1: Linear Programming

Linear programming is perhaps the best known optimization model. It deals with optimal allocation of resources among competing activities. The allocation problem is presented in the model as follows:

The problem is to find the value of the decision variables X_1, X_2, and so on such that the value of the result variable Z is maximized, subject to a set of linear constraints that express the technology, market conditions, and other uncontrollable variables. The mathematical relationships are all linear equations and inequalities. Theoretically, there are an infinite number of possible solutions to any allocation problem of this type. Using special mathematical procedures, the linear programming approach applies a unique search procedure that finds the best solution(s) in a matter of seconds. Furthermore, the solution approach provides automatic sensitivity analysis (see Section 2.8).

The objective is to maximize total profit.

Z = Total profit: $8,000 X_1 + 12,000 X_2$

Uncontrollable variables (constraints):

    Labor constraint: $300 X_1 + 500 X_2 \leq 200,000$ (in days)

    Budget constraint: $10,000 X_1 + 15,000 X_2 \leq 8,000,000$ (in dollars)

    Marketing requirement: $X_1 \geq 100$ (in units)

    This information is summarized in Figure 2.4.

    Solution. The solution to this problem (derived by a computer) is $X_1 = 666,667$, $X_2 = 0$, Profit = $\$5,333,333$.

    The model of the product mix just presented has an infinite number of possible solutions. Assuming that a production plan is not restricted to whole numbers—which is a reasonable assumption in a monthly production plan—we are searching for a solution that maximizes total profit. Determining which model to use (linear programming in this case) relates to the discussion of the principle of choice.

Rational Decision Makers versus Satisfiers. In order to understand the search methods used in making a choice, it is helpful to review the major approaches to choice. Generally speaking, we distinguish between a *rational decision maker* and *satisfier*. It is assumed that a rational decision maker knows exactly what the goal of making a decision is and how its attainment is going to be measured. It is also assumed that this decision maker knows all the alternatives and their precise relationships to various goal attainment levels. Finally, it is assumed that the decision maker will always prefer an alternative with a high level of goal attainment over an alternative with a lower level of goal attainment. In other words, an attempt will be made to maximize the attainment level. Most management science models are structured on the assumption of rationality. However, in real life, people usually make decisions that are based on an attempt to attain only a *satisfactory* level of goal attainment.

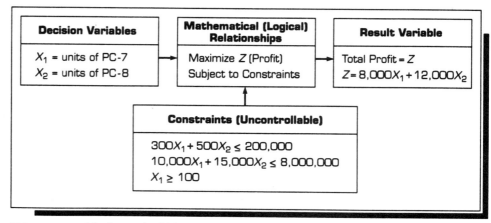

FIGURE 2.4 Mathematical Model of a Product Mix.

The concept of a satisfactory solution rather than a best one was introduced by Simon [1977], who coined the term *satisficing* to describe the typical choices made by decision makers. Simon argued that it is basically impossible to make decisions in a completely rational manner since human rationality is basically *bounded* by its inability to obtain all the information needed to make rational decisions, due to economic, technological, political, or time pressures or other factors. The rational approach to problem solving is important, since even if it is impossible to implement the solution it recommends, it provides a yardstick or a benchmark against which satisfactory solutions can be compared. If the difference is small, then the practical, good enough solution should be adopted; otherwise a search should be continued.

The Principle of Choice

The evaluation of alternatives and the final choice depend on the type of criteria we want to use. Are we trying to find the best solution? Or will a "good enough" result be sufficient? This issue is discussed next.

Selection of a Principle of Choice. A principle of choice refers to a decision regarding the acceptability of a solution approach. Are we willing to assume risk or do we prefer a conservative low risk approach? Are we attempting to optimize or not? Of the various principles of choice, two are of prime interest: normative and descriptive.

Normative Models. *Normative* implies that the chosen alternative is demonstrably the best of all possible alternatives. To find it, one should examine all alternatives and *prove* that the one selected is indeed the best. This process is basically what we call optimization (see Box 2.2). In operational terms, optimization can be achieved in one of three ways:

Box 2.2: Optimization Models

- Assignment (best matching of objects)
- Dynamic programming
- Goal programming
- Investment (maximize rate of return)
- Linear programming
- Maintenance (minimize cost of maintenance)
- Network models for planning and scheduling
- Nonlinear programming
- Replacement (capital budgeting)
- Simple inventory models (e.g., economic order quantity)
- Transportation (minimize cost of shipments)

- Get the highest level of goal attainment (maximization) from a given set of resources. For example, which alternative will yield the maximum profit from an investment of $1,000,000?
- Find the alternative with the highest ratio (maximization) of goal attainment to cost (e.g., profit per dollar invested), or in other words, maximize productivity.
- Find the alternative with the lowest cost (or other resources) that will fulfill a required level of goal(s) (minimization). For example, if your task is to build a product to certain specifications, which method will accomplish this goal with the least cost?

Normative decision theory is based on the following assumptions:

- Humans are economic beings whose objective is to maximize the attainment of goals; that is, the decision maker is rational.
- In a given decision situation, all viable alternative courses of action and their consequences, or at least the probability and the values of the consequences, are known.
- Decision makers have an order or preference that enables them to rank the desirability of all consequences of the analysis.

Suboptimization. By definition, optimization requires the decision maker to consider the impact of each alternative course of action on the entire organization. The reason for this is that a decision made in one area may have significant effects (positive or negative) in other areas. Take as an example a production department that plans its own schedule. For that department it would be beneficial to produce only a few products but in large quantities to reduce manufacturing costs. However, such a plan may result in large, costly inventories and marketing difficulties owing to the lack of a variety of products.

Using a systems point of view affords consideration of the impact on the entire system. Thus the production department should make its plans in conjunction with other departments. Such an approach, however, may require a complicated, expensive, and time-consuming analysis. As a matter of practice the MSS builder may "close" the system within narrow boundaries, considering only part of the organization under study (the production department in this case). Such an approach is called *suboptimization.*

If a suboptimization decision is made in one part of the organization without consideration of the rest of the organization, then a solution that is optimal from the point of view of that part may be inferior from the point of view of the whole.

Suboptimization, however, may still be a very practical approach, and many problems are first approached from this perspective. The primary reason for this is that analyzing only a portion of a system allows some tentative conclusions to be made without bogging down the organization in a deluge of details. Once a solution is proposed, its potential effects on the remaining departments of the organization can be checked. If no significant negative effects are found, the solution may then be adopted. This approach fits nicely with the iterative (step-by-step) development approach to DSS.

Descriptive Models. Descriptive models (see Box 2.3) describe things as they are, or as they are believed to be. Such models are extremely useful in DSS for investigating the consequences of various alternative courses of action under different configurations of *inputs* and processes. However, because a descriptive analysis checks the performance of the system for a given set of alternatives (rather than for *all* alternatives), there is no guarantee that an alternative selected with the aid of a descriptive analysis is optimal. In many cases it is only satisfactory or "good enough." Simulation is probably the most recognized example of descriptive modeling.

Good Enough or "Satisficing." Most human decision making, according to Simon [1977], whether organizational or individual, involves a willingness to settle for a satisfactory solution, "something less than the best." In a **"satisficing"** mode the decision maker sets up an aspiration, goal, or desired level of performance and then searches the alternatives until one is found that achieves this level. The usual reasons for satisficing are lack of time or ability to achieve optimization as well as unwillingness to pay the price for the required information.

A related concept is that of *bounded rationality*. Humans have a limited capacity for rational thinking; they generally construct a simplified model of the real situation in order to deal with it. Their behavior with respect to the simplified model may be rational. However, it does not follow that the rational solution for the simplified model will be rational in the real-world situation. Rationality is bounded not only by limitations on human processing capacities but also by individual differences such as age, education, and attitudes. Bounded rationality is the cause of many models being descriptive rather than normative.

Box 2.3: Descriptive Models

- Information flow
- Scenario analysis
- Financial planning
- Inventory management (complex)
- Markov analysis (predictions)
- Environmental impact analysis
- Simulation (different types)
- Technological forecasting
- Waiting line management

Developing (Generating) Alternatives

A significant part of the process of model building is generating alternatives. In optimization models (such as linear programming) the alternatives may be generated automatically by the model. In most MSS situations, however, it is necessary to generate alternatives. This can be a lengthy process that involves search and creativity, and it takes time and costs money. Issues such as when to stop generating alternatives can be very important. Generating alternatives is heavily dependent on the availability and cost of information and requires expertise in the problem area. This is the least formal portion of problem solving. When creativity is used to generate alternatives it can be enhanced by brainstorming, group dynamics sessions, checklists, and special training.

Notice that the search for alternatives usually comes *after* the criteria for evaluating the alternatives were determined. This sequence can reduce the search for alternatives and the efforts involved in the evaluation of the alternatives. Alternatives can be generated by using heuristics. For example, real estate is a viable alternative in inflationary periods. Generating alternatives is done manually in most DSS; however, as will be shown in Chapters 8 and 9, this activity can be supported by creativity or idea generation software.

Predicting the Outcome of Each Alternative

To evaluate and compare alternatives it is necessary to predict the future outcome of each proposed alternative. Decision situations are frequently classified on the basis of what the decision maker knows (or believes) about the forecasted results. It is customary to classify this knowledge into three categories (see Figure 2.5), ranging from complete knowledge, on the left, to ignorance, on the right. Specifically, these categories are

- Certainty
- Risk
- Uncertainty

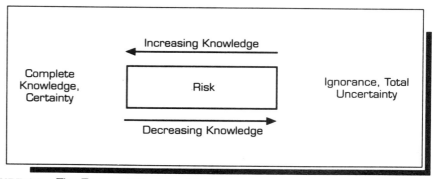

FIGURE 2.5 The Zones of Decision Making.

Decision Making Under Certainty. In decision making under certainty, it is *assumed* that complete information is available so that the decision maker knows exactly what the outcome of each course of action will be. The decision maker is viewed as a perfect predictor of the future, because it is assumed that there is only one outcome for each alternative. For example, the alternative of investing in U.S. Treasury bills is one for which it is reasonable to assume complete availability of information about the future return on the investment. Such a situation is also termed *deterministic.* It occurs most often with structured problems with short time horizons (up to one year). Some problems under certainty are not structured enough to be approached by management science; they thus require a DSS approach.

Decision Making Under Risk (Risk Analysis). A decision made under risk (also known as a probabilistic or stochastic decision situation) is one in which the decision maker must consider several possible outcomes for each alternative, each with a given probability of occurrence. In addition, it is assumed that the long-run probabilities of the occurrences of the given outcomes are known or can be estimated. Under these assumptions, the decision maker can assess the degree of risk assumed (termed *calculated* risk).

Risk analysis is usually executed by computing the expected value of each alternative and selecting the alternative with the best expected value.

Decision Making Under Uncertainty. In decision making under **uncertainty,** * the decision maker considers situations in which several outcomes are possible for each course of action. In contrast to the risk situation, the decision maker does not know, or cannot estimate, the probability of occurrence of the possible outcomes.

Decision making under uncertainty is more difficult to evaluate because of insufficient information. Modeling of such situations involves the assessment of the decision maker's (and/or the organizational) attitude toward risk (e.g., being a conservative or a risk taker).

Measuring Outcomes (Goals' Attainment Level)

The value of an alternative is judged in terms of goals' attainment. Sometimes an outcome is expressed directly in terms of a goal. For example, profit is an outcome, whereas profit maximization is a goal, and both are expressed in dollar terms. In other cases an outcome may be expressed in other terms than that of the goal.

---

*The definitions of the terms *risk* and *uncertainty,* as presented here, were suggested by Professor F. H. Knight of the University of Chicago in 1933. Several other definitions are being used by different organizations and authors.

Scenarios

A **scenario** is a statement of assumptions about the operating environment of a particular system at a given time. In other words, a scenario is a narrative description of the *setting* in which the decision situation is to be examined. A scenario describes the decision and uncontrollable variables and parameters for a specific modeling situation. It also may provide the procedures and constraints for the modeling itself.

Scenarios were originated in the field of drama. The term was then borrowed for war gaming and large-scale simulations. More recently scenarios have entered the realm of MSS. For example, a scenario may describe the set of assumptions about the behaviors, intentions, and effects of the various processes represented in a merger proposal to be evaluated by a DSS.

A scenario is especially helpful in simulation and in "what-if" analysis. In both cases we keep changing scenarios. For example, one can change the anticipated demand for hospitalization (which is an input variable for planning), thus creating a new scenario. Then one can measure the anticipated cash flow of the hospital for each scenario.

Scenarios play an important role in MSS because they:

- Help identify potential opportunities and/or problem areas
- Provide flexibility in planning
- Identify the leading edges of changes that management should monitor
- Help *validate* major assumptions used in the modeling
- Help to check the sensitivity of the proposed solutions to changes in the scenarios.

Possible Scenarios. Thousands of possible scenarios may exist for every decision situation. However, the following are of a special value:

- The "worst possible" scenario
- The "best possible" scenario
- The "most likely" scenario.

The scenario sets the context of the analysis (or the evaluation) to be performed, defines many of the inputs, and to a large degree establishes the evaluation criteria.

2.7 The Choice Phase

The boundary between the design and the choice phases is frequently unclear because certain activities may be performed both during the design and the choice phases and because one may return frequently from the choice activities to the design. For example, one may generate new alternatives while performing an evaluation of existing ones. The choice phase includes search, evaluation, and recommending an appropriate solution to the model.

A *solution* to a model is a specific set of values for the decision variables in a selected alternative.

Note: Solving the model is not the same as solving the problem that the model represents. The solution to the model yields a recommended solution to the problem. Only if this recommended solution is successfully implemented is the problem considered to be solved.

Search Approaches

The choice phase involves the search for an appropriate course of action (among those identified during the design phase) that will solve the real problem. Several major search approaches exist, depending on the criteria of choice. For normative models either an analytical approach is used or a complete, exhaustive enumeration (comparing all alternatives to one another) is applied. For descriptive models a comparison of a limited number of alternatives is used, either blindly, or by using heuristics. These search approaches are shown in Figure 2.6.

Analytical Techniques. **Analytical techniques** use mathematical formulas to directly either derive an *optimal solution* or predict a certain result. Analytical techniques are used mainly for solving structured problems, usually of a tactical or operational nature, in areas like allocation of resources or inventory management. For more complex problems that are addressed by MSS, the blind or heuristic search approaches are generally used.

Algorithms. Analytical techniques may use algorithms to increase the efficiency of the search. An **algorithm** is a step-by-step search process (see Figure 2.7) for arriving at an optimal solution. Solutions are generated and tested for possible improvements. An improvement is made whenever possible and the new solution is subjected to an improvement test. The process continues until no further improvement is possible.

Blind and Heuristic Search Approaches

In conducting a search, a description of a desired solution may be given. This is called a *goal.* A set of possible steps leading from initial conditions to the goal is viewed as the *search steps.* **Problem solving** is carried out by searching through the space of possible solutions. Two search methods are considered: the blind search and the heuristic search.

Blind Search. Blind search techniques refer to a search approach which is arbitrary and not guided. Two types of blind search exist: *complete enumeration,* in

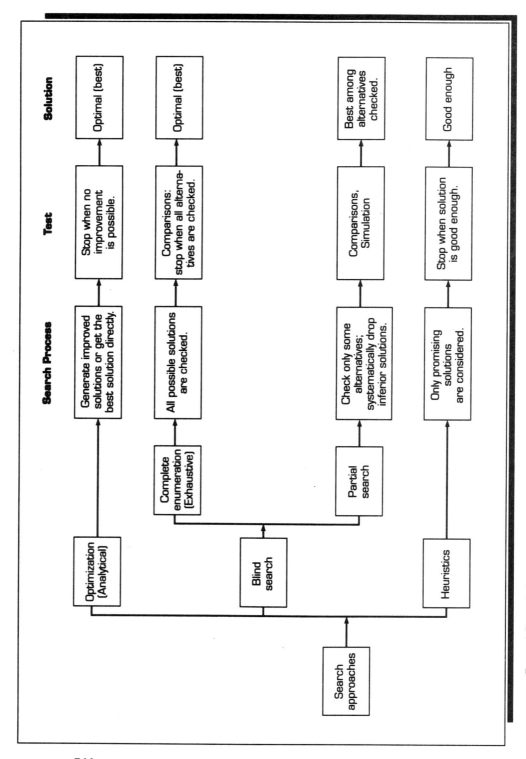

FIGURE 2.6 Formal Search Approaches.

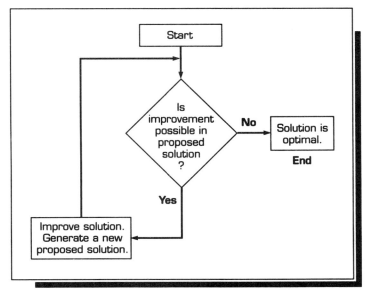

FIGURE 2.7 The Process of Using an Algorithm.

which case all the alternatives are considered, and therefore an optimal solution is discovered; and *incomplete,* partial search, which continues until a "good enough" solution is found.

There are practical limits on the amount of time and computer storage available for blind searches. Although in principle blind search methods can eventually find an optional solution to most search situations, the method is not practical for large problems because too many nodes must be visited before a solution is found.

Heuristic Search. For many applications, it is possible to find specific information to guide the search process and reduce the amount of necessary computations. This is called heuristic information, and the search procedures that use it are called heuristic search methods.

Heuristics (derived from the Greek word for "discovery") are decision rules regarding how a problem should be solved. Heuristics are developed on a basis of solid, rigorous analysis of the problem, sometimes involving designed experimentation. In contrast, "rules of thumb" are usually developed as a result of a trial-and-error experience. Some heuristics were derived from rules of thumb. *Heuristic searches* (or *programming*) are step-by-step procedures that are repeated until a satisfactory solution is found. In practice, such a search is much faster and cheaper than a blind search, while the solutions can be very close to the best ones. For details see Pearl [1984] and Zanakis, et al. [1989]. Examples of heuristics are given in Table 2.3. For the role of heuristics in modeling see Chapter 5.

TABLE 2.3 Examples of Heuristics and Rules of Thumb.

Sequence jobs through a machine	Do the jobs that require the least time first.
Purchase stocks	Do not buy stocks whose price-to-earnings ratio is larger than 10.
Travel	Do not go on the freeway between 8 and 9 A.M.
Capital investment in high-tech projects	Consider only those projects whose estimated payback period is less than two years.
Purchase of a house	Buy only in a good neighborhood, but buy there only in the lower price range.

2.8 Evaluation: Multiple Goals, Sensitivity Analysis, "What-If," and Goal Seeking

The search process described earlier is coupled with evaluation. The evaluation is the final step that leads to the recommended solution. Several topics are important in the evaluation of MSS solutions: multiple goals, sensitivity analysis, "what-if" analysis, and goal seeking. They are discussed next.

Multiple Goals

The analysis of management decisions aims at evaluating, to the greatest possible extent, how far each alternative advances management toward its goals. Unfortunately, managerial problems are seldom evaluated in terms of a single goal such as profit maximization. Today's management systems are becoming more and more complex, and a single goal is rare. Instead, managers want to attain simultaneous goals, some of which conflict with each other. Therefore it is often necessary to analyze each alternative in light of its potential impact on several goals.

For example, consider a profit-making firm. In addition to making money, the company wants to grow, to develop its products and its employees, to provide job security to its workers, and to serve the community. Managers want to satisfy the shareholders and at the same time enjoy high salaries and expense accounts, while employees wish to increase their take-home pay and fringe benefits. Needless to say, some of these goals complement each other while others are in direct conflict. Add to this social and ethical considerations, and the system of goals begins to look quite complex.

Most quantitative approaches to decision theory are based on comparing a single measure of effectiveness. Therefore, it is necessary to transform, mathematically, the multiple-goal problem into a single-measure-of-effectiveness problem prior to the final comparison.

Several methods of handling multiple goals can be used when working with MSS. The most common ones are:

- Use of utility theory
- Goal programming
- Expression of goals as constraints, using linear programming
- Using a point system.

For further details, see Keeney and Raiffa [1976] or Tabucanon [1989].

The analysis of multiple goals involves the following difficulties:

1. It is usually difficult to obtain an explicit statement of the organization's goals.
2. Various participants assess the importance (priorities) of the various goals differently.
3. The decision maker may change the importance assigned to specific goals with the passage of time or for different decision situations.
4. Goals and subgoals are viewed differently at various levels of the organization and in various departments.
5. The goals themselves are dynamic in response to changes in the organization and its environment.
6. The relationship between alternatives and their impact on goals may be difficult to quantify.
7. Complex problems are solved by groups of decision makers.

Computerized models are used extensively to support multiple goal decision making. These will be discussed in detail in Chapter 5.

Sensitivity Analysis

Sensitivity analysis attempts to help managers when they are not certain about the accuracy or the relative importance of information, or when they want to know the impact of changes in input information of a model on some results or measures of performance.

The topic of sensitivity analysis is extremely important in MSS because (a) it enables flexibility and adaptation to changing conditions and to the requirements of different decision-making situations, and (b) it provides a better understanding of the model and the world it purports to describe. Sensitivity analysis checks relationships such as:

- Effect of uncertainty in estimating external variables
- Effects of different interactions among variables
- Robustness of decisions under changing conditions
- The impact of changes in external (uncontrollable) variables and parameters on the outcome variable(s)
- The impact of changes in the decision variables on the outcome variable(s).

Sensitivity analyses are used to:

- Revise models to eliminate too large sensitivities
- Add details about sensitive variables or scenarios
- Obtain better estimates of sensitive external variables
- Alter the real-world system to reduce actual sensitivities
- Live with a sensitive (and hence vulnerable) real world, monitoring actual results continuously and closely.

Two types of sensitivity analysis exist: automatic and trial and error.

Automatic Sensitivity Analysis. This kind of analysis is provided with some standard quantitative models such as linear programming. It tells the manager, for example, the range within which a certain input variable (e.g., unit cost) can vary without any significant impact on the proposed solution. Automatic sensitivity analysis is usually limited to one change at a time, and only for certain variables. It is, however, very powerful because of its ability to establish ranges and limits very fast (and with little or no additional computational efforts).

Trial and Error. The impact of changes in any variable, or in several variables, can be determined through a trial-and-error approach. One simply changes some input data and resolves the problem. By repeating the changes several times, better and better solutions are discovered. Such experimentation appears in two forms: "what-if" and goal seeking.

"What-If" Analysis. A model builder makes predictions and assumptions regarding the input data, many of which deal with the assessment of uncertain futures. When the model is solved, the results depend, of course, on these data. Sensitivity analysis attempts to check the impact of a change in the input data on the proposed solution (the result variable). This type of sensitivity analysis is called **"what-if" analysis,** because it is structured as *"What* will happen to the solution *if* an input variable, an assumption, or a parameter value is changed?"

Examples include the following:

- *What* will happen to the total inventory cost *if* the cost of carrying inventories increases by 10 percent?
- *What* will be the market share *if* the advertising budget increases by 5 percent?

Assuming the appropriate user interface, managers can easily ask the computer these types of questions. Furthermore, they can repeat the question and change the percentage or change any other data in the question, as desired.

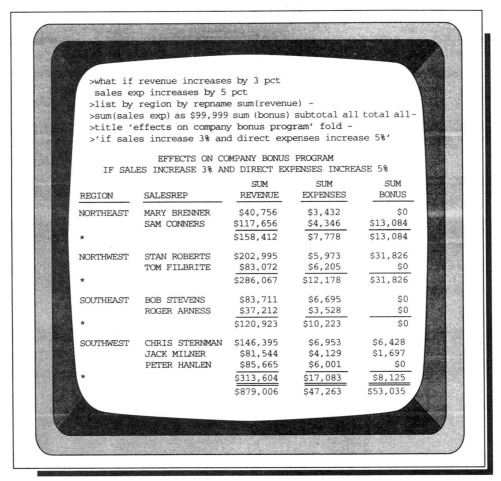

```
>what if revenue increases by 3 pct
 sales exp increases by 5 pct
>list by region by repname sum(revenue) -
>sum(sales exp) as $99,999 sum (bonus) subtotal all total all-
>title 'effects on company bonus program' fold -
>'if sales increase 3% and direct expenses increase 5%'
```

EFFECTS ON COMPANY BONUS PROGRAM
IF SALES INCREASE 3% AND DIRECT EXPENSES INCREASE 5%

REGION	SALESREP	SUM REVENUE	SUM EXPENSES	SUM BONUS
NORTHEAST	MARY BRENNER	$40,756	$3,432	$0
	SAM CONNERS	$117,656	$4,346	$13,084
*		$158,412	$7,778	$13,084
NORTHWEST	STAN ROBERTS	$202,995	$5,973	$31,826
	TOM FILBRITE	$83,072	$6,205	$0
*		$286,067	$12,178	$31,826
SOUTHEAST	BOB STEVENS	$83,711	$6,695	$0
	ROGER ARNESS	$37,212	$3,528	$0
*		$120,923	$10,223	$0
SOUTHWEST	CHRIS STERNMAN	$146,395	$6,953	$6,428
	JACK MILNER	$81,544	$4,129	$1,697
	PETER HANLEN	$85,665	$6,001	$0
*		$313,604	$17,083	$8,125
		$879,006	$47,263	$53,035

FIGURE 2.8 Example of "What If" Analysis Done by NOMAD 2. The upper part of the figure shows the commands as programmed with NOMAD 2; the lower part shows the projections and their impacts. (*Source:* Courtesy of Must Software Int'l.)

Figure 2.8 shows a "what-if" query in the case of a bonus computation. The user asks "what if" sales increase by 3 percent and expenses increase by 5 percent. The computer recomputes the value of the bonus by region and by salesperson. "What-if" analysis can be executed with expert systems as well. Users are given the opportunity to change their answers to some of the computer's questions; then a revised recommendation is shown and compared to the previous one.

Goal Seeking. **Goal-seeking** analysis checks the inputs necessary to achieve a desired level of an output (goal). It represents a "backward" solution approach.

Other examples of goal seeking are:

- What is the annual R&D budget needed for an annual growth rate of 15 percent by 1998?
- How many nurses are needed to reduce the average waiting time of a patient in the emergency room to less than 10 minutes?
- How many auditors are needed to complete an audit by November 15?

A computer printout of a goal-seeking dialogue is shown in Figure 2.9.

Computing a Break-even Point Using Goal Seeking. An interesting application of goal seeking for computing break-even points is available in some computer packages. This application can be done by finding what quantity is needed to be produced in order to generate zero profit.

Sensitivity analysis is important because it can be used to improve confidence in the model and thus increase the success of implementing quantitative analysis.

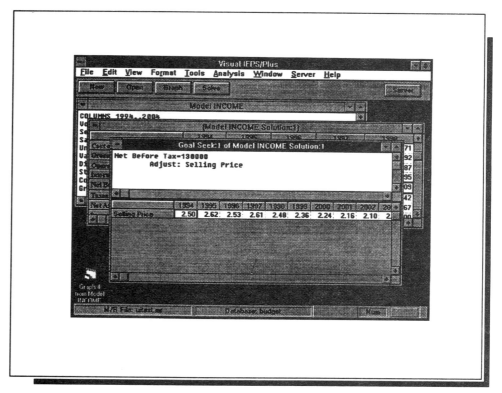

FIGURE 2.9 Goal-Seeking Analysis. The goal to be achieved is net before tax of $130,000. The variable to be adjusted is selling price. The new selling price for the next 8 years is recalculated. (*Source:* Screen from IFPS/PLUS. Courtesy of Comshare, Inc.)

In many regular computer-based decision systems, it is difficult to conduct such an analysis because the prewritten routines usually present only a limited opportunity for "what-if" questions. In a DSS the "what-if" and the goal-seeking options are easy to execute and provide ample opportunity for flexibility and adaptability.

2.9 Critical Success Factors

A final issue that relates to "choice" is the technique of critical success factors. **Critical success factors** (CSF) is a diagnostic technique for identifying the factors that are the most critical to the achievement of organizational objectives. The process involves conducting interviews with individual executives, followed by a structured group discussion for the purpose of identifying success factors and agreeing on their importance. The identification of such factors is essential both for determining the information needs required by management to achieve their objectives and for prioritizing the criteria used in evaluating alternative courses of action.

Once the critical factors are determined, it is possible to identify information gaps, that is, to find out which critical factors are not being adequately supported by the current information system. The lack of such information prevents management from measuring the effectiveness of areas that are critical to the organization. Therefore it is necessary to identify the critical factors and structure the appropriate information system before developing the MSS. In addition to its use in determining information requirements, CSF has been used in feasibility studies of MSS and in other phases of the development process of these techniques. For example, it was used in DSS software selection (Shank, et al. [1985]).

Once the choice phase has been completed, the recommended solution must be implemented. This issue is discussed next.

2.10 Implementation

What is implementation? Machiavelli astutely noted more than 400 years ago that there was "nothing more difficult to carry out, nor more doubtful of success, nor more dangerous to handle, than to initiate a new order of things." The **implementation** of a proposed solution to a problem is, in effect, the initiation of a new order of things, or in modern language—the introduction of a change.

The definition of implementation is somewhat complicated because implementation is a long and involved process whose boundaries are vague. In a simplistic manner, it may be defined as putting a recommended solution to work.

Many of the generic issues of implementation, such as resistance to change, degree of support of top management, and user's training, are important in dealing with MSS. Implementation is discussed in detail in Chapter 21.

The decision-making process described in Sections 2.5 through 2.10 is conducted by people, but it can be improved if supported by computers. The manner in which such support can be provided is the subject of the next section.

2.11 How Decisions Are Being Supported

The discussion in this chapter has centered so far on decisions and systems; equally important is the notion of *support* in MSS. Chapter 1 illustrated, in general terms, how computers have supported management decisions since the early 1950s (Table 1.1). Now that we are familiar with the decision process, we will discuss the support from this point of view. Simon's phases of intelligence, design, and choice will be used as a framework, with the addition of the implementation phase.

As noted by Sprague and Carlson [1982], a DSS may support all phases of the decision-making process (see Figure 2.10). In contrast, MIS supports mainly the intelligence phase, whereas management science supports mainly the choice phase. EIS would support the intelligence phase while ES can support any of the phases. The figure also shows the potential support of the other MSS tools.

Support for the Intelligence Phase

The primary requirement of decision support for the intelligence phase is the ability to scan external and internal databases for opportunities and problems and interpretation of what the scanning discovers. Computerized systems store large volumes of information. An EIS, as will be described later, helps in accessing databases rapidly and efficiently. Furthermore, a DSS, through its modeling capabilities, can analyze data very fast. That is, the scanning done during the intelligence phase can be executed much faster with the aid of a DSS and EIS.

FIGURE 2.10 DSS Support. [*Source:* Based on Sprague, R. H., Jr., "A Framework for the Development of DSS." *MIS Quarterly* [Dec. 1980], Fig. 5, p. 13. Reprinted by special permission of the *MIS Quarterly* © 1980 by the Society for Information Management and the Management Information Systems Research Center at the University of Minnesota.]

Another area of support is that of reporting. Both routine and ad hoc reports can aid in the intelligence phase. For example, regular reports can be designed to assist in the problem-finding activity by comparing expectations with current and projected performance. Table 2.4 lists report elements that can assist in problem finding.

The major purpose of an EIS is to support the intelligence phase. This is done by continuously monitoring both internal and external information, looking for early signs of problems and/or opportunities. For example, EIS will detect below normal performance and through a detailed investigation will attempt to pinpoint its sources.

Finally, ES can render advice regarding the nature of the problem, its classification, its seriousness, and the like. ES can advise on the suitability of a solution approach and on the likelihood of successfully solving the problem. One of the primary areas of ES success, as will be shown later, is in *interpreting* information and in *diagnosing* problems. This capability can be utilized during the intelligence phase.

The phase of intelligence, according to a study conducted by Lucas [1980], is a primary target for DSS and for other computer-based information systems that deal with nonstructured problems.

Support for the Design Phase

The design phase involves generating alternative courses of action, discussing the criteria for choice and their relative importance, and forecasting the future consequences of using various alternatives. Several of these activities could use standard models provided by the DSS (e.g., forecasting). Generation of alternatives for

TABLE 2.4 Report Elements. (Condensed from Brookes [1984].)

Report Elements	Problem-Finding Use
Summarization	Current performance is summarized by expectations provided by the user of the report.
Comparison	The report has explicit comparisons with current performance expectations: Comparison with plans, budgets, or standards. Variance (from standards) reports. Comparison with competitors, industry averages, and other extraorganizational standards and measures. Exceptions reports.
Prediction	Forecasts of future performance: Prediction based on budget, planning models, or historical ratios. Prediction based on seasonally adjusted (or other method) data. Forecast of current performance to the end of the planning period.
Confirmation	Data items that allow the user to validate or audit the report to provide assurance that it corresponds to underlying detail or other data available to the user. Confirmation may use historical data, planning data, or data from elsewhere in the organization.

structured problems could be provided through the use of either standard or special models. However, generation of alternatives for complex problems requires expertise that could be provided by a human, an idea generation software, or an expert system. Information about technology, availability of resources, market conditions, and the like could be provided to the decision maker by the computer's database. This information is essential for the development of alternative solutions to the problems and for the prediction of decision consequences. Most DSS have forecasting capabilities while an added-on ES can assist with qualitative methods of forecasting as well as with expertise required in applying quantitative forecasting models.

Support for the Choice Phase

A decision support system, by definition, recommends but does not make a choice. In addition to the use of models that rapidly identify the best or "good enough" alternative, a DSS can support the choice phase through the "what-if" and goal-seeking analyses. Different scenarios can be tested for the selected option to reinforce the final decision. An ES can be used to assess the desirability of certain solutions as well as to recommend an appropriate solution.

Support for the Decision Implementation

Interviews conducted by Mittman and Moore [1984] suggest that the DSS benefits provided during implementation are frequently as important or even more important than those mentioned in the previously discussed phases. Respondents reported numerous uses of DSS in implementation activities like decision communication, explanation, and justification. For example, a copy containing DSS results was frequently sent to parties who were both internal and external to companies. The recipients included senior managers' peers and subordinates, the board of directors, bankers and financial analysts, customers and clients, suppliers, and others from whom cooperation and coordination are needed.

Benefits of DSS in the implementation phase are due in part to the vividness and detail of the analysis and resulting output. For example, one CEO gives subordinates and external parties not only the aggregate financial goals and cash needs for the near term, but includes the calculations, intermediate results, and statistics used in determining the aggregate figures. In addition to communicating the financial goals unambiguously, the CEO signals other messages. Subordinates know that the CEO has thought through the assumptions behind the financial goals and is serious about their importance and attainability. Bankers and directors are shown that the CEO was personally involved in analyzing cash needs, and is aware of and responsible for the implications of the financing requests prepared by the finance department. Each of these messages improves decision implementation in some way.

The evidence just discussed indicates that senior managers are using computers primarily in support of the implementation aspects of the decision process—

explaining, justifying, and communicating decisions. Numerous indications of the DSS role in decision implementation appear in other studies (e.g., see Alter [1980] and Keen and Scott-Morton [1978]).

All phases of the decision-making process can be supported by improved communication in cases of *group decision making*. Computerized systems can facilitate communication by allowing people to explain and justify their suggestions and opinions, usually with graphic support. Quantitative support can also be quickly provided for various possible scenarios while a meeting is in session.

Decision implementation can also be supported by ES. Some ES include, like a DSS, a "what-if" mechanism that intends to increase the *confidence* in the system. Furthermore, an ES can be used as an advisory system regarding implementation problems (e.g., handling resistance to change). Finally, an ES can provide training that may smooth the course of implementation.

2.12   Human Cognition and Decision Styles

Cognition Theory. Cognition refers to the activities by which an individual resolves differences between an internalized view of the environment and what actually exists in that same environment. In other words, it is the ability to perceive and understand information. Cognitive models are attempts to explain or understand various human cognitive processes. For instance, they explain how individuals revise previous opinions to conform with a particular choice after they have made that choice.

Cognitive Style. Cognitive style refers to the *subjective* process through which individuals perceive, organize, and change information during the decision-making process. Cognitive style may be important because in many cases it determines people's preference for human-machine interface. For example, should data be raw or aggregate, should they be detailed or summarized, should they be tabulated or presented as graphs? Furthermore, cognitive styles impact on preferences for qualitative versus quantitative analysis as well as on the preferences for decision-making aids.

The research on cognitive styles is directly relevant to the design of management information systems. MIS and transaction processing systems tend to be designed by individuals who perceive the decision-making process to be systematic. Systematic managers are generally willing to use such systems; they are typically looking for a standard technique and view the system designer as an expert with a catalog of methods. However, such systems do not conform to the natural style of a heuristic decision maker. For this individual, a system should allow for exploration of a wide range of alternatives, permit changes in priorities or in processing, allow the user to shift easily between levels of detail, and permit some user control over the output form (e.g., visual, verbal, graphic, and so on). And this is precisely what DSS is attempting to do. Other interesting implications of cognitive style will be presented when MSS implementation issues are discussed.

Although cognitive style is a useful concept, it may be overemphasized in the MIS literature. There are difficulties in applying it to information systems and decision making (see Huber [1983]). For one thing, cognitive style is a continuous variable. Many people are not completely heuristic nor analytic, but are somewhere in between. Related to the cognitive styles is the concept of decision styles.

Decision Styles. The manner in which decision makers think and react to problems, the way they perceive, their cognitive response, their values and beliefs vary from individual to individual and from situation to situation. As a result, people make decisions differently. Although there is a general process of decision making, it is far from being linear. People do not follow the same steps of the process in the same sequence, nor do they use all of the steps. Furthermore, the emphasis, time allotment, and priorities given to each step vary significantly—not only from one person to another, but also from one situation to the next. The manner in which managers make decisions (and the way they interact with other people) describes their **decision style.** Because decision styles depend on the factors described earlier, there are many decision styles. For example, Gordon, et al. [1975] identified 40 processes in looking at nine types of decisions, and Mintzberg [1973] identified seven basic styles with many variations.

In addition to the heuristic and analytic styles discussed earlier, one can distinguish autocratic versus democratic styles; another style is consultative (with individuals or groups). Of course, there are many combinations and variations of styles. For example, one can be analytic and autocratic, or consultative (with individuals) and heuristic. For further details on how decision styles relate to DSS and the provided support, see Wedley and Field [1984].

For a computerized system to successfully support a manager, it should fit the decision situation as well as the decision style. Therefore the system should be flexible and adaptable to different users. The capability of asking "what-if" and goal-seeking questions provides flexibility in this direction. Availability of graphics is also desirable in supporting certain decision styles. If an MSS is to support varying styles, skills, and knowledge, it should not attempt to enforce a specific process. Rather, the MSS should help decision makers use and develop their own styles, skills, and knowledge.

Different decision styles require different types of support. A major factor that determines the type of required support is whether the decision maker is an individual or a group.

2.13 Making Decisions in Groups

The discussion of decision making in this chapter is basically centered around a rational approach to decision making, which is usually considered a normative model for an individual decision maker. However, many complex and major decisions are made in organizations by groups. Computerized technologies developed to support such decisions are described in Chapters 9 and 10.

However, computer support can be provided even at a broader level that surpasses the group, moving up to departments, divisions, and even entire organizations. Such support requires specialized architecture and procedures and it is labeled *organizational DSS*. For details see Chapter 8.

Chapter Highlights

- Managerial decision making is synonymous with the whole process of management.
- Problem solving also refers to opportunity's evaluation.
- Systems are composed of inputs, outputs, processes, and a decision maker.
- All systems are separated from their environment by a boundary.
- Systems can be open, interacting with their environment, or closed.
- DSS deals primarily with open systems.
- Models are used extensively in MSS; they can be iconic, analog, or mathematical.
- Models enable fast and inexpensive experimentation with systems.
- Modeling can employ simulation, optimization, or heuristic techniques.
- Decision making involves four major phases: intelligence, design, choice, and implementation.
- In the intelligence step, the problem (opportunity) is identified, classified, and decomposed (if needed).
- In the design phase, a model of the system is built, criteria for selection are agreed upon, alternatives are generated, results are predicted, and decision methodology is created.
- In the choice phase, alternatives are compared and a search for the best (good enough) solution is launched. Many search techniques are available.
- In evaluating alternatives, one should consider multiple goals and sensitivity analysis issues.
- "What-if" and goal seeking are the two most common sensitivity analysis approaches.
- Critical success factors is a methodology for diagnosing problems and identifying information requirements.
- Computers can support all phases of decision making by automating many of the required tasks.
- Humans' decision styles need to be recognized in designing MSS.
- Decisions made by individuals or by groups can be supported by MSS.

Key Words

algorithm
analog model
analytical techniques
cognitive style
critical success factors
decision styles
descriptive models
effectiveness
efficiency
goal seeking
heuristics
iconic model

implementation
independent variables
inputs
linear programming
mathematical
   (quantitative) model
normative models
optimization
outputs
principle of choice
problem solving
programmed problems

risk analysis
satisficing
scenario
sensitivity analysis
simulation
suboptimization
system
uncertainty
uncontrollable
   variables
"what-if" analysis

Questions for Review

1. What is the difference between making decisions and solving problems?
2. Define a system.
3. List the major components of a system.
4. Explain the role of feedback in a system.
5. Define an environment of a system.
6. Define open and closed systems. Give an example of each.
7. What is meant by a "black box"?
8. Define efficiency and contrast it with effectiveness.
9. Define the phases of intelligence, design, and choice.
10. Define a problem and distinguish it from the symptoms of the problem.
11. Define programmed versus nonprogrammed problems; give one example of each in each of the following areas: accounting, marketing, personnel administration.
12. List the major components of a mathematical model.
13. Define optimization and contrast it with suboptimization.
14. Compare and contrast normative versus descriptive approaches to decision making.
15. Why do people have a bounded rationality?
16. Distinguish between decision making under risk and under uncertainty.
17. What is the major advantage of optimization?
18. What is the major disadvantage of complete enumeration?
19. Define heuristics.
20. Why is a heuristic search superior to a blind one?
21. Compare decision style to cognitive style.
22. Discuss the various types of computerized support.
23. Define "what-if" analysis and provide an example.

24. Define goal-seeking analysis and provide an example.
25. Define critical success factors (CSF) and describe the steps in this process.
26. Define implementation.
27. Define a scenario. How is it used in decision making?
28. Define cognition and cognitive style.
29. Compare simulation and optimization.
30. Define sensitivity analysis.

Questions for Discussion

1. Specify in a table the inputs, process, and output of the following systems:
   a. post office
   b. elementary school
   c. social service agency
   d. paper mill.
2. List possible modes of feedback for the systems in the previous question.
3. A hospital includes dietary, radiology, housekeeping, and nursing (patient care) departments, and an emergency room. List four system interfaces between pairs of these departments.
4. How would you measure the productivity of:
   a. a letter carrier
   b. a salesperson
   c. a professor
   d. a social worker?
5. Give an example of five elements in the environment of a university.
6. Analyze a managerial system of your choice and identify the following:
   a. the components, inputs, and outputs
   b. the environment
   c. the processes
   d. the system's goals
   e. the feedback.
7. What are some of the "measures of effectiveness" in a toy manufacturing plant, a restaurant, an educational institution, and the U.S. Congress?
8. What are some of the controllable and uncontrollable variables in the following systems: automotive manufacturing, hospital, courthouse, airline, restaurant, hotel, bank, oil refinery, atomic power plant? Specify a typical decision in each of the above.
9. Assume a marketing department is an open system. How would you "close" this system?
10. What could be the major advantages of a mathematical model that would be used to support a major investment decision?
11. Your company is considering opening a branch in China. List typical activities in each phase of the decision to open or not to open (intelligence, design, choice, implementation).

12. Many farm equipment manufacturers have had major losses in recent years because farmers have had no money to purchase farm equipment. What is the problem that the manufacturing companies are faced with?

13. You are about to sell your car. What criteria (or principles of choice) are you most likely to employ in deciding about accepting or rejecting offers? Why?

14. You are about to decide on driving to work via the freeway or via the parallel road. There is no immediate traffic information. Is your decision under certainty? Risk? Uncertainty? Why?

15. There are $n!$ (n factorial) ways to schedule n jobs through one machine. You have 50 jobs to schedule. You must decide which job to run first, second, etc. There is no analytical solution to the problem. How many feasible solutions exist? What type of search would you use in your analysis and why?

16. List five heuristics (or rules of thumb) that are in use in your company, in a university, a bank, or a fast-food restaurant.

17. A hospital desires to know what level of demand for its services will guarantee an 85 percent bed occupancy. What type of sensitivity analysis should the hospital use and why?

18. Apply the method of critical success factors to determine which computer to buy for your home. Assume that at least three people will use the computer and you can afford only one PC.

19. The use of scenarios is becoming popular in computerized decision making. Why? For what type of decisions is this technique most appropriate?

20. Explain how cognitive style relates to decision style. How might these concepts impact the development of information systems?

21. What is the major advantage of a goal-seeking over a "what-if" analysis?

22. Explain, through an example, the support given to decision makers by computers in each phase of the decision process.

23. Some experts believe that the major contribution of DSS is to the implementation of the decision and not to the intelligence, design, or choice. Why is this so?

24. Table 2.5 shows the differences between heuristic and analytic cognitive styles.
    a. Would you consider yourself heuristic or analytic? Why?
    b. Read Huber's article (*Management Science*, May 1983). Do you agree with Huber's position? Why or why not?
    c. Assume you are making a presentation to two managers—one heuristic, the other analytic—regarding a decision about adding a service by the bank you work for. How would you appeal to their cognitive styles? (Be specific.)

25. How is the term *model* used in this text? What are the strengths and weaknesses of modeling?

26. Most managers are capable of utilizing the telephone without understanding or even considering the electrical and magnetic theories involved. Why then is it necessary for managers to understand MSS tools to use them wisely?

27. Decision-making styles vary from analytical to heuristic-intuitive. Does a decision maker consistently use the same style? Give examples from your own experience.

TABLE 2.5 Cognitive-style Decision Approaches.

Problem-solving Dimension	Heuristic	Analytic
Approach to learning	Learns more by acting than by analyzing the situation and places more emphasis on feedback.	Employs a planned sequential approach to problem solving; learns more by analyzing the situation than by acting and places less emphasis on feedback.
Search	Uses trial and error and spontaneous action.	Uses formal rational analysis.
Approach to analysis	Uses common sense, intuition, and feelings.	Develops explicit, often quantitative, models of the situation.
Scope of analysis	Views the totality of the situation as an organic whole rather than as a structure constructed from specific parts.	Reduces the problem situation to a set of underlying causal functions.
Basis for inferences	Looks for highly visible situational differences that vary with time.	Locates similarities or commonalities by comparing objects.

Source: G. B. Davis; *Management Information Systems: Conceptual Foundations, Structure, and Development.* New York: McGraw-Hill, 1974, p. 150. Reproduced with permission of McGraw-Hill, Inc.

References and Bibliography

Alter, S. L. (1980). *Decision Support Systems: Current Practice and Continuing Challenge.* Reading, MA: Addison-Wesley.

Bell, D. E., et al. (1988). *Decision Making.* New York: Cambridge University Press.

Churchman, C. West. (1975). *The Systems Approach,* Rev. ed. New York: Delacorte.

Courtney J. F., et al. (1993). "Studies in Managerial Problem Formulation Systems." *Decision Support Systems,* Vol. 9, 413–423.

Etzioni, A. (1989, July-August). "Humble Decision Making." *Harvard Business Review.*

Flood, R. L., and M. C. Jackson. (1991). *Creative Problem Solving.* New York: Wiley.

Gordon, L. A., et al. (1975). *Normative Models in Managerial Decision Making.* New York: National Association of Accounting.

Huber, G. P. (1983). "Cognitive Style as a Basis for MIS and DDS Designs: Much Ado About Nothing?" *Management Science,* Vol. 29, No. 5.

Keen, P. G. W., and M. S. Scott-Morton. (1978). *Decision Support Systems: An Organizational Perspective.* Reading, MA: Addison-Wesley.

Keeney, R., and H. Raiffa. (1976). *Decisions with Multiple Objectives, Preferences, and Value Tradeoffs.* New York: Wiley.

Lucas, H. C. (1980). "Top Management Problem Solving and Information Systems." Working Papers CRIS #11, Center for Research on Information Systems; New York University.

Mintzberg, H. (1973). *The Nature of the Managerial Work.* New York: Harper & Row.

Mittman, B. S., and J. H. Moore. (1984, April). *Senior Management Computer Use: Implications for DSS Design and Goals.* Paper presented at the DSS-84 meetings, Dallas, Texas.

Pearl, J. (1984). *Heuristics: Intelligent Search Strategies for Computer Problem Solving.* Reading, MA: Addison-Wesley.

Rios, Insua D. (1990). *Sensitivity Analysis in Multi-objective Decision Making.* Berlin, New York Springer-Verlag.

Robbins, S. R. (1991). *Management,* 3rd ed. Englewood Cliffs, NJ: Prentice-Hall.

Shank, M. E., et al. (1985, June). "Critical Success Factor Analysis as a Methodology for MIS Planning." *MIS Quarterly.*

Simon, H. (1977). *The New Science of Management Decisions,* Rev. ed. Englewood Cliffs, NJ: Prentice-Hall.

Sprague, R. H., and E. D. Carlson. (1982). *Building Effective Decision Support Systems.* Englewood Cliffs, NJ: Prentice-Hall.

Tabucanon, M. T. (1989). *Multiple Criteria Decision Making in Industry.* New York: Elsevier.

Turban, E., and J. Meredith. (1994). *Fundamentals of Management Science,* 6th ed. Homewood, IL: Irwin.

Tylor, A. (1991). *Applied Decision Analysis.* Boston: PWS-Kent.

Van Gigch, J. P. (1978). *Applied General Systems Theory,* 2nd ed. New York: Harper & Row.

Wedley, W. K., and R. H. C. Field. (1984, October). "A Predecision Support System." *Academy of Management Review.*

Zanakis, S. H., et al. (1989). "Heuristic Methods and Applications: A Categorized Survey." *European Journal of Operations Research,* No. 43.

Chapter 15

Decision Support Systems: An Overview

In Chapter 1, we introduced DSS and stressed its support for the solution of complex managerial problems. The methodology of decision making was presented in Chapter 2. In this chapter, we show how DSS superiority is achieved by examining its capabilities, structure, and classifications. The following sections are presented:

3.1 The Case of Gotaas-Larsen Shipping Corp. (GLSC)*

Strategic planning is one of the most difficult tasks of modern management. It involves all functional areas in an organization and several relevant outside factors, a fact that complicates the planning process, especially when one deals with the uncertainties of the long run. As such, strategic planning is clearly not a structured decision situation; therefore it is a potential candidate for DSS applications.

GLSC, a subsidiary of International Utilities (IU), operates cargo ships all over the world. The company developed a comprehensive decision support system for executing both short- and long-term planning in the mid-1970s. The system is composed of two major parts: data and models.

The data include both external data (port or canal characteristics, competitors' activities, and fares) and internal data (existing plans, availability of resources, and individual ships' characteristics). In addition, users can utilize their own data or express their attitudes (e.g., add their own risk preferences).

The models include routine standard accounting and financial analysis models (like cash flow computations and pro forma income and expenses) organized on a per ship, per voyage, per division, and per entire company basis. These models permit elaborate financial analyses. A simulation model is used to analyze short- and long-term plans and to evaluate the desirability of projects. In addition, the system interfaces with a commercially available time-sharing application program for analyzing individual voyages (time-charter analysis).

A highly decentralized, 15-month operational planning and control document is prepared within the framework of the long-term strategic plan. This 15-month document is used as the basis for detailed goal formation for the various ships and the individual voyages. A detailed monitoring and control mechanism is also provided, including a regular variance report and diagnostic analysis. In addition, a detailed performance tracking report is executed (by voyage, ship, division, and entire corporation).

Once the assessment of the opportunity of individual projects (such as contracting a specific voyage) is examined by a charter analysis, an aggregation is performed. The objective is to determine whether a series of individually profitable projects adds up to a feasible and effective long-range plan. The DSS utilizes a simulation model that examines various configurations of projects in an attempt to conduct a "fine tuning" of the aggregate plan. Specifically, when several projects are executed, the resources (like labor and finance) might be insufficient for all the projects. Therefore modifications in scheduling and financial arrangements might be necessary. This fine tuning provides a trial-and-error approach to feasibility testing and sensitivity analyses. The "what-if" capabilities of the DSS are especially important in this case. The strategic plan of GLSC is very detailed and accurate be-

---

*For a complete description, see Alter [1980].

cause of the contractual nature of both the sales and some of the expenses. The model is geared to a traditional business policy structure, which helps in assessing the threats and risks in the general operating environment and makes possible an examination of the impacts of new opportunities on existing plans.

The GLSC case is an example of large-scale DSS. We refer to this case in the forthcoming sections.

3.2 Introduction

The early definitions of a DSS identify it as a system intended to support managerial decision makers in semistructured decision situations. DSS were meant to be an adjunct to decision makers, to extend their capabilities but not to replace their judgment. They were aimed at decisions where judgment was required, or at decisions that could not be completely supported by algorithms. Not specifically stated, but implied in the early definitions, was the notion that the system would be computer-based, would operate on-line, and preferably would have graphic-output capabilities.

The early definitions were open to several interpretations. Soon several other definitions appeared that occasioned considerable disagreement as to what a DSS is. Some skeptics even suggested that DSS was just another buzz word. The purpose of this chapter is to show that this is not the case, and that there is a significant amount of content behind the label DSS. To do so we present the essential characteristics that could help in determining whether a system is a DSS or not. Also, the structure of DSS is presented as well as the various types of systems. Let us begin by reviewing some definitions (based on Ginzberg and Stohr [1982]), and then delve into the DSS content and structure.

3.3 What Is a DSS?

A refinement of Gorry and Scott-Morton's DSS definition (which was given in Chapter 1) was provided by Little [1970], who defines DSS as a "model-based set of procedures for processing data and judgments to assist a manager in his decision making." He argues that in order to be successful, such a system must be (1) simple, (2) robust, (3) easy to control, (4) adaptive, (5) complete on important issues, and (6) easy to communicate with. Implicit in this definition, too, is the assumption that the system is computer-based and serves as an extension of the user's problem-solving capabilities.

Throughout most of the 1970s, definitions of DSS, like those just presented, were accepted by practitioners and researchers. By the end of the decade new definitions began to emerge. Alter [1980] defines DSS by contrasting them with traditional EDP systems on five dimensions, as shown in Table 3.1.

TABLE 3.1   DSS versus EDP.

Dimension	DSS	EDP
Use	Active	Passive
User	Line and staff management	Clerical
Goal	Effectiveness	Mechanical efficiency
Time Horizon	Present and future	Past
Objective	Flexibility	Consistency

Three other definitions of DSS were offered by Moore and Chang [1980], Bonczek, Holsapple, and Whinston [1980], and Keen [1980]. Moore and Chang argue that the "structuredness" concept, so much a part of early DSS definitions (i.e., that DSS can handle semistructured and unstructured situations), is not meaningful in general; a problem can be described as structured or unstructured only with respect to a particular decision maker (i.e., structured decisions are structured because we choose to treat them as such). Thus, they define DSS as (1) extendable systems, (2) capable of supporting ad hoc data analysis and decision modeling, (3) oriented toward future planning, and (4) used at irregular, unplanned intervals.

Note: Computerized systems for decision support are being developed today by end-users on microcomputers for dealing with fairly structured problems for which commercial software is not available. The advantage here is that the user can build systems with little or no help from information systems people.

Bonczek, et al. [1980] define a DSS as a computer-based system consisting of three interacting components: (1) a language system—a mechanism to provide communication between the user and other components of the DSS, (2) a knowledge system—the repository of problem domain knowledge embodied in DSS, either as data or procedures, and (3) a problem-processing system—the link between the other two components, containing one or more of the general problem-manipulatory capabilities required for decision making.

Note: The concepts provided by this definition are important for understanding the structures of DSS and ES and the interrelationship between the two technologies.

Finally, Keen [1980] applies the term DSS "to situations where a `final' system can be developed only through an **adaptive process** of learning and *evolution.*" Thus, he defines DSS as the product of a developmental process in which the DSS user, the DSS builder, and the DSS itself are all capable of influencing one another, resulting in an evolution of the system and the pattern of its use.

These definitions are compared and contrasted by examining the types of concepts employed to define DSS (see Table 3.2). It seems that the basis for defining DSS has been developed from the perceptions of what a DSS does (e.g., support decision making in unstructured problems) and from ideas about how the

590

TABLE 3.2 Concepts
Underlying DSS Definitions.

Source	DSS Defined in Terms of
Gorry and Scott-Morton [1971]	Problem type, system function (support)
Little [1970]	System function, interface characteristics
Alter [1980]	Usage pattern, system objectives
Moore and Chang [1980]	Usage pattern, system capabilities
Bonczek, et al. [1980]	System components
Keen [1980]	Development process

DSS's objective can be accomplished (e.g., components required, appropriate usage pattern, and the necessary development processes).

One result of these definitions is a narrowing of the population of systems that each author would identify as a DSS. For example, Keen would exclude systems built without following an evolutionary strategy, and Moore and Chang would exclude systems used at regular, planned intervals to support decisions about current operations. The narrowing of a population is indeed a proper function of a definition. By dealing with a smaller population of objects, we can identify those characteristics that the population members have in common, as well as characteristics that differentiate one population from another.

Unfortunately, the definitions of DSS do not provide a consistent focus, because each tries to narrow the population in a different way. Furthermore, they collectively ignore the central issue in DSS; that is, support and improvement of decision making. There seems to have been a retreat from the consideration of out-

Box 3.1: What Is a DSS?—A Working Definition

It depends. At minimum we can say: A DSS is an interactive, flexible, and adaptable CBIS, specially developed for supporting the solution of a non-structured management problem for improved decision making. It utilizes data, it provides easy user interface, and it allows for the decision maker's own insights.

The most sophisticated DSS definition will add to this: DSS also utilizes models (either standard and/or custom-made), it is built by an interactive process (frequently by end-users), it supports all the phases of the decision making, and it includes a knowledge base.

puts, and a focus on the inputs instead. A very likely reason for this change in emphasis is the difficulty of measuring the outputs of a DSS (e.g., decision quality).

We provide in Box 3.1 a working definition that basically defines a range, from a basic to an ideal DSS. It is much more beneficial, however, to deal with the characteristics and capabilities of DSS, which are presented next.

3.4   Characteristics and Capabilities of DSS

Because there is no consensus on what a DSS is, there is obviously no agreement on the characteristics and capabilities of DSS. Therefore we label the list in Figure 3.1 as an ideal set. Most DSS have only *some* of the listed features.

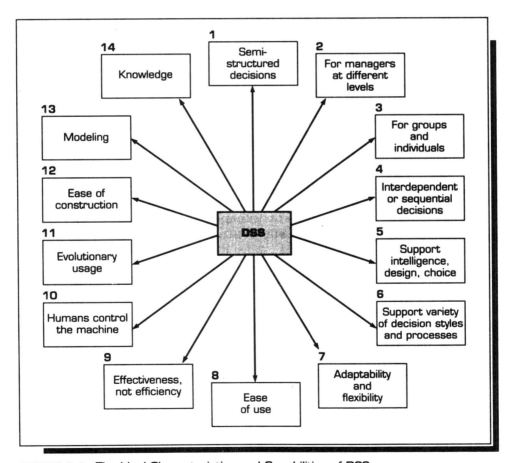

FIGURE 3.1   The Ideal Characteristics and Capabilities of DSS.

1. DSS provides support for decision makers mainly in semistructured and unstructured situations by bringing together human judgment and computerized information. Such problems cannot be solved (or cannot be solved conveniently) by other computerized systems, such as EDP or MIS, nor by standard quantitive methods or tools.

2. Support is provided for various managerial levels, ranging from top executives to line managers.

3. Support is provided to individuals as well as to groups. Many organizational problems involve group decision making. The less structured problems frequently require the involvement of several individuals from different departments and organizational levels.

4. DSS provides support to several interdependent and/or sequential decisions. (See Section 3.12 for definitions.)

5. DSS supports all phases of the decision-making process: intelligence, design, choice, and implementation.

6. DSS supports a variety of decision-making processes and styles; there is a fit between the DSS and the attributes of the individual decision makers (e.g., the vocabulary and decision style).

7. DSS is adaptive over time. The decision maker should be reactive, being able to confront changing conditions quickly and adapt the DSS to meet these changes. DSS are flexible, so users can add, delete, combine, change, or rearrange basic elements (providing fast response to unexpected situations). This capability makes possible timely and quick ad hoc analyses.

8. DSS is easy to use. Users must feel "at home" with the system. User-friendliness, flexibility, strong graphic capabilities, and an English-like human-machine interface language can greatly increase the effectiveness of DSS. This ease of use implies an interactive mode.

9. DSS attempts to improve the effectiveness of decision making (accuracy, timeliness, quality), rather than its efficiency (cost of making the decision, including the charges for computer time).

10. The decision maker has complete control over all steps of the decision-making process in solving a problem. A DSS specifically aims to support and not to replace the decision maker. The decision maker can override the computer's recommendation at any time in the process.

11. DSS leads to learning, which leads to new demands and the refinement of the system, which leads to additional learning, and so forth, in a continuous process of developing and improving the DSS.

12. End-users should be able to construct simple systems by themselves. Larger systems could be built in users' organizations with only minor assistance from information systems (IS) specialists.

13. A DSS usually utilizes models (standard or custom-made) for analyzing decision situations. The modeling capability enables experimenting with different strategies under different configurations. Such experimentations can provide new insights and learning.

14. Advanced DSS are equipped with a knowledge component that enables the efficient and effective solution of very difficult problems.

These characteristics and capabilities provide some major benefits (see Box 3.2).

Box 3.2: The Major Benefits of DSS

1. Ability to support the solution of complex problems.
2. Fast response to unexpected situations that result in changed conditions. A DSS enables a thorough, quantitative analysis in a very short time. Even frequent changes in complex scenarios can be evaluated objectively in a timely manner.
3. Ability to try several different strategies under different configurations, quickly and objectively.
4. New insights and learning. The user can be exposed to new insights through the composition of the model and an extensive sensitivity "what-if" analysis. The new insights can help in training inexperienced managers and other employees as well.
5. Facilitated communication. Data collection and model construction experimentations are executed with active users' participation, thus greatly facilitating communication among managers. The decision process can make employees more supportive of organizational decisions. The "what-if" analysis can be used to satisfy skeptics, in turn improving teamwork.
6. Improved management control and performance. DSS can increase management control over expenditures and improve performance of the organization.
7. Cost savings. Routine applications of a DSS may result in considerable cost reduction, or in reducing (eliminating) the cost of wrong decisions.
8. Objective decisions. The decisions derived from DSS are more consistent and objective than decisions made intuitively.
9. Improving managerial effectivensss, allowing managers to perform a task in less time and/or with less effort. The DSS provides managers with more "quality" time for analysis, planning, and implementation.
10. Improved productivity of analysts.

3.5 Components of DSS

DSS is composed of the following subsystems:

1. Data Management. The data management includes the database(s), which contains relevant data for the situation and is managed by software called **database management systems (DBMS).***
2. Model Management. A software package that includes financial, statistical, management science, or other quantitative models that provide the system's analytical capabilities, and an appropriate software management.
3. Communication (dialog subsystem). The user can communicate with and command the DSS through this subsystem. It provides the *user interface.*
4. Knowledge Management. This optional subsystem can support any of the other subsystems or act as an independent component.

These components constitute the software portion of the DSS. They are housed in a computer and could be facilitated by additional hardware and software pieces. Finally, the user is considered to be a part of the system. Researchers assert that some of the unique contributions of DSS are derived from the interaction between the computer and the decision maker.

---

*DBMS is both singular and plural (system or systems).

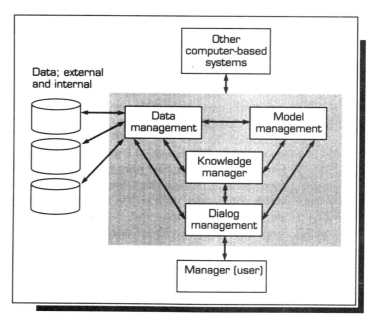

FIGURE 3.2 Conceptual Model of DSS.

A conceptual model of the DSS is given in Figure 3.2. It provides a basic understanding of the general structure and components of a DSS. A more detailed look at each of the components is given in the forthcoming sections and in Chapters 4–6 and 13.

3.6   The Data Management Subsystem

The data management subsystem is composed of the following elements:

- DSS database
- Database management system
- Data directory
- Query facility.

These elements are shown schematically in Figure 3.3 (inside the shaded area). The figure also shows the interaction of the data management subsystem with the other parts of the DSS, as well as the interaction with several data sources. A brief discussion of these elements and their function follows.

The Database

A **database** is a collection of interrelated data organized in such a way that it corresponds to the needs and structure of an organization and can be used by more than one person for more than one application. To understand better what a database is, let us consider information kept in separate files.

A file traditionally contains information regarding one application. For example, a company may have a personnel file listing all employees, a customer file listing all customers, and so on. Such files may contain extensive information such as addresses, telephone numbers, and volume of purchases for each customer. In a computerized system, a file can be on an auxiliary storage device, such as a tape or disk.

Example. Let us assume that a company has four files: a parts inventory file, a product file, a parts usage file (quantity used), and a customer file. Although each file has a different purpose, the data within the files are interrelated. For example, the parts usage file is required in preparing the monthly inventory report. And the purchasing data of products recorded in the customer files are used to forecast the demand for these products.

In addition to routine reports, management may require special reports from time to time (called **ad hoc reports**) based on information available in two or more files. In some companies, as much as 80 percent of all reporting is ad hoc. In the past, programmers and system analysts had to sort files, create new programs, and manipulate data to meet management's needs, usually at tremendous cost. These needs are now being met quickly and inexpensively by

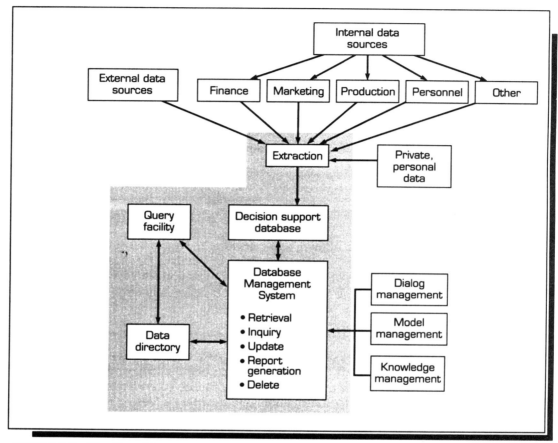

FIGURE 3.3 The Data Management Subsystem.

the database and its management. Many times, users can create the reports by themselves.

The data in the database are stored together with a minimum of redundancy to serve multiple applications, so the database is independent of the computer program that uses it and the type of hardware where it is stored. The database is organized so that the firm's files still exist, but they are linked in certain ways so that they form an integrated unit. This arrangement is very important when information is updated. In addition, there could be a considerable savings of storage space.

The data in the DSS database, as shown in Figure 3.3, may include internal data sources, external data, and private (personal) data belonging to one or more users.

Internal data come from the organization's transaction processing system. Depending on the needs of the DSS, data from functional areas like accounting, finance, marketing, production, and personnel might be included. Transaction data are the major source of information regarding internal company operations. A typical example of such data is the monthly payroll.

Other internal data might also be important to the DSS. Examples include planned dividend rates, machine maintenance scheduling, forecasts of future sales, cost of out-of-stock items, and future hiring plans.

External data may include industry data, marketing research data, census data, regional employment data, government regulations, tax rate schedules, or national economic data. These data might come from the U.S. government, trade associations, marketing research firms, econometric forecasting firms, and the organization's own efforts in collecting external data. Like internal data, the external data may be permanently maintained in the DSS database or may be entered when the DSS is used. External data are provided, in many cases, by computerized online services, a topic discussed in Chapter 4.

Private data may include rules of thumb used by specific decision makers and assessments of specific data and/or situations.

Organization. The data in the database can be organized in different configurations. For details, see Chapter 4. Should a DSS have an independent database? Most large DSS have their own fully integrated, multiple-source DSS database. A separate DSS database does not have to be physically separated from the corporate database. It can be located at the same place as the corporate database for economic reasons. It also can share a DBMS with other databases (see Figure 3.4).

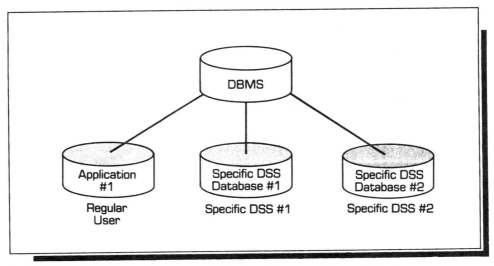

FIGURE 3.4 Database Management System Manages Several Databases.

The major advantages and disadvantages of a separate DSS database are summarized as follows:

Advantages:

1. A greater control exists over the data.
2. A better fit exists with the software that manages the database.
3. Most organizational databases are oriented toward transaction processing; therefore a separate database may be more efficient for a DSS.
4. A DSS may be cross-functional, requiring input from several databases. Once extracted into one database, the use of the data is much more efficient and simpler.
5. Changes and updates are faster, easier, and cheaper.
6. Easier access and data manipulation are provided.
7. Can adopt a database structure that is optimal for the specific DSS use (like relational or object-oriented).

Disadvantages:

1. A special additional database is more expensive to build, secure, and maintain than one database.
2. Separate databases can be individually modified by different users. If redundant data are stored in different places, and if the data are modified differently, we may have inconsistent data in the organization.

Extraction. In order to create a DSS database it is often necessary to capture data from several sources. This operation is called **extraction.** It is basically importing of files, summarization, filtration, and condensation of data. Extraction also occurs when the user produces reports from the data in the DSS database. The extraction process is managed by a DBMS.

Database Management System

The database is created, accessed, and updated by a DBMS, ranging in price from $99 for a microcomputer to $100,000 for complex mainframe software. DBMS have varied capabilities and are fairly complex so that only a few users can program and develop their own DBMS software. Instead, usually a standard software package is purchased. Examples of micro DBMS are dBASE IV, R base 5000, and ORACLE. On the mainframe one can use DB2. The data management capabilities in DSS (see Box 3.3) are provided by either a standard or a custom-made DBMS.

A DBMS performs three basic functions. It enables storage of data in the database, retrieval of data from the database, and control of the database.

Storage. DBMS vary in the configuration of the stored data. Mainframe systems store many large files, each file containing many records, each record containing many data items, and the data items containing many characters. The systems for

Box 3.3: The Capabilities of DBMS in a DSS

- Captures/extracts data for inclusion in a DSS database.
- Quickly updates (adds, deletes, edits, changes) data records and files.
- Interrelates data from different sources.
- Quickly retrieves data from a database for queries and reports.
- Provides comprehensive data security (protection from unauthorized access, recovery capabilities, etc.).
- Handles personal and unofficial data so that users can experiment with alternative solutions based on their own judgment.
- Performs complex retrieval and data manipulation tasks based on queries.
- Tracks usage of data.

microcomputers offer more constrained capacities because of limited primary and secondary storage space. (This limitation is becoming less and less of a factor.)

Retrieval. The feature of the DBMS most visible to the user is data retrieval. Current DBMS offer great flexibility in terms of how the information is retrieved and displayed. With a sophisticated DBMS, the user can specify certain processing of data and customize the output (e.g., reports or graphs) in terms of heading and spacing.

Control. Much of the control activity of the DBMS is invisible to users. The users ask for some information and receive it without knowing the processes that the DBMS has performed. The DBMS can be designed to screen each request for information and determine that (1) the person making the request is indeed an authorized user, (2) the person has access to the requested file, and (3) the person has access to the requested data items in the file. A mainframe DBMS might perform all the control functions very well. The micro DBMS may perform some. This is an area of great variety among the various commercial DBMS.

The manager can obtain information from the DSS in the form of periodic reports, special reports, and output of mathematical models. In all three of these instances, the DBMS serves as a gatekeeper and makes the data available (see Figure 3.5). The periodic reports are frequently prepared by application programs. These programs make requests of the DBMS for data needed from the database. The DBMS might offer a query language that can be manipulated by the user to create special reports. The user enters a few instructions, and this is all that is needed to trigger the preparation of a report.

An effective database and its management can provide support for many managerial activities; general navigation among records, support for a diverse set

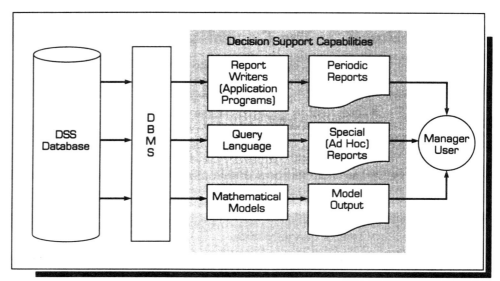

FIGURE 3.5 The Role of DBMS. (*Source:* Adapted by permission of the publisher from *Decision Support Software for the IBM Personal Computer* by R. McLeod, Jr. Copyright © 1985 by Science Research Associates, Inc.)

of data relationships, and report generation are typical examples. However, the real power of the DSS is provided when the database is integrated with models. The data management subsystem is revisited in Chapter 4.

The Query Facility

The **query facility** element provides the basis for access to data. It accepts requests for data (from other DSS components; see Figure 3.3), determines how these requests can be filled (consulting, if necessary, the data directory), formulates the detailed requests, and returns the results to the issuer of the request. The query facility includes a special query language. Important functions of a DSS query system are the "selection" and "manipulation" operations (for example, the ability to follow an instruction such as "search for all sales in zone *B* during January 1992 and summarize sales by salesperson").

The Directory (Dictionary)

The data **directory** is a catalog of all the data in the database. It contains the data definitions, and its main function is to answer questions about the availability of data items, their source, or their exact meaning. The directory is especially appropriate for supporting the intelligence phase of the decision-making process by helping to scan data and identify problem areas or opportunities. The directory, as does any other catalog, supports the addition of new entries, deletion of entries, and retrieval of information on specific objects.

3.7   The Model Management Subsystem

The model management subsystem of the DSS is composed of the following elements:

- Model base
- Model base management system
- Modeling language
- Model directory
- Model execution, integration, and command.

These elements and their **interface** with the other DSS components are shown in Figure 3.6.

The definition and function of each of these elements is described next.

Model Base

A **model base** contains routine and special statistical, financial, management science, and other quantitative models that provide the analysis capabilities in a DSS. (For details, see Chapter 5.) The ability to invoke, run, change, combine, and inspect models is a key capability in DSS that differentiates it from the traditional **computer-based information system** (CBIS). A CBIS refers to an information system supported by computers. Traditional systems are TPS and MIS (see Chapter 1). The models in the model base can be divided into four major categories: strategic, tactical, operational, and **model building blocks** and subroutines.*

Strategic models are used to support top management's strategic planning responsibilities. Potential applications include developing corporate objectives, planning for mergers and acquisitions, plant location selection, environmental impact analysis, and nonroutine capital budgeting. Strategic models tend to be broad in scope, with many variables expressed in a compressed form. The time horizons for these models are expressed in years. The GLSC case includes a long-range planning model. For details regarding planning models, see Naylor [1983].

Tactical models are employed mainly by middle management to assist in allocating and controlling the organization's resources. Examples of tactical models include labor requirement planning, sales promotion planning, plant layout determination, and routine capital budgeting. Tactical models are usually applicable only to an organizational subsystem like the accounting department. Their time horizon varies from one month to less than two years. Some external data are needed, but the greatest requirements are for internal data. The GLSC case includes mainly tactical models for their 15-month plan.

Operational models are used to support the day-to-day working activities of

---

*The details of these are based on Kroeber and Watson [1986].

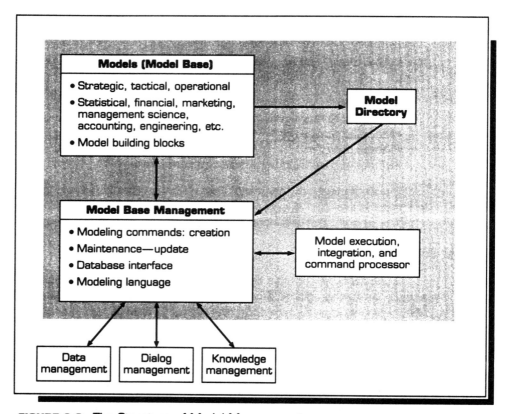

FIGURE 3.6 The Structure of Model Management.

the organization. Approving personal loans by a bank, production scheduling, inventory control, maintenance planning and scheduling, and quality control are all examples of operational areas with potential DSS application. Operational models support mainly first-line managers' decision making with a daily to monthly time horizon. The models normally use internal data.

In addition to strategic, tactical, and operational models, the model base could contain model building blocks and subroutines. Examples include a "random number generator mechanism," "curveline fitting routine," "present-value computational routine," or "regression analysis." Such building blocks can be used in several ways. They can be used on their own for applications like data analysis. They can also be employed as components of larger models. For example, a present-value component can be part of a "make or buy" model. Some of these building blocks are used to determine the values of variables and parameters in a model, as in the use of regression analysis to create trend lines in a forecasting model. They are frequently referred to as *built-in-functions*.

The models in the model base can also be classified by functional areas (e.g., financial models, production control models) or by discipline (e.g., statistical models, management science allocation models). A list of representative models is given in Chapter 5. The number of models in a DSS can vary from a few to several hundred. For example, a DSS for a large transportation company includes over 175 models (see Oliff [1984]).

Modeling Languages

Although some of the models in the model base are prewritten, it is frequently necessary to write a model. This can be done with high-level languages (COBOL) or better with fourth-generation languages (4GL) and special modeling languages (see Chapters 5 and 7).

The Model Base Management System (MBMS)

The **model base management system (MBMS)** is a software system with the following functions: model creation, using subroutines and other building blocks; generation of new routines and reports; model updating and changing; and data manipulation. The MBMS is capable of interrelating models with the appropriate linkages through a database. (See Box 3.4.)

Box 3.4: Major Functions (or Capabilities) of the MBMS

- Creates models easily and quickly, either from scratch or from existing models or from the building blocks.
- Allows users to manipulate the models so that they can conduct experiments and sensitivity analyses ranging from "what-if" to goal seeking.
- Stores and manages a wide variety of different types of models in a logical and integrated manner.
- Accesses and integrates the model building blocks.
- Catalogs and displays the directory of models for use by several individuals in the organization.
- Tracks models, data, and application usage.
- Interrelates models with appropriate linkages through the database.
- Manages and maintains the model base with management functions analogous to database management: store, access, run, update, link, catalog, and query.

The Model Directory

The role of the model directory is similar to that of a database directory. It is a catalog of all the models in the model base. It contains the model definitions, and its main function is to answer questions about the availability and capability of the models.

An interesting issue in a DSS might be, "Which models should be used for what occasion?" Such model selection cannot be done by the MBMS because it requires expertise; it is a potential area for a knowledge component "assisting" the MBMS.

Model Execution, Integration, and Command

The following activities are usually controlled by model management:

- Model execution—controlling the actual running of the model.
- Model integration—combining the operations of several models when needed (e.g., directing the output of one model to be processed by another one).

A modeling command processor is used to accept and interpret modeling instructions as they flow out of the dialog component, and to route them to the MBMS, the model execution, or to the integration functions.

The execution of computations with the models requires retrieval of data items from the DSS's database or from other databases. This activity is performed through a database interface.

3.8   The Knowledge Subsystem

Many unstructured and semistructured problems are so complex that they require expertise for their solution in addition to the regular DSS capabilities. Such an expertise can be provided by an expert system. Therefore, the more advanced DSS are equipped with a component that we call knowledge management. Such a component can provide the required expertise for solving some aspects of the problem and/or providing knowledge that can enhance the operation of the other DSS components.

The knowledge management component is composed of one or more expert systems. Like data and model management, knowledge management software provides the necessary execution and integration of the expert system (see Chapter 20). The capabilities of this component are discussed in Chapter 13.

A decision support system that includes such a component is referred to as an intelligent DSS, a DSS/ES, or a knowledge-based DSS.

3.9   The User Interface (Dialog) Subsystem

The dialog component of a DSS is the software and hardware that provides the user interface for DSS. The term **user interface** covers all aspects of the communications between a user and the DSS. It includes not only the hardware and software, but also factors that deal with ease of use, accessibility, and human-machine interactions. Some DSS experts feel that user interface is the most important component because much of the power, flexibility, and ease-of-use characteristics of DSS are derived from this component (e.g., Sprague and Carlson [1982, p. 29]). An inconvenient user interface is one of the major reasons why managers have not used computers and quantitative analyses to the extent that these technologies have been available.

Management of the Dialog Subsystem

The dialog subsystem is managed by software called **dialog generation and management system (DGMS).** The DGMS is composed of several programs that provide the capabilities listed in Box 3.5. The DGMS is also known as *user interface management-system* (UIMS), and it is further discussed in Chapter 6.

Box 3.5: Major Capabilities of DGMS

- Interacts in several different dialog styles.
- Captures, stores, and analyzes dialog usage (tracking), which can be used for improving the dialog system.
- Accommodates the user with a variety of input devices.
- Presents data with a variety of formats and output devices.
- Gives users "help" capabilities, prompting, diagnostic and suggestion routines, or any other flexible support.
- Provides user interface with database and model base.
- Creates data structures to describe outputs (output formatter).
- Stores input and output data.
- Provides color graphics, three-dimensional graphics, and data plotting
- Has windows to allow multiple functions to be displayed concurrently.
- Can support communication among and between users and builders of DSS.
- Provides training by examples (guiding users through the input and modeling process).
- Provides flexibility and adaptiveness so the DSS will be able to accommodate different problems and technologies.

The Dialog Process

The dialog process for a DSS is shown schematically in Figure 3.7. The user interacts with the computer via an action language processed via the DGMS. In advanced systems the dialog component includes a natural language processor. The DGMS provides the capabilities listed in Box 3.5, and enables the user to interact with the model management and the data management subsystems.

The dialog management subsystem offers a user interface system, which includes the input-output devices and provides the physical means of communication with the DSS; a function that controls the flow of information through the dialog subsystem as data are being inputted and outputted; and a function that transforms the input from the user into languages that can be read by the DBMS

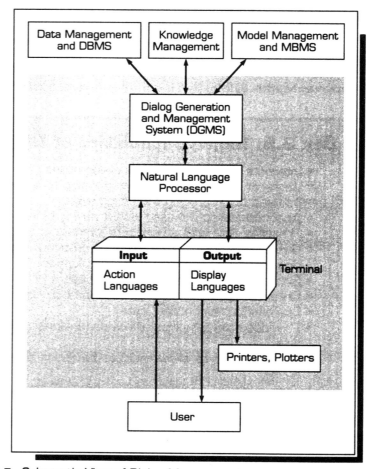

FIGURE 3.7 Schematic View of Dialog Management.

and the MBMS and that can translate output from the DBMS, the MBMS, and the knowledge management subsystem into a form that can be understood by the user. For further discussion see Chapter 6.

3.10   The User

The person faced with the problem or decision that the DSS is designed to support has been referred to as the *user*, the *manager*, or the *decision maker*.* These terms fail to reflect, however, the heterogeneity that exists among users and the usage patterns (see Box 3.6) of DSS. There are differences in the positions that the users hold, the way in which a final decision is reached, the users' cognitive preferences and abilities, and ways of arriving at a decision (decision styles).

A DSS has two broad classes of users: managers and staff specialists. Staff specialists, like financial analysts, production planners, and marketing researchers, outnumber managers by about three to two and are using computers by a much larger ratio. Knowing who will actually have hands-on use of the DSS is important when one is designing it. In general, managers expect systems to be more user-friendly than do staff specialists. Staff specialists tend to be more detail-oriented, are more willing to use complex systems in their day-to-day work, and are interested in the computational capabilities of the DSS. In many cases the staff analysts are the intermediaries between management and the DSS.

Even within the categories of managers and staff specialists, there are important subcategories that influence DSS design. For example, managers differ by organizational level, functional area, educational background, and need for analytic support. Staff specialists differ in areas such as education, the functional area that they operate, and relationship to management.

3.11   DSS Hardware and Software

Decision support systems have evolved simultaneously with advances in computer hardware and software technologies. Hardware affects the functionality and the usability of the DSS. Although the choice of hardware may be made before, during, or after the design of the DSS software, in many cases the hardware choice is predetermined by what is already available within the organization. A DSS runs on standard hardware. The major hardware options are a time-sharing network, the organization's mainframe computer, a minicomputer, a personal computer, or

*The material in Sections 3.10 and 3.11 was adapted from Kroeber and Watson [1986].

608

Box 3.6: DSS Usage Patterns

The ultimate "user" of a decision support system is the decision maker. However, he or she may not actually run the system. Based on his research on 56 decision support systems, Alter ([1980], p. 115) identified the following distinct usage patterns:

1. *Subscription mode.* The decision maker receives reports generated on a regular basis. Although some data analysis systems or accounting models might be used in this way, it is not typical for decision support systems.
2. *Terminal mode.* The decision maker is the direct user of the system through online access. This is becoming the dominant mode.
3. *Intermediary mode.* The decision maker uses the system through intermediaries, who perform the analysis and interpret and report the results. The decision maker does not need to know how the intermediary used the system to arrive at the requested information.

The role of an intermediary is still common in the use of decision support systems and merits separate attention. The use of an intermediary allows the manager to benefit from the decision support system without actually having to use the keyboard. Some managers resist using the keyboard, and until speech understanding devices become more widely available, there will continue to be some resistance to the terminal mode.

There are several types of intermediaries that reflect different support for the manager:

1. *Staff assistant.* This person has specialized knowledge about management problems and some experience with the decision support technology.
2. *Expert tool user.* This person is skilled in the application of one or more types of specialized problem-solving tools. The expert tool user performs tasks that the problem solver does not have the skills or training to perform.
3. *Business (system) analyst.* This person has a general knowledge of the application area, formal business administration education (not computer science), and considerable skill in DSS construction tools.
4. *Facilitator in Group DSS.* This intermediary controls and coordinates the software of group DSS (see Chapter 9).

(*Source:* Stephen L. Alter, *Decision Support Systems,* © 1980 by Addison-Wesley Publishing Company, Inc. Reprinted with permission of the publisher.)

a distributed system. Each option offers advantages and disadvantages. These are briefly discussed next.

Time-sharing Network

Companies like Boeing Computer Services, Tymshare, and CompuServe offer national time-sharing networks on which DSS software can be placed. In addition, several DSS vendors offer tools for building DSS via time-sharing. Time-sharing is an ideal option if you do not have a mainframe computer, but you need its capabilities. It is also used by companies that already have a mainframe because in some instances better response times can be obtained from a time-sharing network than from an in-house computer system. Another benefit is the quickness with which a DSS can be constructed when the vendor is the DSS builder, because the vendor has experience in using the software and building similar DSS.

The major disadvantage of a time-sharing network is cost control. If a DSS is frequently used, time-sharing costs can become quite high. What frequently happens in this case is that the DSS is then brought in-house.

Mainframe, Workstation, Mini-, or Personal Computer

If the DSS is located in-house, a mainframe, workstation, mini-, or personal computer might be used (or a combination of these if a distributed DSS is used). A variety of factors influence the type of computer used, including what kind of computers are available in-house, the type of decision support to be provided, the data needs of the DSS, the computational power that is needed, the existing network system, and the software demands of the DSS.

A major reason for placing a DSS in-house is that the required hardware and software may already be available there. However, this situation need not be the limiting consideration. It is not unusual for software and sometimes hardware to be purchased specifically for DSS.

The range of DSS users also influences what hardware is to be used and where it is placed. If the system is to support users throughout an organization, an enterprise client/server architecture might be required. On the other hand, if the DSS is to provide decision support for one person, a personal computer might be used (e.g., see Hackathorn and Keen [1981]). Developments in the area of client/server architecture, parallel processing, and networks of computers could have a major impact on hardware selection.

The data needs of the DSS may also play a role in determining the hardware selection. Some DSS require considerable data from the organization's database. Then it may be advantageous to place the DSS on the same system where the database is maintained. However, this may not be as important a consideration as it might first seem. Experience has shown that the data needs of many decision support systems differ considerably from what is maintained in existing databases. Therefore, it may be more practical to download and extract data from the corporate database to the DSS database, or even directly to a microcomputer's memory.

610

Some decision support systems require significant computational power, which necessitates the use of large, fast machines. Some simulation models especially require a large number of calculations. Multidimensional reports constructed from a large number of files also require a significant memory and/or access to several databases.

The DSS software, as outlined earlier, is composed of the DBMS, MBMS, and dialog management. There may also be additional software for added capabilities (e.g., knowledge-base, multimedia).

Distributed DSS

An increased number of DSS is available on networks, either LANs and/or wide area networks. The advantages of such systems are the availability of the DSS to users in many locations and the accessibility of the DSS to data and models in many locations. This important topic is revisited in Chapter 4.

3.12 Classifications of DSS and Their Support

There are several ways to classify DSS, some of which overlap. The design process, as well as the operation and implementation of DSS, depends in many cases on the type of DSS involved. Representative classification schemes are presented next.

Type of Support: Data-oriented versus Model-oriented (Alter [1980])

This classification is based on the "degree of action implication of system outputs"; that is, the extent to which system outputs can directly support (or determine) the decision (see Box 3.7). According to this classification, there are seven categories of DSS (see Table 3.3). The first three types are *data-oriented*, performing data retrieval and/or analysis. The remaining four are *model-oriented*, providing either simulation capabilities, optimization, or computations that "suggest an answer." Not every DSS fits neatly into a single classification system; some have equally strong data and modeling orientation (e.g., the GLSC case).

Institutional versus Ad Hoc DSS (Donovan and Madnick [1977])

This classification is based on the nature of the decision situation that the DSS are designed to support. There are two categories:

Institutionalized DSS. This type of DSS deals with decisions of a *recurring* nature. A typical example is a portfolio management system (PMS), which has been used by several large banks (see Alter [1980]). Another example is the GLSC case presented earlier. An **institutionalized DSS** may be developed and refined over a

Box 3.7: Support Provided by DSS

DSS may provide several types of support. The following structure is based on Alter [1980]. Each level of support contains and adds on the previous level (but may also contribute to the previous level).

DSS Provides:	Answers to Questions:
Raw data and status access	What is . . . ?
↓	
General analysis capabilities	What is/Why . . . ?
↓ ↑	
Representation models (financial statements), Causal models (forecasting, diagnosis)	What will be . . . ? Why . . . ?
↓	
Solution suggestions, evaluation	What if . . . ?
↓	
Solution selection	What is best/What is good enough . . . ?

number of years because the DSS will be used over and over (with appropriate updating of the database and models) to solve identical or similar problems. Institutionalized DSS deal mainly with operational and management control problems.

Ad Hoc DSS. This type of DSS deals with specific problems that are usually neither anticipated nor recurring. For example, the Houston Minerals DSS was created specifically to evaluate the feasibility of a joint venture. To economically justify this type of situation it is necessary to use general-purpose software for information retrieval, data analysis, modeling, and the like, that can be quickly and inexpensively customized for each specific application. The concept of DSS generators, which will be introduced later, was developed to provide a means for satisfying ad hoc needs for decision-making support. Ad hoc decisions frequently involve strategic planning issues and sometimes management control problems.

TABLE 3.3 Characteristics of Different Classes of Decision Support Systems.

Category	Type of Operation	Type of Task	User	Usage Pattern	Time Frame
File drawer systems	Access data items	Operational	Nonmanagerial line personnel	Simple inquiries	Irregular
Data analysis systems	Ad hoc analysis of files of data	Operational, analysis	Staff analysts or managerial line personnel	Manipulation and display of data	Irregular or periodic
Analysis information systems	Ad hoc analysis involving multiple databases and small models	Analysis, planning	Staff analyst	Programming special reports, developing small models	Irregular, on request
Accounting models	Standard calculations that estimate future results on the basis of accounting definitions	Planning, budgeting	Analyst or manager	Input estimates of activity; receive estimated monetary results as output	Periodic (e.g., weekly, monthly, yearly)
Representational models	Estimating consequences of particular actions	Planning, budgeting	Staff analyst	Input possible decisions; receive estimated results as output	Periodic or irregular (ad hoc analysis)
Optimization models	Calculating an optimal solution to a combinatorial problem	Planning, resource allocation	Staff analyst	Input constraints and objectives; receive answer	Periodic or irregular (ad hoc analysis)
Suggestion models	Performing calculations that generate a suggested decision	Operational	Nonmanagerial line personnel	Input a structured description of the decision situation; receive a suggested decision as output	Daily or periodic

Source: Condensed from Alter [1980], pp. 90–91.

Many of the DSS developed up to about 1983 were institutionalized in nature (see Alter [1980] and Meador et al, [1984]), mainly owing to the high cost of developing a DSS for nonrecurring use. However, with the increased availability of general purpose DSS tools, with their steadily decreasing costs and increasing capabilities, and with the appearance of DSS software for microcomputers, it is possible to build ad hoc DSS in an economically justifiable manner.

Degree of Nonprocedurality (Bonczek, et al. [1980])

This classification is based on the degree of nonprocedurality of the data retrieval and modeling languages provided by the DSS. Procedural languages, such as BASIC and COBOL, require step-by-step specifications of how data are to be retrieved and how computations are to be performed. In nonprocedural languages the system itself is programmed so that programmers are required to specify only what results are needed. There is no need to specify the sequence of execution. At an intermediate level of procedurality are systems that utilize a command language allowing users to call up a desired prespecified report, model, or function. Most DSS users find nonprocedural languages more convenient for both data retrieval and modeling activities. Nonprocedural languages (also called fourth-generation languages) are discussed in Chapter 7.

Personal, Group, and Organizational Support (Hackathorn and Keen [1981])

The support given by DSS can be separated into three distinct but interrelated categories:

Personal Support. Here the focus is on an individual user (or a group of users) performing an activity in a discrete task or decision (e.g., recommending stocks). The task is relatively independent of other tasks.

Group (Team) Support. The focus here is on a group of people, each of whom is engaged in separate but highly interrelated tasks. An example is a typical finance department where one DSS may serve several employees, all working on the budget.

Organizational Support. Here the focus is on organizational tasks or activities involving a *sequence* of operations, different functional areas, different locations, and massive resources. For example, the GLSC case illustrates a sequence of decisions composed of long-term planning, short-term planning, resource allocation, and job assignment decisions. For further discussion, see organizational DSS in Chapter 8.

Individual versus Group DSS

Many decision support systems are used to support an individual decision maker. However, many DSS researchers and practitioners (e.g., Keen [1980]) point out that the fundamental model of DSS—the lonely decision maker striding down the hall at high noon to make a decision—is true only for minor decisions. In most organizations, be they public or private, Japanese, European, or American, most *major* decisions are made collectively. In making decisions collectively one introduces a new dimension, namely the manner in which the group works together, communicates, and eventually arrives at a decision. This is a complicated *process* and it can be supported by computers. This is basically what is called group DSS.

Note: The term *group support* introduced earlier should not be confused with the concept of **group DSS.** In group support the decisions are made by individuals whose tasks are interrelated. Therefore they should check the impact of their decision on others, but not necessarily make decisions as a group. In a group DSS each decision (sometimes only one decision) is made by the group.

Custom-made versus Ready-made Systems

Many DSS are custom made for individual users and organizations. In such cases, the problem is nonroutine and not structured. However, a similar problem may exist in similar organizations. For example, hospitals, banks, and universities share many such problems. Similarly, certain nonroutine problems in a functional area (finance, accounting, etc.) can repeat themselves in the same functional area of different organizations. Therefore, it makes sense to build generic DSS that can be used (sometimes with modifications) in several organizations of a similar nature. Such DSS are called *ready-made*. They are sold by various vendors and sometimes are available on time-sharing. Recently we have seen an increased number of ready-made DSS, due to their increased flexibility and reduced cost. An example of two such systems is given in Appendix 3-A to this chapter.

3.13 The Big Picture

So far we have introduced you to the fundamentals of DSS. We started the chapter with a discussion of the GLSC case. Now that you have learned about the various components of the DSS, we can superimpose the details of the case on the general structure of the DSS (Figure 3.2 minus the knowledge component). The result is shown in Figure 3.8. Also, we have summarized the major capabilities of the DSS components (excluding the knowledge component) in Figure 3.9.

3.14 Technology Levels

A useful framework for understanding DSS construction issues was devised by Sprague and Carlson [1982], who identified **three levels of DSS technology:** specific DSS, DSS generators, and DSS tools.

Specific DSS (DSS applications)

The "final product," or the DSS application that actually accomplishes the work, is called a **specific DSS** (SDSS). For example, the Houston Minerals case presented earlier is a specific DSS for analyzing a joint venture.

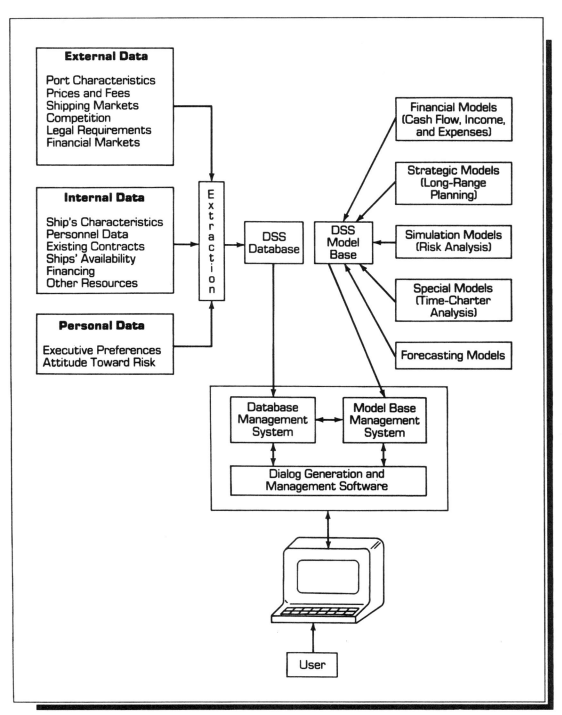

FIGURE 3.8 The GLSC DSS—An Overview.

616

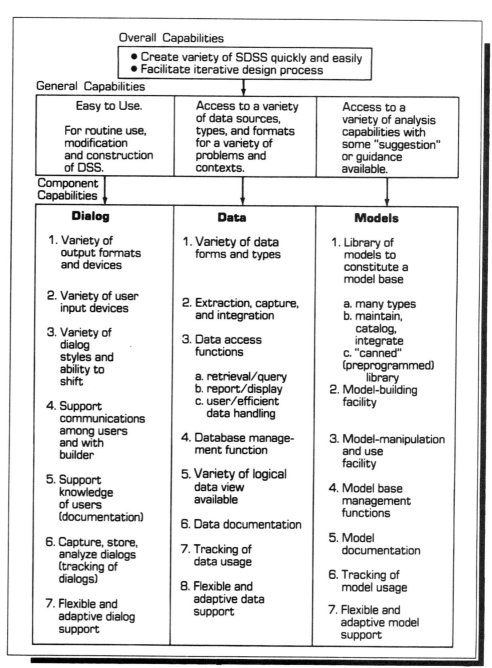

FIGURE 3.9 Summary of DSS Capabilities. (*Source:* Ralph Sprague/Eric Carlson, *Building Effective Decision Support Systems*, © 1982, p. 313. Reprinted by permission of Prentice-Hall, Inc., Englewood Cliffs, NJ).

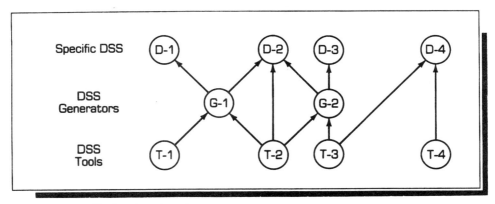

FIGURE 3.10 Technology Levels.

A well-known example of a specific DSS is the police-beat allocation system, which was implemented by IBM in San Jose, California. This system allows a police officer to display a map outline on a video display terminal and call up data by geographical zones showing police calls for service, response times, and activity level. An officer can manipulate the map, zones, and data, and experiment with a variety of police patrol alternatives. Incidentally, this DSS yielded superior results (in terms of acceptance by users and consistency with the problem requirements) over a solution derived by linear programming.

Examples of specific DSS are given as cases at the end of this chapter.

DSS Generators (or Engines)

A **DSS generator (engine)** (see Box 3.8) is an integrated development software that provides a set of capabilities to build a specific DSS quickly, inexpensively, and easily. A popular microcomputer-based generator is Lotus 1-2-3. A generator possesses diverse capabilities ranging from modeling, report generation, and graphical display to performing risk analysis. These capabilities, which have been available separately for some time, are integrated into an easy-to-use package.

There has been an evolutionary growth from two directions toward what might be described as an "ideal" DSS generator. One direction is *special-purpose languages* initially developed for mainframes. In fact, many commercial DSS generators evolved from planning (or modeling) languages, usually with added report generation and graphic display capabilities. Examples of such languages are the Interactive Financial Planning System (IFPS Plus) and Express. Other types of specialized languages are those initially developed around strong DBMS capabilities. Examples of such languages are Nomad 2, Ramis II, and Focus. The second direction is microbased *integrated software* systems like Lotus 1-2-3, Quattro Pro, and Excel, which are constructed around spreadsheet technology. DSS generators are discussed in Chapter 7, and their relationships to other technology levels is shown in Figure 3.10.

Box 3.8: DSS Generator

The term *DSS generator* emerged from the concept of application (or program) generator. Application generators are tools used by programmers and system analysts to expedite programming and systems development. For example, an application generator can be used to build an inventory control system.

Application generators add convenience and reduce costs for the creation of programs. The programs produced are not as efficient, in terms of processing throughout, as those coded from scratch by experienced programmers. Therefore generators are more suitable for applications that run infrequently or that do not involve large-volume data processing.

DSS Tools

At the lowest level of DSS technology are the software utilities or tools. These elements facilitate the *development* of either a DSS generator or a specific DSS. Examples of **DSS tools** are graphics (hardware and software), editors, query systems, random number generators, and spreadsheets.

Relationships Among the Three Levels

The relationships among the three levels are presented in Figure 3.10. The tools are used to construct generators, which in turn are used to construct specific DSS. However, tools can also be used directly to construct specific DSS. In addition (not shown in the figure), there may be simpler tools for constructing more complicated tools.

The use of DSS generators is extremely helpful in constructing specific DSS and enabling them to quickly adapt to changes. Using generators can save a significant amount of time and money, thus making a DSS financially feasible. Constructing DSS only with tools, without generators, can be a very lengthy and expensive proposition, especially if the tools themselves need to be developed. Although most of the early DSS were developed without generators, the opposite is true today.

Significance. The classification of technology levels is not only important for understanding the construction of DSS (and also ES) but also for developing a framework for their use. A field study revealed that DSS generators and tools are extremely useful even for senior managers. There is a wide range of decision situations faced by senior management that require ad hoc DSS. Ad hoc DSS can be developed economically, and in a timely manner, only with the aid of generators.

Chapter Highlights

- There are many definitions of DSS.
- At the minimum, DSS is designed to support complex managerial problems that other computerized techniques cannot. DSS is user-oriented, utilizes data, and frequently models.
- It is possible to add a component to the DSS to make it intelligent.
- DSS may provide support to all phases of the decision-making process and to all managerial levels, both for individuals and groups.
- DSS is a user-oriented tool. It can be constructed by end-users.
- DSS can improve the effectiveness of decision making, decrease the need for training, improve management control, facilitate communication, save effort by the user, reduce costs, and allow for more objective decision making.
- The major components of a DSS are: database and its management, model base and its management, and friendly user interface. An intelligent (knowledge) component can be added.
- The data management subsystem includes: a DSS database (optional), a DBMS, a data directory, and a query facility.
- Data are extracted from several sources, internal and external.
- The DBMS provides many capabilities to the DSS, ranging from storage to retrieval and report generation.
- The model base includes standard models and models specifically written for the DSS.
- Custom-made models can be written with third- and fourth-generation languages. End-user DSS are usually written with 4GL-based DSS tools and generators.
- The user interface (or dialog) is of utmost importance. It is managed by a special software that provides the needed capabilities.
- DSS can be used directly by managers (and analysts) or it can be used via intermediaries.
- DSS can be built for all types of hardware and can be placed on networks (distributed DSS).
- DSS can be used to support individuals or it can be used to support decisions made by groups.

Key Words

adaptive process
ad hoc reports
computer-based
  information system
database
database management
  system (DBMS)

dialog generation and
  management system
  (DGMS)
directory
DSS generators
  (engines)
DSS tools

extraction
group DSS
institutionalized
  DSS
interdependent
  decisions
interface

620

model base	operational models	technology levels of
model base	query facility	DSS
management system	specific DSS	user interface
(MBMS)	strategic models	
model building blocks	tactical models	

Questions for Review

1. Give two definitions of DSS.
2. Why do people attempt to narrow the definition of DSS?
3. Give your own definition of DSS.
4. List the major components of DSS and define each of them briefly.
5. How does a database differ from a collection of files?
6. What are the major functions (capabilities) of DBMS?
7. What is meant by "extraction"?
8. What is the function of a query facility?
9. What is the function of a directory?
10. Models are classified as strategic, tactical, or operational. What is the purpose of such classifications? Give an example of each.
11. List some of the major functions of MBMS.
12. What is the major purpose of the user interface system?
13. Define a ready-made DSS.
14. List the major user patterns.
15. What is meant by "dialog style"?
16. What are the major functions of a dialog management system?
17. List the major classes of DSS users.
18. What types of support are provided by DSS?
19. What are the major advantages of time-sharing?
20. What are the major disadvantages of time-sharing?
21. What are the major software components included in a DSS?
22. Define a procedural computer language and contrast it with a nonprocedural one.
23. Compare a custom-made DSS with ready-made. List advantages and disadvantages of each.
24. List and discuss the various technology levels.
25. Define DSS generators and discuss their objectives.

Questions for Discussion

1. Review the major characteristics and capabilities of DSS. Relate each of them to the major components of DSS.
2. List some internal data and external data that could be found in a DSS for selecting a portfolio of stocks for an investor.
3. List some internal and external data in a DSS that will be constructed for a decision regarding the expansion of a hospital.

4. Provide a list of possible strategic, tactical, and operational models in a university, in a restaurant, in a chemical plant.
5. Show the similarity between DBMS and MBMS. What is common to both?
6. Compare an individual DSS to a group DSS.

Exercise

1. Susan Lopez was promoted to be a director of the transportation department in a medium-size university. She controlled the following vehicles: 17 sedans, 15 vans, and 3 trucks. The previous director was fired because there were too many complaints concerning not getting vehicles when needed. Susan was told not to expect any increase in budget for the next two years (no replacement or additional vehicles). Susan's major job was to schedule vehicles for employees, and to schedule the maintenance and repair of the vehicles. All this was accomplished manually.

   Your job is to consult with Susan regarding the possibility of using a DSS to improve this situation. Susan has a 486 PC, Lotus 1-2-3, Paradox, and Harvard Graphics, but she is using the computer only as a word processor.

   Prepare:

   1. A justification for the use of the DSS, namely, what the DSS can do to support Susan's job.
   2. What will be included in the data management, model management, and dialog (interface)?
   3. What type of support do you expect this DSS to render (consult Table 3.3)?
   4. How would you classify this DSS (consult Section 3.12)?
   5. Does it make sense to have a knowledge component?

CASE APPLICATION 1: Financial Planning at the Louisiana National Bank*

The Louisiana National Bank (LNB) is located in Baton Rouge, Louisiana. In 1958, Charles McCoy became the bank's chief executive officer. Under his leadership, the LNB has developed a reputation for innovation. By 1978 the LNB became the largest bank in Baton Rouge.

In the fall of 1973, the LBN was facing serious problems. Profits had been declining for over a year. Traditional policies for managing the bank were failing. There was a lack of coordination among decision makers. The bank was slow to react to market and regulation changes.

*Condensed from Ralph H. Sprague, Jr., and Ronald L. Olson, "The Financial Planning Systems at Louisiana National Bank," *MIS Quarterly*, September 1979, pp. 35–46.

In response to this deteriorating situation, McCoy designated Gil Urban as corporate planner and charged him with the responsibility of developing a system to help analyze the bank's performance and to support top management decision making. Urban was an excellent choice for this position because he had extensive banking experience and a personal interest in planning and analysis activities.

The Development of FPS

After an intensive six-week study, Urban began developing the financial planning system (FPS). The initial system was designed to produce reports of the type and format that top management had been receiving in the past. Over time, management understanding of FPS grew, and the capabilities of the system were refined and expanded.

System Components

FPS has three components: data, reports and analyses, and forecasts. Each component plays an important role in the functioning of FPS.

Data. On a monthly basis, summary data from the bank's general ledger accounting system are extracted and entered into the FPS. The data are added to a matrix of historical data in which the rows are items in the summary chart of accounts and the columns are time periods. The database maintains up to three years of monthly figures and up to 7.5 years of quarterly figures. The database also stores 12 periods of forecasted data.

Reports and Analyses. Each month, FPS produces a complete set of summary financial statements, including the balance sheet, the income statement, and standard operating reports. Data from the current month are compared with the forecast, the budget, and the actual data for the previous year. A number of special reports are also generated. Of particular importance to the LNB management are the interest rate-volume-mix analysis and the line-of-business-analysis reports.

Forecasts. The system produced a forecast of the information included in the reports for a period of 12 months. The system contains a built-in linear programming submodel that can be used to identify the optimal projected earnings with respect to yields, subject to constraints or guidelines defined by management.

Use of the System

FPS is utilized in several ways. On the first Tuesday of each month, FPS is used to supply the planning committee with reports and graphs that show the previous month's activities and the forecast.

During the meeting of the planning committee, anticipated changes and pending issues are discussed. Frequently, there are questions and possibilities that need to be explored further at the next meeting after additional runs of FPS.

Urban also uses FPS to prepare forecasts for other bank officers who wish to investigate the consequences of possible strategies.

Urban also uses FPS on his own initiative. He investigates areas such as the impact of pending changes in money market rates, banking regulations, market trends, and internal policy changes.

FPS also plays an important role in the bank's budgeting process. Each fall a "grass roots" budget, as it is called, is prepared. It is composed of about 9,000 data items: one for each budget line item, for each of the cost centers, for each of the 12 months of the coming year. Once the tentative budget is prepared, summaries are extracted and entered into the FPS the same way that actual data are transferred after the end of each month. FPS is then used to assess the combined impact of the budget estimates, to examine the reasonableness of the estimates compared with top management's judgment, and to search for any inconsistencies in interrelated areas. Any adjustments in the tentative budget are made through a process of negotiation between top management and the cost center managers. The detailed final budget is approved by mid-December and is then carried in the automated accounting system, which produces monthly budget variance reports for each cost center during the coming year.

Benefits

The LNB has benefited considerably from the use of FPS. Most importantly, it has made the bank profitable. After-tax profit grew from 2 to 6 million dollars between 1974 and 1978.

The use of FPS has led to new policies for asset-liability management. An example of this occurred in 1975 when the government authorized consumer certificates of deposit (CDs) in small denominations for four- and six-year maturities. Many banks hesitated to offer these CDs because of the fear that savers would shift their regular savings to higher-yield CDs. By using FPS, the management at the LNB became convinced that the CDs were an excellent way to obtain long-term funds on which to build their consumer loan portfolio. Consequently, they gave heavy promotion to the CDs, which resulted in increased funds, increased loans, and increased profitability in the retail segment of the LNB's business.

FPS has also provided a framework, a structure, and a discipline for unified decision making. Later on, the LNB experienced a growth in credit card loans and decided to sell a large portion of the loans to a New York bank. Without the convincing analysis provided by FPS, this move would have been strongly opposed by several of the bank's managers because of the bank's history as the leading regional credit card lender.

Reporting and negotiating with bank regulators has been facilitated by FPS. In 1978, management noted that FPS forecasted a need for additional capital because of a growing demand for loans. Using FPS, management developed a "balanced growth" plan.

The use of FPS has made it possible to respond to changes faster. In March 1978, after several years of liquidity shortages, the LNB was experiencing an average excess liquidity of 30 million dollars a day. FPS forecasted, however, that loan growth and deposit shrinkage would create liquidity problems by early fall of that year. Based on this forecast, the planning committee set maximum growth goals for all departments and took some other preemptive actions. By October, it was clear that the LNB had averted a major liquidity crisis because of the early warning provided by FPS.

FPS produces the normal monthly reports less expensively than when they were prepared manually. However, the cost of additional runs to explore alternative plans and assumptions more than consumes this saving.

This additional cost does not bother management. As McCoy has said, "FPS clearly paid for itself in helping us generate that first set of strategic plans. Now we don't even think about what it costs, because we couldn't run the bank without it."

Case Questions

1. Discuss the data, models, software interface, and user components in this case.
2. Is the financial planning system at the Louisiana National Bank best categorized as an MIS or a DSS? Why? Is the distinction clear? Why?
3. Decision support systems have the potential for supporting top-, middle-, and lower-management decision making. To what extent is decision making at these levels supported by the decision support systems described in this case?
4. Decision support systems can be used for ad hoc and for repetitive decision making. How would you classify the decision support systems described in this case?
5. Decision support systems have the potential for supporting the intelligence, design, and choice phases of decision making. To what extent are these decision-making phases supported by the decision support systems described in this case?
6. Decision support systems can support independent and sequential interdependent decision making. What kind of decision support is provided by the decision support systems described in this case?
7. Explain the following statement: "Values for the independent variables were entered by management or statistically estimated by FPS with a management override capability." What is the significance of this statement?
8. An evolutionary developmental approach is best for most decision support systems. To what extent was an evolutionary approach used with the decision support systems described in this case? Do you agree with the approaches that were used? Why?
9. The objective of a DSS is to create organizational benefits. Describe the benefits generated by the decision support systems described in this case.

CASE APPLICATION 2: Decision Support for Military Housing Managers*

The Problem

The Department of the Army often enters into agreements for long-term leasing or even for building appropriate housing facilities close to or on military bases. The decision of where, what, when, and how to build or lease is a complex one, and it requires a formal segmented housing market analysis (SHMA) that costs about $50,000 to prepare and whose purpose is to justify the decision. The SHMA analysis must meet not only the available budget but also the requirements of several auditing agencies. Furthermore, the analysis takes into account the economy around each base and the existing housing market (e.g., availability of rental units that the military may utilize). The problem is even more complex because there are 20 military ranks (the higher your rank, the nicer accommodations you can get, of course). Housing is available in six sizes, ranging from a studio to a five-bedroom unit. A family's size is also a determining factor. The SHMA analysis uses several quantitative models, including econometric models. Execution of such computation, in each of the 200 military installations, is lengthy and is subject to errors, especially when it is done manually.

The Solution

The DSS which was developed with IFPS (see Instructor's Manual book) runs on a PC and is intended to support the SHMA analysis. A simplified diagram of the DSS is shown in Figure 3.11.

The Components of the DSS

On the left side of the figure, two basic components are listed: database and model base.

- The database is composed of:
  1. Off-post data: economic characteristics of the area around the military installation
  2. On-post data: profile of the military personnel seeking housing.

Sources for the internal data are internal databases and reports. Sources for the external data are Rand McNally's *Places Rated Almanac*, statistical abstracts of the United States, chambers of commerce, banks, real estate boards, and on-line databases.

---

*Condensed from G.A. Forgionne, "HANS: A Decision Support System for Military Housing Managers," *Interfaces*, November–December 1991.

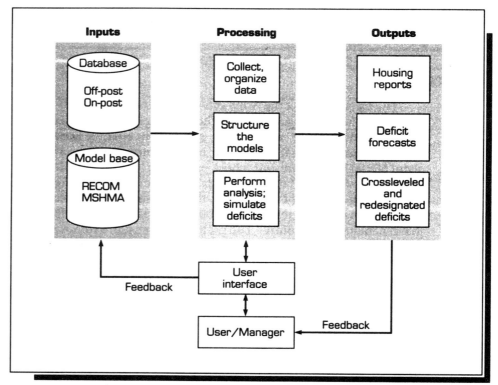

FIGURE 3.11 The Housing Management DSS.

- The model base is composed of two parts:
  1. RECOM (a regional econometric model for the area). This model uses many variables and constraints (such as value of housing, consumer price index, median rent, median per capita income, annual utility bill, and military allowances).
  2. MSHMA (Modified Segmented Housing Market Analysis). This model has many variables, and it also uses on-post and off-post data. The on-post data include: the military share of the housing market, housing available at the base (post), housing occupancy levels, demographics of military people, and housing needs. The off-post data are derived from the RECOM sources, consisting of median selling price, taxes paid, household income, and total population.

Operation

The user receives the DSS on a disk (including all the documentation). The processing starts with data entry. The data are recorded on forms from manuals. The DSS organizes the database, structures the model, and performs analysis (using simulation). All this is done interactively in a user-friendly environment.

The DSS executes all the calculations requested by the housing manager (several options are available). The user can review and modify values as needed.

Outputs

Three major outputs are produced: first, housing reports as desired by army managers (e.g., reports that identify market conditions); second, housing deficit (demand over supply) forecasts; and third, cross-leveled and redesignated deficit forecasts. These outputs are synthesized into two major reports. The output of tested cases was found to be accurate in 95 percent of the cases.

Feedback

Decision making is a continuous process. Managers learn from reality. Thus, corrective actions can take place. As shown in Figure 3.11, there is a feedback from the manager's actions (processing) to the database and the models (adjustment, changes). The second feedback goes from the outputs to the decision maker so that processing can be improved. This feedback may include sensitivity analysis. The DSS can also be used to determine how much SHMA is needed (from "needed" to "strongly needed").

Sensitivity Analysis

The model provides "what-if" and goal-seeking capabilities. These capabilities are included in IFPS.

Benefits

The system provides both monetary and managerial benefits.

1. Monetary benefits. Savings are estimated at about $16,500 per housing project that runs SHMA (or about 2 million dollars per year for the U.S. Army). In addition, there will be a savings of 1 million dollars per year, due to reduced training requirements.

2. Managerial benefits. The tedious manual procedures that often resulted in inaccurate, incomplete, and redundant data were eliminated. The decision-making process has been considerably improved thanks to: quicker analysis of the housing market, impact analysis, error free computation, and rapid sensitivity analyses. In addition, the auditing process has been standardized, and it is done faster, resulting in earlier release of funds and alleviation of housing shortages in many locations.

Enhancements

The DSS is enhanced with an intelligent component, a market-share model, and an improved DBMS.

Case Questions

1. Why was this DSS needed?
2. What factors, in your opinion, contributed to the success of the DSS?
3. Discuss the role of forecasting in this DSS.
4. Discuss the role of sensitivity analysis in this DSS.

References and Bibliography

Adelman L. (1993). *Evaluating Decision Support Systems.* New York: Wiley.

Alter, S. L. (1980). *Decision Support Systems: Current Practices and Continuing Challenges.* Reading, MA: Addison-Wesley.

Bonczek, R. H., C. W. Holsapple, and A. B. Whinston. (1980). "The Evolving Roles of Models in Decision Support Systems." *Decision Sciences,* Vol. 11, No. 2.

Donovan, J. J., and S. E. Madnick. (1977). "Institutional and Ad Hoc Decision Support Systems and Their Effective Use." *Data Base,* Vol. 8, No. 3.

Ginzberg, M. J., and E. Stohr. (1982). "Decision Support Systems: Issues and Perspectives." In M. J. Ginzberg, et al. (ed.). *Decision Support Systems.* Proceedings, NYU Symposium on DSS; New York, 1981. Amsterdam: North-Holland.

Gorry, G. A., and M. S. Scott-Morton. (1971). "A Framework for Management Information Systems." *Sloan Management Review,* Vol. 13, No. 1.

Gray, P. (ed.). (1994). *Decision Support and Executive Information Systems.* Englewood Cliffs, NJ: Prentice Hall.

Hackathorn, R. D., and P. G. W. Keen. (1981, September). "Organizational Strategies for Personal Computing in Decision Support Systems." *MIS Quarterly.*

Keen, P. G. W. (1980). "Adaptive Design for Decision Support Systems." *Data Base,* Vol. 12, Nos. 1 and 2.

Kroeber, D. W., and H. J. Watson. (1986). *Computer-Based Information Systems,* 2nd ed. New York: Macmillan.

Little, J. D. C. (1970). "Models and Managers: The Concept of a Decision Calculus." *Management Science,* Vol. 16, No. 8.

McLeod, R., Jr. (1985). *Decision Support Software for IBM Personal Computer.* Chicago: SRA.

Meador, C. L., et al. (1984, June). "Setting Priorities for DSS Development." *MIS Quarterly.*

Moore, J. H., and M. G. Chang. (1980). "Design of Decision Support Systems." *Data Base,* Vol. 12, Nos. 1 and 2.

Naylor, T. H. (1983). "Strategic Planning Models." *Managerial Planning,* Vol. 30, No. 1.

Oliff, M. D. (1984, November). "FAST Decision Support." *Proceedings of the American Institute of Decision Sciences,* National Meeting, Toronto, Canada.

Palvia, S., and S. R. Gordon. (1992, October). "Tables, Trees and Formulas in Decision Analysis." *Communications of the ACM.*

Sprague, R. H., Jr., and E. D. Carlson. (1982). *Building Effective Decision Support Systems.* Englewood Cliffs, NJ: Prentice-Hall.

Sprague, R. H., and H. J. Watson (eds.). (1993). *Decision Support Systems*, 3rd ed. Englewood Cliffs, NJ: Prentice Hall.

Sprague, R. H., Jr., and J. J. Watson. (1976). "A Decision Support System for Banks." *Omega*, Vol. 4, No. 6.

APPENDIX 3-A: Examples of Ready-Made Systems

1. Hewlett Packard (HP) Quality Decision Management*

HP Quality Decision Management is an applications software package for analyzing manufacturing processes and product quality. The package provides control and Pareto charts that help production and quality assurance engineers identify and prioritize statistically significant product defects and manufacturing process problems. Engineering departments can use data collected on-line to generate scattergrams, histograms, and tabular reports.

The package differs from conventional MIS application packages because of many added-on DSS capabilities. For example, a menu and prompt/response approach allows engineers without programming experience to configure data collection transactions, specify report and graph formats, archive data, and perform system maintenance functions. The database is designed for workstation-oriented production environments. The system provides data collection, validation, and storage to the database. It also allows "what-if" analysis, sensitivity analysis, and simulation capabilities. Engineers can statistically analyze the data and output the results in tabular or graphical format.

The HP Quality Decision Management System may be used in the following application areas:

1. *Incoming inspection:* displays of inspection instructions, vendor rating reports, control charts of defect rates, and vendor's quality.
2. *Product test:* manual and automatic on-line data collection, test procedure display, statistical monitoring of defect levels, and decision support graphics and reports.
3. *Statistical process and product monitoring:* on-line data collection from incoming inspection, manufacturing process and test areas, statistical graphs and reports to monitor manufacturing process quality, correlation between product defect data, and defect cause data (in a real-time environment).

Source: Condensed from "HP Quality Decision Management/1000," Hewlett Packard advertisement brochure, San Jose, CA.

2. Equitable Life Insurance—Real Estate Application Via Time Sharing*

The Realty Group of this large insurance company buys, sells, and manages hundreds of real estate properties for the insurance company and for clients. The DSS (Tymcom 370) provides the following capabilities:

1. Database management including preparation of periodic reports and preparation of real estate closing transactions.
2. Cash flow projections (itemized by expense and income categories) for properties that are candidates for acquisitions.
3. Computations of the rate of return on investments and other measures of performance of existing and proposed properties.
4. Access to the corporate database and execution of standard manipulations.
5. User access to the system through telephone lines.

System Benefits. This type of DSS provides several advantages. Latest software and hardware technologies are available to the user. This system is being constantly updated for increased capabilities and reduced cost.

Notes:

1. The major benefits reported are reduction of report turnaround time (by as much as 75 percent), capability of making faster (and more consistent) acquisition decisions, downloading of information from the corporate database to PCs for manipulation by decision makers, and comparative analysis of hundreds of managers and properties.
2. Time-sharing is mainly appropriate for infrequent use. With the decreased cost of software and hardware and the increased capabilities of microcomputers, there is a trend away from time-sharing to in-house computing.

Source: Condensed from *Computerworld*, February 22, 1982, p. 34.

Chapter 16

Group Decision Support Systems

Most complex decisions in organizations are made by groups of people. As complexity of organizational decision making increases, the need for meetings and for working in groups increases. The preparations for such meetings and the conduct of them can be a complex process. Therefore, a computerized support may be appropriate. Such a support appears under several names; it is referred to in this chapter as Group Decision Support Systems (GDSS). The specific sections of this chapter are:

9.1   Case: Quality Improvement Teams*

Many organizations, private and public, are placing increased emphasis on business process reengineering, use of technology, and introduction of quality improvement programs as means to increase productivity and to better cope with increased competition, customer demands, decreased budgets, and the emergence of global markets. In Manhattan, the management and employees of the Internal Revenue Service (IRS), with the help of the University of Minnesota, implemented a quality improvement program based on participative management (quality teams), which is supported by a **group decision support system (GDSS).**

A major part of any quality improvement program is the *quality team* structure, which is similar to the Japanese *quality circles* concept. Groups, composed of managers and employees, meet as small units (of three to twelve people) to chart out methods for solving problems and for using opportunities to improve quality.

The Problem

Participants in quality teams often come from different functional areas or supervisory levels, and bring a variety of perspectives to the team. Although such variety can enrich the meetings, it can slow work as well. In addition, groups are subject to generic phenomena that inhibit the success of teamwork. These phenomena include domination by one or a few members, poor interpersonal communication, and fear to express innovative ideas. To reduce such negative effects, the IRS introduced extensive training and professional facilitation. However, as the number of teams increases, the training and facilitation budget becomes a problem and it also becomes difficult to find high-quality facilitators.

The Solution

GDSS is a new technology that could support the various activities carried out by the members of the group, the leader, and the facilitator (see Table 9.1). GDSS offers teams the potential to reduce their effort in applying quality improvement methods by providing automated means to enter, record, and operate on team members' ideas during face-to-face meetings. Specifically, support is provided to idea generation, issue prioritization, problem analysis, strategy selection, and so on. In addition, GDSS helps to reduce many of the negative phenomena of face-to-face teamwork (e.g., fear to express ideas). Finally, the technology provides extensive documentation on team meetings and decision procedures.

---

*Condensed from DeSanctis, et al. [1991].

TABLE 9.1   The Decision Support Needs of the Quality Teams

Quality Team Roles and Responsibilities	Decision Support Needs
Members: ■ Identify problems ■ Generate and evaluate ideas ■ Develop and implement solutions Leader: ■ Plans meetings ■ Coordinates team activities ■ Monitors and reports team progress Facilitator: ■ Promotes use of problem-solving techniques ■ Encourages consensus building ■ Serves as a liasion between team and quality steering committee	Access to group problem-solving techniques Methods for encouraging open participation by all members Efficient use of team meeting time (for example, agenda management) Documentation of team decision-making processes and outputs

Implementation

GDSS started as a research project. Special laboratories were built during the late 1980s in several universities, including the University of Minnesota, which worked with the IRS as of 1988. At that time there was no commercially available hardware and software on the market. Therefore, it was necessary to bring the participating IRS team members to the GDSS facility at the University of Minnesota. (The University of Minnesota software is called SAMM, for Software-aided Meeting Management. The details of similar software will be described later.) Team leaders and members were trained to use the software, and were shown how to enhance the quality improvement process by using several features of SAMM.

Results

During the period of September 1989–January 1991, SAMM was used for several hundred meetings. The SAMM was used by members for:

- Idea generation and evaluation (in 19.4 percent of the meetings)
- Use of sophisticated decision aid tools (in 59.4 percent of the meetings)
- Creating and managing the agenda (in 36.5 percent of the meetings)
- Group writing and record keeping (in 15.3 percent of the meetings).

On a scale of 1 to 7 (1 low, 7 high), team members expressed a satisfaction level of about 5.5 in these areas: "being comfortable with the technology," "improvement of the teamwork," "GDSS was *easy* for the group to use," and "GDSS played a major role in meetings." Almost no negative effects were reported. Overall, the GDSS had a tremendous positive impact on the work of the groups.

Epilogue

The GDSS in the IRS case was so successful that its capabilities have been enhanced. Expansions enable team members to access the system modules at different times and from different locations. It is expected that in the future the GDSS will be able to support even emotional aspects of quality teamwork (e.g., social exchanges, negotiations).

9.2   Decision Making in Groups

The case of the quality improvement teams introduces some of the features of electronically supporting the work of groups. The following are some fundamentals of group decision making:

1. *Groups.* The term "group" (or workgroup) refers to two or more (usually up to about twenty-five) individuals whose mission is to perform some task and who act as one unit. The group can be permanent or temporary. The group can be in one location or in several locations, and it can meet concurrently or at different times. A group can be a committee, a review panel, a task force, an executive board, a team, or a permanent unit.

2. *The Nature of Group Decision Making.* Although most business organizations are hierarchical, decision making is usually a shared process. Face-to-face meetings among groups of managers are an essential element of reaching a consensus. The group may be involved in a decision or in a decision-related task like creating a short list of acceptable alternatives or deciding on criteria for accepting an alternative. These group meetings are characterized by the following activities and processes:

- Meetings are a joint activity, engaged in by a group of people, usually of equal or near equal status, typically involving five to twenty-five individuals.
- The outcome of the meeting depends partly on the knowledge, opinions, and judgments of its participants.
- The outcome of the meeting also depends on the composition of the groups and on the decision-making process used by the groups.
- Differences in opinion are settled either by the ranking person present or, more often, by negotiation or arbitration.

3. *The Benefits and Limitations of Working in Groups.* For years, people have recognized the benefits of collaborative work. Typical benefits of such collaboration are shown in Table 9.2. Despite the many benefits of group interaction, the results of people working in groups are not always successful. The reason is that the *process* of collaborative work is frequently plagued with dysfunctions (see Table 9.3). To reconcile the dilemma of having significant benefits on one side and dysfunctions on the other, researchers have developed methods for improving the work of groups.

TABLE 9.2   The Benefits of Working in a Group.

- Groups are better than individuals at understanding problems.
- People are accountable for decisions that they participate in.
- Groups are better than individuals at catching errors.
- A group has more information (knowledge) than any one member. Groups can combine that knowledge and create new knowledge. As a result, there are more alternatives for problem solving, and better solutions can be derived.
- Synergy may be produced.
- Working in a group may stimulate the participants and the process.
- Group members will have their egos embedded in the decision, so they will be committed to the implementation.
- The participation of the members in a decision means less liklihood to resist implementation.
- Risk propensity is balanced. Groups moderate high-risk takers and encourage conservatives.

4. *Improving the Work of Groups.* For many years there were attempts to improve the work of groups. If we can eliminate or lessen some of the phenomena that cause the dysfunctions, the benefits would be greatly enhanced. Behavioral scientists, personnel experts, efficiency experts, and others have developed several approaches to solve these problems. Some of the approaches are labeled "group dynamics." Two representative methods are described next.

The Nominal Group Technique

The **nominal group technique (NGT),** a method developed by Delbec and Van de Ven (see Lindstone and Turroff [1975]), includes a sequence of activities in the process of decision making : (1) silent generation of ideas in writing, (2) round-

TABLE 9.3   The Dysfunctions of Group Process.

- Social pressures of conformity that may result in **"groupthink"** (where people begin to think alike, and where new ideas are not tolerated)
- Time-consuming, slow process
- Lack of coordination of the work done by the group and poor planning of meetings
- Inappropriate influence of group dynamics (e.g., domination of time, topic, or opinion by one or few individuals; fear to speak; rigidity)
- Tendency of group members to rely on others to do most of the work
- Tendency toward compromised solutions of poor quality
- Incomplete task analysis
- Nonproductive time (socializing, getting ready, waiting for people)
- Tendency to repeat what already was said
- Larger cost of making decisions (many hours of participation, travel expenses, etc.)
- Tendency of groups to make riskier decisions than they should
- Incomplete or inappropriate use of information
- Inappropriate representation in the group

robin listing of ideas on a flip chart, (3) serial discussion of ideas, (4) silent listing and ranking of priorities, (5) discussion of priorities, and (6) silent re-ranking and rating of priorities. The nominal group process is based on social-psychological research which indicates that this procedure is superior to conventional discussion groups in terms of generating higher quality, greater quantity, and improved distribution of information on fact-finding tasks.

The success of the NGT and similar methods is heavily dependent on the quality of the facilitator (all group dynamic approaches require a facilitator) and on the training given to the participants. Also, the approach does not solve several of the dysfunctions of group process (such as the fear to speak, poor planning and organization of the meeting, compromises, and lack of appropriate analysis).

The Delphi Method

The **Delphi method** was developed by the RAND Corporation (see Lindstone and Turroff [1975]) as a technique for managing groups of experts making decisions, in order to eliminate the undesirable effects of interaction between members of the group. The experts need not meet face-to-face; they do not know who the other experts are. The method generally begins by having each expert provide an individually written assignment or opinion (e.g., a forecast) regarding the issue of concern along with any supporting arguments and assumptions. These opinions are submitted to the Delphi coordinator who edits, clarifies, and summarizes the data. These opinions are then provided as anonymous feedback to all experts along with a *second round* of issues or questions. Questions and feedback continue in writing for several rounds, becoming increasingly more specific, until consensus among the panel members is reached, or until the experts no longer change their positions.

The Delphi method benefits from anonymity, multiple opinions, and group communication among members representing diverse opinions and assumptions. At the same time it avoids several negative effects such as dominant behavior, "groupthink," and stubbornness to change one's mind, that are often associated with face-to-face solutions.

Although the Delphi method provides anonymity and may encourage some original ideas, it has several limitations. It is slow, expensive, and usually limited to one issue (e.g., technological forecasting, "go" or "no go" of a program).

9.3   The Use of Information Technology: Groupware

The limited success of methods such as the nominal group technique and Delphi, led to attempts to use information technology to support groups. An emerging name that covers the area is **group support systems (GSS).** The name for the software products is **groupware.**

Group Decision Support Systems (GDSS)

Group DSS is considered a subset of a broader field titled *group support systems* or **electronic meeting systems (EMS)**. This field is defined by Dennis, et al. [1988] as:

> An information technology (IT)-based environment that supports group meetings, which may be distributed geographically and temporally. The IT environment includes, but is not limited to, distributed facilities, computer hardware and software, audio and video technology, procedures, methodologies, facilitation, and applicable group data. Group tasks include, but are not limited to, communication, planning, idea generation, problem solving, issue discussion, negotiation, conflict resolution, system analysis and design, and collaborative group activities such as document preparation and sharing (page 593).

GSS support more tasks than just decision making; they focus on the *processes* used by working groups.

Groupware

The term *groupware* refers to software products that support groups of people engaged in a common task or goal. The software provides a mechanism to share opinions and resources (Ellis, et al. [1991]). The term groupware is known in the computer industry to be very ambiguous. It seems that every vendor tries to manipulate the term to its own advantage, and indeed there are dozens of products on the market (e.g., see Briere [1991]), some of which may not be true groupware. Johansen [1988] has identified seventeen different approaches for computer support in groups.

A Time/Place Framework

A framework for classifying IT communication support technologies was proposed by DeSanctis and Gallupe [1985]. According to this framework, communication is divided into four cells, which are shown together with representative IS support technologies in Figure 9.1. The four cells are organized along two dimensions: time and place.

Time. Messages can be sent at a certain time and received almost simultaneously. In such a case, communication is **synchronous**. Telephones, televisions, and face-to-face meetings are examples of synchronous communication. **Asynchronous communication** refers to communication where the receiver gets the message at a different time than it was sent.

Place. The sender(s) and receiver(s), can be in the same room, in different rooms but in the same location, or in different locations.

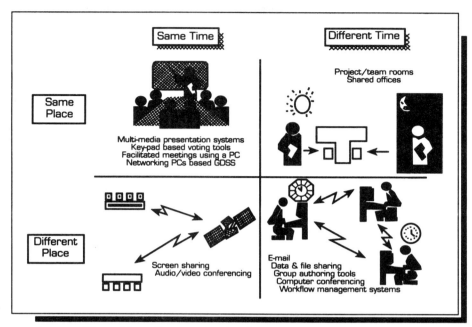

FIGURE 9.1 Time/Place Communication Framework. (*Source:* Chen [1993]. Reproduced with permission.)

These cells are:

Same Time/Same Place. In this setting, participants meet face-to-face in one place and at the same time. An example is a decision room (facility).

Same Time/Different Place. This setting refers to a meeting where the participants are in different places, but they communicate at the same time; a conference telephone call, or video conferencing are examples of such situations.

Different Time/Same Place. This setting can materialize when people work in shifts. The first shift leaves messages for the second shift.

Different Time/Different Place. In this setting participants are in different places and they send and/or receive messages at different times.

The discussion in this chapter concentrates on the first setting: same time/same place. This is the decision room setting. Chapter 10 is devoted to the other three settings, and especially to the different-place/same-time scenario. Chapter 10 also presents the technologies shown in Figure 9.1.

9.4   What Is a GDSS?*

GDSS can be defined in different ways. According to Huber [1984], a GDSS consists of a set of software, hardware, language components, and procedures that support a group of people engaged in a decision-related meeting.

A group decision support system (GDSS), according to DeSanctis and Gallupe [1987], is an interactive computer-based system that facilitates the solution of unstructured problems by a group of decision makers. Components of a GDSS include hardware, software, people, and procedures. These components are arranged to support the *process* of arriving at a decision. Important characteristics of a GDSS can be summarized as follows:

- The GDSS is a specially designed information system, not merely a configuration of already existing system components.
- A GDSS is designed with the goal of supporting groups of decision makers in their work. As such, the GDSS should *improve* the decision-making process and/or the decision outcomes of groups as compared with those that would occur if the GDSS were not present.
- A GDSS is easy to learn and to use. It accommodates users with varying levels of knowledge regarding computing and decision support.
- The GDSS may be designed for one type of problem or for a variety of group-level organizational decisions.
- The GDSS is designed to encourage activities such as generation of ideas, resolution of conflicts, and freedom of expression.
- The GDSS contains built-in mechanisms that discourage development of negative group behaviors, such as destructive conflict, miscommunication, or "groupthink."

Appropriate settings for a GDSS range from an executive group meeting that occurs in a single location for the purpose of considering a specific problem (such as a merger/acquisition decision) to a sales manager's meeting held via telecommunications channels for the purpose of considering a variety of problems (such as hiring of sales representatives, product offerings, and sales call schedules). Because the contexts of group decision making vary so greatly, it is useful to think of a GDSS in terms of the common "group" activities that, therefore, are in need of computer-based support. They are information retrieval, which includes selection of data values from an existing database as well as simple retrieval of information (including attitudes, opinions, and informal observations) from other group members; information sharing, which refers to the display of data to the total group on a viewing screen or sending of data to selected group members' terminal sites for viewing; and information use, which involves the application of software technology (such as modeling packages or

---

*This section is based in part on DeSanctis and Gallupe [1987].

specific application programs), procedures, and group problem-solving techniques for reaching a group decision.

9.5   The Goal of GDSS and Its Levels

The goal of GDSS is to improve productivity and effectiveness of decision-making meetings, either by speeding up the decision-making process or by improving the quality of the resulting decisions. This is accomplished by providing support to the exchange of ideas, opinions, and preferences within the group (Finholt and Sproull [1990]).

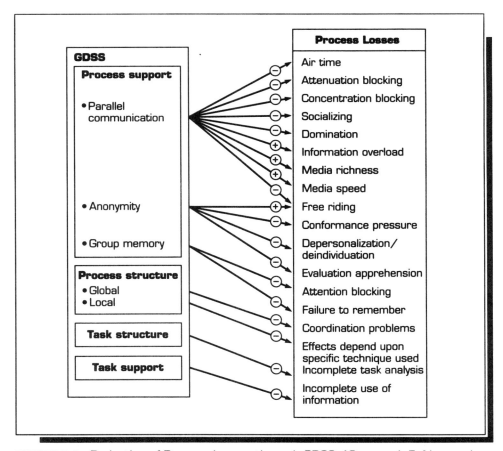

FIGURE 9.2 Reduction of Process Losses through GDSS. (*Source:* J. F. Nunamaker, Jr., et al., "Electronic Meeting Systems to Support Group Work: Theory and Practice at Arizona," Working paper, College of Business, University of Arizona, March 27, 1990. Used by permission.) Note: a plus sign (+) indicates an increase in process losses; a minus sign (-) indicates a decrease in process losses.

This goal can be achieved due to the potential benefits of GDSS. GDSS can reduce the process losses (see Figure 9.2) and can increase process gains (see Table 9.4). This was shown in experiments conducted by the University of Arizona. For example, one study reported a person-hour savings of more than 50 percent, and a 92 percent reduction in the time required to complete a project by the team using the Arizona GDSS room. Several hundred corporations have used the Arizona room and have reported dramatic results (DeSanctis and Gallupe [1987]).

DeSanctis and Gallupe [1987] divide the GDSS technologies into three levels:

- Level 1: Process support
- Level 2: Decision-making support
- Level 3: Rules of order

Level 1: Process Support. This is basically what the IRS system, presented earlier, provides. Items that are supported by such a system are:

- Electronic messaging between group members
- Networks linking each member's personal computer terminal to those of the other group members, the facilitator, the public screen, databases, or any other common CBIS
- A public screen available at each group member's terminal or visible to all members in a central place
- Anonymous input of votes and ideas to enhance participation of group members who prefer anonymity
- Active solicitation of ideas or votes from each group member to encourage participation and induce creativity
- Summary and display of ideas and opinions, including statistical summaries and vote displays (on the public screen)

TABLE 9.4 Process Gains from GDSS

GDSS:
- Supports parallel processing of information and idea generation by the participants.
- Enables larger groups with more complete information, knowledge, and skills to participate in the same meeting.
- Permits the group to use structured or unstructured techniques and methods to perform the task.
- Offers rapid and easy access to external information.
- Allows nonsequential computer discussion (unlike verbal discussions, computer discussions do not have to be serial or sequential).
- Helps participants deal with the larger picture.
- Produces instant anonymous voting results (summaries).
- Provides structure to planning process which keeps the group on track.
- Enables several users to interact simultaneously
- Records automatically all information that passes through the system for future analysis (develops organization memory).

- A format for an agenda that can be agreed upon by the group to aid organization of meetings
- Continuous display of the agenda, as well as other information, to keep meetings on schedule.

Level 2: Decision-making Support. At this level the software adds capabilities for modeling and decision analysis (see Figure 9.3). Features in this category include:

- Planning and financial models
- Decision trees
- Probability assessment models
- Resource allocation models
- Social judgment models.

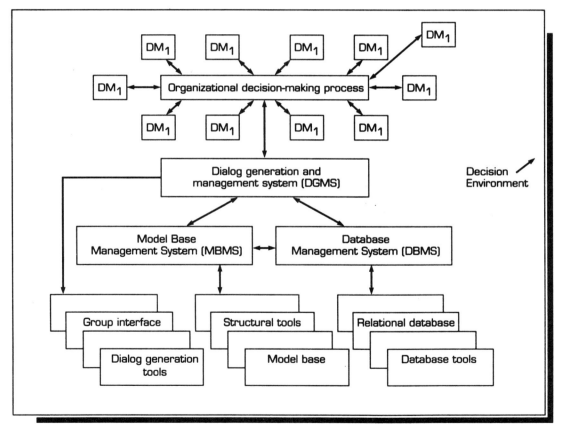

FIGURE 9.3 A Structure of GDSS at Level 2. (*Source:* P.A. Sage, *Decision Support Systems Engineering*, New York: Wiley, 1991. Copyright © 1991. Reprinted by permission of John Wiley & Sons, Inc.)

Such models may exist in regular DSS packages and can be added on to Level 1 software. In addition, one can add idea generation software or software support to Delphi or to the nominal group technique.

Level 3: Rules of Order. At this level a special software containing rules of order is added. For example, some rules could determine the sequence of speaking, the appropriate response, or voting rules.

9.6 The Technology of GDSS

A typical GDSS configuration, and a rather basic one, includes a group of decision makers, who meet in a special facility called a decision room, with access to GDSS software and possibly a database and a model base, during the course of a decision-related meeting. A group facilitator coordinates the group's use of the technology, and there is a flexible, friendly, user-interface language available for use by the facilitator and each group member.

DeSanctis and Gallupe [1987] define the components of GDSS as being *hardware, software, people,* and *procedures.* (See Figure 9.4.)

Hardware. Several basic types of hardware configurations can be used by a group:

1. *Single PC.* In such a case, participants gather around a single PC, while one person enters data. The screen leads the groups to a series of questions, prioritizing and consolidating answers. Finally a decision is indicated. Such a system has very few benefits.
2. *PCs and Keypads.* This is basically a collection of workstations, each equipped with keypads for voting. The machines can be portable so they travel easily. They are simple to operate but very limited in their capabilities. Such PCs can be connected via E-mail or a network.
3. *A Decision Room.* This is a GDSS facility dedicated for electronic meetings and designed as such. A detailed description of such a system is given in Section 9.7.
4. *Distributed GDSS.* In this case the participants are in different locations using existing PCs, networks, and operating systems (e.g., Windows). Supported by special software, such as Lotus Notes, they can work cooperatively. This configuration could be the most commonly used GDSS of the future (see Microsoft [1993] and Chapter 10).

Software. GDSS software includes packages to support *the individual, the group, the process,* and *specific tasks.* For a detailed discussion see Section 9.8.

The software component of the GDSS includes special packages for improvements of the decision-making process and an easy-to-use, flexible, user interface.

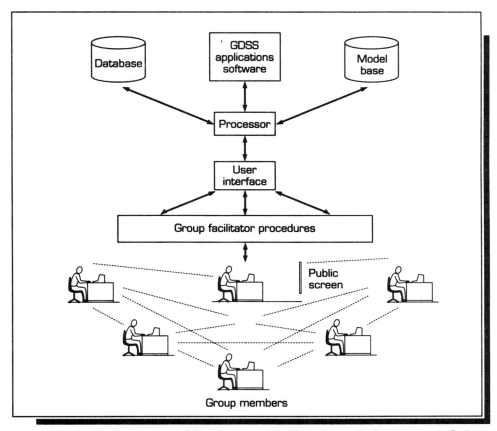

FIGURE 9.4 A Model of GDSS. (*Source:* Modified from DeSanctis and Gallupe [1987].)

(See Macra and Bock [1992].) The software allows each individual to do private work; the usual collection of text and file creation, graphics, spreadsheet, database, and help routines are provided at the individual workstations. Typical *group* features include:

1. Numerical and graphical summarization of group members, ideas, and votes
2. Programs for calculation of weights for decision alternatives; anonymous recording of ideas; formal selection of a group leader; progressive rounds of voting toward consensus building; or elimination of redundant input during brainstorming
3. Text and data transmission among the group members, between the group members and the facilitator, and between the members and a central computer processor. See Box 9.1.

Box 9.1: How to Represent Expressions without Face-to-Face Interaction

Making "faces" during an electronic meeting is not a problem. All you have to do is to agree on a set of symbols like this:

:) = smile	;) = wink	:O = bored
:D = laughter	:(= frown	:X = angry

People. The people component of the GDSS includes the group members and a facilitator who is responsible for the smooth operation of the GDSS technology. The facilitator is usually present at all group meetings and serves as the group's "chauffeur," operating the GDSS hardware and software and displaying requested information to the group as needed.

Procedures. The final component of the GDSS consists of procedures that enable ease of operation and effective use of the technology by group members. These procedures may apply only to the operation of the hardware and software, or they may extend to include rules regarding verbal discussion among members and the flow of events during a group meeting.

9.7 The Decision (Electronic Meeting) Room

Electronic meeting rooms can be constructed in different shapes. A common design includes a large, usually U-shaped table equipped with 12 to 30 networked microcomputers recessed into a table to facilitate face-to-face interaction among participants. A microcomputer that is used as a server attached to a large-screen projection system is connected to the network and permits the display of work done at individual workstations and aggregated information from the total group. Breakout rooms equipped with microcomputers that are connected to the server may be adjacent to the decision room. Small groups can use them for consultation. The output from these small group sessions can also be displayed on the large "public" screen projector for group presentations.

A well known example is the decision support laboratory at the University of Arizona (see Figure 9.5).

A more modern room is shown in Figure 9.6. Notice that the U shape has been changed.

An electronic decision room requires a trained facilitator. The success of any GDSS is largely dependent on the quality of such facilitator.

FIGURE 9.5 University of Arizona Original GDSS Facility Group System. (*Source:* Nunamanker, et al. [1990]. Used by permission.)

9.8   GDSS Software

The following are the major comprehensive software packages available for GDSS and are used primarily in a decision room environment:

1. *GroupSystems* (from Ventana Corporation, Tuscon, AZ). This product is described in detail later in this section.
2. *VisionQuest* (from Collaborative Technologies Corporation, Austin, TX). This product supports a wide range of interactive team functions such as control over the agenda, prioritizing, idea generation, and documentation of activities. It also supports meetings in which the participants are in different locations and can even communicate at different times.

FIGURE 9.6 The Group System 24-Station Decision Center, Located at the University of Arizona. (*Source:* Courtesy Center for the Management of Information Systems, Univeristy of Arizona, College of Business and Public Administration.)

3. *TeamFocus.* This product is what IBM marketed in the early 1990s. It is basically an early version of *GroupSystem.*
4. *SAMM.* This product from the University of Minnesota (see Section 9.1) has been installed in several corporate decision rooms.

In order to illustrate the GDSS software, we elected to use the example of GroupSystems (from Ventana Corporation).

GroupSystems V offers a comprehensive toolset to support a wide variety of group processes. An overview of the various tools and their relationship to the various activities of a GDSS are given in Figure 9.7. The tools in GroupSystems V are divided into basic tools and advanced tools.

The basic tools are the following:

1. *Electronic Brainstorming* is designed to gather ideas and comments in an unstructured manner. Participants respond to a question or to the comments of others in a divergent process. Participants contribute simultaneously and anonymously to a discussion that can be used as is or sorted by

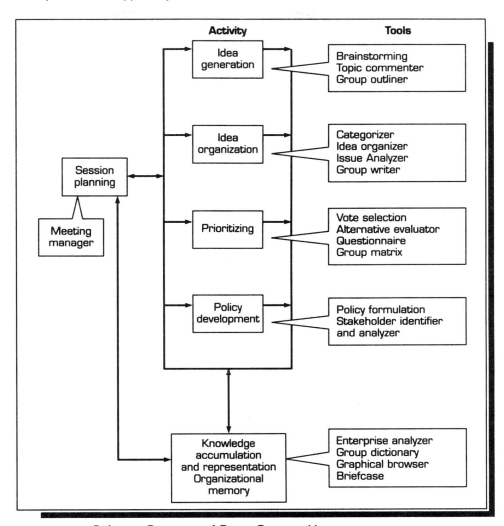

FIGURE 9.7 Software Structure of Group Systems V.

keywords. In addition, the comments can be imported into other Group-Systems V tools where they can be categorized and evaluated.

2. *Topic Commenter* supports idea generation in a structured format. Participants use multiple windows which resemble file folders. Participants may open each file, write relevant comments privately, and then submit them to the specified file for the group to review.

3. *Categorizer* allows participants to cut and paste from a list or reference file and refine, rearrange, categorize, and consolidate the items from the file. This file can be a list generated in another tool or any ASCII file the group chooses.

4. *Vote* supports consensus development through group evaluation of issues. Participants can be polled in seven quantifiable ways: Rank Order, Multiple Choice, Agree/Disagree, Yes/No, True/False, 10-Point Scale, and Allocation. Results are tabulated electronically and displayed graphically and in text.

5. *Alternative Evaluation* allows the group to weight or rate a list of alternatives against a list of criteria. Like Vote, the results of the evaluation can be viewed in a variety of formats, including scatter plots, bar charts, and text reports. Additionally, the group can test "what if" assumptions by adjusting the weighting of the criteria.

6. *Policy Formation* enables groups to develop and edit a statement through an iterative process of review and revision. This "wordsmithing" process supports the development of policies, statements, or action plans—any time a high degree of consensus is desired.

7. *Group Dictinary* supports information management by letting the group build, define, and store a list of terms that have the same meaning for all participants.

8. *Briefcase* incorporates a memory resident set of utilities available to team members while using GroupSystems V. It includes Quick Vote, Mood Meter, Calculator, File Reader, Notepad, Calendar, and Clipboard.

The advanced tools are the following:

1. *Group Outliner* allows a group to develop a tree or outline structure. At each level of the outline participants may attach comments. Participants may view others' comments while creating their own, so comments are integrated and collaborative. A team may use Group Outliner to draft a final report, gather ideas about a project, or describe a business process in detail.

2. *Idea Organization* is a multi-faceted tool that can be used for idea generation and idea organization. Idea Organization allows participants to build a list of key ideas or categories and attach comments to any item on the list. This list can be consolidated, rearranged, and edited.

3. *Group Writer* allows group members to create, edit, and annotate the same document. Group members can scroll through the document and block off a section for individual editing. Viewing, scrolling, and editing are independent of other group members, although all members see when a section is unavailable.

4. *Group Matrix* allows the group to establish relationships between rows and columns in a matrix format. Participants characterize the nature of these relationships by choosing from a predefined word list or by entering a numeric value. A group display of the matrix dynamically reflects the average group results of each cell. Consensus and disagreement are indicated by the color of the cell so the group can focus on building well-focused consensus.

5. *Questionnaire* allows a prepared questionnaire to be distributed to participant workstations. The data collected from participants' responses can be
compiled into a single report.

6. *Stakeholder Identification* is an analysis and issue exploration tool that provides structure for a process that includes stakeholder (an entity who is impacted by the impact of a plan) identification, assumption surfacing, rating
of assumptions, and a graphical representation of the rating results. Groups
use this tool to analyze the impact of a plan, policy, or other set of issues being considered for implementation.

Accessing the Tools. The tool can be assessed from two software environments: Meeting Manager and Group Link

Meeting Manager offers a rich collection of features to support the session
leader and the group as they work together to accomplish objectives during a face-
to-face meeting. Creating agendas, initiating activities, accessing remote files, and
printing and saving session reports and data are just a few of the available features.

Group Link is the home base for GroupSystems V in a distributed environment. Group Link is a project-oriented interface that allows the group to collaborate with other people from their desks, using the same GroupSystems V tools
used in the meeting room environment.

9.9   Idea Generation

Idea generation software helps to generate a free flow of turbulent creative thinking: ideas, words, pictures, and concepts set loose with fearless enthusiasm by intelligent people (Gallupe and DeSanctis [1988]). Some packages are designed to
mimic the creative thought process of the human mind and can be used to create
new product ideas, marketing strategies, promotional campaigns, names, titles,
slogans, stories, or just brainstorming in general.

By definition, idea generation in GDSS is a collaborative effort. One person's
idea triggers the other's ideas, which triggers even more ideas. With electronic
tools, the individual does all the thinking, but the software encourages the individual and pushes him along. Joanne Gallitano, Personal Systems director at the
Decision Support Center at the US Marketing and Services Business Systems facility in Southbury, CT, says that electronic brainstorming is for most people a very
exhilarating experience. This is because the technology is an anonymous, safe way
to get out ideas that have been lurking in the back of people's minds but which
they were reluctant to express in a more conventional setting. Then, by building
on each other's ideas, individuals get creative insights they didn't have before
(Gray [1986]).

The results of each idea generation session can be electronically stored so they
can be carried over from one meeting to another to enhance the creativity of more
people.

652

Research on how a group should organize itself to generate ideas clearly shows that, in contrast to findings from non-computer-mediated idea generation, one single GDSS-supported group generates more ideas with higher quality than the same number of participants working as individuals or in several smaller groups (Bostrom, et al. [1992]). Group DSS participants probably use the idea generation software more frequently than they use any other software (e.g., see the opening case in Section 9.1).

In addition to the idea generation module which is part of the GDSS software kit, it is possible to connect the GDSS with any stand-alone idea generation package (such as IdeaFisher) described in Chapter 8. Such integration can be done for the entire group simultaneously, or each participant can call a creativity-aid tool whenever needed. Such an arrangement is especially easy to build if the GDSS software and the idea generation packages are Windows-based.

9.10 Negotiation Support Systems (NSS)

Conflict resolution mechanisms form an important aspect of GDSS design. When a conflict is present, finding compromised solutions is a key support activity of **negotiation support systems (NSS).**

Conflicts among decision makers can arise from differences in interest or in objectives, and from cognitive limitations. Negotiation is one of the best approaches for conflict resolution, especially in the GDSS environment (see Nunamaker, et al. [1991]).

The need for negotiations arises from different types of disputes (Greif [1988]):

1. Negotiators' interests are fundamentally opposed (e.g., contract negotiations—labor dispute)(see Box 9.2).
2. Negotiators share basic objectives but they differ in their assessment of the priorities of the objectives (e.g., resource allocation—budgeting problems and planning for catastrophic events) (see Belardo and Harrold [1992]).

Intragroup conflict has been studied extensively in game-theory, social, psychological, and political science frameworks. Common to most of these studies is the belief that conflicts arise primarily because of differences in interests among individuals. However, conflicts often arise simply because group members differ in their understanding (or misunderstanding) of the problem, even when their respective interests converge. Such conflicts are a routine feature in group decision making and, consequently, even if differences in motives among group members are eliminated, conflict in a group may persist. In the presence of cognitive conflict, groups behave inconsistently and, as a result, arrive at low-quality decisions (Grohowski and McGoff [1990]). Therefore, it is important to develop decision aids that can help the facilitator to diagnose cognitive conflicts and reduce them.

Box 9.2: Labor-Management Contract Negotiations

San Trans, a Tucson, AZ, bus company, used the University of Arizona GDSS facility to negotiate a labor contract with the Teamsters union, which represents 300 of the blue-collar employees. Management and union representatives met for nine sessions, concluding with a new contract after only 30 hours of electronic meetings. The university's GDSS tools were customized to handle the negotiations.

El Rio Health Care facility of Tuscon, AZ, used the same facility to negotiate a labor contract with their union. The union and management teams have had a history of difficult negotiation. Consequently, personal animosities occasionally surfaced and made the negotiations ardous and lengthy. After 13 sessions that totaled 57 hours in the decision room, the parties reached a mutually agreed-upon contract.

For additional information and descriptions of the process see Herniter, et al. [1993] and Carmel, et al.[1993].

Decision Aids for Negotiations

MEDIATOR, Co-op, and NEGO are examples of systems that span from modeling individual interests to seeking negotiated solutions. They assist in situations where conflicts arise from interest differentials. However, there is little research on building systems to support group decision making in situations involving cognitive conflict.

NSS should help emerge as common ground for people to accept recommendations, instead of blindly accepting proposals sponsored by interested parties. Concession-making procedures may lead to a compromising solution or a break-off (at which point the negotiation conceivably could be restructured). Here, redefining the negotiation problem is the key approach.

Two methods that could provide knowledge for restructuring are:

1. *AI restructuring methods.* Such methods involve case-based reasoning, situational assessment packets, persuasive argumentation, and goal graph procedures.
2. *Rule-based approaches* (utilization of expert systems). Such methods provide advice and strategies about restructuring, based on rules developed for certain scenarios. On the whole, much more research is needed validating NSS software and assessing its impact on negotiations.

9.11 How a GDSS Meeting Runs

Electronic meetings generally follow a superficially similar formula, independent of the topics, which can vary widely: *First,* the group leader meets with the facilitator to plan the meeting, select the software tools to be used, and develop an agenda. *Second,* the participants are gathered in the decision room and the leader poses a question or problem to the group. *Third,* the participants type their ideas or comments, so the results can be publicly displayed. Since the participants can see what others are saying, they can provide comments (positive or negative) or generate new ideas. *Fourth,* the facilitator, using the idea organization software,

FIGURE 9.8 One Sequence of Use. (*Source:* Nunamaker, et al. [1990]. Used by permission.)

searches for common themes, topics, and ideas and organizes them into rough categories (key ideas) with appropriate comments. The results are publicly displayed. *Fifth,* the leader starts a discussion, either vocal or electronic. At that point the participants *prioritize* the ideas. (Software support can be of great help at this step.) *Sixth,* the top five to ten topics are routed to idea generation, after being discussed. *Finally,* the process can repeat itself (idea generation, idea organization, prioritization) or a final vote takes place. A topic commenter software can be used to support this step. The major activities of a simple GDSS session are shown in Figure 9.8. An example of use is shown in Appendix 9-A.

9.12 Constructing a GDSS and the Determinants of Its Success

Constructing a GDSS

Developing a GDSS differs considerably from developing an application of DSS or an expert system. Implementing GDSS implies constructing (or renting) a decision room, developing (or acquiring) the software, developing the procedures, training a facilitator, and putting it all together. Many organizations prefer to use someone else's facility. Unless you have a constant use for the facility, why not rent one?

Several GDSS vendors offer extensive consulting services on how to build such a facility, how to install the software, and how to operate the facility. These vendors can do the entire job for you.

A distributed GDSS can be developed using existing hardware, networks, operating systems, and software utilities. In such a case the GDSS is usually constructed with commercially available software (see Chapter 10).

Having a facility is, of course, necessary but not sufficient for the success of GDSS. Some helpful suggestions for successful implementation are offered next.

Determinants of GDSS Success for a Decision Room Setting

The experience gained from almost two years of experimentations at various universities and at IBM's sites indicates that the success of GDSS depends on many factors. A summary of the major factors is provided in Box 9.3.

More on Critical Success Factors for GDSS

Buckley and Yen studied the critical success factors for GDSS [1990] and categorized them into three major groups: design, implementation, and management.

1. *Design.* Four factors are included:

Box 9.3: Critical Success Factors of GDSS:

1. Organizational commitment—a must
2. Executive sponsor who is committed and informed
3. Operating sponsor to provide quick feedback
4. Dedicated facilities with attention to aesthetics and user comfort
5. Reciprocal site visits that recognize the need for informed personnel who understand the EMS environment
6. Communication and liaison extending beyond site visits—important in maintaining responsiveness to questions arising
7. Fast iteration of software changes—critical to meet evolving needs
8. Training for site personnel at technical, facilitation, and end-user levels
9. Transfer of control to site personnel
10. Cost/benefit evaluation—crucial to expansion of EMS beyond initial trials
11. Software usage flexibility—essential for meeting the evolving needs of groups
12. Appropriate planning—essential (suggestions for structured planning sessions are provided by some vendors)
13. Meeting managerial expectations—the ultimate indicator of successful EMS implementation
14. A seductive user interface (see Gray and Olfman [1989])
15. Anonymity—very important (see Jessup et al [1990])
16. Facilitation—very important (see Dickson et al [1993])
17. Selection of an appropriate task (issue)—very important.

(*Source:* Based on IBM's experience (Grohowski and McGoff [1990]) and on the University of Arizona experimentation.)

- Enhance the structuredness of unstructured decisions (e.g., by providing database access for added information).
- Preserve anonymity of the participant as needed.
- Provide organizational involvement (from all affected individuals and groups), mainly by top management, end-users, and the IS department.
- Include ergonomic considerations that create a comfortable and productive environment.

2. *Implementation.* Four factors are included:
   - Provide extensive and proper user training.
   - Assure the support of top management (not just their involvement).
   - Provide a qualified facilitator.

- Execute trial runs by conducting experiments to assure appropriate operations.
3. *Management.* Three factors are considered:
   - The system must be reliable. Appropriate maintenance, smooth operation, and quality support are a must.
   - The system must be incrementally improved. Using feedback of the participants and hardware and software innovations, the GDSS facility needs to be enhanced constantly.
   - To implement the previous factor, it is necessary for the GDSS staff to keep up with the state of the art of the technology.

Building Decision Rooms Using Off-the-Shelf Software

The cost of building GDSS rooms can be drastically reduced if, instead of comprehensive toolkits and specialized software, one will use standard off-the-shelf software. The idea is promoted by Microsoft [1993], whose aim is to provide the necessary operating systems so their customers can implement workgroup solutions using off-the-shelf products from a variety of vendors and be assured of seamless connectivity and compatibility. Roth, et al. [1993] describes how to implement the Microsoft idea with low-cost off-the-shelf software, much of which is available in many organizations anyway. While the assembled system may not be as powerful as one constructed with GroupSystems V, it sure costs much less. An empirical case study by Mcleod and Liker [1992] summarizes the benefits of such a system.

9.13 GDSS Research Challenges

GDSS is a state-of-the-art technology. Unlike other technologies in IS research, such as end-user computing or system development techniques, it cannot yet be widely investigated for its use in the hands of practitioners. Few organizations use GDSS technology as researchers know it today. Findings from GDSS lab experimentations have been distinctly different from those of GDSS field studies. (For example, see Jessup and Valacich [1993].) The first step toward closing the gap between the laboratory experiments and field studies is to embark on multimethodological research programs that provide individual researchers with first-hand understanding of the key GDSS issues from both the experimental and field research perspectives. The absence of either experiments or field studies in a research program reduces the strength within which conclusions can be drawn, and the applicability of those conclusions to actual organizations. A second challenge would be to understand the effects that these differences have on the process and outcome of group meetings, and to use this understanding in interpreting and applying the conclusions of experiments to the use of GDSS by business organizations. From this understanding, we can develop new research designs: field studies with greater rigor (internal validity) and experiments with greater relevancy to the organizational use of GDSS (external validity).

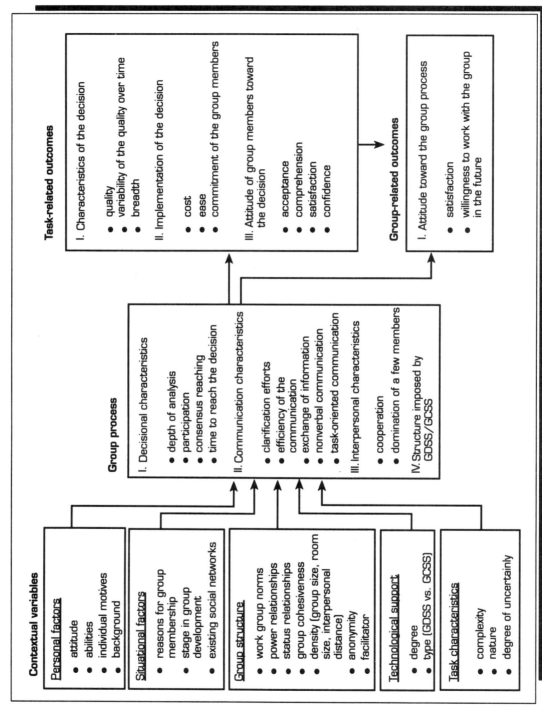

FIGURE 9.9 Details of the Pinsonneault-Kraemer Categorization. (*Source:* E.A. Stohr and B.R. Konsynski [eds.], *Information Systems and Design Processes*, Los Alamitos, CA: IEEE Society Press, 1992.©1992 IEEE.)

658

Research Models. GDSS research is one of the most fertile areas for academic research. Several reseachers proposed a framework for organizing the increasing number of studies. Two approaches were used: (1) outline all the variables in the study of GDSS, and (2) list research topics.

1. *GDSS Variables.* This approach divides the variables into three groups: inputs, processes, and outcome. The initial work was done by DeSanctis and Gallupe. Using this framework, there were several attempts to list the specific variables. (see Gray [1986]; Dennis, et al. [1988]; and Pinsonneault and Kraemer [1989]. A summary of the latter is provided in Figure 9.9)
2. *GDSS Research Topic.* A proposal for specific research topics made by DeSanctis and Gallupe is summarized in Table 9.5.

Additional suggestions were provided by Dickson [1991]. He suggests topics such as: (1) tradeoffs on advanced features versus simplicity, (2) interface studies, (3) supporting groups with difficulties, (4) research on anytime/anyplace configu-

TABLE 9.5 Research Issues in GDSS.

I. GDSS DESIGN
- Human factors design (e.g., spatial arrangement, public screens, informal communications channels)
- Database design
- User interface design
- Interface with DSS
- Design methodologies

II. APPROPRIATENESS OF GDSS
- When should a GDSS be used and when should it not be used?
- When is a GDSS preferred to a DSS?
- Selecting the right GDSS design

III. GDSS SUCCESS FACTORS
- Measures of success (e.g., reduction in group conflict, degree of consensus, group norms)
- Effects of hardware, software, user motivation, and top management support on GDSS's success

IV. IMPACT OF GDSS
- Communication patterns
- Confidence in decision
- Costs
- Level of consensus
- User satisfaction

V. MANAGING THE GDSS
- Responsibility for GDSS in organization
- Planning requirements for GDSS
- Training, maintenance, and other support needed

Source: Based on G. DeSanctis and R. B. Gallupe, "Information System Support for Group Decision Making," Unnumbered working paper, Department of Management Science, University of Minnesota (undated).

660

ration, (5) GDSS benefit identification, (6) the level of support required, (7) embedded knowledge bases (intelligent GDSS), and (8) training issues.

Research Directions. A comprehensive list of GDSS ideas and research topics was compiled by Gray and other GDSS researchers (see Chapter 4 in Stohr and Konsynski [1992]). The several hundred ideas and topics are classified into the following categories:

1. What groups do
2. Effects of GDSS on group work
3. Effects of GDSS on organizations
4. Effects of hardware on GDSS performance
5. Effects of software on GDSS performance
6. Cultural effects of GDSS
7. Training people to use GDSS
8. Cost-benefit analysis for GDSS
9. Critical success factors for implementation an industry
10. Robustness of research results
11. Innovative uses of GDSS
12. Theoretical foundations of GDSS
13. Barriers to research
14. Research methodologies
15. Other ideas and research topics.

Chapter Highlights

- There are many benefits to the work groups ("two heads are better than one"), but there are many dysfunctions due to process loss.
- There are several noncomputerized methods that attempt to improve the process of group decision making. Such methods depend heavily on a facilitator and can be lenghty and expensive.
- Group support systems, electronic meeting systems, computer-supported cooperative work, groupware, and other names designate various types of computer support to groups.
- Computers can support the work of groups in many ways. Here the interest is in supporting decisions made by groups.
- GDSS attempts to reduce process losses and increase the process gains.
- The Delphi method is a non-face-to-face, nonelectronic method that assures anonymity of the participants and provides equal chances to participate.
- There are four settings for GSS: same time/same place, same time/different place, different time/same place, and different time/different place.
- High level GDSS can support decision making in addition to process support. A very high level GDSS utilizes knowledge in terms of rules.

- A group DSS is usually structured on a LAN and is conducted in a decision room environment.
- A GDSS software includes the following main modules: idea generation, idea organization, stakeholder identification, topic commentor, voting tool, policy formulation, enterprise analyzer, and negotiation support system.
- Idea generation is achieved by allowing participants to generate ideas simultaneously and to share them (yet keeping anonymity).
- Resolving conflicts in groups is an essential task. The software supports negotiation for conflict resolution.
- GDSS software is generic. Several commercial packages offer different capabilities.
- GDSS can easily fail. There are many important determinants of its success.
- GDSS research is very diversified. Areas of interest range from individual-level characteristics (of the participants) to types of decision-making techniques used.

Key Words

asynchronous communication	group support systems (GSS)	nominal group technique (NGT)
Delphi method	groupthink	synchronous communication
electronic meeting systems (EMS)	groupware	
	idea generation	
group decision support systems (GDSS)	negotiation support systems (NSS)	

Questions for Review

1. List the major characteristics of GDSS.
2. List three benefits of GDSS.
3. Describe a decision room and contrast it with other GDSS scenarios.
4. Define GDSS.
5. List some of the dysfunctions (or losses) when working in groups.
6. What are the benefits of making decisions in a group?
7. Describe the nominal group technique approach.
8. Describe the Delphi method.
9. Define groupware.
10. List methods, other than GDSS, that support groups.
11. Describe an electronic meeting room.
12. Describe the major software components (modules) in GroupSystems.
13. What is meant by electronic brainstorming?
14. Describe the role of negotiation support systems.
15. Describe the process of building GDSS.

Questions for Discussion

1. Compare GDSS to noncomputerized group decision making.
2. It is said that GDSS supports the process while DSS supports the task. Comment.
3. How can GDSS support creativity?
4. Relate GDSS to groupware.
5. Describe the deficiencies of NGT and Delphi.
6. Describe the differences between the three levels of GDSS technologies.
7. Describe the following GDSS components: hardware, software, people, and procedures.
8. Explain how the various software modules in GroupSystems can support the work of a group.
9. Compare the idea generation activities here with that of IdeaFisher (see Chapter 8).
10. Discuss the major role of a negotiated software.
11. Many factors are necessary to the success of GDSS. Review all of them. Which, in your opinion, are the most important ones (list three)? Why?
12. Distinguish between comprehensive GDSS software and functional tools.
13. It is said that TeamFocus and GroupSystems are conceptually similar to CASE (Computer Aided Software Engineering) tools. Why?
14. If you were to do research on GDSS, what would you do and why?

Exercises

1. Review the case in Section 9.1 and answer the following questions:
   a. Why was there need to use a GDSS in a decision room in this case?
   b. Compare the concept of quality circles to quality teams. What are the major similarities? Differences?
2. Prepare a list of topics that in your opinion are most suitable for a decision room. List one each in the areas of: accounting, finance, marketing, manufacturing, government, educational institution, and hospital.

Case Application 1: GDSS In City Government *

Problem

In Louisville, KY, one volunteer group called Third Century is working to define a future for the inner city. Nearly 500 community members from all neigh-

*Reprinted with permission, "GDSS as a Tool of Public Policy: The Louisville Experience," Robert L. Taylor and Renee A. Beauclair, *DSS-89 Transactions*, Ninth International Conference on Decision Support Systems, George R. Widmeyer (ed.), The Institute of Management Sciences, 290 Westminster Street, Providence, RI 02903. ©1990 the Institute of Management Sciences.

borhoods, public and private sector business organizations, and education meet regularly to identify the major issues confronting the city. Their activities include open forums to discuss critical issues, gathering data to understand the opportunities and problems facing the city, and sponsoring meetings and festivals to help revitalize the downtown as a viable place to live, work, and shop. Third Century's major goal is to develop a set of policy priorities for the future of the community.

The problem, common to every community, is to provide an arena in which each agenda can be dealt with openly while sharing realistic expectations regarding what is possible, given existing resources and competing agendas.

Third Century first identified a list of critical community concerns, which included a wide variety of issues. From their data gathering they found education was at the top of the list in terms of community interest. Third Century planners then refined a list of ten specific education-related items most often cited in the community surveys. They identified executives, neighborhood and community leaders, and key government people who were the opinion leaders, and invited them to participate in a consensus-building exercise. The task was to rank the ten issues. This ranking could then be used for planning and resource allocation purposes.

The University of Louisville developed a limited GDSS to help the large, dispersed, heterogenous group to arrive at consensus goals.

Design and Implementation

The first step was to design the GDSS to assure that all of the leaders had an opportunity to make a case for the educational priorities they felt appropriate.

A flow chart was developed to clarify the GDSS process to technical and nontechnical users (see Figure 9.10). A programmer then translated the chart into usable code. Because of excessive costs and the unavailability of commercial software (this was in 1989), university faculty developed the GDSS software necessary to support the process.

Representatives from Third Century visited each group leader (representatives from the local school board, teachers, parents, parochial and private school heads, business people, political leaders, and individuals from higher education). From these interviews, a list of the ten most frequently cited educational concerns was identified and each was rephrased as an action item. The action items were short statements clarifying each main concern. The cost to fully implement all ten action items far exceeded the available resources of the community; furthermore, some actions had to be taken before others could be accomplished. Priorities had to be established.

The Third Century representatives were invited to discuss the list in the GDSS research room, which included seven networked microcomputers in a comfortable discussion setting. They participated in a pilot exercise to determine whether consensus could be achieved and whether the GDSS configuration was "user-friendly." From the testing, the action items and software were revised.

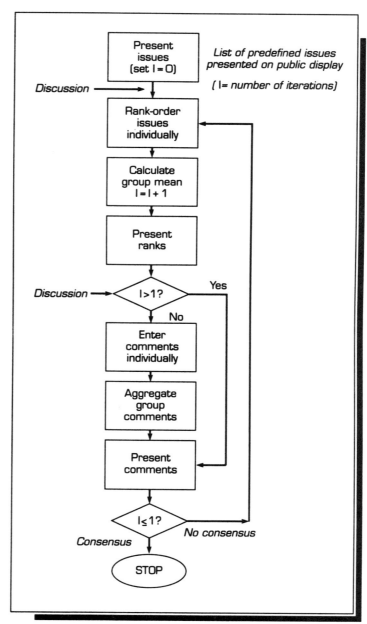

FIGURE 9.10 System Flowchart.

Group Process

Fifty individuals were identified by Third Century to participate. They included the U.S. senator from Louisville, school superintendents from public and private schools, university administrators, outstanding teachers, principals, community leaders, neighborhood advocates, minority leaders, and citizen activists. They were invited to participate in one of four GDSS sessions. Because of scheduling constraints, the number of participants was reduced to 28.

Four sessions of seven participants each were conducted. After a brief orientation to the GDSS process, each of the ten issues was discussed. Participants often advocated their position during this discussion but, more importantly, everyone seemed to achieve a common understanding about the nature and scope of the issues. The ten specific issues were:

1. Corporate and Community Involvement
2. Curriculum
3. Early Childhood Education
4. Funding
5. Higher Education
6. Holding Power (reducing dropout rate)
7. Literacy
8. Research and Technology
9. Responsiveness to Student Needs
10. Professional Teaching Issues.

Each session was scheduled for three hours. The orientation and discussion took about an hour, and then the first iteration of the GDSS process began.

The university provided facilitators and technical assistants so that the process would go smoothly and the participants could overcome any fears they might have about using a computer or an unfamiliar program. Deliberations were tape recorded to provide a record of the session and for researchers to analyze the process. An electronic log of each session was compiled by the system.

In the first iteration, participants were asked to rank-order the issues, assigning a value of 10 to the most important and 1 to the least important. The system collected this information and calculated mean ranks for the group. A consensus list was displayed to the group in order of ranking. Group members were then asked to enter comments about their rankings relative to the group ranking for each of the ten issues. The system collected these comments and then presented them *by issue* back to the group. Lively electronic discussion followed. In general, the first iteration took approximately one hour.

Substantive arguments were made for each of the issues. It was found that the participants spent more time listening than they did advocating their own points of view. There seemed to be a greater degree of understanding about others' points of view and a willingness to rethink initial positions. Although the artificiality of the process seemed to encourage participants to be on their best behavior, it is unlikely that this accounts for all of the activity expressed by group members;

the GDSS appeared to have a positive effect. Much of the discussion in this first iteration centered on what could realistically be done given limited resources.

A second iteration was then initiated, and participants reprioritized the issues on the basis of prior discussion. There was a greater degree of consensus the second time around. A brief discussion was then held, but comments were not collected electronically. This second iteration took no more than 30 minutes.

A final iteration allowed participants to prioritize the issues once more. In this case, there was a surprising degree of consensus, and participants felt they had accomplished something significant. A wrap-up discussion was then held to talk about the list and highlight the importance of advocating this priority list to implement change.

Case Questions

1. Why is this a "limited GDSS"?
2. The decision room accommodates the participants in shifts, due to the small size of the facility. What could be the impact of such a restriction?
3. Compare this case to a Delphi process.
4. What are some of the major advantages of this GDSS?
5. How would a GDSS for public policy compare with one in a for-profit organization?

References and Bibliography

Applegate, L. M. (1991). "Technology Support for Cooperative Work: A Framework for Studying Introduction and Assimilation in Organization." *Journal of Organizational Computing,* Vol. 1, No. 1.

Belardo, S., and J. Harrald. (1992, November). "A Framework for the Application of Group Decision Support Systems to the Problem of Planning for Catastrophic Events." *IEEE Transactions on Engineering Management.*

Bostrom, R., et al. (1992). *Computer Augmented Teamwork: A Guided Tour.* New York: Van Nostrand Reinhold.

Briere, D. (1991, September 16). "Groupware: A Spectrum of Productivity Boosters." *Network World.*

Buckley, S. R., and D. Yen. (1990). "Group Decision Support Systems: Concerns for Success." *The Information Society,* Vol. 7, pp. 109–123.

Carme E., et al. (1993). "Labor-Management Contract Negotiations in an Electronic Meeting Room: A Case Study." *Group Decision and Negotiations,* Vol. 2, pp. 29–60.

Chen, M. (1993). *Group Work and Groupware: A Tutorial,* Unpublished manuscript. Fairfax, VA: George Mason University.

Dennis, A., et al. (1988, December). "Information Technology to Support Electronic Meetings." *MIS Quarterly.*

DeSanctis, G., and B. Gallupe. (1985, Winter). *"Group Decision Support Systems: A New Frontier."* *Data Base.* See also *Management Science,* May 1987.

DeSanctis, G., et al. (1991, November–December). "Using Computing to Facilitate the Quality Improvement Process: The IRS-Minnesota." *Interfaces*.

Dickson, G. W., et al. (1993, June). "Exploring Modes of Facilitative Support for GDSS Technology." *MIS Quarterly*.

Dickson, G. W. (1991 June). "Futures in Computer Supported Collaborative Work: A Look at GDSS Practice & Research." *DSS-91 Transactions*. Providence, RI: The Institute of Management Sciences.

Ellis, C. A., et al. (1991, January). "Groupware: Some Issues and Experiences (Using Computers to Facilitate Human Interaction)." *Communication of the ACM*, Vol. 34.

Finholt, T., and L. S. Sproull. (1990). "Electronic Groups at Work." *Organization Science*, Vol. 1, No. 1.

Gallupe, B., and G. DeSanctis. (1988, June). "Computer-Based Support for Group Problem-Finding: An Experimental Investigation." *MIS Quarterly*.

Gray, P. (1986, April 21–23). "Group Decision Support Systems." *DSS-86 Transactions*. Washington, DC: The Institute of Management Sciences.

Gray, P., and L. Olfman. (1989). "The User Interface in Group Decision Support Systems." *Decision Support Systems*, Vol. 5, No. 2.

Greif, I. (1989). *Computer Supported Cooperative Work: A Book of Readings*. San Mateo, CA: Morgan-Kaufman.

Grohowski, R., and C. McGoff. (1990, December). "Implementing Electronic Meeting Systems at IBM: Lessons Learned and Success Factors." *MIS Quarterly*.

Herniter, B. C., et al. (1993, April). "Computers Improve Efficiency of the Negotiation Process." *Personnel Journal*.

Huber, G. P. (1984, September). "Issues in the Design of Group Decision Support Systems." *MIS Quarterly*.

Jelassi, M., and A. Foroughi. (1989). "Negotiation Support Systems: An Overview of Design Issues and Existing Software." *Decision Support Systems*, Vol. 5, pp. 167–181.

Jessup, L. M., et al. (1990). "The Effects of Anonymity on GDSS Group Process with an Idea-Generating Task." *MIS Quarterly*, Vol. 14, No. 3.

Jessup, L. M., and J. Valacich (eds.). (1993). *Group Support Systems: New Perspectives*. New York: Macmillan.

Johansen, R. (1988). *Groupware: Computer Support for Business Teams*. New York: Free Press.

Lindstone, H., and M. Turroff. (1975). *The Delphi Method: Technology and Applications*. Reading, MA: Addison-Wesley.

Macra, D, and G. Bock, (eds.). (1992). *Groupware: Software for Computer Supported Cooperative Work*. Lot Alamitos CA: IEEE Computer Society Press.

Mcleod, P. L., and Liker J. K. (1992, September). "Electronic Meeting Systems: Evidence from a Law Structure Environment." *Information Systems Research*.

Microsoft Corporation. (1993). "The Microsoft Workgroup Computing Strategy." Stategic white paper, No. 098-39129, Redmond, WA.

Mockler, R. J. (1992). *Computer Software to Support Strategic Management Decision Making*. New York: Macmillan.

Nunamaker, J. F., Jr., et al. (1990, March 27). "Electronic Meeting Systems to Support Group Work: Theory and Practice at Arizona." Working paper, College of Business, University of Arizona.

Nunamaker, J. F., Jr., et al. (1991, October). "Information Technology for Negotiating Groups: Generating Options for Mutual Gain." *Management Science.*

Phillips, L. D. and M. C. Phillips. (1993, June). *"Facilitated Work Groups: Theory and Practice."* Journal of the Operational Research Society.

Pinsonneault, A., and K. L. Kraemer. (1989, June). "The Impact of Technological Support on Groups: An Assessment of the Empirical Research." *Decision Support Systems.* (See also European Journal of Operations Research, 1990.)

Roth, R. M., et al. (1993, May). "Building Group Decision Support Rooms Using 'Off-the-Shelf' Computing Resources: Prospects and Issues." *Database.*

Sage, P. A., (1991). *Decision Support Systems Engineering.* New York: Wiley.

Stohr, E. A. and B. R. Konsynski. (eds.) (1992). *Information Systems and Decision Processes.* Los Alamitos, CA:IEEE Computer Society Press.

Taylor, R. L., and R. A. Beauclair. (1990). "GDSS as a Tool in Public Policy: The Louisville Experience." *DSS-89 Transactions.* The Providence, RI Institute of Management Sciences.

Vickers, B. (1992, October). "Using GDSS to Examine the Future European Automobile Industry." *Futures.*

Walsh, J. P. and G. R. Ungson. (1991). "Organizational Memory." *Academy of Management Review,* Vol. 16, No. 1.

APPENDIX 9-A: An Example of a GDSS Meeting

The Topic: What to Do with the Queen Mary?

On March 6, 1992, the Walt Disney Company advised the city of Long Beach that it would end its lease for operation of the Queen Mary.

The city of Long Beach called an emergency meeting at the Electronic Decision Support Facility at California State University, Long Beach, to discuss what to do with the Queen Mary. (The Facility is equipped with TeamFocus software, from IBM.)

In round one, participants were asked to make suggestions, using the electronic brainstorming module. Since people make these anonymously, they are free to make any type of suggestion. These are made one at a time, and they are transmitted one at a time to another participant.

Some Ideas

Issue: How can we make the Queen Mary profitable?

1.1 Make it into senior citizen housing.
2.1 Take it to the ocean and sink it; it can be used for a skin diving attraction.

3.1 Make it into low-income housing.
4.1 Make it into a casino.
5.1 Turn it into a whorehouse.
6.1 Sink it, make it into an underwater hotel.

Here are some anonymous responses:

1.2 Hell, no. (Response to 1.1)
1.3 Why not?(Response to 2.1).
1.4 Enough seniors in Long Beach. (Response to 3.1)
4.2 Gambling is illegal in California. (Response to 4.1)
5.2 You are a stupid low life who has no respect for your peers. You should be gassed. (Response to 5.1)

The Procedure

In round two the generated ideas were organized, using the idea orginization software, into eight groups (key ideas). In round three these were ranked by each participant in a descending order. The results are shown in Table 9-A.1. Notice that at that time there was very little agreement (0.21 on a scale of 1.0).

The specific ideas in each category can be accessed by each participant at any time.

In round four a discussion occurred in order to achieve greater consensus. The facilitator used both electronic and verbal communication. The result was re-ordering of the key issues and an increased level of agreement to 0.68.

TABLE 9-A.1 The First Vote

| | Number of Votes in Each Position | | | | | | | | | |
	1	2	3	4	5	6	7	8	Mean	STD
Management options	3	4	4	2	1	1	2	—	3.29	1.96
Promotions	4	2	4	2	3	—	—	2	3.47	2.21
Operational budget	3	2	2	4	2	2	—	2	3.94	2.22
Advertising	1	3	2	5	2	3	1	—	4.00	1.70
Alternative uses	2	4	2	1	2	4	2	—	4.00	2.12
Housing	2	—	1	2	2	3	6	1	5.35	2.12
Casino	2	—	2	—	2	4	4	3	5.53	2.27
Scrap	—	2	—	1	3	—	2	9	6.41	2.15

Coefficient of concordance (1.0 = most agreement): 0.21

Chapter 17

Distributed Group Support Systems

The support of groups whose members are at different locations is becoming an increasingly important topic due to the increased emphasis of workgroups and teams. Also, escalating travel and transportation costs and the need to make quick decisions make the distributed GSS a viable technology. The GSS topics discussed in this chapter are:

10.1   Case: Using Notes at Price Waterhouse*

Price Waterhouse (PW) is one of the six largest accounting CPA firms in the United States. In March 1989, PW named Sheldon Laube as the director of information technology. In a few months, in a bold, unorthodox move, Laube licensed 10,000 copies of Lotus Notes at a cost of $2 million, while it was still in beta testing. By 1992, Notes had fundamentally altered PW business processes and brought an end to the chaos that existed in 1989.

Here are typical scenes from "before Notes":

- Highly paid associates shuffling between floors with stacks of paperwork, desperately trying to get sign-offs on top-priority products
- Partners in regional offices struggling to decipher complex accounting rules without the aid of centralized databases
- Out-of-town partners unable to use local offices to print out data from their 3.5-inch disks
- Partners waiting weeks to find information about specific tax court rulings
- Local offices setting their own technology without a strategy for data sharing.

Here is a sample of what Notes enabled PW's employees to do:

- View, from inside a database, a collection of the firm's analysis of IRS rulings and opinions
- Share, within hours, all information describing a court ruling and read the ruling itself
- Tap the labors of others by accessing every business proposal PW has submitted to clients since 1989, thus reducing preparation time and improving the chance of winning contracts (see *Fortune*, December 27, 1993).

The system, which is built with the client/server architecture, includes about 125 servers and 11,000 PC's residing on PW's worldwide network.

Notes is a real success. In addition to its information-sharing capabilities, the system is used to create new applications. More than 500 were created by end-users and 100 by the IS department. These applications include generation of billing reports and compilation of marketing data by the partners themselves. "The system puts knowledge in the senior managers' fingertips, that is why they use it," commented Laube. Notes can also put the knowledge of many experts to the service of clients very quickly.

Notes also changed PW's organizational culture. People who never used computers now use them extensively.

---

*Based on M. Mehler, "Notes Fanatic," *Corporate Computing*, August 1992; and on D. Kirkpatrick, "Groupware Goes Boom," *Fortune*, December 27, 1993.

10.2 Why Distributed GSS?

The decision room facility, while extremely helpful, is used by very few organizations. The major reasons are:

- There is a need for a large investment in the facility (a situation that may be changed due to software availability).
- The facility may be used very infrequently.
- There is a need for a trained facilitator.
- The software support is designed for handling conflicting issues, such as resource allocation. Thus, support for anonymity, voting, negotiation, and conflict resolution is critical. However, the vast majority of groupwork tasks involve *cooperating* rather than *conflicting* issues. Thus, the facility may seldom be utilized.
- More and more groupwork is done while members are in different locations. To use a decision room it is necessary to bring all participants to the same place at the same time. This may be expensive, time consuming, and not practical.
- Renting a decision room may cost several thousand dollars per day. The benefits may be difficult to justify.

Box 10.1: Winning a Multimillion-Dollar Consulting Contract by Using Notes

Price Waterhouse was invited to bid on a multimillion-dollar consulting job regarding a complex securities trading operation. The proposal was due in four days. The four executives who were needed to write the proposal were in three different states. Not only did they work on the same document with Notes in the different locations, but they also extracted key components of the proposal from various databases. For example, they pulled resumes of the company's experts from around the world who could be consulted with when needed. They also borrowed passages from similar previously successful proposals. A draft was written, and each executive modified it or made comments. Other executives looked at the proposal via Notes and contributed valuable suggestions. The proposal was ready on time and the consulting job was awarded to Price Waterhouse. In addition, the company was awarded a multiple-year contract to audit the complex trading system that they helped to create in the initial consulting job.

(*Source:* Based on a story in *Fortune*, December 27, 1993.)

- In some organizations, there are several meetings going on simultaneously. Therefore, there may be a need for several decision rooms in one company.

While the use of decision rooms is spreading slowly, with the reduced cost of hardware and software, an increasing number of companies are implemented **distributed GSS,** also known as **distributed workgroup computing.** For an overview, see McGrath and Hollingshead [1994].

There are other reasons that favor the use of distributed GSS. For example, there is an increased emphasis on team-based organizations and autonomous teams. These teams may be in different locations. Furthermore, frequently there is a time pressure for executing projects and the members are in different locations and so are the databases and other resources (see Box 10.1). Finally, there is an increased cost of travel, and distributed GSS can reduce travel or even eliminate it completely.

Distributed GSS are designed to support people working in groups in different locations and possibly times. The support can be directly related to decision making or it may be indirectly related (e.g., provides information, supports the preparation of a document).

10.3 The Distributed GSS Technologies

Several technologies can support the work of groups whose members are in different places. The major technologies are listed in Table 10.1.

TABLE 10.1 Computer Support to Groups.

1. Integrated conferencing services (computerized plus video and audio)
2. Electronic mail
3. Negotiation support systems
4. Coordination systems
5. Workgroup project management
6. Message systems
7. Computerized bulletin boards
8. Document interchange services
9. Information analysis services
10. Distributed GDSS
11. Electronic data interchange (EDI)
12. Voice technologies
13. Cost/flow systems
14. Idea generation systems

Source: Based on Sprague and McNurlin [1992] and on Ellis [1991].

In this chapter we will review only those technologies that are used more frequently to support decision making. However, before we describe the technologies, we present the most popular operating system for integrating various GSS tools, Windows for Workgroups.

10.4 Windows for Workgroups

Recognizing the importance of supporting people working in groups, Microsoft Corporation is enhancing its operating systems to facilitate groupworks. See Opper and Fresko-Weiss [1992]. Their lead product is Windows for Workgroups.

Windows for Workgroups is an operating system that is embedding fundamental workgroup services in Windows operating systems to provide an open workgroup computing foundation. These services include information sharing, a messaging system, standard directory service, a common data access model, and security, among others. It is an enhanced version of Windows 3.1 that includes several workgroup capabilities (such as resource and information sharing). Windows for Workgroups includes electronic mail, group scheduling, and network-enabled DDE.

Windows NT includes all the workgroup features of Windows for Workgroups and, in addition, it runs 32-bit applications and includes many powerful features that can be helpful for supporting groups.

Future versions of the Windows family will include object-oriented technology to enable users to access and manipulate information regardless of its location or the software application it is in. It will also include features for managing documents, charts, and data files across the enterprise. Finally, future enhancements will include applications of artificial intelligence.

Microsoft has many applications software packages that can be used to support groups. These include electronic messaging, group scheduling, form routing (workflow), and group conferencing.

10.5 Lotus Notes

In the opening case and in Box 10.1 a reference was made to Notes. Notes is presently the most popular distributed GSS software.*

Lotus Notes is software that acts as a group communications environment that lets users access and create shared information. It provides a workgroup E-mail, distributed databases, bulletin boards, text editing, document management, workflow capabilities, and various applications development tools, all inte-

---

*Contribution to this section was made by Gary Grinham, an MBA student at California State University, Long Beach.

grated into an environment with a graphical menu-based user interface. Notes is used for many applications including fostering the virtual corporation and similar intercompany alliances.

Lotus's program allows data to be collected, stored, organized, and disseminated among many users on one or several networks. It employs the Windows interface and extensive networks.

What Is Lotus Notes?

Lotus Notes can best be described as a distributed document database. In a client/server environment, clients communicate over a local area network with a document database that resides on one or more servers. Notes *replicates* the data on each server as needed so users have access to the same information. Notes is a product with a wide variety of capabilities that enable users to work together and to enter and share information with other people. Notes is designed to handle the following four main types of applications:

Tracking helps users follow what is happening in their business such as sales trends, purchasing, and so forth. *Broadcast* is used to deliver announcements or post information to a large group. *Reference* stores and helps users sift through information. It can also be used to store standardized forms. *Discussion* enables groups to discuss issues either formally or informally.

Notes updates its distributed databases at regular intervals, unlike on-line transaction processing, which is constantly updated.

Where to Use Notes?

Notes is best suited for disseminating information that relies on documents and text such as in sales, production, and human resources. Notes is basically a tool designed to share information and improve communication between work groups and among members of one group whether they are in the same building or thousands of miles apart. Proper use of Notes requires a thorough understanding of what application the product is being used for. Deciding to purchase and install Notes before identifying the root causes of a business problem will surely fail in correcting the situation. One must completely understand Notes's capabilities and limitations before deciding that it is the answer to a problem.

Notes was designed with three primary business activities in mind: customer service, product development, and account management. For example, in customer service, Notes can be used to track calls. Each call and its resolution is placed in a common database that would inform others of the outcome. With product development, knowledge workers can freely exchange information, which could greatly improve productivity and reduce time to market. In account management, customer information and action taken can be recorded in a central database that would give all users access to critical information.

Advantages of Notes

Notes utilizes information repositories, or databases, that allow users to store and organize information so others can retrieve it. Notes's database capabilities differ from E-mail systems in that Notes does not require the user to know exactly who the recipient is. Instead, the information is forwarded to the appropriate bulletin board. Any user can access the information and read, update, or respond to it.

At the heart of Notes's success is its distributed document database capability. There are three basic types of databases used in Notes:

- *Discussion Databases:* The most common type of database, these enable users to participate in written meetings and are usually classified by subject.
- *Document Libraries:* Store written information normally printed on paper. Databases can be created containing reports, memos, forms, et cetera.
- *Information Services:* Enable users to obtain the latest information about selected topics.

In addition to its database functions, Notes also has conventional E-mail (cc:Mail, from Lotus) features that allow users to send messages directly to specific individuals.

The use of Notes as a *forms generator* has several advantages. A user can select any form contained in the forms database and create and send the document to another user. Many companies are using this capability to replace paper forms for things such as travel authorizations, purchase orders, and expense reports. One such company is Ryder Systems, Inc., which is known for its commitment to information technology. One of Notes's strongest points is its graphical user interface, which allows users who are already familiar with Windows and OS/2 menu screens to quickly adapt. Overall, Notes can provide a large competitive advantage for users, as was shown in Box 10.1.

Disadvantages of Notes

Notes is not inexpensive to operate. Ed Catlett, assistant vice president of Johnson & Higgins, an insurance brokerage firm, utilizes Notes extensively. The firm uses Notes to exchange information between branch offices and hundreds of insurers worldwide. Catlett says, "You need the people to administer and support the database. You have to have technical people who understand how the servers talk to one another. You have to do disk capacity planning, because you are keeping duplicates of your database in various locations." Lotus recommends that companies using Notes should assign four standard administrative positions. A Notes administrator maintains the servers, supports users, loads software, and performs replication. The Notes support engineer installs and tests Notes and handles troubleshooting. The database manager handles access control, which determines what users can do within Notes. The Notes certifier creates IDs for Notes users, ensuring that proper security precautions are taken.

Accessing Notes

One important aspect of the use of groupware is authorized access. With Notes, the creator of each database controls who has access to the information contained within it. The creator, or database manager, can choose one of the seven following access levels:

- No Access—No access of any kind allowed.
- Depositor—Can create new documents, but cannot read existing documents.
- Reader—Can only read documents.
- Author—Can create and read documents.
- Editor—Can create, modify, and delete documents.
- Designer—Has all capabilities of author, and can create and modify forms.
- Manager—Can perform all possible operations.

Other Notes-related Products

There are several add-on products available from Lotus and other vendors, such as *document imaging, subscription services,* and *workflow management.*

Video Notes. Available soon, this product allows two Notes users to conduct real-time, full-motion videoconferencing across a fiber optic network. It allows users to integrate data from Notes and SQL databases. The important feature of the product is that it allows users to query and update Notes and SQL databases.

AT&T Network Notes. Lotus reached an agreement with AT&T that will make Notes available to business users by dialing into an AT&T public network. AT&T Network Notes will allow users to dial in over telephone lines to a network where they can use Notes to share documents that include text, image, and video; exchange electronic mail; and replicate documents and files for customers, suppliers, or business partners. AT&T Network Notes will be used initially to access on-line newsletters as well as broadcast news, much the same as Prodigy and Compuserve. Eventually, AT&T plans to use the Notes interface to sell movies, music CDs, and other products to consumers.

Intelligent Agent. Intelligent agents reside on Notes servers to filter, abstract, and deliver customized data to users. One drawback to using regular Notes is that users can be bombarded with information. Sorting relevant information can be very time consuming. The intelligent agent allows users to instruct the Notes server about the information they need. It scans the information coming into the server and extracts and/or combines data, meeting predefined criteria, and forwards the information to the user.

1. This is Michelle's Notes desktop. Each icon represents a different Notes application. She uses these to work with people all over the world including the field sales team, manufacturing, engineering, R&D, key customers and senior management. She regularly scans activities in the field by double clicking on ACCOUNT STATUS.

2. Today, she notices a number of entries regarding a slow-down in closing first quarter reorders for their most popular model, the MountainMaster off-road bike. It seems the market for this high-priced bike is beginning to dry up. This could be a major problem.

3. She decides to recommend a price-reduction and double clicks into the STRATEGIC PRODUCT DISCUSSION database. This provides an organization-wide forum to discuss issues and brainstorm solutions. She links the report from the Atlanta rep directly into her Notes document. Then she uses DDE to embed some 1-2-3® charts into her document as well.

4. Later in the day she re-enters the DISCUSSION database looking for responses. Her boss, John, has logged on from his hotel room in San Francisco. Rather than cut the margin, he suggests she explore the feasibility of adding a mid-priced bike to their line. He wants an initial presentation for Friday.

5. The next morning she checks into the DISCUSSION database and this time finds an entry from Reggie in R&D. Reggie had also read Jim's message and is responding with a possible solution his people have been playing with. He pastes in an autocad illustration faxed to him from the U.K. using a Notes incoming fax gateway.

6. With a presentation on Friday, Michelle gets down to some quick market research by opening up the CYCLING INDUSTRY NEWS database. An organized source of live industry data, it provides a news report on a French company that has a couple months head start developing a hybrid bike.

7. A few days after routing her proposal to the product team, she wants to find out where it stands within the organization. She opens the ROUTING STATUS application to find that it has worked its way through the organization to Desmond, the senior decision-maker, and has been finally approved. So she's on her way.

8. Michelle closes the loop by communicating the news to their customers. Double clicking into the CUSTOMER FEEDBACK database, she faxes a memo directly from Notes to all retailers. In it she explains that the company has heard their problems and responded with the Hill Hopper. And with delivery in 60 days, they can order now.

FIGURE 10.1 Using Notes. (*Source:* Screen shot ©1993 Lotus Development Corporation. Used with permission of Lotus Development Corporation.)

Competing Products. Two new products compete with Notes, Touchdown from Microsoft, and Novell Groupware from Novell Corporation.

The eight-step scenario shown in Figure 10.1 (taken from Lotus's advertisement) illustrates Notes' capabilities. Each step is executed with a different module. Step 7 is a part of the workflow capability.

10.6   Electronic Teleconferencing

Telephone Conferencing. Teleconferencing refers to the use of electronic communication to allow two or more people from different locations to have a conference. There are several variations of teleconferencing (see LaPlante [1993]). The oldest and the simplest is a telephone conference. In such a case, several people are talking to each other from three or more locations. Telephone conference calls are available to customers at very low cost. Their biggest disadvantage is that they do not allow for face-to-face communication nor for performing work together on a computer screen. Also, participants in one location cannot see graphs, charts, and pictures available in other locations. While the latter deficiency can be overcome with the support of a fax, it is a time-consuming and expensive process. One solution is videoteleconferencing.

Videoteleconferencing. In a **videoteleconference**, participants in one location can see the other participants in one or several locations. The pictures of the participants can appear on a large screen or on a small CRT (see Figure 10.2).

Originally, videoconferencing used to be a transmission of live, compressed TV sessions between two or more points. Videoconferencing today is a digital technology capable of linking various types of computers. Once videoconferences are digitized and transmitted over networks, they become computer applications. Therefore, in videoconferencing, one can present data, voice, picture, graphics, and animation (see Figure 10.2).

Video mail is an example of how videoconferencing is becoming a computer application. Video mail is similar to voice mail; however, the voice/image contents of the video mail can be created from portions of videoconferences and can be stored on a file server. It is possible to simultaneously transmit data, voice, and pictures during conferences. It is also possible to work on documents and exchange computer files during conferences. This allows the possibility of high quality presentations using computer graphics.

While the first generation of computerized videoconferencing was conducted in special rooms with large screens, cameras, and coder/recorders, the second generation moved to the worker's desktop, using special equipment, such as PC Videophone and LANs. As interactive video moves to the desktop, it can become a valuable item that can be used in conjunction with other desktop facilities.

The major benefits of videoteleconferencing are:

FIGURE 10.2 A Typical Videoteleconference Setup. (*Source:* Reprinted with permission from "Better Than Being Here." *BYTE Magazine*, March 1993. ©1993 by McGraw-Hill, Inc., New York, N. Y. All rights reserved.)

Box 10.2: Videoconferencing Saves Money

Bull HN Information Systems Inc. (Billerca, MA) used to spend several million dollars a year on travel between its headquarters in Billerca and its Phoenix office. To save money, Bull installed, in 1989, a PictureTel System 4000 videoconferencing unit at the two locations. Bull was then able to greatly increase the number of meetings and contain costs, since no travel was required. Many other companies reported significant savings. For example, BASF Corporation's fiber division (Williamsburg, VA) saves over $1 million a year in travel expenses alone.

Videoconferencing is used not only within one company but also among several companies. For example, Sun Health Corporation (Charlotte, NC) purchases supplies for 250 hospitals in 15 states. The member hospitals decided to install videoconferencing equipment in all hospitals, so they can conduct face-to-face meetings without the need to travel. By the end of 1993, 22 hospitals were equipped with videoconferencing equipment.

- Providing opportunity for face-to-face communication for individuals in different locations
- Enabling several members to communicate simultaneously
- Providing the possibility of using several types of media to support conferencing
- Enabling usage of voice (which is more natural than using the keyboard).

Several factors are limiting the growth of videoconferencing. These range from lack of standards to connectivity problems with networks. However, using face-to-face voice communication is an extremely appealing option to management, and with the reduced cost and increased capabilities, the technology will spread throughout the corporate world (see Box 10.2).

One of the largest users of videoconferencing is JCPenney, which uses the technology in several hundred of its stores.

10.7   Electronic Mail

Electronic mail (E-mail) allows multiple access communication delivered exclusively on a computer network. With E-mail, a person can send letters to anyone connected to the system. When a message is sent, it enters an individual's "mailbox." The receiver, when connected to the network, is notified that he or she has mail. The receiver can then read the mail, send a reply, edit the mail, or forward the letter to another person.

E-mail is becoming an important communication tool in many organizations. The primary advantages of E-mail are:

- The ability to send and receive messages very quickly
- Paperless communication
- The ability to connect to the network (using a portable computer and a modem) from any location that has a telephone line. Recently, it became possible to connect to the networks with wireless technologies
- The ability to send messages to many users in a very short time
- The ability to trace any correspondence (who sent, to whom, when, etc.)

Box 10.3: Internet and the Business World

Internet is the world's largest computer network. It is composed of over 18,000 connected networks with over 2 million computers and 20 million users (in 1995). Internet, which initially served the academic world (e.g., for accessing supercomputers), is now serving the business world as well, providing speedy low-cost global communication. About 500 specialty databases are accessed through Internet. Dialog, one of the largest commercial services that provides database and sophisticated retrieval mechanisms, is also connected to Internet. You can read on Internet, without any fee, books whose copyrights have expired. Other books can be reached via Internet and Online BookStore for a minimal fee. Internet E-mail is most efficient. It maximizes bandwidth use and permits continuous connection. Users can send messages to groups (many mailing lists are available), including members of specialized newsgroups. Companies can receive information from experts in narrow specialties. A company can register in any interest-group mailing list and get information that flows continuously to members. For example, there is an oil and gas industry list of new explorations. All together, there are about 2,000 newsgroups that receive messages and news articles according to their specific group profile.

It is also possible to conduct collaborative work over Internet. Professionals can write papers jointly, share data, or design new products as a team whose members are in different locations. Authors and publishers can develop manuscripts very quickly. Also, people can produce business and legal documents as participating members of a team. Companies can retrieve publicly available software from files in Internet. There are thousands of packages, including some given away free by major vendors. Internet is privately owned by about 18,000 organizations and operates in about 50 countries.

(*Source:* Based on material published by J.S. Quarterman in *Computerworld*, February 22, 1993. For more information about Internet see Kehoe [1993].)

- The ability to communicate to millions of people, worldwide
- The ability to work with others on the same task
- The ability to rapidly access information stored in databases from many locations.

The limitations of E-mail are:

- The inability to conduct face-to-face communication
- Most E-mails are not user friendly
- It is necessary to know how to type
- It may involve a problem of confidentiality (see Chapter 22).

It is very likely that the LAN you use is connected to Internet (Box 10.3). If you are connected to a Bitnet or Telnet, you are in the Internet family. In such a case,

Box 10.4: Enabled E-mail at Hughes Aircraft Corporation

Hughes Aircraft Corporation is a multinational aerospace and electronic company that employs 25,000 people worldwide. A leader in electronics, the company was using more than ten different E-mail systems. In order to link all its employees, the company embarked on a six-year integration project that ended in a unified E-mail system in 1992. Not only are the 25,000 employees linked together, they also are connected with 75,000 employees of General Motors (Hughes's parent company). The real value of the system is the provision of infrastructure for company-wide applications, streamlining business processes, and speeding the dissemination of critical information. The infrastructure supports what is called *mail-enabled* applications, which provide a focal point to re-engineer business processes. The E-mail is integrated with a videotext database network that can be accessed for a variety of applications, including electronic routing and approval (ERA). ERA provides electronic forms and routes among employees. The user imports standard information from the database to complete the forms. Thus, the time needed for data entry and approval has been significantly reduced. For example, documents that used to take weeks to get around, now get around in minutes (reducing the cycle time). Employees are getting individually tailored information extracted from sources such as Commerce Business Daily. People get the right information fast, and they are not charged for the service. On the contrary, they are encouraged to use it as much as possible.

(*Source:* Condensed from *CIO*, January 1992, p. 68.)

you can communicate with people all over the world, and access a vast amount of information.

Once the E-mail infrastructure is in place it can be used for many applications. Such E-mail is called **enabled E-mail** (see Box 10.4).

E-Mail on Networks

E-mail systems were used for many years in the mainframe environment. For example, IBM's PROFS enables employees to communicate all over the world. With today's distributed systems, E-mail is capable of connecting people at different locations who are working on different LANs using different hardware, operating systems, and communication systems. The LAN can be simple, or it can be of the client/server architecture. On E-mail, one can send text, files, graphics, or faxes. People can connect to such systems from home or while they are on the road, using the regular telephone lines or a form of wireless equipment.

An E-mail system can interface with other E-mail systems, private or public. For example, a company can connect to public systems which operate all over the world, such as MCI MAIL and IBM's X.400. The company's clients are also connected to the same public systems; therefore, communication is possible among all the companies, regardless of their location.

Several vendors produce E-mail software. A well-known software is cc:Mail (from Lotus Development Corporation). Windows-based E-mail and mail-enabled applications enterprise-wide are increasing the attractiveness and capabilities of E-mail.

10.8   Electronic Data Interchange (EDI)

Electronic Data Interchange (EDI) can be classified as a special category of E-mail. Like E-mail, EDI enables the sending and receiving of messages between computers connected by a communication link (such as a telephone line). However, EDI has some special characteristics. These are:

1. *Business Transactions Messages.* EDI is used primarily to transfer *repetitive business transactions*. These include purchase orders, invoices, approvals of credit, shipping notices, and confirmations. In contrast, E-mail is used mainly for nonstandard correspondence.

2. *Data Formatting Standards.* Since the messages are repetitive, it is sensible to use some standards. These standards can shorten the length of the messages and can eliminate data entry errors. Therefore, data are formatted according to agreed-upon standards. In the United States and Canada, these standards are called ANSI X.12. An international standard developed by the United Nations is called EDI-FACT. In contrast, there are no data formatting standards for E-mail.

3. *Data Formatting and EDI Translators.* The conversion of data sent into standard formats is done by special EDI translators. These translators are programmed to translate to standards such as X.12.

How EDI Works. Information flows from corporation A's information system into an EDI station which includes a PC, an EDI translator, a modem, and a link to the corporate mainframe or LAN (see Figure 10.3). From there, the information moves to a value-added network (VAN) via telephone or other communication lines. The VAN transfers the formatted information to corporation B, where the EDI translator converts it to a desired format (or transmits it as it is). The modems play the usual role of changing digital signals to analog and vice versa. Information then can flow from B to A in a similar manner.

The Advantages of EDI. The following are the major advantages of EDI:

- EDI enables companies to send and receive large amounts of information around the world in real time.
- There are very few errors in the transformed data due to data formatting.
- Information can flow among several trading partners consistently and freely.
- Companies access partners' computers to retrieve and deposit standard transactions.
- EDI fosters a true (and strategic) partnership relationship since it involves a commitment to a long-term investment and to the refinement of the system over time.
- EDI creates a completely paperless TPS environment.
- The time for collecting payments can be shortened by several weeks.

FIGURE 10.3   How EDI Works.

- EDI can save a considerable amount of money. For example, the Health Industry Business Communication Council estimates that EDI can reduce the cost of an order in a hospital from $70 to $14 (a savings of $840,000 annually for an average hospital).

10.9 GSS Software and Workflow Systems

According to Microsoft [1993] there were, in 1993, more than 3,000 software vendors, offering more than 6,000 Windows-based applications and development tools that can be workgroup-enabled and used as components in customer solutions. The many needs facing an organization today require, in most cases, the use of several software products and vendors, working together within an open architecture, to deliver the best solutions for real-world business problems.

The following are some examples of both groupware development tools and applications:

1. *Idea generation.* These products were discussed in Chapter 8.
2. *Managing sessions.* Two expert system products were developed for managing group sessions: Expert Session Manager and Expert System Planner. (For details contact Robert Mockler at St. John's University, New York.)
3. *Multiple criteria decision making products.* These are listed in Chapter 5.
4. *Strategic Planning Planner.* (From Ronin Development Corporation of Princeton, NJ; see Mockler [1992] for details.) A simple stand-alone brainstorming tool (from Experience in Software Inc., Berkeley, CA) guides users through three levels of problem solving.
5. *Innovator.* This meeting-enhancement keypad system polls an audience and provides feedback (from Wilson Learning Corp., Eden Prairie, MN); it is specifically geared toward idea generation, consensus building, and focus research for strategic planning.
6. *One Touch.* This multimedia-based package (from One Touch System, Santa Clara, CA) is designed to support remote teaching and conferencing. It has voting keypads, one-way satellite-relayed video, and two-way audio.
7. *OptionFinder.* This "X-Y Window"-based package (from Option Technology, Mendota Heights, MN) allows groups to brainstorm, weigh alternatives, identify priorities, vote, and work toward consensus in a non-decision room setting.
8. *Higgins.* This is basically a group scheduler software (from Enable Software Higgins Group, Ballston Lake, NY). To do its job, the software interacts with personal calendars of the participants. It works via E-mail to confirm schedules.
9. *Consensus Builder.* This product has a knowledge base for supporting decision making in a group (from Magic 7 Software, Los Altos, CA). It helps in resolving conflicts and taking prompt action. The product weights each

participant's judgment in accordance with his or her own personal standards, capabilities, and biases. It points to similarities among the participants, as well as to differences.

10. *For Comment.* This server-based software (from Access Technology Inc., Natick, MA) manages all the documents related to group meetings and conferences.
11. *Together.* This is an application integrator that enables multiple users to access multiple applications through a windowed desktop screen (from Coordination Technology, Inc., Trumbell, CT). It enables users to work with each other on one task (at the same time or at different times).
12. *Coordinator.* This is an integrated E-mail, scheduling, and calendaring package (from DaVinci Systems Inc.).
13. *Cooperations.* This is an enterprise-wide integrated environment with workflow, control, E-mail, and scheduling features (from NCR Corporation).
14. *Meeting Maker.* This is a leading groupware scheduler (from ON Technology Inc.).
15. *Vineyard.* This is a workgroup-based system for Windows. It transforms a LAN into a repository of shared information available to all group members (from Data Fellows, Inc.).

For further information on these and some other groupware products see Kaplan [1992].

A special type of groupware software that deserves attention is workflow systems.

Workflow Systems. Workflow software is a powerful business process automation tool that places system controls in the hands of end-user departments. It is highly flexible and can be designed to automate almost any information processing system. Not only does workflow automate business processes, it also provides a quality interface between operating systems. As a result, workflow installations have evolved into enterprise-wide computing solutions at major companies.

There are three types of workflow software:

1. *Administrative.* These include expense reports, travel requests, and messages.
2. *Ad hoc.* These include product brochures, sales proposals, and strategic plans.
3. *Production.* These include credit card mailings, mortgage loans, and insurance claims.

The primary purpose of workflow systems is to offer workflow automation capabilities that provide end-users with tracking, routing, document imaging, and other facilities designed to improve business processes (see Box 10.5).

There are many workflow software packages on the market (see Buyer's Guide in *PC Week,* April 5, 1993). Some of them are based on E-mail capabilities; others use a shared database or a file on a server that people can log into. The most

---

Box 10.5: Workflow Software Automates Business Processes

Bankers Trust Company of New York replaced their manual customer requests system with an automated one. The system is based on Action (from Action Technologies Inc.) and it works together with Lotus Notes. Cases are placed into Notes, then Action routes the cases to appropriate employees who work on them. The progress in dealing with each request is monitored. Action pays attention to whether the employees complete each task as scheduled. In case of deviations, a reminder is automatically generated. The software tracks every case and knows where it is.

---

notable software of the latter category is Lotus Notes. As discussed earlier, Notes is not just a workflow package; it is an integrated groupware software that has many other capabilities.

10.10   Distributed Interactive Desktop Groupware

Computer programs can enable people to work together on the same screen, but at different locations, exchanging voice and/or keyed ideas and comments. One such product is Fujitsu's Desktop Conferencing software. The product runs on Windows across a NetWare LAN (from Novell Inc.) and has many applications (see Box 10.6).

Box 10.6: Global Marine (Houston, TX) Uses Interactive Software

In an attempt to cut trips to their offshore drilling sites and to their European office in Aberdeen, Scotland, Global Marine installed Fujitsu's system. One application was to train the MIS employees in Aberdeen in a new client/server system that replaced the mainframe. Other applications include enabling managers at different locations to review contracts, spreadsheets, and proposals. For example, a manager can change a cell value and discuss with his or her colleagues in other locations the impact of the change.

(*Source: Computerworld,* May 3, 1993, p. 4.)

Fujitsu's system works like this: A chairperson or a coordinator sets up the application and the conference time. The other participants all see the same screen, which is controlled by the coordinator. Any update in the chairperson's screen is reflected automatically on the participant's screens. The software includes support for a light pen interface to make handwritten notes on screens, a flip chart function for presentations, a text-messaging feature for sending notes to specific members, and a file-transfer utility. Fujitsu's system is only the beginning of desktop applications in the area of live interactive conferencing (see Box 10.7).

Box 10.7: Painting Together

The figures below show: (a) a screen designed by one person, (b) a screen designed by a second person. The combined design is shown in (c). Each participant can see the design of the other designer (if authorization is given), as well as the combined design. The designers can exchange notes electronically regarding the product, colors, size, shape, and so on. Changes can be made while both designers see the same screen.

The screens were created with software called Group Paint, which was developed by the Center for Group Support Systems at the National Sun Yat-Sen University in Taiwan. (Screens are provided courtesy of the Center in Taiwan.)

(a)

(b)

(c)

10.11   Telecommuting (Working at Home)

Groupware can be used to support groups of employees that are working at their homes. This phenomenon, called *cottage industry* in the past, is now referred to as *telecommuting* or *teleworking*. Employees work at home on a computer or a terminal linked to their place of employment. The first telecommuters were typists and bookkeepers, but now a growing number of professionals do a significant portion of their work at home (see Cross and Raizman [1986], and O'Leary [1991]). Telecommuting, which is used by many corporations in large cities, is also appealing to small entrepreneurs (see Box 10.8). Lately, there is increased evidence of teams whose members are working at their homes.

The advantages of telecommuting are:

- People work with fewer interruptions and can better concentrate on their work, resulting in increased productivity. Also, they are not tired from the travel.

Box 10.8: The Virtual Entrepreneur

While many telecommuters work for other companies, there are people who run their own businesses from home. A third kind of telecommuters are people who work for others in specially designed telecommuting centers. Henricks [1993] provides the following examples of all three kinds:

- Brenda Clamera Brimages develops math textbooks (millions of copies are sold) and manages an ever-shifting stable of writers and designers spread across the country.
- An Ophthalmologist, Dr. J. Garden, examines inmates without traveling the 40 miles to the prison. Instead, she tests eyes using a PC, modem, and video camera, all from her living room.
- Frank Cottle has built nine telecommuting centers in Southern California, where close to 1,000 tenants rent a space, computers, faxes, and phones to work with colleagues thousands of miles away.
- Michael Kouloaroudis of Brooklyn, NY gets leads on overseas companies looking for American products. Using one computer and operating from his home, he grossed over $100,000 on one deal alone by selling American-made window air conditioners to Japan.
- All 14 employees of Journal Graphics Inc. work from home in several states. The company produces transcriptions of broadcast news and talk shows. Employees can relocate as they wish.

- Expensive office and parking space can be saved.
- Housebound people (mothers of young children, handicapped) can be gainfully employed.
- Employees can work flexible hours.
- Driving time for the employees is saved.
- Pollution, traffic congestion, and use of fossil fuels are reduced.
- The advent of the just-in-time workforce can be deployed at will. People can be hired for specific tasks.
- Better workers can be found in different locations, thus improving the quality of the workforce.
- A happier, more motivated workforce results.
- The entrepreneur gains freedom to operate from anywhere.

The major disadvantages are: difficulties in supervising work, lack of human interaction, and increased isolation.

Almost all the technologies can be used to support telecommuting. In addition, the regular and overnight mail, special messengers, and fax are extensively used to support telecommuting.

Chapter Highlights

- Supporting groups whose members are in different locations has many advantages. Such support is referred to as distributed GSS.
- There are several computerized products that can support group members in different locations.
- The major operating system that supports the work of groups is Windows for Workgroups.
- Lotus Notes is the major software that supports the work of dispersed groups.
- Videoteleconferencing utilizes several technologies that allow people to communicate and see each other as well as see and transfer documents.
- Electronic mail allows quick communication across the globe at minimal cost.
- EDI is a special electronic mail that transmits standard transactions (such as purchasing orders) very rapidly and with minimum errors.
- Internet is the largest worldwide electronic mail system.
- Workflow systems can help many routine business processes.
- People can work at home not only as individuals but also as participating team members, supported by GSS.
- Telecommuting is growing rapidly due to its many advantages.

692

Key Words

distributed DSS
distributed workgroup
  computing
electronic data
  interchange (EDI)

enabled E-mail
E-mail
telecommuting
teleconferencing

video mail
videoteleconference
workflow systems

Questions for Review

1. Describe the factors that discourage the use of decision rooms.
2. Describe the factors that encourage the use of distributed GSS.
3. List the major GSS technologies.
4. Describe the major capabilities of Windows for Workgroups.
5. List the major capabilities of Notes.
6. List the major capabilities of teleconferencing.
7. Define E-mail and describe its capabilities.
8. Define EDI and describe its capabilities.
9. What is Internet?
10. Define workflow systems.
11. Define telecommuting and list its major advantages.

Questions for Discussion

1. Explain why there are so few companies that are using decision rooms.
2. Why is Lotus Notes such a successful product?
3. It is said that Notes can change organizational culture; explain how.
4. How can computers support a team whose members work at different times?
5. Based on what you know about Notes, can it support different place/different time work?
6. How is electronic teleconferencing related to computers?
7. Explain how the various technologies are integrated in videoteleconferencing.
8. Explain the advantages of electronic mail over regular mail.
9. Compare and contrast EDI and E-mail.
10. Explain how EDI works.
11. Explain how workflow software can support decision making.
12. Explain the importance of the Fujitsu Desktop system.

Exercises

1. From your own experience or from the vendor's information, list all the major capabilities of Notes and explain how they can be used to support decision making.

2. Read Mehler's case on Notes (*Corporate Computing,* August 1992). Explain how Notes helped in reengineering Price Waterhouse.
3. Review the capabilities of Windows for Workgroups and indicate which ones support group members working in different locations.
4. Find some information about Internet. Explain its importance for world business.
5. The University of Arizona is adopting GroupSystems (see Chapter 9) for use in a distributed mode. Describe which software modules are especially suitable for a distributed mode.

CASE APPLICATION 1: General Mills Uses EDI*

Bob Gaffney, the EDI manager of General Mills (Minneapolis, MN), needed an answer from a transportation company regarding the feasibility of transferring large quantities of Cheerios from a warehouse to a customer. He used the EDI and transferred a standard request. The company had been using EDI for two years. However, the EDI was decentralized; the sales, transportation, and warehousing units were practicing EDI independently. As a result, acknowledgements took about 24 hours.

This response time was unacceptable. It was necessary to change the technology to improve response time. As a part of the corporate reengineering effort, such a change would alter the manner in which General Mills conducted its business. This became the strategic goal of the company. The technical goal was to centralize the EDI and to integrate it seamlessly with the company's business applications. The company uses the EDI for about 5,000 transactions each day. General Mills is also involved with Efficient Consumer Response (ECR), a program sponsored by the grocery industry to remove unnecessary costs from the food distribution cycle. EDI was found to be a key enabler to making ECR work. Several General Mills executives are involved in the industrywide ECR committees.

To build the EDI the company needed:

1. VAN suppliers (four are used)
2. EDI translators (a product from TSI International), a VAN-independent product
3. Select codes (Ansi x.12 and UPC of the grocery industry)
4. To integrate, internally, the EDI with business applications on its mainframe and its LANs, and with communication software
5. To enlist trading partners (suppliers and customers, about 400)

General Mills helped their partners to select VAN, EDI translators and so on. Some of the partners had a mainframe, others used LANs.

---

*Source: Based on *Software Magazine,* June 1993, pp. 95–101.

The system has been implemented successfully. It no longer takes 24 hours to get an answer from a trading partner. The response time has been shortened and it soon will be close to zero (real time).

Case Questions

1. Why was the EDI response time 24 hours?
2. Compare the use of EDI to that of Notes.
3. Why do they need two EDI codes?
4. Why do they need several VAN vendors?
5. Why was it important to select a translator which is VAN-independent?
6. Why was "enlisting trading partners" the last step in the process, and what difficulties may one encounter?
7. From what you learned about EDI, what kind of transactions can take place between a food manufacturer and its suppliers and customers?

References and Bibliography

Applegate, L. M. (1991). "Technology Support for Cooperative Work: A Framework for Studying Introduction and Assimilation in Organization." *Journal of Organizational Computing,* Vol. 1, No. 1.

Bostrom, R., et al. (1992). *Computer Augmented Teamwork: A Guided Tour.* New York: Van Nostrand Reinhold.

Briere, D. (1991, September 16). "Groupware: A Spectrum of Productivity Boosters." *Networkworld.*

Cross, T. B. and H. Raizman. (1986). *Telecommuting: The Future Technology at Work.* Homewood, IL: Dow-Jones/IRWIN.

Ellis, C. A., et al. (1991, January). "Groupware: Some Issues and Experiences (Using Computers to Facilitate Human Interaction)." *Communication of the ACM,* Vol. 34.

Galagher, J., et al. (1990). *Intellectual Teamwork: Social and Technological Foundation of Cooperative Teams.* New York: Lawrence Erlbaum Associates.

Grief, I. (1988). *Computer Supported Cooperative Work: A Book of Readings.* San Mateo, CA: Morgan-Kaufman.

Henricks, M. (1993, June). "The Virtual Entrepreneur." *Success.*

Hindus, L. A. (1992, August 15). "What MIS Should Know About Videoconferencing." *Datamation.*

Hsu, J., and T. Lockwood (eds.). (1993, March). "Collaborative Computing." *Byte.*

Johansen, R. (1988). *Groupware: Computer Support for Business Teams.* New York: Free Press.

Kaplan, A., et al. (1992, March). "Groupware." *PC World.*

Kehoe, B. P. (1993). *Zen and the Art of Internet: A Beginner's Guide.* Prentice Hall.

LaPlante, E. (1993, September 13). "Teleconferencing." *Forbes ASAP.*

McGrath J. E., and A. B. Hollingshead, (1994). *Groups Interacting with Technology: Ideas, Evidence and an Agenda,* Thousand Oak, CA: Sage Pub.

Mockler, R. J. (1992). *Computer Software to Support Strategic Management Decision Making*. New York: Macmillan.

O'Leary, M. (1991, July). "Home Sweet Office." *CIO*.

Opper S., and H. Fersko-Weiss (1992), *Technology for Teams: Enhancing Productivity in Networked Organizations*, New York: Van Nostrand Reinhold.

Sprague R. and B. McNurlin (1993), *Information Systems Management In Practice*, 3rd ed., Prentice Hall.

Yager, T. (1993, March). *"Better Than Being There—Desktop Teleconferencing."* Byte.

Chapter 18

Executive Information and Support Systems

Most DSS users are professionals (e.g., financial analysts, loan officers, auditors, or production schedulers) or middle managers. Very seldom, however, are DSS used directly by top executives. Why is this so? What are the needs of top executives and what is needed in computer-based information systems to make them more appropriate for the upper managerial levels? For answers let us examine a unique MSS tool—the executive information and support system. This chapter is divided into the following sections:

11.1 Executive Information System at Hertz Corporation*

The Problem

The car rental industry is characterized by cutthroat competition and fast-shifting opportunities. Hertz, the largest company in the industry, competes against dozens of competitors in hundreds of locations. The key to success is marketing. Several marketing decisions must be made almost instantaneously (e.g., whether to follow a competitor's price discount or not). These decisions, which are made on a daily basis, are decentralized, and are based on information about cities, climates, holidays, business cycles, tourist activities, past promotions, and competitors' and customers' behavior. Also, it is necessary to know, every day, the rental prices set by all the competitors, in all cities. This is a time-consuming data collection task. The amount of such information is huge, and the only way to process it is to use a large mainframe computer. The problem faced by Hertz was how to provide accessibility to this information and use it properly.

The Initial Solution: A DSS

A DSS was developed in 1987 to allow fast analysis by executives and managers. The system was constructed on the corporate mainframe with System W (from Comshare Inc.). The DSS was very helpful in analyzing information, but when a marketing manager had a question, he or she had to go to a staff assistant, tell that person what was needed, and then wait for the result. There were some problems with this method: the staff assistant was not always available, sometimes there were problems of misunderstanding, and quite often managers needed answers to additional questions—all of which made the process lengthy and cumbersome. When time is of essence, late information is useless to the manager. The need for a better system was obvious.

The EIS

In 1988 Hertz decided to add an EIS—a PC-based system that is used as a front-end to the DSS. The EIS was built with Commander EIS (also from Comshare Inc.). The combined system gave executives tools to analyze the mountains of stored information and make real-time decisions without the help of assistants. Now marketing executives can answer their own questions and plug in their own variables. The system is extremely user-friendly and is maintained by the marketing staff, who continuously upgrade and improve it. Since its assimilation into the corporate culture conformed to the way Hertz executives work, implementation

*Condensed from M. O'Leary, "Putting Hertz Executives in the Driver's Seat," *CIO Magazine*, February, 1990. See also, *Business Month*, July 1989.

was no problem. The system allows Hertz to better use its information and IS resources.

Executives can manipulate and refine data to be more meaningful and strategically significant to them. Further, the work load on the mainframe programming resources has been reduced, since the EIS allows executives to draw information from the mainframe, store the needed data on their own PCs, and perform a DSS-type analysis on their own PCs without tying up valuable mainframe time. The people at Hertz feel that the EIS creates synergy in decision making. It triggers questions, a greater influx of creative ideas, and more cost-effective marketing decisions. The latest enhancement of this EIS is its ability to monitor, in almost real time, competitors' marketing strategies such as pricing and promotions.

11.2 Concepts and Definitions

Hertz's case indicated that neither MIS nor the addition of DSS were sufficient in supporting executives. What is needed is a tool that can handle the many needs for timely information. (See Box 11.1.) The published information about DSS shows that the majority of personal DSS support the work of professionals and

---

Box 11.1: Why EIS?

The following factors were identified by Watson, et al. [1991] (arranged in descending order of importance):

External:

- Increased competition
- Rapidly changing environment
- Need to be more proactive
- Need to access external databases
- Increasing government regulations.

Internal:

- Need for timely information
- Need for improved communications
- Need for access to operational data
- Need for rapid status updates on different activities
- Need for increased effectiveness
- Need to be able to identify historical trends
- Need for access to corporate databases
- Need for more accurate information.

middle-level managers. Organizational DSS provide support primarily to planners, analysts, and researchers. Rarely do we see a DSS used directly by top executives. In many cases, DSS tools are employed by analysts in finding answers to managers' questions.

Executive information systems (EIS), also known as executive support systems (ESS) (see Rockart and Treacy [1982]), is a new technology emerging in response to the situation just described. In a survey conducted by the Center for Information Systems Research (CISR) at MIT, it was found that more than half of the EIS systems were used by people with titles of CEO, CFO, and COO.

The growth of EIS was evident in a study released in 1986 by MIT's CISR. This study showed that about one-third of large U.S. corporations have had EIS programs installed or were developing programs. This figure had grown to more than 50 percent in 1989 (*Computerworld*, February 27, 1989).

Definitions. The terms **executive information systems** and **executive support systems** mean different things to different people. In many cases, the terms are being used interchangeably. The following definitions, based on Rockart and DeLong [1988], distinguish between EIS and ESS.

- *Executive Information System (EIS).* An EIS is a computer-based system that serves the information needs of top executives. It provides rapid access to timely information and direct access to management reports. EIS is very user-friendly, supported by graphics, and provides exceptions reporting and

Box 11.2: ESS in the Persian Gulf War

The Second Marine Aircraft Wing had to plan its activities in a fast-changing political and military environment. The commanding general and his staff of about 100 needed large amounts of information, such as personnel availability, logistics status, and aviation weather conditions and forecasts. Getting all this information via telephones and paper reports was a slow and possibly inaccurate task.

Using RediMaster (from American Information Systems), a local area network, and information downloaded from a mainframe or PCs, an ESS was constructed that could provide the commanders with the needed information in seconds. The ESS included: E-mail, calendar, word processing, spreadsheet, graphics software, and anything else that could be used to support the commanders.

By mid-January, 1991, when the war started, the system was up and running and the Marine's commanding general was able to receive online, real-time reports on subjects ranging from target lists to casualty reports. Indeed, computer technology such as ESS contributed to the success of Desert Storm.

"drill-down" capabilities. It is also easily connected with online information services and electronic mail. *Note:* **Drill down** is an important capability that enables the user to break down data to details. For example, a report on daily corporate rates can be drilled down to find the daily sales in a region, or by product, or by salesperson. A drill down helps the user to identify problems (opportunities).

- *Executive Support System (ESS).* An ESS is a comprehensive support system that goes beyond EIS to include communications, office automation, analysis support, and intelligence. (See Box 11.2.)

11.3   The Nature of the Executive's Work

In order to build an information system for an executive it is first necessary to understand the nature of the executive's work. A well-known study on this topic was conducted by Mintzberg [1975], who divided the manager's roles into three categories:

1. *Interpersonal Roles.* Figurehead, leader, liaison
2. *Informational Roles.* Monitor, disseminator, spokesperson
3. *Decisional Roles.* Entrepreneur, disturbance handler, resource allocator, negotiator.

Early EIS mainly supported some of the informational roles, while the purpose of the second-generation EIS is to support as many roles as possible.

TABLE 11.1 Executive Activities and Information Support.

Nature of Activity (Decision Role)	Percentage of Support
Handling disturbances. A disturbance is something that happens unexpectedly and demands immediate attention, but might take weeks or months to resolve.	42
Entrepreneural activity. Such an activity is intended to make improvements that will increase performance levels. They are strategic and long-term in nature.	32
Resource allocation. Managers allocate resources within the framework of the annual and monthly budgets. Resource allocation is tied with budget and activity planning tasks.	17
Negotiations. The manager attempts to resolve conflicts and disputes, either internal or external to the organization. Such attempts usually involve some negotiations.	3
Other.	6

Source: R. McLeod and J. W. Jones, "Making Executive Information Systems More Effective," *Business Horizons,* September–October, 1986.

To determine the information needs of executives, it is necessary to specify the activities that are performed in each role. Table 11.1 presents the findings of a study conducted by McLeod and Jones [1986]. Notice that the table provides the percentage of information transactions that were used to support the specific activities (decision roles). The table indicates that most information is used in two roles: handling disturbances and entrepreneurial activities.

We divide the executive work, as it is related to decisional roles, into two phases. Phase I is the identification of problems and/or opportunities. Phase II is the decision of what to do about it. Figure 11.1 provides a flow chart of this process and the flow of information in it.

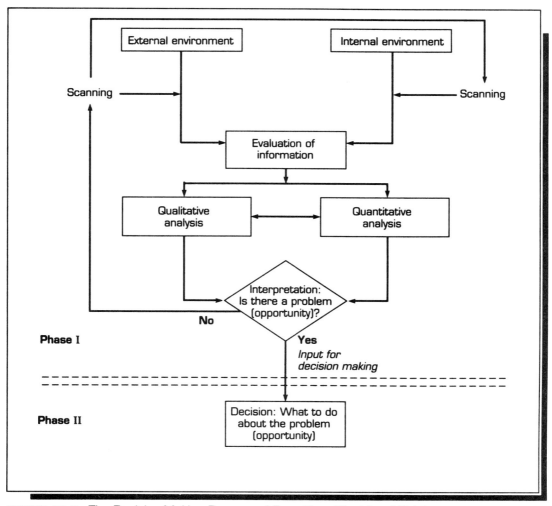

FIGURE 11.1 The Decision-Making Process of Executives (Decisional Role).

702

11.4 Executives' Information Needs

As shown in Figure 11.1, information flows to the executive from the external and the internal environment. Internal information is generated from the functional units (finance, marketing, production, accounting, personnel, etc.). The external information comes from sources such as online databases, newspapers, industry newsletters, government reports, personal contacts, and so on. It is clear that the combined information is extremely valuable; it is an important organizational resource needed for successful competition and survival. Due to the large amount of information available, it is necessary to **scan the environment** and data sources to find the *relevant* pieces. Scanning can be done by the executives themselves, by staff, and/or by machines. The collected information is then evaluated and channeled to quantitative and qualitative analysis (which is carried out by experts whenever needed). Then, a decision (by the executive or by a team) is made on whether a problem or opportunity exists. This is basically an *interpretation* of the information. If it is decided that there is a problem, then this interpretation is an input to the next step: a decision made by the executive, or by a group, on what to do about the problem. Not shown in the figure is the extensive communication that

---

Box 11.3: How to Find Executives' Information Needs

1. Ask senior executives what questions they would ask upon their return from a three-week vacation.
2. Use the critical success factor methodology (see Table 11.2).
3. Interview all senior managers to determine what data they think is most important.
4. List the major objectives in the short- and long-term plans and identify their information requirements.
5. Ask the executives what information they would least like for their competition to see.
6. Either through an interview or observation process, determine what information from current management reports is actually being used by the executive.
7. Provide more immediate, online access to current management reports, and then ask executives how you can better tailor the system to their needs. (Executives are much better at telling you what is wrong with what you have given them than telling you what they need.)
8. Use prototyping (show, criticize, improve). (This approach will be described later.)

may take place among executives, managers, and staff. The basic purpose of EIS is to support Phase I of the process shown in Figure 11.1, as well as to support the specific roles described earlier.

Methods for Finding Information Needs

There are several methods for finding executives' **information needs** (see Box 11.3). Three formal procedures are described next.

a. Wetherbe's Approach [1991]. This approach consists of a two-phase process (see Figure 11.2). In Phase I, *structured interviews* are conducted to determine the executives' perceived information needs. Wetherbe suggested three methods for conducting the structured interviews. They are: IBM's Business System Planning (BSP), critical success factors (CSF), and ends/means (E/M) analysis. Table 11.2 illustrates sample questions raised in each method.

In Phase II (see Figure 11.2), **prototyping** is used. Based on the conceptual information requirements found in Phase I, a prototype of the EIS is quickly constructed (in a couple of days or weeks). The prototyped system is shown to the executives, who then make suggestions for improvements. The system is modified and shown again to the executives. The testing and modification goes through several rounds of trial-and-error until the detailed requirements are established. The best sources of information are then determined and the EIS can be finished.

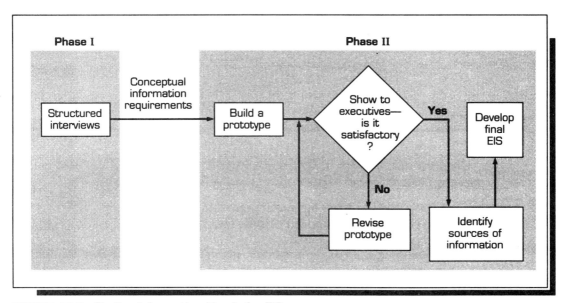

FIGURE 11.2 Finding Information Needs for EIS.

TABLE 11.2 Methods and Sample Questions for Structured Interviews.

Method	Sample Interview Questions
1. *The executive interview portion of IBM's Business System Planning (BSP):* Specify problems and decisions	a. What are the major problems encountered in accomplishing the purposes of the organizational unit you manage? b. What are good solutions to those problems? c. How can information play a role in any of those solutions? d. What are the major decisions associated with your management responsibilities? e. What improvements in information could result in better decisions?
2. *Critical success factors (CSF):* Specify critical factors	a. What are the critical success factors of the organizational unit you manage? Most managers have four to eight of these. b. What information is needed to ensure that critical success factors are under control? c. How do you measure the specific CSFs? For example: Prompt shipment of orders (a CSF) is measured by the percentage of time shipments are delivered on schedule.
3. *End/means (E/M) analysis:* Specify effectiveness criteria or outputs and efficiency criteria for processes used to generate outputs	a. What are the resulting goods or services provided by the business process? b. What makes these goods or services effective to recipients or customers? c. What information is needed to evaluate that effectiveness? d. What are the key means or processes used to generate or provide goods or services? e. What constitutes efficiency in the providing of these goods or services? f. What information is needed to evaluate that efficiency?

b. Watson and Frolick's Approach [1992]. This approach is based on the following basic strategies for determining information requirements:

1. Asking (the interview approach presented earlier)
2. Deriving the needs from an existing information system
3. Synthesis from characteristics of the systems
4. Discovering from experimentation with evolving systems that are utilized (prototyping).

Based on these approaches, the authors suggested ten specific methods that are organized along two dimensions: (1) the source of information (either direct or

TABLE 11.3 Methods for Assessing Information Requirements.

Interaction	Noncomputer Related	Computer Related
Direct Executive Interaction	■ Participation in strategic planning sessions ■ Formal CSF sessions ■ Informal discussions of information needs ■ Tracking executive activity	■ Collaborative work system sessions (Chapter 9)
Indirect Executive Interaction	■ Discussions with support personnel ■ Examination of noncomputer-generated information ■ Attendance at meetings	■ Software tracking of EIS usage ■ Examinations of computer-generated information

Source: H. J. Watson and M. Frolick, "Determining Information Requirements for an Executive Information System," *Information System Management,* Spring 1992. Reprinted from *Journal of Information Systems Management* (New York: Auerbach Publications). © 1992 Research Institute of America Inc. Used with permission.

indirect interaction with the executive) and (2) the primary method of determining requirements (supported by computers versus noncomputerized). The ten methods are shown in Table 11.3.

11.5 The Characteristics of EIS

The desired characteristics of EIS as well as its benefits are presented in Table 11.4. Not all implemented systems possess all of these characteristics and benefits.

Discussion of Important Terms Related to the Characteristics

Drill Down. One of the most useful capabilities of an EIS is to provide details of any given information. For example, an executive may notice a decline in corporate sales in a daily (or weekly) report. To find the reason, the executive may like to see sales in each region. If a problematic region is identified, the executive may like to see further details (e.g., by product or by salesperson). In certain cases, this "drill-down" process may continue into several levels of detail.

Drill-down paths, which are manually constructed and maintained, typically use hypertext-style connections rather than menus in systems with GUI (that is, the "button" for requesting a drill-down path is typically defined as a "hot spot" directly over the high-level data to be explained). This frees more of the screen space for delivering information, and can speed access to drill-down information by eliminating the additional mouse movements typically required by pull-down or pop-up menus.

TABLE 11.4   The Characteristics and Benefits of EIS.

Quality of information:
- Is flexible
- Produces correct information
- Produces timely information
- Produces relevant information
- Produces complete information
- Produces validated information.

User interface:
- Includes sophisticated graphic user interface (e.g., GUI)
- Includes a user-friendly interface
- Allows secure and confidential access to information
- Has a short response time (timely information)
- Is accessible from many places
- Includes a reliable access procedure
- Minimizes keyboard use; alternatively uses infrared controllers, mouse, touch pads, and touch screen
- Provides quick retrieval of desired information
- Is tailored to management styles of individual executives
- Contains self-help menu.

Technical capability provided:
- Access to aggregate (global) information
- Access to electronic mail
- Extensive use of external data
- Written interpretations
- Highlights problem indicators
- Hypertext and hypermedia
- Ad hoc analysis
- Multidimentional presentation and analysis
- Information presented in hierarchical form
- Incorporates graphics and text in the same display
- Provides management by exception reports
- Shows trends, ratios, and deviations
- Provides access to historical and most current data
- Organized around critical success factors
- Provides forecasting capability
- Produces information at various levels of details ("drill down")
- Filters, compresses, and tracks critical data
- Supports open-ended problem explanation.

Benefits:
- Facilitates the attainment of organizational objectives
- Facilitates access to information
- Allows the user to be more productive
- Increases the quality of decision making
- Provides a competitive advantage
- Saves time for the user
- Increases communication capacity
- Increases communication quality
- Provides better control in the organization
- Allows the anticipation of problems/opportunities
- Allows planning
- Allows finding the cause of a problem
- Meets the needs of executives.

Source: Based on Bergerson, et al. [1991].

Menu-driven drill-down is generally a characteristic of ad hoc query applications, and the menus in these applications are almost always automatically generated by the software based on: (1) the user's logical "position" within the database, and (2) "knowledge" of the structure of the database. This "knowledge" of the database structure may have been specified in advance, or it may have been obtained dynamically by having the application directly query the dictionary of the database.

It may be conceivable that a query application could potentially generate several hundred menus and submenus covering all possible combinations of logical position and valid drill-down path.

Critical Success Factors (CSF). Critical factors that *must* be considered in attaining the organization's goals are called CSFs. Such factors can be strategic or operational, and are derived mainly from three sources: organizational factors, industry factors, and environmental factors. Success factors can be at the corporate level as well as other levels (division, plant, department). Sometimes it is necessary to consider the CSFs of individuals.

Critical success factors, once identified, can be monitored by five types of information (per Kogan [1986]). They are: **key problems narratives, highlight charts,** top-level financials, key factors, and detailed responsibility reports. A brief description of each follows.

1. *Key Problems Narratives.* These reports highlight overall performance, key problems, and the possible reasons for the problems within an organization. Explanations are often combined with tables, graphs, or tabular information.
2. *Highlight Charts.* These summary displays show high-level information based on the user's own judgment or preference. Because they are designed from the user's perspective, these displays quickly highlight areas of concern, visually signaling the state of organizational performance against CSF.
3. *Top-level Financials.* These displays provide information on the overall financial health of the company in the form of absolute numbers and comparative performance ratios.
4. *Key Factors.* These factors provide specific measures of CSF, called **key performance indicators (KPI),** at the corporate level. The displays are often used on an exceptional basis to examine specific measures of CSF that are flagged as problems on the highlight charts (see Box 11.4).
5. *Detailed KPI Responsibility Reports.* These reports indicate the detailed performance of individuals or business units in those areas critical to the success of the company.

Status Access. In this mode the *latest data* or reports on the status of key variables can be accessed at any time, by using networks. The *relevance* of information is important here. Emphasis is placed on the latest data. This may require daily or

Box 11.4: Typical Key Performance Indicators

Profitability	Profitability measures for each department, product, region, and so on; comparisons among departments and products and with competitors
Financial	Financial ratios, balance sheet analysis, cash reserve position, rate of return on investment
Marketing	Market share, advertisement analysis, product pricing, weekly (daily) sales results, customer sales potential
Human Resources	Turnover rate, level of job satisfaction
Planning	Corporate partnership ventures, sales growth/market share analysis
Economic Analysis	Market trends, foreign trades and exchange rates, industry trends, labor cost trends
Consumer Trends	Consumer confidence level, purchasing habits, demographic data

even hourly operational tracking and reporting. In extreme cases, real-time reporting may be required. Although **status access** allows executives to pursue the information requested (e.g., to conduct a drill down), it is not geared to *data manipulation*.

Analysis. Analytical capabilities are available in executive support systems (ESS). Instead of merely having access to the data, executives can use the ESS to do analysis on their own. Analysis can be performed in the following ways:

1. *Using built-in functions.* Several EIS products include built-in analytical functions, similar to those available in DSS generators. For example, Commander EIS includes its own ad hoc analysis capabilities that allow executives to easily compute trends and variances. Also, it is possible to perform a multidimensional flipping on data and convert tables into graphics. (See Section 11.10.)

2. *Integration with DSS products.* Several EIS products have easy interfaces to DSS tools. For example, Commander EIS includes an open scripting language that allows it to easily integrate with many mainframe, server, or workstation DSS tools ranging from Lotus 1-2-3 to Comshare's System W.

Here is how the analysis is done: First, the executives in the regular course of using the ESS, come across some information that they want to analyze in more depth. Then, the executives either directly request the analysis action from an ESS menu (for example, to convert the currently displayed table into a graph), or export the current display into a separate product that offers the desired analysis capability. Depending on the ESS, the process of exporting to and starting up another tool may simply be a menu-pick within the ESS, or could require the executive to overtly save the display to a file, exit the ESS, start up the other tool, and read in the file written out by the ESS. Once the executive is in the other tool, analysis features are typically selected from menus. Whether the analysis is performed within the ESS or by an external tool, the results of the analysis are displayed in a default format, and the executive may then have options to modify the display to improve its understandability.

Exception Reporting. Exception reporting is based on the concept of *management by exception*. According to this concept, attention should be given by the executive to exceptions from the standards. Thus, in exception reporting the executive's attention will be called only to cases of very bad (or very good) performance. For example, the EIS can compute variances, and if the variances exceed a certain threshold they will be highlighted. This approach saves considerable time for the producers and readers of reports.

Navigation of Information. This is a capability that allows large amounts of data to be explored easily and quickly. To enhance this capability one can use hypermedia tools (see Frolick and Ramarapo [1993]).

11.6   Comparing EIS and MIS

In examining the EIS characteristics in the previous section one may come to the conclusion that an EIS is nothing but a fancy MIS. However, as indicated by Millet, et al. [1992], this is really not the case; their view of the relationship between MIS and EIS is shown in Figure 11.3.

According to their view, MIS provides managers with detailed and summarized information from operational databases, which are created by the various functional transaction processes (TPS) activities in the various business areas (e.g., accounting, finance, marketing). Therefore, the capabilities of MIS are constrained by the limitations of TPS, which are relatively inflexible. For example, transactions may be updated only once a week. Also, MIS are basically geared to *internal* data, usually in one functional area (accounting information systems, marketing information systems). Thus, MIS lacks data integration *across* functional areas. This may result in a serious limitation when attempting to satisfy the needs of top management for comprehensive organization-wide information. Millet, et al., summarized the major differences between MIS and EIS in a tabular form (see Table 11.5)

In addition, several EIS capabilities, such as making presentations that fit the decision styles of specific users, are simply too expensive to be designed in an MIS system that serves hundreds or thousands of users, whose population changes continuously. Another deficiency of a traditional MIS is *slow response time.* This is

FIGURE 11.3 The EIS Role. (*Source:* Reprinted with permission, I. Millet, et al., "Alternative Paths to EIS," *DSS-91 Transactions,* Eleventh International Conference on Decision Support Systems, Ilze Zigurs [Ed.], The Institute of Management Sciences, 290 Westminster Street, Providence, Rhode Island 02903.)

TABLE 11.5 MIS and EIS: A Comparison.

System	Primary Purpose	Primary Users	Primary Output	Primary Operations	Time Orientation	Example
MIS	Internal monitoring	Managers and executives	Predefined periodic reports	Summarize information	Past	Sales report
EIS	Internal and external monitoring	Executives	Predefined customized periodic or ad hoc reports, presentations, and queries	Integrate present, track CSF	Past and present	Market share tracking

Source: Reprinted with permission, Millet et al. [1991], *DSS-91 Transactions,* Eleventh International Conference on Decision Support Systems, Ilze Zigurs (Ed.), The Institute of Management Sciences, 290 Westminster Street, Providence, Rhode Island 02903.

mainly due to the fact that the information they process is not oriented to the format, content, or organization of the executive's need. Furthermore, executive decision making, especially that of a strategic nature, is complex and multidimensional. Conventional MIS are usually designed to deal with fairly structured and much simpler configurations. Finally, conventional MIS are *not* usually designed to combine data from different sources. However, development of multidimensional flipping tools (see Section 11.10) could provide MIS some capabilities provided by EIS.

11.7 Comparing and Integrating EIS and DSS

The above characteristics and capabilities are unique to EIS primarily because an EIS is designed to support top executives, helping them to discover problems and opportunities. A DSS, on the other hand, supports an analysis that aims at giving an answer to the question of what to do with a problem (or an opportunity). Tables 11.6 and 11.7 compare the two systems. Table 11.6 contains portions of typical DSS definitions as they relate to EIS. Table 11.7 compares EIS and DSS along several dimensions (which are derived from the characteristics and capabilities of EIS).

Examination of the two tables points out that in a general sense, EIS is really part of the decision support field. That is, it is designed to support some tasks of the top management decision process. However, in a functional sense, EIS and DSS are two different, although complementary, applications. The differences are simple but profound. Fundamentally, EIS is a structured, automated tracking system that operates continuously to keep management abreast of what is happening

TABLE 11.6 Definitions of DSS as They Relate to EIS.

Relevant Portion of DSS Definition	Comparison to EIS	Author
"CBIS consisting of three subsystems: a problem-solving subsystem . . ."	No problem-solving subsystem exists in an EIS.	Bonczek, et al. [1980]
"DSS can be developed *only* through an adaptive process . . ."	EIS may or may not be developed through an adaptive process.	Keen [1980]
"Model-based set of procedures . . ."	EIS is not model-based.	Little [1970]
"Extendable system . . . supporting decision modeling . . . used at irregular intervals."	EIS is not extendable, may not have modeling capabilities, and is used at regular intervals.	Moore and Chang [1980]
"Utilizes data and models . . ."	EIS does not utilize models.	Scott-Morton [1971]

712

TABLE 11.7 A Comparison of EIS and DSS.

Dimension	EIS	DSS
Focus	Status access, drill down	Analysis, decision support
Typical users served	Senior executives	Analysts, professionals, managers (via intermediaries)
Impetus	Expediency	Effectiveness
Application	Environmental scanning, performance evaluation, identification of problems and opportunities	Diversified areas where managerial decisions are made
Decision support	Indirect support, mainly high-level and unstructured decisions and policies	Supports semistructured and unstructured decision making, and ad hoc, but some repetitive, decisions
Type of information	News items, external information on customers, competitors, and the environment; scheduled and demand reports on internal operations	Information to support specific situations
Principle use	Tracking and control	Planning, organizing, staffing, and control
Adaptability to individual users	Tailored to the decision-making style of each individual executive, offers several options of outputs	Permits individuals' judgment, what-if capabilities, some choice of dialog style
Graphics	A must	Important part of many DSS
User-friendliness	A must	A must if no intermediaries are used
Processing of information	Filters and compresses information, tracks critical data and information	EIS triggers questions, answers are worked out by the DSS and fed into the EIS
Supporting detailed information	Instant access to the supporting details of any summary ("drill down")	Can be programmed into the DSS, but usually is not
Model base	Limited built-in functions	The core of the DSS
Construction	By vendors or IS specialists	By users, either alone or with specialists from the Information Center or the IS department
Hardware	Mainframe, LANs, or distributed systems	Mainframe, micros, or distributed systems
Nature of software packages	Interactive, easy access to multiple databases, online access, sophisticated DBMS capabilities, complex linkages	Large computational capabilities, modeling languages and simulation, application and DSS generators
Nature of information	Displays pregenerated information about the past and present, creates new information about the past, present, and future	Creates new information about the past, present, and future

in all important areas both inside and outside the corporation. EIS is designed to support the complex and multidimensional nature of top-level decision making.

EIS delivers information that managers need in their day-to-day job responsibilities. The information is typically presented in a structured, easy-to-access manner with only limited capability for *direct* ad hoc analysis. If there are analytical capabilities in EIS, they tend to be of a repetitive nature (e.g., trend analysis), as opposed to the unique ad hoc analysis of DSS. Although this is the usual case, both DSS and EIS may center on the investigation and understanding of problems that are not necessarily predictable, structured, or repetitive.

EIS is designed very differently from DSS. For example, a good EIS must offer a high-speed, nontechnical method for managers to investigate business dynamics (i.e., to understand where and why things are happening, so tactical changes and course corrections can be made). This is also a major area that distinguishes EIS from a standard MIS reporting system. Any summary coming up on an EIS screen must offer instant access to the supporting detail; otherwise, it is just a glorified slide show. In addition, the supporting details must be meaningful (e.g., time-series orientation with graphic and numerical content or written narratives from those "in the know"). In this fashion, a simple analysis or investigation can be quickly and easily accomplished by the nontechnical manager.

DSS overlaps this process when more complex analysis is required to understand *why* things are happening the way they are or to investigate alternative solutions to a problem or a prospective opportunity. These appraisals are done as needed, usually require evaluation of much raw data, consume more time, and almost always require an analyst who is technically proficient with the tools at hand.

Integrating EIS and DSS: An Executive Support System (ESS)

Previously, we concluded that EIS differs from DSS. And indeed, they are being used as two independent applications by many organizations. However, in some cases it makes sense to integrate the two technologies.

For example, at a large drug company, product managers download from an EIS the previous day's orders of their products. The download creates a Lotus-readable file on their PC. Then they run a Lotus DSS model against the data to predict where they will be at the end of the month. The results of this model are then uploaded to the EIS. So, by 11 A.M. every morning, senior managers can get on their EIS and see where each brand manager thinks he or she is going to be at the end of the month.

The integration of EIS and DSS can be accomplished in several ways. One alternative is that the output of the EIS is used to trigger the DSS. For instance, executives at GE's Major Appliance Division decided that an immediate marketing response was needed to a competitor's action reported by the EIS. Exactly what that response should be is determined by DSS models and simulation tools. In this case the DSS is fed from the same reservoir of raw data that fed the EIS, but the DSS action is triggered by the EIS. More sophisticated systems include feedback from the

714

DSS to the EIS, and even an explanation capability. If an intelligent module with explanation and interpretation capabilities is added, then the system can be defined as an "intelligent ESS." (See Chapter 20.)

Another dimension along which EIS and DSS can be assessed is the users' roles. Executive roles differ substantially from the roles of the typical users of DSS, namely middle-line and functional supervisory levels and functional analysts, such as financial and marketing analysts. Although lower level managers focus much of their time on pursuing predetermined strategies, executives are faced with developing these strategies. Ambiguity and uncertainty characterize an executive's environment, resulting in a need for "what-if" and "goal-seeking" analyses that are provided by most DSS. Yet, studies have shown that many senior executives leave this technical analysis to lower-level, functional managers and staff analysts. It is possible that this cost-effective occurrence results because functional managers have less of a need for status updates, due to their proximity to the functional areas of business. Top-level executives, on the other hand, are more isolated from functional operations, and need to be informed of these activities on a timely basis. It is only with these reports that senior executives can pursue planning functions and set corporate strategy.

Another point is that although much of this information is internal, the demand for external data exists as well. Whatever the needed information is about, be it industry, competitors, or general environmental scanning, executives need systems that can provide timely external information. To address the needs of the executive, an ESS must be able to provide not only reporting capability, but user-friendly DSS capabilities as well.

Finally, the ESS includes productivity tools (such as personal calendar) and communication tools (e.g., E-mail) designed to meet the divergent needs of executives. The integration of EIS and DSS is reflected in the development tools offered by the major vendors, as seen in Box 11.5.

The integration of EIS and DSS, which will be revisited in Chapter 20, is closely related to the role of spreadsheet and multidimensional analysis. In a study conducted by Thiriez [1992] among some major DSS and EIS vendors, a strong trend toward the integration of traditional DSS and EIS tools was found. Furthermore, this integration is based on a distributed database and the role of the spreadsheet will be that of a front-end interface. Finally, all this will take place in a client/server environment supported by strong GUI. The conclusion of Thiriez's study are already evidenced in the new EIS developments discussed in Sections 11.10 through 11.14.

Integrating EIS and Group Support Systems

As shown in Figure 11.1, the information generated in Phase I flows to Phase II, where determination is made on what to do about the problem. A DSS supports the quantitative analysis of Phase I and can support Phase II as well. Therefore, it makes sense to integrate an EIS (which supports most of the tasks in Phase I) with DSS. In Phase II, however, the decision may be made by a group. Therefore, it is

Box 11.5: Representative ESS Integrated Products

1. *Commander EIS*. This system has several built-in analytical tools, such as forecasting. In addition, it is designed for easy interface with DSS tools.
2. *EIS Tool Kit*. This PC-based product (from Ferox Microsystems Inc.) works with Encore Plus, a financial modeling DSS from the same vendor. The EIS/DSS combination is designed primarily to support financial and accounting planning.
3. *Command Center EIS*. This product (from Pilot Software Inc.), which is linked with a DSS engine called FCS and with LightShip's Modular (see Section 11.10), is also linked with a software called Advantage/G.
4. *Express/EIS*. This product (from Information Resources Inc.) is an enterprise-wide system that integrates the powerful Express DSS generator with EIS II. This product is based on a multidimensional relational data model and it provides single, unifying, and flexible architecture.
5. *EIS-EPIC*. This LAN- and UNIX-based product (from EPIC Software Inc.) integrates, at the PC level, DSS capabilities with EIS.
6. *Holos*. This product (from Holistic Systems) combines EIS and DSS activities into one system, together with dynamic links to operational data.
7. *TRACK EIS*. This product (from Intelligent Office Co., London, U.K.; marketed by IBM) interfaces with IBM's DSS tools.
8. *PowerPlay*. This product (from Cognos Inc.) incorporates statistical analysis to analyze data.

likely that the EIS will be integrated with some groupware applications. Several EIS vendors have developed easy interfaces with GSS. For example, IMRS has enhanced its On Track product with a Lotus Notes application called Executive Forum. Both Comshare Inc. and Pilot Inc. have Note-based enhancements to their major products. EIS applications can also be used to provide information in a decision room setting.

11.8   Hardware

There are at least four options for hardware configurations for an EIS. The simplest option is to support executives from mainframe computers using graphics terminals. In general, this approach is difficult to implement successfully, because the options for implementing the user interface are much more limited than is acceptable for executive users. A second configuration is to have personal computers connected to a mainframe or a minicomputer. In this situation, the PCs handle the interface and some of the data reduction functions, while the large system handles the data management and the bulk of the analysis. The third option involves a departmental LAN or a client/server architecture. In this case, information is downloaded onto stand-alone LANs, and then it is delivered to PCs. (See Davis [1989].) In the fourth configuration, which seems to be the configuration of the future, the EIS is constructed on an enterprise-wide network, or on a client/server enterprise-wide system. In such a case, workstations are used in a network, so that the interface is handled on high-speed graphics display devices, and so that the data management and analysis can be distributed over the network. This environment offers the potential of providing maximum performance and flexibility.

The four alternatives are summarized in Table 11.8. The table highlights the dual role of the hardware as an information source and as a user interface.

The difference between the third and fourth options has less to do with the actual EIS delivery software, and more to do with the inevitable trend towards connecting all enterprise information sources into a high-speed network. For example, Comshare Inc. created PC/LAN versions of the Commander host components to support local PC/LAN environments. For the enterprise-wide architecture, Comshare Inc. had to initially open up their information-access architecture to exploit third-party "middleware" products that provide direct access to networked data sources. (For a discussion about middleware products see *InformationWeek*, November 1, 1993.)

Note: To overcome some of the problems of enterprise computing discussed in Chapter 4, EIS vendors are developing special solutions. For example, Comshare Inc. introduced the Administrator's Workstation that enables centralized maintenance of their main product, Commander, an application whose use is spread over multiple PCs and/or LANs.

TABLE 11.8 Hardware Alternatives.

Option	EIS Information Source	User Interface
1	Mainframe (or mini)	Graphical terminal (dumb)
2	Mainframe (or mini)	PCs
3	LAN-based PCs (or servers) on a departmental client/server	PCs (regular, GUI)
4	Enterprise-wide network (many possible databases)	PCs (regular, GUI)

The key to an effective hardware decision is to try to match the actual delivery of the system with the computational philosophy of the organization. This ensures that the support of whichever system is installed will be within the capabilities of the organization itself. It also makes it easier to implement an ESS that will match with the corporate culture of the implementing organization.

Organizations that go with option 3 EIS are typically smaller than organizations that use option 4. They have fewer executives to serve, and manage smaller EIS information bases.

Larger organizations tend to prefer the micro/mainframe products such as EIS III, Command Center, or Commander EIS, because these tools leverage their existing investment in minicomputer/mainframe technology and databases. Larger organizations require the additional horsepower and connectivity of a shared computer to deliver acceptable response time for complex queries and analyses, to permit shared access to large information bases, and to connect executives in a geographically distributed E-mail network.

The usefulness of option 3 and especially option 4 will increase with the increased capabilities of PCs and networks. These systems will also benefit from the transparent connectivity that will be available through advances in communications and database technology. The growth in distributed database software, peer-to-peer communications, and standardized network protocols should eventually permit the option 3 and 4 solutions to offer all of the capabilities of today's micro/mainframe architectures (option 2).

EIS architectures can be hybrids of several options.

11.9   Software

Commercially available software products typically address one or more of the following functional areas: office automation, electronic mail, information management, remote information access, and information analysis. No single product currently offers extensive features in all of these areas, although some of the more open-ended products permit ESS applications to directly incorporate additional software tools that specialize in some of these areas, such as office automation and E-mail. Like DSS tools, some of these products have many integrated parts analogous to DSS generators (or engines), whereas other tools are specialized and provide only one or few capabilities. A representative list of EIS software products is given in Table 11.9. One of these systems, the Command Center, is described next.

Command Center. Command Center includes sophisticated communications software on both the mainframe and PCs. Consequently, performance is exceptionally fast even over lower-speed communications links. The structure of the Command Center is shown in Figure 11.4. Notice that the Command Center does not have a model base. However, it does have an interface that allows it to receive and transmit data to and from DSS, freestanding model(s), or other CBIS.

TABLE 11.9 Representative EIS Products.

Product	Vendor
Control	KCI Computing Inc.
Command Center	Pilot Software
Commander EIS, EIS LAN	Comshare Inc.
Easel Workbench, ENFIN	Easel Corp.
EIS Tool Kit	Ferox Microsystems, Inc.
EIS ToolKit	Micro Strategy Inc.
Epic EIS	Planning Science, Inc.
Executive Decisions	IBM Corp.
Express/EIS	Information Resources, Inc.
Focus/EIS; EDA/EIS	Information Builders, Inc.
Forest and Trees	Channel Computing (now Trinzic)
Holos	Holistic Systems, Inc.
IDIS	Intelligence Ware Inc.
IMRS On Track	IMRS Inc.
LightShip	Pilot Software
Metaphor Data	Metaphor Inc; IBM Corp.
Miten View	Miten Corp.
Notebook	Lotus Development Corp.
PowerPlay	Cognos Inc.
Redi-Master	American Information Systems Inc.; Computer Associates
Track/EIS	Intelligent Office Systems; IBM Corp.
The SAS System	SAS Institute Inc.

Capabilities of EIS: The Commander EIS Example. Some EIS software products are designed to provide extensive capabilities. They are usually structured in a modular fashion. An example of five EIS screens representing five modules is provided in Box 11.6 as explained below:

- *Screen A.* Status report (with possibility of drill down and exception reporting): textual explanation and trend graph
- *Screen B.* Reminder: notes, calendar, tracking information about messages
- *Screen C.* Investigation: comparisons, calculations, drill down, personalized analysis, graphics
- *Screen D.* Electronic mail: alerts if mail is pending, monitoring mail, can transmit any screen of the other modules
- *Screen E.* News service: both external and internal with capability to drill down for details; hypertext capabilities are available.

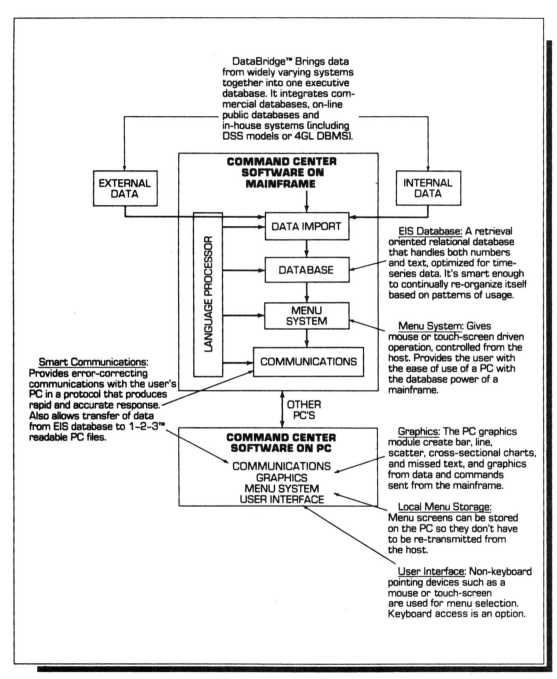

FIGURE 11.4 Command Center. (*Source:* Courtesy of Pilot Software Inc., Boston, MA. Used with permission.)

720

Box 11.6: Sample Screens from Commander EIS.

Screen A: Status report (Briefing Book Module)

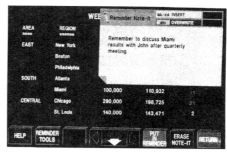

Screen B: Reminder note, attached in appropriate place (Reminder Module)

Screen C: Investigation, analysis, exceptions (Execu-View Module)

Screen D: Electronic mail (Redi-Mail Module)

Screen E: News service, external and internal (Newswire Module)

(*Source:* Courtesy of Comshare Inc. [One screen from each major module.])

Note: Several other EIS products are structured in a modular fashion. Notable are EIS II, SAS EIS, and Command Center. For a complete EIS software review, see *Computer World,* July 22, 1991. For a software selection methodology, see Frolick and Jeanings [1993].

11.10 Multidimensional Analysis and Presentation

The data multidimensionality issue, discussed in Chapter 4, is best illustrated by the latest developments in EIS tools and enhancements. As can be seen in Table 11.9, there are a large number of products that provide **business intelligence (BI)** capabilities. Business intelligence refers to the capability of CBIS to quickly provide answers to questions posed by managers about the current status of the business, the business and economic trends, and the potential impact of changes in strategy and in the environment. (See Box 11.7.)

11.11 Data Access EIS: LightShip

The issue of accessing data in an enterprise was discussed in Chapter 4. When data are viewed by an executive they become part of an EIS.

Box 11.7: Quaker Oats Uses Multidimensional Data Analysis.

Quaker Oats is a large food processor that packs the supermarkets with dozens of products. As a multinational corporation, the company needs to have an overall worldwide competitive picture in almost real time. It needs to know what products are being sold and where and how sales compare to the competition's. Such information allows Quaker to decide almost instantly which products should be marketed, in which country (or part of it), and at what price in order to beat its competitors. Using Express (from IRI Software) and a second-generation EIS, the company provided the system to 60 managers in marketing, sales, and finance. Express, which provides for up to 10-dimensional analysis, enables an instant drill down. Express also is replacing Excel for conducting financial consolidations and analysis.

Quaker Oats is reorganizing the database to be multidimensional, so users can tap into the database using multidimensional tools.

(*Source:* Based on *Datamation,* February 15, 1994, p. 26.)

Of special interest is a client/server, LAN-based, Windows-based software product called LightShip (from Pilot Software Inc.). LightShip (LS) enables an end-user to extract data from various sources and turns it into intuitive screen-based information (see Box 11.8). The on-screen view of the data allows the user to drill down into deeper levels of information.

LightShip's interface is based on objects, such as documents, menus, images, charts, and text. These can have data or actions (an SQL query, for example) associated with them. Building an LS interface includes selecting an object, pasting it to the work space, sizing it, and then tying a desired action or predefined function to it. Generally, various objects combine to produce a particular result.

Any object or area on the screen—a button, graph, or bitmapped image—can be designated a hot spot. Clicking on one can trigger almost any function. This allows for considerable creativity and flexibility.

The base LS package can accesss various data sources including Windows applications (via DDE). LightShip is supported by a family of products such as LS Link, which provides connectivity to many databases/servers, and LS Lens, which enables the creation of multidimensional reports. LS Server is a multidimensional data structure, and LS Modeler allows modeling and budgeting applications. LS Modeler is a DSS engine with enterprise-wide capabilities. The entire LS family can operate as a stand-alone EIS software or can be combined with Command Center Plus (which is used as a server) to create powerful enterprise solutions.

Note: A LightShip demo, tutorial, and limited development tool are provided with this book courtesy of Pilot Software Inc. A similar product is Forest and Trees (from Trinzic Corp.). Both products are reviewed in *Computerworld*, June 19, 1992.

11.12   System Development

Like any other system, EIS can be developed in-house, or it can be purchased. If developed in-house it can be programmed from scratch, or it can be developed with special tools such as those shown in Table 11.9.

Another approach is an attempt to modify an existing information system to serve EIS goals. Several companies attempted to turn their MIS or DSS into a dual-purpose system. This usually does not work, especially when a DSS/EIS attempt is involved. The reason is that a DSS that is productive for an analyst may be counterproductive for the executive. All the design criteria and the capabilities are completely different as well. These two systems are designed differently and they perform different functions.

Another interesting issue is who is going to be the EIS developer. In contrast with DSS, which can be built by the information system people and even by end-users, EIS and ESS are usually constructed by vendors or information system consultants.

Box 11.8: Screens from LightShip.

Screen (a) shows the visual programming environment. Various EIS routines are activated once icons are defined. Appropriate reports or presentations appear as a result ((b) and (c)). Queries are answered with scrolled bars (c).

(a)

(b)

(c)

[*Source:* Courtesy of Pilot Software, Inc.]

724

Working with Data Dippers. In contrast with comprehensive EIS, the construction of front-end/EIS systems can be done by IS people or by end-users, using tools such as LightShip.

The Process. The process of building an ESS can be very complex and lengthy. The general phases are similar to those that are used in other management support systems (see Chapters 7 and 17). The complexity of the process can be seen in Table 11.10, which summarizes an EIS development framework. The framework is divided into three modules—first, structural perspective, then a development process, and finally a user-system dialog development, which is extremely important (a good EIS interface is said to be "seductive" to attract users).

The EIS developer needs to consider the issues discussed earlier, and especially the establishment of information needs.

The appropriate development of EIS requires attention to EIS implementation factors. These are presented in Section 11.14.

11.13 Enterprise EIS

Providing relational and multidimensional analysis and presentation, data access, drill down, user-friendly graphical interface, imaging, E-mail, and analysis are certainly helpful for any executive. However, it is much more important to remember that the most important goal is the *overall solution* to the enterprise. While drill down or data multidimensionality presentation are important, they are done for the purpose of serving the enterprise. For this reason, one can distinguish two types of EIS: first, the one designed specially to support top executives; and second, an EIS that is intended to serve a wider community of users.

The executive-only EIS can be a part of the enteprise-wide system. As such, EIS will become less strictly defined, and EIS applications will embrace a range of products targeted to support professional decision makers *throughout the enterprise.* (See Box 11.9.) Tools such as those discussed in Sections 11.10 and 11.11 are already providing some of the needed capabilities. In addition, there is an increasing number of tools that are designed to help the functional managers (finance, marketing), and these tools are integrated with EIS.

For this reason, some people define the acronym EIS to mean Enterprise Information Systems, or Everybody's Information Systems. Comshare Inc. uses the term Management Support Systems (MSS) to describe the new role of EIS.

To better understand these changes in EIS, one could read the *Computerworld* white paper on the topic (see Gillan and McPherson [1992]), the Comshare report [1993], and the Gartner Group report (see Dresner [1993]).

EIS-style Technology

There is a trend to deliver EIS-style technology (such as superb graphs and accessibility to data) to a large community of users. As such, the traditional EIS be-

TABLE 11.10 Aspects of the
EIS Development Framework.

STRUCTURAL
Personnel
EIS Initiator
Executive Sponsor
Operating Sponsor
EIS Builder/Support Staff
EIS Users
Functional Area Personnel
IS Personnel
Data
Internal
External

DEVELOPMENT PROCESS
External and Internal Pressures
Cost/Benefit Analysis
Costs
Development Costs
Annual Operating Costs
Development Time
Development Methodology
Hardware
Software
Spread
Evolution
Information Provided
EIS Capabilities

USER-SYSTEM DIALOG
Knowledge Base
Training
User Documentation
System User
Action Language
User-System Interface
System Response Time
Presentation Language
Multiple Information Formats
Color

Source: H. J. Watson, et al., *Executive Information Systems: A Framework for Development and a Survey of Current Practices,* Working Paper #41, Department of Management, University of Georgia, Athens, 1991. Used with permission.

Box 11.9 Banc One Is Shifting to Enterprise Support Systems

For 25 years, Banc One, one of the most profitable U.S. banks, used a home-grown profit tracking and management information system. The system was used by about 200 managers and financial analysts to evaluate their units' performance on a variety of profit indexes.

As of the end of 1994, the bank is using one of the largest client/server decision support networks in the banking industry. The profit monitoring system is from Treasury Services Corp. (Santa Monica, CA). It distributes financial information to over 2,000 corporatewide employees. The technology allows Banc One to disseminate information not only to the privileged few but to anyone who needs it.

The new system, which can be regarded as a combination of EIS and ESS, gives the employees more detailed financial information, right down to the revenue, costs, and profits for an individual customer. It allows users to deliver much more detailed data to support decision making throughout the bank.

(*Source:* Based on a story published in *Information Week*, November 1, 1993, p. 14; and on information provided by Treasury Services Corp.)

---

comes a general enterprise support system. It should be clear that an information-delivery application designed for a small number of top executives must be different in some respects from an information-delivery application designed for a broad cross-section of managers and analysts throughout the corporation. The suggestion of an EIS growing, over time, into a general support system is a myth. Either the original application was delivering MIS information to begin with, and therefore was not an EIS; or, more typically, the EIS technology (but *not* the EIS information or application) was exploited to support a larger community of users.

11.14 EIS Implementation: Success or Failure

The implementation of an EIS could be different from the implementation of a DSS or any other CBIS, since it involves executives. DeLong and Rockart [1986] offer the following list of factors that they feel are critical for the successful implementation of EIS:

1. *A committed and informed executive sponsor.* There must be an executive who has both a realistic understanding of the capabilities (and limitations)

of EIS, and who really wants the system so badly that he or she is willing to put considerable time and energy into seeing that a system gets developed. There should also be commitment of company resources for a long period.

2. *An operating sponsor.* Because the executive sponsor usually lacks sufficient time to devote to the project, it appears very worthwhile to have an "operating sponsor" designated to manage the details of implementation from the user's side.

3. *A clear link to business objective(s).* The EIS must help in solving business problems or meet a need that is addressed most effectively with information systems (IS) technology. There should be a clear benefit to using the technology. It must provide something that would not otherwise be available, such as very rapid access to external databases, superb graphical displays, or data with textual annotations.

4. *Appropriate IS resources.* The quality of the EIS project manager on the IS side is most critical. This person should have not only technical knowledge, but also business knowledge and the ability to communicate effectively with senior management.

5. *Appropriate technology.* The choice of hardware and software has a major bearing on the acceptance or rejection of a system. One of the early barriers to executive support systems has been the lack of hardware and software that could meet the demands of highly variable executive work styles and environments. Things are improving, however, as more and more products are being designed specifically for the EIS market.

6. *Management of data problems.* The physical and technical ability to provide reliable access to data can be a major issue in EIS development. Aggregating, accessing, and managing databases in a corporation with multiple divisions can be the biggest physical roadblock to the EIS implementation.

7. *Management of organizational resistance.* Political resistance to EIS is one of the most common causes of implementation failure. An EIS alters information flows, and this always has the potential to significantly shift power relationships in a company.

8. *Management of spread and system evaluation.* An installation that is successful and used regularly by the executive sponsor will almost inevitably produce demand by peers or subordinates for access to a similar system.

Other suggestions for successful implementation are:

- Develop a small, but significant, prototype and plan its evaluation properly.
- Communicate to overcome resistance (change management).
- Use MIS experts.
- Correctly define executives' information requirements.

For further discussion of EIS implementation see D. Raths, "The Politics of EIS," *Infoworld*, May 15, 1989. For a successful implementation at British Airways see Cottrell and Rapley [1991].

11.15   The Future of EIS and Research Issues*

Executives place substantial requirements on EIS. *First,* they often ask questions that require complex, real-time analyses for their answers. This is why many EIS/ESS are being built on top of mainframe DSS systems, which provide the necessary analytical tools for performing these requisite analyses. But even these systems often lack the ability to respond in real time. Delay in the delivery of information can mean loss of competitive position, loss of sales, and loss of profits. *Second,* like other infrequent, untrained, or uncooperative users, executives require systems that are "easy to use," "easy to learn," and "easy to navigate." Current EIS/ESS systems generally possess these qualities. However, "ease of use" can also mean that the system has enough intelligence to automatically determine which tasks need to be performed, and either performs the tasks directly or guides the user through the tasks. Although current systems provide executives with the capabilities to monitor the present state of affairs, the systems typically lack the ability to automate the processes of interpreting or explaining information. The automation of these tasks requires the integration of current EIS/ESS capabilities with those of an expert system. *Third,* executives tend to have highly individualized workstyles. Although the current generation of EIS/ESS can be molded to the needs of the executive, it is very difficult to alter the "look-and-feel" of the system or to alter the basic way in which the user interacts with the system. *Finally,* any information system is essentially a social system. One of the key elements of an EIS/ESS is the E-mail capabilities that it provides for members of the executive team. In the current generation of systems, however, these capabilities are again limited.

Therefore, the EIS/ESS of the future will look substantially different from today's systems. Like most other systems, EIS/ESS will migrate to the networked world of the technical workstation. Within five years, these will have at least ten times the speed and memory of today's PCs; will have at least four to eight times the disk capacity; will possess a very high-resolution, bitmapped screen; will be multitasking; and will be connected with other workstations over a high-speed network. The advantages of such a configuration are that data and programs can be distributed and shared as needed. Individual workstations will have the ability to house and run mainframe versions of most DSS and DBMS software. In fact, because of their multitasking capabilities, these programs can run simultaneously (in separate windows), if need be.

The following list briefly describes some of the features that are likely to appear in the next generation on EIS/ESS:

  - *A toolbox for building customized systems.* In order to quickly configure a system for an executive, the builder of the system needs a toolbox of graphic and analytical objects that can be easily linked together to produce the system. In the future, EIS/ESS systems are likely to provide toolkits like Hyper-

*This section was condensed from an unpublished work of D. King of Comshare Inc. (courtesy of D. King), 1991.

Card for building visual and graphic front-ends. Commander EIS LAN, Forest and Trees, and LightShip are examples of such tools.

- *Multimedia support.* The requirement that an EIS/ESS be configurable also requires support of multiple modes of input and output. The current generation basically provides text and graphic output with touch screen, mouse, or keyboard input. The rapid proliferation of databases supporting image data and the slow, but sure, appearance of video as well as voice I/O, will probably mean that future EIS/ESS will be multimedia in nature. For example, in the next generation of systems an executive may be sitting in front of a high-resolution map of the company's sales regions. By touching one of these regions the executive might be presented with an animated display of the region's revenue and expense figures over the past few years along with a voice summary of the results mailed by the regional sales directors. Not only does this mean that the workstation will have to support the storage and display of multimedia objects but also that the network will support the transfer of these objects.

- *Merging of analytical systems with desktop publishing.* Many of the reports prepared for executives contain tables, graphs, and text. To support the preparation of these reports, some software companies are now beginning to merge desktop publishing capabilities with various analytical capabilities. Examples are the Wingz product from Informix and the Trapeze program for the Macintosh. In keeping with the multimedia features, coming EIS/ESS are likely to have the capability to at least cut and paste data and graphs from various windows into a document, and to ship that document via E-mail to other executives.

- *Automated support and intelligent assistance.* Expert systems and other AI technologies (e.g., natural language) are currently being embedded or integrated with existing DSS or DBMS systems. This will clearly add more automated support and assistance to the analytical engines underlying EIS/ESS. However, we are also likely to see other forms of intelligent or automated assistance. One such form is the "agent." We might think of an "agent" as a small, individualized, knowledge-based system designed to carry out a few rudimentary tasks. For example, we might have a mail "agent" that monitors incoming E-mail, and, based on various built-in rules, places the mail in appropriate slots. Thus, instead of thinking of an EIS/ESS as a single program or system, we might think of the system as a society of cooperating agents whose actions need to be coordinated. Although the concept of an agent may appear a bit foreign, it is currently being touted as the foundation for Apple's Knowledge Navigator—the ultimate ESS of the future.

- *Client/server architecture.* This approach, described in Chapter 4, could be extremely important for EIS. For additional discussion see Thiriez [1992].

Research Issues. The following research issues were suggested by Watson, et al. [1991]:

- Is the organizational position and level of commitment of the executive sponsor related to EIS success?
- What considerations are most important when selecting an operating sponsor?
- How can the benefits of an EIS be assessed in advance?
- How does the software used in building an EIS affect the development process and system success?
- What level of staffing and organizational structure are best for the EIS builder/support staff?
- What methods can be most effectively used to identify executives' information requirements?
- What are the major EIS data management problems and their solutions?
- What impact does the inclusion of soft data have on EIS success?
- What are the major problems associated with EIS "spread" and its evolution?
- How can EIS functionality be increased while maintaining ease of use?
- What emerging technologies (e.g., voice, optical disc) can be effectively used with EIS?
- What are the most effective screen presentation formats for an EIS?

Research activities will help in creating more effective and efficient executive information systems.

Chapter Highlights

- Many internal and external factors create the need for EIS.
- EIS serves the information needs of top executives.
- EIS provides rapid access to timely information at various levels of details. It is very user friendly.
- ESS is basically an EIS with analysis capabilities.
- Executives play three major roles: interpersonal, informational, and decisional.
- Executives' work can be divided into two major phases: finding problems (opportunities) and deciding what to do about them.
- Finding information needs of executives is a very difficult process. Methods such as CSF and BSP (Business System Planning) are effective, especially if they are followed by prototyping.
- If properly designed and operated, EIS has many benefits, but most of them are intangible.
- Drill down is an important capability of EIS. It allows the executive to look at details (and details of details).
- EIS uses a management by exception approach. It centers around CSF, key performance indicators, and highlight charts.

- In contrast with MIS, EIS has an overall organizational perspective and it uses external data extensively.
- There is a trend to integrate EIS and DSS tools.
- EIS requires either a mainframe or a LAN.
- Constructing an EIS is a difficult task. Using vendors or consultants is a viable approach.
- EIS success depends on many factors ranging from appropriate technology to managing organizational resistance.
- Multidimensional analysis and presentation is becoming an important part in EIS.
- Data access to database information by end-users, throughout the enterprise, is an essential part of EIS.

Key Words

business intelligence (BI)
critical success factors
drill down
exception reporting
executive information system (EIS)
executive support system (ESS)

highlight charts
information requirements (needs)
key performance indicators (KPI)
key problems narratives
multidimensional analysis

navigation of information
prototyping
scanning the environment
status access

Questions for Review

1. Define EIS.
2. Define ESS.
3. List the pressures for the creation of EIS.
4. Define the executive's interpersonal, informational, and decisional roles.
5. List a few methods of soliciting executives' information needs.
6. Describe the interviewing approach to information discovery.
7. List the major characteristics and capabilities of EIS in the following categories: quality of information, user-interface, and technical capabilities.
8. List the major benefits of EIS.
9. Define "drill down" and list its advantages.
10. Define status access.
11. Define exception reporting.
12. List the major differences between MIS and EIS.
13. List the major differences between EIS and DSS.
14. List the major hardware configuration for EIS.

15. Define multidimensional presentation.
16. Describe how LightShip helps in accessing enterprise data.

Questions for Discussion

1. If a DSS is employed in finding answers to management questions, what is the EIS used for?
2. Explain how the CSF approach is used in an interviewing approach for finding information needs.
3. Discuss the concept of status access and contrast it with ad hoc analysis.
4. Review the five types of information essential to senior management. Relate these to a fast-food company and to a hospital. (Be specific and imaginative in your response.)
5. Prepare a table that shows the differences between a traditional reporting system and an EIS.
6. American Can Company announced in early 1986 that it was interested in acquiring a company in the health maintenance organization (HMO) field. Two decisions are involved in this act: (1) the decision to acquire an HMO, and (2) the decision of which one to acquire. How can a DSS and EIS be used in such a situation?
7. Why is a typical office automation system insufficient for providing for executives' needs?
8. Compare the structure of EIS with that of a typical DSS and comment on the differences.
9. Why is it advantageous to include both a mainframe and PCs in an EIS?
10. It is said that EIS supports unstructured decisions. It is also said that EIS is used to perform structured, somewhat repetitive analyses. Use Simon's phases of the decision-making process, described in Chapter 2, to reconcile these statements.
11. What is the difference between EIS and ESS?
12. Why can't a conventional MIS fulfill the information needs of executives?
13. Why is it advisable to use vendors or consultants to build an EIS?
14. List a few approaches that can be used to discover the information needs of executives.
15. Describe the logic of Wetherbe's two-phase information discovery approach.
16. Why is it so difficult to find the information needs of executives?
17. Explain how CSF are monitored.
18. Relate CSF to key performance indicators.
19. What are the major benefits of integrating EIS and DSS?
20. What are the relationships between EIS and GDSS?
21. Why is it difficult to build an EIS in-house?
22. Why is it desirable to use a vendor or a consultant to build an EIS?
23. Explain the statement in the Hertz case: "The company added an EIS that is used as a front-end to the DSS."
24. Data access (data dipping) is becoming critical for enterprise-wide EIS. Explain why.

Exercises

1. Implementing EIS may mean reengineering a corporation; for example, redefining relationships among departments and senior executives, or changing the manner in which strategic information is used. Survey the literature and find EIS application cases, such as that of British Airways (see Cottrell and Rapley [1991]). Identify the business processes that have been changed due to the introduction of EIS.

2. Debate: The Clients and Philosophy of EIS.

   - *Position A* (supported by Comshare Inc.): EIS is an executives' tool. It should be designed, operated, and maintained as such. It could be customized to a specific executive. The emphasis here is on *executive support.*
   - *Position B* (supported by Pilot Software Inc. and Information Resources, Inc.): EIS is everybody's information system that could serve hundreds or even thousands of users. It is an enterprise intelligence system. The emphasis here is on a *very large number of users.*
   - *Position C* (supported by SAS Institute Inc.): An EIS is a component in a data management, access, analysis, and presentation system. Such an enterprise-wide information delivery system is supported by a set of software products that easily interface with each other. The emphasis here is on *data delivery.*

   The Issues:

   a. Most organizations can adopt only one architecture, that goes with one of the previous positions. Examine the pros and cons of each.
   b. Present some scenarios in which each of the three positions might excel.
   c. Can the positions be reconciled?

3. Debate: Whose Fault Is It?—The Lockheed Corp.

   Developed in-house in the late 1970s and early 1980s, Lockheed's EIS is considered one of the first successful EIS (e.g., see Houdeshel and Watson in Watson, et al. [1991]). Lockheed believed that its EIS tracked all critical factors, until a critical error was discovered. The weight of the P-7 aircraft that Lockheed was building for the U.S. Navy was never programmed into the EIS. This omission cost the company millions of dollars (possibly $300 million). The designers of the EIS claim that the system works fine. However, the information requirements were established improperly. Decisions about what was to be included in the EIS involved both the executives and information systems staff. Such decisions are complicated by the fact that the potentially critical information is not obvious. Did the problem occur because the information system professional did not understand the business side of Lockheed? Or was it because the executives failed to mention weight as being a critical factor?

   The builders blamed the executives, the executives blamed the builders. Whose fault is it anyway? *Note:* The Lockheed case is presented in Appendix A to this book.

References and Bibliography

Bergerson, F., et al. (1991). "Top Managers Evaluate the Attributes of EIS." *DSS-91 Transactions*. Providence, RI: The Institute of Management Sciences.

Bonczek, R. H., C. W. Holsapple, and A B. Whinston. (1980). "The Evolving Role of Models in Decision Support Systems." *Decision Sciences*, Vol. 11, No. 2.

Brandel, M. (1991, July 22). "Executive Information Systems (LAN-based vs. Host-based EISs)." *Computerworld*.

Burkan, W. C. (1991). *Executive Information Systems*. New York: Van Nostrand Reinhold.

Carrol, C., and C. Larkin. (1992, Summer). "Executive Information Technology." *Information Systems Management*.

Comshare Inc. (1993, September). *Commander EIS: Delivering the Complete EIS Solution*. Report No. 629721. Ann Arbor, MI: Comshare Inc. (available free on request).

Cottrell N., and K. Rapley. (1991). "Factors Critical to the Success of EIS in British Airways." *European Journal of Information Systems*, Vol. 1, No. 1, pp. 65–71.

Davis, S. G. (1989, July 1). "Can Stand-Alone EIS's Stand Up?" *Datamation*.

DeLong, D. W., and J. F. Rockart. (1986). "Identifying the Attributes of Successful Executive Support System Implementation." In Fedorowicz [1986].

Dresner, H. (1993, May 5–7). *Business Intelligence: Competing Against Time*. Stamford, CT: The Gartner Group.

Fedorowicz, J. (ed.). (1986, April). *DSS-86 Transactions*. Sixth Annual Conference on DSS. Washington, DC: The Institute of Management Sciences.

Frolick, M., and N. K. Ramarapo. (1993, July). "Hypermedia: The Future of EIS." *Journal of Systems Management*.

Frolick, M. N., and S. Jeanings. (1993, Spring). "EIS Software Selection at Georgia Power: A Structured Approach." *Information Strategy: The Executive Journal*.

Gillan, C., and K. McPherson. (1992, October 26). *"EIS: A White Paper."* Supplement to *Computerworld*.

Keen, P. G. W. (1980, Fall). "Adaptive Design for Decision Support Systems." *Data Base*, Vol 12, Nos. 1, 2.

Kogan, J. M. (1986). "Information for Motivation: A Key to Executive Information Systems that Translate Strategy Into Results for Management." In Fedorowicz [1986].

Little, J. D. C. (1970, April). "Models and Managers: The Concept of a Decision Calculus." *Management Science*, Vol. 16, No. 2.

McCartney, L. (1989, July). "How ESS Keeps Hertz Managers Out In Front." *Business Month*.

McLeod, R., Jr., and J. W. Jones. (1986, September–October). "Making Executive Information Systems More Effective." *Business Horizons*.

Millet, I., and C. H. Mawhinney. (1992). "Executive Information Systems." *Information and Management*, Vol. 23.

Mintzberg, H. (1975, July–August). "The Manager's Job: Folklore and Fact." *Harvard Business Review*.

Moore, J. H., and M. G. Chang. (1980, Fall). "Design of Decision Support Systems." *Data Base*, Vol. 12, Nos. 1, 2.

Moynihan, G. P. (1993, July). "An Executive Information System: Planning for Post-Implementation at NASA." *Journal of Systems Management*.

Rockart, J. F., and M. E. Treacy. (1982, January–February). "The CEO Goes On-Line." *Harvard Business Review*.

Rockart, J. F., and D. DeLong. (1988). *Executive Support Systems*. Homewood, IL: Dow Jones-Irwin.

Scott-Morton, M. S. (1971). *Management Decision Systems: Computer-Based Support for Decision Making*. Cambridge, MA: Harvard University, Division of Research.

Thiriez, H. (1992, August). "Towards a DEISS." *European Journal of Operational Research*.

Turban, E., and J. Walls (eds.). (1994, May/June). "Executive Information Systems." Special issue of *Decision Support Systems*.

Watson, H. J., et al. (1991, March). "Executive Information Systems: A Framework for Development and a Survey of Current Practices." *MIS Quarterly*.

Watson, H. J., et al. (eds) (1992). *Executive Information Systems*. New York: Wiley.

Watson, H. J., et al. (1992, April). "Executive Information Systems: An Ongoing Study of Current Practices." *International Information Systems*.

Watson, H. J., and M. Frolick. (1992, Spring). "Determining Information Requirements for an Executive Information System." *Information System Management*.

Watson, H. J., et al. (1991). *Executive Information Systems: A Framework for Development and Survey of Current Practices*. Working paper 41, Department of Management, University of Georgia, Athens, GA.

Wetherbe, J. C. (1991, March). "Executive Information Requirements: Getting It Right." *MIS Quarterly*.

GLOSSARY

AI: *See* Artificial intelligence, Expert systems shell.

Analog network: The electronic linking of devices, where messages are sent over the links by having some analogous physical quantity (e.g., voltage) continuously vary as a function of time. Historically, the telephone network has been an analog network.

Application independence: The separation of data from applications. Application independence means that applications are built separate from the databases from which applications draw their data; application independence results in lower long term costs for systems development.

Application system: *See* Information system.

Applications architecture: That part of an IT architecture that defines the process for applications development and management.

Applications software: All programs written to accomplish particular tasks for computer users. Examples include programs for payroll computation, inventory record-keeping, word processing, and producing a summarized report for top management.

Architecture: *See* Information technology architecture.

Arithmetic/logical unit: The portion of a computer system in which arithmetic operations (such as addition and multiplication) and logical operations (such as comparing two numbers for equality) are carried out.

Artificial intelligence (AI): The study of how to make computers do things that are presently done better by people. AI research includes five separate but related areas: natural languages, robotics, perceptive systems (vision and hearing), expert systems, and neural networks.

Artificial intelligence (AI) shell: *See* Expert system shell.

Assembler: A program (software) that translates an assembly language program—a program containing mnemonic operation codes and symbolic addresses—into an equivalent machine language program.

Assembly language: Second-generation computer language in which the programmer uses easily remembered mnemonic operation codes instead of machine language operation codes and symbolic addresses instead of memory cell addresses. Such a language is considerably easier to use than machine language, but it still requires the programmer to employ the same small steps that the computer has been built to understand.

Audit trail: A list of references that allows a business transaction to be traced from the time of input through all the reports in which the transaction data are used. An audit trail is used to identify where errors are introduced or security breaches may have occurred.

Backbone: The underlying foundation of a telecommunications network, to which the other elements attach. For example, the backbone of a local area network serving multiple buildings on a campus may be high-capacity fiber optic cabling connecting all the buildings in a ring topology; within each building, less expensive twisted pair wiring may be used to connect specific devices to the backbone.

Bandwidth: The difference between the highest and the lowest frequencies (cycles per second) that can be transmitted on a single medium. Bandwidth is important because it is a measure of the capacity of the transmission medium.

Baseband coax: A simple-to-use and inexpensive-to-install type of coaxial cable that offers a single digital transmission channel with maximum transmission speeds ranging from 10 million bits per second (mbps) up to 264 mbps. Baseband coax has been widely used for local area networks and telephone long-distance transmission.

Batch processing: A mode of transaction processing in which a group or "batch" of transactions (of a particular type) is accumulated and then processed as a single batch at one time. For example, all sales for a firm would be accumulated during the day and then processed as a single batch at night.

Batch total: The sum of values in a specific field across all transactions in a group.

Baud: Number of signals sent per second; one measure of data transmission speed. Baud is often equivalent to Hertz (another measure of transmission speed) and to bits per second.

Benchmarking: A procedure to compare the capabilities of various computers in a particular organizational setting by running a representative set of real jobs (jobs regularly run on the organization's existing computer) on each of the machines and comparing the resulting elapsed times.

Bit: Widely-used abbreviation for a *bi*nary digi*t*, i.e., a 0 or a 1. Coding schemes used in computer systems employ particular sequences of bits to represent the decimal numbers, alphabetic characters, and special characters.

Bottom-up approach: A way to develop the IS plan by concentrating on the current and expected problems, and ideas for change at the operating level in an organization. *See also* Top-down approach.

Boundary: Marks the inside and the outside (scope) of a system. A boundary segregates the environment from the system.

Broadband coax: A type of coaxial cable—more expensive and harder to use than baseband coax—that uses analog transmission; can be divided into multiple channels, and can achieve transmission speeds up to 550 million bits per second.

Bus: *See* Communications bus, Bus topology.

Bus topology: A network topology in which a single length of cable (coax, fiber optic, or twisted pair)—not connected at the ends—is shared by all network devices; also called a linear topology.

Business process reengineering: The radical redesign of business processes to achieve dramatic improvements by taking advantage of information technology.

Byte: A memory cell that can store only one character of data. *See also* Memory.

Cache memory: A very high-speed storage unit used as an intermediary between elements of a computer system that have a significant mismatch in speeds (e.g., the very fast data channel and relatively slow DASD). An entire block of data is moved from the slower element to cache memory, so that most requests for data from the faster element can be satisfied directly from the very high-speed cache memory.

CAD: *See* Computer-aided design.

CAE: *See* Computer-aided engineering.

CAM: *See* Computer-aided manufacturing.

CAPP: *See* Computer-aided process planning.

CASE: *See* Computer-aided software engineering.

Cellular telephone: A telephone instrument that can be installed in a car or carried in a pocket or briefcase; this instrument can be used anywhere as long as it is within the 8 to 10 mile range of a cellular switching station.

Central processing unit (CPU): The name given to the combination of the control unit, which controls all other components of a computer, and the arithmetic/logical unit, in which computations and logical comparisons are carried out; also referred to as the processor.

Champion: A person who has the motivation and/or power to push a system through to successful implementation, avoiding or overcoming the obstacles that arise along the way.

Change management: A function within IS that attempts to manage changes to information systems so as to minimize the problems caused by these changes.

Chargeback: The process that IS follows to internally charge client units for services provided. These internal charges may be established to recover costs or may represent market prices.

Check digit: One or more digits appended to a critical value; the check digit has some mathematical relationship to the other digits in the number.

Chief information officer (CIO): The most senior organizational officer who is responsible for only information technology. The CIO leads all usage of information technology from a general business perspective, much like a chief financial officer does for finance, but often does not have operating responsibility for the IS organization.

CIM: *See* Computer-integrated manufacturing.

Client/server system: A particular type of distributed system in which the processing power is distributed between a central server computer, such as a minicomputer or a powerful workstation, and a number of client computers, which are usually desktop microcomputers. The split in responsibilities between the server and the client varies considerably between applications, but the client often handles data entry and the immediate output, while the server maintains the larger database against which the new data are processed. *See also* Distributed systems.

Coaxial cable (coax): A common transmission medium that consists of a heavy copper wire at the center, surrounded by insulating material, then a cylindrical conductor such as a woven braided mesh, and finally an outer protective plastic covering. The two kinds of coaxial cable in widespread use are baseband coax for digital transmission and broadband coax for analog transmission.

Code generator: *See* Computer-aided software engineering.

Cohesion: *See* Functional cohesion.

COM: *See* Computer output microfilm.

Commercial IS planning systems: A variety of productized approaches to IS planning offered by consultants and vendors.

Communications bus: A communications cable (conventional or fiber optics) to which various information technologies can be easily attached, providing a flexible way of building or modifying a computer and communications system.

Compiler: A program (software) that translates a third- or fourth-generation language program into an equivalent machine language program, translating the entire program into machine language before any of the program is executed.

Computer-aided design (CAD): The use of computer graphics (both two-dimensional and three-dimensional) and database to create and modify engineering designs.

Computer-aided engineering (CAE): The analysis

of the functional characteristics of an engineering design by simulating the product performance under various conditions.

Computer-aided manufacturing (CAM): The use of computers to plan and control manufacturing processes. CAM incorporates computer programs to control automated equipment on the shop floor, automated guided vehicles (AGVs) to move material, and a communications network to link all the pieces.

Computer-aided process planning (CAPP): A computer-based system that plans the sequence of processes that produce or assemble a part. During the design process, the engineer retrieves the closest standard plan from a database and modifies that plan rather than starting from scratch.

Computer-aided software engineering (CASE): A collection of support software tools (designed to be used by computer professionals) to help automate software development. CASE can include tools for managing the development process; facilities for production of the documentation; a database that manages all the information produced about the project and makes it available to the project team; tools to support analysis and modeling; support for the data dictionary; code generators that produce code (usually COBOL) from diagrams, screen designs, and text commands; and program maintenance and code analysis tools which help to restructure, convert, or rewrite programs into a standard form. *See also* Upper-case, Lower-case, Integrated-case, Software reengineering.

Computer-integrated manufacturing (CIM): A broad term which encompasses many uses of the computer to help manufacturers operate more effectively and efficiently. CIM systems fall into three major categories: engineering systems, which are aimed at increasing the productivity of engineers; manufacturing administration, which includes systems that develop production schedules and monitor production; and factory operations, which include those systems that actually control the operation of machines on the factory floor.

Computer output microfilm (COM): A computer output method using microfilm or microfiche (a sheet of film) as the output medium. A computer output device called a COM recorder accepts the data from memory and prepares the microfilm output at very high speeds.

Computer telecommunications network: The type of network emanating from a single medium, large, or very large computer or a group of closely linked computers; usually arranged in a tree topology.

Computer virus: A small unit of code that invades a computer program, and, when the invaded program is executed, the virus makes copies of itself that are released to attack other computer programs. Hundreds of virus programs have been created, some of which are intended as jokes that do little harm, but some of them degrade performance by using up computer memory, and others wipe out memory or destroy files.

Contention bus: A design standard for a local area network based on a bus topology and contention for the use of the bus by all devices on the network, i.e., any device may transmit a message if the bus is idle, but if two devices start to transmit at the same time a collision will occur and both messages will be lost. *See also* CSMA/CD protocol.

Controller: A hardware unit to link input/output or file devices to the CPU and memory of large computer systems (through the data channel). The controller is a highly specialized microprocessor which manages the operation of its attached devices to free the CPU from these tasks (e.g., a DASD controller handles direct access devices, while a communications controller handles multiple terminals).

Conversion: The process of changing to the use of a new system.

Cordless telephone: A portable telephone instrument that can be used up to about 1,000 feet from its wired telephone base unit; this permits the user to carry the instrument to various rooms in a house or take it outdoors on the patio.

Corporate data model: A chart that describes all the data requirements of a given organization. This chart shows what data entities and relationships between the entities are important for the organization.

Counterimplementation: Actions taken to resist or prevent the successful implementation of a new system.

CPU: *See* Central processing unit.

Critical success factor (CSF): One of a few organizational activities that, if done well, should result in the strategic success of an organization.

CSMA/CD protocol: An abbreviation for Carrier Sense Multiple Access with Collision Detection, the protocol used in the contention bus design for a local area network. With this protocol, any device may transmit a message if the bus is idle. But if two devices start to transmit at the same time, a collision will occur and the messages will become garbled. Both devices must recognize that this collision has occurred, stop transmitting, wait some random period of time, and then try again.

Customer resource life cycle: An approach to identify stategic uses of information technology.

DASD: *See* Direct access storage device.

Data administration: The organizational unit that leads the efforts to plan, control, define, justify, and account for organizational data as a resource. Data administration has both managerial and technical interests in data and databases. *See also* Database administration.

Data analysis and presentation application: An application that manipulates data and then distributes information to authorized users. These applications concentrate on creating useful information from established data sources and, because they are separate from data capture and transfer systems, can be individually changed without having to modify the more costly to change data capture and transfer systems.

Data architecture: *See* Data model.

Data capture application: An application that gathers data and populates databases. These applications simplify all other applications that then transfer or report data and information.

Data center: A large mainframe computer installation that stores, maintains and provides access to vast quantities of data; includes computer hardware, communications facilities, system software, and technical support and operations staff.

Data channel: A specialized input/output processor (hardware) that takes over the function of device communication from the CPU. The data channel corrects for the significant speed mismatch between the slow input/output and file devices and the fast and expensive CPU.

Data dictionary/directory (DD/D): Support software that provides a repository of data definitions—including the meaning, storage format, integrity rules, security clearances, and physical location of data—that is used by the DBMS and system users.

Data flow diagram (DFD): A common diagrammatic technique for showing the movement, storage, and processing of data in a system and with its environment.

Data model: A map or blueprint for organizational data. A data model shows the data entities and relationships that are important to an organization.

Data-oriented approach: An approach to systems development that concentrates on the ideal and natural organization of data, independent of how or where data are used. *See also* Process-oriented approach.

Data steward: A business manager responsible for the quality and viability of a particular data entity (like customer, product, or employee).

Data transfer application: An application that moves data from one database to another. These applications permit one source of data to serve many localized systems within an organization.

Database: A shared collection of files and associations between these files. A database reduces redundancy and inconsistency compared to file processing, but this lack of natural redundancy can cause risks from loss of data or breaches of authorized data access or manipulation.

Database administration (DBA): The part of the data administration unit that is responsible for computerized databases. A DBA is concerned with efficiency, integrity, and security of database processing.

Database machine: *See* Database server.

Database management system (DBMS): Support software that is used to create, manage, and protect organizational data. A DBMS is the software that manages a database; it works with the operating system to store and modify data and to make data accessible in a variety of meaningful and authorized ways.

Database server: A separate computer, attached to another computer, that is responsible for only processing database queries and updates. A database server is usually part of a local area network and serves the database needs of all the personal and larger computers on this network.

DBA: *See* Database administration.

DBMS: *See* Database management system.

DBMS engine: A computer program that handles the detailed retrieving and updating of data for a wide variety of other DBMSs, electronic spreadsheet, and other software. Use of a DBMS engine allows the other software to concentrate on providing a convenient user interface while the DBMS engine handles the common database access functions.

DDD: *See* Direct Distance Dialing.

DD/D: *See* Data dictionary/directory.

Decentralized system development: Systems development done by people who are not part of the central IS group; may involve user application development, or development that involves IS professionals reporting to a department, plant, or other business unit.

Decision analysis: A requirements definition approach in which analysts identify the key decisions made by those who will use the system, formulate models that describe how these decisions are (or should be) made, and thus determine what information is needed to improve the decision-making process.

Decision support system (DSS): A computer-based system, almost always interactive, designed to assist managers in making decisions. A DSS incorporates both data and models and is usually intended to assist in the solution of semi- or unstructured problems. An actual application that assists in the decision-making process is properly called a specific DSS; examples of specific DSS include a police-beat allocation system, a capacity planning and production scheduling system, and a capital investment decision system.

Decision support system (DSS) generator: Computer software that provides a set of capabilities to build a specific DSS quickly and easily. For example, IFPS, a financial modeling language, is a DSS generator that permits the construction of specific financial models that can be used in decision-making.

Decoupling of system components: Reducing the need to coordinate two system components. Decoupling is accomplished by creating slack and flexible resources, buffers, sharing resources, and standards.

DFD: *See* Data flow diagram.

Digital network: The electronic linking of devices, where messages are sent over the links by directly transmitting the zeros and ones used by computers and other digital devices. Computer telecommunications networks are digital networks, and the telephone network is gradually being shifted from an analog to a digital network.

Direct access file: A basic type of computer file from which it is possible for the computer to obtain a record immediately, without regard to where the record is located on the file; usually stored on magnetic disk. Computer files, also called secondary memory or secondary storage, are added to a computer system to keep vast quantities of data accessible within the computer system at more reasonable costs than main memory.

Direct access storage device (DASD): The device on which direct access files are stored. *See also* Direct access file.

Direct Distance Dialing (DDD): The normal way of using the long-distance telephone network in the United States in which the user directly dials the number with which he wishes to communicate and pays for the service based on the duration of the call and the geographical distance;

may be used for voice and data communications between any two spots served by the telephone network.

Direct file organization: *See* Direct access file.

Disposable system: A system that can be discarded when it becomes obsolete without affecting the operation of any other information system.

Distributed data processing: *See* Distributed systems.

Distributed database: A database that is physically located across several computer systems. A goal of managing a distributed database is to give the impression to all database programmers and users that the database is actually in one location.

Distributed systems: Application systems in which the processing power is distributed to multiple sites, which are then tied together via telecommunications lines. Distributed systems have computers (of some size) located at various physical sites at which the organization does business, and these computers are linked by telecommunications lines in order to support some business process.

Documentation: The written descriptions produced during the systems development process; includes documents produced as deliverables at each stage of the development process, as well as descriptions for the users of the system, those who operate the hardware, and those who will maintain the system.

Downsizing: A term that usually means making something smaller. When referring to computer hardware, downsizing refers to the substitution of minicomputers, workstations, or PC networks for mainframes as the platform to support applications.

DSS: *See* Decision support system.

EDI: *See* Electronic data interchange.

EDP auditing: A variety of methods to ensure the correct processing of data. EDP auditing combines data processing controls with classical accounting auditing methods.

EIS: *See* Executive information system.

Electronic data interchange (EDI): A set of standards and hardware and software technology that permit computers in separate organizations to transfer documents electronically. The data transferred is typically purchase orders, invoices, account balances, or price listing, but any document can potentially be exchanged in EDI.

Electronic mail: A system whereby users send and receive messages electronically at their workstations, which are usually microcomputers connected to a minicomputer or mainframe computer or a local area network. Electronic mail permits asynchronous communication, thus eliminating telephone tag, and usually incorporates such features as sending a message to a distribution list, resending a message to someone else with an appended note, and filing messages in electronic file folders for later recall.

E-mail: *See* Electronic mail.

End-user computing: Hands-on use of computer resources by employees throughout the organization to enter data, make inquiries, release orders into production, prepare reports, communicate, perform statistical analysis, analyze problems, design products, and so forth; may even involve decentralizing control of computer resources and system development to users.

Enterprise data planning and modeling: A top-down approach to detailing the data requirements of an organization. Enterprise modeling describes data at a very general level and indicates how data relates to various business activities. *See also* Top-down approach.

Entity-relationship (ER) diagramming: A popular notation for modeling organizational data requirements. ER diagramming uses specific symbols to represent data entities, relationships, and elements.

Ethernet: The name of the original Xerox version of a contention bus local area network design, which has come to be used as a synonym for a contention bus design. *See also* Local area network, Contention bus.

Evolutionary development: Any development approach that does not depend upon defining the final requirements early in the development process, but (like prototyping) evolves the system

by building successive versions that eventually result in a system that is acceptable. *See also* Prototyping, Rapid application development.

Executive information system (EIS): A computer application designed to be used directly by top managers, without the assistance of intermediaries, to provide the executive easy on-line access to current information about the status of the organization and its environment. Such information would include filtered and summarized internal transactions data, but it would also incorporate "soft" data such as assessments, rumors, opinions, and ideas.

Expanded storage: A type of storage unit that is slower and less expensive than main memory, but with a much faster data transfer rate than is possible from DASD. Expanded storage provides performance similar to additional main memory at a greatly reduced cost.

Expert systems: The branch of artificial intelligence concerned with building systems that incorporate the decision-making logic of a human expert. Expert systems have been developed to diagnose and prescribe treatment for diseases, to analyze proposed bank loans, and to determine the sequence of stops on a truck route.

Expert systems shell: Computer software which provides the basic framework of an expert system and a limited but user-friendly special language to develop the expert system. With the purchase of such a shell, the organization's system builder can concentrate on the details of the business decision being modeled and the development of the knowledge base.

Factory automation: The use of information technology to automate various aspects of factory operations. Factory automation includes numerically controlled machines, material requirements planning (MRP) systems, computer-integrated manufacturing (CIM), and computer-controlled robots.

FDDI: *See* Fiber Distributed Data Interface.

Feasibility analysis: A thorough analysis of the economic, technical, and organizational feasibility of a proposed system; includes a description of what the system would do and how it would operate, an analysis of its costs and benefits, and a rough plan for the development of the system.

Fiber Distributed Data Interface (FDDI): An American National Standards Institute (ANSI) standard for building a local area network that offers a transmission speed of 100 million bits per second and fault tolerance because of its double-ring architecture; FDDI utilizes either fiber optic cabling or shielded twisted pair wiring.

Fiber optics: A transmission medium in which data are transmitted by sending pulses of light through a thin fiber of glass or fused silica. Although expensive to install and difficult to work with, the high transmission speeds possible with fiber optic cabling—500 thousand bits per second (bps) to 30 billion bps—are leading to its use in most new long distance telephone lines.

File processing: An approach to managing data in which each application system separately maintains its own set of computer files. File processing permits different systems to remain independent of one another, but redundant and inconsistent data across systems can cause other severe and costly problems.

Formal system: The way an organization was designed to work. *See also* Informal system.

Fourth-generation language: A computer language in which the user gives a precise statement of what is to be accomplished, not how to do it. No procedure is necessary; the order of statements is usually inconsequential. Examples include IFPS, SAS, FOCUS, and NOMAD.

Full-duplex transmission: A type of data transmission in which data can travel in both directions at once over the communication line.

Functional cohesion: A property of a system by which each component has a well-defined function and all components cooperate to achieve an overall system goal. *See also* Subsystem, Module, Hierarchical decomposition.

Functional information system: An information system, usually composed of multiple interrelated subsystems, that provides the information necessary to accomplish various tasks within a specific functional area of the business, such as production, marketing, accounting, personnel, or engineering. For example, the marketing information system may include subsystems for promotion and advertising, new product development, sales forecasting, product planning, product pricing, market research, and sales information.

Geographic information system (GIS): A computer-based system designed to collect, store, retrieve, manipulate, and display spatial data; a GIS links data to maps so that the spatial characteristics of the data can be easily comprehended.

GIS: *See* Geographic information system.

Graphical user interface (GUI): An interface between a computer (usually a microcomputer or workstation) and a human user based on graphical screen images, such as icons. With a GUI (pronounced gooey), the user selects an application or makes other choices by using a mouse to click on an appropriate icon or label appearing on the screen. Both Windows (used with PC-DOS or MS-DOS) and the OS/2 operating system employ a GUI.

Group support system (GSS): A variant of a decision support system (DSS) in which the system is designed to support a group rather than an individual. The purpose of a GSS is to make group sessions more productive by supporting such group activities as brainstorming, issue structuring, voting, and conflict resolution.

Group technology (GT): A computer-based system that logically groups parts according to physical characteristics, machine routings through the factory, and similar machine operations. Based on these logical groupings, GT is able to identify existing parts that engineers can use or modify rather than design new parts.

GSS: *See* Group support system.

GT: *See* Group technology.

GUI: *See* Graphical user interface.

Half-duplex transmission: A type of data transmission in which data can travel in both directions over the communication line, but not simultaneously.

Hardware: The physical pieces of a computer or telecommunications system, such as a central processing unit, a printer, and a terminal.

Hertz: Cycles per second; one measure of data transmission speed. Hertz is often equivalent to baud (another measure of transmission speed) and to bits per second.

Hierarchical decomposition: The process of breaking down a system into successive levels of subsystems. This recursive decomposition allows a system to be described at various levels of detail, each appropriate for a different kind of analysis or for a different audience.

Human information processing: A model of how humans receive stimuli from the senses. This model contains four components: reception of stimuli, effecting actions, processing, and memory.

I-CASE: *See* Integrated-case.

Imaging: A computer input/output method by which any type of paper document—including business forms, reports, charts, graphs, and photographs—can be read by a scanner and translated into digital form so that it can be stored in the computer system; this process can also be reversed so that the digitized image stored in the computer system can be displayed on a video display unit, printed on paper, or transmitted to another computer or workstation.

In-line system: A computer system in which data entry is accomplished on-line (i.e., a transaction is entered directly into the computer via some input device) but the processing is deferred until a suitable batch of transactions has been accumulated.

Indexed file organization: A method of organizing a computer file or database in which the control keys only are arranged in sequence in a separate table, along with a pointer to the complete records associated with each key. The records themselves can then be arranged in any order.

Informal system: The way the organization actually works. *See also* Formal system.

Information: Data (usually processed data) that are useful to a decision-maker.

Information center: An organizational unit whose mission is to support users in exploiting information technology by providing education and training, consulting on the use of selected hardware and software, assistance in selecting hardware and software, assistance in locating and accessing computerized data, and so forth. In some organizations, an information center also includes the software, hardware, and methods used to support end-user computing.

Information economics: An approach to justifying systems that attempts to assess the impact of a new system upon the business by using a scoring system based upon corporate objectives and the risks associated with the system. Top management is involved in defining the objectives and risks, and in assigning relative weights to them.

Information intensity: The amount of dependence a product or firm has on information and information technology. High information intensity is usually associated today with service or financial organizations in which information is an integral part of the service rendered.

Information range: Shows the information and information-based services that can be directly shared through an organization's IT platform.

Information reach: Shows who (both internal and external to the organization) can access information through an organization's IT platform.

Information system (IS): The collection of computer programs, hardware, people, procedures, documentation, forms, inputs, and outputs used in or generated by handling business data. An information system consists of these components and their interrelationships.

Information technology architecture: A written set of guidelines for a company's desired future for information technology within which people can make individual decisions that will be compatible with that desired future; should include components relating to beliefs or values, data, the technology infrastructure, applications, and the management system for information technology.

Information vision: A written expression of the desired future for information use and management in an organization.

Infrastructure architecture: A structure that describes the technical components of the IS infrastructure and the relationships between these components. The technical architecture is concerned with such things as the types of computer hardware, telecommunications network topologies, communications protocols, requirements for interfacing local equipment with the network, and so on.

Innovation adoption: The process followed by an individual or organization to use a new idea, method, system, or technology.

Instruction: An individual step or operation in a program, particularly in a machine language program. *See also* Machine language, Program.

Integrated-case (I-CASE): A full-cycle case system that combines the facilities provided by both upper- and lower-case to support automation of the entire development process. The integrated-case tools are integrated so that the system specifications expressed in the form supported by the front-end tools can be converted into computer code by the back-end tools included in the system. *See also* Computer-aided software engineering, Upper-case, Lower-case.

Integrated Services Digital Network (ISDN): An emerging set of international standards by which the public telephone network will offer extensive new telecommunications capabilities—including simultaneous transmission of both voice and data over the same line—to telephone users worldwide.

Interactive system: A computer system in which the user directly interacts with the computer. In such a system, the user would enter data into the computer via some type of input device and the computer would provide a response almost immediately (e.g., an airline reservation system). An interactive system is an on-line system in which the computer provides an immediate response to the user.

Interface: The point of contact where the environment meets a system or where two subsystems meet. Special functions (filtering, coding/decoding, error detection and correction, buffering, security, summarizing) occur at an interface, which allow the environment and system or two subsystems to work together (or be compatible).

Interorganizational information system (IOS): An integrated data processing and data communi-

cations system used by two or more participant organizations. An IOS links the information systems within each participant so that only a minimal amount of paperwork and manual handling of data is required to transmit information between the participant organizations.

Interpreter: A program (software) that translates a third- or fourth-generation language program into an equivalent machine language program, executing each source program statement as soon as that single statement is translated.

Invisible queue: Those systems development requests that are not formally submitted because their sponsors are discouraged by the pool of projects that are already approved and awaiting development, or because the sponsors doubt that they would be approved if submitted. These requests are in addition to the official backlog of work.

IOS: *See* Interorganizational information system.

IS: *See* Information system.

IS coordinator: A position in a user organization whose role is to serve as a liaison between the organization and the IS organization. The IS coordinator must understand the business and the user organization, but must also understand the technology and the IS organization's perspective.

IS mission: The reason(s) for the existence of the IS organization. Typical reasons include: reducing the costs of the organization, creating an effective information technology system, and exercising leadership in creating competitive advantage for the organization.

IS operational plan: Part of the IS plan that focuses on IS project selection and prioritization.

IS plan: A statement of the objectives and initiatives that relate information systems to business priorities. The plan can be divided into a strategic plan, a long-term plan, and a short-term plan and budget.

IS steering committee: A committee of business managers whose function is to advise the head of IS on policy matters and often to decide which proposed systems will be developed by IS.

IS strategic planning process: Setting objectives,

conducting internal and external analyses, and establishing strategic initiatives.

ISDN: *See* Integrated Services Digital Network.

IT platform: The set of hardware, software, and standards an organization uses to build its information systems.

JAD: *See* Joint application design.

Job control language (JCL): The specialized computer language by which computer users communicate with the operating system. The term JCL is used primarily in the context of IBM mainframe computers.

Joint application design (JAD): An intensive effort to define the requirements of a system by using a full-time team of users, IS specialists, and a trained facilitator. Often uses special joint development facilities, including meeting rooms supported by computers with CASE tools, so that the participants are away from the distractions of their normal environment.

LAN: *See* Local area network.

Lewin/Schein change model: Describes planned change in an organization as consisting of three stages: unfreezing, moving, and refreezing.

Local area network (LAN): A local data-only network, usually within a single organization and generally operating within an area no more than two or three miles in diameter, that contains a number of intelligent devices (usually microcomputers) capable of data processing. LANs are usually arranged in one of three topologies: contention bus, token bus, and token ring (see these entries).

Logical system: A depiction of the function and purpose (the what) of a system without reference to or implications for how the system is implemented. *See also* Physical system.

Lower-case: The back-end CASE tools that support system construction, such as code generators to produce computer code (usually in COBOL) from high-level specifications such as diagrams, screen designs, models, and high-level specifications. *See also* Computer-aided software engineering, Upper-case, Integrated-case.

Machine language: The form of a computer program that the control unit of the computer has been built to understand. In general, each machine language instruction consists of an operation code that tells the control unit what basic machine function is to be performed and one or more addresses that identify the specific memory cells whose contents will be involved in the operation.

Magnetic ink character recognition (MICR): A computer input method used for check processing in the United States. Identifying information and the amount are recorded in magnetizable ink at the bottom of the check; a computer input device called a magnetic ink character reader magnetizes the ink, recognizes the numbers, and transmits the data to the memory of the bank's computer to permit the check to be processed.

Magnetic tape unit: A computer file device that stores (writes) data on magnetic tape and retrieves (reads) data from tape back into memory; the usual device on which sequential access files are stored. *See also* Sequential access file.

Mainframes: The kind of computer that is used as the main, central computing system of most major corporations and government agencies, ranging in cost from $500,000 to $20,000,000 and above, and power from 20 to 400 MIPS; used for large business general processing and a wide range of other applications.

Maintenance: Any changes made to a system after it has been placed in operation, including changes required to correct errors, those required to adapt the system to changes in its environment, and enhancements to the system.

Managed free economy: A comprehensive approach to managing end-user computing that involves a stated end-user strategy, a user/IS working partnership, targeting of critical end-user systems and applications, an integrated support organization, and an emphasis on education throughout the organization.

Management systems architecture: The portion of an information technology architecture that specifies the management process for IS in an organization.

Manufacturing automation protocol (MAP): A communications protocol (a set of rules) for communicating between automated equipment on a factory floor. MAP, which was pioneered by General Motors and has now been accepted by most major IT manufacturers and vendors, insures an "open" manufacturing system in which communication between equipment from various vendors will be possible.

Manufacturing resources planning (MRP II): A computer-based manufacturing administration system that usually incorporates three major components—the master production schedule, which sets the overall production goals; material requirements planning, which develops the detailed production schedule; and shop floor control, which releases orders to the shop floor based on the detailed schedule and actual production to date.

MAP: *See* Manufacturing automation protocol.

Massively parallel processor (MPP): A parallel processor computer with some large number of parallel CPUs; in general, 32 or more parallel CPUs is considered an MPP if the different CPUs are capable of performing different instructions at the same time, or a thousand or more parallel CPUs is considered an MPP if the different CPUs must all carry out the same instruction at the same time. *See also* Parallel processor.

Material requirements planning (MRP): A computer-based system that accepts the master production schedule for a factory as input and then develops a detailed production schedule, using parts explosion, production capacity, inventory, and lead time data; usually a component of a manufacturing resources planning (MRP II) system.

MegaFLOPS (MFLOPS): Shorthand for millions of floating point operations per second, a commonly used speed rating for computers. MegaFLOPS ratings are derived by running a particular set of programs in a particular language on the machines being investigated.

Memory: The primary area for storage of data in a computer system; also referred to as main memory or primary memory. All data flows in a computer system are to and from memory.

Memory is divided into cells, and a fixed amount of data can be stored in each cell.

MFLOPS: *See* MegaFLOPS.

MICR: *See* Magnetic ink character recognition.

Microcomputers: The category of computers with the least cost ($1,000 to $5,000) and the least power (0.5 to 20 MIPS), generally used for personal computing, small business processing, and as a workstation attached to large computers; also called micros or personal computers.

Microwave: Considered as a transmission medium, although strictly speaking it is line-of-sight broadcast technology in which radio signals are sent out into the air. With transmission speeds of 56 thousand bits per second (bps) to 50 million bps, microwave is widely used for long distance telephone communication and for corporate voice and data networks.

Middle-out approach: A way to develop the IS plan through the use of prototypical systems solutions to suspected problems of the organization.

Minicomputers: The next category of computers above microcomputers in terms of cost ($10,000 to $750,000) and power (1 to 50 MIPS), generally used for departmental computing, specific applications such as CAD or office automation, and midsized business general processing. Minicomputers overlap in price and power with workstations, but tend to have less power for the same price.

Minisupercomputers: Small supercomputers; the newest and most innovative category of computers, ranging in cost from $500,000 to $5,000,000 and power from 200 to 4000 MIPS; used for numerically-intensive scientific computing.

MIPS: An acronym for *millions* of *instructions per second* executed by the control unit of a computer, a commonly used maximum speed rating for computers.

Modem: An abbreviation for *modulator/demodulator*, a device that converts data from digital form to analog form so that it can be sent over the analog telephone network (as well as reconverts data from analog to digital form after it has been transmitted).

Module: A self-contained unit of software that performs one or more functions. Ideally it has well-defined interfaces with the other modules in the program so that changes in a module only affect the rest of the program through the outputs from that module. *See also* Subsystem, Functional cohesion.

MRP: *See* Manufacturing resources planning, material requirements planning.

Multimedia: The use of a microcomputer system to coordinate many types of communication media—text, graphics, sound, still images, animations, and video. The purpose of a multimedia system is to enhance the quality of and interest in a presentation, whether it is a corporate briefing or a school lesson.

Multiprocessing: The method of processing when two or more CPUs are installed as part of the same computer system. Each CPU works on its own job or set of jobs (often using multiprogramming), with all the CPUs under control of a single operating system.

Multiprocessor: A computer configuration in which multiple processors (CPUs) are installed as part of the same computer system, with each processor or CPU operating independently of the others. *See* Multiprocessing.

Multiprogramming: A procedure by which the operating system switches back and forth among a number of programs, all located in memory at the same time, to keep the CPU busy while input/output operations are taking place.

Natural language: A computer language (often termed a fifth-generation language) in which the user writes his program in ordinary English (or something very close to it). Little or no training is required to use a natural language.

Needs-based IS planning: The process of assembling the IS plan by addressing only the stated needs of users.

Network protocol: An agreed-upon set of rules or conventions governing communication among elements of a network, or, more specifically, among layers or levels of a network.

Networking: The electronic linking of geographically dispersed devices.

Neural networks: The branch of articificial intelligence concerned with recognizing patterns from vast amounts of data by a process of adaptive learning; named after the study of how the human nervous system works, but in fact uses extensive statistical analysis to identify meaningful patterns from the data.

Nonprocedural language: *See* Fourth-generation language.

Object-oriented programming (OOP): A type of computer programming based on the creation and use of a set of objects (each object is a chunk of program code) and the development of relationships among the objects. The most popular OOP languages are C++ and Smalltalk.

Object-oriented technology: A broader term than object-oriented programming that includes object-oriented analysis and design as well as programming.

Object program: The machine language program that is the result of translating a second-, third-, or fourth-generation source program.

OCR: *See* Optical character recognition.

Office automation: The use of information technology to automate various aspects of office operations. Office automation involves a set of office-related functions, which may or may not be integrated in a single system, including electronic mail, word processing, photocopying, document preparation, voice mail, desktop publishing, personal databases, and electronic calendaring.

On-line processing: A mode of transaction processing in which each transaction is entered directly into the computer when it occurs and the associated processing is carried out immediately. For example, sales would be entered into the computer (probably via a terminal) as soon as they occurred, and sales records would be updated immediately.

On-line system: *See* On-line processing.

Open systems: Systems (usually operating systems) that are not tied to a particular computer system or hardware manufacturer. An example is the UNIX operating system, with versions available for a wide variety of hardware platforms.

Open Systems Interconnection (OSI) Reference Model: An evolving set of network protocols, developed by the International Standards Organization (ISO), which deals with connecting all systems that are open for communication with other systems (i.e., systems that conform to certain minimal standards) by defining seven layers, each of which will have one or more protocols.

Operating system: A very complex program (software) that controls the operation of the computer hardware and coordinates all the other software. The purpose of an operating system is to get as much work done as possible with the available resources, and to be convenient to use.

Optical character recognition (OCR): A computer input method that directly scans typed, printed, or hand-printed material. A computer input device called an optical character reader scans and recognizes the characters and then transmits the data to the memory or records them on magnetic tape.

Optical disk: A relatively new medium upon which computer files can be stored. Data are recorded on an optical disk by using a laser to burn microscopic pits on its surface. Optical disks have a much greater capacity than magnetic disks but are typically much slower.

Organizational design: Design of an organization, including such aspects as organization structure, job content, communication patterns, and reward systems.

Organizational system: A system that serves the organization rather than just an individual.

OSI: *See* Open Systems Interconnection Reference Model.

Outsourcing: The elimination of part of the internal IS organization by hiring an outside organization to perform these functions. Outsourcing has most often involved the operation of data centers, but may include applications system design or programming, and data communications network management. Outsourcing is done to achieve economies of scale by combining the functions of several organizations into one highly-qualified professional staff.

Packet switching: A method of operating a digital telecommunications network (especially a value added network) in which information is divided into packets of some fixed length that are then sent over the network separately. Rather than tying up an entire end-to-end circuit for the duration of the session, the packets from various users can be interspersed with one another to permit more efficient use of the network.

Parallel processor (PP): A multiprocessor configuration (multiple CPUs installed as part of the same computer system) designed to give a separate piece of the same program to each of the processors so that work on the program can proceed in parallel on the separate pieces.

Partnership: A coordinating strategy for IS management. Partnership creates strong working relationships between IS personnel and peer managers in business functions, and often results in more effective information systems and IS management.

PBX network: The type of network emanating from a *private branch exchange*, or PBX, which is a digital switch operated by a built-in computer with the capability of simultaneously handling communications with internal analog telephones, digital microcomputers and terminals, mainframe computers, and the external telephone network; usually arranged in a star or a tree topology.

Personal system: A system that serves the needs of an individual rather than the organization. For example, a system that enables a salesman to maintain information on his customer contacts would be a personal system as long as it does not report this information to anyone else.

Physical system: A depiction which shows the physical form (the how) in which a system operates. *See also* Logical system.

Political perspective: The view that decisions in organizations are influenced by political considerations rather than always being entirely rational. It holds that the interests of the decision-makers, rather than just what is best for the organization, influence the outcomes of decisions. *See also* Rational perspective.

Problem management: A function within the data center that accepts reports of problems from users and technical personnel, identifies the cause of the problem, identifies the person or unit that can resolve the problem, and follows up to verify that the problem has been resolved. It also attempts to identify and upgrade problem systems and components to reduce the level of problems.

Procedural language: *See* Third-generation language.

Process-oriented approach: An approach to systems development that concentrates on the flow, use, and transformation of information. *See also* Data-oriented approach.

Processor: *See* Central processing unit.

Productivity language: Another name for a fourth-generation language. This type of language tends to make the programmer or user more productive, which explains the name.

Program: A complete listing of what the computer is to do for a particular application, expressed in a form that the control unit of the computer has been built to understand or that can be translated into such a form. A program is made up of a sequence of individual steps or operations called instructions.

Project-oriented IS planning: An approach to building the IS plan that assembles the IS plan from individual projects.

Proprietary systems: Systems (usually operating systems) that were written expressly for a particular computer system. Examples are PC-DOS and MS-DOS, which are the same operating system written by Microsoft for IBM microcomputers and IBM compatibles, respectively; MVS and VM, which are the two alternative large machine operating systems offered by IBM; and VMS, which is the operating system offered by Digital Equipment Corporation for its VAX computers.

Prototyping: An approach to systems development in which an initial version of the system is built very quickly using fourth-generation tools, then it is tried out by users to determine how it is

inadequate, an improved version is built, and this process of trial and improvement is continued until the result is satisfactory. *See also* Rapid application development.

Query-by-example (QBE): A specific kind of relational DBMS programming language in which examples of the desired output are entered onto table templates on the terminal screen. This "what you see is what you get" approach makes it very easy for novice users to query a database.

Query language: Fourth-generation software that allows one to produce reports without writing procedural programs by specifying their contents and format.

Queueing system: A system in which one or more servers provide service to customers who may have to wait in a queue for a server who is busy with another customer. The customers may be people waiting for service at a check-out counter, but they may also be other entities such as messages, raw materials or work-in-process in a factory, or programs in computer memory.

Rapid application development (RAD): A development methodology based upon a combination of prototyping and the information engineering methodology. It is based on the use of I-CASE tools and reusable code to quickly prototype the system and the enterprise modeling aspects of information engineering. *See also* Prototyping.

Rational perspective: A traditional view of how organizations function, with decision-making based upon maximizing organizational objectives using rational analysis. *See also* Political perspective.

Reengineering: *See* Software reengineering.

Relational DBMS: A particular style of database management system (DBMS) that views each data entity as a simple table, with the columns as data elements and the rows as different instances of the entity. Relational DBMSs are the most popular type of DBMS today, especially for data analysis and presentation systems.

Request for proposal (RFP): A document that is sent to potential vendors inviting them to submit a proposal to furnish a system. It describes the objectives and requirements of the desired system and the environment in which it must operate, specifies what the vendor must provide as input to the selection process, and explains the conditions for submitting proposals and the general criteria that will be used to evaluate them.

Response time: The elapsed time between when a user presses a key to send data to a computer and when the response from the computer appears on the terminal screen.

Reverse engineering: A term used to describe the generation of program specifications by starting with the existing source program code.

RFP: *See* Request for proposal.

Rightsizing: A strategy used to fit the type of computer technology to diverse needs within an organization. Rightsizing typically involves use of a combination of mainframes, intelligent workstations, and client/server software that blends aspects of centralized and decentralized computing.

Ring topology: A network topology in which a single length of cable—with the ends of the cable connected to form a ring—is shared by all network devices.

Ripple effect: When a change in one part of a program or system causes problems in another part of it. Then changes necessary to correct that problem may cause problems somewhere else, and so on.

SAA: *See* Systems Application Architecture.

Satellite communications: A variation of microwave transmission in which a communications satellite is used to relay microwave signals over long distances.

SDLC: *See* System development life cycle.

Sequential access file: A basic type of computer file in which all of the records that make up the file are stored in sequence according to the control key of the file (e.g., a payroll file will contain individual employee records stored in sequence according to the employee identification number); usually stored on magnetic tape. Computer files, also called secondary memory or secondary storage, are added to a computer system

to keep vast quantities of data accessible within the computer system at more reasonable costs than main memory.

Sequential file organization: *See* Sequential access file.

Service level agreement: An agreement between IS and a client that specifies a set of services to be provided, the amount of those services to be provided, the quality or these services and how it is to be measured, and the price to be charged for these services.

Shop floor control (SFC): A computer-based system which releases orders to the shop floor based on the detailed production schedule and the actual production accomplished thus far; usually a component of a manufacturing resources planning (MRP II) system.

Simplex transmission: A type of data transmission in which data can travel only in one direction over the communication line. Simplex transmission might be used from a monitoring device at a remote site back to a central computer.

SIS: *See* Strategic information system.

SNA: *See* Systems Network Architecture.

Sociotechnical approach: A system development methodology that uses a group of managers, workers, and facilitators trained in this approach to define a new system that attempts to simultaneously improve the performance of the organization and the quality of working life of the workers.

Software: The set of programs (made up of instructions) that control the operations of the computer system.

Software package: Software that is "packaged" to be self-contained so that it may be distributed widely. In addition to the computer programs, a package may include comprehensive documentation of the system, assistance in installing the system, training, a hot-line consulting service for dealing with problems, and even maintenance of the system.

Software reengineering: Upgrading an existing system to improve its functionality and changeability by evaluating the structure and components of the system to create a new structure if necessary, continuing to use those components that are satisfactory, rehabilitating those components that can be modified to be satisfactory, replacing those components that cannot be rehabilitated, and adding components that are needed to enhance the functionality of the system.

Source program: A program written in a second-, third-, or higher generation language.

Spaghetti code: Programs with complex logic, where the flow of control may take many intertwined paths through the various parts of the program. Logically, it resembles a plate of spaghetti where the many strands are tangled in a confusing jumble. The opposite of structured code.

Specific DSS: *See* Decision support system.

Sponsoring manager: The manager who is the responsible party in the development or acquisition of a new system. Responsibilities include acquiring the necessary resources, managing user aspects of the project, making sure requirements are properly defined, managing implementation in the user organization, obtaining the promised benefits of the system, and championing the system.

SQL: A standard query and data definition language for relational DBMSs. This standard, endorsed by the American National Standards Institute (ANSI), is used in many personal computer, minicomputer, and mainframe computer DBMSs.

Stages of growth: A framework for viewing the management of technology that assumes that organizations go through an organizational learning curve that can be described in terms of stages such as initiation, contagion, control, and maturity.

Star topology: A network topology that has some primary device at its center with cables radiating from the primary device to all the other network devices.

Steering committee: *See* IS steering committee.

Stored-program concept: The concept of preparing a precise list of exactly what the computer is to do (this list is called a program), loading or storing this program in the memory of the computer, and then letting the control unit carry out

the program at electronic speed. The listing or program must be in a form that the control unit of the computer has been built to understand.

Strategic information system (SIS): The use of information, information processing, and/or communications for implementing business strategy. A SIS often includes the use of an organization's computer systems by its customers or suppliers. Further, a system is strategic if it changes an organization's product or service or the way it competes in its industry.

Strategic thrusts: An approach used to identify strategic uses of information technology.

Structure chart: A tree-structured diagram that shows the logic (flow of information and control) within one computer program.

Structured design: *See* Structured programming.

Structured development: A top-down development approach based upon the use of hierarchical decomposition in analysis, design, programming, construction, and testing of a new system.

Structured programming: A technique of writing programs so that each program is divided into modules or blocks, where each block has only one entry point and one exit point. In this form, the program logic is easy to follow and understand, and thus the maintenance and correction of such a program should be easier than for a nonstructured program.

Subsystem: A component of a system that is itself viewed as a set of interrelated components. A subsystem has a well defined purpose which must contribute to the purpose of the system as a whole. *See also* Module, Hierarchical decomposition.

Supercomputers: The most expensive and most powerful category of computers, ranging in cost from $5,000,000 to $30,000,000 and power from 400 to 10,000 MIPS; used for numerically-intensive computing.

Superminicomputers: Large minicomputers; the upper end of the minicomputer category, generally used for departmental computing in large departments, midsized business general processing, and by universities.

Support software: Programs that do not directly produce output needed by users, but instead support other applications software in producing the needed output. Support software provides a computing environment in which it is relatively easy and efficient for humans to work, enables applications programs written in a variety of languages to be carried out, and ensures that computer hardware and software resources are used efficiently. Support software includes operating systems, language compilers, and sort utilities.

SWOT analysis: Part of IS planning, referring to strengths, weaknesses, opportunities, and threats.

System: A set of interrelated components that work together to achieve some common purpose.

System development life cycle (SDLC): The traditional methodology used by the IS department to build a system—define and test the feasibility of the requirements; design, build, and test the system; and finally install, operate, maintain, and dispose of it. The SDLC methodology defines the activities necessary to build a system, and therefore allows one to plan and manage a development project.

System flow chart: A diagram which shows the relationship between major system components, not detailed logic.

System release: An identified version of a software system. Maintenance changes to the current release (say 4.2) are batched to produce version 4.3 that is released to replace the previous version.

Systems analysis and design (SA&D): The process followed to develop a system. *See also* System development life cycle.

Systems Application Architecture (SAA): An evolving set of specifications, under development by IBM, defining programming, communications, and a common end-user interface that will allow applications to be created and moved among the full range of IBM computers. IBM has stated its intention of supporting both SNA and OSI protocols in its future efforts under the SAA umbrella.

Systems development portfolio: The mix of IS development projects arrayed by risk and return.

Systems integrator: A firm that will take overall responsibility for managing the development or integration of large, complex systems involving the use of components from a number of different vendors.

Systems Network Architecture (SNA): A set of network protocols created by IBM to allow its customers to construct their own private networks using the wide variety of IBM communication products, teleprocessing access methods, and data link protocols. SNA was first created in 1974 and is still in widespread use.

Systems software: *See* Support software.

T-1 lines: The most common leased communication lines, operating at a data transmission rate of 1.544 million bits per second. These lines, which may be leased from AT&T or another long distance carrier, often provide the basis for a wide area network (WAN).

TCP/IP: *See* Transmission Control Protocol/Internet Protocol.

Telecommunications: Communications at a distance, including voice (telephone) and data (text/image) communications. Other similar terms used almost interchangeably with telecommunications include data communications, datacom, teleprocessing, telecom, and networking.

Telemarketing: The use of the telephone, customer databases, direct mail, and data processing to market and support a product or service. Telemarketing is used by many organizations as a strategic information system.

Terminal: A computer input/output device, usually incorporating a keyboard for input and a video display unit for output; does not incorporate a processor (CPU) and thus operates as a "slave" to a "master" computer, usually a minicomputer or a mainframe.

Text data management system (TDMS): A type of database management system for storing and retrieving textual data in reports, memos, correspondence, agendas, and other documents.

Third-generation language: A programming language in which the programmer expresses a step-by-step procedure devised to accomplish the desired task. Examples include FORTRAN, COBOL, BASIC, PASCAL, and C.

Time-sharing: A procedure by which the operating system switches among a number of programs, all stored in memory at the same time, giving each program a small slice of CPU time before moving on to the next program.

Token bus: A design standard for a local area network based on a bus topology and the passing of a token around the bus to all devices in a specified order. In this design, a given device can only transmit when it has the token and thus collisions can never occur. The token bus design is central to the Manufacturing Automation Protocol, or MAP.

Token ring: A design standard for a local area network based on a ring topology and the passing of a token around the ring to all devices in a specified order. In this design, a given device can only transmit when it has the token and thus collisions can never occur.

Top-down approach: A way to develop the IS plan by identifying those areas that senior management believes would be most helpful to the organization for the application of information technology. *See also* Bottom-up approach.

Transaction processing system: A very common type of computer application in which transactions (of a particular type) are processed in order to provide desired output. Examples include the processing of employee work records (transactions) to produce payroll checks and accompanying reports and the processing of orders (transactions) to produce invoices and associated reports. Transaction processing systems may be batch, on-line, or in-line.

Transborder data flow: Electronic movement of data across a country's national boundary. Such data flows may be restricted by laws that protect a country's economic, political, or personal privacy interests.

Transmission Control Protocol/Internet Protocol (TCP/IP): A popular network protocol used in the Berkeley version of the UNIX operating system and several value-added networks, including NSFNET and ARPANET. Although not part of the OSI model, TCP/IP corresponds

roughly to the network and transport layers of the seven-layer model.

Tree topology: A network topology that has some primary device at the top of the tree, with cables radiating from this primary device to devices further down the tree that, in turn, may have cables radiating from them to other devices still further down the tree, and so on; also called an hierarchical topology.

Twisted pair: The most common transmission medium, with two insulated copper wires (about 1 millimeter thick) twisted together in a long helix. Data transmission speeds of 300 to 14,400 bits per second (bps) are possible with twisted pairs on the voice telephone network, with higher speeds of 56,000 to 144,000 bps attainable on conditioned lines or 4 million bps to 16 million bps on local area networks.

Upper-case: The front-end CASE tools that support the project management, requirements definition, and design activities of systems development. Upper-case does not include tools for automation of the system construction activities. *See also* Computer-aided software engineering, Lower-case, Integrated-case.

User application development: Development of applications systems by people who are not IS professionals, but rather are primarily in traditional business roles such as managers, accountants, financial analysts, production schedulers, engineers, brand managers, and so forth.

User interface: That part of a system through which the user interacts with the system. As examples, it may use a mouse, a touch-screen, menus, commands, voice recognition, a telephone keypad, output screens, voice response, and printed reports. *See also* Graphical user interface.

Value-added network (VAN): A data-only, private, nonregulated telecommunications network that uses packet switching. An organization may choose to buy the services of a VAN to implement its wide area network (WAN).

Value chain analysis: A method, developed by

Porter, to identify possible strategic uses of information technology.

Value of information: The net benefits obtained in a decision situation (total benefits minus total costs) when a particular piece of information is known, less the net benefits that would have been obtained in the same decision situation without the information.

Values architecture: That part of an IT architecture that specified the basic beliefs of the people about IT in the organization.

VAN: *See* Value-added network.

Vector facility: A specialized multiprocessor configuration (multiple CPUs installed as part of the same computer system) to handle calculations involving vectors. The same operation is performed simultaneously on each element of the vector by parallel microprocessors. A vector facility can be attached to a mainframe or super-minicomputer to handle numeric- or compute-intensive parts of programs.

Vertically integrated information system: An information system that serves more than one vertical level in an organization or an industry, such as a system designed to be used by an automobile manufacturer and the associated independent dealers.

View integration: A bottom-up approach to detailing the data requirements of an organization. View integration analyzes each report, screen, form, and document in the organization and combines each of these views into one consolidated and consistent picture of all organizational data.

Virtual memory: A procedure by which the operating system switches portions of programs (called pages) between main memory and DASD so that portions of enough programs are stored in main memory to enable efficient multiprogramming. To the user, it appears as though he has an unlimited amount of main memory available, while in fact most of each program is stored in DASD.

Virtual reality: The use of computer-based systems to create an environment that seems real to one or more more senses (usually including sight) of the human user or users. Examples of practical

uses of virtual reality include tank crew training for the U.S. Army, the design of an automobile dashboard and controls, and retail store layout.

Virus: *See* Computer virus.

Voice response unit: A computer output method using the spoken voice to provide a response to the user. This output method is gaining increasing acceptance as a provider of limited, tightly programmed computer output, often in conjunction with touch-tone telephone input.

WAN: *See* Wide area network.

WATS: *See* Wide Area Telephone Service.

Wide area network (WAN): A type of network over which both voice and data for a single organization are communicated among the multiple locations (often far apart) where the organization operates, usually employing point-to-point transmission over facilities owned by several organizations, including the public telephone network; also called a long-haul network.

Wide Area Telephone Service (WATS): A service available from the telephone company in which an organization pays a monthly fee for (typically) unlimited long distance telephone service, using the ordinary voice circuits. WATS is an easy way to set up a wide area network (WAN), and it costs less per hour than standard Direct Distance Dialing (DDD).

Wireless: Considered as a transmission medium, although strictly speaking it is broadcast technology in which radio signals are sent out into the air. Wireless transmission speeds vary from 2 million bits per second (bps) to 50 million bps. Four examples are: cordless telephone, cellular telephone, wireless LAN, and microwave.

Wireless LAN: A local area network employing wireless communication between the various devices in the network. Compared to a wired LAN, a wireless LAN is easier to plan and install, generally more expensive, less secure, and usually slower with transmission speeds from 2 million bits per second (bps) to 4 million bps for a radio signal LAN.

Word: A memory cell that can store two or more characters of data (see memory); alternatively, the amount of data handled by the central processing unit (CPU) as a single unit.

Workstations: General meaning: any computer-related device at which an individual may work, such as a personal computer or a terminal. Specific meaning: the category of computers based on powerful microprocessor chips, with costs from $5,000 to $100,000 and power ranging from 20 to 400 MIPS; generally used as the server in client/server applications, the server for a local area network, or for specific applications such as computer-aided design or graphics.

X.25 protocol: A network protocol, formally adopted as part of the OSI model, employed to handle the packet switching in many value added networks (VANs). X.25 encompasses the physical, data link, and network layers of the seven-layer OSI model.

Glossary

Action Language   User's action (e.g., input data, query, etc.) in communication.

Active DSS   A special type of intelligent DSS that can respond to changes and is viewed as proactive rather than reactive.

AI Workstations   *See* LISP Machines.

Algorithm   A step-by-step search, where improvement is made in every step until the best solution is found.

Analogical Reasoning   Determining the outcome of a problem by the use of analogies. A procedure for drawing conclusions about a problem by using past experience.

Artificial Intelligence (AI)   The subfield of computer science that is concerned with symbolic reasoning and problem solving.

Artificial Neural Network (ANN)   An experimental computer technology that attempts to build computers that will operate like a human brain. The machines possess simultaneous memory storage and work with ambiguous information. (*See* Neural Computing Networks.)

Assembly Language   Computer language that replaces the binary digits of machine language with abbreviations to indicate processing operations.

Asynchronous Communication   Communication between parties that takes place at different times. That is, the message is sent at one time and the reply is provided later.

Axon   Outgoing terminal from a biological neuron.

Backpropagation   The best-known learning algorithm in neural computing. Learning is done by comparing inputs to desired outputs of historical cases.

Backtracking   A technique used in tree searches. The process of working backward from a failed objective or an incorrect result to examine unexplored alternatives.

758

Backward Chaining A search technique used in production ("IF-THEN" rule) systems that begins with the action clause of a rule and works "backward" through a chain of rules in an attempt to find a verifiable set of condition clauses.

Belief Function Representation of uncertainty without the need to specify exact probabilities.

Blind Search A search approach that makes use of no knowledge or heuristics to help speed up the search process. A time-consuming and arbitrary search process that attempts to exhaust all possibilities.

Brainstorming (Electronic) Methodology of idea generation by association. This group process uses analogy and synergy. In this text, it is computer supported.

Breadth-first Search A search technique that evaluates every item at a given level of the search space before proceeding to the next level.

Business Intelligence An information system that allows users to view data in databases and interpret them easily and quickly. It is usually related to an EIS.

Business Processes Reengineering A methodology for introducing a fundamental change in specific business processes. It is usually supported by an information system.

Case-based Reasoning Methodology in which knowledge and/or inferences are derived from historical cases.

Certainty Factor A percentage supplied by an expert system that indicates the probability that the conclusion reached by the system is correct. Also, the degree of belief of the expert that a certain conclusion will occur if a certain premise is true.

Chunk of Information A collection of facts stored and retrieved as a single unit. The limitations of working memory are usually defined in terms of the number of chunks that can be handled simultaneously.

Class Term used in object-oriented programming to designate a group of items with the same characteristics. (For example, the car Mustang is in a class of transportation.)

Classification Model (for ES) A model used in building expert systems that uses production rules and covers a highly bounded problem with few known possible solutions.

Client/Server Architecture A network system where several PCs (clients) share the memory and other capabilities of a larger computer or that of printers, databases, etc. (the servers).

Cognitive Style (Cognition) The subjective process through which individuals organize and change information during the decision-making process.

Combinatorial Explosion Problem in which adding one variable, or even one value to a variable, increases the size of the problem exponentially, resulting in an astronomical number of potential solutions to the problem.

Complete DSS A strategy for constructing a full-service DSS generator and an organization to manage it. Contrasted with a quick-hit strategy.

Complete Enumeration Process of checking *every* feasible solution to a problem.

Computer-aided Instruction In general, the use of the computer as a teaching tool. Synonymous with Computer-based Instruction, Computer-assisted Learning, and Computer-based Training.

Computer Graphics The presentation of data in the form of bar charts, histograms, pie charts, or grids on a display screen or plotter to highlight data variations. Graphics are available in black and white or in color and can be presented in two or three dimensions.

Conflict Resolution (of Rules) Selecting a procedure from a conflicting set of applicable competing procedures or rules.

Consultation Environment The part of the expert system that is used by the nonexpert to obtain expert knowledge and advice. It includes the workplace, inference engine, explanation facility, the recommended action, and the user interface.

Controllable Variables Decision variables such as quantity to produce, amounts of resources to be allocated, etc. that can be changed and manipulated by the decision maker.

Cooperative Processing Sharing of computing work among several CPUs, usually a mainframe and PCs.

Cottage Industry Factory employees who are doing the work in their homes. The modern version of the cottage industry is telecommuting.

Critical Success Factors (CSF) A methodology developed at MIT for identifying the factors that are most critical to the success of an organization.

Crossover Combination of parts from two superior solutions in a genetic algorithm in an attempt to produce even better solutions.

Data Access Ability to easily access data regardless of where it is stored and how it is organized in the storage area.

Database The organizing of files into related units that are then viewed as a single storage concept. The data are then made available to a wide range of users.

Database Management System (DBMS) The software to establish, update, or query a database.

Data Dipping Accessing different databases from the user's PC to retrive desirable data.

Decision Room An arrangement for a group DSS in which terminals are available to some or all participants. The objective is to enhance the decision-making process (e.g., by tabulating secret ballots).

Decision Styles The manner in which decision makers think and react to problems. It includes their perceptions, cognitive responses, values, and beliefs.

Decision Support Systems (DSS) Computer-based information systems that combine models and data in an attempt to solve nonstructured problems with extensive user involvement.

Decision Table Table that is used to represent knowledge and prepare it for analysis.

Decision Tree A graphical presentation of a sequence of interrelated decisions to be made under assumed risk.

Declarative Knowledge Representation Representation of facts and assertions.

Deductive Reasoning In logic, reasoning from the general to the specific. Conclusions follow premises. Consequent reasoning.

Deep Representation Model that captures all the forms of knowledge used by experts in their reasoning.

Default Value A value given to a symbol or variable automatically if no other value is defined by the programmer or user.

Delphi A qualitative forecasting methodology using anonymous questionnaires. Effective for technological forecasting and forecasting involving sensitive issues.

Demon A procedure that is automatically activated if a specific, predefined state is recognized.

Dependent Variables Systems' measure of effectiveness.

Depth-first Search A search procedure that explores each branch of a search tree to its full vertical length. Each branch is searched for a solution and if none is found, a new vertical branch is searched to its depth, and so on.

Descriptive Models Models that describe things as they are.

Deterministic Models Models that are constructed under assumed certainty, namely, there is only one possible (and known) result to each alternative course of action.

Development Environment That part of the expert system that is used by the builder. It includes the knowledge base, the inference engine, knowledge acquisition, and improving reasoning capability. The knowledge engineer and the expert are considered a part of this environment.

Dialog Generation and Management System (DGMS) A software management package in a DSS whose functions in the dialog subsystem are similar to that of a DBMS in a database.

Dialog Style The combination of the action languages, the display language, and knowledge base that determines input and provides output. Examples of styles include menu-driven and command language.

Dialog System The hardware and software that provide the user interface for DSS. It also includes the ease-of-use, accessibility, and human-machine interface.

Disbelief Degree of belief that something is *not* going to happen.

Distributed AI Splitting of a problem to multiple cooperating systems for deriving a solution.

Distributed DSS A DSS system accessible to people at various locations. The databases are in different locations as well.

Distributed GSS A computerized support for people who are located in different places but work as a group on the same task.

Drill Down The ability to investigate information in details. For example, find not only total sales, but also sales by region, by product, or by salesperson.

DSS Generator   Computer software that provides a set of capabilities to quickly build a specific DSS.

DSS Tools   Software elements (such as languages) that facilitate the development of a DSS, or a DSS generator.

Dynamic Models   Models whose input data are being changed over time; for example, a five-year profit (loss) projection.

Effectiveness   The degree of goal attainment. Doing the right things.

Efficiency   Ratio of output to input. Appropriate use of resources.

Electronic Bulletin Boards   Public electronic mail message centers where authorized people can leave messages for everyone to read.

Electronic Data Interchange (EDI)   A computer-to-computer direct communication of standard transactions, such as placing orders, between two or more organizations.

Embedded Systems   Inclusion of one system inside another one. No distinction among the composing parts is visible.

EMYCIN   Nonspecific part (called shell) of MYCIN consisting of what is left when the knowledge is removed. EMYCIN becomes a new problem solver by adding the knowledge (using rules) for a different problem domain.

Encapsulation   Coupling of data and procedures in object-oriented programming.

End-user Computing   Development of one's own information system by a computer user.

English-like Language   A computer language that is very similar to the everyday, ordinary English.

Enterprise Computing   An organization-wide system that enables people to communicate with each other and to access data throughout the enterprise.

Enumeration (Complete)   A listing of *all* possible solutions and the comparison of their results in order to find the best solution.

Evolutionary (Iterative) Process   A systematic process for system development that is used in DSS. A portion of the system is quickly constructed, then tested, improved, and enlarged in steps. Similar to prototyping.

Exception Reporting   Reports that call attention to deviation larger than an agreed upon threshold (e.g. 10 percent, or $200,000).

Executive Information Systems (EIS)   Computerized systems that are specifically designed to support executive work.

Executive Support System   An executive information system that includes some analytical and communication capabilities.

Expert Support System   Expert system whose primary mission is to support problem solving and decision making.

Expert System (ES)   Computer system that applies reasoning methodologies on knowledge in a specific domain in order to render advice or recommendations, much like a human expert. A computer system that achieves a high level of performance in task areas that, for human beings, require years of special education and training.

Expertise   The set of capabilities that underlines the performance of human experts, including extensive domain knowledge, heuristic rules that simplify and improve approaches to problem-solving, metaknowledge and metacognition, and compiled forms of behavior that afford great economy in skilled performance.

Explanation Facility   The component of an expert system that can explain the system's reasoning and justify its conclusions.

Extraction   To capture data from several sources, synthesize them, summarize, find the relevant data, and organize them.

Facet   An attribute or a feature that describes the content of a slot in a frame.

Factory of the Future   Highly automated factory that is managed and controlled by intelligent computers.

Fault-tolerance   A computing system that continues to operate satisfactorily in the presence of faults.

Feasibility Study   A preliminary investigation to develop plans for construction of a new information system. The major aspects of the study are cost/benefit, technological, human, organizational, and financial.

Federal Privacy Act   Federal legislation (1974) that prohibits governmental agencies from providing information about individuals without the consent of the individuals.

Fifth-generation Languages   Artificial Intelligence languages such as LISP and PROLOG and their variants.

Fifth-generation Project   The research project in which the Japanese are investigating parallel processing and other advanced computing techniques in an attempt to develop a "fifth generation" of computer systems, which will be both efficient and intelligent.

Firing a Rule   Obtaining information on either the IF or THEN part of a rule, which makes this rule an assertion (true or false).

Flexibility in DSS   System ability to react to changes in the environment, tasks, or users of the DSS. It is the ability to modify, adapt, solve problems, and evolve.

Form Interaction   Input data into designated spaces (fields) in forms displayed on the CRT.

Forward Chaining   Data-driven search in a rule-based system.

Fourth-generation Languages (4GLs)   Nonprocedural, user-oriented languages that enable quick programming by specifying only the desired results.

Frames   A knowledge representation scheme that associates one or more features with an object in terms of various slots and particular slot values.

Front-end Systems   Software systems (sometimes with hardware) that are used to simplify the accessibility to other computerized systems (e.g., to a database).

Fuzzy Logic   Ways of reasoning that can cope with uncertain or partial information; characteristic of human thinking and many expert systems.

General-purpose Problem Solver   A procedure developed by Newell and Simon in an attempt to create an intelligent computer. Although unsuccessful, the concept itself made a valuable contribution to the AI field.

Genetic Algorithm   Software program that learns from experience in a similar (simplified) manner to the way in which biological systems learn.

Geographical Information System   An information system that uses spatial data such as digitized maps. A combination of text, graphics, icons, and symbols on maps.

Goal-seeking   The capability of asking the computer what values certain variables must have in order to attain desired goals.

Graphical User Interface (GUI)   An interactive user-friendly interface, in which by using icons and similar devices the user can control the communication with the computer.

Group DSS   An interactive, computer-based system that facilitates solution of unstructured problems by a set of decision makers working together as a group.

Group Support Systems (GSS)   Information systems that support the works of groups (communication, decision making).

Groupware   Several computerized technologies and methods that aim to support the work of people working in groups.

Hardware   The physical equipment of a computer system, including processor, memory, input/output devices, and other components.

Heuristics   Informal, judgmental knowledge of an application area that constitutes the "rules of good judgement" in the field. Heuristics also encompass the knowledge of how to solve problems efficiently and effectively, how to plan steps in solving a complex problem, how to improve performance, and so forth.

Hidden Layer   Middle layer of an artificial neural network with three or more layers.

Hidden Unemployment   Refers to cases in which people are considered employed but are working only part of the time. Thus, the same amount of work can be executed by fewer employees.

Highlight Charts   Summary displays that show only important information based on the user's own judgment.

Human-Machine Interface   *See* User Interface.

Hybrid Environment   A software package for expediting the construction of expert systems that includes several knowledge representation schemes.

Hypermedia   Combination of several types of media such as text, graphics, audio, and video, using the concept of links by association.

Hypertext   An approach for handling text and other information by allowing the user to jump from a given topic, whenever he or she wishes, to related topics. The jumps are supported by associations.

Icon   A visual, graphic representation of an object, word, or concept.

Iconic Model   A physical, scaled replica.

Idea Generation   A process of generating ideas by people, usually supported by some software. For example, developing alternative solutions to a problem.

IF-THEN   A conditional rule in which a certain action is taken only if some condition is satisfied.

Implementation   The introduction of a change; putting things to work.

Independent Variables   Variables in a model that are controlled by the decision maker and/or by the environment and that determine the result of a decision (also called Input Variables).

Inductive Reasoning   In logic, reasoning from the specific to the general. Conditional or antecedent reasoning.

Inexact (Approximate) Reasoning   Used when the expert system must make decisions based on partial or incomplete information.

Inference   The process of drawing a conclusion from given evidence. To reach a decision by reasoning.

Inference Engine   That part of an expert system that actually performs the reasoning function.

Inference Tree   A schematic view of the inference process that shows the order in which rules are being tested.

Influence Diagram   A diagram that shows the various types of variables (decision, independent, result) in a problem and how they are related to each other.

Information Center   Facility with end-user tools that is staffed by end-user oriented specialists who first train and then support business users.

Information Overload   Large amounts of information; too heavy a load.

Inheritance   The process by which one object takes on or is assigned the characteristics of another object higher up in a hierarchy.

Inputs   The resources introduced into a system for transformation into outputs.

Instantiation   The process of assigning (or substituting) a specific value or name to a variable in a frame (or in a logic expression) making it a particular "instance" of that variable.

Institutionalization   The process through which an MSS system becomes incorporated as an ongoing part of organizational procedures.

Institutionalized MSS   One that is a permanent fixture in the organization with continuing financial support. It deals with decisions of a recurring nature.

Integrated Circuits   Circuits composed of many tiny transistors that have been placed together in a single physical element, typically into a silicon chip.

Integrated Computer Systems   Software packages that perform several different functions. For example Lotus 1-2-3 provides modeling capability, database management, and graphics.

Intelligent Agent   Expert or knowledge-based system that is embedded in computer-based information systems (or their components) to make them smarter.

Intelligent Computer-aided Instruction (ICAI)   Using AI techniques for training or teaching with a computer.

Intelligent DSS   A DSS that includes one or more components of expert systems or other AI technologies. This component makes the DSS behave in a better (more "intelligent") manner.

Interactive Visual Decision Making (IVDM)   Graphic animation in which systems and processes are presented dynamically to the decision maker. It enables visualization of the results of different potential actions.

Interactive Visual Simulation   A special case of IVDM in which a simulation approach is used in the decision-making process.

Interdependent Decisions   A series of interrelated decisions. Sequential decisions are usually interdependent.

Interface   The portion of a computer system that interacts with the user, accepting commands from the computer keyboard and displaying the results generated by other portions of the computer system.

Intermediary   A person who uses the computer to fulfill requests made by other people. Example: a financial analyst uses the computer to answer questions for top management.

Iterative Process   *See* Evolutionary Process; Prototyping.

Justification Facility   *See* Explanation Facility. Also called justifier.

Key Performance Indicators (KPI)   Specific measures of the critical success factors in an Executive Information System.

Knowledge   Understanding, awareness, or familiarity acquired through education or experience. Anything that has been learned, perceived, discovered, inferred, or understood. The ability to use information.

Knowledge Acquisition   The extraction and formulation of knowledge derived from various sources, especially from experts.

Knowledge Base   A collection of facts, rules, and procedures organized into schemas. The assembly of all of the information and knowledge of a specific field of interest.

Knowledge-based Management   Management of the stored knowledge in terms of storing, accessing, updating, and reasoning with (analogous to a database management system).

Knowledge Engineer   An AI specialist responsible for the technical side of developing an expert system. The knowledge engineer works closely with the domain expert to capture the expert's knowledge in a knowledge base.

Knowledge Engineering (KE)   The engineering discipline whereby knowledge is integrated into computer systems in order to solve complex problems normally requiring a high level of human expertise.

Knowledge Refining   The ability of the program to analyze its own performance, learn, and improve itself for future consultations.

Knowledge Representation   A formalism for representing facts and rules in the computer about a subject or a specialty.

Knowledge Worker   Employee who uses knowledge as a significant input to his or her work.

Lexicon A dictionary.

Life Cycle (in System Development) Structured approach to the development of information systems with several distinct steps.

Linear Programming A mathematical model for optimal solution of resource allocation problems.

LISP (List Processor) An AI programming language, created by AI pioneer John McCarthy, that is especially popular in the United States.

LISP Machines (or AI Workstations) A single-user computer designed primarily to expedite the development of AI programs.

Machine Language A language for writing instructions in a form to be executed directly by the computer. The language is composed of two values: zeros and ones.

Machine Learning Computer that can learn from experience (e.g., programs that can learn from historical cases).

Management by Exception A control system in which performance is monitored and action is taken only if the performance is outside a designated range.

Management Information Systems (MIS) A business information system designed to provide past, present, and future information appropriate for planning, organizing, and controlling the operations of the organization.

Management Science (MS) The application of scientific approach and mathematical models to the analysis and solution of managerial decision problems.

Mathematical Model A system of symbols and expressions representing a real situation.

Megachip Chip with more than 1 million components.

Metaknowledge Knowledge in an expert system about how the system operates or reasons. More generally, knowledge about knowledge.

Metarules A rule that describes how other rules should be used or modified.

Microelectronics Miniaturization of electronic circuits and components.

Model Base A collection of preprogrammed quantitative models (e.g., statistical, financial, optimization) organized as a single unit.

Model Base Management System (MBMS) A software to establish, update, combine, etc. a model base.

Model-based System (or Reasoning) Application whose knowledge is derived by mathematical (or other type of) model.

Model Building Blocks Preprogrammed software elements that can be used to build computerized models. For example, a random number generator can be used in the construction of a simulation model.

Modeling Tools Software programs that enable the building of mathematical models quickly. A spreadsheet and a planning language are modeling tools.

Modified Turing Test Test in which a manager is shown two solutions, one derived by a computer and one by a human, and is asked to compare the two.

Modus Ponens   An inference rule type which from "A implies B" justifies B by the existence of A.

Monte Carlo Simulation   A mechanism that uses random numbers in order to predict the behavior of an event whose probabilities are known.

Multidimensional Analysis   Analyzing data by three or more dimensions. See Multidimensionality.

Multidimensionality   Organizing, presenting, and analyzing data by several dimensions, such as sales by region, by product, by salesperson, and by time (four dimensions).

Multimedia   Several human-machine communication media (e.g., voice, text).

Multiple Experts   A case in which two or more experts are used as the source of knowledge for an expert system.

Multiple Goals   A decision situation in which alteratives are being evaluated in light of several sometimes conflicting goals.

Mutation   Genetic operator that causes a change in a situation.

MYCIN   Early rule-based expert system, developed by Dr. Edward H. Shortliffe, that helps to determine the exact identity of an infection of the blood and that helps to prescribe the appropriate antibiotic.

Natural Language   A language spoken by humans on a daily basis, such as English, French, Japanese, or German.

Natural Language Processors (NLP)   An AI-based user interface that allows the user to carry on a conversation with a computer-based system in much the same way as he or she would converse with another human.

Navigation of Information   The ability to access and identify required data using intelligent software that makes the search efficient and effective.

Neural Computing (Networks)   An experimental computer design that aims at building intelligent computers that will operate much like the human brain.

Nonprocedural Languages   The programmer specifies only the desired results rather than the detailed steps of how to get there.

Normative   Prescribes how a system should operate.

Numerical Processing   The traditional use of computers to manipulate numbers.

Object-oriented Programming   A language for representing objects and processing those representations by sending messages and activating methods.

Open System   Computer systems on a network, which permit the software and hardware of any vendor to be used by any user.

Operations Research   *See* Management Science.

Optimization   Identification of the best possible solution.

Organizational Culture (Climate)   The aggregate attitudes in the organization concerning a certain issue (such as technology, computers, and DSS).

Organizational DSS (ODSS)   A network DSS that serves people, at several locations, usually dealing with several decisions.

Parallel Processing An advanced computer processing technique that allows the computer to perform multiple processes at the same time, in "parallel."

Parsing The process of breaking down a character string of natural language input into its component parts so that it can be more readily analyzed, interpreted, or understood.

Pattern Matching *See* Pattern Recognition. However, sometimes it refers specifically to matching the IF and THEN parts in rule-based systems. In such a case, pattern matching can be considered as one area of pattern recognition.

Pattern Recognition The technique of matching an external pattern to one stored within a computer's memory, used in inference engines, image processing, neural computing, and speech recognition (e.g., the process of classifying data into predetermined categories).

Planning Language A software package designed to expedite the construction of a financial and/or operational computerized planning system.

Predicate Calculus A logical system of reasoning used in AI programs to indicate relationships among data items. The basis for the computer language PROLOG.

Presentation Language The information displayed; output.

Principle of Choice The criterion for making a choice among alternatives.

Problem Solving A process in which one starts from an initial state and proceeds to search through a problem space in order to identify a desired goal.

Procedural Knowledge (contrasted with Declarative Knowledge) Information about courses of action.

Procedural Languages A language in which the programmer must define the detailed procedures that the computer is to follow.

Production Rules A knowledge representation method in which knowledge is formalized into "rules" containing an IF part and a THEN part (also called a condition and an action).

Productivity The ratio of outputs (results) to inputs (resources).

PROLOG A high-level computer language designed around the concepts of predicate calculus.

Propositional Logic A formal logical system of reasoning in which conclusions are drawn from a series of statements according to a strict set of rules.

Protocols A set of instructions governing the format and control of data in moving from one medium to another.

Prototyping A strategy in system development in which a scaled-down system or portion of a system is constructed in a short time, tested, and improved in several iterations.

Query Language A language provided as part of a DBMS for easy access to data in the database.

Random Number A number sampled from a uniform distribution in an unbiased manner (each number has exactly the same chance of being selected).

Rapid Prototyping   In expert systems development, a prototype is an initial version of an expert system, usually a system with 25 to 200 rules, that is quickly developed to test the effectiveness of the overall knowledge representation and inference mechanisms being employed to solve a particular problem.

Ready-made Expert System   Mass-produced packages that may be purchased from software companies. These are very general in nature.

Real-time   In synchronization with the actual occurrence of events; results are given rapidly enough to be useful in directly controlling a physical process or guiding a human user.

Relational Database   A database whose records are organized into tables that can be processed by either relational algebra or relational calculus.

Report Generation   The ability to use a few commands to generate an entire report. At the extreme, one command can generate an entire report patterned according to a template.

Repertory Grid Technique   A tool used by psychologists to represent a person's view of a problem in terms of its elements and constructs.

Reusability   Self-sufficiency of an object that enables it to be used as an independent component (in object-oriented programming).

Risk Analysis   Analysis of decision situations in which results are dependent on events whose probabilities of occurrence are assumed to be known.

Robotics   The science of using a machine (a robot) to perform manual functions without human intervention.

Role Ambiguity   A situation in which the role to be performed by an employee is not clear. Lack of job description and changing conditions often result in role ambiguity.

ROMC (Representation, Operations, Memory Aids, Mechanism Control)   A systematic approach for developing large-scale DSS. It is a user-oriented approach for articulating system performance requirements.

Rule   A formal way of specifying a recommendation, directive, or strategy, expressed as IF premise THEN conclusion.

Rule-based System   A system in which knowledge is represented completely in terms of rules (e.g., a system based on production rules).

Rule Induction   Rules are created by a computer from examples of problems where the outcome is known in a process called *induction*. These rules are generalized to other cases.

Rule Interpreter   Inference mechanism in a rule-based system.

Runtime System   Part of an expert system shell that provides a consultation by interfacing with a user and an *existing knowledge base* and inference engine.

Satisficing   A process during which one seeks a solution that will satisfy a set of constraints. In contrast to optimization, which seeks the best possible solution; when one satisfices, one simply seeks a solution that will work. (Good enough.)

Scenario   A statement of assumptions and configurations concerning the operating environment of a particular system at a particular time.

Schema   A data structure for knowledge representation. Examples of schemas are frames and rules.

Script   Framelike structure representing a stereotyped sequence of events (such as eating at a restaurant).

Search Space   Set of all possible solutions to a problem.

Search Tree   Graphic presentation that shows the problem, its alternative solutions, and the progress of a search for the best (acceptable) solution.

Self-evolving DSS   A special type of intelligent DSS.

Semantic Networks   A knowledge representation method consisting of a network of nodes, standing for concepts or objects, connected by arcs describing the relations between the nodes.

Semantics   The meaning in language. The relationship between words and sentences.

Semistructured Decisions   Decisions in which some aspects of the problem are structured and others are unstructured.

Sensitivity Analysis   A study of the effect of a change in one or more input variables on a proposed solution.

Sensory System   Any system that monitors the external environment for a computer.

Sequential Processing   The traditional computer processing technique of performing actions one at a time, in a sequence.

Shallow (Surface) Representation   Model that does not capture all of the forms of knowledge used by experts in their reasoning. Contrasted with Deep Representation.

Shell   A complete expert system stripped of its specific knowledge. In rule-based systems, it is a kind of expert system development tool consisting of two stand-alone pieces of software: a rule set manager and an inference engine capable of reasoning with the rule set built with the rule set manager.

Sigmoid Function   Transfer function of an S shape in the range of zero to one.

Simulation   An imitation of reality.

Slot   A sub-element of a frame of an object. A particular characteristic, specification, or definition used in forming a knowledge base.

Specific DSS   A system that actually accomplishes a specific task. It is similar to "application software" in conventional MIS.

Specific Expert Systems   An expert system that advises users on a specific issue.

Speech Understanding   An area of AI research that attempts to allow computers to recognize words or phrases of human speech.

Spreadsheet (Electronic)   Computer technology that is similar to columns-and-rows worksheets used by accountants. It is a modeling tool.

SQL (Structured Query Language)   A data definition and management language of relational databases. It front-ends most relational DBMS.

Status Access   Rapid access to current information, provided by a computer.

Structured Decisions   Standard or repetitive decision situations for which solution techniques are already available.

Symbolic Processing Use of symbols, rather than numbers, combined with rules of thumb (or heuristics), in order to process information and solve problems.

Synchronous Communication Communication conducted among people conversing at the same time (instantaneous reply). People may be at the same place.

Syntax The manner in which words are assembled to form phrases and sentences. Putting words in a specific order.

System A set of elements that is considered to act as a single, goal-oriented entity.

System Analysis The investigation and recording of existing systems and the conceptual design and feasibility study of new systems.

System Design Specification of appropriate hardware and software components required to implement an information system.

System Development Life Cycle (SDLC) A systematic process for constructing large information systems in an effective manner.

Technology Levels of DSS (or ES) Classification of software as basic development tools, integrated development tools, and completed applications (DSS or ES).

Telecommunication The transfer of information over distance by means of computer, telephone, radio, or other transmission.

Telecommuting Employees work at home, usually using a computer or a terminal that is linked to their place of employment.

Template A piece of presentation knowledge that indicates the visual layout of a report's contents and the sources of values that can appear in particular locations.

Time-series Analysis A technique that analyzes historical data over a period of a few years and then makes a forecast.

Turing Test A test that is designed to measure the degree of a computer's "intelligence."

Uncertainty In the context of expert systems, uncertainty refers to a value that cannot be determined during a consultation. Many expert systems can accommodate uncertainty. That is, they allow the user to indicate if he or she does not know the answer.

Uncontrollable Variations Factors that affect the result of a decision but are not under the control of the decision maker. These can be internal (technology, policies) or external (legal, climate).

Unstructured Decisions Complex decisions for which no standard solutions exist.

User-friendly Term used to describe a facility designed to make interaction with a computer system easy and comfortable for the user.

User Interface (or Human-Machine Interface) The component of a computer system that allows bidirectional communication between the system and its user.

User Interface Management System (UIMS)   *See* Dialog Generation and Management System.

Validation   Determination of whether the right system was built.

Verification   Confirmation that the system was built to specifications (correctly).

Videoteleconferencing   Communication among people who are in different locations but are able to see each other on TV screens or desktop computers.

Virtual Reality   A 3-D interactive technology which provides the user a feeling that he or she is physically present in the real world.

Visual Simulation   *See* Interactive Visual Simulation.

Visual Spreadsheet   Programming and presentation of spreadsheet data as influence diagrams.

VLSI (Very-Large-Scale Integration)   The process of combining several hundred thousand electronic components into a single integrated circuit (chip).

Voice Recognition   The ability of a computer to understand the meaning of spoken words (sentences as input).

Voice Synthesis   A transformation of computer output to an audio (voice); for example, a telephone number given as a response to a request from 411.

Weight   Value assigned on each connection at the input to a neuron. Analogous to a synapse in the brain. Weights control the inflow to the processing elements in neural networks.

"What-If" Analysis   The capability of "asking" the computer what the effect will be of changing some of the input data.

Workflow Systems   Group support software for scheduling, routing, and monitoring specific tasks throughout an organization.

Workplace (or Blackboard)   A globally accessible database used in expert systems for recording intermediate, partial results of problem solving.

WYSIWYG   "What you see is what you get." A capability of creating reports (or other outputs) on the computer screen and then printing the results in the format seen on the screen.